Feltre

Udine

Vicenza Treviso VENICE Aquilea

Padua

ste

Venice

EPUBLIC Chioggia Parenzo

OF

ISTRIA

Rovigno

rrara Rovigo
Po R. Pola
FERRARA

ologna

LIA Ravenna

Faenza
Forli Rimini
Cesena Pesaro

ole San Marino

ce ROMAGNA Urbino

Senigallia

FLORENCE STATES Ancona

Arezzo Fabriano

ortona

IC Perugia OF THE
Assisi
NA Foligno

CHURCH

Orvieto Spoleto

Bolsena Terni

Viterbo Pescara

Chieti

ecchia

Tagliacozzo

Tiber R.

Rome Tivoli KINGDOM

Anagni Mt. Gargano

Ostia Molise
Lucera Foggia

S. Germano

OF

Sea Grandella Cerignola
Benevento

Gaeta Capua NAPLES

Naples

Amalfi Salerno

Adriatic Sea

Zara DALMATIA

W E

N

S

BY WILL DURANT

The Story of Philosophy
Transition
The Pleasures of Philosophy
Adventures in Genius

BY WILL AND ARIEL DURANT

THE STORY OF CIVILIZATION:

I. *Our Oriental Heritage*
II. *The Life of Greece*
III. *Caesar and Christ*
IV. *The Age of Faith*
V. *The Renaissance*
VI. *The Reformation*
VII. *The Age of Reason Begins*
VIII. *The Age of Louis XIV*
IX. *The Age of Voltaire*
X. *Rousseau and Revolution*
XI. *The Age of Napoleon*

The Lessons of History
Interpretations of Life

THE STORY OF CIVILIZATION: PART V

THE
RENAISSANCE

A History of Civilization in Italy
from 1304-1576 A.D.

By Will Durant

SIMON AND SCHUSTER
NEW YORK: 1953

ISBN 0-671-61600-5
LIBRARY OF CONGRESS CATALOG CARD NUMBER 53-10016
MANUFACTURED IN THE UNITED STATES OF AMERICA
BY THE HADDON CRAFTSMEN, INC., SCRANTON, PA.

15 16 17 18 19 20 21 22 23 24 25

TO MY WIFE

Who has shared in a hundred ways
in writing this book

To the Reader

THIS volume, while complete and independent in itself, forms Part V in a history of civilization written on the "integral method" of uniting in one narrative all phases of human activity. The series began in 1935 with *Our Oriental Heritage*—a history of Egypt and the Near and Middle East to 323 B.C., and of India, China, and Japan to 1930. Part II, *The Life of Greece* (1939), recorded Greek history and culture from the beginnings, and the history of the Near and Middle East from 323 B.C., to the Roman Conquest in 146 B.C. Part III, *Caesar and Christ* (1944), carried the story of white civilization to A.D. 325, centered around the rise and fall of Rome, and the first centuries of Christianity. Part IV, *The Age of Faith* (1950), continued the narrative to 1300, including Byzantine civilization, Islam, Judaism, and Latin Christendom.

The present work aims to give a rounded picture of all phases of human life in the Italy of the Renaissance—from the birth of Petrarch in 1304 to the death of Titian in 1576. The term "Renaissance" will in this book refer only to Italy. The word does not properly apply to such native maturations, rather than exotic rebirths, as took place in France, Spain, England, and the Lowlands in the sixteenth and seventeenth centuries; and even in Italy the designation lays undue stress on that revival of classic letters which was of less importance to Italy than the ripening of its economy and culture into their own characteristic forms.

In order to avoid a superficial repetition of the excellent books already in print on this subject, the scale of treatment has been enlarged as compared with the previous volumes in the series. Moreover, as we approach our own epoch our interests are more widely engaged; we still feel in our blood the sap of those effervescent centuries in which modern Europe began; and their ideas, events, and personalities are especially vital to an understanding of our own minds and times.

I have studied at first hand nearly all the works of art mentioned in this book, but I lack the technical training that would give me the right to express any critical judgments. I have ventured, however, to voice my impressions and preferences. Modern art is absorbed in a forgivable reaction against the Renaissance, and is zealously experimenting to find new forms of beauty or significance. Our appreciation of the Renaissance should not deter us from welcoming every sincere and disciplined attempt to imitate not its products but its originality.

If circumstances permit, a sixth volume, probably under the title of *The Age of the Reformation*, will appear three or four years hence, covering the history of Christian, Islamic, and Judaic civilization outside of Italy from 1300, and in Italy from 1576 to 1648. The enlarged scale of treatment, and the imminence of senility, make it advisable to plan an end of the series with a seventh volume, *The Age of Reason*, which may carry the tale to the beginning of the nineteenth century.

Acknowledgments are due to Mr. Joseph Auslander for permission to quote his fine translation of a sonnet by Petrarch; to the Cambridge University Press for permission to quote a paragraph by Richard Garnett from Volume I of *The Cambridge Modern History*; to my wife for a hundred illuminating suggestions and conversations; to Dr. C. Edward Hopkin for aid in classifying the material; to Miss Mary Kaufman and Miss Flora Kaufman for varied clerical assistance; to Mrs. Edith Digate for her highly competent typing of a difficult manuscript; and to Wallace Brockway for expert editing and advice.

A tardy acknowledgment is due to my publishers. In my long association with them I have found them ideal. They have given me every consideration, have shared with me the expenses of research, and have never let calculations of profit or loss determine our relations. In 1926 they published my *Story of Philosophy* hoping only to "break even." We have been together now for twenty-seven years; and it has been for me a fortunate and happy union.

Notes on the Use of This Book

1. Dates of birth and death are omitted from the text, but will be found in the index.

2. Passages in reduced type are for students and may be safely omitted by the general reader.

3. In locating works of art the name of the city will be used to indicate its leading picture gallery, e.g.:

Bergamo, the Accademia Carrara;

Berlin, the Kaiser-Friedrich Museum;

Brescia, the Pinacoteca Martinengo;

Chicago, the Art Institute;

Cleveland, the Museum of Art;
Detroit, the Institute of Art;
Leningrad, the Hermitage;
London, the National Gallery;
Madrid, the Prado;
Mantua, the Palazzo Ducale;
Milan, the Brera Gallery;
Modena, the Pinacoteca Estense;
Naples, the Museo Nazionale;
New York, the Metropolitan Museum of Art;
Parma, the Royal Gallery;
Venice, the Academy;
Washington, the National Gallery; but the great galleries of Florence will be distinguished by their names, Uffizi and Pitti, as will the Borghese in Rome.

WILL DURANT

Los Angeles, December 1, 1952

Table of Contents

BOOK I: PRELUDE: 1300-77

BOOK II: THE FLORENTINE RENAISSANCE: 1378-1534

BOOK III: ITALIAN PAGEANT: 1378-1534

BOOK V: DEBACLE

BOOK VI: FINALE: 1534-76

List of Illustrations

The page number referred to in the captions is for a discussion of the particular painting or the artist, and sometimes both.

BOOK I

PRELUDE

1300-77

CHAPTER I

The Age of Petrarch and Boccaccio

1304-75

I. THE FATHER OF THE RENAISSANCE

IN that same year 1302 in which the aristocratic party of the *neri* (Blacks), having seized the government of Florence by force, exiled Dante and other middle-class *bianchi* (Whites), the triumphant oligarchy indicted a White lawyer, Ser (i.e., Messer or Master) Petracco on the charge of having falsified a legal document. Branding the accusation as a device for ending his political career, Petracco refused to stand for trial. He was convicted in absence, and was given the choice of paying a heavy fine or having his right hand cut off. As he still refused to appear before the court, he was banished from Florence, and suffered the confiscation of his property. Taking his young wife with him, he fled to Arezzo. There, two years later, Francesco Petrarca (as he later euphonized his name) burst upon the world.

Predominantly Ghibelline—yielding political allegiance to the emperors of the Holy Roman Empire rather than to the popes—little Arezzo experienced in the fourteenth century all the tribulations of an Italian city. Guelfic Florence—supporting the popes against the emperors in the struggle for political authority in Italy—had overwhelmed Arezzo at Campaldino (1289), where Dante fought; in 1340 all Aretine Ghibellines between thirteen and seventy were exiled; and in 1384 Arezzo fell permanently under Florentine rule. There, in ancient days, Maecenas had been born; there the fifteenth and sixteenth centuries would see the birth of Giorgio Vasari, who made the Renaissance famous, and of Pietro Aretino, who for a while made it infamous. Every town in Italy has fathered genius, and banished it.

In 1312 Ser Petracco rushed north to welcome the Emperor Henry VII as one who would save Italy, or at least its Ghibellines. As sanguine as Dante in that year, Petracco moved his family to Pisa, and awaited the destruction of the Florentine Guelfs.

Pisa was still among the splendors of Italy. The shattering of her fleet by the Genoese in 1284 had reduced her possessions and narrowed her com-

3

merce; and the strife of Guelf and Ghibelline within her gates left her with scant strength to elude the imperialistic grasp of a mercantile Florence eager to control the Arno to its mouth. But her brave burghers gloried in their majestic marble cathedral, their precarious campanile, and their famous cemetery, that Campo Santo, or Sacred Field, whose central quadrangle had been filled with soil from the Holy Land, and whose walls were soon to receive frescoes by Giotto's pupils and the Lorenzetti, and whose sculptured tombs gave a moment's immortality to the heroic or lavish dead. In Pisa's university, soon after its establishment, the subtle jurist Bartolus of Sassoferrato adapted Roman law to the needs of the age, but phrased his legal science in such esoteric verbiage as brought both Petrarch and Boccaccio down upon his head. Perhaps Bartolus found obscurity prudent, since he justified tyrannicide, and denied the right of governments to take a man's property except by due process of law.[1]

Henry VII died (1313) before he could make up his mind to be or not to be a Roman emperor. The Guelfs of Italy rejoiced; and Ser Petracco, unsafe in Pisa, emigrated with his wife, his daughter, and his two sons to Avignon on the Rhone, where the newly established papal court, and a rapidly expanding population, offered opportunities for a lawyer's skill. They sailed up the coast to Genoa, and Petrarch never forgot the unfolding splendor of the Italian Riviera—towns like diadems on mountain brows, slipping down to green blue seas; this, said the young poet, "is liker to heaven than to earth."[2] They found Avignon so stuffed with dignitaries that they moved some fifteen miles northeast to Carpentras (1315); and there Francesco spent four years of happy carelessness. Bliss ended when he was sent off to Montpellier (1319-23), and then to Bologna (1323-6) to study law.

Bologna should have pleased him. It was a university town, full of the frolic of students, the odor of learning, the excitement of independent thought. Here in this fourteenth century were given the first courses in human anatomy. Here were women professors, some, like Novella d'Andrea (d. 1366), so attractive that tradition, doubtless fanciful, described her as lecturing behind a veil lest the students should be distracted by her beauty. The commune of Bologna had been among the first to throw off the yoke of the Holy Roman Empire and proclaim its autonomy; as far back as 1153 it had chosen its own podesta or city manager; and for two centuries it had maintained a democratic government. But in 1325, while Petrarch was there, it suffered so disastrous a defeat by Modena that it placed itself under the protection of the papacy, and in 1327 accepted a papal vicar as its governor. Thereby would hang many a bitter tale.

Petrarch liked the spirit of Bologna, but he hated the letter of the law. "It went against my bent painfully to acquire an art that I would not practise dishonestly, and could hardly hope to practise otherwise."²ᵃ All that he cared for in the legal treatises was their "numberless references to Roman antiquity." Instead of studying law he read all that he could find of Virgil, Cicero, and Seneca. They opened to him a new world, both of philosophy and of literary art. He began to think like them, he longed to write like them. When his parents died (1326) he abandoned law, returned to Avignon, and steeped himself in classic poetry and romantic love.

It was on Good Friday of 1327, he tells us, that he saw the woman whose withheld charms made him the most famous poet of his age. He described her in fascinating detail, but kept the secret of her identity so well that even his friends thought her the invention of his muse, and counted all his passion as poetic license. But on the flyleaf of his copy of Virgil, jealously treasured in the Ambrosian Library at Milan, may still be seen the words that he wrote in 1348:

> Laura, who was distinguished by her virtues, and widely celebrated by my songs, first appeared to my eyes . . . in the year of Our Lord 1327, on the sixth day of April, at the first hour, in the church of Santa Clara at Avignon. In the same city, in the same month, on the same sixth day, at the same first hour, in the year 1348, that light was taken from our day.

Who was this Laura? A will was filed in Avignon on April 3, 1348, by one Laura de Sade, wife of Count Hugues de Sade, to whom she had given twelve children; presumably this was the lady of the poet's love, and her husband was a distant ancestor of the most famous sadist in history. A miniature attributed to Simone Martini, and now in the Laurentian Library at Florence, is described by tradition as a portrait of Petrarch's Laura; it shows a face of delicate beauty, fine mouth, straight nose, and lowered eyes suggesting a pensive modesty. We do not know if Laura was married, or already a young mother, when Petrarch first saw her. In any case she received his adoration calmly, kept him at a distance, and gave his passion all the encouragement of denial. The occasional sincerity of his feeling for her is suggested by his later remorse over its sensual elements, and his gratitude for the refining influence of this unrequited love.

Meanwhile he lived in Provence, the land of the troubadours; the echoes of their songs still lingered in Avignon; and Petrarch, like the young Dante a generation before him, became unconsciously a troubadour, wedding his passion to a thousand tricks of verse. The writing of poetry was then a popular pastime; Petrarch complained, in one of his letters, that lawyers and theologians, nay, even his own valet, had taken to rhyming; soon, he feared, "the very cattle would begin to low in verse."[3] From his own country he inherited the sonnet form, and bound it into the difficult rhyme-pattern that for centuries molded and hampered Italian poetry. Walking along the streams or among the hills, kneeling distracted at Vespers or Mass, groping his way among verbs and adjectives in the silence of his room, he composed during the next twenty-one years 207 sonnets and sundry other poems on the living, breeding Laura. Gathered in manuscript copies as a *Canzoniere* or Songbook, these compositions caught the fancy of Italian youth, of Italian manhood, of the Italian clergy. No one was disturbed by the fact that the author, seeing no road to advancement except in the Church, had taken the tonsure and minor orders, and was angling for a benefice; but Laura may have blushed—and thrilled—on hearing that her hair and brow and eyes and nose and lips . . . were sung from the Adriatic to the Rhone. Never before, in the salvaged literature of the world, had the emotion of love been expounded in such diverse fullness, or with such painstaking artifice. Here were all the pretty conceits of versified desire, the fitful flame of love miraculously trimmed to meter and rhyme:

> No rock, however cold, but with my theme
> Shall henceforth kindle and consume in sighs!

But the Italian people received these bonbons in the most exquisite music that their language had yet heard—subtle and delicate and melodious, gleaming with bright imagery, making even Dante seem at times crude and harsh; now, indeed, that glorious language—the triumph of the vowel over the consonant—reached a height of beauty that even to our day remains unscaled. An alien can translate the thought, but who shall translate the music?

> *In qual parte del ciel, in quale idea*
> *Era l'essempio, onde Natura tolse*
> *Quel bel viso leggiadro, in ch' ella volse*
> *Mostrar qua giú quanto lassú potea?*
> *Qual ninfa in fonti, in selve mai qual dea,*
> *Chiome d'oro so fino a l'aura sciolse?*
> *Quando un cor tante in sé vertuti accolse?*
> *Benché la somma è di mia morte rea.*

Per divina bellezza indarno mira
   Chi gli occhi de costei già mai non vide
   Come soavemente ella gli gira;
Non sa come Amor sana, e come ancide,
   Chi non sa come dolce ella sospira,
   E come dolce parla, e dolce ride.[4]*

His poems, his gay wit, his sensitivity to beauty in woman, nature, conduct, literature, and art, made a place for Petrarch in cultured society; and his condemnation of ecclesiastical morals in Avignon did not deter great churchmen like Bishop Giacomo Colonna, and a brother Cardinal Giovanni Colonna, from offering him hospitality and patronage. Like most of us he enjoyed and condoned before he tired and condemned; between sonnets to Laura he dallied with a mistress, and begot two illegitimate children. He had leisure for travel, and apparently substantial funds; we find him in Paris in 1331, then in Flanders and Germany, then in Rome (1336) as the guest of the Colonnas. He was deeply moved by the ruins of the Forum, revealing an ancient power and grandeur that shamed the poverty and squalor of the abandoned medieval capital. He pled with five successive popes to leave Avignon and return to Rome. He himself, however, left Rome and returned to Avignon.

For seven years, between his travels, he lived in the palace of Cardinal Colonna there, meeting the finest scholars, churchmen, lawyers, and statesmen of Italy, France, and England, and conveying to them some of his enthusiasm for classical literature. But he resented the simoniacal corruption of Avignon, the consuming leisure of ecclesiastical litigation, the confusion of cardinals and courtesans, the conversion of Christianity to the world. In 1337 he bought a small house at Vaucluse—"Closed Valley"—some fifteen miles east of Avignon. Traveling through majestic views to

---

* An excellent translation by Joseph Auslander:
   In what bright realm, what sphere of radiant thought
     Did Nature find the model whence she drew
     That delicate dazzling image where we view
   Here on this earth what she in heaven wrought?
   What fountain-haunting nymph, what dryad sought
     In groves, such golden tresses ever threw
     Upon the gust? What heart such virtues knew?—
   Though her chief virtue with my death is fraught.
   He looks in vain for heavenly beauty, he
     Who never looked upon her perfect eyes,
   The vivid blue orbs burning brilliantly—
     He does not know how Love yields and denies;
   He only knows who knows how sweetly she
     Can talk and laugh, the sweetness of her sighs.[5]

locate that hideaway, one is surprised to find it a tiny cottage built against a cliff, oppressed by massive crags, but caressed by the quiet flow of the undulant Sorgue. Petrarch foreshadowed Rousseau not only in the sentimental involution of his love, but in the pleasure he derived from natural scenery. "Would that you could know," he wrote to a friend, "with what delight I wander, free and alone, among the mountains, forests, and streams." Already in 1336 he had set a fashion by climbing Mt. Ventoux (6214 feet high), purely for the exercise, the view, and the vanity of victory. Now at Vaucluse he dressed like a peasant, fished in the brook, puttered in two gardens, and contented himself "with a single dog and only two servants." His sole regret (for his passion for Laura had spent itself in hunting rhymes) was that he was too far from Italy and too near Avignon.

From that foot of land he moved half the literary world. He loved to write long letters to his friends, to popes and kings, to dead authors, to unborn posterity. He kept copies of this correspondence, and in his declining years he amused his pride by revising it for posthumous publication. These epistles, in vigorous but hardly Ciceronian Latin, are the most vital relics of his pen. Some of them so harshly criticized the Church that Petrarch kept them secret till he was safely dead. While accepting with apparent sincerity the full doctrine of Catholic Christianity, he dwelt in spirit with the ancients; he wrote to Homer, Cicero, Livy as if they were living comrades, and complained that he had not been born in the heroic days of the Roman Republic. He habitually called one of his correspondents Laelius, and another Socrates. He inspired his friends to search for lost manuscripts of Latin or Greek literature, to copy ancient inscriptions, and collect ancient coins, as precious documents of history. He urged the establishment of public libraries. He practised what he preached: on his travels he sought and bought classic texts as "more valuable merchandise than anything offered by the Arabs or the Chinese";[6] he transcribed unpurchasable manuscripts with his own hand; and at home he hired copyists to live with him. He gloried in a Homer sent him from Greece, begged the sender for a copy of Euripides, and made his copy of Virgil a *vade mecum* on whose flyleaf he entered events in the careers of his friends. The Middle Ages had preserved, and some medieval scholars had loved, many pagan classics; but Petrarch knew from references in these works that numberless masterpieces had been forgotten or mislaid; and it became his passion to recover them.

Renan called him "the first modern man," as having "inaugurated in the

Latin West a tender feeling for ancient culture."[7] This will not do as a definition of modernity, which did not merely rediscover the classic world, but replaced the supernatural with the natural as the focus of human concern. In this sense too Petrarch may deserve the epithet "modern"; for though moderately pious, and occasionally worried about the afterlife, his revival of interest in antiquity fostered the Renaissance emphasis on man and the earth, on the legitimacy of sensory pleasure, and on mortal glory as a substitute for personal immortality. Petrarch had some sympathy for the medieval view, and in his dialogues *De contemptu mundi* he let St. Augustine expound it well; but in those imaginary conversations he made himself the defender of secular culture and earthly fame. Though Petrarch was already seventeen when Dante died, an abyss divided their moods. By common consent he was the first humanist, the first writer to express with clarity and force the right of man to concern himself with this life, to enjoy and augment its beauties, and to labor to deserve well of posterity. He was the Father of the Renaissance.

II. NAPLES AND BOCCACCIO

At Vaucluse Petrarch began the poem by which he aspired to rival Virgil —an epic, *Africa*, on the liberation of Italy through the victory of Scipio Africanus over Hannibal. Like the humanists of a century after him, he chose Latin as his medium, not, like Dante, Italian; he wished to be understood by the whole literate Western world. As the poem progressed he became more and more doubtful of its merit; he never completed it, never published it. While he was absorbed in Latin hexameters his Italian *Canzoniere* was spreading his fame through Italy, and a translation carried his name through France. In 1340—not without some sly manipulations on his part[8]—two invitations reached him, one from the Roman Senate, the other from the University of Paris, to come and receive at their hands the poet's laurel crown. He accepted the Senate's offer, and the suggestion of Robert the Wise that he should stop at Naples on the way.

After the overthrow of Frederick II and the Hohenstaufens by the arms and diplomacy of the popes, his *Regno*—Italy south of the Papal States— had been given to the house of Anjou in the person of Charles, Count of Provence. Charles ruled as King of Naples and Sicily; his son Charles II lost Sicily to the house of Aragon; his grandson Robert, though failing in his war to recapture Sicily, earned his cognomen by competent government, wise diplomacy, and a discriminating patronage of literature and art. The Kingdom was poor in industry, and its agriculture was dominated by myopic landowners who, as now, exploited the peasantry to the edge of revolution; but the commerce of Naples gave the court an income that made the royal Castel Nuovo ring with frequent festivities. The well-to-do imitated the court; marriages became ruinous ceremonies; periodic regattas animated the historic bay; and in the city square young blades jousted in perilous tournaments while their garlanded ladies smiled upon them from bannered balconies. Life was pleasant in Naples, and morals were comfortably loose; women were beautiful and accessible; and poets found in this atmosphere of amorous dalliance many a theme and stimulus for their verse. In Naples Boccaccio was formed.

Giovanni had begun life in Paris as the unpremeditated result of an *entente cordiale* between his father, a Florentine merchant, and a French lass of doubtful name and morals;[9] perhaps his bastard birth and half-French origin shared in determining his character and history. He was brought in infancy to Certaldo, near Florence, and suffered an unhappy childhood under a stepmother. At the age of ten (1323) he was sent to Naples, where he was apprenticed to a career of finance and trade. He learned to hate business as Petrarch hated law; he announced his preference for poverty and poetry, lost his soul to Ovid, feasted on the *Metamorphoses* and the *Heroides*, and learned by heart most of the *Ars amandi*, wherein, he wrote, "the greatest of poets shows how the sacred fire of Venus may be made to burn in the coldest" breast.[10] The father, unable to make him love money more than beauty, allowed him to quit business on condition that he study canon law. Boccaccio agreed, but he was ripe for romance.

The gayest lady in Naples was Maria d'Aquino. She was the natural daughter of King Robert the Wise,[11] but her mother's husband accepted her as his own child. She was educated in a convent, and was married at fifteen to the Count of Aquino, but found him inadequate to her needs. She encouraged a succession of lovers to supply his deficiencies, and to spend their substance upon her finery. Boccaccio first saw her at Mass on Holy Saturday (1331) four Easters after Petrarch's discovery of Laura under similarly sacred auspices. She seemed to him fairer than Aphrodite; the world held nothing lovelier than her blonde hair, nothing more alluring than her roguish eyes. He called her Fiammetta—Little Flame—and longed to singe himself in her fire. He forgot canon law, forgot all the commandments he had ever learned; for months he thought only of how he might be near her. He went to church solely in the hope that she might appear; he paced the street before her window; he went to Baiae on hearing that she was there. For five years he pursued her; she let him wait until other purses were empty; then she allowed him to persuade her. A year of costly assignations dulled the edge of adultery; she complained that he looked at other women; besides, his funds ran out. The Little Flame sought other food, and Boccaccio retired to poetry.

Very probably he had read Petrarch's *Canzoniere* and Dante's *Vita Nuova;* his first poems were like theirs, sonnets of yearning, burning, churning love. Most of them were addressed to Fiammetta, some celebrated lesser flames. For her he wrote a long and dreary prose version—*Filocopo* —of a medieval romance, *Fleur et Blancfleur.* Finer was his *Filostrato;* here he told in glowing verse how Criseida vowed eternal fidelity to Troilus, was captured by the Greeks, and soon yielded herself to Diomed on the plea that he was so "tall and strong and beautiful," and at hand. For his medium Boccaccio chose an eight-line stanza—*ottava rima*—that set a form for Pulci, Boiardo, and Ariosto. It is a frankly sensual story, whose 5400 lines reach their climax when Criseida, "throwing away her shift, sprang naked into her lover's arms."[12] But it is also a remarkable psychological study of one type of woman—lightly false and gayly vain; and it ends with phrases now familiar in opera:

> *Giovane donna è mobile, e vogliosa*
> *E negli amanti molti, e sua bellezza*
> *Estima più ch' allo specchio, e pomposa. . . .*
> *Virtù non sente ni conoscimento,*
> *Volubil sempre come foglia al vento.**

Soon afterward, as if to break down resistance with sheer weight, Boccaccio presented to Fiammetta an epic poem, *Teseide*, precisely as long as the *Aeneid.* It told of the bloody rivalry of two brothers, Palemon and Arcite, for Emilia; the death of the victor in her loving arms; and her acceptance of the loser after a proper delay. But even heroic love palls after half the 9896 lines; and the English reader may content himself with Chaucer's judicious abbreviation of the story in *The Knight's Tale.*

Early in 1341 Boccaccio abandoned Naples for Florence. Two months later Petrarch arrived at King Robert's court. He basked awhile in the royal shade, and then went on to seek a crown in Rome.

---

* "A young woman is flighty, eager for many lovers; she rates her beauty beyond what the mirror shows; and is proud. . . . She knows neither virtue nor intelligence, always giddy like a leaf in the wind."

III. THE POET LAUREATE

It was a pitiful capital of the world. The papacy having moved to Avignon in 1309, no economic means remained of supporting even such moderate splendor as the city had known in the thirteenth century. The wealth that had trickled from a thousand bishoprics into streams from a dozen states no longer flowed into Rome; no foreign embassies kept palaces there; and rare was the cardinal who showed his face amid the ruins of the Empire and the Church. Christian shrines rivaled classic colonnades in dilapidation; shepherds grazed their flocks on the slopes of the seven hills; beggars roamed the streets and highwaymen lurked along the roads; wives were abducted, nuns were raped, pilgrims were robbed; every man carried arms.[13] The old aristocratic families—Colonna, Orsini, Savelli, Annibaldi, Gaetani, Frangipani—contested with violence and intrigue for political mastery in the oligarchic Senate that ruled Rome. The middle classes were small and weak; and the motley masses, mingled of a score of peoples, lived in a poverty too stupefying to generate self-government. The hold of the absent papacy upon the city was reduced to the theoretical authority of a legate, who was ignored.

Amid this chaos and penury the mutilated remains of a proud antiquity nourished the visions of scholars and the dreams of patriots. Some day, the Romans believed, Rome would again be the spiritual and political capital of the world, and the barbarians beyond the Alps would send imperial tribute as well as Peter's pence. Here and there men could still spare a pittance for art: Pietro Cavallini adorned Santa Maria in Trastevere with remarkable mosaics, and in Santa Cecilia he inaugurated a Roman school of fresco painting almost as important as Duccio's in Siena or Giotto's in Florence. Even in Rome's destitution poets sang, forgetting the present for the past. After Padua and Prato had restored Domitian's rite of placing a laurel wreath upon the brow of a favorite bard, the Senate thought it befitting the traditional primacy of Rome to crown the man who by universal consent was the leading poet of his nation and his time.

And so, on April 8, 1341, a colorful procession of youths and senators escorted Petrarch—clad in the purple robe that King Robert had given him —to the steps of the Capitol; there a laurel crown was laid upon his head, and the aged Senator Stefano Colonna pronounced a eulogy. From that day Petrarch had new fame and new enemies; rivals plucked at his laurels with their pens, but kings and popes gladly received him at their courts.

Soon Boccaccio would rank him with "the illustrious ancients"; and Italy, proud of his renown, proclaimed that Virgil had been born again.

What sort of man was he at this apex of his curve? In his youth he had been handsome, and vain of his looks and clothes; in later years he laughed at his once meticulous ritual of toilette and dress, and curling of the hair, and squeezing of the feet into fancy shoes. In middle age he grew a bit stout and doubled his chin, but his face had still the charm of refinement and animation. He remained vain to the end, merely pluming himself on his achievements instead of his appearance; but this is a fault that only the greatest saints can shun. His letters, so fascinating and brilliant, would have been more so without their sham modesty and honest pride. Like all of us he relished applause; he longed for fame, for literary "immortality"; so early, in this presage of the Renaissance, he struck one of its most sustained notes, the thirst for glory. He was a little jealous of his rivals, and descended to answer their slurs. He fretted some (though he denied it) at Dante's popularity; he shuddered at Dante's ferocity as Erasmus would at Luther's crudity; but he suspected that there was something in the dour Florentine too deep to be fathomed by a facile pen. Himself now half French in spirit, he was too urbane to curse half the world; he lacked the passion that exalted and exhausted Italy.

Equipped with several ecclesiastical benefices, he was affluent enough to despise wealth, and timid enough to like the literary life.

> There is no lighter burden, nor more agreeable, than a pen. Other pleasures fail us, or wound us while they charm; but the pen we take up rejoicing, and lay down with satisfaction; for it has the power to advantage not only its lord and master but many others as well, even though they be not born for thousands of years to come. . . . As there is none among earthly delights more noble than literature, so there is none more lasting, none gentler or more faithful; none that accompanies its possessor through the vicissitudes of life at so small a cost of effort or anxiety.[14]

Yet he speaks of his "varying moods, which were rarely happy and usually despondent."[15] To be a great writer he had to be sensitive to beauty in form and sound, in nature and woman and man; that is, he had to suffer more than most of us from the noises and deformities of the world. He loved music, and played the lute well. He admired fine painting, and numbered Simone Martini among his friends. Women must have attracted him, for at times he spoke of them with almost anchoritic fear. After forty, he assures us, he never touched a woman carnally. "Great must be the powers of both body and mind," he wrote, "that may suffice both to literary activity and to a wife."[16]

He offered no novel philosophy. He rejected Scholasticism as vain logic-chopping far removed from life. He challenged the infallibility of Aristotle, and dared to prefer Plato. He went back from Aquinas and Duns Scotus to the Scriptures and the Fathers, and relished the melodious piety of Augustine and the Stoic Christianity of Ambrose; however, he quoted Cicero and Seneca as reverently as he cited the saints, and drew his arguments for Christianity most often from pagan texts. He smiled at the discord of philosophers, among whom he found "no more agreement than among clocks."[17] "Philosophy," he complained, "aims only at hair-splitting, subtle distinctions, quibbles of words."[18] Such a discipline could make clever debaters, but hardly wise men. He laughed at the high degree of Master and Doctor with which such studies were crowned, and marveled how a ceremony could make a pundit out of a fool. Almost in modern terms he rejected astrology, alchemy, demoniac possession, prodigies, auguries, dream prophecies, and the miracles of his time.[19] He had the courage to praise Epicurus[20] in an age when that name was used as a synonym for atheist. Now and then he spoke like a skeptic, professing Cartesian doubt: "Distrustful of my own faculties . . . I embrace doubt itself as truth . . . affirming nothing, and doubting all things except those in which doubt is sacrilege."[21]

Apparently he made this exception in all sincerity. He expressed no doubt as to any dogma of the Church; he was too genial and comfortable to be a heretic. He composed several devotional works, and wondered had it not been better for him, like his brother, to ease his way into heaven through monastic peace. He had no use for the near-atheism of the Averroists in Bologna and Padua. Christianity seemed to him an indisputable moral advance upon paganism, and he hoped that men would find it possible to be educated without ceasing to be Christians.

The election of a new pope, Clement VI (1342), made it advisable for Petrarch to return to Avignon and present his compliments and expectations. Following the precedent of awarding some benefices—i.e., the income from ecclesiastical properties—for the support of writers and artists, Clement gave the poet a priorate near Pisa, and in 1346 made him a canon of Parma. In 1343 he sent him on a mission to Naples, and there Petrarch met one of the most unruly rulers of the age.

Robert the Wise had just died, and his granddaughter Joanna I had inherited his throne and dominions, including Provence and therefore Avignon. To please her father she had married her cousin Andrew, son of the king of Hungary. Andrew thought he should be king as well as consort; Joanna's lover, Louis of Taranto, slew him (1345), and married the Queen. Andrew's brother Louis, succeeding to the throne of Hungary, marched his army into Italy, and took Naples (1348). Joanna fled to Avignon, and sold that city to the papacy for 80,000 florins ($2,000,000?); Clement declared her innocent, sanctioned her marriage, and ordered the invader back to Hungary. King Louis ignored the order, but the Black Death (1348) so withered his army that he was compelled to withdraw. Joanna regained her throne (1352), and ruled in splendor and vice until deposed by Pope Urban VI (1380); a year later she was captured by Charles, Duke of Durazzo, and in 1382 she was put to death.

Petrarch touched this bloody romance only at its source, in the first year of Joanna's reign. He soon resumed his wandering, staying for a while at Parma, then at Bologna, then (1345) at Verona. There, in a church library, he found a manuscript of Cicero's lost letters to Atticus, Brutus, and Quintus. In Liége he had already (1333) disentombed Cicero's speech *Pro Archia*—a paean to poetry. These were among the most fruitful explorations in the Renaissance discovery of antiquity.

Verona, in Petrarch's time, might have been classed among the major powers of Italy. Proud of her antiquity and her Roman theater (where one may still, of a summer evening, hear opera under the stars), enriched by the trade that came over the Alps and down the Adige, Verona rose under the Scala family to a height where she threatened the commercial supremacy of Venice. After the death of the terrible Ezzelino (1260) the commune chose Mastino della Scala as podesta; Mastino was assassinated in due course (1277), but his brother and successor Alberto firmly established the rule of the Scaligeri ("ladder bearers," from the apt emblem of a climbing family), and inaugurated the heyday of Verona's history. During his reign the Dominicans began to build the lovely church of Sant' Anastasia; an obscure copyist unearthed the lost poems of Catullus, Verona's most famous son; and the Guelf family of the Capelletti fought the Ghibelline family of the Montechi, never dreaming that they would become Shakespeare's Capulets and Montagues. The strongest and not the least noble of the Scala "despots" was Can Grande della Scala, who made his court an asylum for exiled Ghibellines and a haven for poets and scholars; there Dante for several years indignantly climbed the shaky stairs of patronage. But Can Grande brought Vicenza, Padua, Treviso, Belluno, Feltre, and

Cividale under his power; Venice saw herself threatened with a strangling encirclement; when Can Grande was succeeded by the less ardent Mastino II she declared war, brought in Florence and Milan as her allies, and forced Verona to surrender all but one of the conquered towns. Can Grande II built the majestic Scaligero Bridge over the Adige, with an arch whose span of 160 feet was then the largest in the world. He was assassinated by his brother Consignorio, who followed this fratricide with a wise and beneficent rule, and built the most ornate of the famous tombs of the Scaligers. His sons divided the throne and quarreled to the death; and in 1387 Verona and Vicenza were absorbed into the duchy of Milan.

IV. RIENZO'S REVOLUTION

Back in Avignon and Vaucluse (1345-7), Petrarch, still enjoying the friendship of the Colonnas, rejoiced to hear that revolution had flared up in Rome, and that the son of a tavern keeper and a washerwoman[22] had deposed the Colonnas and other aristocrats from power, and had restored the glorious republic of the Scipios, the Gracchi, and Arnold of Brescia.

Niccola di Rienzo Gabrini, known by the economy of popular speech as Cola di Rienzo, and by a careless posterity as Rienzi, had met Petrarch in 1343 when, as a young notary of thirty years' age, he had come to Avignon to acquaint Clement VI with the dire condition of Rome, and to solicit for the Roman people the support of the papacy against the feuding, marauding nobles who dominated the capital. Clement, though skeptical, had sent him back with encouragement and florins, hoping to use the fervent lawyer in the recurrent conflict of the popes with the aristocracy.

Rienzo, like Petrarch, had had his imagination fired by the ruins and classics of Rome. Dressed in the white toga of an ancient senator, and speaking with the ardor of the Gracchi and almost the eloquence of Cicero, he pointed to the remains of the majestic forums and colossal baths, and reminded the Romans of the time when consuls or emperors, from these hills, had given laws and order *urbi et orbi*, to the city and to the world; and he challenged them to seize the government, to restore the popular assembly, and to elect a tribune strong enough to protect them against the usurping nobility. The poor listened in awe; merchants wondered might this potential tribune make Rome safe for industry and trade; aristocrats laughed, and made Rienzo the butt of their dinner jollity. He promised to hang a selection of them when the revolution came.

To their consternation it came. On May 20, 1347 a concourse of Romans crowded to the Capitol. Rienzo appeared before them escorted by the bishop of Orvieto as vicar of the pope; he proclaimed the restoration of the Republic and a distribution of alms; they elected him dictator, and at a later meeting allowed him to take the old popular title of tribune. The aged Senator Stefano Colonna protested; Cola ordered him and the other nobles to leave the city; furious, but respecting the armed revolutionaries, they withdrew to their country estates. Delirious with success, Rienzo began to speak of himself as the divinely inspired "Illustrious Redeemer of the Holy Roman Republic by the authority of . . . Jesus Christ."[23]

His administration was excellent. Food prices were regulated to check profiteering; surplus corn was stored in the granaries; work was begun to drain the malarial marshes and put the Campagna under cultivation. New courts dealt out justice with impartial severity; a monk and a baron were beheaded for equal felonies; a former senator was hanged for robbing a merchant vessel; the cutthroats hired by noble factions were arrested; a court of conciliation pacified in a few months 1800 feuds. Aristocrats accustomed to being their own law were shocked to find themselves held responsible for crimes committed on their estates; some paid heavy fines; Pietro Colonna, dripping dignity, was led on foot to jail. Judges guilty of malfeasance were exposed in public pillories. Peasants tilled their fields in unwonted security and peace; merchants and pilgrims en route to Rome kissed the insignia of the resurrected Republic that made the highways safe after half a century of brigandage.[24] All Italy marveled at this intrepid transformation, and Petrarch raised to Rienzo a paean of gratitude and praise.

Seizing his opportunity with bold statesmanship, the tribune despatched envoys throughout the peninsula, inviting the cities to send representatives who would form a great parliament to unite and govern "the whole of sacred Italy" in a federation of municipalities, and to make Rome again the capital of the world. To a preliminary council of judges gathered from all Italy he submitted a question: might the Roman Republic, now reconstituted, rightfully reclaim all the privileges and powers that in its decay had been delegated to other authorities? Answered in the affirmative, Rienzo put through the popular assembly a law restoring to the Republic all such grants of power. This grandiose declaration, sweeping away a millennium of donations, abdications, and coronations, threatened alike the Holy Roman Empire, the autonomous cities, and the temporal power of the Church. Twenty-five communes sent representatives to Rienzo's parliament, but the major city-states—Venice, Florence, Milan—hesitated to submit their sovereignty to a federation. Clement VI was pleased with the tribune's piety, his formal sharing of his authority with the bishop of Orvieto, the protection he gave to pilgrims, the prospects he held out of a lucrative jubilee in 1350; but—he began to wonder—was not this sanguine republican an impractical idealist who would outreach himself to ruin?

Amazing and pitiful was the collapse of the noble dream. Power, like freedom, is a test that only a sober intelligence can meet. Rienzo was too great an orator to be a realistic statesman; he came to believe his own magnificent phrases, promises, and claims; he was poisoned by his own periods. When the federative assembly met (August, 1347), he had arranged that it should begin by conferring knighthood upon him. That evening he proceeded with his escort to the baptistery of St. John Lateran, and plunged bodily into the great basin wherein, according to legend, Constantine had washed away his paganism and his sins; then, clad in white, he slept through the night on a public couch set up amid the pillars of the church. On the morrow he issued to the assembly and the world a decree declaring all the cities of Italy to be free, endowing them with Roman citizenship, and reserving exclusively to the people of Rome and Italy the authority to elect an emperor. Drawing his sword, he flourished it in three directions, saying, as the representative of Rome, "That belongs to me, that to me, and that." He began now to indulge in ostentatious extravagance. He rode about on a white horse under a royal banner, preceded by one hundred armed men, and dressed in a white silk robe with fringes of gold.[25] When Stefano Colonna twitted him about the gold fringe he announced that the nobles were conspiring against him (which was probably true), ordered the arrest of several, had them led in chains to the Capitol, proposed to the assembly that they should be beheaded, relented, pardoned them, and ended by appointing them to offices of state in the Campagna. They rewarded him by raising a force of mercenaries against the Republic; the city's militia went out to meet them, and defeated them; and Stefano Colonna and his son died in the battle (November 20, 1347).

Rienzo, exalted by success, more and more ignored and thrust aside the papal representative whom he had associated with himself in office and authority. Cardinals from Italy and from France warned Clement that a unified Italy—and much more an empire ruled from Rome—would make the Italian Church a prisoner of the state. On October 7 Clement commissioned his legate Bertrand de Deux to offer Rienzo a choice between deposition and the restriction of his powers to the secular affairs of the city of Rome. After some resistance Cola yielded; he promised obedience to the

Pope, and withdrew the edicts that had annulled imperial and papal privileges. Unmollified, Clement resolved to unseat the incalculable tribune.
On December 3 he published a bull stigmatizing Cola as a criminal and a
heretic, and called upon the Romans to banish him. The legate suggested
that if this should not be done no jubilee would be proclaimed. Meanwhile
the nobles had raised another army, which now advanced upon Rome.
Rienzo had the tocsin rung to call the people to arms. Only a few came;
many resented the taxes he had levied; some preferred the profits of a jubilee to the responsibilities of freedom. As the forces of the aristocracy neared
the Capitol Rienzo's wonted courage waned; he discarded the insignia of
his office, said good-by to his friends, broke into tears, and shut himself up
in the Castello Sant' Angelo (December 15, 1347). The triumphant nobles
re-entered their city palaces, and the papal legate named two of them as
senators to rule Rome.

Unmolested by the nobles but still under the ban of the Church, Rienzo
fled to Naples, and then to the mountain forests of the Abruzzi near Sul-
mona; there he donned the garb of a penitent, and for two years lived as
an anchorite. Then, surviving a thousand hardships and tribulations, he
made his way, secretly and in disguise, through Italy and the Alps and
Austria to the Emperor Charles IV at Prague. He pronounced before him
an angry indictment of the popes; to their absence from Rome he attributed
the anarchy and poverty of that city, and to their temporal power and
policy the abiding division of Italy. Charles rebuked him and defended the
popes; but when Clement demanded that Cola be sent as a papal prisoner
to Avignon Charles kept him in protective confinement in a fortress on the
Elbe. After a year of unbearable inactivity and isolation Cola asked to be
sent to the papal court. On his journey to Avignon crowds flocked to see
him, and gallant knights offered to guard him with their swords. On August 10, 1352, he reached Avignon in such miserable raiment that all men
pitied him. He asked for Petrarch, who was at Vaucluse; the poet responded by issuing to the people of Rome a clarion call to protect the man
who had offered them liberty.

> To the Roman people . . . invincible . . . conquerors of nations!
> . . . Your former tribune is now a captive in the power of strangers;
> and—a sad spectacle indeed!—like a nocturnal thief or a traitor to his
> country, he pleads his cause in chains. The highest of earthly
> tribunals refuses him the opportunity of a legitimate defense. . . .
> Rome assuredly does not merit such treatment. Her citizens, once
> inviolable by alien law . . . are now indiscriminately maltreated; and

this is done not only without the guilt that attaches to a crime, but even with the high praise of virtue. . . . He is accused not of betraying but of defending liberty; he is guilty not of surrendering but of holding the Capitol. The supreme crime with which he is charged, and which merits expiation on the scaffold, is that he dared affirm that the Roman Empire is still at Rome, and in possession of the Roman people. O impious age! O preposterous jealousy, malevolence without precedent! What dost thou, O Christ! ineffable and incorruptible judge of all? Where are thine eyes with which thou art wont to scatter the clouds of human misery? . . . Why dost thou not, with thy forked lightning, put an end to this unholy trial?[26]

Clement did not ask for Cola's death, but ordered him kept in custody in the tower of the papal palace at Avignon. While Rienzo studied Scripture and Livy there, a new tribune, Francesco Baroncelli, seized power in Rome, banished the nobles, flouted the papal legate, and allied himself with the Ghibelline supporters of the emperors against the popes. Clement's successor, Innocent VI, released Cola, and sent him to Italy as an aide to Cardinal Albornoz, whom he charged with restoring the papal authority in Rome. As the subtle cardinal and the subdued dictator neared the capital a revolt was staged; Baroncelli was deposed and killed, and the Romans turned over the city to Albornoz. The populace welcomed Rienzo with arches of triumph and joyful acclamations in crowded streets. Albornoz appointed him senator, and delegated to him the secular government of Rome (1353).

But years of imprisonment had fattened the body, broken the courage, and dulled the mind of the once brilliant and fearless tribune. His policies cleaved to the papal line, and shunned the grand emprises of his younger reign. The nobility still hated him, and the proletariat, seeing in him now a cautious conservative cured of Utopia, turned against him as disloyal to their cause. When the Colonna declared war upon him, and besieged him in Palestrina, his unpaid troops verged on mutiny; he borrowed money to pay them, raised taxes to redeem the debt, and alienated the middle class. Hardly two months after his return to power a revolutionary mob marched to the Capitol shouting "Long live the people! Death to the traitor Cola di Rienzo!" He came out of his palace in knightly armor, and tried to control the crowd with eloquence. But the rebels drowned his voice with noise, and showered him with missiles; an arrow struck him in the head, and he withdrew into the palace. The mob set fire to the doors, broke through them, and plundered the rooms. Hiding in one of these, Rienzo hastily cut off his beard, donned a porter's cloak, and piled some bedding upon his head. Emerging, he passed through part of the crowd unrecognized. But his gold bracelet betrayed him, and he was led as a prisoner to the steps of the Capitol, where he himself had condemned men to death. He asked for a hearing, and began to move the people with his speech; but an artisan fearful of eloquence cut him short with a sword thrust in the stomach. A hundred demiheroes plunged their knives into his dead body. The bloody corpse was dragged through the streets, and was hung up like carrion at a butcher's stall. It remained there two days, a target for public contumely and urchins' stones.[27]

V. THE WANDERING SCHOLAR

Rienzo failed to restore ancient Rome, which was dead to all but poetry; Petrarch succeeded in restoring Roman literature, which had never died. He had so openly supported Cola's revolt that he had forfeited the favor of the Colonna in Avignon. For a time he thought of joining Rienzo in Rome; he was as far on the way as Genoa when he heard that the tribune's position and conduct were deteriorating. He changed his course to Parma (1347). He was in Italy when the Black Death came, taking many of his friends, and killing Laura in Avignon. In 1348 he accepted the invitation of Iacopo II da Carrara to be his guest in Padua.

The city had a burdensome antiquity; it was already hundreds of years old when Livy was born there in 59 B.C. It became a free commune in 1174, suffered the tyranny of Ezzelino (1237-56), recovered its independence, sang litanies to liberty, and subjected Vicenza to its domination. Attacked and almost overcome by Can Grande della Scala of Verona, it abandoned its freedom and chose as dictator Iacopo I da Carrara (1318), a man as hard as the marble that bore his name. Later members of the family succeeded to his power by inheritance or assassination. Petrarch's host seized the reins in 1345 by murdering his predecessor, tried to atone by good government, but was stabbed to death after four years of rule. Francesco I da Carrara (1350-89), in a remarkable reign of almost forty years, raised Padua to a passing rivalry with Milan, Florence, and Venice. He made the mistake of joining Genoa against Venice in the bitter war of 1378; Venice won, and subjected Padua to her rule (1404).

Meanwhile the city contributed more than its share to the cultured life of Italy. The majestic church of St. Anthony, known affectionately as Il Santo, was completed in 1307. The great Salone, or Sala della Ragione

(Hall of Parliament), was repaired in 1306 by the monastic architect Fra Giovanni Eremitano, and still stands. The Reggia, or Royal Palace (1345f), had 400 rooms, many with frescoes that were the pride of the Carraresi; nothing remains of them but a tower whose celebrated clock first chimed in 1364. At the beginning of the century an ambitious merchant, Enrico Scrovegni, bought a palace in the old Roman amphitheater known as the Arena, and summoned Italy's most famous sculptor, Giovanni Pisano, and her most famous painter, Giotto, to decorate the chapel of his new home (1303-5); as a result the little Arena Chapel is now known throughout the educated world. Here the genial Giotto painted half a hundred murals, roundels, and medallions, telling again the wondrous story of the Virgin and her Son, surrounding the main frescoes with the heads of prophets and saints, and with ample female forms symbolizing the virtues and vices of mankind. Over the inner portal his pupils, with half-hearted seriousness, depicted the Last Judgment in a carnal confusion of gargoyle-like grotesques. Mantegna, decorating a chapel in the near-by church of the Eremitani a century and a half later, may have smiled at the simple draftsmanship, the primitive perspective, the monotonous similarity of faces, poses, and figures, the imperfect sense and command of anatomy, the blonde heaviness of nearly all the figures, as if the Lombards of Padua were still Longobards freshly come from well-fed Germany. But the lovely features of the Virgin in the *Nativity*, the noble head of Jesus in the *Raising of Lazarus*, the stately high priest in *The Wooers*, the calm Christ and coarse Judas of *The Betrayal*, the serene grace, harmonious composition, and developing action of the spacious panorama in color and form, make these paintings—still fresh and clear after six centuries—the first pictorial triumph of the fourteenth century.

Petrarch may have seen the Arena frescoes; certainly he appreciated Giotto, for in his will he left to Francesco da Carrara a Madonna "by that excellent painter, Giotto, a picture whose beauty . . . surprises the masters of the art."[28] But at the time he was more interested in literature than in art. He must have been stimulated by hearing that Albertino Mussato, a humanist even before Petrarch, had been crowned as Padua's poet laureate in 1314 for writing a Latin drama, *Ecerinis*, in the style of Seneca; this, so far as we know, was the first Renaissance play. Surely Petrarch visited the university that was the city's noble pride. It was at this time the most celebrated school in Italy, rivaling Bologna as a center of legal training, and Paris as a hotbed of philosophy. Petrarch was shocked by the frank "Averroism" of some Paduan professors, who questioned the immortality of the individual soul, and spoke of Christianity as a useful superstition privately discarded by educated men.

In 1348 we find our restless poet at Mantua, then at Ferrara. In 1350 he joined the flow of pilgrims bound for the jubilee in Rome. On the way he visited Florence for the first time, and established a cordial friendship with Boccaccio. Thereafter, said Petrarch, they "shared a single heart."[29] In 1351, on Boccaccio's urging, the Florentine Signory repealed the edict that had confiscated Ser Petracco's property, and sent Boccaccio to Padua to offer Petrarch a money recompense and a professorship in the University of Florence. When he rejected the offer Florence repealed the repeal.

VI. GIOTTO

It is difficult to love medieval Florence,* she was so hard and bitter in industry and politics; but it is easy to admire her, for she devoted her wealth to the creation of beauty. There, in the very youth of Petrarch, the Renaissance was in full swing.

It developed in a stimulating atmosphere of business competition, family feuds, and private violence unparalleled in the rest of Italy. The population was divided by class war, and each class itself was split into factions merciless in victory and vengeful in defeat. At any moment the defection of a few families from one *parte* to another would tip the scales of power. At any moment some discontented element might take to arms and try to oust the government; if successful it exiled the leaders of the beaten party, usually confiscated their property, sometimes burned down their homes. But this economic strife and political agitation were not all of Florentine life. Though more devoted to their party than to their city, the citizens had a proud civic sense, and spent much of their substance for the common good. Rich individuals or guilds would pay for paving a street, constructing sewers, improving the water supply, housing a public market, establishing or improving churches, hospitals, or schools. An esthetic sense as keen as that of the ancient Greeks or the modern French dedicated public and private funds to the embellishment of the city with architecture, sculpture, and painting, and to the interior adornment of homes with these and a dozen minor arts. Florentine pottery led all Europe in this period. Florentine goldsmiths decorated necks, bosoms, hands, wrists, girdles, altars, tables, armor, coins with jewelry or intarsia or engraved or embossed designs unsurpassed in that or any other age.

---

* The term *medieval* is used in these volumes as denoting European history and civilization between A.D. 325 and 1492—between Constantine and Columbus.

And now the artist, reflecting the new emphasis on personal ability or *virtù*, stood out from the guild or the group, and identified his product with his name. Niccolò Pisano had already freed sculpture from limitation to ecclesiastical motives, and subservience to architectural lines, by uniting a sturdy naturalism with the physical idealism of the Greeks. His pupil Andrea Pisano cast for the Florentine Baptistery (1300-6) two bronze half-doors depicting in twenty-eight reliefs the development of the arts and sciences since Adam delved and Eve span; and these fourteenth-century works survive comparison with Ghiberti's fifteenth-century "doors to Paradise" on the same building. In 1334 the Florentine Signory approved the designs of Giotto for a tower to bear the weight and scatter the chimes of the cathedral bells, and a decree was passed, in the spirit of the age, that "the campanile should be built so as to exceed in magnificence, height, and excellence of workmanship everything of the kind achieved of old by the Greeks and Romans when at the zenith of their greatness."[30] The loveliness of the tower lies not in its square and undistinguished form (which Giotto had wished to top with a spire), but in the Gothic traceried windows, and the reliefs, in colored marble, carved on the lower panels by Giotto, Andrea Pisano, and Luca della Robbia. After Giotto's death the work was carried on by Pisano, Donatello, and Francesco Talenti, to whom the tower owes the culminating beauty of its highest arcade (1359).

Giotto di Bondone dominated the painting of the fourteenth century as Petrarch dominated its poetry; and the artist rivaled the poet in ubiquity. Painter, sculptor, architect, capitalist, man of the world, equally ready with artistic conceptions, practical devices, and humorous repartee, Giotto moved through life with the confidence of a Rubens, and spawned masterpieces in Florence, Rome, Assisi, Ferrara, Ravenna, Rimini, Faenza, Pisa, Lucca, Arezzo, Padua, Verona, Naples, Urbino, Milan. He seems never to have worried about obtaining commissions; and when he went to Naples it was as the palace guest of the king. He married and had ugly children, but this did not disturb the placid grace of his compositions, or the cheerful tenor of his life. He leased looms to artisans at twice the ordinary rental;[31] however, he told the story of St. Francis, the apostle of poverty, in one of the outstanding works of the Renaissance.

He was still a youth when Cardinal Stefaneschi called him to Rome to design a mosaic—the celebrated *Navicella*, or Little Ship, showing Christ saving Peter from the waves; it survives, considerably altered, in the vestibule of St. Peter's, inconspicuous above and behind the portico colonnade. It was probably the same Cardinal who commissioned the polyptych preserved in the Vatican. These products show an immature Giotto, vigorous in conception, weak in execution. Possibly a study of Pietro Cavallini's mosaics in Santa Maria in Trastevere, and his fresco in Santa Cecilia, helped to form Giotto in those Roman years; while the naturalistic sculpture of Niccolò Pisano may have moved him to turn his eyes from the works of his predecessors to the actual features and feelings of living women and men. "Giotto appeared," said Leonardo da Vinci, "and drew what he saw,"[32] and the Byzantine petrifaction faded from Italian art.

Moving to Padua, Giotto painted in three years the famous frescoes of the Arena Chapel. Perhaps at Padua he met Dante; he may have known him in Florence; Vasari, always interesting and sometimes accurate, calls Dante the "close companion and friend" of Giotto,[33] and ascribes to Giotto a portrait of Dante that formed part of a fresco in the Florentine Bargello or Palace of the Podesta. The poet, with exceptional amiability, celebrates the painter in *The Divine Comedy*.[34]

In 1318 two banking families, the Bardi and the Peruzzi, engaged Giotto to tell in frescoes the stories of St. Francis, St. John the Baptist, and St. John the Evangelist, in the chapels that they were dedicating in the church of Santa Croce in Florence. These paintings were whitewashed in later years; they were uncovered in 1853 and were repainted, so that only the drawing and the composition are Giotto's. A like fate befell the celebrated frescoes in the double church of St. Francis at Assisi. That hilltop shrine is one of the major goals of pilgrimage in Italy, and those visitors who come to view the paintings attributed to Cimabue and Giotto seem as numerous as those who come to honor or solicit the saint. It was probably Giotto who planned the subjects and drew the outlines for the lower frescoes of the Upper Church; for the rest he seems to have confined himself to supervising the work of his pupils. These frescoes of the Upper Church narrate in detail the life of St. Francis; Christ Himself had rarely received so extensive a painted biography. They are masterly in their conception and composition, pleasant in their gentle mood and flowing harmony; they end once and for all the hieratic stiffness of Byzantine forms; but they lack depth and force and individuality, they are graceful tableaux without the color of passion or the blood of life. The frescoes in the Lower Church, less mangled by time, mark an advance in Giotto's power. He seems to have been directly responsible for the pictures in the Magdalen Chapel, while his aides painted the allegories illustrating the Franciscan vows of poverty, obedience, and chastity. In this duplex church the legend of Francis gave a mighty stimulus, almost a new birth, to Italian painting, and generated a tradition ideally completed in the work of the Dominican Fra Angelico.

All in all, Giotto's work was a revolution. We feel his faults because we know of the painting skills that were developed by the movement that he began. His drawing, modeling, perspective, and anatomy are painfully inadequate; art, like the medical science of Giotto's time, was just beginning to dissect the human body, to learn the place, structure, and function of each muscle, bone, tendon, nerve; men like Mantegna and Masaccio would master these elements, and Michelangelo would perfect them, almost make a fetish of them; but in Giotto's day it was still unusual to study, scandalous to represent, the nude. What is it, then, that makes the work of Giotto in Padua and Assisi a landmark in the history of art? It is the rhythmic composition, drawing the eye from every angle to the center of interest; the dignity of quiet motion, the soft and luminous coloring, the majestic flow of the narrative, the restraint of expression even in deep feeling, the grandeur of the calm that bathes these troubled scenes; and, now and then, the naturalistic portraiture of men, women, and children not as studied in past art but as seen and felt in the movement of life. These were the components of Giotto's triumph over Byzantine rigidity and gloom, these were the secrets of his enduring influence. For a century after him Florentine art lived on his example and his inspiration.

In his wake came two generations of Giotteschi, who imitated his themes and style, but rarely touched his excellence. His godson and pupil, Taddeo Gaddi, almost inherited art; Taddeo's father, and three of Taddeo's five sons, were painters; the Italian Renaissance, like German music, tended to run in families, and prospered there through the transmission and accumulation of techniques in homes, studios, and schools. Taddeo began as an apprentice to Giotto; by 1347 he was at the head of Florentine painters; even then, however, he signed himself devotedly "Discepol di Giotto il buon maestro."[35] He became so rich through his industry as painter and architect that his descendants could afford to be patrons of art.

An impressive work long attributed to him but now ascribed to Andrea da Firenze shows how, in this first century of the Renaissance, Italy was still medieval. In the Capella degli Spagnuoli, or Chapel of the Spaniards, in the church of Santa Maria Novella, the Dominican friars set up about 1370 a pictorial apotheosis of their famous philosopher. St. Thomas Aquinas, comfortably substantial but too devoted to be proud, stands in triumph, with the heretics Arius, Sabellius, and Averroes groveling at his feet; around him Moses, Paul, John the Evangelist, and other saints seem but accessories; below them fourteen figures symbolize seven sacred and seven profane sciences—Donatus grammar, Cicero rhetoric, Justinian law, Euclid geometry, and so on. The thought is still completely medieval; only the art, in design and color, shows the emergence of a new age from the old. The transition was so gradual that not for a century yet would men feel themselves to be in a different world.

The advance in technique is clearer in Orcagna, who stands second only to Giotto among the Italian artists of the fourteenth century. Named originally Andrea di Cione, he was called Arcagnolo—Archangel—by his admiring contemporaries, and lazy tongues shortened the appellation to Orcagna. Though often listed among Giotto's followers, he was rather a pupil of the sculptor Andrea Pisano. Like the greatest geniuses of the Renaissance he was a master of many arts. As a painter he made a colorful altarpiece of *Christ Enthroned* for the Strozzi Chapel in Santa Maria Novella, while his elder brother Nardo executed on the walls vivid frescoes of heaven and hell (1354-7). As an architect he designed the Certosa or Carthusian monastery near Florence, famous for its graceful cloisters and its Acciaiuoli tombs. As architects and sculptors he and his brother executed the ornate tabernacle in the Or(atory) San Michele in Florence. A picture of the Virgin there was believed to work miracles; after the Black Death of 1348 the votive offerings of survivors enriched the fraternity that managed the building, and it was decided to house the picture in a sumptuous shrine of marble and gold. The Cioni designed it as a miniature Gothic cathedral, with columns, pinnacles, statues, reliefs, precious metal, and costly stone; it is a jewel of *trecento* decoration.* Andrea, acclaimed for it, was appointed *capomaestro* at Orvieto, and shared in designing the façade of the cathedral. In 1362 he returned to Florence, and worked there on the great *duomo* till his death.

The immense fame of Santa Maria del Fiore—the largest church that had as yet been built in Italy—had been begun by Arnolfo di Cambio in 1296. A succession of masters—Giotto, Andrea Pisano, Francesco Talenti, and many others —labored on it till our time; its present façade dates from 1887; even now the cathedral is incomplete, and must in good measure be rebuilt by every century. Architecture was the least successful of the arts in Renaissance Italy; it took half-heartedly from the north some elements of Gothic like the pointed arch, combined them with classic columns, and sometimes, as in Florence, topped the whole with a Byzantine dome. The mixture was incongruous and—barring some small churches by Bramante—lacked unity and grace. The façade of Orvieto and Siena were superb displays of sculpture and mosaic rather than honest architecture; and the accentuation of horizontal lines by the alternating strata of black and white marble in the walls depresses eye and soul, when the very meaning of the church should have been a prayer or paean rising to the

---

* The Italians call the fourteenth century *trecento*, three hundred; the fifteenth century *quattrocento*, four hundred; the sixteenth century *cinquecento*, etc.

skies. Santa Maria del Fiore—as the Florentine cathedral was called after 1412 from the lily in the heraldic emblem of the city—is hardly a flower; it is, but for Brunellesco's illustrious dome, a cavern, whose dark vacuity might be the mouth of Dante's Inferno instead of a vestibule to God.

It was the inexhaustible Arnolfo di Cambio who in 1294 began the Franciscan church of Santa Croce, or the Holy Cross, and in 1298 the loveliest structure in Florence, the Palazzo della Signoria, known to later generations as the Palazzo Vecchio. The church was finished in 1442 except for the façade (1863); the Palace of the Signory, or Old Palace, was completed in its main features by 1314. Those were the years that saw the banishment of Dante and Petrarch's father; factional strife was in its heyday; so Arnolfo built for the Signory a fortress rather than a palace, and designed its roof with machicolated battlements; while the unique campanile, by the diverse ringing of its bell, served to call the citizens to parliament or to arms. Here the city fathers (*priori, signori*) not only governed but lived; and the temper of the time appears in the law that during their two months of office they were not to leave the building on any pretext whatever. In 1345 Neri di Fioravante spanned the Arno with one of the world's famous bridges, the Ponte Vecchio, now cracked with age and many wars, but still precariously bearing impatient traffic and twenty-two shops. Around these proud achievements of the Florentine civic spirit, in the narrow streets that led from the cathedral and Signoria squares, rose the as yet modest mansions of the worried rich, the noble churches that transmuted merchants' gold into art, the noisy shops of traders and artisans, and the crowded tenements of an industrious, rebellious, excitable, intelligent populace. In that frenzy of egos the Renaissance was born.

VII. "THE DECAMERON"

It was in Florence that Italian literature achieved its first and greatest triumphs. There Guinizelli and Cavalcanti, in the late thirteenth century, gave the sonnet its finished form; not there, but longing for it, Dante the Florentine struck the first and last true note of Italian epic poetry; there Boccaccio composed the supreme work of Italian prose, and Giovanni Villani wrote the most modern of medieval chronicles. Visiting Rome for the jubilee of 1300, and moved like Gibbon by the ruins of a mighty past, Villani thought for a while of recording its history; then, judging that Rome had been sufficiently commemorated, he turned back to his native haunts, and resolved "to bring into this volume . . . all the events of the city of Florence . . . and give in full the deeds of the Florentines, and briefly the notable affairs of the rest of the world."[36]

He began with the Tower of Babel and ended on the verge of the Black

Death, in which he died; his brother Matteo and his nephew Filippo continued the story to 1365. Giovanni was well prepared; he came of a prosperous mercantile family, commanded a pure Tuscan speech, traveled in Italy, Flanders, and France, served thrice as prior and once as master of the mint. He had for those times an uncommon sense of the economic bases and influences of history; and he was the first to salt his narrative with statistics of social conditions. The first three books of his *Croniche Fiorentine* are mostly legend; but in later books we learn that in 1338 Florence and its hinterland had 105,000 inhabitants, of whom seventeen thousand were beggars and four thousand were on public relief; that there were six primary schools, teaching ten thousand boys and girls, and four high schools, in which six hundred boys and a few girls studied "grammar" (literature) and "logic" (philosophy). Unlike most historians Villani included notices of new books, paintings, buildings; seldom has a city been so directly described in all the departments of its life. Had Villani brought all these phases and details into one united narrative of causes, phenomena, personalities, and effects he would have transformed his chronicle into history.

Settling down in Florence in 1340, Boccaccio continued to pursue woman in life and verse and prose. The *Amorosa Visione* was dedicated to Fiammetta, and recalled in 4400 lines of *terza rima* the happier days of their liaison. In a psychological novel, *Fiammetta*, the bastard princess is made to tell the story of her deviation with Boccaccio; she analyzes the emotions of love, the torments of desire and jealousy and desertion, in Richardsonian detail; and when her conscience rebukes her infidelity she imagines Aphrodite chiding her for cowardice: "Make not thyself so timorous in saying, 'I have a husband, and holy laws and promised faith forbid me these things.' These are but vain conceits and frivolous objections against the power of Eros. For like a strong and mighty prince he plants his eternal laws; not caring for other laws of lower state, he accounts them base and servile rules."[37] Boccaccio, abusing the power of the pen, ends the book by having Fiammetta proclaim, to his glory, that it was he who deserted her, not she who deserted him. Returning to poetry, he sang in the *Ninfale Fiesolano* the love of a shepherd for a priestess of Diana; his triumph is described in fond detail, with some enthusiasm spared for natural scenery. This is almost the working formula of *The Decameron*.

It was shortly after the plague of 1348 that Boccaccio began to write this renowned concatenation of seductive tales. He was now thirty-five; the temperature of desire had fallen from poetry to prose; he could begin to see the humor of the mad pursuit. Fiammetta herself seems to have died in the plague, and Boccaccio was calm enough to use the name that he had given her for one of the least finicky *raconteuses* of his book. Though the whole was not published till 1353, some of it must have been issued in installments, for in the introduction to the Fourth Day the author replies to the criticism that had reproved the earlier narratives. As we have the book now it is a "century" of stories—a full hundred; they were not meant to be read in any great number at one time; published seriatim, they must have provided topics for many a Florentine evening.

The prelude describes the effects, in Florence, of the Black Death that struck all Europe in 1348 and afterward. Born apparently of the fertility and filth of Asiatic populations impoverished by war and weakened by famine, the infection crossed Arabia into Egypt, and the Black Sea into Russia and Byzantium. From Constantinople, Alexandria, and other ports of the Near East the merchants and vessels of Venice, Syracuse, Pisa, Genoa, and Marseille, aided by fleas and rats, brought it to Italy and France.[38] A succession of famine years in western Europe—1333-4, 1337-42, 1345-7—probably sapped the resistance of the poor, who then communicated the disease to all classes.[39] It took two forms: pulmonary, with high fever and spitting of blood, bringing death in three days; or bubonic, with fever, abscesses, and carbuncles, leading to death in five days. Half the population of Italy was carried off in the successive visitations of the plague from 1348 to 1365.[40] A Sienese chronicler wrote, about 1354:

> Neither relatives nor friends nor priests nor friars accompanied the corpses to the grave, nor was the office of the dead recited. . . . In many places of the city trenches were dug, very broad and deep, and into these the bodies were thrown, and covered with a little earth; and thus layer after layer until the trench was full; and then another trench was begun. And I, Agniolo di Tura . . . with my own hands buried five of my children in a single trench; and many others did the like. And many dead were so ill covered that the dogs dug them up and ate them, dispersing their limbs throughout the city. And no bells rang, and nobody wept no matter what his loss, because almost everyone expected death. . . . And people said and believed, "This is the end of the world."[41]

In Florence, according to Matteo Villani, three out of five of the population died between April and September of 1348. Boccaccio estimated the Florentine dead at 100,000, Machiavelli at 96,000;[42] these are transparent exaggerations, since the total population hardly exceeded 100,000. Boccaccio opens *The Decameron* with a frightful description of the plague:

Not only did converse and consorting with the sick give the infection to the sound, but the mere touching of the clothes, or of whatsoever had been touched or used by the sick, appeared of itself to communicate the malady. . . . A thing which had belonged to a man sick or dead of the sickness, being touched by an animal . . . in a brief time killed it . . . of this mine own eyes had experience. This tribulation struck such terror to the hearts of all . . . that brother forsook brother, uncle nephew . . . oftentimes wife husband; nay (what is yet more extraordinary and well nigh incredible), some fathers and mothers refused to visit or tend their very children, as though they had not been theirs. . . . The common people, being altogether untended and unsuccored, sickened by the thousand daily, and died well nigh without recourse. Many breathed their last in the open street, whilst other many, for all they died in their houses, made it known to the neighbors that they were dead rather by the stench of their rotting bodies than otherwise; and of these and others who died the whole city was full. The neighbors, moved more by fear lest the corruption of the dead bodies should imperil themselves than by any charity for the departed . . . brought the bodies forth from the houses and laid them before the doors, where, especially in the morning, those who went about might see corpses without number. Then they fetched biers, and some, in default thereof, they laid upon a board; nor was it only one bier that carried two or three corpses, nor did this happen but once; nay, many might have been counted which contained husband and wife, two or three brothers, father and son, and the like. . . . The thing was come to such a pass that folk reckoned no more of men that died than nowadays they would of goats.[43]

Out of this scene of desolation Boccaccio pictures his *Decameron* as taking form. The plan for the pagan outing is made in "the venerable church of Santa Maria Novella" by "seven young ladies, all knit one to another by friendship or neighborhood or kinship," who had just heard Mass. They ranged between eighteen and twenty-eight years of age. "Each was discreet and of noble blood, fair of favor and well-mannered, and full of honest sprightliness." One proposes that they should lessen their chances of infection by retiring to their country houses, not separately but together, with their servants, moving from one villa to another, "taking such pleasance and diversion as the season may afford. . . . There may we hear the small birds sing, there may we see the hills and plains clad in green and the fields full of corn wave even as doth the sea; there may we see trees, a thousand sorts; and there is the face of heaven more open to the view, the which, angered against us though it be, denieth not unto us its eternal beauties."[44] The suggestion is accepted, but Filomena improves upon it: since "we women are fickle, willful, suspicious, and timorous," it might be well to have some men in the party. Providentially at that moment "there entered the church three young men . . . in whom neither the perversity of the time, nor loss of friends and kinsfolk . . . had availed to cool . . . the fire of love. . . . All were agreeable, well-bred, and they went seeking their supreme solace . . . to see their mistresses, who, as it chanced, were all three among the seven ladies aforesaid." Pampinia recommends that the young gentlemen be invited to join the outing. Neifile fears that this will lead to scandal. Filomena answers: "So but I live honestly, and conscience prick me not of aught, let who will speak to the contrary."

So, on the Wednesday following, they set out, preceded by servants and victuals, to a villa two miles from Florence, "with a goodly and great court-yard in its midst, and galleries and saloons and bedchambers, each in itself most fair, and adorned with jocund paintings; with lawns and grassplots round about, and wondrous-goodly gardens, and wells of very cold water, and cellars full of wines of price."[45] The ladies and gentlemen sleep late, breakfast leisurely, walk in the gardens, dine at length, and amuse themselves by matching stories. It is agreed that each of the ten shall tell a story on each day of the outing. They stay in the country ten days (whence the title of the book, from the Greek *deka hemerai*, ten days); and the result is that Boccaccio's *commedia umana* counters each of Dante's gloomy cantos with a merry tale. Meanwhile a rule forbids any member of the group to "bring in from without any news other than joyous."

The narratives, averaging six pages in length, were seldom original with Boccaccio; they were collected from classical sources, Oriental writers, medieval *gesta*, French *contes* and *fabliaux*, or the folklore of Italy itself. The last and most famous story in the book is that of the patient Griselda, which Chaucer adopted for one of the best and most absurd of *The Canterbury Tales*. The finest of Boccaccio's *novelle* is the ninth of the fifth day —of Federigo, his falcon, and his love, almost as self-sacrificing as Griselda's. The most philosophical is the legend of the three rings (I, 3). Saladin, "Soldan of Babylon," needing money, invites the rich Jew Melchisedek to dinner, and asks him which of the three religions is the best—the Jewish, the Christian, or the Mohammedan. The wise old moneylender, fearing to speak his mind directly, answers with a parable:

> There was once a great man and a rich, who, among other very precious jewels in his treasury, had a goodly and costly ring. . . .

Wishing to leave it in perpetuity to his descendants, he declared that whichever of his sons should, at his death, be found in possession thereof, by his bequest unto him, should be recognized as his heir, and be held by all the others in honor and reverence as chief and head. He to whom the ring was left held a like course with his own descendants, and did even as his father had done. In brief, the ring passed from hand to hand, through many generations, and came at last into the possession of a man who had three goodly and virtuous sons all very obedient to their father, whereof he loved all three alike. The young men knowing the usance of the ring, each desiring to be the most honored among his folk . . . besought his father, who was now an old man, to leave him the ring. . . . The worthy man, who knew not himself how to choose to which he had liefer leave the ring, bethought himself . . . to satisfy all three, and privily let make by a good craftsman other two rings which were so like unto the first that he himself scarce knew which was the true. When he came to die he secretly gave each one of his sons his ring, wherefore each of them, seeking, after their father's death, to occupy the inheritance and the honor and denying it to the others, produced his ring in witness of his right, and the three rings being found so like one another that the true might not be known, the question which was the father's very heir abode pending and yet pendeth. And so I say to you, my lord: of the three Laws given by God the Father to the three peoples, each people deemeth itself to have His inheritance, His true Law and His commandments; but of which in very deed hath them, even as of the rings, the question yet pendeth.

Such a story suggests that in his thirty-seventh year Boccaccio was not a dogmatic Christian. Contrast his tolerance with the bitter bigotry of Dante, who condemns Mohammed to perpetually repeated vivisections in hell.[46] In the second story of *The Decameron* the Jew Jehannat is converted to Christianity by the argument (adapted by Voltaire) that Christianity must be divine, since it has survived so much clerical immorality and simony. Boccaccio makes fun of asceticism, purity, the confessional, relics, priests, monks, friars, nuns, even the canonization of saints. He thinks most monks are hypocrites, and laughs at the "simpletons" who give them alms (VI, 10). One of his most hilarious stories tells how the friar Cipolla, to raise a good collection, promised his audience to display "a very holy relic, one of the angel Gabriel's feathers, which remained in the Virgin Mary's chamber after the Annunciation" (VI, 10). The most obscene of the stories tells how the virile youth Masetto satisfied an entire nunnery (III,

1). In another tale Friar Rinaldo cuckolds a husband; whereupon the narrator asks, "What monks are there that do not do thus?" (VII, 3)

The ladies in *The Decameron* blush a bit at such stories, but enjoy the Rabelaisian-Chaucerian humor; Filomena, a girl of especially nice manners, tells the tale of Rinaldo; and sometimes, says Boccaccio's least happy image, "the ladies kept up such a laughing that you might have drawn all their teeth."[47] Boccaccio had been reared in the loose gaiety of Naples, and most often thought of love in sensual terms; he smiled at chivalric romance, and played Sancho Panza to Dante's Don Quixote. Though twice married he seems to have believed in free love.[48] After recounting a score of stories that would today be unfit for a male gathering, he makes one of the men say to the ladies: "I have noted no act, no word, in fine nothing blameworthy, either on your part or on that of us men." In concluding his book the author acknowledges some criticism of the license he has used, and especially because "I have in sundry places written the truth about the friars." At the same time he congratulates himself on his "long labor, thoroughly accomplished with the aid of the Divine favor."

The Decameron remains one of the masterpieces of world literature. Its fame may be due more to its morals than to its art, but even if immaculate it would have merited preservation. It is perfectly constructed—superior in this respect to *The Canterbury Tales*. Its prose set a standard that Italian literature has never surpassed, a prose sometimes involved or flowery, but for the most part eloquent and vigorous, pungent and vivacious, and clear as a mountain stream. It is a book of the love of life. In the greatest disaster that had befallen Italy in a thousand years Boccaccio could find in his vitals the courage to see beauty, humor, goodness, and joy still walking the earth. At times he was cynical, as in his unmanly satire on women in the *Corbaccio*; but in *The Decameron* he was a hearty Rabelais, relishing the give and take, the rough and tumble, of life and love. Despite caricature and exaggeration the world recognized itself in the book; every European language translated it; Hans Sachs and Lessing, Molière and La Fontaine, Chaucer and Shakespeare, took leaves from it admiringly. It will be enjoyed when all of Petrarch's poetry has entered the twilight realm of the praised unread.

VIII. SIENA

Siena would have challenged the claim of Florence to have begotten the Renaissance. There too the violence of faction raised the temperature of thought, and communal pride nourished art. The woolen industry, the export of Sienese products to the Levant, and the trade of the Via Flaminia between Florence and Rome gave the city a moderate affluence; by 1400 the squares and principal streets were paved with brick or stone; and the poor were rich enough to stage a revolution. In 1371 the woolworkers besieged the Palazzo Pubblico, broke down its doors, expelled the businessmen's government, and set up the rule of the *riformatori*. A few days later an army of two thousand men, fully equipped by the mercantile interests, made its way into the city, invaded the quarters of the proletariat, and slew men, women, and children without discrimination or mercy, spitting some on the lance, hacking others with the sword. The nobility and the lower middle class came to the rescue of the commons, the counterrevolution was defeated, and the reform government gave Siena the most honest administration that the citizens could recall. In 1385 the rich merchants rose again, overthrew the *riformatori*, and expelled four thousand rebel workmen from the city. From that date industry and art declined in Siena.*

It was in this turbulent fourteenth century that Siena reached the zenith of her art. On the west side of the spacious Campo—the main square of the city—rose the Palazzo Pubblico (1288-1309); the adjoining campanile, the Torre de Mangia, rearing its slender height to 334 feet, is the most beautiful tower in Italy. In 1310 the Sienese architect and sculptor Lorenzo Maitani went to Orvieto and designed the lordly façade of the cathedral there; he and other Sienese artists, and Andrea Pisano, engaged in a frenzy of decoration on the portals, pilasters, and pediments, and produced a miracle in marble to commemorate the miracle of Bolsena. In 1377 the great *duomo* of Siena received a similar façade from designs left by Giovanni Pisano, perhaps too ornate, but still one of the wonders of inexhaustible Italy.

Meanwhile a brilliant band of Sienese painters had carried on where Duccio di Buoninsegna had left off. In 1315 Simone Martini was commissioned to decorate the Hall of the Great Council in the Palazzo Pubblico with a *maestà*, i.e., a *Coronation of the Virgin;* for Mary was, in law as well as in theology, the crowned queen of the city, and might properly preside at meetings of the municipal government. The picture dared comparison with the *maestà* that Duccio had painted for the cathedral five years before; it was not so large, nor so overlaid with gold; like that "majesty" it betrayed the Byzantine derivation of Sienese painting by the immobile features and

---

* The revolt of the Sienese workers in 1371, the Ciompi revolt in Florence in 1378, the almost simultaneous rebellion of Wat Tyler in England, and the uprisings in France about 1380 suggest a Continental wave of revolution, and a greater measure of intercommunication and mutual influence, among the working classes in Western Europe, than has generally been supposed.

lifeless pose of its crowded characters; perhaps it made some advance in color and design. But in 1326 Simone went to Assisi; there he studied the frescoes of Giotto; and when he was invited to picture in a chapel of the Lower Church the life of St. Martin he escaped from the stereotyped faces of his earlier work, and achieved a memorable individualization of the great Bishop of Tours. At Avignon he met Petrarch, painted portraits of the poet and Laura, and won an appreciative mention in the *Canzoniere*. These brief lines, said Vasari, "have given more fame to Simone than all his own works have done . . . for a day will come when his paintings will be no more, whereas the writings of such a man as Petrarch endure for all time"; no geologist would be so optimistic. Benedict XII made Simone official painter to the papal court (1339); and in that capacity he illustrated the life of the Baptist in the papal chapel, and of the Virgin and the Saviour in the portico of the cathedral. He died at Avignon in 1344.

That secularization of art which Simone had essayed in his lay portraits was extended by Pietro and Ambrogio Lorenzetti. Perhaps after studying in Florence, Pietro abandoned the sentimental traditions of Sienese painting, and produced a series of altar pictures of unprecedented power, sometimes of savage realism. In the Hall of the Nine (Councilors) in the Palazzo Pubblico Ambrogio painted four famous frescoes (1337-43): *Evil Government*, *The Consequences of Evil Government*, *Good Government*, and *The Consequences of Good Government*. Here the medieval habit of symbolism, superseded by Giotto, is retained; majestic figures represent Siena, Justice, Wisdom, Concord, the Seven Virtues, and Peace—the last reclining gracefully like a Pheidian deity. In *Evil Government* Tyranny is enthroned, and Terror is his vizier; merchants are plundered on the road; faction and violence incarnadine the town. Against the same architectural background *Good Government* shows a population happily busy with handicrafts, amusements, and trade; farmers and merchants lead into the city mules laden with food and goods; children play, maidens dance, viols make silent music; and over the scene a winged spirit flies, figuring Security. Perhaps it was these energetic brothers—or Orcagna, or Francesco Traini —who painted the immense fresco, *The Triumph of Death*, in the Campo Santo at Pisa. A hunting party of lords and ladies richly attired comes upon three open coffins in which royal corpses lie festering; one hunter holds his nose at their smell; above the scene hovers the Angel of Death, wielding an enormous scythe; in the air ministers of grace escort saved souls to paradise, while winged demons drag most of the dead into hell; serpents and black vultures entwine and consume the naked bodies of women and men; and below, kings, queens, princes, bishops, cardinals writhe in the pit of the damned. On a neighboring wall the same authors, in another immense fresco, painted on the left a *Last Judgment*, and on the right a second vision of hell. All the terrors of medieval theology here take physical form; it is Dante's *Inferno* visualized without mercy and without stint.

Siena never emerged from the Middle Ages; there, as in Gubbio, San Gimignano, and Sicily, they survived the Renaissance. They never die, but patiently, subtly bide their time to come again.

IX. MILAN

In 1351 Petrarch returned to Avignon. Probably at Vaucluse he wrote a pretty essay, *De vita solitaria*, lauding the solitude that he could bear as a healing medicine but not as a sustaining food. It was shortly after this return to Avignon that he brought the medical fraternity down upon his head by exhorting Pope Clement VI, who was in failing health, to beware of doctors' prescriptions. "I have always begged my friends, and ordered my servants, never to let any of these doctors' tricks to be tried on my body, but always to do the exact contrary of what they advise."[49] In 1355, exasperated by some therapeutic fiasco, he composed an intemperate *Invective Against a Physician*. He was not much better disposed toward lawyers, "who spend their entire time in disputations . . . . over trival questions. Hear my verdict upon the whole pack of them. Their fame will die with their flesh, and a single grave will suffice for their names and their bones."[50] To make Avignon completely distasteful to him Pope Innocent VI proposed to excommunicate Petrarch as a necromancer, on the ground that the poet was a student of Virgil. Cardinal Talleyrand came to Petrarch's rescue, but the air of saintly ignorance that now perfumed Avignon sickened the laureate. He visited his monk brother Gherardo, wrote a wistful treatise *De otio reliogiosorum (On the Leisure of Monks)*, and toyed with the idea of entering a monastery. But when an invitation came to him to be the palace guest of the dictator of Milan (1353), he accepted with a readiness that shocked his republican friends.

The ruling family in Milan bore the name Visconti from having often filled the post of *vicecomites*, or archiepiscopal judges. In 1311 the Emperor Henry VII appointed Matteo Visconti his vicar in Milan, which, like most cities in northern Italy, loosely acknowledged itself as part of the Holy Roman Empire. Though Matteo made serious blunders he governed so ably that his descendants held power in Milan till 1447. They were seldom scrupulous, often cruel, sometimes extravagant, never stupid. They taxed the people heavily for the numerous campaigns that brought most of northwestern Italy under their rule, but their skill in finding competent administrators and generals brought victory to their arms and prosperity to Milan. To the woolen manufactures of the city they added a silk industry; they multiplied the canals that extended the city's trade; they gave to life and property a security that made their subjects forgetful of liberty. Under their tyranny Milan became one of the richest cities of Europe; its palaces, faced with marble, lined avenues paved with stone. With Giovanni Visconti, handsome, indefatigable, ruthless or generous at need or whim, Milan reached its zenith; Lodi, Parma, Crema, Piacenza, Brescia, Bergamo, Novara, Como, Vercelli, Alessandria, Tortona, Pontremoli, Asti, Bologna acknowledged his rule; and when the Avignon popes contested his claim to Bologna, and visited him with excommunication, he fought Clement VI with courage and bribery, and with 200,000 florins won Bologna, absolution, and peace (1352). He paid for his crimes with gout, and adorned his despotism with the patronage of poetry, learning, and art. When Petrarch, arriving at his court, asked what duties would be expected of him, Giovanni replied handsomely: "Only your presence, which will grace both myself and my reign."[51]

Petrarch remained eight years at the Visconti court in Pavia or Milan. During this comfortable subjection he composed in Italian *terza rima* a series of poems that he called *Trionfi:* the triumph of desire over man, of chastity over desire, of death over chastity, of fame over death, of time over fame, of eternity over time. Here he sang his final word of Laura; he asked pardon for the sensuality of his love, conversed with her chaste ghost, and dreamed of being united with her in paradise—her husband having apparently gone elsewhere. These poems, challenging comparison with Dante, represent the triumph of vanity over art.

Giovanni Visconti, dying in 1354, bequeathed his state to three nephews. Matteo II was a sensual incompetent, and was fraternally assassinated for the honor of the house (1355). Bernabò governed part of the duchy from Milan, Galeazzo II the remainder from Pavia. Galeazzo II was a capable ruler who wore his golden hair in curls and wedded his children to royalty. When his daughter Violante married the Duke of Clarence, son of King Edward III of England, Galeazzo dowered the bride with 200,000 gold florins ($5,000,000), and gave the two hundred English attendants of the groom such presents as outshone the generosity of the wealthiest contemporary kings; the leavings of the wedding banquet, we are assured, could have fed ten thousand men. So rich was *trecento* Italy, at a time when England was bankrupting herself, and France was bleeding herself white, in the Hundred Years' War.

X. VENICE AND GENOA

In 1354 Duke Giovanni Visconti sent Petrarch to Venice to negotiate peace between Venice and Genoa.

"You see in Genoa," the poet had written, "a city in the act of ruling, seated on rough hillsides, superb in walls and men."[52] The merchant's itch for gain, pitting the sailor's pluck against the sea, had plowed lanes of Genoese commerce through the Mediterranean to Tunis, Rhodes, Acre, and Tyre, to Samos, Lesbos, and Constantinople, through the Black Sea to the Crimea and Trebizond, through Gibraltar and the Atlantic to Rouen and Bruges. These enterprising businessmen developed double-entry book-keeping by 1340, and marine insurance by 1370;[53] they borrowed money from private investors at seven to ten per cent, while in most Italian cities the rate ranged from twelve to thirty. For a long time the fruits of trade were divided, never amicably, among a few rich families—the Doria, the Spinola, the Grimaldi, the Fieschi. In 1339 Simone Boccanera led the sailors and other workers in a successful revolution, and became the first of a line of doges that ruled Genoa till 1797; Verdi commemorated him in an opera. The victors in their turn divided into hostile family groups, and disordered the city with costly strife, while Genoa's great rival, Venice, thrived on order and unity.

Next to Milan, Venice was the richest and strongest state in Italy, and without exception the most ably governed. Its craftsmen were famous for the elegance of their products, mostly made for the luxury trade. Its great arsenal employed 16,000 men; 36,000 seamen manned its 3300 vessels of war or trade; and in the galleys freemen, not slaves as in the sixteenth century, plied the oars. Venetian merchants invaded every market from Jerusalem to Antwerp; they traded impartially with Christians and Mohammedans, and papal excommunications fell upon them with all the force of dew upon the earth. Petrarch, who had ranged from Naples to Flanders in his "love and zeal for seeing many things," marveled at the shipping he saw in the Venetian lagoons:

> I see vessels . . . as big as my mansion, their masts taller than its towers. They are as mountains floating on the waters. They go to face incalculable dangers in every portion of the globe. They bear

wine to England, honey to Russia, saffron, oil, and linen to Assyria, Armenia, Persia, and Araby, wood to Egypt and Greece. They return heavily laden with products of all kinds, which are sent hence to every part of the world.[54]

This lusty trade was financed by private funds collected and invested by moneylenders who began in the fourteenth century to take the name of bankers, *bancherii*, from the *banco* or bench on which they sat before their tables of exchange. The chief monetary units were the lira (a shortening of *libra*, pound) and the ducat (from *duca*, duke, doge), a gold coin of 3560 grams. This and the Florentine florin were the most stable and most widely honored currencies in Christendom.*

Life here was almost as gay as in the Naples of Boccaccio's youth. The Venetians celebrated their holidays and victories with majestic ceremonies, carved and colored their pleasure vessels and their men-o'-war, draped their flesh in Oriental silks, brightened their tables with Venetian glass, and made much music on their waters and in their homes. In 1365 the Doge Lorenzo Celsi, accompanied by Petrarch, presided over a competition among the best musicians in Italy; poems were chanted to various accompaniments, great choruses sang, and the first prize was awarded to Francesco Landino of Florence, a blind composer of ballads and madrigals. Lorenzo Veneziano and others were making the transition from medieval severity to Renaissance grace in frescoes and polyptychs already presaging the colorfulness of Venetian painting. Houses, palaces, and churches rose like corals out of the sea. There were no castles in Venice, no fortified dwellings, no massive forbidding walls, for here private feud soon submitted to public law, and, besides, almost every mansion had a natural moat. Architectural design was still Gothic, but light and graceful as northern Gothic dared not be. In this period the majestic church of Santa Maria Gloriosa dei Frari was built; St. Mark's continued, every now and then, to lift its aging face with youthful decorations of sculpture, mosaic, and arabesques, and superimposed Gothic ogives upon some round arches of the old Byzantine form. Though the Piazza San Marco had not yet received its full encirclement of architecture, Petrarch doubted "if it has an equal within the bounds of the world."[55]

All this beauty, quivering in the reflection of the Grand Canal, all this monolithic structure of economy and government, ruling an Adriatic and Aegean empire from an Archimedean fragment of the earth, met a mortal

---

* All three of these coins, prior to 1490, will be loosely reckoned in this volume as having the purchasing power of $25 in the currency of the United States of America in 1952; after 1490 at $12.50. A slow inflation cut the value of Italian currencies by approximately fifty per cent between 1400 and 1580.[54a]

challenge in 1378, when the old strife with Genoa reached its peak. Luciano Doria led a Genoese armada up to Pola, found the main Venetian fleet weakened by an epidemic among the sailors, and in an overwhelming victory captured fifteen galleys and nearly two thousand men. Luciano lost his life in the battle, but his brother Ambrogio, succeeding him as admiral, took the town of Chioggia—on a narrow promontory some fifteen miles south of Venice—formed an alliance with Padua, blocked all Venetian shipping, and prepared, with Genoese seamen and Paduan mercenaries, to invade Venice itself. The proud city, apparently defenseless, asked for terms; these were so insolent and severe that the Great Council resolved to fight for every foot of water in the lagoons. The rich poured their hidden wealth into the coffers of the state; the people labored day and night to build another fleet; floating fortresses were raised around the islands, and were equipped with cannon, now for the first time appearing in Italy (1379). But the Genoese and Paduans, having already blockaded Venice from the sea, stretched a cordon of troops across its land approaches, and shut off the city's food supply. While some of the population starved, Vittore Pisani trained recruits for the new navy. In December, 1379, Pisani and the Doge Andrea Contarini led the reconstituted fleet—thirty-four galleys, sixty large craft, four hundred small boats—to besiege the Genoese and their ships at Chioggia. The Genoese fleet was too small to face the new Venetian navy; Venetian cannon shot into the Genoese vessels, fortresses, and barracks stones weighing 150 pounds, killing, among many, the Genoese admiral Pietro Doria. The Genoese, starving, asked leave to evacuate the women and children from Chioggia; the Venetians consented; but when the Genoese offered to yield if their fleet should be allowed to depart, it was the turn of Venice to demand unconditional surrender. For six months the siege of Chioggia continued; at last, reduced by disease and death, the Genoese gave up; and Venice treated them humanely. When Amadeus VI, Count of Savoy, offered mediation the exhausted rivals agreed; they made mutual concessions, exchanged prisoners, and resigned themselves to peace (1381).

XI. TWILIGHT OF THE "TRECENTO"

Petrarch, sampling every city and every host, took up his residence in Venice in 1361, and lived there for seven years. He brought his library with him, containing almost all the Latin classics except Lucretius. In an eloquent letter he deeded the precious collection to Venice, but reserved its use to himself till his death. As a gesture of appreciation the Venetian government assigned to him the Palazzo Molina, furnished for his comfort. However, Petrarch took his books with him on his later wanderings; at his death they fell into the hands of his last host, Francesco I da Carrara, an enemy of Venice; some were kept at Padua, most were sold or otherwise dispersed.

It was probably at Venice that he wrote an essay *De officio et virtutibus imperatoris* (*On the Duty and Virtues of an Emperor*), and a long concatenation of dialogues *De remediis utriusque fortunae* (*Remedies for Both [Good and Bad] Fortune*). He counsels modesty in prosperity and courage in adversity; warns against hitching one's happiness to earthly victories or goods; teaches how to bear with toothache, obesity, the loss of a wife, the fluctuations of fame. It is all good advice, but it is all in Seneca. About this time, too, he composed his greatest prose work, *De viris illustribus*, thirty-one biographies of Roman celebrities from Romulus to Caesar; the 350 octavo pages devoted to Caesar constituted the most thorough life of that statesman till the nineteenth century.

Petrarch left Venice in 1368 for Pavia, hoping to negotiate a peace there between Galeazzo II Visconti and Pope Urban V, only to learn that eloquence without guns finds no ears among diplomats. In 1370 he accepted the invitation of Francesco I da Carrara to live for the second time as a royal guest in Padua. But his aging nerves resented the city's bustle, and he soon retired to a modest villa at Arqua, in the Euganean hills, twelve miles southwest of Padua. There he passed the remaining four years of his life. He gathered and edited his letters for posthumous publication, and wrote a charming miniature autobiography, *Epistola ad posteros* (1371). Again he yielded to the philosopher's ancient failing—to tell statesmen how to manage states. In *De republica optime administranda* (1372) he advised the lord of Padua to "be not the master but the father of thy subjects, and to love them as thy children"; to drain marshes, ensure a food supply, maintain churches, support the sick and helpless, and give protection and patronage to men of letters—on whose pens all fame depends. Then he took up *The Decameron*, and translated the story of Griselda into Latin to win for it a European audience.

Boccaccio was now in a mood to regret that he had ever written *The Decameron* or the sensual poems of his youth. In 1361 a dying monk had sent him a message reproaching him with his evil life and merry tales, and prophesying for him, in case he deferred reform, a speedy death and everlasting agonies in hell. Boccaccio had never been an assiduous thinker; he accepted the delusions of his time in regard to casting horoscopes and telling the future through dreams; he believed in a multitude of demons, and thought that Aeneas had veritably visited Hades.[56] He turned now to orthodoxy, and thought of selling his books and becoming a monk. Petrarch, advised of this, besought him to take a middle course: to turn from the writing of amorous Italian poems and *novelle* to the earnest study of the Latin and Greek classics. Boccaccio accepted the counsel of his "venerable master," and became the first Greek humanist in Western Europe.

Urged on by Petrarch, he collected classical manuscripts; rescued books XI-XVI of the *Annals*, and books I-V of the *Histories*, of Tacitus from their oblivion in the neglected library of Monte Cassino; restored the texts of Martial and Ausonius, and contrived to give Homer to the Western world. Some scholars in the Age of Faith had carried on a knowledge of Greek, but in Boccaccio's day Greek had almost totally disappeared from the ken of the West except in half-Greek Southern Italy. In 1342 Petrarch began to study Greek with the Calabrian monk Barlaam. When a bishopric in Calabria fell vacant Petrarch successfully recommended Barlaam for it; the monk departed, and Petrarch dropped Greek for lack of a teacher, a grammar, or a lexicon; no such books were then available in Latin or Italian. In 1359 Boccaccio met at Milan one of Barlaam's pupils, Leon Pilatus. He invited him to Florence, and persuaded the university—which had been founded eleven years before—to establish a chair of Greek for Pilatus. Petrarch helped to pay his salary, sent copies of the *Iliad* and the *Odyssey* to Boccaccio, and commissioned Pilatus to translate them into Latin. The work was frequently delayed, and involved Petrarch in a troublesome correspondence; he complained that the letters of Pilatus were even longer and dirtier than his beard;[57] only through Boccaccio's exhortations and cooperation was Pilatus prodded to complete the task. This inaccurate and prosaic version was the only Latin translation of Homer known to Europe in the fourteenth century.

Meanwhile Pilatus had taught Boccaccio enough Greek to read the Greek classics haltingly. Boccaccio confessed that he understood the texts only partly, but described what he did understand as surpassingly beautiful. Inspired by these books and Petrarch, he devoted almost all his remaining literary work to the purpose of promoting in Latin Europe a knowledge of Greek literature, mythology, and history. In a series of brief biographies *De casibus virorum illustrium* (*On the Vicissitudes of Famous Men*) he ranged from Adam to King John of France; in *De claris mulieribus* he told the stories of famous women from Eve to Queen Joanna I of Naples; in *De montibus, silvis, fontibus*, etc., he described in alphabetical order the mountains, forests, springs, rivers, and lakes named in Greek literature; and in *De genealogiis deorum* he composed a handbook of classical mythology. So deeply did he become absorbed in his subject that he spoke of the Christian God as Jove, of Satan as Pluto, of Venus and Mars as if they were as real as Mary and Christ. These books seem now intolerably dull, written in bad Latin and with middling scholarship; but in their time they were precious manuals for students of Greece, and played an important role in implementing the Renaissance.

So Boccaccio moved from the escapades of youth to the dignity of old age. Florence used him now and then as a diplomat, sending him on missions to Forlì, Avignon, Ravenna, and Venice. At sixty he was physically weak, suffering from dry scab and "more maladies than I know how to enumerate."[58] He lived in suburban Certaldo in bitter poverty. Perhaps it was to aid him financially that some friends in 1373 persuaded the Florentine Signory to create a *cathedra Dantesca*, or chair of Dante, and to pay Boccaccio a hundred florins ($2500) to give a course of lectures on Dante in the Badia. His health broke down before the course was complete, and he turned to Certaldo reconciled to death.

Petrarch had written, "I desire that death find me ready and writing, or, if it please Christ, praying and in tears."[59] On his seventieth birthday, July 20, 1374, he was found leaning over a book, apparently sleeping, actually dead. In his will he left fifty florins to buy a mantle for Boccaccio as protection against the cold during the long winter nights. On December 21, 1375, Boccaccio too died, aged sixty-one. For fifty years now Italy would lie fallow, till the seeds that these men had planted would come to flower.

XII. PERSPECTIVE

We have followed Petrarch and Boccaccio through Italy. But politically there was no Italy; there were only city-states, fragments free to consume themselves in hate and war. Pisa destroyed its commercial rival Amalfi; Milan destroyed Piacenza; Genoa and Florence destroyed Pisa; Venice destroyed Genoa; and half of Europe would join most of Italy to destroy Venice. The collapse of central government in the barbarian invasions, the "Gothic War" of the sixth century, the Lombard-Byzantine dichotomy of the peninsula, the decay of the Roman roads, the contest of Lombards and popes, the conflict of papacy and Empire, the papal fear that one secular power sovereign from the Alps to Sicily would make the pope a prisoner, subjecting the spiritual head of Europe to the political leader of a state: all

these had wrought the disunity of Italy. Partisans of the popes and partisans of the emperors not only divided Italy, they split almost every city into
Guelf and Ghibelline; and even when that strife subsided the old labels
were used by new rivalries, and the lava of hate flowed into all the avenues
of life. If Ghibellines wore feathers on one side of their caps, Guelfs wore
them on the other; if Ghibellines cut fruit crosswise, Guelfs cut it straight
down; if Ghibellines wore white roses, Guelfs wore red. In Crema the
Ghibellines of Milan tore a statue of Christ from a church altar and burned
it becaused its face was turned in what was considered a Guelf direction;
in Ghibelline Bergamo some Calabrians were murdered by their hosts, who
discovered from their way of eating garlic that they were Guelfs.[60] The
timid weakness of individuals, the insecurity of groups, and the delusion of
superiority generated perpetual fear, suspicion, dislike, and contempt of
the different, the alien, and the strange.

Out of these impediments to unity rose the Italian city-state. Men
thought in terms of their city, and only a few philosophers like Machiavelli,
or a poet like Petrarch, could think of Italy as a whole; even in the sixteenth
century Cellini would refer to Florentines as "men of our nation," and to
Florence as "my fatherland." Petrarch, freed by foreign residence from a
merely local patriotism, mourned the petty wars and divisions of his native
country, and in an eloquent ode—*Italia Mia!*—besought the princes of Italy
to give her unity and peace.

> O my own Italy!—though words are vain
>   The mortal wounds to close
> Innumerable that thy bosom stain—
> Yet may it soothe my pain
>   To sing of Tiber's woes
> And Arno's wrongs, as on Po's saddened shore
> Mournful I wander, and my numbers pour. . . .
>
> Oh, is this not the soil my foot first pressed?
> And here, in cradled rest
> Was I not softly hushed and fondly reared?
> Oh, is not this my country—so endeared
> By every filial tie—
> In whose earth shrouded both my parents lie?
> Oh, by this tender thought
> Your hard hearts to some pity wrought,
> Look on the people's grief,
> Who, under God, of you expect relief,

> And, if ye but relent,
>   Virtue shall rouse her in embattled might,
> Against blind fury bent,
>   Nor long shall doubtful hang the unequal fight.
> No, no! The ancient flame
> Is not extinguished yet, that raised the Italian name!

Petrarch had dreamed that Rienzo might make Italy one; when that bubble burst he turned like Dante to the head of the Holy Roman Empire, theoretically the secular heir to all the temporal powers of the pagan Roman Empire in the West. Soon after Rienzo's retirement (1347) Petrarch addressed a stirring message to Charles IV, King of Bohemia and, as "King of the Romans," heir apparent to the Imperial throne. Let the King come down to Rome and be crowned emperor, the poet pleaded; let him make Rome, not Prague, his capital; let him restore unity, order, and peace to "the garden of the Empire"—Italy.[61] When Charles crossed the Alps in 1354 he invited Petrarch to meet him at Mantua, and listened courteously to appeals echoing the impassioned pleas of Dante to Charles's grandfather Henry VII. But Charles, having no force adequate to conquer all the despots of Lombardy and all the citizens of Florence and Venice, hurried to Rome, got himself crowned by a papal prefect for lack of a pope, and then hastened back to Bohemia, sedulously selling Imperial vicariates on the way. Two years later Petrarch went to him in Prague as Milanese ambassador, but with no significant results for Italy.

Perhaps there would have been no Renaissance if Petrarch had had his way. The fragmentation of Italy favored the Renaissance. Large states promote order and power rather than liberty or art. The commercial rivalry of the Italian cities inaugurated and completed the work of the Crusades in developing the economy and wealth of Italy. The variety of political centers multiplied interurban strife, but these modest conflicts never totaled the death and destruction caused in France by the Hundred Years' War. Local independence weakened the capacity of Italy to defend herself against foreign invasion, but it generated a noble rivalry of the cities and princes in cultural patronage, in the zeal to excel in architecture, sculpture, painting, education, scholarship, poetry. Renaissance Italy, like Goethe's Germany, had many Parises.

We need not exaggerate, to appreciate, the degree in which Petrarch and Boccaccio prepared the Renaissance. Both were still mortgaged to medieval ideas. The great storyteller, in his lusty youth, laughed at clerical immorality and relicmongering, but so had millions of medieval men and women; and he became more orthodox and medieval in those very years in which he studied Greek. Petrarch properly and prophetically described himself as standing between two eras.[62] He accepted the dogmas of the Church even while he flayed the morals of Avignon; he loved the classics with a troubled conscience at the close of the Age of Faith as Jerome had loved them at its opening; he wrote excellent medieval essays on contempt of the secular world and on the holy peace of the religious life. Nevertheless, he was more faithful to the classics than to Laura; he sought and cherished ancient manuscripts, and inspired others to do the same; he overleaped nearly all medieval authors except Augustine to regain continuity with Latin literature; he formed his manner and style on Virgil and Cicero; and he thought more of the fame of his name than of the immortality of his soul. His poems fostered a century of artificial sonneteering in Italy, but they helped to mold the sonnets of Shakespeare. His eager spirit passed down to Pico, his polished form to Politian; his letters and essays threw a bridge of classical urbanity and grace between Seneca and Montaigne; his reconciliation of antiquity and Christianity matured in Popes Nicholas V and Leo X. He was truly, in these ways, the Father of the Renaissance.

But again it would be an error to overrate the contributions of antiquity to this Italian apogee. It was a fullfillment rather than a revolution, and the medieval maturation played a far greater role than the recovery of classic manuscripts and art. Many medieval scholars had known and loved the pagan classics; it was the monks who had preserved them; it was clerics who in the twelfth and thirteenth centuries had translated or edited them. The great universities had since 1100 passed down to the youth of Europe some measure of the mental and moral heritage of the race. The growth of a critical philosophy in Erigena and Abelard, the introduction of Aristotle and Averroes into university curriculums, the brave proposal of Aquinas to prove nearly all Christian dogmas by reason, so soon followed by Duns Scotus' confession that most of these doctrines were beyond reason, had reared and shattered the intellectual edifice of Scholasticism, and had left the educated Christian free to attempt a new synthesis of pagan philosophy and medieval theology with the experience of life. The liberation of the towns from feudal hindrances, the widening of commerce, the spread of a money economy—all these had preceded Petrarch's birth. Roger of Sicily and Frederick II, not to speak of Moslem caliphs and sultans, had taught rulers to give glamour to power by patronizing art and poetry, science and philosophy. Medieval men and women, despite an otherworldly minority, had kept, unabashed, the natural human relish for the simple and sensual pleasures of life. The men who conceived, built, and carved the cathedrals had their own sense of beauty, and a sublimity of thought and form never surpassed.

Therefore all the bases of the Renaissance had been established by the time of Petrarch's death. The amazing growth and zest of Italian trade and industry had gathered the wealth that financed the movement, and the passage from rural peace and stagnation to urban vitality and stimulus had begotten the mood that nourished it. The political basis had been prepared in the freedom and rivalry of the cities, in the overthrow of an idle aristocracy, in the rise of educated princes and a virile bourgeoisie. The literary basis had been prepared in the improvement of the vernacular languages, and in the zeal for recovering and studying the classics of Greece and Rome. The ethical bases had been laid: increasing wealth was breaking down old moral restraints; contact with Islam in commerce and Crusades had encouraged a new tolerance for doctrinal and moral deviations from traditional beliefs and ways; the rediscovery of a pagan world relatively free in thought and conduct shared in undermining medieval dogmas and morality; interest in a future life gave ground before secular, human, earthly concerns. Esthetic development proceeded; the medieval hymns, the cycles of romance, the songs of the troubadours, the sonnets of Dante and his Italian predecessors, the sculptured harmony and form of *The Divine Comedy*, had left a heritage of literary art; the classic models transmitted a refinement of taste and thought, a polish and politeness of speech and style, to Petrarch, who would bequeath it to an international dynasty of urbane genius from Erasmus to Anatole France. And a revolution in art had begun when Giotto abandoned the mystic rigor of Byzantine mosaics to study men and women in the actual flow and natural grace of their lives.

In Italy all roads were leading to the Renaissance.

CHAPTER II

The Popes in Avignon

1 3 0 9 - 7 7

I. THE BABYLONIAN CAPTIVITY

IN 1309 Pope Clement V removed the papacy from Rome to Avignon. He was a Frenchman, the former bishop of Bordeaux; he owed his elevation to Philip IV of France, who had startled all Christendom by not only defeating Pope Boniface VIII but arresting him, humiliating him, and almost starving him to death. Clement's life would be unsafe in a Rome that reserved to itself the right to maltreat a pope, and resented the insolent irreverence of the King; moreover, the French cardinals formed now a large majority in the Sacred College, and refused to entrust themselves to Italy. So Clement stayed awhile at Lyons and Poitiers; then, hoping to be less subject to Philip in a territory owned by the king of Naples as count of Provence, he took up his residence in Avignon, just across the Rhone from fourteenth-century France.

The immense effort of the papacy from Gregory VII (1073-85) to Boniface VIII (1294-1303) to form a European world state by subordinating the kings to the popes had failed; nationalism had triumphed over a theocratic federalism; even in Italy the republics of Florence and Venice, the city-states of Lombardy, and the Kingdom of Naples rejected ecclesiastical control; a republic twice raised its head in Rome; and in the other Papal States* military adventurers or feudal magnates—Baglioni, Bentivogli, Malatestas, Manfredi, Sforzas—were replacing the vicars of the Church with their own swashbuckling authority. The papacy in Rome had wielded the prestige of centuries, and the nations had learned to do it homage and send it fees; but a papacy of continuously French pontiffs

---

* The Papal States may be listed under four provinces:
I. LATIUM, containing the cities of Tivoli, Civita Castellana, Subiaco, Viterbo, Anagni, Ostia, and Rome;
II. UMBRIA, with Narni, Spoleto, Foligno, Assisi, Perugia, and Gubbio;
III. THE MARCHES, with Ascoli, Loreto, Ancona, Senigallia, Urbino, Camerino, Fabriano, and Pesaro; and
IV. THE ROMAGNA, with Rimini, Cesena, Forlì, Faenza, Ravenna, Imola, Bologna, and Ferrara.

49

(1305-78), almost imprisoned by the kings of France, and lending them great sums to carry on their wars, seemed to Germany, Bohemia, Italy, and England a hostile power, the psychological weapon of the French monarchy. Increasingly those nations ignored its excommunications and interdicts, and only with rising reluctance yielded it a declining reverence.

Against these difficulties Clement V labored with patience, if not with fortitude. He bowed as little as he could to Philip IV, who held over Clement's head the threat of a scandalous post-mortem inquest into the private conduct and beliefs of Boniface VIII. Harassed for funds, the Pope sold ecclesiastical benefices to the highest bidder; but he lent tacit approval to the merciless reports that the mayor of Angers and the bishop of Mende presented on the subject of clerical morals and Church reform to the Council of Vienne (1311).[1] He himself led a clean and frugal life, and practised an undemonstrative piety. He protected the great physician and critic of the Church, Arnold of Villanova, from persecution for heresy; he reorganized medical studies at Montpellier on Greek and Arabic texts, and tried—though he failed—to establish chairs of Hebrew, Syriac, and Arabic in the universities. To all his troubles was added a painful disease—*lupulus*, probably a fistula— which compelled him to shun society, and killed him in 1314. In a better environment he would have been an ornament to the Church.

The chaotic interregnum that followed revealed the temper of the times. Dante wrote to the Italian cardinals urging them to hold out for an Italian pope and a return to Rome; but only six of the twenty-three cardinals were Italian; and when the conclave met in a locked room* at Carpentras, near Avignon, it was surrounded by a Gascon populace that shouted: "Death to the Italian cardinals!" The houses of these prelates were attacked and destroyed; the crowd set fire to the building that housed the conclave; the cardinals broke a passage through the rear wall, and fled from the fire and the mob. For two years no further attempt was made to choose a pope. Finally at Lyons, under the protection of French soldiery, the cardinals raised to the papacy a man already seventy-two years of age, who might reasonably be expected to die soon, but who was destined to rule the Church for eighteen years with rugged zeal, insatiable avidity, and imperial will. John XXII had been born at Cahors in southern France, the son of a cobbler; it was the second time that a cobbler's son

---

* Since 1274 it had been the custom to lock up the cardinals when they met in conclave (*con clave*, with a key) to choose a pope.

had risen, by the remarkable democracy of an authoritarian Church, to the highest place in Christendom; Urban IV (1261-4) had shown the way. Employed as a teacher for the children of the French king of Naples, John studied civil and canon law with such aptitude that the king took him into favor. On the king's recommendation Boniface VIII made him bishop of Fréjus, and Clement V raised him to the see of Avignon. At Carpentras the gold of Robert of Naples silenced the patriotism of the Italian cardinals, and the cobbler's son became one of the strongest of the popes.

He displayed abilities rarely combined: scholarly studies and administrative skill. Under his leadership the Avignon papacy developed a competent, if corrupt, bureaucratic organization, and a fiscal staff that shocked the envious chancelleries of Europe with its capacity for gathering revenues. John undertook a dozen major conflicts that called for funds; like his predecessor he sold benefices, but without a blush; by sundry devices this scion of the banking town of Cahors so fattened the papal treasury that at his death it held 18,000,000 gold florins ($450,000,000), and 7,000,-000 in plate and jewelry.[2] He explained that the papal Curia had lost much of its income from Italy, and had to build its offices, staff, and services anew. John seems to have felt that he could serve God best by winning Mammon to his side. His personal habits tended to an abstemious simplicity.[3]

Meanwhile he patronized learning, shared in establishing medical schools at Perugia and Cahors, helped universities, founded a Latin college in Armenia, fostered the study of Oriental languages, fought alchemy and magic, spent days and nights in scholastic studies, and ended as a theologian suspected of heresy. Perhaps to check the spread of a mysticism that claimed direct contact with God, John ventured to teach that no one—not even the Mother of God—can attain to the Beatific Vision until the Last Judgment. A storm of protest arose among the eschatological experts; the University of Paris denounced the Pope's view, a church synod at Vincennes condemned it as heresy, and Philip VI of France ordered him to reform his theology.[4] The crafty nonagenarian eluded them all by dying (1334).

John's successor was a man of gentler mold. Benedict XII, the son of a baker, tried to be a Christian as well as a pope; he resisted the temptation to distribute offices among his relatives; he earned an honorable hostility by bestowing benefices for merits, not for fees; he repressed bribery and corruption in all branches of Church administration; he alienated the mendicant orders by commanding them to reform; he was never known to be cruel or to shed blood in war. All the forces of corruption rejoiced at his early death (1342).

Clement VI, born of a noble house in Limousin, was accustomed to luxury, gaiety, and art, and could not understand why a pope should be austere when the papal treasury was full. Almost all who came to him for appointments secured them; no one, he said, should depart from him unsatisfied. He announced that any poor clergyman who should come to him within the next two months would partake of his bounty; an eyewitness reckoned that 100,000 came.[5] He gave rich gifts to artists and poets; maintained a stud of horses equal to any in Christendom; admitted women freely to his court, enjoyed their charms, and mingled with them in Gallic gallantry. The countess of Turenne was so close to him that she sold ecclesiastical preferments with careless publicity.[6] Hearing of Clement's good nature, the Romans sent an embassy inviting him to reside in Rome. He did not relish the prospect, but he appeased them by declaring that the jubilee, which Boniface VIII had established in 1300 for every hundred years, should be celebrated every half century. Rome rejoiced at the news, deposed Rienzo, and renewed its political submission to the popes.

Under Clement VI Avignon became the capital not only of the religion but of the politics, culture, pleasure, and corruption of the Latin world. Now the administrative machinery of the Church took its definitive form: an Apostolic Chamber (*camera apostolica*) in charge of finances, and headed by a papal chamberlain (*camerarius*) who was second in dignity to the pope alone; a Papal Chancery (*cancelleria*) whose seven agencies, directed by a cardinal vice-chancellor, handled the complex correspondence of the See; a Papal Judiciary composed of prelates and laymen learned in canon law, and including the Consistory—the pope and his cardinals acting as a court of appeals; and an Apostolic Penitentiary—a college of clergy who dealt with marital dispensations, excommunication and interdict, and heard the confessions of those seeking papal absolution.

To house the pope and his aides, these ministries and agencies, their staffs and servants, Benedict XII began, and Urban V completed, the immense Palace of the Popes, a congeries of Gothic buildings—living chambers, council halls, chapels, and offices—enclosing two courts, and themselves enclosed by mighty ramparts whose height and breadth and massive towers suggest that the popes, if besieged, would rely on no miracle for their defense. Benedict XII invited Giotto to come and decorate the palace and the adjoining cathedral; Giotto planned to come, but died; and in 1338

Benedict summoned from Siena Simone Martini, whose frescoes, now obliterated, marked the zenith of painting in Avignon. Around this palace, in lesser palaces, mansions, tenements, and hovels, gathered a great population of prelates, envoys, lawyers, merchants, artists, poets, servants, soldiers, beggars, and prostitutes of every grade from cultured courtesans to tavern tarts. Here, for the most part, dwelt those bishops *in partibus infidelium* who were appointed to sees that had fallen into the hands of non-Christians.

We, who are inured to colossal figures, can imagine the amount of money required to support this complex administrative establishment and its entourage. Several sources of income were nearly dried up: Italy, deserted by the papacy, sent hardly anything; Germany, at odds with John XXII, sent half its usual tribute; France, holding the Church almost at its mercy, appropriated for secular purposes a large part of French ecclesiastical revenues, and borrowed heavily from the papacy to finance the Hundred Years' War; England severely restricted the flow of money to a Church that was in effect an ally of France. To meet this situation the Avignon popes were driven to develop every trickle of revenue. Each bishop or abbot, whether appointed by pope or secular prince, transmitted to the Curia, as an inaugural fee, one third of his prospective income for a year, and paid exasperating gratuities to the numerous intermediaries who had supported his nomination. If he became an archbishop he had to pay a substantial fee for the archiepiscopal pallium—a circular band of white wool, worn over the chasuble as the insignia of his office. When a new pontiff was elected, every ecclesiastical benefice or office sent him its full revenue for one year (annates), and thereafter a tenth of its revenue in each year; additional voluntary contributions were expected from time to time. On the death of any cardinal, archbishop, bishop, or abbot, his personal possessions and effects belonged to the papacy. In the interim between such death and the installation of a new appointee the popes received the revenues, and paid the expenses, of the benefice; and they were accused of deliberately extending this interval. Every ecclesiastical appointee was held responsible for dues unpaid by his predecessors. As bishops and abbots were in many cases feudal proprietors of estates received in fief from the king, they had to pay him tribute and provide him with soldiery, so that many were hard pressed to meet their combined ecclesiastical and secular obligations; and as the papal exactions were more severe than the state's, we find the hierarchy sometimes supporting the king against the pope. The Avignon pontiffs almost completely ignored the ancient rights of cathedral chapters or monastic councils to choose bishops or abbots; and these by-passed collators joined in the accumulating resentment. Cases tried in the Papal Judiciary usually required the expensive help of lawyers, who had to pay an annual fee for license to plead in the papal courts. Every judgment or favor received from the Curia expected a gift in acknowledgment; even permission to be ordained had to be bought. The secular governments of Europe looked with awe and fury upon the fiscal machinery of the popes.[7]

Protests arose from every quarter, and not least vigorously from churchmen themselves. The Spanish prelate Alvaro Pelayo, though thoroughly loyal to the papacy, wrote *On the Lamentation of the Church*, in which he mourned that "Whenever I entered the chambers of the ecclesiastics of the papal court, I found brokers and clergy engaged in weighing and reckoning the money that lay in heaps before them. . . . Wolves are in control of the Church, and feed on the blood" of the Christian flock.[8] Cardinal Napoleone Orsini was disturbed to find that nearly all the bishoprics of Italy were the object of barter or family intrigue under Clement V. Edward III of England, himself adept in taxation, reminded Clement VI that "the successor of the Apostles was commissioned to lead the Lord's sheep to the pasture, not to fleece them,"[9] and the English parliament passed several statutes to check the taxing power of the popes in Britain. In Germany papal collectors were hunted down, imprisoned, mutilated, in some cases strangled. In 1372 the clergy of Cologne, Bonn, Xanten, and Mainz bound themselves by oath not to pay the tithe demanded by Gregory XI. In France many benefices were ruined by a tragic combination of war, the Black Death, pillage by brigands, and the exactions of papal collectors; many pastors abandoned their parishes.

To such complaints the popes replied that ecclesiastical administration required all these funds, that incorruptible agents were hard to find, and that they themselves were in a sea of troubles. Probably under duress, Clement VI lent Philip VI of France 592,000 gold florins ($14,800,000), and 3,517,000 more ($87,925,000) to King John II.[10] Great outlays were required to reconquer the lost papal states in Italy. Despite all taxes the popes suffered dire deficits. John XXII rescued the papal treasury by paying into it 440,000 florins from his personal funds; Innocent VI sold his silver plate, his jewelry and works of art; Urban V had to borrow 30,000 florins from his cardinals; Gregory XI owed 120,000 francs when he died.

Critics retorted that deficits were caused not by legitimate outlays but by the worldly luxury of the papal court and its hangers-on. Clement VI was surrounded by male and female relatives attired in precious stuffs and furs; by knights, squires, sergeants at arms, chaplains, ushers, chamberlains, musicians, poets, artists, doctors, scientists, tailors, philosophers, and chefs who were the envy of kings—all in all, some four hundred persons, all fed, clothed, lodged, and salaried by a lovably lavish Pope who had never known the cost of money. Clement thought of himself as a ruler who had to awe his subjects and impress ambassadors by "conspicuous consumption" after the custom of kings. The cardinals too, as the royal council of a state as well as the princes of the Church, had to maintain establishments befitting their dignity and power; their retinues, equipages, banquets were the talk of the town. Perhaps Cardinal Bernard of Garves overdid it, who hired fifty-one dwellings to house his retainers; and Cardinal Peter of Banhac, five of whose ten stables sheltered thirty-nine horses in comfort and style. Even bishops fell in line, and, despite remonstrances from provincial synods, kept rich establishments with jesters, falcons, and dogs.

Avignon now assumed the morals, as well as the manners, of royal courts. Venality there was notorious. Guillaume Durand, Bishop of Mende, reported to the Council of Vienne:

> The whole Church might be reformed if the Church of Rome would begin by removing evil examples from itself . . . by which men are scandalized, and the whole people, as it were, infected. . . . For in all lands . . . the holy Church of God, and especially the most holy Church of Rome, is in evil repute; and all cry and publish it abroad that within her bosom all men, from the greatest unto even the least, have set their hearts upon covetousness. . . . That the whole Christian folk take from the clergy pernicious examples of gluttony is clear and notorious, since the said clergy feast more luxuriously and splendidly, and with more dishes, than princes and kings.[11]

And Petrarch, a master of words, exhausted his vocabulary of vituperation to brand Avignon as

> the impious Babylon, the hell on earth, the sink of vice, the sewer of the world. There is in it neither faith nor charity nor religion nor the fear of God. . . . All the filth and wickedness of the world have run together here. . . . Old men plunge hot and headlong into the arms of Venus; forgetting their age, dignity, and powers, they rush into every shame, as if all their glory consisted not in the cross of

Christ but in feasting, drunkenness, and unchastity. . . . Fornication, incest, rape, adultery are the lascivious delights of the pontifical games.[12]

Such testimony, from an eyewitness who never veered from orthodoxy,
cannot be entirely disregarded, but it has the ring of exaggeration and
personal resentment. Some discount must be made from it as the cry of
a man who hated Avignon for snatching the papacy from Italy; who
begged for benefices from the Avignon popes, received many, and asked
for more; who consented to live with the murderous and antipapal Visconti, and had two bastards of his own. Morals in Rome, to which Petrarch
importuned the popes to return, were then no better than in Avignon,
except as poverty is an aid to chastity. St. Catherine of Siena was not as
vivid as the poet in describing Avignon, but she told Gregory XI that at
the papal court "her nostrils were assailed by the odors of hell."[13]

Amid the moral decay there were many prelates who were worthy of
their calling, and preferred the morals of Christ to those of their time.
When we reflect that of the seven Avignon popes only one lived a life of
worldly pleasure, and another, John XXII, however rapacious and severe,
disciplined himself to ascetic austerity, and another, Gregory XI, though
merciless in war was in peace a man of exemplary morals and piety, and
three—Benedict XII, Innocent VI, and Urban V—were men of almost
saintly life, we cannot hold the popes responsible for all the vice that
gathered in papal Avignon. The cause was wealth, which has had like
results in other times—in the Rome of Nero, the Rome of Leo X, the
Paris of Louis XIV, the New York and Chicago of today. And as in these
last cities we perceive that the vast majority of men and women lead
decent lives, or practise their vices modestly, so we may presume that
even in Avignon the lecher and the courtesan, the glutton and the thief,
the crooked lawyer and the dishonest judge, the worldly cardinal and the
faithless priest, were exceptions standing out more vividly than elsewhere
because surveyed, and sometimes condoned, by the Apostolic See.

The scandal was real enough to share with the flight from Rome in
undermining the prestige and authority of the Church. As if to confirm
the suspicion that they were no longer a world power but merely the
tools of France, the Avignon popes named 113 Frenchmen to the college
of cardinals in a total of 134 nominations.[14] Hence the connivance of the
English government at Wyclif's uncompromising attacks upon the papacy.
The German electors repudiated any further interference of the popes in
the election of their kings and emperors. In 1372 the abbots of the arch-

diocese of Cologne, in refusing the tithe to Pope Gregory XI, publicly proclaimed that "the Apostolic See has fallen into such contempt that the Catholic faith in these parts seems to be seriously imperiled. The laity speak slightingly of the Church because, departing from the custom of former days, she hardly ever sends forth preachers or reformers, but rather ostentatious men, cunning, selfish, and greedy. Things have come to such a pass that few are Christians in more than name."[15]

It was the Babylonian Captivity of the popes in Avignon, and the ensuing Papal Schism, that prepared the Reformation; and it was their return to Italy that restored their prestige and deferred catastrophe for a century.

II. THE ROAD TO ROME

The status of the Church was lowest in Italy. In 1342 Benedict XII, to weaken the rebellious Louis of Bavaria, confirmed to all the despots of the Lombard cities the authority they had assumed in defiance of Imperial claims; Louis, in revenge, gave the Imperial sanction to the despots who had seized the Papal States.[16] Milan openly flouted the popes. When Urban V sent two legates to Milan (1362), bearing bulls of excommunication to the Visconti, Bernabò compelled them to eat the bulls—parchment, silken cords, and leaden seals.[17] Sicily, ever since its "Vespers" (1282), had remained in open enmity to the popes.

Clement VI engaged an army to recapture the Papal States, but it was his successor, Innocent VI, who for a time restored them to obedience. Innocent was almost a model pope. After indulging a few relatives with appointments, he determined to stop the current of nepotism and corruption. He put an end to the epicurean splendor and wasteful outlay of the papal court, dismissed the horde of servants that had ministered to Clement VI, scattered the swarm of place seekers, ordered every priest to reside in his benefice, and himself led a life of integrity and modesty. He saw that the authority of the Church could be restored only by liberating her from the power of France and returning the papacy to Italy. But a Church alienated from France could hardly maintain herself without the revenues that had formerly come to her from the Papal States. Innocent, a man of peace, decided that these could be reclaimed only by war.

He entrusted the task to a man with the fervent faith of a Spaniard, the energy of a Dominic, and the chivalry of a Castilian grandee. Gil Álvarez Carrillo de Albornoz had been a soldier under Alfonso XI of Castile, and had not abandoned war on becoming archbishop of Toledo; now, as Cardinal Egidio d'Albornoz, he became a brilliant general. He persuaded the republic of Florence—which feared the despots and brigands that surrounded her—to advance him the funds to organize an army. By clever and yet honorable negotiation, rather than by force, he deposed one after another of the petty tyrants that had seized the Papal States. He gave to these states the "Egidian Constitutions" (1357) that remained their basic law till the nineteenth century, and that provided a workable compromise between self-government and allegiance to the papacy. He outwitted the famous English adventurer John Hawkwood, took him prisoner, and threw the fear if not of God at least of the papal legate into the *condottieri*. He recovered Bologna from a rebellious archbishop, and persuaded the Visconti of Milan to make their peace with the Church. The way was now open for the popes to return to Italy.

Urban V continued the austerity and reforms of Innocent VI. He labored to restore discipline and honesty in the clergy and at the papal court, discountenanced luxury among the cardinals, checked the chicanery of the lawyers and the extortions of the moneylenders, punished simony, and won to his service men of excellence in character and mind. He maintained at his own expense a thousand students in the universities, founded a new college at Montpellier, and supported many savants. To crown his pontificate he resolved to restore the papacy to Rome. The cardinals were horrified at the prospect; most of them had their roots and affections in France, and were hated in Italy. They begged him not to heed the pleas of St. Catherine or the eloquence of Petrarch. Urban pointed out to them the chaotic condition of France—its king a prisoner in England, its armies shattered, the English conquering the southern provinces and coming ever nearer to Avignon; what would a victorious England do to a papacy that had served and financed France?

So on April 30, 1367, he sailed from Marseille, joyously escorted by Italian galleys. On October 16 he entered Rome amid the wild acclaim of the populace, the clergy, and the aristocracy; Italian princes held the bridle of the white mule on which he rode; and Petrarch poured out his gratitude to the French Pope who dared to live in Italy. It was a desolate though happy Rome: impoverished by its long separation from the papacy, half of its churches deserted and decayed, St. Paul's in ruins, St. Peter's threatening at any minute to collapse, the Lateran palace but recently destroyed by fire, palaces rivaling the tenements in dilapidation, swamps where there had been dwellings, rubbish lying ungathered in the squares and streets.[18] Urban gave orders and allotted funds for rebuilding the papal palace; unable to bear the sight of Rome, he went to live at Montefiascone; but even there his memories of luxurious Avignon and beloved France made him miserable. Petrarch heard of his hesitations, and urged him to persevere; St. Bridget of Sweden predicted that he would die soon if he left Italy. The Emperor Charles IV sought to strengthen him, gave the Imperial sanction to the papal recovery of central Italy, came humbly to Rome (1368) to lead the Pope's horse from Sant' Angelo to St. Peter's, served him at Mass, and was crowned by him in a ceremony that seemed happily to heal the old strife of Empire and papacy. Then, on September 5, 1370, perhaps yielding to his French cardinals, and saying that he wished to make peace between England and France, Urban embarked for Marseille. On September 27 he reached Avignon, and there, on December 19, he died, clothed in the habit of a Benedictine monk, lying on a miserable couch, and having ordered that all who cared to enter should be admitted, so that all might see how vain and brief is the splendor of the most exalted man.[19]

Gregory XI had been made a cardinal at eighteen by his genial uncle Clement VI; on December 29, 1370, he was ordained a priest, and on December 30, aged thirty-nine, he was elected pope. He was a man of learning, in love with Cicero; fate made him a man of war, and consumed his pontificate in violent revolt. Urban V, fearing that a French pope could not yet trust Italians, had named too many Frenchmen as legates to govern the Papal States. Finding themselves in a hostile environment, these prelates had built fortresses against the people, had imported numerous French aides, had taxed exorbitantly, and had preferred tyranny to tact. At Perugia a nephew of the legate pursued a married lady so voraciously that in trying to escape him she fell from a window and was killed. When a deputation demanded punishment for the nephew, the legate replied, "Why all this fuss? Do you mistake a Frenchman for a eunuch?"[20] By a variety of means the legates earned such hatred that in 1375 many of the states rose against them in successive revolutions. St. Catherine made herself the voice of Italy, and urged Gregory to remove these "evil pastors who poison and devastate the garden of the Church."[21] Florence, usually an ally of the papacy, took the lead of the movement, and unfurled a red flag bearing in golden letters the word *Libertas*. At the beginning of 1375 sixty-four cities had acknowledged the pope as their civic as well as their spiritual head; in 1376 only one remained loyal to him. It seemed that all the work of Albornoz was undone, and that central Italy was again lost to the papacy.

Gregory, prodded by the French cardinals, charged the Florentines with being the head of the revolt, and ordered them to submit to the papal legates. When they refused he excommunicated them, forbade religious services in their city, and declared all Florentines to be outlaws, whose goods might be seized, and whose persons might be enslaved, by any man anywhere. The whole structure of Florentine commerce and finance was threatened with collapse. England and France at once laid hands upon the Florentines and their property there. Florence responded by confiscating all Church property in its territory, tearing down the buildings of the Inquisition, closing the ecclesiastical courts, jailing—in some cases hanging —obstinate priests, and sending an appeal to the people of Rome to join the revolution, and end all temporal power of the Church in Italy. While Rome hesitated, Gregory despatched to its leaders a solemn promise that if the city remained loyal to him he would return the papacy to Rome. The Romans accepted the pledge, and kept the peace.

Meanwhile the Pope had sent to Italy a force of "wild Breton mercenaries" under the command of "the fierce Cardinal Legate Robert of Geneva."[22] Robert waged the war with incredible barbarity. Having taken Cesena with the promise of an amnesty, he put every man, woman, and child there to the sword.[23] John Hawkwood, leading his mercenaries in the service of the Church, slew 4000 in Faenza on suspicion that the town intended to join the revolt. St. Catherine of Siena was shocked by these brutalities, by the mutual confiscations, by the cessation of religious services in so much of Italy. She wrote to Gregory:

> You are indeed bound to win back the territory which has been lost to the Church; but you are even more bound to win back all the lambs which are the Church's real treasure, and whose loss will truly impoverish her. . . . You must strike men with the weapons of goodness, love, and peace, and you will gain more than by the weapons of war. When I inquire of God what is best for your salvation, for the restoration of the Church, and for the whole world, there is no other answer but the word Peace! Peace! For the love of the Crucified Saviour, Peace![24]

Florence invited her to be one of its envoys to Gregory; she went, and took the occasion to condemn the morals of Avignon; she was so outspoken that many called for her arrest, but Gregory protected her. The mission had no immediate result. But when word reached him that unless he came soon Rome would join the revolt, Gregory—perhaps moved also by Catherine's pleas—set out from Marseille, and reached Rome on January 17, 1377. He was not unanimously welcomed; the appeal of Florence had stirred old republican memories in the degenerate city, and Gregory was warned that his life was unsafe in the ancient capital of Christendom. In May he re- tired to Anagni.

And now, as if at last yielding to Catherine, he turned from war to diplomacy. His agents encouraged the populace of the cities, who longed for peace with the Church, to overthrow their rebel governments; and to all towns that returned to his allegiance he promised self-government un- der a papal vicar of their own choice. City after city accepted these terms. In 1377 Florence agreed with Gregory to let Bernabò Visconti arbitrate their dispute. Bernabò, having persuaded the Pope to give him half of any penalty he might lay upon Florence, bade the city pay an indemnity of 800,000 florins ($20,000,000) to the Holy See. Deserted by her allies, Florence angrily submitted; but Pope Urban VI reduced the penalty to 250,000 florins.

Gregory had not lived to see his victory. On November 7, 1377, he re- turned to Rome. He had been an invalid even in Avignon, and had not borne well his winter in central Italy. He felt the approach of death, and feared that the conflict between France and Italy for possession of the papacy would tear the Church to pieces. On March 19, 1378, he made ar- rangements for the speedy election of his successor. Eight days later he died, longing for *le beau pays de France*.[25]

III. THE CHRISTIAN LIFE: 1300-1424

Deferring to a later chapter a consideration of the faith of the people and the morals of the clergy, let us note two contrasting features of Chris- tian life in fourteenth-century Italy: the Inquisition and the saints. Fairness requires us to remember that the great majority of Christians then believed that the Church had been instituted, and that her basic doctrines had been laid down, by the Son of God; hence—whatever might be the faults of her human personnel—any active movement to overthrow her was rebellion against divine authority as well as treason against the secular state of which the Church was the upholding moral arm. Only with this thought in mind can we understand the ferocity with which Church and laity joined in suppressing the heresy preached (*c.* 1303) by Dolcino of Novara and his comely sister Margherita.

Like Joachim of Flora, Dolcino divided history into periods, of which the third, from Pope Sylvester I (314-35) to 1280, saw the gradual corruption of the Church through worldly wealth; since Sylvester (said Dolcino) all the popes except Celestine V had been unfaithful to Christ; Benedict, Francis, and Dominic had nobly tried to win the Church back from Mammon to God, but had failed; and the papacy had now, under Boniface VIII and Clement V, become the harlot of the Apocalypse. Dolcino made himself the head of a new fraternity, the "Apostolic Brethren of Parma," who rejected the authority of the popes, and inherited a medley of doctrines from the Patarines, the Waldenses, and the Spiritual Franciscans. They professed absolute chastity, but each man among them lived with a woman whom he called his sister. Clement V ordered the Inquisition to examine them; they refused to appear before the tribunal; instead they armed themselves, and took up positions at the foot of the Piedmontese Alps. The inquisitors led an army against them; bloody battles were fought; the Brethren retreated into mountain passes, where they were blockaded and starved; they ate rats, dogs, hares, grass; at last their mountain stronghold was stormed, a thousand fell fighting, thousands were burned to death (1304). When Margherita was led to the stake she was still so beautiful, despite emaciation, that men of rank offered her marriage if she would abjure her heresies; she refused, and was slowly consumed. Dolcino and an associate, Longino, were reserved for special treatment. They were mounted on a cart and were paraded through Vercelli; during this procession their flesh was torn from them bit by bit with hot pincers; their limbs and genitals were wrenched from their bodies; finally they were allowed to die.[26]

It is pleasant to turn from such barbarism to the continuing efficacy of Christianity in inspiring men and women to saintliness. The same century that saw the tribulations and corruptions of Avignon produced missionaries like Giovanni da Monte Corvino and Oderic of Pordenone, who tried to convert the Hindus and Chinese; but the Chinese, says a Franciscan chronicler, clung to the "error that any man could be saved in his own sect."[27] Unwittingly these missionaries contributed less to religion than to the science of geography.

St. Catherine of Siena was born, lived, and died in a modest room still shown to visitors. From that foot of earth she helped to move the papacy, and to revive in the people of Italy a piety that has survived *Rinascita* and *Risorgimento* alike. At fifteen she joined the Order of Penance of St. Dominic; this was a "tertiary" organization, composed not of monks or nuns, but of men and women living a secular life, yet dedicating themselves as much as possible to works of religion and charity. Catherine dwelt with her parents, but she made her room almost an anchoritic cell, lost herself in prayer and mystical contemplation, and hardly left her home except to go to church. Her parents were disturbed by her preoccupation with religion, and feared for her health. They laid upon her the heaviest drudgery of the household, which she performed without complaint. "I make a little corner apart in my heart for Jesus," she said,[28] and maintained a childlike serenity. All the joy, doubt, and ecstasy that other girls might derive from "profane" love Catherine sought and found in devotion to Christ. In the growing intensity of these solitary meditations she thought and spoke of Christ as her heavenly lover, she exchanged hearts with Him, saw herself, in vision, married to Him; and like St. Francis she thought so long about the five wounds of the Crucified that it seemed to her that she felt them in her own hands and feet and side. All temptations of the flesh she rejected as the wiles of Satan to withdraw her from her one engrossing love.

After three years of almost solitary piety she felt that she could safely venture into the life of the city. As she had devoted her womanhood to Christ, so she devoted her maternal tenderness to the sick and needy of Siena; she stayed to the last moment with the victims of plague, and stood in spiritual consolation beside condemned criminals until the hour of their execution.[29] When her parents died and left her a modest patrimony, she distributed it among the poor. Though she was disfigured by smallpox, her face was a blessing to all who saw her. Young men at her word abandoned their wonted blasphemies, and older men heard with melting skepticism her simple and trusting philosophy. All the evils of human life, she thought, were the result of human wickedness; but all the sins of mankind would be swallowed up and lost in the ocean of God's love; and all the ills of the world would be cured if men could be persuaded to practise Christian love. Many believed her; Montepulciano sent for her to come and reconcile its feuding families; Pisa and Lucca sought her counsel; Florence invited her to join an embassy to Avignon. Gradually she was drawn into the world.

She was horrified by what she saw in Italy and France: Rome filthy and desolate; Italy divorcing itself from a Church that had deserted to France; a clergy whose worldly living had forfeited the respect of the laity; a France already half ruined with war. Confident in her divine mission, she denounced prelates and pontiffs to their faces, and told them that only a return to Rome and to decency could save the Church. Herself unable to write, she, a girl of twenty-six, dictated stern but loving letters, in her simple and melodious Italian, to popes, princes, and statesmen; and on almost every page appeared the prophetic word *Riformazione*.[30] She failed with the statesmen, but she succeeded with the people. She rejoiced when Urban V came to Rome, mourned when he left, lived again when Gregory XI came; she gave good advice to Urban VI, but was shocked by his brutality; and when the Papal Schism tore Christendom in two she was among the first casualties of that incredible conflict. She had reduced her meals to a mere mouthful of food; she carried asceticism so far, said legend, that the consecrated wafer received by her in communion was her only nourishment. She lost all power to resist disease; the Schism broke her will to live; and two years after its outbreak she passed away, aged thirty-three (1380). To this day she is a force for good in the Italy that she loved only next to Christ and the Church.

In the year (1380) and city of her death St. Bernardino was born. The tradition of Catherine molded him; in the plague of 1400 he gave his days and nights to caring for the sick. Having joined the Franciscans, he set the example of obeying the strict rule of the Order. Many monks followed him; with these he founded (1405) the Observantine Franciscans, or Brethren of the Strict Observance; and before he died three hundred monastic communities had accepted his rule. The purity and nobility of his life gave an irresistible eloquence to his preaching. Even in Rome, whose population was more lawless than that of any other city in Europe, he drew criminals to confession, sinners to repentance, and habitual feudists to peace. Seventy years before Savonarola's Burning of the Vanities in Florence, Bernardino persuaded Roman men and women to throw their playing cards, dice, lottery tickets, false hair, indecent pictures and books, even their musical instruments, into a giant funeral pyre on the Capitol (1424). Three days later a young woman accused of witchcraft was burned on the same square, and all Rome crowded to the spectacle.[31] Saint Bernardino himself was "a most conscientious persecutor of heretics."[32]

So the good and the evil, the beautiful and the horrible, mingled in the flux and chaos of the Christian life. The simple folk of Italy remained contentedly medieval, while the middle and upper classes, half drunk with the long-cellared wine of classic culture, moved forward with a noble ardor to create the Renaissance, and modern man.

Fig. 1—GIOTTO: *Flight into Egypt;* Arena Chapel, Padua   PAGE 22

Fig. 2—SIMONE MARTINI: *The Annunciation;* Uffizi Gallery, Florence   PAGE 35

Fig. 3—Lorenzo Ghiberti· *Doors of the Baptistery;* Florence PAGE 91

Fig. 4—DONATELLO: *Crucifixion*,
wood; Santa Croce, Florence

PAGE 95

Fig. 5—DONATELLO: *David*, bronze; Bargello,
Florence   PAGE 93

Fig. 6—DONATELLO: *Annunciation*, sandstone; Santa Croce, Florence   PAGE 95

Fig. 7—LUCA DELLA ROBBIA: *Madonna and Child*, terra cotta; relief over a
portal of the Badia, Florence

Fig. 8—DONATELLO: *Gattamelata;* Padua

Fig. 9—MASACCIO: *The Tribute Money;* Brancacci Chapel, Florence PAGE 100

Fig. 10—FRA ANGELICO: *The Annunciation;* San Marco, Florence PAGE 102

Fig. 11—Fra Filippo Lippi:
Virgin Adoring the Child;
Kaiser Friedrich Museum,
Berlin   PAGE 105

Fig. 12—Andrea del
Verrochio: *The
Baptism of Christ;*
Uffizi   Gallery,
Florence PAGE 131

Fig. 13 — DOMENICO GHIR-
LANDAIO: *Portrait of
Count Sassetti(?) and
Grandson;* Louvre,
Paris PAGE 130

Fig. 14—SANDRO BOTTICELLI: *The Birth of Venus;* Uffizi Gallery, Florence
PAGE 137

BOOK II

THE FLORENTINE RENAISSANCE

1378-1534

CHAPTER III

The Rise of the Medici

1378-1464

I. THE SETTING

THE Italians called this coming of age *la Rinascita,* Rebirth, because to them it seemed a triumphant resurrection of the classic spirit after a barbarous interruption of a thousand years.* The classic world, the Italians felt, had died in the German and Hun invasions of the third, fourth, and fifth centuries; the heavy hand of the Goth had crushed the fading but still fair flower of Roman art and life; "Gothic" art had repeated the invasion with an architecture precariously unstable and decoratively bizarre, and a sculpture coarse, crude, and gloomy with dour prophets and emaciated saints. Now, by the grace of time, those bearded Goths and those "long-beard" Lombards had been absorbed into the dominant Italian blood; by the grace of Vitruvius and the instructive ruins of the Roman Forum the classic column and architrave would again build shrines and palaces of sòber dignity; by the grace of Petrarch and a hundred Italian scholars the rediscovered classics would restore the literature of Italy to the pure idiom and precision of Cicero's prose, and the mellow music of Virgil's verse. The sunshine of the Italian spirit would break through the northern mists; men and women would escape from the prison of medieval fear; they would worship beauty in all its forms, and fill the air with the joy of resurrection. Italy would be young again.

The men who spoke so were too near the event to see the "Rebirth" in historical perspective, or in the confusing diversity of its constituents. But it took more than a revival of antiquity to make the Renaissance. And first of all it took money—smelly bourgeois money: the profits of skillful managers and underpaid labor; of hazardous voyages to the East, and laborious crossings of the Alps, to buy goods cheap and sell them dear; of careful calculations, investments, and loans; of interest and dividends accumulated

---

* Vasari, in his *Vite de' più eccelenti architetti, pittori, e scultori Italiani* (1550), established the term *Rinascita,* and the French *Encyclopédie* of 1751-72 first definitely used the word *Renaissance,* to denote the flowering of letters and arts in the fourteenth, fifteenth, and sixteenth centuries.

until enough surplus could be spared from the pleasures of the flesh, from the purchase of senates, signories, and mistresses, to pay a Michelangelo or a Titian to transmute wealth into beauty, and perfume a fortune with the breath of art. Money is the root of all civilization. The funds of merchants, bankers, and the Church paid for the manuscripts that revived antiquity. Nor was it those manuscripts which freed the mind and senses of the Renaissance; it was the secularism that came from the rise of the middle classes; it was the growth of the universities, of knowledge and philosophy, the realistic sharpening of minds by the study of law, the broadening of minds by wider acquaintance with the world. Doubting the dogmas of the Church, no longer frightened by the fear of hell, and seeing the clergy as epicurean as the laity, the educated Italian shook himself loose from intellectual and ethical restraints; his liberated senses took unabashed delight in all embodiments of beauty in woman, man, and art; and his new freedom made him creative for an amazing century (1434-1534) before it destroyed him with moral chaos, disintegrative individualism, and national slavery. The interlude between two disciplines was the Renaissance.

Why was northern Italy the first to experience this spring awakening? There the old Roman world had never been quite destroyed; the towns had kept their ancient structure and memories, and now renewed their Roman law. Classic art survived in Rome, Verona, Mantua, Padua; Agrippa's Pantheon still functioned as a place of worship, though it was fourteen hundred years old; and in the Forum one could almost hear Cicero and Caesar debating the fate of Catiline. The Latin language was still a living tongue, of which Italian was merely a melodious variant. Pagan deities, myths, and rites lingered in popular memory, or under Christian forms. Italy stood athwart the Mediterranean, commanding that basin of classic civilization and trade. Northern Italy was more urban and industrial than any other region of Europe except Flanders. It had never suffered a full feudalism, but had subjected its nobles to its cities and its merchant class. It was the avenue of trade between the rest of Italy and transalpine Europe, and between Western Europe and the Levant; its commerce and industry made it the richest region in Christendom. Its adventurous traders were everywhere, from the fairs of France to the farthest ports of the Black Sea. Accustomed to dealing with Greeks, Arabs, Jews, Egyptians, Persians, Hindus, and Chinese, they lost the edge of their dogmas, and brought into the literate classes of Italy that same indifference to creeds which in nineteenth-century Europe came from widening contacts with alien faiths. Mercantile wisdom, however, conspired with national traditions, temperament, and pride to keep Italy Catholic even while she became pagan. Papal fees trickled to Rome along a thousand rivulets from a score of Christian lands, and the wealth of the Curia overflowed throughout Italy. The Church rewarded Italian loyalty with a generous lenience to the sins of the flesh, and a genial tolerance (before the Council of Trent, 1545) of heretical philosophers who refrained from undermining the piety of the people. So Italy advanced, in wealth and art and thought, a century ahead of the rest of Europe; and it was only in the sixteenth century, when the Renaissance faded in Italy, that it blossomed in France, Germany, Holland, England, and Spain. The Renaissance was not a period in time but a mode of life and thought moving from Italy through Europe with the course of commerce, war, and ideas.

It made its first home in Florence for much the same reasons that gave it birth in northern Italy. Through the organization of her industry, the extension of her commerce, and the operations of her financiers, Fiorenza—the City of Flowers—was in the fourteenth century the richest town in the peninsula, excepting Venice. But while the Venetians in that age gave their energies almost entirely to the pursuit of pleasure and wealth, the Florentines, possibly through the stimulus of a turbulent semidemocracy, developed a keenness of mind and wit, and a skill in every art, that made their city by common consent the cultural capital of Italy. The quarrels of the factions raised the temperature of life and thought, and rival families contended in the patronage of art as well as in the pursuit of power. The final—not the first—stimulus was given when Cosimo de' Medici offered the resources of his own and other fortunes and palaces to house and entertain the delegates to the Council of Florence (1439). The Greek prelates and scholars who came to that assembly to discuss the reunion of Eastern and Western Christianity had a far better knowledge of Greek literature than any Florentine could then possess; some of them lectured in Florence, and the elite of the city crowded to hear them. When Constantinople fell to the Turks many Greeks left it to make their home in the city where they had found such hospitality fourteen years before. Several of them brought manuscripts of ancient texts; some of them lectured on the Greek language or on Greek poetry and philosophy. So, by the concourse of many streams of influence, the Renaissance took form in Florence, and made it the Athens of Italy.

II. THE MATERIAL BASIS

Florence, in the fifteenth century, was a city-state ruling not only Florence but (with interruptions) Prato, Pistoia, Pisa, Volterra, Cortona, Arezzo, and their agricultural hinterland. The peasants were not serfs but partly small proprietors, mostly tenant farmers, who lived in houses of crude cemented stone much as today, and chose their own village officials to govern them in local affairs. Machiavelli did not disdain to chat and play with these hardy knights of the field, the orchard, or the vine. But the magistrates of the cities regulated sales, and, to appease a troublesome proletariat, kept food prices too low for peasant happiness; so the ancient strife of country and city added its somber obbligato to the songs of hate that rose from embattled classes within the city walls.

According to Villani the city of Florence proper had in 1343 a population of some 91,500 souls; we have no equally reliable estimate for later Renaissance years, but we may presume that the population grew as commerce expanded and industry thrived. About a fourth of the city dwellers were industrial workers; the textile lines alone, in the thirteenth century, employed 30,000 men and women in two hundred factories.[1] In 1300 Federigo Oricellarii earned his surname by bringing from the East the secret of extracting from lichens a violet pigment (*orchella*, archil). This technique revolutionized the dye industry, and made some woolen manufacturers into what today would be millionaires. In textiles Florence had already reached by 1300 the capitalistic stage of large investment, central provision of materials and machinery, systematic division of labor, and control of production by the suppliers of capital. In 1407 a woolen garment passed through thirty processes, each performed by a worker specializing in that operation.[2]

To sell its products Florence encouraged its merchants to maintain trade with all ports of the Mediterranean, and along the Atlantic as far as Bruges. Consuls were stationed in Italy, the Baleares, Flanders, Egypt, Cyprus, Constantinople, Persia, India, and China to protect and promote Florentine trade. Pisa was conquered as an indispensable outlet of Florentine goods to the sea, and Genoese merchant vessels were hired to carry them. Foreign products competitive with Florentine manufactures were excluded from the markets of Florence through protective tariffs set by a government of merchants and financiers.

To finance this industry and commerce, and much else, the eighty banking houses of Florence—chiefly the Bardi, Peruzzi, Strozzi, Pitti, and Medici

—invested the savings of their depositors. They cashed checks (*polizze*),[3] issued letters of credit (*lettere di pagamenti*),[4] exchanged merchandise as well as credit,[5] and supplied governments with funds for peace or war. Some Florentine firms lent 1,365,000 florins ($34,125,000?) to Edward III of England,[6] and were ruined by his default (1345). Despite such catastrophes Florence became the financial capital of Europe from the thirteenth through the fifteenth century; it was there that rates of exchange were fixed for the currencies of Europe.[7] As early as 1300 a system of insurance protected the cargoes of Italy on their voyages—a precaution not adopted in England till 1543.[8] Double-entry bookkeeping appears in a Florentine account book of 1382; probably it was already a century old in Florence, Venice, and Genoa.[9] In 1345 the Florentine government issued negotiable gold-redeemable bonds bearing the low interest rate of five per cent—a proof of the city's reputation for commercial prosperity and integrity. The revenue of the government in 1400 was greater than that of England in the heyday of Elizabeth.

The bankers, merchants, manufacturers, professional men, and skilled workers of Europe were organized in guilds. In Florence seven guilds (*arti*, arts, trades) were known as *arti maggiori* or greater guilds: clothing manufacturers, wool manufacturers, silk goods manufacturers, fur merchants, financiers, physicians and druggists, and a mixed guild of merchants, judges, and notaries. The remaining fourteen guilds of Florence were the *arti minori* or minor trades: clothiers, hosiers, butchers, bakers, vintners, cobblers, saddlers, armorers, blacksmiths, locksmiths, carpenters, innkeepers, masons and stonecutters, and a motley conglomeration of oil sellers, pork butchers, and ropemakers. Every voter had to be a member of one or another of these guilds; and the nobles who had been disfranchised in 1282 by a bourgeois revolution joined the guilds to regain the vote. Below the twenty-one guilds were seventy-two unions of voteless workingmen; below these, thousands of day laborers forbidden to organize, and living in impotent poverty; below these—or above them as better cared for by their masters—were a few slaves. The members of the greater guilds constituted in politics the *popolo grasso,* the fat or well-fed people; the rest of the population composed the *popolo minuto* or little people. The political history of Florence, like that of modern states, was first the victory of the business class over the old landowning aristocracy (1293), and then the struggle of the "working class" to acquire political power.

In 1345 Cinto Brandini and nine others were put to death for organizing the poorer workers in the woolen industry, and foreign laborers were imported to break up these unions.[10] In 1368 the "little people" attempted a revolution but were suppressed. Ten years later the *tumulto dei Ciompi*—the revolt of the wool carders—brought the working classes for a dizzy moment into control of the commune. Led by a barefoot workingman, Michele di Lando, the carders surged into the Palazzo Vecchio, dispersed the Signory, and established a dictatorship of the proletariat (1378). The laws against unionization were repealed, the lower unions were enfranchised, a moratorium of twelve years was declared on the debts of wage earners, and interest rates were reduced to further ease the burdens of the debtor class. Business leaders retaliated by shutting down their shops and inducing the landowners to cut the city's food supply. The harassed revolutionists split into factions—an aristocracy of labor consisting of skilled craftsmen, and a "left wing" moved with communistic ideas. Finally the conservatives brought in strong men from the countryside, armed them, overthrew the divided government, and restored the business class to power (1382).

The triumphant bourgeoisie revised the constitution to consolidate its victory. The *Signoria*, or municipal council of *signori* or gentlemen, was composed of eight *priori delle arti*—priors or leaders of the guilds—chosen by lot from bags containing the names of those eligible for office. They in turn chose as their executive head a *gonfaloniere di giustizia*—a "standard-bearer of justice" or executor of the law. Of the eight priors four had to be from the greater guilds, though these *arti maggiori* included but a small minority of the adult male population. The same proportion was required in the advisory *Consiglio del Popolo* or Council of the People; *popolo*, however, meant only the members of the twenty-one guilds. The *Consiglio del Comune* was chosen from any guild membership, but its function was confined to assembling when summoned by the Signory, and to voting yes or no on proposals put before it by the priors. On rare occasions the priors called a *parlamento* of all voters to the Piazza della Signoria by ringing the great bell in the Palazzo Vecchio tower. Usually such a general assembly chose a *balia* or commission of reform, gave it supreme power for a stated period, and adjourned.

It was a generous error of nineteenth-century historians to credit pre-Medicean Florence with a degree of democracy quite unknown in that plutocratic paradise. The subject cities, though themselves fertile in genius and proud of their heritage, had no voice in the Florentine Signory that governed them. In Florence only 3200 males could vote; and in both councils the representatives of the business class were a rarely challenged majority.[11] The upper classes were convinced that the illiterate masses could form no sound or safe judgment of the community good in domestic crises or foreign affairs. The Florentines loved freedom, but it was, among the poor, the freedom to be commanded by Florentine masters, and, among the rich, the liberty to rule the city and its dependencies without imperial or papal or feudal impediment.

The indisputable defects of the constitution were the brevity of its terms of office, and the frequent changes in the constitution itself. The evil results were faction, conspiracy, violence, confusion, incompetence, and the inability of the republic to design and execute such consistent and long-term policies as made for the stability and power of Venice. The pertinent good result was an electric atmosphere of conflict and debate that quickened the pulse, sharpened sense and mind and wit, stirred the imagination, and lifted Florence for a century to the cultural leadership of the world.

III. COSIMO "PATER PATRIAE"

Politics in Florence was the conflict of wealthy families and factions—the Ricci, Albizzi, Medici, Ridolfi, Pazzi, Pitti, Strozzi, Rucellai, Valori, Capponi, Soderini—for control of the government. From 1381 to 1434, with some interruptions, the Albizzi maintained their ascendancy in the state, and valiantly protected the rich against the poor.

The Medici family can be traced back to 1201, when Chiarissimo de' Medici was a member of the Communal Council.* Averardo de' Medici, great-great-grandfather of Cosimo, founded the fortune of the family by bold commerce and judicious finance, and was chosen gonfalonier in 1314. Averardo's grandnephew, Salvestro de' Medici, gonfalonier in 1378, established the popularity of the family by espousing the cause of the rebel poor. Salvestro's grandnephew, Giovanni di Bicci de' Medici, gonfalonier in 1421, further endeared the family to the people by supporting—though he himself would suffer heavily from it—an annual tax (*catasto*) of one half of one per cent on income, which was reckoned at seven per cent of a man's capital (1427).[12] The rich, who had previously enjoyed a poll or head tax merely equal to that paid by the poor, vowed vengeance on the Medici.

---

* The origin of their name is a mystery. There is no evidence that they were physicians, though they may at one time have joined a medical guild in the loose way of Florentine guild demarcations. Nor do we know the meaning of their famous emblem, the six red balls (*palle*) on a field of gold. These balls, reduced to three, became the insignia of pawn-brokers in later times.

Giovanni di Bicci died in 1428, bequeathing to his son Cosimo a good name and the largest fortune in Tuscany—179,221 florins ($4,480,525?).[13] Cosimo was already thirty-nine years old, fully fit to carry on the far-flung enterprises of the firm. These were not confined to banking; they included the management of extensive farms, the manufacture of silk and woolen goods, and a varied trade that bound Russia and Spain, Scotland and Syria, Islam and Christendom. Cosimo, while building churches in Florence, saw no sin in making trade agreements, and exchanging costly presents, with Turkish sultans. The firm made a specialty of importing from the East articles of little bulk and great value, like spices, almonds, and sugar, and sold these and other products in a score of European ports.

Cosimo directed all this with quiet skill, and found time left for politics. As a member of the *Dieci*, or War Council of Ten, he guided Florence to victory against Lucca, and as a banker he financed the war by lending large sums to the government. His popularity excited the envy of other magnates, and in 1433, Rinaldo degli Albizzi launched an attack upon him as planning to overthrow the Republic and make himself dictator. Rinaldo persuaded Bernardo Guadagni, then gonfalonier, to order Cosimo's arrest; Cosimo surrendered himself, and was confined in the Palazzo Vecchio. Since Rinaldo, with his armed retainers, dominated the *parlamento* in the Piazza della Signoria, a decree of death seemed imminent. But Cosimo managed to convey a thousand ducats ($25,000?) to Bernardo, who suddenly became more humane, and compromised by having Cosimo, his sons, and his chief supporters banished for ten years.[14] Cosimo took up his residence in Venice, where his modesty and his means made him many friends. Soon the Venetian government was using its influence to have him recalled. The Signory elected in 1434 was favorable to him, and reversed the sentences of exile; Cosimo returned in triumph, and Rinaldo and his sons fled.

A *parlamento* appointed a *balia*, and gave it supreme power. After serving three short terms Cosimo relinquished all political positions; "to be elected to office," he said, "is often prejudicial to the body and hurtful to the soul."[15] Since his enemies had left the city, his friends easily dominated the government. Without disturbing republican forms, he managed, by persuasion or money, to have his adherents remain in office to the end of his life. His loans to influential families won or forced their support; his gifts to the clergy enlisted their enthusiastic aid; and his public benefactions, of unprecedented scope and generosity, easily reconciled the citizens to his rule. The Florentines had observed that the constitution of the Republic did not protect them from the aristocracy of wealth; the defeat of the

Ciompi had burned this lesson into the public memory. If the populace had to choose between the Albizzi, who favored the rich, and the Medici, who favored the middle classes and the poor, it could not long hesitate. A people oppressed by its economic masters, and weary of faction, welcomed dictatorship in Florence in 1434, in Perugia in 1389, in Bologna in 1401, in Siena in 1477, in Rome in 1347 and 1922. "The Medici," said Villani, "were enabled to attain supremacy in the name of freedom, and with the support of the *popolo* and the populace."[16]

Cosimo used his power with shrewd moderation, tempered with occasional violence. When his friends suspected that Baldaccio d'Anghiari was forming a conspiracy to end Cosimo's power, they threw Baldaccio out of a sufficiently high window to ensure his termination, and Cosimo did not complain; it was one of his quips that "states are not ruled with paternosters." He replaced the fixed income tax with a sliding scale of levies on capital, and was accused of adjusting these assessments to favor his friends and discourage his enemies. These levies totaled 4,875,000 florins ($121,875,000) in the first twenty years of Cosimo's ascendancy; and those who balked at paying them were summarily jailed. Many aristocrats left the city and resumed the rural life of the medieval nobility. Cosimo accepted their departure with equanimity, remarking that new aristocrats could be made with a few yards of scarlet cloth.[17]

The people smiled approval, for they noted that the levies were devoted to the administration and adornment of Florence, and that Cosimo himself contributed 400,000 florins ($10,000,000?) to public works and private charities;[18] this was almost double the sum that he left to his heirs.[19] He labored assiduously to the end of his seventy-five years, managing at once his own properties and the affairs of the state. When Edward IV of England asked for a substantial loan, Cosimo obliged him, ignoring the faithlessness of Edward III, and the King repaid him with coin and political support. Tommaso Parentucelli, Bishop of Bologna, ran out of funds and asked for aid; Cosimo supplied him; and when Parentucelli became Pope Nicholas V Cosimo was given charge of all papal finances. To keep the varied threads of his activity from tangling, he rose early, and went nearly every day to his office, like an American millionaire. At home he pruned his trees and tended his vines. He dressed simply, ate and drank temperately, and (after begetting an illegitimate son by a slave girl) lived a quiet and orderly family life. Those who were admitted to his home were astonished at the contrast between the homely fare of his private table and the lavish feasts that he provided for foreign dignitaries as a lure to comity and peace. He was normally humane, mild, forgiving, reticent and yet known for his dry wit. He was generous to the poor, paid the taxes of impoverished friends, and hid his charity, like his power, in a gracious anonymity. Botticelli, Pontormo, and Benozzo Gozzoli have pictured him for us: of middle stature and olive complexion, with gray receding hair, long, sharp nose, and a grave, kindly countenance bespeaking shrewd wisdom and calm strength.

His foreign policy was dedicated to the organization of peace. Coming to power after a series of ruinous conflicts, Cosimo noted how war, actual or imminent, hobbled the march of trade. When the rule of the Visconti in Milan collapsed in chaos at Filippo Maria's death, and Venice threatened to absorb the duchy and dominate all nothern Italy to the very gates of Florence, Cosimo sent Francesco Sforza the means to establish himself in Milan and check the Venetian advance. When Venice and Naples formed an alliance against Florence, Cosimo called in so many loans made to their citizens that their governments were induced to make peace.[20] Thereafter Milan and Florence stood against Venice and Naples in a balance of power so even that neither side dared to risk a war. This policy of balanced powers, conceived by Cosimo and continued by Lorenzo, gave Italy those decades of peace and order, from 1450 to 1492, during which the cities grew rich enough to finance the early Renaissance.

It was the good fortune of Italy and mankind that Cosimo cared as much for literature, scholarship, philosophy, and art as for wealth and power. He was a man of education and taste; he knew Latin well, and had a smattering of Greek, Hebrew, and Arabic; he was broad enough to appreciate the piety and painting of Fra Angelico, the engaging rascality of Fra Filippo Lippi, the classical style of Ghiberti's reliefs, the bold originality of Donatello's sculpture, the grandiose churches of Brunellesco, the restrained power of Michelozzo's architecture, the pagan Platonism of Gemistus Pletho, the mystic Platonism of Pico and Ficino, the refinement of Alberti, the learned vulgarity of Poggio, the bibliolatry of Niccolò de' Niccoli; and all these men experienced his generosity. He brought Joannes Argyropoulos to Florence to instruct its youth in the language and literature of ancient Greece, and for twelve years he studied with Ficino the classics of Greece and Rome. He spent a large part of his fortune collecting classic texts, so that the most costly cargoes of his ships were in many cases manuscripts carried from Greece or Alexandria. When Niccolò de' Niccoli had ruined himself in buying ancient manuscripts, Cosimo opened for him an unlimited credit at the Medici bank, and supported him till death. He engaged forty-five copyists, under the guidance of the enthusiastic bookseller Vespasiano da Bisticci, to transcribe such manuscripts as could not be bought. All these "precious minims" he placed in rooms at the monastery of San Marco, or in the abbey of Fiesole, or in his own library. When Niccoli died (1437), leaving eight hundred manuscripts valued at 6000 florins ($150,000), along with many debts, and naming sixteen trustees to determine the disposal of the books, Cosimo offered to assume the debts if he might allocate the volumes. It was so agreed, and Cosimo divided the collection between San Marco's library and his own. All these collections were open to teachers and students without charge. Said the Florentine historian Varchi, with patriotic exaggeration:

> That Greek letters were not completely forgotten, to the great loss of humanity, and that Latin letters have been revived to the infinite benefit of the people—this all Italy, nay all the world, owes solely to the high wisdom and friendliness of the house of the Medici.[21]

Of course the great work of revival had been inaugurated by the translators in the twelfth and thirteenth centuries, and by Arabic commentators, and by Petrarch and Boccaccio. It had been continued by scholars and collectors like Salutati, Traversari, Bruni, and Valla before Cosimo; it was carried forward independently of him by Niccoli, Poggio, Filelfo, King Alfonso the Magnanimous of Naples, and a hundred other contemporaries of Cosimo, even by his exiled rival, Palla Strozzi. But if we embrace in our judgment not only Cosimo *Pater Patriae*, but his descendants Lorenzo the Magnificent, Leo X, and Clement VII, we may admit that in the patronage of learning and art the Medici have never been equaled by any other family in the known history of mankind.

IV. THE HUMANISTS

It was under the Medici, or in their day, that the humanists captivated the mind of Italy, turned it from religion to philosophy, from heaven to earth, and revealed to an astonished generation the riches of pagan thought and art. These men mad about scholarship received, as early as Ariosto,[22] the name of *umanisti* because they called the study of classic culture *umanità*—the "humanities"—or *literae humaniores*—not "more humane" but more human letters. The proper study of mankind was now to be man, in all the potential strength and beauty of his body, in all the joy and pain of his senses and feelings, in all the frail majesty of his reason; and in these as most abundantly and perfectly revealed in the literature and art of ancient Greece and Rome. This was humanism.

Nearly all the Latin, and many of the Greek classics now extant were known to medieval scholars here and there; and the thirteenth century was acquainted with the major pagan philosophers. But that century had almost ignored Greek poetry; and many ancient worthies now honored by us lay neglected in monastic or cathedral libraries. It was mostly in such forgotten corners that Petrarch and his successors found the "lost" classics, "gentle prisoners," he called them, "held in captivity by barbarous jailers." Boccaccio, visiting Monte Cassino, was shocked to find precious manuscripts rotting in dust, or mutilated to make psalters or amulets. Poggio, visiting the Swiss monastery of St. Gall while attending the Council of Constance, found the *Institutiones* of Quintilian in a foul dark dungeon, and felt, as he reclaimed the rolls, that the old pedagogue was stretching out his hands, begging to be saved from the "barbarians"; for by that name the culture-conscious Italians, like the ancient Greeks and Romans, called their virile conquerors beyond the Alps. Poggio alone, undeterred by winter's cold or snow, exhumed from such tombs the texts of Lucretius, Columella, Frontinus, Vitruvius, Valerius Flaccus, Tertullian, Plautus, Petronius, Ammianus Marcellinus, and several major speeches of Cicero. Coluccio Salutati unearthed Cicero's letters *ad familiares* at Vercelli (1389); Gherardo Landriani found Cicero's treatises on rhetoric in an old chest at Lodi (1422); Ambrogio Traversari rescued Cornelius Nepos from oblivion in Padua (1434); the *Agricola, Germania,* and *Dialogi* of Tacitus were discovered in Germany (1455); the first six books of Tacitus' *Annales,* and a full manuscript of the younger Pliny's letters were recovered from the monastery of Corvey (1508), and became a prize possession of Leo X.

In the half century before the Turks took Constantinople a dozen humanists studied or traveled in Greece; one of them, Giovanni Aurispa, brought back to Italy 238 manuscripts, including the plays of Aeschylus and Sophocles; another, Francesco Filelfo, salvaged from Constantinople (1427) texts of Herodotus, Thucydides, Polybius, Demosthenes, Aeschines, and Aristotle, and seven dramas of Euripides. When such literary explorers returned to Italy with their finds they were welcomed like victorious generals, and princes and prelates paid well for a share of the spoils. The fall of Constantinople resulted in the loss of many classics previously mentioned by Byzantine writers as in the libraries of that city; nevertheless thousands of volumes were saved, and most of them came to Italy; to this day the best manuscripts of Greek classics are in Italy. For three centuries, from Petrarch to Tasso, men collected manuscripts with philatelic passion. Niccolò de' Niccoli spent more than he had in this pursuit; Andreolo de Ochis was ready to sacrifice his home, his wife, his life to add to his library; Poggio suffered when he saw money being spent on anything else than books.

An editorial revolution ensued. The texts so recovered were studied, compared, corrected, and explained in a campaign of scholarship that ranged from Lorenzo Valla in Naples to Sir Thomas More in London. Since these labors in many cases required a knowledge of Greek, Italy—and later France, England, and Germany—sent out a call for teachers of Greek. Aurispa and Filelfo learned the language in Greece itself. After Manuel Chrysoloras came to Italy (1397) as Byzantine envoy, the University of Florence persuaded him to join its faculty as professor of Greek language and literature. Among his pupils there were Poggio, Palla Strozzi, Marsuppini, and Manetti. Leonardo Bruni, studying law, abandoned it, under the spell of Chrysoloras, for the study of Greek; "I gave myself to his teaching with such ardor," he tells us, "that my dreams at night were filled with what I had learned from him during the day."[23] Who now could imagine that Greek grammar was once an adventure and a romance?

In 1439 Greeks met Italians at the Council of Florence, and the lessons they exchanged in language had far more result than their laborious negotiations in theology. There Gemistus Pletho gave the famous lectures that ended the reign of Aristotle in European philosophy and enthroned Plato as almost a god. When the Council dispersed, Joannes Bessarion, who had come to it as Bishop of Nicaea, remained in Italy and gave part of his time to teaching Greek. Other cities contracted the fever; Bessarion brought it to Rome; Theodorus Gaza taught Greek at Mantua, Ferrara (1444), and Rome (1451); Demetrius Chalcondyles taught at Perugia (1450), Padua, Florence, and Milan (c. 1492-1511); Joannes Argyropoulos at Padua (1441), Florence (1456-71), and Rome (1471-86). All these men came to Italy before the fall of Constantinople (1453), so that that event played a minor role in the transit of Greek from Byzantium to Italy; but the gradual encirclement of Constantinople by the Turks after 1356 shared in persuading Greek scholars to go west. One of those who fled at the collapse of the Eastern capital was Constantine Lascaris, who came to teach Greek at Milan (1460-5), Naples, and Messina (1466-1501). The first Greek book printed in Renaissance Italy was his Greek grammar.

With all these scholars and their pupils enthusiastically active in Italy, it was but a short time when the classics of Greek literature and philosophy were rendered into Latin with more thoroughness, accuracy, and finish than in the twelfth and thirteenth centuries. Guarino translated parts of Strabo and Plutarch; Traversari, Diogenes Laertius; Valla, Herodotus, Thucydides, and the *Iliad;* Perotti, Polybius; Ficino, Plato and Plotinus. Plato, above all, amazed and delighted the humanists. They gloried in the fluid grace of his style; they found in the *Dialogues* a drama more vivid and contemporary than anything in Aeschylus, Sophocles, or Euripides; they envied and marveled at the freedom with which the Greeks of Socrates' time discussed the most crucial problems of religion and politics; and they thought they had found in Plato—clouded with Plotinus—a mystical philosophy that would enable them to retain a Christianity that they had ceased to believe in, but never ceased to love. Moved by the eloquence of Gemistus Pletho and the enthusiasm of his pupils at Florence, Cosimo established there (1445) a Platonic Academy for the study of Plato, and provided handsomely for Marsilio Ficino to give half a lifetime to the translation and exposition of Plato's works. Now, after a reign of four hundred years, Scholasticism lost its domination in the philosophy of the West; the dialogue and essay replaced the *scholastica disputatio* as the form of philosophical exposition, and the exhilarating spirit of Plato entered like an energizing yeast into the rising body of European thought.

But as Italy recovered more and more of its own classic heritage, the admiration of the humanists for Greece was surpassed by their pride in the literature and art of ancient Rome. They revived Latin as a medium of living literature; they Latinized their names, and Romanized the terms of Christian worship and life: God became *Iuppiter,* Providence *fatum,* the saints *divi,* nuns *vestales,* the pope *pontifex maximus.* They fashioned their prose style on Cicero, their poetry on Virgil and Horace; and some, like Filelfo, Valla, and Politian, achieved an almost classic elegance. So, in its course, the Renaissance moved back from Greek to Latin, from Athens to Rome; fifteen centuries appeared to fall away, and the age of Cicero and Horace, of Ovid and Seneca, seemed reborn. Style became more important than substance, form triumphed over matter; and the oratory of majestic periods rang again in the halls of princes and pedagogues. Perhaps it would have been better if the humanists had used Italian; but they looked down upon the speech of the *Commedia* and the *Canzoniere* as a corrupt and degenerate Latin (which almost it was), and deplored Dante's choice of the vernacular tongue. As a penalty the humanists lost touch with the living sources of literature; and the people, leaving their works to the aristocracy, preferred the jolly tales—*novelle*—of Sacchetti and Bandello, or the exciting mixture of war and love in the romances that were being translated or adapted into Italian from the French. Nevertheless this passing infatuation with a dying language and an "immortal" literature helped Italian authors to recapture the architecture, sculpture, and music of style, and to formulate the canons of taste and utterance that lifted the vernaculars to literary form, and set a goal and a standard for art. In the field of history it was the humanists who ended the succession of medieval chronicles—chaotic and uncritical—by scrutinizing and harmonizing sources, marshaling the matter into order and clarity, vitalizing and humanizing the past by mingling biography with history, and raising their narratives to some level of philosophy by discerning causes, currents, and effects, and studying the regularities and lessons of history.

The humanist movement spread throughout Italy, but until the accession of a Florentine Medici to the papacy its leaders were almost all citizens or graduates of Florence. Coluccio Salutati, who became executive secretary or chancellor (*cancellarius*) to the Signory in 1375, was a bridge from Petrarch and Boccaccio to Cosimo, knowing and loving all three. The public documents drawn up by him were models of classical Latinity, and set an example that officials in Venice, Milan, Naples, and Rome bestirred themselves to follow; Giangaleazzo Visconti of Milan said that Salutati had done him more harm by excellence of style than could have come from an army of mercenaries.[24] The fame of Niccolò de' Niccoli as a Latin stylist rivaled his renown as a collector of manuscripts; Bruni called him the "censor of the Latin tongue," and, like other authors, submitted his own writings to Niccoli for correction before publishing them. Niccoli filled his house with ancient classics, statuary, inscriptions, vases, coins, and gems. He avoided marriage lest it distract him from his books, but found time for a concubine stolen from his brother's bed.[25] He opened his library to all who cared to study there, and urged young Florentines to abandon luxury for literature. Seeing a wealthy youth idling the day away, Niccoli asked him, "What is your object in life?" "To have a good time," was the frank reply. "But when your youth is over, of what consequence will you be?"[26] The youth saw the point, and put himself under Niccoli's tutelage.

Leonardo Bruni, secretary to four popes and then (1427-44) to the Florentine Signory, translated several dialogues of Plato into a Latin whose excellence for the first time fully revealed the splendor of Plato's style to Italy; he composed a Latin *History of Florence* for which the Republic exempted him and his children from taxation; and his speeches were com-

pared with those of Pericles. When he died the priors decreed him a public funeral after the manner of the ancients; he was buried in the church of
Santa Croce, with his *History* on his breast; and Bernardo Rossellino designed for his resting place a noble and sumptuous tomb.

Born like Bruni in Arezzo, and succeeding him as secretary to the
Signory, Carlo Marsuppini awed his time by carrying half the classics of
Greece and Rome in his head; he left hardly one ancient author unquoted
in his inaugural address as professor of literature in the University of
Florence. His admiration for pagan antiquity was such that he felt called
upon to reject Christianity;[27] nevertheless he became for a time apostolic
secretary to the Roman See; and though he was said to have died without
bothering to receive the sacraments,[28] he too was buried in Santa Croce
under gorgeous oratory by Giannozzo Manetti and an ornate tomb by
Desiderio da Settignano (1453). Manetti, who pronounced this eulogy
over an atheist, was a man whose piety rivaled his learning. For nine years
he hardly stirred from his house and garden, steeping himself in classical
literature, and learning Hebrew as well as Latin and Greek. Sent as ambassador to Rome, Naples, Venice, Genoa, he charmed all, and won friendships precious to his government by his culture, his liberality, and his integrity.

All these men except Salutati were members of the circle that gathered
in the city house or country villa of Cosimo, and led the movement of
scholarship during his ascendancy. Another friend of Cosimo almost
equaled him as a host to learning. Ambrogio Traversari, general of the
Camaldulite order, lived in a cell in the monastery of Santa Maria degli
Angeli near Florence. He mastered Greek, and suffered qualms of conscience in his affection for the classics; he refrained from quoting them in
his writings, but revealed their influence in a Latin style whose idiomatic
purity would have shocked all the famous Gregories. Cosimo, who knew
how to reconcile the classics, as well as high finance, with Christianity,
loved to visit him. Niccoli, Marsuppini, Bruni, and others made his cell a
literary rendezvous.

The most active and troublesome of the Italian humanists was Poggio
Bracciolini. Born poor near Arezzo (1380), he was educated at Florence,
studied Greek under Manuel Chrysoloras, supported himself by copying
manuscripts, was befriended by Salutati, and secured appointment, at
twenty-four, as a secretary in the papal chancery at Rome. For the next
half century he served the Curia, never taking even minor orders, but
wearing ecclesiastical dress. Valuing his energy and his learning, the Curia

sent him on a dozen missions. From these he digressed, time and again, to search for classic manuscripts; his credentials as a papal secretary won him access to the most jealously guarded, or most carelessly neglected, treasures in the monastic libraries at St. Gall, Langres, Weingarten, and Reichenau; and his spoils were so rich that Bruni and other humanists hailed them as epochal. Back in Rome he wrote for Martin V vigorous defenses of Church dogmas, and then, in private gatherings, joined with other employees of the Curia in laughing at the Christian creed.[29] He composed dialogues and letters in rough but breezy Latin, satirizing the vices of the clergy even while practising them to the extent of his means. When Cardinal Sant' Angelo reproved him for having children, which hardly befitted a man in ecclesiastical dress, and for maintaining a mistress, which seemed unbecoming in a layman, Poggio replied with his usual insolence: "I have children, which is becoming to a layman, and I have a mistress, which is an old custom of the clergy."[30] At fifty-five he abandoned the mistress who had given him fourteen children, and married a girl of eighteen. Meanwhile he almost founded modern archeology by collecting ancient coins, inscriptions, and statuary, and by describing with scholarly precision the surviving monuments of classic Rome. He accompanied Pope Eugenius IV to the Council of Florence, quarreled with Francesco Filelfo, and exchanged with him enthusiastic invectives of the coarsest indecency, peppered with accusations of theft, atheism, and sodomy. Again in Rome, he worked with especial pleasure for the humanist Pope Nicholas V. At seventy he composed his famous *Liber facetiarum*, a collection of stories, satires, and obscenities. When Lorenzo Valla joined the papal secretariat Poggio attacked him in a new series of *Invectivae*, charging him with larceny, forgery, treachery, heresy, drunkenness, and immorality. Valla replied by laughing at Poggio's Latin, quoting his sins against grammar and idiom, and setting him aside as a fool in his dotage.[31] No one but the immediate victim took such literary assaults seriously; they were competitive essays in Latin composition; indeed Poggio proclaimed, in one of them, that he would show how well classic Latin could express the most modern ideas and the most private concerns. He was so adept in the art of erudite scurrility that "the whole world," said Vespasiano, "was afraid of him."[32] His pen, like that of a later Aretine, became an instrument of blackmail. When Alfonso of Naples delayed in acknowledging Poggio's gift of Xenophon's *Cyropaedia* translated into Latin, the irate humanist hinted that a good pen could stab any king, and Alfonso hastily sent him 500 ducats to hold his tongue. After enjoying every instinct and impulse for seventy years, Poggio composed a treatise *De miseriis humanae conditionis*, in which he reckoned that the ills of life outweigh the joys, and concluded, like Solon, that the luckiest people are those who escape being born.[33] At seventy-two he returned to Florence, was soon made secretary to the Signory, and finally was elected to the Signory itself. He expressed his appreciation by writing a history of Florence in the style of the ancients—politics, war, and imaginary speeches. Other humanists breathed relief when at last, aged seventy-nine, he died (1459). He too was buried in Santa Croce; his statue by Donatello was erected on the façade of the *duomo;* and in 1560, in the confusion of some alterations, it was set up inside the cathedral as one of the twelve Apostles.[34]

It is clear that Christianity, in both its theology and its ethics, had lost its hold on perhaps a majority of the Italian humanists. Several, like Traversari, Bruni, and Manetti in Florence, Vittorino da Feltre in Mantua, Guarino da Verona in Ferrara, and Flavio Biondo in Rome, remained loyal to the faith. But to many others the revelation of a Greek culture lasting a thousand years, and reaching the heights of literature, philosophy, and art in complete independence of Judaism and Christianity, was a mortal blow to their belief in the Pauline theology, or in the doctrine of *nulla salus extra ecclesiam*—"no salvation outside the Church." Socrates and Plato became for them uncanonized saints; the dynasty of the Greek philosophers seemed to them superior to the Greek and Latin Fathers, the prose of Plato and Cicero made even a cardinal ashamed of the Greek of the New Testament and the Latin of Jerome's translation; the grandeur of Imperial Rome seemed nobler than the timid retreat of convinced Christians into monastic cells; the free thought and conduct of Periclean Greeks or Augustan Romans filled many humanists with an envy that shattered in their hearts the Christian code of humility, otherworldliness, continence; and they wondered why they should subject body, mind, and soul to the rule of ecclesiastics who themselves were now joyously converted to the world. For these humanists the ten centuries between Constantine and Dante were a tragic error, a Dantesque losing of the right road; the lovely legends of the Virgin and the saints faded from their memory to make room for Ovid's *Metamorphoses* and Horace's ambisexual odes; the great cathedrals now seemed barbarous, and their gaunt statuary lost all charm for eyes that had seen, fingers that had touched, the *Apollo Belvedere*.

So the humanists, by and large, acted as if Christianity were a myth conformable to the needs of popular imagination and morality, but not to be taken seriously by emancipated minds. They supported it in their public pronouncements, professed a saving orthodoxy, and struggled to harmonize Christian doctrine with Greek philosophy. The very effort betrayed them; implicitly they accepted reason as the supreme court, and honoured Plato's *Dialogues* equally with the New Testament. Like the Sophists of pre-Socratic Greece, they directly or indirectly, willfully or unwittingly undermined their hearers' religious faith. Their lives reflected their actual creed; many of them accepted and practised the ethics of paganism in the sensual rather than in the Stoic sense. The only immortality they recognized was that which came through the recording of great deeds; they with their pens, not God, would confer it, would destine men to everlasting glory or shame. A generation after Cosimo they would agree to share this magic power with the artists who carved or painted the effigies of patrons, or built noble edifices that preserved a donor's name. The desire of patrons to achieve such mundane immortality was one of the strongest generative forces in the art and literature of the Renaissance.

The influence of the humanists was for a century the dominant factor in the intellectual life of Western Europe. They taught writers a sharper sense of structure and form; they taught them also the artifices of rhetoric, the frills of language, the abracadabra of mythology, the fetishism of classical quotation, the sacrifice of significance to correctness of speech and beauty of style. Their infatuation with Latin postponed for a century (1400-1500) the development of Italian poetry and prose. They emancipated science from theology, but impeded it by worshiping the past, and by stressing erudition rather than objective observation and original thought. Strange to say, they were least influential in the universities. These were already old in Italy; and at Bologna, Padua, Pisa, Piacenza, Pavia, Naples, Siena, Arezzo, Lucca, the faculties of law, medicine, theology, and "arts"—i.e., language, literature, rhetoric, and philosophy—were too mortised in medieval custom to allow a new emphasis on ancient cultures; at most they yielded, here and there, a chair of rhetoric to a humanist. The influence of the "revival of letters" operated chiefly through academies founded by patron princes in Florence, Naples, Venice, Ferrara, Mantua, Milan, and Rome. There the humanists dictated in Greek or Latin the classic text they proposed to discuss; at each step they commented in Latin on the grammatical, rhetorical, geographical, biographical, and literary aspects of the text; their students took down the dictated text, and, in the margins, much of the commentary; in this way copies of the classics, and of commentaries as well, were multiplied and were scattered into the world. The age of Cosimo was therefore a period of devoted scholarship, rather than of creative literature. Grammar, lexicography, archeology, rhetoric, and the critical revision of classical texts were the literary glories of the time. The form, machinery, and substance of modern erudition were established; a bridge was built by which the legacy of Greece and Rome passed into the modern mind.

Not since the days of the Sophists had scholars risen to so high a place in society and politics. The humanists became secretaries and advisers to senates, signories, dukes, and popes, repaying their favors with classic eulogies, and their snubs with poisoned epigrams. They transformed the ideal of a gentleman from a man with ready sword and clanking spurs into that of the fully developed individual attaining to wisdom and worth by absorbing the cultural heritage of the race. The prestige of their learning and the fascination of their eloquence conquered transalpine Europe at the very time when the arms of France, Germany, and Spain were preparing to conquer Italy. Country after country was inoculated with the new culture, and passed from medievalism to modernity. The same century that saw the discovery of America saw the rediscovery of Greece and Rome; and the literary and philosophical transformation had far profounder results for the human spirit than the circumnavigation and exploration of the globe. For it was the humanists, not the navigators, who liberated man from dogma, taught him to love life rather than brood about death, and made the European mind free.

Humanism influenced art last because it appealed rather to intellect than to sense. The chief patron of art was still the Church, and the chief purpose of art was still to convey the Christian story to the letterless, and to adorn the house of God. The Virgin and her Child, the suffering and crucified Christ, the prophets, Apostles, Fathers, and saints remained the necessary subjects of sculpture and painting, even of the minor arts. Gradually, however, the humanists taught the Italians a more sensual sense of beauty; a frank admiration for the healthy human body—male or female, preferably nude—permeated the educated classes; the reaffirmation of life in Renaissance literature, as against the medieval contemplation of another world, gave art a secret secular leaning; and by finding Italian Aphrodites to pose as Virgins, and Italian Apollos to serve as Sebastians, the painters of Lorenzo's age, and later, introduced pagan motives into Christian art. In the sixteenth century—when secular princes rivaled ecclesiastics in financing artists—Venus and Ariadne, Daphne and Diana, the Muses and the Graces challenged the rule of the Virgin; but Mary the modest mother continued her wholesome dominance to the end of Renaissance art.

V. ARCHITECTURE: THE AGE OF BRUNELLESCO

"Cursed be the man who invented this wretched Gothic architecture!" cried Antonio Filarete in 1450; "only a barbarous people could have brought it to Italy."[35] Those walls of glass hardly suited the sun of Italy; those flying buttresses—though at Notre Dame de Paris they had been forged into a frame of beauty, like fountain jets petrified in their flow— seemed to the South unsightly scaffoldings left by builders who had failed to give their structures a self-contained stability. The Gothic style of pointed arch and soaring vault had well expressed the aspirations of tender spirits turning from the laborious soil to the solacing sky; but men new dowered with wealth and ease wished now to beautify life, not to escape or malign it; earth would be heaven, and they themselves would be gods.

The architecture of the Italian Renaissance was not basically a revolt against Gothic, for Gothic had never conquered Italy. Every kind of style and influence spoke its piece in the experiments of the fourteenth and fifteenth centuries: the heavy columns and round arches of Lombard Romanesque, the Greek cross of some ground plans, the Byzantine pendentive and dome, the stately grace of campaniles echoing Moslem minarets, the slender columns of Tuscan cloisters remembering mosque or classic porticoes, the beamed ceilings of England and Germany, the groined vault and ogive and tracery of Gothic, the harmonious majesty of Roman façades, and, above all, the simple strength of the basilican nave flanked by its supporting aisles: all these, in Italy, were mingling fruitfully when the humanists turned architectural vision to the ruins of Rome. Then the shattered colonnades of the Forum, rising through the medieval mist, seemed to Italian eyes more beautiful than the Byzantine bizarreries of Venice, the somber majesty of Chartres, the fragile audacity of Beauvais, or the mystic reaches of Amiens' vault. To build again with columns finely turned, firmly mortised into massive plinths, gayly crowned with flowering capitals, and bound to stability by imperturbable architraves— this became, by the groping emergence of the buried but living past, the dream and passion of men like Brunellesco, Alberti, Michelozzo, Michelangelo, and Raphael.

"Of Filippo Brunellesco," wrote the patriotic Vasari, "it may be said that he was given by heaven to invest architecture with new forms, after it had wandered astray for many centuries."[36] Like so many artists of the Italian Renaissance, he began as a goldsmith. He graduated into sculpture, and for a time entered into friendly rivalry with Donatello. He competed with him and Ghiberti for a commission to sculpture the bronze doors of the Florentine Baptistery; when he saw Ghiberti's sketches he pronounced them superior to his own, and with Donatello he left Florence to study perspective and design in Rome. He was fascinated by the ancient and medieval architecture there; he measured the major buildings in all their elements; he marveled above all at the dome of Agrippa's Pantheon, 142 feet wide; and he conceived the idea of crowning with such a dome the unfinished cathedral of Santa Maria del Fiore in the city of his birth. He returned to Florence in time to take part in a conference of architects and engineers on the problem of roofing the cathedral's octagonal choir, 138½ feet across. Filippo proposed a dome, but the expansive pressure that so immense a cupola would exert upon walls unsupported by external but-tresses or internal beams seemed to the conferees a forbidding obstacle. All the world knows the story of Brunellesco's egg: how he challenged the other artists to make an egg stand on end, and, after all the rest had failed, himself succeeded by pressing the blunt and empty end down upon the table. When they protested that they could have done the the same, he answered that they would make similar claims *after* he had domed the cathedral. He received the commission. For fourteen years (1420-34) he labored intermittently at the task, fighting a thousand tribulations, rais-ing the cupola precariously 133 feet above the summit of its supporting walls. At last it was finished, and stood firm; all the city gloried in it as the first major achievement—and with one exception the boldest—in the architecture of the Renaissance. When Michelangelo, a century later, planned the dome of St. Peter's, and was told that he had an opportunity to surpass Brunellesco's, he answered: "I will make a sister dome, larger, but not more beautiful."[37] The lordly colorful cupola still dominates, for leagues around, the panorama of a red-roofed Florence nestling like a bed of roses in the lap of the Tuscan hills.

Though Filippo had taken his conception from the Pantheon, he had compromised gracefully with the Tuscan Gothic style of the Florentine cathedral by curving his dome along the lines of the Gothic pointed arch. But in buildings that he was allowed to design from the ground he made his classic revolution more explicit and complete. In 1419 he had begun, for Cosimo's father, the church of San Lorenzo; he finished only the "Old Sacristy"; but there he chose the basilican form, the colonnade and en-tablature, and the Romanesque arch as the elements of his plan. In the cloisters of Santa Croce he built for the Pazzi family a pretty chapel again recalling the dome and colonnaded portico of the Pantheon; and in those same cloisters he designed a rectangular portal—of fluted columns, flowered capitals, sculptured architrave, and lunette reliefs—which formed the style of a hundred thousand Renaissance doors, and survives everywhere in western Europe and America. He began on classic lines the church of Santo Spirito, but died while the walls had barely left the ground. In 1446 the corpse of the passionate builder lay in state in the cathedral under the dome that he had raised; and from Cosimo to the simple workingman who had labored there the people of Florence came to mourn that geniuses must die. "He lived as a good Christian," said Vasari, "and left to the world the savor of his goodness. . . . From the time of the ancient Greeks and Romans until now there has been no man more rare or more excellent."[38]

In his architectural enthusiasm Brunellesco had designed for Cosimo a palace so extensive and ornate that the modest dictator, fearing envy, denied himself the luxury of seeing it take form. Instead he commissioned Michelozzo di Bartolommeo (1444) to build for him, his family, and his offices, the existing Palazzo Medici or Riccardi, whose thick stone walls, bare of ornament, reveal the social disorder, the family feuds, the daily dread of violence or revolt, that gave a zest to Florentine politics. Immense iron gates opened to friends and diplomats, artists and poets, access to a court decorated with statuary by Donatello, and thence to rooms of moderate splendor, and a chapel brightened by the stately and colorful frescoes of Benozzo Gozzoli. There the Medici lived till 1538, with interludes of banishment; but surely they often left those gloomy walls to take the sun at the villas that Cosimo built outside the city in Careggi and Cafaggiolo, and on the slopes of Fiesole. It was in those rural retreats that Cosimo and Lorenzo, with their friends and protégés, took refuge from politics in poetry, philosophy, and art; and to Careggi father and grandson retired for their rendezvous with death. Glancing now and then beyond the grave, Cosimo gave substantial sums to raise an abbey at Fiesole, and to rebuild more commodiously the old convent of San Marco. There Michelozzo designed graceful cloisters, a library for Niccoli's books, and a cell where, occasionally, Cosimo withdrew even from his friends, and spent a day in meditation and prayer.

In these enterprises Michelozzo was his favorite architect and the unfailing friend who accompanied him into exile, and returned with him. Soon thereafter the Signory gave Michelozzo the delicate task of reinforcing the Palazzo Vecchio against threatened collapse. He restored the church of Santissima Annunziata, made a lovely tabernacle for it, and showed himself a sculptor too by adorning it with a statue of St. John the

Baptist. For Cosimo's son Piero he built a magnificent marble chapel in the hillside church of San Miniato. He pooled his skill with Donatello's to design and carve the charming "pulpit of the girdle" on the façade of the Prato cathedral. In any other country in that age Michelozzo would have led his architectural tribe.

Meanwhile the merchant aristocracy was raising proud civic halls and palaces. In 1376 the Signory commissioned Benci di Cione and Simone di Francesco Talenti to build a portico opposite the Palazzo Vecchio as a rostrum for governmental oratory; in the sixteenth century it came to be known as the Loggia dei Lanzi from the German lancers that Duke Cosimo I stationed there. The most magnificent private palace in Florence was built (1459) for the banker Luca Pitti by Luca Fancelli from plans made by Brunellesco nineteen years before. Pitti was almost as rich as Cosimo, but not so wisely modest; he contested Cosimo's power, and drew from him some sharp counsel:

> You strive toward the indefinite, I toward the definite. You plant your ladder in the air, I place mine on the ground. . . . It seems to me but just and natural that I should desire the honor and reputation of my house to surpass yours. Let us therefore do like two big dogs, which sniff at one another when they meet, show their teeth, and then go their separate ways. You will attend to your affairs, I to mine.[39]

Pitti continued to plot; after Cosimo's death he conspired to displace Piero de' Medici from power. He committed the only crime universally condemned in the Renaissance—he failed. He was banished and ruined, and his palace remained unfinished for a century.

VI. SCULPTURE

1. Ghiberti

The imitation of classic forms was more thorough in sculpture than in architecture. The sight and study of Roman ruins, and the occasional recovery of some Roman masterpiece, stirred the sculptors of Italy to an emulative ecstasy. When the *Hermaphrodite* that now lies in the Borghese Gallery—with its neutral back modestly turned to the spectator—was found in the vineyard of San Celso, Ghiberti wrote of it: "No tongue could describe the learning and art displayed in it, or do justice to its masterly style"; the perfection of such works, he said, eluded the eye, and could be appreciated only by passing the hand over the marble surface and curves.[40] As these exhumed relics grew in number and familiarity, the Italian mind slowly accustomed itself to the nude in art; the study of anatomy became as much at home in artists' *botteghe* as in medical halls; soon nude models were used without fear and without reproach. So stimulated, sculpture graduated from subservience to architecture, and from stone or stucco reliefs to statues of bronze or marble in the round.

But it was in relief that sculpture won its first and most famous triumph in the Florence of Cosimo's time. The ugly striated Baptistery that fronted the cathedral could only be redeemed by incidental ornament. Iacopo Torriti had adorned the tribune, and Andrea Tafi the cupola, with crowded mosaics; Andrea Pisano had molded a double bronze portal for the south façade (1330-6); now (1401) the Florentine Signory, in conjunction with the Guild of Wool Merchants, and to persuade the Deity to end a plague, voted a generous sum to provide the Baptistery with a bronze door for the north side. A competition was opened; all the artists of Italy were invited to submit designs; the most successful—Brunellesco, Iacopo della Quercia, Lorenzo Ghiberti, and a few others—were commissioned and paid to cast in bronze a sample panel showing the sacrifice of Isaac by Abraham. A year later the completed panels were submitted to thirty-four judges—sculptors, painters, and goldsmiths. It was generally agreed that Ghiberti's was the best; and the youth of twenty-five began the first pair of his famous bronze doors.

Only those who have closely studied this north portal can understand why it took the better part of twenty-one years to design and cast. Ghiberti was aided, in generous fellowship, by Donatello, Michelozzo, and a large corps of assistants; it was as if all were resolved, and all Florence expected, that these should be the finest bronze reliefs in the history of art. Ghiberti divided the pair into twenty-eight panels: twenty told the life of Christ, four pictured Apostles, four represented Doctors of the Church. When all these had been designed, criticized, redesigned, cast, and set in place on the door, the donors, not grudging the 22,000 florins ($550,000) already spent, engaged Ghiberti to make a corresponding double door for the east side of the Baptistery (1425). In this second undertaking, covering twenty-seven years, Ghiberti had as assistants men already renowned or soon to be: Brunellesco, Antonio Filarete, Paolo Uccello, Antonio del Pollaiuolo, and others; his studio became in the process a school of art that nurtured a dozen geniuses. As the first pair of doors had illustrated the New Testament, so now, in ten panels, Ghiberti presented Old Testament scenes, from the creation of man to the visit of the Queen of Sheba to Solomon; in the borders he added twenty figures in almost full relief, and varied ornament—animal and floral—of surpassing loveliness. Here the Middle Ages and the Renaissance met in perfect harmony: in the very first panel the medieval themes of the creation of Adam, the temptation of Eve, and the expulsion from Eden were treated with a classic flow of drapery and a bold exuberance of nudes; and Eve emerging from Adam's flesh rivaled the Hellenistic relief of Aphrodite rising from the sea. Men were astonished to find, in the background of the actions, landscapes almost as precise in perspective, and as rich in detail, as in the best painting of the time. Some complained that this sculpture infringed too much on painting, and overstepped the traditions of classical relief; it was academically true, but the effect was vivid and superb. This second double door was by common consent even finer than the first; Michelangelo considered it "so fine that it would grace the entrance of paradise"; and Vasari, doubtless thinking only of reliefs, pronounced it "perfect in every particular, the finest masterpiece in the world, whether among the ancients or the moderns."[41] Florence was so pleased that it elected Ghiberti to the Signory, and gave him a substantial property to support his declining years.

2. *Donatello*

Vasari thought that Donatello had been among the artists chosen to make trial panels for the Baptistery doors; but Donatello was only a lad of sixteen at the time. The affectionate diminutive by which his friends and posterity named him denoted Donato di Niccolò di Betto Bardi. He learned his art only partly in Ghiberti's studio; he soon struck out for himself, passed from the feminine grace of Ghibertian relief to virile statuary in the round, and revolutionized sculpture not so much by adopting classic methods and aims as by his uncompromising fidelity to nature, and the blunt force of his original personality and style. He was an independent spirit as tough as his *David*, as bold as his *St. George*.

His genius did not develop as rapidly as Ghiberti's, but it reached greater scope and heights. When it matured it spawned masterpieces with reckless fertility, until Florence was populated with his statues, and countries beyond the Alps echoed his fame. At twenty-two he rivaled Ghiberti by carving for Or San Michele a figure of St. Peter; at twenty-seven he surpassed him by adding to that edifice a *St. Mark* so strong and simple and sincere that "it would have been impossible," said Michelangelo, "to reject the Gospel preached by such a straightforward man as this."*⁴² At twenty-three Donatello was engaged to carve a *David* for the cathedral; it was only the first of many *Davids* made by him; the subject never ceased to please his fancy; perhaps his finest work is the bronze *David* ordered by Cosimo, cast in 1430, set up in the courtyard of the Medici palace, and now in the Bargello. Here the nude figure in the round made its unblushing debut in Renaissance sculpture: a body smooth with the firm texture of youthful flesh, a face perhaps too Greek in profile, a helmet certainly too Greek; in this instance Donatello put realism aside, indulged his imagination richly, and almost equaled Michelangelo's more famous figure of the future Hebrew king.

He was not so successful with the Baptist; it was a dour subject alien to his earthly spirit; the two statues of John in the Bargello are lifeless and absurd. Far finer is a stone relief of a child's head, named for no good reason *San Giovannino*—the youthful St. John. In the same Salone Donatelliano *St. George* unites all the idealism of a militant Christianity with the restrained lines of Greek art: a figure firmly and confidently poised, a body mature and strong, a head Gothically oval and yet prefiguring the classic *Brutus* of Buonarotti. For the cathedral façade at Florence he made two powerful figures—of Jeremiah and Habbakuk, the latter so bald that Donatello called him *lo Zuccone*, "the big pumpkin." On the Loggia dei Lanzi Donatello's bronze *Judith*, commissioned by Cosimo, still brandishes her sword over Holofernes; the wine-drugged general sleeps placidly before his decapitation; he is masterfully conceived and cast; but the young tyrannicide, overwhelmed with drapery, approaches her deed with inopportune calm.

On a brief trip to Rome (1432) Donatello designed a classic tabernacle in marble for the old St. Peter's. Probably in Rome he studied the portrait busts that had survived from the days of the Empire; in any case it was he who developed the first significant portrait sculpture of the Renaissance. His *chef-d'oeuvre* in portraiture was his bust, in painted terra cotta, of the politician Niccolò da Uzzano; here he amused and expressed himself with a realism that offered no compliments but revealed a man. Donatello made his own discovery of the old truth that art need not always pursue beauty,

---

* Or San Michele, erected by Francesco and Simone Talenti and Benci di Cione (1337-1404), was the religious shrine of the Greater Guilds. Each guild was represented by a statue placed in a niche on the outer walls. Figures were contributed to this series by Ghiberti, Verrocchio, Nanni di Banco, and Gian Bologna.

but must seek to select and reveal significant form. Many dignitaries risked the veracity of his chisel, sometimes to their discomfiture. A Genoese merchant, dissatisfied with himself as Donatello saw him, haggled about the price; the matter was referred to Cosimo, who judged that Donatello had asked too little. The merchant complained that the artist had taken only a month for the work, so that the fee demanded came to half a florin ($12.50) per day—too much, he thought, for a mere artist. Donatello smashed the bust into a thousand pieces, saying that this was a man who could bargain intelligently only about beans.[43]

The cities of Italy appreciated him better, and competed for his services. Siena, Rome, and Venice lured him for a time, but Padua saw him fashion his masterpiece. In the church of St. Anthony he carved a marble screen for the altar that covered the bones of the great Franciscan; and over it he placed moving reliefs and a bronze *Crucifixion* most tenderly conceived. In the piazza before the church he set up (1453) the first important equestrian statue of modern times; inspired, doubtless, by the mounted *Aurelius* in Rome, but thoroughly Renaissance in face and mood; no idealized philosopher-king, but a man of visibly contemporary character, fearless, ruthless, powerful—Gattamelata, "the honeyed cat," the Venetian general. It is true that the chafing, foaming horse is too big for his legs, and that the pigeons, innocent of Vasari, daily bespatter the bald head of the conquering *condottiere;* but the pose is proud and strong, as if all the *virtù* of Machiavelli's longing had here passed with the fused bronze to harden in Donatello's mold. Padua gazed in astonishment and glory at this hero rescued from mortality, gave the artist 1650 golden ducats ($41,250) for his six years of toil, and begged him to make their city his home. He whimsically demurred: his art could never improve at Padua, where all men praised him; he must, for art's sake, return to Florence, where all men criticized all.

In truth he returned to Florence because Cosimo needed him, and he loved Cosimo. Cosimo was a man who understood art, and gave him intelligent and bountiful commissions; so close was the entente between them that Donatello "divined from the slightest indication all that Cosimo desired."[44] At Donatello's suggestion Cosimo collected ancient statuary, sarcophagi, arches, columns, and capitals, and placed them in the Medici gardens for young artists to study. For Cosimo, with Michelozzo's collaboration, Donatello set up in the Baptistery a tomb of the refugee Antipope John XXIII. For Cosimo's favorite church, San Lorenzo, he carved two pulpits, and adorned them with bronze reliefs of the Passion; from those pulpits, among others, Savonarola would launch his bolts against later Medici. For the altar he molded a lovely terra-cotta bust of St. Lawrence; for the Old Sacristy he designed two pairs of bronze doors, and a simple but beautiful sarcophagus for Cosimo's parents. Other works came from him as if they were child's play: an exquisite stone relief of the Annunciation for the church of Santa Croce; for the cathedral a *Cantoria* of Singing Boys—plump *putti* violently chanting hymns (1433-8); a bronze bust of a *Young Man*, the incarnation of healthy youth (in the Metropolitan Museum of Art); a *Santa Cecilia* (possibly by Desiderio da Settignano), fair enough to be the Christian muse of song; a bronze relief of the Crucifixion (in the Bargello) overpowering in its realistic detail; and in Santa Croce another *Crucifixion*, a gaunt and solitary figure in wood, one of the most moving representations of this scene, despite Brunellesco's criticism of it as "a crucified peasant."

Patron and artist grew old together, and Cosimo took such care of the sculptor that Donatello rarely thought about money. He kept his funds, says Vasari, in a basket suspended from the ceiling of his studio, and bade his aides and friends take from it according to their needs, without consulting him. When Cosimo was dying (1464) he recommended Donatello to the care of his son Piero; Piero gave the old artist a house in the country, but Donatello soon returned to Florence, preferring his accustomed studio to the sunshine and insects of the countryside. He lived in simplicity and content till the age of eighty. All the artists—nearly all the people—of Florence joined in the funeral that laid him to rest, as he had asked, in the crypt of San Lorenzo, beside Cosimo's own tomb (1466).

He had immeasurably advanced the sculptural art. Now and then he poured too much force into his poses and designs; often he fell short of the finished form that exalts Ghiberti's doors. But his faults were due to his resolve to express not beauty so much as life, not merely a strong and healthy body but a complex character or mental state. He developed sculptural portraiture by extending it from the religious to the secular field, and by giving his subjects an unprecedented variety, individuality, and power. Overcoming a hundred technical difficulties, he created the first great equestrian statue left to us by the Renaissance. Only one sculptor would reach greater heights, and then by inheriting what Donatello had learned, achieved, and taught. Bertoldo was Donatello's pupil, and the teacher of Michelangelo.

3. Luca della Robbia

The picture that takes form in our minds, as we read Vasari's biographies of Ghiberti and Donatello, shows the studio of a Renaissance sculptor as the co-operative enterprise of many hands, directed by one mind, but transmitting the art, day by day, from master to apprentice, generation after generation. From such studios came minor sculptors who left to history a less imperious fame, but in their degree contributed to give to passing beauty a lasting form. Nanni di Banco inherited a fortune, and had the means to be worthless; but he fell in love with sculpture and Donatello, and served a faithful apprenticeship under him until he could set up his own studio. He carved a *St. Philip* for the niche of the shoemakers' guild in Or San Michele, and for the cathedral a *St. Luke* seated with the Gospel in his hand, and looking out with all the confidence of fresh faith upon a Renaissance Italy just beginning to doubt.

In another studio the brothers Bernardo and Antonio Rossellino combined their skills in architecture and sculpture. Bernardo designed a classic tomb in Santa Croce for Leonardo Bruni; then, on the accession of Nicholas V he went to Rome, and consumed himself in the great Pope's architectural revolution. Antonio reached his zenith at thirty-four (1461) with his marble tomb in San Miniato, at Florence, for Don Jayme, Cardinal of Portugal; here is the victory of the classic style in all but the angel's wings, the Cardinal's vestments, and his crown of virginity—for James had startled his time by his chastity. America has two lovely examples of Antonio's work—the marble bust of *The Christ Child* in the Morgan Library, and *The Young St. John the Baptist* in the National Gallery. And is there anywhere a nobler example of realistic portraiture than the powerful head—corrugated with veins and furrowed with thought—of the physician Giovanni di San Miniato, in the Victoria and Albert Museum?

Desiderio da Settignano came to Florence from the nearby village that gave him his cognomen. He joined Donatello's staff, saw that the master's work lacked only patient finish, and distinguished his own productions with elegance, simplicity, and grace. His tomb for Marsuppini did not quite equal Rossellino's for Bruni, but the tabernacle that he designed for the church of San Lorenzo (1464) pleased all who saw it; and his incidental portraits* and reliefs augmented his fame. He died at thirty-six; what might he have done if given, like his master, eighty years?

---

* Cf. his busts of Marietta Strozzi in the Morgan Library, New York, and in the National Gallery at Washington.

Luca della Robbia was granted eighty-two, and used them well; he raised terra-cotta work almost to the level of a major art, and his fame out-journeyed Donatello's; there is hardly a museum in Europe that does not display the tenderness of his Madonnas, the cheerful blue and white of his painted clay. Beginning as a goldsmith like so many artists of the Renaissance, and learning in that minuscule field all the delicacies of design, he passed on to sculptural relief, and carved five marble plaques for Giotto's Campanile. Perhaps the wardens of the cathedral did not tell Luca that these reliefs excelled Giotto's, but they soon commissioned him to adorn the organ loft with a relief picturing choir boys and girls in the ecstasy of song. Two years later (1433) Donatello carved a similar *Cantoria*. The rival reliefs now face each other in the *Opera di duomo* or Works of the Cathedral; both of them powerfully convey the exuberant vitality of childhood; here the Renaissance rediscovered children for art. In 1446 the wardens engaged him to make reliefs for the bronze doors of a cathedral sacristy. These could not rival Ghiberti's but they saved Lorenzo de' Medici's life in the Pazzi conspiracy. All Florence now acclaimed Luca as a master.

So far he had followed the traditional methods of the sculptor's art. Meanwhile, however, he had been experimenting with clay, seeking to find a way in which this tractable material could be made as beautiful in texture as marble. He molded the clay into the form designed, covered it with a glaze of divers chemicals, and baked it in a specially constructed kiln. The wardens admired the result, and commissioned him to place terra-cotta representations of the Resurrection and the Ascension over the doors of the cathedral sacristies (1443, 1446). These tympanums, though in monochrome white, made a stir by the novelty of their material and the refinement of their finish and design. Cosimo and his son Piero ordered similar terra cottas for the Medici palace and for Piero's chapel in San Miniato; in these Luca added blue to the dominant white. Orders came to him now in an abundance that tempted him to rapid facility. He brightened with a terra-cotta *Coronation of the Virgin* the portal of the church of the Ognissanti, and the portal of the Badia with a tenderly graceful *Madonna and Child*, between such angels as might reconcile us to an eternity of heaven. For the church of San Giovanni in Pistoia he attempted a large terra-cotta *Visitation*; it was a fresh departure in the aged features of Elizabeth and the youthful innocence and diffidence of Mary. So Luca created a new realm of art, and founded a della Robbia dynasty that would flourish till the end of the century.

VII. PAINTING

1. Masaccio

In fourteenth-century Italy painting dominated sculpture; in the fifteenth century sculpture dominated painting; in the sixteenth painting again took the lead. Perhaps the genius of Giotto in the *trecento*, of Donatello in the *quattrocento*, of Leonardo, Raphael, and Titian in the *cinquecento* played some part in this alteration; and yet genius is more a function than a cause of the spirit of an age. Perhaps in Giotto's time the recovery and revelation of classic sculpture had not yet provided such stimulus and direction as they were to give to Ghiberti and Donatello. But that stimulus reached its height in the sixteenth century; why did it not lift the Sansovinos and Cellinis, as well as Michelangelo, above the painters of that time? —and why was Michelangelo, primarily a sculptor, forced more and more into painting?

Was it because Renaissance art had tasks and needs too wide and deep for sculpture? Art, liberated by intelligent and opulent patronage, wished to cover the whole field of representation and ornament. To do this with statuary would have taken time, toil, and money prohibitively; painting could more readily express the double gamut of Christian and pagan ideas in a hurried and exuberant age. What sculptor could have portrayed the life of St. Francis as rapidly as Giotto and with Giotto's excellence? Moreover, Renaissance Italy included a majority of persons whose feelings and ideas were still medieval, and even the emancipated minority harbored echoes and memories of the old theology, of its hopes and fears and mystic visions, its devotion and tenderness and pervasive spiritual overtones; all these, as well as the beauties and ideals expressed in Greek and Roman sculpture, had to find vent and form in Italian art; and painting offered to do it at least more conveniently, if not also with greater fidelity and subtlety, than sculpture. Sculpture had studied the body so long and lovingly that it was not at home in representing the soul, though Gothic carvers had now and then made spiritual stone. Renaissance art had to portray both body and soul, face and feeling; it had to be sensitive to, take the impress of, all the range and moods of piety, affection, passion, suffering, skepticism, sensualism, pride, and power. Only laborious genius could accomplish this with marble, bronze, or clay; when Ghiberti and Donatello attempted it they had to carry into sculpture the methods, perspectives, and nuances of painting, and sacrificed to vivid expression the ideal form and placid repose required of Greek statuary in the Golden Age. Finally, the painter spoke a language more easily understood by the people, in colors that seized the eye, in scenes or narratives that told beloved tales; the Church found that painting moved the people more quickly, touched their hearts more intimately, than any carving of cold marble or casting of somber bronze. As the Renaissance progressed, and art broadened its scope and aim, sculpture receded into the background, painting advanced; and as sculpture had been the highest art expression of the Greeks, so now painting, widening its field, varying its forms, improving its skills, became the supreme and characteristic art, the very face and soul, of the Renaissance.

In this period it was still groping and immature. Paolo Uccello studied perspective until nothing else interested him. Fra Angelico was the perfection, in life and art, of the medieval ideal. Only Masaccio felt the new spirit that would soon triumph in Botticelli, Leonardo, and Raphael.

Certain minor talents had transmitted the techniques and traditions of the art. Giotto taught Gaddo Gaddi, who taught Taddeo Gaddi, who taught Agnolo Gaddi, who, as late as 1380, adorned Santa Croce with frescoes still in Giottesque style. Agnolo's pupil, Cennino Cennini, gathered into a *Libro dell' arte* (1437) the accumulated knowledge of his time in drawing, composition, mosaic, pigments, oils, varnishes, and other phases of the painter's work. "Here," says page one, "begins the Book of the Art, made and composed in the reverence of God and the Virgin Mary . . , and all the saints . . . and in the reverence of Giotto, of Taddeo, and of Agnolo";[45] art was becoming a religion. Agnolo's greatest pupil was a Camaldulese monk, Lorenzo Monaco. In the magnificent altarpiece—*The Coronation of the Virgin*—that Lawrence the Monk painted (1413) for his monastery "of the Angels," a fresh vigor of conception and execution appeared; the faces were individualized, the colors were brilliant and strong. But in that triptych there was no perspective; the figures in the rear rose taller than those in the foreground, like heads in an audience seen from the stage. Who would teach Italian painters the science of perspective?

Brunellesco, Ghiberti, Donatello had made approaches to it. Paolo Uccello almost gave his life to the problem; night after night he pored over it, to the fury of his wife. "How charming a thing is this perspective!" he told her; "ah, if I could only get you to understand its delights!"[46] Nothing seemed to Paolo more beautiful than the steady approximation and distant merging of parallel lines in the furrows of a pictured field. Aided by a Florentine mathematician, Antonio Manetti, he set himself to formulate the laws of perspective; he studied how to represent accurately the receding arches of a vault, the ungainly enlargement of objects as they advanced into the foreground, the peculiar distortion of columns arranged in a curve. At last he felt that he had reduced these mysteries to rules; through these rules one dimension could convey the illusion of three; painting could represent space and depth; this, to Paolo, seemed a revolution as great as any in the history of art. He illustrated his principles in his painting, and colored the cloisters of Santa Maria Novella with frescoes that startled his contemporaries but have yielded to the erosion of time. Still surviving is his vivid portrait of Sir John Hawkwood on a wall of the cathedral (1436); the proud *condottiere*, having turned his arms from attacking to defending Florence, now joined, in the *duomo*, the company of scholars and saints.

Meanwhile another line of development had reached from the same origin to the same end. Antonio Veneziano was a follower of Giotto; Gherardo Starnina was a pupil of Veneziano; from Starnina stemmed Masolino da Panicale, who taught Masaccio. Masolino and Masaccio made their own studies of perspective; Masolino was one of the first Italians to paint nudes; Masaccio was the first to apply the new principles of perspective with a success that opened the eyes of his generation, and began a new era in pictorial art.

His real name was Tommaso Guidi di San Giovanni; Masaccio was a nickname meaning Big Thomas, as Masolino meant Little Thomas; Italy was fond of giving such identifying marks to her children. Taking to the brush at an early age, he so lost himself in devotion to painting that he neglected everything else—his clothes, his person, his income, his debts. He worked a while with Ghiberti, and may have learned in that *bottega*-academy the anatomical precision that was to be one mark of his drawing. He studied the frescoes that Masolino was painting in the Brancacci Chapel at Santa Maria del Carmine, and noted with special delight their experiments in perspective and foreshortening. On a pillar in the abbey church known as the Badia he represented St. Ivo of Brittany with feet foreshortened as seen from below; the spectators refused to believe that a saint could have such mighty feet. In Santa Maria Novella, as part of a fresco of the Trinity, he pictured a barrel vault in such perfect diminishing perspective that the eye seemed to see the painted ceiling as sunk into the church wall.

The epochal masterpiece that made him the teacher of three generations was his continuation of Masolino's Brancacci Chapel frescoes on the life of St. Peter (1423). The incident of the tribute money was represented by the young artist with a new power of conception and veracity of line: Christ with stern nobility, Peter in angry majesty, the tax collector with the lithe frame of a Roman athlete, every Apostle individualized in feature, raiment, and pose. Buildings and background hills illustrated the young science of perspective; and Tommaso himself, self-portrayed by posing to a mirror, became a bearded apostle in the crowd. While he was working on this series the chapel was consecrated with processional ceremony; Masaccio watched the ritual with sharp retentive eye, then reproduced it in a fresco in the cloister; Brunellesco, Donatello, Masolino, Giovanni di Bicci de' Medici, and Antonio Brancacci, sponsor of the chapel, had taken part, and now found themselves in the picture.

In 1425, for reasons now unknown, Masaccio left his work unfinished, and went to Rome. We do not hear of him again, and we can only surmise that some accident or disease prematurely ended his life. But even though incomplete those Brancacci frescoes were recognized at once as an immense step forward in painting. In those bold nudes, graceful draperies, startling perspectives, realistic foreshortenings, and precise anatomical details, in this modeling in depth through subtle gradations of light and shade, all sensed a new departure, which Vasari called the "modern" style. Every ambitious painter within reach of Florence came to study the series: Fra Angelico, Fra Lippo Lippi, Andrea del Castagno, Verrocchio, Ghirlandaio, Botticelli, Perugino, Piero della Francesca, Leonardo, Fra Bartolommeo, Andrea del Sarto, Michelangelo, Raphael; no dead man had ever had such distinguished pupils, no artist since Giotto had wielded, unwittingly, such influence. "Masaccio," said Leonardo, "showed by perfect works that those who are led by any guide except Nature, the supreme mistress, are consumed in sterile toil."[47]

2. Fra Angelico

Amid these exciting novelties Fra Angelico went quietly his own medieval way. Born in a Tuscan village and named Guido di Pietro, he came to Florence young, and studied painting, probably with Lorenzo Monaco. His talent ripened quickly, and he had every prospect of making a comfortable place for himself in the world, but the love of peace and the hope of salvation led him to enter the Dominican order (1407). After a long novitiate in various cities, Fra Giovanni, as he had been renamed, settled down in the convent of San Domenico in Fiesole (1418). There, in happy obscurity, he illuminated manuscripts, and painted pictures for churches and religious confraternities. In 1436 the friars of San Domenico were transferred to the new convent of San Marco, built by Michelozzo at Cosimo's order and expense. During the next nine years Giovanni painted half a hundred frescoes on the walls of the monastery church, chapter house, dormitory, refectory, hospice, cloisters, and cells. Meanwhile he practised religion with such modest devotion that his fellow friars called him the Angelic Brother—Fra Angelico. No one ever saw him angry, or succeeded in offending him. Thomas à Kempis would have found fully realized in him the *Imitation of Christ*, except for one smiling lapse: in a *Last Judgment* the angelic Dominican could not resist placing a few Franciscan friars in hell.[48]

Painting, with Fra Giovanni, was a religious exercise as well as an esthetic release and joy; he painted in much the same mood in which he prayed, and he never painted without praying first. Protected from the harsh competitions of life, he saw it all as a hymn of divine atonement and love. His subjects were invariably religious—the life of Mary and Christ, the blessed in heaven, the lives of the saints and the generals of his order. His aim was not so much to create beauty as to inspire piety. In the chapter house where the friars held their assemblies he painted the picture that the prior thought should most frequently be in their minds—the Crucifixion; a powerful representation, in which Angelico showed his study of the nude, and at the same time the all-embracing quality of his Christianity; here, at the foot of the cross, along with St. Dominic, were the founders of rival orders—Augustine, Benedict, Bernard, Francis, John Gualberto of the Vallombrosans, Albert of the Carmelites. In a lunette over the entrance to the hospice, where the friars were required to offer hospitality to any wayfarer, Angelico told the story of the pilgrim who proved to be Christ; every pilgrim was to be treated as if he might be so revealed. Within the hospice are now gathered some of the subjects painted by Angelico for divers churches and guilds: the *Madonna of the Linaioli* (linen workers), where the angel choristers have the pliant figures of women and the smiling faces of guileless children; a *Descent from the Cross*, equal in beauty and tenderness to any of the thousand representations of that scene in the art of the Renaissance; and a *Last Judgment*, a bit too symmetrical, and crowded with lurid and repellent fantasies, as if to forgive were human and to hate were divine. At the top of the staircase leading to the cells stands Angelico's masterpiece, *The Annunciation*—an angel of infinite grace already in his obeisance revering the future Mother of God, and Mary bowing and crossing her hands in humble incredulity. In each of the half hundred cells the loving friar, aided by his friar pupils, found time to paint a fresco recalling some inspiring Gospel scene—the Transfiguration, the communion of the Apostles, Magdalen anointing the feet of Christ. In the double cell where Cosimo played monk, Angelico painted a *Crucifixion*, and an *Adoration of the Kings* gorgeous with such Eastern costumes as perhaps the artist had seen in the Council of Florence. In his own cell he pictured the Coronation of the Virgin. It was his favorite subject, which he painted time and again; the Uffizi Gallery has one form of it, the Academy at Florence another, the Louvre a third; best of all is that which Angelico painted for the dormitory of San Marco, wherein the figures of Christ and Mary are among the most exquisite in the history of art.

The fame of these devout creations brought Giovanni hundreds of proffered commissions. To all such seekers he replied that they must first obtain the consent of his prior; that secured, he would not fail them. When Nicholas V asked him to come to Rome he left his Florentine cell and went to decorate the chapel of the Pope with scenes from the lives of St. Stephen and St. Lawrence; they are still among the most pleasant sights in the Vatican. Nicholas so admired the painter that he offered to make him archbishop of Florence; Angelico excused himself, and recommended his beloved prior; Nicholas accepted the suggestion, and Fra Antonino remained a saint even under the pallium.

No painter except El Greco ever made a style so uniquely his own as Fra Angelico; even a novice can identify his hand. A simplicity of line and form going back to Giotto; a narrow but ethereal assemblage of colors— gold, vermilion, scarlet, blue, and green—reflecting a bright spirit and happy faith; figures perhaps too simply imaged, and almost without anatomy; faces beautiful and gentle, but too pale to be alive, too monotonously alike in monks, angels, and saints, conceived rather as flowers in paradise; and all redeemed by an ideal spirit of tender devotion, a purity of mood and thought recalling the finest moments of the Middle Ages, and never to be captured again by the Renaissance. This was the final cry of the medieval spirit in art.

Fra Giovanni worked for a year in Rome, for a time in Orvieto; served for three years as prior of the Dominican convent in Fiesole; was called back to Rome, and died there at the age of sixty-eight. Probably it was Lorenzo Valla's classic pen that wrote his epitaph:

Non mihi sit laudi quod eram velut alter Apelles,
sed quod lucra tuis omnia, Christe, dabam;

altera nam terris opera extant, altera coelo.
urbs me Ioannem Flos tulit Etruriae:—

"Let it not be to my praise that I was as another Apelles, but that I gave all my gains, O Christ, to your faithful; for some works are for the earth, some for heaven. I, Giovanni, was a child of the Tuscan City of Florence."

3. *Fra Filippo Lippi*

From the gentle Angelico, crossed with the lusty Masaccio, came the art of a man who preferred life to eternity. Filippo, son of the butcher Tommaso Lippi, was born in Florence in a poor street behind the convent of the Carmelites. Orphaned at two, he was reluctantly reared by an aunt, who rid herself of him when he was eight by entering him into the Carmelite order. Instead of studying the books assigned to him he covered their margins with caricatures. The prior, noting their excellence, set him to drawing the frescoes that Masaccio had just painted in the Carmelite church. Soon the lad was painting frescoes of his own in that same church; they have disappeared, but Vasari thought them as good as Masaccio's. At the age of twenty-six (1432) Filippo left the monastery; he continued to call himself Fra, brother, friar, but he lived in the "world" and supported himself by his art. Vasari tells a story that tradition has accepted, though we cannot test its truth.

Filippo is said to have been so amorous that when he saw a woman who pleased him he would have given all his possessions to have her; and if he could not succeed in this he quieted the flame of his love by painting her portrait. This appetite so took possession of him that while the humor lasted he paid little or no attention to his work. Thus, on one occasion when Cosimo was employing him, he shut him up in the house so that he might not go out and waste time. Filippo remained so for two days; but, overcome by his amorous and bestial desires, he cut up his sheet with a pair of scissors, and letting himself out of the window, devoted many days to his pleasures. When Cosimo could not find him he caused a search to be made for him, until at length Filippo returned to his labors. From that time forward Cosimo gave him liberty to go and come as he chose, repenting that he had shut him up . . . for, he said, geniuses are celestial forms and not pack asses. . . . Ever afterward he sought to hold Filippo by the bonds of affection, and was thus served by him with greater readiness.[49]

In 1439 "Fra Lippo" described himself, in a letter to Piero de' Medici, as the poorest friar in Florence, living with, and supporting with difficulty, six nieces anxious to be married.[50] His work was in demand, but apparently not as well paid as the nieces wished. His morals could not have been notoriously bad, for we find him engaged to paint pictures for various nunneries. At the convent of Santa Margherita in Prato (unless Vasari and tradition err) he fell in love with Lucrezia Buti, a nun or a ward of the nuns; he persuaded the prioress to let Lucrezia pose for him as the Virgin; soon they eloped. Despite her father's reproaches and appeals she remained with the artist as his mistress and model, sat for many Virgins, and gave him a son, the Filippino Lippi of later fame. The wardens of the cathedral at Prato did not hold these adventures against Filippo; in 1456 they engaged him to paint the choir with frescoes illustrating the lives of St. John the Baptist and St. Stephen. These paintings, now much damaged by time, were acclaimed as masterpieces: perfect in composition, rich in color, alive with drama—coming to a climax on one side of the choir with the dance of Salome, on the other with the stoning of Stephen. Filippo found the task too wearisome for his mobility; twice he ran away from it. In 1461 Cosimo persuaded Pius II to release the artist from his monastic vows; Filippo seems to have thought himself also freed from fidelity to Lucrezia, who could no longer pose as a virgin. The Prato wardens exhausted all schemes for luring him back to his frescoes; at last, ten years after their inception, he was induced to finish them by Carlo de' Medici, Cosimo's illegitimate son, now an apostolic notary. In the scene of Stephen's burial Filippo exercised all his powers—in the deceptive perspective of the architectural background, in the sharply individualized figures surrounding the corpse, and in the stout proportions and calm rotund face of Cosimo's bastard reading the services for the dead.

Despite his sexual irregularities, and perhaps because of his amiable sensitivity to the loveliness of woman, Filippo's finest pictures were of the Virgin.* They missed the ethereal spirituality of Angelico's Madonnas, but they conveyed a deep sense of soft physical beauty and infinite tenderness. In Fra Lippo the Holy Family became an Italian family, surrounded

---

* E.g., the *Annunciation* in San Lorenzo at Florence—a peasant girl in modest deprecation; the *Virgin Adoring the Child* (Berlin), rich in the blue of the Virgin's gown and the green bed of flowers beneath the Child; a *Madonna* in the Uffizi, with grave blonde face, flowing veil, and beautifully drawn robe; the *Madonna* of the Pitti Gallery; the *Madonna and Child* of the Medici Palace; the *Virgin and Child Between Saints Frediano and Augustine*, in the Louvre; the *Coronation of the Virgin*, in the Vatican Pinacoteca; and the *Coronation* in the Uffizi, with its graceful auxiliary figures, and Filippo himself, kneeling in prayer, penitent at last.

with homely incidents, and the Virgin took on a sensuous loveliness herald-
ing the pagan Renaissance. To these feminine charms Filippo in his Madonnas added an airy grace that passed down to his apprentice Botticelli.

In 1466 the city of Spoleto invited him to tell the story of the Virgin
again in the apse of its cathedral. He labored conscientiously, passion having cooled; but his powers failed with his passion, and he could not repeat
the excellence of his Prato murals. Amid this effort he died (1469),
poisoned, Vasari thought, by the relatives of a girl whom he had seduced.
The story is improbable, for Filippo was buried in the Spoleto cathedral;
and there, a few years later, his son, on commission from Lorenzo de'
Medici, built for his father a splendid marble tomb.

Everyone who creates beauty deserves remembrance, but we must pass
in shameful haste by Domenico Veneziano and his supposed murderer
Andrea del Castagno. Domenico was called from Perugia (1439) to paint
murals in Santa Maria Nuova; he had as aide a promising youth from
Borgo San Sepolcro—Piero della Francesca; and in these works—now lost
—he made one of the earliest Florentine experiments with paints mixed in
oil. He has left us one masterpiece—the *Portrait of a Woman* (Berlin)
with upswept hair, wistful eyes, obtrusive nose, and bulging bosom. According to Vasari, Domenico taught the new technique to Andrea del
Castagno, who was also painting murals in Santa Maria Nuova. Rivalry
may have marred their friendship, for Andrea was a dour and passionate
man; Vasari tells how he murdered Domenico; but other records relate
that Domenico outlived Andrea by four years. Andrea reached fame by
his picture of the scourging of Christ, in the cloister of Santa Croce, where
his tricks of perspective astonished even his fellow artists. Hidden away
in the old monastery of Sant' Apollonia in Florence are his imaginary portraits of Dante, Petrarch, Boccaccio, Farinata degli Uberti, a vivid representation of the swashbuckler Pippo Spana, and a *Last Supper* (1450) that
seems poorly drawn and lifeless, but may have suggested an idea or two to
Leonardo none the less.

VIII. A MISCELLANY

To feel with any vividness the life of art in Cosimo's Florence we must
not only contemplate those major geniuses whom we have here commemorated so hurriedly. We must enter the side streets and alleys of art and
visit a hundred shops and studios where potters shaped and painted clay,
or glassmakers blew or cut glass into forms of fragile loveliness, or gold-

smiths fashioned precious metals or stone into gems and medals, seals and coins, and a thousand ornaments of dress or person, home or church. We must hear noisy intent artisans beating or chasing iron, copper, or bronze into weapons and armor, vessels and utensils and tools. We must watch the cabinet makers designing, carving, inlaying, or surfacing wood; engravers cutting designs into metal; and other workers chiseling chimney pieces, or tooling leather, or carving ivory, or producing delicate textiles to make flesh seductive or adorn a home. We must enter convents and see patient monks illuminating manuscripts, placid nuns stitching storied tapestries. Above all we must picture a population developed enough to understand beauty, and wise enough to give honor, sustenance, and stimulus to those who consumed themselves in its making.

Metal engraving was one of the inventions of Florence; and its Gutenberg died in the same year as Cosimo. Tommaso Finiguerra was a worker in niello—i.e., he cut designs into metal or wood, and filled the cavities with a black compound of silver and lead. One day, says a pretty story, a stray piece of paper or cloth fell upon a metal surface just inlaid; removed, it was found imprinted with the design. The tale has the earmarks of an afterthought; in any case Finiguerra and others deliberately took such impressions on paper in order to judge of the effect of the engraved patterns. Baccio Baldini (*c.* 1450), a Florentine goldsmith, was apparently the first to take such impressions, from incised metal surfaces, as a means of preserving and multiplying the drawings of artists. Botticelli, Mantegna, and others supplied him with designs. A generation later Marcantonio Raimondi would develop the new technique of engraving into a means of broadcasting all but the color of Renaissance paintings to the world.

We have kept for the last a man who defies classification, and can best be understood as the embodied synthesis of his time. Leon Battista Alberti lived every phase of his century except the political. He was born in Venice of a Florentine exile, returned to Florence when Cosimo was recalled, and fell in love with its art, its music, its literary and philosophical coteries. Florence responded by hailing him as almost a monstrously perfect man. He was both handsome and strong; excelled in all bodily exercises; could, with feet tied, leap over a standing man; could, in the great cathedral, throw a coin far up to ring against the vault; amused himself by taming wild horses and climbing mountains. He was a good singer, an eminent organist, a charming conversationalist, an eloquent orator, a man of alert but sober intelligence, a gentleman of refinement and courtesy, generous to all but women, whom he satirized with unpleasant persistence and possibly artificial indignation. Caring little about money, he committed the care of his property to his friends, and shared its income with them. "Men can do all things if they will," he said; and indeed there were few major artists in the Italian Renaissance who did not excel in several arts. Like Leonardo half a century later, Alberti was a master, or at least a skilled practitioner, in a dozen fields—mathematics, mechanics, architecture, sculpture, painting, music, poetry, drama, philosophy, civil and canon law. He wrote on nearly all these subjects, including a treatise on painting that influenced Piero della Francesca and perhaps Leonardo; he added two dialogues on women and the art of love, and a famous essay on "The Care of the Family." After painting a picture he would call in children and ask them what it meant; if it puzzled them he considered it a failure.[51] He was among the first to discover the possibilities of the camera obscura. Predominantly an architect, he passed from city to city raising façades or chapels in the Roman style. In Rome he shared in planning the buildings with which, as Vasari put it, Nicholas V was "turning the capital upside down." In Rimini he transformed the old church of San Francesco into almost a pagan temple. In Florence he raised a marble front for the church of Santa Maria Novella, and built for the Rucellai family a chapel in the church of San Pancrazio, and two palaces of simple and stately design. In Mantua he adorned the cathedral with a chapel of the Incoronata, and faced the church of Sant' Andrea with a façade in the form of a Roman triumphal arch.

He composed a comedy, *Philodoxus*, in such idiomatic Latin that no one doubted him when, as a hoax on his time, he passed it off as the newly discovered work of an ancient author; and Aldus Manutius, himself a scholar, printed it as a Roman classic. He wrote his treatises in chatty dialogue form, and in "bare and simple" Italian so that even a busy businessman might read him. His religion was rather Roman than Christian, but he was always a Christian when he heard the cathedral choir. Looking far ahead, he expressed the fear that the decline of Christian belief would plunge the world into a chaos of conduct and ideas. He loved the countryside around Florence, retired to it whenever he could, and made the title character of his dialogue *Teogenio* say:

> The society of the illustrious dead can be enjoyed by me at leisure here; and when I choose to converse with sages, statesmen, or great poets, I have but to turn to my bookshelves, and my company is better than any that your palaces can afford with all their crowd of clients and flatterers.

Cosimo agreed with him, and found no greater solace in his old age than his villas, his intimates, his art collection, and his books. He suffered severely from gout, and in his final years left the internal affairs of the state to Luca Pitti, who abused the opportunity to add to his wealth. Cosimo's own fortune had not been diminished by his numerous charities; he whimsically complained that God kept always a step ahead of him in returning his benefactions with interest.[52] In his country seats he applied himself to the study of Plato, under the tutelage of his protégé Ficino. When Cosimo lay dying it was on the authority of Plato's Socrates, not on that of Christ, that Ficino promised him a life beyond the grave. Friends and enemies alike grieved over his death (1464), fearing chaos in the government; and almost the entire city followed his corpse to the tomb that he had commissioned Desiderio da Settignano to prepare for him in the church of San Lorenzo.

Patriots like Guicciardini, angered by the conduct of the later Medici, thought of him as Brutus thought of Caesar;[53] Machiavelli honored him as he honored Caesar.[54] Cosimo had overthrown the Republic, but the freedom he had checked was the liberty of the rich to rule the state with factious violence. Though he sullied his record with occasional cruelty, his reign was by and large one of the most genial, peaceful, and orderly periods in the history of Florence; and the other was that of the grandson who had been trained by his precedents. Rarely had any prince been so wisely generous, or so genuinely interested in the advancement of mankind. "I owe much to Plato," said Ficino, "but to Cosimo no less; he realized for me the virtues of which Plato gave me the conception."[55] Under him the humanist movement flowered; under him the diverse genius of Donatello, Fra Angelico, and Lippo Lippi received bountiful encouragement; under him Plato, so long overshadowed by Aristotle, returned into the mindstream of humanity. When a year had passed after Cosimo's death, and time had had a chance to dull his glory and reveal his faults, the Florentine Signory voted to inscribe upon his tomb the noblest title it could confer: *Pater Patriae*, Father of His Country. And it was deserved. With him the Renaissance lifted its head; under his grandson it reached its purest excellence; under his great-grandson it conquered Rome. Many sins may be forgiven to such a dynasty.

CHAPTER IV

The Golden Age

1464-92

I. PIERO "IL GOTTOSO"

COSIMO'S son Piero, aged fifty, succeeded to his wealth, his authority, and his gout. Even from boyhood this disease of the prosperous had afflicted Piero, so that his contemporaries, to distinguish him from other Peters, called him *Il Gottoso*. He was a man of fair ability and good morals; he had performed reasonably well some diplomatic missions entrusted to him by his father; he was generous to his friends, to literature, religion, and art; but he lacked Cosimo's intelligence, geniality, and tact. To cement political support Cosimo had lent large sums to influential citizens; Piero now suddenly called in these loans. Several debtors, fearing bankruptcy, proclaimed a revolution under "the name of liberty, which," says Machiavelli, "they adopted as their ensign to give their purpose a graceful covering."[1] For a brief interval they controlled the government; but the Medicean party soon recaptured it; and Piero continued a troubled reign until his death (1469).

He left two sons, Lorenzo aged twenty, Giuliano sixteen. Florence could not believe that such youths could successfully direct the business of their family, much less the affairs of the state. Some citizens demanded the restoration of the Republic in fact as well as form; and many feared a generation of chaos and civil war. Lorenzo surprised them.

II. THE DEVELOPMENT OF LORENZO

Noting Piero's ill health, Cosimo had done his best to prepare Lorenzo for the tasks of power. The boy had learned Greek from Joannes Argyropoulos, philosophy from Ficino, and he had absorbed education unconsciously by hearing the conversation of statesmen, poets, artists, and humanists. He learned also the arts of war, and at nineteen, in a tournament displaying the sons of Florence's leading families, he won the first prize "not by favor, but by his own valor."[2] On his armor, in that contest, was a French motto, *Le temps revient*, which might have been the theme of the Renaissance—"The [Golden] Age returns." Meanwhile he had taken to writing sonnets in the style of Dante and Petrarch; and bound by fashion to write of love, he sought among the aristocracy some lady whom he might poetically desire. He chose Lucrezia Donati, and celebrated all her virtues except her regrettable chastity; for she seems never to have allowed more than the passions of the pen. Piero, thinking marriage a sure cure for romance, persuaded the youth to wed Clarice Orsini (1469), thus allying the Medici with one of the two most powerful families in Rome. On that occasion the entire city was feasted by the Medici for three successive days, and five thousand pounds of sweetmeats were consumed.

Cosimo had given the lad some practice in public affairs, and Piero, in power, widened the range of his responsibilities in finance and government. When Piero died Lorenzo found himself the richest man in Florence, perhaps in Italy. The management of his fortune and his business might have been a sufficient burden for his young shoulders, and the Republic had now a chance to reassert its authority. But the clients, debtors, friends, and appointees of the Medici were so numerous, and so anxious for the continuance of Medicean rule, that, two days after Piero's death, a deputation of leading citizens waited upon Lorenzo at his home, and asked him to assume the guidance of the state. He was not hard to convince. The finances of the Medici firm were so entangled with those of the city that he feared ruin if the enemies or rivals of his house should capture political power. To quiet criticism of his youth, he appointed a council of experienced citizens to advise him on all matters of major concern. He consulted this council throughout his career, but he soon showed such good judgment that it rarely questioned his leadership. He offered his younger brother a generous share of power; but Giuliano loved music and poetry, jousts and love; he admired Lorenzo, and gladly resigned to him the cares and honors of government. Lorenzo ruled as Cosimo and Piero had ruled, remaining (till 1490) a private citizen, but recommending policies to a *balia* in which the supporters of his house had a secure majority. The *balia*, under the constitution, had absolute but only temporary power; under the Medici it became a permanent Council of Seventy.

The citizens acquiesced because prosperity continued. When Galeazzo Maria Sforza, Duke of Milan, visited Florence in 1471, he was amazed at the signs of wealth in the city, and still more at the art that Cosimo, Piero, and Lorenzo had gathered in the Medici palace and gardens. Here already was a museum of statuary, vases, gems, paintings, illuminated manuscripts, and architectural remains. Galeazzo averred that he had seen a greater number of fine paintings in this one collection than in all the rest of Italy; so far had Florence forged ahead in this characteristic art of the Renaissance. The Medici fortunes were further enhanced when (1471) Lorenzo led a delegation of Florentines to Rome to congratulate Sixtus IV on his elevation to the papacy; Sixtus responded by renewing the Medici management of the papal finances. Five years earlier Piero had obtained for his house the lucrative right to develop the papal mines near Civitavecchia, which produced the precious alum used in dyeing and finishing cloth.

Soon after his return from Rome Lorenzo met, not too successfully, his first major crisis. An alum mine in the district of Volterra—a part of the Florentine dominion—had been leased to private contractors probably connected with the Medici. When it proved extremely lucrative the citizens of Volterra claimed a share of the profits for their municipal revenue. The contractors protested, and appealed to the Florentine Signory; the Signory doubled the problem by decreeing that the profits should go to the general treasury of the whole Florentine state. Volterra denounced the decree, declared its independence, and put to death several citizens who opposed the secession. In the Council of Florence Tommaso Soderini recommended conciliatory measures; Lorenzo rejected them on the ground that they would encourage insurrection and secession elsewhere. His advice was taken, the revolt was suppressed by force, and the Florentine mercenaries, getting out of hand, sacked the rebellious city. Lorenzo hurried down to Volterra and labored to restore order and make amends, but the affair remained a blot on his record.

The Florentines readily forgave his severity to Volterra, and they applauded the energy with which, in 1472, he averted famine in the city by quickly securing heavy imports of grain. They were happy, too, when Lorenzo arranged a triple alliance with Venice and Milan to preserve the peace of northern Italy. Pope Sixtus was not so well pleased; the papacy could never be comfortable in its weak temporal power if a strong and united northern Italy bounded the Papal States on one side, and an extensive Kingdom of Naples hedged it in on the other. When Sixtus learned that Florence was trying to purchase the town and territory of Imola (between Bologna and Ravenna), he suspected Lorenzo of planning to extend Florentine territory to the Adriatic. Sixtus himself soon bought Imola as a necessary link in the chain of cities legally—seldom actually—subject to the popes. In this transaction he used the services and funds of the Pazzi banking firm, now the strongest rival of the Medici; he transferred from

Lorenzo to the Pazzi the lucrative privilege of managing the papal revenues; and he appointed two enemies of the Medici—Girolamo Riario and Francesco Salviati—to be respectively governor of Imola and archbishop of Pisa, then a Florentine possession. Lorenzo reacted with an angry haste that Cosimo would have deplored: he took measures to ruin the Pazzi firm, and he ordered Pisa to exclude Salviati from its episcopal see. The Pope was so enraged that he gave his consent to a plot of the Pazzi, Riario, and Salviati to overthrow Lorenzo; he refused to sanction the assassination of the youth, but the conspirators did not consider such squeamishness an impediment. With remarkable indifference to religious propriety, they planned to kill Lorenzo and Giuliano at Mass in the cathedral on Easter Sunday (April 26, 1478), at the moment when the priest should elevate the Host. At the same time Salviati and others were to seize the Palazzo Vecchio and eject the Signory.

On the appointed day Lorenzo entered the cathedral unarmed and unguarded, as was his wont. Giuliano was delayed, but Francesco de' Pazzi and Bernardo Bandini, who had undertaken to murder him, went to his house, amused him with jests, and persuaded him to come to the church. There, as the priest raised the Host, Bandini stabbed Giuliano in the breast. Giuliano fell to the ground, and Francesco de' Pazzi, leaping upon him, stabbed him repeatedly and with such fury that he severely cut his own leg. Meanwhile Antonio da Volterra and Stefano, a priest, attacked Lorenzo with their daggers. He protected himself with his arms, and received but a slight cut; friends surrounded him and led him into a sacristy, while his assailants fled from the hostile crowd. Giuliano was carried dead to the Medici palace.

While these ceremonies were taking place in the cathedral, Archbishop Salviati, Iacopo de' Pazzi, and a hundred armed followers proceeded against the Palazzo Vecchio. They tried to rouse the populace to their aid by shouting *Popolo! Libertà!* But the people, in this crisis, rallied to the Medici with the cry, *Vivano le palle!*—"Long live the balls!"—the emblem of the Medici family. When Salviati entered the palace he was struck down by the gonfalonier Cesare Petrucci; Iacopo di Poggio, son of the humanist, was hanged from a palace window; and several other conspirators, who had climbed the stairs, were seized by the resolute priors and were thrown out of the windows to be finished by the stone pavement or the crowd. When Lorenzo appeared, now with a numerous escort, the joy of the people at his safety expressed itself in violent rage against all who were suspected of sharing in the conspiracy. Francesco de' Pazzi, weak from loss of blood, was snatched from his bed and hanged beside the Archbishop, who gnawed at Francesco's shoulder in his dying agony. The body of Iacopo de' Pazzi, the old honored head of his family, was drawn naked through the streets and flung into the Arno. Lorenzo did what he could to mitigate the blood-thirst of the mob, and saved several men unjustly accused; but instincts stealthily latent even in civilized men could not forego this opportunity of safe expression in the anonymity of the crowd.

Sixtus IV, shocked by the hanging of an archbishop, excommunicated Lorenzo, the gonfalonier, and the magistrates of Florence, and suspended all religious services throughout the Florentine dominions. Some of the clergy protested against this interdict, and issued a document condemning the Pope in terms of unmeasured vituperation.[3] At Sixtus' suggestion Fer-rante—King Ferdinand I—of Naples sent an envoy to Florence, urging the Signory and the citizens to deliver up Lorenzo to the Pope, or at least to banish him. Lorenzo advised the Signory to comply; instead it answered Ferdinand that Florence would suffer every extremity rather than betray its leader to his enemies. Sixtus and Ferrante now declared war upon Florence (1479). The King's son Alfonso defeated the Florentine army near Poggibonsi, and ravaged the countryside.

Soon the people of Florence began to complain of the taxes levied to finance the campaign, and Lorenzo realized that no community will long sacrifice itself for an individual. He made a characteristic and unprece-dented decision in this turning point of his career. Embarking at Pisa, he sailed to Naples, and asked to be taken to the King. Ferrante admired his courage; the two men were at war; Lorenzo had no safe-conduct, no weapons, no guard; only recently the *condottiere* Francesco Piccinino, invited to Naples as guest of the King, had been treacherously murdered at the royal command. Lorenzo frankly admitted the difficulties that Florence faced; but he pointed out how dangerous it would be to Naples that the papacy should be so strengthened by the dismemberment of the Florentine dominions as then to be able to press its old claim upon Naples as a papal and tributary fief. The Turks were advancing westward by land and sea; they might at any moment invade Italy, and attack Ferrante's Adriatic provinces; it would not do, in that crisis, for Italy to be divided with internal hate and war. Ferrante did not commit himself, but he gave orders that Lorenzo should be detained as both a prisoner and an honored guest.

Lorenzo's mission was made more difficult by the continued victories of Alfonso against the Florentine troops, and by the repeated request of Sixtus that Lorenzo should be sent to Rome as a papal prisoner. For three months the Florentine was kept in suspense, knowing that failure probably meant his death and an end to the independence of Florence. Meanwhile he made friends by his hospitality and generosity, his good manners and good cheer. Count Caraffa, minister of state, was won over, and supported his cause. Ferrante appreciated the culture and character of his prisoner; here, apparently, was a man of refinement and integrity; peace made with such a man would assure the friendship of Florence for Naples through at least Lorenzo's life. He signed a treaty with him, gave him a splendid horse, and allowed him to take ship from Naples. When Florence learned that Lorenzo brought peace it gave him a grateful and tumultuous welcome. Sixtus raged, and wished to continue the war alone; but when Mohammed II, the conqueror of Constantinople, landed an army at Otranto (1480), and threatened to overrun Italy and capture the very citadel of Latin Christianity, Sixtus invited the Florentines to discuss terms. Their envoys made the due obeisances to the Pope; he scolded them properly, forgave them, persuaded them to equip fifteen galleys against the Turks, and made peace. From that time forward Lorenzo was the unchallenged lord of Tuscany.

III. LORENZO THE MAGNIFICENT

He ruled now with a milder hand than in his youth. He had just entered the thirties, but men matured quickly in the hothouse of the Renaissance. He was not handsome: his large flat nose overhung his upper lip and then turned outward curiously; his complexion was dark; and his stern brow and heavy jaw belied the geniality of his spirit, the charm of his courtesy, the vivacity of his wit, the poetic sensitivity of his mind. Tall, broad-shouldered, and robust, he looked more like an athlete than a statesman; and indeed he was seldom surpassed in physical games. He carried himself with the moderate dignity indispensable to his station, but in private he made his many friends immediately forget his power and his wealth. Like his son Leo X he enjoyed the subtlest art and the simplest buffoons. He was a humorist with Pulci, a poet with Politian, a scholar with Landino, a philosopher with Ficino, a mystic with Pico, an esthete with Botticelli, a musician with Squarcialupi, a reveler with the gayest in festival time. "When my mind is disturbed with the tumults of public business," he wrote to Ficino, "and my ears are stunned with the clamors of turbulent citizens, how could I support such contention unless I found relaxation in science?"—by which he meant the pursuit of knowledge in all its forms.[4]

His morals were not as exemplary as his mind. Like many of his contemporaries he did not allow his religious faith to hamper his enjoyment of
life. He wrote devout hymns with apparent sincerity, but turned from
them, without evident qualm, to poems celebrating licentious love. He
seems rarely to have known remorse except for pleasures missed. Having
reluctantly accepted, for political reasons, a wife whom he respected rather
than loved, he amused himself with adultery after the fashion of the time.
But it was accounted one of his distinctions that he had no illegitimate
children. Debate is still warm as to his commercial morality. No one questions his liberality; it was as lavish as Cosimo's. He never rested till he had
repaid every gift with a greater gift; he financed a dozen religious undertakings, supported countless artists, scholars, and poets, and lent great sums
to the state. After the Pazzi conspiracy he found that his public and private
disbursements had left his firm unable to meet its obligations; whereupon a
complaisant Council voted to pay his debts out of the state treasury (1480).
It is not clear whether this was a fair return for services rendered and
private funds spent for public purposes,[5] or a plain embezzlement;[6] the fact
that the measure, though openly known, did no harm to Lorenzo's popularity, suggests the more lenient interpretation. It was his liberality, as
well as his wealth and his luxurious menage, that men had in mind when
they called him *Il Magnifico*.

His cultural activities involved some neglect of the far-flung business of
his firm. His agents took advantage of his preoccupation, and indulged in
extravagance and chicanery. He rescued the family fortune by gradually
withdrawing it from commerce and investing it in city realty and large-
scale agriculture; he took pleasure in personally supervising his farms and
orchards, and was as familiar with fertilizer as with philosophy. Scientifi-
cally irrigated and manured, the lands near his villas at Careggi and
Póggio a Caiano became models of agricultural economy.

The economic life of Florence prospered under his government.[7] The
rate of interest fell as low as five per cent, and commercial enterprise,
readily financed, flourished until, toward the close of Lorenzo's career,
England became a troublesome competitor in the textile export trade. Even
more conducive to prosperity was his policy of peace, and the balance of
power that he maintained in Italy during the second decade of his rule.
Florence joined with other Italian states in ejecting the Turks from Italy;
this accomplished, Lorenzo induced Ferrante of Naples and Galeazzo
Sforza of Milan to sign with Florence an alliance for mutual defense; when
Pope Innocent VIII joined this league most of the minor states adhered to

it too; Venice held aloof, but was persuaded to good behavior by fear of
the allies; in this way, with some minor interruptions, the peace of Italy
was maintained until Lorenzo's death. Meanwhile he exerted all his tact
and influence to protect weak states against the strong, to adjudicate and
reconcile interstate interests and disputes, and to nip every *casus belli* in the
bud.[8] In that happy decade (1480-90) Florence reached the apogee of her
glory in politics, literature, and art.

Domestically Lorenzo ruled through the *Consiglio di Settanta*. By the
constitution of 1480 this Council of Seventy was composed of thirty members chosen by the Signory of that year, and forty others chosen by these
thirty. Membership was for life, and vacancies were filled by co-optation.
Under this arrangement the Signory and the gonfalonier had authority only
as executive agents of the Council. Popular *parlamenti* and elections were
dispensed with. Opposition was difficult, for Lorenzo employed spies to
detect it, and had means of troubling his opponents financially. The old
factions slept; crime hid its head; order prospered while liberty declined.
"We have here," wrote a contemporary, "no robberies, no nocturnal com-
motions, no assassinations. By night or by day every person may transact
his affairs in perfect safety."[9] "If Florence was to have a tyrant," said
Guicciardini, "she could never have found a better or more delightful
one."[10] The merchants preferred economic prosperity to political freedom;
the proletariat was kept busy with extensive public works, and forgave
dictatorship so long as Lorenzo supplied it with bread and games. Tournaments allured the rich, horse races thrilled the bourgeoisie, and pageants
amused the populace.

It was the custom of the Florentines, in carnival days, to promenade the
streets in gay or frightful masks, singing satiric or erotic songs, and to organize *trionfi*—parades of painted and garlanded floats representing mythological or historical characters or events. Lorenzo relished the custom, but
distrusted its tendency to disorder; he resolved to bring it under control by
lending it the approval and order of government; under his rule the pageants became the most popular feature of Florentine life. He engaged leading artists to design and paint the chariots, banners, and costumes; he and
his friends composed lyrics to be sung from the *carri;* and these songs reflected the moral relaxation of carnival. The most famous of Lorenzo's
pageants was the "Triumph of Bacchus," wherein a procession of floats
carrying lovely maidens, and a cavalcade of richly garbed youths on
prancing steeds, came over the Ponte Vecchio to the spacious square before
the cathedral, while voices in polyphonic harmony, to the accompaniment

of cymbals and lutes, sang a poem composed by Lorenzo himself, and hardly becoming a cathedral:

1. *Quanto è bella giovinezza,*
   Che si fuge tutta via!
   Chi vuol esser lieto sia!
   Di doman non c'è certezza.

1. Fair is youth and void of sorrow,
   But it hourly flies away.
   Youths and maids, enjoy today;
   Nought ye know about tomorrow.

2. This is Bacchus and the bright
   Ariadne, lovers true!
   They, in flying time's despite,
   Each with each finds pleasures new;

3. These, their nymphs, and all their crew
   Keep perpetual holiday.
   Youths and maids, enjoy today;
   Nought ye know about tomorrow. . . . . .

14. Ladies and gay lovers young!
    Long live Bacchus, live Desire!
    Dance and play, let songs be sung;
    Let sweet love your bosoms fire.

15. In the future come what may
    Youths and maids enjoy today;
    Nought ye know about tomorrow.[11]

Such poems and pageants lend some pale color to the charge that Lorenzo corrupted Florentine youth. Probably it would have been "corrupt" without him; morals in Venice, Ferrara, and Milan were no better than in Florence; they were better in Florence under the Medici bankers than later in Rome under the Medici popes.

Lorenzo's esthetic sensibilities were too keen for his morals. Poetry was one of his prime devotions, and his compositions rivaled the best of his time. While his only superior, Politian, still hesitated between Latin and Italian, Lorenzo's verses restored to the vernacular the literary primacy that Dante had established and the humanists had overthrown. He preferred Petrarch's sonnets to the love poetry of the Latin classics, though he could read these easily in the original; and more than once he himself composed a sonnet that might have graced Petrarch's *Canzoniere.* But he did not take poetic love too seriously. He wrote with finer sincerity about the rural scenes that gave exercise to his limbs and peace to his mind; his best poems celebrate the woods and streams, trees and flowers, flocks and shepherds, of the countryside. Sometimes he wrote humorous pieces in *terza rima* that lifted the simple language of the peasantry into sprightly verse; sometimes he composed satirical farces Rabelaisianly free; then, again, a religious play for his children, and some hymns that catch here and there a note of honest piety. But his most characteristic poems were the *Canti carnascialeschi*—Carnival Songs—written to be sung in festival time and mood, and expressing the legitimacy of pleasure and the discourtesy of maidenly prudence. Nothing could better illustrate the morals and manners, the complexity and diversity of the Italian Renaissance than the picture of its most central character ruling a state, managing a fortune, jousting in tournament, writing excellent poetry, supporting artists and authors with discriminating patronage, mingling at ease with scholars and philosophers, peasants and buffoons, marching in pageants, singing bawdy songs, composing tender hymns, playing with mistresses, begetting a pope, and honored throughout Europe as the greatest and noblest Italian of his time.

IV. LITERATURE: THE AGE OF POLITIAN

Encouraged by his aid and example, Florentine men of leters now wrote more and more of their works in Italian. Slowly they formed that literary Tuscan which became the model and standard of the whole peninsula—"the sweetest, richest, and most cultured, not only of all the languages of Italy," said the patriotic Varchi, "but of all the tongues that are known today."[12]

But while reviving Italian literature, Lorenzo carried on zealously his grandfather's enterprise of gathering for the use of scholars in Florence all the classics of Greece and Rome. He sent Politian and John Lascaris to various cities in Italy and abroad to buy manuscripts; from one monastery at Mt. Athos Lascaris brought two hundred, of which eighty were as yet unknown to Western Europe. According to Politian, Lorenzo wished that he might be allowed to spend his entire fortune, even to pledge his furniture, in the purchase of books. He paid scribes to make copies for him of manuscripts that could not be purchased, and in return he allowed other collectors, like King Matthias Corvinus of Hungary and Duke Federigo of Urbino, to send their copyists to transcribe manuscripts in the Medicean Library. After Lorenzo's death this collection was united with that which Cosimo had placed in the convent of San Marco; together, in 1495, they included 1039 volumes, of which 460 were Greek. Michelangelo later designed a lordly home for these books, and posterity gave it Lorenzo's name—Bibliotheca Laurentiana, the Laurentian Library. When Bernardo Cennini set up a printing press in Florence (1471) Lorenzo did not, like his friend Politian or Federigo of Urbino, turn up his nose at the new art; he seems to have recognized at once the revolutionary possibilities of movable type; and he engaged scholars to collate diverse texts in order that the classics might be printed with the greatest accuracy possible at that time. So encouraged, Bartolommeo di Libri printed the *editio princeps* of Homer (1488) under the careful scholarship of Demetrius Chalcondyles; John Lascaris issued the *editiones principes* of Euripides (1494), the *Greek Anthology* (1494), and Lucian (1496); and Cristoforo Landino edited Horace (1482), Virgil, Pliny the Elder, and Dante, whose language and allusions already required elucidation. We catch the spirit of the time when we learn that Florence rewarded Cristoforo, for these labors of scholarship, with the gift of a splendid home.

Lured by the reputation of the Medici and other Florentines for generous patronage, scholars flocked to Florence and made it the capital of literary learning. Vespasiano da Bisticci, after serving as bookseller and librarian at Florence, Urbino, and Rome, composed an eloquent but judicious series of *Lives of Illustrious Men*, commemorating the writers and patrons of the age. To develop and transmit the intellectual legacy of the race Lorenzo restored and enlarged the old University of Pisa, and the Platonic Academy at Florence. The latter was no formal college but an association of men interested in Plato, meeting at irregular intervals in Lorenzo's city palace or in Ficino's villa at Careggi, dining together, reading aloud part or all of a Platonic dialogue, and discussing its philosophy. November 7, the supposed anniversary of Plato's birth and death, was celebrated by the Academy with almost religious solemnity; a bust believed to be of Plato was crowned with flowers, and a lamp was burned before it as before the image of a deity. Cristoforo Landino used these meetings as the basis for the imaginary conversations that he wrote as *Disputationes Camaldulenses* (1468). He told how he and his brother, visiting the monastery of the Camaldulese monks, met the young Lorenzo and Giuliano de' Medici, Leon Battista Alberti, and six other Florentine gentlemen; how they reclined on the grass near a flowing fountain, compared the worried hurry of the city with the healing quiet of the countryside, and debated the active versus the contemplative career, and how Alberti praised a life of rural meditation, while Lorenzo urged that the mature mind finds its fullest functioning and satisfaction in the service of the state and the commerce of the world.[13]

Among those who attended the discussions of the Platonic Academy were Politian, Pico della Mirandola, Michelangelo, and Marsilio Ficino. Marsilio had been so faithful to Cosimo's commission as to devote almost all his life to translating Plato into Latin and to studying, teaching, and writing about Platonism. In youth he was so handsome that the maidens of Florence eyed him possessively, but he cared less for them than for his books. For a time he lost his religious faith; Platonism seemed superior; he addressed his students as "beloved in Plato" rather than "beloved in Christ";[14] he burned candles before a bust of Plato, and adored him as a saint.[15] Christianity appeared to him, in this mood, as but one of the many religions that hid elements of truth behind their allegorical dogmas and symbolic rites. St. Augustine's writings, and gratitude for recovery from a critical illness, won him back to the Christian faith. At forty he became a priest, but he remained an enthusiastic Platonist. Socrates and Plato, he argued, had expounded a monotheism as noble as that of the Prophets; they, too, in their minor way, had received a divine revelation; so, indeed, had all men in whom reason ruled. Following his lead, Lorenzo and most of the humanists sought not to replace Christianity with another faith, but to reinterpret it in terms that a philosopher could accept. For a generation or two (1447-1534) the Church smiled tolerantly on the enterprise. Savonarola denounced it as humbug.

Next to Lorenzo himself, Count Giovanni Pico della Mirandola was the most fascinating personality in the Platonic Academy. Born in the town (near Modena) made famous by his name, he studied at Bologna and Paris, and was received with honor at almost every court in Europe; finally Lorenzo persuaded him to make Florence his home. His eager mind took up one study after another—poetry, philosophy, architecture, music—and achieved in each some outstanding excellence. Politian described him as a paragon in whom Nature had united all her gifts: "tall and finely molded, with something of divinity shining in his face"; a man of penetrating glance, indefatigable study, miraculous memory, and ecumenical erudition, eloquent in several languages, a favorite with women and philosophers, and as lovable in character as he was handsome in person and eminent in all qualities of intellect. His mind was open to every philosophy and every faith; he could not find it in him to reject any system, any man; and though in his final years he spurned astrology, he welcomed mysticism and magic as readily as he accepted Plato and Christ. He had a good word to say for the Scholastic philosophers, whom most other humanists repudiated as having barbarously expressed absurdities. He found much to admire in Arabic and Jewish thought, and numbered several Jews among his teachers and honored friends.[16] He studied the Hebrew Cabala, innocently accepted its alleged antiquity, and announced that he had found in it full proofs for the divinity of Christ. As one of his feudal titles was Count of Concordia, he assumed the high duty of reconciling all the great religions of the West —Judaism, Christianity, and Islam—and these with Plato, and Plato with Aristotle. Though flattered by all, he retained to the end of his brief life a charming modesty that was impaired only by his ingenuous trust in the accuracy of his learning and the power of human reason.

Going to Rome at the age of twenty-four (1486), he startled priests and pundits by publishing a list of nine hundred propositions, covering logic, metaphysics, theology, ethics, mathematics, physics, magic, and the Cabala, and including the generous heresy that even the greatest mortal sin, being finite, could not merit eternal punishment. Pico proclaimed his readiness to defend any or all of these propositions in public debate against any person, and offered to pay the traveling expenses of any challenger from whatever land he might come. As a preface to this proposed tournament of philosophy he prepared a famous oration, later entitled *De hominis dignitate* (*On the Dignity of Man*), which expressed with youthful ardor the high opinion that the humanists—contradicting most medieval views—held of the human species. "It is a commonplace of the schools," wrote Pico, "that man is a little world, in which we may discern a body mingled of earthly elements, and a heavenly spirit, and the vegetable soul of plants, and the senses of the lower animals, and reason, and the mind of angels, and the likeness of God."[17] And then Pico put into the mouth of God Himself, as words spoken to Adam, a divine testimony to the limitless potentialities of man: "I created thee as being neither heavenly nor earthly . . . that thou mightest be free to shape and to overcome thyself. Thou mayest sink into a beast, or be born anew to the divine likeness." To which Pico added, in the high spirit of the young Renaissance:

> This is the culminating gift of God, this is the supreme and marvelous felicity of man . . . that he can be that which he wills to be. Animals, from the moment of their birth, carry with them, from their mothers' bodies, all that they are destined to have or be; the highest spirits [angels] are from the beginning . . . what they will be forever. But God the Father endowed man, from birth, with the seeds of every possibility and every life.[18]

No one cared to accept Pico's multifarious challenge, but Pope Innocent VIII condemned three of the propositions as heretical. Since these formed so tiny a proportion of the whole, Pico might have expected mercy, and indeed, Innocent did not press the matter. But Pico issued a cautious retraction, and departed for Paris, where the University offered him protection. In 1493 Alexander VI, with his wonted geniality, notified Pico that all was forgiven. Back in Florence Pico became a devout follower of Savonarola, abandoned his pursuit of omniscience, burned his five volumes of love poetry, gave his fortune to provide marriage dowries for poor girls, and himself adopted a semimonastic life. He thought of joining the Dominican order, but died before he could make up his mind—still a youth of thirty-one. His influence survived his brief career, and inspired Reuchlin to continue, in Germany, those Hebrew studies which had been among the passions of Pico's life.

Politian, who admired Pico generously, and corrected his poetry with the most gracious apologies, was a man of less meteoric lure, but of deeper penetration and more substantial accomplishment. Angelus Bassus, as he originally called himself—Angelo Ambrogini, as some called him—took his more famous name from Monte Poliziano, in the Florentine hinterland. Coming to Florence he studied Latin under Cristoforo Landino, Greek under Andronicus of Salonica, Platonism under Ficino, and the Aristotelian philosophy under Argyropoulos. At sixteen he began to translate Homer into a Latin so idiomatic and vigorous that it seemed the product of at least the Silver Age of Roman poetry. Having finished the first two books, he sent them to Lorenzo. That prince of patrons, alert to every excellence, encouraged him to continue, took him into his home as tutor of his son Piero, and provided for all his needs. So freed from want, Politian edited ancient texts—among them the *Pandects* of Justinian—with a learning and judgment that won universal praise. When Landino published an edition of Horace, Politian prefaced it with an ode comparable in Latinity, phrasing, and complex versification with the poems of Horace himself. His lectures on classic literature were attended by the Medici, Pico della Mirandola, and foreign students—Reuchlin, Grocyn, Linacre, and others—who had heard, beyond the Alps, the echo of his fame as scholar, poet, and orator in three tongues. It was not unusual for him to prelude a lecture with an extensive Latin poem composed for the occasion; one such piece, in sonorous hexameters, was nothing less than a history of poetry from Homer to Boccaccio. This and other poems, published by Politian under the title of *Sylvae*, revealed a Latin style so facile and fluent, so vivid in imagery, that the humanists acclaimed him as their master despite his youth, and rejoiced that the noble language which they aspired to restore had been taught to live again.

While making himself almost a Latin classic, Politian issued with fertile ease a succession of Italian poems that stand unrivaled between Petrarch and Ariosto. When Lorenzo's brother Giuliano won a joust in 1475, Politian described *La giostra* in *ottava rima* of melodious elegance; and in *La bella Simonetta* he celebrated the aristocratic beauty of Giuliano's beloved with such eloquence and finesse that Italian love poetry took on thereafter a new delicacy of diction and feeling. Giuliano tells how, going out to hunt, he came upon Simonetta and other lasses dancing in a field.

> The beauteous nymph who feeds my soul with fire
>   I found in gentle, pure, and prudent mood,
>   In graceful attitude,
> Loving and courteous, holy, wise, benign.
> So sweet, so tender was her face divine,
>   So gladsome, that in those celestial eyes
>   Shone perfect paradise,
> Yea, all the good that we poor mortals crave. . . .
> Down from her royal head and lustrous brow
>   The golden curls fell joyously unpent,
>   While through the choir she went
> With feet well lessoned to the rhythmic sound.
> Her eyes, though scarcely raised above the ground,
>   Sent me by stealth a ray divinely fair;
>   But still her jealous hair
> Broke the bright beam, and veiled her from my gaze.
> She, born and nursed in heaven for angels' praise,
>   No sooner saw this wrong than back she drew—
>   With hand of purest hue—
> Her truant curls with kind and gentle mien;
> Then from her eyes a soul so fiery keen,
>   So sweet a soul of love, she cast on mine
>   That scarce can I divine
> How then I 'scaped from burning utterly.[19]

For his own mistress, Ippolita Leoncina, Politian composed love songs of exquisite grace and tenderness; and, overflowing with rhymes, he fashioned similar lyrics to be used by his friends as charms to exorcise modesty. He learned the ballads of the peasantry, and reshaped them into finished literary form; so rephrased they passed back into popularity, and have left echoes in Tuscany to this day. In *La brunettina mia* he described a village beauty bathing her face and bosom at a fountain, and crowning her hair with flowers; "her breasts were as May roses, her lips were as strawberries"; it is a hackneyed theme that never palls. Trying to recapture that union of drama, poetry, music, and song which had been accomplished in the Dionysian Theater of the Greeks, Politian composed—in two days, he vows—a little lyric drama of 434 lines, which was sung for Cardinal Francesco Gonzaga at Mantua (1472). It was called *La favola di Orfeo*— *The Fable of Orpheus*—and told how Orpheus' wife Eurydice died of a snake bite as she fled from an amorous shepherd; how the disconsolate Orpheus made his way down to Hades, and so charmed Pluto with his lyre that the lord of the underworld restored Eurydice to him on condition that he should not look upon her until quite emerged from Hades. He had led her but a few steps when, in the ecstasy of his love, he turned to look upon her; whereupon she was snatched back to Hades, and he was barred from following her. In an insane reaction Orpheus became a misogynist, and recommended that men should ignore women and satisfy themselves with boys after the example of sated Zeus with Ganymede. Woodland maenads, furious at his contempt of women, beat him to death, flayed him, tore him limb from limb, and rejoiced tunefully in their revenge. The music that accompanied the lines is lost; but we may safely rank the *Orfeo* among the harbingers of Italian opera.

Politian fell short of greatness as a poet because he avoided the pitfalls of passion and never plumbed the depths of life or love; he is always charming and never profound. His love for Lorenzo was the strongest feeling that he knew. He was at his patron's side when Giuliano was killed in the cathedral; he saved Lorenzo by slamming and bolting the doors of the sacristy in the face of the conspirators. When Lorenzo returned from his perilous journey to Naples Politian welcomed him with verses almost scandalously affectionate. When Lorenzo passed away Politian mourned him inconsolably, and then gradually faded out. He died two years later, like Pico, in the fateful year 1494, when the French discovered Italy.

Lorenzo would not have been the full man that he was had he not enjoyed some humor with his philosophy, some doubt with his faith, some license with his loves. As his son would welcome jesters and smile at risqué comedies at the papal court, so the banker prince of Florence invited to his friendship and his table Luigi Pulci, and relished the rough satire of the *Morgante maggiore*. That famous poem, so admired by Byron, was read aloud, canto by canto, to Lorenzo and his household guests. Luigi was a man of robust and uninhibited wit, who convulsed a palace and a nation by applying the language, idioms, and views of the bourgeoisie to the romances of chivalry. The legends of Charlemagne's adventures in France, Spain, and Palestine had entered Italy in the twelfth century or before, and had been spread through the peninsula by minstrels and *im-provisatori* to the delight of every class. But there has always been, in the common male of the species, a bluff and lusty self-ridiculing realism, accompanying and checking the romantic spirit given to literature and art by woman and youth. Pulci combined all these qualities, and put together— from popular legends, from the manuscripts in the Laurentian Library, and from the conversation at Lorenzo's table—an epic that laughs at the giants, demons, and battles of chivalric tales, and recounts, in sometimes serious, sometimes mocking verse, the adventures of the Christian knight Orlando and the Saracen giant who gives the poem half its name.*

Attacked by Orlando, Morgante saves himself by announcing his sudden conversion to Christianity. Orlando teaches him theology; explains to him that his two brothers, just slain, are now in hell as infidels; promises him heaven if he becomes a good Christian; but warns him that in heaven he will be required to look without pity upon his burning relatives. "The doctors of our Church," says the Christian knight, "are agreed that if those who are glorified in heaven were to feel pity for their miserable kindred, who lie in such horrible confusion in hell, their beatitude would come to nothing." Morgante is not disturbed. "You shall see," he assures Orlando, "if I grieve for my brethren, and whether or no I submit to the will of God and behave myself like an angel . . . I will cut off the hands of my brothers, and take the hands to these holy monks, that they may be sure that their enemies are dead."

In the eighteenth canto Pulci introduces another giant, Margute, a jolly thief and mild murderer, who ascribes to himself every vice but that of betraying a friend. To Morgante's question whether he believes in Christ or prefers Mohammed, Margute answers:

> I don't believe in black more than in blue,
>   But in fat capons, boiled or maybe roasted;
> And I believe sometimes in butter, too,
>   In beer and must, where bobs a pippin toasted; . . .
> But mostly to old wine my faith I pin,
> And hold him saved who firmly trusts therein. . . .
> Faith, like the itch, is catching; . . .
> Faith is as man gets it—this, that, or another.
>   See then what sort of creed I'm bound to follow:
> For you must know a Greek nun was my mother,
>   My sire, at Brusa mid the Turks, a mullah.[21]

---

* Pulci published first the cantos referring to Morgante; the completed poem was called *Morgante maggiore—The Greater Morgante*.

Margute dies of laughter after rollicking through two cantos; Pulci wastes no tear over him, but pulls from his magic fancy a demon of the first order, Astarotte, who rebelled with Lucifer. Summoned from hell by the sorcerer Malagigi to bring Rinaldo swiftly from Egypt to Roncesvalles, he accomplishes the matter deftly, and wins such affection from Rinaldo that the Christian knight proposes to beg God to free Astarotte from hell. But the courteous devil is an excellent theologian, and points out that rebellion against infinite Justice was an infinite crime, requiring eternal punishment. Malagigi wonders why a God who foresaw everything, including Lucifer's disobedience and everlasting damnation, proceeded to create him; Astarotte confesses that this is a mystery which even a wise devil cannot resolve.[22]

He was in truth a wise devil, for Pulci, writing in 1483, puts into his mouth an astonishing anticipation of Columbus. Referring to the old warning, at the Pillars of Hercules (Gibraltar), *ne plus ultra*—"go no further"— Astarotte says to Rinaldo:

> Know that this theory is false; his bark
> The daring mariner shall urge far o'er
> The western wave, a smooth and level plain
> Albeit the earth is fashioned like a wheel.
> Man was in ancient days of grosser mold,
> And Hercules might blush to learn how far
> Beyond the limits he had vainly set
> The dullest sea-boat soon shall wing her way,
> Men shall descry another hemisphere.
> Since to one common center all things tend,
> So earth, by curious mystery divine
> Well balanced, hangs amid the starry spheres.
> At our antipodes are cities, states,
> And throngéd empires, ne'er divined of yore.
> But see, the Sun speeds on his western path
> To glad the nations with expected light.[23]

It was part of Pulci's method to introduce each canto, however full of buffoonery, with a pious invocation of God and the saints; the more profane the matter, the more solemn the prologue. The poem ends with a declaration of faith in the goodness of all religions—a proposition sure to offend every true believer. Now and then Pulci allows himself a timid heresy, as when he quotes Scripture to argue that Christ's foreknowledge did not equal that of God the Father, or when he allows himself to hope that all souls, even Lucifer, will in the end be saved. But like a good Florentine, and the other members of Lorenzo's circle, he remained externally faithful to a Church inextricably bound up with Italian life. Ecclesiastics were not deceived by his obeisance; when he died (1484) his body was refused burial in consecrated ground.

If Lorenzo's group could produce so varied a literature in one generation, we may reasonably suppose—and shall find—a like awakening in other cities —Milan, Ferrara, Naples, Rome. In the century between Cosimo's birth and Lorenzo's death Italy had accomplished and transcended the first stage in her Renaissance. She had rediscovered ancient Greece and Rome, had established the essentials of classical scholarship, and had made Latin again a language of masculine splendor and pithy force. But more: in the generation between Cosimo's death and Lorenzo's, Italy rediscovered her own language and soul, applied the new standards of diction and form to the vernacular, and composed poetry classical in spirit, but indigenous and "modern" in tongue and thought, rooted in the affairs and problems of its own day, or in the scenes and persons of the countryside. And again: Italy in one generation, through Pulci, had lifted the humorous romance into literature, had prepared the way for Boiardo and Ariosto, had even anticipated Cervantes' smiles at chivalric fustian and pretense. The age of the scholars receded, imitation gave way to creation; Italian literature, which had languished after Petrarch's choice of Latin for his epic, was reborn. Soon the revival of antiquity would be almost forgotten in the exuberance of an Italian culture leading the world in letters, and flooding it with art.

V. ARCHITECTURE AND SCULPTURE: THE AGE OF VERROCCHIO

Lorenzo continued enthusiastically the Medicean tradition of supporting art. "He was such an admirer of all the remains of antiquity," wrote his contemporary Valori, "that there was nothing with which he was more delighted. Those who wished to oblige him were accustomed to collect, from every part of the world, medals, coins . . . statues, busts, and whatever else bore the stamp" of ancient Greece or Rome.[24] Uniting his architectural and sculptural collections with those left by Cosimo and Piero, he placed them in a garden between the Medici palace and the monastery of San Marco, and admitted to them all responsible scholars and visitors. To students who showed application and promise—among whom was the young Michelangelo—he gave a stipend for their maintenance, and awards for special proficiency. Says Vasari: "It is highly deserving of notice that all those who studied in the gardens of the

Medici, and were favored by Lorenzo, became excellent artists. This can only be ascribed to the exquisite judgment of this great patron . . . who could not merely distinguish men of genius, but had the will and power to reward them."[25]

The key event in the art history of Lorenzo's regime was the publication (1486) of Vitruvius' treatise *De architectura* (first century B.C.), which Poggio had unearthed in the monastery of St. Gall some seventy years before. Lorenzo succumbed completely to that rigid classic, and used his influence to spread the style of Imperial Rome. Perhaps in this matter he did as much harm as good, for he discouraged in architecture what he was fruitfully practising in literature—the development of native forms. But his spirit was generous. Through his encouragement, and in many cases with his funds, Florence was now adorned with elegant civic buildings and private residences. He completed the church of San Lorenzo and the abbey at Fiesole, and he engaged Giuliano da Sangallo to design a monastery outside the San Gallo gate that gave the architect his name. Giuliano built for him a stately villa at Póggio a Caiano, and so handsomely that Lorenzo recommended him when King Ferdinand of Naples asked him for an architect. How well such artists loved him appears in the subsequent generosity of Giuliano, who sent as presents to Lorenzo the gifts that Ferrante gave him—a bust of the Emperor Hadrian, a *Sleeping Cupid*, and other ancient sculptures. Lorenzo added these to the collections in his garden, which were later to form the nucleus of the statuary in the Uffizi Gallery.

Other rich men rivaled—some surpassed—him in the splendor of their residences. About 1489 Benedetto da Maiano built for Filippo Strozzi the Elder the most perfect embodiment of that "Tuscan" style of architecture which Brunellesco had developed in the Pitti Palace—internal splendor and luxury behind a massive front of "rustic" or unfinished stone blocks. It was begun with careful astrological timing, with religious services in several churches, and with a conciliatory distribution of alms. After Benedetto's death (1497) Simone Pollaiuolo* completed the building, and added a fine cornice on the model of one that he had seen in Rome. How excellent the interior of these seeming prisons might be we may surmise from their magnificent fireplaces—mighty marble entablatures supported by floral-carved pillars and surmounted with reliefs. Meanwhile the Signory continued to improve its unique and beautiful home, the Palazzo Vecchio.

Most of the architects were sculptors too, for sculpture played the leading part in architectural ornament, carving cornices and moldings, pilasters and capitals, door jambs and chimney pieces, wall reliefs, altars, choir stalls, pulpits, and baptismal fonts. Giuliano da Maiano carved the stalls in the sacristy of the cathedral and in the abbey at Fiesole. His brother Benedetto developed the

---

* Called Il Cronaca from the lively record he wrote of his travels and studies.

art of intarsia, and became so famous for it that King Matthias Corvinus of Hungary ordered from him two coffers of inlaid wood, and invited him to his court. Benedetto went, and had the coffers sent after him; when these arrived at Budapest and were unpacked in the presence of the King the inlaid pieces fell out, the glue having been loosened by the damp sea air; and Benedetto, though he replaced the pieces successfully, took a distaste to marquetry, and devoted himself thereafter to sculpture. There are few sculptured Virgins lovelier than his *Enthroned Madonna*, few busts that surpass his honest and revealing *Filippo Strozzi*, few tombs so fine as that of the same Strozzi in Santa Maria Novella, no pulpit more elegantly carved than that which Benedetto made for the church of Santa Croce, and few altars so near perfection as that of Santa Fina in the Collegiate Church of San Gimignano.

Sculpture and architecture tended to run in families—the della Robbias, the Sangalli, the Rossellini, the Pollaiuoli. Antonio Pollaiuolo, uncle of Simone, learned accuracy and delicacy of design as a goldsmith in the studio of his father Iacopo. The bronze, silver and gold products of Antonio made him the Cellini of his time, and a favorite of Lorenzo, the churches, the Signory, and the guilds. Noting how rarely such small objects retained the name of their maker, and sharing the Renaissance mirage of immortal fame, Antonio turned to sculpture, and cast in bronze two magnificent figures of Hercules, rivaling the strained power of Michelangelo's *Captives*, and the tortured passion of the *Laocoön*. Passing to painting, he told the story of Hercules in three murals for the Medici palace, challenged Botticelli in *Apollo and Daphne*, and equaled the absurdity of a hundred artists in showing how calmly St. Sebastian could receive into his flawless body the arrows launched at him by leisurely bowmen. In his final years Antonio returned to sculpture and cast for the old church of St. Peter in Rome two superb sepulchral monuments—of Sixtus IV and Innocent VIII—with a vigor of chiseling and a precision of anatomy again presaging Michelangelo.

Mino da Fiesole was not so versatile nor so tempestuous; he was content to learn the sculptor's art from Desiderio da Settignano, and when his master died, to carry on his tradition of smooth elegance. If we may believe Vasari, Mino was so affected by Desiderio's early death that he found no happiness in Florence, and sought new scenes in Rome. There he made a name for himself with three masterpieces: tombs of Francesco Tornabuoni and Pope Paul II, and a marble tabernacle for Cardinal d'Estouteville. His confidence and solvency restored, he returned to Florence, and adorned with exquisite altars the churches of Sant' Ambrogio and Santa Croce, and the Baptistery. In the cathedral of his native Fiesole he set up in classical style an ornate tomb for Bishop Salutati, and for the abbey of Fiesole he molded a similar monument, more restrained in ornament, to commemorate the Count Ugo who had founded that monastery. The cathedral of Prato boasts a pulpit by him, and a dozen museums display one or more of the busts by which his patrons were less flattered than embalmed: the face of Niccolò Strozzi, swollen as with the mumps, the weak features of Piero the Gouty, the fine head of Dietisalvi Neroni, a pretty relief of Marcus Aurelius as a youth, a splendid bust of St. John the Baptist in infancy, and several lovely reliefs of the Virgin and Child. Nearly all these works have the feminine grace that Mino had learned from Desiderio; they are pleasing, but not arresting or profound; they do not grip our interest as do the sculptures of Antonio Pollaiuolo or Antonio Rossellino. Mino loved Desiderio too much; he could not turn his back upon his master's exemplars and seek in the merciless neutrality of Nature the significant realities of life.

Verrocchio—"True Eye"—was brave enough to do this, and produced two of the greatest sculptures of his time. Andrea di Michele Cione (for that was his real name) was a goldsmith, a sculptor, a bell-caster, a painter, a geometrician, a musician. As a painter his chief claim to fame lies in having taught and influenced Leonardo, Lorenzo di Credi, and Perugino; his own paintings are mostly stiff and dead. There are few Renaissance pictures more unpleasant than the famous *Baptism of Christ;* the Baptist is a dour Puritan, Christ, presumably thirty, looks like an old man, and the two angels at the left are effeminately insipid, including the one traditionally ascribed to Leonardo. But *Tobias and the Three Angels* is excellent; the central angel foreshadows the grace and mood of Botticelli, and the young Tobias is so fair that we must either attribute him to Leonardo, or confess that da Vinci received more of his pictorial style from Verrocchio than we supposed. A drawing of a woman's head, in Christ Church, Oxford, again suggests the vague and pensive ethereality of Leonardo's women; and Verrocchio's dark landscapes already feature the gloomy rocks and mystic streams of Leonardo's dreamy masterpieces.

Probably there is mostly fable in Vasari's tale that when Verrocchio saw the angel that Leonardo had painted in *The Baptism of Christ* he "resolved never to touch the brush again, because Leonardo, though so young, had so far surpassed him."[26] But though Verrocchio continued to paint after the *Baptism*, it is true that he gave most of his mature years to sculpture. He worked for a while with Donatello and Antonio Pollaiuolo, learned something from each of them, and then developed his own style of stern and angular realism. He took his career in his hands by molding in terra cotta an unflattering bust of Lorenzo—nose and bangs and worried brow. In any case Il Magnifico was well pleased with two bronze reliefs —of Alexander and Darius—made for him by Verrocchio; he sent them to

Matthias Corvinus of Hungary, and engaged the sculptor (1472) to design, in the church of San Lorenzo, a tomb for his father Piero and his uncle Giovanni. Verrocchio carved the sarcophagus in porphyry, and decorated it with bronze supports and wreaths in exquisite floral form. Four years later he cast a boyish *David* standing in calm pride over the severed head of Goliath; the Signory liked it so much that it placed the statue at the head of the main stairway in the Palazzo Vecchio. In the same year it accepted from him a bronze *Boy Holding a Dolphin*, and used it as a fountain spout in the courtyard of the palace. At the height of his powers Verrocchio designed, and cast in bronze for a niche on the exterior of Or San Michele, a group of *Christ and Doubting Thomas* (1483). The Christ is a figure of divine nobility, Thomas is portrayed with understanding sympathy, the hands are finished with a perfection seldom attained in statuary, the robes are a triumph of sculptural art; the whole group has a living and mobile reality.

So obvious was Verrocchio's superiority in bronze that the Venetian Senate invited him (1479) to come to Venice and cast a statue of Bartolommeo Colleoni, the *condottiere* who had won so many victories for the island state. Andrea went, made a model for the horse, and was preparing to cast it in bronze when he learned that the Senate was considering the advisability of confining his commission to the horse and letting Vellano of Padua make the man. Andrea, according to Vasari, broke the head and legs of his model and returned to Florence in a rage. The Senate warned him that if he ever put foot on Venetian soil again he would lose his head in no figurative way; he replied that they should never expect him there, since senators were not as skillful as sculptors in replacing broken heads. The Senate thought better of the matter, restored the total commission to Verrocchio, and persuaded him to return at twice the original fee. He repaired the model of the horse, and cast it successfully; but in the process he became overheated, caught a chill, and died within a few days, at the age of fifty-six (1488). In his last hours a rude crucifix was placed before him; he begged the attendants to take it away and bring him one by Donatello, so that he might die, as he had lived, in the presence of beautiful things.

The Venetian sculptor Alessandro Leopardi completed the great statue in so vivid a style, with such mastery of motion and command, that the *Colleoni* suffered no loss by Verrocchio's death. It was set up (1496) in the Campo di San Zanipolo—the Field of Sts. John and Paul; and it struts there to this day, the proudest and finest equestrian statue surviving from the Renaissance.

VI. PAINTING

1. Ghirlandaio

Verrocchio's thriving studio was characteristic of Renaissance Florence —it united all the arts in one workshop, sometimes in one man; in the same *bottega* one artist might be designing a church or a palace, another might be carving or casting a statue, another sketching or painting a picture, another cutting or setting gems, another carving or inlaying ivory or wood, or fusing or beating metal, or fashioning floats and pennons for a festival procession; men like Verrocchio, Leonardo, or Michelangelo could do any of these. Florence had many such studios, and art students went wild in the streets,[27] or lived Bohemianly in the tenements, or became rich men honored by popes and princes as inspired spirits beyond price and—like Cellini—above the law. More than any other city except Athens, Florence attached importance to art and artists, talked and fought about them, and told anecdotes about them,[28] as we do now of actors and actresses. It was Renaissance Florence that formed the romantic concept of the genius—the man inspired by a divine spirit (the Latin *genius*) dwelling within him.

It is worthy of note that Verrocchio's studio left no great sculptor (except one side of Leonardo) to carry on the master's excellence, but taught two painters of high degree—Leonardo and Perugino—and one of lesser but notable talent, Lorenzo di Credi. Painting was gradually ousting sculpture as the favorite art. Probably it was an advantage that the painters were uninstructed and uninhibited by the lost murals of antiquity. They knew that there had been such men as Apelles and Protogenes, but few of them saw even the Alexandrian or Pompeian remnants of ancient painting. In this art there was no revival of antiquity, and the continuity of the Middle Ages with the Renaissance was most visible: the line was devious but clear from the Byzantines to Duccio to Giotto to Fra Angelico to Leonardo to Raphael to Titian. So the painters, unlike the sculptors, had to forge through trial and error their own technology and style; originality and experiment were forced upon them. They labored over the details of human, animal, and plant anatomy; they tried circular, triangular, or other schemes of composition; they explored the tricks of perspective and the illusions of *chiaroscuro* to give depth to their backgrounds and body to their figures; they scoured the streets for Apostles and Virgins, and drew from models clothed or nude; they passed from fresco to tempera and back again, and appropriated the new techniques of oil painting introduced into northern Italy by Rogier van der Weyden and Antonio da Messina. As their skill and courage grew, and their lay patrons multiplied, they added to the old religious subjects the stories of classic mythology and the pagan glories of the flesh. They took Nature into the studio, or betook themselves to Nature; nothing human or natural seemed in their view alien to art, no face so ugly but art could reveal its illuminating significance. They recorded the world; and when war and politics had made Italy a prison and a ruin, the painters left behind them the line and color, the life and passion, of the Renaissance.

Formed by such studies, inheriting an ever richer tradition of methods, materials, and ideas, men of talent painted better now than men of genius had painted a century before. Benozzo Gozzoli, says Vasari in an ungracious moment, "was not of great excellence . . . yet he distanced all the others of his age in his perseverance; for among the multitude of his works some could hardly help but be good."[29] He began as a pupil of Fra Angelico, and followed him to Rome and Orvieto as assistant. Piero the Gouty recalled him to Florence and invited him to portray, on the walls of the chapel in the Medici Palace, the journey of the Magi from the East to Bethlehem. These frescoes are Benozzo's *chef-d'oeuvre:* a stately and yet lively procession of kings and knights in gorgeous robes, of squires, pages, angels, hunters, scholars, slaves, horses, leopards, dogs, and half a dozen Medici—and Benozzo himself slyly introduced into the parade—and all against backgrounds and landscapes marvelous and picturesque. Flushed with triumph, Benozzo went to San Gimignano, and decorated the choir of Sant' Agostino with seventeen scenes from the life of its patron saint. In the Campo Santo at Pisa he labored for sixteen years, covering vast walls with twenty-one Old Testament scenes from Adam to the Queen of Sheba; some, like *The Tower of Babel*, were among the major frescoes of the Renaissance. Benozzo diluted his excellence through eager haste; he drew carelessly, made many of his figures depressingly uniform, and crowded his pictures with a confusing multitude of persons and details; but he had in him the blood and joy of life, he loved its lusty panorama and the glory of the great; and the imperfections of his line are half forgotten in the splendor of his color and the enthusiasm of his fertility.

The benign influence of Fra Angelico passed down to Alesso Baldovinetti and Cosimo Roselli, and through Alesso to one of the major painters of the Renaissance—Domenico Ghirlandaio. Domenico's father was a goldsmith who had received the nickname of Ghirlandaio from the gold and silver garlands that he had fashioned for the pretty heads of Florence. Under this father and Baldovinetti Domenico studied with zest and zeal; spent many hours before the frescoes of Masaccio in the Carmine; learned by indefatigable practice the arts of perspective, foreshortening, modeling, and composition; "he would draw everyone who passed the shop," says Vasari, "making extraordinary likenesses" after a fleeting view. He was barely twenty-one when he was charged to paint the story of Santa Fina in her chapel in the cathedral at San Gimignano. At thirty-one (1480) he earned the title of master by four frescoes in the church and refectory of the Ognissanti in Florence—a *St. Jerome*, a *Descent From the Cross*, a *Madonna della Misericordia* (which included a portrait of the donor, Amerigo Vespucci), and a *Last Supper* that gave some hints to Leonardo.

Summoned to Rome by Sixtus IV, he painted in the Sistine Chapel *Christ Calling Peter and Andrew from Their Nets*—especially beautiful in its background of mountains, sea, and sky. During this stay in Rome he studied and drew the arches, baths, columns, aqueducts, and amphitheaters of the ancient city, and with so practiced an eye that he was able to seize at once, without rule or compass, the just proportions of each part. A Florentine merchant in Rome, Francesco Tornabuoni, mourning his dead wife, employed Ghirlandaio to paint frescoes for her memorial in Santa Maria sopra Minerva, and Domenico succeeded so well that Tornabuoni sent him back to Florence armed with florins and a letter attesting his excellence. The Signory soon entrusted to him the decoration of the Sala del Orologio in their palace. In the next four years (1481-5) he painted scenes from the life of St. Francis in the Sassetti Chapel of Santa Trinità. All the progress of the painter's art, except the use of oil, was embodied in these frescoes: harmonious composition, accurate line, gradations of light, perspective fidelity, realistic portraiture (of Lorenzo, Politian, Pulci, Palla Strozzi, Francesco Sassetti), and at the same time the Angelesque tradition of ideality and piety. From the near-perfection of the altarpiece—the *Adoration of the Shepherds*—there would be but a step of deeper imagination and subtler grace to Leonardo and Raphael.

In 1485 Giovanni Tornabuoni, chief of the Medici bank in Rome, offered Ghirlandaio twelve hundred ducats ($30,000) to paint a chapel in Santa Maria Novella, and promised him two hundred more if the work should prove fully satisfactory. Aided by several pupils, including Michelangelo, Ghirlandaio gave most of the following five years to this high moment of his career. On the ceiling he painted the four Evangelists; on the walls St. Francis, Peter Martyr, John the Baptist, and scenes from the lives of Mary and Christ, from an *Annunciation* to a magnificent *Coronation of the Virgin.* Here again he delighted in contemporary portraits: the stately Lodovica Tornabuoni, fit to be a queen, the saucy beauty of Ginevra de' Benci, the scholars Ficino, Politian, and Landino, the painters Baldovinetti, Mainardi, and Ghirlandaio himself. When, in 1490, the chapel was opened to the public, all the dignitaries and literati of Florence flocked to examine the paintings; the realistic portraits were the talk of the town; and Tornabuoni expressed himself as completely satisfied. Financially pressed at the time, he begged Domenico to forgive him the extra two hundred ducats; the artist replied that the satisfaction of his patron was more precious to him than any gold.

He was a lovable character, so adored by his brothers that one of them, David, almost slew an abbot with an aged loaf of bread for bringing to Domenico and his aides food that David held unworthy of his brother's genius. Ghirlandaio opened his studio to all who cared to work or study there, making it a veritable school of art. He accepted all commissions, great or small, saying that none should be denied; he left the care of his household and finances to David, saying that he would not be content till he had painted the whole circuit of Florence's wall. He produced many mediocre paintings, and yet some incidental pieces of great charm, like the Louvre's delightful *Grandfather* with the bulbous nose, and the lovely *Portrait of a Woman* in the Morgan Collection in New York—pictures full of the character that year by year records itself upon the human face. Great critics of unquestionable learning and repute yield him only a minor rank;[30] and it is true that he excelled rather in line than in color, that he painted too rapidly, and crowded his pictures with irrelevant detail, and took a step backward, perhaps, in preferring tempera after Baldovinetti's experiments with oil. Even so, he brought the accumulated technology of his art to the highest point that it would reach in his country and his century; and he bequeathed to Florence and the world such treasures that criticism hangs its head in gratitude.

2. Botticelli

Only one Florentine surpassed him in his generation. Sandro Botticelli was as different from Ghirlandaio as ethereal fancy from physical fact. Alessandro's father, Mariano Filipepi, unable to persuade the boy that life would be impossible without reading, writing, and arithmetic, apprenticed him to the goldsmith Botticelli, whose name, through the affection of the pupil or the whim of history, became permanently attached to Sandro's own. From this *bottega* the lad passed at sixteen to that of Fra Filippo Lippi, who came to love the restless and impetuous youth. Filippo's Filippino later painted Sandro as a sullen fellow with deep-set eyes, salient nose, sensual fleshy mouth, flowing locks, purple cap, red mantle, and green hose;[31] who would have guessed such a man from the delicate fantasies that Botticelli has left to the museums? Perhaps every artist must be a sensualist before he can paint ideally; he must know and love the body as the ultimate source and standard of the esthetic sense. Vasari describes Sandro as "a merry fellow," who played pranks upon fellow artists and obtuse citizens. Doubtless, like all of us, he was many men, turned on one or another of his selves as occasion required, and kept his real self a frightened secret from the world.

About 1465 Botticelli set up his own studio, and soon received commissions from the Medici. It was apparently for Lorenzo's mother, Lucrezia Tornabuoni, that he painted *Judith;* and for Piero Gottoso, her husband, he made his *Madonna of the Magnificat* and his *Adoration of the Magi*—hymns in color to three Medici generations. In the *Madonna* Botticelli pictured Lorenzo and Giuliano as boys of sixteen and twelve, holding a book upon which the Virgin—borrowed from Fra Lippo—writes her noble song of praise; in the *Adoration* Cosimo kneels at Mary's feet, Piero kneels at a lower level before them, and Lorenzo, now seventeen, holds a sword in his hand as a sign that he has reached the age of legitimate killing.

Lorenzo and Giuliano carried on Piero's patronage of Botticelli. His finest portraits are of Giuliano and Giuliano's beloved Simonetta Vespucci. He still painted religious pictures, like the powerful *St. Augustine* in the church of the Ognissanti; but in this period, perhaps under the influence of Lorenzo's circle, he turned more and more to pagan subjects, usually from classical mythology, and favoring the nude. Vasari reports that "in many houses Botticelli painted . . . plenty of naked women," and accuses him of "serious disorders in his living";[32] the humanists, and animal spirits, had won Sandro for a time to an epicurean philosophy. It was apparently for Lorenzo and Giuliano that he painted (1480) *The Birth of Venus.* A demure nude rises from a golden shell in the sea, using her long blonde tresses as the only fig leaf at hand; on her right winged zephyrs blow her to the shore; on her left a pretty maid (Simonetta?), clad in a gown of flowered white, offers the goddess a mantle to enhance her loveliness. The painting is a masterpiece of grace, in which design and composition are everything, color is subordinate, realism is ignored, and everything is directed to evoking an ethereal fancy through the flowing rhythm of the line. Botticelli had taken the theme from a passage in Politian's *La giostra*. From a description, in the same poem, of Giuliano's victories in jousts and love the artist took his second pagan picture, *Mars and Venus;* here Venus is clothed, and may again be Simonetta; Mars lies exhausted and asleep, no rude warrior but a youth of unblemished flesh, who might almost be mistaken for another Aphrodite. Finally, in his *Spring* (*Primavera*) Botticelli expressed the mood of Lorenzo's hymn to Bacchus ("Who would be happy, let him be!"): the auxiliary lady of the *Birth* reappears with her flowing robe and pretty feet; at the left Giuliano (?) plucks an apple from a tree to give to one of the three graces standing half nude beside him; on the right a lusty male seizes a maiden dressed in a little mist; Simonetta presides modestly over the scene; and in the air above her Cupid shoots his quite superfluous darts. These three pictures symbolized many things, for Botticelli loved to allegorize; but perhaps without his realizing it they represented also the victory of the humanists in art. The Church would now for half a century (1480-1534) struggle to regain her dominance over pictorial themes.

As if to meet the issue squarely, Sixtus IV called Botticelli to Rome (1481), and commissioned him to paint three frescoes in the Sistine Chapel. They are not among his masterpieces; he was in no mood for piety. But when he returned to Florence (1485) he found the city astir with Savonarola's sermons, and went to hear him. He was deeply moved. He had always harbored a strain of austerity, and whatever skepticism he might have caught from Lorenzo, Pulci, and Politian had been lost in the secret well of his youthful faith. Now the fiery preacher at San Marco's pressed upon him and Florence the awful implications of that faith: God had allowed Himself to be insulted, scourged, and crucified to redeem mankind from the guilt of Adam and Eve's sin; only a life of virtue or sincere repentance could win some grace from that sacrifice of God to God, and so escape eternal hell. It was about this time that Botticelli illustrated Dante's *Divine Comedy*. He turned his art again to the service of religion, and told once more the marvelous story of Mary and Christ. For the church of St. Barnabas he painted a masterly group of the Virgin enthroned, with divers saints; she was still the tender and lovely maiden whom he had drawn in Fra Lippo's studio. Soon afterward he painted the *Madonna of the Pomegranate*—the Virgin surrounded by singing cherubim, the Child holding in His hand the fruit whose innumerable seeds symbolized the dissemi-

nation of the Christian faith. In 1490 he recapitulated the epic of the
Divine Mother in two pictures: the *Annunciation* and the *Coronation*.
But he was aging now, and had lost the fresh clarity and grace of his art.

In 1498 Savonarola was hanged and burned. Botticelli was horrified at
this most distinguished murder of the Renaissance. Perhaps it was shortly
after that tragedy that he painted his complex symbolism, *Calumny*.
Against a background of classic archways and distant sea three women—
Fraud, Deception, Calumny—led by a ragged male (Envy), drag a nude
victim by the hair to a tribunal where a judge with the long ears of an ass,
advised by females personifying Suspicion and Ignorance, prepares to yield
to the fury and bloodthirst of the crowd and condemn the fallen man;
while at the left Remorse, garbed in black, looks in sorrow upon naked
Truth—Botticelli's Venus once more, clad in the same reptilian hair. Was
the victim intended to represent Savonarola? Perhaps, though the nudes
might have startled the monk.

The *Nativity* in the National Gallery at London is Botticelli's final
masterpiece, confused but colorful, and capturing for the last time his
rhythmic grace. Here all seems to breathe a heavenly happiness; the ladies
of the *Spring* return as winged angels, hailing the miraculous and saving
birth, and dancing precariously on a bough suspended in space. But on the
picture Botticelli wrote in Greek these words, savoring of Savonarola, and
recalling the Middle Ages in the height of the Renaissance:

> This picture I, Alessandro, painted at the end of the year 1500, in
> the troubles of Italy . . . during the fulfillment of the Eleventh
> [Chapter] of St. John, in the second woe of the Apocalypse, in the
> loosing of the Devil for three years and a half. Later he shall be
> chained, according to the Twelfth of St. John, and we shall see him
> trodden down as in this picture.

After 1500 we have no paintings from his hand. He was only fifty-six,
and might have had some art left in him; but he yielded place to Leonardo
and Michelangelo, and lapsed into a morose poverty. The Medici who had
been his mainstay gave him charity, but they themselves were in a fallen
state. He died alone and infirm, aged sixty-six, while the forgetful world
hurried on.

Among his pupils was his teacher's son, Filippino Lippi. This "love
child"* was loved by all who knew him: a man gentle, affable, modest,
courteous, whose "excellence was such," says Vasari, "that he obliterated

---

* Crowe and Cavalcaselle have labored to restore Filippino's legitimacy, but their argument reduces itself to a gallant wish.[33]

the stain of his birth, if any there be." Under his father's tutelage and
Sandro's he learned the painter's art so rapidly that already at twenty-three
he produced in *The Vision of St. Bernard* a portrait that in Vasari's judgment "lacked only speech." When the Carmelite monks decided to complete the frescoes begun in their Brancacci Chapel sixty years before, they
awarded the commission to Filippino, still but twenty-seven. The result did
not equal Masaccio, but in *St. Paul Addressing St. Peter in Prison* Filippino
achieved a memorable figure of simple dignity and quiet power.

In 1489, at Lorenzo's suggestion, Cardinal Caraffa called him to Rome to
decorate a chapel in Santa Maria sopra Minerva with scenes from the life
of St. Thomas Aquinas. In the main fresco the artist, perhaps recalling a
similar picture by Andrea da Firenze a century before, showed the philosopher in triumph, with Arius, Averroes, and other heretics at his feet;
meanwhile, in the universities of Bologna and Padua, the doctrines of
Averroes were gaining ground over the orthodox faith. Back in Florence,
in the chapel of Filippo Strozzi in Santa Maria Novella, Filippino recorded
the careers of the Apostles Philip and John in frescoes so realistic that
legend told how a boy tried to hide a secret treasure in a hole that Filippino
had represented in a pictured wall. Interrupting this series for a time, and
replacing the dilatory Leonardo, he painted an altarpiece for the monks
of Scopeto; he chose the old subject of the Magi adoring the Child, but
enlivened it with Moors, Indians, and many Medici; one of these last, serving as an astrologer with a quadrant in his hands, is among the most human
and humorous portraits of the Renaissance. Finally (1498), as if to say
that his father's sins had been forgiven, Filippino was invited to Prato to
paint a *Madonna;* Vasari praised it, the Second World War destroyed it.
He settled down to marriage at forty, and knew for a few years the joys
and tribulations of parentage. Suddenly, at forty-seven, he died of so
simple an ailment as quinsy sore throat (1505).

VII. LORENZO PASSES

Lorenzo himself was not among the few who in those centuries reached
old age. Like his father he suffered from arthritis and gout, to which was
added a stomach disorder that frequently caused him exhausting pain.
He tried a dozen remedies, and found nothing better than the passing al-
leviation given by warm mineral baths. For some time before his death he
perceived that he, who had preached the gospel of joy, had not much
longer to live.

His wife died in 1488; and though he had been unfaithful to her he sincerely mourned her loss and missed her helping hand. She had given him a numerous progeny, of whom seven survived. He had sedulously supervised their education; and in his later years he labored to guide them into marriages that might redound to the happiness of Florence as well as their own. The oldest son, Piero, was affianced to an Orsini to win friends in Rome; the youngest, Giuliano, married a sister of the duke of Savoy, received from Francis I the title of duke of Nemours, and so helped to build a bridge between Florence and France. Giovanni, the second son, was directed into an ecclesiastical career, and took to it amiably; he pleased everyone by his good nature, good manners, and good Latin. Lorenzo persuaded Innocent VIII to violate all precedents by making him a cardinal at fourteen; the Pope yielded for the same reason that made most marriages of royalty—to bind one government to another in the amity of one blood.

Lorenzo retired from active participation in the government of Florence, delegated more and more of his public and private business to his son Piero, and sought comfort in the peace of the countryside and the conversation of his friends. He excused himself in a characteristic letter.

> What can be more desirable to a well-regulated mind than the enjoy-
> ment of leisure with dignity? This is what all good men wish to
> obtain, but which great men alone accomplish. In the midst of
> public affairs we may indeed be allowed to look forward to a day
> of rest; but no rest should totally seclude us from an attention to the
> concerns of our country. I cannot deny that the path which it has
> been my lot to tread has been arduous and rugged, full of dangers,
> and beset with treachery; but I console myself in having contributed
> to the welfare of my country, the prosperity of which may now
> rival that of any other state, however flourishing. Nor have I been
> inattentive to the interests and advancement of my own family,
> having always proposed to my imitation the example of my grand-
> father Cosmo, who watched over his public and private concerns
> with equal vigilance. Having now obtained the object of my cares,
> I trust I may be allowed to enjoy the sweets of leisure, to share the
> reputation of my fellow-citizens, and to exult in the glory of my
> native place.

But little time was left him to enjoy his unaccustomed peace. He had hardly moved to his villa at Careggi (March 21, 1492) when his stomach pains became alarmingly intense. Specialist physicians were summoned, who made him drink a mixture of jewels. He became rapidly worse, and reconciled himself to death. He expressed to Pico and Politian his sorrow that he could not live long enough to complete his collection of manuscripts for their accommodation and the use of students. As the end approached he sent for a priest, and with his last strength insisted on leaving his bed to receive the sacrament on his knees. He thought now of the uncompromising preacher who had denounced him as a destroyer of liberty and a corrupter of youth, and he longed to have that man's forgiveness before he died. He despatched a friend to beg Savonarola to come to him to hear his confession and give him a more precious absolution. Savonarola came. According to Politian he offered absolution on three conditions: that Lorenzo should have a lively faith in God's mercy, should promise to mend his life if he recovered, and should meet death with fortitude; Lorenzo agreed, and was absolved. According to Savonarola's early biographer, G. F. Pico (not the humanist), the third condition was that Lorenzo should promise "to restore liberty to Florence"; in Pico's account Lorenzo made no response to this demand, and the friar left him unabsolved.[34] On April 9, 1492, Lorenzo died, aged forty-three.

When the news of this premature death reached Florence almost the entire city mourned, and even Lorenzo's opponents wondered how social order could now be maintained in Florence, or peace in Italy, without his guiding hand.[35] Europe recognized his stature as a statesman, and sensed in him the characteristic qualities of the time; he was "the man of the Renaissance" in everything but his aversion to violence. His slowly acquired prudence in policy, his simple but persuasive eloquence in debate, his firmness and courage in action, had made all but a few Florentines forget the liberty that his family had destroyed; and many who had not forgotten remembered it as the freedom of rich clans to compete in force and chicanery for an exploitive dominance in a "democracy" where only a thirtieth of the population could vote. Lorenzo had used his power with moderation and for the good of the state, even to the neglect of his private fortune. He had been guilty of sexual looseness, and had given a bad example to Florentine youth. He had given a good example in literature, had restored the Italian language to literary standing, and had rivaled his protégés in poetry. He had supported the arts with a discriminating taste that set a standard for Europe. Of all the "despots" he was the gentlest and the best. "This man," said King Ferdinand of Naples, "lived long enough for his glory, but too short a time for Italy."[36] After him Florence declined, and Italy knew no peace.

CHAPTER V

Savonarola and the Republic

1492-1534

I. THE PROPHET

THE advantage of hereditary rule is continuity; its nemesis is mediocrity. Piero di Lorenzo succeeded without trouble to his father's power, but his character and his misjudgments forfeited the popularity upon which the rule of the Medici had been based. He was endowed with a violent temper, a middling mind, a vacillating will, and admirable intentions. He continued Lorenzo's generosity to artists and men of letters, but with less discrimination and tact. He was physically strong, excelled in sports, and took part more frequently and prominently in athletic competitions than Florence thought becoming in the head of an endangered state. It was among his many misfortunes that Lorenzo's enterprises and extravagance had depleted the city's treasury; that the competition of British textiles was causing economic depression in Florence; that Piero's Orsini wife turned up her Roman nose at the Florentines as a nation of shopkeepers; that the collateral branch of the Medici family, derived from Cosimo's brother Lorenzo "the Elder," began now to challenge the descendants of Cosimo, and led a party of opposition in the name of liberty. It was Piero's crowning misery that he was contemporary with Charles VIII of France, who invaded Italy, and of Savonarola, who proposed to replace the Medici with Christ. Piero had not been built to withstand such strains.

The Savonarola family came from Padua to Ferrara about 1440, when Michele Savonarola was invited by Niccolò III d'Este to be his court physician. Michael was a man of piety rare in medicos; he was wont to rebuke the Ferrarese for preferring romances to religion.[1] His son Niccolò was a mediocre physician, but Niccolò's wife Elena Bonacossi was a woman of strong character and high ideals. Girolamo was the third of their seven children. They set him in his turn to study medicine, but he thought Thomas Aquinas more absorbing than anatomy, and solitude with his books more pleasant than the sports of youth. At the University of Bologna he was horrified to find no student so poor as to do virtue reverence. "To be considered a man here," he wrote, "you must defile your mouth with the most filthy, brutal, and tremendous blasphemies. . . . If you study philosophy and the good arts you are considered a dreamer; if you live chastely and modestly, a fool; if you are pious, a hypocrite; if you believe in God, an imbecile."[2] He left the University, and returned to his mother and solitude. He became self-conscious, fretted over the thought of hell and the sinfulness of men; his earliest known composition was a poem denouncing the vices of Italy, including the popes, and pledging himself to reform his country and his Church. He passed long hours in prayer, and fasted so earnestly that his parents mourned his emaciation. In 1474 he was stirred to even severer piety by the Lenten sermons of Fra Michele, and he rejoiced to see many Ferrarese bringing masks, false hair, playing cards, unseemly pictures, and other worldly apparatus to fling them upon a burning pyre in the market place. A year later, aged twenty-three, he fled secretly from home, and entered a Dominican monastery in Bologna.

He wrote a tender letter to his parents begging their forgiveness for disappointing the expectations they had had of his advancement in the world. When they importuned him to return he answered angrily: "Ye blind! Why do you still weep and lament? You hamper me, though you should rejoice. . . . What can I say if you grieve yet, save that you are my sworn enemies and foes to Virtue? If so, then I say to you, 'Get ye behind me, all ye who work evil!' "[3] Six years he stayed in the Bologna convent. He proudly asked that the most humble tasks should be given him, but his talent as an orator was discovered, and he was set to preaching. In 1481 he was transferred to San Marco in Florence, and was assigned to preach in the church of San Lorenzo. His sermons there proved unpopular; they were too theological and didactic for a city that knew the eloquence and polish of the humanists; his congregation dwindled week by week. The prior set him to instructing novices.

It was probably in the next five years that his final character was formed. As the intensity of his feelings and purposes increased they wrote themselves upon his features in the furrowed and frowning forehead, the thick lips tight with determination, the immense nose curving out as if to encompass the world, a countenance somber and severe, expressing an infinite capacity for love and hate; a small frame racked and haunted with visions, frustrated aspirations, and introverted storms. "I am still flesh like you," he wrote to his parents, "and the senses are unruly to reason, so that I must struggle cruelly to keep the Demon from leaping upon my back."[4] He fasted and flogged himself to tame what seemed to him the inherent corruption of human nature. If he personified the promptings of flesh and pride as Satanic voices, he could with equal readiness personify the admonitions of his better self. Alone in his cell, he glorified his solitude by conceiving himself as a battleground of spirits hovering over him for evil or for good. Finally it seemed to him that angels, archangels, were speaking to him; he accepted their words as divine revelations; and suddenly he spoke to the world as a prophet chosen to be a messenger of God. He avidly absorbed the apocalyptic visions attributed to the Apostle John, and inherited the eschatalogy of the mystic Joachim of Flora. Like Joachim he announced that the reign of Antichrist had come, that Satan had captured the world, that soon Christ would appear to begin His earthly rule, and that divine vengeance would engulf the tyrants, adulterers, and atheists who seemed to dominate Italy.

When his prior sent him to preach in Lombardy (1486), Savonarola abandoned his youthful pedagogic style, and cast his sermons into the form of denunciations of immorality, prophecies of doom, and calls to repentance. Thousands of people who could not have followed his earlier arguments listened with awe to the newly impassioned eloquence of a man who seemed to be speaking with authority. Pico della Mirandola heard of the friar's success; he asked Lorenzo to suggest to the prior that Savonarola should be brought back to Florence. Savonarola returned (1489); two years later he was chosen prior of San Marco; and Lorenzo found in him an enemy more forthright and powerful than any that had ever crossed his path.

Florence was surprised to discover that the swarthy preacher who a decade before had chilled them with argument, could now awe them with apocalyptic fantasies, thrill them with vivid descriptions of the paganism, corruption, and immorality of their neighbors, lift up their souls to repentance and hope, and renew in them the full intensity of the faith that had inspired and terrified their youth.

> Ye women, who glory in your ornaments, your hair, your hands, I tell you you are all ugly. Would you see true beauty? Look at the pious man or woman in whom spirit dominates matter; watch him when he prays, when a ray of the divine beauty glows upon him when his prayer is ended; you will see the beauty of God shining in his face, you will behold it as it were the face of an angel.[5]

Men marveled at his courage, for he flayed the clergy and the papacy more than the laity, the princes more than the people; and a note of political radicalism warmed the hearts of the poor:

> In these days there is no grace, no gift of the Holy Spirit, that may not be bought or sold. On the other hand, the poor are oppressed by grievous burdens; and when they are called to pay sums beyond their means the rich cry unto them, "Give me the rest." There be some who, having an income of fifty [florins per year], pay a tax on one hundred, while the rich pay little, since the taxes are regulated at their pleasure. Bethink ye well, O ye rich, for affliction shall smite ye. This city shall no more be called Florence but a den of thieves, of baseness and bloodshed. Then shall ye all be poverty-stricken . . . and your name, O priests, shall be changed into a terror.[6]

After the priests the bankers:

> You have found many ways of making money, and many exchanges which you call lawful but which are most unjust; and you have corrupted the offices and magistrates of the city. No one can persuade you that usury [interest] is sinful; you defend it at the peril of your souls. No one is ashamed of lending at usury; nay, those who do otherwise pass for fools. . . . Your brow is that of a whore, and you will not blush. You say, a good and glad life lies in gain; and Christ says, Blessed are the poor in spirit, for they shall inherit heaven.[7]

And a word for Lorenzo:

> Tyrants are incorrigible because they are proud, because they love flattery, and will not restore ill-gotten gains. . . . They hearken not unto the poor, and neither do they condemn the rich. . . . They corrupt voters, and farm out taxes to aggravate the burdens of the people[8]. . . . The tyrant is wont to occupy the people with shows and festivals, in order that they may think of their own pastimes and not of his designs, and, growing unused to the conduct of the commonwealth, may leave the reins of government in his hands.[9]

Nor shall that dictatorship be excused on the ground that it finances literature and art. The literature and art, said Savonarola, are pagan; the humanists merely pretend to be Christians; those ancient authors whom they so sedulously exhume and edit and praise are strangers to Christ and the Christian virtues, and their art is an idolatry of heathen gods, or a shameless display of naked women and men.

Lorenzo was disturbed. His grandfather had founded and enriched the monastery of San Marco; he himself had given to it lavishly; it seemed to him unreasonable that a friar who could know little of the difficulties of government, and who idealized a liberty that had been merely the right of the strong to use the weak without hindrance by law, should now undermine, from a Medici shrine, that public support upon which the political power of his family had been built. He tried to appease the friar; he went to Mass in San Marco's, and sent the convent rich gifts. Savonarola scorned them, and remarked in a subsequent sermon that a faithful dog does not leave off barking in his master's defense because a bone is thrown to him. When he found an unusually large sum, in gold, in the alms box, he suspected that it came from Lorenzo, and gave it to another monastery, saying that silver sufficed the needs of his brethren. Lorenzo sent five leading citizens to argue with him that his inflammatory sermons would lead to useless violence, and were unsettling the order and peace of Florence; Savonarola answered by telling them to bid Lorenzo do penance for his sins. A Franciscan friar famous for eloquence was encouraged to preach popular sermons with a view to drawing the Dominican's audience away; the Franciscan failed. Greater throngs than ever before came to San Marco, until its church could no longer hold them. For his Lenten sermons of 1491 Savonarola moved his pulpit into the cathedral; and though that edifice had been designed to contain a city, it was crowded whenever the friar was scheduled to speak. The ailing Lorenzo made no further effort to interfere with his preaching.

After Lorenzo's death the weakness of his son Piero made Savonarola the greatest power in Florence. With the reluctant consent of the new pope, Alexander VI, he separated his convent from the Lombard Congregation (of Dominican monasteries) of which it had been a part, and made himself in practice the independent head of his monastic community. He reformed its regulations, and raised the moral and intellectual level of the friars under his rule. New recruits joined his flock, and most of its 250 members developed for him a love and fidelity that upheld him in all but his final ordeal. He became bolder in his criticism of the laic and clerical immorality of the time. Inheriting, however unwittingly, the anticlerical views of the Waldensian and Patarine heretics who still lurked here and there in northern Italy and central Europe, he condemned the worldly wealth of the clergy, the pomp of ecclesiastical ceremony, "the great prelates with splendid miters of gold and precious stones on their heads . . . with fine copes and stoles of brocade"; he contrasted this affluence with the simplicity of the priests in the early Church; these "had fewer gold miters and fewer chalices, for what few they possessed were broken up to relieve the needs of the poor; whereas our prelates, for the sake of obtaining chalices, will rob the poor of their sole means of support."[10] To these denunciations he added prophecies of doom. He had predicted that Lorenzo and Innocent VIII would die in 1492; they did. Now he predicted that presently the sins of Italy, of her despots and her clergy, would be avenged by a dire disaster; that thereafter Christ would lead the nation in a glorious reform; and that he himself, Savonarola, would die a violent death. Early in 1494 he foretold that Charles VIII would invade Italy, and he welcomed the invasion as the chastening hand of God. His sermons at this time, says a contemporary, were "so full of terrors and alarms, cries and lamentations, that everyone went about the city bewildered, speechless, and, as it were, half dead."[11]

In September, 1494, Charles VIII crossed the Apennines into Italy, resolved to add the Kingdom of Naples to the French crown. In October he entered Florentine territory and besieged the fortress of Sarzana. Piero thought he could save Florence from France as his father had saved it from Naples, by going in person to the enemy. He met Charles at Sarzana, and yielded to all demands: Pisa, Leghorn, and every bastion of Florence in the west were surrendered to the French for the duration of the war, and Florence was to advance 200,000 florins ($5,000,000) to help finance Charles's campaign.[12] When news of these concessions reached Florence the Signory and the Council were shocked; contrary to Lorenzo's precedents, they had not been consulted in these negotiations. Led by the Medici opponents of Piero, the Signory decided to depose him and restore the old republic. When Piero returned from Sarzana he found the gates of the Palazzo Vecchio closed in his face. As he rode to his home the people jeered him, and urchins pelted him with stones. Fearing for his life, he fled from the city with his family and his brothers. The populace sacked the Medici palace and gardens, and the homes of Piero's financial agents; the art collection gathered by four generations of Medici was plundered and scattered, and its remains were sold at auction by the government. The Signory offered a reward of five thousand florins for the delivery of Piero and Cardinal Giovanni de' Medici alive, two thousand for their delivery dead. It sent five men, including Savonarola, to Charles at Pisa to ask for better terms; Charles met them with noncommittal courtesy. When the delegation had left, the Pisans tore the lion and lilies of Florence from their buildings, and declared their independence. Charles entered Florence, consented to some slight modification of his demands, and, eager to get to Naples, led his army

to the south. Florence addressed itself now to one of history's most spec-
tacular experiments in democracy.

II. THE STATESMAN

On December 2, 1494 the citizens were summoned to a *parlamento* by
the great bell in the Palazzo Vecchio tower. The Signory asked and received the power to name twenty men who would appoint a new Signory
and new magistrates for a year, after which all offices were to be filled by
lot from a register of the approximately three thousand enfranchised males.
The Twenty dismissed the councils and agencies which under the Medici
had considered and administered public affairs, and divided the diverse
functions among themselves. They were inadequately experienced for
these tasks, and were torn by family factions; the new governmental machinery broke down, and chaos was imminent; commerce and industry
hesitated, men were thrown out of work, and angry crowds gathered in the
streets. Piero Capponi persuaded the Twenty that order could be saved
only by inviting Savonarola into their councils.

The friar summoned them to his monastery, and expounded to them an
ambitious program of political, economic, and moral legislation. Under his
leadership and that of Pietro Soderini, the Twenty devised a new constitution, partly modeled on that which was so successfully maintaining stability
in Venice. A *Maggior Consiglio* or Great Council was to be formed of men
who—or their ancestors in the preceding three generations—had held a major office in the state; and these initial members were to choose twenty-
eight additional councilors in each year. The executive organs of the government were to remain essentially as under the Medici: a Signory of eight
priors and a gonfalonier, chosen by the Council for a term of two months,
and various committees—The Twelve, The Sixteen, The Ten, The Eight—
to carry on administration, taxation, and war. Complete democracy was
postponed as impractical in a society still largely illiterate and subject to
waves of passion; but the Great Council, numbering almost three thousand
members, was considered to be a representative body. Since no room in
the Palazzo Vecchio could house so large an assemblage, Simone Pollaiuolo
—Il Cronaca—was engaged to redesign part of the interior into a *Sala dei
Cinquecento*, or Hall of the Five Hundred, where the Council could meet
in sections; here, eight years later, Leonardo da Vinci and Michelangelo
would be commissioned to paint opposed walls in a famous rivalry.
Through Savonarola's influence and eloquence the proposed constitution

received public acclaim, and the new Republic came into operation on June 10, 1495.

It began amiably by issuing amnesty to all supporters of the deposed Medici regime. With self-respecting generosity it abolished all taxes except a ten-per-cent levy on income from real property; the merchants who dominated the Council thus exempted commerce from taxation, and laid the whole burden on the landowning aristocracy and the land-using poor. At Savonarola's urging the government established a *monte di pietà*, or state loan office, which lent money at five to seven per cent, and freed the poor from dependence on private moneylenders, who had charged up to thirty per cent. Again at the friar's prompting, the Council attempted to reform morals with laws: it forbade horse races, gross carnival songs, profanity, and gambling; servants were encouraged to inform against masters who gambled, and convicted offenders were punished with torture; blasphemers had their tongues pierced, and homosexuals were degraded with merciless penalties. To aid in the enforcement of these reforms Savonarola organized the boys of his congregation into a moral police. They pledged themselves to attend church regularly, to avoid races, pageants, acrobatic displays, loose company, obscene literature, dancing, and music schools, and to wear their hair short. These "bands of hope" roamed the streets soliciting alms for the Church; they dispersed groups that had gathered to gamble, and tore from the bodies of women what they judged to be indecent dress.

For a time the city accepted these reforms; many women gave them enthusiastic support, behaved modestly, dressed plainly, and put aside their jewelry. A moral revolution transformed what had been the gay Florence of the Medici. People sang hymns, not Bacchic lyrics, in the streets. Churches were filled, and alms were given in unprecedented quantity. Some bankers and merchants restored illegal gains.[13] Savonarola called upon all the population, rich and poor, to shun idleness and luxury, to work assiduously, and to give a good example with their lives. "Your reform," he said, "must begin with the things of the spirit . . . your temporal good must serve your moral and religious welfare, on which it depends. And if you have heard it said that 'states are not ruled by paternosters,' remember that this is the rule of tyrants . . . a rule for oppressing, not for liberating, a city. If you desire a good government you must restore it to God."[14] He proposed that Florence should think of its government as having an invisible king—Christ Himself; and under this theocracy he predicted Utopia: "O Florence! then wilt thou be rich with spiritual and temporal wealth; thou wilt achieve the reformation of Rome, of Italy, of all countries; the wings of thy greatness shall spread over the world."[15] And in truth Florence had seldom been so happy before. It was a bright moment in the hectic history of virtue.

But human nature remained. Men are not naturally virtuous, and social order maintains itself precariously amid the open or secret conflict of egos, families, classes, races, and creeds. A powerful element in the Florentine community itched for taverns, brothels, and gambling halls as outlets for instincts or as sources of gain. The Pazzi, the Nerli, the Capponi, the younger branch of the Medici, and other aristocrats who had effected the expulsion of Piero were furious at seeing the government fall into the hands of a friar. Remnants of Piero's party survived, and watched for a chance to restore him and their fortunes. The Franciscan friars worked with religious zeal against the Dominican Savonarola, and a small group of skeptics called for a plague on both their houses. These diverse enemies of the new order agreed in satirizing its supporters as *Piagnoni* or weepers (for many wept at Savonarola's sermons), *Collitorti* or wry-necks, *Stropiccioni* or hypo-crites, *Masticapaternostri* or prayer-munchers; and the recipients of these titles denominated their opponents, from the virulence of their hostility, *Arrabiati*, mad dogs. Early in 1496 the *Arrabiati* succeeded in electing their candidate for gonfalonier, Filippo Corbizzi. Having assembled in the Pa-lazzo Vecchio a council of ecclesiastics, he summoned Savonarola before it, and accused him of political activities improper in a friar; and several churchmen, including one of his own Dominican order, joined in the charge. He replied: "Now the words of the Lord are fulfilled: 'The sons of my mother have fought against me.' . . . To be concerned with the af-fairs of this world . . . is no crime in a monk unless he should mix in them without any higher aim, and without seeking to promote the cause of re-ligion."[16] They challenged him to say whether his sermons were inspired by God, but he refused to answer. He returned to his cell a sadder man.

He might have overcome his enemies had foreign affairs favored him. The Florentines, who praised liberty, were furious at Pisa for demanding and securing it. Even Savonarola dared not defend the rebellious city; and a cathedral canon who remarked that the Pisans too had a right to be free was severely punished by a *Piagnone* Signory. Savonarola promised to re-store Pisa to Florence, and rashly claimed that he held Pisa in the hollow of his hand; but he was, as Machiavelli scornfully said, a prophet without arms. When Charles VIII was chased from Italy, Pisa consolidated its in-dependence by an alliance with Milan and Venice; and the Florentines mourned that Savonarola had tied them to Charles's falling star, and that they alone had not shared in the glorious expulsion of the French from Italy.[17] Before abandoning the lately Florentine fortresses of Sarzana and

Pietra Santa, their French commandants had sold one to Genoa and the other to Lucca. Montepulciano, Arezzo, Volterra, and other Florentine dependencies were agitated by movements for liberation; the once proud and powerful city seemed on the verge of losing nearly all its outlying possessions, and all its trade outlets by the Arno, the Adriatic, and the roads to Milan and Rome. Trade suffered, tax revenues fell. The Council tried to finance the war against Pisa by forced loans from rich citizens, offering them government bonds in return; but as bankruptcy neared these bonds declined to eighty to fifty to ten per cent of their face value. In 1496 the treasury was exhausted, and the government imitated Lorenzo by borrowing money from a fund confided to the state to provide dowries for poor brides. In the administration of government funds, whether by *Arrabiati* or *Piagnoni*, corruption and incompetence rose and spread. Francesco Valori, made gonfalonier (January, 1497) by a *Piagnone* majority in the Council, maddened the Mad Dogs by excluding them from all magistracies, denying them membership in the Council if they were delinquent in taxes, allowing none but *Piagnoni* to address the Council, and expelling from Florence any Franciscan friar who preached against Savonarola. For eleven months in 1496 rain fell almost daily, ruining the crops of the narrowed hinterland; in 1497 people dropped dead of hunger in the streets. The government opened relief stations to provide grain for the poor; women were crushed to death in the multitudes that applied. The Medicean party plotted to restore Piero; five leaders were detected and were condemned to death (1497); appeal to the Council, guaranteed by the constitution, was refused them; they were executed within a few hours of their condemnation; and many Florentines contrasted the faction, violence, and severity of the Republic with the order and peace of Lorenzo's time. Hostile crowds repeatedly demonstrated before Savonarola's monastery; *Piagnoni* and *Arrabiati* stoned each other in the streets. When the friar preached on Ascension Day of 1497 his sermon was interrupted by a riot in which his enemies tried to seize him and were repulsed by his friends. A gonfalonier proposed to the Signory that he should be banished as a means of quieting the city, and the proposal was lost by a single vote. Amid this bitter collapse of his dream Savonarola faced and defied the strongest power in Italy.

III. THE MARTYR

Pope Alexander VI was not deeply disturbed by Savonarola's criticism of the clergy or of the morals of Rome. He had heard the like before;

hundreds of ecclesiastics, for centuries past, had complained that many priests lived immoral lives, and that the popes loved wealth and power more than became the vicars of Christ.[18] Alexander was of a genial temperament; he did not mind a little criticism so long as he felt secure in the Apostolic chair. What disturbed him in Savonarola was the friar's politics. Not the semidemocratic nature of the new constitution; Alexander had no special interest in the Medici, and perhaps preferred in Florence a weak republic to a strong dictatorship. Alexander feared another French invasion; he had joined in forming a league of Italian states to expel Charles VIII and to discourage a second French attack; he resented the adherence of Florence to its alliance with France, considered Savonarola the power behind this policy, and suspected him of secret correspondence with the French government. Savonarola wrote to Charles VIII about this time three letters seconding the proposal of Cardinal Giuliano della Rovere that the King should call a general council of ecclesiastics and statesmen to reform the Church and depose Alexander as "an infidel and a heretic."[19] Cardinal Ascanio Sforza, representing Milan at the papal court, urged the Pope to end the friar's preaching and influence.

On July 21, 1495 Alexander wrote a brief note to Savonarola:

> To our well-beloved son, greeting and the apostolic benediction. We have heard that of all the workers in the Lord's vineyard thou art the most zealous; at which we deeply rejoice, and give thanks to Almighty God. We have likewise heard that thou dost assert thy predictions proceed not from thee but from God.* Therefore we desire, as behooves our pastoral office, to have speech with thee considering these things; so that, being by these means better informed of God's will, we may be better able to fulfill it. Wheretofore, by thy vow of holy obedience, we enjoin thee to wait on us without delay, and shall welcome thee with loving kindness.[20]

This letter was a triumph for Savonarola's enemies, for it placed him in a situation where he must either end his career as a reformer, or flagrantly disobey the Pope. He feared that once in the papal power he would never be allowed to return to Florence; he might end his days in a Sant' Angelo dungeon; and if he did not come back his supporters would be ruined. On their advice he replied to Alexander that he was too ill to travel to Rome. That the Pope's motives were political appeared when he wrote to the Signory on September 8 protesting against the continued alliance of Flor-

---

* The Church, to check false prophets, had pronounced such claims to be heretical.

ence with France, and exhorting the Florentines not to endure the reproach of being the only Italians allied with the enemies of Italy. At the same time he ordered Savonarola to desist from preaching, to submit to the authority of the Dominican vicar-general in Lombardy; and to go wherever the vicar-general should bid him. Savonarola replied (September 29) that his congregation was unwilling to subordinate itself to the vicar-general, but that meanwhile he would refrain from preaching. Alexander, in a conciliatory response (October 16), repeated his prohibition of preaching, and expressed the hope that when Savonarola's health should permit he would come to Rome, to be received in "a joyful and fatherly spirit."[21] There, for a year, Alexander let the problem rest.

Meanwhile the prior's party had recaptured control of the Council and the Signory. The emissaries of the Florentine government in Rome besought the Pope to withdraw his interdict on the friar's preaching, urging that Florence needed his moral stimulus in Lent. Alexander seems to have given a verbal consent, and on February 17, 1496, Savonarola resumed his preaching in the cathedral. About this time Alexander commissioned a learned Dominican bishop to examine Savonarola's published sermons for heresy. The bishop reported: "Most Holy Father, this friar says nothing that is not wise and honest; he speaks against simony and the corruption of the priesthood, which in truth is very great; he respects the dogmas and authority of the Church; wherefore I would rather seek to make him my friend—if need be by offering him the cardinal's purple."[22] Alexander complaisantly sent a Dominican to Florence to offer Savonarola the red hat. The friar felt not complimented but shocked; this, to him, was but another instance of simony. His answer to Alexander's emissary was: "Come to my next sermon, and you will have my reply to Rome."[23]

His first sermon of the year reopened his conflict with the Pope. It was an event in the history of Florence. Half the excited city wished to hear him, and even the vast *duomo* could not contain all who sought entry, though within they were crowded so tightly that no one could move. A group of armed friends escorted the prior to the cathedral. He began by explaining his long absence from the pulpit, and affirming his full loyalty to the teachings of the Church. But then he issued an audacious challenge to the Pope:

> The superior may not give me any command contrary to the rules of my order; the pope may not give any command opposed to charity or the Gospel. I do not believe that the pope would ever seek to do so; but were he so to do I should say to him, "Now thou

art no pastor, thou art not the Church of Rome, thou art in error."
... Whenever it be clearly seen that the commands of superiors are
contrary to God's commandments, and especially when contrary
to the precepts of charity, no one is in such case bound to obedience.
... Were I to clearly see that my departure from a city would be
the spiritual and temporal ruin of the people, I would obey no living
man that commanded me to depart . . . forasmuch as in obeying
him I should disobey the commands of the Lord.[24]

In a sermon for the second Sunday in Lent he denounced the morals of
Christendom's capital in harsh terms: "One thousand, ten thousand, fourteen thousand harlots are few for Rome, for there both men and women are
made harlots."[25] These sermons were spread throughout Europe by the
new marvel, the printing press, and were read everywhere, even by the
sultan of Turkey. They aroused a war of pamphlets in and out of Florence, some of them accusing the friar of heresy and indiscipline, others defending him as a prophet and a saint.

Alexander sought an indirect escape from open war. In November,
1496, he ordered the union of all Tuscan Dominican monasteries in a new
Tuscan-Roman Congregation, to be directly under the authority of Padre
Giacomo da Sicilia. Padre Giacomo was favorably disposed toward Savonarola, but would presumably accept a papal suggestion to transfer the friar
to another environment. Savonarola refused to obey the order of union,
and took his case over the head of the Pope to the public at large in a pamphlet called "An Apology of the Brethren of San Marco." "This union,"
he argued, "is impossible, unreasonable, and hurtful, nor can the brethren
of San Marco be bound to agree to it, inasmuch as superiors may not issue
commands contrary to the rules of the order, nor contrary to the law of
charity or the welfare of our souls."[26] Technically all monastic congregations were directly subject to the popes; a pope might compel the merger
of congregations against their will; Savonarola himself, in 1493, had approved Alexander's order uniting the Dominican Congregation of St. Catherine's at Pisa, against its will, with Savonarola's Congregation of St. Mark.[27]
Alexander, however, took no immediate action. Savonarola continued to
preach, and issued to the public a series of letters defending his defiance of
the Pope.

As the Lenten season of 1497 approached, the *Arrabiati* prepared to celebrate carnival by such festivities, processions, and songs as had been sanc-
tioned under the Medici. To counter these plans Savonarola's loyal aide,
Fra Domenico, instructed the children of the congregation to organize a

quite different celebration. During the week of Carnival—preceding Lent —these boys and girls went about the city in bands, knocked at doors, and asked for—sometimes demanded—the surrender of what they called "vanities" or cursed objects (*anathemase*)—pictures considered immoral, love songs, carnival masks and costumes, false hair, fancy dresses, playing cards, dice, musical instruments, cosmetics, wicked books like the *Decameron* or the *Morgante maggiore*. . . . On the final day of Carnival, February 7, the more ardent supporters of Savonarola, singing hymns, marched in solemn procession, behind a figure of the Infant Jesus carved by Donatello and borne by four children in the guise of angels, to the Piazza della Signoria. There a great pyramid of combustible material had been raised, 60 feet high and 240 feet in circumference at the base. Upon the seven stages of the pyramid the "vanities" collected during the week, or now brought to the sacrifice, were arranged or thrown, including precious manuscripts and works of art. Fire was set to the pyre at four points, and the bells of the Palazzo Vecchio were rung to acclaim this first Savonarolan "burning of the vanities."*

The Lenten sermons of the friar carried the war to Rome. While accepting the principle that the Church should have some *terra firma* of temporal power, he argued that the wealth of the Church was the source of her deterioration. His invective now knew no bounds.

> The earth teems with bloodshed, yet the priests take no heed; rather, by their evil example, they bring spiritual death upon all. They have withdrawn from God, and their piety consists in spending their nights with harlots. . . . They say that God hath no care of the world, that all cometh by chance; neither believe they that Christ is present in the sacrament. . . . Come hither, thou ribald Church. The Lord saith: I gave thee beautiful vestments, but thou hast made idols of them. Thou hast dedicated the sacred vessels to vainglory, the sacraments to simony. Thou hast become a shameless harlot in thy lusts; thou art lower than a beast; thou art a monster of abomination. Once thou felt shame for thy sins, but now thou art shameless. Once anointed priests called their sons nephews, but now they speak of their sons.†. . . And thus, O prostitute Church, thou hast displayed thy foulness to the whole world, and stinkest unto heaven.[28]

Savonarola suspected that such tirades would earn him excommunication. He welcomed it.

---

* Such bonfires of vanities were an old custom with mission friars.
† A reference to Alexander VI's candor about his children.

Many of ye say that excommunication will be decreed. . . . For my part I beseech Thee, O Lord, that it may come quickly. . . . Bear this excommunication aloft on a lance, open the gates to it! I will reply to it: and if I do not amaze thee, then thou mayest say what thou wilt. . . . O Lord, I seek only Thy cross! Let me be persecuted; I ask this grace of Thee. Let me not die in my bed, but let me give my blood for Thee, even as Thou gavest thine for me.[29]

These passionate sermons created a furore throughout Italy. Men came from distant cities to hear them; the duke of Ferrara came in disguise; the crowd overflowed from the cathedral into the square, and each striking sentence was relayed from those within to those without. In Rome the people turned almost unanimously against the friar, and called for his punishment.[30] In April, 1497 the *Arrabiati* secured control of the Council, and —on pretext of danger from the plague—forbade all preaching in the churches after May 5. Urged on by Roman agents of the *Arrabiati*, Alexander signed a decree excommunicating the friar (May 13); but he let it be known that he would rescind the excommunication if Savonarola would obey the summons to Rome. The prior, fearing imprisonment, still refused, but for six months he held his peace. Then on Christmas Day he sang High Mass at San Marco, gave the Eucharist to his friars, and led them in a solemn procession around the square. Many were scandalized at an excommunicate celebrating Mass, but Alexander made no protest; on the contrary he intimated that he would withdraw the excommunication if Florence would join the league to resist a second invasion from France.[31] The Signory, gambling on the success of the French, rejected the proposal. On February 11, 1498, Savonarola completed his rebellion by preaching in San Marco. He denounced the excommunication as unjust and invalid, and charged with heresy any man who should uphold its validity. Finally he issued an excommunication himself:

Therefore, on him that giveth commands opposed to charity *anathema sit* [let there be a curse]. Were such a command pronounced by an angel, even by the Virgin Mary herself and all the saints (which is certainly impossible), *anathema sit*. . . . And if any pope hath ever spoken to the contrary, let him be declared excommunicate.[32]

On the last day before Lent Savonarola read Mass in the open square before San Marco's, administered the sacrament to a great multitude, and publicly prayed: "O Lord, if my deeds be not sincere, if my words be not

inspired by Thee, strike me dead on this instant." That afternoon his followers staged a second burning of the vanities.

Alexander informed the Signory that unless it could dissuade Savonarola
from further preaching he would lay an interdict upon the city. Though
now thoroughly hostile to the prior, the Signory refused to silence him,
preferring to let the onus of such a prohibition remain with the Pope; besides, the eloquent friar might be useful in combating a pope who was
organizing the Papal States into a power too strong for the comfort of its
neighbors. Savonarola continued to preach, but only in the church of his
monastery. The Florentine ambassador reported that feeling against the
friar was so intense in Rome that no Florentine was safe there; and he feared
that if the Pope issued the threatened interdict all Florentine merchants in
Rome would be thrown into jail. The Signory yielded, and ordered Savonarola to quit preaching (March 17). He obeyed, but predicted great
calamities for Florence. Fra Domenico filled the convent pulpit in his stead,
and served as the voice of his prior. Meanwhile Savonarola wrote to the
sovereigns of France, Spain, Germany, and Hungary, begging them to call
a general council for the reform of the Church:

> The moment of vengeance has arrived. The Lord commands
> me to reveal new secrets, and make manifest to the world the peril
> by which the bark of St. Peter is threatened, owing to your long
> neglect. The Church is all teeming with abomination, from the
> crown of her head to the soles of her feet; yet not only do ye apply
> no remedy, but ye do homage to the cause of the woes by which she
> is polluted. Wherefore the Lord is greatly angered, and hath long
> left the Church without a shepherd. . . . For I hereby testify . . . that
> this Alexander is no pope, nor can be held as one; inasmuch as, leav-
> ing aside the mortal sin of simony, by which he hath purchased the
> papal chair, and daily selleth the benefices of the Church to the high-
> est bidder, and likewise putting aside his other manifest vices, I
> declare that he is no Christian, and believes in no God.[33]

If, he added, the kings will call a council he will appear before it and give
proof of all these charges. One of these letters was intercepted by a Milanese agent, and was sent to Alexander.

On March 25, 1498 a Franciscan friar, preaching in the church of Santa
Croce, turned the drama of the case upon himself by challenging Savonarola to an ordeal of fire. He stigmatized the Dominican as a heretic and
false prophet, and offered to walk through fire if Savonarola would do the
same. He expected, he said, that both of them would be burned, but hoped

by his sacrifice to free Florence from the disorders that had been caused by a proud Dominican's disobedience of the Pope. Savonarola rejected the challenge; Domenico accepted it. The hostile Signory seized the chance to discredit a prior who in its view had become a troublesome demagogue. It approved of the resort to medieval methods, and arranged that on April 7 Fra Giuliano Rondinelli of the Franciscans and Fra Domenico da Pescia should enter a fire in the Piazza della Signoria.

On the appointed day the great square was filled with a crowd eager to enjoy a miracle or the sight of human suffering. Every window and roof overlooking the scene was occupied with spectators. In the center of the square, athwart a passage two feet wide, twin pyres had been erected of wood mixed with pitch, oil, resin, and gunpowder, guaranteed to make a searing flame. The Franciscan friars took their stand in the Loggia dei Lanzi; the Dominicans marched in from the opposite direction; Fra Domenico carried a consecrated Host, Savonarola a crucifix. The Franciscans complained that Fra Domenico's red cape might have been charmed into incombustibility by the prior; they insisted on his discarding it; he protested; the crowd urged him to yield; he did. The Franciscans asked him to remove other garments which they thought might have been charmed; Domenico consented, went into the palace of the Signory, and changed clothes with another friar. The Franciscans urged that he should be forbidden to approach Savonarola, lest he be re-enchanted; Domenico submitted to being surrounded by Franciscans. They objected to his carrying either a crucifix or a consecrated Host into the fire; he surrendered the crucifix but kept the Host, and a long theological discussion ensued between Savonarola and the Franciscans as to whether Christ would be burned along with the appearances of bread. Meanwhile the Franciscan champion remained in the palace, begging the Signory to save him by any ruse. The priors allowed the discussions to go on till darkness fell, and then announced that the ordeal could no longer take place. The crowd, cheated of blood, attacked the palace, but was repulsed; some *Arrabiati* tried to seize Savonarola, but his guard protected him. The Dominicans returned to San Marco, jeered by the populace, though apparently the Franciscans had been the chief cause of delay. Many complained that Savonarola, after claiming that he was inspired by God and that God would protect him, had allowed Domenico to represent him in the ordeal, instead of facing it himself. These thoughts spread through the city, and almost overnight the prior's following faded away.

On the morrow, Palm Sunday, a mob of *Arrabiati* and others marched to attack the monastery of San Marco. On the way they killed some *Piagnoni*, including Francesco Valori; his wife, drawn to a window by his cries, was shot through with an arrow; his house was pillaged and burned; one of his grandchildren was smothered to death. The bell of San Marco tolled to call the *Piagnoni* to the rescue, but they did not come. The friars prepared to defend themselves with swords and clubs; Savonarola in vain bade them lay down their arms, and himself stood unarmed at the altar, awaiting death. The friars fought valiantly; Fra Enrico wielded his sword with secular delight, accompanying each blow with a lusty cry, *Salvum fac populum tuum, Domine*—"Save thy people, Lord!" But the hostile crowd was too numerous for the friars; Savonarola finally prevailed upon them to lay down their arms; and when an order came from the Signory for his arrest and that of Domenico, the two surrendered, and were led through a mob that jeered, struck, kicked, and spat upon them, to cells in the Palazzo Vecchio. On the following day Fra Silvestro was added to the prisoners.

The Signory sent to Pope Alexander an account of the ordeal and arrest, begged his absolution for the violence committed on an ecclesiastic, and asked his authorization to subject the prisoners to trial, and, if necessary, to torture. The Pope urged that the three friars should be sent to Rome to be tried before an ecclesiastical court; the Signory refused, and the Pope had to be content with having two papal delegates share in examining the accused.[34] The Signory was resolved that Savonarola should die. As long as he lived his party would live; only his death, they thought, could heal the strife of factions that had so divided the city and its government that alliance with Florence had become worthless to any foreign power, and Florence lay open to internal conspiracy or external attack.

Following the custom established by the Inquisition, the examiners put the three friars to torture on various occasions between April 9 and May 22. Silvestro succumbed at once, and answered so readily as the examiners wished that his confession was too facile to be useful. Domenico resisted to the last; tortured to the verge of death, he continued to avow that Savonarola was a saint without guile or sin. Savonarola, high-strung and exhausted, soon collapsed under torture, and gave whatever replies were suggested to him. Recovering, he retracted the confession; tortured again, he yielded again. After three ordeals his spirit broke, and he signed a confused confession that he had no divine inspiration, that he had been guilty of pride and ambition, that he had urged foreign and secular powers to call a general council of the Church, and that he had plotted for the deposition of the Pope. On charges of schism and heresy, of revealing confessional secrets as pretended visions and prophecies, of causing faction and disorder in the state, the three friars were condemned to death by the united sentence of state and Church. Alexander graciously sent them absolution.

On May 23, 1498, the parricide Republic executed its founder and his comrades. Unfrocked and barefoot, they were led to the same Piazza della Signoria where twice they had burned the "vanities." As then, and as for the trial by ordeal, a great crowd gathered for the sight; but now the government supplied it with food and drink. A priest asked Savonarola, "In what spirit do you bear this martyrdom?" He answered, "The Lord has suffered much for me." He kissed the crucifix that he carried, and did not speak again. The friars walked bravely to their doom, Domenico almost joyfully, singing a *Te Deum* in gratitude for a martyr's death. The three men were hanged from a gibbet, and boys were allowed to stone them as they choked. A great fire was lighted under them, and burned them to ashes. The ashes were thrown into the Arno, lest they be worshiped as the relics of saints. Some *Piagnoni*, braving incrimination, knelt in the square and wept and prayed. Every year until 1703, on the morning after the 23rd of May, flowers were strewn on the spot where the hot blood of the friars fell. Today a plaque in the pavement marks the site of the most famous crime in Florentine history.

Savonarola was the Middle Ages surviving into the Renaissance, and the Renaissance destroyed him. He saw the moral decay of Italy under the influence of wealth and a declining religious belief, and he stood bravely, fanatically, vainly against the sensual and skeptical spirit of the times. He inherited the moral fervor and mental simplicity of medieval saints, and seemed out of place and key in a world that was singing the praises of rediscovered pagan Greece. He failed through his intellectual limitations and a forgivable but irritating egotism; he exaggerated his illumination and his capacity, and naïvely underestimated the task of opposing at once the power of the papacy and the instincts of men. He was understandably shocked by Alexander's morals, but intemperate in his denunciations and intransigeant in his policy. He was a Protestant before Luther only in the sense of calling for a reform of the Church; he shared none of Luther's theological dissents. But his memory became a force in the Protestant mind; Luther called him a saint. His influence on literature was slight, for literature was in the hands of skeptics and realists like Machiavelli and Guicciardini; but his influence on art was immense. Fra Bartolommeo signed his portrait of the friar, "Portrait of Girolamo of Ferrara, prophet sent by

God." Botticelli turned from paganism to piety under Savonarola's preaching. Michelangelo heard the friar frequently, and read his sermons devotedly; it was the spirit of Savonarola that moved the brush over the ceiling of the Sistine Chapel, and traced behind the altar the terrible *Last Judgment*.

The grandeur of Savonarola lay in his effort to achieve a moral revolution, to make men honest, good, and just. We know that this is the most difficult of all revolutions, and we cannot wonder that Savonarola failed where Christ succeeded with so pitiful a minority of men. But we know, too, that such a revolution is the only one that would mark a real advance in human affairs; and that beside it the bloody overturns of history are transient and ineffectual spectacles, changing anything but man.

IV. THE REPUBLIC AND THE MEDICI: 1498-1534

The chaos that had almost nullified government in the later years of Savonarola's ascendancy was not mitigated by his death. The brief term of two months allowed to each Signory and gonfalonier made for a hectic discontinuity in the executive branch, and inclined the priors to irresponsibility and corruption. In 1502 the Council, dominated by a triumphant oligarchy of rich men, sought to overcome part of this difficulty by electing the gonfalonier for life, so that while still subject to Signory and Council, he might face the popes and the secular rulers of Italy on terms of equal tenure. The first man to receive this honor was Pietro Soderini, a millionaire friendly to the people, an honest patriot whose powers of mind and will were not so eminent as to threaten Florence with dictatorship. He enlisted Machiavelli among his advisers, governed prudently and economically, and used his private fortune to resume that patronage of art which had been interrupted under Savonarola. With his support Machiavelli replaced the mercenary troops of Florence with a citizen militia, which finally (1508) forced Pisa to yield again to a Florentine "protectorate."

But in 1512 the foreign policy of the Republic brought on the disaster that Alexander VI had foretold. Through all the efforts of the "Holy League" of Venice, Milan, Naples, and Rome to rid Italy of its French invaders Florence had persisted in its alliance with France. When victory crowned the League it turned in revenge upon Florence, and sent its troops to replace the republican oligarchy with a Medicean dictatorship. Florence resisted, and Machiavelli labored strenuously to organize its defense. Its outpost, Prato, was taken and sacked, and Machiavelli's militia turned and

fled from the trained mercenaries of the League. Soderini resigned to avoid
further bloodshed. Giuliano de' Medici, son of Lorenzo, having contributed 10,000 ducats ($250,000) to the League treasury, entered Florence
under the protection of Spanish, German, and Italian arms; his brother,
Cardinal Giovanni, soon joined him; the Savonarolan constitution was abolished, and the Medicean ascendancy was restored (1512).

Giuliano and Giovanni behaved with moderation, and the public, surfeited with excitement, readily accepted the change. When Giovanni
became Leo X (1513), Giuliano, having proved too gentle to be a successful
ruler, yielded the government of Florence to his nephew Lorenzo. This
ambitious youth died after six years of reckless rule. Cardinal Giulio de'
Medici, son of the Giuliano who had been slain in the Pazzi conspiracy,
now gave Florence an excellent administration; and after he became Clement VII (1521) he ruled the city from the papal chair. Florence took advantage of his misfortunes to expel his representatives (1527), and for four
years it again enjoyed the trials of liberty. But Clement tempered defeat
with diplomacy, and used the troops of Charles V to avenge his ousted
relatives; an army of Spanish and German troops marched upon Florence
(1529), and repeated the story of 1512; resistance was heroic but vain; and
Alessandro de' Medici began (1531) a regime of oppression, brutality, and
lechery unprecedented in the annals of the family. Three centuries would
pass before Florence would know freedom again.

V. ART UNDER THE REVOLUTION

An age of political excitement is usually a stimulant to literature; and we
shall study later two writers of the first rank—Machiavelli and Guicciardini
—who belonged to this period. But a state always verging on bankruptcy,
and engaged in almost permanent revolution, does not favor art—and least
of all architecture. Some rich men, skilled in floating on a flood, still gave
hostages to fortune by building palaces; so Giovanni Francesco and Aris-
totele da Sangallo, working on plans by Raphael, raised a palatial mansion
for the Pandolfini family. In 1520-4 Michelangelo designed for Cardinal
Giulio de' Medici a Nuova Sagrestia, or New Sacristy, for the church of
San Lorenzo—a simple quadrangle and modest dome, known to all the
world as the home of Michelangelo's finest sculptures, the tombs of the
Medici.

Among the Titan's rivals was the sculptor Pietro Torrigiano, who
worked with him in Lorenzo's garden of statuary, and broke his nose to

win an argument. Lorenzo was so incensed by this violence that Torrigiano took refuge in Rome. He became a soldier in Caesar Borgia's service, fought bravely in several battles, found his way to England, and designed there one of the masterpieces of English art, the tomb of Henry VII in Westminster Abbey (1519). Wandering restlessly to Spain, he carved a handsome *Madonna and Child* for the duke of Arcos. But the duke underpaid him; the sculptor smashed the statue to bits; the vengeful aristocrat denounced him to the Inquisition as a heretic; Torrigiano was sentenced to severe punishment, but cheated his foes by starving himself to death.

Florence had never had so many great artists at one time as in 1492; but many of them fled from her turbulence, and lent their renown to other scenes. Leonardo went to Milan, Michelangelo to Bologna, Andrea Sansovino to Lisbon. Sansovino took his cognomen from Monte San Savino, and made it so famous that the world forgot his real name, Andrea di Domenico Contucci. Born the son of a poor laborer, he developed a passion for drawing and for modeling in clay; a kindly Florentine sent him to the studio of Antonio del Pollaiuolo. Maturing rapidly, he built for the church of Santo Spirito a Chapel of the Sacrament, with statues and reliefs "so vigorous and excellent," said Vasari, "that they are without a flaw"; and before it he placed a bronze grille that halts the breath with its beauty. King John II of Portugal begged Lorenzo to send the young artist to him; Andrea went, and labored nine years there in sculpture and architecture. Lonesome for Italy, he returned to Florence (1500), but soon passed to Genoa and finally to Rome. In Santa Maria del Popolo he built two marble tombs—for Cardinals Sforza and Basso della Rovere—which won high acclaim in a city then (1505-7) buzzing with geniuses. Leo X sent him to Loreto, and there (1523-8) Andrea adorned the church of Santa Maria with a series of reliefs from the life of the Virgin, so beautiful that the angel in the *Annunciation* seemed to Vasari "not marble but celestial." Soon afterward Andrea retired to a farm near his native Monte San Savino, lived energetically as a peasant, and died in 1529, aged sixty-eight.

Meanwhile the della Robbia family had faithfully and skillfully carried on the work of Luca in glazed clay. Andrea della Robbia exceeded in longevity even the eighty-five years of his uncle, and had time to train three sons in the art—Giovanni, Luca, and Girolamo. Andrea's terra cottas have a brilliance of tone and a tenderness of sentiment that snare the eye and still the feet of the museum traveler. A room in the Bargello is rich with him, and the Hospital of the Innocents is distinguished by his decorative lunette of the Annunciation. Giovanni della Robbia rivaled his father Andrea's excellence, as one may see in the Bargello and the Louvre. The della Robbias almost confined themselves to religious subjects through three generations; they were among the most fervent supporters of Savonarola; and two of Andrea's sons joined the Brethren of San Marco to seek salvation with the friar.

The painters felt Savonarola's influence most deeply. Lorenzo di Credi learned his art from Verrocchio, imitated the style of his fellow student Leonardo, and took the tenderness of his religious pictures from the piety nurtured in him by Savonarola's eloquence and fate. He spent half his life painting Madonnas; we find them almost everywhere—in Rome, Florence, Turin, Avignon, Cleveland; the faces poor, the robes magnificent; perhaps the best is the *Annunciation* in the Uffizi. At the age of seventy-two, feeling it time to take on the savor of sanctity, Lorenzo went to live with the monks of Santa Maria Nuova; and there, six years later, he died.

Piero di Cosimo took his cognomen from his teacher Cosimo Rosselli, for "he who instructs ability and promotes well-being is as truly a father as the one who begets."[35] Cosimo came to the conclusion that his pupil surpassed him; summoned by Sixtus IV to decorate the Sistine Chapel, he took Piero with him; and Piero painted there *The Destruction of Pharaoh's Troops in the Red Sea*, with a gloomy landscape of water, rocks, and cloudy sky. He has left us two magnificent portraits, both in the Hague: of Giuliano da Sangallo and Francesco da Sangallo. Piero was all artist, caring little for society or friendship, loving nature and solitude, absorbed in the pictures and scenes that he painted. He died unconfessed and alone, having transmitted his art to two pupils who followed his example by surpassing their master: Fra Bartolommeo and Andrea del Sarto.

Baccio della Porta took his last name from the gate of San Piero where he lived; when he became a friar he received the name Fra Bartolommeo— Brother Bartholomew. Having studied with Cosimo Rosselli and Piero di Cosimo, he opened a studio with Mariotto Albertinelli, painted many pictures in collaboration with him, and remained bound to him in a fine friendship till parted by death. He was a modest youth, eager for instruction and receptive to every influence. For a time he sought to catch the subtle shading of Leonardo; when Raphael came to Florence Baccio studied perspective with him, and better blending of colors; later he visited Raphael in Rome and painted with him a noble *Head of St. Peter*. Finally he fell in love with the majestic style of Michelangelo; but he lacked the terrible intensity of that angry giant; and when Bartolommeo attempted the monumental he lost in the enlargement of his simple ideas the charm of his qualities—the rich depth and soft shading of his colors, the stately symmetry of his composition, the piety and sentiment of his themes.

He was deeply stirred by the sermons of Savonarola. He brought to the burning of the vanities all his paintings of the nude. When the enemies of the friar attacked the convent of San Marco (1498) he joined in its defense; in the course of the melee he vowed to become a monk if he survived; he kept his pledge, and in 1500 he entered the Dominican monastery at Prato. For five years he refused to paint, giving himself up to religious exercises. Transferred to San Marco, he consented to add his masterpieces in blue, red, and black to the rosy frescoes of Fra Angelico. There, in the refectory, he painted a *Madonna and Child* and a *Last Judgment;* in the cloisters a *St. Sebastian;* and in Savonarola's cell a powerful portrait of the friar in the guise of St. Peter Martyr. The *St. Sebastian* was the only nude that he painted after becoming a monk. Originally it was placed in the church of San Marco, but it was so handsome that some women confessed to having been stirred to wicked thoughts by it, and the prior sold it to a Florentine who sent it to the king of France. Fra Bartolommeo continued to paint until 1517, when disease so paralyzed his hands that he could no longer hold the brush. He died in that year, at the age of forty-five.

His only rival for supremacy among the Italian painters of this period was another disciple of Piero di Cosimo. Andrea Domenico d'Agnolo di Francesco Vannuci is known to us as Andrea del Sarto because his father was a tailor. Like most Renaissance artists he developed quickly, beginning his apprenticeship at seven. Piero marveled at the lad's skill in design, and noted with warm approval how Andrea, when a holyday closed the studio, spent his time drawing the figures in the famous cartoons made by Leonardo and Michelangelo for the Hall of the Five Hundred in the Palazzo Vecchio. When Piero became in old age too eccentric a master, Andrea and his fellow student Franciabigio set up their own *bottega,* and for some time worked together. Andrea seems to have begun his independent career by painting, in the court of the Annunziata Church (1509), five scenes from the life of San Filippo Benizzi, a Florentine noble who had founded the order of the Servites for the special worship of Mary. These frescoes, though sorely injured by time and exposure, are so remarkable for draughtsmanship, composition, vividness of narrative, and the soft merging of warm and harmonious colors, that this atrium is now one of the goals of art pilgrims in Florence. For one of the female figures Andrea used as model the woman who in the course of these paintings became his wife—Lucrezia del

Fede, a sensuously beautiful shrew whose dark face and raven hair haunted the artist to all but his dying days.

In 1515 Andrea and Franciabigio undertook a series of frescoes in the cloisters of the Scalzo fraternity. They chose as subject the life of St. John the Baptist; but it was surely Andrea's hand that in several figures displayed one of his specialties, picturing the female breast in all the perfection of its texture and form. In 1518 he accepted the invitation of Francis I to come to France; there he painted the figure of Charity that hangs in the Louvre. But his wife, left behind in Florence, begged him to come back; the king granted permission on Andrea's pledge to return, and entrusted him with a considerable sum to buy works of art for him in Italy. Andrea, in Florence, spent the royal funds in building himself a house, and never went back to France. Facing bankruptcy nevertheless, he resumed his painting, and produced for the cloisters of the Annunziata a masterpiece which, said Vasari, "in design, grace, excellence of coloring, vivacity, and relief, proved him far superior to all his predecessors"—who included Leonardo and Raphael.[36] This *Madonna del Sacco*—absurdly so called because Mary and Joseph are shown leaning against a sack—is now damaged and faded, and no longer conveys the full splendor of its color; but its perfect composition, soft tones, and quiet presentation of a family—with Joseph, suddenly literate, reading a book—make it one of the great pictures of the Renaissance.

In the refectory of the Salvi monastery Andrea challenged Leonardo with a *Last Supper* (1526), choosing the same moment and theme—"One of you shall betray me." Bolder than Leonardo, Andrea finished the face of his Christ; even he, however, fell far short of the spiritual depth and understanding gentleness that we associate with Jesus. But the Apostles are strikingly individualized, the action is vivid, the colors are rich and soft and full; and the picture as seen from the entrance of the refectory conveys almost irresistibly the illusion of a living scene.

The Virgin Mother remained the favorite subject of Andrea, as of most artists of Renaissance Italy. He painted her again and again in studies of the Holy Family, as in the Borghese Gallery in Rome, or the Metropolitan Museum in New York. He pictured her, in one of the treasures of the Uffizi Gallery, as *Madonna delle Arpie, Madonna of the Harpies;** this is the fairest of the Lucrezia Virgins, and the Child is the finest in Italian art. Across the Arno, in the Pitti Gallery, the *Assumption of the Virgin* shows Apostles and holy women looking up in amazement and adoration as cheru-

---

* So named from the avenging fates represented on the pedestal.

bim raise the praying Madonna—again Lucrezia—to heaven. So, in Andrea's colorful illumination, the moving epos of the Virgin is complete.

There is seldom any sublimity in Andrea del Sarto, no majesty of Michelangelo, nor the unfathomable nuances of Leonardo, nor the finished perfection of Raphael, nor yet the range or power of the great Venetians. Yet he alone of the Florentines rivals the Venetians in color and Correggio in grace; and his mastery of tones—in their depth and modulation and transparency—might well be preferred to the lavishment of color in Titian, Tintoretto, and Veronese. We miss variety in Andrea; his paintings move within too small a circle of subject and sentiment; his hundred Madonnas are always the same young Italian mother, modest and lovely and at last cloyingly sweet. But no one has surpassed him in composition, few in anatomy, modeling, and design. "There is a little fellow in Florence," said Michelangelo to Raphael, "who will bring sweat to your brow if ever he is engaged in great works."[37]

Andrea himself never lived to reach full maturity. The victorious Germans, capturing Florence in 1530, infected it with plague, and Andrea was one of its victims. His wife, who had aroused in him all the heartaches of jealousy that beauty brings to marriage, shunned his room in those last fevered days; and the artist who had given her an almost deathless life died with no one by his side, at the age of forty-four. About 1570 Iacopo da Empoli went to the court of the Annunziata to copy del Sarto's *Nativity*. An old lady who had come to Mass stopped beside him and pointed to a figure in the foreground of the painting. "It is I," she said. Lucrezia had outlived herself by forty years.

The few artists whom we have here commemorated must be viewed not as a record but as representatives of the plastic and graphic genius of this period. There were other sculptors and painters of the time, who still lead a ghostly existence in the museums—Benedetto da Rovezzano, Franciabigio, Ridolfo Ghirlandaio, and hundreds more. There were half-secluded artists, monastic and secular, who still practised the intimate art of illuminating manuscripts, like Fra Eustachio and Antonio di Girolamo; there were calligraphers whose handwriting might excuse Federigo of Urbino for regretting the invention of print; there were mosaicists who despised painting as the perishable pride of a day; wood carvers like Baccio d'Agnolo, whose carved chairs, tables, chests, and beds were the glory of Florentine homes; and nameless other workers in the minor arts. Florence was so rich in art that she could bear the depredations of invaders, pontiffs, and millionaires from Charles VIII to our own times, and still retain so much of delicate workmanship that no man has ever compassed all the treasures deposited in that one city by the two centuries of the Renaissance. Or by one century; for just as the great age of Florence in art had begun with Cosimo's return from exile in 1434, so it ended with Andrea del Sarto's death in 1530. Civil strife, Savonarola's puritan regime, siege and defeat and plague, had destroyed the joyful spirit of Lorenzo's day, had broken the frail lyre of art.

But the great chords had been struck, and their music echoed throughout the peninsula. Orders came to Florentine artists from other Italian cities, even from France, Spain, Hungary, Germany, and Turkey. To Florence flocked a thousand artists to learn her lore and form their styles—Piero della Francesca, Perugino, Raphael. . . . From Florence a hundred artists took the gospel of art to half a hundred Italian cities and to foreign lands. In those half-hundred cities the spirit and taste of the age, the generosity of wealth, the heritage of technique worked together with the Florentine stimulus. Presently all Italy, from the Alps to Calabria, was painting, carving, building, composing, singing, in a creative frenzy that seemed to know, in the fever of its haste, that soon the wealth would vanish in war, and the pride of Italy would be humbled under an alien tyranny, and the prison doors of dogma would close again upon the marvelous exuberant mind of Renaissance man.

BOOK III

ITALIAN PAGEANT

1378-1534

CHAPTER VI

Milan

I. BACKGROUND

W E do injustice to the Renaissance when we concentrate our study on Florence, Venice, and Rome. For a decade it was more brilliant in Milan, under Lodovico and Leonardo, than in Florence. Its liberation and exaltation of woman found their best embodiment in Isabella d'Este at Mantua. It glorified Parma with Correggio, Perugia with Perugino, Orvieto with Signorelli. Its literature reached an apex with Ariosto at Ferrara, and its cultivation of manners at Urbino in the days of Castiglione. It gave name to a ceramic art at Faenza, and to the Palladian architectural style at Vicenza. It revived Siena with Pinturicchio and Sassetta and Sodoma, and made Naples a home and symbol of joyous living and idyllic poetry. We must pass leisurely through the incomparable peninsula from Piedmont to Sicily, and let the varied voices of the cities merge in the polyphonic chorus of the Renaissance.

The economic life of the Italian states in the fifteenth century was as diverse as their climate, dialects, and costumes. The north—i.e., above Florence—could have severe winters, sometimes freezing the Po from end to end; yet the coastal region around Genoa, sheltered by the Ligurian Alps, enjoyed mild weather in almost every month. Venice could shroud its palaces and towers and liquid streets in clouds and mist; Rome was sunny but miasmic; Naples was a climatic paradise. Everywhere, at one time or another, the cities and their countryside suffered those earthquakes, floods, droughts, tornadoes, famines, plagues, and wars that a Malthusian Nature sedulously provides to compensate for the reproductive ecstasies of mankind. In the towns the old handicrafts supplied the poor with a living and the rich with superfluities. Only the textile industry had reached the factory and capitalist stage; one silk mill at Bologna contracted with the city authorities to do "the work of 4000 spinning women."[1] Petty tradesmen, merchants of import and export, teachers, lawyers, physicians, administrators, politicians, made up a complex middle class; a wealthy and worldly clergy added their color and grace to the courts and the streets; and monks and friars, somber or jovial, wandered about seeking alms or romance. The aristocracy of landowners and financiers lived for the most part within the city walls, occasionally in rural villas. At the top a banker, *condottiere*, marquis, duke, doge, or king, with his wife or mistress, presided over a court hampered with luxuries and gilded with art. In the countryside the peasant tilled his modest acres or some lord's domain, and lived in a poverty so traditional that it seldom entered his thoughts.

Slavery existed on a minor scale, chiefly in domestic service among the rich; occasionally as a supplement and corrective to free labor on large estates, especially in Sicily; but here and there even in northern Italy.[2] From the fourteenth century onward the slave trade grew; Venetian and Genoese merchants imported them from the Balkans, southern Russia, and Islam; male or female Moorish slaves were considered a shining ornament of Italian courts.[3] In 1488 Pope Innocent VIII received a hundred Moorish slaves as a present from Ferdinand the Catholic, and distributed them as gratuities among his cardinals and other friends.[4] In 1501, after the capture of Capua, many Capuan women were sold as slaves in Rome.[5] But these stray facts illustrate the morals rather than the economy of the Renaissance; slavery rarely played a significant role in the production or transport of goods.

Transport was chiefly on muleback or by cart, or by river, canal, or sea. The well-to-do traveled on horseback or in horse-drawn carriages. Speed was moderate but exciting; it took two days and a good spine to ride from Perugia to Urbino—sixty-four miles; a boat might take fourteen days from Barcelona to Genoa. Inns were numerous, noisy, dirty, and uncomfortable. One at Padua could house 200 guests and stable 200 horses. Roads were rough and perilous. The main streets of the cities were paved with flagstones, but were only exceptionally lighted at night. Good water was brought in from the mountains, rarely to individual homes, usually to public fountains artistically designed, by whose cooling flow simple women and idle men gathered and distributed the news of the day.

The city-states that divided the peninsula were ruled in some cases— Florence, Siena, Venice—by mercantile oligarchies; more often by "despots" of diverse degree, who had superseded republican or communal institutions vitiated by class exploitation and political violence. Out of the competition of strong men one emerged—almost always of humble birth —who subdued and destroyed or hired the rest, made himself absolute ruler, and in some cases transmitted his power to his heir. So the Visconti or Sforzas ruled in Milan, the Scaligeri in Verona, the Carraresi in Padua, the Gonzagas in Mantua, the Estensi in Ferrara. Such men enjoyed a precarious popularity because they laid a lid upon faction, and made life and property safe within their whim and the city's walls. The lower classes accepted them as a last refuge from the dictatorship of ducats; the surrounding peasantry reconciled itself to them because the commune had given it neither protection nor justice nor freedom.

The despots were cruel because they were insecure. With no tradition of legitimacy to support them, subject at any moment to assassination or revolt, they surrounded themselves with guards, ate and drank in fear of poison, and hoped for a natural death. In their earlier decades they governed by craft, corruption, and quiet murder, and practised all the arts of Machiavelli before he was born; after 1450 they felt more secure through sanctification by time, and contented themselves with pacific means in domestic government. They suppressed criticism and dissent, and maintained a horde of spies. They lived luxuriously, and affected an impressive pomp. Nevertheless they earned the tolerance and respect, even, in Ferrara and Urbino, the devotion, of their subjects, by improving administration, executing impartial justice where their own interests were not involved, helping the people in famine and other emergencies, relieving unemployment with public works, building churches and monasteries, beautifying their cities with art, and supporting scholars, poets, and artists who might polish their diplomacy, brighten their aura, and perpetuate their name.

They waged frequent but usually petty war, seeking the mirage of security through the advancement of their frontiers, and having an expansive appetite for taxable terrain. They did not send their own people to war, for then they would have had to arm them, which might be suicidal; instead they hired mercenaries, and paid them with the proceeds of conquests, ransoms, confiscations, and pillage. Dashing adventurers came down over the Alps, often with bands of hungry soldiers in their train, and sold their services as *condottieri* to the highest bidder, changing sides with the fluctuations of the fee. A tailor from Essex, known in England as Sir John Hawkwood and in Italy as Acuto, fought with strategic subtlety and tactical skill against and for Florence, amassed several hundred thousand florins, died as a gentleman farmer in 1394, and was buried with honors and art in Santa Maria del Fiore.

The despot financed education as well as war, built schools and libraries, supported academies and universities. Every town in Italy had a school, usually provided by the Church; every major city had a university. Under the schooling of humanists, universities, and courts, public taste and manners improved, every second Italian became a judge of art, every important center had its own artists and its own architectural style. The joy of life spread, for the educated classes, from one end of Italy to the other; manners were relatively refined, and yet instincts were unprecedentedly free. Never since the days of Augustus had genius found such an audience, such stimulating competition, and such liberty.

II. PIEDMONT AND LIGURIA

In northwestern Italy and what is now southeastern France lay the principality of Savoy-Piedmont, whose ruling house was till 1945 the oldest royal family in Europe. Founded by Count Humbert I as a dependency of the Holy Roman Empire, the proud little state expanded to a moment of glory under the "Green Count" Amadeus VI (1343-83), who annexed Geneva, Lausanne, Aosta, and Turin, which he made his capital. No other ruler of his time enjoyed so fair a reputation for wisdom, justice, and generosity. The Emperor Sigismund raised the counts to dukes (1416), but the first duke, Amadeus VIII, lost his head when he accepted nomination as Antipope Felix V (1439). A century later Savoy was conquered by Francis I for France (1536). Savoy and Piedmont became a battleground between France and Italy; Apollo surrendered them to Mars; they remained in the backwater of the Italian torrent, and never felt the full flow of the Renaissance. In the rich Turin Gallery, and in his native Vercelli, are the pleasant but mediocre paintings of Defendente Ferrari.

South of Piedmont, Liguria embraces all the glory of the Italian Riviera: on the east the Riviera di Levante, or Coast of the Rising (Sun); on the west the Riviera di Ponente, or Coast of the Setting; and at their junction Genoa, almost as resplendent as Naples on a throne of hills and a spreading pedestal of blue sea. To Petrarch it had seemed "a city of Kings, the very temple of prosperity, the gate of joy";[6] but that was before the Genoese debacle at Chioggia (1378). While Venice recovered rapidly through the orderly and devoted co-operation of all classes in restoring commerce and solvency, Genoa continued its tradition of civil strife between noble and noble, nobles and commoners. Oligarchic oppression provoked a minor revolution (1383); the butchers, armed with the persuasive cutlery of their trade, led a crowd to the palace of the doge, and compelled a reduction of taxes and the exclusion of nobles from the government. In five years (1390-4) Genoa had ten revolutions, ten doges rose and fell; finally order ~med more precious than freedom, and the harassed republic, fearing absorption by Milan, gave itself over, with its Rivieras, to France (1396).

Two years later the French were expelled in a passionate revolt; five bloody battles were fought in the streets; twenty palaces were burned, government buildings were sacked and demolished, property to the value of a million florins was destroyed. Genoa again found the chaos of freedom unbearable, and surrendered itself to Milan (1421). The Milanese rule became intolerable, revolution restored the republic (1435), and the strife of factions was resumed.

The one element of stability amid these fluctuations was the Bank of St. George. During the war with Venice the government had borrowed money from its citizens, and had given them promissory notes. After the war it was unable to redeem these pledges, but it turned over to the lenders the customs dues of the port. The creditors organized themselves into the Casa di San Giorgio, the House of St. George, chose a directorate of eight governors, and received from the state a palace for their use. The House or Company was well managed, being the least corrupt institution in the republic. It was entrusted with the collection of taxes; it lent some of its funds to the government, and received in return substantial properties in Liguria, Corsica, the eastern Mediterranean, and the Black Sea. It became both the state treasury and a private bank, accepting deposits, discounting notes, making loans to commerce and industry. As all factions were financially tied to it, all respected it, and left it unharmed in revolution and war. Its magnificent Renaissance palace still stands in the Piazza Caricamento.

The fall of Constantinople was an almost fatal blow to Genoa. The rich Genoese settlement at Pera, near Constantinople, was taken over by the Turks. When the impoverished republic once more submitted to France (1458), Francesco Sforza financed a revolution that expelled the French and made Genoa again a dependency of Milan (1464). The confusion that weakened Milan after the assassination of Galeazzo Maria Sforza (1476) allowed the Genoese a brief interlude of freedom; but when Louis XII seized Milan (1499), Genoa too succumbed to his power. At last, in the long conflict between Francis I and Charles V, a Genoese admiral, Andrea Doria, turned his ships against the French, drove them out of Genoa, and established a new republican constitution (1528). Like the governments of Florence and Venice, it was a commercial oligarchy; only those families were enfranchised whose names were inscribed in *il libro d'oro* (*The Golden Book*). The new regime—a senate of 400, a council of 200, a doge elected for two years—brought a disciplined peace to the factions, and maintained the independence of Genoa till the coming of Napoleon (1797).

Amid this passionate disorder the city contributed far less than her due share to Italian letters, science, and art. Her captains explored the seas avidly, but when her son Columbus appeared among them Genoa was too timid or too poor to finance his dream. The nobles were absorbed in politics, the merchants in gain; neither class spared much for the adventures of the mind. The old cathedral of San Lorenzo was remodeled in Gothic (1307) with a majestic interior; its chapel of San Giovanni Battista (1451f) was adorned with a handsome altar and canopy by Matteo Civitali and a somber statue of the Baptist by Iacopo Sansovino. Andrea Doria effected almost as significant a revolution in Genoese art as in government. He brought Fra Giovanni da Montorsoli from Florence to remodel the Palazzo Doria (1529), and Perino del Vaga from Rome to adorn it with frescoes and stucco reliefs, grotesques, and arabesques; the result was one of the most ornate residences in Italy. Leone Leoni, rival and foe of Cellini, came from Rome to cast a fine medallion of the admiral, and Montorsoli designed his tomb. In Genoa the Renaissance did not long antedate Doria, and did not long survive his death.

III. PAVIA

Between Genoa and Milan the ancient city of Pavia lay quietly along the Ticino. Once it had been the seat of the Lombard kings; now, in the fourteenth century, it was subject to Milan, and was used by the Visconti and the Sforzas as a second capital. There Galeazzo Visconti II began (1360), and Gian (i.e., Giovanni, John) Galeazzo Visconti completed, the majestic Castello that served as a ducal residence for its second founder, and as a pleasure palace for later dukes of Milan. Petrarch called it "the noblest product of *modern* art," and many contemporaries ranked it first among the royal dwellings of Europe. The library contained one of the most precious collections of books in Europe, including 951 illuminated manuscripts. Louis XII, having taken Milan in 1499, carried off this Pavia library among his spoils; and a French army destroyed the interior of the castle with the latest artillery (1527). Nothing remains but the walls.

Though the Castello is ruined, the finest jewel of the Visconti and the Sforzas survives intact—the Certosa, or Carthusian monastery, hidden off the highway between Pavia and Milan. Here, in a placid plain, Giangaleazzo Visconti undertook to build cells, cloisters, and a church in fulfillment of a vow made by his wife. From that beginning until 1499 the dukes of Milan continued to develop and embellish the edifice as the favorite embodiment of their piety and their art. There is nothing more exquisite in Italy. The Lombard-Romanesque façade of white Carrara marble was designed, carved, and erected (1473f) by Cristoforo Mantegazza and Giovanni Antonio Amadeo of Pavia sponsored by Galeazzo Maria Sforza and Lodovico il Moro. It is too ornate, too fondly gifted with arches, statues, reliefs, medallions, columns, pilasters, capitals, arabesques, carved angels, saints, sirens, princes, fruits, and flowers to convey a sense of unity and harmony; each part importunes attention regardless of the whole. But each part is a labor of love and skill; the four Renaissance windows by Amadeo would of themselves entitle him to the remembrance of mankind. In some Italian churches the façade is a brave front on an otherwise undistinguished exterior; but in this Certosa di Pavia every external feature and aspect is arrestingly beautiful: the stately attached buttresses, the noble towers, arcades, and spires of the north transept and the apse, the graceful columns and arches of the cloisters. Within the court the eye rises from these slender columns through three successive stories of arcades to the four superimposed colonnades of the cupola; this is an ensemble harmoniously conceived and admirably wrought. Within the church everything is of unsurpassed excellence: columns rising in clusters and Gothic arches to carved and coffered vaults; bronze and iron grilles as delicately designed as royal lace; doors and archways of elegant form and ornament; altars of marble studded with precious stones; paintings by Perugino, Borgognone, and Luini; the magnificent inlaid choir stalls; the luminous stained glass; the careful carving of pillars, spandrels, archivolts, and cornices; the stately tomb of Giangaleazzo Visconti by Cristoforo Romano and Benedetto Briosco; and, as the last relic of a pathetic romance, the tomb and figures of Lodovico il Moro and Beatrice d'Este, here united in exquisite marble, though they died ten years and five hundred miles apart. In a like union of diverse moods the Lombard, Gothic, and Renaissance styles are here wedded in the most nearly perfect architectural product of the Renaissance. For under Lodovico the Moor Milan had gathered fair women to create an unrivaled court, and supreme artists like Bramante, Leonardo, and Caradosso to snatch the leadership of Italy, for one bright decade, from Florence, Venice and Rome.

IV. THE VISCONTI: 1378-1447

Galeazzo II, dying in 1378, bequeathed his share of the Milanese realm to his son Giangaleazzo Visconti, who continued to use Pavia as a capital.

Here was a man who would have warmed Machiavelli's heart. Immersed in the great library of his palace, taking care of a delicate constitution, winning his subjects by moderate taxation, attending church with impressive piety, filling his court with priests and monks, he was the last prince in Italy whom diplomats would have suspected of planning to unite the entire peninsula under his rule. Yet this was the ambition that seethed in his brain; he pursued it to the end of his life, and almost realized it; and in its service he used craft, treachery, and murder as if he had studied the unwritten *Prince* with reverence, and had never heard of Christ.

Meanwhile his uncle Bernabò was ruling the other half of the Visconti realm from Milan. Bernabò was a candid villain; he taxed his subjects to the edge of endurance, compelled the peasantry to keep and feed the five thousand hounds that he used in the chase, and stilled resentment by announcing that criminals would be tortured for forty days. He laughed at Giangaleazzo's piety, and schemed how to dispose of him and make himself master of all the Visconti heritage. Gian, equipped with the spies necessary to any competent government, learned of these plans. He arranged a meeting with Bernabò, who came conveniently with two sons; Gian's secret guard arrested all three, and apparently poisoned Bernabò (1385). Gian now ruled Milan, Novara, Pavia, Piacenza, Parma, Cremona, and Brescia. In 1387 he took Verona, in 1389 Padua; in 1399 he shocked Florence by buying Pisa for 200,000 florins; in 1400 Perugia, Assisi, and Siena, in 1401 Lucca and Bologna, submitted to his generals; and Gian was master of nearly all north Italy from Novara to the Adriatic. The Papal States were now weakened by the Schism (1378-1417) that had followed the return of the papacy from Avignon. Gian played pope against rival pope, and dreamed of absorbing all the lands of the Church. Then he would send his armies against Naples; his control of Pisa and other outlets would force Florence into submission; Venice alone would remain unbound, but helpless against a united Italy. However in 1402 Giangaleazzo, aged fifty-one, died.

All this time he had hardly moved from Pavia or Milan. He liked intrigue better than war, and achieved by subtlety more than his generals won for him by arms. Nor could these political enterprises exhaust the fertility of his mind. He issued a code of laws including the regulation of public health and the compulsory isolation of infectious disease.[7] He built the Castello of Pavia, and began the Certosa di Pavia and the cathedral of Milan. He called Manuel Chrysoloras to the chair of Greek in the University of Milan, fostered the University of Pavia, helped poets, artists, scholars, and philosophers, and relished their company. He extended the Naviglio Grande, or Great Canal, from Milan to Pavia, thereby opening an inland waterway across the breadth of Italy from the Alps through Milan and the Po to the Adriatic Sea, and providing irrigation for thousands of acres of soil. The agriculture and commerce so promoted encouraged industry; Milan began to rival Florence in woolen goods; her smiths made weapons and armor for warriors throughout western Europe; in one crisis two master armorers forged arms for six thousand soldiers in a few days.[8] In 1314 the silk weavers of Lucca, impoverished by faction and war, had migrated by hundreds to Milan; by 1400 the silk industry was well developed there, and moralists complained that clothing had become shamefully beautiful. Giangaleazzo protected this flourishing economy with wise administration, equable justice, and reliable currency, and a tolerable taxation that extended to clergy and nobility as well as laymen and commoners. Under his prodding the postal service was expanded; in 1425 over a hundred horses were regularly employed by the post; private correspondence was accepted at post offices, and traveled all day—in emergency, all night as well. In 1423 Florence had an annual state revenue of 4,000,000 gold florins ($100,000,000), Venice 11,000,000, Milan 12,000,000.[9] Kings were glad to have their sons and daughters marry into the Visconti family. Emperor Wenceslas merely crowned fact with form when (1395) he gave imperial sanction and legitimacy to Gian's title of duke, and invested him and his heirs with the duchy of Milan "forever."

This proved to be fifty-two years. Gian's oldest son, Gianmaria Visconti,* was thirteen when his father died (1402). The generals who had led Gian's victorious armies competed for the regency. While they fought for Milan, Italy resumed her fragmentation: Florence recaptured Pisa; Venice took Verona, Vicenza, and Padua; Siena, Perugia, and Bologna submitted to individual despots. Italy was as before, and worse, for Gianmaria, leaving the government to oppressive regents, devoted himself to his dogs, trained them to eat human flesh, and joyfully watched them feed on the live men whom he had condemned as political offenders or social criminals.[10] In 1412 three nobles stabbed him to death.

His brother Filippo Maria Visconti seemed to have inherited the subtle intelligence, the patient industry, the ambitious and farseeing policies of his father. But what had been sedentary courage in Giangaleazzo became in Filippo sedentary timidity, a perpetual fear of assassination, a haunting

---

* Giangaleazzo, who had prayed to the Virgin for a son, was so grateful for his success in begetting one that he vowed that all his progeny should bear her name.

belief in universal human perfidy. He shut himself up in the castle of Porta Giovia at Milan, ate and grew fat, cherished superstitions and astrologers, and yet by pure craft remained to the end of his long reign the absolute master of his country, his generals, and even of his family. He married Beatrice Tenda for her money, and condemned her to death for infidelity. He married Maria of Savoy, kept her secluded from all but her ladies in waiting, brooded over his lack of a son, took a mistress, and became partly human in his affection for the pretty daughter Bianca who was born of this liaison. He continued his father's patronage of learning, called noted scholars to the University of Pavia, and gave commissions to Brunellesco and the incomparable medalist Pisanello. He ruled Milan with efficient autocracy, suppressing faction, maintaining order, protecting peasants against feudal exactions, and merchants against brigandage. By deft diplomacy and adroit manipulation of his armies he restored to Milanese allegiance Parma and Piacenza, all of Lombardy to Brescia, all the lands between Milan and the Alps; and in 1421 he persuaded the Genoese that his dictatorship was milder than their civil wars. He encouraged marriages between rival families, so ending many feuds. For a hundred petty tyrannies he set up one; and the population, shorn of liberty but free from internal strife, grumbled, prospered, and multiplied.

He had a flair for finding able generals; suspected them all of wishing to replace him; played them off against one another; and kept war brewing in the hope of regaining all that his father had won and his brother had lost. A breed of powerful *condottieri* developed in his wars with Venice and Florence: Gattamelata, Colleoni, Carmagnola, Braccio, Fortebraccio, Montone, Piccinino, Muzio Attendolo. . . . Muzio was a country lad, one of a large family of male and female fighters; he won the cognomen Sforza by the strength of body and will with which he served Queen Joanna II of Naples; he lost her favor and was thrown into prison; his sister, in full armor, forced his jailers to set him free; he was given command of one of the Milanese armies, but was drowned soon afterward while crossing a stream (1424). His bastard son, then twenty-two, leaped into his father's place, and fought and married his way to a throne.

V. THE SFORZAS: 1450-1500

Francesco Sforza was the ideal of Renaissance soldiers: tall, handsome, athletic, brave; the best runner, jumper, wrestler in his army; sleeping little, marching bareheaded winter and summer; winning the devotion of his men by sharing their hardships and rations, and leading them to lucrative victories by strategy and tactics rather than by superior numbers or arms. So unrivaled was his reputation that enemy forces, on more than one occasion, laid down their arms at sight of him, and greeted him with uncovered heads as the greatest general of his time. Ambitious to found a state of his own, he allowed no scruple to hinder his policy; he fought alternately for Milan, Florence, and Venice until Filippo won his loyalty by giving him Bianca in marriage, with Cremona and Pontremoli as her dowry (1441). When, six years later, Filippo died heirless, bringing the Visconti dynasty to an end, Francesco felt that the dowry should include Milan.

The Milanese thought differently; they proclaimed a republic named Ambrosian from the masterful bishop who had chastened Theodosius and converted Augustine a thousand years before. But the rival factions in the city could not agree; the dependencies of Milan snatched the opportunity to declare themselves free; some of them fell before Venetian arms; danger was imminent of a Venetian or Florentine attack; moreover the Duke of Orléans, the Emperor Frederick III, and King Alfonso of Aragon all claimed Milan as their own. In this crisis a deputation sought Sforza, gave him Brescia, and begged him to defend Milan. He fought off its enemies with resourceful energy; but when the new government made peace with Venice without consulting him he turned his troops against the Republic, besieged Milan to the edge of starvation, accepted its surrender, entered the city amid the acclamations of a hungry populace, and dulled the lust for liberty by distributing bread. A general assembly was summoned, composed of one man from each household; it invested him with the ducal authority over the protests of the Emperor, and the Sforza dynasty began its brief and brilliant career (1450).

His elevation did not change his character. He continued to live simply and to work hard. Now and then he was cruel or treacherous, alleging the good of the state as his excuse; generally he was a man of justice and humanity. He suffered from a lawless sensitivity to the beauty of women. His accomplished wife killed his mistress, and then forgave him; she bore him eight children, advised him wisely in politics, and won the people to his rule by succoring the needy and protecting the oppressed. His administration of the state was as competent as his leadership of its armies. The social order that he enforced brought back to the city a prosperity that dimmed the memory of its suffering and its fitful liberty. As a citadel against revolt or siege he began to build the enormous Castello Sforzesco. He cut new canals through the land, organized public works, and built the

Ospedale Maggiore, or Great Hospital. He brought the humanist Filelfo to Milan, and encouraged education, scholarship, and art; he lured Vincenzo Foppa from Brescia to develop a school of painting. Threatened by the intrigues of Venice, Naples, and France, he held them all at bay by winning the decisive support and firm friendship of Cosimo de' Medici. He disarmed Naples by wedding his daughter Ippolita to Ferdinand's son Alfonso; he checkmated the Duke of Orléans by signing an alliance with Louis XI of France. Some nobles continued to seek his death and his power, but the success of his government disordered their plans, and he lived to die, in peace, the traditional death of generals (1466).

Born to the purple, his son Galeazzo Maria Sforza never knew the discipline of poverty and struggle. He gave himself up to pleasure, luxury, and pomp, seduced with special relish the wives of his friends, and punished opposition with a cruelty that seemed to have descended to him, deviously and mysteriously, through the kindly Bianca from the hot Visconti blood. The people of Milan, inured to absolute rule, offered no resistance to his despotism, but private vengeance punished what public terror brooked. Girolamo Olgiati grieved over a sister seduced and then discarded by the Duke; Giovanni Lampugnani thought himself despoiled of property by the same lord; together with Carlo Visconti they had been trained by Niccolò Monteno in Roman history and ideals, including tyrannicide from Brutus to Brutus. After imploring the help of the saints, the three youths entered the church of St. Stephen, where Galeazzo was worshiping, and stabbed him to death (1476). Lampugnani and Visconti were killed on the spot. Olgiati was tortured till almost every bone in his body was broken or torn from its socket; he was then flayed alive; but to his last breath he refused to repent, called upon pagan heroes and Christian saints to approve his deed, and died with a classic and Renaissance phrase on his lips: *Mors acerba, fama perpetua*—"Death is bitter, but fame is everlasting."[11]

Galeazzo left his throne to a seven-year-old boy, Giangaleazzo Sforza. For three chaotic years Guelf and Ghibelline factions competed in force and fraud to capture the regency. The victor was one of the most colorful and complex personalities in all the crowded gallery of the Renaissance. Lodovico Sforza was the fourth of Francesco Sforza's sons. His father gave him the cognomen Mauro; his contemporaries jokingly transformed this into *il Moro*—"the Moor"—because of his dark hair and eyes; he himself good-humoredly accepted the nickname, and Moorish emblems and costumes became popular at his court. Other wits found in the name a synonym for the mulberry tree (in Italian, *moro*); this too became a symbol for him, made the mulberry color fashionable in Milan, and provided a theme and motive for some of Leonardo's decorations in the Castello rooms. Lodovico's chief teacher was the scholar Filelfo, who gave him a rich grounding in the classics; but his mother Bianca warned the humanist that "we have princes to educate, not merely scholars"; and she saw to it that her sons should also be skilled in the arts of government and war. Lodovico was seldom physically brave; but in him the intelligence of the Visconti freed itself from their cruelty, and with all his faults and sins, he became one of the most civilized men in history.

He was not handsome; like most great men, he was spared this distracting handicap. His face was too full, his nose too long and curved, his chin too ample, his lips too firmly closed; and yet in the profile attributed to Boltraffio, in the busts in Lyons and the Louvre, there is a quiet strength in the features, a sensitive intelligence, an almost soft refinement. He earned the reputation of being the craftiest diplomat of his time, sometimes vacillating, often devious, not always scrupulous, occasionally unfaithful; these were the common faults of Renaissance diplomacy; perhaps they are the hard necessities of all diplomacy. Nevertheless few Renaissance princes equaled him in mercy and generosity; cruelty was against his grain, and countless men and women enjoyed his beneficence. Mild and courteous, sensually susceptible to every beauty and every art, imaginative and emotional and yet rarely losing perspective or his temper, skeptical and superstitious, the master of millions and the slave of his astrologer—all this was Lodovico, the unstable culminating heir of clashing strains.

For thirteen years (1481-94) he governed Milan as regent for his nephew. Giangaleazzo Sforza was a timid retiring spirit, dreading the responsibilities of rule; he was subject to frequent illness, and incapable of serious affairs —*incapacissimo*, Guicciardini called him; he gave himself to amusement or idleness, and gladly left the administration of the state to the uncle whom he admired with envy and trusted with doubt. Lodovico resigned to him all the pomp and splendor of the ducal title and office; it was Gian who sat on the throne, received homage, and lived in regal luxury. But his wife, Isabella of Aragon, resented Lodovico's retention of power, urged Gian to take the reins of office in his own hands, and begged her father Alfonso, heir to the throne of Naples, to come with his army and give her the powers of an actual ruler.

Lodovico governed efficiently. Around his summer cottage at Vigevano he developed a vast experimental farm and cattle-breeding station; experiments were made there in cultivating rice, the vine, and the mulberry tree;

the dairies made butter and cheese of such excellence as even Italy had never known before; the fields and hills pastured 28,000 oxen, cows, buffaloes, sheep, and goats; the spacious stables sheltered the stallions and mares that bred the finest horses in Europe. Meanwhile, in Milan, the silk industry employed twenty thousand workers, and captured many foreign markets from Florence. Ironmongers, goldsmiths, woodcarvers, enamelers, potters, mosaicists, glass painters, perfumers, embroiderers, tapestry weavers, and makers of musical instruments contributed to the busy din of Milanese industry, adorned the palaces and personages of the court with ornaments, and exported sufficient surplus to pay for the softer luxuries that came from the East. To ease the traffic of men and goods, and "give the people more light and air,"[12] Lodovico had the principal streets widened; the avenues leading to the Castello were lined with palaces and gardens for the aristocracy; and the great cathedral, which now took its definitive form, rose as a rival focus of the city's throbbing life. Milan had in 1492 a population of some 128,000 souls.[13] It prospered under Lodovico as not even under Giangaleazzo Visconti, but complaints were heard that the profits of this flourishing economy went rather to strengthen the regent and glorify his court than to raise the populace from its immemorial poverty. Householders groaned at the heavy taxes, and riots of protest disturbed Cremona and Lodi. Lodovico answered that he needed the money to build new hospitals and care for the sick, to support the universities of Pavia and Milan, to finance experiments in agriculture, breeding, and industry, and to impress with the art and lavish magnificence of his court ambassadors whose governments respected only those states that were rich and strong.

Milan was not convinced, but it seemed to share Lodovico's happiness when he brought to it as his bride the tenderest and most lovable of the Ferrara princesses (1491). He made no pretense that he could match the vivacious virginity of Beatrice d'Este; he was already thirty-nine, and had served a number of mistresses, who had given him two sons and a daughter —the gentle Bianca whom he loved as his father had loved the passionate lady from whom she took her name. Beatrice raised no difficulties about these usual preparations of the Renaissance male for monogamy; but when she reached Milan she was shocked to find her lord's latest mistress, the beautiful Cecilia Gallerani, still lodged in a Castello suite. Worse yet, Lodovico continued to visit Cecilia for two months after his marriage; he explained to the Ferrarese ambassador that he had not the heart to send away the cultured poetess who had so graciously entertained his body and soul. Beatrice threatened to return to Ferrara; Lodovico yielded, and persuaded Count Bergamini to marry Cecilia.

Beatrice was a girl of fourteen when she came to Lodovico. She was not especially pretty; her charm lay in the innocent gaiety with which she approached and appropriated life. She had grown up at Naples and learned its joyous ways; she had left it before it could spoil her guilelessness, but it had imparted to her a carefree extravagance which now, in the lap of Lodovico's wealth, so indulged itself that Milan caller her *amantissima del lusso*—madly in love with luxury.[14] Everybody forgave her, for she diffused such innocent merriment—"spending day and night," reports a contemporary chronicler,[15] "in singing and dancing and all manner of delights" —that the whole court caught her spirit, and joy was unconfined. The grave Lodovico, some months after their marriage, fell in love with her, and confessed for a while that all power and wisdom were negligible things beside his new felicity. Under his care she added graces of mind to the lure of her youthful *esprit:* she learned to make Latin speeches, dizzied her head with affairs of state, and at times served her lord well as an irresistible ambassadress. Her letters to her still more famous sister, Isabella d'Este, are fragrant flowers in the Machiavellian jungle of Renaissance strife.[16]

With playful Beatrice to lead the dance, and hard-working Lodovico to pay the bills, the court of Milan became now the most splendid not only in Italy but in all Europe. The Castello Sforzesco expanded to its fullest glory, with its majestic central tower, its endless maze of luxurious rooms, its inlaid floors, its stained-glass windows, its embroidered cushions and Persian carpets, its tapestries telling again the legends of Troy and Rome; here a ceiling by Leonardo, there a statue by Cristoforo Solari or Cristoforo Romano, and almost everywhere some luscious relic of Greek or Roman or Italian art. In that resplendent setting scholars mingled with warriors, poets with philosophers, artists with generals, and all with women whose natural charms were enhanced by every refinement of cosmetics, jewelry, and dress. The men, even the soldiers, were carefully coiffured and richly garbed. Orchestras played a combination of musical instruments, and song filled the halls. While Florence trembled before Savonarola and burned the vanities of love and art, music and loose morals reigned in Lodovico's capital. Husbands connived at their wives' amours in exchange for their own excursions.[17] Masked balls were frequent, and a thousand gay costumes covered a multitude of sins. Men and women danced and sang as if poverty were not stalking the city walls, as if France were not planning to invade Italy, as if Naples were not plotting the ruin of Milan.

Bernardino Corio, who came from his native Como to this court, described it with classic flourishes in his lively *Historia di Milano* (*c.* 1500):

> The court of our princes was splendid exceedingly, full of new fashions, dresses, and delights. Nevertheless, at this time virtue was so much lauded on every side that Minerva had set up great rivalry with Venus, and each sought to make her school the most brilliant. To that of Cupid came the most beautiful youths. Fathers yielded to it their daughters, husbands their wives, brothers their sisters, and so thoughtlessly did they thus flock to the amorous hall that it was reckoned a stupendous thing by those who had understanding. Minerva, she too, sought with all her might to adorn her gentle Academy. Wherefore that glorious and most illustrious Prince Lodovico Sforza had called into his pay—as far as from the uttermost parts of Europe—men most excellent in knowledge and art. Here was the learning of Greece, here Latin verse and prose flourished resplendently, here were the poetic Muses; hither the masters of the sculptor's art and those foremost in painting had gathered from distant countries, and here songs and sweet sounds of every kind and such dulcet harmonies were heard, that they seemed to have descended from Heaven itself upon this excelling court.[17a]

Perhaps it was Beatrice who, in the fervor of maternal love, brought disaster to Lodovico and Italy. In 1493 she bore him a son, who was named Maximilian after his godfather, the heir apparent to the Imperial throne. Beatrice wondered what her future, and the boy's, would be should Lodovico die. For her lord had no legal right to rule Milan; Giangaleazzo Sforza, with Neapolitan aid, might at any moment depose, exile, or kill him; and if Gian should manage to have a son, the duchy would presumably descend to that son, regardless of Lodovico's fate. Lodovico, sympathizing with these worries, sent a secret embassy to King Maximilian, offering him his niece, Bianca Maria Sforza, in marriage, with a tempting dowry of 400,000 ducats ($5,000,000), provided that Maximilian, on becoming emperor, would confer upon Lodovico the title and powers of duke of Milan. Maximilian agreed. We should add that the emperors, who had given the ducal title to the ruling Visconti, had refused to sanction its assumption by the Sforzas. Legally Milan was still subject to Imperial authority.

Giangaleazzo was too busy with his dogs and doctors to bother his head with these developments, but his fuming Isabella sensed their trend, and renewed her pleas to her father. In January, 1494, Alfonso became King of Naples, and adopted a policy frankly hostile to the regent of Milan.

Pope Alexander VI was not only allied with Naples, he was anxious to unite the town of Forlì—then ruled by a Sforza—with other cities in a powerful papal state. Lorenzo de' Medici, who had been friendly to Lodovico, had died in 1492. Driven to desperate measures to protect himself, Lodovico allied Milan with France, and consented to give Charles VIII and the French army an unhindered passage through northwestern Italy when Charles should undertake to assert his rights to the Neapolitan throne.

So the French came. Lodovico played host to Charles, and bade him Godspeed on his expedition against Naples. While the French marched south Giangaleazzo Sforza died of a combination of ailments. Lodovico was wrongly suspected of poisoning him, but gave some support to the rumor by the haste with which he had himself invested with the ducal title (1495). Meanwhile Louis, Duke of Orléans, invaded Italy with a second French army, and announced that he would take Milan as his rightful possession through his descent from Giangaleazzo Visconti. Lodovico saw now that he had made a tragic error in welcoming Charles. Swiftly reversing his policy, he helped to form, with Venice, Spain, Alexander VI, and Maximilian, a "Holy League" to expel the French from the peninsula. Charles hastily retraced his steps, suffered an indecisive defeat at Fornovo (1495), and barely managed to bring his battered army back to France. Louis of Orléans decided to wait for a better day.

Lodovico prided himself on the apparent success of his tortuous policy: he had taught Alfonso a lesson, had foiled Orléans, and had led the League to victory. His position now seemed safe; he relaxed the vigilance of his diplomacy, and again enjoyed the splendor of his court and the liberties of his youth. When Beatrice became pregnant a second time he freed her from marital obligations, and formed a liaison with Lucrezia Crivelli (1496). Beatrice bore his infidelity with impatient grief; she no longer spread song and merriment about her, but immersed herself in her two sons. Lodovico vacillated between his mistress and his wife, pleading that he loved both. In 1497 Beatrice was a third time confined in childbirth. She was delivered of a stillborn son; and half an hour later, after great agony, she died, aged twenty-two.

From that moment everything changed in the city and the Duke. The people, says a contemporary, "showed such grief as had never been known before in Milan." The court put on mourning; Lucrezia Crivelli fled into obscurity; Lodovico, overcome with remorse and sorrow, passed days in solitude and prayer; and the strong man who had hardly thought of religion now asked for only one boon—that he might die, see Beatrice again, earn her forgiveness, and regain her love. For two weeks he refused to receive officials, his envoys, or his children; he attended three Masses daily, and daily visited the tomb of his wife in the church of Santa Maria delle Grazie. He commissioned Cristoforo Solari to carve a recumbent effigy of Beatrice; and as he wished, when dead, to be buried with her in one tomb, he asked that his own effigy should be placed beside hers. It was so done; and that simple monument in the Certosa di Pavia still commemorates the brief bright day that for Lodovico and Milan, as well as for Beatrice and Leonardo, had now come to an end.

The tragedy ripened rapidly. In 1498 the Duke of Orléans became Louis XII of France, and at once reaffirmed his intention of taking Milan. Lodovico sought allies, but found none; Venice bluntly reminded him of his invitation to Charles VIII. He gave command of his army to Galeazzo di San Severino, who was too handsome for a general; Galeazzo fled at sight of the enemy, and the French marched unhindered upon Milan. Lodovico appointed his trusted friend Bernardino da Corte to guard the well-fortified Castello, and bade him hold it till Lodovico could secure aid from Maximilian. Then Lodovico, in disguise and through a hundred vicissitudes, made his way (September 2, 1499) to Innsbruck and Maximilian. When Gian Trivulzio, a Milanese general whom Lodovico had offended, led the French into Milan, Bernardino surrendered the Castello and its treasures to him without resistance for a bribe of 150,000 ducats ($1,875,-000). "Since Judas," mourned Lodovico, "there was no greater treason,"[18] and all Italy agreed with him.

Louis bade Trivulzio make the conquered pay for the conquest; the general levied heavy taxes; the French soldiers behaved with coarse insolence; the people began to pray for Lodovico's return. He came, with a small force of Swiss, German, and Italian mercenaries; the French troops retired into the Castello, and Lodovico entered Milan in triumph (February 5, 1500). During his brief stay there a distinguished French prisoner was brought to him, the Chevalier Bayard, renowned for courage and courtesy; Lodovico restored to him his sword and horse, freed him, and sent him back under escort to the French camp. The French did not return the courtesy; the garrison in the Castello bombarded the streets of Milan until Lodovico, to protect or appease the population, changed his headquarters to Pavia. His funds began to run out, and he fell behind in paying his troops. They proposed to compensate themselves by pillaging the Italian towns, and fumed when he forbade them. He engaged Gianfrancesco Gonzaga, husband of Beatrice's sister Isabella, to lead his little army; Francesco agreed,

but secretly negotiated with the French.[19] When the French appeared at
Novara, Lodovico led his motley force to battle; it turned at the first shock
and fled; its leaders arranged terms with the French; and when Lodovico
tried to escape in disguise his Swiss mercenaries betrayed him to the enemy
(April 10, 1500). He accepted his fate quietly, merely asking that his copy
of *The Divine Comedy* should be brought to him from his library in Pavia.
White-haired but still proud, he was led through hostile mocking crowds
in the streets of Lyons, and was imprisoned in the castle of Lys-Saint-
Georges in Berry. Louis XII refused to see him, and ignored the pleas of
the Emperor Maximilian to set the broken captive free, but he allowed
Lodovico to stroll in the castle grounds, to fish in the moat, and to receive
friends. When Lodovico fell seriously ill Louis sent him his own doctor,
Maître Salomon, and brought one of Lodovico's dwarfs from Milan to
amuse him. In 1504 he transferred Lodovico to the château of Loches, and
allowed him still wider liberty. In 1508 Lodovico tried to escape; he made
his way out of the castle precincts in a load of straw; he lost himself in the
woods, was tracked by bloodhounds, and thereafter suffered a stricter
imprisonment. He was deprived of books and writing materials, and was
confined in a subterranean dungeon. There, on May 17, 1508, in a dark
solitude all the world away from the bright life of his once gay capital,
Lodovico, aged fifty-seven, died.[20]

He had sinned against man and woman and Italy, but he had loved
beauty, and had cherished the men who brought art and music, poetry
and learning to Milan. Said one of Italy's greatest historians, Girolamo
Tiraboschi, a century ago:

> If we consider the immense number of learned men who flocked
> to his court from all parts of Italy in the certainty of receiving great
> honors and rich rewards; if we recall how many famous architects
> and painters he invited to Milan, and how many noble buildings he
> raised; how he built and endowed the magnificent University of
> Pavia, and opened schools of every kind of science in Milan; if be-
> sides all this we read the splendid eulogies and dedicatory epistles
> addressed to him by scholars of every nationality, we feel inclined
> to pronounce him the best prince that ever lived.[21]

VI. LETTERS

Lodovico and Beatrice gathered about them many poets, but life was too
pleasant at this court to inspire in a poet the arduous and persevering de-

votion that produces a masterpiece. Serafino of Aquila was short and ugly, but his lyrics, sung by himself to the lute he played, were a delight to Beatrice and her friends. When she died he slipped away from Milan, unable to bear the heavy silence of rooms that had rung with her laughter and known the lightness of her feet. Lodovico invited the Tuscan poets Camelli and Bellincione to his court in the hope that they would refine the rude diction of Lombardy. The result was a war of Tuscan vs. Lombard poets, in which venomous sonnets ousted honest poetry. Bellincione was so quarrelsome that when he died a rival wrote an inscription for his tomb, warning the passer-by to tread quietly, lest the corpse should rise and bite him. Therefore Lodovico made a Lombard, Gasparo Visconti, his court poet. In 1496 Visconti presented to Beatrice 143 sonnets, and other poems, written in letters of silver and gold on ivory vellum, illuminated with delicate miniatures, and bound in silver-gilt boards enameled with flowers. He was a real poet, but time has withered him. He loved Petrarch, and engaged in an earnest but friendly debate with Bramante, in verse, on the relative merits of Petrarch and Dante, for the great architect loved to think himself a poet as well. Such jousts of rhyme were a favorite amusement of Renaissance courts; almost everybody took part in them, and even generals became sonneteers. The best poems written under the Sforzas were those of a polished courtier, Niccolò da Correggio; he had come to Milan in Beatrice's bridal train, and had been detained there by love for her and Lodovico; he served them as poet and diplomat, and composed his noblest verses on Beatrice's death. Lodovico's mistress, Cecilia Gallerani, herself a poetess, presided over a distinguished salon of poets, scholars, statesmen, and philosophers. All the refinements of life and culture that marked the eighteenth century in France flourished in Lodovico's Milan.

Lodovico did not match Lorenzo's interest in scholarship, nor his discrimination in patronage; he brought a hundred scholars to his city, but their learned intercourse produced no outstanding native savant. Francesco Filelfo, who made all Italy resound with his erudition and vituperation, was born in Tolentino, studied at Padua, became a professor there at eighteen, taught for a while at Venice, and rejoiced at the opportunity to visit Constantinople as secretary to the Venetian consulate (1419). There he studied Greek under John Chrysoloras, married John's daughter, and served for years as a minor official at the Byzantine court. When he returned to Venice he was an expert Hellenist; he boasted, with some truth, that no other Italian had so thorough a knowledge of classic letters and tongues; he wrote poetry, and delivered orations, in Greek and Latin; and Venice paid him, as professor of those languages and their literature, the unusually high stipend of 500 sequins ($12,500) a year. A still fatter fee lured him to Florence (1429), where he became a scholastic lion. "The whole city," he assured a friend, "turns to look at me. . . . My name is on every lip. Not only civic leaders, but women of the noblest birth make way for me, paying me so much respect that I am ashamed of their worship. My audience numbers every day four hundred persons, mostly men advanced in years, and of the dignity of senators."[22] All this soon ended, for Filelfo had a flair for quarreling, and alienated the very men—Niccolò de' Niccoli, Ambrogio Traversari, and others—who had invited him to Florence. When Cosimo de' Medici was imprisoned in the Palazzo Vecchio, Filelfo urged the government to put him to death; when Cosimo triumphed Filelfo fled. For six years he taught at Siena and Bologna; finally (1440) Filippo Maria Visconti drew him to Milan with the unprecedented fee of 750 florins per year. There Filelfo spent the remainder of his long and tempestuous career.

He was a man of awesome energy. He lectured four hours a day, in Greek, Latin, or Italian, expounding the classics or Dante or Petrarch; he delivered public orations for governmental ceremonies or private celebrations; he wrote a Latin epic on Francesco Sforza, ten "decades" of satires, ten "books" of odes, and twenty-four hundred lines of Greek poetry. He composed ten thousand lines *De seriis et iocis* (1465), which were never printed and are often unprintable. He buried two wives, married a third, and had twenty-four children in addition to the bastards that plagued his infidelities. Amid these labors he found time to carry on gigantic literary wars with poets, politicians, and humanists. Despite his handsome salary and incidental fees, he pled intermittent poverty, and asked his patrons, in classic couplets, for money, food, clothing, horses, and a cardinal's hat. He made the mistake of including Poggio among his targets, and found that jolly scoundrel his master in scurrility.*

Even so, his learning made him the most sought-for scholar of the age. In 1453 Pope Nicholas V, receiving him in the Vatican, gave him a purse of 500 ducats ($12,500); Alfonso I at Naples crowned him poet laureate and knighted him; Duke Borso was his host at Ferrara, the Marchese Lodovico Gonzaga at Mantua, the dictator Sigismondo Malatesta at Rimini. When the death of Francesco Sforza, and the ensuing chaos, made his position insecure in Milan, he had no difficulty securing a post in the University of

---

* A precious but untranslatable sample by Poggio about Filelfo: *Itaque Chrysoloras, moerore confectus, compulsus precibus, malo coactus, filiam tibi nuptui dedit a te corruptam, quae si extitisset integra, ne pilum quidem tibi abrasum ab illius natibus ostendisset.*[23]

Rome. But the papal treasurer was remiss in his payments, and Filelfo returned to Milan. Nevertheless he longed to end his days near Lorenzo de'
Medici, to be one of the illustrious group that surrounded the grandson of
the man whom he had nominated for death. Lorenzo forgave him, and
offered him the chair of Greek literature in Florence. Filelfo was so poor
now that the government of Milan had to lend him money for the trip.
He managed to reach Florence, but died of dysentery a fortnight after his
arrival, aged eighty-three (1481). His career is one of a hundred that,
taken together, convey the unique aroma of the Italian Renaissance, in
which scholarship could be a passion, and literature could be war.

VII. ART

Despotism was a boon to Italian art. A dozen rulers competed in seeking
architects, sculptors, and painters to adorn their capitals and their memory;
and in this rivalry they spent such sums as democracy rarely spares to
beauty, and such as would never have been available to art had the proceeds
of human labor and genius been equitably shared. The result was, in Renaissance Italy, an art of courtly distinction and aristocratic taste, but too
often circumscribed, in form and theme, to the needs of secular potentates
or ecclesiastical powers. The noblest art is that which, out of the toil and
contributions of multitudes, creates for them a common gift and glory;
such were the Gothic cathedrals and the temples of classic Greece and
Rome.

Every critic denounces the *duomo* of Milan as a plethora of ornament
confusing structural line; but the people of Milan have for five centuries
gathered fondly in its cool immensity, and, even in this doubting day, cherish it as their collective achievement and pride. Giangaleazzo Visconti
began it (1386), and planned it on a scale befitting the capital of the united
Italy of his dreams; 40,000 people should find room there to worship God
and admire Gian. Tradition tells how, at that time, the women of Milan
were afflicted with a mysterious disease in their pregnancies, and many
of their babies died in infancy; Gian himself mourned three sons painfully
born and all soon dead; and he dedicated the great shrine as an offering
Mariae nascenti, "to Mary in her birth," praying that he might have an heir,
and that the mothers of Milan might bear a wholesome progeny. He summoned architects from France and Germany as well as from Italy; the
northerners dictated the Gothic style, the Italians lavished ornament; harmony of style and form faded in a conflict of counsels and two centuries of

delay; the mood and taste of the world changed during the process; and those who finished the structure no longer felt as those who had begun it. When Giangaleazzo died (1402) only the walls had been built; then the work marked time for lack of funds. Lodovico called in Bramante, Leonardo, and others to design a cupola that should bring the proud wilderness of pinnacles to some crowning unity; their ideas were rejected; finally (1490) Giovanni Antonio Amadeo was drawn from his labors on the Certosa di Pavia, and was given full charge of the whole cathedral enterprise. He and most of his aides were rather sculptors than architects; they could not bear that any surface should remain uncarved or unadorned. He consumed in the task the last thirty years of his life (1490-1522); even so the cupola was not finished till 1759; and the façade, begun in 1616, was not completed till Napoleon made that consummation an imperial command (1809).

In Lodovico's day it was the second largest church in the world, covering 120,000 square feet; today it yields the specious honor of size to St. Peter's and the cathedral of Seville; but it is still proud of its length and breadth (486 by 289 feet), its height of 354 feet from the ground to the head of the Virgin on the spire of the cupola, the 135 pinnacles that splinter its glory, and the 2300 statues that people its pinnacles, pillars, walls, and roof. All of it—even the roof—was built of white marble laboriously transported from a dozen quarries in Italy. The façade is too low for its width, and yet hides the exquisite cupola. One must be poised in midair to see this maze of praying stalagmites rising from the earth; or one must travel again and again around the great dolmen, amid a shower of buttresses, to feel the extravagant majesty of the mass; or one must come through the narrow and swarming streets of the city, and suddenly emerge into the vast open square of the Piazza del Duomo, to catch the full splendor of façade and spire turning the sun of Italy into a radiance of stone; or one must crowd with the people through the portals on some holyday, and let all those spaces, pillars, capitals, arches, vaults, statues, altars, and colored panes convey without words the mystery of faith, hope, and adoration.

As the cathedral is the monument of Giangaleazzo Visconti, and the Certosa of Pavia is the shrine of Lodovico and Beatrice, so the Ospedale Maggiore, or Great Hospital, is the simple and stately memorial of Francesco Sforza. To design it in a manner "worthy of the ducal dominion and of so great and illustrious a city," Sforza brought in from Florence (1456) Antonio Averulino, known as Filarete, who chose for it a stately form of Lombard Romanesque. Bramante, the probable architect of the inner court or cortile, faced this with a double tier of round arches, each tier surmounted by an elegant cornice. The Great Hospital remained one of Milan's chief glories till the Second World War left most of it in ruins.

In the judgment of Lodovico and his court the supreme artist in Milan was not Leonardo but Bramante, for Leonardo revealed only a part of himself to his time. Born at Castel Durante near Urbino, Donato d'Agnolo began his career as a painter, and received the nickname Bramante as meaning one consumed with insatiable desires. He went to Mantua to study with Mantegna; he learned enough to paint some mediocre frescoes, and a splendid portrait of the mathematician Luca Pacioli. Perhaps in Mantua he met Leon Battista Alberti, who was designing the church of Sant' Andrea; in any case repeated experiments in perspective led Bramante from painting to architecture. In 1472 he was in Milan, studying the cathedral with the intensity of a man resolved to do great things. About 1476 he was given a chance to show his mettle by designing the church of Santa Maria around the little church of San Satiro. In this modest masterpiece he revealed his peculiar architectural style—semicircular apses and sacristies, octagonal cupolas, and circular domes, all crowned with elegant cornices, and all crowded one upon another in an engaging ensemble. Lacking space for an apse, Bramante, frolicking with perspective, painted the wall behind the altar with a pictured apse whose converging lines gave the full illusion of spatial depth. To the church of Santa Maria delle Grazie he added an apse, a cupola, and the handsome cloister porticoes that were another casualty of the Second World War. After Lodovico fell Bramante went south, ready to tear down and rebuild Rome.

The sculptors at Lodovico's court were not such giants as Donatello and Michelangelo, but they carved for the Certosa, the cathedral, and the palaces a hundred figures with fascinating grace. Cristoforo Solari the hunchback (*il Gobbo*) will be remembered as long as his tomb of Lodovico and Beatrice survives. Gian Cristoforo Romano won all hearts by his gentle manner and beautiful singing; he was a major sculptor at the Certosa, but after Beatrice died he yielded to a year of urging and went to Mantua. There he carved for Isabella the pretty doorway of her Paradiso study, and cut her likeness in one of the finest medallions of the Renaissance. Then he moved on to Urbino to work for the Duchess Elisabetta Gonzaga, and became a leading figure in Castiglione's *Courtier*. The greatest medallion carver of Milan was Cristoforo Foppa, nicknamed Caradosso, who cut the gleaming gems that Beatrice wore, and earned the envy of Cellini.

There were good painters in Milan a generation before Leonardo came. Vincenzo Foppa, born at Brescia and formed in Padua, worked chiefly in Milan; his frescoes in Sant' Eustorgio were renowned in their day, and his *Martyrdom of St. Sebastian* still adorns a Castello wall. His follower Ambrogio Borgognone has left us a more pleasing legacy: Madonnas in the Brera and Ambrosiana galleries at Milan, in Turin, and Berlin, all in the pure tradition of warm piety; a delectable portrait of Giangaleazzo Sforza as a child, in the Wallace Collection in London; and, in the church of the Incoronata at Lodi, an *Annunciation* which is one of the most successful renderings of that difficult theme. Ambrogio de Predis was court painter to Lodovico when Leonardo arrived; he seems to have had a brush in Leonardo's *Virgin of the Rocks;* he may have painted the captivating angel musicians in the London National Gallery; but his finest relics are two portraits now in the Ambrosiana: one of a very serious young man, identity unknown;* the other of a young woman, now generally identified with Lodovico's natural daughter Bianca. Rarely has an artist caught the conflicting charms of a girl innocently demure and yet proudly conscious of her simple beauty.

The cities subject to Milan suffered from the luring of their talent to the capital, but several of them managed to earn a place in the history of art. Como was not satisfied to be merely a Milanese gate to the lake that gave it fame; it was proud, too, of its Torre del Comune, its Broletto, above all of its majestic marble cathedral. The superb Gothic façade rose under the Sforza rule (1457-87); Bramante designed a pretty doorway on the south side, and on the east Cristoforo Solari built a charming apse in Bramantean style. More interesting than these features is a pair of statues adjoining the main portal: on the left Pliny the Elder, on the right Pliny the Younger, ancient citizens of Como, civilized pagans finding a place on a Christian cathedral façade in the tolerant days of Lodovico the Moor.

The jewel of Bergamo was the Cappella Colleoni. The Venetian *condottiere*, born here, desired a chapel to receive his bones, and a sculptured cenotaph to commemorate his victories. Giovanni Antonio Amadeo designed the chapel and the tomb with splendor and taste; and Sixtus Siry of Nuremberg surmounted the sepulcher with an equestrian statue in wood, which would have won a wider fame had not Verrocchio cast the great captain in prouder bronze. Bergamo was too near to Milan to keep its paint-

---

* This portrait is by some students ascribed to Leonardo da Vinci, and may represent Franchino Gaffuri, a musician at Lodovico's court.

ers home; but one of them, Andrea Previtali, after studying with Giovanni Bellini in Venice, returned to Bergamo (1513) to bequeath to it some paintings of exemplary piety and modest excellence.

Brescia, subject at times to Venice, at times to Milan, held a balance between the two influences, and developed its own school of art. After disseminating his talent among half a dozen cities, Vincenzo Foppa returned to spend his declining years in his native Brescia. His pupil Vincenzo Civerchio shared with Floriano Ferramolo the honor of forming the Brescian school. Girolamo Romani, called Romanino, studied with Ferramolo, later in Padua and Venice; then, making Brescia his center, he painted there, and in other towns of northern Italy, a long series of frescoes, altarpieces, and portraits, excellent in color, less laudable in line; let us name only the *Madonna and Child*, in a magnificent frame by Stefano Lamberti, in the church of San Francesco. His pupil Alessandro Bonvicino, known as Moretto da Brescia, brought this dynasty to its zenith by blending the sensuous glory of the Venetians with the warm religious sentiment that marked Brescian painting to its end. In the church of SS. Nazaro e Celso, where Titian placed an *Annunciation*, Moretto painted an equally beautiful *Coronation of the Virgin*, whose archangel rivals in delicacy of form and feature the most graceful figures of Correggio. Like Titian he could paint, when he wished, an appetizing Venus; and his *Salome*, instead of revealing a murderess by proxy, shows us one of the sweetest, gentlest faces in the whole gamut of Renaissance art.

Cremona gathered her life around her twelfth-century cathedral and its adjoining Torrazo—a campanile almost challenging Giotto's and the Giralda. Within the *duomo* Giovanni de' Sacchi—named Il Pordenone from his native town—painted his masterpiece, *Jesus Carrying His Cross*. Three remarkable families contributed successive generations of talent to Cremonese painting: the Bembi (Bonifazio, Benedetto, Gian Francesco), the Boccaccini, and the Campi. Boccaccio Boccaccini, after studying in Venice and burning his fingers in a competition with Michelangelo in Rome, returned to Cremona and won acclaim by his frescoes of the Virgin in the Cathedral; and his son Camillo continued his excellence. In like manner the work of Galeazzo Campi was carried on by his sons Giulio and Antonio, and by Giulio's pupil Bernardino Campi. Galeazzo designed the church of Santa Margherita in Cremona, and then painted in it a magnificent *Presentation in the Temple*. So the arts, in Renaissance Italy, tended to mate in one mind, and flowered under geniuses of such versatility as not even Periclean Greece had known.

CHAPTER VII

Leonardo da Vinci

1452-1519

I. DEVELOPMENT: 1452-1482

THE most fascinating figure of the Renaissance was born on April 15, 1452 near the village of Vinci, some sixty miles from Florence. His mother was a peasant girl, Caterina, who had not bothered to marry his father. Her seducer, Piero d'Antonio, was a Florentine attorney of some means. In the year of Leonardo's birth Piero married a woman of his own rank. Caterina had to be content with a peasant husband; she yielded her pretty love child to Piero and his wife; and Leonardo was brought up in semiaristocratic comfort without maternal love. Perhaps in that early environment he acquired his taste for fine clothing, and his aversion to women.

He went to a neighborhood school, took fondly to mathematics, music, and drawing, and delighted his father by his singing and his playing of the lute. In order to draw well he studied all things in nature with curiosity, patience, and care; science and art, so remarkably united in his mind, had there one origin—detailed observation. When he was turning fifteen his father took him to Verrocchio's studio in Florence, and persuaded that versatile artist to accept him as an apprentice. All the educated world knows Vasari's story of how Leonardo painted the angel at the left in Verrocchio's *Baptism of Christ*, and how the master was so overwhelmed by the beauty of the figure that he gave up painting and devoted himself to sculpture. Probably this abdication is a post-mortem legend; Verrocchio made several pictures after the *Baptism*. Perhaps in these apprentice days Leonardo painted the *Annunciation* in the Louvre, with its awkward angel and its startled maid. He could hardly have learned grace from Verrocchio.

Meanwhile Ser Piero prospered, bought several properties, moved his family to Florence (1469), and married four wives in turn. The second was only ten years older than Leonardo. When the third presented Piero with a child Leonardo eased the congestion by going to live with Verrocchio. In that year (1472) he was admitted to membership in the Company of St. Luke. This guild, composed chiefly of apothecaries, physicians, and artists, had its headquarters in the hospital of Santa Maria Nuova. Presumably Leonardo found there some opportunities to study internal as well as external anatomy. Perhaps in those years he—or was it he?—painted the gaunt anatomical *St. Jerome* ascribed to him in the Vatican Gallery. And it was probably he who, toward 1474, painted the colorful and immature *Annunciation* of the Uffizi.

A week before his twenty-fourth birthday Leonardo and three other youths were summoned before a committee of the Florentine Signory to answer a charge of having had homosexual relations. The result of this summons is unknown. On June 7, 1476, the accusation was repeated; the committee imprisoned Leonardo briefly, released him, and dismissed the charge as unproved.[1] Unquestionably he was a homosexual. As soon as he could afford to have his own studio he gathered handsome young men about him; he took some of them with him on his migrations from city to city; he referred to one or another of them in his manuscripts as *amantissimo* or *carissimo*—"most beloved," "dearest."[2] What his intimate relations with these youths were we do not know; some passages in his notes suggest a distaste for sexual congress in any form.* Leonardo might reasonably doubt why he and a few others had been singled out for public accusation when homosexuality was so widespread in the Italy of the time. He never forgave Florence for the indignity of his arrest.

Apparently he took the matter more seriously than the city did. A year after the accusation he was invited, and agreed, to accept a studio in the Medici gardens; and in 1478 the Signory itself asked him to paint an altarpiece for the chapel of St. Bernard in the Palazzo Vecchio. For some reason he did not carry out the assignment; Ghirlandaio took it over; Filippino Lippi completed it. Nevertheless the Signory soon gave him—and Botticelli—another commission: to paint—we cannot say to the life—full-length portraits of two men hanged for the conspiracy of the Pazzi against Lorenzo and Giuliano de' Medici. Leonardo, with his half-morbid interest in human deformity and suffering, may have felt some fascination in the gruesome task.

But indeed he was interested in everything. All postures and actions of

---

* "And they will go wild for the things that are most beautiful to seek after, to possess and make use of their vilest parts. . . .[3] The act of procreation and the members employed therein are so repulsive that if it were not for the beauty of the faces, and the adornment of the actors, and the pent-up impulse, nature would lose the human species."[4]

the human body, all expressions of the face in young and old, all the organs and movements of animals and plants from the waving of wheat in the field to the flight of birds in the air, all the cyclical erosion and elevation of mountains, all the currents and eddies of water and wind, the moods of the weather, the shades of the atmosphere, and the inexhaustible kaleidoscope of the sky—all these seemed endlessly wonderful to him; repetition never dulled for him their marvel and mystery; he filled thousands of pages with observations concerning them, and drawings of their myriad forms. When the monks of San Scopeto asked him to paint a picture for their chapel (1481), he made so many sketches for so many features and forms of it that he lost himself in the details, and never finished *The Adoration of the Magi.*

Nevertheless it is one of his greatest paintings. The plan from which he developed it was drawn on a strictly geometrical pattern of perspective, with the whole space divided into diminishing squares; the mathematician in Leonardo always competed— often co-operated—with the artist. But the artist was already developed; the Virgin had the pose and features that she would keep in Leonardo's work to the end; the Magi were drawn with a remarkable understanding—for a youth—of character and expression in old men; and the "Philosopher" at the left was literally a brown study of half-skeptical meditation, as if the painter had so soon come to view the Christian story with a spirit unwillingly incredulous and still devout. And around these figures half a hundred others gathered, as if every kind of man and woman had hurried to this crib seeking hungrily the meaning of life and some Light of the World, and finding the answer in a stream of births.

The unfinished masterpiece, almost erased by time, hangs in the Uffizi at Florence, but it was Filippino Lippi who executed the painting accepted by the Scopetini brotherhood. To begin, to conceive too richly, to lose himself in experimenting with details; to see beyond his subject a boundless perspective of human, animal, plant, and architectural forms, of rocks and mountains, streams and clouds and trees, in a mystic chiaroscuro light; to be absorbed in the philosophy of the picture rather than in its technical accomplishment; to leave to others the lesser task of coloring the figures so drawn and placed for revealing significance; to turn in despair, after long labor of mind and body, from the imperfection with which the hand and the materials had embodied the dream: this was to be Leonardo's character and fate, with a few exceptions, to the end.

II. IN MILAN: 1482-99

There was nothing hesitant, no sense yet of the merciless brevity of time, only youth's limitless ambitions fed by burgeoning powers, in the letter that Leonardo, now thirty, sent in 1482 to Lodovico, regent of Milan. He had had enough of Florence; the desire to see new places and faces mounted in his blood. He had heard that Lodovico wanted a military engineer, an architect, a sculptor, a painter; well, he would offer himself as all these in one. And so he wrote his famous letter:

Most Illustrious Lord, having now sufficiently seen and considered the proofs of all those who count themselves masters and inventors of instruments of war, and finding that their invention and use of the said instruments does not differ in any respect from those in common practice, I am emboldened without prejudice to anyone else to put myself in communication with your Excellency, in order to acquaint you with my secrets, thereafter offering myself at your pleasure effectually to demonstrate at any convenient time all those matters which are in part briefly recorded below.

1. I have plans for bridges, very light and strong and suitable for carrying very easily. . . .

2. When a place is besieged I know how to cut off water from the trenches, and how to construct an infinite number of . . . . scaling ladders and other instruments. . . .

4. I have plans for making cannon, very convenient and easy of transport, with which to hurl small stones in the manner almost of hail. . . .

5. And if it should happen that the engagement is at sea, I have plans for constructing many engines most suitable for attack or defense, and ships which can resist the fire of all the heaviest cannon, and powder and smoke.

6. Also I have ways of arriving at a certain fixed spot by caverns and secret winding passages, made without any noise even though it may be necessary to pass underneath trenches or a river.

7. Also I can make covered cars, safe and unassailable, which will enter the serried ranks of the enemy with artillery, and there is no company of men at arms so great as not to be broken by it. And behind these the infantry will be able to follow quite unharmed and without any opposition.

8. Also, if need shall arise, I can make cannon, mortars, and light ordance. of very beautiful and useful shapes, quite different from those in common use.

9. Where it is not possible to employ cannon, I can supply catapults, mangonels, traps, and other engines of wonderful efficacy not in general use. In short, as the variety of circumstances shall necessitate, I can supply an infinite number of different engines of attack and defense.

10. In time of peace I believe that I can give you as complete satisfaction as anyone else in architecture, in the construction of buildings both public and private, and in conducting water from one place to another.

Also I can execute sculpture in marble, bronze, or clay, and also painting, in which my work will stand comparison with that of anyone else whoever he may be.

Moreover, I would undertake the work of the bronze horse, which shall endue with immortal glory and eternal honor the auspicious memory of the Prince your father and of the illustrious house of Sforza.

And if any of the aforesaid things should seem impossible or impracticable to anyone, I offer myself as ready to make trial of them in your park or in whatever place shall please your Excellency, to whom I commend myself with all possible humility.

We do not know how Lodovico replied, but we know that Leonardo reached Milan in 1482 or 1483, and soon made his way into the heart of "the Moor." One story has it that Lorenzo, as a diplomatic bonbon, had sent him to Lodovico to deliver a handsome lute; another that he won a musical contest there, and was retained not for any of the powers that he had claimed "with all possible humility," but for the music of his voice, the charm of his conversation, the soft sweet tone of the lyre that his own hands had fashioned in the form of a horse's head.[5] Lodovico seems to have accepted him not at his own valuation but as a brilliant youth who—even though he might be less of an architect than Bramante, and too inexperienced to be entrusted with military engineering—might plan court masques and city pageants, decorate dresses for wife or mistress or princess, paint murals and portraits, and perhaps construct canals to improve the irrigation of the Lombard plain. It offends us to learn that the myriad-minded man had to spend irrecoverable time making curious girdles for Lodovico's pretty bride, Beatrice d'Este, conceiving costumes for jousts and festivals, organizing pageants, or decorating stables. But a Renaissance artist was expected to do all these things between Madonnas; Bramante too shared in this courtlery; and who knows but the woman in Leonardo delighted in designing dresses and jewelry, and the accomplished equestrian in him enjoyed painting swift horses on stable walls? He adorned the ballroom of the Castello for the marriage of Beatrice, built a special bathroom for her, raised in the garden a pretty pavilion for her summer joy, and painted other rooms—*camerini*—for palace celebrations. He made portraits of Lodovico, Beatrice, and their children, of Lodovico's mistresses Cecilia Gallerani and Lucrezia Crivelli; these paintings are lost, unless *La Belle Ferronière* of the Louvre is Lucrezia. Vasari speaks of the family portraits as "marvelous," and the picture of Lucrezia inspired a poet to a fervid eulogy of the lady's beauty and the artist's skill.[6]

Perhaps Cecilia was Leonardo's model for *The Virgin of the Rocks*. The painting was contracted for (1483) by the Confraternity of the Conception as the central part of an altarpiece for the church of San Francesco. The original was later bought by Francis I and is in the Louvre. Standing before it, we note the softly maternal face that Leonardo would use a dozen times in later works; an angel recalling one in Verrocchio's *Baptism of Christ*; two infants exquisitely drawn; and a background of jutting, overhanging rocks that only Leonardo could have conceived as Mary's habitat. The colors have been darkened by time, but possibly the artist intended a darkling effect, and suffused his pictures with a hazy atmosphere that Italy calls *sfumato*—"smoked." This is one of Leonardo's greatest pictures, surpassed only by *The Last Supper, Mona Lisa*, and *The Virgin, Child, and St. Anne.*

The Last Supper and *Mona Lisa* are the world's most famous paintings. Hour after hour, day after day, year after year, pilgrims enter the refectory that holds Leonardo's most ambitious work. In that simple rectangular building the Dominican friars who were attached to Lodovico's favorite church—Santa Maria delle Grazie—took their meals. Soon after the artist arrived in Milan Lodovico asked him to represent the Last Supper on the farthest wall of this refectory. For three years (1495-8), on and off, Leonardo labored or dallied at the task, while Duke and friars fretted over his incalculable delays. The prior (if we may believe Vasari) complained to Lodovico of Leonardo's apparent sloth, and wondered why he would sometimes sit before the wall for hours without painting a stroke. Leonardo had no trouble explaining to the Duke—who had some trouble explaining to the prior—that an artist's most important work lies in conception rather than in execution, and (as Vasari put it) "men of genius do most when they work least." There were in this case, said Leonardo to Lodovico, two special difficulties—to conceive features worthy of the

Son of God, and to picture a man as heartless as Judas; perhaps, he slyly suggested, he might use the too frequently seen face of the prior as a model for Iscariot.* Leonardo hunted throughout Milan for heads and faces that might serve him in representing the Apostles; from a hundred such quarries he chose the features that were melted in the mintage of his art into those astonishingly individualized heads that make the wonder of the dying masterpiece. Sometimes he would rush from the streets or his studio to the refectory, add a stroke or two to the picture, and depart.[8]

The subject was superb, but from a painter's point of view it was pitted with hazards. It had to confine itself to male figures and a modest table in a simple room; there could be only the dimmest landscape or vista; no grace of women might serve as foil to the strength of the men; no vivid action could be brought in to set the figures into motion and convey the sense of life. Leonardo let in a glimpse of landscape through the three windows behind Christ. As a substitute for action he portrayed the gathering at the tense moment Christ has prophesied that one of the Apostles will betray Him, and each is asking, in fear or horror or amazement, "Is it I?" The institution of the Eucharist might have been chosen, but that would have frozen all thirteen faces into an immobile and stereotyped solemnity. Here, on the contrary, there is more than violent physical action; there is a searching and revelation of spirit; never again, so profoundly, has an artist revealed in one picture so many souls. For the Apostles Leonardo made numberless preliminary sketches; some of these—for James the Greater, Philip, Judas—are drawings of such finesse and power as only Rembrandt and Michelangelo have matched. When he tried to conceive the features of Christ, Leonardo found that the Apostles had exhausted his inspiration. According to Lomazzo (writing in 1557), Leonardo's old friend Zenale advised him to leave the face of Christ unfinished, saying: "Of a truth it would be impossible to imagine faces lovelier or gentler than those of James the Greater or James the Less. Accept your misfortune, then, and leave your Christ incomplete; for otherwise, when compared with the Apostles, He would not be their Saviour or their Master."[9] Leonardo took the advice. He or a pupil made a famous sketch (now in the Brera Gallery) for the head of Christ, but it pictured an effeminate sadness and resignation rather than the heroic resolve that calmly entered Gethsemane.

---

* The story may be a legend; we have only Vasari's evidence for it. There is no evidence against it except a tradition which reports that *The Last Supper* contained no likenesses of living men.[7]

Perhaps Leonardo lacked the reverent piety that, had it been added to his sensitivity, his depth, and his skill, might have brought the picture nearer to perfection.

Because he was a thinker as well as an artist, Leonardo shunned fresco painting as an enemy to thought; such painting on wet and freshly laid plaster had to be done rapidly before the plaster dried. Leonardo preferred to paint on a dry wall with tempera—colors mixed in a gelatinous substance, for this method allowed him to ponder and experiment. But these colors did not adhere firmly to the surface; even in Leonardo's lifetime— what with the usual dampness of the refectory and its occasional flooding in heavy rains—the paint began to flake and fall; when Vasari saw the picture (1536) it was already blurred; when Lomazzo saw it, sixty years after its completion, it was already ruined beyond repair. The friars later helped decay by cutting a door through the legs of the Apostles into the kitchen (1656). The engraving by which the painting has been reproduced throughout the world was taken not from the spoiled original but from an imperfect copy made by one of Leonardo's pupils, Marco d'Oggiono. Today we can study only the composition and the general outlines, hardly the shades or subtleties. But whatever were the defects of the work when Leonardo left it, some realized at once that it was the greatest painting that Renaissance art had yet produced.

Meanwhile (1483) Leonardo had undertaken a work completely different and still more difficult. Lodovico had long wished to commemorate his father, Francesco Sforza, with an equestrian statue that would bear comparison with Donatello's *Gattamelata* at Padua and Verrocchio's *Colleoni* in Venice. Leonardo's ambition was stirred. He set himself to studying the anatomy, action, and nature of the horse, and drew a hundred sketches of the animal, nearly all of snorting vivacity. Soon he was absorbed in making a plaster model. When some citizens of Piacenza asked him to recommend an artist to design and cast bronze doors for their cathedral he wrote characteristically in reply: "There is no one who is capable except Leonardo the Florentine, who is making the bronze horse of the Duke Francesco, and you need take no count of him, for he has work that will last his whole lifetime; and I fear that it is so great an undertaking that he will never finish it."[10] Lodovico at times thought so too, and asked Lorenzo for other artists to come and complete the task (1489). Lorenzo, like Leonardo, could not think of anybody better than Leonardo himself.

At last (1493) the plaster model was finished; all that remained was to cast it in bronze. In November the model was set up publicly under an arch to adorn the wedding procession of Lodovico's niece Bianca Maria. Men marveled at its size and splendor; horse and rider rose to twenty-six feet; poets wrote sonnets in its praise; and no one doubted that when cast it would surpass in power and life the masterpieces of Donatello and Verrocchio. But it was never cast. Apparently Lodovico could not spare funds for the fifty tons of bronze required. The model was left in the open while Leonardo busied himself with art and boys, with science and experiments, with mechanisms and manuscripts. When the French captured Milan (1499) their bowmen made a target of the plaster *cavallo*, and broke off many pieces of it. Louis XII, in 1501, expressed a desire to cart it off to France as a trophy. We do not hear of it again.

The great fiasco unnerved and exhausted Leonardo for a time, and may have disturbed his relations with the Duke. Normally Lodovico paid his "Apelles" well; a cardinal was surprised to learn that Leonardo received 2000 ducats ($25,000?) a year, in addition to many gifts and privileges.[11] The artist lived like an aristocrat: he had several apprentices, servants, pages, horses; engaged musicians; dressed in silks and furs, embroidered gloves, and fancy leather boots. Though he produced works beyond price, he seemed at times to dally with his assignments, or to interrupt them for his private researches and compositions in science, philosophy, and art. In 1497, tired of such delays, Lodovico invited Perugino to come and decorate some rooms in the Castello. Perugino could not come, and Leonardo took over the assignment, but the incident left hurt feelings on both sides. About this time Lodovico, straitened in his finances by diplomatic and military expenses, fell behind in paying Leonardo's salary. Leonardo paid his own costs for almost two years, and then sent the Duke a gentle reminder (1498). Lodovico excused himself graciously, and a year later gave Leonardo a vineyard as a source of revenue. By that time Lodovico's political edifice was falling about him; the French captured Milan, Lodovico fled, and Leonardo found himself uncomfortably free.

He moved to Mantua (December, 1499), and there made a remarkable drawing of Isabella d'Este. She let her husband give it away as the first stage of its journey to the Louvre; and Leonardo, not relishing such generosity, passed on to Venice. He marveled at its proud beauty, but found its rich colors and Gothic-Byzantine ornaments too bright for his Florentine taste. He turned his steps back to the city of his youth.

III. FLORENCE: 1500-1, 1503-6

He was forty-eight when he tried to take up again the cords of life that he had snapped some seventeen years before. He had changed; Florence had, too, but divergently. She had become in his absence a half-democratic, half-puritan republic; he was accustomed to ducal rule and to soft aristocratic luxuries and ways. The Florentines, always critical, looked askance at his silks and velvets, his gracious manners, and his retinue of curly-headed youths. Michelangelo, twenty-two years his junior, resented the good looks that so contrasted with his own broken nose, and wondered, in his poverty, where Leonardo found the funds to maintain so rich a life. Leonardo had salvaged some six hundred ducats from his Milan days; now he refused many commissions, even from the imperious Marchesa of Mantua; and when he worked it was with his wonted leisureliness.

The Servite friars had engaged Filippino Lippi to paint an altarpiece for their church of the Annunziata; Leonardo casually expressed his desire to do a similar work; Filippino courteously surrendered the assignment to the man then generally considered to be the greatest painter in Europe. The Servites brought Leonardo and his "household" to live at the monastery, and paid their expenses for what seemed a very long time. Then one day in 1501 he unveiled the cartoon for his proposed picture of *The Virgin and Child with St. Anne and the Infant St. John*. It "not only filled every artist with wonder," says Vasari, "but when it was set up . . . men and women, young and old, flocked for two days to see it, as if in festival time, and they marveled exceedingly." We do not know if this was the full-size drawing that is now a treasured possession of the Royal Academy of Arts in Burlington House, London; probably it was, though French authorities[12] like to believe that it was the first form of the quite different picture in the Louvre. The smile of tender pride that softens and brightens the face of the Virgin in the cartoon is one of Leonardo's miracles; beside it the smile of Mona Lisa is earthly and cynical. Nevertheless, though this is among the greatest of Renaissance drawings, it is unsuccessful; there is something ungainly, and in poor taste, in seating the Virgin unstably across the widespread legs of her mother. Leonardo apparently neglected to transform this sketch into a picture for the Servites; they had to turn back to Lippi, and then to Perugino, for their altarpiece. But soon afterward, perhaps from a variant of the Burlington cartoon, Leonardo painted *The Virgin, St. Anne, and the Infant Jesus* of the Louvre. This is a technical triumph, from Anne's diademed head to Mary's feet—scandalously naked but divinely fair. The triangular composition that had failed in the cartoon here came to full success: the four heads of Anne, Mary, the Child, and the lamb make one rich line; the Child and His grandmother are intent on Mary, and the incomparable draperies of the women fill out the divergent space. The characteristic *sfumato* of Leonardo's brush has softened all outlines, as shadows soften them in life. The Leonardesque smile, on Mary in the cartoon but on Anne in the painting, set a fashion that would continue in Leonardo's followers for half a century.

From the mystic ecstasy of these tender evocations Leonardo passed, by an almost incredible transition, to serve Caesar Borgia as military engineer (June, 1502). Borgia was beginning his third campaign in the Romagna; he wanted a man who could make topographical maps, build and equip fortresses, bridge or divert streams, and invent weapons of offense and defense. Perhaps he had heard of the ideas that Leonardo had expressed or drawn for new engines of war. There was, for example, his sketch for an armored car or tank, whose wheels were to be moved by soldiers within its walls. "These cars," Leonardo had written, "take the place of elephants . . . one may tilt with them; one may hold bellows in them to terrify the horses of the enemy; one may put carabineers in them to break up every company."[13] Or, said Leonardo, you can put terrible scythes on the flanks of a chariot, and a still more lethal revolving scythe on a forward projecting shaft; these would mow down men like a field of grain.[14] Or you can make the wheels of the chariot turn a mechanism that will swing deadly flails at four ends.[15] You can attack a fort by placing your soldiers under some protective covering;[16] and you can repel besiegers by throwing down upon them bottles of poison gas.[17] Leonardo had planned a "book of how to drive back armies by the fury of floods caused by releasing waters," and a "book of how to inundate armies by closing the outlets" of waters flowing through valleys.[18] He had designed devices for mechanically discharging a succession of arrows from a revolving platform, for raising cannon upon a carriage, for toppling over the crowded ladders of a besieging force attempting to scale the walls.[19] Borgia put most of these contraptions aside as impracticable; he tried one or two in the siege of Ceri in 1503. Nevertheless he issued the following patent of authority (August, 1502):

> To all our lieutenants, castellans, captains, *condottieri*, officials, soldiers, and subjects. We constrain and command that the bearer, our most excellent and well-beloved servant, architect, and engineer-in-chief, Leonardo Vinci—whom we have appointed to inspect

strongholds and fortresses in our dominions to the end that according to their need and his counsel we may be enabled to provide for
their necessities—to accord a passage absolutely free from any toll
or tax, a friendly welcome both for himself and his company; freedom to see, examine and take measurements precisely as he may
wish; and for this purpose assistance in men as many as he may desire; and all possible aid and favor. It is our will that in the execution
of any works in our dominions every engineer will be bound to confer with him and follow his advice.[20]

Leonardo wrote much, but rarely about himself. We should have
relished his opinion of Borgia, and might have put it illuminatingly beside
that of the envoy whom Florence was sending to Caesar at this time—Niccolò Machiavelli. But all that we know is that Leonardo visited Imola,
Faenza, Forlì, Ravenna, Rimini, Pesaro, Urbino, Perugia, Siena, and other
cities; that he was in Senigallia when Caesar snared and strangled there four
treasonable captains; and that he presented Caesar with six extensive maps
of central Italy, showing the direction of the streams, the nature and contours of the terrain, the distances between rivers, mountains, fortresses,
and towns. Then suddenly he learned that Caesar was almost dead in
Rome, the Caesarian empire was collapsing, and an enemy of the Borgias
was mounting the papal throne. Once more Leonardo, his new world of
action fading before him, turned back to Florence (April, 1503).

In October of that year Pietro Soderini, head of the Florentine government, proposed to Leonardo and Michelangelo that each should paint a
mural in the new Hall of the Five Hundred in the Palazzo Vecchio. Both
men accepted, strict contracts were drawn up, and the artists retired to
separate studios to design their guiding cartoons. Each was to picture
some triumph of Florentine arms: Angelo an action in the war with Pisa,
Leonardo the victory of Florence over Milan at Anghiari. The alert citizens followed the progress of the work as a contest of gladiators; argument rose excitedly on the rival merits and styles; and some observers
thought that any definite superiority of one picture over the other would
decide whether later painters would follow Leonardo's bent toward delicate and subtle representation of feeling, or Michelangelo's penchant for
mighty muscles and demonic force.

Perhaps it was at this time (for the incident has no date) that the
younger artist let his dislike of Leonardo come to flagrant insult. One day
some Florentines in the Piazza Santa Trinità were discussing a passage in
The Divine Comedy. Seeing Leonardo pass, they stopped him and asked

for his interpretation. At that moment Michelangelo appeared, who was known to have studied Dante zealously. "Here is Michelangelo," said Leonardo; "he will explain the verses." Thinking that Leonardo was making fun of him, the unhappy Titan broke out in violent scorn: "Explain them yourself! You who made the model of a horse to be cast in bronze and could not cast it, and left it unfinished, to your shame! And those Milanese capons thought you could do it!" Leonardo, we are told, flushed deeply, but made no reply; Michelangelo marched off fuming.[21]

Leonardo prepared his cartoon carefully. He visited the scene of the engagement at Anghiari, read reports of it, made innumerable sketches of horses and men in the passion of battle or the agony of death. Now, as seldom in Milan, he found an opportunity to put movement into his art. He took full advantage of it, and depicted such a fury of mortal conflict that Florence almost shuddered at the sight; no one had supposed that this most refined of Florentine artists could conceive or picture such a vision of patriotic homicide. Perhaps Leonardo used here his experience in Caesar Borgia's campaign; the horrors that he may then have witnessed could be expressed in his drawing and exorcised from his mind. By February of 1505 he had finished his cartoon, and began to paint its central picture— *The Battle of the Standard*—in the Sala dei Cinquecento.

But now again he who had studied physics and chemistry, and had not yet learned the fate of his *Last Supper*, made a tragic mistake. Experimenting with encaustic techniques, he thought to fix the colors into the stucco wall by heat from a brazier on the floor. The room was damp, the winter was cold, the heat did not reach high enough, the stucco failed to absorb the paint, the upper.colors began to run, and no frenzied effort availed to halt the ruin. Meanwhile financial difficulties arose. The Signory was paying Leonardo fifteen florins ($188?) per month, hardly to be compared with the 160 or so that Lodovico had assigned him in Milan. When a tactless official offered the month's payment in coppers, Leonardo rejected them. He abandoned the enterprise in shame and despair, only moderately consoled by the fact that Michelangelo, after completing his cartoon, made no painting from it at all, but accepted a call from Pope Julius II to come and work in Rome. The great competition was a sorry mess that left Florence ill disposed toward the two greatest artists in her history.

On and off, during the years 1503-6, Leonardo painted the portrait of Mona Lisa—i.e., Madonna Elisabetta, third wife of Francesco del Giocondo, who in 1512 was to be a member of the Signory. Presumably a child of Francesco, buried in 1499, was one of Elisabetta's children, and this loss may have helped to mold the serious features behind La Gioconda's smile. That Leonardo should call her back to his studio so many times during those three years; that he should spend upon her portrait all the secrets and nuances of his art—modeling her softly with light and shade, framing her in a fanciful vista of trees and waters, mountains and sky—clothing her in raiment of velvet and satin woven into folds whose every wrinkle is a masterpiece—studying with passionate care the subtle muscles that form and move the mouth—bringing musicians to play for her and to evoke upon her features the disillusioned tenderness of a mother remembering a departed child: these are inklings of the spirit in which he came to this engaging merger of painting and philosophy. A thousand interruptions, a hundred distracting interests, the simultaneous struggle with the Anghiari design, left unbroken the unity of his conception, the unwonted pertinacity of his zeal.

This, then, is the face that launched a thousand reams upon a sea of ink. Not an unusually lovely face; a shorter nose would have launched more reams; and many a lass in oil or marble—as in any Correggio—would by comparison make Lisa only moderately fair. It is her smile that has made her fortune through the centuries—a nascent twinkle in her eyes, an amused and checked upcurving of her lips. What is she smiling at? The efforts of the musicians to entertain her? The leisurely diligence of an artist who paints her through a thousand days and never makes an end? Or is it not just Mona Lisa smiling, but woman, all women, saying to all men: "Poor impassioned lovers! A Nature blindly commanding continuance burns your nerves with an absurd hunger for our flesh, softens your brains with a quite unreasonable idealization of our charms, lifts you to lyrics that subside with consummation—and all that you may be precipitated into parentage! Could anything be more ridiculous? But we too are snared; we women pay a heavier price than you for your infatuation. And yet, sweet fools, it is pleasant to be desired, and life is redeemed when we are loved." Or was it only the smile of Leonardo himself that Lisa wore—of the inverted spirit that could hardly recall the tender touch of a woman's hand, and could believe in no other destiny for love or genius than obscene decomposition, and a little fame flickering out in man's forgetfulness?

When at last the sittings ended, Leonardo kept the picture, claiming that this most finished of all portraits was still incomplete. Perhaps the husband did not like the prospect of having his wife curl up her lips at him and his guests, hour after hour from his walls. Many years later Francis I bought it for 4000 crowns ($50,000),[22] and framed it in his palace at Fontaine-bleau. Today, after time and restorations have blurred its subtleties, it hangs in the majestic Salon Carré of the Louvre, daily amused by a thousand worshipers, and waiting for time to efface and confirm Mona Lisa's smile.

IV. IN MILAN AND ROME: 1506-16

Contemplating such a picture, and reckoning how many hours of thought must have guided so many minutes of the brush, we revise our judgment of Leonardo's seeming sloth, and perceive again that his work embodied the meditations of numberless inactive days; as when an author on an evening's stroll, or lying sleepless in the night, molds the next day's chapter, page, or verse, or rolls on the mind's tongue some savory adjective or bewitching phrase. And in those same five years at Florence that saw *The Virgin, Child, and St. Anne* in all its forms, and *Mona Lisa,* and the ferocious cartoon and melting *Battle,* Leonardo found time to paint other pictures, like the lovely portrait of Ginevra de' Benci now in Vienna, and the lost *Youthful Christ* that at last he yielded to the importunate Marchioness of Mantua (1504). But her agent sent her a revealing note: "Leonardo grows very impatient of painting, and spends most of his time on geometry."[23] Perhaps in those outwardly idle hours Leonardo was burying the artist in the scientist, the Apelles in the Faust.

However, science brought no fees; and though he was living simply now, he must have mourned the passing of those days when he had been the artist prince of Milan. When Charles d'Amboise, viceroy of Milan for Louis XII, invited him to return, Leonardo asked Soderini might he be excused for a few months from his commitments to Florence. Soderini complained that Leonardo had not yet earned the money paid him for *The Battle of Anghiari;* Leonardo raised the unearned sum and brought it to Soderini, who refused it. Finally (1506) Soderini, anxious to keep the good will of the French King, let Leonardo go on condition that he return to Florence after three months, or pay a penalty of 150 ducats ($1875?). He went; and though he revisited Florence in 1507, 1509, and 1511, he remained in the employ of Amboise and Louis in Milan till 1513. Soderini protested, but Louis overruled him with the gracious courtesy of confident strength. To make matters quite clear, Louis in 1507 appointed Leonardo *peintre et ingénieur ordinaire*—painter and engineer in ordinary—to the King of France.

It was no sinecure; Leonardo earned his keep. We hear of him again

decorating palaces, designing or building canals, preparing pageants, painting pictures, planning an equestrian monument of Marshal Trivulzio, and
collaborating in anatomical studies with Marcantonio della Torre. Probably during this second stay at Milan he painted two pictures that came
from the lower levels of his genius. The *St. John* of the Louvre has the
rounded contours of a woman, and such flowing curls and delicate features
as might have graced a Magdalen. *Leda and the Swan* (in a private collection in Rome) has a face and fleshly softness recalling the *St. John* and
the *Bacchus* formerly ascribed to Leonardo; but it is most likely a copy
from a lost painting or cartoon by the master. His fame would have
gained had these pictures died at birth.

In 1512 the French were chased out of Milan, and Lodovico's son Maximilian began a brief reign. Leonardo stayed a while, writing illegibile
notes on science and art while Milan burned with fires set by the Swiss.
But in 1513, hearing that Leo X had been chosen pope, he thought there
might be, in Medicean Rome, a place even for an artist of sixty-one years;
and he set out with four of his pupils. At Florence Leo's brother, Giuliano
de' Medici, attached Leonardo to his retinue, and assigned him a monthly
stipend of thirty-three ducats ($412?). Arrived in Rome, Leonardo was
welcomed by the art-loving Pope, who gave him rooms in the Belvedere
Palace. Presumably Leonardo met—certainly he influenced—Raphael and
Sodoma. Leo may have given him a commission for a picture, for Vasari
tells how surprised the Pope was to find Leonardo mixing varnish before
doing any painting; "this man," Leo is reported to have said, "will never do
anything, for he begins to think of the last stage before the first."[24] In
truth Leonardo had now ceased to be a painter; science more and more absorbed him; he studied anatomy at the hospital, worked on problems of
light, and wrote many pages on geometry. He amused his leisure by constructing a mechanical lizard with beard, horns, and wings, which he made
to flutter by an injection of quicksilver. Leo lost interest in him.

But meanwhile Francis I, a royal lover of art, had succeeded Louis XII.
In October 1515 he recaptured Milan. Apparently he invited Leonardo to
join him there. Early in 1516 Leonardo bade farewell to Italy, and accompanied Francis to France.

V. THE MAN

What sort of man was this prince of art? There are several alleged
portraits of him, but none before fifty. Vasari speaks with unusual fervor

of "the never adequately praised beauty of his body," and "the splendor of his appearance, which was extremely beautiful, and made every sorrowful soul serene"; but Vasari spoke from hearsay, and we have no representation of this godlike stage. Even in middle age Leonardo wore a long beard, carefully perfumed and curled. A portrait of Leonardo by himself, in the Royal Library at Windsor, shows a broad and benign face, with long flowing hair and a vast white beard. A magnificent painting in the Uffizi Gallery, by an unknown artist, pictures him with a strong face, searching eyes, white hair and beard, and soft black hat. The noble figure of Plato in Raphael's *School of Athens* (1509) has by tradition and some scholars been called a portrait of Leonardo.[24a] A self-portrait in chalk, in the Turin Gallery, shows him bald to the mid-pate, wrinkled in forehead, cheeks, and nose, and almost lost in hair. He seems to have grown old before his time, and died at sixty-seven, despite a careful vegetarian regimen, while Michelangelo, who scorned hygiene and entertained one ailment after another, reached eighty-nine. He dressed in luxurious clothing, while Michelangelo lived in his boots. Yet Leonardo in his prime was known for his strength, bending a horseshoe with his hands; he was an expert fencer, and skilled in riding and managing horses, which he loved as the noblest and fairest of animals. Apparently he drew, painted, and wrote with his left hand; this, rather than a desire to be illegible, made him write from right to left.

We have suggested that his homosexuality was not innate, but grew out of the unpleasant relation of a burdened stepmother with a bastard stepson. His need for receiving and returning affection found satisfaction with the handsome youths whom he later collected. He drew women much less frequently than men; he acknowledged their beauty, but seems to have shared Socrates' preference for boys. In all the jungle of his manuscripts there is no word of love or tenderness for women. Yet he understood well many phases of woman's nature; no one has surpassed him in representing virginal delicacy, motherly solicitude, or feminine subtlety. It may be that his sensitiveness, his secretive anagrams and codes, his double locking of his studio at night, had a root in his consciousness of abnormality as well as in his fear of being charged with heresy. He was not anxious to be read by the many. "The truth of things," he wrote, "is a supreme food for fine intelligences, but not for wandering wits."[25]

His sexual inversion may have influenced other elements of his character. He was the soul of gentle kindness to his friends. He protested against killing animals, "would not allow anyone to hurt any living thing";[26] he bought caged birds to free them.[27] In other aspects he seemed morally insensitive. He was apparently fascinated by the problem of designing instruments of war. He appears to have felt no strong resentment against the French for condemning to a dungeon the Lodovico who for sixteen years had maintained him handsomely in Milan. He went off without visible qualm to serve a Borgia whom Florence feared as a threat to her liberty. Like every artist, every author, and every homosexual, he was unusually self-conscious, sensitive, and vain. *Se tu sarai solo tu sarai tutto tuo,* he wrote; "if you are alone, you are all your own; with a companion you are half yourself; so you squander yourself according to the indiscretion of your company."[28] He could shine in company as a musician or a conversationalist, but he liked rather to isolate himself in rapt concentration on his tasks. "The chief gift of nature," he said (never having starved), "is liberty."[29]

His virtues were the better side of his faults. His aversion to sexual behavior may have left him free to spend his blood upon his work. His painful sensitivity opened up to him a thousand facets of reality unseen by the common eye. He would follow through a dozen streets, or all day long, some unusual face, and then, in his studio, draw it as well as if he had brought the model with him. His mind leaped at peculiarities—strange forms, actions, ideas. "The Nile," he wrote, "has discharged more water into the sea than is at present contained in all the waters of the earth"; consequently "all the sea and the rivers have passed through the mouth of the Nile an infinite number of times."[30] By a kindred bent he indulged himself in queer pranks; so one day he hid the cleaned gut of a ram in a room, and when his friends had gathered there, he inflated the gut by a bellows in an adjoining chamber, until the swelling skin crowded his guests against the walls. He recorded in his notebooks a variety of second-class fables and jokes.

His curiosity, his inversion, his sensitivity, his passion for perfection, all entered into his most fatal defect—the inability or unwillingess to complete what he had begun. Perhaps he entered upon each work of art with a view to solve a technical problem of composition, color, or design, and lost interest in the work when the solution had been found. Art, he said, lies in conceiving and designing, not in the actual execution; this was labor for lesser minds. Or he pictured to himself some subtlety, significance, or perfection that his patient, and at last impatient, hand could not realize, and he abandoned the effort in despair, as in the case of the face of Christ.[31] He passed too quickly from one task or subject to another; he was interested in too many things; he lacked a unifying purpose, a dominating idea; this "universal man" was a medley of brilliant fragments; he was possessed of and by too many abilities to harness them to one goal. In the end he mourned, "I have wasted my hours."[32]

He wrote five thousand pages, but never completed one book. Quantitatively he was more an author than an artist. He speaks of having composed 120 manuscripts; fifty remain. They are written from right to left in a half-Oriental script that almost lends color to the legend that at one time he traveled in the Near East, served the Egyptian sultan, and embraced the Mohammedan faith.[33] His grammar is poor, his spelling is individualistic. His reading was varied and desultory. He had a little library of thirty-seven volumes: the Bible, Aesop, Diogenes Laertius, Ovid, Livy, Pliny the Elder, Dante, Petrarch, Poggio, Filelfo, Ficino, Pulci, the *Travels* of "Mandeville," and treatises on mathematics, cosmography, anatomy, medicine, agriculture, palmistry, and the art of war. He remarked that "the knowledge of past times and of geography adorns and nourishes the intellect,"[34] but his many anachronisms show only a scattering acquaintance with history. He aspired to be a good writer; made several attempts at eloquence, as in his repeated descriptions of a flood;[35] and wrote vivid accounts of a tempest and a battle.[36] He clearly intended to publish some of his writings, and often began to put his notes into order for this purpose. So far as we know he published nothing during his lifetime; but he must have allowed some friends to see selected manuscripts, for there are references to his writings in Flavio Biondo, Jerome Cardan, and Cellini.

He wrote equally well on science and art, and divided his time almost evenly between them. The most substantial of his manuscripts is the *Trattato della pittura*, or *Treatise on Painting*, first published in 1651. Despite devoted modern editing, it is still a loose aggregation of fragments, in poor array, and often repetitious. Leonardo anticipates those who argue that painting can be learned only by painting; he thinks a sound knowledge of theory helps; and he laughs off his critics as being like "those of whom Demetrius declared that he took no more account of the wind that came from their mouths than of that which they expelled from their lower parts."[37] His basic precept is that the student of art should study nature rather than copy the works of other artists. "See to it, O painter, that when you go into the fields you give your attention to the various objects, looking carefully in turn first at one object then at another, making a bundle of different things selected among those of less value."[38] Of course the painter must study anatomy, perspective, modeling by light and shade; boundaries sharply defined make a picture seem wooden. "Always make the figure so that the bosom is not turned in the same direction as the head";[39] here is one secret of the grace in Leonardo's own compositions. Finally he urges: "Make figures with such action as may suffice to show what the figure has in mind."[40] Did he forget to do this with Mona Lisa, or did he exaggerate our ability to read the soul in the eyes and the lips?

Leonardo the man appears more clearly and variously in his drawings than in his paintings or his notes. Their number is legion; one manuscript alone—the *Codice Atlantico* in Milan—has seventeen hundred. Many are hasty sketches; many are such masterpieces that we must rank Leonardo as the ablest, subtlest, profoundest draughtsman of the Renaissance; there is nothing in the drawings of Michelangelo or Rembrandt that can match the amazing *Virgin, Christ, and St. Anne* in Burlington House. Leonardo used silverpoint, charcoal, red chalk, or pen and ink to draw almost every phase of physical, many of spiritual life. A hundred *putti* or *bambini* spread their fat and dimpled legs in his sketches; a hundred youths, half Greek in profile, half woman in soul; a hundred pretty maidens, of demure and tender mien, hair waving in the wind; athletes proud of their muscles, and warriors breathing battle or gleaming with armor and arms; saints from the soft beauty of Sebastian to the haggard skin of Jerome; gentle madonnas seeing the world redeemed in their babes; complex drawings of costumes for masquerades; and studies of shawls and scarves and laces and robes caressing the head or the neck, curling on the arm, or falling from shoulder or knee in folds that catch the light, invite the touch, and seem more real than the garments on our flesh. All these forms sing the zest and marvel of life; but scattered among them are horrible grotesques and caricatures—deformed heads, leering imbeciles, bestial faces, crippled bodies, shrews contorted with fury, a Medusa with snakes for hair, men desiccated and corrugated with age, women in the last stages of decay; this was another side of reality, and Leonardo's impartial universal eye caught it, fixed it, put it down resolutely on his sheets, as if to look ugly evil squarely in the face. He kept these horrors out of his paintings, which owed some loyalty to beauty, but he had to find room for them in his philosophy.

Perhaps nature pleased him more than man did, for nature was neutral, and could not be accused of evil as malice; everything in her was forgivable to an unbiased eye. So Leonardo drew many landscapes, and scolded Botticelli for ignoring them; he followed the tendrils of flowers faithfully with his pen; he hardly painted a picture without giving it added magic and depth by a background of trees, streams, rocks, mountains, clouds, and sea.

He almost banished architectural forms from his art so that he might leave more room for nature to enter and absorb the painted individual or group into the reconciling totality of things.

Sometimes Leonardo tried his hand at architectural design, but with chastening unsuccess. There are architectural fantasies among his drawings, quaint and half Syrian. He liked domes, and made a pretty sketch for a kind of St. Sophia that Lodovico might build in Milan; it never rose from the ground. Lodovico sent him to Pavia to help redesign the cathedral there, but Leonardo found the mathematicians and anatomists of Pavia more interesting than the cathedral. He mourned the noise, filth, and narrow congestion of Italian towns, studied town planning, and submitted to Lodovico a sketch for a city of two levels. On the lower level would move all commercial traffic, "and loads for the service and convenience of the common people"; the upper level would be a roadway twenty *braccia* (some forty feet) wide, upheld by colonnaded arcades, and "not to be used by vehicles, but solely for the convenience of the gentlefolk"; spiral staircases would occasionally connect the two levels, and every here and there a fountain would cool and cleanse the air.[41] Lodovico had no funds for such an upheaval, and the Milanese aristocracy remained on the earth.

VI. THE INVENTOR

It is hard for us to realize that to Lodovico, as to Caesar Borgia, Leonardo was primarily an engineer. Even the pageants that he planned for the Duke of Milan included ingenious automata. "Every day," says Vasari, "he made models and designs for the removal of mountains with ease, and to pierce them to pass from one place to another; and by means of levers, cranes, and winches to raise and draw heavy weights; he devised methods for cleaning harbors, and for raising water from great depths."[42] He developed a machine for cutting threads in screws; he worked along correct lines towards a water wheel; he devised frictionless roller-bearing band brakes.[43] He designed the first machine gun, and mortars with cog gears to elevate their range; a multiple-belt drive; three-speed transmission gears; an adjustable monkey wrench; a machine for rolling metal; a movable bed for a printing press; a self-locking worm gear for raising a ladder.[44] He had a plan for underwater navigation, but refused to explain it.[45] He revived the idea of Hero of Alexandria for a steam engine, and showed how steam pressure in a gun could propel an iron bolt twelve hundred yards. He invented a device for winding and evenly distributing yarn on a revolving spindle,[46] and scissors that would open and close with one movement of the hand. Often he let his fancy bemuse him, as when he suggested inflated skis for walking on water, or a water mill that would simultaneously play several musical instruments.[47] He described a parachute: "If a man have a tent made of linen, of which the apertures have all been stopped up, and it be twelve cubits across and twelve in depth, he will be able to throw himself down from any great height without sustaining any injury."[48]

Through half his life he pondered the problem of human flight. Like Tolstoi he envied the birds as a species in many ways superior to man. He studied in detail the operation of their wings and tails, the mechanics of their rising, gliding, turning, and descending. His sharp eye noted these movements with passionate curiosity, and his swift pencil drew and recorded them. He observed how birds avail themselves of air currents and pressures. He planned the conquest of the air:

> You will make an anatomy of the wings of a bird, together with the muscles of the breast, which move these wings. And you will do the same for a man, in order to show the possibility of a man sustaining himself in the air by the beating of wings.[49]... The rising of birds without beating their wings is not produced by anything other than their circular movement amid the currents of the wind.[50]... Your bird should have no other model than the bat, because its membranes serve as . . . . a means of binding together the framework of the wings.[51].... A bird is an instrument working according to mechanical law. This instrument it is within the power of man to reproduce with all its movements, but not with a corresponding degree of strength.[52]

He made several drawings of a screw mechanism by which a man, through the action of his feet, might cause wings to beat fast enough to raise him into the air.[53] In a brief essay *Sul volo, On Flight*, he described a flying machine made by him with strong starched linen, leather joints, and thongs of raw silk. He called this "the bird," and wrote detailed instructions for flying it.[54]

> If this instrument made with a screw . . . be turned swiftly, the said screw will make its spiral in the air, and it will rise high.[55]. . . Make trial of the machine over the water, so that if you fall you do not do yourself any harm.[56]. . . The great bird will take its first flight . . . filling the whole world with amazement and all records with its fame; and it will bring eternal glory to the nest where it was born.[57]

Did he actually try to fly? A note in the *Codice Atlantico*[58] says: "To-morrow morning, on the second day of January, 1496, I will make the thong and the attempt"; we do not know what this means. Fazio Cardano, father of Jerome Cardan the physicist (1501-76), told his son that Leonardo himself had essayed flight.[59] Some have thought that when Antonio, one of Leonardo's aides, broke his leg in 1510, it was in trying to fly one of Leonardo's machines. We do not know.

Leonardo was on the wrong tack; human flight came not by imitating the bird, except in gliding, but by applying the internal combustion engine to a propellor that could beat the air not downward but backward; forward speed made possible upward flight. But the noblest distinction of man is his passion for knowledge. Shocked by the wars and crimes of mankind, disheartened by the selfishness of ability and the perpetuity of poverty, saddened by the superstitions and credulities with which the nations and generations gild the brevity and indignities of life, we feel our race in some part redeemed when we see that it can hold a soaring dream in its mind and heart for three thousand years, from the legend of Daedalus and Icarus, through the baffled groping of Leonardo and a thousand others, to the glorious and tragic victory of our time.

VII. THE SCIENTIST

Side by side with his drawings, sometimes on the same page, sometimes scrawled across a sketch of a man or a woman, a landscape or a machine, are the notes in which this insatiable mind puzzled over the laws and operations of nature. Perhaps the scientist grew out of the artist: Leonardo's painting compelled him to study anatomy, the laws of proportion and perspective, the composition and reflection of light, the chemistry of pigments and oils; from these researches he was drawn to a more intimate investigation of structure and function in plants and animals; and from these inquiries he rose to a philosophical conception of universal and invariable natural law. Often the artist peered out again in the scientist; the scientific drawing might be itself a thing of beauty, or terminate in a graceful arabesque.

Like most scientists of his time, Leonardo tended to identify scientific method with experience rather than experiment.[60] "Remember," he counsels himself, "when discoursing about water, to adduce first experience and then reason."[61] Since any man's experience can be no more than a microscopic fragment of reality, Leonardo supplemented his with reading, which can be experience by proxy. He studied carefully but critically the writ-ings of Albert of Saxony,[62] gained a partial acquaintance with the ideas of Roger Bacon, Albertus Magnus, and Nicholas of Cusa, and learned much from association with Luca Pacioli, Marcantonio della Torre, and other professors in the University of Pavia. But he tested everything with his own experience. "Whoever refers to authorities in disputing ideas works with his memory rather than with his reason."[63] He was the least occult of the thinkers of his age. He rejected alchemy and astrology, and hoped for a time when "all astrologers will be castrated."[64]

He tried his hand at almost every science. He took enthusiastically to mathematics as the purest form of reasoning; he felt a certain beauty in geometrical figures, and drew some on the same page with a study for *The Last Supper*.[65] He expressed vigorously one of the fundamental principles of science: "There is no certainty where one can neither apply any of the mathematical sciences nor any of those that are based upon them."[66] And he proudly echoed Plato: "Let no man who is not a mathematician read the elements of my work."[67]

He was fascinated by astronomy. He proposed to "make glasses in order to see the moon large,"[68] but apparently he did not make them. He writes: "The sun does not move . . . the earth is not in the center of the circle of the sun, nor in the center of the universe."[69] "The moon has every month a winter and a summer."[70] He discusses acutely the causes of spots on the moon, and combats, on that matter, the views of Albert of Saxony.[71] Taking a lead from the same Albert, he argues that since "every heavy substance presses downward, and cannot be upheld perpetually, the whole earth must become spherical," and will ultimately be covered with water.[72]

He noticed on high elevations the fossil shells of marine animals, and concluded that the waters had once reached those altitudes[73] (Boccaccio had suggested this about 1338 in his *Filocopo*[74]). He rejected the notion of a universal flood,[75] and ascribed to the earth an antiquity that would have shocked the orthodoxy of his time. He assigned to the accumulations brought down by the Po a duration of 200,000 years. He made a map of Italy as he imagined it to have been in an early geological era. The Sahara Desert, he thought, had once been covered with salt water.[76] Mountains have been formed through erosion by rain.[77] The bottom of the sea is con-tinually rising with the detritus of all the streams that flow into it. "Very great rivers flow underground";[78] and the movement of life-giving water in the body of the earth corresponds to the movement of the blood in the body of man.[79] Sodom and Gomorrah were destroyed not by human wickedness but by slow geological action, probably the subsidence of their soil into the Dead Sea.[80]

Leonardo followed avidly the advances made in physics by Jean Buridan and Albert of Saxony in the fourteenth century. He wrote a hundred pages on motion and weight, and hundreds more on heat, acoustics, optics, color, hydraulics, and magnetism. "Mechanics is the paradise of the mathematical sciences, for by its means one comes to the fruit of mathematics" in useful work.[81] He delighted in pulleys, cranes, and levers, and saw no end to what they could lift or move; but he laughed at seekers for perpetual motion. "Force with material movement, and weight with percussion, are the four accidental powers in which all the works of mortals have their being and their end."[82] Despite these lines he was not a materialist. On the contrary he defined force as "a spiritual capacity . . . spiritual because the life in it is invisible and without body . . . impalpable because the body in which it is produced is increased neither in size nor in weight."[83]

He studied the transmission of sound, and reduced its medium to waves of air. "When the string of a lute is struck it . . . conveys a movement to a similar string of the same tone on another lute, as one may convince oneself by placing a straw on the string similar to the one struck."[84] He had his own notion of a telephone. "If you cause your ship to stop, and place the head of a long tube in the water, and place the other extremity to your ear, you will hear ships at a great distance from you. You can also do the same by placing the head of the tube upon the ground, and you will then hear anyone passing at a distance."[85]

But sight and light interested him more than sound. He marveled at the eye: "Who would believe that so small a space could contain the images of all the universe?"[86]—and he wondered even more at the power of the mind to recall an image long past. He gave an excellent description of the means by which spectacles compensate for the weakening of the muscles of the eyes.[87] He explained the operation of the eye by the principle of the *camera obscura:* in the *camera* and in the eye the image is inverted because of the pyramidal crossing of the light rays that come from the object into the *camera* or the eye.[88] He analyzed the refraction of sunlight in the rainbow. Like Leon Battista Alberti he had a good notion of complementary colors four centuries before the definitive work of Michel Chevreul.[89]

He planned, began, and left countless notes for, a treatise on water. The movements of water captivated his eye and mind; he studied placid and turbulent streams, springs and falls, bubbles and foam, torrents and cloudbursts, and the simultaneous fury of wind and rain. "Without water," he wrote, repeating Thales after twenty-one hundred years, "nothing can exist among us."[90] He anticipated Pascal's fundamental principle of hydrostatics—that the pressure exerted upon a fluid is transmitted by it.[91] He noted that the liquids in communicating vessels keep the same level.[92] Inheriting Milan's tradition of hydraulic engineering, he designed and built canals, suggested ways of conducting navigable canals under or over the rivers that crossed them, and proposed to free Florence from her need of Pisa as a port by canalizing the Arno from Florence to the sea.[93] Leonardo was not a Utopian dreamer, but he planned his studies and works as if he had a dozen lives to live.

Armed with the great text of Theophrastus on plants, he turned his alert mind to "natural history." He examined the system on which leaves are arranged about their stalks, and formulated its laws. He observed that the rings in a cross section of a tree trunk record the years of its growth by their number, and the moisture of the year by their width.[94] He seems to have shared several delusions of his time as to the power of certain animals to heal some human diseases by their presence or their touch.[95] He atoned for this uncharacteristic lapse into superstition by investigating the anatomy of the horse with a thoroughness to which recorded history had no precedent. He prepared a special treatise on the subject, but it was lost in the French occupation of Milan. He almost inaugurated modern comparative anatomy by studying the limbs of men and animals in juxtaposition. He set aside the superannuated authority of Galen, and worked with actual bodies. The anatomy of man he described not only in words but in drawings that excelled anything yet done in that field. He planned a book on the subject, and left for it hundreds of illustrations and notes. He claimed to "have dissected more than thirty human cadavers,"[96] and his countless drawings of the foetus, the heart, lungs, skeleton, musculature, viscera, eye, skull, and brain, and the principal organs in woman, support his claim. He was the first to give—in remarkable drawings and notes—a scientific representation of the uterus, and he described accurately the three membranes enclosing the foetus. He was the first to delineate the cavity of the bone that supports the cheek, now known as the antrum of Highmore. He poured wax into the valves of the heart of a dead bull to get an exact impression of the chambers. He was the first to characterize the moderator band (*catena*) of the right ventricle.[97] He was fascinated by the network of bloodvessels; he divined the circulation of the blood, but did not quite grasp its mechanism. "The heart," he wrote, "is much stronger than the other muscles. . . . The blood that returns when the heart opens

Fig. 15 — ANDREA DEL
SARTO: *Madonna delle
Arpie;* Uffizi Gallery,
Florence   PAGE 167

Fig. 16 — CRISTOFORO SOLARI:
*Tomb Effigies of Lodovico
il Moro and Beatrice d'Este;*
Certosa di Pavia   PAGE 190

Fig. 17—AMBROGIO DA PREDIS or LEO-
NARDO DA VINCI: *Portrait of Bianca
Sforza;* Pinacoteca Ambrosiana, Milan
PAGE 197

Fig. 18—LEONARDO DA VIN-
CI: *Virgin of the Rocks;*
Louvre, Paris   PAGE 204

Fig. 19—LEONARDO DA VINCI: *Self-portrait*, red chalk; Turin Gallery

PAGE 215

Fig. 20—LEONARDO DA VINCI: *Mona Lisa;* Louvre, Paris

PAGE 211

Fig. 21—PIERO DELLA FRAN-
CESCA: *Portrait of Duke
Federigo da Montefeltro;*
Uffizi Gallery, Florence

PAGE 232

Fig. 22—LUCA SIGNORELLI:
The End of the World
(detail), fresco; Ca-
thedral of Orvieto,
Chapel of San Brizio

PAGE 234

Fig. 23—Iacopo della Quercia: *The Nativity*, one of four reliefs from the main portal; San Petronio, Bologna   PAGE 237

Fig. 24—Iacopo della Quercia: *Noah's Ark*, relief; San Petronio, Bologna   PAGE 237

Fig. 25—PERUGINO: *Self-portrait;* Sistine Chapel, Rome   PAGE 245

Fig. 26 — PINTURICCHIO: *The Nativity;* Santa Maria del Popolo, Rome   PAGE 244

Fig. 27—ANDREA MANTEGNA: *Lodovico Gonzaga and His Family;* Castello, Mantua

PAGE 253

Fig. 28—ANDREA MANTEGNA: *Adoration of the Shepherds;* Metropolitan Museum of Art, New York

PAGE 253

Fig. 29—LEONARDO DA VINCI: *Portrait of Isabella d'Este;* Louvre, Paris   PAGE 255

Fig. 30—TITIAN: *Portrait of Isabella d'Este;* Kunsthistorisches Museum, Vienna   PAGE 256

is not the same as that which closes the valves."[98] He traced the blood-vessels, nerves, and muscles of the body with fair accuracy. He attributed old age to arteriosclerosis, and this to lack of exercise.[99] He began a volume *De figura umana*, on the proper proportions of the human figure as an aid to artists, and some of his ideas were incorporated in his friend Pacioli's treatise *De divina proportione*. He analyzed the physical life of man from birth to decay, and then planned a survey of mental life. "Oh, that it may please God to let me also expound the psychology of the habits of man in such fashion as I am describing his body!"[100]

Was Leonardo a great scientist? Alexander von Humboldt considered him "the greatest physicist of the fifteenth century,"[101] and William Hunter ranked him as "the greatest anatomist of his epoch."[102] He was not as original as Humboldt supposed; many of his ideas in physics had come down to him from Jean Buridan, Albert of Saxony, and other predecessors. He was capable of egregious errors, as when he wrote that "no surface of water that borders upon the air will ever be lower than that of the sea";[103] but such slips are remarkably few in so vast a production of notes on almost everything on the earth or in the sky. His theoretical mechanics were those of a highly intelligent amateur; he lacked training, instruments, and time. That he achieved so much in science, despite these handicaps and his labors in art, is among the miracles of a miraculous age.

From his studies in so many fields Leonardo rose at times to philosophy. "O marvelous Necessity! Thou with supreme reason constrainest all effects to be the direct result of their causes, and by a supreme and irrevocable law every natural action obeys thee by the shortest possible process."[104] This has all the proud ring of nineteenth-century science, and suggests that Leonardo had shed some theology. Vasari, in the first edition of his life of the artist, wrote that he was of "so heretical a cast of mind that he conformed to no religion whatever, accounting it perchance better to be a philosopher than a Christian"[105]—but Vasari omitted this passage in later editions. Like many Christians of the time, Leonardo took a fling now and then at the clergy; he called them Pharisees, accused them of deceiving the simple with bogus miracles, and smiled at the "false coin" of celestial promissory notes which they exchanged for the coinage of this world.[106] On one Good Friday he wrote: "Today all the world is in mourning because one man died in the Orient."[107] He seems to have thought that dead saints were incapable of hearing the prayers addressed to them.[108] "I could wish that I had such power of language as should avail me to censure those who would extol the worship of men above that of the sun. . . . Those who have wished to worship men as gods have made a very grave error."[109] He took more liberties with Christian iconography than any other Renaissance artist: he suppressed halos, put the Virgin across her mother's knee, and made the infant Jesus try to bestride the symbolic lamb. He saw mind in matter, and believed in a spiritual soul, but apparently thought that the soul could act only through matter, and only in harmony with invariable laws.[110] He wrote that "the soul can never be corrupted with the corruption of the body,"[111] but he added that "death destroys memory as well as life,"[112] and "without the body the soul can neither act nor feel."[113] He addressed the Deity with humility and fervor in some passages;[114] but at other times he identified God with Nature, Natural Law, and "Necessity."[115] A mystic pantheism was his religion until his final years.

VIII. IN FRANCE: 1516-19

Arrived in France, Leonardo, sixty-four and ill, was established with his faithful companion Francesco Melzi, twenty-four, in a pretty house at Cloux, between the town and château of Amboise on the Loire, then the frequent residence of the King. His contract with Francis I designated him as "painter, engineer, and architect of the King, and state mechanician," at an annual salary of seven hundred crowns ($8750). Francis was generous, and appreciated genius even in its decline. He enjoyed conversation with Leonardo, and "affirmed," reported Cellini, "that never had any man come into the world who knew so much as Leonardo, and that not only in sculpture, painting, and architecture, for in addition he was a great philosopher."[116] Leonardo's anatomical drawings amazed the physicians at the French court.

For a time he labored manfully to earn his salary. He arranged masques and pageants for royal displays; worked on plans to bind the Loire and the Saône with canals and to drain the marshes of Sologne,[117] and may have shared in designing parts of the Loire châteaux; some evidence links his name with the jewel loveliness of Chambord.[118] Probably he did little painting after 1517, for in that year he suffered a paralytic stroke that immobilized his right side; he painted with his left hand, but needed both hands for careful work. He was now a wrinkled wreck of the youth whose repute for beauty of body and face came down to Vasari across half a century. His once proud self-confidence faded, his serenity of spirit yielded to the pains of decay, his love of life gave place to religious hope. He made a simple will, but he asked for all the services of the Church at his funeral.

Once he had written: "As a day well spent makes it sweet to sleep, so a life well used makes it sweet to die."[119]

Vasari tell a touching story of how Leonardo died, on May 2, 1519, in the arms of the King; but apparently Francis was elsewhere at the time.[120] The body was buried in the cloister of the Collegiate Church of St. Florentin in Amboise. Melzi wrote to Leonardo's brothers informing them of the event, and added: "It would be impossible for me to express the anguish that I have suffered from this death; and while my body holds together I shall live in perpetual unhappiness. And for good reason. The loss of such a man is mourned by all, for it is not in the power of Nature to create another. May Almighty God rest his soul forever!"[121]

How shall we rank him?—though which of us commands the variety of knowledge and skills required to judge so multiple a man? The fascination of his polymorphous mind lures us into exaggerating his actual achievement; for he was more fertile in conception than in execution. He was not the greatest scientist or engineer or painter or sculptor or thinker of his time; he was merely the man who was all of these together and in each field rivaled the best. There must have been men in the medical schools who knew more of anatomy than he; the most notable works of engineering in the territory of Milan had been accomplished before Leonardo came; both Raphael and Titian left a more impressive total of fine paintings than has survived from Leonardo's brush; Michelangelo was a greater sculptor; Machiavelli and Guicciardini were profounder minds. And yet Leonardo's studies of the horse were probably the best work done in the anatomy of that age; Lodovico and Caesar Borgia chose him, from all Italy, as their engineer; nothing in the paintings of Raphael or Titian or Michelangelo equals *The Last Supper;* no painter has matched Leonardo in subtlety of nuance, or in the delicate portrayal of feeling and thought and pensive tenderness; no statue of the time was so highly rated as Leonardo's plaster *Sforza;* no drawing has ever surpassed *The Virgin, Child, and St. Anne;* and nothing in Renaissance philosophy soared above Leonardo's conception of natural law.

He was not "the man of the Renaissance," for he was too gentle, introverted, and refined to typify an age so violent and powerful in action and speech. He was not quite "the universal man," since the qualities of statesman or administrator found no place in his variety. But, with all his limitations and incompletions, he was *the fullest man* of the Renaissance, perhaps of all time. Contemplating his achievement we marvel at the distance that man has come from his origins, and renew our faith in the possibilities of mankind.

IX. THE SCHOOL OF LEONARDO

He left behind him at Milan a bevy of younger artists who admired him too much to be original. Four of them—Giovanni Antonio Boltraffio, Andrea Salaino, Cesare da Sesto, and Marco d'Oggiono—are figured in stone at the base of the patriarchal statue of Leonardo in the Piazza della Scala in Milan. There were others—Andrea Solari, Gaudenzio Ferrari, Bernardino de' Conti, Francesco Melzi. . . . All had worked in Leonardo's studio, and learned to imitate his grace of line without reaching his subtlety or depth. Two other painters acknowledged him as their teacher, though we are not sure that they knew him in the flesh. Giovanni Antonio Bazzi, who allowed himself to come down in history under the name of Sodoma, may have met him in Milan or Rome. Bernardino Luini exalted sentiment, but with an engaging straightforwardness that charms away reproach. He chose as his repeated subject the Madonna and her Child; perhaps he rightly saw in this most hackneyed of all pictorial themes the supreme embodiment of life as a stream of births, of love as surmounting death, and of womanly beauty that is never mature except in motherhood. More than any other follower of Leonardo he caught the master's effeminate delicacy and the tenderness—not the mystery—of the Leonardesque smile; the *Holy Family* in the Ambrosiana at Milan is a delectable variation on the Master's *Virgin, Child, and St. Anne;* and the *Sposalizio* at Saronno has all the grace of Correggio. He seems never to have doubted, as Leonardo did, the touching story of the peasant maid who bore a god; he softened the lines and colors of his paintings with a simple piety that Leonardo could hardly feel or represent; and the unwilling skeptic who can still respect a lovely and inspiring myth will pause longer, in the Louvre, before Luini's *Sleep of the Infant Jesus* and *Adoration of the Magi* than before Leonardo's *St. John,* and will find in them a profounder satisfaction and truth.

With these elegant epigoni the great age of Milan died away. The architects, painters, sculptors, and poets that had made Lodovico's court surpassingly brilliant had seldom been natives of the city, and many of them sought other pastures when the gentle despot fell. No outstanding talent rose in the ensuing chaos and servitude to take their place; and a generation later the castle and the cathedral were the sole reminders that for a magnificent decade—the last of the fifteenth century—Milan had led the pageant of Italy.

CHAPTER VIII

Tuscany and Umbria

I. PIERO DELLA FRANCESCA

IF now we cross back into Tuscany, we find that Florence, like another Paris, absorbed the talents of her dependencies, and left only here and there among them a figure that bids us pause in our pilgrimage. Lucca bought a charter of autonomy from the Emperor Charles IV (1369), and managed to remain a free city till Napoleon. The Lucchesi were properly proud of their eleventh-century cathedral; they kept it in form with repeated restorations, and made it a veritable museum of art. There eye and soul may still feast on the lovely stalls (1452) and stained glass (1485) of the choir; on a noble tomb by Iacopo della Quercia (1406); on one of Fra Bartolommeo's profoundest pictures—*Madonna with St. Stephen and St. John the Baptist* (1509); and on one handsome work after another by Lucca's own son, Matteo Civitali.

Pistoia preferred Florence to freedom. The conflict of "Whites" and "Blacks" so disordered the city that the government appealed to the Florentine Signory to take over its management (1306). Thereafter Pistoia received its art as well as its laws from Florence. For the Ospedale del Ceppo—named from the hollow stump into which one might drop contributions for the hospital—Giovanni della Robbia and some aides designed (1514-25) a frieze of gleaming terra-cotta reliefs of the Seven Works of Mercy: clothing the naked, feeding the hungry, nursing the sick, visiting prisons, receiving strangers, burying the dead, and comforting the bereaved. Here religion was at its best.

Pisa, once so rich that it could transform mountains of marble into a cathedral, baptistery, and Leaning Tower, had owed its wealth to its strategic position at the mouth of the Arno. For that reason Florence beat it into subjection (1405). Pisa never reconciled itself to this servitude; it rebelled again and again. In 1431 the Florentine Signory expelled from Pisa all males capable of bearing arms, and kept their women and children as hostages for their good behavior.[1] Pisa took advantage of the French invasion (1495) to reassert its independence; for fourteen years it fought off the Florentine mercenaries; finally, after a fanatically heroic resistance, it succumbed. Many leading families, choosing exile rather than vassalage, migrated to France or Switzerland—among them the Sismondi ancestors of the historian who in 1838 wrote an eloquent account of these events in his *History of the Italian Republics*. Florence tried to atone for her despotism by financing the University of Pisa, and sending her artists to adorn the cathedral and the Campo Santo; but not even the famous frescoes of Benozzo Gozzoli in that Holy Field of the dead could comfort a city geologically doomed to decay. For the detritus of the Arno gradually and mercilessly advanced the shore line, creating a new port at Livorno—Leghorn—six miles away; and Pisa lost the commercial situation that had made its fortune and its tragedy.

San Gimignano took its name from St. Geminian, who saved the incipient village from the hordes of Attila about 450. It rose to some prosperity in the fourteenth century; but its rich families divided into murderous factions, and built the fifty-six fortress towers (now reduced to thirteen) that gave the town its fame as San Gimignano delle Belle Torri. In 1353 the strife grew so violent that the city accepted with resigned relief its absorption into the Florentine dominion. Thereafter life seems to have gone out of it. Domenico Ghirlandaio made the Santa Fina Chapel of the Collegiata famous with his finest frescoes, and Benozzo Gozzoli rivaled his Medici Chapel cavalcades with scenes from the life of St. Augustine in the church of Sant' Agostino, and Benedetto da Maiano carved superb altars for those shrines. But commerce took other routes, industry starved, stimulus died; San Gimignano remained becalmed in her narrow streets and disintegrating towers; and in 1928 Italy made the city a national monument, preserved as a half-living picture of medieval life.

Forty miles up the Arno from Florence, Arezzo was a vital spot in the web of Florentine defense and trade. The Signory itched and angled to control it; in 1384 Florence bought the city from the duke of Anjou; Arezzo never forgot the indignity. It gave birth to Petrarch, Aretino, and Vasari, but failed to hold them, for its soul still belonged to the Middle Ages. Luca Spinello, also called Aretino, went from Arezzo to paint in the Campo Santo at Pisa lively frescoes stirring with the shock of battle (1390-2), but also portraying Christ and Mary and the saints with an intense and moving piety. If we wish to believe Vasari, Luca portrayed Satan so repulsively that the Devil appeared to him in a dream and reprimanded him with such violence that Luca died of fright—at ninety-two.[2]

Northeast of Arezzo, on the upper Tiber, the town of Borgo San Sepolcro seemed too small to have and to hold an artist of high rank.

Piero di Benedetto was called della Francesca after his mother; for she, left pregnant with him after his father's death, reared him lovingly, and guided and aided him to an education in mathematics and art. Though we know that he was born in the Town of the Holy Sepulcher, the earliest notice of him places him in Florence in 1439. That was the year in which Cosimo brought the Council of Ferrara to Florence; presumably Piero saw the gorgeous costumes of the Byzantine prelates and princes who had come to negotiate the reunion of the Greek with the Roman Church. We may more confidently presume that he studied the frescoes of Masaccio in the Brancacci Chapel; this was routine for any art student in Florence. The dignity, power, and resolute perspective of Masaccio mingled in Piero's art with the picturesque grandeur and majestic beards of the Eastern potentates.

When he returned to Borgo (1442) Piero was elected, aged thirty-six, to the town council. Three years later he received his first recorded commission: to paint a *Madonna della Misericordia* for the church of San Francesco. It is still preserved in the Palazzo Comunale: a strange assemblage of somber saints, a semi-Chinese Virgin enfolding eight praying figures in the robe of her mercy, a stiff Archangel Gabriel making a very formal announcement of her motherhood to Mary, an almost peasant Christ in a grimly realistic *Crucifixion*, and vivid forms of the Mater Dolorosa and the Apostle John. This is half-primitive painting, but powerful: no pretty sentiment, no delicate decoration, no idealized refinement of the tragic tale; but bodies soiled and consumed with the struggle of life, and yet rising to nobility in the silence of their suffering, their prayers, and their forgiveness.

His fame now spread through Italy, and Piero was in demand. At Ferrara (1449?) he painted murals in the Ducal Palace. Rogier van der Weyden was then court painter there; probably Piero learned from him something of the new technique of painting with pigments mixed in oil. At Rimini (1451) he pictured Sigismondo Malatesta—tyrant, murderer, and patron of art—in an attitude of pious prayer, redeemed by the presence of two magnificent dogs. In Arezzo, at intervals between 1452 and 1464, Piero painted for the church of San Francesco a series of frescoes that mark the zenith of his art. They told mainly the story of the True Cross, culminating in its capture by Khosru II, and its recovery and restoration to Jerusalem by the Emperor Heraclius; but they found place also for such episodes as the death of Adam, the Queen of Sheba's visit to Solomon, and the victory of Constantine over Maxentius at the Milvian Bridge. The emaciated figure of the dying Adam, the worn face and drooping breasts of Eve, the powerful bodies of their sons and their almost equally virile daughters, the flowing majesty of the Queen of Sheba's retinue, the profound and disillusioned face of Solomon, the startling incidence of light in *The Dream of Constantine*, the fascinating turmoil of men and horses in *The Victory of Heraclius*—these are among the most impressive frescoes of the Renaissance.

Probably in the interludes of this major effort Piero painted an altarpiece at Perugia, and some murals in the Vatican—later whitewashed to make more space for Raphael's conquering brush. At Urbino in 1469 he produced his most famous picture—the arresting profile of Duke Federigo da Montefeltro. Federigo's nose had been broken, and his right cheek scarred, in a tournament. Piero showed the left side, intact but hilly with moles, and portrayed the crooked nose with dauntless realism; he made the firm lips and half-closed eyes and sober face reveal the administrator, the stoic, the man who has plumbed the shallowness of wealth and power; we miss, however, in these features, the refinement of taste that guided Federigo in organizing music at his court and collecting his celebrated library of classical and illuminated manuscripts. Paired with this portrait in the Uffizi diptych is a profile of Federigo's wife, Battista Sforza—a face almost Dutch, and pale to sallowness—against a background of fields, hills, sky, and battlemented walls. On the obverse of the portraits Piero painted two "triumphs"—one chariot drawing Federigo, the other Battista, in solemn state; both elegantly absurd.

About 1480 Piero, now sixty-four, began to suffer from eye trouble. Vasari thought he became blind, but apparently he could still draw well. In those declining years he wrote a manual of perspective, and a treatise *De quinque corporibus regolaribus*, in which he analyzed the geometrical relations and proportions involved in painting. His pupil Luca Pacioli adopted Piero's ideas in his own book *De divina proportione;* and perhaps through this mediation Piero's mathematical ideas influenced Leonardo's studies in the geometry of art.

The world has forgotten Piero's books and has rediscovered his paintings. When we place him in time, and note that his work was completed when Leonardo's had just begun, we must assign him a rank with the leading Italian painters of the fifteenth century. His figures seem crude, their faces coarse; many seem cast in a Flemish mold. What ennobles them is their quiet dignity, their grave mien and stately carriage, the restrained and yet dramatic force of their action. What transfigures them is the harmonious flow of the design, and, above all, the uncompromising faithfulness with which Piero's hand, disdaining idealization and sentimentality, has represented what his eye has seen and his mind has conceived.

He lived too far from the intense centers of the Renaissance to attain the potential perfection, or to exert the full influence, of his art. Nevertheless he numbered Signorelli among his pupils, and shared in forming Luca's style. It was Raphael's father who invited Piero to Urbino; and though this was fourteen years before Raphael's birth, that blessed youth must have seen and studied the paintings left by Piero there and in Perugia. Melozzo da Forlì learned from Piero something of strength and grace in design; and Melozzo's angel musicians in the Vatican recall those which Piero painted in one of his final works—the *Nativity* of the London National Gallery—even as Piero's angel choristers recall Luca della Robbia's *Cantoria*. So men hand down to their successors their heritage—their lore and codes and skills; and transmission becomes half the technique of civilization.

II. SIGNORELLI

When Piero della Francesca was painting his masterpieces at Arezzo, Lazzaro Vasari, great-grandfather of the historian, invited a young art student, Luca Signorelli, to come and live in the Vasari home and study with Piero. Luca had first seen the light at Cortona, some fourteen miles southeast of Arezzo (1441). He was only eleven when Piero came, but he was twenty-four when Piero finished. In the interval the youth, taking with passion to the painter's art, learned from Piero to draw the nude body with merciless veracity—with a stern rigor that went back to his teacher, and a masculine force that pointed forward to Michelangelo. In the studio and the hospitals, under the gibbet and in the cemeteries, he sought the human body, as naked as he could find it; and he asked of it not beauty but strength. He seems to have cared for nothing else; if he painted anything else it was by impatient concession; and then, as often as not, he would use nude figures for incidental ornament. Like Michelangelo he was not at home (if we may speak so carelessly) with female nudes; he drew them with scant success; and among males he preferred not the young and fair, as Leonardo did and Sodoma, but the middle-aged man in the full development of musculature and virility.

Carrying this passion with him, Signorelli moved about among the cities of central Italy depositing nudes. After some early works in Arezzo and

San Sepolcro he moved on to Florence (*c.* 1475), and there painted, and presented to Lorenzo, *The School of Pan,* a canvas crowded with naked pagan gods. Probably for Lorenzo he painted the *Virgin and Child* now in the Uffizi: the Virgin ample but beautiful, the background largely composed of naked men; here Michelangelo would find a hint for his Doni *Holy Family.*

And yet this carnal pagan could paint piously. The Virgin in his Uffizi *Holy Family* is one of the fairest figures in Renaissance art. At the behest of Pope Sixtus IV he went to Loreto (*c.* 1479), and adorned the sanctuary of Santa Maria with excellent frescoes of the evangelists and other saints. Three years later we find him in Rome contributing to the Sistine Chapel a scene from the life of Moses—admirable in its male figures, ungainly in its women. Called to Perugia (1484), he painted some minor frescoes in the cathedral. Thenceforth he seems to have made Cortona his home, producing pictures there for delivery elsewhere, and leaving it chiefly for major assignments in Siena, Orvieto, and Rome. In the cloister of the monastery of Monte Oliveto at Chiusuri, near Siena, he depicted scenes from the life of St. Benedict. For the church of Sant' Agostino in Siena he completed an altarpiece which was ranked among his best works; only the wings remain. For the palace of the Sienese dictator, Pandolfo Petrucci, he painted episodes from classic history or legend. Then he passed on to Orvieto for his culminating achievement.

The cathedral council there had waited in vain for Perugino to come and decorate the chapel of San Brizio. It had considered and rejected Pinturicchio. Now (1499) it summoned Signorelli, and bade him complete the work that Fra Angelico had begun in that chapel half a century before. It was the favorite altar in the great cathedral, for over it hung an old picture of the Madonna di San Brizio, who (the people liked to believe) could ease the pains of childbirth, keep lovers and husbands faithful, ward off the ague, and quiet a storm. Under the ceiling frescoes where Fra Angelico had pictured the Last Judgment in the full spirit of medieval hopes and fears, Signorelli painted similar themes—*Antichrist, The End of the World, The Resurrection of the Dead, Paradise,* and *The Descent of the Damned Into Hell.* But these old themes were for him merely a frame wherein to show the naked bodies of men and women in a hundred different attitudes, and in a hundred varieties of joy and pain. Not until Michelangelo's *Last Judgment* would the Renaissance see again such an orgy of human flesh. Bodies handsome or deformed, faces bestial or celestial, the grimaces of devils, the agony of the condemned sprayed by jets of fire, the torturing of one sinner by breaking his teeth and his thighbone with a club—did Signorelli delight in these scenes, or was he instructed to paint them as encouragement to piety? In any case he pictured himself (in a corner of the *Antichrist*) looking upon the melee with the equanimity of the saved.

After spending three years on these frescoes, Signorelli returned to Cortona, and painted a *Dead Christ* for the church of Santa Margherita. It was about this time that tragedy overtook him in the violent death of his favorite son. When the corpse was brought to him, says Vasari, "he caused it to be stripped, and with extraordinary fortitude, without shedding a tear, he made a drawing of the body, so that he might always behold in this work of his hands what Nature had given him and cruel Fortune had taken away."[3]

In 1508 a different misfortune came. With Perugino, Pinturicchio, and Sodoma he was commissioned by Julius II to decorate the papal chambers in the Vatican. While their labors were progressing Raphael arrived, and so pleased the Pope with his initial frescoes that Julius turned over all the rooms to him, and dismissed the other artists. Signorelli was then sixty-seven, and perhaps his hand had lost its skill or steadiness. Nevertheless, eleven years later, he painted with success and acclaim an altarpiece commissioned by the Company of San Girolamo at Arezzo; when it was finished the brothers of the Company came to Cortona and carried this *Madonna and Saints* on their shoulders all the way to Arezzo. Signorelli accompanied them, and again lodged in the house of the Vasari. There Giorgio Vasari, a lad of eight, saw him, and received from him long-remembered words of encouragement in the study of art. Once a youth of impetuous passion, Signorelli was now a kindly old gentleman, nearing eighty, living in moderate prosperity in his native town, and honored by all. At the age of eighty-three he was elected for the last time to the governing council of Cortona. In that year, 1524, he died.

Excellent scholars[4] have thought that Signorelli's fame is inadequate to his deserts; but perhaps it exceeds them. He was a facile draftsman, who amazes us with his studies of anatomy, posture, perspective, and foreshortening, and amuses us with his use of human figures in composition and ornament. Sometimes in his Madonnas he reaches a note of tenderness, and the musician angels at Loreto have charmed discriminating minds. But for the rest he was the apostle of the body as anatomy; he gave it no sensual softness, no voluptuous grace, no glory of color, no magic of light and shade; he seldom realized that the function of the body is to be the outward expression and instrument of a subtle and intangible spirit or character, and that the sovereign task of art is to find and reveal that soul through its veil of flesh. Michelangelo took from Signorelli this idolatry of anatomy, this loss of the end in the means, and in the *Last Judgment* of the Sistine Chapel he repeated on a larger scale the physiological frenzy of the Orvieto frescoes; but on the ceiling of that same chapel, and in his sculpture, he used the body as the voice of the soul. In Signorelli painting passed at one step from the terrors and tenderness of medieval art to the strained and soulless exaggerations of baroque.

III. SIENA AND SODOMA

In the fourteenth century Siena had almost kept pace with Florence in commerce, government, and art. In the fifteenth she exhausted herself with such fanatical factional violence as no other city in Europe could match. Five parties—*monti*, hills, the Sienese called them—ruled the city in turn; each in turn was overthrown by revolution, and its more influential members, sometimes numbering thousands, were exiled. We may judge the bitterness of this strife from the oath that two of the factions swore to end it (1494). An awed eyewitness describes them as gathering solemnly at dead of night, in separate aisles, in their vast and dimly lit cathedral.

> The conditions of the peace were read, which took up eight pages, together with an oath of the most horrible sort, full of maledictions, imprecations, excommunications, invocations of evil, confiscations of goods, and so many other woes that to hear it was a terror; even in the hour of death no sacrament should save, but should rather add to the damnation of, those who should break the conditions; so that I . . . believe that never was made or heard a more awful or horrible oath. Then the notaries, on either side of the altar, wrote down the names of all the citizens, who swore upon the crucifix, of which there was one on each side; and every couple of the one or other faction kissed, and the church bells rang, and *Te Deum laudamus* was sung with the organs and the choir while the oath was being sworn.[5]

From this turmoil a dominant family emerged, the Petrucci. In 1497 Pandolfo Petrucci made himself dictator, took the title *il Magnifico*, and proposed to give Siena the order, peace, and gentlemanly autocracy that had been the fortune of Florence under the Medici. Pandolfo was clever, and always landed on his feet after any crisis, even eluding the vengeance of Caesar Borgia; he patronized art with some discrimination; but he so often resorted to secret assassination that his death (1512) was celebrated with universal acclaim. In 1525 the desperate city paid the Emperor Charles V 15,000 ducats to take it under his protection.

In the lucid intervals of peace Sienese art had its final fling. Antonio Barile continued the medieval tradition of the wondrous carving of wood. Lorenzo di Mariano built in the church of Fontegiusta a high altar of classic beauty. Iacopo della Quercia took his cognomen from a village in Siena's hinterland. His early sculptures were financed by Orlando Malevolti, who thus belied his name of Evil Faces. When Orlando was banished for taking the losing side in politics, Iacopo left Siena for Lucca (1390), where he designed a stately tomb for Ilaria del Carretto. After competing unsuccessfully against Donatello and Brunellesco in Florence, he went on to Bologna, and carved over and alongside the portal of San Petronio marble statues and reliefs which are among the finest sculptures of the Renaissance (1425-8). Michelangelo saw them there seventy years later, admired the vigor of the nude and virile figures, and found in them for a time inspiration and stimulus. Returning to Siena, Iacopo spent much of the next ten years on his masterpiece, the Fonte Gaia. On the base of this Gay Fountain he cut in marble a relief of the Virgin as the official sovereign of the city; around her he represented the Seven Cardinal Virtues; for good measure he added scenes from the Old Testament, and filled the surviving spaces with children and animals—all with a power of conception and execution that presaged Michelangelo. For this work Siena renamed him Iacopo della Fonte, and paid him 2200 crowns ($55,000?). He died at sixty-four, exhausted by his art and mourned by the citizens.

Through most of the fourteenth and fifteenth centuries the proud city engaged a hundred artists, of any provenance, to make its cathedral the architectural jewel of Italy. From 1413 to 1423 Domenico del Coro, a master of intarsia, was superintendent of the cathedral work; he and Matteo di Giovanni and Domenico Beccafumi and Pinturicchio and many others inlaid the floor of the great shrine with marble marquetry picturing episodes from Scripture, and making this the most remarkable church pavement in the world. Antonio Federighi carved for the cathedral two handsome baptismal fonts, and Lorenzo Vecchietta cast for it a dazzling tabernacle in bronze. Sano di Matteo raised the Loggia della Mercanzia in the Campo (1417-38), and Vecchietta and Federighi faced its pillars with harmonious statuary. The fourteenth century saw a dozen famous palaces take form—the Salimbeni, the Buonsignori, the Saracini, the Grottanelli . . . and about 1470 Bernardo Rossellino supplied plans for the Florentine-style palace of the Piccolomini family. Andrea Bregno designed for the Piccolomini an altar in the cathedral (1481); and Cardinal Francesco Piccolomini built, as an adjunct to the *duomo*, a library (1495) to house the books and manuscripts bequeathed to him by his uncle Pius II. Lorenzo di Mariano gave the library one of the handsomest portals in Italy; and Pinturicchio and his aides (1503-8) painted on the walls, within superb architectural frames, delightful frescoes picturing scenes in the life of the scholar Pope.

Siena in the fifteenth century was rich in painters of secondary excellence. Taddeo Bartoli, Domenico di Bartolo, Lorenzo di Pietro called Vecchietta, Stefano di Giovanni called Sassetta, Sani di Pietro, Matteo di Giovanni, Francesco di Giorgio—all continued the strong religious tradition of Sienese art, painting devout themes and somber saints, often in stiff and cramping polyptychs, as if resolved to prolong the Middle Ages forever. Sassetta, recently restored to fame by a passing whim of critical opinion, painted in simple line and color a charming procession of Magi and attendants moving sedately through mountain passes to the crib of Christ; he described in a graceful triptych the birth of the Virgin; celebrated the wedding of St. Francis to poverty; and died in 1450, "stabbed through and through by the sharp southwest wind."[5a]

Only toward the end of the century did Siena produce an artist whose name, for good or evil, rang through Italy. His real name was Giovanni Antonio Bazzi, but his ribald contemporaries rechristened him Sodoma because he was so candid a catamite. He accepted the cognomen with good humor as a title that many deserved but failed to obtain. Born at Vercelli (1477), he moved to Milan, and may have learned painting and pederasty from Leonardo. He put a Vincian smile on his Brera *Madonna*, and copied Leonardo's *Leda* so well that for centuries his imitation was taken for the Master's original. Migrating to Siena after Lodovico's fall, he developed a style of his own, picturing Christian subjects with a pagan joy in the human form. Perhaps it was during this first stay at Siena that Bazzi painted a powerful *Christ at the Column*—about to be scourged, yet physically perfect. For the monks of Monte Oliveto Maggiore he told the story of St. Benedict in a series of frescoes, some carelessly done, some so seductively beautiful that the abbot insisted, before paying Sodoma, that the nude figures should be prefaced with clothing to preserve peace of mind in the monastery.[6]

When the banker Agostino Chigi visited his native Siena in 1507 he took a fancy to Sodoma's work, and invited him to Rome. Pope Julius II set the artist to work painting one of the rooms of Nicholas V in the Vatican, but Sodoma spent so much time living up to his name that the old Pope soon turned him out. Raphael replaced him, and Sodoma, in a modest moment, studied the young master's style, and absorbed something of his smooth finish and delicate grace. Chigi rescued Sodoma by engaging him to paint in the Villa Chigi the story of Alexander and Roxana, and soon Leo X, succeeding Julius, restored Sodoma to papal favor. Giovanni painted for the jolly Pope a nude Lucretia stabbing herself to death; Leo rewarded him well, and made him a Cavalier of the Order of Christ.

Returning to Siena with these laurels, Sodoma received numerous commissions from clergy and laity. Though apparently a skeptic, he painted Madonnas almost as lovely as Raphael's. The martyrdom of St. Sebastian was a subject especially to his taste; and his rendering of the theme in the Pitti Palace has never been excelled. In the church of San Domenico at Siena he pictured St. Catherine fainting, so realistically that Baldassare Peruzzi pronounced the painting incomparable in its kind. While engaged on these religious subjects, Sodoma scandalized Siena with what Vasari calls his "bestial pursuits."

> His manner of life was licentious and dishonorable; and as he always had boys and beardless youths about him, of whom he was inordinately fond, this earned him the name of Sodoma. Instead of feeling shame, he gloried in it, writing verses about it, and singing them to the accompaniment of the lute. He loved to fill his house with all kinds of curious animals: badgers, squirrels, apes, catamounts, dwarf asses, Barbary race horses, Elba ponies, jackdaws, bantams, turtle doves, and similar creatures. . . . In addition to these he had a raven which he had taught to speak so well that it imitated his voice, especially in answering the door, and many mistook it for its master. The other animals were so tame that they were always about him, with their strange gambols, so that his house resembled a veritable Noah's ark.[7]

He married a woman of good family; but after giving him one child she left him. Having worn out his welcome and his income in Siena, he went to Volterra, Pisa, and Lucca (1541-2), seeking new patrons. When these too ran out, Sodoma went back to Siena, shared his poverty for seven years with his animals, and died at seventy-two. He had accomplished in art all that a skilled hand could do without a deepened soul to guide it.

The man who superseded him at Siena was Domenico Beccafumi. When

Perugino came there in 1508 Domenico studied his style. When Perugino left, Domenico sought further instruction in Rome, familiarized himself with the remains of classic art, and sought the secrets of Raphael and Michelangelo. In Siena again, he first imitated Sodoma, then rivaled him. The Signory asked him to decorate the Sala del Consistorio; he painted its walls during six laborious years (1529-35) with scenes from Roman history; the result was technically excellent, spiritually dead.

When Beccafumi died (1551) the Sienese Renaissance was finished. Baldassare Peruzzi was of Siena, but left it for Rome. Siena fell back into the arms of the Virgin, and adjusted itself without discomfort to the Counter Reformation. To this day it is contentedly orthodox, and lures tired or curious spirits with its simple piety, its picturesque annual *palio* or tournament of races (from 1659), and its precious immunity to modernity.

IV. UMBRIA AND THE BAGLIONI

Hemmed in by Tuscany on the west, Latium on the south, and the Marches on the north and east, mountainous Umbria lifts up, here and there, the cities of Terni, Spoleto, Assisi, Foligno, Perugia, Gubbio. We preface them here with Fabriano—across the border in the Marches—because Gentile da Fabriano was a prelude to the Umbrian school.

Gentile is an obscure but dominating figure: painting medieval pictures in Gubbio and Perugia and the Marches, feeling vaguely the influence of the early Sienese painters, and slowly maturing to such prominence that Pandolfo Malatesta, says a quite incredible tradition, paid him 14,000 ducats to fresco the chapel of the Broletto in Brescia (*c.* 1410).[8] Some ten years later the Venetian Senate commissioned him to paint a battle scene in the Hall of the Great Council; Gentile Bellini seems to have been among his pupils at that time. We find him next in Florence, painting for the church of Santa Trinità an *Adoration of the Magi* (1423) which even the proud Florentines acclaimed as a masterpiece. It is still preserved in the Uffizi: a bright and picturesque cavalcade of kings and retinues, stately horses, musing cattle, squatting monkeys, alert dogs, a lovely Mary, all compellingly focused upon a charming Infant who places an explorative hand upon the bald head of kneeling royalty; it is a picture admirable in gay color and flowing line, but almost primitively innocent of perspective and foreshortening. Pope Martin V called Gentile to Rome, where the artist deposited some frescoes in San Giovanni Laterano; they have disappeared, but we may surmise their quality from the enthusiasm of Rogier van der Weyden, who, on seeing them, pronounced Gentile the greatest painter in Italy.[9] In the church of Santa Maria Nuova Gentile painted other lost frescoes, one of which led Michelangelo to say to Vasari, "he had a hand like his name."[10] Gentile died in Rome in 1427, at the height of his renown.

His career is evidence that Umbria, to which he culturally belonged, was generating its own geniuses and style in art. By and large, however, the Umbrian painters took their lead from Siena, and continued the religious mood without a break from Duccio to Perugino and the early Raphael. Assisi was the spiritual source of Umbrian art. The churches and legends of St. Francis disseminated through the neighboring provinces a devotion that dominated painting as well as architecture, and discountenanced the pagan or secular themes that were elsewhere invading Italian art. Portraits were seldom asked of Umbrian painters, but private individuals, sometimes using the savings of a lifetime, commissioned an artist, usually local, to paint a Madonna or a Holy Family for their favorite chapel; and there was hardly a church so poor but it could raise funds for such a symbol of hopeful piety and community pride. So Gubbio had her own painter, Ottaviano Nelli, and Foligno had Niccolò di Liberatore, and Perugia boasted Bonfigli, Perugino, and Pinturicchio.

Perugia was the oldest, largest, richest, and most violent of the Umbrian towns. Placed sixteen hundred feet high on an almost inaccessible summit, it commanded a spacious view of the surrounding country; the site was so favorable for defense that the Etruscans built—or inherited—a city there before the foundation of Rome. Long claimed by the popes as one of the Papal States, Perugia declared itself independent in 1375, and enjoyed over a century of passionate factionalism surpassed only by Siena. Two wealthy families fought for control of the city—its commerce, its government, its benefices, its 40,000 souls. The Oddi and the Baglioni murdered one another by stealth or openly in the streets; their conflicts fertilized with blood the plain that smiled beneath their towers. The Baglioni were noted for their handsome faces and physiques, their courage and their ferocity. In the heart of pious Umbria they scorned the Church, and gave themselves pagan names—Ercole, Troilo, Ascanio, Annibale, Atalanta, Penelope, Lavinia, Zenobia. In 1445 the Baglioni repelled an attempt of the Oddi to seize Perugia; thereafter they ruled the city as despots, though formally acknowledging it to be a papal fief. Let Perugia's own historian, Francesco Matarazzo, describe the Baglioni government:

From the day the Oddi were expelled, our city went from bad to worse. All the young men followed the trade of arms. Their lives were disorderly, and every day divers excesses were divulged, and the city had lost all reason and justice. Every man administered right unto himself, by his own authority and with royal hand. The pope sent many legates, if so be the city could be brought to order. But all who came went back in dread of being hewn to pieces; for the Baglioni threatened to throw some from the windows of the palace, so that no cardinal or other legate durst approach Perugia unless he were their friend. And the city was brought to such misery that the most lawless men were most prized; and those who had slain two or three men walked as they pleased through the palace, and went with sword or poignard to speak to the podesta and other magistrates. Every man of worth was trodden down by bravos whom the nobles favored, nor could a citizen call his property his own. The nobles robbed first one and then another of goods and land. All offices were sold or else suppressed; and taxes and extortions were so grievous that everyone cried out.[11]

What can be done, a cardinal asked of Pope Alexander VI, with "these demons who have no fear of holy water"?[12]

Having disposed of the Oddi, the Baglioni divided into new factions, and fought one of the bloodiest feuds of the Renaissance. Atalanta Baglioni, being left a widow through the assassination of her husband, consoled herself with the beauty of her son Grifonetto, whom Matarazzo describes as another Ganymede. Her happiness seemed fully restored when he married Zenobia Sforza, whose beauty matched his own. But a minor branch of the Baglioni plotted to overthrow the ruling branch—Astorre, Guido, Simonetto, and Gianpaolo. Valuing Grifonetto's bravery, the conspirators won him to their plan by deluding him into the belief that Gianpaolo had seduced his young wife. One night in the year 1500, when the dominant Baglioni families had left their castles and assembled in Perugia for the wedding of Astorre and Lavinia, the conspirators attacked them in their beds, and killed all but one of them. Gianpaolo escaped by clambering over roofs, hiding through the night with some frightened university students, disguising himself in a scholastic gown, and so passing out through the city gates at dawn. Atalanta, horrified to learn that her son had shared in these murders, drove him from her presence with curses. The assassins dispersed, leaving Grifonetto homeless and alone in the city. On the morrow Gianpaolo, with an armed escort, re-entered Perugia, and came upon Grifonetto in a public square. He wished to spare the youth, but the soldiers wounded Grifonetto mortally before Gianpaolo could restrain them. Atalanta and Zenobia came from their concealment to find son and husband dying in the street. Atalanta knelt by him, took back her curses, gave him her blessing, and asked him to forgive those who had slain him. Then, says Matarazzo, "the noble youth extended his right hand to his young mother, pressing her white hand, and forthwith he breathed his soul from his beautiful body."[13] Perugino and Raphael were painting in Perugia at this time.

Gianpaolo had a hundred men massacred, in the streets or in the cathedral, on suspicion of complicity in the plot; he had the Palazzo Comunale decorated with the heads of the slain, and with their portraits hung head downward; here was a substantial commission for Perugian art. Thereafter he ruled the city unchallenged until he yielded to Julius II (1506), and consented to govern as vicar of the popes. But he did not know how to govern except by assassination. In 1520 Leo X, tired of his crimes, lured him to Rome with a safe-conduct, and had him beheaded in the Castel Sant' Angelo; this was one form of Renaissance diplomacy. Other Baglioni maintained themselves in power for a time; but after Malatesta Baglioni had murdered a papal legate Pope Paul III sent forces to take final possession of the city as an appanage of the Church (1534).

V. PERUGINO

Under this cloak-and-dagger government literature and art prospered surprisingly; the same passionate temperament that worshiped the Virgin, flouted cardinals, and murdered close kin could feel the fever of creative writing, or steel itself to the discipline of art. Matarazzo's *Cronaca della Città di Perugia*, describing the zenith of the Baglioni, is one of the most vivid literary products of the Renaissance. Commerce, before the Baglioni came to power, had accumulated enough wealth to build the massive Gothic Palazzo Comunale (1280-1333), and to adorn it and the adjoining Collegio del Cambio (1452-6)—Chamber of Commerce—with some of the finest art in Italy. The Collegio had a judicial throne and a moneychangers' bench so exquisitely carved that no one could reproach the businessmen of Perugia with lack of taste. The church of San Domenico had choir stalls (1476) almost as elegant, and a celebrated chapel of the Rosary designed by Agostino di Duccio. Agostino hesitated between sculpture and architecture; usually he combined them, as in the *oratorio* or prayer chapel of San Bernardino (1461), where he covered almost the entire façade with statues, reliefs, arabesques, and other ornament. An unadorned surface always aroused an Italian artist.

At least fifteen painters were busy meeting such challenges in Perugia. Their leader in Perugino's youth was Benedetto Bonfigli. Apparently through association with Domenico Veneziano or Piero della Francesca, or through studying the frescoes painted by Benozzo Gozzoli at Montefalco, Benedetto learned something of the new techniques that Masolino, Masaccio, Uccello, and others had developed in Florence. When he painted frescoes for the Palazzo Comunale he displayed a knowledge of perspective new among Umbrian artists, though his figures borrowed stereotyped faces and were shrouded in shapeless drapery. A younger rival, Fiorenzo di Lorenzo, equaled Benedetto in dullness of color, surpassed him in delicacy of sentiment and occasional grace. Both Bonfigli and Fiorenzo, in Perugian tradition, taught the two masters who brought Umbrian painting to its culmination.

Bernardino Betti, called Pinturicchio, learned the arts of tempera and fresco from Fiorenzo, but never adopted the oil technique that came to Perugino from the Florentines. In 1481, aged twenty-seven, he accompanied Perugino to Rome, and covered a panel in the Sistine Chapel with a lifeless *Baptism of Christ*. But he improved; and when Innocent VIII bade him decorate a loggia of the Belvedere Palace he struck out on a new line by painting views of Genoa, Milan, Florence, Venice, Naples, and Rome. His drawing was imperfect, but there was a pleasant plein-air quality in his painting that attracted Alexander VI. That genial Borgia, wishing to adorn his own chambers in the Vatican, commissioned Pinturicchio and some aides to paint the walls and ceilings with frescoes of prophets, sibyls, musicians, scientists, saints, Madonnas, and perhaps a mistress. These again so pleased the Pope that when an apartment was designed for his use in the Castel Sant' Angelo he engaged the artist to portray there some episodes in the Pope's conflict with Charles VIII (1495). By this time Perugia had heard of Pinturicchio's fame; it called him home; and the church of Santa Maria de' Fossi asked him for an altarpiece. He responded with a *Virgin, Child, and St. John* that satisfied all but the professionals. In Siena, as we have seen, he made the Piccolomini Library radiant with a vivid portrayal of the life and legend of Pius II; and despite many technical faults, this pictorial narrative makes that room one of the most delightful remains of Renaissance art. After spending five years on this work Pinturicchio went to Rome, and shared in the humiliation of Raphael's success. Thereafter he faded from the artistic scene, perhaps through illness, perhaps because

Perugino and Raphael so obviously excelled him. A doubtful story reports that he died of hunger in Siena, aged fifty-nine (1513).[14]

Pietro Perugino received that surname because he made Perugia his home; Perugia itself always called him by his family name, Vannucci. Born in nearby Città della Pieve (1446), he was sent to Perugia at the age of nine and was there apprenticed to an artist of uncertain identity. According to Vasari his teacher ranked the painters of Florence as the best in Italy, and advised the youth to go and study there. Pietro went, carefully copied the frescoes of Masaccio, and enrolled as an apprentice or assistant to Verrocchio. Leonardo entered Verrocchio's studio about 1468; very probably Perugino met him, and, though six years older, did not disdain to learn from him some qualities of finish and grace, and a better handling of perspective, coloring, and oils. These skills already appear in Perugino's *St. Sebastian* (Louvre), together with a pretty architectural setting, and a landscape as placid as the face of the perforated saint. After leaving Verrocchio, Perugino returned to the Umbrian style of demure and tender Madonnas; and through him the harder and more realistic traditions of Florentine painting may have been softened into the warmer idealism of Fra Bartolommeo and Andrea del Sarto.

By 1481 Perugino, now thirty-five, had won sufficient repute to be invited by Sixtus IV to Rome. In the Sistine Chapel he painted several frescoes, of which the finest survivor is *Christ Giving the Keys to Peter.* It is too formal and conventional in its symmetrical composition; but here, for the first time in painting, the air, with its subtle gradations of light, becomes a distinct and almost palpable element in the picture; the drapery, so stereotyped in Bonfigli, is here tucked and wrinkled into life; and a few of the faces are finished to striking individuality—Jesus, Peter, Signorelli, and, not least, the large, rotund, sensual, matter-of-fact countenance of Perugino himself, transformed for the occasion into a disciple of Christ.

In 1486 Perugino was again in Florence, for the archives of the city record his arrest for criminal assault. He and a friend disguised themselves, and, armed with clubs, waited in the dark of a December night to waylay some chosen enemy. They were detected before they could commit any injury. The friend was banished, Perugino was fined ten florins.[15] After another interlude in Rome he set up a *bottega* in Florence (1492), hired assistants, and began to turn out pictures, not always carefully finished, for customers near and far. For the Gesuati brotherhood he made a *Pietà* whose melancholy Virgin and pensive Magdalen were to be repeated by him and his aides in a hundred variations for any prosperous institution or individual. A *Madonna and Saints* found its way to Vienna, another to Cremona, another to Fano, another—the *Madonna in Glory*—to Perugia, another to the Vatican; another is in the Uffizi. Rivals charged him with turning his studio into a factory; they thought it scandalous that he should grow so rich and fat. He smiled and raised his prices. When Venice invited him to paint two panels in the Ducal Palace, offering 400 ducats ($5000?), he demanded 800; and when these were not forthcoming he remained in Florence. He clung to cash, and let the credit go. He made no pretense of despising wealth; he was resolved not to starve when his brush began to tremble; he bought property in Florence and Perugia, and was bound to land on at least one foot after any overturn. His self-portrait in the Cambio at Perugia (1500) is a remarkably honest confession. A pudgy face, large nose, hair flowing carelessly from under a close red cap, eyes quiet but penetrating, lips slightly contemptuous, heavy neck and powerful frame: here was a man hard to deceive, ready for battle, sure of himself, and holding no high opinion of the human race. "He was not a religious man," says Vasari, "and would never believe in the immortality of the soul."[16]

His skepticism and commercialism did not prevent him from occasional generosity,[17] or from producing some of the tenderest devotional pictures of the Renaissance. He painted a lovable *Madonna* for the Certosa di Pavia (now in London); and the *Magdalen* attributed to him in the Louvre is so fair a sinner that one would not need divine mercy to forgive her. For the nuns of Santa Clara at Florence he painted an *Entombment* in which the women had a rare beauty of features, and the faces of the old men summarized their lives, and the lines of composition met on the bloodless corpse of Christ, and a landscape of slender trees on rocky slopes, and distant town on a quiet bay, shed an atmosphere of calm over the scene of death and grief. The man could paint as well as sell.

His success in Florence finally convinced the Perugians of his worth. When the merchants of the Cambio decided to adorn their Collegio they emptied their pockets with tardy largesse and offered the assignment to Pietro Vannucci. Following the mood of the age and the suggestions of a local scholar, they asked that their hall of audience should be decorated with a medley of Christian and pagan subjects: on the ceiling the seven planets and the signs of the zodiac; on one wall a Nativity and a Transfiguration; on another the Eternal Father, the prophets, and six pagan sibyls, prefiguring Michelangelo's; and on another wall the four classical virtues, each illustrated by pagan heroes: Prudence by Numa, Socrates, and Fabius;

Justice by Pittacus, Furius, and Trajan, Fortitude by Lucius, Leonidas, and Horatius Cocles; Temperance by Pericles, Cincinnatus, and Scipio. All this, it seems, was accomplished by Perugino and his aides—including Raphael—in the one year 1500, the very year when the feuds of the Baglioni incarnadined the streets of Perugia. When the blood had been washed away the citizens could stream in to see the new beauty of the Cambio. Perhaps they found the pagan worthies a bit wooden, and wished that Perugino had shown them not posing but engaged in some action that would have given them life. But the *David* was majestic, the *Erythrean Sibyl* almost as gracious as a Raphael *Madonna*, and the *Eternal Father* a remarkably good conception for an atheist. On those walls, in his sixtieth year, Perugino reached the fullness of his powers. In 1501 the grateful city made him a municipal prior.

From that zenith he rapidly declined. In 1502 he painted a *Marriage of the Virgin*, which Raphael imitated two years later in the *Sposalizio*. About 1503 he returned to Florence. He was not pleased to find the city in much ado about Michelangelo's *David;* he was among the artists summoned to consider where the figure should be placed, and his opinion was overruled by the sculptor himself. The two men, meeting shortly afterward, traded insults; Michelangelo, then a lad of twenty-nine, called Perugino a blockhead, and informed him that his art was "antiquated and absurd."[18] Perugino sued him for libel, and won nothing but ridicule. In 1505 he agreed to finish for the Annunziata a *Deposition* that the late Filippino Lippi had begun, and to add to it an *Assumption of the Virgin*. He completed Filippino's work with skill and dispatch; but in the *Assumption* he repeated so many figures that he had used in previous pictures that the artists of Florence (still jealous of his quondam fees) condemned him for dishonesty and sloth. He left the city in anger, and took up his residence in Perugia.

The inevitable defeat of age by youth was repeated when he accepted an invitation from Julius II to decorate a room in the Vatican (1507). When he had made some progress his former pupil, Raphael, appeared, and swept everything before him. Perugino left Rome wtih heavy heart. Back in Perugia, he prospected for commissions, and kept on working to the end. He began (1514) and apparently finished (1520) a complex altarpiece for the church of Sant' Agostino, recounting again the story of Christ. For the church of the Madonna delle Lagrime at Trevi he painted (1521) an *Adoration of the Magi* which, despite some palsied drawing, is an astonishing product for a man of seventy-five. In 1523, while he was painting at neighboring Fontignano, he fell a victim to the plague, or perhaps died of old age and weariness. According to tradition he refused the last sacraments, saying that he preferred to see what would happen, in the other world, to an obstinately impenitent soul.[19] He was buried in unhallowed ground.[20]

Everyone knows the defects of Perugino's painting—the exaggerated sentiment, the dolorous and artificial piety, the stereotyped oval faces and ribboned hair, the heads regularly bent forward in modesty, even those of stern Cato and bold Leonidas. Europe and America can show a hundred Peruginos of this repetitious type; the master was more fertile than inventive. His pictures want action and vitality; they reflect the needs of Umbrian devotion rather than the realities and significance of life. And yet there is much in them that can please the soul mature enough to surmount its sophistication: the living quality of their light, the modest loveliness of their women, the bearded majesty of their old men, the soft and quiet colors, the gracious landscapes covering all tragedies with peace.

When Perugino returned to Perugia in 1499, after long stays in Florence, he brought into Umbrian painting the technical skill, without the critical faculty, of the Florentines. When he died he had faithfully passed down those skills to his associates and pupils—to Pinturicchio, Francesco Ubertino "Il Bachiacca," Giovanni di Pietro "Lo Spagna," and Raphael. The master had served his purpose: he had enriched and transmitted his heritage, and had trained a pupil to surpass him. Raphael is Perugino faultless, perfected, and complete.

CHAPTER IX

Mantua

1378-1540

I. VITTORINO DA FELTRE

MANTUA was fortunate: throughout the Renaissance it had but one ruling family, and was spared the turmoil of revolutions, court murders, and *coups d'état*. When Luigi Gonzaga became *capitano del popolo* (1328) the ascendancy of his house was so well established that he could occasionally leave his capital and hire himself out to other cities as general—a custom followed by his successors through several generations. His great-great-grandson Gianfrancesco I was raised to the dignity of marquis (1432) by their theoretical sovereign the Emperor Sigismund, and this title became hereditary in the Gonzaga family until it was exchanged for the still loftier title of duke (1530). Gian was a good ruler. He drained marshes, promoted agriculture and industry, supported art, and brought to Mantua, to tutor his children, one of the noblest figures in the history of education.

Vittorino took his surname from his native town of Feltre, in northeast Italy. Catching the itch for classical erudition that swept like an epidemic through the Italy of the fifteenth century, he went to Padua and studied Latin, Greek, mathematics, and rhetoric under divers masters; he paid one of them by serving as his domestic. After being graduated from the university he opened a school for boys. He chose his pupils by their talent and eagerness rather than by their pedigree or funds; he made the richer students pay according to their means, and charged the poor students nothing. He tolerated no idlers, exacted hard work, and maintained strict discipline. As this proved difficult in the roistering atmosphere of a university town, Vittorino transferred his school to Venice (1423). In 1425 he accepted the invitation of Gianfrancesco to come to Mantua and teach a selected group of boys and girls. These included four sons and a daughter of the Marquis, a daughter of Francesco Sforza, and some other scions of Italian ruling families.

The Marquis provided for the school a villa known as Casa Zojosa, or

Joyous House. Vittorino turned it into a semimonastic establishment, in which he and his students lived simply, ate sensibly, and devoted themselves to the classic ideal of a healthy mind in a healthy body. Vittorino himself was an athlete as well as a scholar, an expert fencer and horseman, so at home in weather that he wore similar clothing winter and summer, and walked in nothing but sandals in the severest cold. Inclined to sensuality and anger, he controlled his flesh by periodic fasting and by flogging himself every day; his contemporaries believed that he remained a virgin till his death.

To chasten the instincts and form sound character in his pupils, he first of all required of them a regularity of religious devotions, and instilled in them a strong religious feeling. He sternly rebuked all profanity, obscenity, or vulgarity of language, punished any lapse into angry dispute, and made lying almost a capital crime. However, he did not have to be told, as Lorenzo's wife warned Politian, that he was educating princes who might some day face the tasks of administration or war. To make their bodies healthy and strong he trained them in gymnastics of many kinds, in running, riding, leaping, wrestling, fencing, and military exercises; he accustomed them to bear hardships without injury or complaint; though medieval in his ethics, he rejected the medieval scorn of the body, and recognized with the Greeks the role of physical health in the rounded excellence of man. And as he formed the bodies of his pupils with athletics and toil, and their characters with religion and discipline, so he trained their taste with instruction in painting and music, and their minds with mathematics, Latin, Greek, and the ancient classics; he hoped to unite in his pupils the virtues of Christian conduct with the sharp clarity of the pagan intellect and the esthetic sensitivity of Renaissance men. The Renaissance ideal of the complete man—*l'uomo universale*—health of body, strength of character, wealth of mind—reached its first formulation in Vittorino da Feltre.

The fame of his methods spread through Italy and beyond. Many visitors came to Mantua to see not its Marquis but its pedagogue. Fathers begged from Gianfrancesco the privilege of enrolling their sons in this "School of Princes." He agreed, and such later notables as Federigo of Urbino, Francesco da Castiglione, and Taddeo Manfredi came under Vittorino's formative hand. The most promising students enjoyed the master's personal attention; they lodged with him under his own roof, and received the priceless instruction of daily contact with integrity and intelligence. Vittorino insisted that poor but qualified applicants should also be admitted; he persuaded the Marquis to provide funds, facilities, and assistant teachers for the education and maintenance of sixty poor scholars at a time; and when such funds did not suffice, Vittorino made up the difference out of his modest means. When he died (1446) it was found that he had not left enough to pay for his funeral.

Lodovico Gonzaga, who succeeded Gianfrancesco as marquis of Mantua (1444), was a credit to his teacher. When Vittorino took him in hand Lodovico was a lad of eleven years, fat and indolent. Vittorino taught him to control his appetite and to make himself fit for all the tasks of government. Lodovico performed these duties well, and left his state flourishing at his death. Like a true Renaissance prince, he used part of his wealth to nourish literature and art. He collected an excellent library, largely of Latin classics; he employed miniaturists to illuminate the *Aeneid* and *The Divine Comedy;* he established the first printing press in Mantua. Politian, Pico della Mirandola, Filelfo, Guarino da Verona, Platina were among the humanists who at one time or another accepted his bounty and lived at his court.[1] At his invitation Leon Battista Alberti came from Florence and designed the Incoronata Chapel in the cathedral, and the churches of Sant' Andrea and San Sebastiano. Donatello came too, and made a bronze bust of Lodovico. And in 1460 the Marquis brought into his service one of the greatest artists of the Renaissance.

II. ANDREA MANTEGNA: 1431-1506

He was born at Isola di Cartura, near Padua, thirteen years before Botticelli; we must here retrace our steps in time if we are to appreciate Mantegna's achievement. He was enrolled in the painters' guild in Padua when he was but ten years old. Francesco Squarcione was then the most famous teacher of painting not only in Padua but in Italy. Andrea entered his school, and progressed so rapidly that Squarcione took him into his home and adopted him as a son. Inspired by the humanists, Squarcione collected into his studio all the significant remains of classic sculpture and architecture that he could appropriate and transport, and bade his students copy them over and over again as models of strong, restrained, and harmonious design. Mantegna obeyed with enthusiasm; he fell in love with Roman antiquity, idealized its heroes, and so admired its art that half his pictures have Roman architectural backgrounds, and half his figures, of whatever nation or time, bear a Roman stamp and garb. His art profited and suffered through this youthful infatuation; he learned from these exemplars a majestic dignity and a stern purity of design, but he never fully emancipated his painting from the petrified calm of sculptural forms. When Donatello came to Padua Mantegna, still a lad of twelve, felt again the influence of sculpture, together with a powerful impulse toward realism. At the same time he was fascinated by the new science of perspective, so recently developed in Florence by Masolino, Uccello, and Masaccio; Andrea studied all its rules, and shocked his contemporaries with foreshortenings ungracious in their truth.

In 1448 Squarcione received a commission to paint frescoes in the church of the Eremitani friars at Padua. He assigned the work to two favorite pupils: Niccolò Pizzolo and Mantegna. Niccolò finished one panel in excellent style, then lost his life in a brawl. Andrea, now seventeen, continued the work, and the eight panels that he painted in the next seven years made him a name from one end of Italy to the other. The themes were medieval, the treatment was revolutionary: the backgrounds of classical architecture were carefully detailed, the virile physique and gleaming armor of Roman soldiers were mingled with the somber features of Christian saints; paganism and Christianity were more vividly integrated in these frescoes than in all the pages of the humanists. Drawing reached here a new accuracy and grace; perspective appeared in painstaking perfection. Rarely had painting seen a figure as splendid in form and bearing as that of the soldier guarding the saint before the Roman judge; or anything so grimly realistic as the executioner raising his club to beat out the martyr's brains. Artists came from distant cities to study the technique of the amazing Paduan youth.—All but two of these frescoes were destroyed in the Second World War.

Iacopo Bellini, himself a painter of renown, and already (in 1454) father of painters fated to eclipse his fame, saw these panels in the making, took a fancy to Andrea, and offered him his daughter in marriage. Mantegna accepted. Squarcione opposed the union, and punished Mantegna's flight from his adoptive home by condemning the Eremitani frescoes as stiff and pallid imitations of marble antiques. More remarkable, the Bellinis succeeded in conveying to Andrea a hint that there was some truth in the charge.[2] Most remarkable, the hot-tempered artist accepted the criticism, and profited from it by turning from the study of statuary to the intent observation of life in all its actuality and details. In the last two panels of the Eremitani series he included ten portraits of contemporaries; and one, squat and fat, was Squarcione.

Canceling his contract with his teacher, Mantegna was now free to accept some of the invitations that besieged him. Lodovico Gonzaga offered him a commission in Mantua (1456); Andrea held him off for four years, and meanwhile, in Verona, he painted for the church of San Zeno a polyptych that to this day makes that noble edifice a goal of pilgrimage. In the central panel, amid a stately framework of Roman columns, cornice, and pediment, the Virgin holds her Child, while angel musicians and choristers envelop them; beneath this a powerful *Crucifixion* shows Roman soldiers throwing dice for the garments of Christ; and at the left the *Garden of Olives* presents a rugged landscape that Leonardo may have studied for his *Virgin of the Rocks*. This polyptych is one of the great paintings of the Renaissance.*

After three years in Verona Mantegna finally agreed to go to Mantua (1460); and there, except for brief stays in Florence and Bologna, and two years in Rome, he remained till his death. Lodovico gave him a home, fuel, corn, and fifteen ducats ($375) a month. Andrea adorned the palaces, chapels, and villas of three successive marquises. The sole survivors in Mantua of his labors there are the famous frescoes in the Ducal Palace, specifically in the Sala degli Sposi—the Hall of the Betrothed—named and decorated for the engagement of Lodovico's son Federigo to Margaret of Bavaria. The subject was simply the ruling family—the Marquis, his wife, his children, some courtiers, and Cardinal Francesco Gonzaga welcomed by his father Lodovico on the young prelate's return from Rome. Here was a gallery of remarkably realistic portraits, among them Mantegna himself, looking older than his forty-three years, with lines in his face and pouches under his eyes.

Lodovico too was aging rapidly, and his last years were dark with troubles. Two of his daughters were deformed; wars consumed his revenues; in 1478 plague so devastated Mantua that economic life almost stopped, state revenues fell, and Mantegna's salary was one of many that went for a time unpaid. The artist wrote Lodovico a letter of reproach; the Marquis answered with a gentle plea for patience. The plague passed; Lodovico did not survive it. Under his son Federigo (1478-84) Mantegna began, and under Federigo's son Gianfrancesco (1484-1519) he completed, his finest work, *The Triumph of Caesar*. These nine pictures, painted in tempera on canvas, were designed for the Corte Vecchia of the

---

* In 1797 the lower panels were appropriated by French conquerors; the *Garden of Olives* and the *Resurrection* are in Tours, the *Crucifixion* is in the Louvre; good copies have replaced these originals in the Verona polyptych.

Ducal Palace; they were sold to Charles I of England by a needy duke of Mantua, and are now in Hampton Court. The enormous frieze, eighty-eight feet long, depicts a procession of soldiers, priests, captives, slaves, musicians, beggars, elephants, bulls, standards, trophies, and spoils, all escorting Caesar riding on a chariot and crowned by the Goddess of Victory. Here Mantegna returns to his first love, classic Rome; again he paints like a sculptor; nevertheless his figures move with life and action; the eye is drawn along, despite a hundred picturesque details, to the culminating coronation; all the painter's artistry of composition, drawing, perspective, and meticulous observation enters into the work, and makes it the master's masterpiece.

During the seven years that elapsed between the undertaking and the completion of *The Triumph of Caesar*, Mantegna accepted a call from Innocent VIII, and painted (1488-9) several frescoes that vanished in the later vicissitudes of Rome. Complaining of the Pope's parsimony—while the Pope complained of his impatience—Mantegna returned to Mantua, and rounded out his prolific career with a hundred pictures on religious themes; he was forgetting Caesar and returning to Christ. The most famous and disagreeable of these paintings is the *Cristo morto* (Brera), the dead Christ lying on His back with His vast foreshortened feet toward the spectator, and looking more like a sleeping *condottiere* than like an exhausted god.

A final pagan picture came from Mantegna's old age. In the *Parnassus* of the Louvre he put aside his usual resolve to capture reality rather than picture beauty; he surrendered himself for a moment to an unmoral mythology, and portrayed a nude Venus throned on Parnassus beside her soldier lover Mars, while at the mountain's base Apollo and the Muses celebrate her loveliness in dance and song. One of the Muses was probably the Marquis Gianfrancesco's wife, the peerless Isabella d'Este, now the leading lady in the land.

It was Mantegna's last great painting. His final years were saddened by ill health, bad temper, and mounting debts. He resented Isabella's presumption to lay down the precise details of the pictures she asked of him; he retired into an angry solitude, sold most of his art collection, finally sold his house. In 1505 Isabella described him as "tearful and agitated, and with so sunken a face that he seemed to me more dead than alive."[3] A year later he died, aged seventy-five. Over his tomb, in Sant' Andrea, a bronze bust—perhaps by Mantegna himself—portrayed with angry realism the bitterness and exhaustion of a genius who had used himself up in his art for half a century. Those who desire "immortality" must pay for it with their lives.

III. THE FIRST LADY OF THE WORLD

La prima donna del mondo—so the poet Niccolò da Correggio called Isabella d'Este.[4] The novelist Bandello considered her "supreme among women";[5] and Ariosto did not know which to praise most highly in "the liberal and magnanimous Isabella"—her gracious beauty, her modesty, her wisdom, or her fostering of letters and arts. She possessed most of the accomplishments and charms that made the educated woman of the Renaissance one of the masterpieces of history. She had a wide and varied culture without being an "intellectual" or ceasing to be an attractive woman. She was not extraordinarily beautiful; what men admired in her was her vitality, her high spirits, the keenness of her appreciation, the perfection of her taste. She could ride all day and then dance all night, and remain every moment a queen. She could rule Mantua with a tact and good sense alien to her husband; and in the debility of his later years she held his little state together despite his blunders, his wanderings, and his syphilis. She corresponded on equal terms with the most eminent personalities of her time. Popes and dukes sought her friendship, and rulers came to her court. She subpoenaed nearly every artist to work for her, she inspired poets to sing of her; Bembo, Ariosto, and Bernardo Tasso dedicated works to her, though they knew that her purse was small. She collected books and art with the judgment of a scholar and the discrimination of a connoisseur. Wherever she went she remained the cultural focus and sartorial exemplar of Italy.

She was one of the Estensi—the brilliant family that gave dukes to Ferrara, cardinals to the Church, and a duchess to Milan. Isabella, born in 1474, was a year older than her sister Beatrice. Their father was Ercole I of Ferrara, their mother was Eleonora of Aragon, daughter of King Ferrante I of Naples; they were well equipped with lineage. While Beatrice was sent to Naples to learn vivacity at the court of her grandfather, Isabella was brought up amid the scholars, poets, dramatists, musicians, and artists that were making Ferrara for a time the most brilliant of Italian capitals. At six she was an intellectual prodigy who made diplomats gape; "though I had heard much of her singular intelligence," wrote Beltramino Cusatro to Marquis Federigo of Mantua in 1480, "I could never have imagined such a thing to be possible."[6] Federigo thought she would be a good catch for his son Francesco, and so proposed to her father. Ercole, needing the support of Mantua against Venice, agreed, and Isabella, aged six, found herself engaged to a boy of fourteen. She remained for ten years more at Ferrara, learning how to sew and sing, to write Italian poetry and Latin prose, to play the clavichord and the lute, and to dance with a sprightly grace that seemed to attest invisible wings. Her complexion was clear and fair, her black eyes sparkled, her hair was a mesh of gold. So, at sixteen, she left the haunts of her happy childhood, and became, proudly and seriously, the Marchioness of Mantua.

Gianfrancesco was swarthy, bushy-haired, fond of hunting, impetuous in war and love. In those early years he attended zealously to government, and faithfully maintained Mantegna and several scholars at his court. He fought with more courage than wisdom at Fornovo, and chivalrously or prudently sent to Charles VIII most of the spoils that he had captured in the tent of the fleeing King. He used the soldier's privilege of promiscuity, and began his infidelities with the first confinement of his wife. Seven years after his marriage he allowed his mistress Teodora to appear in almost regal raiment at a tournament in Brescia, where he rode in the lists. Isabella may have been partly to blame: she became a bit plump, and went on long visits to Ferrara, Urbino, and Milan; but doubtless the Marquis was not inclined to monogamy in any case. Isabella bore with his adventures patiently, took no public notice of them, remained a good wife, gave her husband excellent advice in politics, and supported his interests by her diplomacy and her charm. But in 1506 she wrote to him—then leading papal troops—a few words warm with the hurt she felt: "No interpreter is needed to make me aware that Your Excellency has loved me little for some time past. Since this, however, is a disagreeable subject, I will . . . say no more.'" Her devotion to art, letters, and friendship was in part an attempt to forget the bitter emptiness of her married life.

There is nothing more pleasant in all the rich diversity of the Renaissance than the tender relations that bound together Isabella, Beatrice, and Isabella's sister-in-law Elisabetta Gonzaga; and few passages finer in Renaissance literature than the affectionate letters they exchanged. Elisabetta was grave and weak, and often ill; Isabella was merry, witty, brilliant, more interested in literature and art than either Elisabetta or Beatrice; but these differences of character were made complementary by good sense. Elisabetta loved to come to Mantua, and Isabella worried more about her sister-in-law's health than about her own, and took every measure to make her well. Yet there was a selfishness in Isabella quite absent from Elizabeth. Isabella could ask Caesar Borgia to give her Michelangelo's *Cupid*, which

Borgia had stolen after seizing Elisabetta's Urbino. After the fall of Lodovico il Moro, the brother-in-law who had lavished every courtesy upon her, she went to Milan and danced at a ball given by Lodovico's conqueror, Louis XII; perhaps, however, it was her feminine way of saving Mantua from the resentment aroused in Louis by the injudicious candor of her husband. Her diplomacy accepted the interstate amorality of that time and ours. Otherwise she was a good woman, and there was hardly a man in Italy that would not have been glad to serve her. Bembo wrote to her that he "desired to serve her and please her as if she were pope."[8]

She spoke Latin better than any other woman of her time, but she never mastered the language. When Aldus Manutius began to print his choice editions of the classics she was among his most enthusiastic customers. She employed scholars to translate Plutarch and Philostratus, and a learned Jew to translate the Psalms from the Hebrew so that she might assure herself of their original magnificence. She collected Christian classics too, and read the Fathers with courage. Probably she treasured books more as a collector than as a reader or a student; she respected Plato, but really preferred the chivalric romances that entertained even the Ariostos of her generation and the Tassos of the next. She loved finery and jewelry more than books and art; even in her later years the women of Italy and France looked to her as the glass of fashion and the queen of taste. It was part of her diplomacy to move ambassadors and cardinals with the combined allure of her person, her dress, her manners, and her mind; they thought they were admiring her erudition or her wisdom when they were relishing her beauty, her costume, or her grace. She was hardly profound, except perhaps in statesmanship. Like practically all her contemporaries she listened to astrologers, and timed her enterprises by the concurrence of the stars. She amused herself with dwarfs, maintained them as part of her entourage, and had six rooms and a chapel built to their measure for them in the Castello. One of these favorites was so short (said a wit) that if it had rained an inch more he would have been drowned. She was fond, too, of dogs and cats, chose them with the finesse of a fancier, and buried them with solemn funerals in which the surviving pets joined with the ladies and gentlemen of the court.

The Castello—or Reggia, or Palazzo Ducale—over which she reigned was a medley of buildings of various dates and authorship, but all in that style of outer fortress and inner palace which raised similar structures in Ferrara, Pavia, and Milan. Some components, like the Palazzo del Capitano, went back to the Buonacolsi rulers in the thirteenth century; the harmonious Castello San Giorgio was a creation of the fourteenth; the Camera degli

Sposi was the work of Lodovico Gonzaga and Mantegna in the fifteenth; many rooms were rebuilt in the seventeenth and eighteenth; some, like the sumptuous Sala degli Specchi, or Hall of Mirrors, were redecorated during the rule of Napoleon. All were elegantly fitted out; and the vast congeries of residential chambers, reception halls, and administrative offices looked out on courts, or gardens, or Virgil's meandering Mincio, or the lakes that bordered Mantua. In this labyrinth Isabella occupied different quarters at different times. In her later years she loved best a little apartment of four rooms (*camerini*), known as *il Studiolo* or *il Paradiso;* here, and in another room called *il Grotto*, she gathered her books, her *objets d'art*, and her musical instruments—themselves finished works of art.

Next to her care for the preservation of Mantua's independence and prosperity, and sometimes above her friendships, the ruling passion of her life was the collection of manuscripts, statues, paintings, majolica, antique marbles, and little products of the goldsmith's art. She used her friends, and employed special agents, in cities from Milan to Rhodes, to bargain and buy for her, and to be on the alert for "finds." She haggled because the treasury of her modest state was too narrow for her ideas. Her collection was small, but every item in it stood high in its class. She had statuary by Michelangelo, paintings by Mantegna, Perugino, Francia; not content, she importuned Leonardo da Vinci and Giovanni Bellini for a picture, but they held her off as one who paid more in praise than in cash, and doubtless, too, because she specified too immutably what each picture should represent and contain. In some cases, as when she paid 115 ducats ($2875) for Jan van Eyck's *Passage of the Red Sea*, she borrowed heavily to satisfy her eagerness for a masterpiece. She was not generous to Mantegna, but when that ogre of a genius died she persuaded her husband to lure Lorenzo Costa to Mantua with a handsome salary. Costa decorated Gianfrancesco Gonzaga's favorite retreat, the palace of St. Sebastian, made portraits of the family, and painted a mediocre *Madonna* for the church of Sant' Andrea.

In 1524 Giulio Pippi, called Romano, the greatest of Raphael's pupils, settled at Mantua, and astonished the court with his skill as architect and painter. Almost the entire Ducal Palace was redecorated according to his designs, and by the brushes of himself and his pupils—Francesco Primaticcio, Niccolò dell' Abbate, and Michelangelo Anselmi. Federigo, Isabella's son, was ruler now; and since he, like Romano, had acquired at Rome a taste for pagan subjects and decorative nudes, he had the walls and ceilings of several rooms in the Castello painted with inviting pictures of Aurora, Apollo, the Judgment of Paris, the Rape of Helen, and other phases of classic myth. In 1525, on the outskirts of the town, Giulio began to build his most famous work, the Palazzo del Te.* A vast rectangle of one-storied structures, in a simple design of stone blocks and Renaissance windows, surrounds what was once a pleasant garden but is now a neglected waste in the impoverished aftermath of war. The interior is a succession of surprises: rooms tastefully adorned with pilasters, carved cornices, painted spandrels, and coffered vaults; walls, ceilings, and lunettes picturing the story of the Titans and the Olympians, Cupid and Psyche, Venus and Adonis and Mars, Zeus and Olympia, all in a revel of splendid nudes, in the amorous and reckless taste of the later Renaissance. To crown these masterpieces of sexual license and gigantic strife, Primaticcio carved in stucco a grand processional relief of Roman soldiers in the manner of Mantegna's *Triumph of Caesar*, and almost with the chiseled excellence of Pheidias. When Primaticcio and dell' Abbate were summoned to Fontainebleau by Francis I they brought to the royal palaces of France this style of decoration—with rosy nudes—which Giulio Romano had brought to Mantua from his work with Raphael in Rome. From the citadel of Christianity pagan art radiated to the Christian world.

The last years of Isabella mingled sweet and bitter in her cup. She helped her invalid husband to govern Mantua. Her diplomacy saved it from falling prey to Caesar Borgia, then to Louis XII, then to Francis I, then to Charles V; one after another she humored, flattered, charmed, when Gianfrancesco or Federigo seemed on the edge of political disaster. Federigo, who succeeded his father in 1519, was an able general and ruler, but he allowed his mistress to displace his mother as ruler of the Mantuan court. Perhaps retreating from this indignity, Isabella went to Rome (1525) to seek a red hat for her son Ercole. Clement VII was noncommittal, but the cardinals welcomed her, made her suite in the Colonna Palace a salon, and kept her there so long that she found herself imprisoned in the palace during the sack of Rome (1527). She escaped with her usual adroitness, won the coveted cardinalate for Ercole, and returned to Mantua in triumph.

In 1529, attractive at fifty-five, she went to the Congress of Bologna, courted Emperor and Pope, helped the lords of Urbino and Ferrara to keep their principalities from being absorbed into the Papal States, and persuaded Charles V to make Federigo a duke. In that same year Titian came to Mantua and painted a famous portrait of her; the fate of this picture is uncertain, but the copy made of it by Rubens shows a woman still in the

---

* The derivation and significance of this word are uncertain.

vigor and love of life. Bembo, visiting her eight years later, was amazed by her vivacity, the alertness of her mind, the scope of her interests. He called her "the wisest and most fortunate of women,"[9] but her wisdom fell short of accepting old age cheerfully. She died in 1539, aged sixty-four, and was buried with preceding rulers of Mantua in the Capella dei Signori in the church of San Francesco. Her son ordered a handsome tomb to be raised to her memory, and joined her in death a year later. When the French pillaged Mantua in 1797 the tombs of the Mantuan princes and princesses were shattered, and the ashes they contained were mingled in the indiscriminate dust.

CHAPTER X

Ferrara

1378-1534

I. THE HOUSE OF ESTE

IN the first quarter of the sixteenth century the most active centers of the Renaissance were Ferrara, Venice, and Rome. The student who wanders through Ferrara today can hardly believe—until he enters the mighty Castello—that this slumbering city was once the home of a powerful dynasty, whose court was the most splendid in Europe, and whose pensioners included the greatest poet of the time.

The city owed its existence partly to its position on the route of commerce between Bologna and Venice, partly to the agricultural hinterland that used it as a mart and was itself enriched by three branches of the Po. It was included in the territory given to the papacy by Pepin III (756) and Charlemagne (773), and was again deeded to the Church by the Countess Matilda of Tuscany (1107). While formally acknowledging itself to be a papal fief it governed itself as an independent commune, dominated by rival mercantile families. Disordered by these feuds it accepted Count Azzo VI of Este as its podesta (1208), and made this office hereditary in his progeny. Este was a small Imperial fief, some forty miles north of Ferrara, which had been given to Count Azzo I of Canossa by the Emperor Otho I (961); in 1056 it became the seat of the family, and soon gave it its name. From this historic house came the later royal families of Brunswick and Hanover.

From 1208 to 1597 the Estensi ruled Ferrara technically as vassals of the Empire and the papacy, but practically as independent lords, with the title of marquis or (after 1470) duke. Under their government the people prospered tolerably, and supplied the needs and luxuries of a court that entertained emperors and popes, and supported a notable retinue of scholars, artists, poets, and priests. Despite lawless cruelties and frequent wars, the Estensi retained the loyalty of their subjects through four centuries. When a legate of Pope Clement V expelled the Estensi and proclaimed Ferrara a papal state (1311), the people found ecclesiastical rule more irksome than secular exploitation; they drove out the legate, and restored the Estensi to power (1317). Pope John XXII laid an interdict upon the city; soon the people, deprived of the sacraments, began to murmur. The Estensi sought reconciliation with the Church, and obtained it on hard conditions: they acknowledged Ferrara to be a papal fief, which they would rule as vicars of the popes; and they pledged themselves and their successors to pay, from the revenues of the state, an annual tribute of 10,000 ducats ($250,000?) to the papacy.[1]

During the long rule (1393-1441) of Niccolò III the house of Este reached the acme of its power, governing not only Ferrara but also Rovigo, Modena, Reggio, Parma, and even, briefly, Milan. Niccolò married as widely as he ruled, having a long succession of wives and mistresses. One especially pretty and popular wife, Parisina Malatesta, committed adultery with her stepson Ugo; Niccolò had them both beheaded (1425), and ordered that all Farrarese women convicted of adultery should be put to death. When it became clear that this edict threatened to depopulate Ferrara, it was no longer enforced. For the rest Niccolò ruled well. He reduced taxes, encouraged industry and commerce, summoned Theodorus Gaza to teach Greek in the university, and engaged Guarino da Verona to establish at Ferrara a school rivaling in fame and result the school of Vittorino da Feltre at Mantua.

Niccolò's son Leonello (1441-50) was a rare phenomenon—a ruler both gentle and virile, refined and competent, intellectual and practical. Trained in all the arts of war, he cherished peace, and became the favored arbiter and peacemaker among his fellow rulers in Italy. Taught letters and literature by Guarino, he became—a generation before Lorenzo de' Medici—one of the most cultivated men of the age; the learned Filelfo was astonished by Leonello's mastery of Latin and Greek, rhetoric and poetry, philosophy and law. This Marquis was the scholar who first suggested that the supposed letters of St. Paul to Seneca were spurious.[2] He established a public library, provided fresh funds and inspiration for the University of Ferrara, brought to its staff the best scholars that he could find, and participated actively in their discussions. No scandal or bloodshed or tragedy marred his reign, except its tragic brevity. When he died at forty, all Italy mourned.

A succession of able rulers continued the Golden Age that Leonello had begun. His brother Borso (1450-71) was a man of sterner stuff, but he maintained the policy of peace, and Ferrara's prosperity became the envy of other states. He did not care for literature or art, yet he supported them amply. He administered his realm with skill and comparative justice, but he taxed his people heavily, and spent much of their substance on court pageants and displays. He loved rank and title, and longed to be a duke like the Visconti of Milan; by expensive gifts he persuaded the Emperor Frederick III to invest him with the dignity of Duke of Modena and Reggio (1452), and marked the occasion with a costly festival. Nineteen years later he secured from his other feudal lord, Pope Paul II, the title of Duke of Ferrara. His fame spread throughout the Mediterranean world; the Moslem sovereigns of Babylonia and Tunis sent him gifts, presuming him to be the greatest ruler in Italy.

Borso was fortunate in his brothers: Leonello, who had given him the best of examples; and Ercole, who had refused to sanction a conspiracy to depose him, had remained his loyal aide to the end, and now succeeded to his power. For six years Ercole continued the reign of peace, pageantry, poetry, art, and taxation. He cemented friendship with Naples by marrying King Ferrante's daughter Eleonora of Aragon, and welcomed her with the most lavish festivities that Ferrara had ever seen (1473). But in 1478, when Sixtus IV declared war on Florence because of its punishment of the Pazzi conspirators, Ercole joined Florence and Milan against Naples and the papacy. That war having ended, Sixtus induced Venice to join him in attacking Ferrara (1482). While Ercole lay sick in bed the Venetian forces advanced to within four miles of the city; the dispossessed peasantry crowded within the gates, and joined in the general starvation. Then the temperamental Pope, fearing that Venice, not the papacy or his nephew, would get Ferrara, made peace with Ercole; and the Venetians, retaining Rovigo, retired to their lagoons.

The fields were planted again, food came into the city, trade was resumed, taxes could be gathered. Ercole complained that the fines levied for blasphemous profanity were falling away from the normal total of 6000 crowns a year ($150,000?); he could not believe that profanity was any less popular than before; he demanded strict enforcement of the law.[3] Every penny was needed, for Ercole, perceiving that the people had multiplied beyond their housing, built an extension as large as the older city. He had this Addizione Erculea designed with such wide straight streets as no Italian town had known since Roman days; the new Ferrara was "the first really modern city in Europe."[4] Within a decade the growth and influx of population had filled the added space. Ercole raised churches, palaces, and convents, and coaxed holy women to make Ferrara their home.

The focus of the people's life was the twelfth-century cathedral. The elite preferred the giant Castello that Niccolò II had built (1385) to protect the government from foreign attack or domestic revolt. Restored and transformed through seven generations, its massive towers still dominate the central square of the city. Below are the dungeons in which Parisina and many others died; above are the spacious halls, adorned by Dosso Dossi and his assistants, where duke and duchess held court, musicians played and sang, dwarfs pranced, poets recited their verses, buffoons put on their antic jests, male sought female, ladies and cavaliers danced through the night, and on quieter days, in quieter rooms, dames and lasses read romances of chivalry. Isabella and Beatrice d'Este, born to Ercole and Eleonora in 1474 and 1475, grew up like fairy princesses in this environment of wealth and festival, war and song and art. But a fond grandfather lured Beatrice to Naples, a betrothed called her to Milan; and in that same year 1490 Isabella left for Mantua. Their departure saddened many hearts in Ferrara, but their marriages strengthened the alliance of the Estensi with the Sforzas and Gonzagas. Ippolito, one of several sons, was made an archbishop at eleven, a cardinal at fourteen, and became one of the most cultured and dissolute prelates of the age.

We should in fairness note again that such ecclesiastical appointments, ignoring fitness and age, were part of the diplomatic alliances of the time. Alexander VI, pope since 1492, was eager to please Ercole, for he aimed at making his daughter, Lucrezia Borgia, the duchess of Ferrara. When he proposed to Ercole that Alfonso, son and heir of the Duke, should marry Lucrezia, Ercole received the proposal coldly, for Lucrezia had not then the fumigated reputation that she has now. He finally consented, but after wringing from the eager father such concessions as made Alexander call him a haggling shopkeeper. The Pope was to give Lucrezia a dowry of 100,000 ducats ($1,250,000?); the annual tribute of Ferrara to the papacy was to be reduced from four thousand to one hundred florins ($1250?); and the duchy of Ferrara was to be settled by papal confirmation upon Alfonso and his heirs forever. Despite all this Alfonso was reluctant, until he saw the bride. We shall see later how he welcomed her.

In 1505 he succeeded to the ducal throne. He was a new type among the Estensi. He had traveled through France, the Lowlands, and England, studying industrial and commercial techniques. Leaving to Lucrezia the patronage of arts and letters, he devoted himself to government, machinery, and pottery. With his own hands he made a painted fine majolica, and founded the best cannon of the time. He studied the art of fortification until he was the leading authority on the subject in Europe. He was nor-

mally a just man; he treated Lucrezia kindly, despite her epistolary flirta-
tions; but when he dealt with external enemies or internal revolt he gave
scant play to sentiment.

One of Lucrezia's ladies, Angela, charmed two of Alfonso's brothers:
Ippolito and Giulio. In a moment of thoughtless arrogance Angela taunted
Ippolito by telling him that his whole person was worth less to her than
the eyes of his brother. The Cardinal, with a band of bravos, waylaid
Giulio, and looked on while these pierced Giulio's eyes with stakes (1506).
Giulio appealed to Alfonso to avenge him; the Duke banished the Cardinal,
but soon allowed him to return. Stung by Alfonso's apparent indifference,
Giulio conspired with another brother, Ferrante, to murder both the Duke
and the Cardinal. The plot was discovered, and Giulio and Ferrante were
imprisoned in the cells of the Castello. Ferrante died there in 1540; Giulio
was freed by Alfonso II in 1558, after fifty years of genteel confinement;
he emerged an old man, white of hair and beard, and dressed in the fashion
of half a century before. He died shortly after his release.

Alfonso's qualities were what his government needed, for Venice was
expanding into the Romagna and was plotting to absorb Ferrara; while
Julius II, the new Pope, resenting the concessions made to the Estensi in
connection with Lucrezia's marriage, was resolved to reduce the principality to the status of an obedient and profitable fief. In 1508 Julius persuaded
Alfonso to join with him and France and Spain in subduing Venice; Alfonso agreed because he yearned to recover Rovigo. The Venetians concentrated their attack upon Ferrara. Their fleet, sailing up the Po, was
destroyed by Alfonso's concealed artillery; and their soldiers were routed
by Ferrarese troops under Cardinal Ippolito, who enjoyed war only next
to venery. When Venice seemed on the verge of defeat, Julius, not wishing
to weaken irreparably the strongest Italian bulwark against the Turks,
made peace with her, and ordered Alfonso to do the same. Alfonso refused,
and found himself at war with both his enemy and his late ally. Reggio and
Modena fell to the papal forces, and Alfonso seemed lost. In desperation he
went to Rome and asked the Pope for terms; Julius demanded the complete
abdication of the Estensi and the absorption of Ferrara into the Papal States.
When Alfonso rejected these demands Julius tried to arrest him; Alfonso
escaped, and after three months of disguises, wanderings, and perils, reached
his capital. Julius died (1513); Alfonso retook Reggio and Modena. Leo X
resumed the war of the papacy for Ferrara; Alfonso, always improving his
artillery and shifting his diplomacy, held his own obstinately until Leo too

died (1521). Pope Adrian VI gave the indomitable Duke an honorable settlement, and Alfonso was allowed, for a spell, to turn his talents to the arts of peace.

II. THE ARTS IN FERRARA

Ferrarese culture was purely aristocratic, and its arts sedulously served the few. The ducal family, so often at war with the papacy, had no stronger stimulus to piety than to give a devout example to the people. Some new churches were built, but of no memorable quality. The cathedral received in the fifteenth century an unprepossessing campanile, a choir in the Renaissance style, and a pretty Gothic loggia and Virgin in its façade; *non ragionam di lor, ma guarda e passa.* The architects of the time, and their patrons, preferred palaces. About 1495 Biagio Rossetti designed one of the finest, the Palazzo di Lodovico il Moro; according to a doubtful tradition Lodovico had commissioned it in the thought that he might some day be driven from Milan; it was left unfinished when he was taken to France; its cortile, with simple but graceful arcades, is among the lesser jewels of the Renaissance. Lovelier still was the court of the palace built for the Strozzi (1499), and now named Bevilacqua (Drinkwater) from a later occupant. Imposing is the Palazzo de' Diamanti, designed by Rossetti (1492) for Duke Ercole's brother Sigismondo, and faced with 12,000 marble bosses whose diamond shape gave the building its name.

Pleasure palaces were in fashion, and had fancy names: Belfiore, Belriguardo, La Rotonda, Belvedere, and, above all, the summer palace of the Estensi, the Palazzo di Schifanoia—"Skip Annoyance," or, as Frederick the Great would say, Sans Souci ("Without Care"). Begun in 1391, finished by Borso about 1469, it served as one home of the court, and as a dwelling for minor members of the ducal family. When Ferrara declined, the palace was turned into a tobacco factory, and the murals that Cossa, Tura, and others had painted in the main hall were covered with calcimine. In 1840 this was removed, and seven of the twelve panels were salvaged. They constitute a remarkable record of the costumes, industries, pageantry, and sports of Borso's time, strangely mingled with personages from pagan mythology. These frescoes are the happiest product of a school of painting that for half a century made Ferrara a busy center of Italian art.

Ferrarese painters humbly followed the Giottesque tradition until Niccolò III stirred the stagnant waters by bringing in foreign artists to compete with them —Iacopo Bellini from Venice, Mantegna from Padua, Pisanello from Verona. Leonello added stimulus by welcoming Rogier van der Weyden (1449), who helped to turn Italian painters to the use of oil. In the same year Piero della Francesca came from Borgo San Sepolcro to paint murals (now lost) in the Ducal Palace. What really formed the Ferrara school was Cosimo Tura's zealous study of Mantegna's frescoes at Padua, and of the techniques taught there by Francesco Squarcione.

Tura became court painter to Borso (1458), made portraits of the ducal family, shared in decorating the Schifanoia palace, and won such acclaim that Raphael's father ranked him among the leading painters of Italy. Giovanni Santi apparently relished Cosimo's dignified and somber figures, his ornate architectural backgrounds, his landscapes of fantastic rocks; but Raffaello Santi would have missed in these pictures any element of tenderness or grace. We find those elements in Tura's pupil Ercole de' Roberti, who succeeded his teacher as court painter in 1495; but this Hercules lacked power and vitality, unless we except the Frans-Halsian *Concert* once ascribed to him in the London Gallery. Francesco Cossa, the greatest of Tura's pupils, painted in the Schifanoia two masterpieces rich in both vitality and grace: *The Triumph of Venus* and *The Races*, revealing the charm and joy of life at the Ferrara court. When Borso paid him for these at the official rate—ten *bolognini* per foot of painted space—Cossa protested; and when Borso failed to see the point Francesco took his talents to Bologna (1470). Lorenzo Costa did likewise thirteen years later, and the school of Ferrara lost two of its best men.

Dosso Dossi revitalized it by studying in Venice in the heyday of Giorgione (1477-1510). Returning to Ferrara, he became the favorite painter of Duke Alfonso I. Ariosto, his friend, ranked him and a forgotten brother among the immortals:

> *Leonardo, Andrea Mantegna, Gian Bellino,*
> *Duo Dossi, e quel ch'a par sculpe e colora*
> *Michel, più che mortale, angel divino,*
> *Bastiano, Rafael, Tizian.*[5]

We can understand why Ariosto liked Dosso, who brought into his pictures an outdoor quality almost illustrative of Ariosto's sylvan epic, and bathed them in the warm colors that he had borrowed from the sumptuous Venetians. It was Dosso and his pupils who decorated the Sala di Consiglio in the Castello with lively scenes of athletic contests in the ancient style, for Alfonso liked athletics more than poetry. In his later years Dosso painted with uneven hand the allegorical and mythological scenes on the ceiling of the Sala dell' Aurora. Here the pagan motives rampant in Italy triumphed in a celebration of physical beauty and sensuous life. Perhaps the decadence that now began in Ferrarese art—due chiefly to the exhausting cost of Alfonso's wars—had one source in this victory of flesh over spirit; the passion and grandeur of the old religious themes faded from a largely secular art, leaving it predominantly decoration.

The most brilliant figure in this decline was Benvenuto Tisi, named Garofalo from his native town. On two visits to Rome he became so enamored of Raphael's art that, though two years his senior, he enrolled as an assistant in the young master's studio. When family affairs recalled him to Ferrara he promised Raphael to return, but Alfonso and the nobility gave him so many commissions that he could never tear himself away. He consumed his energy, and divided his ability, in producing a multitude of paintings, of which some seventy remain. They lack both force and finish; and yet one *Holy Family*, in the Vatican, shows how even the minor artists of the Renaissance could now and then touch greatness.

The painters and the architects were only a fraction of the artists who labored to please the fortunates of Ferrara. Miniaturists produced there, as elsewhere in that eager age, works of a delicate beauty on which the eye rests longer and more contentedly than on many a famous painting; the Schifanoia palace has preserved several of these gems of illumination and calligraphy. Niccolò III brought in tapestry weavers from Flanders; Ferrarese artists furnished designs; the patient art flourished under Leonello and Borso; the resulting tapestries decorated palace walls, and were lent to princes and nobles for their special festivities. Goldsmiths were kept busy making ecclesiastical vessels and personal ornaments. Sperandio of Mantua and Pisanello of Verona made here some of the finest medallions of the Renaissance.

Last and least was sculpture. Cristoforo da Firenze molded the man, Niccolò Baroncelli the horse, for a bronze statue of Niccolò III; it was set up in 1451, two years before Donatello's *Gattamelata* rose in Padua. Beside it, in 1470, was placed a bronze statue of Duke Borso, calmly seated as became a man of peace. In 1796 both monuments were destroyed by revolutionists who branded the bronzes as mementos of tyranny, and melted them into cannon to end all tyranny and all wars. Alfonso Lombardi adorned the "Alabaster Chambers" of the Castello with stately statuary; then, like so many Ferrarese artists, he decamped to Bologna, where we shall find him in glory. The court of Ferrara was too narrow in its ideas, tastes, and fees to transmute evanescent wealth into immortal art.

III. LETTERS

The intellectual life of Ferrara had two roots: the University, and Guarino da Verona. Founded in 1391, the University had soon closed for lack of funds; reopened by Niccolò III, it led a half-starved existence until Leonello (1442) reorganized and refinanced it with an edict whose prelude deserves commemoration:

> It is an ancient opinion, not only of the Christians but of the Gentiles, that the heavens, the sea, and the earth must some day perish; in like manner, of many magnificent cities nothing but ruins leveled with the ground can now be seen, and Rome the conqueror herself

lies in the dust and is reduced to fragments; while only the understanding of things divine and human, which we call wisdom, is not
extinguished by length of years, but retains its rights in perpetuity.[6]

By 1474 the University had forty-five well paid professors, and the faculties of astronomy, mathematics, and medicine were rivaled in Italy only by
those at Bologna and Padua.

Guarino, born at Verona in 1370, went to Constantinople, lived there
five years, mastered the Greek language, and returned to Venice with a
cargo of Greek manuscripts; a legend told how, when a box of these was
lost in a storm, his hair turned white overnight. He taught Greek at Venice,
where he had Vittorino da Feltre among his pupils, and then at Verona,
Padua, Bologna, and Florence, absorbing the classical scholarship of each
city in turn. He was already fifty-nine when he accepted an invitation to
Ferrara. There, as tutor to Leonello, Borso, and Ercole, he trained three of
the most enlightened rulers in Renaissance history. As professor of Greek
and rhetoric in the University his success was the talk of Italy. So popular
were his lectures that students made their way through any rigor of winter
to wait outside the unopened doors of the room in which he was scheduled
to speak. They came not only from Italian cities, but from Hungary, Germany, England, and France; and many of them went forth from his instruction to fill vital posts in education, law, and statesmanship. Like
Vittorino, he supported poor students out of his personal funds; he lived
in humble quarters, ate but one meal a day, and used to invite his friends
not to feasts but to *fave e favole*—beans and conversation.[7] He was not
quite the equal of Vittorino as a moral paragon; he could pen virulent
invectives like any humanist, perhaps as a literary game; but his thirteen
children were apparently begotten on one wife, he was temperate in everything but study, and he maintained health, vigor, and mental clarity till his
ninetieth year.[8] It was chiefly due to him that the dukes of Ferrara supported education, scholarship, and poetry, and made their capital one of
the most renowned cultural centers in Europe.

The revival of antiquity brought with it a renewed acquaintance with
classic drama. Plautus, son of the people, and Terence, manumitted darling
of the aristocracy, came alive again after fifteen centuries, and were acted
on temporary stages at Florence and Rome, above all at Ferrara. Ercole I,
in particular, loved the old comedies, and spared no revenues in producing
them; one representation of the *Menaechmi* cost him a thousand ducats.
When Lodovico of Milan saw a performance of this play at Ferrara he
begged Ercole to send the players to repeat it at Pavia; Ercole not only

sent them but went with them (1493). When Lucrezia Borgia came to Ferrara, Ercole celebrated her hymeneals with five of Plautus' comedies performed by 110 actors, with lavish interludes of music and ballet. Guarino, Ariosto, and Ercole himself translated Latin plays into Italian, and performances were given in the vernacular. It was through imitation of these classic comedies that Italian drama took form. Boiardo, Ariosto, and others wrote plays for the ducal company. Ariosto drew up plans, and Dosso Dossi painted the fixed scenery, for the first permanent theater of Ferrara and modern Europe (1532).

Music and poetry also won the patronage of the court. Tito Vespasiano Strozzi needed no ducal subsidies for his verse, for he was the scion of a rich Florentine family. He composed in Latin ten "books" of a poem in praise of Borso; leaving it unfinished at his death, he bequeathed to his son Ercole the task of completing it. Ercole was well fitted for the assignment; he wrote excellent lyrics, Latin and Italian, and a longer poem, *La caccia* —*The Hunt*—dedicated to Lucrezia Borgia. In 1508 he married a poetess, Barbara Torelli; thirteen days later he was found dead near his home, his body savagely pierced with twenty-two wounds. This is a mystery story still unsolved after four centuries. Some have thought that Alfonso had approached Barbara, had been repulsed, and revenged himself by hiring assassins to kill his successful rival. It is unlikely, for Alfonso, as long as Lucrezia lived, showed her every sign of fidelity. The desolate young widow composed an elegy whose ring of sincerity is rare in the usually artificial literature of the Ferrara court. "Why may I not go down to the grave with thee?" she asks the slain poet:

> *Vorrei col foco mio quel freddo ghiaccio*
> *Intorpidire, e rimpastar col pianto*
> *La polve, e ravivarla a nuove vita!*
> *E vorrei poscia, baldanzosa e ardita,*
> *Mostrarlo a lui che ruppe il caro laccio,*
> *E dirgli: amor, mostro crudel, può tanto.**

In this courtly society, dowered with leisure and fair women, the French romances of chivalry were a daily food. In Ferrara Provençal troubadours

---

* Would that my fire might warm this frigid ice,
  And turn, with tears, this dust to living flesh,
  And give to thee anew the joy of life!
  Then would I boldly, ardently, confront
  The man who snapped our dearest bond, and cry,
  "O cruel monster! See what love can do!"

had sung their lays in Dante's time, and had left a mood of fanciful, not onerous, chivalry. Here, and throughout northern Italy, the legends of Charlemagne, his knights, and his wars with the Moslem infidels had become almost as familiar as in France. The French trouvères had spread and swelled these legends as *chansons de geste;* and their recitals, piling episode upon episode, hero upon heroine, had become a mass of fiction monumental and confused, crying out for some Homer to weave the tales into sequence and unity.

As an English knight, Sir Thomas Malory, had recently accomplished this with the legends of Arthur and the Round Table, so now an Italian nobleman took up the task for the cycle of Charlemagne. Matteo Maria Boiardo, Count of Scandiano, was among the most distinguished members of the Ferrara court. He served the Estensi as ambassador on important missions, and was entrusted by them with the administration of their largest dependencies, Modena and Reggio. He governed poorly but sang well. He addressed passionate verses to Antonia Caprara, soliciting and publishing her charms, or reproaching her for lack of fidelity in sin. When he married Taddea Gonzaga he turned his muse to graze in safer pastures, and began an epic—*Orlando innamorato* (1486f)—recounting the troubled love of Orlando (i.e., Roland) for the enchantress Angelica, and mingling with this romance a hundred scenes of tilt, tournament, and war. A humorous legend tells how Boiardo sought far and wide to find a properly resounding name for the boastful Saracen in his tale, and how, when he hit upon the mighty cognomen of Rodomonte, the bells of the Count's fief, Scandiano, were set ringing for joy, as if aware that their lord was unwittingly giving a word to a dozen languages.

It is hard for us, in our own exciting times, agitated even in peace with the tilts and tournaments of hostile words, to interest ourselves in the imaginary wars and loves of Orlando, Rinaldo, Astolfo, Ruggiero, Agramante, Marfisa, Fiordelisa, Sacripante, Agricane; and Angelica, who might have stirred us by her beauty, disconcerts us by the supernatural enchantments that she practises; we are no longer bewitched by sorceresses. These are tales that befitted a comely audience in some palace bower or garden close; and indeed, we are told, the Count read these cantos at the Ferrara court[9]— doubtless a canto or two at a sitting; we do Boiardo and Ariosto injustice when we try to take them an epic at a time. They wrote for a leisurely generation and class, and Boiardo for one that had not yet seen the invasion of Italy by Charles VIII. When that disillusioning humiliation came, and Italy saw how helpless she was, with all her art and poetry, against the ruthless powers of the North, Boiardo lost heart, and after writing 60,000 lines he dropped his pen with a stanza of despair:

> *Mentre che io canto, o Dio redentore,*
> *Vedo l'Italia tutto a fiamma e foco,*
> *Per questi Galli, che con gran valore*
> *Vengon, per disertar non so che loco . . .**

He did well to end, and wisely died (1494) before the invasion had reached full force. The noble sentiment of chivalry that had found rough utterance in his poetry evoked only the rarest response in the troubled generation that ensued. Though he had earned a niche in history by developing the modern romantic epic, his voice was soon forgotten in the wars and turmoil of Alfonso's reign, in the alien rape of Italy, and in the seductive beauty of Ariosto's gentler verse.

IV. ARIOSTO

As we approach the supreme poet of the Italian Renaissance, we must remind ourselves that poetry is an untranslatable music, and that those of us to whom the Italian language is not a native boon must not expect to understand why Italy ranks Lodovico Ariosto only next to Dante among her bards, and reads the *Orlando furioso* with an affectionate delight surpassing that which Englishmen take in Shakespeare's plays. We shall hear the words but miss the melody.

He was born on September 14, 1474, at Reggio Emilia, where his father was governor. In 1481 the family moved to Rovigo, but apparently Lodovico received his education in Ferrara. Like Petrarch he was set to study law, but preferred to write poetry. He was not much disturbed by the French invasion of 1494; and when Charles VIII prepared a second descent into Italy (1496), Ariosto composed an ode, in Horatian style, putting the matter in what seemed to him a proper perspective:

> What signifies to me the coming of Charles and his hosts? I shall rest in the shade, hearkening to the gentle murmur of the waters, watching the reapers at work; and thou, O my Phyllis, wilt stretch thy white hand among the enameled flowers, and weave me garlands to the music of thy voice.[10]

In 1500 the father died, leaving to his ten children a patrimony sufficient

---

* O God Redeemer! even while I sing
I see all Italy in flame and fire,
Brough by these Gauls who, spurred with courage high,
Advance to make a desert everywhere.

to support one or two. Lodovico, the oldest, became father of the family, and began a long struggle with economic insecurity. His anxieties warped his character into a timidity and angry subservience unintelligible to those who have never hungered between rhymes. In 1503 he entered the service of Cardinal Ippolito d'Este. Ippolito had little taste for poetry, and kept Ariosto uncomfortably busy with diplomatic errands and trivia, for which the poet received 240 lire ($3000?) a year, irregularly paid. He sought to improve his position by writing lauds of the Cardinal's courage and chastity, and defending the blinding of Giulio. Ippolito offered to raise his salary if he would take holy orders and become eligible for certain available benefices; but Ariosto disliked the clergy, and preferred to philander rather than to burn.

It was during his service with Ippolito that he wrote most of his plays. He had begun as an actor, and had been one of the company that Ercole sent to Pavia. When he himself devised dramas they bore the stamp of Terence or Plautus, and were frankly offered as imitations.[11] His *Cassaria* was performed at Ferrara in 1508, his *Suppositi* at Rome in 1519 before an approving Leo X. He continued to write plays till his last year, and left the best of them, *Scolastica*, unfinished at his death. Nearly all turn on the classic theme of how one or more young men, usually through the wits of their servants, may possess themselves, by marriage or seduction, of one or more young women. Ariosto's plays rank high in Italian comedy, low in the history of drama.

It was again during his employment with Ippolito that the poet wrote most of his enormous epic, *Orlando furioso;* apparently the Cardinal was no hard taskmaster after all. When Ariosto showed Ippolito the manuscript the realistic prelate, according to an uncertain tradition—*se non vero, ben trovato*—asked him, "Where, Messer Lodovico, have you found so much nonsense (*tante corbellerie*)?"[12] But the laudatory dedication seemed to make more sense, and the Cardinal paid the cost of publishing the poem (1515), and secured all rights and profits of its sale to Ariosto. Italy did not think the poem nonsense, or thought it delectable nonsense; nine printings were bought up between 1524 and 1527. Soon the choicest passages were being recited or sung throughout the peninsula. Ariosto himself read much of it to Isabella d'Este in her illness at Mantua, and rewarded her patience with a eulogy in later editions. He spent ten years (1505-15) writing the *Furioso*, sixteen more in polishing it; every now and then he added a canto, until the whole ran to almost 39,000 lines, equivalent to the *Iliad* and the *Odyssey* combined.

At first he merely proposed to continue and expand Boiardo's *Orlando innamorato*. He took from his predecessor the chivalric setting and theme, the loves and battles of Charlemagne's knights, the central characters, the loose episodic construction, the suspension of one narrative to pass to another, the magic operations that often turn the tale, even the idea of tracing the pedigree of the Estensi to the marriage of the mythical Ruggiero and Bradamante. And yet, while praising a hundred others, he never mentions Boiardo's name; no man is a hero to his debtor. Perhaps Ariosto felt that the theme and characters belonged to the cycle of legends themselves, rather than to Boiardo.

Like the Count, and unlike the legends, he stressed the role of love above that of war, and so proclaimed in his opening lines:

> *Le donne, i cavalier, l'arme, gli amori,*
> *Le cortesie, l'audaci imprese io canto—*

"Women I sing, and knights, and arms, and loves, and deeds of chivalry and bold emprise." The story carries out this program faithfully: it is a series of combats, some for Christianity against Islam, most for women. A dozen counts and kings contest Angelica; she flirts with them all, plays them one against another, and is caught in an anticlimax when she falls in love with a handsome mediocrity, and marries him before she has time to make the usual examination of his income. Orlando, who enters the story after eight cantos have rolled by, pursues her over three continents, neglecting meanwhile to go to the aid of his sovereign Charlemagne when the Saracens attack Paris. He goes mad on learning that he has lost her (canto XXIII), and recovers sanity sixteen cantos later when his lost wits are found in the moon and brought back to him by a predecessor of Jules Verne's lunar navigators. This central theme is confused and obfuscated by the interpolated adventures of a dozen other knights, who pursue their respective women through forty-six cantos of seductive verse. The women enjoy the chase, perhaps excepting Isabella, who persuades Rodomonte to cut off her head rather than to deflower her, and earns a monument. The old legend of St. George is included: the beautiful Angelica is chained to the rocks beside the sea as a propitiatory offering to a dragon who hungers for a virgin annually; and before Ruggiero can arrive to rescue her the poet contemplates her with Correggian appreciation:

> *La fiera gente inospitale e cruda*
> *Alla bestia crudel nel lito espose*
> *La bellissima donna così ignuda*

Come Natura prima la compose.
Un velo non ha pure in che rinchiuda
I bianchi gigli e le vermiglie rose,
Da non cader per luglio o per Decembre,
Di che non sparse le polite membre.

Creduta avria che fosse statua finta
O d'alabastro o d'altri marmi illustri
Ruggiero, e su lo scoglio così avvinta
Per artificio di scultori industri;
Se non videa la lachrima distinta
Tra fresche rose e candidi ligustri
Far rugiadose le crudette pome,
E l'aura sventolar l'aurate chiome.[13]

Which may be rendered, musicless:

A people fierce, inhospitable, crude
Exposed upon the shore, to savage beast,
A woman fairest of the fair, and nude
As when first Nature her sweet form composed.
No smallest veil enclosed the lilies white
And vermeil roses of her flesh, that bear
Midsummer's ardor and December's cold
Unhurt, and gleam on her resplendent limbs.

She might have seemed to him a statue made
Of alabaster, or some marble form
Bound to the stone by sculptor's artifice,
Had he not seen a bright tear fall between
The roses and white privets of her cheeks,
Bedewing breasts like apples firm, and seen
The breezes breathing on her golden hair.

Ariosto does not take all this too seriously; he is writing to amuse; he deliberately charms us, by the incantation of his verse, into an unreal world, and mystifies his tale with fairies, magic weapons and enchantments, winged horses touring the clouds, men turned into trees, fortresses melting at an imperious word. Orlando spits six Dutchmen on one spear; Astolfo creates a fleet by throwing leaves into the air, and catches the wind in a bladder. Ariosto laughs with us at all this, and smiles tolerantly, not sarcastically, at the tilts and shams of chivalry. He has an excellent sense of humor, salted with gentle irony; so he includes, in the waste deposited by the earth upon the moon, the prayers of hypocrites, the flatteries of poets (*peccavit*), the services of courtiers, the Donation of Constantine (XXXIV). Only now and then, in a few moral exordiums, does Ariosto pretend to philosophy. He was so completely the poet that he lost and consumed himself in forging and polishing a beautiful form for his verse; he had no energy left to pour into it an ennobling purpose or a philosophy of life.[13a]

Italians love the *Furioso* because it is a treasury of exciting stories—with never a pretty woman too far away—told in melodious and yet unaffected language, and in racy stanzas that lure us swiftly on from scene to scene. They forgive the long detours and descriptions, the innumerable and sometimes labored similes, for these too are dressed in sparkling verse. They are rewarded, and silently shout "Bravo!" when the poet hammers out a striking line, as when he says of Zerbino,

Natura il fece, e poi roppe la stampa,—[14]

"Nature made him, and then broke the mold." They are not long disturbed by Ariosto's expectant flattery of the Estensi, his paeans to Ippolito, his praise of Lucrezia's chastity. These obeisances were in the manner of the times; Machiavelli would stoop as low to conquer a subsidy; and a poet must live.

But this became difficult when the Cardinal decided to campaign in Hungary, and desired Ariosto to accompany him. Ariosto demurred, and Ippolito freed him from further service and recompense (1517). Alfonso saved the poet from penury by giving him an annual stipend of eighty-four crowns ($1050?), plus three servants and two horses, and requiring almost nothing in return. After forty-seven years of obstinate but hardly celibate bachelordom, Ariosto now married Alessandra Benucci, whom he had loved when she was still the wife of Tito Vespasiano Strozzi. By her he had no children, but two natural sons had rewarded his premarital efforts.

For three years (1522-5) he served unhappily as governor of the Garfagnana, a mountainous region racked with brigandage. But he was unfit for action or command, and gladly retired to spend the remaining eight years of his life in Ferrara. In 1528 he bought a plot of land on the outskirts of the city, and built a pretty house, still shown in the Via Ariosto, and maintained by the state. Across the front he inscribed Horatian lines of proud simplicity: *Parva sed apta mihi, sed nulli obnoxia, sed non sordida, parta meo sed tamen aere domus*—"Small but suitable for me, hurtful to no one, not mean, yet acquired by my own funds: home." There he lived quietly, working occasionally in his garden, and revising or expanding the *Furioso* every day.

Meanwhile, further emulating Horace, he had written to various friends seven poetical epistles that have come down to us under the name of satires. They are not as sharp and compact as those of his model, nor as bitter and lethal as Juvenal's; they were the product of a mind loving and never quite finding peace, bearing fretfully the whips and scorns of time, the proud man's contumely. They describe the faults of the clergy, the simony rampant in Rome, the nepotism of worldly popes (Satire i). They excoriate Ippolito for paying his menials better than his poet (ii). They expound a cynical conception of women as rarely faithful or honest, and offer the advice of a tardy expert on choosing and taming a wife (iii). They lament the indignities of a courtier's life, and wryly recount an unsuccessful visit to Leo X (iv):

> I kissed his foot, he bent down from the holy seat, took my hand, and saluted me on both cheeks. Besides, he made me free of half the stamp dues I was bound to pay. Then, breast full of hope but body soaked with rain and smirched with mud, I went and had my supper at the Ram.

Two satires mourn his narrow life at Garfagnana, his days "spent in threatening, punishing, persuading, or acquitting," his muse frightened and paralyzed into silence by crimes, lawsuits, and brawls; and his mistress so many miles away! (v-vi) The last epistle asks Bembo to recommend a Greek tutor for Ariosto's son Virginio:

> The Greek must be learned but also of sound principles, for erudition without morality is worse than worthless. Unhappily, in these days, it is difficult to find a teacher of this sort. Few humanists are free from the most infamous of vices, and intellectual vanity makes most of them skeptics also. Why is it that learning and infidelity go hand in hand?[15]

Ariosto himself had through most of his life taken religion lightly; but, like nearly all the intellects of the Renaissance, he made his peace with it in the end. Even from youth he had suffered from a bronchial catarrh, which was probably aggravated by his travels as courier for the Cardinal. In 1532 the trouble sank deeper, and became tuberculosis. He struggled against it as if not satisfied with a mere immortality of fame. He was only fifty-eight when he died (1533).

He had become a classic long before his death. Twenty-three years earlier Raphael had painted him, in the *Parnassus* fresco of the Vatican, with Homer and Virgil, Horace and Ovid, Dante and Petrarch, among the unforgettable voices of mankind. Italy calls him her Homer, and the *Furioso* her *Iliad;* but even to an idolater of Italy this appears more generous than just. The world of Ariosto seems light and fantastic beside the ruthless siege of Troy; his knights—some as indistinguishable in their character as in their armor—hardly rise to the majesty of Agamemnon, the passion of Achilles, the wisdom of Nestor, the nobility of Hector, the tragedy of Priam; and who will equate the fair and flighty Angelica with the *dia gynaikon*, the goddess among women, Helen conqueror in defeat? And yet the last word must be as the first: only those can judge Ariosto who know his language thoroughly, who can catch the nuances of his gaiety and his sentiment, and can respond to all the music of his melodious dream.

V. AFTERMATH

It was the Italians themselves, with their lusty sense of humor, who provided an antidote to the romanticism of the two *Orlandos*. Six years before Ariosto's death Girolamo Folengo published an *Orlandino* in which the absurdities of the epics were caricatured with hilarious exaggerations. Girolamo heard the skeptical lectures of Pomponazzi at Bologna, adopted a curriculum of amours, intrigues, fisticuffs, and duels, and was expelled from the University. His father disowned him, and he became a Benedictine monk (1507), perhaps as a means of subsistence. Six years later he fell in love with Girolama Dieda, and eloped with her. In 1519 he published a volume of burlesques under the title of *Maccaronea*, which thenceforth gave its name to a swelling literature of rough and ribald satire in mingled Latin and Italian verse. The *Orlandino* was a riotous mock epic, in coarse and popular vernacular, pursuing a serious vein for a stanza or two, then startling the reader with a thought and phrase worthy of the most scatophilic privy councilor. The knights, armed with kitchen utensils, rush into the lists on limping mules. The leading churchman of the tale is the monk Griffarosto—Abbot Grab-the-Roast—whose library consists of cook books interspersed with victuals and wine, and "all the tongues he knew were those of oxen and swine";[16] through him Folengo satirizes the clergy of Italy to any Lutheran's content. The work was received with guffaws of applause, but the author continued to starve. Finally he retired again to a monastery, wrote pious poetry, and died in the odor of sanctity at fifty-three (1544). Rabelais relished him,[17] and perhaps Ariosto, in his final years, joined in the merriment.

Alfonso I kept his little state secure against all the assaults of the papacy, and at last took a reckless revenge by encouraging and abetting the German-Spanish army that besieged, captured, and plundered Rome (1527).[18] Charles V expressed appreciation by restoring to him Ferrara's ancient fiefs, Modena and Reggio, so that Alfonso transmitted his duchy undiminished to his heirs. In 1528 he sent his son Ercole to France to bring home a diplomatic bride from the royal family—Renée or Renata—tiny, somber, deformed, and secretly won by the heresy of Calvin. Alfonso, after Lucrezia's passing, consoled himself with a mistress, Laura Dianti, and perhaps married her before his death (1534). He had outwitted every enemy but time.

CHAPTER XI

Venice and Her Realm

1378-1534

I. PADUA

UNDER the dictatorship of the Carraresi Padua was a major Italian power, rivaling and threatening Venice. In 1378 Padua joined Genoa in attempting to subjugate the island republic. In 1380 Venice, exhausted by her war with Genoa, ceded to the duke of Austria the city of Treviso, strategically situated on her north. In 1383 Francesco I da Carrara bought Treviso from Austria; soon afterward he tried to take Vicenza, Udine, and Friuli; had he succeeded he would have commanded the roads from Venice to her iron mines at Agordo, and the routes of Venetian trade with Germany; i.e., Padua would have controlled vital sources of Venetian industry and commerce. Venice was saved by the skill of her diplomats. They persuaded Giangaleazzo Visconti to join Venice in war against Padua; Gian, while doubtless distrusting Venice, seized the opportunity to extend his frontier eastward with Venetian connivance. Francesco I da Carrara was defeated and abdicated (1389); and his son, namesake, and successor renewed (1399) a treaty of 1338 that had acknowledged Padua to be a dependency of Venice. When Francesco II da Carrara resumed the struggle and attacked Verona and Vicenza, Venice declared war to the death, captured and executed him and his sons, and brought Padua under direct rule by the Venetian Senate (1405). The weary city abandoned the luxury of a native exploiter, prospered under an alien but competent administration, and became the educational center of the Venetian domain. From all quarters of Latin Christendom students came to its renowned university—Pico della Mirandola, Ariosto, Bembo, Guicciardini, Tasso, Galileo, Gustavus Vasa who would be King of Sweden, John Sobieski who would be King of Poland. . . . The chair of Greek was founded in 1463 and occupied by Demetrius Chalcondyles sixteen years before he went to Florence. A century later Shakespeare could still speak of "Fair Padua, nursery of arts."

One Paduan was himself a famous educational institution. Trained as a tailor, Francesco Squarcione developed a passion for classic art, traveled widely in Italy and Greece, copied or sketched Greek and Roman sculpture and architecture, collected ancient medals, coins, and statuary, and returned to Padua with one of the best classical collections of his time. He opened a school of art, installed his collection there, and gave his pupils two main directives: to study ancient art and the new science of perspective. Few of the 137 artists whom he formed remained in Padua, since most of them came from outside. But in return Giotto came from Florence to paint the Arena frescoes; Altichiero came from Verona (*c.* 1376) to adorn a chapel in St. Anthony's; and Donatello left memorials of his genius in the cathedral and its square. Bartolommeo Bellano, a pupil of Donatello, set up two lovely female statues for Gattamelata's chapel in the same church; Pietro Lombardo of Venice added a fine figure of the *condottiere's* son, and a splendid tomb for Antonio Roselli. Andrea Briosco—"Riccio"—and Antonio and Tullio Lombardo carved for the Gattamelata chapel some superb marble reliefs; and Riccio set up in the choir of the church one of the most imposing candelabra in Italy. He shared with Alessandro Leopardi of Venice and Andrea Morone of Bergamo in designing the unfinished church of Santa Giustina (1502f), a chaste example of the Renaissance architectural style.

It was from Padua and Verona that Iacopo Bellini and Antonio Pisanello brought to Venice the seeds of that Venetian school of painting through which the splendor of Venice was blazoned to the world.

II. VENETIAN ECONOMY AND POLICY

In 1378 Venice was at nadir: her Adriatic trade was bottled up by a victorious Genoese fleet, her communications with the mainland were blocked by Genoese and Paduan troops, her people were starving, her government contemplated surrender. Half a century later she ruled Padua, Vicenza, Verona, Brescia, Bergamo, Treviso, Belluno, Feltre, Friuli, Istria, the Dalmatian coast, Lepanto, Patras, and Corinth. Secure in her many-moated citadel, she seemed immune to the political vicissitudes of the Italian mainland; her wealth and power mounted until she sat like a throned queen at the head of Italy. Philippe de Comines, arriving as French ambassador in 1495, pictured her as "the most triumphant city that I have ever seen."[1] Pietro Casola, coming from hostile Milan about the same time, found it "impossible to describe the beauty, magnificence, and wealth"[2] of this unique assemblage of 117 islands, 150 canals, 400 bridges, all dominated by the flowing promenade of the Grand Canal, which the traveled Comines pronounced "the most beautiful street in the world."

Whence came the wealth that supported this magnificence? Partly from a hundred industries—shipbuilding, iron manufactures, glass blowing, leather dressing and tooling, gem cutting and setting, textiles . . . all organized in proud guilds (*scuole*) that united master and man in patriotic fellowship. But perhaps more of Venetian opulence came from the mercantile marine whose sails flapped on the lagoons, whose galleys took the products of Venice and her mainland dependencies, and the German and other wares that scaled the Alps, and carried them to Egypt, Greece, Byzantium, and Asia, and returned from the East with silks, spices, rugs, drugs, and slaves. The exports of an average year were valued at 10,000,000 ducats ($250,000,000?);[3] no other city in Europe could equal this trade. The Venetian vessels could be seen in a hundred ports, from Trebizond in the Black Sea to Cadiz, Lisbon, London, Bruges, even in Iceland.[4] On the Rialto, the commercial center of Venice, merchants could be seen from half the globe. Marine insurance covered this traffic, and a tax on imports and exports was the mainstay of the state. The annual income of the Venetian government in 1455 was 800,000 ducats ($20,000,000?); in the same year the revenue of Florence was some 200,000 ducats, of Naples 310,000, of the Papal States 400,000, of Milan 500,000, of all Christian Spain, 800,000.[5]

This commerce dictated the policies, as it so largely financed the operations, of the Venetian Republic. It raised to power a mercantile aristocracy that made itself hereditary and controlled all the organs of the state. It kept a population of 190,000 (in 1422) profitably employed, but it left them dependent upon foreign markets, materials, and food. Imprisoned in her labyrinth, Venice could feed her people only by importing food; she could supply her industries only by importing lumber, metals, minerals, leather, cloth; and she could pay for these imports only by finding markets for her products and her trade. Dependent on the mainland for food, outlets, and raw materials, she fought a succession of wars to establish her control over northeastern Italy; dependent likewise on non-Italian areas, she was anxious to dominate the regions that supplied her wants, the markets that took her goods, the routes by which her vital commerce passed. She became by "manifest destiny" an imperialistic power.

So the political history of Venice turned on her economic needs. When the Scaligeri at Verona, or the Carraresi at Padua, or the Visconti at Milan attempted to spread their sway over northeastern Italy, Venice felt endangered and took to arms. Fearful that Ferrara might control the mouths of the Po, she tried to determine the choice or policy of the ruling marquis there, and resented the claims of the papacy to Ferrara as its fief. Her own westward expansion angered Milan, which had expansive ideas of its own. When Filippo Maria Visconti attacked Florence (1423), the Tuscan Republic appealed to Venice for aid, and pointed out that a Milan master over Tuscany would soon absorb all Italy north of the Papal States. In a debate often repeated in history, Doge Tommaso Mocenigo, dying, pled in the Venetian Senate the cause of peace; Francesco Foscari argued for an offensive war of defense; Foscari won, and Venice began with Milan a series of wars that lasted, with some lucid intervals, from 1425 to 1454. The death of Filippo Maria (1447), the chaos of the Ambrosian Republic in Milan, and the capture of Constantinople by the Turks inclined the rival states to sign at Lodi a treaty that left the island Republic exhausted but victorious.

Her expansion in the Adriatic began with a legitimate excuse. Her geographical position as the northernmost port of the Mediterranean was the fortune of Venice, but it was of no worth without control of the Adriatic. The eastern coast offered in its isles and bays convenient lairs for pirate vessels, whose raids were a frequent loss and constant peril to Venetian shipping. When Venice bribed the Crusaders to help her take Zara in 1202, she acquired a post from which year by year to clear out these pirate nests, until all the Dalmatian coast accepted her sovereignty. When those same Crusaders raped Constantinople (1204), Venice received, as her share of the spoils, Crete, Salonika, the Cyclades, and the Sporades, precious links in a golden chain of trade. With leisurely pertinacity she took Durazzo, the Albanian coast, the Ionian Islands (1386-92), Friuli and Istria (1418-20), Ravenna (1441); she was now indisputably Queen of the Adriatic, and charged tolls to all non-Venetian vessels plying that sea.[6] As the advance of the Ottoman Turks toward Constantinople made it difficult for that capital to defend the outlying possessions of Byzantium, many Greek islands and cities submitted themselves to Venice as the only power ready to protect them. In Cyprus a stately queen, Caterina Cornaro, last of the Lusignan line, was persuaded that she could not hold her island against the Turks; she abdicated in favor of a Venetian governor (1489) and a Venetian pension of 8000 ducats a year; she retired to an estate at Asolo, near Treviso, set up an unofficial court, patronized literature and art, and became the subject or dedicatee of poems and operas, and paintings by Gentile Bellini, Titian, and Veronese.

All these laborious conquests of diplomacy or arms, these outlets, guardians, and tributaries of Venetian trade faced in their turn the rising tide of the Ottomans. At Gallipoli (1416) a Turkish garrison attacked a Venetian fleet; the Venetians fought with their usual courage and won a decisive victory; for a generation the rival powers lived in a truce and commercial amity that shocked a Europe anxious to have Venice fight Europe's battle against the Turks. Even the fall of Constantinople did not disrupt this entente; Venice arranged a tolerable commercial treaty with the victorious Turks, and exchanged courtesies with the conqueror. But now Venetian access to the lucrative trade of the Black Sea ports was dependent on Turkish permission, and soon met with irritating limitations. When Pius II, voicing the sentiments of a Christian and the commercial interests of Europe, proclaimed a crusade against the Turks, and received pledges of arms and men from the European powers, Venice responded to the call, hoping to repeat the strategy of 1204. But the powers welched on their promises, and Venice found herself alone at war with the Turks (1463). For sixteen years she carried on this struggle. She was defeated and despoiled; by the peace that she signed in 1479 she ceded Negroponte (Euboea), Scutari, and Morea to the Turks, paid 100,000 ducats as a war indemnity, and pledged 10,000 ducats a year for the privilege of trading in Turkish ports. Europe denounced her as a traitor to Christendom. When another pope proposed another crusade against the Turks Venice turned a deaf ear. She agreed with Europe that trade was more important than Christianity.

III. VENETIAN GOVERNMENT

Even her enemies admired her government, and sent agents to study its structure and functioning. Its military organs were the most efficient navy and army in Italy. Besides her merchant fleet, which in need could be converted to men-of-war, Venice had in 1423 a navy of forty-three galleys and 300 auxiliary vessels.[7] These were used even in wars with land powers in Italy; in 1439 they were dragged overland on rollers across mountains and valleys to be launched on the Lago di Garda, where they bombarded the possessions of Milan.[8] While other Italian states still waged their wars with mercenaries, Venice built her army around a militia of her own loyal population, well seasoned and trained, and armed with the latest muskets and artillery. For generals, however, she relied on *condottieri* schooled in the Renaissance style of campaign by strategy. In her wars with Milan Venice developed the talents of three famous *condottieri*: Francesco Carmagnola,

Erasmo da Narni "Gattamelata," and Bartolommeo Colleoni; the last two distinguished by historic statues, the other by having his head cut off, in the Venetian Piazzetta, on a charge of privately negotiating with the enemy.

This government, which even Florentines sought to emulate, was a closed oligarchy of old families so long enriched by commerce that only the initiate could smell the money in their nobility. These families had managed to restrict membership in the *Maggior Consiglio* to male descendants of persons who had sat in this Great Council before 1297. In 1315 the names of all eligibles were inscribed in a *Libro d'oro*, or Book of Gold. Out of its 480 members the Council named sixty—later 120—*Pregadi* ("invited men") to serve in yearly terms as a legislative Senate; it appointed the heads of the numerous governmental departments, who together constituted an administrative *Collegio;* and it selected as chief executive—always subject to the Council—a doge or leader who presided over it and the Senate, and held office for life unless the Council cared to depose him. The doge was aided by six privy councilors, who with him composed the *Signoria*. This Signory and the Senate were in practice the real government of Venice; the Great Council proved too large for effective action, and became a body of electors exercising appointive and supervisory powers. It was an efficient constitution, which normally maintained the people in a reasonable degree of prosperity; and it was capable of long-term and well calculated policies that might have been impossible in a government subject to the fluctuations of public emotion or sentiment. The great majority of the population, though excluded from office, showed no active resentment against the ruling minority. In 1310 a group of excluded nobles under Bajamante Tiepolo rose in revolt; and in 1355 Doge Marino Faliero conspired to make himself dictator. Both attempts were easily suppressed.

To guard against internal or external conspiracies, the *Maggior Consiglio* yearly chose from its membership a Council of Ten as a committee of public safety. Through its secret sessions and trials, its spies and swift procedure, this *Consiglio di Dieci* became for a time the most powerful body in the government. Ambassadors often reported to it secretly, and held its instructions more binding than those of the Senate; and any edict of the Ten had the full force of law. Two or three of its members were delegated, each month, as *Inquisitori di stato*, to search among the people and the officials for any suspicion of malfeasance or treason. Many legends arose around this Council of Ten, usually exaggerating its secrecy and severity. It published its decisions and sentences to the Great Council;

though it allowed secret denunciations to be placed in the mouths of lions' heads scattered about the city, it refused to consider any unsigned charges, or any that did not offer two witnesses;[9] and even then a four-fifths vote was required before the accusation could be put on the agenda.[10] Any person arrested had the right to choose two counsel for his defense before the Ten.[11] A condemnatory sentence had to receive a majority vote on five successive ballots. The number of persons imprisoned by the Ten was "very small."[12] However, it was not above arranging the assassination of spies, and of enemies of Venice in foreign states.[13] In 1582 the Senate, feeling that the Council had served its purpose and had often exceeded its authority, reduced its powers; and from that date the Council of Ten existed only in name.

The forty judges appointed by the Great Council provided an efficient and severe judiciary. The laws were clearly formulated, and were strictly enforced against nobles and commoners alike. Penalties reflected the cruelty of the times. Imprisonment was often in narrow cells admitting a minimum of light and air. Flogging, branding, mutilation, blinding, cutting out the tongue, breaking limbs on the wheel, and other delicacies were included among legal punishments. Persons condemned to death could be strangled in jail, or secretly drowned, or hanged from a window of the Doges' Palace, or burned at the stake. Persons guilty of atrocious crimes or sacrilegious theft were tortured with red-hot pincers, dragged along the streets by a horse, and then beheaded and quartered.[14] As if to compensate for this ferocity, Venice opened her doors to political and intellectual refugees, and dared to shelter Elisabetta Gonzaga and her Guidobaldo against the terrible Borgia, when her sister-in-law Isabella had been frightened into letting her depart from her native Mantua.

The administrative organization was probably the best in Europe in the fifteenth century, though corruption found openings here as in every government. A bureau of public sanitation was established in 1385; measures were taken to provide clean drinking water and to prevent the formation of swamps. Another bureau fixed the maximum prices that might be charged for food. A postal and courier service was set up not only for the government but also for private correspondence and parcel transportation.[15] Retired public servants were pensioned, and provision was made for their widows and orphans.[16] The administration of dependent territories on the Italian mainland was relatively so just and competent that these districts prospered better under Venetian rule than ever before, and readily returned to Venetian allegiance after being detached from it by the chances of war.[17] Venetian administration of overseas dependencies was not so laudable; they were used chiefly as prizes of war, much of their soil was awarded to Venetian noblemen and generals, and the native population, while retaining their local institutions of government, seldom reached the higher offices. In her relations with other states Venice was especially well served by her diplomats. Few governments possessed such acute observers and intelligent negotiators as Bernardo Giustiniani. Guided by the informed reports of her ambassadors, the careful statistical records of her bureaucracy, and the astute statesmanship of her senators, Venice repeatedly won in diplomacy what she had lost in war.[18]

Morally this government was no better than the others of the time, in penal legislation worse. It made and broke alliances according to fluctuations of advantage, allowing no scruple, no sentiment of fidelity, to hamper policy: such was the code of all Renaissance powers. The citizens readily accepted this code; they approved every Venetian victory, however won; they gloried in the strength and stability of their state, and offered it, in its need, a patriotism and fullness of service unmatched among their contemporaries. They honored the doge only next to God.

The doge was usually the agent, quite exceptionally the master, of the Council and the Senate; his splendor far outshone his power. In his public appearances he was clothed in magnificent raiment and was heavy with gems; his official bonnet alone contained jewels to the value of 194,000 ducats ($4,850,000?).[19] Venetian painters may have learned from his garb the gorgeous colors that flowed from their brushes; and some of their most brilliant portraits are of doges in official robes. Venice believed in ceremony and display, partly to impress ambassadors and visitors, partly to awe the population, partly to give it pageantry in place of power. Even the *dogaressa* received a sumptuous coronation. The doge received foreign dignitaries, and signed all important documents of state; his influence was pervasive and continuous through his lifelong tenure amid persons elected for a year; in theory, however, he was merely the servant and spokesman of the government.

A long and colorful succession of doges marches through Venetian history, but only a few impressed their personalities upon the character or fortunes of the state. Despite the dying eloquence of Tommaso Mocenigo, the Great Council chose the expansionist Francesco Foscari to succeed him. Coming to the throne at the age of fifty, the new Doge, in a reign of thirty-four years (1423-57), carried Venice through blood and turmoil to the zenith of her power. Milan was defeated, Bergamo, Brescia, Cremona, Crema were won. But the growing autocracy of the victorious Doge aroused the jealousy of the Ten. They charged him with having won his election by bribery; and unable to prove this they accused his son Iacopo of treasonable communication with Milan (1445). Under the agony of the wheel Iacopo admitted or pretended his guilt. He was exiled to Rumania, but was soon permitted to live near Treviso. In 1450 one of the Inquisitors of the Ten was assassinated; Iacopo was credited with the crime; he denied it even under extreme torture; he was exiled to Crete, where he went mad with loneliness and grief. In 1456 he was brought back to Venice, charged again with secret correspondence with the government of Milan; he admitted it, was tortured to the verge of death, and was returned to Crete, where he died soon afterward. The old Doge, who had borne the perils and responsibilities of a long and unpopular war with stoic fortitude, broke down before these trials, which not all his dignity could prevent. At eighty-six he became incapable of carrying the burdens of his office; he was deposed by the Great Council with a life annuity of 2000 ducats. He retired to his home, and there, a few days later, he died of a burst blood vessel as the bells of the campanile announced the accession of a new doge.

Foscari's victories had earned Venice the hatred of all the Italian states; none could any longer feel secure in the nearness of her grasping power. A dozen combinations were formed against her; finally (1508) Ferrara, Mantua, Julius II, Ferdinand of Spain, Louis XII of France, and the Emperor Maximilian joined in the League of Cambrai to destroy her. Leonardo Loredano (1501-21) was Doge in that crisis; he led the people through it with an incredible tenacity only partly revealed in the handsome portrait of him by Giovanni Bellini. Nearly all that Venice had won on the mainland by a century of forceful expansion was taken from her; Venice herself was surrounded. Loredano minted his plate; the aristocracy brought forth its hidden wealth to finance resistance; the armorers forged a hundred thousand weapons; and every man armed himself to fight for island after island in what seemed to be a hopeless cause. Miraculously, Venice saved herself, and recovered part of her mainland realm. But the effort exhausted her finances and her spirit; and when Loredano died— though fifty-seven years of Titian, and most of Tintoretto and Veronese, were still to come—Venice knew that in wealth and power her zenith and glory had passed.

IV. VENETIAN LIFE

The last decades of the fifteenth century, and the early decades of the sixteenth, were the period of greatest splendor in Venetian life. The profits

of a world trade that had made its peace with the Turks, and had not yet
suffered severe curtailment from the rounding of Africa or the opening of
the Atlantic, poured into the islands, crowned them with churches, walled
the canals with palaces, filled the palaces with precious metals and costly
furniture, glorified the women with finery and jewelry, supported a brilliant galaxy of painters, and overflowed in bright festivals of tapestried
gondolas, masked liaisons, and babbling waters echoing with song.

The life of the lower classes was the normal routine of toil, eased by
Italian leisureliness and loquacity, and the inability of the rich to monop-
olize any but the most perfumed delights of love. Every humpbacked
bridge, and the Grand Canal, teemed with men transporting the products
of half the world. There were more slaves here than in other European
cities; they were imported, chiefly from Islam, not as laborers but as domestic servants, personal guards, wet nurses, concubines. Doge Pietro
Mocenigo, at the age of seventy, kept two Turkish slaves for his sexual
entertainment.[20] One Venetian record tells of a priest who sold a female
slave to another priest, who on the following day had the contract annulled
because he had found her with child.[21]

The upper classes, though so well served, were not idlers. Most of them,
in their mature years, were active in commerce, finance, diplomacy, government, or war. The portraits we have of them show men rich in conscious personality, proud of their place, but also serious with a sense of
obligation. A minority of them dressed in silks and furs, perhaps to please
the artists who painted them; and a set of young bloods—La Compagnia
della Scalza, "the Company of the Hose"—flaunted tight doublets, silk
brocades, and striped hose embroidered with gold or silver or inset with
gems. But every young patrician sobered his dress when he became a
member of the Great Council; then he was required to wear a toga, for by
a robe almost any male may be endowed with dignity, and any woman with
mystery. Occasionally, in their magnificent palaces, or in their villa gardens
at Murano or other suburbs, the nobles betrayed their secret wealth to lavishly entertain a visitor, or to celebrate some vital event in the history of
their city or their family. When Cardinal Grimani, high in both the nobility and the Church, gave a reception for Ranuccio Farnese (1542), he
invited three thousand guests; most of them came in cabined gondolas
smoothed with velvet and eased with cushions; and he provided them with
music, acrobatics, ropewalking, dancing, and dinner. Normally, however,
the Venetian nobility in this period lived, ate, and dressed in moderate style,
and earned some fraction of their keep.

Perhaps the middle classes were the happiest of all, and joined most light-heartedly in private and public merriment. They provided the lower hierarchy of the Church, the bureaucracy of the government, the professions of physician, attorney, and pedagogue, the management of industry and the guilds, the mathematical operations of foreign commerce, the control of local trade. They were neither so harassed as the rich to preserve a fortune, nor so worried as the poor to feed and clothe their young. Like the other classes they played cards, threw dice, and deployed chessmen across the hours, but they rarely gambled into ruin. They loved to play musical instruments, to sing and dance. As their houses or apartments were small, they made promenades and patios of the streets; these were almost free of horses and vehicles, since transport preferred the canals. So it was not unusual for the less sedate classes, of an evening or on some festal day, to form impromptu dances and choruses in the public squares. Every family had musical instruments and included some bearable voice. And when Adrian Willaert led the great double choir in St. Mark's, the thousands who could get in to hear reversed their famous boast, and became for a moment Christians first and Venetians afterward.

The festivals of Venice, in their unrivaled setting of churches, palaces, and sea, were the most gorgeous in Europe. Every excuse was used for pomp and pageantry: the inauguration of a doge, some religious holyday or national holiday, the visit of a foreign dignitary, the conclusion of a favorable peace, the Gharingello or Women's Holiday, the anniversary of St. Mark or the patron saint of a guild. In the fourteenth century the joust was still the crowning event of a festival; indeed, as late as 1491, when Venice received with stately ceremony the abdicated Queen of Cyprus, some troops from Crete held a joust on the frozen Grand Canal. But the joust seemed inappropriate to a naval power, and it was gradually replaced with some form of water festival, usually a regatta. The greatest feast of all the year was the *Sposalizio del Mare*, the solemn and colorful rite of marrying Venice—*La Serenissima*, the most serene—to the Adriatic. When Beatrice d'Este came to Venice in 1493 as the captivating emissary of Lodovico of Milan, the Grand Canal was adorned throughout its length like some splendid avenue in Christmas time; the ship *Bucentaur*, symbolizing the Venetian state and all decorated in purple and gold, sailed to meet her; a thousand boats rowed or sailed around it, each adorned with garlands and bunting; so many were the vessels, said an enthusiastic chronicler, that for a mile around the water could not be seen.

In a letter written from Venice on this occasion Beatrice described a

momaria given in her honor in the Palace of the Doges. It was a dramatic
spectacle, mostly in pantomime, presented by masked actors called *momari*,
mummers. The Venetians were fond of divers such performances. They
retained till 1462 the medieval "mysteries"; but popular demand caused
these religious plays to be prefaced or interrupted with comic interludes of
so loose and disorderly a character that they were forbidden in that year.
Meanwhile the humanist movement renewed Italian acquaintance with
classic comedy; Plautus and Terence were staged by the Compagnia della
Scalza and other groups; and in 1506 Fra Giovanni Armonio, monk, actor,
and musician, presented in Latin, in the convent of the Eremitani, *Stepha-
nium*, the first modern comedy. From these beginnings Venetian comedy
progressed toward Goldoni, always competing with the Harlequin and
Pantaloon of the *commedia dell' arte*, and at times so rivaling this in uninhibited humor that Church and state engaged in a running war with the
Venetian stage.

An earthy licentiousness and profanity sat side by side, in the Venetian
or Italian character, with orthodox belief and hebdomadal piety. The
populace crowded St. Mark's on Sundays and holydays, and drank homeo-
pathic doses of the religion of terror and hope pictured in the mosaics or
sculptured in statue or relief; the deliberate darkness of the pillared cavern
intensified the effect of the icons and sermons; and even the prostitutes,
hiding for a time the yellow handkerchief which the law required them to
display as the badge of their tribe, came here, after a weary night, to cleanse
themselves with prayer. The Venetian Senate favored this popular piety,
and surrounded the doge and the state with all the awe of religious ritual.
It imported at great cost, after the fall of Constantinople, the relics of Eastern saints, and offered to pay ten thousand ducats for the seamless coat of
Christ.

And yet that same Senate, which Petrarch likened to an assembly of the
gods,[22] repeatedly flouted the authority of the Church, ignored the most
terrible papal decrees of excommunication and interdict, offered asylum to
prudent skeptics (till 1527),[23] sharply reproved a friar for attacking the
Jews (1512), and sought to make the Church in Venice an appanage of the
state. Bishops for Venetian sees were chosen by the Senate, and were presented to Rome for confirmation; such appointments were in many cases
put into effect despite papal refusal to confirm them; after 1488 none but a
Venetian could be appointed to a Venetian episcopate; and no revenues
could be collected or used by any ecclesiastic, in the Venetian realm, who
had not been approved by the government. Churches and monasteries were

subject to state supervision, but no churchman could hold a public office.[24] All legacies to monastic establishments paid a tax to the state. Ecclesiastical courts were carefully watched to see to it that guilty ecclesiastics should receive the same penalties as guilty laymen. The Republic long resisted the introduction of the Inquisition; when it yielded it made all verdicts of the Venetian inquisitors subject to review and sanction by a senatorial commission; and only six sentences of death were issued in all the history of the Inquisition in Venice.[25] The Republic proudly took the stand that in temporal matters it "recognized no superior except the Divine Majesty."[26] It openly accepted the principle that a general council of the bishops of the Church is above the pope, and that an appeal may be made from a pope to a future council. When Sixtus IV laid an interdict on the city (1483) the Council of Ten ordered all clergy to continue their services as usual. When Julius II renewed the interdict as part of his war against Venice, the Ten forbade the publication of the edict in Venetian territory, and had their agents in Rome affix to the doors of St. Peter's an appeal from the Pope to a future council (1509).[27] Julius won that war, and forced Venice to accept his spiritual authority as absolute.

All in all, Venetian life was more attractive in its setting than in its spirit. The government was competent, and showed high courage in adversity; but it was sometimes brutal and always selfish; it never thought of Venice as part of Italy, and seemed to care little what tragedy might befall that divided land. It developed powerful personalities—self-reliant, shrewd, acquisitive, valiant, proud; we know a hundred of them in their portraits by artists whom they had just enough refinement to patronize. It was a civilization that, compared with the Florentine, lacked subtlety and depth; that, compared with the Milanese under Lodovico, lacked finesse and grace. But it was the most colorful, sumptuous, and sensually bewitching civilization that history has ever known.

V. VENETIAN ART

1. Architecture and Sculpture

Sensuous color is the essence of Venetian art, even of its architecture. Many Venetian churches and mansions, some business buildings, had mosaics or frescoes on their fronts. The façade of St. Mark's gleamed with gilt and almost haphazard ornament; every decade brought to it new spoils and forms, until the face of the great fane became a bizarre medley of architecture, sculpture, and mosaic, in which decoration drowned structure, and the parts forgot the whole. To admire that façade with something fonder than wonder one must take his stand 576 feet away, at the farther end of the Piazza San Marco; in that perspective the brilliant conglomeration of Romanesque portals, Gothic ogees, classical columns, Renaissance railing, and Byzantine domes blends into one exotic phantasm, an Aladdin's magic dream.

The Piazza was not then as ample and majestic as now. In the fifteenth century it was still unpaved; part of it was occupied by vines and trees, a stonecutter's yard, and a latrine. In 1495 it was paved with brick; in 1500 Alessandro Leopardi cast for the three flagstaffs such pedestals as no later ones would ever surpass; and in 1512 Bartolommeo Buon the Younger raised the majestic campanile. (It fell in 1902, but was rebuilt on the same design.) Not so pleasing are the offices of the Procurators of St. Mark— the Procuratie Vecchie and Nuove, built between 1517 and 1640, and hemming in the Piazza on north and south with their immense and monotonous façades.

Between St. Mark's and the Grand Canal stood the chief glory of civic Venice, the Palace of the Doges. It underwent in this period so many renovations that little remained of its earlier form. Pietro Baseggio rebuilt (1309-40) the southern wing facing the Canal; Giovanni Buon and his son Bartolommeo Buon the Elder raised a new wing (1424-38) on the western or Piazzetta front, and set up the Gothic Porta della Carta (1438-43)* at the northwestern corner. These southern and western façades, with their graceful Gothic arcades and balconies, are among the happiest products of the Renaissance. To the fourteenth and fifteenth centuries belong most of the sculptures on the façades, and the superb carvings of the column capitals; Ruskin thought one of these capitals—beneath the figures of Adam and Eve—the finest in Europe. Within the court Bartolommeo Buon the Younger and Antonio Rizzo built an ornate arch, named after Francesco Foscari, and mingling three architectural styles in unexpected harmony: Renaissance columns and lintels, Romanesque arches, Gothic pinnacles. In the niches of the arch Rizzo placed two strange statues: Adam protesting his innocence, and Eve wondering at the penalties of knowledge. Rizzo planned, and Pietro Lombardo completed, the eastern façade of the court, a delightful marriage of round and pointed arches with Renaissance cornices and balconies. It was Rizzo again who designed the Scala de' Giganti,

* Called "Door of the Paper" because on a bulletin board near it the Signory posted its decrees.

or Giants' Stairs, from the court to the first floor—a simple, stately structure named from the gigantic statues of Mars and Neptune set up by Iacopo Sansovino at the head of the steps to symbolize Venetian mastery of land and sea. In the interior were prison cells, administrative offices, reception rooms, assembly halls for the Great Council, the Senate, and the Ten. Many of these rooms were, or were soon to be, decorated with the proudest murals in the history of art.

While the Republic glorified itself in this architectural gem, the richer nobles . . . Giustiniani, Contarini, Gritti, Barbari, Loredani, Foscari, Vendramini, Grimani . . . bounded the Grand Canal with their palaces. We must picture these not in their present deterioration but in their fifteenth- and sixteenth-century heyday: with their façades of white marble, porphyry, or serpentine; their Gothic windows and Renaissance colonnades; their carved portals opening on the water; their hidden courtyards adorned with statuary, fountains, gardens, frescoes, urns; their interiors with tile or marble floors, mighty fireplaces, inlaid furniture, Murano glass, silken canopies, hangings of gold or silver cloth, bronze chandeliers gilded, enameled, or chased, coffered ceilings, and murals by men whose names have gone around the world. So, for example, the Palazzo Foscari was decorated with paintings by Gian Bellini, Titian, Tintoretto, Paris Bordone, Veronese. Perhaps these rooms were more magnificent than comfortable, the chairs too straight-backed, the windows drafty, and no mode of heating that could warm both sides of a room or a man at the same time. Some Venetian palaces cost 200,000 ducats; a law of 1476 tried to limit expenditure to 150 ducats per room, but we hear of rooms whose fixtures and furnishings cost 2000. Probably the most ornate of the palaces was the Ca d'Oro, named the House of Gold because the owner, Marino Contarini, ordered that almost every inch of the marble façade should be covered with decoration, much of it in gilt. Its Gothic balconies and tracery still make it the prettiest front on the Canal.

These millionaires, while feathering their own nests, spared something for the citadels of their incidental faith. Strange to say, St. Mark's was not till 1807 the cathedral of Venice; formally it was the private chapel of the doge and the shrine of the city's patron saint; it belonged, so to speak, to the religion of the state. The episcopal see was attached to the minor church of San Pietro di Castello, in the northeastern corner of the city. In the same remote section the Dominican friars had their seat, in the church of San Giovanni e Paolo; there Gentile and Giovanni Bellini found their final rest. More important to history is the church of the Franciscans—Santa Maria

Gloriosa dei Frari (1330-1443), known in fond abbreviations as I Frari, the Friars. Externally it made no show, but its interior gathered fame through the years as the tomb of celebrated Venetians—Francesco Foscari, Titian, Canova—and as a gallery of art. Here Antonio Rizzo designed a noble monument for the Doge Niccolò Tron; Gian Bellini set up his *Frari Madonna*, and Titian his *Madonna of the Pesaro Family*; here, above all, Titian's *Assumption of the Virgin* rises in majesty behind the altar. Lesser masterpieces adorned lesser fanes: San Zaccaria offered its congregation inspiring Madonnas by Giovanni Bellini and Palma Vecchio; Santa Maria dell' Orto had Tintoretto's *Presentation of the Virgin*, and his bones; San Sebastiano received Veronese's remains and some of his finest paintings; and for San Salvatore Titian painted an *Annunciation* in his ninety-first year.

In the construction and decoration of the churches and palaces of Venice a remarkable family of architects and sculptors played a persistent part. The Lombardi came to Venice from northwestern Italy, and so earned their cognomen, but their real name was Solari. They included the Cristoforo Solari who carved the effigies of Lodovico and Beatrice, and his brother Andrea, a painter; both men worked in Venice as well as Milan. Pietro Lombardo left his mark upon a score of buildings in Venice. He and his sons Antonio and Tullio designed the churches of San Giobbe and Santa Maria de' Miracoli—hardly to our current taste; the tombs of Pietro Mocenigo and Niccolò Marcello in Santi Giovanni e Paolo, of Bishop Zanetti in Treviso Cathedral, and of Dante in Ravenna; and the Palazzo Vendramin-Calergi, in which Wagner died; and in most of these enterprises they supplied the sculpture as well as the architectural plans. Pietro himself did much architectural and sculptural work in the Palace of the Doges. Tullio and Antonio, aided by Alessandro Leopardi, set up the tomb of Andrea Vendramin in Santi Giovanni e Paolo—the greatest work of sculpture in Venice excepting only the *Colleoni* of Verrocchio and Leopardi in the square before that church. For the adjoining Scuola di San Marco, or Fraternity of St. Mark, Pietro Lombardo designed a rich portal and a strange façade. Finally a Sante Lombardo shared in building the Scuola di San Rocco, famous for its fifty-six paintings by Tintoretto. Largely through the work of this family the Renaissance style of columns, architraves, and decorated pediments prevailed over Gothic ogives and pinnacles, and Byzantine domes. In Venice, however, Renaissance architecture, still unsteady under Oriental influence, was too ornate, and obscured its lines with ornament. The atmosphere and classic traditions of Rome were needed to give the new style its definitive and harmonious form.

2. *The Bellini*

Next to St. Mark's and the Ducal Palace, the glory of Venetian art was in painting. Many forces conspired to make the painters the favorites of Venetian patronage. The Church, here as elsewhere, had to tell the Christian story to its people, of whom only a few could read; she needed pictures and statuary to continue the passing effect of speech; so each generation, and many churches and monasteries, had to have Annunciations, Nativities, Adorations, Visitations, Presentations, Massacres of the Innocents, Flights into Egypt, Transfigurations, Last Suppers, Crucifixions, Entombments, Resurrections, Ascensions, Assumptions, Martyrdoms. When detachable paintings faded, or grew stale to a congregation, they might be sold to collectors or museums; they were periodically cleaned and occasionally repainted or retouched; their authors, if reincarnated, might not recognize them today. This, of course, did not apply to murals, which usually disintegrated on their walls. Sometimes, to avoid this fatality, the picture was painted upon canvas and this was then fixed to the wall, as in the Hall of the Great Council. In Venice the state rivaled the Church in appetite for murals, for these could feed patriotism and pride by celebrating the grandeur and ceremonies of the government, the triumphs of trade or war. The *scuole*, too, might order murals and painted banners to commemorate their patron saints or their annual pageantry. Rich men wanted scenes of outdoor beauty or indoor love pictured on the walls of their palaces; and they sat for portraits to cheat for a while the ironic brevity of fame. The Signory ordered a portrait of every doge in turn; even the Procurators of St. Mark so preserved their features for a careless posterity. It was in Venice that the portrait and the easel picture achieved most popularity.

Until the middle of the fifteenth century painting developed slowly in Venice; then, like some flower catching the morning sun, it burst into unparalleled radiance as Venetians found in it a vehicle of the color and life that they had learned to love. Perhaps some of that Venetian flair for color had come to the lagoons from the East, with merchants who imported Oriental ideas and tastes as well as goods, who brought back with them memories of gleaming tiles and gilded domes, and displayed in Venetian markets, churches, or homes Oriental silks, satins, velvets, brocades, and cloth of silver or gold. Indeed Venice never quite made up its mind whether it was an Occidental or an Oriental state. On the Rialto East and West did meet; Othello and Desdemona could become man and wife. And if Venice and her painters could not learn color from the East, they could get it from the Venetian sky, observing its infinite variety of light and mist, and the splendor of sunsets touching campaniles and palaces, or mirrored in the sea. Meanwhile the victories of Venetian arms and fleets, and the heroic recovery from threatened ruin, roused the pride and imagination of patrons and painters, and commemorated themselves in art. Wealth discovered that it was meaningless unless it could transform itself into goodness, beauty, or truth.

An external stimulus was added to generate a Venetian school of painting. In 1409 Gentile da Fabriano was brought to Venice to decorate the Hall of the Great Council, and Antonio Pisano, called Pisanello, came from Verona to collaborate. We cannot say how well they performed, but it is probable that they stirred the Venetian painters to replace with softer contours and richer colors the dark and rigid hieratic forms of the Byzantine tradition, and the pale and lifeless forms of the Giottesque school. Perhaps some minor influence came down over the Alps with Giovanni d'Alamagna (d. 1450); but Giovanni seems to have grown up, and learned his art, in Murano and Venice. With his brother-in-law Antonio Vivarini he painted for the church of San Zaccaria an altarpiece whose figures begin to have the grace and tenderness that would make the work of the Bellini a revelation to Venice.

The greatest influence of all came from Sicily, or Flanders. Antonello da Messina grew up as a businessman, and presumably had no thought, in his youth, that his name would be carried down for centuries in the history of art. While in Naples he saw (if we accept Vasari's perhaps romantic account) an oil painting that had been sent to King Alfonso by some Florentine merchants in Bruges. From Cimabue (c. 1240-c. 1302) to Antonello (1430-79) Italian painting on wood or canvas had relied on tempera—mixing the colors with a gelatinous substance. Such colors left a rough surface, were maladapted to blending for delicate shades and gradations, and tended to crack and slake off even before the artist's death. Antonello saw the advantages of mixing pigments with oil: readier blending, easier handling and cleaning, brighter finish, greater permanence. He went to Bruges, and there studied the oil technique of the Flemish painters, then basking in the heyday of Burgundy. Having occasion to go to Venice, he became so enamored of the city—being himself "greatly addicted to women and pleasure"[28]—that he spent there the remainder of his life. He abandoned business, and gave all his industry to painting. For the church of San Cassiano he painted in oil an altarpiece that became a model for a hundred similar pictures: the Madonna enthroned between four saints, with musician angels at her feet, and full Venetian colors on the brocades and satins of the drapery. Antonello shared his knowledge of the new method with other artists, and the great age of Venetian painting began. Many nobles sat to him for their portraits, and several of these pictures survive: the crude, strong *Poet* at Pavia, the *Condottiere* in the Louvre, the *Portrait of a Man*, plump and quizzical, in the Johnson Collection in Philadelphia, the *Portrait of a Young Man* in New York, and the *Self-Portrait* in London. At the height of his success Antonello fell sick, developed pleurisy, and died at the age of forty-nine. The artists of Venice gave him a sumptuous funeral, and acknowledged their debt in a generous epitaph:

> In this ground is buried Antoninus the painter, the highest orna-
> ment of Messina and all Sicily; celebrated not only for his pictures,
> which were distinguished by singular skill and beauty, but because,
> with high zeal and tireless technique, through mixing colors with oil,
> he first brought splendor and permanence to Italian painting.[29]

Among the pupils of Gentile da Fabriano at Venice was Iacopo Bellini, founder of a brief but major dynasty in Renaissance art. After this tutelage Iacopo painted in Verona, Ferrara, and Padua. There his daughter married Andrea Mantegna; and through him, as well as more directly, Iacopo came under Squarcione's influence. When he returned to Venice he brought with him, if we may mingle metaphors, a rubbing of the Paduan technique, and an echo of the Florentine. All this, and the Venetian heritage, and, later, Antonello's tricks with oil, passed down to Iacopo's sons, the rival geniuses Gentile and Giovanni Bellini.

Gentile was twenty-three when the family moved to Padua (1452). He felt intimately the influence of his brother-in-law Mantegna; when he painted the shutters for the organ in the Padua cathedral he followed too carefully the hard figures and bold foreshortenings of the Eremitani frescoes. But in Venice a new gentleness appeared in his portrait of San Lorenzo Giustiniani. In 1474 the Signory assigned to him and his half-brother Giovanni the task of painting or repainting fourteen panels in the Hall of the Great Council. These canvases were among the earliest Venetian pictures painted in oil.[30] They were destroyed by fire in 1577, but the sketches that remain show that Gentile used for the pictures his characteristic narrative style, in which some major incident is portrayed at the center, and a dozen episodes play at the side. Vasari saw the paintings, and marveled at their realism, variety, and complexity.[31]

When Sultan Mohammed II sent a request to the Signory for a good portrait painter, Gentile was chosen. In Constantinople (1474) he enlivened the Sultan's chambers and spirits with erotic pictures, and made of him a portrait (London) and a medallion (Boston), both showing a powerful character drawn by an expert hand. Mohammed died in 1481; his successor, more orthodox, obeyed the Moslem ban on the painting of human figures, and scattered into oblivion all but those two of the works done by Gentile in the Turkish capital. Luckily Gentile had returned to Venice in 1480, heavy with gifts and decorations from the old Sultan. He rejoined Giovanni in the Ducal Palace, and completed his contract with the Signory. It rewarded him with a pension of two hundred ducats a year.

In his old age he painted his greatest pictures. The guild of St. John the Evangelist had what it believed to be a miracle-working relic of the True Cross. It solicited Gentile to describe in three paintings the healing of an invalid by the relic, a Corpus Christi procession carrying it, and the miraculous finding of the lost fragment. The first panel has yielded its splendor to time. The second, painted when Gentile was seventy, is a brilliant panorama of dignitaries, choristers, and candle bearers parading around the Piazza San Marco, with St. Mark's in the background, appearing very much as it is today. In the third picture, painted at seventy-four, the relic has fallen into the San Lorenzo Canal; the people crowding the bywalks and bridges are panic-stricken, and many kneel in prayer; but Andrea Vendramin plunges into the water, recovers the relic, and then, buoyed up by it, moves with uninfected dignity toward the shore. Every figure in these crowded canvases is drawn with realistic fidelity. And again the artist delights in surrounding the main event with engaging episodes: a boat slipping away from its dock while the gondolier watches the recovery of the relic; and a nude black Moor poised to dive into the stream.

Gentile's last great picture (Brera) was painted at the age of seventy-six for his own confraternity of St. Mark, and showed the Apostle preaching in Alexandria. As usual it is a crowd; Gentile preferred to take humanity wholesale. He died at seventy-eight (1507), leaving the picture to be finished by his brother Gian.

Giovanni Bellini (Gian Bellini, Giambellino) was only two years younger than Gentile, but outlived him by nine. In this span of eighty-six years he ranged the whole gamut of his art, tried and mastered a rich variety of genres, and brought Venetian painting to its first peak. At Padua he absorbed Mantegna's technical teaching without imitating his hard and statuesque style; and in Venice he adopted with unprecedented success the new method of mixing pigments with oil. He was the first Venetian to reveal the glory of color; and at the same time he attained to a grace and accuracy of line, a delicacy of feeling, a depth of interpretation, that, even in the lifetime of his brother, made him the greatest and most sought-for painter in Venice.

Churches and guilds and private patrons seemed never to tire of his Madonnas; he bequeathed the Virgin in a hundred forms to a dozen lands. The Venetian Academy alone has a host of them: *Madonna with the Sleeping Child*, *Madonna with Two Holy Women*, *Madonna con Bambino*, *Madonna degli Alberetti*, *Madonna with St. Paul and St. George*, *Madonna Enthroned* . . . and, best of this group, the *Madonna of St. Job*; this, we are told, is the first picture that Giovanni painted in oils, and it is one of the most brilliantly colored works in Venice—which is to say in the world. The little Museo Correr at the western end of the Piazza San Marco has another Giambellino *Madonna*, tender and sad and lovely; San Zaccaria has a variation on the *Madonna of St. Job*; the church of the Frari has a *Madonna Enthroned*, a little stiff and severe and hemmed in by gloomy saints, but appealing in her rich blue robes. The zealous wanderer will find many more of Gian's Virgins, in Verona, Bergamo, Milan, Rome, Paris, London, New York, Washington. What more, in color, could be said of Our Lady after this polygraphic devotion? Perugino and Raphael would rival this multiplicity, and Titian, in that same church of the Frari, would find something more to say.

Giovanni did not do so well with the Son. *Christ Blessing*, in the Louvre, is middling, but the *Sacred Conversation* near it is movingly beautiful. The famous *Pietà* in the Brera at Milan has been warmly praised,[32] but it shows a duet of charmless faces holding up a dead Christ who seems to need nothing more, for perfect physical condition, than to be freed from too much attention; this harsh and crude burial picture—undated—belongs to Bellini's Mantegnesque youth. How much more pleasing is the *Santa Justina* in a private collection in Milan!—again somewhat stylized and posed, but with a delicacy of features, a modest drooping of the eyelids, a splendor of costume, that make this one of Gian's most successful efforts. It was apparently a portrait, and Gian was now so skilled in rendering a living face and soul that a hundred patrons begged to share his immortality. Look again at *Doge Loredano*; with what depth of understanding, and keenness of eye, and dexterity of hand Bellini has caught the unfaltering, serene power of the man who could lead his people to victory in a war for survival against the united assault of nearly all the great states of Italy and transalpine Europe!—And then, rivaling the Leonardo who was creeping up on him in skill and fame, Giovanni tried his palette at bizarre landscapes like that medley of rocks, mountains, castles, sheep, water, riven tree, and clouded sky which St. Francis (in the Frick Collection) calmly confronts as he receives the stigmata.

In his old age the master tired of repeating the usual sacred themes, and experimented with allegory and classic mythology. He turned Knowledge, Happiness, Truth, Slander, Purgatory, the Church herself, into persons or stories, and sought to bring them to life with alluring landscapes. Two of his pagan pictures hang in the Washington National Gallery: *Orpheus Charming the Beasts*, and *The Feast of the Gods*—a picnic of bare-breasted women and half-naked, half-drunken men. The picture is dated 1514; it was painted for Duke Alfonso of Ferrara when the artist was eighty-four years old. We are reminded again of Alfieri's boast—that the man-plant grows more vigorously in Italy than elsewhere on the earth.

Giovanni lived only a year after signing that testament of youth. His was a full and reasonably happy life: an astonishing procession of masterpieces, a kaleidoscope of warm colors on soft robes, an immense advance in grace, composition, and vitality upon the Giotteschi and the Byzantophiles, a power of perception and individualization unseen in the arid figures and indiscriminate masses of Gentile's pictures, a fruitful mediation, in time and style, between a Mantegna who knew only Romans and a Titian who felt and pictured every phase of life from Flora to Charles V. One of Gian's pupils was Giorgione, who developed his master's idyls of wood and stream; Titian worked with Giorgione, and received the great tradition. Generation by generation Venetian art was accumulating its knowledge, varying its experiments, and preparing its culmination.

3. From the Bellini to Giorgione

The success of the Bellini made painting popular in Venice, where mosaics had held so long a sway. Studios multiplied, patrons opened their purses, and artists developed who, though they were not Bellini or Giorgiones, would have been the brightest stars in lesser galaxies. Vincenzo Catena painted so well that many of his pictures were credited to Gian Bellini or to Giorgione. Antonio Vivarini's younger brother, Bartolommeo, met a conservative demand by applying to medieval themes the technique of Squarcione and the fuller colors that painting had learned to mix and convey. Bartolommeo's nephew and pupil, Alvise Vivarini, threatened for a time to rival Gian Bellini with pretty Madonnas, and achieved a monumental altarpiece—*Madonna with Six Saints*—which passed from Italy to the Kaiser-Friedrich Museum in Berlin. Alvise was a good teacher, for three of his pupils found moderate fame. Bartolommeo Montagna we leave to Vicenza. Giovanni Battista Cima da Conegliano worked for the Madonna market; one at Parma has a handsome figure of the Archangel Michael, while another in Cleveland redeems itself with brilliant color. Marco Basaiti painted a fine *Calling of the Sons of Zebedee* (Venice), and a delightful portrait—*A Youth*—in the London National Gallery.

Carlo Crivelli may also have been a pupil of the Vivarini; however, he had to abscond from Venice soon after his seventeenth year (1457): having abducted the wife of a sailor, he was fined and jailed; released, he sought safety in Padua, where he studied in Squarcione's school. In 1468 he moved to Ascoli, and spent his remaining twenty-five years painting pictures for the churches there and thereabouts. Perhaps because he left Venice so soon, Crivelli hardly shared in the progressive movement of Venetian painting; he preferred tempera to oil, kept to the traditional religious subjects, and adopted an almost Byzantine scheme of subordinating representation to decoration. He gave his pictures an enamel finish, which went well with the gilded frames of the polyptychs he filled; and though his Madonnas seem cold, there is a delicate grace in their drawing that presages Giorgione.

Vettor (Vittore) Carpaccio was a major among these minors. Starting with studies in perspective and design in the manner of Mantegna, he adopted the narrative style of Gentile Bellini, added to it a youthful preference for imaginary idyls rather than contemporary events, and applied to his romantic themes a fully developed technique. Quite alien to his usually blithe spirit is an early picture (in New York), *Meditation on the Passion*—a macabre study of Sts. Jerome and Onofrius imagining Christ seated before them dead, with skull and crossbones at their feet, and a background of lowering clouds. When he was thirty-three (1488) Carpaccio received an important commission: to paint for the School of St. Ursula a series of pictures illustrating her history. In nine picturesque panels he told how the handsome Prince Conon of England had come to Brittany to wed Ursula, daughter of its king; how she begged him to postpone the wedding until, with a train of 11,000 virgins, she could make a pilgrimage to Rome;

how Conon accompanied her lovingly, and all received the papal blessing; how, then, an angel appeared to Ursula and announced that she and her virgins must go to Cologne and be martyred; how she leaves the sorrowing Conon and, with her train, goes in calm dignity to Cologne; how its pagan kinglet proposes marriage to her, and, when she refuses, slays all 11,001. The legend suited Carpaccio's fancy; he delighted in picturing the crowds of maidens and courtiers, and made nearly every one of them aristocratic and fair and colorfully dressed; and to the various scenes he brought not only his pictorial science but his knowledge of actual things—the forms of architecture, the shipping in a bay, the patient procession of the clouds.

In an interval of his nine years' labor with Ursula, Carpaccio painted for the School of St. John the Evangelist *The Healing of the Demoniac* by a relic of the Holy Cross. Daring comparison with Gentile Bellini, Vittore described a scene on a Venetian canal, crowded with people, gondolas, and palaces. Here was all of Gentile's realism and detail, done with a brilliant finish beyond the older man's reach. Stirred by Carpaccio's success, the School of St. George of the Slavonians asked him to commemorate their patron saint on the walls of their Venetian oratory. Again he took nine years, and painted nine scenes. They do not quite equal the Ursula series, but Carpaccio, now in his fifties, had not lost his flair for representing graceful figures in harmonious combinations, and architectural backgrounds fanciful in conception but convincing in presentation. St. George attacks the dragon in an impetuous charge; in contrast St. Jerome is shown as the quiet scholar immersed in study in a surprisingly handsome room, with no other company than his lion. Every feature in the room is pictured with minute fidelity, even to the musical score so legible on a fallen scroll that Molmenti transcribed it for the piano.

In 1508 Carpaccio and two obscure artists were appointed to set a value on a strange mural painted by a rising young artist on an outer wall of the Fondaco dei Tedeschi—the warehouse of the Teuton merchants near the Rialto bridge. He judged it worth a fee of 150 ducats ($1875?). Though Carpaccio still had eighteen years of life in him, he painted only one more great picture—a *Presentation in the Temple* (1510) for the chapel of the Sanudo family in the church of San Giobbe. There it had to compete with Gian Bellini's *Madonna of St. Job;* and though the Virgin and her attendant ladies are lovely, Giovanni, not Vittore, is victor in this silent contest. Carpaccio, in a later century, might have been the master of the age; it was his misfortune that he came between Giovanni Bellini and Giorgione.

4. Giorgione

It might seem strange that artists should be hired at high fees to paint a warehouse wall. But in 1507 the Venetians felt that life without color was dead; and the German traders there, some from the great Dürer's Nuremberg, had their own lusty sense of art. So they sublimated part of their profits into two murals, and had the luck to choose immortals for the task. The paintings soon succumbed to salt moisture and the sun, and only vague blotches remain, but even these attest the early fame of Giorgione da Castelfranco. He was then twenty-nine years old. We do not know his name; an old story made him the love child of an aristocratic Barbarelli and a woman of the people; but this may be an afterthought.[33] In his thirteenth or fourteenth year (*c.* 1490) he was sent from Castelfranco to Venice to serve as apprentice to Gian Bellini. He developed rapidly, won substantial commissions, bought a house, painted a fresco on its front, and filled his home with music and revelry; for he played the lute well, and preferred gay women in the flesh to the loveliest of them on canvas. What influences formed his wistful style it is hard to say, for he was unlike the other painters of his day, except that he may have learned from Carpaccio some grace and charm. Probably the decisive influence came from letters rather than from art. When Giorgione was twenty-seven or twenty-eight Italian literature was taking a bucolic turn; Sannazaro published his *Arcadia* in 1504; perhaps Giorgione read these poems and found in their pleasant fancies some suggestions of idealized landscapes and amours. From Leonardo—passing through Venice in 1500—Giorgione may have acquired a taste for a mystic, dreamy softness of expression, a delicacy of nuance, a refinement of manner that made him, for a tragically brief moment, the summit of Venetian art.

Among the earliest works attributed to him—for in hardly any case can we be sure of his authorship—are two wood panels describing the exposure and rescue of the infant Paris; the story is an excuse for painting shepherds and rural landscapes breathing peace. In the first picture that is by common consent his—*The Gypsy and the Soldier*—we get a typically Giorgionesque fancy: a casual woman, naked except for a shawl around her shoulders, sits on her discarded dress on the mossy bank of a rushing stream, nurses a child, and looks anxiously about her; behind her stretches a landscape of Roman arches, a river and a bridge, towers and a temple, curious trees, white lightning, and green storm-laden clouds; near her is a comely youth holding a shepherd's staff—but richly garbed for a shepherd!—and so pleased with the scene that he ignores the gathering storm. The story is uncertain;

what the picture means is that Giorgione liked handsome youths, soft-contoured women, and nature even in its moods of wrath.

In 1504 he painted, for a bereaved family in the town of his birth, the *Madonna of Castelfranco*. It is absurd and beautiful. In the forefront St. Liberale, in the shining armor of a medieval knight, holds a lance for the Virgin, and St. Francis preaches to the air; high aloft on a double pedestal Mary sits with her babe, who leans recklessly out from his high perch. But the green and violet brocade at Mary's feet is a wonder of color and design; Mary's robes fall about her in wrinkles as lovely as wrinkles can ever be; her face has the gentle tenderness that poets picture in the mates of their dreams; and the landscape recedes with Leonardesque mystery till the sky melts into the sea.

When Giorgione and his friend Tiziano Vecelli received the assignment to paint the Fondaco dei Tedeschi, Giorgione chose the wall fronting the Grand Canal, and Titian took the Rialto side. Vasari, examining Giorgione's fresco half a century later, found it impossible to make head or tail of what another spectator described as "trophies, nude bodies, heads in chiaroscuro . . . geometricians measuring the terrestrial globe, perspectives of columns, and between them men on horseback, and other fantasies." However, the same writer adds: "It may be seen how accomplished Giorgione was in handling colors in fresco."[34]

But his genius lay in conception rather than coloring. When he painted the *Sleeping Venus* that was a priceless treasure of the Dresden Gallery, he might have thought of her in purely sensual terms as an inviting formation of molecules. Doubtless she is that, too, and marks the passage of Venetian art from Christian to pagan themes and sentiment. But there is nothing immodest or suggestive about this Venus. She lies asleep, precariously nude in the open air, on a red cushion and a white silken robe, her right arm under her head, her left hand serving as a fig leaf, one perfect limb outstretched over another raised beneath it; seldom has art so simulated the velvet texture of feminine surfaces, or so conveyed the grace of a natural pose. But on her face is a look of such innocence and peace as rarely accord with naked beauty. Giogione here has put himself beyond good and evil, and lets the esthetic sense transiently dominate desire. In another piece— the *Fête champêtre* or *Pastoral Symphony* of the Louvre—the pleasure is frankly sexual, and yet again has all the innocence of nature. Two nude women and two clothed men are enjoying a holiday in the countryside: a patrician youth, in a doublet of gleaming red silk, strumming a lute; beside him a disheveled shepherd painfully trying to bridge the gap between a sim-

ple and a cultivated mind; the aristocrat's lady, in a graceful motion, empty-
ing a crystal pitcher into a well; the shepherd's lass waiting patiently for
him to attend to her charms or her flute. No notion of sin has entered their
heads; the lute and the flute have sublimated sex into harmony. Behind the
figures rises one of the richest landscapes in Italian art.

Finally, in *The Concert* of the Pitti Palace, desire seems forgotten as
irrelevantly primitive, and music is all, or becomes a bond of friendship
subtler than desire. Until the nineteenth century this "most Giorgionesque" of all pictures[35] was regularly accredited to Giorgione; many critics
now ascribe it to Titian; since the matter is still doubtful let us leave the
authorship to Giorgione, because he loved music only next to woman, and
because Titian is rich enough in masterpieces to spare one to his friend. At
the left a plumed youth stands, a bit lifeless and negative; a monk sits at a
clavichord, his beautifully rendered hands on the keys, his face turned
round to a bald cleric on our right; the cleric lays one hand on the monk's
shoulder, and holds in the other a cello resting on the floor. Has the music
ended, or not yet begun? It does not matter; what moves us is the silent
depth of feeling in the countenance of the monk, whose every fiber has
been refined, and his every sentiment ennobled, by music; who hears it long
after all the instruments have been mute. That face, not idealized but profoundly realized, is one of the miracles of Renaissance painting.

Giorgione lived a short life, and apparently a merry one. He seems to
have had many women, and to have healed each broken romance with a
new one soon begun. Vasari reports that Giorgione caught the plague from
his latest love; all that we know is that he died in the epidemic of 1511 at the
age of thirty-four. His influence was already extensive. A dozen "Giorgionesque" minor artists painted rural idyls, conversation pieces, musical
interludes, masque costumes, in vain efforts to capture the refinement and
finish of his style, the airy overtones of his landscapes, the guileless eroti-
cism of his themes. He left two pupils who were to make a stir in the
world: Sebastiano del Piombo, who went off to Rome, and Tiziano Vecelli,
the greatest Venetian of all.

5. Titian: The Formative Years: 1477-1533

He was born in the town of Pieve, in the Cadoric range of the Dolomites,
and those rugged mountains were well remembered in his landscapes.
When he was nine or ten he was brought to Venice, and was apprenticed
successively to Sebastiano Zuccato, Gentile Bellini, and Giovanni Bellini.

In Giovanni's studio he worked side by side with Giorgione, who was his senior by only a year. When that Keats of the brush set up his own studio Titian probably went with him as assistant or associate. He was so deeply influenced by Giorgione that some of his early pictures have been ascribed to Giorgione, and some of Giorgione's later pictures to Titian; the inimitable *Concert* probably belongs to this period. Together they painted the Fondaco walls.

From the plague that took Giorgione's life—or from the moratorium laid upon Venetian art by the war of the League of Cambrai—Titian fled to Padua (1511). There he painted three frescoes for the Scuola del Santo, recording miracles of St. Anthony; if we may judge from their crudity, Titian at thirty-five had far to go before equaling the best work of Giorgione; Goethe, however, with penetrating hindsight, saw in them "the promise of great things."[36] Returning to Venice, Titian addressed to the doge and the Council of Ten (May 31, 1513) a letter that recalls Leonardo's appeal to Lodovico a generation before:

> Illustrious Prince! High and mighty lords! I, Titian of Cadore, have from childhood upwards studied the art of painting, desirous of a little fame rather than of profit. . . . And although in the past, and also in the present, I have been urgently invited by His Holiness the Pope and other lords to enter their service, I, as the faithful subject of your Excellencies, have rather cherished the wish to leave behind me a memorial in this famous city. Therefore, if it seem good to your Excellencies, I am anxious to paint in the Hall of the Great Council, employing therein all my powers; and to begin with a canvas of the battle on the side of the Piazzetta, which is so difficult that no one has yet had the courage to attempt it. I should be willing to accept for my labor any reward that may be thought proper, or even less. Therefore, being, as aforesaid, studious only of honor and to please your Excellencies, I beg to ask for the first broker's patent, for life, that shall fall vacant in the Fondaco de' Tedeschi, irrespective of all promised reversions of such patent, and on the same conditions and with the same charges and exemptions as Messer Zuan Belin [Gian Bellini], besides two assistants to be paid by the Salt Office, as well as all colors and necessaries. . . . In return for which I promise to do the work above named with such speed and excellence as will satisfy the Signori.[37]

A "broker's patent" (*senseria*) was formally an appointment as trade intermediary between Venetian and foreign merchants; actually, in the case of the broker's patent with the German merchants in Venice, it made the holder the official painter of the state, and paid him 300 crowns ($3750) a year for painting a portrait of the doge and such other pictures as the government might require. Apparently Titian's proposal was tentatively accepted by the Council; in any case he began to paint *The Battle of Cadore* in the Ducal Palace. But his rivals persuaded the Council to withhold the patent from him, and to suspend the pay of his assistants (1514). After negotiations that irritated all concerned, he received the post and pay of the patent without the title (1516). He in his turn procrastinated, and did not complete till 1537 the two canvases that he had begun in the Sala del Maggior Consiglio. They were destroyed by fire in 1577.

Titian developed leisurely, like any organism dowered with a century of life. But as early as 1508 he showed the spiritual penetration and technical power that were to put him above all his rivals in portraiture. A nameless portrait once named *Ariosto* has in it a memory of Giorgione's style— a poetic face, and subtle eyes a little malicious, and sumptuous raiment that set a model for a thousand later works. And in this period (1506-16) the maturing artist already knew how to paint women of ample loveliness, stemming from Giorgione and expanding toward Rubens. The movement from the Virgin to Venus continued in Titian, even while he painted religious pictures of great spendor and renown. The same hand that stirred piety with a *Gypsy Madonna* and an *Adoration of the Shepherds* could turn to a *Woman at Her Toilet*, and that incarnation of voluptuous innocence, the *Flora* of the Uffizi Gallery. This gentle face and generous bosom probably served again in *The Daughter of Herodias;* Salome is as thoroughly Venetian as the severed head is powerfully Hebraic.

In or near the year 1515 Titian produced two of his most celebrated pictures. *The Three Ages of Man* shows a group of naked infants sleeping beneath a tree; a Cupid so soon inoculating them with the mad pursuit; a bearded octogenarian contemplating a skull; and a young couple happy in the spring of love, yet looking at each other wistfully, as if foreseeing the erosive pertinacity of time. *Sacred and Profane Love* has a modern title that would surprise a resurrected Titian. When first mentioned (1615), the picture was called *Beauty Adorned and Unadorned;*[38] probably it aimed not to point a moral but to adorn a tale. The "profane" nude is the most perfect figure in Titian's repertoire, the very *Venus de Milo* of the Renaissance. But the "sacred" lady is secular too; her jeweled girdle draws the eye, her silken gown tempts the touch; probably she is the same buxom courtesan who posed for *Flora* and the *Woman at Her Toilet*. If the spectator looks long enough he will see a complex landscape behind the figures:

plants and flowers and a thick clump of trees, a shepherd tending his flock, two lovers, hunters and dogs chasing a hare, a town and its towers, a church and its campanile, a green Giorgionesque sea, a clouded sky. What difference does it make that we cannot know just what the picture "means"? It is beauty made to "stay awhile"; and is that not what Faust thought worth a soul?

Having learned that female beauty, adorned or natural, would always find customers, Titian pursued the theme joyously. Early in 1516 he accepted the invitation of Alfonso I to paint some panels in the Castello at Ferrara. The artist was lodged there, with two assistants, for some five weeks, and presumably came frequently thereafter from Venice. For the Alabaster Hall Titian painted three pictures that continued Giorgione's pagan mood. In *The Bacchanal* men and women, some of them naked, drink, dance, and make love before a landscape of brown trees, blue lake, and silver clouds; a scroll on the ground bears a French motto: "He who drinks and does not drink again does not know what drinking is." In the distance an old Noah sprawls naked and drunk; closer a lad and lass join in dance, their garments whirling in the breeze; in the foreground a woman whose firm breasts display her youth lies nude and sleeping on the grass; and near her an anxious child raises his dress to ease his bladder and bring the Bacchic cycle to completion. In *Bacchus and Ariadne* the abandoned woman is startled by a Bacchic procession bursting through the woods— drunken satyrs, a naked male entwined with snakes, the nude god of wine leaping from his chariot to capture the fleeing princess. In these pictures, and *The Worship of Venus*, the Pagan Renaissance is in full command.

Meanwhile Titian painted an arresting portrait of his new patron, the Duke Alfonso: a handsome intelligent face, a corpulent body dignified with robes of state, a beautiful hand (hardly that of a potter and gunner) resting on a beloved cannon; this is the picture that stirred even Michelangelo to praise. Ariosto sat for a portrait, and returned the compliment with a line in a later edition of the *Furioso*. Lucrezia Borgia too sat for the great portraitist, but no trace of that painting remains; and Laura Dianti, Alfonso's mistress, may have posed for a picture that survives only in a copy in Modena. It was probably for Alfonso that Titian made one of his finest pictures, *The Tribute Money:* a Pharisee with the head of a philosopher, asking his question sincerely, and a Christ answering without resentment, brilliantly.

It is characteristic of the times that Titian could pass from Bacchus to Christ, from Venus to Mary, and back again, with no apparent loss to his peace of mind. In 1518 he painted for the church of the Frari his greatest work, *The Assumption of the Virgin*. When it was placed behind the high altar, in a majestic marble frame, the Venetian diarist Sanudo thought the event worth noting: "May 20, 1518: Yesterday the panel painted by Titian for . . . the Minorites was put up."[39] To this day the sight of the Frari *Assumption* is an event in any sensitive life. Near the center of the immense panel is the figure of the Virgin, full and strong, clothed in a robe of red and a mantle of blue, rapt in wonder and expectation, lifted up through the clouds by an inverted halo of winged cherubim. Above her is an inevitably futile attempt to portray the Deity—all raiment and beard, and hair disheveled by the winds of heaven; finer is the angel that brings Him a crown for Mary. Below are the Apostles, a variety of magnificent figures, some gazing in astonishment, some kneeling in adoration, some reaching up as if to be taken with her into paradise. Standing before this powerful evocation, the unwilling skeptic mourns his doubts, and acknowledges the beauty and aspiration of the myth.

In 1519 Iacopo Pesaro, Bishop of Paphos in Cyprus, in gratitude for the victory of his Venetian fleet over a Turkish squadron, commissioned Titian to paint another altarpiece for the Frari—for the chapel that had been dedicated there by his family. Titian knew the risk he was running in challenging comparison between this *Madonna of the Pesaro Family* and his masterpiece so lately acclaimed. He worked for seven years on the new picture before he released it from his studio. He chose to represent the Virgin enthroned; but, defying precedent, he placed her at the right in a diagonal scheme that put the donor at the left, with St. Peter between them, and St. Francis at her feet. The composition would have been thrown off balance but for the bright illumination focusing the Mother and her Child. Many an artist, tired of the traditional centralized or pyramidal structure of such pictures, welcomed and imitated the experiment.

About 1523 Marquis Federigo Gonzaga invited Titian to Mantua. The artist did not stay long, for he had commitments in Venice and Ferrara; but he began a series of eleven paintings representing Roman emperors; these have been lost. On one of his visits he painted an attractive portrait of the young bearded Marquis. Federigo's mother, the splendid Isabella, was still living, and sat for a picture. Finding the result uncomfortably realistic, she put it among her antiquities, and asked Titian to copy a portrait that Francia had made of her forty years before. It was from this that Titian produced (c. 1534) the famous picture with the turban hat, the ornate sleeves, the stole of fur, the pretty face. Isabella protested that she had never been so beautiful, but she arranged to have this reminiscent portrait descend to posterity.

Here for a while we leave Tiziano Vecelli. To understand his later career we must fill in the background of political events in which his greatest patron after 1533—Charles V—was intimately concerned. Titian was fifty-six in 1533. Who would have supposed that he had still forty-three years to live, and that he would paint as many masterpieces in his second half-century as in the first?

6. Minor Artists and Arts

We must retrace our steps now, and briefly honor two painters who were born after Titian but died long before his death. We bow, in passing, to Girolamo Savoldo, who came to Venice from Brescia and Florence, and painted pictures of high excellence: the *Madonna and Saints* now in the Brera Gallery; an ecstatic *St. Matthew* in the Metropolitan Museum of Art; and a *Magdalen* in Berlin, far more tempting than the stout lady of that name in Titian.

Giacomo Nigreti was named Palma from some hills near his birthplace, Serina, in the Bergamasque Alps; he became Palma Vecchio when his grand-nephew Palma Giovane also acquired fame. For a time he was considered the equal of Titian by their contemporaries. Perhaps some jealousy arose between them, which was not eased by Titian's stealing of Giacomo's mistress. Giacomo had painted her as *Violante;* Titian had her pose for his *Flora.* Like Titian, Palma handled sacred and profane themes with equal skill if not with equal zest; he specialized in Sacred Conversations or Holy Families, but probably owed his fame to his portraits of Venetian blondes—full-bosomed women who dyed their hair to an auburn hue. Nevertheless his finest pictures are religious: a *Santa Barbara* in the church of Santa Maria Formosa, the patron saint of the Venetian bombardiers; and the *Jacob and Rachel* of the Dresden gallery—a handsome shepherd sharing a kiss with a buxom lass. Palma's portraits would have ranked with the best of his time and city had not Titian produced half a hundred deeper ones.

His pupil Bonifazio de' Pitati, called Veronese from his birthplace, adopted the style of Giorgione's *Fête champêtre* and Titian's *Diana* to adorn Venetian walls and furniture with attractive landscapes and nudes; and his *Diana and Actaeon* is worthy of these masters.

Lorenzo Lotto, less popular than Bonifazio in their day, has gained repute with the years. A shy, pious, melancholy spirit, he was not quite at home in Venice, where paganism resumed its sway as soon as the church bells and choirs ceased to sing. At the age of twenty (1500) he produced one of the most original paintings of the Renaissance, the *St. Jerome* in the Louvre: no hackneyed image of the emaciated eremite, but an almost Chinese study of somber chasms and mountainous rocks, amid which the old scholar is a minor element, at first hardly seen; this is the first European painting that reproduces nature in its wild dominance rather than as an imaginary background.[40] Passing to Treviso, Lorenzo painted for the church of Santa Cristina a monumental altar back of *The Madonna Enthroned*, which made his fame throughout northern Italy. Another success with a *Madonna* for the church of San Domenico at Recanati earned him a call to Rome. There Julius II commissioned him to paint some rooms in the Vatican; but when Raphael came the frescoes that Lotto had begun were destroyed. Perhaps this humiliation helped to darken Lorenzo's mood. Bergamo better appreciated his peculiar talent for moderating the warm colors of Venetian art into softer tones more congruous with piety; twelve years he labored there, modestly paid but content to be first in Bergamo rather than fourth in Venice. For the church of San Bartolommeo he painted an overcrowded but still beautiful altarpiece, *The Madonna in Majesty*. Lovelier is an *Adoration of the Shepherds* at Brescia; the color, while full and pervasive, has a subdued tone more restful to eye and spirit than the brilliant effects of the great Venetians.

A sensitive soul like Lotto's could at times penetrate more deeply into a personality than Titian. Few artists have caught the glow of healthy youth so intimately as in Lotto's *Portrait of a Boy* in the Castello at Milan. His *Self-Portrait* shows Lorenzo himself apparently well and strong, but he must have known much sickness and pain to represent illness so sympathetically as in *The Sick Man* of the Borghese Gallery, or in another of the same title in the Galleria Doria at Rome—an emaciated hand pressed over the heart, a look of pain and bewilderment on the face, as if asking why should he, so good or so great, be chosen by the germ? A more famous portrait, *Laura di Pola*, shows a woman of quiet beauty, also puzzled by life, and finding no answer except in religious faith.

Lotto too came to that consolation. Restless, solitary, unmarried, he wandered from place to place, perhaps from philosophy to philosophy, until in his final years (1552-6) he settled down as a resident in the convent of the Santa Casa at Loreto, near the Holy House that pilgrims believed to have once sheltered the Mother of God. In 1554 he gave all his property to the convent, and took an oblate's vows. Titian called him "as good as goodness, and as virtuous as virtue."[41] Lotto had outlived the Pagan Renaissance, and had sunk to rest, so to speak, in the arms of the Council of Trent.

In that vibrant century—1450-1550—during which Venetian commerce suffered so many defeats, and Venetian painting scored so many victories, the minor arts shared in the cultural exuberance. It was not for them a Renaissance, for they were old and mature in Italy by Petrarch's time, and merely continued their medieval excellence. Perhaps the mosaicists had lost some of their skill or patience; even so their work on St. Mark's was at least abreast of their age. The potters were now learning to make porcelain; Marco Polo had brought some from China; a sultan had sent fine specimens of it to the doge (1461); by 1470 the Venetians were making their own. The glass blowers at Murano reached in this period the acme of their art, making *cristallo* of exquisite purity and design. The names of the leading glass blowers were known throughout Europe, and every royal house competed for their wares. Most of them used a mold or model; some put the mold aside, blew a bubble into the molten glass as it poured from the furnace, and shaped the substance into cups, vases, chalices, ornaments of a hundred colors and a thousand forms. Sometimes, learning from the Moslems, they painted the surface with colored enamel or gold. The glass artisans kept jealously in their families the secret processes by which they achieved their miracles of fragile beauty, and the Venetian government passed stern laws to prevent these esoteric subleties from becoming known in other lands. In 1454 the Council of Ten decreed that

> if a workman carry into another country any art or craft to the detriment of the Republic, he will be ordered to return; if he disobeys, his nearest relatives will be imprisoned, in order that the solidarity of the family may persuade him to return; if he persists in his disobedience, secret measures will be taken to have him killed wherever he may be.[42]

The only known case of such an assassination was at Vienna in the eighteenth century. Despite the law, Venetian artists and artisans found their way over the Alps in the sixteenth century, and brought their technique to France and Germany as gifts to the conquerors of Italy.

Half the artisans of Venice were artists. The pewterers embellished dishes, platters, beakers, and cups with graceful borders and floral designs. The armorers were famous for damascened cuirasses, helmets, shields, swords, and daggers, and sheaths chased or engraved with elegant patterns; and other masters might make for short weapons ivory handles studded

with gems. In Venice, about 1410, Baldassare degli Embriachi, a Florentine, carved in bone the great altarpiece, in thirty-nine sections, now in the
Metropolitan Museum in New York. The wood carvers not only made fine
sculptural figures and reliefs, like the *Circumcision* in the Louvre, or the
chest painted by Bartolommeo Montagna and formerly in the bombed
Poldi-Pezzoli Museum in Milan; they decorated the ceilings and doors and
furniture of Venetian aristocrats with carvings, bosses, and intarsia, and
chiseled the choir stalls of such churches as the Frari and San Zaccaria.
Venetian jewelers met a heavy foreign as well as domestic demand, but
took time to rise from quantity to quality. The goldsmiths, now under
German instead of Oriental influence, turned out tons of plate, personal
adornment, and decorative fixtures for everything from cathedrals to shoes.
The illumination and calligraphy of manuscripts continued, slowly yielding
to print. French and Flemish influences entered into the designs of Venetian textiles, but Venetian dyes and skills gave the products their favored
texture and hues. It was from Venice that the queen of France ordered
three hundred pieces of dyed satin (1532); and it was in the soft and luxurious stuffs worked in Venetian shops, and in the colors given them in
Venetian vats, that the great painters of Venice found models for the lordly
and glowing robes that made half the brillance of their art. Venice almost
realized Ruskin's ideal of an economy in which every industry would be an
art, and every product would proudly express the personality and artistry
of the artisan.

VI. VENETIAN LETTERS

1. *Aldus Manutius*

Venice was in this period too busy living to care much for books; and still
its scholars, libraries, poets, and printers shared in giving it a fair name. It
took no prominent part in the humanist movement; nevertheless humanism
had here one of its noblest exemplars—Ermolao Barbaro, who was crowned
poet by an emperor at fourteen, taught Greek, translated Aristotle, served
his fellow men as a physician, his country as a diplomat, and his Church as a
cardinal, and was killed by the plague at thirty-nine. Venetian women
made as yet little pretense to education; they were content to be physically
alluring, or maternally fertile, or finally venerable; but in 1530 Irene of
Spilimbergo opened a salon for men of letters, studied painting under Titian, sang sweetly, played well on viol, harpsichord, and lute, and talked

learnedly about ancient and modern literature. Venice gave protection to intellectual refugees from the Turks in the East and from the Christians in the West; here Aretino would laugh securely at popes and kings, as, centuries later, Byron would here celebrate their decay. Aristocrats and prelates formed clubs or academies for the cultivation of music and letters, and opened their homes and libraries to the assiduous, the melodious, and the erudite. Monasteries, churches, and private families collected books; Cardinal Domenico Grimani had eight thousand, which he gave to Venice; Cardinal Bessarion did the same with his precious hoard of manuscripts. To house these, and the remnants of Petrarch's bequest, the government twice ordered the erection of a public library; war and other distractions foiled the plan; at last (1536) the Senate engaged Iacopo Sansovino to build the Libreria Vecchia, architecturally the most handsome library in Europe.

Meanwhile Venetian printers were producing the finest printed books of the age, perhaps of all time. They were not the first in Italy. Sweynheim and Pannartz, once aides to Johann Fust in Mainz, set up the first Italian press in a Benedictine monastery at Subiaco in the Apennines (1464); in 1467 they transferred their equipment to Rome, and published twenty-three books in the next three years. In 1469, or earlier, printing began in Venice and Milan. In 1471 Bernardo Cennini opened a printing establishment in Florence, to the dismay of Politian, who mourned that "now the most stupid ideas can in a moment be transferred into a thousand volumes and spread abroad."[43] Copyists thrown out of work vainly denounced the new gadget. By the end of the fifteenth century 4987 books had been printed in Italy: 300 in Florence, 629 in Milan, 925 in Rome, 2835 in Venice.[44]

The superiority of Venice in this regard was due to Teobaldo Manucci, who changed his name to Aldo Manuzio, and later Latinized it into Aldus Manutius. Born at Bassiano in the Romagna (1450), he learned Latin at Rome and Greek at Ferrara, both under Guarino da Verona; and then himself lectured at Ferrara on the classics. Pico della Mirandola, one of his pupils, invited him to come to Carpi and tutor his two nephews, Lionello and Alberto Pio. Teacher and pupils developed a lasting mutual affection; Aldus added the name Pio to his own, and Alberto and his mother, Countess of Carpi, agreed to finance the first large-scale adventure in publishing. Aldus' plan was to collect, edit, print, and broadcast at nominal cost all the significant Greek literature that had been salvaged from the storms of time. It was a heady enterprise for a dozen reasons: manuscripts were hard to get; different manuscripts of the same classic varied dishearteningly in their text;

nearly all manuscripts were heavy with errors of transcription; editors would have to be found and paid to collate and revise texts; fonts of Latin and Greek type would have to be designed and cast; paper would have to be imported in large quantities; typesetters and pressmen would have to be engaged and trained; a machinery of distribution would need to be improvised; a book-buying public would have to be coaxed into existence on a wider base than ever before; and all this would have to be financed without the protection of copyright laws.

Aldus chose Venice for his headquarters because its commercial connections made it an excellent center for distribution; because it was the richest city in Italy, and had many magnates who might want to adorn their rooms with uncut books; and because it harbored scores of refugee Greek scholars who would be glad to be employed as editors or proofreaders. John of Speyer had already established the first printing press in Venice (1469?); Nicholas Jensen of France, who had learned the new art in Gutenberg's Mainz, set up another a year later. In 1479 Jensen sold his press to Andrea Torresano. In 1490 Aldus Manutius settled in Venice, and in 1499 he married Torresano's daughter.

In his home near the church of Sant' Agostino Aldus gathered Greek scholars, fed them, bedded them, and set them to editing classic texts. He talked Greek with them, and wrote in Greek his dedications and prefaces. In his house the new type was molded and cast, the ink was made, the books were printed and bound. His first publication (1495) was a Greek and Latin grammar by Constantine Lascaris, and in that same year he began to issue the works of Aristotle in the original. In 1496 he published the Greek grammar of Theodorus Gaza, and in 1497 a Greek-Latin dictionary compiled by himself. For he continued to be a scholar even amid the hazards and tribulations of publishing. So in 1502, after years of study, he printed his own *Rudimenta grammaticae linguae Latinae*, with an introduction to Hebrew for good measure.

From these technical beginnings he went on to publish one after another of the Greek classics (1495f): Musaeus (*Hero and Leander*), Hesiod, Theocritus, Theognis, Aristophanes, Herodotus, Thucydides, Sophocles, Euripides, Demosthenes, Aeschines, Lysias, Plato, Pindar, Plutarch's *Moralia*. . . . In those same years he put forth a large number of Latin and Italian works, from Quintilian to Bembo, and the *Adagia* of Erasmus, who, sensing the vital import of Aldo's enterprise, came in person to live with him for a time, and edit not only his own *Adagia* or Dictionary of Quotations, but Terence, Plautus, and Seneca too. For the Latin books Aldus had a graceful semiscript type designed, not, as legend said, from the handwriting of Petrarch, but by Francesco da Bologna, an expert calligrapher; this is the type that we now, from that origin, call *italic*. For the Greek texts he cut a font based on the careful handwriting of his chief Greek scholar, Marcus Musurus of Crete. He marked all his publications with a motto, *Festina lente*—"Make haste slowly"—and accompanied it with a dolphin symbolizing speed and an anchor standing for stability; this symbol, along with the pictured tower that Torresano had used, established the custom of the printer's or publisher's colophon.*

Aldus worked at his enterprise quite literally night and day. "Those who cultivate letters," he wrote, in his preface to Aristotle's *Organon*, "must be supplied with the books necessary for their purpose; and until this supply is secured I shall not rest." Over the door of his study he placed a warning inscription: "Whoever thou art, thou art earnestly requested by Aldus to state thy business briefly, and to take thy departure promptly. . . . For this is a place of work."[45] He was so absorbed in his publishing campaign that he neglected his family and his friends, and ruined his health. A thousand tribulations sapped his energy: strikes disrupted his schedule, war suspended it for a year during the Venetian struggle for survival against the League of Cambrai; rival printers in Italy, France, and Germany pirated the editions whose manuscripts had cost him dearly, and whose texts he had paid scholars to revise. But the sight of his small and handy volumes, clearly typed and neatly bound, going forth to a widening public at a modest price (about two dollars in the currency of today) gladdened his heart and repaid his toil. Now, he told himself, the glory of Greece would shine upon all who cared to receive it.[46]

Inspired by his devotion, Venetian scholars joined with him to found the *Neacademia*, or New Academy (1500), dedicated to the acquisition, editing, and publishing of Greek literature. The members, at their meetings, spoke only Greek; they changed their names to Greek forms; they shared the tasks of editing. Distinguished men labored in this Academy—Bembo, Alberto Pio, Erasmus of Holland, Linacre of England. Aldus gave them much credit for the success of his enterprise, but it was his own energy and passion that carried it through. He died exhausted and poor (1515), but fulfilled. His sons continued the work; but when their son, Aldo the second, died (1597), the firm dissolved. It had served its purpose faithfully. It had taken Greek literature from the half-hidden shelves of rich collec-

---

* Cf. the seed-sower on the title page of this volume.

tors, and had scattered it so widely that even the ravaging of Italy in the third decade of the sixteenth century, and the desolation of northern Europe by the Thirty Years' War, could lose that heritage as it had been so largely lost in the dying ages of ancient Rome.

2. Bembo

Besides helping to revive the literature of Greece, the members of the New Academy contributed vigorously to the literature of their time. Antonio Coccio, called Sabellicus, chronicled Venetian history in his *Decades*. Andrea Navagero composed Latin poems so nearly perfect in form that his proud countrymen hailed him as having snatched the leadership of letters from Florence to Venice. Marino Sanudo kept a lively diary of current events in politics, literature, art, manners, and morals; the fifty-eight volumes of these *Diarii* picture the life of Venice more fully and vividly than any history of any city in Italy.

Sanudo wrote in the racy language of daily speech; his friend Bembo devoted half a long life to polishing an artificial style in Latin and Italian. Pietro imbibed culture in his cradle, for he was the child of rich and lettered Venetians. Moreover, as if to confirm his literary purity, he was born in Florence, proud home of the Tuscan dialect. He studied Greek in Sicily under Constantine Lascaris, and philosophy at Padua under Pomponazzi. Perhaps, if we may judge from his conduct—for he seldom took sin very seriously—he imbibed some skepticism from Pomponazzi, who doubted the immortality of the soul; but he was too much of a gentleman to disturb the consolations of the faithful; and when the reckless professor was accused of heresy Bembo persuaded Leo X to deal with him leniently.

Bembo's happiest days were spent at Ferrara, from his twenty-eighth to his thirty-sixth year (1498-1506). There he fell in love, if only in a literary way, with Lucrezia Borgia, queen of that courtly court. He forgot her dubious background at Rome in the lure of her quiet grace, the glow of her "Titian" hair, the fascination of her fame; for fame too, like beauty, can intoxicate. He wrote her, in scholarly diction, letters as tender as might comport with his safety in the precincts of that excellent gunner, her husband Alfonso. He dedicated to her an Italian dialogue on Platonic love, *Gli asolani* (1505); and he composed in her praise Latin elegiacs as elegant as any in Rome's Silver Age. She wrote to him carefully, and may have sent him that tress of her hair which is preserved, with her letters to him, in the Ambrosian Library at Milan.[47]

When Bembo moved from Ferrara to Urbino (1506) he was at the height of his charm. He was tall and handsome, of noble birth and breeding, of distinguished presence without obtrusive pride; he could write poetry in three languages, and his letters were already prized; his conversation was that of a Christian, a scholar, and a gentleman. His *Asolani*, published during his stay at Urbino, fell in with the spirit of that court. What topic could be more pleasant than love?—what *mise en scène* fitter for such discourse than the gardens of Caterina Cornaro at Asolo?—what occasion more suitable than the wedding of one of her maids of honor?— who could better speak of love, however Platonic, than the three youths and three maidens into whose mouths Bembo put his savory mixture of philosophy and poetry? Venice, whose artists took hints and scenes from the book, Ferrara, whose Duchess received the adoring dedication, Rome, where ecclesiastics were glad *ragionar d'amore*, Urbino, which boasted the author in the flesh—all Italy acclaimed Bembo as a master of delicate sentiment and polished style. When Castiglione idealized in *The Courtier* the discussions he had heard or imagined in the Ducal Palace at Urbino, he gave to Bembo the most distinguished role in the dialogue, and chose him to phrase the famed concluding passages on Platonic love.

In 1512 Bembo accompanied Giuliano de' Medici to Rome. A year later Giuliano's brother became Leo X. Bembo was soon lodged in the Vatican as a secretary to the Pope. Leo liked his wit, his Ciceronian Latin, his easygoing ways. For seven years Bembo was an ornament of the papal court, an idol of society, an intellectual father to Raphael, a favorite with millionaires and generous women. He was only in minor orders, and accepted the opinion current in Rome that his trial marriage with the Church did not forbid a little gracious venery. Vittoria Colonna, purest of the pure, doted on him.

Meanwhile, at Venice, Ferrara, Urbino, Rome, he wrote such Latin poetry as Catullus or Tibullus might have penned—elegies, idyls, epitaphs, odes; many frankly pagan, some, like his *Priapus*, in the best vein of Renaissance licentiousness. The Latin of Bembo and Politian was idiomatically perfect, but it came at the wrong time; had they been born fourteen centuries earlier they would have been *de rigueur* in the schools of modern Europe; writing in the fifteenth and sixteenth centuries, they could not be the voice of their country, their epoch, even of their class. Bembo realized this, and in an essay *Della volgar lingua* he defended the use of Italian for literary purposes. He tried to show the way by composing *canzoni* in the manner of Petrarch; but here his passion for polish devitalized his verse, and turned his amours into poetic conceits. Nevertheless many of these poems were set to music as madrigals, some by the great Palestrina himself.

The sensitive Bembo found Rome a ghostly city after the death of his friends Bibbiena, Chigi, and Raphael. He retired from his papal post (1520), and, like Petrarch, sought health and ease in a rural home near Padua. Now, at fifty, he fell in love in no mild Platonic way. For the next twenty-two years he lived in a free union with Donna Morosina, who gave him not only three children but such comforts and consolations, such solicitude and care, as had never graced his fame, and now came doubly welcome to his declining years. He still enjoyed the income of several ecclesiastical benefices. He used his wealth largely to collect fine paintings and sculptures, and among them Venus and Jove held an honored place beside Mary and Christ.[48] His home became a goal of literary pilgrimage, a salon of artists and wits; and from that throne he laid down the laws of style for Italy. Even while papal secretary he had cautioned his associate Sadoleto to avoid reading the Epistles of St. Paul, lest their unpolished speech of the commonalty should mar his taste; "put away these trifles," Bembo told him, "for such absurdities do not become a man of dignity."[49] All Latin, he told Italy, must be modeled upon Cicero, all Italian upon Petrarch and Boccaccio. He himself, in his old age, wrote histories of Florence and Venice; they are beautiful and dead. But when his Morosina died the great stylist forgot his rules, forgot Plato and Lucrezia and Castiglione, and wrote to a friend a letter that, perhaps alone of all that flowed from his pen, invites remembrance:

> I have lost the dearest heart in the world, a heart which tenderly watched over my life—which loved it and sustained it neglectful of its own; a heart so much the master of itself, so disdainful of vain embellishments and adornments, of silk and gold, of jewels and treasures of price, that it was content with the single and (so she assured me) supreme joy of the love I bore it. This heart, moreover, had for vesture the softest, gracefulest, daintiest of limbs; it had at its service pleasant features, and the sweetest, most graciously endowed form that I have ever met in this land.

He can never forget her dying words:

> "I commend our children to you, and beseech you to have care of them, both for my sake and for yours. Be sure they are your own, for I have never deceived you; that is why I could take Our Lord's body just now with a soul at peace." Then, after a long pause, she

added, "Rest with God," and a few minutes afterward closed her
eyes forever, those eyes that had been the clear-shining faithful stars
of my weary pilgrimage through life.[50]

Four years later he was still mourning her. Losing his ties with life, he
became pious at last; and in 1539 Paul III could make him a priest and a
cardinal. For his remaining eight years he was a pillar and exemplar of the
Church.

VII. VERONA

If now, leaving the egregious Aretino to a later chapter, we move out of
Venice to her northern and western dependencies, we shall find there too
some radiance of the Golden Age. Treviso could boast that it had begotten
Lorenzo Lotto and Paris Bordone; and its cathedral had an *Annunciation*
by Titian and a fine choir designed by the innumerable Lombardi. The
little town of Pordenone gave its name to Giovanni Antonio de' Sacchi, and
still shows in its *duomo* one of his *chefs-d'oeuvre*, a *Madonna with Saints
and Donor*. Giovanni was a man of buoyant energy and self-confidence,
ready of wit and sword, willing to undertake anything anywhere. We find
him painting in Udine, Spilimbergo, Treviso, Vicenza, Ferrara, Mantua,
Cremona, Piacenza, Genoa, Venice, forming his style on Giorgione's landscapes, Titian's architectural backgrounds, and Michelangelo's muscles. He
gladly accepted an invitation to Venice (1527), anxious to pit his brush
against Titian's; his *St. Martin and St. Christopher*, painted for the church
of San Rocco, achieved an almost sculptural effect by modeling with light
and shade; Venice hailed him as a worthy rival of Titian. Pordenone resumed his travels, married thrice, was suspected of killing his brother, was
knighted by King John of Hungary (who had never seen any of his pictures), and returned to Venice (1533) to resume his duel with Titian.
Hoping to prod Titian on to finishing his battle picture in the Ducal Palace,
the Signory engaged Pordenone to do a panel on the opposite wall. The
competition between Leonardo and Michelangelo was here repeated
(1538), with a dramatic supplement: Pordenone wore a sword at his belt.
His canvas—splendid in color, too violent in action—was adjudged second
best, and Pordenone moved on to Ferrara to design some tapestries for
Ercole II. Two weeks after arrival he died. His friends said it was poisoning; his enemies said it was time.

Vicenza too had heroes. Bartolommeo Montagna founded a school of
painting rich in middling Madonnas. Montagna's best is the *Madonna En-*

throned in the Brera; it cleaves safely to Antonello's model of two saints on the right, two on the left, and angels making music at the Virgin's feet; but these angels deserve their name, and the Virgin, with comely features and graceful robe, is one of the finest figures in the crowded gallery of Renaissance *Madonnas*. Vicenza's heyday, however, awaited Palladio.

Verona, after a proud history of fifteen hundred years, became a Venetian dependency in 1404, and remained so till 1796. Nevertheless she had a healthy cultural life of her own. Her painters fell behind those of Venice, but her architects, sculptors, and woodworkers were not surpassed in the "Most Serene" capital. The fourteenth-century tombs of the Scaligers, though too ornate, suggest no lack of sculptors; and the equestrian statue of Can Grande della Scala, with the flowing caparison of the horse so vividly portraying motion, falls short only of the masterpieces of Donatello and Verrocchio. The most sought-for wood carver in Italy was Fra Giovanni da Verona. He worked in many cities, but he devoted a large part of his life to carving and inlaying the choir stalls of Santa Maria in Organo in his native city.

The great name in Veronese architecture was "that rare and universal genius" (Vasari calls him), Fra Giocondo. Hellenist, botanist, antiquarian, philosopher, and theologian, this remarkable Dominican friar was also one of the leading architects and engineers of his time. He taught Latin and Greek to the famous scholar Julius Caesar Scaliger, who practised medicine in Verona before moving to France. Fra Giocondo copied the inscriptions on the classic remains in Rome, and presented a book on the subject to Lorenzo de' Medici. His researches led to the discovery of the greater part of Pliny's letters in an old collection in Paris. While in that city he built two bridges over the Seine. When the detritus of the River Brenta threatened to fill up the lagoons that made Venice possible, Fra Giocondo persuaded the Signory to order, at great cost, the diversion of the river to empty farther south; but for this procedure Venice would not be today a miracle of liquid streets; hence Luigi Cornaro called Giocondo the second founder of the city. In Verona his masterpiece is the Palazzo del Consiglio, a simple Romanesque loggia surmounted by an elegant cornice, and crowned with statues of Cornelius Nepos, Catullus, Vitruvius, Pliny the Younger, and Emilius Macer—all ancient gentlemen of Verona. In Rome Giocondo was made architect of St. Peter's with Raphael and Giuliano da Sangallo, but died in that year (1514), aged eighty-one. It was a well-spent life.

Giocondo's work on the ruins of Rome excited another Veronese architect. Giovanmaria Falconetto, after drawing all the antiquities of his own locality, marched off to Rome to do the same thing there, and devoted twelve years, on and off, to the task. Returning to Verona, he took the losing side in politics, and had to move to Padua. There Bembo and Cornaro encouraged him in the application of classical design to architecture; and the generous centenarian housed, fed, financed, and loved Giovanmaria to the end of the artist's seventy-six years. Falconetto designed a loggia for Cornaro's palace in Padua, two of that city's gates, and the church of Santa Maria delle Grazie. Giocondo, Falconetto, and Sanmicheli constituted a trio of architects rivaled only in Rome.

Michele Sanmicheli gave himself chiefly to fortification. Son and nephew of Veronese architects, he went to Rome at sixteen, and carefully measured the ancient buildings. After making a name for himself in designing churches and palaces, he was sent by Clement VII to build defenses for Parma and Piacenza. The distinguishing feature of his military architecture was the pentagonal bastion, from whose projecting balcony guns could be fired in five directions. When he examined the fortifications of Venice he was arrested as a spy; but his examiners were so impressed by his knowledge that the Signory engaged him to construct fortresses in Verona, Brescia, Zara, Corfu, Cyprus, and Crete. Back in Venice, he built a massive fort on the Lido. In preparing for the foundations he soon struck water. Following the example of Fra Giocondo, he sank a double cordon of connected piles, pumped the water from between the two circles, and set the foundations in this dry ring. It was a hazardous undertaking, whose success was in doubt to the last minute. Critics predicted that when heavy artillery should be fired from this fort the structure would shake itself loose from its foundations and collapse. The Signory placed in it the stoutest cannon in Venice, and ordered them all fired at once. Pregnant women fled from the neighborhood to avoid premature deliveries. The cannon were fired, the fort stood firm, the mothers returned, and Sanmicheli was the toast of Venice.

In Verona he designed two majestic city gates, adorned with Doric columns and cornices; Vasari ranked these structures, architecturally, with the Roman theater and amphitheater that had survived in Verona from Roman days. He built the Palazzo Bevilacqua there, and the Grimani and Mocenigo palaces; he reared a campanile for the cathedral, and a dome for San Giorgio Maggiore. His friend Vasari tells us that though Michele in youth had indulged in some moderate adultery, he became in later life a model Christian, taking no thought for material gains, and treating all men with kindness and courtesy. He bequeathed his skills to Iacopo Sansovino and a nephew whom he loved exceedingly. When news came to him that this nephew had fallen in Cyprus while fighting for Venice against the Turks, Sanmicheli developed a fever, and died in a few days, aged seventy-three (1559).

To Verona belonged the finest medalist of the Renaissance, perhaps of all time.[51] Antonio Pisano, known to history as Pisanello, always signed himself *Pictor*, and thought of himself as a painter. Half a dozen of his paintings survive, and they are of excellent quality;* but it is not these that have sustained his name through the centuries. Recapturing the skill and compact realism of Greek and Roman coin designs, Pisanello molded little circular reliefs, seldom more than two inches in diameter, combining finesse of workmanship with such fidelity to truth that his medallions are the most trustworthy representations we have of several Renaissance notables. These are not profound works; they have no philosophical overtones; but they are treasures of painstaking workmanship and historical illumination.

Excepting Pisanello and the Carotos, Verona, in painting, remained medieval. After the fall of the Scaligers it subsided quietly into a secondary role. It was not, like Venice, a Rialto where merchants from a dozen lands rubbed elbows and faiths and wore out one another's dogmas with mutual attrition. It was not, like Lodovico's Milan, a political power, nor like Florence a focus of finance, nor like Rome an international house. It was not so close to the Orient, nor so captivated by humanism, as to tincture its Christianity with paganism; it continued content with medieval themes, and rarely reflected in its art the sensuous zest that evoked the nudes of Giorgione and Titian, Correggio and Raphael. In a later period one of its sons, who indeed is known by its name, entered gaily into the pagan mood; but Paolo Veronese became in life a Venetian rather than a Veronese. Verona was becalmed.

In the fourteenth century its painters were still abreast of their times; note how Padua called one of them—Altichiero da Zevio—to decorate the chapel of San Giorgio. Toward the end of that century Stefano da Zevio went to Florence and learned the Giottesque tradition from Agnolo Gaddi; returning to Verona he painted frescoes that Donatello pronounced the

---

* Cf. the honest portrait of Leonello d'Este (Bergamo); the pensive *Princess of the House of Este* (Louvre), in a pretty entourage of flowers and shells; the *Profile of a Lady* (Washington); an impressive fresco, *St. George*, in St. Anastasia, Verona; and a striking study in light and shade, *St. Eustachius* (London).

best yet done in those parts. His pupil Domenico Morone advanced upon him by studying the works of Pisanello and the Bellini; the *Defeat of the Buonacolsi*, in the Castello at Mantua, emulates the multitudinous panoramas of Gentile. Domenico's son Francesco, by his murals, helped Fra Giovanni's woodwork to make the sacristy of Santa Maria in Organo one of the treasure rooms of Italy. Domenico's pupil Girolamo dai Libri, at the age of sixteen (1490), painted in the same favorite church an altarpiece— *Deposition from the Cross*—"which when uncovered," reports Vasari, "excited such wonder that the whole city ran to congratulate the artist's father";[52] its landscape was one of the best in fifteenth-century art. In another of Girolamo's pictures (New York) a tree was so realistically portrayed that—on the word of a holy Dominican—birds tried to perch on its branches; and the grave Vasari himself avers that in a *Nativity* that Girolamo painted for Santa Maria in Organo you might count the hairs on the rabbits.[53] Girolamo's father had received the name dai Libri from his skill in illuminating manuscripts; the son carried on the art, and came to excel in it all other miniaturists in Italy.

About 1462 Iacopo Bellini painted in Verona. One of the boys who served him was Liberale, who later received the name of his city; through this Liberale da Verona a touch of Venetian color and vitality entered Veronese painting. Liberale, like Girolamo, found that he prospered best by illuminating manuscripts; he earned 800 crowns ($20,000?) in Siena by his miniatures. Badly treated in his old age by his married daughter, he bequeathed his estate to his pupil Francesco Torbido, went to live with him, and died at the reasonable age of eighty-five (1536). Torbido studied also with Giorgione, and improved upon Liberale, who forgave him. Another of Liberale's pupils, Giovanfrancesco Caroto, was strongly influenced by Mantegna's masterly polyptych in San Zeno. He went to Mantua to study with the old master, and made such progress that Mantegna sent out Caroto's work as his own. Giovanfrancesco made excellent portraits of Guidobaldo and Elisabetta, Duke and Duchess of Urbino. He returned to Verona a rich man, who could afford, now and then, to speak his mind. When a priest accused him of making lascivious figures, he asked, "If painted figures move you so, how can you be trusted with flesh and blood?"[54] He was among the few Veronese painters who wandered from religious themes.

If to these men we add Francesco Bonsignori, Paolo Morando, called Cavazzolo, Domenico Brusasorci, and Giovanni Caroto (Giovanfrancesco's younger brother), the roster of Veronese painters in the Renaissance is relatively complete. They were almost all good men; Vasari has a moral pat on the back for nearly every one of them; their lives were orderly for artists, and their work had a placid and wholesome beauty that reflected their natures and their environment. Verona sang a pious and tranquil minor chord in the song of the Renaissance.

CHAPTER XII

Emilia and the Marches

1378-1534

I. CORREGGIO

FIFTY miles south of Verona one comes to the old Via Emilia, or Emilian Way, which ran 175 miles from Piacenza through Parma, Reggio, Modena, Bologna, Imola, Forlì, and Cesena to Rimini.* We pass over Piacenza and (for the moment) Parma, to note a little commune eight miles northeast of Reggio, and sharing its name. Correggio is one of several towns in Italy that are remembered only through some genius to whom they gave a cognomen. Its ruling family also was called Correggio; one member was the Niccolò da Correggio who wrote genteel verses for Beatrice and Isabella d'Este. It was a place where you might expect genius to be born and to die, but not to stay, for it had no significant art, or clear tradition, to give to ability instruction and form. But in the first decades of the sixteenth century the house of Correggio was headed by Count Gilbert X, and his wife, Veronica Gambara, was one of the great ladies of the Renaissance. She could speak Latin, knew Scholastic philosophy, wrote a commentary on patristic theology, composed delicate Petrarchian verses, was called "the tenth Muse." She made her little court a salon for artists and poets, and helped to spread that romantic worship of woman which was now replacing, among the upper classes of Italy, the medieval worship of Mary, and was molding Italian art toward the representation of feminine charms. On September 3, 1528, she wrote to Isabella d'Este that "our Messer Antonio Allegri has just finished a masterpiece picturing Magdalen in the desert, and expressing in full the sublime art of which he is a great master."[1]

It was this Antonio Allegri who unwittingly stole the name and made the fame of his town, though his family name might have well expressed the joyous nature of his art. His father was a small landed proprietor, prosperous enough to win for his son a bride with a dowry of 257 ducats ($6425?).

---

* All these, with Ferrara and Ravenna, constitute the modern *compartimento* of Emilia. Southeast of Rimini are the Marches, or frontier provinces, of Pesaro and Urbino, Ancona, Macerata, and Ascoli Piceno.

When Antonio showed a flair for drawing and painting he was apprenticed to his uncle Lorenzo Allegri. Who taught him further we do not know; some say that he went to Ferrara to study with Francesco de' Bianchi-Ferrari, then to the studios of Francia and Costa at Bologna, then with Costa to Mantua, where he felt the influence of the massive frescoes of Mantegna. In any case he spent most of his life in Correggio in comparative obscurity, and presumably he was the only one in the town who suspected that he would be ranked among the "immortals." He seems to have studied the engravings that Marcantonio Raimondi had made from Raphael, and probably saw, if only in copy, the chief works of Leonardo. All these influences entered into his completely individual style.

The sequence of his subjects corresponds to the decline of religion among the literate classes of Italy in the first quarter of the sixteenth century, and the rise of secular patronage and themes. His early works, even when painted for private purchasers, told again, and mostly for churches, the Christian story: *The Adoration of the Magi*, where the Virgin has the pretty, girlish face that Correggio later confined to subordinate characters; *The Holy Family*; *The Madonna of St. Francis*, still traditional in all its features; *The Repose on the Return from Egypt*, freshly original in composition, coloring, and characterization; *La Zingarella*, where the Virgin, leaning fondly over her babe, is drawn with full Correggian grace; and *The Madonna Adoring Her Child*, which makes the infant the radiant source of the scene's illumination.

His pagan turn came through an odd commission. In 1518 Giovanna da Piacenza, abbess of the convent of San Paolo in Parma, engaged him to decorate her apartment. She was a lady of more pedigree than piety; she chose as theme of the frescoes chaste Diana, goddess of the hunt. Over the fireplace Correggio portrayed Diana in a splendid chariot; above her, in sixteen radial sections converging in the cupola, he painted scenes from classical mythology; in one a dog, too passionately hugged by a child, expresses with a remarkably pictured eye his fear of being choked with love, and shames by his alert beauty all the human and divine figures scattered about. From this time forward the human body, mostly nude, became for Correggio the chief element in pictorial decoration, and pagan motives entered into even his Christian themes. The abbess had converted him from Christianity.

His success made a stir in Parma, and brought him lucrative assignments. About 1519 he painted *The Mystic Marriage of St. Catherine* (Naples); the Virgin and the saint were here unspeakably beautiful; and yet, four years later, Correggio surpassed them when he used the same subject for the picture that is one of the treasures of the Louvre—lovely faces, an alluring landscape, the magic play of light and shade upon flowing raiment and waving hair.

In 1520 Correggio accepted an arduous commission from Parma—to paint frescoes in the cupola and over the tribune and side chapels of a new Benedictine abbey church, San Giovanni Evangelista. He toiled on this task for four years, and in 1523 he moved with his wife and children to Parma to be nearer his work. In the dome he represented the Apostles, seated comfortably in a circle on soft clouds, and fixing their gaze upon a Christ whose foreshortened figure, seen from below, gives an astonishing illusion of distance. The splendor of this dome is in the superbly modeled figures of the Apostles, some of them quite nude, rivaling the gods of Pheidias, and perhaps echoing in their muscular splendor the figures that Michelangelo had painted on the Sistine Chapel ceiling twelve years before. In a spandrel between two arches a powerful St. Ambrose discusses theology with an Apostle John who is as handsome as any Parthenon ephebus. Luscious youthful forms, theoretically angels, fill the interstices with angelic faces, buttocks, legs, and thighs. The Greek revival, already old in humanism and Manutius, is here in full swing in Christian art.

In 1522 the great cathedral of Parma opened its doors to the young artist, and contracted to pay him a thousand ducats ($12,500) to paint the chapels, apse, choir, and dome. On this assignment he worked at intervals through eight years, from 1526 till his death. For the dome he chose the Assumption of the Virgin, and shocked many of the cathedral canons by making this culminating picture a whirling panorama of human flesh. In the center the Virgin, reclining on the air, floats up to heaven with arms outstretched to meet her Son; around and beneath her a heavenly host of Apostles, disciples, and saints—magnificent figures worthy of Raphael at his best—seems to puff her upward with the breath of adoration; and supporting her is a choir of angels looking remarkably like healthy boys and girls in all the splendor of youthful nudity; these are the loveliest adolescent nudes in Italian art. One of the canons, confused by so many arms and legs, denounced the painting as "a fricassee of frogs"; apparently other members of the chapter were dubious about this melee of human flesh celebrating a virgin; and Correggio's work on the cathedral seems to have been interrupted for a time.

He was now (1530) advancing in middle age, and longed for the peace of a settled life. He bought some acres outside Correggio, became, like his father, a landed proprietor, and strove to support his family and his farm with his brush. During and after his major enterprises he produced a series of religious pictures, almost every one of them masterly: *Magdalen Reading; The Virgin of St. Sebastian*—the fairest Virgin in Correggio; *The Madonna della Scodella*—"with a bowl" and an incomparable Bambino; *The Madonna di San Girolamo*, sometimes called *Il Giorno* or *Day*, in which the Jerome is worthy of Michelangelo, and the angel holding a book before the Child is a vision of girlish beauty, and the Magdalen laying her cheek upon the Child's thigh is the purest and tenderest of sinners, and the warm rich reds and yellows make a canvas worthy of Titian at his best; and finally a companion picture, *The Adoration of the Shepherds*, which fancy has called *La Notte, Night*. What interested Correggio in these pictures was not the religious sentiment but the esthetic values—the adoring devotion of the young mother, herself so comely with oval face, glossy hair, dropped eyelids, slender nose, thin lips, full bosom; or the masculine muscles of athletic saints; or the demure loveliness of Magdalen, or the rosy flesh of a child. Correggio, coming down from cathedral scaffolds, refreshed himself with composite visions of beauties that might be.

About 1523 a series of commissions from Federigo II Gonzaga invited the full expression of the pagan element in his art. Wishing to court the favor of Charles V, the Marquis ordered picture after picture, sent them as gifts to the Emperor, and received his coveted bauble, the title of duke. For him, schooled in the paganism of Rome, Correggio painted a succession of mythological subjects, commemorating Olympian triumphs of love or desire. In *The Education of Eros* Venus blindfolds Cupid (lest the human race should die); in *Jupiter and Antiope* the god, disguised as a satyr, advances upon the lady as she lies in naked slumber on the grass; in *Danaë* a winged herald prepares for Jupiter's coming by undraping the fair maid, while beside her bed two *putti* play in happy indifference to the morality of the gods; in *Io* Jupiter descends from his boredom in a concealing cloud and clasps with omnipotent hand a plump lady who hesitates gracefully and ends by yielding to the compliment of desire. In *The Rape of Ganymede* a pretty boy is flown to heaven by an eagle in haste to meet the needs of the ambidextrous god of gods. In *Leda and the Swan* the lover is a swan, but the motive is the same. Even in *The Virgin and St. George* two naked Cupids romp before the Virgin, and St. George, in his flashing mail, is the physical ideal of Renaissance youth.

We must not conclude that Correggio was merely a sensualist with a flair for painting flesh. He loved beauty perhaps immoderately, and in these mythologies he stressed the surface of it too exclusively; but in his *Madon-nas* he had done justice to a profounder beauty. He himself, while his brush romped through Olympus, lived like an orderly bourgeois, devoted to his family, and seldom leaving home except to work. "He was content with little," Vasari tells us, "and lived as a good Christian should." He is reported to have been timid and melancholy; who would not be melan-choly coming every day into a world of deformed adults from a haunting dream of loveliness?

Perhaps some quarrel arose about payment for the work in the cathedral. When Titian visited Parma he heard echoes of the dispute, and gave his opinion that if the dome could be inverted and filled with ducats they would not adequately pay for what Correggio had painted there. In any case the payments were curiously involved in the artist's premature death. In 1534 he received an installment of sixty crowns ($750?), all in coppers. Carrying this weight of metal, he set out from Parma on foot; he became overheated, drank too much water, took a fever, and died on his farm March 5, 1534, in the fortieth (some say forty-fifth) year of his age.

For so short a life his achievement was stupendous, far greater than all that Leonardo, or Titian, or Michelangelo, or anyone but Raphael could show in their first forty years. Correggio equals them all in grace of line, the soft modeling of contours, in portraying the living texture of human flesh. His coloring has a liquid and radiant quality, alive with reflections and transparencies, softer—with its violet, orange, rose, blue, and silver hues —than the glaring brilliance of the later Venetians. He was a master of chiaroscuro, of light and shade in their endless combinations and revela-tions; in some of his Madonnas matter becomes almost a form and function of light. He experimented bravely with schemes of composition—pyra-midal, diagonal, circular; but in his cupola frescoes he let unity slip through a superabundance of Apostolic and angelic legs. He played too fondly with foreshortenings, so that the figures in his cupolas, though drawn as science might require, seem huddled and cramped and ungainly, like the ascending Christ of San Giovanni Evangelista. On the other hand he cared nothing for mechanics, so that many of his characters, like Micawber, lack all visible means of support. He painted some religious subjects with ex-quisite tenderness, but his prevailing interest was in the body—its beauty, movements, attitudes, joys; and his later pictures symbolized the triumph of Venus over the Virgin in sixteenth-century Italian art.

His influence in Italy and France was rivaled only by Michelangelo's. In the later sixteenth century the Bolognese school of painting, led by the

Carracci, took him as their model; and their followers, Guido Reni and Domenichino, founded upon Correggio an art of physical excellence and sensual sentiment. Charles Le Brun and Pierre Mignaud imported into France, and deployed in Versailles, a rosy voluptuous style of decoration through pagan figures, darting Cupids, and chubby cherubim. Correggio, rather than Raphael, conquered France, and left upon its art an influence that lasted till Watteau.

In Parma itself his work was continued, and then transformed, by Francesco Mazzuoli, called by Italian whim il Parmigianino—the Parmesan. Born an orphan (1504), he was reared by two uncles who were painters, so that his talent ripened rapidly. At seventeen he was commissioned to decorate a chapel of that same church—San Giovanni Evangelista—in which Correggio was painting the dome; in these frescoes his style achieved an almost Correggian grace, to which he added his own peculiar love of fine raiment. About this time he painted a remarkable portrait of himself as seen in a mirror; this is one of the most engaging *autorittrati* in art, revealing a lad of refinement, sensitivity, and pride. When Parma was besieged by papal troops his uncles packed up this and others of his pictures, and sent Francesco with them to Rome (1523) to study the works of Raphael and Michelangelo, and seek the favor of Pope Clement VII. He was on the way to full success when the sack of Rome forced him to flee to Bologna (1527). There a fellow artist robbed him of all his engravings and designs. Presumably by this time his protective uncles had died. He earned his bread by painting for Pietro Aretino the queenly *Madonna della Rosa*, formerly in Dresden, and for some nuns the *Santa Margherita*, which still survives in Bologna. When Charles V came there to reorganize a devastated Italy, Francesco made a portrait of him in oils; the Emperor liked it, and might have made the artist's fortune, but Parmigianino took the portrait back to his studio to give it a few finishing touches, and never saw Charles again.

He returned to Parma (1531), and received a commission to paint a vault in the church of the Madonna della Steccata. He was now at the top of his powers, and his incidental products were of a high order: a *Turkish Slave* who looks more like a princess; a *Marriage of St. Catherine* matching Correggio's handling of this theme, with children of unearthly beauty; and an anonymous portrait allegedly of his mistress Antea, described as one of the most famous courtesans of the time, but here angelically demure, with robes too gorgeous for anyone less than a queen.

But now Parmigianino, perhaps goaded on by his misfortunes and poverty, became ardently interested in alchemy, and neglected his painting to set up furnaces for the improvisation of gold. The ecclesiastics of San Giovanni, unable to recall him to his work there, ordered his arrest for violation of contract. The painter fled to Casalmaggiore, lost himself in alembics and crucibles, let his beard grow, neglected his person and his health, caught a chill and fever, and died as suddenly as Correggio (1540).

II. BOLOGNA

If we pass over Reggio and Modena in unseemly haste it is not because they had no cherished heroes of sword or brush or pen. In Reggio an Augustinian monk, Ambrogio Calepino, compiled a dictionary of Latin and Italian, which in successive editions grew into a polyglot lexicon of eleven languages (1590). Little Carpi had a handsome cathedral designed by Baldassare Peruzzi (1514). Modena had a sculptor, Guido Mazzoni, who shocked his townsmen by the realism of a terra-cotta *Cristo morto;* and the fifteenth-century choir stalls of the eleventh-century cathedral matched the beauty of the façade and campanile. Pellegrino da Modena, who worked with Raphael in Rome and then returned to his native city, might have become a painter of note had he not been murdered by ruffians bent upon killing his son. Doubtless Renaissance violence snuffed out in their growth a regiment of potential geniuses.

Bologna, standing at a main crossing of Italy's trade routes, continued to prosper, though her intellectual leadership was passing to Florence as humanism dethroned Scholasticism. Her university was now only one of many in Italy, and could no longer read the law to pontiffs and emperors; but its medical school was still supreme. The popes claimed Bologna as one of the Papal States, and Cardinal Albornoz had passingly enforced the claim (1360); but the schism of the Church between rival popes (1378-1417) reduced papal control to a technicality. A rich family, the Bentivogli, rose to political mastery, and maintained throughout the fifteenth century a mild dictatorship, which observed republican forms and acknowledged but ignored the overlordship of the popes. As *capo* or head of the Senate, Giovanni Bentivoglio governed Bologna for thirty-seven years (1469-1506) with sufficient wisdom and justice to win the admiration of princes and the affection of the people. He paved streets, improved roads, and built canals; he helped the poor with gifts, and organized public works to mitigate unemployment; he actively supported the arts. It was he who brought Lorenzo Costa to Bologna; for him and his sons Francia painted; Filelfo, Guarino, Aurispa, and other humanists were welcomed to his court. During the later years of his rule, embittered by a conspiracy to depose him, he used harsh methods to maintain his ascendancy, and forfeited the good will of the people. In 1506 Pope Julius II advanced upon Bologna with a papal army, and demanded his abdication. He yielded peaceably, was allowed to depart intact, and died in Milan two years later. Julius agreed that Bologna should thenceforth be ruled by its Senate, subject to veto, by a papal legate, of legislation opposed by the Church. The rule of the popes proved more orderly and liberal than that of the Bentivogli; local self-government was unhindered; and the university enjoyed remarkable academic freedom. Bologna remained a papal state, in fact as well as name, till the advent of Napoleon (1796).

Renaissance Bologna was proud of its civic architecture. The guild of merchants raised an elegant Mercanzia, or Chamber of Commerce (1382f), and the lawyers rebuilt (1384) their imposing Palazzo dei Notari. The nobles built handsome palaces like the Bevilacqua, where the Council of Trent would hold its sittings in 1547, and the Palazzo Pallavicini, described by a contemporary as "not unworthy of kings."[3] The massive Palazzo del Podestà, seat of the government, received a new façade (1492), and Bramante designed a stately spiral staircase for the Palazzo Comunale. Many façades had arcades on the street level, so that one might walk for miles in the heart of the city without being exposed—except at crossings—to sun or rain.

While in the university skeptics like Pomponazzi questioned the immortality of the soul, the people and their rulers built new churches, adorned or repaired old ones, and brought hopeful offerings to miracle-working shrines. The Franciscan friars added to their picturesque church of San Francesco one of the fairest campaniles in Italy. The Dominicans enriched their church of San Domenico with choir stalls painstakingly carved and inlaid by Fra Damiano of Bergamo; and they engaged Michelangelo to carve four figures for the ornate *arca* or tabernacle in which the bones of their founder were zealously preserved. The great pride and tragedy of Bolognese art was the cathedral of San Petronio. Far back in the fifth century this Petronius had served the city as its bishop, and had been deeply loved for his beneficence. In 1307 many worshipers claimed to have been healed of blindness, deafness, or other infirmities by washing the diseased parts with water from the well beneath his shrine. Soon the city had to provide accommodations for hundreds of pilgrims seeking cures. In 1388

the communal council decreed that a church should be built for San Petronio, and on a scale that would humble the Florentines and their *duomo;*
it was to be 700 by 460 feet, with a dome rising to 500 feet from the ground.
Money proved less ample than pride; only nave and aisles to the transept
were completed, and only the lower part of the façade. But that lower
part is a masterpiece that attests the noble aspirations and taste of Renaissance art. The portal jambs and architrave were carved with reliefs (1425-
38) challenging in subjects and surpassing in power Ghiberti's gates to the
Florentine Baptistery, and yielding to them only in refinement of finish;
and in the pediment, along with unprepossessing figures of Petronius and
Ambrose, a *Madonna and Child,* carved in the round, worthy of comparison with Michelangelo's *Pietà.* These works of Iacopo della Quercia of
Siena were an inspiration to Michelangelo, and he might have been saved
from the muscular exaggerations of his sculptural style had he accepted
more of the classic purity in della Quercia's designs.

Sculpture rivaled architecture in Bologna. Properzia de' Rossi carved a
bas-relief for the façade of San Petronio; it won such praise that when
Clement VII came to Bologna he asked to see her; but she had died in that
week. Alfonso Lombardi, whose reliefs won Michelangelo's praise, stepped
into history on the coattails of Titian. Learning that Charles V, during the
conference at Bologna (1530), was to sit for Titian, he persuaded the
painter to take him along as a servant; and while Titian painted, Alfonso,
partly concealed behind him, modeled the Emperor in stucco. Charles spied
him, and asked to see his work; he liked it, and asked Alfonso to copy it in
marble. When Charles paid Titian a thousand crowns he bade him give half
to Alfonso. Lombardi brought the finished marble to Charles at Genoa,
and received an additional three hundred crowns. Now famous, Alfonso
was taken to Rome by Cardinal Ippolito de' Medici, and was commissioned
by him to carve tombs for Leo X and Clement VII. But the Cardinal died
in 1535; and Alfonso, losing his commissions and his patron, followed him,
within a year, to the grave.

Painting, in fourteenth-century Bologna, was chiefly illumination; and
when it graduated into murals it followed a stiff Byzantine style. It was
apparently two artists from Ferrara who aroused Bolognese painters from
the *rigor mortis* of Byzantium. When Francesco Cossa came to make his
home in Bologna (1470) there was still in his painting a certain Mantegnesque severity and sculptural hardness of line, but he had learned to in-
fuse his figures with feeling as well as dignity, to set them in motion, and to
bathe them in a living play of light. Lorenzo Costa arrived in Bologna

when he was a lad of twenty-three (1483), and he stayed there for twenty-six years. He took a studio in the same house as Francia; the two men became fast friends, and influenced each other to mutual advantage; sometimes they painted a picture together. Costa won the praise and ducats of Giovanni Bentivoglio by painting an excellent *Madonna Enthroned* in San Petronio. When Giovanni fled at the approach of the terrible Julius (1506), Costa accepted an invitation to succeed Mantegna at Mantua.

Meanwhile Francesco Francia was making himself the head and crown of the Bolognese school. His father was Marco Raibolini, but as surnames were loose in Italy, Francesco became known by the name of the goldsmith to whom he was apprenticed. For many years he practised the goldsmith's art, silverwork, niello, enameling, and engraving. He was made master of the mint, and engraved the coins of the city for both Bentivoglio and the popes; and his coins were so distinguished by their beauty that they became collectors' items, bringing high prices soon after his death. Vasari describes him as a lovable man, "so pleasant in conversation that he could divert the most melancholy individuals, and won the affection of princes and lords and all who knew him."[4]

We cannot say what turned Francia to painting. Bentivoglio discovered his talent, and commissioned him—already forty-nine—to paint an altarpiece for a chapel in San Giacomo Maggiore (1499). The dictator was pleased, and engaged Francia to decorate his palace with murals. They were destroyed when the populace sacked the palace in 1507, but we have Vasari's word for it that these and other frescoes "brought Francia such reverence in the city that he was reckoned as a god."[5] Commissions poured in upon him, and perhaps he accepted too many to allow his best potentialities to mature. Mantua, Reggio, Parma, Lucca, and Urbino received panels from his brush; the Pinacoteca Bolognese has a roomful of them; Verona has a *Holy Family*, Turin an *Entombment*, the Louvre a *Crucifixion*, London a *Dead Christ* and a striking portrait of Bartolommeo Bianchini, the Morgan Library a *Virgin and Child*, the Metropolitan Museum of Art a delightful portrait of Federigo Gonzaga in youth. None of these is of the first order, but each is gracefully drawn, softly colored, and suffused with a tenderness and piety that makes them heralds of Raphael.

Francia's epistolary friendship with Raphael is one of the pleasantest episodes of the Renaissance. Timoteo Viti was among Francia's pupils at Bologna (1490-5), and became at Urbino one of Raphael's early teachers; possibly some quality of Francia passed to the young artist.[6] When Raphael had achieved fame in Rome he invited Francia to visit him. Francia ex-

cused himself as too old, but he wrote a sonnet in Raphael's praise. Raphael
sent him a letter (September 5, 1508) rich in Renaissance courtesy:

> M. Francesco *mio caro:*
>
> I have just received your portrait, brought to me in good con-
> dition . . . for which I thank you very warmly. It is most beautiful,
> so lifelike that I sometimes mistake, believing myself to be with you
> and to hear your words. I pray you to excuse and pardon the delay
> and postponement of my self-portrait, which, because of important
> and incessant occupation, I have not yet been able to execute with
> my own hand in accordance with our agreement. . . . However, I
> send you meanwhile another drawing, of the Nativity, done amid
> so many other things that I blush for it; I do this trifle rather in sign
> of obedience and love than for anything else. If in exchange I shall
> receive [the drawing of] your story of Judith I shall place it among
> the things that are dearest and most precious to me.
>
> Monsignor il Datario expects your little *Madonna* with great anx-
> iety, and Cardinal Riario the large one. . . . I look for them with
> that pleasure and satisfaction with which I see and praise all your
> works, never seeing any others more beautiful, or more devout and
> well done, than yours.
>
> Meanwhile take courage, take care of yourself with your wonted
> prudence, and be assured that I feel your afflictions as if they were
> my own. Continue to love me as I love you with all my heart.
>
> Always entirely at your service,
Your Raffaelle Sancio.[7]

We may allow here for some mannerly flourish, but that this mutual affection was real appears from another letter, in which Raphael sent his
famous *St. Cecilia* to Francia, to be placed in a chapel at Bologna, and asked
him, "as a friend, to correct any errors he might find in it."[8] Vasari relates
that when Francia saw the picture he was so overwhelmed by its beauty,
and so painfully recognized his own inferiority, that he lost all will to paint,
grew ill, and presently died, in the sixty-seventh year of his age (1517).
This is one of many dubious deaths in Vasari; but he adds, graciously, that
there were other theories.

Perhaps, before his death, Francia saw some engravings made in Rome by
his pupil Marcantonio Raimondi from the drawings of Raphael. Visiting
Venice, Mark saw some engravings by Albrecht Dürer on copper or wood.
He spent almost all his travel money buying thirty-six wood engravings by
the Nuremberg master on the Passion of Christ; he copied them on copper,

made prints from the copies, and sold the prints as Dürer's works. Going to Rome, he engraved on copper a drawing by Raphael, so faithfully that the painter allowed a great number of his drawings to be engraved, and prints to be made and sold. Raimondi copied also the paintings of Raphael and others, transferred the copy to copper, and sold the prints. While he made a living in this novel way, the artists of Europe, without visiting Italy, could now know the design of the famous paintings of the Renaissance masters. Finiguerra, Raimondi, and their successors did for art what Gutenberg and Aldus Manutius and others did for scholarship and literature: they built new lines of communication and transmission, and offered to youth at least the outlines of its heritage.

III. ALONG THE EMILIAN WAY

Eastward from Bologna lies a string of minor towns that contributed their commensurate luster to the total splendor of the Renaissance. Little Imola had its Innocenzo da Imola, who studied with Francia, and left a *Holy Family* almost worthy of Raphael. Faenza gave its name and partial industry to faience; there—as in Gubbio, Pesaro, Castel Durante, and Urbino—Italian potters in the fifteenth and sixteenth centuries perfected the art of coating earthenware with opaque enamel, and painting thereon, with metallic oxides, designs that on firing became brilliant purples, greens, and blues. Forlì (anciently Forum Livii) was made famous by two painters and one virile heroine. Melozzo da Forlì we defer to Rome, his favorite theater of operations. His pupil Marco Palmezzano painted the old Christian themes for a hundred churches or patrons, and left us a deceptively charming portrait of Caterina Sforza.

Born out of wedlock to Galeazzomaria Sforza, Duke of Milan, Caterina married the cruel and rapacious Girolamo Riario, despot of Forlì. In 1488 his subjects rebelled, killed him, and captured Caterina and her children; but troops loyal to her held the citadel. She promised her captors, if released, to go and persuade these soldiers to surrender; they agreed, but kept her children as hostages. Once in the castle she had its gates closed, and vigorously directed the resistance of the garrison. When the rebels threatened to kill her children unless she and her men submitted, she defied them, and told them from the ramparts that she had another child in her womb, and could easily conceive more. Lodovico of Milan sent troops who effected her rescue; the rebellion was mercilessly suppressed; and Caterina's son Ottaviano was made lord of Forlì under his mother's iron thumb. We shall meet her again.

North and south of the Emilian Way two ancient capitals survive: Ravenna, once the retreat of Roman emperors, and San Marino, the inextinguishable republic. Around the ninth-century convent of St. Marinus (d. 366) a tiny settlement formed, which, from its once easily defensible perch on a rocky mountain top, remained immune to all the *condottieri* of the Renaissance. Its independence was formally recognized by Pope Urban VIII in 1631, and endures by the courtesy of the Italian government, which finds little there to tax. Ravenna recaptured a passing prosperity after the Venetians took it in 1441; Julius II reclaimed it for the papacy in 1509; and three years later a French army, having won a famous battle near by, felt entitled to sack the city so thoroughly that it never recovered until the Second World War, which shattered it again. There, on a commission from Bernardo Bembo, father of the poet cardinal, Pietro Lombardo designed the tomb (1483) that houses Dante's bones.

Rimini—where the Emilian Way, just south of the Rubicon, reached its Adriatic end—entered violently into Renaissance history through its ruling family, the Malatestas—Evil Heads. They appear first toward the end of the tenth century as lieutenants of the Holy Roman Empire, governing the Marches of Ancona for Otho III. By playing Guelf and Ghibelline factions against each other, and making obeisance now to the emperor, now to the pope, they acquired actual, though not formal, sovereignty over Ancona, Rimini, and Cesena, and ruled them as despots acknowledging no morals except those of intrigue, treachery, and the sword. Machiavelli's *Prince* was a feeble echo of their reality—blood and iron turned into ink, like Bismarck into Nietzsche. It was a Malatesta, Giovanni, who, in a monogamous moment, killed his wife Francesca da Rimini and his brother Paolo (1285). Carlo Malatesta established the repute of the family in the patronage of arts and letters. Sigismondo Malatesta carried the dynasty to its zenith of power, culture, and assassination. His many mistresses gave him several children, in some instances with disturbing simultaneity.[9] He married thrice, and killed two wives on pretext of adultery.[10] He was alleged to have made his daughter pregnant, to have attempted sodomy with his son, who repelled him with drawn dagger,[11] and to have wreaked his lust upon the corpse of a German lady who had preferred death to his embrace;[12] however we have for these exploits only the word of his foes. To his final mistress, Isotta degli Atti, he gave unwonted devotion and ultimately marriage; and after her death he set up in the church of San Francesco a monument marked *Divae Isottae sacrum*—"Sacred to the Divine Isotta." He seems to have denied God and immortality; he thought it a merry prank to fill with ink the holy-water stoup of a church, and to watch the worshipers bespatter themselves as they entered.[13]

Crime had not enough varieties to exhaust his energy. He was an able general, known for reckless bravery, and for resolute endurance of all the hardships incident to military life. He wrote poetry, studied Latin and Greek, supported scholars and artists, and delighted in their company. He was especially fond of Leon Battista Alberti, the Leonardo before da Vinci, and commissioned him to transform the cathedral of San Francesco into a Roman temple. Leaving the thirteenth-century Gothic church intact, Alberti fronted it with a classic façade modeled on the Arch of Augustus erected at Rimini 27 B.C.; he planned to cover the choir with a dome, but this was never built; the result is an unpleasant torso, called by contemporaries Tempio Malatestiano. The art with which Sigismondo had the interior refinished was a paean to paganism. In a brilliant fresco by Piero della Francesca, Sigismondo was shown kneeling before his patron saint; but this was almost the only Christian symbol left in the church. In one of the chapels Isotta was buried; and on the tomb an inscription was placed twenty years before her death: "To Isotta of Rimini, in beauty and virtue the glory of Italy." In another chapel were representations of Mars, Mercury, Saturn, Diana, and Venus. The walls of the church were carved with marble reliefs of a high order, chiefly by Agostino di Duccio, representing satyrs, angels, singing boys, and personified arts and sciences, and emblazoned with the initials of Sigismondo and Isotta. Pope Pius II, a lover of the classics, described the new structure as a *"nobile templum . . .* so filled with pagan symbols that it seemed the shrine not of Christians but of infidels worshiping heathen deities."[14]

At the Peace of Mantua (1459) Pius compelled Sigismondo to restore his principalities to the Church. When the doughty despot renewed his hold upon them, Pius hurled a bull of excommunication at him, charging him with heresy, parricide, incest, adultery, rape, perjury, treason, and sacrilege.[15] Sigismondo laughed at the bull, saying that it had not perceptibly lessened his enjoyment of food and wine.[16] But the patience, arms, and strategy of the scholar Pope proved too much for him; in 1463 he knelt in penitence before a papal legate, surrendered his realm to the Church, and received absolution. Still afire with energy, he took command of a Venetian army, won several victories against the Turks, and returned to

Rimini with what seemed to him a prize as precious as the bones of the greatest saint—the ashes of the philosopher Gemistus Pletho, the Greek Platonist who had in effect proposed the replacement of Christianity with a Neoplatonic pagan faith. Sigismondo buried his treasure in a splendid tomb alongside his Tempio. Three years later (1468) he died. We must not forget him in our composite image of the Renaissance.

If Sigismondo represented that small but influential minority which had more or less openly ceased to accept the medieval Christian creed, we need only follow the Adriatic down from Rimini into the Marches to Loreto to find a living symbol of the old religion still warm in Italian hearts. Every year during the Renaissance, as in our times, thousands of earnest pilgrims traveled to Loreto to visit the Casa Santa, or Holy House, in which, they were told, Mary and Joseph and Jesus had lived in Nazareth, and which, said the marvelous legend, had been miraculously transported by angels first to Dalmatia (1291), then (1294) over the Adriatic to a laurel grove (*lauretum*) near Recanati. Around the little stone house a marble screen was built from designs by Bramante, and Andrea Sansovino added sculptural decorations; and over the Casa a church called the *santuario* was raised by Giuliano da Maiano and Giuliano da Sangallo (1468f). On a small altar inside the Holy House was a figure of Mary and her Child in black cedar, which piety ascribed to the artist hand of Luke the Evangelist. Consumed by fire in 1921, the group was replaced by a reproduction, adorned with jewels and precious stones; and silver lamps keep lights burning before it day and night. This too was part of the Renaissance.

IV. URBINO AND CASTIGLIONE

Twenty miles inland from the Adriatic, midway between Loreto and Rimini, hidden aloft on a scenic spur of the Apennines, the little principality of Urbino—forty miles square—was in the fifteenth century one of the most civilized centers on the earth. That fortunate territory, two hundred years before, had come into the possession of a family—the Montefeltri—that made fortunes as *condottieri*, and spent them as wisely as they were darkly earned. In a remarkable reign of thirty-eight years (1444-82) Federigo da Montefeltro ruled Urbino with a skill and justice unequaled even by Lorenzo the Magnificent. He began judiciously by being a pupil of Vittorino da Feltre, and his life was the finest encomium that noble teacher ever received. While governing Urbino he hired himself out as a general to

Naples, Milan, Florence, and the Church. He never lost a battle, and never allowed war to touch his own soil. He captured a town by forging a letter, and sacked Volterra with superfluous thoroughness; yet he was reputed the most merciful commander of the time. In civil life he was a man of high honor and fidelity. He earned enough as a *condottiere* to administer his state without oppressively taxing his people; he walked unarmed and unprotected among them, confident of their affectionate loyalty. Every morning he gave audience, in a garden open on all sides, to any who wished to speak to him; in the afternoon he rendered judgment, in the Latin tongue. He relieved the destitute, dowered orphan girls, filled his granaries in time of plenty, sold grain cheaply in time of dearth, and forgave the debts of impoverished purchasers. He was a good husband, a good father, a generous friend.

In 1468 he built for himself, his court, and the five hundred members of his government a palace that served not so much as a bastion of defense as a center of administration and a citadel of letters and arts. Luciano Laurana, a Dalmatian, designed it so well that Lorenzo de' Medici sent Baccio Pontelli to make drawings of it. A façade of four stories, with four superimposed arches in the center and a machicolated tower at each side; an inner *cortile* of graceful arcades; rooms now mostly bare but still revealing, by their irremovable carvings and magnificent fireplaces, the taste and luxury of the time; this was the center of the court where Castiglione molded his *Courtier*. The rooms that most delighted Federigo were those in which he gathered his library, and discoursed with the artists, scholars, and poets who enjoyed his friendship and patronage. He himself was the most widely accomplished man in the state. He preferred Aristotle to Plato, and knew the *Ethics*, *Politics*, and *Physics* thoroughly. He put history above philosophy, doubtless feeling that he could learn more about life by studying the record of human behavior than by tracing the web of human theory. He loved the classics without surrendering his Christianity; he read the Fathers and the Scholastics, and heard Mass every day; in peace as well as war he was a foil to Sigismondo Malatesta. His library was as well provided with patristic and medieval literature as with classic works. For fourteen years he kept thirty copyists transcribing Greek and Latin manuscripts, until his library was the fullest in Italy outside the Vatican. He agreed with his librarian, Vespasiano da Bisticci, that no printed book should be allowed entry to the collection; for they thought of a book as a work of art in binding, lettering, and illumination, as well as a vehicle of ideas; and almost every book in the palace was carefully handwritten on vellum, illustrated with miniatures, and bound in crimson leather with silver clasps.

Miniature painting was a favorite art at Urbino. The Vatican Library, which purchased Federigo's collection, prizes particularly two volumes of the "Urbino Bible" which the Duke commissioned Vespasiano and others to illustrate, bidding them, says Vespasiano, to "make this most excellent of all books as rich and worthy as possible."[17] To adorn the palace walls Federigo brought in tapestry weavers and the painters Justus van Ghent from Flanders, Pedro Berruguete from Spain, Paolo Uccello from Florence, Piero della Francesca from Borgo San Sepolcro, and Melozzo da Forlì; here Melozzo painted two of his finest pictures (one now in London, the other in Berlin), showing the cultivation of the "sciences" (i.e., literature and philosophy) at the court of Urbino, with a splendid portrait of Federigo. From these painters, and from Francia and Perugino, came the stimulus that developed Urbino's own school, led by the father of Raphael. When Caesar Borgia appropriated the art treasures of the palace in 1502 they were valued at 150,000 ducats ($1,875,000?).[18]

Federigo had few enemies, many friends. Pope Sixtus IV made him a duke (1474), Henry VII of England made him a Knight of the Garter. When he died (1482) he bequeathed a flourishing principality and an inspiring tradition of justice and peace. His son Guidobaldo did his best to follow in his steps, but disease interfered with his military pursuits, and left him an invalid through most of his life. In 1488 he married Elisabetta Gonzaga, sister-in-law of Isabella, Marchioness of Mantua. Elisabetta too was a frequent invalid, made timid and gentle by physical weakness. Perhaps she was relieved to find that her husband was impotent;[19] she was content, she said, to live with him as a sister;[20] and on that basis they avoided the quarrels of man and wife. She became his mother rather than his sister, cared for him tenderly, never deserted him in his tragic tribulations. Her letters to Isabella are all the more precious because they reveal a delicacy of feeling, a warmth of family attachment, that are sometimes ignored in moral appraisals of the Renaissance. When, after a fortnight's visit at Urbino in 1494, the lively Isabella returned to Mantua, Elisabetta sent after her this touching note:

> Your departure made me feel not only that I had lost a dear sister, but that life itself had gone from me. I know not how else to soften my grief, except by writing every hour to you, and telling you on paper all that my lips desire to say. If I could express the sorrow I feel, I believe that you would come back out of compassion for me.

And if I did not fear to vex you, I would follow you myself. But since both these things are impossible from the respect which I owe to Your Highness, all I can do is to beg you earnestly to remember me sometimes, and to know that I bear you always in my heart.[21]

One of the questions discussed at the court of Guidobaldo and Elisabetta was, "After perseverance, what is the best proof of love?" The answer was, "The sharing of joys and griefs."[22] The young couple gave plentiful proof. In November, 1502, Caesar Borgia, after flourishing protestations of friendship for Guidobaldo, suddenly turned his army up the road to Urbino, claiming that principality as a fief of the Church. The ladies of Urbino brought to the Duke their diamonds and pearls, their necklaces, bracelets, and rings, to finance an impromptu mobilization for defense. But Borgia's treachery had left no time for effective resistance; what troops could now be mustered would be easy victims of the trained and ruthless force that was advancing; the bloodshed would be useless. Duke and Duchess left their power and wealth, fled to Città del Castello and thence to Mantua, where Isabella received them with loving commiseration. Borgia, fearing that Guidobaldo would organize an army there, demanded that Isabella and her Marquis should dismiss the exiles; and to protect Mantua Guidobaldo and Elisabetta moved on to Venice, whose fearless Senate gave them protection and sustenance. A few months later Borgia and his father, Alexander VI, were struck down with acute malarial fever in Rome; the Pope died; Caesar recovered, but his finances collapsed. The people of Urbino rose against his garrison, drove it from the city, and joyously welcomed the return of Guidobaldo and Elisabetta (1503). The Duke adopted his nephew Francesco Maria della Rovere as heir to his throne; and as Francesco was nephew also to Pope Julius II, the little principality remained for a decade secure.

In the five ensuing years (1504-8) the court of Urbino became the cultural model and paragon of Italy. Though fond of the classics, Guidobaldo encouraged the literary use of Italian; and it was at his court that one of the earliest Italian comedies—Bibbiena's *Calandra*—received its first performance (c. 1508). Sculptors and painters carved and painted scenery for the occasion; the spectators sat on carpets; an orchestra, hidden behind the stage, provided music; children sang a prelude; ballets were danced between the acts; at the close a Cupid recited some verses, viols played a song without words, and a quartet sang a hymn to love. For though Urbino's was the most moral court in Italy, it was also the center of the movement that raised

woman upon a pedestal, and liked to talk of love—Platonic or unphilosophi-
cal. The leading spirits in the cultural life of the court were Elisabetta, who
had no viable alternative to Platonic love, and Emilia Pio, who remained to
the end of her life the chaste and grieving widow of Guidobaldo's brother.
A livelier element was contributed to the circle by Bembo the poet and
Bibbiena the dramatist; an esthetic dash by a famous singer, Bernardino
Accolti, called Unico Aretino—"the one and only Arezzian"—and the
sculptor Cristoforo Romano, whom we have met in Milan. A seasoning
of noble blood was provided by Giuliano de' Medici, son of Lorenzo;
Ottaviano Fregoso, soon to be Doge of Genoa; his brother Federigo, destined to be a cardinal; Louis of Canossa, soon to be papal nuncio to France.
Others now and then joined the group: high ecclesiastics, generals, bureau-
crats, poets, scholars, artists, philosophers, musicians, distinguished visitors.
This varied company gathered in the evening in the salon of the Duchess,
gossiped, danced, sang, played games, and conversed. There the art of
conversation—the polite and urbane, serious or humorous consideration of
significant matters—reached its Renaissance peak.

It was this genteel company that Castiglione described and idealized in
one of the most famous books of the Renaissance—*Il Cortigiano, The Courtier*, by which he meant the gentleman. He was himself an exemplary
gentleman: a good son and husband, a man of honor and decency even
amid the dissolute society of Rome, a diplomat esteemed by friend and foe,
a loyal friend who never had an unkind word for anyone, a gentleman in
the best definition as a man always considerate of all. Raphael caught his
inmost character astonishingly well in the superb portrait that hangs in
the Louvre: a wistful meditative face, dark hair and soft blue eyes; too
guileless to be successful in diplomacy except by the sheer charm of his
integrity; clearly a man who would love beauty, in woman and art, in
manners and style, with the sensitiveness of a poet and the comprehension
of a philosopher.

He was the son of Count Cristoforo Castiglione, who held an estate in
the territory of Mantua, and had married a Gonzaga relative of the Marquis
Francesco. At eighteen (1496) he was sent to the court of Lodovico at
Milan, and pleased everyone by his good nature, good manners, and versatile excellence in athletics, letters, music, and art. When his father died his
mother urged him to marry and attend to the perpetuation of his line; but
though Baldassare could write most elegantly of love, he was too Platonic
for matrimony; and he kept his mother waiting seventeen years before he
yielded to her counsel. He joined the army of Guidobaldo, achieved noth-

ing but a broken ankle, convalesced in the ducal palace at Urbino, and remained there for eleven years, enamored of the mountain air, the courtly company, the gracious conversation, and Elisabetta. She was not beautiful, she was six years older than he, and almost as heavy, but her gentle spirit captivated his; he kept her picture behind a mirror in his room, and composed secret sonnets in her praise.[23] Guidobaldo eased the situation by sending him on a mission to England (1506); but Baldassare seized the first excuse to hurry back. The Duke perceived that there was no harm in him, and graciously consented to form with him and Elisabetta a Platonic *ménage à trois*. Castiglione stayed on till the Duke's death (1508), continued in chaste devotion to the widow, and remained at Urbino until Leo X deposed the nephew of Guidobaldo and put upon the ducal throne a nephew of his own (1517).

He returned to his little patrimony near Mantua, and disinterestedly married Ippolita Torelli, twenty-three years his junior. Then he began to fall in love with her, first as a child, then as a mother; he perceived that he had never really known woman, or himself, before, and the new experience brought him a profound and unprecedented happiness. But Isabella persuaded him to serve as Mantuan ambassador in Rome; he went reluctantly, leaving his wife behind in the care of his mother. Soon across the divisive Apennines a tender letter came:

> I have given birth to a little girl. I do not think you will be disappointed. But I have been much worse than before. I have had three bad spells of fever; I am better now, and I hope it will not return. I will write no more, as I am not very well yet, and I commend myself to you with all my heart.—From your wife who is a little exhausted with the pain, from your Ippolita.[24]

Ippolita died shortly after writing this letter, and Castiglione's love of life died with her. He continued to serve Isabella and the Marquis Federigo in Rome; but even at the polished court of Leo X he missed not only the peace of his Mantuan home but the integrity, kindliness, and grace that had made the Urbino circle almost the embodiment of his ideals.

He had begun in Urbino (1508), he finished in Rome, the book that carried him down to posterity. Its purpose was to analyze the conditions that produced, and the conduct that distinguished, a gentleman. Castiglione imagined that fine company at Urbino discussing the subject; perhaps he reported, nicely refined, some of the conversations he had heard there; he used the names of the men and women who had spoken there, and gave them sentiments agreeing with their characters; so he put into the mouth of Bembo a paean to Platonic love. He sent the manuscript to Bembo, asking if the now exalted secretary of the pope had objections to this use of his name; the genial Bembo had none. Even so the timid author kept his book unpublished till 1528; then, a year before his death, he surrendered it to the world only because some friends forced his hand by circulating copies of it in Rome. Within ten years it was translated into French; and in 1561 Sir Thomas Hoby made it a quaint and piquant English classic, which every educated Elizabethan read.

Castiglione was not quite sure, but he inclined to believe that the first requisite of a gentleman must be gentle birth; i.e., it would be very difficult for one to acquire good manners, and an easy grace of body and mind, except by being reared among persons already possessing these qualities; aristocracy seemed a necessary depository, nursery, and vehicle of manners, standards, and taste. Secondly, the gentleman must, early in life, become a good horseman, and learn the arts of war; enthusiasm for peaceful arts and letters must not be carried to the point of weakening in the citizens the martial qualities without which a nation is soon enslaved. Too much war, however, can make a man a brute; he needs, along with the hardening hardships of soldiering, the refining influence of women. "No court, how great soever it be, can have any sightliness or brightness in it, or mirth, without women; nor any courtier can be gracious, pleasant, or hardie [brave], nor at any time undertake any gallant enterprise of chivalrie, unless he be stirred with the conversation and love . . . of women."[25] To wield this civilizing influence woman must as far as possible be feminine, avoiding all imitation of the male in carriage, manners, speech, or dress. She must discipline her body to comeliness, her speech to kindness, her soul to gentleness; therefore she should learn music, dancing, literature, and the art of entertaining; in this way she may achieve that inner beauty of spirit which is the stimulating object and genesis of true love. "The body, where beauty shineth, is not the fountain whence beauty springeth . . . because beauty is bodiless."[26] "Love is nothing else but a certain coveting to enjoy beauty";[27] but "whoso thinketh in possessing the body to enjoy beauty, he is far deceived."[28] The book ends by transforming the lusty chivalry of the Middle Ages into that pale Platonic love which is the last disappointment that a woman will forgive.

The ideal world of refined culture and mutual consideration that Castiglione had conceived collapsed in the brutal sack of Rome (1527). "Many times," reads a passage toward the end of his book, "abundance of wealth is cause of great destruction, as in poor Italy, which hath been, and still is, a prey and booty in the teeth of strange nations, as well for the ill government as for the abundance of riches in it."[29] He could in some measure reproach himself for the disaster. Clement VII sent him (1524) as papal nuncio to Madrid to reconcile Charles V to the papacy; Clement's own behavior made the mission difficult, and it failed. When the news reached Spain that the troops of the Emperor had invaded Rome, imprisoned the Pope, and destroyed half the wealth and grace that Julius and Leo and a thousand artists had created there, life flowed out of Baldassare Castiglione as from a severed vein; and at Toledo in 1529, aged but fifty-one, the gentlest gentleman of the Renaissance passed away.

His body was taken to Italy, and his mother, "who against her will survives her son," raised a tomb to his memory in the church of Santa Maria delle Grazie outside of Mantua. Giulio Romano designed the monument, and Bembo composed for it an elegent inscription; but the finest words engraved on the stone were the verses that Castiglione himself had composed for the grave of his wife, whose remains were now, in accordance with his will, brought to lie beside his own:

> *Non ego nunc vivo coniunx dulcissima vitam*
> *corpore namque tuo fata meam abstulerunt,*
> *sed vitam tumulo cum tecum condar in isto,*
> *iungenturque tuis ossibus ossa mea:*

"I do not live now, O sweetest spouse, for fate has taken my life from your body; but I shall live when I am laid in the same tomb with you, and my bones are joined with yours."[30]

CHAPTER XIII

The Kingdom of Naples

1378-1534

I. ALFONSO THE MAGNANIMOUS

SOUTHEAST of the Marches and the Papal States all mainland Italy constituted the Kingdom of Naples. On the Adriatic side it included the ports of Pescara, Bari, Brindisi, and Otranto; a bit inland the city of Foggia, once the lively capital of the wondrous Frederick II; on the "instep" the ancient port of Taranto; on the "toe" another Reggio; and on the southwestern coast one scenic splendor after another, rising to the glory of Salerno, Amalfi, Sorrento, and Capri, and culminating in busy, noisy, loquacious, passionate, joyous Naples. It was the only great city in the realm. Outside of it and the ports the country was agricultural, medieval, feudal: the land was tilled by serfs or slaves, or by peasants "free" to starve or to work for bread and a shirt, under barons whose ruthless rule of their great estates defied the authority of the throne. The king had little revenue from those lands, but had to finance his government and court from the returns of his own feudal domains, or by exploiting to the point of diminishing returns the royal control of commerce.

The house of Anjou had begun a rapid decline with the escapades of Queen Joanna I, which ended when Charles of Durazzo had her strangled with a silken cord (1382). Joanna II, though forty at her accession (1414), was as excitable as the first. She married thrice, banished her second husband, and had the third murdered. Faced by revolt, she called to her aid King Alfonso of Aragon and Sicily, and adopted him as her son and heir (1420). Rightly suspecting him of planning to replace her, she disowned him (1423), and left her state to René of Anjou at her death (1435). A long war of succession followed, in which Alfonso, having sampled Naples, fought to seize its throne. While he was besieging Gaeta he was captured by the Genoese, and was brought before Filippo Maria Visconti at Milan. With consummate logic surely never learned in schools, he persuaded the Duke that French power re-established in Naples, added to French power already pressing upon Milan from the north and Genoa from the west, would hold half of Italy in a vise, which the Visconti would be the first to feel. Filippo understood, freed his prisoner, and bade him Godspeed to Naples. After many battles and intrigues Alfonso won; the rule of the house of Anjou at Naples (1268-1442) ended, that of the house of Aragon (1442-1503) began. This usurpation provided the legal basis for the French invasion of Italy in 1494, which was the first act in the tragedy of Italy.

Alfonso was so pleased with his new royal seat that he left the rule of Aragon and Sicily to his brother John II. He was not an easy ruler; he taxed with a hard hand; allowed financiers to squeeze the people, then squeezed them in turn; and extorted money from Jews by threatening to baptize them. But most of his taxation fell upon the merchant class; Alfonso reduced the taxes levied from the poor, and helped the destitute. The Neapolitans thought him a good king; he walked among them unarmed, unattended, and unafraid. Having no children by his wife, he begot some on the ladies of his court; his wife killed one of these rivals, and Alfonso never admitted the Queen to his presence thereafter. He was a zealous churchgoer, and listened to sermons faithfully.

Nevertheless he caught the humanist fever, and supported classical scholars with so open a hand that they named him *il Magnanimo*. He welcomed Valla, Filelfo, Manetti, and other humanists to his table and his treasury. He paid Poggio 500 crowns ($12,500?) for a translation of Xenophon's *Cyropaedia* into Latin; paid Bartolommeo Fazio 500 ducats a year for writing an *Historia Alfonsi*, and 1500 more when it was finished; in the one year 1458 he distributed 20,000 ducats ($500,000) among literary men. He carried some classic with him wherever he went; at home and on campaigns he had a classic read to him at meals; and students who wished to hear these readings were admitted to them. When the supposed remains of Livy were discovered at Padua, he sent Beccadelli to Venice to buy a bone, and he received it with all the awe and devotion of a good Neapolitan watching the flow of St. Januarius' blood. When Manetti orated to him in Latin Alfonso was so fascinated by the Florentine scholar's idiomatic style that he allowed a fly to feast on the royal nose till the oration was complete.[1] He gave his humanists full freedom of speech, even to heresy and pornography, and protected them from the Inquisition.

The most remarkable of the scholars at Alfonso's court was Lorenzo Valla. Born in Rome (1407), he studied the classics with Leonardo Bruni, and became an enthusiastic, even a fanatical, Latinist, among whose many wars was a campaign to destroy Italian as a literary language, and make good Latin live again. While teaching Latin and rhetoric at Pavia he wrote a violent diatribe against the famous jurist Bartolus, laughing at his laborious Latinity, and contending that only a man skilled in Latin and in Roman history could understand Roman law. The law students in the university defended Bartolus, the art students rallied around Valla; the debate graduated into riots, and Valla was asked to leave. Later, in *Notes on the New Testament* (*Adnotationes ad novum testamentum*), he applied his linguistic learning and fury to Jerome's Latin translation of the Bible, and revealed many an error in that heroic undertaking; Erasmus would later praise, epitomize, and use Valla's critique. In another treatise, *Elegantiae linguae Latinae*, Valla gave his rules for Latin elegance and purity, ridiculed the Latin of the Middle Ages, and joyfully exposed the bad Latin of many humanists. In an age that adored Cicero he preferred Quintilian. He was left with hardly a friend in the world.

To confirm his isolation he published (1431) a dialogue *On Pleasure and the True Good* (*De voluptate et vero bono*), which expounded the amoralism of the humanists with astonishing temerity. He used as persons of the dialogue three men still living: Leonardo Bruni to defend Stoicism, Antonio Beccadelli to vindicate Epicureanism, and Niccolò de' Niccoli to reconcile Christianity and philosophy. Beccadelli was made to speak with such force that readers rightly assumed that his views were Valla's own. We must suppose, argued Beccadelli, that human nature is good, for it was created by God; indeed Nature and God are one. Consequently our instincts are good, and our natural desire for pleasure and happiness is in itself a justification of the pursuit of these as the proper object of human life. All pleasures, whether of the senses or of the intellect, are to be held legitimate until proved injurious. Now we have an imperious instinct to mate, and certainly no instinct for lifelong chastity. Such continence is therefore unnatural; it is an intolerable torment, and should not be preached as virtue. Virginity, Beccadelli was made to conclude, is a mistake and a waste; and a courtesan is of more value to mankind than a nun.[2]

So far as his means allowed, Valla lived this philosophy. He was a man of promiscuous passion, hot temper, and extreme speech. He wandered from city to city, seeking literary employment. He asked for a place in the papal secretariat, and was turned away. When Alfonso took him up (1435), the King of Aragon and Sicily was fighting for the throne of Naples, and counted among his foes Pope Eugenius IV (1431-47), who claimed Naples as a lapsed papal fief. A reckless scholar like Valla, learned in history, skilled in polemics, and with nothing to lose, was a handy tool against the Pope. Under Alfonso's protection Valla wrote (1440) his most famous treatise, *On the Falsely Believed and Lying Donation of Constantine* (*De falso credita et ementita Constantini donatione*). He assailed as a ridiculous forgery the *Constitutum Constantini* by which the first Christian emperor transferred to Pope Sylvester I (314-35) full secular dominion over all Western Europe. Nicholas of Cusa had recently (1433) exposed the falsity of the Donation in his *De concordantia Catholica*, written for a Council of Basel also at odds with Eugenius IV; but Valla's historical and linguistic criticism of the document was so devastating (though he himself made many errors) that the question was settled once and for all.

Valla and Alfonso were not content with scholarship; they waged war. "I attack not only the dead but the living," said Valla; and he excoriated the relatively decent Eugenius with the most idiomatic abuse. "Even were the Donation authentic, it would be null and void, for Constantine could have no power to make it, and in any case the crimes of the papacy would already have annulled it."[3] And if the Donation was a forgery, Valla concluded (ignoring the territorial donations of Pepin and Charlemagne to the papacy), then the temporal power of the popes had been a thousand-year-long usurpation. From that temporal power had come the corruption of the Church, and the wars of Italy, and the "overbearing, barbarous, tyrannical priestly domination." Valla appealed to the people of Rome to rise and overthrow the papal government of their city, and invited the princes of Europe to deprive the popes of all territorial possessions.[4] It sounded like the voice of Luther, but it was Alfonso who inspired the pen; humanism had become a weapon of war.

Eugenius fought back with the Inquisition. Valla was summoned before its agents at Naples; he ironically professed his complete orthodoxy, and refused to say more. Alfonso ordered the Inquisitors to let him alone, and they dared not disobey. Valla continued his attacks on the Church: he showed that the works attributed to Dionysius the Areopagite were unauthentic; that the letter of Abgarus to Jesus, published by Eusebius, was a forgery; and that the Apostles had had no hand in composing the Apostles' Creed. However, when he surmised that Alfonso was moving toward reconciliation with the papacy he decided that he too had better make peace. He addressed an apology to Eugenius, retracting his heresies, reaffirming his orthodoxy, and asking pardon for his sins. The Pope made no answer. But when Nicholas V ascended the papal throne, and sent out a call for scholars, Valla was made a secretary to the Curia (1448), and was employed to make Latin translations from the Greek. He ended his life as a canon of St. John Lateran, and was buried in holy ground (1457).

His friendly rival, Antonio Beccadelli, illustrated the morals of his time by writing an obscene book and receiving acclaim for it from the leading men of Italy. Born at Palermo (1394), and therefore nicknamed il Panormita, he imbibed his higher education, and perhaps his ambiguous morals, in Siena. About 1425 he composed, under the title of *Hermaphroditus*, a series of Latin elegies and epigrams rivaling Martial in Latinity and pornography. Cosimo de' Medici accepted the dedication, probably without reading the book; the virtuous Guarino da Verona praised the eloquence of its language; a hundred others added encomiums; finally the Emperor Sigismund placed a poet's crown upon Beccadelli's head (1433). Priests denounced the volume, Eugenius proclaimed the excommunication of all who read it, friars publicly burned it at Ferrara, Bologna, Milan. Nevertheless Beccadelli lectured *summa cum laude* in the universities of Bologna and Pavia, received a stipend of eight hundred scudi from the Visconti, and was invited to Naples as court historiographer. His history *Of the Memorable Words and Deeds of King Alfonso* was written in such idiomatic Latin that Aeneas Sylvius Piccolomini—Pope Pius II—himself no middling Latinist, considered it a model of Latin style. Beccadelli lived to be seventy-seven, and died rich in honors and property.

II. FERRANTE

Alfonso left his kingdom to his putative son Ferdinand (r. 1458-94). Ferrante, as his people called him, was of dubious parentage. His mother was Margaret of Hijar, who had other lovers besides the King; Pontano, Ferrante's secretary, affirmed that the father was a Valencian marrano—i.e., a Christianized Spanish Jew. Valla was his tutor. Ferrante was not known for sexual profligacy, but he had most of the vices that can come from a passionate nature untamed by a firm moral code, and aroused by apparently unreasonable hostility. Pope Calixtus III legitimated his birth but refused to recognize him as king; he declared the Aragonese line in Naples extinct, and claimed the Kingdom as a fief of the Church. René of Anjou made another attempt to regain the throne bequeathed him by Joanna II. While he landed forces on the Neapolitan coast, the feudal barons rose in revolt against the house of Aragon, and allied themselves with the foreign foes of the King. Ferrante confronted these simultaneous challenges with angry courage, overcame them, and revenged himself with somber ferocity. One by one he lured his enemies with pretended reconciliation, gave them excellent dinners, killed some of them after dessert, imprisoned others, let several starve to death in his dungeons, kept some of them in cages for his occasional delectation, and, when they died, had them embalmed and dressed in their favorite costumes, and preserved them as mummies in his museum;[5] these stories, however, may be "war atrocities" manufactured by historians in a hostile camp. It was this king who dealt so fairly with Lorenzo de' Medici in 1479. Revolution nearly upset him in 1485, but he recovered his footing, completed a long reign of thirty-six years, and died amid general rejoicing. The rest of the story of Naples belongs to the collapse of Italy.

Ferrante did not continue Alfonso's patronage of scholars, but he engaged as his prime minister a man who was at once a poet, a philosopher, and a skillful diplomat. Giovanni Pontano developed—Beccadelli had founded—the Neapolitan Academy. Its members were men of letters who met periodically to exchange verses and ideas. They took Latin names (Pontano became Jovianus Pontanus), and loved to think that they were continuing, after a long and cruel interlude, the stately culture of Imperial Rome. Several of them wrote a Latin worthy of the Silver Age. Pontanus composed Latin treatises on ethics, praising the virtues that Ferrante allegedly ignored, and an eloquent essay *De principe*, recommending to a ruler those amiable qualities which Machiavelli's *Prince*, twenty years later, would contemn. Giovanni dedicated this exemplary tract to his pupil, Ferrante's son and heir Alfonso II (1494-5), who practised all that Machiavelli preached. Pontano taught in verse as well as in prose, and expounded in Latin hexameters the mysteries of astronomy and the proper cultivation of oranges. In a series of pleasant poems he celebrated every species of normal love: the mutual itching of healthy youth, the tender attachment of newlyweds, the reciprocal satisfactions of marriage, the joys and griefs of parental love, the merger of mates into one being by the accumulation of the years. He described in verses seemingly as spontaneous as Virgil's, and with a surprising command of the Latin lexicon, the holiday life of the Neapolitans: the workers sprawling on the grass, the athletes at their games, the picnickers in their carts, the seductive girls dancing the tarantella to the clash of their tambourines, the lads and lasses flirting on the bayside promenade, the lovers keeping tryst, the bluebloods taking the baths at Baiae as if fifteen centuries had not passed since Ovid's raptures and despairs. Had Pontano written in Italian with the same felicity and grace with which he composed Latin verse, we should have ranked him with the bilingual Petrarch and Politian, who had the good sense to march with the present as well as roam in the past.

After Pontano the most prominent member of the Academy was Iacopo Sannazaro. Like Bembo he could write Italian in the purest Tuscan dialect —far different from the Neapolitan speech; like Politian and Pontano he could mold Latin elegies and epigrams that would not have shamed Tibullus or Martial. For one epigram praising Venice Venice sent him six hundred ducats.[6] Alfonso II, at war with Alexander VI, took Sannazaro with him on his campaigns to shoot poetic darts into Rome. When the lusty Pope, whose Borgia family carried a Spanish bull on its coat of arms, took Giulia Farnese as his alleged mistress, Sannazaro gored him with two lines that must have made Alfonso's soldiers regret their ignorance of Latin:

> *Europen Tyrio quondam sedisse iuvenco*
> *quis neget? Hispano Iulia vecta tauro est;*[7]

which is to say:

> That once on Tyrian bull Europa sat,
> Who doubts? A Spanish bull bears Julia.

And when Caesar Borgia took the field against Naples, a barb went his way:

> *Aut nihil aut Caesar vult dici Borgia; quidni?*
> *cum simul et Caesar possit et esse nihil;*[8]

i.e.,

> Caesar or nothing Borgia would be called;
> But why not both, since he is both at once?

Such sallies passed from mouth to ear in Italy, and shared in forming the legend of the Borgias.

In a gentler mood Sannazaro composed (1526) a Latin epic *On the Virgin Birth* (*De partu Virginis*). It was an astonishing *tour de force:* it used the classical machinery of the pagan gods, but brought them in as adjuncts to—eavesdroppers on—the Gospel narrative; and it dared comparison with Virgil by quoting the famous Fourth Eclogue in the body of the poem. It was excellent Latin, and delighted Clement VII, but not even a pope will lose himself in it today.

The masterpiece of Sannazaro was written in the living tongue of his people, in a medley of prose and verse—*Arcadia* (1504). Like Theocritus in ancient Alexandria, the poet had grown tired of cities, and had learned to love rural fragrance and peace. It was an urban sentiment that Lorenzo and Politian had expressed, with evident sincerity, some twenty years before. The landscapes in the painting of the time marked a growing appreciation of the countryside; and men of the world began to babble of woods and fields, limpid streams, and virile shepherds piping amorous lays. Sannazaro's book caught these fancies at their flow, and was carried to such fame and popularity as favored no other book of the Italian Renaissance. He led his readers into an imaginary world of strong men and beautiful women—none of these old, and most of them nude; he described their splendor, and that of natural scenes, in a poetic prose that set a fashion in Italy, and later in France and England; and he interspersed his prose with pardonable poetry. In this book the modern pastoral was born, perhaps less graceful than the ancient, more elongated and windy, but with interminable effect upon literature and art. Here Giorgione, Titian, and a hundred artists after them would find themes for their pigments; here Edmund Spenser and Sir Philip Sidney would take impressions for their faery queens and an English *Arcadia*. Sannazaro had rediscovered a continent more enchanting than the New World of Columbus, a melodious Utopia where any soul might enter at no other cost than literacy, and might build its castle to its taste and whim without lifting a finger from the page.

The art of the *Regno* was more masculine than its poetry, though there too the soft Italian touch showed its hand. Donatello and Michelozzo came down from Florence and set the pace with an imposing mausoleum for Cardinal Rinaldo Brancacci in the church of San Angelo a Nilo. For the Castel Nuovo, begun by Charles I of Anjou (1283), Alfonso the Magnanimous ordered a new gate (1443-70), which Francesco Laurana designed, and for which Pietro di Martino, and probably Giuliano da Maiano, carved handsome reliefs of the King's achievements in war and peace. The church of Santa Chiara, built for Robert the Wise (1310), still contains the lovely Gothic monument set up by the brothers Giovanni and Pace da Firenze soon after the King's death in 1343. The cathedral of San Gennaro (1272) received a new Gothic interior in the fifteenth century. There, in the costly Cappella del Tesoro, the blood of St. Januarius, protective patron of Naples, flows three times a year, insuring the prosperity of a city weary with commerce and burdened with centuries, but consoled by faith and love.

Sicily remained aloof from the Renaissance. She produced a few scholars like Aurispa, a few painters like Antonello da Messina, but they soon migrated to the wider opportunities of the mainland. Palermo, Monreale, Cefalù had great art, but only as the relic of Byzantine, Moslem, or Norman days. The feudal lords who owned the land preferred the eleventh to the fifteenth century, and lived in knightly scorn or ignorance of letters. The people whom they exploited were too poor to have any cultural expression beyond their colorful dress, their religion of bright mosaics and somber hope, their songs and simple poetry of love and violence. The lovely island enjoyed its own Aragonese kings and queens from 1295 to 1409; thereafter, for three centuries, it was a jewel in the crown of Spain.

Lengthy as this brief survey of non-Roman Italy has seemed, it has done scant justice to the full and varied life of the passionate peninsula. Consideration of morals and manners, of science and philosophy, may be deferred till we have spent some chapters with the Renaissance popes; but even in those cities that we have touched how many precious byways of life and art have escaped our eyes! We have said nothing of a whole branch of Italian literature, for the greatest *novelle* belong to a later period. We have inadequately visualized the major role that the minor arts played in the adornment of Italian bodies, minds, and homes. What deformed or inflated botches were majestically transformed by the textile arts! What would some of the grandees and grand dames glorified by Venetian painting have been without their velvets, satins, silks, and brocades? They did well to cover their nakedness and brand nudity as a sin. Wise it was of them, too, to cool their summers with gardens, even though so formal; to beautify their homes with colored tiles on roof and floor, with iron wrought into lacery and arabesques, and copper vessels gleaming smooth, and figurines of bronze or ivory reminding them how fair might men and women be, and woodwork carved and marquetried and built to last a thousand years, and lustrous pottery brightening table and cupboard and mantelpiece, and the miraculous embroidery of Venetian glass offering its fragile challenge to time, and the golden dies and silver clasps of leather bindings around treasured classics illuminated by happy bondsmen of the pen. Many painters, like Sano di Pietro, chose to ruin their eyesight with drawing and coloring miniatures rather than spread their subtle and intimate dreams of beauty crudely over panels and walls. And sometimes, weary of walking through galleries, one could sit gladly for hours over the illumination and calligraphy of such manuscripts as still hide in the Schifanoia palace at Ferrara, or in the Morgan Library at New York, or in the Ambrosiana at Milan.

All these, as well as the greater arts, and the labor and love, chicanery and statesmanship, devotion and war, faith and philosophy, science and superstition, poetry and music, hatreds and humor, of a lovable and volcanic people combined to make the Italian Renaissance, and to bring it to fulfillment and destruction in Medicean Rome.

BOOK IV

THE ROMAN RENAISSANCE

1378-1521

CHAPTER XIV

The Crisis in the Church

1378-1447

I. THE PAPAL SCHISM: 1378-1417

GREGORY XI had brought the papacy back to Rome; but would it stay there? The conclave that met to name his successor was composed of sixteen cardinals, only four of whom were Italians. The municipal authorities petitioned them to choose a Roman, or at least an Italian; and to support the suggestion a crowd of Romans gathered outside the Vatican, threatening to kill all non-Italian cardinals unless a Roman were made pope. The frightened conclave, by a vote of fifteen to one, hastily elected (1378) Bartolommeo Prignano, Archbishop of Bari, who took the name of Urban VI; then they fled in fear of their lives. But Rome accepted the compromise.[1]

Urban VI ruled the city and the Church with impetuous and despotic energy. He appointed senators and municipal magistrates, and reduced the turbulent capital to obedience and order. He shocked the cardinals by announcing that he proposed to reform the Church, and to begin at the top. Two weeks later, preaching publicly in their presence, he condemned the morals of the cardinals and the higher clergy in unmeasured terms. He forbade them to accept pensions, and ordered that all business brought to the Curia should be dispatched without fees or gifts of any kind. When the cardinals murmured he commanded them to "cease your foolish chattering"; when Cardinal Orsini protested the Pope called him a "blockhead"; when the Cardinal of Limoges objected Urban rushed at him to strike him. Hearing of all this, St. Catherine sent the fiery Pontiff a warning: "Do what you have to do with moderation . . . with good will and a peaceful heart, for excess destroys rather than builds up. For the sake of the crucified Lord keep these hasty movements of your nature a little in check."[2] Urban, heedless, announced his intention to appoint enough Italian cardinals to give Italy a majority in the College.

The French cardinals gathered in Anagni, and planned revolt. On August 9, 1378, they issued a manifesto declaring Urban's election invalid as having been made under duress of the Roman mob. All the Italian cardinals joined them, and at Fondi on September 20 the entire College proclaimed Robert of Geneva to be the true pope. Robert, as Clement VII, took up his residence at Avignon, while Urban clung to his pontifical office in Rome. The Papal Schism so inaugurated was one more result of the rising national state; in effect it was an attempt by France to retain the vital aid of the papacy in her war with England and in any future contest with Germany or Italy. The lead of France was followed by Naples, Spain, and Scotland; but England, Flanders, Germany, Poland, Bohemia, Hungary, and Portugal accepted Urban, and the Church became the political plaything of the rival camps. The confusion reached a pitch that aroused the scornful laughter of expanding Islam. Half the Christian world held the other half to be heretical, blasphemous, and excommunicate. St. Catherine denounced Clement VII as a Judas; St. Vincent Ferrer applied the same term to Urban VI.[3] Each side claimed that sacraments administered by priests of the opposite obedience were invalid, and that the children so baptized, the penitents so shriven, the dying so anointed, remained in a state of mortal sin, doomed to hell or limbo if death should supervene. Mutual hatred rose to a fervor equaled only in the bitterest wars. When many of Urban's newly appointed cardinals plotted to place him in confinement as a dangerous incompetent, he had seven of them arrested, tortured, and put to death (1385).

His own death (1389) brought no compromise; the fourteen cardinals surviving in his camp made Piero Tomacelli Pope Boniface IX, and the divided nations prolonged the divided papacy. When Clement VII died (1394) the cardinals at Avignon named Pedro de Luna to be Benedict XIII. Charles VI of France proposed that both popes should resign; Benedict refused. In 1399 Boniface IX proclaimed a jubilee for the following year. Realizing that many potential pilgrims would be kept at home by the chaos and insecurity of the times, he empowered his agents to give the full indulgence of the jubilee to any Christian who, having confessed his sins and done due penance, should contribute to the Roman Church the sum that a trip to Rome would have cost him. The collectors were not scrupulous theologians; many of them offered the indulgence without requiring confession; Boniface reproved them, but he felt that no one could make better use than he of money so secured; even amid the acute pains of the stone, said his secretary, Boniface "did not cease to thirst for gold."[4] When some collectors tried to cheat him he had them tortured till they disgorged. Other collectors were torn to pieces by the Roman mob for letting Christians get the jubilee indulgence without coming to spend money in Rome.[5] Amid the jubilee celebrations and solemnities the Colonna family aroused the people to demand the restoration of republican government. When Boniface refused, the Colonna led an army of eight thousand against him; the aging pope stood siege resolutely in Sant' Angelo; the people turned against the Colonna, the rebel army dispersed, and thirty-one leaders of the revolt were jailed. One of them was promised his life if he would serve as executioner of the rest; he consented, and hanged thirty men, including his father and his brother.[6]

On the death of Boniface and the election of Innocent VII (1404), revolt broke out again, and Innocent fled to Viterbo. The Roman mob, led by Giovanni Colonna, sacked the Vatican, smeared the emblems of Innocent with mud, and scattered papal registers and historic bulls through the streets (1405).[7] Then the people, bethinking themselves that Rome without the popes would be ruined, made their peace with Innocent, who returned in triumph and, a few days later, died (1406).

His successor, Gregory XII, invited Benedict XIII to a conference. Benedict offered to resign if Gregory would do likewise; Gregory's relatives dissuaded him from consent. Some of his cardinals withdrew to Pisa, and called for a general council to elect a pope acceptable to all Christendom. The King of France again urged Benedict to resign; when Benedict again refused, France renounced its allegiance, and adopted an attitude of neutrality. Deserted by his cardinals, Benedict fled to Spain. His cardinals joined with those who had left Gregory, and together they issued a call for a council to be held at Pisa on March 25, 1409.

II. THE COUNCILS AND THE POPES: 1409-18

Rebellious philosophers, almost a century before, had laid the foundations of the "conciliar movement." William of Occam protested against identifying the Church with the clergy; the Church, he said, is the congregation of all the faithful; that whole has authority superior to any part; it may delegate its authority to a general council, which should have the power to elect, reprove, punish, or depose the pope.[8] A general council, said Marsilius of Padua, is the gathered intelligence of Christendom; how shall any one man dare set up his own intelligence above it? Such a council should be composed not only of clergy but also of laymen elected by the people; and its deliberations should be free from domination by the pope.[9] Heinrich von Langenstein, a German theologian at the University of Paris, in a tract *Concilium pacis* (1381), applied these ideas to the Papal Schism. Whatever logic there might be (said Heinrich) in the arguments of the popes for their supreme, God-derived authority, a crisis had arisen from which logic offered no escape; only a power outside the popes, and superior to the cardinals, could rescue the Church from the chaos that was crippling her; and that authority could only be a general council. Jean Gerson, chancellor of the University of Paris, in a sermon preached at Tarascon before Benedict XIII himself, reasoned that since the exclusive power of the pope to call a general council had failed to end the Schism, that rule must be abrogated for the emergency, and a general council must be otherwise summoned, and must assume the authority to end the crisis.[10]

The Council of Pisa met as scheduled. In the majestic cathedral gathered twenty-six cardinals, four patriarchs, twelve archbishops, eighty bishops, eighty-seven abbots, the generals of all the great monastic orders, delegates from all major universities, three hundred doctors of canon law, ambassadors from all the governments of Europe except those of Hungary, Naples, Spain, Scandinavia, and Scotland. The Council declared itself canonical (valid in Church law) and ecumenical (representing the whole Christian world)—a claim which ignored the Greek and Russian Orthodox Church. It summoned Benedict and Gregory to appear before it; neither appearing, it declared them deposed, and named the Cardinal of Milan as Pope Alexander V (1409). It instructed the new Pope to call another general council before May, 1412, and adjourned.

It had hoped to end the Schism, but as both Benedict and Gregory refused to recognize its authority, the result was that there were now three popes instead of two. Alexander V did not help matters by dying (1410); his cardinals chose as his successor John XXIII, the most unmanageable man to occupy the papal throne since his predecessor of that name. Baldassare Cossa had been made papal vicar of Bologna by Boniface IX; he had governed the city like a *condottiere*, with absolute and unscrupulous power; he had taxed everything, including prostitution, gambling, and usury; according to his secretary, he had seduced two hundred virgins, matrons, widows, and nuns.[11] But he was a man of precious ability in politics and war; he had accumulated great wealth, and commanded a force of troops personally loyal to him; perhaps he could conquer the Papal States from Gregory, and reduce Gregory to impecunious submission.

John XXIII delayed as long as he could to call the council decreed at Pisa. But in 1411 Sigismund became King of the Romans, and the uncrowned but generally acknowledged head of the Holy Roman Empire.

He compelled John to call a council, and chose Constance for its seat as free from Italian intimidation and open to Imperial influence. Taking the initiative from the Church like another Constantine, Sigismund invited all prelates, princes, lords, and doctors in Christendom to attend. Everybody in Europe responded except the three popes and their retinues. So many dignitaries came, at their own dignified leisure, that half a year was spent in assembling them. When, finally, John XXIII consented to open the Council on November 5, 1414, only a fraction had arrived of the three patriarchs, twenty-nine cardinals, thirty-three archbishops, one hundred and fifty bishops, one hundred abbots, three hundred doctors of theology, fourteen university deputies, twenty-six princes, one hundred and forty nobles, and four thousand priests who were to make the completed Council the largest in Christian history, and the most important since the Council of Nicaea (325) had established the creed of the Church. Where normally Constance had sheltered some six thousand inhabitants, it now successfully housed and fed not only some five thousand delegates to the Council, but, to attend to their wants, a host of servants, secretaries, pedlars, physicians, quacks, minstrels, and fifteen hundred prostitutes.[12]

The Council had hardly formulated its procedure when it was faced with the dramatic desertion of the Pope who had convened it. John XXIII was shocked to learn that his enemies were preparing to present to the assembly a record of his life, crimes, and incontinence. A committee advised him that this ignominy could be averted if he would agree to join Gregory and Benedict in a simultaneous abdication.[13] He agreed; but suddenly he fled from Constance disguised as a groom (March 20, 1415), and found refuge in a castle at Schaffhausen with Frederick, Archduke of Austria and foe to Sigismund. On March 29 he announced that all the promises made by him in Constance had been drawn from him through fear of violence, and could have no binding force. On April 6 the Council issued a decree—*Sacrosancta*—which one historian has called "the most revolutionary official document in the history of the world":[14]

> This holy synod of Constance, being a general council, and legally assembled in the Holy Spirit for the praise of God and for ending the present Schism, and for the union and reform of the Church of God in its head and its members . . . ordains, declares, and decrees as follows: First, it declares that this synod . . . represents the Church Militant, and has its authority directly from Christ; and everybody, of whatever rank or dignity, including also the pope, is bound to obey this council in those things that pertain to the faith, to

the ending of this Schism, and to a general reform of the Church in its head and members. Likewise it declares that if anyone, of whatever rank, condition, or dignity, including also the pope, shall refuse to obey the commands, statutes, ordinances, or orders of this holy council, or of any other holy council properly assembled, in regard to the ending of the Schism or to the reform of the Church, he shall be subject to proper punishment . . . and, if necessary, recourse shall be had to other aids of justice.[15]

Many cardinals protested against this decree, fearing that it would end the power of the college of cardinals to elect the pope; the Council overrode their opposition, and thereafter they played but a minor role in its activities.

The Council now sent a committee to John XXIII to ask for his abdication. Receiving no definite answer, it accepted (May 25) the presentation of fifty-four charges against him as a pagan, an oppressor, a liar, a simoniac, a traitor, a lecher, and a thief;[16] sixteen other accusations were suppressed as too severe.[17] On May 29 the Council deposed John XXIII; and broken at last, he accepted the decree. Sigismund ordered him confined in the castle of Heidelberg for the duration of the Council. He was released in 1418, and found asylum and sustenance, as an old man, with Cosimo de' Medici.

The Council celebrated its triumph with a parade through Constance. When it returned to business it found itself in a quandary. If it should choose another pope it would be restoring the threefold division of Christendom, for many districts still obeyed Benedict or Gregory. Gregory rescued the Council by an act at once subtle and magnanimous: he agreed to resign, but only on condition that he should be allowed to reconvene and legitimate the Council by his own papal authority. On July 4, 1415, the Council, so reconvened, accepted Gregory's resignation, confirmed the validity of his appointments, and named him legate governor of Ancona, where he lived quietly the two remaining years of his life.

Benedict continued to resist, but his cardinals left him and made their peace with the Council. On July 26, 1417, the Council deposed him. He retired to his family stronghold near Valencia, and died there at ninety, still counting himself pope. In October the Council passed a decree—*Frequens* —requiring that another general council should be convened within five years. On November 17 an electoral committee of the Council chose Cardinal Oddone Colonna as Pope Martin V. All Christendom accepted him, and after thirty-nine years of chaos the Great Schism came to an end.

The Council had now accomplished its first purpose. But its victory on this point defeated its other purpose—to reform the Church. When Martin V found himself pope he assumed all the powers and prerogatives of the papacy. He displaced Sigismund as president of the Council, and with courteous and subtle address negotiated with each national group in the Council a separate treaty of ecclesiastical reform. By playing off each group against the others he persuaded each to accept a minimum of reform, couched in carefully obscure language which each party might interpret to save its emoluments and its face. The Council yielded to him because it was tired. It had labored for three years, it longed for home, and felt that a later synod could take up in sharper detail the problem of reform. On April 22, 1418, it declared itself dissolved.

III. THE TRIUMPH OF THE PAPACY: 1418-47

Martin V, though himself a Roman, could not go at once to Rome; the roads were held by the *condottiere* Braccio da Montone; Martin thought it safer to stay in Geneva, then Mantua, then Florence. When at last he reached Rome (1420), he was shocked by the condition of the city, by the dilapidation of the buildings and the people. The capital of Christendom was one of the least civilized cities in Europe.

If Martin continued a characteristic abuse by appointing his Colonna relatives to places of income and power, it may be because he had to strengthen his family in order to have some physical security in the Vatican. He had no army, but upon the Papal States, from every side, pressed the armed forces of Naples, Florence, Venice, and Milan. The Papal States, for the most part, had again fallen into the hands of petty dictators who, though they called themselves vicars of the pope, had assumed practically sovereign powers during the division of the papacy. In Lombardy the clergy had for centuries been hostile to the bishops of Rome. Beyond the Alps lay a disordered Christendom that had lost most of its respect for the papacy, and grudged it financial support.

Martin faced these difficulties with courage and success. Though he had inherited an almost empty treasury, he allotted funds for the partial rebuilding of his capital. His energetic measures drove the brigands from the roads and Rome; he destroyed a robber stronghold at Montelipo, and had its leaders beheaded.[18] He restored order in Rome, and codified its communal law. He appointed one of the early humanists, Poggio Bracciolini, to be a papal secretary. He engaged Gentile da Fabriano, Antonio Pisanello, and Masaccio to paint frescoes in Santa Maria Maggiore and St. John in the Lateran. He named men of intellect and character, like Giuliano Cesarini, Louis Allemand, Domenico Capranica, and Prospero Colonna, to the college of cardinals. He reorganized the Curia to effective functioning, but found no way to finance it except by selling offices and services. Since the Church had survived for a century without reform, but could hardly survive a week without money, Martin judged money to be more urgently needed than reform. Pursuant to the *Frequens* decree of Constance, he called a council to meet at Pavia in 1423. It was sparsely attended; plague compelled its transference to Siena; when it proposed to assume absolute authority Martin ordered it to dissolve; and the bishops, fearing for their sees, obeyed. To soothe the spirit of reform Martin issued (1425) a bull detailing some admirable changes in the procedure and financing of the Curia; but a thousand obstacles and objections arose, and the proposals faded in the quick oblivion of time. In 1430 a German envoy to Rome sent to his prince a letter that almost sounded the tocsin of the Reformation:

> Greed reigns supreme in the Roman court, and day by day finds new devices . . . for extorting money from Germany under pretext of ecclesiastical fees. Hence much outcry . . . and heartburnings; . . . also many questions in regard to the papacy will arise, or else obedience will at last be entirely renounced, to escape from these outrageous exactions of the Italians; and this latter course, as I perceive; would be acceptable to many countries.[19]

Martin's successor faced the accumulated problems of the papacy from the background of a devout Franciscan monk ill equipped for statesmanship. The papacy was a government more than a religion; the popes had to be statesmen, sometimes warriors, and could rarely afford to be saints. Eugenius IV was sometimes a saint. True, he was obstinate and dourly inflexible, and the gout that gave him almost constant pain in his hands helped his sea of troubles to make him impatient and unsociable. But he lived ascetically, ate sparingly, drank nothing but water, slept little, worked hard, attended conscientiously to his religious duties, bore no malice against his enemies, pardoned readily, gave generously, kept nothing for himself, and was so modest that in public he seldom raised his eyes from the ground.[20] Yet few popes have earned so many foes.

The first were the cardinals who had elected him. As the price of their votes, and to protect themselves from such one-man rule as that of Martin, they had induced him to sign *capitula*—literally, headings—promising them freedom of speech, guarantees for their offices, control over half the revenues, and consultation with them on all important affairs; such "capitulations" set a precedent regularly followed in papal elections throughout the Renaissance. Furthermore, Eugenius made powerful enemies of the Colonna. Believing that Martin had transferred too much Church property to that family, he ordered restoration of many parcels, and had Martin's former secretary tortured almost to death to elicit information in the matter. The Colonna made war upon the Pope; he defeated them with soldiery sent him by Florence and Venice, but in the process he aroused the hostility of Rome. Meanwhile the Council of Basel, called by Martin, met in the first year (1431) of the new pontificate, and proposed again to assert the supremacy of the councils over the popes. Eugenius ordered it to dissolve; it refused, commanded him to appear before it, and sent Milanese troops to attack him in Rome. The Colonna seized the chance for revenge; they organized a revolution in the city, and set up a republican government (1434). Eugenius fled down the Tiber in a small boat pelted by the populace with arrows, pikes, and stones.[21] He found refuge in Florence, then in Bologna; for nine years he and the Curia were exiles from Rome.

The majority of the delegates to the Council of Basel were French. They aimed, as the bishop of Tours frankly said, "either to wrest the Apostolic See from the Italians, or so to despoil it that it will not matter where it abides." The Council therefore assumed one after another the prerogatives of the papacy: it issued indulgences, granted dispensations, appointed to benefices, and required that annates should be paid to itself and not to the pope. Eugenius again ordered its dissolution; it countered by deposing him (1439) and naming Amadeus VIII of Savoy as Antipope Felix V; the Schism was renewed. To complete the apparent defeat of Eugenius, Charles VII of France convened at Bourges (1438) an assembly of French prelates, princes, and lawyers, which proclaimed the supremacy of councils over popes, and issued the Pragmatic Sanction of Bourges: ecclesiastical offices were henceforth to be filled through election by the local chapter or clergy, but the king might make "recommendations"; appeals to the Papal Curia were forbidden except after exhausting all judicial possibilities in France; the collection of annates by the pope was prohibited.[22] This Sanction in effect established an independent Gallican Church, and made the king its master. A year later a diet at Mainz adopted measures for a similar national church in Germany. The Bohemian Church had separated itself from the papacy in the Hussite revolt; the archbishop of Prague called the pope "the Beast of the Apocalypse."[23] The whole edifice of the Roman

Church seemed shattered beyond repair; the nationalistic Reformation seemed established a century before Luther.

Eugenius was rescued by the Turks. As the Ottomans came ever nearer to Constantinople, the Byzantines decided that Constantinople was worth a Roman Mass, and that a reunion of Greek with Roman Christianity was an indispensable prelude to securing military aid from the West. The Emperor John VIII sent an embassy to Martin V (1431) to propose a council of both churches. The Council of Basel despatched envoys to John (1433), explaining that the Council was superior in power to the pope, was under the protection of the Emperor Sigismund, and would procure money and troops for the defense of Constantinople if the Greek Church would deal with the Council rather than with the Pope. Eugenius sent his own embassy, offering aid on condition that the proposal of union should be laid before a new council to be called by him at Ferrara. John decided for Eugenius. The Pope summoned to Ferrara such of the hierarchy as were still loyal to him; many leading prelates, including Cesarini and Nicholas of Cusa, abandoned Basel for Ferrara, feeling that the matter of prime importance was the negotiation with the Greeks. The Council at Basel lingered on, but with mounting exasperation and declining prestige.

The news that Christendom, divided between the Greek and the Roman Churches since 1054, was now to be united stirred all Europe. On February 8, 1438, the Byzantine Emperor, the Patriarch Joseph of Constantinople, seventeen Greek metropolitans, and a large number of Greek bishops, monks, and scholars, arrived at Venice, still partly a Byzantine city. At Ferrara Eugenius received them with a pomp that must have meant little to the ceremonious Greeks. After the opening of the Council various commissions were appointed to reconcile the divergences of the two Churches on the primacy of the pope, the use of unleavened bread, the nature of the pains of purgatory, and the procession of the Holy Ghost from the Father and/or the Son. For eight months the pundits argued these points, but could come to no agreement. Meanwhile plague broke out in Ferrara; Cosimo de' Medici invited the Council to move to Florence and be housed at the expense of himself and his friends; it was so ordered; and some would date the Italian Renaissance from that influx of learned Greeks into Florence (1439). There it was agreed that the formula acceptable to the Greeks—that "the Holy Ghost proceeds from the Father through the Son" (*ex Patre per Filium procedit*)—meant the same as the Roman formula, "proceeds from the Father and the Son" (*ex Patre Filioque procedit*); and by June 1439 an accord was reached on purgatorial pains. The primacy of the pope led to hot debates, and the Greek Emperor threatened to break up the Council. The conciliatory Archbishop Bessarion of Nicaea contrived a compromise that recognized the universal authority of the pope, but reserved all the existing rights and privileges of the Eastern churches. The formula was accepted; and on July 6, 1439, in the great cathedral that only three years before had received from Brunellesco its majestic dome, the decree uniting the two Churches was read in Greek by Bessarion and in Latin by Cesarini; the two prelates kissed; and all the members of the Council, with the Greek Emperor at their head, bent the knee before that same Eugenius who had seemed, so recently, the despised and rejected of men.

The joy of Christendom was brief. When the Greek Emperor and his suite returned to Constantinople they were met with insults and ribaldry; the clergy and population of the city repudiated the submission to Rome. Eugenius kept his part of the bargain; Cardinal Cesarini was sent to Hungary at the head of an army to join the forces of Ladislas and Hunyadi; they were victorious at Nish, entered Sofia in triumph on Christmas Eve of 1443, and were routed at Varna by Murad II (1444). The antiunion party in Constantinople won the upper hand, and the Patriarch Gregory, who had supported union, fled to Italy. Gregory fought his way back to St. Sophia, and read the decree of union there in 1452; but from that time the great church was shunned by the people. The antiunion clergy anathematized all adherents of union, refused absolution to those who had attended the reading of the decree, and exhorted the sick to die without the sacraments rather than receive them from a "Uniate" priest.[24] The patriarchs of Alexandria, Antioch, and Jerusalem repudiated the "robber synod" of Florence.[25] Mohammed II simplified the situation by making Constantinople a Turkish capital (1453). He gave the Christians full freedom of worship, and appointed as patriarch Gennadius, a devoted foe of unity.

Eugenius returned to Rome in 1443, after his legate general, Cardinal Vitelleschi, had suppressed the chaotic republic and the turbulent Colonna with a ferocity unequaled by the Vandals or the Goths. The Pope's stay at Florence had acquainted him with the development of humanism and art under Cosimo de' Medici, and the Greek scholars who had attended the Council of Ferrara and Florence had aroused in him an interest in the preservation of the classic manuscripts that the imminent fall of Constantinople might forfeit or destroy. He added to his secretariat Poggio, Flavio Biondo, Leonardo Bruni, and other humanists who could negotiate with the Greeks in Greek. He brought Fra Angelico to Rome, and had him paint frescoes in the Chapel of the Sacrament at the Vatican. Having admired the bronze gates that Ghiberti had cast for the Florentine Baptistery, Eugenius commissioned Filarete to make similar doors for the old church of St. Peter (1433). It was significant—though already it aroused hardly any comment—that the sculptor placed upon the portals of the chief church in Latin Christendom not only Christ and Mary and the Apostles, but Mars and Roma, Hero and Leander, Jupiter and Ganymede, even Leda and the swan. In the hour of his victory over the Council of Basel Eugenius brought the pagan Renaissance to Rome.

CHAPTER XV

The Renaissance Captures Rome

1447-92

I. THE CAPITAL OF THE WORLD

WHEN Pope Nicholas V mounted the oldest throne in the world,* Rome was hardly a tenth of the Rome that had been enclosed by the walls of Aurelian (A.D. 270-5), and was smaller in area and population (80,000)[1] than Venice, Florence, or Milan. Since the ruin of the major aqueducts by the barbarian invasions, the seven hills had been without a reliable water supply; some minor aqueducts remained, some springs, many cisterns and wells; but a large proportion of the inhabitants drank the water of the Tiber.[2] Most of the people lived in the unhealthy plains, subject to inundation from the river and to malarial infection from the neighboring swamps. The Capitoline hill was now called Monte Caprino, from the goats (*capri*) that nibbled its slopes. The Palatine hill was a rural retreat, almost uninhabited; the ancient palaces from which it derived its name were dusty quarries. The Borgo Vaticano, or Vatican Town, was a small suburb across the river from the central city, and huddled about the decaying shrine of St. Peter. Some churches, like Santa Maria Maggiore or Santa Cecilia, were beautiful within but plain without; and no church in Rome could compare with the *duomo* of Florence or Milan, no monastery could rival the Certosa di Pavia, no town hall rose to the dignity of the Palazzo Vecchio, or the Castello Sforzesco, or the Palace of the Doges, or even the Palazzo Pubblico of Siena. Nearly all the streets were muddy or dusty alleys; some were paved with cobblestones; only a few were lit at night; they were swept only on extraordinary occasions like a jubilee, or the formal entry of some very important person.

The economic support of the city came partly from pasturage and the production of wool, and the cattle that grazed in the environing fields, but chiefly from the revenues of the Church. There was little agriculture, and only petty trade; industry and commerce had well-nigh disappeared through lack of protection from brigand raids. There was almost no mid-

---

* Rejecting as legend the alleged foundation of the Japanese imperial dynasty in 660 B.C.

dle class—only nobles, ecclesiastics, and commoners. The nobles, who owned nearly all the land that had not fallen to the Church, exploited their peasantry without Christian compunction or hindrance. They suppressed revolt, and waged their feuds, with *bravi*—strong-arm ruffians kept in their employ and trained to beat or kill. The great families—above all the Colonna and the Orsini—seized tombs, baths, theaters, and other structures in or near Rome and turned them into private fortresses; and their rural castles were designed for war. The nobles were usual hostile to the popes, or strove to name and govern them. Time and again they created such disorder that the popes fled; Pius II prayed that any other city might be his capital.[3] When Sixtus IV and Alexander VI warred against such men it was in a forgivable effort to win some security for the Papal See.

Normally the ecclesiastics ruled Rome, for they had the Church's varied revenue to spend. The inhabitants were dependent upon that influx of gold from a dozen countries, upon the employment it enabled churchmen to provide, and upon the charity that it allowed the popes to dispense. The people of Rome could not be enthusiastic about any reform of the Church that would lessen that golden flow. Precluded from rebellion, they substituted for it a sharpness of satire unequaled elsewhere in Europe. A statue in the Piazza Navona, probably a Hellenistic *Hercules*, was renamed *Pasquino*—perhaps from a nearby tailor—and became the bulletin board of the latest squibs, usually in the form of Latin or Italian epigrams, and often against the reigning pope. The Romans were religious, at least on occasion; they crowded to receive the papal blessing, and were proud to imitate ambassadors by kissing the papal feet; but when Sixtus IV, suffering from gout, failed to appear for a scheduled benediction they cursed him with Roman virulence. Moreover, since Eugenius IV had abrogated the Roman Republic, the popes were the secular rulers of Rome, and received the contumely usually awarded to governments. It was the misfortune of the papacy to be seated amid the most lawless population in Italy.

The popes felt themselves thoroughly justified in claiming a degree and area of temporal power. As the heads of an international organization they could not afford to be the captives of any one state, as they had been in effect in Avignon; so trammeled, they could hardly serve all peoples impartially, much less realize their majestic dream of being the spiritual governors of every government. Though the "Donation of Constantine" was a palpable forgery (as Nicholas admitted by hiring Valla), the donation of central Italy to the papacy by Pepin (755), confirmed by Charlemagne (773), was an historical fact. The popes had coined their own money at least as far back as 782,[4] and for centuries no one had questioned their right. The unification of local powers, feudal or martial, in a central government was taking place in the Papal States as in the other nations of Europe. If the popes from Nicholas V to Clement VII ruled their states as absolute monarchs they were following the fashion of the times; and they could with reason complain when reformers like Chancellor Gerson of the University of Paris proposed democracy in the Church but deprecated it in the state. Neither state nor Church was ready for democracy at a time when printing had not yet begun or spread. Nicholas V became pope seven years before Gutenberg printed his Bible, thirty years before printing reached Rome, forty-eight years before the first publication of Aldus Manutius. Democracy is a luxury of disseminated intelligence, security, and peace.

The secular rule of the popes directly applied to what antiquity had called Latium (now Lazio), a small province lying between Tuscany, Umbria, the Kingdom of Naples, and the Tyrrhenian Sea. Beyond this they claimed also Umbria, the Marches, and the Romagna (the ancient Romania). These four regions together made a broad belt across central Italy from sea to sea; they contained some twenty-six cities, which the popes, when they could, ruled by vicars, or divided among provincial governors. Furthermore, Sicily and the whole Kingdom of Naples were claimed as papal fiefs on the basis of an agreement between Pope Innocent III and Frederick II; and the payment of an annual feudal fee by these states to the papacy became a major source of quarrels between the *Regno* and the popes. Finally the Countess Matilda had bequeathed to the popes (1107), as her feudal domain, practically all of Tuscany, including Florence, Lucca, Pistoia, Pisa, Siena, and Arezzo; over all these the popes claimed the rights of a feudal sovereign, but were rarely able to give effect to their claim.

Harassed by internal corruption, military and fiscal incompetence, and the confusion of European with Italian politics, and of ecclesiastical with secular affairs, the papacy struggled through centuries to preserve its traditional territories from internal usurpation by *condottieri*, and from external encroachment by other Italian states; so Milan repeatedly tried to appropriate Bologna, Venice seized Ravenna and sought to absorb Ferrara, and Naples stretched tentative tentacles into Latium. To meet these attacks the popes seldom depended on their little army of mercenaries, but played the covetous states one against another in a balance-of-power policy, striving to keep any one of them from growing strong enough to swallow papal terrain. Machiavelli and Guicciardini rightly traced the disunion of Italy in part to this policy of the popes; and the popes rightly pursued it as their only means of sustaining their political and spiritual independence through their temporal power.

As political rulers the popes felt compelled to adopt the same methods as their secular compeers. They distributed—sometimes they sold—offices or benefices to influential persons, even to minors, to pay political debts, or to advance political purposes, or to reward or support men of letters or artists. They arranged marriages for their relatives into politically poweful families. They used armies like Julius II, or the diplomacy of deceit like Leo X.[5] They put up with—sometimes profited from—a degree of bureaucratic venality probably no greater than that which prevailed in most governments of the time. The laws of the Papal States were as severe as those of others; thieves and counterfeiters were hanged by papal vicars as a more or less bitter necessity of government. Most of the popes lived as simply as the supposedly requisite display of official ceremony would permit; the worst tales we read of them were legends set afloat by irresponsible satirists like Berni, or disappointed place hunters like Aretino, or the Roman agents—e.g., Infessura—of powers in violent or diplomatic conflict with the papacy. As for the cardinals who administered the ecclesiastical and political affairs of the Church, they thought of themselves as senators of a wealthy state, and lived accordingly; many of them built palaces, many patronized letters or arts, some indulged themselves with mistresses; they genially accepted the easy moral code of their reckless time.

As a spiritual power the Renaissance popes faced the problem of reconciling humanism with Christianity. Humanism was half pagan, and the Church had once set herself to destroy paganism root and branch, creed and art. She had encouraged or countenanced the demolition of pagan temples and statuary; the cathedral of Orvieto, for example, had only recently been built with marbles taken partly from Carrara, partly from Roman ruins; a papal legate had sold marble blocks from the Colosseum to be burned for lime;[6] as late as 1461 the Palazzo Venezia had been begun with further spoliation of that Flavian Amphitheater; Nicholas himself, in his architectural enthusiasm, used twenty-five hundred cartloads of marble and travertine from the Colosseum, the Circus Maximus, and other ancient structures to rebuild the churches and palaces of Rome.[7] To reverse that attitude, to preserve and collect and cherish the remaining art and classics of Rome and Greece, required a revolution in ecclesiastical thought. The prestige of humanism was already so high, the impetus of the neopagan movement was so strong, her own leaders were so deeply tinged with it, that the Church had to find place for these developments in the Christian life, or risk losing the intellectual classes of Italy, perhaps later of Europe. Under Nicholas V she opened her arms to humanism, placed herself bravely and generously on the side, at the head, of the new literature and art. And for an exhilarating century (1447-1534) she gave to the mind of Italy such ample freedom—*incredibilis libertas*, said Filelfo[8] —and to the art of Italy such discriminating patronage, opportunity, and stimulus that Rome became the center of the Renaissance, and enjoyed one of the most brilliant epochs in the history of mankind.

II. NICHOLAS V: 1447-55

Raised in poverty at Sarzana, Tommaso Parentucelli somehow found means to attend the University of Bologna for six years. When his funds ran out he went to Florence and served as tutor in the homes of Rinaldo degli Albizzi and Palla de' Strozzi. His purse replenished, he returned to Bologna, continued his studies, and received at twenty-two the doctorate in theology. Niccolò degli Albergati, Archbishop of Bologna, made him controller of the archiepiscopal household, and took him to Florence to attend Eugenius IV in the Pope's long exile there. In these Florentine years the priest became a humanist without ceasing to be a Christian. He developed a warm friendship with Bruni, Marsuppini, Manetti, Aurispa, and Poggio, and joined their literary gatherings; soon Thomas of Sarzana, as the humanists called him, was aflame with their passion for classical antiquity. He spent almost all his income on books, borrowed money to buy costly manuscripts, and expressed the hope that some day his funds would suffice to gather into one library all the great books in the world; in that ambition the Vatican Library had its origin.[9] Cosimo engaged him to catalogue the Marcian Library, and Tommaso was happy among the manuscripts. He could hardly know that he was preparing himself to be the first Renaissance pope.

For twenty years he served Albergati in Florence and Bologna. When the Archbishop died (1443) Eugenius appointed Parentucelli to succeed him; and three years later the Pope, impressed by his learning, his piety, and his administrative ability, made him a cardinal. Another year passed; Eugenius passed away; and the cardinals, deadlocked between the Orsini and Colonna factions, raised Parentucelli to the papacy. "Who would have thought," he exclaimed to Vespasiano da Bisticci, "that a poor bell ringer of a priest would be made pope, to the confusion of the proud?"[10] The humanists of Italy rejoiced, and one of them, Francesco Barbaro, proclaimed that Plato's vision had come true: a philosopher had become king.

Nicholas V, as he now called himself, had three aims: to be a good pope, to rebuild Rome, and to restore classical literature, learning, and art. He conducted his high office with modesty and competence, gave audience at almost any hour of the day, and managed to get along amicably with both Germany and France. The Antipope Felix V, realizing that Nicholas would soon win all Latin Christendom to his allegiance, resigned his pretensions and was gracefully forgiven; the rebellious but disintegrating Council of Basel moved to Lausanne and dissolved (1449); the conciliar movement was ended, the Papal Schism was healed. Demands for reform of the Church still came from beyond the Alps; Nicholas felt incapable of achieving that reform in the face of all the office-holders who would lose by it; instead he hoped that the Church would regain, as the leader in the revival of learning, the prestige that she had lost at Avignon and in the Schism. Not that his support of scholarship was motivated by political ends; it was a sincere, almost an amorous passion. He had made arduous trips over the Alps in search of manuscripts; it was he who had unearthed at Basel the works of Tertullian.

Now, dowered with the revenues of the papacy, he sent agents to Athens, Constantinople, and divers cities in Germany and England to seek and buy or copy Greek or Latin manuscripts, pagan or Christian; he installed a large corps of copyists and editors in the Vatican; he called almost every prominent humanist in Italy to Rome. "All the scholars in the world," wrote Vespasiano in fond exaggeration, "came to Rome in the time of Pope Nicholas, partly of their own accord, partly at his request."[11] He rewarded their work with the liberality of a caliph thrilled by music or poetry. The subdued Lorenzo Valla received 500 ducats ($12,500?) for putting Thucydides into Latin dress; Guarino da Verona received 1500 ducats for translating Strabo; Niccolò Perotti 500 for Polybius; Poggio was put to translating Diodorus Siculus; Theodorus Gaza was lured from Ferrara to make a new translation of Aristotle; Filelfo was offered a house in Rome, an estate in the country, and 10,000 ducats to render into Latin the *Iliad* and the *Odyssey;* the Pope's death, however, prevented the execution of this Homeric enterprise. These rewards were so great that some scholars—*mirabile dictu*—hesitated to accept them; the Pope overcame their scruples by playfully warning them: "Don't refuse; you may not find another Nicholas."[12] When an epidemic drove him from Rome to Fabriano he took his translators and copyists with him, lest any of them should succumb to the plague.[13] Meanwhile he did not neglect what might be called the Christian classics. He offered five thousand ducats to anyone who would bring him the Gospel of St. Matthew in the original tongue. He engaged Gianozzo Manetti and George of Trebizond to translate Cyril, Basil, Gregory Nazianzen, Gregory of Nyssa, and other patrological literature; he commissioned Manetti and aides to make a new version of the Bible from the original Hebrew and Greek; this, too, was frustrated by his death. These Latin translations were hurried and imperfect, but they for the first time opened Herodotus, Thucydides, Xenophon, Polybius, Diodorus, Appian, Philo, and Theophrastus to students who could not read Greek. Referring to these translations, Filelfo wrote: "Greece has not perished, but has migrated to Italy—which in former days was called Greater Greece."[14] Manetti, with greater gratitude than accuracy, calculated that more Greek authors were translated during the eight years of Nicholas' pontificate than in all the preceding five centuries.[15]

Nicholas loved the appearance and form as well as the contents of books; himself a calligraphist, he had his translations written carefully upon parchment by expert scribes; the leaves were bound in crimson velvet, secured by silver clasps. As the number of his books mounted—finally to 824 Latin and 352 Greek manuscripts—and these were added to previous papal collections, the problem arose of housing the five thousand volumes—the largest store of books in Christendom—in such a way that their complete transmission to posterity might be assured. The construction of a Vatican Library was one of Nicholas' dearest dreams.

He was a builder as well as a scholar, and from the outset of his pontificate he had resolved to make Rome worthy of leading the world. A jubilee year was at hand in 1450; a hundred thousand visitors were expected; they must not find Rome a shabby ruin; the prestige of the Church and the papacy required that the citadel of Christianity should confront pilgrims with "noble edifices combining taste and beauty with noble proportions," which "would immensely conduce to the exaltation of the chair of St. Peter"; so Nicholas, on his deathbed, apologetically explained his aim. He restored the walls and gates of the city, repaired the Acqua Vergine aqueduct, and had an artist construct an ornamental fountain at its mouth. He engaged Leon Battista Alberti to design palaces, public squares, and spacious avenues shielded from sun and rain by arcaded porticoes. He had many streets paved, many bridges renewed, the Castle of Sant' Angelo repaired. He lent money to prominent citizens to help them build palaces that would be an ornament to Rome. At his bidding Bernardo Rossellino renovated Santa Maria Maggiore, San Giovanni Laterano, San Paolo and San Lorenzo *fuori le mura*—outside the walls—and the forty churches that Gregory I had designated as stations of the cross.[16] He made majestic plans for a new Vatican Palace that, with its gardens, would cover all the Vatican hill, and would house the pope and his staff, the cardinals, and the administrative offices of the Curia; he lived to complete his own chambers (later occupied by Alexander VI and called the Appartamento Borgia), the library (now the Pinacoteca Vaticana), and the rooms or *stanze* later decorated by Raphael. He brought Benedetto Bonfigli from Perugia, and Andrea del Castagno from Florence, to paint frescoes—now lost—on the Vatican walls; and he persuaded the aging Fra Angelico to return to Rome and paint in the Pope's own chapel the stories of St. Stephen and St. Laurence. He planned to tear down the old and crumbling basilica of St. Peter, and raise over the Apostle's tomb the most imposing church in the world; it was left for Julius II to take up this audacious aim.

All this, he hoped, could be financed from the proceeds of the jubilee. Nicholas announced this as a celebration of the restored peace and unity of the Church, and the sentiment went well with the peoples of Europe. The migration of pilgrims from every quarter of Latin Christendom was of unprecedented magnitude; eyewitnesses compared it to the movement of myriads of ants. The crowding in Rome was so extreme that the Pope limited to five, then three, then two days the maximum length of any visitor's stay. On one occasion two hundred persons were killed in a crush that swept many into the Tiber; Nicholas thereafter tore down houses to widen the approaches to St. Peter's. As the pilgrims brought rich offerings, the financial returns from the jubilee exceeded even the Pope's expectations, and covered the expense of his new buildings and his outlay for scholars and manuscripts.[17] The other cities of Italy suffered a shortage of money because—a Perugian complained—"it all flowed into Rome"; but in Rome the innkeepers, moneychangers, and tradesmen profited hugely, and Nicholas was able to deposit 100,000 florins ($2,500,000?) in the bank of the Medici alone.[18] The countries beyond the Alps rumbled with discontent at the efflux of gold into Italy.

Even in Rome some disaffection troubled the new prosperity. Nicholas' government of the city was enlightened and just from his point of view, and he had made a concession to republican hopes by nominating four citizens who were to appoint all municipal officials and control all taxes levied in the city. But the senators and nobles whose class had ruled Rome during the Avignon papacy and the Schism fretted under the papal government, and the populace resented the transformation of the Vatican into a palace fortress secure against such assaults as had driven Eugenius from Rome. The republican ideas preached by Arnold of Brescia and Cola di Rienzo still agitated many minds. In the year of Nicholas' accession a leading burgher, Stefano Porcaro, made a fiery speech demanding the restoration of self-government. Nicholas sent him into comfortable exile as podesta of Anagni, but Porcaro found his way back to the capital, and raised the cry of liberty before an excited carnival crowd. Nicholas banished him to Bologna, but left him full freedom except for the necessity of daily showing himself to the papal legate there. Nevertheless the undiscourageable Stefano managed, from Bologna, to organize a complicated plot among three hundred of his followers in Rome. On the feast of the Epiphany, while the Pope and the cardinals were at Mass in St. Peter's, an attack was to be made on the Vatican, its treasury was to be seized to provide funds for establishing a republic, and Nicholas himself was to be taken prisoner.[19] Porcaro secretly left Bologna (December 26, 1452), and joined the conspirators on the eve of the planned attack. But his absence from Bologna was noted, and a courier brought warning to the Vatican. Stefano was traced, found, and imprisoned, and on January 9 he was beheaded in Sant' Angelo. The republicans denounced the execution as murder, the humanists condemned the plot as monstrous infidelity to a benevolent pope.

Nicholas was shaken and changed by the discovery that a large section of the citizenry looked upon him as a despot, however benevolent. Harrowed with suspicion, embittered by resentment, tortured by gout, he aged rapidly. When news came to him that the Turks had entered Constantinople over the corpses of 50,000 Christians, and had turned St. Sophia into a mosque (1453), all the glory of his pontificate seemed a fitful vanity. He appealed to the European powers to join in a crusade to recapture the fallen citadel of Eastern Christianity; he called for a tenth of all the revenue of Western Europe to finance the effort, and pledged a tenth of papal, Curial, and other ecclesiastical revenues; and all war between Christian nations was to cease on pain of excommunication. Europe hardly listened. People complained that money raised by previous popes for crusades had been used for other purposes; Venice preferred a commercial entente with the Turks; Milan took advantage of Venetian difficulties by retaking Brescia; Florence looked with satisfaction on Venice's loss of Eastern trade.[20] Nicholas bowed to reality, and the lust of life cooled in his veins. Worn out with futile diplomacy, and punished for the sins of his predecessors, he died in 1455, at the age of fifty-eight.

He had restored peace within the Church, he had restored order and splendor to Rome, he had founded the greatest of libraries, he had reconciled the Church and the Renaissance. He had kept his hands free from war, had avoided nepotism, had struggled to turn Italy from suicidal strife. Amid unprecedented revenues he himself had led a simple life, loving the Church and his books, and extravagant only in his gifts. A grieving chronicler expressed the feeling of Italy when he described the scholar Pope as "wise, just, benevolent, gracious, peaceable, affectionate, charitable, humble . . . endowed with every virtue."[21] It was the verdict of love, and Porcaro might have demurred; but we may let it stand.

III. CALIXTUS III: 1455-8

The disunion of Italy determined the papal election that followed: the factions, unable to agree on an Italian, chose a Spanish cardinal, Alfonso Borgia, who took the name of Calixtus III. He was already seventy-seven; he could be depended upon to die soon, and allow the cardinals another and perhaps more profitable choice. A specialist in canon law and diplomacy, he had a legalistic mind, and cared little for the classical scholarship that had enamored Nicholas. The humanists, who had no indigenous root in Rome, languished during his pontificate, except that Valla, now quite reformed, was still a papal secretary.

Calixtus was a good man, who loved his relatives. Ten months after his coronation he raised to the cardinalate two of his nephews—Luis Juan de Mila and Rodrigo Borgia—and Don Jayme of Portugal, respectively twenty-five, twenty-four, and twenty-three years of age. Rodrigo (the future Alexander VI) had the additional handicap of being carelessly candid about his mistresses; however, Calixtus gave him (1457) the most lucrative post at the papal court—that of vice-chancellor; in the same year he made him also commander in chief of the papal troops. So began, or grew, the nepotism by which pope after pope gave church offices to his nephews or other relatives, who were sometimes his sons. To the anger of the Italians, Calixtus surrounded himself with men of his own country; Rome was now ruled by Catalans. The Pope had reasons: he was a foreigner in Rome; the nobles and republicans were plotting against him; he wished to have near him men whom he knew, and who would protect him from intrigue while he attended to his prime interest—a crusade. Moreover, the Pope was resolved to have friends in a College of Cardinals perpetually struggling to make the papacy a constitutional as well as an elective monarchy, subject in all its decisions to the cardinals as a senate or privy council. The popes opposed and overcame this movement precisely as the kings fought and defeated the nobles. In each case absolute monarchy won; but perhaps the replacement of a local with a national economy, and the growth of international relations in scope and complexity, required, for the time, a centralization of leadership and authority.[21a]

Calixtus wore out his last energies in a vain attempt to stir Europe to resist the Turks. When he died Rome celebrated the end of its rule by "barbarians." When Cardinal Piccolomini was named his successor Rome rejoiced as it had not rejoiced over any pope during the last two hundred years.

IV. PIUS II: 1458-64

Enea Silvio de' Piccolomini began his career in 1405 in the town of Corsignano, near Siena, of poor parents with a noble pedigree. The University of Siena taught him law; it was not to his taste, for he loved literature, but it gave keenness and order to his mind, and prepared him for the tasks of administration and diplomacy. At Florence he studied the humanities under Filelfo, and from that time he remained a humanist. At twenty-seven he was engaged as secretary by Cardinal Capranica, whom he accompanied to the Council of Basel. There he fell in with a group hostile to Eugenius IV; for many years thereafter he defended the conciliar movement against the papal power; for a time he served as secretary to the Antipope Felix V. Perceiving that he had hitched his wagon to a falling star, he coaxed a bishop to introduce him to the Emperor Frederick III. Soon he received a post in the royal chancery, and in 1442 he accompanied Frederick to Austria. For a while he remained moored.

In those formative years he seemed quite formless—merely a clever climber who had no sturdy principles, no goal but success. He passed from cause to cause without losing his heart, and from woman to woman with a gay inconstancy that seemed to him—and to most of his contemporaries —the proper training for the obligations of matrimony. He wrote for a friend a love letter designed to melt the obstinacy of a girl who preferred marriage to fornication.[22] Of his several illegitimate children he sent one to his father, asking him to rear it, and confessing that he was "neither holier than David nor wiser than Solomon";[23] the young devil could quote

Scripture to his purpose. He wrote a novel in the manner of Boccaccio; it was translated into almost every European tongue, and plagued him in the days of his sanctity. Though his further advancement seemed to require taking holy orders, he shrank from the step because, like Augustine, he doubted his capacity for continence.[24] He wrote against the celibacy of the clergy.[25]

Amid these infidelities he remained faithful to letters. That same sensitivity to beauty which had corrupted his morals enamored him of nature, delighted him with travel, and formed his style until he had made himself one of the most engaging writers and eloquent orators of the fifteenth century. He wrote, nearly always in Latin, in nearly every species of composition—fiction, poetry, epigrams, dialogues, essays, histories, travel sketches, geography, commentaries, memoirs, a comedy; and always with a verve and grace that rivaled Petrarch's liveliest prose. He could phrase a state paper, prepare or improvise an address, with persuasive subtlety and captivating fluency; it is characteristic of the age that Aeneas Sylvius, beginning almost from nothing, raised himself to the papacy on the point of his pen. His verses had no enduring depth or worth, but they were smooth enough to get him the poet's crown from the hand of the complaisant Frederick III (1442). His essays had a lighthearted charm that glossed over their author's lack of conviction or principle. He could pass from a discourse on "The Miseries of Court Life" ("as rivers flow to the sea, so vices flow to courts"[26]), to a treatise "On the Nature and Care of Horses." It was another sign of the times that his long letter on education—addressed to King Ladislas of Bohemia but intended for publication—quoted, with one exception, only pagan authors and instances, stressed the glory of humanistic studies, and urged the King to fit his sons for the hardships and responsibilities of war; "serious matters are settled not by laws but by arms."[27] His travel notes are the best of their kind in Renaissance literature. He described with avid interest not only cities and rural scenes, but industries, products, political conditions, constitutions, manners, and morals; and not since Petrarch had any Italian written so fondly well of the countryside. He was the only Italian in centuries who loved Germany; he had a good word for the boisterous burghers who filled the air with song and themselves with beer instead of murdering one another in the streets. He called himself *varia videndi cupidus*, eager to see a variety of things;[28] and one of his frequent sayings was: "A miser is never satisfied with his money, nor a wise man with his knowledge."[29] Turning his facile plume to history, he composed short biographies of illustrious contemporaries (*De*

Fig. 31—GIOVANNI BELLINI:
Madonna degli Alberetti;
Academy, Venice

PAGE 300

Fig. 32—GIOVANNI BELLINI:
*Portrait of Doge Leo-
nardo Loredano;* Na-
tional Gallery, London

PAGE 300

Fig. 33—Giorgione: *Sleeping Venus;* Art Gallery, Dresden PAGE 305

Fig. 34—Giorgione: *Concert Champêtre;* Louvre, Paris PAGE 305

Fig. 35—TITIAN: *"Sacred and Profane Love"*; Borghese Gallery, Rome

PAGE 308

FIG. 36—TITIAN: *Venus and Adonis;* Metropolitan Museum of Art, New York

PAGE 310

Fig. 37–VITTORE CARPACCIO: *The Dream of St. Ursula;* Academy, Venice   PAGE 302

Fig. 38–TITIAN: *Assumption of the Virgin;* Frari, Venice

PAGE 310

Fig. 39—CORREGGIO: *Sts. John and Augustine;* from a spandrel in the Church of San Giovanni Evangelista, Parma   PAGE 329

Fig. 40—CORREGGIO: *The Mystic Marriage of St. Catherine;* Art Institute, Detroit   PAGE 328

LIBRARY, METROPOLITAN MUSEUM OF ART

LIBRARY, METROPOLITAN MUSEUM OF ART

Fig. 42—*Majolica from Faenza;* Left and right are vinegar bottles, center is
vase, from Urbino, middle of 16th Century   PAGE 338

Fig. 43—RAPHAEL: *The Pearl Madonna;* Prado, Madrid

PAGE 462

Fig. 44—RAPHAEL: *Portrait of Pope Julius II;* Pitti Palace, Florence

PAGE 441

Fig. 45—MICHELANGELO
BUONARROTI: *Pietà;*
St. Peter's, Rome
PAGE 466

Fig. 46—MICHELANGELO BUONARROTI: *Creation of Adam*, ceiling; Sistine Chapel,
Rome PAGE 474

viris claris), a life of Frederick III, an account of the Hussite wars, and an outline of universal history. He planned a larger *Universal History and Geography*, continued to work on it during his pontificate, and completed the section on Asia, which Columbus read with interest.[30] As pope he composed, from day to day, *Commentarii* or memoirs, giving the history of his reign to his final illness. "He read and dictated till midnight as he lay in bed," says his contemporary Platina, "nor did he sleep above five or six hours."[31] He apologized for giving papal time to literary composition: "Our time has not been taken from our duties; we have given to writing the hours due to sleep; we have robbed our old age of its rest that we might hand down to posterity all that we know to be memorable."[32]

In 1445 the Emperor sent Aeneas Sylvius as envoy to the Pope. He, who had a hundred times written against Eugenius, made his apologies so eloquently that the kindly pontiff readily forgave him; and from that day the soul of Aeneas belonged to Eugenius. He became a priest (1446), and at forty-one reconciled himself to chastity; henceforth he lived an exemplary life. He kept Frederick loyal to the papacy, and by skillful—sometimes devious—diplomacy restored the allegiance of the German electors and prelates to the Apostolic See. His visits to Rome and Siena reawakened his love of Italy; gradually he loosened his ties with Frederick, and attached himself (1455) to the papal court. He had always wanted to be back in the excitement and politics of his native land; in Rome he would be at the very center of things; who could say but in the tumult and shuffle of events he might not become pope? In 1449 he was made bishop of Siena; in 1456 he became Cardinal Piccolomini.

When the time came to choose a successor to Calixtus, the Italians in the conclave, to prevent the election of the French Cardinal d'Estouteville, gave their votes to Piccolomini. The Italian cardinals were resolved to keep the papacy and the Sacred College Italian, not only for their personal reasons but through fear that a non-Italian pope might again disrupt Christendom by favoring his own country or taking the papacy from Italy. No one held against Aeneas the sins of his youth; the merry Cardinal Rodrigo Borgia cast a decisive vote for him; the majority felt that Cardinal Piccolomini, though so recently capped in red, had the qualifications of a man of wide experience, a successful diplomat well posted on troublesome Germany, and a scholar whose learning would heighten the luster of the papacy.

He was now fifty-three, and his adventurous life had taken such toll of his health that he seemed already an old man. On a voyage from Holland to Scotland (1435) he had encountered frighteningly rough seas—taking twelve days from Sluys to Dunbar—and had vowed, if saved, to walk barefoot to the nearest shrine of the Virgin. This proved to be at Whitekirk, ten miles away. He kept his vow, walked the full distance with bare feet on snow and ice, contracted gout, and suffered severely from it all the rest of his life. By 1458 he had stone in the kidneys, and a chronic cough. His eyes were sunken, his face pale; at times, says Platina, "nobody could tell that he was alive but by his voice."[33] As pope he lived simply and frugally; his household expenses in the Vatican were the lowest on record. When his duties allowed he retired to a rural suburb, where "he entertained himself not like a pope but as an honest humble rustic";[34] sometimes he held consistories, or received ambassadors, under shady trees, or amid an olive grove, or by a cooling spring or stream. He called himself—punning on his name—*silvarum amator*, lover of woods.

As pope he took his name from Virgil's recurrent phrase, *pius Aeneas*. If we may with custom moderately mistranslate the adjective, he lived up to it: he was pious, faithful to his duties, benevolent and indulgent, temperate and mild, and won the affection of even the cynics of Rome. He had outgrown the sensualism of his youth, and was morally a model pope. He made no attempt to conceal his early amours, or his propaganda for the councils against the papacy, but he issued a Bull of Retraction (1463) humbly asking God and the Church to forgive his errors and sins. The humanists who had expected lavish patronage from a humanist pope were disappointed to find that while he enjoyed their company, and gave several of them places in the Curia, he dispensed no luscious fees but conserved the papal funds for a crusade against the Turks. He continued, in his leisure moments, to be a humanist: he studied the ancient ruins carefully, and forbade their further demolition; he amnestied the people of Arpino because Cicero had been born there; he commissioned a new translation of Homer, and employed Platina and Biondo in his secretariat. He brought Mino da Fiesole to carve, and Filippino Lippi to paint, in the churches of Rome. He indulged his vanity by building, from designs by Bernardo Rossellino, a cathedral and Piccolomini palace in his native Corsignano, which he renamed Pienza after himself. He had the poor noble's pride of ancestry, and was too loyal to his friends and relatives for the good of the Church; the Vatican became a Piccolomini hive.

Two admirable scholars graced his pontificate. Flavio Biondo, a papal secretary since Nicholas V, was a symbol of the Christian Renaissance: he loved antiquity and spent half his life describing its history and relics, but he never ceased to be a devout, orthodox, and practising Christian. Pius valued him as guide and friend, and profited from his company on tours of the Roman remains; for Biondo had written an encyclopedia in three parts—*Roma instaurata*, *Roma triumphans*, and *Italia illustrata*—recording the topography, history, institutions, laws, religion, manners, and arts of ancient Italy. Greater still was his *Historiarum ab inclinatione Romanorum*, an immense *Decline and Fall of the Roman Empire* from 476 to 1250—the first critical history of the Middle Ages. Biondo was no stylist, but he was a discriminating historian; through his work the legends that Italian cities had cherished of their Trojan or like fancied origins died away. The undertaking was too ambitious even for Biondo's seventy-five years; it was. unfinished at his death (1463); but it set to later historians an example of conscientious scholarship.

John Cardinal Bessarion was a living vehicle of the Greek culture that was entering Italy. Born at Trebizond, he received at Constantinople a thorough schooling in Greek poetry, oratory, and philosophy; he continued his studies under the famous Platonist Gemistus Pletho at Mistra. Coming to the Council of Florence as Archbishop of Nicaea, he took a leading part in the reunion of Greek and Latin Christianity; returning to Constantinople he and other "Uniates" were repudiated by the lower clergy and the people. Pope Eugenius made him a cardinal (1439), and Bessarion moved to Italy, bringing with him a rich collection of Greek manuscripts. At Rome his house became a salon of humanists; Poggio, Valla, and Platina were among his closest friends; Valla called him *latinorum graecissimus, graecorum latinissimus*—the most learned Hellenist among the Latins, the most accomplished Latinist among the Greeks.[35] He spent nearly all his income in purchasing manuscripts or having them copied. He himself made a new translation of Aristotle's *Metaphysics;* but as a disciple of Gemistus he favored Plato, and led the Platonic camp in a hot controversy that raged at the time between Platonists and Aristotelians. Plato won that campaign, and the long rule of Aristotle over Western philosophy came to an end. When Nicholas V appointed Bessarion legate at Bologna, to govern the Romagna and the Marches, Bessarion acquitted himself so well that Nicholas called him "angel of peace." For Pius II he undertook difficult diplomatic missions in a Germany again seething with revolt against the Roman Church. Toward the end of his life he bequeathed his library to Venice, where it now forms a precious part of the Biblioteca Marciana. In 1471 he narrowly missed election to the papacy. He died a year later, honored throughout the world of scholarship.

His missions to Germany failed, partly because the efforts of Pius II to reform the Church were frustrated, and partly because a new attempt to levy a tithe for a crusade revived transalpine antipathy to Rome. At the outset of his pontificate Pius appointed a committee of high prelates to formulate a program of reform. He accepted a plan submitted by Nicholas of Cusa, and embodied it in a papal bull. But he found that no one in Rome wanted reform; almost every second dignitary there profited from one or another immemorial abuse; apathy and passive resistance defeated Pius; and meanwhile his difficulties with Germany, Bohemia, and France used up his energy, and the crusade that he planned absorbed his devotion and cried for funds. He had to content himself with reproving cardinals for licentious lives, and with sporadic improvements of monastic discipline. In 1463 he addressed a final appeal to the cardinals:

> People say that we live for pleasure, accumulate wealth, bear ourselves arrogantly, ride on fat mules and handsome palfreys, trail the fringes of our cloaks after us, and show round plump faces beneath the red hat and the white hood, keep hounds for the chase, spend much on actors and parasites, and nothing in defense of the Faith. And there is some truth in their words: many among the cardinals and other officials of our court do lead this kind of life. If the truth be confessed, the luxury and pomp at our court is too great. And this is why we are so detested by the people that they will not listen to us, even when we say what is just and reasonable. What do you think is to be done in such a shameful state of things? ... We must inquire by what means our predecessors won authority and consideration for the Church. ... We must maintain that authority by the same means. Temperance, chastity, innocence, zeal for the Faith ... contempt of earth, the desire for martyrdom have exalted the Roman Church, and made her mistress of the world.[36]

The Pope, who as Aeneas Sylvius had been so uniformly successful as a diplomat, had to bear one setback after another in his dealings with the European powers. Louis XI gave him a brief triumph by revoking the Pragmatic Sanction of Bourges, but when Pius refused to aid the house of Anjou in its plans for recapturing Naples, Louis in effect revoked his revocation. Bohemia persisted in the revolt that John Huss had started; the Reformation had begun there a century before Luther, and the new king, George Poděbrad, was giving it his powerful support. The German hierarchy continued to league with German princes in resisting collection of the tithe, and renewed the old cry for a general council to reform the

Church and sit in judgment upon the pope. Pius responded by issuing (1460) the bull *Execrabilis*, which condemned and forbade any attempt to convene a general council without papal initiative and consent; if, he argued, such a council could be summoned at any time by opponents of papal policy, papal jurisdiction would be in constant jeopardy, and ecclesiastical discipline would be paralyzed.

These disputes fettered the efforts of the Pope to unify Europe against the Turks. On the very day of his coronation he expressed his horror at the advance of the Moslems along the Danube to Vienna, and through the Balkans into Bosnia. Greece, Epirus, Macedonia, Serbia, Bosnia were falling to the enemies of Christianity; who could say when they would leap across the Adriatic into Italy? A month after his coronation Pius issued an invitation to all Christian princes to join him in a great congress at Mantua and lay plans to rescue Eastern Christendom from the Ottoman tide.

He himself arrived there on May 27, 1459. Arrayed in the most gorgeous vestments of his office, he was borne through the city on a litter held up by the nobles and vassals of the Church. He addressed great throngs in one of the most moving orations of his career. But no king or prince came from beyond the Alps, and none sent representatives with powers to commit his state to war; nationalism, which was to achieve the Reformation, was already strong enough to make the papacy an ineffectual suppliant before the thrones of the kings. The cardinals urged the Pope to return to Rome; neither did they relish the thought of yielding a tithe of their income to the crusade; some decamped to their pleasures; some asked Pius to his face did he wish them to die of fever in Mantua's summer heat? The Pontiff waited patiently for the Emperor, but Frederick III, instead of coming to the aid of the man who in the past had served him well, declared war on Hungary in an effort to add to his realm the very nation that was most actively preparing to resist the Turks. France again made its co-operation conditional on papal support of a French campaign against Naples. Venice held back for fear that her remaining possessions in the Aegean would be the first sacrifice in a war of Christian Europe against the Ottomans. At last, in August, an embassy came from Duke Philip the Good of Burgundy; in September Francesco Sforza appeared; other Italian princes followed his lead, and on the 26th the Congress held its first sitting, four months after the arrival of the Pope. Four months more passed in argument; finally, by agreeing to the division of Turkish and formerly Byzantine territory in Europe among the victorious powers, Pius won Burgundy and Italy to his plan for a holy war. All Christian laymen were to contribute to the cause a thirtieth of their income, all Jews a twentieth, all clergy a tenth. The Pope returned to Rome in almost complete exhaustion; but he gave orders for the construction of a papal fleet, and prepared, despite gout and cough and stone, to lead the crusade himself.

And yet his nature shrank from war, and he dreamed of a peaceful victory. Perhaps encouraged by rumors that Mohammed II, born of a Christian mother, had secret leanings toward Christianity, Pius addressed to the Sultan (1461) an earnest appeal to accept the Gospel of Christ. He had never been more eloquent.

> Were you to embrace Christianity there is no prince on earth who would surpass you in glory or equal you in power. We would acknowledge you as emperor of the Greeks and the East; and what you have now taken by violence, and retain by injustice, would then be your lawful possession.... Oh, what a fullness of peace it would be! The golden age of Augustus, sung by the poets, would return. If you were to join yourself to us the whole of the East would soon turn to Christ. One will could give peace to the entire world, and that will is yours![37]

Mohammed made no reply; whatever his theology, he knew that his final protection against Western arms lay not in the promises of the Pope but in the religious ardor of his people. Pius turned more realistically to collecting the clerical tithe. A windfall sustained him in 1462 when rich deposits of alum were found in papal soil at Tolfa in western Latium; several thousand men were put to work mining the substance so valued by dyers; soon the mines were yielding 100,000 florins per year to the Holy See. Pius announced that the discovery was a miracle, a divine contribution to the Turkish war.[38] The Papal States were now the richest government in Italy, with Venice a close second, Naples third, then Milan, Florence, Modena, Siena, Mantua.[39]

Venice, perceiving the resolute earnestness of the Pope, accelerated its preparations. The other powers held back, or offered merely token aid; the collection of taxes for the crusade met with formidable resistance almost everywhere. Francesco Sforza cooled to the enterprise as promising to strengthen Venice by redeeming her lost possessions and trade. Genoa, which had pledged eight triremes, withheld them. The Duke of Burgundy urged the Pope to wait for a better day. But Pius announced that he would go to Ancona, expect there the union of new papal and Venetian fleets, cross with them to Ragusa, join Skanderbeg of Bosnia and Matthias Corvinus of Hungary, and lead in person the advance against the Turks. Nearly all the cardinals protested; they had no appetite for marching through the Balkans; they warned the Pope that Bosnia was reeking with heretics and plague. The ailing pontiff nevertheless took the cross of a crusader, bade farewell to Rome, not expecting to see it again, and sailed with his fleet for Ancona (June 18, 1464).

Meanwhile the armies that were supposed to meet him faded away as if by Oriental magic; the troops originally promised by Milan did not come; those which Florence sent were so poorly equipped as to be useless; when Pius reached Ancona (July 19) he found that most of the crusaders who had assembled there had deserted, weary of waiting and worried for food. Plague broke out in the Venetian fleet as it left the lagoons, and caused a delay of twelve days. Brokenhearted by the vanishing of his armies and the nonappearance of the Venetian armada, Pius languished at Ancona, sick to the verge of death. Finally the fleet was sighted; the Pope sent his galleys to meet them, and had himself carried to a window from which he could see the harbor. As the combined navies came in sight he died (August 14, 1464). Venice recalled her vessels, the remaining soldiers dispersed, the crusade collapsed. The brilliant and versatile climber who had craved success after success had reached the throne of thrones, had graced it with urbane scholarship and Christian benevolence, and had drunk to the dregs the gall of failure, humiliation, and defeat; but he had redeemed the errors of his youth with the devotion of his maturity, and had shamed the cynicism of his peers with the nobility of his death.

V. PAUL II: 1464-71

The lives of great men oft remind us that a man's character can be formed after his demise. If a ruler coddles the chroniclers about him they may lift him to posthumous sanctity; if he offends them they may broil his corpse on a spit of venom or roast him to darkest infamy in a pot of ink. Paul II quarreled with Platina; Platina wrote the biography upon which most estimates of Paul depend, and handed him down to posterity as a monster of vanity, pomp, and greed.

There was some truth in the indictment, though not much more than might be found in any biography untempered with charity. Pietro Barbo, Cardinal of San Marco, was proud of his handsome appearance, as nearly all men are. When elected pope he proposed, probably in humor, to be called Formosus—good-looking; he allowed himself to be dissuaded, and took the title of Paul II. Simple in his private life, yet knowing the hypnotic effect of magnificence, he kept a luxurious court, and entertained his friends and guests with costly hospitality. On entering the conclave that elected him he, like the other cardinals, had pledged himself, if chosen, to wage war against the Turks, to summon a general council, to limit the number of cardinals to twenty-four and the number of papal relatives among them to one, to create no man a cardinal under thirty years of age, and to consult the cardinals on all important appointments. Paul, elected, repudiated these capitulations as nullifying time-honored traditions and powers. He consoled the cardinals by raising their yearly revenue to a minimum of 4000 florins ($100,000?). He himself, coming of a mercantile family, relished the security of florins, ducats, scudi, and gems that held a fortune in a ray of light. He wore a tiara that outweighed a palace in worth. As cardinal he had kept the goldsmiths busy with orders for jewels, medals, and cameos; these, and costly relics of classic art, he had collected in the sumptuous Palazzo San Marco which he had built for himself at the foot of the Capitol.* With all his acquisitiveness he stooped to no simony, repressed the sale of indulgences, and governed Rome with justice if not with mercy.

He is worst remembered by his quarrel with the Roman humanists. Some of these were secretaries to the pope or the cardinals; most of them filled less dignified positions as *abbreviatores*—writers of briefs, or keepers of records, for the Curia. Whether as a measure of economy, or to rid the Collegium Abbreviatorum of the fifty-eight Sienese whom Pius II had appointed to it, Paul disbanded the whole group, gave its work to other departments, and left some seventy humanists jobless or reduced to less lucrative posts. The most eloquent of these dismissed humanists was Bartolommeo de' Sacchi, who took the Latin name Platina from his native Piadena near Cremona. He appealed to the Pope to re-employ the dismissed men; when Paul refused he wrote him a threatening letter. Paul had him arrested, and kept him for four months in Sant' Angelo, bound with heavy chains. Cardinal Gonzaga secured his release; but Platina, Paul thought, would bear watching.

The leader of the humanists in Rome was Iulio Pomponio Leto, allegedly the natural son of Prince Sanseverino of Salerno. Coming to Rome in youth, he attached himself to Valla as a disciple, and succeeded him as professor of Latin in the university. He became so enamored of pagan literature that he lived and had his being not in the Rome of Nicholas V

---

* Pius IV presented it to Venice; hence its later name of Palazzo Venezia. It was the official headquarters of Benito Mussolini during the Fascist regime.

or Paul II, but in that of the Catos or the Caesars. He was the first to edit the agricultural classics of Varro and Columella, and he sedulously followed their precepts in tending his vineyard. He remained content in learned poverty, spent half his time among the historic ruins, wept at their spoliation and desolation, Latinized his name to Pomponius Laetus, and walked to his classroom in ancient Roman dress. Hardly any hall could hold the crowd that gathered at dawn to hear his lectures; some students came at midnight to secure a place. He despised the Christian religion, denounced its preachers as hypocrites, and trained his scholars in the Stoic rather than the Christian morality. His home was a museum of Roman antiquities, a meeting place for students and teachers of Roman lore. About 1460 he organized them into a Roman Academy, whose members took pagan names, gave such names to their children in baptism, exchanged the Christian faith for a religious worship of the *genius* of Rome, performed Latin comedies, and celebrated the anniversary of Rome's foundation with pagan ceremonies in which the officiating members were termed *sacerdotes*, and Laetus was called *pontifex maximus*. Some enthusiastic members dreamed of restoring the Roman Republic.[40]

Early in 1468 a citizen laid before the papal police a charge that the Academy was plotting to depose and arrest the Pope. Certain cardinals supported the charge, and assured the pontiff that a rumor in Rome was predicting his early death. Paul ordered the arrest of Laetus, Platina, and other leaders of the Academy. Pomponius wrote humble apologies and professions of orthodoxy; after due chastening he was released, and resumed his lecturing, but with such careful conformity that when he died (1498) forty bishops attended his funeral. Platina was tortured to elicit evidence of a conspiracy; no such evidence was anywhere found, but Platina, despite a dozen letters of apology, was kept in prison for a year. Paul decreed the dissolution of the Academy as a nest of heresy, and forbade the teaching of pagan literature in the schools of Rome. His successor allowed the Academy to reopen reformed, and gave the penitent Platina charge of the Vatican Library. There Platina found the materials for his graphic and elegant biographies of the popes (*In vitas summorum pontificum*); and when he came to Paul II he took his revenge. His indictment might with more justice have been reserved for Sixtus IV.

VI. SIXTUS IV: 1471-84

Of the eighteen cardinals who met to choose a new pontiff, fifteen were Italian, Rodrigo Borgia was Spanish, d'Estouteville was French, Bessarion was Greek. One participant later described the election of Cardinal Francesco della Rovere as due to "intrigue and bribery" (*ex artibus et corruptelis*),[41] but this seems to have meant only that various offices were promised to various cardinals for their votes. The new pope illustrated the admirable equality of opportunity (among Italians) to reach the papacy. He was born of a peasant family at Pecorile, near Savona. Repeatedly ill as a child, he was consecrated to St. Francis by his mother in prayer for his recovery. At nine he was sent to a Franciscan convent, and later entered the Minorite order. For a while he served as tutor in the della Rovere family, whose name he took as his own. He studied philosophy and theology at Pavia, Bologna, and Padua, and taught them there and elsewhere to classes so crowded that almost every learned Italian of the next generation was said to have been his pupil.

When, at fifty-seven, he became Sixtus IV, his reputation was that of a scholar distinguished for learning and integrity. Almost overnight, by one of the strangest transformations in papal history, he became a politician and a warrior. Finding Europe too divided, and its governments too corrupt, for a crusade against the Turks, he decided to confine his secular efforts to Italy. There too, of course, he found division—in the Papal States the authority of the pope largely flouted by local rulers, in Latium a rule by noble violence ignoring the papal power, and in Rome a mob so disorderly that at his coronation it stoned his litter in anger at a crush caused by a stoppage of the cavalcade. Sixtus proposed to restore order in Rome, to reinvigorate legatine authority in the Papal States, and to bring Italy under the unifying rule of the pope.

Surrounded by chaos, distrustful of strangers, and subject to family affection, Sixtus appointed his avid nephews to positions of power and revenue. It was the prime curse of his pontificate that those whom he loved best proved worst, and took such venal advantage of their place that all Italy came to despise them. The favorite nephew was Pietro (or Piero) Riario, a youth of some charm—cheerful, witty, courteous, generous—but so fond of luxury and sensual delights that even the rich benefices bestowed upon him by the Pope failed to finance the tastes of this formerly mendicant friar. Sixtus made him a cardinal at twenty-five (1471), and gave him the bishoprics of Treviso, Senigallia, Spalato, Florence, and other dignities, with a total income of 60,000 ducats ($1,500,000?) a year. Pietro spent all, and more, on vessels of silver and gold, fine raiment, tapestries, embroideries, a pretentious retinue, expensive public games, and the patronage of painters, poets, and scholars. The festivities—including a banquet that lasted six hours—with which he and his cousin Giuliano welcomed to Rome Ferrante's daughter Eleonora marked a height of extravagance hardly equaled there since Lucullus or Nero. Dizzy with power, Pietro made a triumphal tour of Florence, Bologna, Ferrara, Venice, and Milan, enjoying regal honors everywhere as a prince of the blood, displaying his mistresses in costly attire, and making plans to become pope on or before the death of his uncle. But on his return to Rome he died (1474) of his excesses at the age of twenty-eight, having spent 200,000 ducats in two years, and owing 60,000 more.[42] His brother Girolamo was made commander of the papal armies and lord of Imola and Forlì; we have already disposed of him there. Another nephew, Leonardo della Rovere, was made prefect of Rome; and when he died his brother Giovanni succeeded him. The ablest of these innumerable nephews was Giuliano della Rovere, who will require a chapter as Julius II; his life was reasonably decent, and he rose to the papacy over every obstacle by force of intellect and character.

The plans of Sixtus to strengthen the Papal States disturbed the other governments of Italy. Lorenzo de' Medici, as we have before related, schemed to get Imola for Florence; Sixtus outplayed him, and replaced the Medici with the Pazzi as bankers for the papacy; Lorenzo tried to ruin the Pazzi, they tried to kill him. Sixtus agreed to the conspiracy but deprecated murder; "go and do what you will," he told the plotters, "provided there be no killing."[43] The result was a war that lasted (1478-80) until the Turks threatened to overrun Italy. When that danger subsided, Sixtus was free to resume his liberation of the Papal States. Late in 1480 the Ordelaffi line of dictators died out at Forlì, and the people asked the Pope to take over the city; Sixtus bade Girolamo govern Imola and Forlì together. Girolamo suggested taking Ferrara next, and persuaded Sixtus and Venice to join in war upon Duke Ercole (1482). Ferrante of Naples sent troops to defend his son-in-law; Florence and Milan also helped Ferrara; and the Pope, who had begun his reign with plans for European peace, found that he had plunged all Italy into war. Harassed by Naples in the south, by Florence in the north, and by disturbances in Rome, Sixtus came to terms with Ferrara after a year of chaos and bloodshed. When the Venetians refused to follow suit he excommunicated them, and joined Florence and Milan in war upon his late ally.

The nobles of the capital had felt justified, by the example of a warlike pontiff, in renewing their exhilarating feuds. It was one of the polite customs of Rome to plunder the palace of a cardinal just elected to the papacy. In so handling the palace of one of the della Rovere cardinals, a young aristocrat, Francesco di Santa Croce, had been wounded by a member of the della Valle family. The youth revenged himself by cutting the tendon of della Valle's heel; della Valle's relatives revenged him by cleaving Francesco's head; Prospero di Santa Croce revenged Francesco by killing Piero Margani. The feud spread through the city, the Orsini and the papal forces supporting the Santa Croce, the Colonna defending the Valle. Lorenzo Oddone Colonna was captured, tried, tortured into a confession, and put to death in Sant' Angelo, though his brother Fabrizio surrendered two Colonna fortresses to Sixtus in the hope of having Lorenzo spared. Prospero Colonna joined Naples in war on the Pope, ravaged the Campagna, raided Rome. Sixtus engaged Roberto Malatesta of Rimini to come and lead the papal troops, Roberto defeated the Neapolitan and Colonna forces at Campo Morto, returned to Rome victorious, and died of fever contracted in the Campagna swamps. Girolamo Riario took his place, and Sixtus officially blessed the artillery that his nephew directed against the Colonna citadels. But while the Pope's spirit willed war, his body collapsed under the strain of successive crises. In June, 1484, he too came down with fever. On August 11 news came to him that his allies had made peace with Venice over his protests; he refused to ratify it. The next day he died.

Sixtus was in many ways a preview of Julius II, as Girolamo Riario rehearsed the career of Caesar Borgia. A stern imperial priest who loved war and art and power, Sixtus pursued his purposes without scruple or finesse, but with wild energy and unhesitating courage to the end. Like later warrior popes, he made enemies who tried to weaken his arms by blackening his name. Some gossips accounted for his lavish support of Pietro and Girolamo Riario by calling them his sons;[44] others, like Infessura, called them his lovers, and did not hesitate to term the Pope "a sodomite."[45]* The picture is bad enough without these incredible and unsupported allegations. After exhausting on his nephews the treasury that Paul II had left full, Sixtus financed his wars by selling ecclesiastical offices to the highest bidder. A hostile Venetian ambassador quotes him as saying that "a pope needs only pen and ink to get whatever sum he wishes";[47] but this is equally true of most modern governments, whose interest-bearing bonds correspond in many ways with the salary-bearing sinecures sold by the popes. Sixtus, however, was not content with this scheme. He kept throughout

---

* Stefano Infessura composed a *Diario della città di Roma*, a history of fifteenth-century Rome from family records and personal observation. He was an ardent republican who looked upon the popes as despots; he was also a partisan of the Colonna; he cannot be trusted when he retails stories, not elsewhere confirmed, about the wickedness of the popes.[46]

the Papal States a monopoly on the sale of corn; he sold the best abroad, and the rest to his people, at a goodly profit.[48] He had learned this trick from the other rulers of his time, like Ferrante of Naples; presumably he charged no more than private engrossers would have done, since it is an unwritten law of economics that the price of a product depends on the gullibility of the purchaser; but the poor grumbled forgivably at the thought that their hunger fed the luxuries of the Riarios. Despite these and other devices for raising revenues, Sixtus left debts totaling 150,000 ducats ($3,750,000?).

A substantial portion of his revenues was spent on art and public works. He tried, unsuccessfully, to drain the pestilential marshes around Foligno, and at least dreamt of draining the Pontine swamps. He had the major streets of Rome straightened, widened, and paved; he improved the water supply; restored bridges, walls, gates, and towers; spanned the Tiber with the Ponte Sisto that bears his name; built a new Vatican Library, and the Sistine Chapel above it; founded the Sistine Choir; and rebuilt the ruined Hospital of Santo Spirito, whose main ward, 365 feet long, could accommodate a thousand patients. He reorganized the University of Rome, and opened to the public the Capitoline Museum that Paul II had established; this was the first public museum in Europe. During his pontificate, and largely under the direction of Baccio Pontelli, the churches of Santa Maria della Pace and Santa Maria del Popolo were erected, and many others were repaired. In Santa Maria del Popolo Mino da Fiesole and Andrea Bregno sculptured a noble tomb for Cardinal Cristoforo della Rovere (c. 1477); and in Santa Maria in Aracoeli Pinturicchio pictured the career of San Bernardino of Siena in some of the finest frescoes in Rome (c. 1484).

The Sistine Chapel was designed by Giovannino de' Dolci, simply and unpretentiously, for semiprivate worship by the popes and high ecclesiastics. It was beautified with a marble sanctuary screen by Mino da Fiesole, and by spacious frescoes recounting on the south wall scenes from the life of Moses, and on the north wall corresponding scenes from the life of Christ. For these paintings Sixtus called to Rome the greatest masters of the time: Perugino, Signorelli, Pinturicchio, Domenico and Benedetto Ghirlandaio, Botticelli, Cosimo Roselli, and Piero di Cosimo. Sixtus offered an additional reward for the best picture of the fifteen painted there by these men. Roselli, knowing his own inferiority in design, decided to stake all on brilliant coloring; his fellow artists laughed at his lavish spread of ultramarine and gold; but Sixtus gave him the prize.

The warrior pope brought other painters to Rome, and organized them into a protective guild under the aegis of St. Luke. It was for Sixtus that Melozzo da Forlì did his best work. Coming to Rome about 1472 after studying with Piero della Francesca, he painted in the church of Santi Apostoli a fresco of the Ascension which aroused the enthusiasm of Vasari; all but a few fragments of it disappeared when the church was rebuilt (1702f). Gracious and tender are the *Angel* and the *Virgin of the Annunciation* in the Uffizi Gallery, but finer still the *Angeli musicanti*—one with a viol, one with a lute—in the Vatican. Melozzo's masterpiece was painted as a fresco in the Vatican Library, and was later transferred to canvas. Against the ornate pillars and ceiling of the Library six figures are portrayed with veracity and power: Sixtus seated, massive and regal; at his right the gay Pietro Riario; standing before him the tall dark Giuliano della Rovere; kneeling before him the high-browed Platina, receiving appointment as librarian; and behind him Giovanni della Rovere and Count Girolamo Riario; it is a living picture of an eventful pontificate.

In 1475 the Vatican Library contained 2527 volumes in Latin and Greek; Sixtus added 1100 more, and for the first time threw the collection open to the public. He restored the humanists to favor, though he paid them with preoccupied irregularity. He called Filelfo to Rome, and that warrior of the pen praised the Pope enthusiastically until his annual salary of 600 florins ($15,000) fell into arrears. Joannes Argyropoulos was invited from Florence to Rome, where his lectures on the Greek language and literature were attended by cardinals, bishops, and foreign students like Reuchlin. Sixtus also brought to Rome the German scientist Johann Müller—Regiomontanus—and commissioned him to correct the Julian calendar; but Müller died a year later (1476), and calendar reform had to wait a century more (1582).

It is remarkable that a Franciscan friar and professor of philosophy and theology should have become the first secularizing pope of the Renaissance —or, more precisely, the first Renaissance pope whose chief interest was to establish the papacy as a strong political power in Italy. Perhaps excepting the case of Ferrara, whose able rulers had faithfully paid their feudal dues, Sixtus was perfectly justified in seeking to make the Papal States papal, and to make Rome and its environs safe for the popes. History might forgive, as it has forgiven Julius II, his use of war for these ends; it might acknowledge that his diplomacy merely followed the amoral principles of other states; but it finds no pleasure in watching a pope conspire with assassins, bless cannon, or wage war with a thoroughness that shocked his time; the death of a thousand men at Campo Morto was a heavier loss of life than any

battle yet fought in Renaissance Italy. The morality of the Roman court
was further lowered by reckless nepotism and unblushing simony, and the
costly indecent revels of his kin; in these and other ways Sixtus IV made
straight the way for Alexander VI, and contributed—as he responded—to
the moral disintegration of Italy. It was Sixtus who appointed Torquemada
to head the Spanish Inquisition; Sixtus who, provoked by the virulence and
license of Roman satire, gave the Inquisitors in Rome power to prohibit
the printing of any book they did not like. At his death he might have admitted many failures—against Lorenzo, Naples, Ferrara, Venice—and even
the Colonna were not yet subdued. Three significant successes he had
achieved: he had made Rome a fairer and healthier city, he had given it
invigorating drafts of fresh art, and he had restored the papacy to its place
among the most powerful monarchies in Europe.

VII. INNOCENT VIII: 1484-92

The failure of Sixtus was confirmed by the chaos that ruled Rome after
his death. Mobs sacked the papal granaries, broke into the banks of the
Genoese, attacked the palace of Girolamo Riario. Vatican attendants
stripped the Vatican of its furniture. The noble factions armed themselves;
barricades were thrown up in the streets; Girolamo was forced to quit his
campaign against the Colonna and lead his troops back to the city; the
Colonna recaptured many of their citadels. A conclave was hastily assembled in the Vatican, and an exchange of promises and bribes[49] between
Cardinal Borgia and Cardinal Giuliano della Rovere secured the election of
Giovanni Battista Cibò of Genoa, who took the name of Innocent VIII.

He was fifty-two; tall and handsome, kindly and peaceable to the point
of complaisant weakness; of moderate intelligence and experience; a contemporary described him as "not wholly ignorant."[50] He had at least one
son and one daughter, probably more;[51] he acknowledged them candidly,
and after taking priestly orders he led an apparently celibate life. Though
the Roman wits wrote epigrams about his children, few Romans held it
againt the Pope that he had been so fertile in his youth. But they raised
eyebrows when he celebrated the marriages of his children and grandchildren in the Vatican.

In truth Innocent was content to be a grandfather, to enjoy domestic
affection and ease. He gave Politian two hundred ducats for dedicating to
him a translation of Herodotus, but for the rest he hardly bothered his head
about the humanists. He continued leisurely, and quite by proxy, the repair

and adornment of Rome. He engaged Antonio Pollaiuolo to build the Villa Belvedere in the Vatican gardens, and Andrea Mantegna to paint frescoes in a chapel adjoining it; but for the most part he left the patronage of letters and art to magnates and cardinals. In a similar mood of genial *laissez-faire* he entrusted foreign policy first to Cardinal della Rovere, then to Lorenzo de' Medici. The powerful banker offered his richly dowered daughter Maddalena as a bride for the Pope's son Franceschetto Cibò; Innocent was agreeable, and signed an alliance with Florence (1487); thereafter he allowed the experienced and pacific Florentine to guide the papal policy. For five years Italy enjoyed peace.

The age of Innocent was amused by one of the strangest comedies in history. After the death of Mohammed II (1481) his sons Bajazet II and Djem fought a civil war for the Ottoman throne. Defeated at Brusa, Djem sought to escape death by surrendering to the Knights of St. John in Rhodes (1482). Their Grand Master, Pierre d'Aubusson, held him as a threat over Bajazet. The Sultan agreed to pay the Knights 45,000 ducats yearly, ostensibly for Djem's maintenance, actually as an inducement not to set up Djem as a pretender to the Turkish sultanate and a useful ally in a Christian crusade. To better safeguard so lucrative a prisoner, d'Aubusson sent him to Knightly custody in France. The Sultan of Egypt, Ferdinand and Isabella of Spain, Matthias Corvinus of Hungary, Ferrante of Naples, and Innocent himself all offered large sums to d'Aubusson to transfer Djem to their care. The Pope won because, in addition to ducats, he promised the Grand Master a red hat, and helped Charles VIII of France to secure the hand and province of Anne of Brittany. So, on March 13, 1489, the "Grand Turk," as Djem was now called, was escorted in princely cavalcade through the streets of Rome to the Vatican, and received courteous and luxurious imprisonment. Bajazet, to ensure the honorable intentions of the Pope, sent him three years' salary for the upkeep of Djem; and in 1492 he dispatched to Innocent what he assured him was the head of the lancet that had pierced the side of Christ. Some cardinals were skeptical, but the Pope arranged that the relic should be brought from Ancona to Rome; when it reached the Porta del Popolo he himself received it and bore it in solemn ceremony to the Vatican. Cardinal Borgia held it aloft for the people's reverence, and then returned to his mistress.

Despite the Sultan's contribution to the support of the Church, Innocent found it troublesome to make ends meet. Like Sixtus IV and most of the rulers of Europe, he replenished his coffers by charging fees for appointment to office; and finding this lucrative, he created new offices to sell. By raising the number of papal secretaries to twenty-six, he realized 62,400 ducats; he increased to fifty-two the *plumbatores* whose heavy task was to place a leaden seal on papal decrees, and received 2500 ducats from each appointee. Such practices might have been no worse than selling annuity insurance, had it not been that the incumbents reimbursed themselves not merely by their salaries but by candid venality in their functions. For example, two papal secretaries confessed that in two years they had forged more than fifty papal bulls granting dispensations; the angry Pope had the men hanged and burned for stealing beyond their station (1489).[52] Everything in Rome seemed purchasable, from judicial pardons to the papacy itself.[53] The unreliable Infessura tells of a man who committed incest with his two daughters, then murdered them, and was let off by paying eight hundred ducats.[54] When Cardinal Borgia was asked why justice was not done, he is reputed to have answered: "God desires not the death of a sinner, but rather that he should pay and live."[55] The Pope's son, Franceschetto Cibò, was an unprincipled scoundrel; he forced his way into private homes "for evil purposes"; he saw to it that of the fines levied in the ecclesiastical courts of Rome a substantial portion should go to himself, and he spent his spoils in gambling. One night he lost 14,000 ducats ($350,000) to Cardinal Raffaelle Riario; he complained to the Pope that he had been cheated, and Innocent tried to recover the sum for him; but the Cardinal professed to have already used up the sum on the immense Palazzo della Cancelleria that he was building.[56]

The secularization of the papacy—its absorption in politics, war, and finance—had filled the college of cardinals with appointees noted for their administrative ability, their political influence, or their capacity to pay for their hats. Despite his promise to keep the College down to twenty-four members, Innocent added to it eight men most of whom were eminently unsuited to such a dignity; so the cardinalate was conferred upon the thirteen-year-old Giovanni de' Medici as part of a bargain with Lorenzo. Many of the cardinals were men of high education, benevolent patrons of literature, music, drama, and art. A few of them were saintly. Several had taken only minor orders, and were not yet priests. Many of them were frankly secular; their political, diplomatic, and fiscal duties required them to be men of the world, capable of meeting on a level of knowledge and subtlety the similar officials of Italian or transalpine governments. Some of them imitated the Roman nobles, fortified their palaces and retained armed men to protect themselves from these nobles, and the Roman mob, and other cardinals.[57]* Perhaps the great Catholic historian Pastor is a bit too severe on them, in view of their secular functions:

> Lorenzo de' Medici's low estimate of the College of Cardinals in the time of Innocent VIII was unfortunately only too well founded. . . . Of the worldly cardinals Ascanio Sforza, Riario, Orsini, Sclafenatus, Jean de la Balue, Giuliano della Rovere, Savelli, and Rodrigo Borgia were the most prominent. All of these were deeply infected with the corruption that prevailed in Italy amongst the upper classes in the age of the Renaissance. Surrounded in their splendid palaces with all the most refined luxury of a highly developed civilization, these cardinals lived the lives of secular princes, and seemed to regard their ecclesiastical garb simply as one of the adornments of their rank. They hunted, gambled, gave sumptuous banquets and entertainments, joined in all the rollicking merriment of the carnival-tide, and allowed themselves the utmost license in morals. This was especially the case with Rodrigo Borgia.[58]

The disorder at the top reflected and enhanced the moral chaos of Rome. Violence, thievery, rape, bribery, conspiracy, revenge were the order of the day. Each dawn revealed, in the alleys, men who had been killed during the night. Pilgrims and ambassadors were waylaid, were sometimes stripped naked, as they approached the capital of Christendom.[59] Women were attacked in the streets or in their homes. A piece of the True Cross, encased in silver, was stolen from the sacristy of Santa Maria in Trastevere; later the wood, shorn of its setting, was found in a vineyard.[60] Such religious skepticism was widespread. Over five hundred Roman families were condemned for heresy, but were let off with fines; perhaps the mercenary Curia of Rome was preferable to the mercenary and murderous inquisitors who were now ravaging Spain. Even priests had their doubts; one was accused of substituting, for the words of transubstantiation in the Mass, his own formula: "O fatuous Christians, who adore food and drink as God!"[61] As the end of Innocent's pontificate approached, prophets appeared who proclaimed impending doom; and in Florence the voice of Savonarola was rising to brand the age as that of Antichrist.

"On September 20," 1492, says a chronicler, "there was a great tumult in the city of Rome, and the merchants closed their shops. People who were in the fields and vineyards returned home in haste, because it was announced

---

* In a consistory of June, 1486, Cardinal Borgia reproached Cardinal Balue for being drunk; to which Balue responded by calling the future Alexander VI "son of a whore."[57a]

that Pope Innocent VIII was dead."[62] Strange stories were told of his dying hours: how the cardinals placed Djem under special guards lest Franceschetto Cibò should appropriate him; how Cardinals Borgia and della Rovere had almost come to blows beside the deathbed; and the dubious Infessura is our oldest authority for the report that three boys died from giving too much of their blood in a transfusion designed to revive the failing Pope.[63] Innocent bequeathed 48,000 ducats ($600,000?) to his relatives, and passed away. He was buried in St. Peter's, and Antonio Pollaiuolo covered his sins with a splendid tomb.

CHAPTER XVI

The Borgias

1492-1503

I. CARDINAL BORGIA

THE most interesting of the Renaissance popes was born at Xativa, Spain, on January 1, 1431. His parents were cousins, both of the Borjas, a family of some slight nobility. Rodrigo received his education at Xativa, Valencia, and Bologna. When his uncle became a cardinal, and then Pope Calixtus III, a straight path was opened for the young man's advancement in an ecclesiastical career. Moving to Italy, he respelled his name Borgia, was made a cardinal at twenty-five, and at twenty-six received the fruitful office of vice-chancellor—head of the entire Curia. He performed his duties competently, earned some repute as an administrator, lived abstemiously, and made many friends in either sex. He was not yet—would not be till his thirty-seventh year—a priest.

He was so handsome in his youth, so attractive in the grace of his manners, his sensual ardor and cheerful temperament, his persuasive eloquence and gay wit, that women found it hard to resist him. Brought up in the easygoing morality of fifteenth-century Italy, and perceiving that many a cleric, many a priest, allowed himself the pleasure of women, this young Lothario in the purple decided to enjoy all the gifts that God had given him and them. Pius II reproved him for attending "an immodest and seductive dance" (1460), but the Pope accepted Rodrigo's apology, and continued him as vice-chancellor and trusted aide.[1] In that year Rodrigo's first son, Pedro Luis, was born or begotten, and perhaps also his daughter Girolama, who was married in 1482;[2] their mothers are not known. Pedro lived in Spain till 1488, came to Rome in that year, and died soon afterward. In 1464 Rodrigo accompanied Pius II to Ancona, and there contracted some minor sexual disease "because," said his doctor, "he had not slept alone."[3]

About 1466 he formed a more permanent attachment with Vanozza de' Catanei, then some twenty-four years old. Unfortunately, she was married to Domenico d'Arignano, but Domenico left her in 1476.[4] To Rodrigo (who had become a priest in 1468) Vanozza bore four children: in 1474

Giovanni, in 1476 Cesare (whom we shall call Caesar), in 1480 Lucrezia, in 1481 Giofre. These four were ascribed to Vanozza on her tombstone, and were at one time or another acknowledged by Rodrigo as his own.[5] Such persistent parentage suggests an almost monogamous union, and perhaps Cardinal Borgia, in comparison with other ecclesiastics, may be credited with a certain domestic fidelity and stability.* He was a tender and benevolent father; it was a pity that his efforts to advance his children did not always bring glory to the Church. When Rodrigo set his eye on the papacy he found a tolerant husband for Vanozza, and helped her to prosperity. She was twice widowed, married again, lived in modest retirement, rejoiced in the rise of her children to fame and wealth, mourned her separation from them, earned a reputation for piety, died at seventy-six (1518), and left all her substantial property to the Church. Leo X sent his chamberlain to attend her ceremonious funeral.[7]

We should betray a lack of historical sense were we to judge Alexander VI from the moral standpoint of our age—or rather of our youth. His contemporaries looked upon his prepapal sexual sins as only canonically mortal, but, in the moral climate of his time, venial and forgivable.[8] Even in the generation between the reproof given him by Pius II and Rodrigo's elevation to the papacy, public opinion had become more lenient toward unobtrusive sexual digressions from clerical celibacy. Pius II himself, besides spawning some love children in his presacerdotal youth, had once advocated the marriage of priests; Sixtus IV had had several children; Innocent VIII had brought his into the Vatican. Some condemned the morals of Rodrigo, but apparently no one mentioned them when the conclave met to choose a successor to Innocent. Five popes, including the reasonably virtuous Nicholas V, had granted him lucrative benefices through all these years, had entrusted him with difficult missions and responsible posts, and had apparently (Pius II for a moment excepted) taken no notice of his philoprogenitive exuberance.[9] What men remarked in 1492 was that he had been vice-chancellor for thirty-five years, had been appointed and reappointed to that office by five successive popes, and had administered the office with conspicuous industry and competence; and that the external magnificence of his palace concealed a remarkable simplicity of private life. Iacopo da Volterra, in 1486, described him as "a man of an intellect capable of anything, and of great sense; he is a ready speaker, is of an astute

---

* Says the judicious Roscoe: "His attachment to Vanozza appears to have been sincere and uniform; and although his connexion was necessarily disavowed, he regarded her as a legitimate wife."[6]

nature, and has wonderful skill in conducting affairs."[10] He was popular with the Romans, having amused them with games; when news reached Rome that Granada had fallen to the Christians, he regaled Rome with a bullfight in Spanish style.

Perhaps the cardinals assembling in conclave on August 6, 1492, were also interested in his wealth, for in five administrations he had become the richest cardinal—excepting d'Estouteville—in the memory of Rome. They relied upon him to make substantial presents to those who should vote for him; and he did not fail them. To Cardinal Sforza he promised the vice-chancellorship, several rich benefices, and the Borgia palace in Rome; to Cardinal Orsini the see and ecclesiastical revenues of Cartagena, the towns of Monticelli and Soriano, and the governorship of the Marches; to Cardinal Savelli Civita Castellana and the bishopric of Majorca; and so on; Infessura described the process as Borgia's "evangelical distribution of his goods to the poor."[11] It was not an unusual procedure; every candidate had used it for many conclaves past, as every candidate uses it in politics today. Whether money bribes were also used is uncertain.[12] The decisive vote was cast by Cardinal Gherardo, ninety-six years old, and "hardly in possession of his faculties."[13] Finally all the cardinals rushed to the winning side, and made the election of Rodrigo Borgia unanimous (August 10, 1492). When asked by what name he wished to be called as pope, he answered, "By the name of the invincible Alexander." It was a pagan beginning for a pagan pontificate.

II. ALEXANDER VI

The choice of the conclave was also the choice of the people. Never had any papal election brought so much rejoicing,[14] never had a coronation been so magnificent. The populace delighted in the panoramic cavalcade of white horses, allegorical figures, tapestries and paintings, knights and grandees, troops of archers and Turkish horsemen, seven hundred priests, cardinals colorfully clad, and finally Alexander himself, sixty-one years old but majestically straight and tall, overflowing with health and energy and pride, "serene of countenance and of surpassing dignity," said an eyewitness,[15] and looking like an emperor even while blessing the multitude. Only a few sober minds, like Giuliano della Rovere and Giovanni de' Medici, expressed some apprehension lest the new Pope, known to be a fond father, would use his power to aggrandize his family rather than to cleanse and strengthen the Church.

He began well. In the thirty-six days between the death of Innocent and the coronation of Alexander there had been two hundred and twenty known murders in Rome. The new Pope made an example of the first captured assassin; the culprit was hanged, his brother was hanged with him, and his house was pulled down. The city approved this severity; crime hid its head; order was restored in Rome, and all Italy was glad that a strong hand was at the helm of the Church.[16]

Art and literature marked time. Alexander did considerable building in and out of Rome; financed a new ceiling for Santa Maria Maggiore with a gift of American gold from Ferdinand and Isabella; remodeled the Mausoleum of Hadrian into the fortified Castle of Sant' Angelo, and redecorated its interior to provide cells for papal prisoners and more comfortable quarters for harassed popes. He built between the Castle and the Vatican a long covered corridor, which gave him refuge from Charles VIII in 1494, and saved Clement VII from a Lutheran noose in the sack of Rome. Pinturicchio was engaged to adorn the Appartamento Borgia in the Vatican. Four of these six rooms were restored and opened to the public by Leo XIII. A lunette in one of them contains a vivid portrait of Alexander—a happy face, a prosperous body, gorgeous robes. In another room a Virgin teaching the Child to read was described by Vasari[17] as a portrait of Giulia Farnese, an alleged mistress of the Pope. Vasari adds that the picture also contained "the head of Pope Alexander adoring her," but no picture of him is there visible.

He rebuilt the University of Rome, called to it several distinguished teachers, and paid them with unheard-of regularity. He liked drama, and was pleased to have the students of the Roman Academy stage comedies and ballets for his family festivals. He preferred light music to heavy philosophy. In 1501 he re-established censorship of publications by an edict requiring that no book might be printed without the approval of the local archbishop. But he allowed a wide freedom of satire and debate. He laughed off the bites of the town wits, and rejected Caesar Borgia's proposal that such snipers should be disciplined. "Rome is a free city," he told the Ferrarese ambassador, "where everyone can say or write whatever he pleases. They say much evil of me, but I don't mind."[18]

His administration of Church affairs was, in the early years of his pontificate, unusually efficient. Innocent VIII had left a debt in the treasury; "it needed all the financial ability of Alexander to restore the papal finances; it took him two years to balance the budget."[18a] The Vatican staff was reduced, and expenses were curtailed, but records were strictly kept, and salaries were promptly paid.[19] Alexander performed the laborious religious ritual of his office with fidelity, but with the impatience of a busy man.[20] His *magister ceremoniarum* was a German, Johann Burchard, who helped to perpetuate the fame and infamy of his employer by recording in a *Diarium* nearly all that he saw, including much that Alexander would have wished unseen. To the cardinals the Pope gave as he had promised in the conclave, and he was even more generous to those who, like Cardinal de' Medici, had longest opposed him. A year after his accession he created twelve new cardinals. Several were men of real ability; some were appointed at the request of political powers that it was wise to conciliate; two were scandalously young—Ippolito d'Este, fifteen, and Caesar Borgia, eighteen; one of them, Alessandro Farnese, owed his elevation to his sister Giulia Farnese, who was believed by many to be a mistress of the Pope. The sharp-tongued Romans, not foreseeing that they would one day acclaim Alessandro as Paul III, called him *il cardinale della gonnella*—the cardinal of the petticoat. The strongest of the older cardinals, Giuliano della Rovere, was displeased to find that he, who had often ruled Innocent VIII, had little influence with Alexander, who made Cardinal Sforza his favorite counselor. In a huff Giuliano retired to his episcopal see at Ostia, and formed a guard of armed men. A year later he fled to France, and besought Charles VIII to invade Italy, summon a general council, and depose Alexander as a shamelessly simoniacal pope.

Meanwhile Alexander was facing the political problems of a papacy caught between the millstones of scheming Italian powers. The Papal States had again fallen into the hands of local dictators who, while calling themselves vicars of the Church, had snatched the opportunity provided by the weakness of Innocent VIII to re-establish the practical independence that they or their predecessors had lost under Albornoz or Sixtus IV. Some papal cities had been seized by neighboring powers; so Naples had taken Sora and Aquila in 1467, and Milan had appropriated Forlì in 1488. Alexander's first task, then, was to bring these states under a centralized papal rule and taxation, as the kings of Spain, France, and England had subdued the feudal lords. This was the mission that he assigned to Caesar Borgia, who accomplished it with such speed and ruthlessness as made Machiavelli gape with admiration.

Closer to Rome, and more immediately harassing, was the turbulent autonomy of the nobles, theoretically subject, actually hostile and dangerous, to the popes. The temporal weakness of the papacy since Boniface VIII (d. 1303) had allowed these barons to maintain a medieval feudal sovereignty on their estates, making their own laws, organizing their own armies, fighting at will their private and reckless wars, to the ruin of order and commerce in Latium. Soon after Alexander's accession Franceschetto Cibò sold to Virginio Orsini, for 40,000 ducats ($500,000), estates left him by his father Innocent VIII. But this Orsini was a high officer in the Neapolitan army; he had received from Ferrante most of the money for the purchase;[21] in effect Naples had secured two strategic strongholds in papal territory.[22] Alexander reacted by forming an alliance with Venice, Milan, Ferrara, and Siena, raising an army, and fortifying the wall between Sant' Angelo and the Vatican. Ferdinand II of Spain, fearing that a combined attack upon Naples would end the Aragon power in Italy, persuaded Alexander and Ferrante to negotiate. Orsini paid the Pope 40,000 ducats for the right to retain his purchases; and Alexander betrothed his son Giofre, then thirteen, to Sancia, the pretty granddaughter of the Neapolitan King (1494).

In return for Ferdinand's happy mediation, Alexander awarded him the two Americas. Columbus had discovered the "Indies" some two months after Alexander's succession, and had presented them to Ferdinand and Isabella. Portugal claimed the New World by virtue of an edict of Calixtus III (1479), which had confirmed her claim to all lands on the Atlantic coast. Spain retorted that the edict had in mind only the eastern Atlantic. The states were near war when Alexander issued two bulls (May 3 and 4, 1493) allotting to Spain all discoveries west, and to Portugal all those east, of an imaginary line drawn from pole to pole a hundred Spanish leagues west of the Azores and Cape Verde Islands, in each case on condition that the lands discovered were not already inhabited by Christians, and that the conquerors would make every effort to convert their new subjects to the Christian faith. The "grant" of the Pope, of course, merely confirmed a conquest of the sword, but it preserved the peace of the peninsular powers. No one seems to have thought that non-Christians had any rights to the lands in which they dwelt.

If Alexander might distribute continents he found it difficult to hold the Vatican. When Ferrante of Naples died (1494), Charles VIII decided to invade Italy and restore Naples to French rule. Fearing deposition, Alexander went to the extraordinary step of soliciting help from the Sultan of the Turks. In July, 1494, he sent a papal secretary, Giorgio Bocciardo to warn Bajazet II that Charles VIII was planning to enter Italy, take Naples depose or control the Pope, and use Djem as a pretender to the Ottoman throne in a crusade against Constantinople. Alexander proposed that Bajazet should make common cause with the papacy, Naples, and perhaps Venice, against the French. Bajazet received Bocciardo with Oriental courtesy, and sent him back with the 40,000 ducats due for the maintenance of Djem, and with an envoy of his own to Alexander. At Senigallia Bocciardo was captured by Giovanni della Rovere, brother to the disaffected cardinal; the 40,000 ducats were seized, together with five letters allegedly from the Sultan to the Pope. One letter proposed that Alexander should put Djem to death and send the dead body to Constantinople; upon its receipt the Sultan would pay the Pope 300,000 ducats ($3,750,000), "with which Your Highness may buy some dominions for your children."[23] Cardinal della Rovere gave copies of the letters to the French King. Alexander claimed that the Cardinal had forged the letters and had invented the whole story. The evidence supports the authenticity of Alexander's message to Bajazet, but discounts the Sultan's reply as probably forged.[24] Venice and Naples had already entered into similar negotiations with the Turks; Francis I would later do likewise. To rulers religion, like almost everything else, is a tool of power.

Charles came, advanced through friendly Milan and frightened Florence, and approached Rome (December, 1494). The Colonna supported him by preparing to invade the capital. A French fleet seized Ostia—Rome's port at the mouth of the Tiber—and threatened to stop the supply of grain from Sicily. Many cardinals, including Ascanio Sforza, declared for Charles; Virginio Orsini opened his castles to the King; half the cardinals in Rome besought him to depose the Pope.[24a] Alexander withdrew to Castel Sant' Angelo, and sent envoys to treat with the conqueror. Charles did not wish, by attempting to remove the Pope, to rouse Spain against him; his goal was Naples, whose wealth was ever in the thoughts of his officers. He made peace with Alexander on condition of an unimpeded passage for his army through Latium, papal forgiveness of the pro-French cardinals, and the surrender of Djem. Alexander yielded, returned to the Vatican, enjoyed Charles's three genuflections before him, graciously prevented him from kissing the papal feet, and received from the King the formal "obedience" of France—i.e., all plans for deposing Alexander were withdrawn. On January 25, 1495, Charles moved on to Naples, taking Djem with him. On February 25 Djem died of bronchitis. Gossip said that the subtle Alexander had given him a slow poison, but no one any longer credits that tale.[25]

Once the French were gone, Alexander recovered his courage. Now, probably, he made up his mind that strong Papal States, a good army, and a good general were necessary to the safety of the popes from secular domination.[26] With Venice, Germany, Spain, and Milan he formed a Holy

League (March 31, 1495), ostensibly for mutual defense and for war against the Turks, secretly for the expulsion of the French from Italy. Charles took the hint, and retreated through Rome to Pisa; Alexander, to avoid him, sojourned in Orvieto and Perugia. When Charles fled back to France Alexander returned in triumph to Rome. He demanded of Florence that it should join the League, and expel or silence Savonarola, friend of France and foe of the Pope. He reorganized the papal army, put his oldest surviving son Giovanni at its head, and bade him conquer for the papacy the revolted Orsini fortresses (1496). But Giovanni was no general; he was defeated at Soriano, returned to Rome in disgrace, and pursued the careless gallantries that probably caused his early death. Nevertheless Alexander recovered the strongholds sold to Virginio Orsini, and recaptured Ostia from the French. Apparently victorious over all obstacles, he bade Pinturicchio paint on the walls of the papal apartment in Sant' Angelo frescoes picturing the triumph of the Pope over the King. Alexander was at the top of his curve.

III. THE SINNER

Rome applauded him for his internal administration, and his successful though hesitant diplomacy. It reproved him mildly for his love affairs, vigorously for feathering the nests of his children, bitterly for appointing to office in Rome a host of Spaniards whose alien mien and speech set Italian teeth on edge. A hundred Spanish relatives of the Pope had flocked to Rome; "ten papacies," said one observer, "would not have sufficed for all these cousins."[27] Alexander himself was by this time fully Italian in his culture, policy, and ways, but he still loved Spain, spoke Spanish too frequently with Caesar and Lucrezia, elevated nineteen Spaniards to the cardinalate, and surrounded himself with Catalan servants and aides. Finally the jealous Romans, half in humor, half in wrath, called him "the marrano Pope,"[28] implying his descent from Christianized Spanish Jews. Alexander excused himself on the ground that many Italians, especially in the college of cardinals, had proved faithless to him, and that he had to have about him a nucleus of supporters bound to him by a personal loyalty based on their awareness that he was their sole protector in Rome.

He—and the princes of Europe down to Napoleon—argued likewise in promoting relatives to positions of trust and power.* He hoped for a while

* Cf. the admirable Creighton: "In the precarious condition of Italian politics allies were not to be trusted unless their fidelity was secured by interested motives; so Alexander VI

that his son Giovanni might help him to protect the Papal States, but Giovanni had inherited his father's sensitivity to women without Alexander's capacity to govern men. Perceiving that of his sons only Caesar had in him the iron and gall necessary to play the game of Italian politics in that violent age, Alexander conferred upon him a maze of benefices whose income would finance the youth's rising power. Even the gentle Lucrezia was an instrument of policy, and found herself promoted to the governorship of a city or the bed of a valuable duke. The Pope's fondness for Lucrezia led him to such shows of affection that cruel gossip accused him of incest, and pictured him as competing with his sons for her love.[29] On two occasions when he had to be absent from Rome, Alexander left Lucrezia in charge of his rooms in the Vatican, with authority to open his correspondence and attend to all routine business. Such delegation of power to a woman was frequent in the ruling houses of Italy—as in Ferrara, Urbino, Mantua—but it mildly shocked even blasé Rome. When Giofre and Sancia arrived from Naples after their wedding, Caesar and Lucrezia went out to meet them; all four then hurried to the Vatican, and Alexander was happy to have them near him. "Other popes, to conceal their infamy," says Guicciardini, "were wont to term their offspring nephews; but Alexander took delight in letting all the world know that they were his children."[30]

The city had forgiven the Pope his pristine Vanozza, but marveled at his current Giulia. Giulia Farnese was noted for her beauty, above all for her golden hair; when she let it down, and it hung to her feet, it was a sight that would have stirred the blood of men less mettlesome than Alexander. Her friends called her La Bella. Sanudo speaks of her as "the Pope's favorite, a young woman of great beauty and understanding, gracious and gentle."[31] In 1493 Infessura described her as attending Lucrezia's nuptial banquet in the Vatican, and called her Alexander's "concubine"; Matarazzo, the Perugian historian, used the same term for Giulia, but probably copied Infessura; and a Florentine wit in 1494 called her *sposa di Cristo*, bride of Christ, a phrase usually reserved for the Church.[32] Some scholars have sought to clear Giulia on the ground that Lucrezia—who has been made respectable by research—remained her friend to the end, and that Giulia's

---

used the marriage connections of his family as a means to secure for himself a strong political party. He had no one whom he could trust save his own children, whom he regarded as instruments for his own plans."—M. Creighton, *History of the Papacy During the Period of the Reformation*, III, 263. The impartiality and learning of the Anglican bishop is matched in this field only by the scholarship and honesty of the Catholic Ludwig von Pastor's *History of the Popes*. The existence of these two remarkable histories should long since have dissipated the mist of legend cast by partisan pamphleteering around the Renaissance popes.

husband, Orsino Orsini, built a chapel to her honored memory.[33] In 1492 Giulia gave birth to a daughter Laura, who was officially listed as begotten by Orsini, but Cardinal Alessandro Farnese recognized the girl as Alexander's child.[34]* By yet another woman the Pope was credited with having a mysterious son, born about 1498, and known in Burchard's diary as *Infans Romanus*.[35] It is not certain, but one more or less hardly matters.

There is no question that Alexander was a sensual man, full-blooded to a degree painfully uncongenial to celibacy. When he gave a public festival in the Vatican, at which a comedy was performed (February, 1503), he rumbled with amusement, and was pleased to have fair women crowd about him and seat themselves gracefully on footstools at his feet. He was a man. He seems to have felt, like many clergymen of the time, that clerical celibacy was a mistake of Hildebrand's, and that even a cardinal should be permitted the pleasures and tribulations of female company. He showed feelings of husbandly tenderness for Vanozza, and perhaps a paternal solicitude for Giulia. On the other hand his devotion to his children, sometimes overriding his fidelity to the interests of the Church, could well be used to argue the wisdom of the canon law requiring celibacy of a priest.

In these middle years of his pontificate, before Caesar Borgia overshadowed it, Alexander had many virtues. Though he bore himself with proud dignity at public functions, in private he was jovial, good-natured, sanguine, eager to enjoy life, capable of a hearty laugh at seeing, from his window, a parade of masked men "with long false noses of great size in the form of the male member."[36] He was a bit stout now, if we may trust Pinturicchio's apparently honest picture of him, praying, on the Appartamento wall; and yet all reports concur that he lived frugally, on so plain a fare that the cardinals shunned his table.[37] He was unsparing of himself in administration, working till late at night, and watching actively over the affairs of the Church everywhere in Christendom.

Was his Christianity a pretense? Probably not. His letters, even those concerning Giulia, are warm with phrases of piety that were not indispensable in private correspondence.[38] He was so much a man of action, and had so thoroughly absorbed the easy morals of his time, that he only sporadically noted any contradiction between Christian ethics and his life. Like most persons completely orthodox in theology, he was completely worldly in conduct. He seems to have felt that in his circumstances the papacy needed a statesman, not a saint; he admired sanctity, but thought it

---

* Pastor (V, 417n) accepts the evidence as conclusive of Alexander's guilt; but the Pope's character was so blackened by hostile gossip that charity may still suspend judgment.

belonged to monasticism and private life rather than to a man compelled to deal at every step with subtle and acquisitive despots or unscrupulous and treacherous diplomats. He ended by adopting all their methods, and the most questionable devices of his predecessors in the papacy.

Needing funds for his government and his wars, he sold offices, took over the estates of dead cardinals, and exploited the jubilee of 1500 to the full. Dispensations and divorces were given as profitable parts of political bargains; so King Ladislaus VII of Hungary paid 30,000 ducats for the annulment of his marriage with Beatrice of Naples; had Henry VIII such an Alexander to deal with he would have remained to the end a Defender of the Faith. When the jubilee threatened to be a financial disappointment because would-be pilgrims stayed home through fear of robbery, pestilence, or war, Alexander, not to be cheated, and following pontifical precedents, issued a bull (March 4, 1500) detailing by what payments Christians might obtain the jubilee indulgence without coming to Rome, at what cost penitents might gain absolution from consanguineous marriages, and how much a clergyman should pay to be forgiven simony and "irregularity."[39] On December 16 he extended the jubilee till Epiphany. The collectors promised payors that the funds gathered in by the jubilee would be used in a crusade against the Turks; the promise was kept in the case of Polish and Venetian collections; but Caesar Borgia used jubilee proceeds to finance his campaigns for the recovery of the Papal States.[40]

To further celebrate the jubilee, Alexander (September 28, 1500) created twelve new cardinals, who paid a total of 120,000 ducats for their appointment; and these promotions, says Guicciardini, were made "not of such as had the most merit, but of those that offered the most money."[41] In 1503 he named nine additional cardinals at a commensurate price.[42] In the same year he created *ex nihilo* eighty new offices in the Curia, and these places, according to the hostile Venetian ambassador Giustiniani, were sold at 760 ducats each.[43] A satirist attached to the statue of Pasquino (1503) a stinging pasquinade:

Vendit Alexander claves, altaria, Christum;
vendere iure potest, emerat ipse prius[44]—

"the keys, the altars, Alexander sells, and Christ; with right, since he has paid for them."

By canon law the property left by an ecclesiastic at his death reverted to the Church, except as the pope might allow otherwise.[45] Alexander regularly gave such dispensations except in the case of cardinals. Under pressure from the victorious but money-consuming Caesar Borgia, Alexander made it a general principle to appropriate the fortunes left by high ecclesiastics; in this way substantial sums came into the treasury. Some cardinals eluded the Pope by making large gifts in expectation of death, and some, during their lives, deliberately squandered great sums on their funeral monuments. When Cardinal Michiel died (1503), his house was immediately stripped of its wealth by the agents of the Pope, who, if we may believe Giustiniani, netted 150,000 ducats; Alexander complained that only 23,832 were in cash.[46]

Deferring fuller consideration of the alleged poisonings, by Alexander or Caesar Borgia, of high ecclesiastics who took too long to die, we may provisionally accept the conclusion of recent research—that "there is no evidence that Alexander VI poisoned anybody."[47] This does not quite clear him; he may have been too clever for history. But he could not escape the satirists, pamphleteers, and other wits who sold their deadly epigrams to his opponents. We have seen how Sannazaro belabored Pope and son with lethal couplets in the strife between the papacy and Naples. Infessura served the Colonna with his scandalmongering pen; and Geronimo Mancione was worth a regiment to the Savelli barons. Alexander, as part of his campaign against the Campagna nobles, issued in 1501 a bull detailing the crimes and vices of the Savelli and the Colonna. Its exaggerations were bettered in Mancione's famous "Letter to Silvio Savelli," retailing the vices and crimes of Alexander and Caesar Borgia. This document was widely circulated, and did much to create the legend of Alexander as a monster of perversions and cruelty.[48] Alexander won the battle of the sword, but his noble foes, unchecked by his enemy Pope Julius II, won the battle of the word, and transmitted their picture of him to history.

He paid too little attention to public opinion, and rarely answered the slanders that so mercilessly multiplied the reality of his faults. He was resolved to build a strong state, and thought that it could not be done by Christian means. His use of the traditional tools of statecraft—propaganda, deception, intrigue, discipline, war—was bound to offend those who preferred a Christian Church to a strong one, and those to whose advantage it was that the papacy and the Papal States should be disorganized and weak among the nobles of Rome and the powers of Italy. Occasionally Alexander stopped to examine his life by evangelical standards, and then he admitted himself to be a simoniac, a fornicator, even—through war—a destroyer of human lives. Once, when his lucky star seemed suddenly to fall, and all his proud and happy world seemed shattered, he lost his Machiavellian amoralism, confessed his sins, and vowed to reform himself and the Church.

He loved his son Giovanni even more than his daughter Lucrezia. When Pedro Luis died, Alexander saw to it that Giovanni should receive the duchy of Gandia in Spain. It was easy to love the lad, he was so handsome, kindly, gay. The fond father did not perceive that the youth was made for Eros, not for Mars; he made him a general, and the young commander proved incompetent. Giovanni thought a beautiful woman more precious than a captured city. On June 14, 1497, he supped with his brother Caesar and other guests at the home of his mother Vanozza. As they were returning, Giovanni parted from Caesar and the rest, saying that he wished to visit a lady of his acquaintance. He was never seen alive again. When his disappearance was noted the anxious Pope sent out an alarm. A boatman confessed that he had seen a body thrown into the Tiber on the night of the 14th; asked why he had not reported it he replied that in the course of his life he had seen a hundred such disposals, and had learned not to trouble himself about them. The river was dragged, the body was found, stabbed in nine places; apparently the young Duke had been attacked by several men. Alexander was so broken with grief that he shut himself up in a private chamber and refused food, and his moans could be heard in the street.

He ordered a search for the murderers, but perhaps he soon reconciled himself to letting the case remain a mystery. The body had been recovered near the castle of Antonio Pico della Mirandola, whose pretty daughter had allegedly been seduced by the Duke; many contemporaries, like the Mantuan ambassador Scalona, ascribed the death to thugs hired by the Count; and this is still the likeliest explanation.[49] Others, including the Florentine and Milanese ambassadors at Rome, attributed the crime to some member of the Orsini clan, then at war with the Pope.[50] Some scandal-sippers said that Giovanni had made love to his sister Lucrezia, and had been killed by retainers of her husband Giovanni Sforza.[51] No one at the time accused Caesar Borgia. Caesar, now twenty-two, had apparently been on the best terms with his brother; he was a cardinal, and was moving in his own line of advancement; not till fourteen months later did he turn to a military career; he derived no advantage from his brother's death; he could hardly have anticipated that Giovanni would leave him on the way home from Vanozza. Alexander, so far from suspecting Caesar at this time, appointed him Giovanni's executor. The first known mention of Caesar as the possible murderer occurs in a letter written by the Ferrarese ambassador Pigna on February 22, 1498, eight months after the event. Not till Caesar had shown his character in all its ruthless force did popular opinion connect him with the crime; then Machiavelli and Guicciardini agreed in laying it at his door. He might have been capable of it at a later stage of his development, had Giovanni opposed him in some vital policy; but of this particular murder he was almost certainly innocent.[52]

When the Pope had recovered his self-control he called a consistory of the cardinals (June 19, 1497), received their condolences, told them that he had "loved the Duke of Gandia more than anyone else in the world," and attributed the blow—"the heaviest that could have befallen" him—to God as a punishment for his sins. He went on: "We on our part are resolved to amend our life, and to reform the Church. . . . Henceforth benefices shall be given only to deserving persons, and in accordance with the votes of the cardinals. We renounce all nepotism. We will begin the reform with ourselves, and so proceed through all ranks of the Church till the whole work is accomplished."[53] A committee of six cardinals was appointed to draw up a program of reform. It labored earnestly, and presented to Alexander a bull of reform so excellent that if its provisions had been put into effect they might have saved the Church from both the Reformation and the Counter Reformation. But when Alexander faced the question how the revenues of the papacy, without the fees paid for ecclesiastical appointments, could finance the papal government, he found no acceptable answer. Meanwhile Louis XII was preparing a second French invasion of Italy, and soon Caesar Borgia proposed to recapture the Papal States from their recalcitrant "vicars." The dream of a powerful political structure that would give the Church a physical and financial leverage in a rebellious and fluent world absorbed the spirit of the Pope; he deferred the reforms from day to day; at last he forgot them in the exciting successes of a son who was conquering a realm for him and making him every ounce a king.

IV. CAESAR BORGIA

Alexander had many reasons to be proud of his now oldest son. Caesar was blonde of hair and beard, as many Italians wanted to be; keen of eye, tall and straight, strong, and a stranger to fear. Of him, as of Leonardo, the story was told that he could twist a horseshoe with his bare hands. He rode with wild control the spirited horses collected for his stable; he went to the hunt with the eagerness of a hound sniffing blood. During the jubilee he astonished a crowd by decapitating a bull with one stroke in a bullbaiting contest in a Roman square; on January 2, 1502, in a formal bullfight ar-

ranged by him in the Piazza San Pietro, he rode into the enclosure with nine
other Spaniards, and attacked singlehanded, with his pike, the more ferocious of two bulls let loose there; dismounting, he played *torero* for a while;
then, having sufficiently proved his courage and skill, he left the arena to
the professionals.[54] He introduced the sport into the Romagna as well as at
Rome; but after a few amateur matadors had been gored it was sent back
to Spain.

To think of him as an ogre is to miss him widely. One contemporary
called him "a young man of great and surpassing cleverness and excellent
disposition, cheerful, even merry, and always in good spirits";[55] another
described him as "far superior in looks and wit to his brother the Duke of
Gandia."[56] Men noted his grace of manner, his simple but costly garb, his
commanding glance, and air of one who felt that he inherited the world.
Women admired but did not love him; they knew that he took them lightly
and lightly cast them aside. He had studied law in the University of Perugia, enough to sharpen the natural shrewdness of his mind. He spared
little time for books or "culture," though like everybody he wrote verses
now and then; later he flaunted a poet on his staff. He had a discriminating
appreciation of the arts; when Cardinal Raffaello Riario refused to buy a
Cupid because it was no antique but the work of an unknown Florentine
youth, Michelangelo Buonarroti, Caesar gave a good price for it.

He was clearly not made for an ecclesiastical career, but Alexander, having bishoprics rather than principalities at his disposal, made him archbishop
of Valencia (1492), then cardinal (1493). No one took such appointments
as religious; they were means of supplying income to youths who had influential relatives, and who might be trained for the practical management
of ecclesiastical property and personnel. Caesar took minor orders, but
never became a priest. Since canon law excluded bastards from the cardinalate, Alexander, in a bull of September 19, 1493, declared him the legitimate son of Vanozza and d'Arignano. It was inconvenient that in a bull
of August 16, 1482, Sixtus IV had described Caesar as the son of "Rodrigo,
bishop and vice-chancellor." The public winked and smiled, accustomed
to see legal fictions veil untimely truths.

In 1497, shortly after Giovanni's death, Caesar went to Naples as papal
legate, and had the thrill of crowning a king. Perhaps the touch of a crown
stirred his blood. On his return to Rome he importuned his father to let
him renounce his ecclesiastical career. There was no way of releasing him
from it except through Alexander's frank admission to the college of cardinals that Caesar was his illegitimate son; it was so done, and the appoint-

ment of the young bastard to the cardinalate was duly declared invalid (August 17, 1498).[57] His illegitimacy restored, Caesar turned with zest to the game of politics.

Alexander hoped that Federigo III, King of Naples, would accept Caesar as husband for his daughter Carlotta, but Federigo had different tastes. Deeply offended, the Pope turned to France, hoping to secure its help in reclaiming the Papal States. An opportunity came when Louis XII asked for the annulment of a marriage that had been forced upon him in his youth, and which, he claimed, had never been consummated. In October, 1498, Alexander sent Caesar to France bearing a decree of divorce for the King, and 200,000 ducats with which to woo a bride. Pleased with the divorce, further pleased by a papal dispensation to marry Anne of Brittany, widow of Charles VIII, Louis offered Caesar the hand of Charlotte d'Albret, sister to the king of Navarre; moreover, he made Caesar duke of Valentinois and Diois, two French territories to which the papacy had some legal claim. In May, 1499, the new Duke—Valentino, as he was henceforth called in Italy—married the good, beautiful, and wealthy Charlotte; and Rome, told the news by Alexander, lit bonfires of rejoicing over the marriage of their prince. The marriage committed the papacy to an alliance with a king who was openly planning to invade Italy and take Milan and Naples. Alexander was as guilty in 1499 as Lodovico and Savonarola had been in 1494. This alliance undid all the work of the Holy League that Alexander had helped to form in 1495, and it prepared the scene for the wars of Julius II. Caesar Borgia was among the notables who escorted Louis XII into Milan on October 6, 1499; Castiglione, who was there, described Duke Valentino as the tallest and handsomest man in all the King's stately retinue.[58] His pride matched his appearance. His ring bore the inscription, *Fays ce que dois, advien que pourra*—"Do what you must, whate'er betide." His sword was engraved with scenes from the life of Julius Caesar, and bore two mottoes: on one side, *Alea iacta est*—"The die is cast"; on the other, *Aut Caesar aut nullus*—"Either Caesar or nobody."[59]

In this bold youth and happy warrior Alexander found at last the general he had long sought to lead the armed forces of the Church in the reconquest of the Papal States. Louis contributed three hundred French lances, four thousand Gascons and Swiss were recruited, and two thousand Italian mercenaries. It was a small army with which to overcome a dozen despots, but Caesar was eager for the adventure. To add spiritual to military weapons, the Pope issued a bull solemnly declaring that Caterina Sforza and her son Ottaviano held Imola and Forlì—Pandolfo Malatesta held Rimini—Giulio

Varano held Camerino—Astorre Manfredi held Faenza—Guidobaldo held Urbino—Giovanni Sforza held Pesaro—only by usurping lands, property, and rights long pertaining in law and justice to the Church; that they were all tyrants who had abused their powers and exploited their subjects; and that they must now resign or be expelled by force.[60] Possibly, as some charged, Alexander dreamed of welding these principalities into a kingdom for his son; it is unlikely, for Alexander must have known that neither his successors nor the other states of Italy would long tolerate a usurpation more illegal and unwelcome than any that it would have replaced. Caesar himself may have dreamed of such a consummation; Machiavelli hoped so, and would have rejoiced to see so strong a hand unite all Italy and expel all invaders. But to the end of his life Caesar protested that he had no other aim than to win the States of the Church for the Church, and would be content to be governor of the Romagna as a vassal of the pope.[61]

In January, 1500, Caesar and his army marched over the Apennines to Forlì. Imola surrendered at once to his deputy, and the citizens of Forlì threw open the gates to welcome him; but Caterina Sforza, as she had done twelve years before, bravely held the citadel with her garrison. Caesar offered her easy terms; she preferred to fight. After a brief siege the papal troops forced their way into the *rocca*, and put the defenders to the sword. Caterina was sent to Rome, and was lodged as an unwilling guest in the Belvedere wing of the Vatican. She refused to resign her right to rule Forlì and Imola; she tried to escape, and was transferred to Sant' Angelo. After eighteen months she was released, and entered a nunnery. She was a brave woman, but quite a virago.[62] "She was a feudal ruler of the worst type, and in her dominions, as elsewhere in the Romagna, Caesar was regarded as an avenger commissioned by Heaven to redress ages of oppression and wrong."[63]

But Caesar's first triumph was brief. His foreign troops mutinied because Caesar had insufficient funds to pay them; they were hardly appeased when Louis XII recalled the French detachment to help him recapture the Milan that Lodovico had for a moment regained. Caesar led his remaining army back to Rome, and received almost the honors of a victorious Roman general. Alexander gloried in his son's success; "the Pope," reported the Venetian ambassador, "is more cheerful than ever."[64] He appointed Caesar papal vicar for the conquered cities, and began to lean fondly on his son's advice. The receipts from the jubilee and from the sale of red hats replenished the treasury, and Caesar could now plan a second campaign. He offered a convincing sum to Paolo Orsini to join the papal forces with his armed men; Paolo came, and several other nobles followed suit; with this clever stroke Caesar enlarged his army and protected Rome from baronial raids during the absence of the papal troops beyond the Apennines. Perhaps by similar inducements, and the promise of spoils, he enlisted the services and soldiers of Gianpaolo Baglioni, lord of Perugia, and engaged Vitellozzo Vitelli to lead the artillery. Louis XII sent him a small regiment of lancers, but Caesar was no longer dependent upon French reinforcements. In September, 1500, at Alexander's urging, he attacked the castles occupied by hostile Colonna and Savelli in Latium. One after another surrendered. Soon Alexander was enabled to make a tour in safety and triumph through regions long lost to the papacy. He was received everywhere with popular acclaim,[65] for the feudal barons had not been loved by their subjects.

When Caesar set out on his second major campaign (October, 1500), he had an army of 14,000 men, with a retinue of poets, prelates, and prostitutes to service his troops. Anticipating their arrival, Pandolfo Malatesta vacated Rimini, and Giovanni Sforza fled from Pesaro; the two cities welcomed Caesar as a liberator. At Faenza Astorre Manfredi resisted, and the people supported him loyally. Borgia offered generous terms, Manfredi rejected them. The siege lasted all winter; finally Faenza surrendered on Caesar's promise of leniency to all. He behaved handsomely to the citizens, and was so warm in praising Manfredi's resolute defense that the defeated apparently fell in love with the victor, and remained with him as part of his staff or retinue. Astorre's younger brother did the same, though both were free to go wherever they wished.[66] For two months they followed Caesar in all his wanderings, and were treated with all respect. Then suddenly, on reaching Rome, they were thrown into the Castel Sant' Angelo. There they remained for a year; then, on June 2, 1502, their bodies were thrown up by the Tiber. What made Caesar—or Alexander—condemn them is not known. Like a hundred other strange events in the history of the Borgias, the case remains a mystery that only the uninformed can solve.

Caesar, now adding duke of Romagna to his titles, studied the map, and decided to complete the task assigned him by his father. Camerino and Urbino remained to be taken. Urbino, though doubtless papal in law, was almost a model state as politics then went; it seemed a disgraceful thing to depose so loved a couple as Guidobaldo and Elisabetta; and perhaps they would now have consented to be papal vicars in fact as well as name. But Caesar argued that the city blocked his easiest avenue to the Adriatic, and might, in hostile hands, cut off his communications with Pesaro and Rimini.

We do not know if Alexander agreed; it seems incredible, for about this time he persuaded Guidobaldo to lend the papal army his artillery.[67] It is more likely that Caesar deceived his father, or changed his own plans. On June 12, 1502, now with Leonardo da Vinci as his chief engineer, he set out on his third campaign, apparently headed for Camerino. Suddenly he turned north, and approached Urbino so rapidly that its invalid ruler had barely time to escape, leaving the city to fall undefended into Caesar's hands (June 21). If this move was made with Alexander's knowledge and consent, it was one of the most despicable treacheries in history, though Machiavelli would have been thrilled by its subtlety. The victor treated the inhabitants with feline gentleness, but appropriated the precious art collection of the fallen Duke, and sold it to pay his troops.

Meanwhile his general Vitelli, apparently on his own authority, seized Arezzo, long since an appanage of Florence. The shocked Signory sent the bishop of Volterra, with Machiavelli, to appeal to Caesar at Urbino. He received them with successful charm. "I am not here to play the tyrant," he told them, "but to extinguish tyrants."[68] He agreed to check Vitelli and restore Arezzo to Florentine allegiance; in return he demanded a definite policy of mutual friendliness between Florence and himself. The bishop thought him sincere, and Machiavelli wrote to the Signory with undiplomatic enthusiasm:

> This lord is splendid and magnificent, and is so bold that there is no enterprise so great that it does not seem to him small. To gain glory and dominions he robs himself of repose, and knows neither danger nor fatigue. He comes to a place before his intentions are understood. He makes himself well liked among his soldiers, and has chosen the best men in Italy. These things make him victorious and formidable, with the aid of perpetual good fortune.[69]

On July 20 Camerino surrendered to Caesar's lieutenants, and the Papal States were papal again. Directly or by proxy Caesar gave them such good government as seemed to vindicate his claim to be a deposer of tyrants; later all of them but Urbino and Faenza would mourn his fall.[70]—Hearing that Gianfrancesco Gonzaga (Elisabetta's brother and Isabella's husband) had gone with several other prominent men to Milan to turn Louis XII against him, Caesar hurried across Italy, confronted his enemies, and quickly regained the favor of the King (August, 1502). It is deserving of note that up to this point, and even after his most questionable exploit, a bishop, a king, and a diplomat later famous for subtlety, should have joined in admiring Caesar, and accepting the justice of his conduct and his aims.

Nevertheless Italy was dotted with men who prayed for his fall. Venice, though it had made him an honorary citizen (*gentiluomo di Venezia*), was not happy to see the Papal States so strong again, and controlling so much of the Adriatic shore. Florence fretted at the thought that Forlì, only eight miles from Florentine territory, was in the hands of an incalculable and unscrupulous young genius of statecraft and war. Pisa offered itself to his rule (December, 1502); he politely refused; but what if he changed his course —as on the way to Camerino? The gifts that Isabella sent him were perhaps a blind to disguise the resentment she and Mantua felt against his rape of Urbino. The Colonna and Savelli, and in less degree the Orsini, had been ruined by his victories, and merely bided their time to raise some coalition against him. His own "best men," who had led his cohorts brilliantly, were not sure but that he might attack their territories next, some of which were also claimed by the Church. Gianpaolo Baglioni trembled for his hold on Perugia, Giovanni Bentivoglio for his rule in Bologna; Paolo Orsini and Francesco Orsini, Duke of Gravina, wondered how long it would be before Caesar would do to the Orsini clan what he had done to the Colonna. Vitelli, raging at being forced to relinquish Arezzo, invited these men, and Oliverotto of Fermo, and Pandolfo Petrucci of Siena, and representatives of Guidobaldo, to meet at La Magione on Lake Trasimene (September, 1502). There they agreed to turn their troops against Caesar, capture and depose him, end his rule in the Romagna and the Marches, and restore the dispossessed lords. It was a formidable plot, whose success would have brought to a sorry issue the best-laid plans of Alexander and his son.

The conspiracy began with brilliant victories. Revolts were organized in Urbino and Camerino, with the support of the people; the papal garrisons there were expelled; Guidobaldo returned to his palace (October 18, 1502); everywhere the fallen lords raised their heads and planned to return to power. Caesar suddenly found that his lieutenants would not obey him, and that his forces were reduced to a point where he could not possibly hold his conquests. In this crisis Cardinal Ferrari opportunely died; Alexander hurriedly appropriated the 50,000 ducats left by him, and sold some of the Cardinal's benefices; he turned over the receipts to Caesar, who rapidly raised a new army of six thousand men. In the meantime Alexander negotiated individually with the conspirators, made them fair promises, and won so many of them back to obedience that by the end of October they had all made their peace with Caesar; it was an astonishing feat of diplomacy. Caesar received their apologies with silent skepticism; and he noted that though Guidobaldo again fled from Urbino, the Orsini still held the duchy's strongholds with their troops.

In December Caesar's lieutenants, at his bidding, besieged Senigallia, on the Adriatic. The town soon yielded, but the governor of the castle refused to surrender it except to Caesar himself. A messenger was sent to the Duke at Cesena; he hastened down the coast, followed by twenty-eight hundred soldiers especially devoted to him. Arriving at Senigallia he greeted with apparent cordiality the four leaders of the conspiracy—Vitellozzo Vitelli, Paolo and Francesco Orsini, and Oliverotto. He invited them to a conference with him in the governor's palace; when they came he had them arrested; and that very night (December 31, 1502) he had Vitelli and Oliverotto strangled. The two Orsini were kept in prison till Caesar could communicate with his father; apparently Alexander's views agreed with his son's; and on January 18 the two men were put to death.[71]

Caesar prided himself on his clever stroke at Senigallia; he thought Italy should thank him for ridding it so neatly of four men who were not only feudal usurpers of Church lands but had been reactionary oppressors of helpless subjects. Perhaps he felt a qualm or two, for he excused himself to Machiavelli: "It is proper to snare those who are proving themselves past masters in the art of snaring others."[72] Machiavelli fully agreed with him, and considered Caesar, at this time, the bravest and wisest man in Italy. Paolo Giovio, historian and bishop, called the quadruple extinction of the conspirators *bellissimo inganno*—a "most lovely ruse."[73] Isabella d'Este, playing safe, sent Caesar congratulations, and a hundred masks to amuse him "after the fatigues and struggles of this glorious expedition." Louis XII hailed the coup as "a deed worthy of the great days of Rome."[74]

Alexander was now free to express his full rage at the conspiracy against his son and the reclaimed cities of the Church. He claimed to have evidence that Cardinal Orsini had plotted with his relatives to assassinate Caesar;[75] he had the Cardinal and several other suspects arrested (January 3, 1503); he seized the Cardinal's palace, and confiscated all his goods. The Cardinal died in prison on February 22, probably through excitement and exhaustion; Rome speculated that the Pope had had him poisoned. Alexander advised Caesar to root out the Orsini completely from Rome and the Campagna. Caesar was not so anxious; perhaps he too was exhausted; he delayed returning to the capital, and then set out unwillingly[76] to besiege Giulio Orsini's mighty fortress at Ceri (March 14, 1503). In this siege—perhaps in others—Borgia used some of Leonardo's war machines; one was a movable tower holding three hundred men and capable of being raised to the top of the enemy's walls.[77] Giulio surrendered, and went with Caesar to the Vatican to ask for peace; the Pope granted it on condition that all Orsini castles in papal territory should be given up to the Church; it was done. In the meantime Perugia and Fermo had quietly accepted the governors sent them by Caesar. Bologna was still unredeemed, but Ferrara had joyfully received Lucrezia Borgia as its duchess. Aside from these two major principalities—which would occupy Alexander's successors—the reconquest of the Papal States was complete, and Caesar Borgia, at twenty-eight, found himself the governor of a realm equaled in size, in the peninsula, only by the Kingdom of Naples. He was now by common consent the most remarkable and powerful man in Italy.

For a time he remained in unwonted quiet at the Vatican. We should have expected him at this point to send for his wife; he did not. He had left her with her family in France, and she had borne him a child during his wars; occasionally he wrote to her and sent her gifts; but he never saw her again. The Duchesse de Valentinois lived a modest and retired life in Bourges, or in the château de La Motte-Feuilly in the Dauphiné, waiting hopefully to be sent for, or to have her husband come to her. When he was ruined and deserted she tried to go to him; when he died she hung her house with black, and remained in mourning for him until her death. Perhaps he would have sent for her later, had he been given more than a few months of peace; more likely he looked upon the marriage as purely political, and felt no obligation to tenderness. There was apparently only a modicum of tenderness in him, and he kept most of that for Lucrezia, whom he loved as much as he could love a woman. Even when hurrying from Urbino to Milan to circumvent his foes with Louis XII, he had gone considerably out of his way to visit his sister at Ferrara, then dangerously ill. Returning from Milan he stopped there again, held her in his arms while physicians bled her, and stayed with her till she was out of danger.[78] Caesar was not made for marriage; he had mistresses, but none for long; he was too consumed by the will to power to let any woman enter possessively into his life.

In Rome he lived in privacy, almost in concealment. He worked at night and was rarely seen by day. But he worked hard, even in this period of seeming rest; he kept close watch on his appointees in the States of the Church, punished those who misused their position, had one appointee put to death for cruelty and exploitation, and always found time to see men who needed his instructions on the government of the Romagna or the maintenance of order in Rome. Those who knew him respected his shrewd intelligence, his capacity for going directly to the heart of the matter, for seizing every opportunity that chance presented, and for taking quick, decisive, and effective action. He was popular with his soldiers, who secretly admired the saving severity of his discipline. They highly approved of the bribes, stratagems, and deceits by which he reduced the number and persistence of his enemies and the battles and casualties of his troops.[79] Diplomats were chagrined to find that this swift-moving and fearless young general could outthink them and outreason them in their shrewdest subtleties, and could, at need, match all their charm and tact and eloquence.[80]

His flair for secrecy made him an easy victim for the satirists of Italy, and for the ugly rumors that hostile ambassadors or deposed aristocrats might invent or spread; it is impossible today to separate fact from fiction in these lurid reports. A favorite story was that Alexander and his son made a practice of arresting rich ecclesiastics on trumped up charges, and releasing them on the payment of large ransoms or fines; so, it was alleged, the bishop of Cesena, for a crime whose nature was not divulged, was cast into Sant' Angelo, and was freed on paying 10,000 ducats to the Pope.[81] We cannot say whether this was justice or robbery; in fairness to Alexander we should bear in mind that it was then the custom of both secular and ecclesiastical courts to make crime pay the court by replacing expensive imprisonment with lucrative fines. According to the Venetian ambassador Giustiniani and the Florentine ambassador Vittorio Soderini, Jews were frequently arrested on charges of heresy, and could prove their orthodoxy only by substantial contributions to the papal treasury.[82] It is possible; but Rome was known for its relatively decent treatment of the Jews, and no Jew was considered a heretic—or was prosecuted by the Inquisition—for being a Jew.

Many rumors charged the Borgias with poisoning rich cardinals to accelerate the reversion of their estates to the Church. Some such casualties seemed so well attested—rather by repetition than by evidence—that Protestant historians generally accepted them as late as the judicious Jacob Burckhardt (1818-97);[83] and the Catholic historian Pastor believed it "extremely probable that Caesar poisoned Cardinal Michiel in order to obtain the money that he wanted."[84] This conclusion was founded on the fact that under Julius II (extremely hostile to Alexander) a subdeacon, Aquino da Colloredo, being put to the torture, confessed that he had poisoned Cardinal Michiel at the behest of Alexander and Caesar.[85] A twentieth-century historian may be excused for being skeptical of confessions elicited by torture.

An enterprising statistician has shown that the death rate among cardinals was no higher in Alexander's pontificate than before or afterward;[86] but there is no doubt that Rome, in the last three years of that reign, thought it dangerous to be a cardinal and rich.[87] Isabella d'Este wrote to her husband to be careful what he said about Caesar, for "he does not scruple to conspire against those of his own blood";[88] apparently she accepted the tale that he had killed the Duke of Gandia. Roman gossip talked about a slow poison, *cantarella*, whose base was arsenic, and which, dropped as a powder upon food or into drink—even into the sacramental wine of the Mass—would produce a leisurely death difficult to trace to its human cause. Historians now generally reject the slow poisons of the Renaissance as legendary, but believe that in one or two cases the Borgias poisoned rich cardinals.[89]* Further research may reduce these cases to zero.

Worse stories were told of Caesar. To amuse Alexander and Lucrezia, we are assured, he released into a courtyard several prisoners who had been sentenced to death, and, from a safe point, showed his bowmanship by shooting fatal arrows into one after another of the convicts as they sought some refuge from his shafts.[90] Our sole authority for this tale is the Venetian envoy Capello; it is rather less probable that Caesar did this than that a diplomat should lie. Much history of the Renaissance popes has been written on the authority of war propaganda and diplomatic lies.

The most incredible of the Borgia horrors appears in the usually reliable diary of Alexander's master of ceremonies, Burchard. Under October 30, 1501, the *Diarium* describes a dinner in the apartment of Caesar Borgia in the Vatican, at which nude courtesans chased chestnuts scattered over the floor while Alexander and Lucrezia looked on.[91] The story appears also in the Perugian historian Matarazzo, who took it not from Burchard (for the *Diarium* was still secret) but from gossip that ranged out of Rome through Italy; "the thing was known far and wide," he says.[92] If so, it is strange that the Ferrarese ambassador, who was in Rome at the time, and was later commissioned to investigate the morals of Lucrezia and her fitness to marry Alfonso, son of Duke Ercole, made no mention of the story in his report, but (as we shall see) gave a most favorable account of her; either he was bribed by Alexander, or he ignored unverified gossip. But how did the story get into Burchard's diary? He does not profess to have been present,

---

* "The general tendency of investigation, while utterly shattering all idle attempts to represent Alexander as a model pope, has been to relieve him of the most odious imputations against his character. There remains the charge of secret poisoning from motives of cupidity, which indeed appears established, or nearly so, only in a single instance; but this may imply others."—Richard Garnett in *The Cambridge Modern History*, I, 242.

and could hardly be, for he was a man of sturdy morals. Normally he included in his notes only such events as he had witnessed, or such as had been reported to him on good authority. Was the story interpolated into the manuscript? Of the original manuscript only twenty-six pages survive, all concerning the period following Alexander's final illness. Of the remainder of the *Diarium* only copies exist. All these copies carry the story. It may have been interpolated by a hostile scribe who thought to liven a dry chronicle with a juicy tale; or Burchard may for once have allowed gossip to creep into his notes, or the original may have marked it as gossip. Probably the story was based on an actual banquet, and the lurid fringe was added by fancy or spite. The Florentine ambassador Francesco Pepi, always hostile to the Borgias since Florence was almost always at odds with them, reported, on the morrow of the affair, that the Pope had stayed up till a late hour in the apartments of Caesar the night before, and there had been "dancing and laughter";[93] there is no mention of the courtesans. It is incredible that a pope who was at this time making every effort to marry his daughter to the heir of the duchy of Ferrara should have risked the marriage and a vital diplomatic alliance by allowing Lucrezia to witness such a spectacle.[94]

But let us look at Lucrezia.

V. LUCREZIA BORGIA: 1480-1519

Alexander admired, perhaps feared, his son, but he loved his daughter with all the emotional intensity of his nature. He seems to have taken profounder pleasure in her moderate beauty, in her long golden hair (so heavy that it gave her headaches), in the rhythm of her light form dancing,[95] and in the filial devotion that she gave him through all contumely and bereavements, than he had ever derived from the charms of Vanozza or Giulia. She was not particularly fair, but she was described in her youth as *dolce ciera*, sweet face; and amid all the coarseness and looseness of her times and her environment, through all the disillusionments of divorce and the horror of seeing her husband murdered almost before her eyes, she kept this "sweet face" to her pious end, for it was a frequent theme in Ferrarese poetry. Pinturicchio's portrait of her, in the Borgia apartment of the Vatican, agrees well with this description of her in her youth.

Like all Italian girls who could afford it, she went to a convent for her education. At an unknown age she passed from the house of her mother Vanozza to that of Donna Adriana Mila, a cousin of Alexander. There she formed a lifelong friendship with Adriana's daughter-in-law Giulia Farnese, alleged mistress of her father. Favored with every good fortune except legitimacy, Lucrezia grew up in a gay and joyous girlhood, and Alexander was happy in her happiness.

This carefree youth was ended by marriage. Probably she was not offended when her father chose a husband for her; that was then normal procedure for all good girls, and produced no more unhappiness than our own reliance on the selective wisdom of romantic love. Alexander, like any ruler, thought that the marriages of his children should advance the interests of the state; this too, doubtless, seemed reasonable to Lucrezia. Naples was then hostile to the papacy, and Milan was hostile to Naples; so her first marriage bound her, at the age of thirteen, to Giovanni Sforza, aged twenty-six, lord of Pesaro and nephew to Lodovico, regent of Milan (1493). Alexander amused himself paternally by arranging a handsome home for the couple in Cardinal Zeno's palace, close to the Vatican.

But Sforza had to live at Pesaro part of the time, and took his young bride with him. She languished on those distant shores, far from her doting father and the excitement and splendor of Rome; and after a few months she returned to the capital. Later Giovanni joined her there; but after Easter of 1497 he stayed at Pesaro and she at Rome. On June 14 Alexander asked him to consent to an annulment on the ground of the husband's impotence—the only ground recognized by canon law for annulling a valid marriage. Lucrezia, whether in grief or in shame, or to circumvent scandalmongers, retired to a convent.[96] A few days later her brother the Duke of Gandia was slain, and the delicate wits of Rome suggested that he had been murdered by agents of Sforza for attempting to seduce Lucrezia.[97] Her husband denied his impotence, and hinted that Alexander was guilty of incest with his daughter. The Pope appointed a committee, headed by two cardinals, to inquire into whether the marriage had ever been consummated; Lucrezia took oath that it had not, and they assured Alexander that she was still a virgin. Lodovico proposed to Giovanni that he should demonstrate his potency before a committee including the papal legate at Milan; Giovanni forgivably refused. However, he signed a formal admission that the marriage had not been consummated; he returned to Lucrezia her dowry of 31,000 ducats; and on December 20, 1497, the marriage was annulled. Lucrezia, who had borne no offspring to Giovanni, bore children to both her later husbands; but Sforza's third wife, in 1505, gave birth to a son presumably his own.[98]

It was formerly assumed that Alexander had broken the marriage in order to make a politically more profitable marriage; there is no evidence for this assumption; it is more likely that Lucrezia told the pitiful truth of the matter. But Alexander could not let her remain husbandless. Seeking a *rapprochement* with the papacy's bitter enemy, Naples, he proposed to King Federigo the union of Lucrezia with Don Alfonso, Duke of Bisceglie, the bastard son of Federigo's heir Alfonso II. The King agreed, and a formal betrothal was signed (June, 1498). Federigo's proxy on this occasion was Cardinal Sforza, uncle to the divorced Giovanni. Lodovico of Milan also had encouraged Federigo to accept the plan.[99] Apparently Giovanni's uncles felt no resentment at the annulment of his marriage. In August the wedding was celebrated in the Vatican.

Lucrezia facilitated matters by falling in love with her husband. It helped that she could mother him, for she was eighteen now, and he was a child of seventeen. But it was their misfortune to be important; politics entered even their marriage bed. Caesar Borgia, rejected in Naples, went to France for a bride (October, 1498); Alexander entered into alliance with Louis XII, the declared enemy of Naples; the young Duke of Bisceglie was increasingly ill at ease in a Rome filling up with French agents; suddenly he fled to Naples. Lucrezia was brokenhearted. To appease her and heal the breach, Alexander appointed her regent of Spoleto (August, 1499); Alfonso rejoined her there; Alexander visited them at Nepi, reassured the youth, and brought them back to Rome. There Lucrezia was delivered of a son, who was named Rodrigo after her father.

But again their happiness was brief. Whether because Alfonso was uncontrollably high-strung, or because Caesar Borgia symbolized the French alliance, Alfonso took a passionate dislike to him, which Borgia disdainfully returned. On the night of July 15, 1500, some bravos attacked Alfonso as he was leaving St. Peter's. He received several wounds, but managed to reach the house of the Cardinal of Santa Maria in Portico. Lucrezia, summoned to him, fainted on seeing his condition; she soon recovered, and, with his sister Sancia, tended him anxiously. Alexander sent a guard of sixteen men to protect him from further injury. Alfonso slowly convalesced. One day he saw Caesar walking in a nearby garden. Convinced that this was the man who had hired his assassins, Alfonso seized bow and arrow, aimed at Caesar, and shot to kill. The weapon narrowly missed its mark. Caesar was not the man to give an enemy a second chance; he called his guards and sent them up to Alfonso's room, apparently with orders to slay him; they pressed a pillow upon his face until he died, perhaps under the eyes of his sister and his wife.[100] Alexander accepted Caesar's account of the matter, gave Alfonso a quiet burial, and did what he could to console the inconsolable Lucrezia.

She retired to Nepi, and there signed her letters *la infelicissima principessa*, "the most miserable princess," and ordered Masses for the repose of Alfonso's soul. Strange to relate, Caesar visited her at Nepi (October 1, 1499) only two and a half months after Alfonso's death, and stayed overnight as her guest. Lucrezia was malleable and patient; she seems to have looked upon the killing of her husband as the natural reaction of her brother to an attempt upon his life. She does not appear to have believed that Caesar had hired the unsuccessful assassins of Alfonso, though this seems the most probable explanation of another Renaissance mystery. During the remainder of her life she gave many proofs that her love for her brother had survived all trials. Perhaps because he too, like her father, loved her with Spanish intensity, the wits of Rome, or rather of hostile Naples,[101] continued to accuse her of incest; one synoptic scribe called her "the Pope's daughter, wife, and daughter-in-law."[102] This, too, she bore with quiet resignation. All students of the epoch are now agreed that these charges were cruel calumnies,[103] but such libels formed her fame for centuries.*

That Caesar killed Alfonso with a view to remating her to better political result is improbable. After a period of mourning she was offered to an Orsini, then to a Colonna—matches hardly as advantageous as that with the son of the heir to the Neapolitan throne. Not till November, 1500, do we hear of Alexander proposing her to Duke Ercole of Ferrara for Ercole's son Alfonso;[104] and not till September, 1501, was she betrothed to him. Presumably Alexander hoped that a Ferrara ruled by a son-in-law, and a Mantua long since bound to Ferrara by marriage, would in effect be papal states; and Caesar seconded the plan as offering greater security for his conquests, and an elegant background for an attack upon Bologna. Ercole and Alfonso hesitated, for reasons already retailed. Alfonso had been offered the hand of the Countess of Angoulême, but Alexander topped his offer with the pledge of an immense dowry, and practical remission of the annual tribute that Ferrara had been paying to the papacy. Even so, it is hardly credible that one of the oldest and most prosperous ruling families in Europe would have received Lucrezia as wife to the future duke had it believed the lurid stories bandied about by the intellectual underworld of Rome. As neither Ercole nor Alfonso had yet seen Lucrezia, they followed customary procedure in such diplomatic matings, and asked the Ferrarese

---

* Cf. *Cambridge Modern History*, I, 239: "Nothing could be less like the real Lucrezia than the Lucrezia of the dramatists and romancers."

ambassador in Rome to send them a report on her person, her morals, and her accomplishments. He replied as follows:

> Illustrious Master: Today after supper Don Gerardo Saraceni and I betook ourselves to the Illustrious Madonna Lucrezia to pay our respects in the name of Your Excellency and His Majesty Don Alfonso. We had a long conversation regarding various matters. She is a most intelligent and lovely, and also an exceedingly gracious, lady. Your Excellency and the Illustrious Don Alfonso—so we were led to conclude—will be highly pleased with her. Besides being extremely graceful in every way, she is modest, lovable, and decorous. Moreover, she is a devout and God-fearing Christian. Tomorrow she is going to confession, and during Christmas week she will receive communion. She is very beautiful, but her charm of manner is still more striking. In short, her character is such that it is impossible to suspect anything "sinister" of her; but on the contrary we look for only the best . . . Rome, December 23, 1501. . . .
>
> Your Excellency's servant,
Joannes Lucas[105]

The Excellent and Illustrious Estensi were convinced, and sent a magnificent body of knights to escort the bride from Rome to Ferrara. Caesar Borgia equipped two hundred cavaliers to accompany her, and supplied musicians and buffoons to amuse the arduous travel hours. Alexander, proud and happy, provided her with a retinue of 180 persons, including five bishops. Vehicles especially built for the trip, and 150 mules, carried her trousseau; and this included a dress valued at 15,000 ducats ($187,500?), a hat worth 10,000 and 200 bodices costing a hundred ducats each.[106] On January 6, 1502, having privately taken leave of her mother Vanozza, Lucrezia began her bridal tour across Italy to join her fiancé. Alexander, after bidding her good-by, went from point to point on the line of procession to catch another glimpse of her as she rode on her little Spanish horse all caparisoned in harness of leather and gold; he watched until she and her retinue of a thousand men and women were out of sight. He suspected that he would never see her again.

Rome had probably never witnessed such an exit before, nor Ferrara such an entry. After twenty-seven days of travel, Lucrezia was met outside the city by Duke Ercole and Don Alfonso with a superb cavalcade of nobles, professors, seventy-five mounted archers, eighty trumpeters and fifers, and fourteen floats carrying highborn ladies sumptuously dressed. When the procession reached the cathedral two ropewalkers descended from its towers and addressed compliments to Lucrezia. As the ducal palace was reached all prisoners were given their liberty. The people rejoiced in the beauty and smiles of their future duchess; and Alfonso was happy to have so splendid and charming a bride.[107]

VI. THE COLLAPSE OF THE BORGIA POWER

The final years of Alexander were apparently happy and prosperous. His daughter was married into a ducal family, and was respected by all Ferrara; his son had brilliantly accomplished his assignments as general and administrator, and the Papal States were flourishing under excellent government. The Venetian ambassador describes the Pope, in those last years, as cheerful and active, apparently quite easy of conscience; "nothing worries him." He was seventy years old on January 1, 1501, but, reported the ambassador, "he seems to grow younger every day."[108]

On the afternoon of August 5, 1503, Alexander, Caesar, and some others dined in the open air at the villa of Cardinal Adriano da Corneto, not far from the Vatican. All remained in the gardens till midnight, for the heat indoors was exhausting. On the 11th the Cardinal was attacked by a severe fever, which lasted three days and then subsided. On the 12th both the Pope and his son were bedded with fever and vomiting. Rome, as usual, talked of poison; Caesar, said gossip, had ordered the poisoning of the Cardinal to secure his fortune; by mistake the poisoned food had been eaten by nearly all the guests. Historians now agree with the physicians who treated the Pope, that the cause was malarial infection, invited by prolonged exposure to the night air of midsummer Rome.[109] In that same month malarial fever laid low half the household of the Pope, and many of these cases proved fatal;[110] in Rome there were hundreds of deaths from the same cause in that season.

Alexander lingered for thirteen days between life and death, occasionally recovering to the extent of resuming the conferences of diplomacy; on August 13 he played cards. The doctors bled him repeatedly, probably once too much, depleting his natural strength. He died on August 18. Soon afterward the body became black and fetid, lending color to hasty rumors of poison. Carpenters and porters, "joking and blaspheming," says Burchard, had trouble forcing the swollen corpse into the coffin designed for it.[111] Gossip added that a little devil had been seen, at the moment of death, carrying Alexander's soul to hell.[112]

The Romans rejoiced at the passing of the Spanish Pope. Riots broke out, the "Catalans" were chased from the city or were killed in their tracks; their houses were plundered by the mob; one hundred dwellings were burned to the ground. The armed troops of the Colonna and the Orsini entered the city on August 22 and 23, over the protests of the college of cardinals. Said Guicciardini, the patriotic Florentine:

> The whole city of Rome ran together with incredible alacrity, and crowded about the corpse in St. Peter's Church, and were not able to satisfy their eyes with the sight of a dead serpent, who, with his immoderate ambition and detestable treachery, with manifold instances of horrid cruelty and monstrous lust, and exposing to sale all things without distinction, both sacred and profane, had intoxicated the whole world.[113]

Machiavelli agreed with Guicciardini: Alexander

> did nothing but deceive, and thought of nothing else during the whole of his life; nor did any man vow with stronger oaths to observe promises which he afterwards broke. Nevertheless he succeeded in everything, for he was well acquainted with this part of the world.[114]

These condemnations were based on two assumptions: that the tales told of Alexander in Rome were true, and that Alexander was unjustified in the methods that he used to reclaim the Papal States. Catholic historians, while defending Alexander's right to restore the temporal power of the papacy, generally join in condemning Alexander's methods and morals. Says the honest Pastor:

> He was universally described as a monster, and every sort of foul crime was attributed to him. Modern critical research has in many points judged him more fairly and rejected some of the worst accusations made against him. But even though we must beware of accepting without examination all the tales told of Alexander by his contemporaries . . . and though the bitter wit of the Romans found its favorite exercises in tearing him to pieces without mercy, and attributing to him in popular pasquinades and scholarly epigrams a life of incredible foulness, still so much against him has been clearly proved that we are forced to reject the modern attempts at whitewashing him as an unworthy tampering with truth. . . . From the Catholic point of view it is impossible to blame Alexander too severely.[115]

Protestant historians have sometimes shown a generous lenience to Alexander. William Roscoe, in his classic *Life and Pontificate of Leo X* (1827), was among the first to say a good word for the Borgia Pope:

> Whatever were his crimes, there can be no doubt that they have been highly overcharged. That he was devoted to the aggrandizement of his family, and that he employed the authority of his elevated station to establish a permanent dominion in Italy in the person of his son, cannot be doubted; but when almost all the sovereigns of Europe were attempting to gratify their ambition by means equally criminal, it seems unjust to brand the character of Alexander with any peculiar and extraordinary share of infamy in this respect. While Louis of France and Ferdinand of Spain conspired together to seize upon and divide the Kingdom of Naples, by an example of treachery that can never be sufficiently execrated, Alexander might surely think himself justified in suppressing the turbulent barons, who had for ages rent the dominions of the Church with intestine wars, and in subjugating the petty sovereigns of the Romagna, over whom he had an acknowledged supremacy, and who had in general acquired their dominions by means as unjustifiable as those which he adopted against them. With respect to the accusation so generally believed, of a criminal intercourse between him and his own daughter . . . it might not be difficult to show its improbability. In the second place the vices of Alexander were accompanied, though not compensated, by many great qualities, which in the consideration of his character ought not to be passed over in silence. . . . Even by his severest adversaries he is allowed to have been a man of elevated genius, of a wonderful memory, eloquent, vigilant, and dexterous in the management of all his concerns.[116]

Bishop Creighton summarized Alexander's character and achievements in general agreement with Roscoe's judgment, and far more mercifully than Pastor.[117] A later judgment is more favorable still—by the Protestant scholar Richard Garnett in *The Cambridge Modern History*:

> Alexander's character has undoubtedly gained by the scrutiny of modern historians. It was but natural that one accused of so many crimes, and unquestionably the cause of many scandals, should alternately appear as a tyrant and a voluptuary. Neither description suits him. The groundwork of his character was extreme exuberance of nature. The Venetian ambassador calls him a carnal man, not implying anything morally derogatory, but meaning a man of sanguine temperament, unable to control his passions and emotions. This per-

plexed the cool unimpassioned Italians of the diplomatic type then prevalent among rulers and statesmen, and their apprehensions have unduly prejudiced Alexander, who in truth was not less but more human than most princes of his time. This excessive "carnality" wrought in him for good and ill. Unrestrained by moral scruples, or by any spiritual conception of religion, he was betrayed by it into gross sensuality of one kind, though in other respects he was temperate and abstemious. In the more respectable guise of family affection it led him to outrage every principle of justice, though even here he only performed a necessary work which could not, as one of his agents said, have been accomplished by "holy water." On the other hand his geniality and joyousness preserved him from tyranny in the ordinary sense of the term. . . . As a ruler, careful of the material weal of his people, he ranks among the best of his age; as a practical statesman he was the equal of any contemporary. But his insight was impaired by his lack of political morality; he had nothing of the higher wisdom which comprehends the characteristics and foresees the drift of an epoch, and he did not know what a principle was.[118]

Those of us who share Alexander's sensitivity to the charms and graces of woman cannot find it in their hearts to throw stones at him for his amours. His prepapal deviations were no more scandalous than those of Aeneas Sylvius, who fares so well with the historians, or of Julius II, whom time has graciously forgiven. It is not recorded that these two Popes took such care of their mistresses and their children as Alexander did of his. Indeed there was something familial and domestic about Alexander that would have made him a relatively respectable man if the laws of the Church, as well as the customs of Renaissance Italy and Protestant Germany and England, had allowed the marriage of the clergy; his sin was not against nature but against a rule of celibacy soon to be rejected by half of Christendom. We cannot say that his relation with Giulia Farnese was carnal; so far as we know, neither Vanozza, nor Lucrezia, nor Giulia's husband expressed any objection to it; perhaps it was the simple delight of a normal man in the lure and vivacity of a beautiful woman.

Our judgment of Alexander's politics must distinguish between his ends and his means. His purposes were entirely legitimate—to recover the "Patrimony of Peter" (essentially the ancient Latium) from disorderly feudal barons, and to regain from usurping despots the traditional States of the Church. The methods used by Alexander and Caesar in realizing these aims were those used by all other states then and now—war, diplomacy, deceit, treachery, violation of treaties, and desertion of allies. Alexander's abandonment of the Holy League, his purchase of French soldiers and support at the price of surrendering Milan to France, were major crimes against Italy. And those secular means that states use, and consider indispensable, in the lawless jungle of international strife, offend us when employed by a pope pledged to the principles of Christ. Whatever danger the Church ran of becoming subject to some domineering government—as to France at Avignon—if she lost her own territories, it would have been better for her to sacrifice all temporal power, and be as poor again as the Galilean fishermen, than to adopt the ways of the world to achieve her political ends. By adopting them, and financing them, she gained a state and lost a third of Christendom.

Caesar Borgia, slowly recovering from the same illness that had killed the Pope, found himself enmeshed in a dozen unanticipated perils. Who could have foreseen that he and his father would be incapacitated at the same time? While the doctors bled him the Colonna and the Orsini quickly recovered the castles that he had taken from them; the deposed lords of the Romagna, with the encouragement of Venice, began to reclaim their principalities; and the Roman mob, already out of hand, might at any moment, now that Alexander was dead, plunder the Vatican and seize the funds upon which Caesar depended for the payment of his troops. He sent some armed men to the Vatican; they compelled Cardinal Casanuova, at swords' points, to give up the treasury; so Caesar repeated Caesar after fifteen centuries. They brought back to him 100,000 ducats in gold, and 300,000 ducats' worth of plate and jewelry. At the same time he sent galleys and troops to prevent his strongest enemy, Cardinal Giuliano della Rovere, from reaching Rome. He felt that unless he could persuade the conclave to elect a pope favorable to him, he was lost.

The cardinals insisted that the troops of Caesar, the Orsini, and the Colonna should leave Rome before an unintimidated election could be held. All three groups yielded. Caesar retired with his men to Civita Castellana, while Cardinal Giuliano entered Rome and led, in the conclave, the forces hostile to all Borgias. On September 22, 1503, the rival factions in the College chose Cardinal Francesco Piccolomini as a compromise pope. He took the name Pius III, in honor of his uncle Aeneas Sylvius. He was a man of learning and integrity, though he was also the father of a large family.[119] He was sixty-four, and suffered from an abscess in his leg. He was friendly to Caesar, and allowed him to return to Rome. But on October 18 Pius III died.

Caesar saw that he could no longer prevent the election of Cardinal della Rovere, who was clearly the ablest man in the College. In a private interview with Giuliano, Caesar effected an apparent reconciliation: he promised Giuliano the support of the Spanish cardinals (who were loyal to Caesar), and Giuliano promised, if elected, to confirm him as Duke of the Romagna and commander of the papal troops. Some other cardinals Giuliano bought with simple bribery.[120] Giuliano della Rovere was chosen pope (October 31, 1503), and took the name Julius II, as if to say that he too would be a Caesar, and better Alexander. His coronation was postponed till November 26 because the astrologers predicted for that day a propitious conjunction of stars.

Venice did not wait for a lucky star; it seized Rimini, besieged Faenza, and gave every sign of taking over as much of the Romagna as possible before the Church could organize her forces. Julius bade Caesar go to Imola and recruit a new army for the protection of the Papal States. Caesar agreed, and proceeded to Ostia with a view to sailing to Pisa. At Ostia a message from the Pope commanded him to surrender his control of the Romagna fortresses. In a crucial error suggesting that sickness had impaired his judgment, Caesar refused, though it should have been obvious that he was now dealing with a man whose will was at least as strong as his own. Julius ordered him to return to Rome; Caesar obeyed, and was subjected to house arrest. There Guidobaldo, who now not only was restored to Urbino but was the newly appointed commander of the papal armies, came to see the fallen Borgia. Caesar humbled himself before the man whom he had deposed and despoiled, gave him the watchwords of the fortresses, returned to him some precious books and tapestries left from the Urbino pillage, and begged his intercession with Julius. Cesena and Forlì refused to honor the watchwords until Caesar was set at liberty; Julius refused to release him until Caesar persuaded the Romagna castles to yield to the Pope. Lucrezia implored her husband to help her brother; Alfonso (still only heir, not occupant, of the ducal throne) did nothing. She appealed to Isabella d'Este; Isabella did nothing; probably she and Alfonso knew that Julius was immovable. Caesar finally gave the word of surrender to his loyal supporters in the Romagna; the Pope freed him, and he fled to Naples (April 19, 1504).

There he was welcomed by Gonzalo de Córdoba, who gave him a safe-conduct. His courage returning sooner than his good sense, he organized a small force, and was preparing to sail with it to Piombino (near Leghorn) when he was arrested by Gonzalo on orders from Ferdinand of Spain; the

"Catholic King" had been urged to the action by Julius, who did not propose to have Caesar start a civil war. In August Caesar was transported to Spain, and fretted in prison there for two years. Lucrezia again sought to have him freed, but in vain. His deserted wife pled for him with her brother Jean d'Albret, King of Navarre; a plan of escape was devised; and in November, 1506, Caesar was again a free man, at the court of Navarre. He soon found a chance to repay d'Albret. The Count of Lerin, a vassal of the King, rebelled; Caesar led part of Jean's army against the Count's fortress at Viana; the Count made a sortie, which Caesar repulsed; Caesar pursued the defeated too recklessly; the Count, reinforced, turned upon him, Caesar's few troops fled; Caesar, with only one companion, stood his ground, and fought till he was cut down and killed (March 12, 1507). He was thirty-one years old.

It was an honorable end to a questionable life. There are many things in Caesar Borgia that we cannot stomach: his insolent pride, his neglect of his faithful wife, his treatment of women as mere instruments of passing pleasure, his occasional cruelty to his enemies—as when he condemned to death not only Giulio Varano, lord of Camerino, but Giulio's two sons, and apparently ordered the death of the two Manfredi; severities that compare shamefully with the calm mercies of the man whose name he bore. Usually he acted on the principle that the achievement of his purpose justified any means. He found himself surrounded with lies, and managed to lie better than the rest until Julius lied to him. He was almost certainly innocent of his brother Giovanni's death; he was probably the man who set the thugs upon the Duke of Bisceglie. He lacked—perhaps through illness—the strength to face his own misfortunes with courage and dignity. Only his death brought a gleam of nobility into his life.

But even he had virtues. He must have had extraordinary ability to rise so rapidly, to learn so readily the arts of leadership, negotiation, and war. Given the difficult task of restoring, with only a small force at his command, the papal power in the Papal States, he accomplished it with surprising rapidity of movement, skill of strategy, and economy of means. Empowered to govern as well as to conquer, he gave the Romagna the fairest rule and most prosperous peace that it had enjoyed in centuries. Ordered to clear the Campagna of rebellious and troublesome vassals, he did it with a celerity that Julius Caesar himself could hardly have surpassed. With such achievements mounting to his head, he may well have played with the dream that Petrarch and Machiavelli entertained: to give Italy, if necessary by conquest, the unity that would enable her to stand against the centralized strength of France or Spain.* But his victories, his methods, his power, his dark secrecy, his swift incalculable attacks, made him the terror instead of the liberator of Italy. The faults of his character ruined the accomplishments of his mind. It was his basic tragedy that he had never learned to love.

Except, again, Lucrezia. What a contrast she offered to her fallen brother in the modesty and prosperity of her final years! She who in Rome had been the subject and victim of every scandalmonger was loved by the people of Ferrara as a model of feminine virtue.[121] She tried there to forget all the horrors and tribulations of her past; she recaptured, with due restraint, the joyousness of her youth, and added to it a generous interest in the needs of others. Ariosto, Tebaldeo, Bembo, Tito and Ercole Strozzi praised her profitably in their verse; they called her *pulcherrima virgo*, "most beautiful maiden," and no one blinked an eye. Perhaps Bembo tried to play Abélard to her Héloïse, and Lucrezia now became something of a linguist, speaking Spanish, Italian, French, and reading a "little Latin and less Greek." We are told that she wrote poetry in all these tongues.[122] Aldus Manutius dedicated to her his edition of the Strozzi poems, and implied, in the preface, that she had offered to underwrite his great printing enterprise.[123]

Amid all these learned concerns she found time to bear to her third husband four sons and a daughter. Alfonso was well pleased with her in his uneffusive way. In 1506, having occasion to leave Ferrara, he appointed her his regent; and she fulfilled her duties with such good judgment that the Ferrarese were inclined to pardon Alexander for having once left her in charge of the Vatican.

In the last years of her brief life she devoted herself to the education of her children, and to works of charity and mercy; she became a pious Franciscan tertiary. On June 14, 1519, she was delivered of her seventh child, but it was stillborn. She never rose from that bed of pain. On June 24, aged thirty-nine, Lucrezia Borgia, more sinned against than sinning, passed away.

---

* "These nations"—France, Spain, England, Hungary—"had now become great military monarchies, for which" Italy's "loose bundle of petty states was no match. A Cesare Borgia might possibly have saved her if he had wrought at the beginning of the fifteenth century instead of the end. . . . The only considerable approach to consolidation was the establishment of the Papal Temporal Power, of which Alexander and Julius were the chief architects. While the means employed in its creation were often most condemnable, the creation itself was justified by the helpless condition of the Papacy without it, and by the useful end it was to serve when it became the only vestige of dignity and independence left to Italy."—*Cambridge Modern History*, I, 252.

CHAPTER XVII

Julius II

1503-13

I. THE WARRIOR

IF we place before us Raphael's searching and profound portrait of Julius II, we shall see at once that Giuliano della Rovere was one of the strongest personalities that ever reached the papal chair. A massive head bent with exhaustion and tardy humility, a wide high brow, a large pugnacious nose, grave, deep-set, penetrating eyes, lips tight with resolution, hands heavy with the rings of authority, face somber with the disillusionments of power: this is the man who for a decade kept Italy in war and turmoil, freed it from foreign armies, tore down the old St. Peter's, brought Bramante and a hundred other artists to Rome, discovered, developed, and directed Michelangelo and Raphael, and through them gave to the world a new St. Peter's and the Sistine Chapel ceiling, and the *stanze* of the Vatican. *Voilà un homme!*—here is a man.

His violent temper presumably characterized him from his first breath. Born near Savona (1443) a nephew of Sixtus IV, he reached the cardinalate at twenty-seven, and fumed and fretted in it for thirty-three years before being promoted to what had long seemed to him his manifest due. He paid no more regard to his vow of celibacy than most of his colleagues;[1] his master of ceremonies at the Vatican later reported that Pope Julius would not allow his foot to be kissed because it was disfigured *ex morbo gallico* —with the French disease.[2] He had three illegitimate daughters,[3] but he was too busy fighting Alexander to find time for the unconcealed parental fondness that in Alexander so offended the cherished hypocrisies of mankind. He disliked Alexander as a Spanish intruder, denied his fitness for the papacy, called him a swindler and a usurper,[4] and did all he could to unseat him, even to inviting France to invade Italy.

He seemed made as a foil and contrast to Alexander. The Borgia Pope was jovial, sanguine, good-natured (if we except a possible poisoning or two); Julius was stern, Jovian, passionate, impatient, readily moved to anger, passing from one fight to another, never really happy except at war.

Alexander waged war by proxy, Julius in person; the sexagenarian Pope became a soldier, more at ease in military garb than in pontifical robes, loving camps and besieging towns, having guns pointed and assaults delivered under his commanding eyes. Alexander could play, but Julius moved from one enterprise to another, never resting. Alexander could be a diplomat; Julius found it extremely difficult, for he liked to tell people what he thought of them; "often his language overstepped all bounds in its rudeness and violence," and "this fault increased perceptibly as he grew older."[5] His courage, like his language, knew no limits; stricken with illness time and again in his campaigns, he would confound his enemies by recovering and leaping upon them once more.

Like Alexander, he had had to buy a few cardinals to ease his way to the papacy, but he denounced the practice in a bull of 1505. If in this matter he did not reform with inconvenient precipitation, he rejected nepotism almost completely, and rarely appointed relatives to office. In selling church benefices and promotions, however, he followed Alexander's example, and his grants of indulgences shared with the building of St. Peter's in angering Germany.[6] He managed his revenues well, financed war and art simultaneously, and left Leo a surplus in the treasury. In Rome he restored social order, which had declined in Alexander's later years, and he governed the States of the Church with wise appointments and policies. He allowed the Orsini and the Colonna to reoccupy their castles, and sought to tie these powerful families to loyalty by marriages with his relatives.

When he came to power he found the States of the Church in turmoil, and half the work of Alexander and Caesar Borgia undone. Venice had seized Faenza, Ravenna, and Rimini (1503); Giovanni Sforza had returned to Pesaro; the Baglioni were again sovereign in Perugia and the Bentivogli in Bologna; the loss of revenues from these cities threatened the solvency of the Curia. Julius agreed with Alexander that the spiritual independence of the Church required her continued possession of the Papal States; and he began with Alexander's mistake by asking the help of France—and of Germany and Spain to boot—against his Italian enemies. France consented to send eight thousand men in exchange for three red hats; Naples, Mantua, Urbino, Ferrara, and Florence pledged small detachments. In August, 1506, Julius left Rome at the head of his own modest force—four hundred cavalry, his Swiss guards, and four cardinals. Guidobaldo, the restored Duke of Urbino, was in military command of the papal troops, but the Pope rode at their head in person—a sight not seen in Italy for many centuries past. Gianpaolo Baglioni, calculating that he could not defeat such a coalition, came to Orvieto, surrendered to the Pope, and asked forgiveness. "I forgive your mortal sins," growled Julius, "but the first venial sin you commit, I will make you pay for them all."[7] Trusting to his religious authority, Julius entered Perugia with only a small guard, and before his soldiers could reach the gates; Baglioni might have ordered his men to arrest him and close the gates, but he dared not. Machiavelli, who was on hand, marveled that Baglioni should lose a chance "to do a deed which would have left an eternal memory. He might have been the first to show priests how little a man is esteemed who lives and rules as they do. He would have done a deed whose greatness would have outweighed all its infamy and all the danger which might have followed."[8] Machiavelli, like most Italians, objected to the temporal power of the papacy, and to popes who were also kings. But Baglioni valued his neck, and possibly his soul, more than his posthumous fame.

Julius spent little time in Perugia; his real goal was Bologna. He led his little army over the rough roads of the Apennines to Cesena, and then turned upon Bologna from the east while the French attacked it from the west. Julius reinforced the attack by issuing a bull of excommunication against the Bentivogli and their adherents, and offering a plenary indulgence to any man who should kill any of them; this was a new brand of war. Giovanni Bentivoglio fled, and Julius entered the city borne in a litter on men's shoulders, and hailed by the people as a liberator from tyranny (Nov. 11, 1506). He bade Michelangelo make a colossal statue of him for the portal of San Petronio, and then returned to Rome. There he rode through the streets in a triumphal car, and was greeted as a victorious Caesar.

But Venice still held Faenza, Ravenna, Rimini, and failed to estimate properly the martial spirit of the Pope. Risking Italy to get the Romagna, Julius invited France, Germany, and Spain to help him subdue the Queen of the Adriatic. We shall see later how vigorously they responded in the League of Cambrai (1508)—seeking not to help Julius but to dismember Italy; in joining them Julius allowed his justifiable resentment against Venice to overcome his love of Italy. While his allies attacked Venice with armies, Julius aimed at her one of the most forthright bulls of excommunication and interdict in history. He won; Venice restored the stolen cities to the Church, and accepted the most humiliating terms; her envoys received absolution, and the removal of the interdict, in a long ceremony that sorely tried their knees (1510). Regretting his invitation to the French, Julius now reversed his policy to expelling them from Italy, and convinced himself that God was reversing the divine policy accordingly. When the

French ambassador announced to him a French victory over the Venetians, and added, "God willed it," Julius angrily retorted, "The devil willed it!"[9]

Now he turned his martial eye to Ferrara. Here was an acknowledged papal fief, but through Alexander's concessions at Lucrezia's betrothal it paid only a token tribute to the papacy; moreover Duke Alfonso, after joining in war against Venice at the Pope's behest, refused to make peace at his behest, and remained an ally of France. Julius resolved that Ferrara must become wholly a papal state. He began his campaign with another bull of excommunication (1510), by which the son-in-law of one pope became to another a "son of iniquity and a root of perdition." Without much difficulty Julius, with Venetian aid, took Modena. While his troops were resting there the Pope made the mistake of going to Bologna. Suddenly news came to him that a French army, instructed to help Alfonso, was at the gates. The papal forces were too distant to help him; within Bologna were only nine hundred soldiers; and the people of the city, who had been oppressed by the papal legate Cardinal Alidosi, could not be relied upon to offer resistance to the French. Sick abed with fever, Julius for a moment despaired, and thought of drinking poison;[10] he was about to sign a humiliating peace with France when Spanish and Venetian reinforcements arrived. The French retreated, and Julius sped them on their way with a lusty excommunication for one and all.

Meanwhile Ferrara had armed itself so strongly that Julius judged his forces inadequate to take it. Not to be cheated of military glory, he led his troops in person to besiege Mirandola, a northern outpost of the Ferrara duchy (1511). Though now sixty-eight he tramped through deep snow, violated precedent by campaigning in winter, presided over councils of strategy, directed operations and the placement of cannon, inspected his troops, relished the life of a soldier, and let no man surpass him in martial oaths and jests.[11] Sometimes the troops laughed at him; more often they applauded his courage. When enemy fire killed a servant at his side, he moved to other quarters; when these too were reached by Mirandola's artillery, he returned to his first station, shrugging his bent shoulders at the danger of death. Mirandola surrendered after two weeks of resistance. The Pope ordered that all French soldiers found in the city should be put to death; perhaps by mutual arrangement none was found. He protected the city from pillage, and preferred to feed and finance his army by selling eight new cardinalates.[12]

He sought rest in Bologna, but there he was soon again besieged by the French. He fled to Rimini, and the French restored the Bentivogli to power. The people cheered the return of their ousted despots; they demolished the castle that Julius had built, threw down the statue that Michelangelo had made of him, and sold it as bronze scrap to Alfonso of Ferrara; the grim Duke cast it into a cannon, which he christened La Giulia in honor of the Pope. Julius launched another bull, excommunicating all who had shared in the overthrow of papal authority at Bologna. The French troops responded by retaking Mirandola. At Rimini Julius found affixed to the door of San Francesco a document signed by nine cardinals, which summoned a general council to meet at Pisa on September 1, 1511, to examine into the conduct of the Pope.

Julius returned to Rome broken in health, overwhelmed with disaster, but not bowing to defeat. Says Guicciardini:

> Though the Pontiff found himself so grossly deceived by his flattering hopes, yet he seemed in his deportment to resemble what the fabulous writers have reported of Antaeus, who, as often as he was disabled by the force of Hercules, on touching the ground recovered still greater strength and vigor. Adversity had the same effect on the Pope; for when he seemed to be most depressed and most dejected, he recovered his spirits, and rose again with greater firmness and constancy of mind, and with more pertinacious resolution.[13]

To counter the disaffected cardinals, he published a call for a general council to meet at the Lateran Palace on April 19, 1512. He labored night and day to build a formidable alliance against France. He was approaching success when he was seized with a severe illness (August 17, 1511). For three days he hovered near death; on August 21 he remained unconscious so long that the cardinals prepared for a conclave to choose his successor; at the same time Pompeo Colonna, Bishop of Rieti, appealed to the Roman people to rise against papal rule of their city, and re-establish Rienzo's republic. But on the 22nd Julius regained consciousness; overruling his doctors, he drank a substantial draft of wine; he surprised all, and disappointed many, by recovering; the republican movement faded away. On October 5 he announced that he had formed a Holy League of the papacy, Venice, and Spain; on November 17 Henry VIII joined it for England. So reinforced, he deposed from their dignities the cardinals who had signed the summons to Pisa, and forbade such a council to meet. At the command of the French king the Florentine Signory gave permission for the banned council to meet at Pisa; Julius declared war upon Florence, and plotted to restore the Medici. A group of twenty-seven ecclesiastics, with representatives of the king of France and some French universities, met at Pisa (November 5, 1511); but the inhabitants were so threatening, and Florence so reluctant, that the council retired to Milan (November 12). There, under the protection of the French garrison, the schismatic councilors could bear in timid safety the taunts of the people.

Having won this battle of the bishops, Julius turned again to war. He purchased the alliance of the Swiss, who despatched an army to attack the French at Milan; the attack failed, and the Swiss returned to their cantons. On Easter Sunday, April 11, 1512, the French under Gaston de Foix, decisively helped by Alfonso's artillery, overwhelmed the composite army of the League at Ravenna; practically all the Romagna passed under French control. Julius' cardinals begged him to make peace; he refused. The council at Milan celebrated the victory by proclaiming the Pope deposed; Julius laughed. On May 2 he was carried in his litter to the Lateran Palace, where he opened the Fifth Lateran Council. He soon left it to its own slow development while he hurried back to battle.

On May 17 he announced that Germany had joined the Holy League against France. The Swiss, repurchased, entered Italy through the Tirol, and advanced to meet a French army disorganized by victory and the death of their leader. Now outnumbered, the French abandoned Ravenna, Bologna, even Milan; and the schismatic cardinals retreated to France. Once more the Bentivogli fled, and Julius was master of Bologna and the Romagna. He seized the opportunity to take also Parma and Piacenza; and now he could hope to win Ferrara, which could no longer rely on aid from France. Alfonso offered to come to Rome and ask for absolution and terms of peace if the Pope would give him a safe-conduct. Julius did, Alfonso came, and was graciously absolved; but when he refused to exchange Ferrara for little Asti, Julius pronounced his safe-conduct invalid, and threatened him with imprisonment and arrest. Fabrizio Colonna, who had conveyed the safe-conduct to the Duke, felt that his own honor was involved; he helped Alfonso to escape from Rome; after arduous adventures Alfonso made his way back to Ferrara, and there resumed the arming of his forts and walls.

And now at last the demonic energy of the warrior Pope ran out. Late in January, 1513, he took to his bed with a complication of ailments. Merciless gossip said that his trouble was an aftermath of the "French disease"; others that it came from immoderate eating and drinking.[14] When no treatment availed to reduce his fever, he reconciled himself to death, gave instructions for his funeral, urged the Lateran Council to go on with its work without interruption, confessed himself a great sinner, bade farewell to his cardinals, and died with the same courage with which he had lived (February 20, 1513). All Rome mourned him, and an unprecedented throng came to bid him good-by, and to kiss the feet of the corpse.

We cannot estimate his place in history until we have studied him as the liberator of Italy, as the builder of St. Peter's, and as the greatest patron of art that the papacy has ever known. But his contemporaries were right in viewing him chiefly as a statesman and a warrior. They feared his incalculable energy, his *terribilità*, his curses and apparently unappeasable wrath; but they sensed behind all his violence a spirit capable of compassion and love.* They saw him defending the Papal States as unscrupulously and ruthlessly as the Borgias, but with no view to aggrandize his family; all but his enemies applauded his aims, even when they shuddered at his language and mourned his means. He did not govern the reclaimed states as well as Caesar Borgia had done, for he was too fond of war to be a good administrator; but his conquests were lasting, and the Papal States remained henceforth loyal to the Church until the revolution of 1870 ended the temporal power of the popes. Julius sinned—like Venice, Lodovico, Alexander—by calling foreign armies into Italy; but he succeeded better than his predecessors and successors in freeing Italy from these powers when they had served his turn. Perhaps he weakened Italy in saving it, and taught the "barbarians" that they might fight out their quarrels on the sunny plains of Lombardy. There were elements of cruelty in his greatness; he was misled by acquisitiveness in attacking Ferrara and in taking Piacenza and Parma; he dreamed not only of preserving the legitimate possessions of the Church but of making himself the master of Europe, the dictator to kings. Guicciardini condemned him for "bringing empire to the Apostolic See by arms and the shedding of Christian blood, rather than troubling himself to set an example of holy life";[16] but it could hardly be expected of Julius, in his place and age, that he should abandon the Papal States to Venice and other assailants, and risk the survival of the Church on purely spiritual grounds, when all the world about him recognized no rights but those that armed themselves with power. He was what he had to be in the circumstances and atmosphere of his time; and his time forgave him.

II. ROMAN ARCHITECTURE: 1492-1513

The most lasting part of his work was his patronage of art. Under him the Renaissance moved its capital from Florence to Rome, and there

---

* Cf. his fondness for Federigo, son of Isabella d'Este. Gossip did not scruple to put the vilest interpretation on this affection.[15]

reached its zenith in art, as under Leo X it would reach its peak in literature and scholarship. Julius did not care much for literature; it was too
quiet and feminine for his temperament; but the monumental in art accorded well with his nature and life. So he subordinated all other arts to
architecture, and left a new St. Peter's as an index of his spirit and a symbol
of the Church whose secular power he had saved. That he should have
financed Bramante, Michelangelo, Raphael, and a hundred more, as well as
a dozen wars, and have left 700,000 florins in the papal treasury, is one of
the wonders of history, and one of the causes of the Reformation.

No other man ever brought so many artists to Rome. It was he, for
example, who invited Guillaume de Marcillat from France to set up the
fine stained-glass windows of Santa Maria del Popolo. It was characteristic
of his vast conceptions that he should try to reconcile Christianity and paganism in art as Nicholas V had done in letters; for what are the *stanze* of
Raphael but a pre-established harmony of classic mythology and philosophy, Hebrew theology and poetry, Christian sentiment and faith? And
what could better represent the union of pagan and Christian art and feeling
than the portico and dome, the interior columns, statuary, paintings, and
tombs of St. Peter's? Prelates and nobles, bankers and merchants, now
crowding into an enriched Rome, followed the Pope's lead, and built palaces with almost imperial splendor in opulent rivalry. Broad avenues were
cut through or from the chaos of the medieval city; hundreds of new streets
were opened; one of them still bears the great Pope's name. Ancient Rome
rose out of its ruins, and became again the home of a Caesar.

St. Peter's aside, it was, in Rome, an age of palaces rather than of
churches. Exteriors were uniform and plain: a vast rectangular façade of
brick or stone or stucco, a portal of stone usually carved in some decorative
design; on each floor uniform rows of windows, topped with triangular or
elliptical pediments; and almost always a crowning cornice whose elegant
configuration was a special test and care of the architect. Behind this
unpretentious front the millionaires concealed a luxury of ornament and
display seldom revealed to the jealous popular eye: a central well, usually
surrounded or divided by a broad staircase of marble; on the ground floor,
simple rooms for transacting business or storing goods; on the first (our
second) floor, the *piano nobile*, the spacious halls for reception and entertainment, and galleries of art, with pavements of marble or sturdy colored
tile; the furniture, carpets, and textiles of exquisite material and form; the
walls strengthened with marble pilasters, the ceilings coffered in circles,
triangles, diamonds, or squares; and on walls and ceilings paintings by

famous artists, usually of pagan themes—for fashion now decreed that Christian gentlemen, even of the cloth, should live amid scenes from classical mythology; and on the upper floors the private chambers for lords and ladies, for liveried lackeys, for children and nurses, tutors and governesses and maids. Many men were rich enough to have, besides their palaces, rural villas as refuges from the city's din or summer heat; and these villas too might conceal sybaritic glories of ornament and comfort, and mural masterpieces by Raphael, Peruzzi, Giulio Romano, Sebastiano del Piombo. . . . This palace and villa architecture was in many ways a selfish art, in which the wealth drawn from unseen and countless laborers and distant lands vaunted itself in gaudy decoration for a few; in this respect ancient Greece and medieval Europe had shown a finer spirit, devoting their wealth not to private luxury but to the temples and cathedrals that were the possession, pride, and inspiration of all, the home of the people as well as the house of God.

Of the architects outstanding at Rome in the pontificates of Alexander VI and Julius II two were brothers, and a third was their nephew. Giuliano da Sangallo began as a military engineer in the Florentine army; passed to the service of Ferrante of Naples; and became a friend of Giuliano della Rovere in the early days of the latter's cardinalate. For Giuliano, the cardinal, Giuliano the architect turned the abbey of Grottaferrata into a castle-fortress; probably at Alexander's behest he designed the great coffered ceiling of Santa Maria Maggiore, and gilded it with the first gold brought from America. He accompanied Cardinal della Rovere into exile, built a palace for him in Savona, went with him to France, and returned to Rome when his patron at last became pope. Julius invited him to submit plans for the new St. Peter's; when those of Bramante were preferred the old architect reproached the new Pope, but Julius knew what he wanted. Sangallo outlived both Bramante and Julius, and was later appointed *administer et coadiutor* to Raphael in the building of St. Peter's; but he died two years later. Meanwhile his younger brother Antonio da Sangallo had also come from Florence, as architect and military engineer for Alexander VI, and had built the imposing church of Santa Maria di Loreto for Julius; and a nephew, Antonio Picconi da Sangallo, had begun (1512) the most magnificent of the Renaissance palaces of Rome—the Palazzo Farnese.

The greatest name in the architecture of this age was that of Donato Bramante. He was already fifty-six when he came from Milan to Rome (1499), but his study of the Roman ruins fired him with youthful zeal to apply classical forms to Renaissance building. In the court of a Franciscan convent near San Pietro in Montorio he designed a circular Tempietto, or Little Temple, with columns and cupola so classical in form that architects studied and measured it as if it had been a newly discovered masterpiece of ancient art. From that beginning Bramante passed through a succession of *chefs-d'oeuvre:* the cloister of Santa Maria della Pace, the elegant *cortile* of San Damaso . . . Julius overwhelmed him with assignments, both as architect and as military engineer. Bramante laid out the Via Giulia, finished the Belvedere, began the Loggie of the Vatican, and designed a new St. Peter's. He was so interested in his work that he cared little for money, and Julius had to command him to accept appointments whose revenue would main-tain him;[17] some rivals, however, accused him of embezzling papal funds and using shoddy materials in his buildings.[18] Others described him as a jovial and generous soul, whose home became a favorite resort of Perugino, Signorelli, Pinturicchio, Raphael, and other artists in Rome.

The Belvedere was a summer palace built for Innocent VIII, and situated on a hill some hundred yards away from the rest of the Vatican. It took its name from the beautiful view (*bel vedere*) that extended before it; and it gave its name to various sculptures that were housed in it or its court. Julius had long been a collector of ancient art; his prize possession was an *Apollo* discovered during the pontificate of Innocent VIII; when he became Pope he placed it in the *cortile* of the Belvedere, and the *Apollo Belvedere* became one of the famous statues of the world. Bramante gave the palace a new façade and garden court, and planned to connect it with the Vatican proper by a series of picturesque structures and gardens, but both he and Julius died before the plan could be carried out.

If we attribute the Reformation proximately to the sale of indulgences for the building of St. Peter's, the most momentous event in the pontificate of Julius was the demolition of the old St. Peter's and the beginning of the new. According to the received tradition the old church had been built by Pope Sylvester I (326) over the grave of the Apostle Peter near the Circus of Nero. In that church many emperors, from Charlemagne on-ward, had been crowned, and many popes. Repeatedly enlarged, it was, in the fifteenth century, a spacious basilica with nave and double aisles, flanked with smaller churches, chapels, and convents. But by the time of Nicholas V it showed the wear of eleven centuries; cracks veined its walls, and men feared that it might at any moment collapse, perhaps upon a con-gregation. So in 1452 Bernardo Rossellino and Leon Battista Alberti were commissioned to strengthen the edifice with new walls. The work had hardly begun when Nicholas died; and succeeding popes, needing funds for crusades, suspended it. In 1505, after considering and rejecting various other plans, Julius II determined to tear down the old church, and build an entirely new shrine over what was said to be St. Peter's grave. He invited several architects to submit designs. Bramante won with a proposal to rear a new basilica on the plan of a Greek cross (with arms of equal length), and to crown its transept crossing with a vast dome; in the famous phrase ascribed to him, he would raise the dome of the Pantheon upon the basilica of Constantine. In Bramante's intent the new majestic edifice would cover 28,900 square yards—11,600 more than the area covered by St. Peter's to-day. Excavation was begun in April, 1506. On April 11 Julius, aged sixty-three, descended a long and trembling rope ladder to a great depth to lay the foundation stone. The work progressed slowly as Julius and his funds were more and more absorbed in war. In 1514 Bramante died, happily not knowing that his design would never be carried out.

Many good Christians were shocked at the thought of destroying the venerable old cathedral. Most of the cardinals were strongly opposed, and many artists complained that Bramante had recklessly shattered the fine columns and capitals of the ancient nave when with better care he might have taken them down intact. A satire published three years after the architect's death told how Bramante, on reaching St. Peter's gate, had been severely rebuked by the Apostle, and had been refused admittance to Paradise. But, said the satirist, Bramante did not like the arrangement of Paradise anyway, nor the steep approach to it from the earth. "I will build a new, broad, and commodious road, so that old and feeble souls may travel on horseback. And then I will make a new Paradise, with delightful residences for the blessed." When Peter rejected this proposal Bramante offered to go down to hell and build a new and better inferno, since the old one must by this time be almost burned out. But Peter returned to the question: "Tell me, seriously, what made you destroy my church?" Bramante tried to comfort him: "Pope Leo will build you a new one." "Well, then," said the Apostle, "you must wait at the gate of Paradise until it is finished."[19]

It was finished in 1626.

III. THE YOUNG RAPHAEL

1. Development: 1483-1508

After Bramante's death Leo X named to succeed him, as architectural director of the work at the new St. Peter's, a young painter thirty-one years old, too young to bear on his shoulders the weight of Bramante's dome, but the happiest, most successful, and best-loved artist in history.

His good fortune began when he was born to Giovanni de' Santi, then the leading painter at Urbino. Some pictures survive from Giovanni's brush; they suggest an indifferent talent; but they show that Raphael— named after the fairest of the archangels—was brought up in the odor of painting. Visiting artists like Piero della Francesca often stayed at Giovanni's home; and Giovanni was sufficiently familiar with the art of his time to write intelligently of a dozen Italian, and some Flemish, painters and sculptors in his *Rhymed Chronicle of Urbino*. Giovanni died when Raphael was only eleven, but apparently the father had already begun to transmit the art to his son. Probably Timoteo Viti, who returned to Urbino from Bologna in 1495 after studying with Francia, continued the instruction, and brought to Raphael what he had learned from Francia, Tura, and Costa. Meanwhile the boy grew up in circles that had access to the court; and that refined society that Castiglione was to describe in *The Courtier* was beginning to spread among the lettered classes of Urbino the graces of character, manners, and speech that Raphael would illuminate with his art and his life. The Ashmolean Museum at Oxford has a remarkable drawing attributed to Raphael in the period between 1497 and 1500, and traditionally supposed to be a self-portrait. The face almost of a girl, the soft eyes of a poet: these are the features that we shall meet again, darker and a little wistful, in the engaging self-portrait (*c.* 1506) in the Pitti Gallery.

Picture the youth of the earlier portrait passing at sixteen from quiet and orderly Urbino to a Perugia where despotism and violence were the order of the day. But Perugino was there, whose fame was filling Italy; Raffaello's guardian uncles felt that the boy's manifest talent deserved instruction from the best painters in Italy. They could have sent him to Leonardo at Florence, where he might have imbibed some deepening strain of that master's esoteric lore; but there was something peculiar about the great Florentine, something a bit left-handed—literally sinister—in his loves, which disturbed all good uncles. Perugia was closer to Urbino, and Perugino was returning to Perugia (1499) with presumably all the technical tricks of Florentine painters at the tips of his brushes. So for three years the handsome lad worked for Pietro Vannucci, helped him to decorate the Cambio, mastered his secrets, and learned how to paint virgins as blue and devout as Perugino's own. The Umbrian hills—above all around the Assisi that Raphael could sight from the Perugian plateau—gave teacher and pupil a full supply of such simple and devoted mothers, fair with the forms of youth, yet molded to a trustful piety by the Franciscan air that they breathed.

When Perugino went again to Florence (1502) Raphael remained in Perugia, and fell heir to the demand that his master had developed for religious pictures. In 1503 he painted for the church of St. Francis a *Coronation of the Virgin*, now in the Vatican: the Apostles and Magdalen, standing around an empty sarcophagus, gaze upward to where, on a pavement of clouds, Christ places a crown upon Mary's head, while graceful angels celebrate her with the music of lute and tambourines. There are many signs of immaturity in the picture: heads insufficiently individualized, faces inexpressive, hands ill formed, fingers rigid, and Christ Himself, obviously older than His pretty mother, moving as awkwardly as a commencement graduate. But in the angel musicians—the grace of their motion, the flow of their draperies, the soft contour of their features—Raphael gives a pledge of his future.

The picture was apparently successful, for in the following year another church of San Francesco, in Città di Castello, some thirty miles from Perugia, ordered from him a similar picture—a *Sposalizio* or *Marriage of the Virgin* (Brera). It repeats some figures from the earlier painting, and copies the form of a similar picture by Perugino. But the Virgin herself has now the peculiar mark and grace of Raphael's women—the head modestly inclined, the oval face tender and demure, the smooth curve of shoulder and arm and raiment; behind her is a woman more buxom and alive, blonde and lovely; to the right a youth in tight garb shows that Raphael has studied the human form sedulously; and now all the hands are well drawn, and some are beautiful.

About this time Pinturicchio, who had made Raphael's acquaintance in Perugia, invited him to Siena as assistant. There Raphael made sketches and cartoons for some of the brilliant frescoes with which Pinturicchio, in the library of the cathedral, told such portions of Aeneas Sylvius' story as befitted a pope. In that library Raphael was struck by an antique statuary group, *The Three Graces*, that Cardinal Piccolomini had brought from Rome to Siena; the young artist made a hasty drawing of it, apparently to help his memory. He seems to have recognized in these three nudes a different world and morality than those that had been impressed upon him in Urbino and Perugia—a world in which woman was a joyful goddess of beauty rather than the sorrowful Mother of God, and in which the worship of beauty was considered as legitimate as the exaltation of purity and innocence. The pagan side of Raphael, which would later paint rosy nudes in the bathroom of a cardinal, and place Greek philosophers beside Christian saints in the chambers of the Vatican, developed now in quiet company with that aspect of his nature and his art which would produce *The Mass of Bolsena* and *The Sistine Madonna*. In Raphael, more than in any other hero of the Renaissance, the Christian faith and the pagan rebirth would live in harmonious peace.

Shortly before or after his visit to Siena he returned briefly to Urbino. There he painted for Guidobaldo two pictures that probably symbolized the Duke's triumph over Caesar Borgia: a *St. Michael* and a *St. George*, both now in the Louvre. Never before, so far as we know, had the artist succeeded so well in representing action; the figure of St. George drawing his sword back to strike, while his horse rears up in terror and the dragon claws at the knight's leg, is startling in its vigor and yet pleasing in its grace. Raphael the draftsman was coming into his own.

And now Florence called him, as it had called Perugino and a hundred other young painters. He seemed to feel that unless he could live for a while in that stimulating hive of competition and criticism, and learn at first hand the latest developments in line and composition and color, in fresco and tempera and oil, he would never be more than a provincial painter, talented but limited, and fated at last for obscure domesticity in the town of his birth. Late in 1504 he set out for Florence.

He behaved there with his usual modesty; studied the ancient sculptures and architectural fragments that had been gathered into the city; went to the Carmine and copied Masaccio; sought out and pored over the famous cartoons that Leonardo and Michelangelo had made for paintings in the Hall of Council in the Palazzo Vecchio. Perhaps he met Leonardo; certainly for a time he yielded to that elusive master's influence. It seemed to him now that beside Leonardo's *Adoration of the Magi, Mona Lisa*, and *The Virgin, Child, and St. Anne*, the paintings of the Ferrara, Bologna, Siena, Urbino schools were struck with the rigor of death, and even the Madonnas of Perugino were pretty puppets, immature young women of the countryside suddenly endowed with an uncongenial divinity. How had Leonardo acquired such grace of line, such subtlety of countenance, such shades of coloring? In a portrait of Maddalena Doni (Pitti) Raphael obviously imitated the *Mona Lisa;* he omitted the smile, for Madonna Doni apparently had none; but he pictured well the robust form of a Florentine matron, the soft, plump, ringed hands of moneyed ease, and the rich weave and color of the garments that dignified her form. About the same time he painted her husband, Angelo Doni, dark, alert, and stern.

From Leonardo he passed to Fra Bartolommeo, visited him in his cell at

San Marco, wondered at the tender expression, the warm feeling, the soft contours, the harmonious composition, the deep, full colors, of the melancholy friar's art. Fra Bartolommeo would visit Raphael in Rome in 1514, and wonder in his turn at the swift ascent of the modest artist to the pinnacle of fame in the capital of the Christian world. Raphael became great partly because he could steal with the innocence of Shakespeare, could try one method and manner after another, take from each its precious element, and blend these gleanings, in the fever of creation, into a style unmistakably his own. Bit by bit he absorbed the rich tradition of Italian painting; soon he would bring it to fulfillment.

Already in this Florentine period (1504-5, 1506-7) he was painting pictures now famous throughout Christendom and beyond. The Budapest Museum has a *Portrait of a Young Man*, perhaps a self-portrait, with the same beret and side glance of the eyes as in the *autoritratto* of the Pitti Gallery. When Raphael was but twenty-three he painted the lovely *Madonna del Granduca* (Pitti), whose perfectly oval face, and silken hair, and small mouth, and Leonardesque eyelids lowered in pensive affection, were framed in a warm contrast of green veil and red robe; Ferdinand II, Grand Duke of Tuscany, found such pleasure in contemplating this picture that he took it with him on his travels—whence its name. Quite as beautiful is the *Madonna del Cardellino*—of the Goldfinch (Uffizi); the Infant Jesus is no masterpiece of conception of design, but the playful St. John, arriving triumphantly with the captured bird, is a delight to mind and eye, and the face of the Virgin is an unforgettable representation of a young mother's tolerant tenderness. Raphael gave this painting as a wedding present to Lorenzo Nasi; in 1547 an earthquake crushed Nasi's mansion and broke the picture into fragments; the pieces were so cleverly reunited that only a Berenson, seeing it in the Uffizi, could surmise its vicissitudes. The *Madonna in the Meadow* (Vienna) is a less successful variant; here, however, Raphael gives us a remarkable landscape, bathed in the soft blue light of an evening falling quietly upon green fields, unruffled stream, towered town, and far-off hills. *La Belle Jardinière* (Louvre) hardly deserves to be the most famous of the Florentine Madonnas; it almost duplicates the *Madonna of the Meadow*, makes the Baptist absurd from nose to foot, and only redeems itself with an ideal Infant standing with chubby feet upon the Virgin's bare foot, and looking up at her with loving confidence. The last and most ambitious of them in this period was the *Madonna del Baldacchino* (Pitti)—the Virgin Mother enthroned under a canopy (*baldacchino*), with two angels parting its folds, two saints at each side, two angels singing at her feet; all in all a conventional performance, famous only because it is Raphael's.

In 1505 he interrupted his stay in Florence to visit Perugia and execute two commissions there. For the nuns of St. Anthony he painted an altar-piece which is now one of the most precious pictures in the Metropolitan Museum of Art in New York. Within a frame beautifully carved, the Virgin sits on a throne, looking like Wordsworth's "nun breathless with adoration"; in her lap the Child raises a hand to bless the infant St. John; two exquisite female figures—St. Cecilia and St. Catherine of Alexandria—flank the Virgin; in the foreground St. Peter frowns and St. Paul reads; and above, in a lunette, God the Father, surrounded by angels, blesses the Mother of His Son, and with one hand upholds the world. In one panel of the predella Christ prays on the Mount of Olives while the Apostles sleep; and in another Mary supports the dead Christ while Magdalen kisses His pierced feet. The perfect composition of the ensemble, the appealing figures of the female saints, meditative and wistful, the powerful conception of the passionate Peter, and the unique vision of Christ on the Mount, make this "Colonna" *Madonna* the first indubitable masterpiece of Raphael. In that same year 1506 he painted a less imposing picture, a *Madonna* (National Gallery, London) for the Ansidei family: the Virgin, straitly enthroned, teaches the Child how to read; at her left St. Nicholas of Bari, gorgeous in his episcopal robes, is also studious; at her right the Baptist, suddenly thirty while his playmate is still an infant, points the traditional finger of the Forerunner at the Son of God.

From Perugia Raphael seems to have gone again to Urbino (1506). Now he painted for Guidobaldo a second *St. George* (Leningrad), this time with a lance; a handsome young knight sheathed in armor whose gleaming blue displays another phase of Raphael's skill. Probably on the same visit he painted for his friends the most familiar of his self-portraits (Pitti): black beret over long black locks; face still youthful, and with no trace yet of beard; long nose, small mouth, soft eyes; altogether a haunting face, that might have been Keats's—revealing a spirit clean and fresh, and sensitive to every beauty in the world.

Late in 1506 he returned to Florence. There he painted some of his less renowned pictures—*St. Catherine of Alexandria* (London), and the "Niccolini Cowper" *Madonna and Child* (Washington). About 1780 the third Earl Cowper smuggled this out of Florence in the lining of his carriage; it is not one of Raphael's finest, but Andrew Mellon paid $850,000 to add it to

his collection (1928).[20] A far greater picture was begun by Raphael at
Florence in 1507: *The Entombment of Christ* (Borghese Gallery). It was
ordered for the church of San Francesco in Perugia by Atalanta Baglioni,
who, seven years before, had knelt in the street over her own dying son;
perhaps through Mary's grief she expressed her own. Taking Perugino's
Deposition as his model, Raphael grouped his figures in a masterly composition, almost with the power of Mantegna: the emaciated dead Christ,
borne in a sheet by a virile and muscular youth and a bearded straining man;
a splendid head of Joseph of Arimathea; a lovely Magdalen leaning in
horror over the corpse; Mary fainting into the arms of attendant women;
every body in a different attitude, yet all rendered with anatomical verity
and Correggian grace; a somber symphony of reds, blues, browns, and
greens mingling in a luminous unity, with a Giorgionesque landscape showing the three crosses of Golgotha under an evening sky.

In 1508 Raphael received at Florence a call that changed the current of
his life. The new Duke of Urbino, Francesco Maria della Rovere, was a
nephew of Julius II; Bramante, a distant relative of Raphael, was now a
favorite with the Pope; apparently both the Duke and the architect recommended Raphael to Julius; soon an invitation was sent the young painter to
come to Rome. He was glad to go, for Rome, not Florence was now the
exciting and stimulating center of the Renaissance world. Julius, who had
lived for four years in the Borgia apartment, had tired of seeing Giulia
Farnese playing Virgin on the wall; he wished to move into the four chambers once used by the admirable Nicholas V; and he wanted these *stanze* or
rooms to be decorated with paintings congenial to his heroic stature and
aims. In the summer of 1508 Raphael went to Rome.

2. Raphael and Julius II: 1508-13

Rarely since Pheidias had so many great artists gathered in one city and
year. Michelango was carving figures for Julius' gigantic tomb, and was
painting the Sistine Chapel ceiling; Bramante was designing the new St.
Peter's; Fra Giovanni of Verona, master woodworker, was carving doors
and chairs and bosses for the *stanze;* Perugino, Signorelli, Peruzzi, Sodoma,
Lotto, Pinturicchio had already painted some of the walls; and Ambrogio Foppa, called Caradosso, the Cellini of his age, was making gold in
every way.

Julius assigned to Raphael the *Stanza della Segnatura*, so called because
usually in this room the Pope heard appeals and signed pardons. He was so

pleased with the youth's first paintings here, and saw in him so excellent and pliable an agent to execute the grand conceptions that seethed in the papal brain, that he dismissed Perugino, Signorelli, and Sodoma, ordered their paintings whitewashed, and offered to Raphael the opportunity to paint all the walls of the four rooms. Raphael persuaded the Pope to retain some of the work done by the earlier artists; most of it, however, was covered over, so that the major paintings might have the unity of one mind and hand. For each room Raphael received 1200 ducats ($15,000?); and on the two rooms that he did for Julius he spent four and a half years. He was now twenty-six.

The plan for the *Stanza della Segnatura* was lordly and sublime: the paintings were to represent the union of religion and philosophy, of classic culture and Christianity, of Church and state, of literature and law, in the civilization of the Renaissance. Probably the Pope conceived the general plan, and chose the subjects in consultation with Raphael and the scholars of his court—Inghirami and Sadoleto, later Bembo and Bibbiena. In the great semicircle formed by one side wall Raphael pictured religion in the persons of the Trinity and the saints, and theology in the form of the Fathers and Doctors of the Church discussing the nature of the Christian faith as centered in the doctrine of the Eucharist. How carefully he prepared himself for this first test of his ability to paint on a monumental scale may be seen from the thirty preliminary studies that he made for this *Disputa del Sacramento*. He recalled Fra Bartolommeo's *Last Judgment* in Santa Maria Nuova at Florence, and his own *Adoration of the Trinity* in San Severo at Perugia; and on them he modeled his design.

The result was a panorama so majestic as almost to convert the most obdurate skeptic to the mysteries of the faith. At the top of the arch, radial lines, converging upward, make the uppermost figures seem to bend forward; at the bottom the converging lines of a marble pavement give the picture depth. At the summit God the Father—a solemn, kindly Abraham —holds up the globe with one hand, and with the other blesses the scene; below Him the Son sits, naked to the waist, as in a shell; on His right Mary in humble adoration, on His left the Baptist still carrying his shepherd's staff crowned with a cross; beneath Him a dove represents the Holy Spirit, third person of the Trinity; everything is here. Seated on a fluffy cloud around the Saviour are twelve magnificent figures of Old Testament or Christian history: Adam, a bearded Michelangelesque athlete, almost nude; Abraham; a stately Moses holding the tables of the Law; David, Judas Maccabaeus, Peter and Paul, St. John writing his evangel, St. James the

Greater, St. Stephen, St. Lawrence, and two others of debated identity; among them, and in the clouds—everywhere except in the beards—cherubim and seraphim dart in and out, and angels weave through the air on the wings of song. Dividing and uniting this celestial assembly from an earthly throng below are two cherubim holding the Gospel, and a monstrance displaying the Host. Around this a varied assemblage of theologians gathers to consider the problems of theology: St. Jerome with his Vulgate and his lion; St. Augustine dictating *The City of God*; St. Ambrose in his episcopal robes; Popes Anacletus and Innocent III; the philosophers Aquinas, Bonaventura, and Duns Scotus; the dour Dante crowned as if with thorns; the gentle Fra Angelico; the angry Savonarola (another Julian revenge on Alexander VI); and finally, in a corner, bald and ugly, Raphael's protecting friend Bramante. In all these human figures the young artist has achieved an astonishing degree of individualization, making each face a credible biography; and in many of them a degree of superhuman dignity ennobles the whole picture and theme. Probably never before had painting so successfully conveyed the epic sublimity of the Christian creed.

But could the same youth, now twenty-eight, represent with equal force and grandeur the role of science and philosophy among men? We have no evidence that Raphael had ever done much reading; he spoke with his brush and listened with his eyes; he lived in a world of form and color in which words were trivial things unless they issued in the significant actions of men and women. He must have prepared himself by hurried study, by dipping into Plato and Diogenes Laërtius and Marsilio Ficino, and by humble conversation with learned men, to rise now to his supreme conception, *The School of Athens*—half a hundred figures summing up rich centuries of Greek thought, and all gathered in an immortal moment under the coffered arch of a massive pagan portico. There, on the wall directly facing the apotheosis of theology in the *Disputa*, is the glorification of philosophy: Plato of the Jovelike brow, deep eyes, flowing white hair and beard, with a finger pointing upward to his perfect state; Aristotle walking quietly beside him, thirty years younger, handsome and cheerful, holding out his hand with downward palm, as if to bring his master's soaring idealism back to earth and the possible; Socrates counting off his arguments on his fingers, with armed Alcibiades listening to him lovingly; Pythagoras trying to imprison in harmonic tables the music of the spheres; a fair lady who might be Aspasia; Heraclitus writing Ephesian riddles; Diogenes lying carelessly disrobed on the marble steps; Archimedes drawing geometries on a slate for four absorbed youths; Ptolemy and Zoroaster bandying globes; a boy at the left running up eagerly with books, surely seeking an autograph; an assiduous lad seated in a corner taking notes; peeking out at the left, little Federigo of Mantua, Isabella's son and Julius' pet; Bramante again; and hiding modestly, almost unseen, Raphael himself, now sprouting a mustache. There are many more, about whose identity we shall let leisurely pundits dispute; all in all, such a parliament of wisdom had never been painted, perhaps never been conceived, before. And not a word about heresy, no philosophers burned at the stake; here, under the protection of a Pope too great to fuss about the difference between one error and another, the young Christian has suddenly brought all these pagans together, painted them in their own character and with remarkable understanding and sympathy, and placed them where the theologians could see them and exchange fallibilities, and where the Pope, between one document and another, might contemplate the co-operative process and creation of human thought. This painting and the *Disputa* are the ideal of the Renaissance—pagan antiquity and Christian faith living together in one room and harmony. These rival panels, in the sum of their conception, composition, and technique, are the apex of European painting, to which no man has ever risen again.

A third wall remained, smaller than the other two, and so broken by a casement window that unity of pictorial subject seemed impossible there. It was a brilliant choice to let that surface picture poetry and music; so a chamber heavily laden with theology and philosophy was made light and bright with the world of harmonious imagination, and gentle melodies could sing silently through the centuries across that room where unappealable decisions gave life or death. In this fresco of Parnassus, Apollo, seated under some laurel trees atop the sacred mount, draws from his viol "ditties of no tone"; and at his right a Muse reclines in graceful ease, baring a lovely breast to the saints and sages on the adjacent walls; and Homer recites his hexameters in blind ecstasy, and Dante looks with unreconciled severity even at this goodly company of graces and bards; and Sappho, too beautiful to be Lesbian, strums her cithara; and Virgil, Horace, Ovid, Tibullus, and other singers chosen by time mingle with Petrarch, Boccaccio, Ariosto, Sannazaro, and lesser voices of more recent Italy. So the young artist suggested that "life without music would be a mistake,"[21] and that the strains and visions of poetry might lift men to heights as lofty as the myopia of wisdom and the impudence of theology.

On the fourth wall, also pierced by a window, Raphael honored the place of law in civilization. In the lunette he painted figures of Prudence, Force, and Moderation; on one side of the casement he represented civil law in the form of *The Emperor Justinian Promulgating the Pandects*, and on the other, canon law in the person of *Pope Gregory IX Promulgating the Decretals*. Here, to flatter his irascible master, he pictured Julius as Gregory, and achieved another powerful portrait. In the circles, hexagons, and rectangles of the ornate ceiling he painted little masterpieces like *The Judgment of Solomon*, and symbolic figures of theology, philosophy, jurisprudence, astronomy, and poetry. With these and similar cameos, and some medallions left by Sodoma, the great *Stanza della Segnatura* was complete.

Raphael had exhausted himself there, and never attained to such colossal excellence again. By 1511, when he began the next room—now called the *Stanza d'Eliodoro* from its central picture—the conceptual inspiration of Pope and artist seemed to lose force and fire. Julius could hardly be expected to dedicate his entire apartment to a glorification of a union between classic culture and Christianity; it was natural now that he should devote a few walls to commemorating scenes in Scriptural and Christian story. Perhaps to symbolize his expected expulsion of the French from Italy, he chose for one side of the chamber the vivid description, in the Second Book of Maccabees, of how Heliodorus and his pagan cohorts, attempting to abscond with the treasury of the Jerusalem Temple (186 B.C.), were overwhelmed by three angel warriors. Against an architectural background of great pillars and receding arches the high priest Onias, kneeling at the altar, begs divine aid. On the right a mounted angel, with irresistible wrath, tramples down the robber general, while two other heavenly rescuers advance to attack the fallen infidel, whose stolen coins spill out upon the pavement. On the left, with sublime disdain of chronology, Julius II sits enthroned in calm majesty, watching the expulsion of the invaders; at his feet a crowd of Jewish women mingle incongruously with Raphael (now bearded and solemn) and his friends Marcantonio Raimondi the engraver and Giovanni di Foliari, a member of the papal secretariat. It is hardly as exalting a fresco as the *Disputa* or *The School of Athens*; it is too visibly devoted, at the cost of compositional unity, to the celebration of one pontiff and a passing theme; but it is still a masterpiece, vibrating with action, stately with architecture, and almost rivaling Michelangelo in the display of angry and muscular anatomies.

On another wall Raphael painted *The Mass of Bolsena*. About 1263 a Bohemian priest of Bolsena (near Orvieto), who had doubted that the sacramental wafer was really transformed into the body and blood of Christ, was amazed to see drops of blood ooze from the Host that he had just consecrated in the Mass. In commemoration of this miracle Pope Urban IV ordered the erection of a cathedral at Orvieto, and the annual celebration of the Corpus Christi feast. Raphael painted the scene with brilliance and mastery. The priestly skeptic gazes at the bleeding Host, while the acolytes behind him start at the sight; women and children at one side, Swiss guards at the other, unable to see the miracle, are visibly unmoved; Cardinals Riario and Schinner and other ecclesiastics stare at the scene in mingled astonishment and terror; across from the altar, kneeling on a *prie-dieu* carved with grotesques, Julius II looks on in quiet dignity, as if he had known all along that the Host would bleed. Technically this is one of the best of the *stanze* frescoes: Raphael has distributed his figures skillfully around and above the window that mounts into the wall; he has designed them with firmness of line and careful execution; and he has brought to flesh and drapery a new depth and warmth of coloring. The figure of the kneeling Julius is a revealing portrait of the Pope in his final year. Still the warrior strong and stern, still the proud King of Kings, he is a man worn with his toils and combats, clearly marked for death.

During these major labors (1508-13) Raphael produced several memorable Madonnas. The *Virgin with the Diadem* (Louvre) reverts to the Umbrian style of modest piety. The *Madonna della Casa Alba*—literally "the Lady of the White House"—is a graceful study in pink and green and gold, with the large and flowing lines of Michelangelo's sibyls; Andrew Mellon contributed $1,166,400 to the Soviet Government in exchange for this picture (1936). The *Madonna di Foligno* (Vatican) shows a lovely Virgin and Child in the clouds, a ghastly Baptist pointing to her, a stout St. Jerome presenting to her the donor of the picture, Sigismondo de' Conti of Foligno and Rome; here Raphael, under the influence of the Venetian Sebastiano del Piombo, achieves a new splendor of luminous color. The *Madonna della Pesce* (Prado) is altogether beautiful: in the face and mood of the Virgin; in the Child—never surpassed by Raphael; in the youthful Tobit presenting to Mary the fish whose liver has restored his father's sight; in the robe of the angel who guides him; in the patriarchal head of St. Jerome. In composition, color, and light this painting can bear comparison with the *Sistine Madonna* itself.

Finally Raphael in this period raised portrait painting to a height that only Titian would reach again. The portrait was a characteristic product of the Renaissance, and corresponds to the proud liberation of the individual in that flamboyant age. Raphael's portraits are not numerous, but they all stand on the highest level of the art. One of the finest is *Bindo Altoviti*. Who could surmise that this gentle but alert youth, healthy and clear-eyed, and as pretty as a girl, was no poet but a banker, and a generous patron of artists from Raphael to Cellini? He was twenty-two when so portrayed; in 1556 he died at Rome after a noble but disastrous and exhausting effort to save the independence of Siena from Florence. And of course to this period belongs the greatest of all portraits, the *Julius II* of the Uffizi Gallery (*c.* 1512). We cannot say that this is the original that first came from Raphael's hand; possibly it is a studio replica; and the marvelous copy in the Pitti Palace was made by none other than that rival portraitist, Titian. The fate of the original is unknown.

Julius himself died before the *Stanza d'Eliodoro* was finished, and Raphael wondered whether the great plan of the four *stanze* would be carried out. But how could a pope like Leo X, wedded to art and poetry almost as deeply as to religion, hesitate? The young man from Urbino was to find in Leo his most loyal friend; the living genius of happiness was to know under a happy pope his happiest years.

IV. MICHELANGELO

1. *Youth: 1475-1505*

We have left to the last Julius' favorite painter and sculptor, a man rivaling him in temper and *terribilità*, in power and depth of spirit—the greatest and saddest artist in the records of mankind.

Michelangelo's father was Lodovico di Lionardo Buonarroti Simoni, podesta or mayor of the little town of Caprese, on the road from Florence to Arezzo. Lodovico claimed distant kinship with the counts of Canossa, one of whom was pleased to acknowledge the relation; Michael always prided himself on having a liter or two of noble blood; but ruthless research has proved him mistaken.[22]

Born at Caprese on March 6, 1475, and named, like Raphael, after an archangel, Michelangelo was the second of four brothers. He was put out to nurse near a marble quarry at Settignano, so that he breathed the dust of sculpture from his birth; he remarked later that he had sucked in chisels and hammers with his nurse's milk.[23] When he was six months old the family moved to Florence. He received some schooling there, enough to enable him, in after years, to write good Italian verse. He learned no Latin, and never fell so completely under the hypnosis of antiquity as did many artists of the time; he was Hebraic not classic, Protestant in spirit rather than Catholic.

He preferred drawing to writing—which is a corruption of drawing. His father mourned the preference, but finally yielded to it, and apprenticed Michael, aged thirteen, to Domenico Ghirlandaio, then the most popular painter in Florence. The contract bound the youth to stay with Domenico three years "to learn the art of painting"; he was to receive six florins the first year, eight the second, ten the third, and presumably shelter and food. The boy supplemented Ghirlandaio's instruction by keeping his eyes open as he wandered through Florence, seeing in everything some object for art. "Thus," reports his friend Condivi, "he used to frequent the fish market and study the shape and hues of fishes' fins, the color of their eyes, and so for every part belonging to them; all which details he reproduced with the utmost diligence in his painting."[24]

He had been with Ghirlandaio hardly a year when a combination of nature and chance turned him to sculpture. Like many other art students he had free access to the gardens in which the Medici had disposed their collections of antique statuary and architecture. He must have copied some of these marbles with especial interest and skill, for when Lorenzo, wishing to develop a school of sculpture in Florence, asked Ghirlandaio to send him some students of promise in that direction, Domenico gave him Francesco Granacci and Michelangelo Buonarroti. The boy's father hesitated to let him make the change from one art to the other; he feared that his son would be put to cutting stone; and indeed Michael was so used for a time, blocking out marble for the Laurentian Library. But soon the boy was carving statues. All the world knows the story of Michael's marble faun: how he chiseled a stray piece into the figure of an old faun; how Lorenzo, passing, remarked that so old a faun would hardly have so complete a set of teeth; and how Michael remedied the fault at one blow by knocking a tooth out of the upper jaw. Pleased with the boy's product and aptitude, Lorenzo took him into his home and treated him as his son. For two years (1490-2) the young artist lived in the Palazzo Medici, regularly ate at the same table with Lorenzo, Politian, Pico, Ficino, and Pulci, heard the most enlightened talk about politics, literature, philosophy and art. Lorenzo assigned him a good room, and allowed him five ducats ($62.50?) a month for his personal expenses. Whatever works of art Michael might produce remained his own, to dispose of as he wished.

These years in the Medici Palace might have been a period of pleasant growth had it not been for Pietro Torrigiano. Pietro one day took offense at Michael's banter, and (so he told Cellini), "clenching my fist, I gave him such a blow on the nose that I felt bone and cartilage go down like biscuit beneath my knuckles; and this mark of mine he will carry to the grave."[25] It was so: Michelangelo for the next seventy-four years showed a nose broken at the bridge. It did not sweeten his temper.

In those same years Savonarola was preaching his fiery gospel of puritan reform. Michael went often to hear him, and never forgot those sermons, or the cold thrill that ran through his youthful blood as the prior's angry cry, announcing the doom of corrupt Italy, pierced the stillness of the crowded cathedral. When Savonarola died, something of his spirit lingered in Michelangelo: a horror of the moral decay about him, a fierce resentment of despotism, a somber presentiment of doom. Those memories and fears shared in forming his character, in guiding his chisel and his brush; lying on his back under the ceiling of the Sistine Chapel, he remembered Savonarola; painting *The Last Judgment*, he resurrected him, and hurled the friar's fulminations down the centuries.

In 1492 Lorenzo died, and Michael returned to his father's house. He continued his sculpture and painting, and now added a strange experience to his education. The prior of the hospital of Santo Spirito allowed him, in a private room, to dissect corpses. Michael performed so many dissections that his stomach revolted, and for a time he could hardly hold any food or drink. But he learned anatomy. He had an absurd chance to show his knowledge when Piero de' Medici asked him to mold a gigantic snow man in the court of the palace. Michael complied, and Piero persuaded him to live again in the Casa Medici (January, 1494).

Late in 1494 Michelangelo, in one of his many hectic moves, fled through the winter snow of the Apennines to Bologna. One story says that he was warned of Piero's coming fall by the dream of a friend; perhaps his own judgment predicted that event; in any case Florence might not then be safe for one so favored by the Medici. At Bologna he studied carefully the reliefs by Iacopo della Quercia on the façade of San Petronio. He was engaged to finish the tomb of St. Dominic, and carved for it a graceful *Kneeling Angel*; then the organized sculptors of Bologna sent him warning that if he, a foreigner and interloper, continued to take work out of their hands, they would dispose of him by one or another of the many devices open to Renaissance initiative. Meanwhile Savonarola had taken charge of Florence, and virtue was in the air. Michael returned (1495).

He found a patron in Lorenzo di Pierfrancesco, of the collateral branch of the Medici. For him he carved a *Sleeping Cupid*, which had a strange history. Lorenzo suggested that he treat the surface to make it look like an antique; Michael complied; Lorenzo sent it to Rome, where it was sold for thirty ducats to a dealer who sold it for two hundred to Raffaello Riario, Cardinal di San Giorgio. The Cardinal discovered the cheat, sent back the *Cupid*, recovered his ducats. It was later sold to Caesar Borgia, who gave it to Guidobaldo of Urbino; Caesar reclaimed it on taking that city, and sent it to Isabella d'Este, who described it as "without a peer among the works of modern times."[26] Its later history is unknown.

With all his versatile ability Michael found it hard to earn a living by art in a city where there were almost as many artists as citizens. An agent of Riario invited him to Rome, assuring him that the Cardinal would give him employment, and that Rome was full of wealthy patrons. So in 1496 Michelangelo moved hopefully to the capital, and received a place in the household of the Cardinal. Riario did not prove generous; but Iacopo Gallo, a banker, commissioned Michael to carve a *Bacchus* and a *Cupid*. One is in the Bargello at Florence, the other in the Victoria and Albert Museum in London. The *Bacchus* is an unpleasant representation of the young god of wine in a state of bibbling intoxication; the head is too small for the body, as may be fitting in a toper; but the body is well designed, and smooth with an androgynous softness of texture. The *Cupid* is a crouching youth, more like an athlete than a god of love; possibly Michelangelo did not name it so incongruously; as sculpture it is excellent. Here, almost at the outset, the artist distinguished his work by showing the figure in a moment and attitude of action. The Greek preference for repose in art was alien to him, except in the *Pietà;* so—with the same exception—was the Greek flair for universality—for depicting general types; Michelangelo chose rather to portray an individual imaginary in conception, realistic in detail. He did not imitate the antique, except in costumes; his work was characteristically his own, no renaissance, but a unique creation.

The greatest product of this first stay in Rome was the *Pietà* that is now one of the glories of St. Peter's. The contract for it was signed by Cardinal Jean de Villiers, French ambassador at the papal court (1498); the fee was to be 450 ducats ($5,625?); the time allowed, one year; and Michael's banker friend added his own generous guarantees:

> I, Iacopo Gallo, pledge my word to his most reverend Lordship that the said Michelangelo will finish the said work within one year, and that it shall be the finest work in marble which Rome today can show, and that no master of our day shall be able to produce a better. And in like manner . . . I pledge my word to the said Michelangelo that the most reverend Cardinal will disburse the payments according to the articles above engrossed.[27]

There are some blemishes in this glorious group of the Virgin Mother holding her dead Son in her lap: the drapery seems excessive, the Virgin's head is small for her body, her left hand is extended in an inappropriate gesture; her face is that of a young woman clearly younger than her Son. To this last complaint Michelangelo, as reported by Condivi, made answer:

> Do you not know that chaste women maintain their freshness far longer than the unchaste? How much more would this be the case with a virgin into whose breast there never crept the least lascivious desire which would affect the body! Nay, I will go further, and hazard the belief that this unsullied bloom of youth, besides being maintained in her by natural causes, may have been miraculously wrought to convince the world of the virginity and perpetual purity of the Mother.[28]

It is a pleasant and forgivable fancy. The spectator is soon reconciled to that gentle face, untorn by agony, calm in her grief and love, the bereaved mother resigned to the will of God, and consoled by holding for some final moments the dear body here cleansed of its wounds, freed from its indignities, resting in the lap of the woman that bore it, and beautiful even in death. All the essence and tragedy and redemption of life are in this simple group: the stream of births by which woman carries on the race; the certainty of death as the penalty for every birth; and the love that ennobles our mortality with kindness, and challenges every death with new birth. Francis I was right when he pronounced this the finest achievement of Michelangelo.[29] In all the history of sculpture no man has ever surpassed it, except, perhaps, the unknown Greek who carved the *Demeter* of the British Museum.

The success of the *Pietà* brought Michelangelo not only fame, which he humanly enjoyed, but money, which his relatives were ready to enjoy with him. His father had lost, with the fall of the Medici, the little sinecure that Lorenzo the Magnificent had given him; Michael's older brother had entered a monastery; the two younger brothers were improvident, and Michael became now the main support of the family. He complained of this necessity, but gave generously.

Probably because the disordered finances of his relatives called him, he returned to Florence in 1501. A unique assignment came to him in August of that year. The Operai or Board of Works at the cathedral owned a block of Carrara marble thirteen and a half feet high, but so irregularly shaped that it had lain unused for a hundred years. The Board asked Michelangelo could a statue be chiseled out of it. He agreed to try; and on August 16 the Operai del Duomo and the Arte della Lana (the Wool Guild) signed the contract:

> That the worthy master Michelangelo . . . has been chosen to fashion, complete, and finish to perfection that male statue called *Il gigante*, of nine cubits in height . . . that the work shall be completed within two years dating from September, at a salary of six golden florins per month; that what is needed for the accomplishment of this task, as workmen, timbers, etc., shall be supplied him by the Operai; and when the statue is finished the Guild consuls and the Operai . . . shall estimate whether he deserve a larger recompense, and this shall be left to their consciences.[30]

The sculptor toiled on the refractory material for two and a half years; with heroic labor he drew from it, using every inch of its height, his *David*. On January 25, 1504, the Operai assembled a council of the leading artists in Florence to consider where *Il gigante*, as they called the *David*, should be placed: Cosimo Roselli, Sandro Botticelli, Leonardo da Vinci, Giuliano and Antonio da Sangallo, Filippino Lippi, David Ghirlandaio, Perugino, Giovanni Piffero (father of Cellini), and Piero di Cosimo. They could not agree, and finally they left the matter to Michelangelo; he asked that the statue be placed on the platform of the Palazzo Vecchio. The Signory consented; but the task of moving *The Giant* from the workshop near the cathedral to the Palazzo took forty men four days; a gateway had to be heightened by breaking a wall above it before the colossus could pass; and twenty-one additional days were spent in raising it into place. For 369 years it stood on the open and uncovered porch of the Palazzo, subject to weather, urchins, and revolution. For in a sense it was a radical pronunciamento, symbol of the proud restored republic, stern threat to usurpers. The Medici, returning to power in 1513, left it untouched; but in the uprising that again deposed them (1527) a bench thrown from a window of the Palace broke the statue's left arm. Francesco Salviati and Giorgio Vasari, then lads of sixteen, gathered and preserved the pieces, and a later Medici, Duke Cosimo, had these fragments put together and replaced. In 1873, after the statue had suffered erosion from the weather, *David* was laboriously transferred to the Accademia delle Belle Arti, where it occupies the place of honor as the most popular figure in Florence.

It was a *tour de force*, and as such can hardly be overpraised; the mechanical difficulties were brilliantly overcome. Esthetically one may pick a few flaws: the right hand is too large, the neck too long, the left leg over-

long below the knee, the left buttock does not swell as any proper buttock
should. Piero Soderini, head of the republic, thought the nose excessive;
Vasari tells the story—perhaps a legend—how Michelangelo, hiding some
marble dust in his hand, mounted a ladder, pretended to chisel off a bit of
the nose while leaving it intact, and let the marble dust fall from his hand
before the Gonfalonier, who then pronounced the statue much improved.
The total effect of the work silences criticism: the splendid frame, not yet
swollen with the muscles of Michelangelo's later heroes, the finished texture
of the flesh, the strong yet refined features, the nostrils tense with excitement, the frown of anger and the look of resolution subtly tinged with diffidence as the youth faces the fearsome Goliath and prepares to fill and cast
his sling—these share in making the *David*, with one exception,* the most
famous statue in the world. Vasari thought it "surpassed all other statues
ancient and modern, Latin or Greek."[31]

The Duomo Board paid Michelangelo a total of 400 florins for the *David*.
Allowing for the depreciation of currency between 1400 and 1500, we may
equate this roughly at $5000 in the money of 1952; it seems a rather small
sum for thirty months' work; presumably he accepted other commissions
during that time. Indeed the Board and Guild themselves, while *David* was
in process, engaged him to carve statues, six and a half feet high, of the
twelve Apostles, to be placed in the cathedral. He was allowed twelve
years for the work, was to be paid two florins a month, and a house was to
be built for his free occupancy. Of these statues the sole survivor is a *St.
Matthew*, only half emerged from the block of stone, like some figure by
Rodin. Looking at it in the Florence Academy, we understand better what
Michelangelo meant when he defined sculpture as the art "that works by
force of taking away"; and again, in one of his poems: "In hard and craggy
stone the mere removal of the surface gives being to a figure, which ever
grows the more the stone is hewn away."[32] He often spoke of himself as
searching to find the figure concealed in the stone, knocking the surface
away as if seeking a miner buried in fallen rock.

About 1505 he carved for a Flemish merchant the *Madonna* that sits in
the church of Notre Dame at Bruges. It has been highly praised, but it is
one of the artist's poorer works—the drapery simple and dignified, the head
of the Child quite out of proportion to the body, the face of the Virgin
pouting and mournful as if she felt that it was all a mistake. Still stranger is
the homely Virgin in the *Madonna* painted (1505) for Angelo Doni. In
truth Michelangelo did not care much for beauty; he was interested in

* Which should be the *Hermes* of Praxiteles but more probably is the Statue of Liberty in
the harbor of New York.

bodies, preferably male, and represented them sometimes with all the defects of their seen forms, sometimes in a way to convey some sermon or idea, but seldom with a view to catching beauty and imprisoning it in lasting stone. In this Doni *Madonna* he offends good taste by placing a row of naked youths on a parapet behind the Virgin. Not that he was paganizing; he was apparently a sincere, even a puritan, Christian; but here, as in *The Last Judgment*, his fascination with the human body triumphed over his piety. He was deeply interested, too, in the anatomy of position, in what happens to limbs, extremities, frame, and muscles when the body changes its pose. So here the Virgin leans backward, apparently to receive the Child over her shoulder from St. Joseph. It is excellent sculpture, but lifeless and almost colorless painting. Michelangelo was to protest, time and again, that painting was not his forte.

Therefore he must have felt no great pleasure when Soderini invited him (1504) to paint a mural in the Hall of the Great Council of the Palazzo Vecchio, while his *bête noire*, Leonardo da Vinci, was to paint an opposite wall. He disliked Leonardo for a hundred reasons—for his aristocratic manners, his costly and pretentious dress, his retinue of pretty youths, perhaps for his greater success and fame, till then, as a painter. Angelo was not sure that he, a sculptor, could rival Leonardo in painting; it was courageous of him to try. For his preliminary cartoon he set up a panel of linen-backed paper 288 square feet in area. He had made some progress on this sketch when a summons came to him from Rome: Julius needed the best sculptor to be found in Italy. The Signory fumed, but let Michelangelo go (1505). Perhaps he was not sorry to leave the pencil and the brush, and return to the laborious art that he loved.

2. *Michelangelo and Julius II: 1505-13*

He must have seen at once that he would be miserable with Julius, they were so much alike. Both had temper and temperament: the Pope imperious and fiery, the artist somber and proud. Both were Titans in spirit and aim, acknowledging no superior, admitting no compromise, passing from one grandiose project to another, stamping their personalities on their time, and laboring with such mad energy that when both were dead all Italy seemed exhausted and empty.

Julius, following the example long since set by the cardinals, wanted for his bones a mausoleum whose size and splendor should proclaim his greatness even to distant and forgetful posterity. He looked with envy upon the beautiful tomb that Andrea Sansovino had just carved for Cardinal Ascanio

Sforza in Santa Maria del Popolo. Michael proposed a colossal monument twenty-seven feet in length and eighteen in width. Forty statues would adorn it: some symbolizing the redeemed Papal States; some personifying Painting, Architecture, Sculpture, Poetry, Philosophy, Theology—all made captive by the irresistible Pope; others depicting his major predecessors, as, for example, Moses; two would picture angels—one weeping at Julius' removal from the earth, the other smiling at his entrance into heaven. At the top would be a handsome sarcophagus for the mortal papal remains. Along the surfaces of the monument would run bronze reliefs recounting the achievements of the Pope in war, government, and art. All this was to stand in the tribune of St. Peter's. It was a design that would use many tons of marble, many thousands of ducats, many years of the sculptor's life. Julius approved, gave Angelo two thousand ducats for the purchase of marble, and sent him off to Carrara instructed to pick the finest veins. While there Michael noted a hill overlooking the sea, and conceived the idea of carving the mount into a colossal human figure, which, lighted at the top, would serve as a beacon to distant mariners; but Julius' tomb called him back to Rome. When the marble that he had bought arrived, and was piled up in a square by his lodgings near St. Peter's, people marveled at its quantity and cost, and Julius rejoiced.

The drama became tragedy. Bramante, desiring money for the new St. Peter's, looked askance at this titanic project; moreover he feared that Michelangelo would replace him as the Pope's favorite artist; he used his influence to divert papal funds and passion from the proposed tomb. For his part Julius was planning war upon Perugia and Bologna (1506), and found Mars an expensive god; the tomb should wait for peace. Meanwhile Angelo had received no salary, had spent on marble all that Julius had advanced him, had paid out of his own pocket to furnish the house that the Pope had provided for him. He went to the Vatican on Holy Saturday, 1506, to ask for money; he was told to return on Monday; he did, and was told to return on Tuesday; like rebuffs met him on Tuesday, Wednesday, and Thursday; on Friday he was turned away with the blunt statement that the Pope did not wish to see him. He went home and wrote a letter to Julius:

> Most Blessed Father: I have been turned out of the Palace today by your orders; wherefore I give you notice that from this time forward, if you want me, you must look for me elsewhere than at Rome.[33]

He gave instructions for the sale of the furniture he had bought, and took horse toward Florence. At Poggibonsi he was overtaken by couriers bearing a letter from the Pope, which commanded him to return at once to Rome. If we may accept his own account (and he was an unusually honest man) he sent back a reply that he would come only when the Pope agreed to fulfill the conditions of their understanding for the tomb. He continued to Florence.

Now he resumed work on the immense cartoon for *The Battle of Pisa*. He chose as his subject no actual warfare, but the moment when the soldiers, who had been swimming in the Arno, were suddenly called to action. Michael was not concerned with battles; he wanted to study and portray the nude male form in every position; here was his chance. He showed some men emerging from the river, others running to their weapons, others struggling to pull up stockings on wet legs, others leaping or riding on horseback, others hurriedly adjusting their armor, some running stark naked to the fight. There was no landscape background; Michelangelo never cared for landscape, or for anything in nature except the human form. When the cartoon was finished it was put alongside Leonardo's in the Hall of the Pope in Santa Maria Novella. There the rival sketches became a school for a hundred artists—Andrea del Sarto, Alonso Berruguete, Raphael, Iacopo Sansovino, Perino del Vaga, and a hundred more. Cellini, who copied Michelangelo's cartoon about 1513, described it with youthful enthusiasm as "so splendid in action that nothing survives of ancient or modern art which touches the same point of lofty excellence. Though the divine Michel Agnolo in later life finished that great [Sistine] Chapel, he never rose halfway to the same pitch of power."[34]

We cannot say as much. The picture was never painted, the cartoon is lost, and only minor fragments survive of the many copies made. While Angelo was working on the sketch Pope Julius sent message after message to the Florentine Signory, commanding them to send him back to Rome. Soderini, loving the artist and fearing for his safety in Rome, temporized. After the third letter from the Pope he begged Angelo to obey, saying that his obstinacy endangered the peaceful relations between Florence and the papacy. Michael demanded a safe-conduct, to be signed by the Cardinal of Volterra. During the delay Julius captured Bologna (November, 1506). Now he sent to Florence a peremptory order that Michelangelo should come to Bologna for an important commission. Armed with a letter from Soderini to Julius, which begged the Pope to "show him love and treat him gently," Michael went once more over the snows of the Apennines. Julius received him with a heavy frown, ordered from the room a bishop who presumed to rebuke the artist for disobedience, gave Angelo a grumbling pardon, and a characteristic assignment. "I wish you to make my statue on a large scale in bronze. I mean to place it on the façade of San Petronio."[35] Michael was glad to get back to sculpture, though not confident of his ability to cast successfully a sitting figure fourteen feet in height. Julius provided a thousand ducats for the work; Angelo reported later that he had spent all but four ducats on materials, so that he had for himself only that reward for two years of labor in Bologna. The task was as heartbreaking as that which Cellini described for casting the Loggia *Perseus*. "I work night and day," the sculptor wrote to his brother Buonarroto; "if I had to begin the whole thing over again I do not think I could survive it."[36] In February, 1508, the statue was raised to its place above the main portal of the cathedral. In March Michael returned to Florence, probably praying that he might never see Julius again. Three years later, as we have seen, the statue was melted into cannon.

Almost at once the Pope sent for him. Angelo went back to Rome, and was chagrined to find that Julius wanted him not to carve the great tomb but to paint the ceiling of the chapel of Sixtus IV. He hesitated to face the problems of perspective and foreshortening in painting a ceiling sixty-eight feet above the floor; he protested again that he was a sculptor, not a painter; in vain he recommended Raphael as a better man for the work. Julius commanded and coaxed, pledging a fee of 3000 ducats ($37,500?); Michael feared the Pope and needed the money. Still murmuring, "This is not my trade," he undertook the arduous and uncongenial task. He sent to Florence for five assistants trained in design; tore down the clumsy scaffolding that Bramante had raised, erected his own, and set to work measuring and charting the ten thousand square feet of the ceiling, planning the general design, making cartoons for each separate space, including spandrels, pendentives, and lunettes; in all there were to be 343 figures. Many preliminary studies were made, some from living models. When the final form of a cartoon was finished it was carried carefully up the scaffolding and was applied, face outward, to the freshly plastered surface of its corresponding place; the lines of the composition were then pricked through the drawing into the plaster, the cartoon was removed, and the sculptor began to paint.

For over four years—from May, 1508, to October, 1512—Angelo worked on the Sistine ceiling. Not continuously; there were interruptions of uncertain length, as when he went to Bologna to besiege Julius for more funds. And not alone: he had helpers to grind the colors, prepare the plaster, perhaps to draw or paint some minor features; parts of the frescoes reveal inferior hands. But the five artists whom he had summoned to Rome were soon dismissed; Angelo's style of conception, design, and coloring was so different from theirs and the traditions of Florence that he found them more hindrance than aid. Besides, he did not know how to get along with others, and it was one of his consolations, up there on the scaffold, that he was alone; there he could think, in pain but in peace; there he could exemplify Leonardo's saying: "If you are alone you will be wholly your own." To the technical difficulties Julius added himself by his impatience to have the great work completed and displayed. Picture the old Pope mounting the frail frame, drawn up to the platform by the artist, expressing admiration, always asking, "When will it be finished?" The reply was a lesson in integrity: "When I shall have done all that I believe required to satisfy art."[37] To which Julius retorted angrily: "Do you want me to hurl you from this scaffold?"[38] Yielding later to the papal impatience, Angelo took down the scaffolding before all final touches had been applied. Then Julius thought that a little gold should be added here and there, but the weary artist persuaded him that gold trimmings would hardly become the Prophets or the Apostles. When for the last time Michael descended from the scaffold he was exhausted, emaciated, prematurely old. A story says that his eyes, long accustomed to the subdued illumination of the chapel, could hardly bear the light of the sun;[39] and another story that he found it now easier to read by looking upward than by holding the page beneath his eyes.[40]

The original plan of Julius for the ceiling had been merely a series of Apostles; Michelangelo prevailed upon him to allow an ampler and nobler scheme. He divided the convex vault into over a hundred panels by picturing columns and moldings between them; and he enhanced the tridimensional illusion with lusty youthful figures upholding the cornices or seated on capitals. In the major panels, running along the crest of the ceiling, Angelo painted episodes from Genesis: the initial act of creation separates light from darkness; the sun, moon, and planets come into being at the command of the Creator—a majestic figure stern of face, powerful of body, with beard and robes flying in the air; the Almighty, even finer in form and feature than in the previous panel, extends His right arm to create Adam, while with the left arm He holds a very pretty angel—this panel is Michelangelo's pictorial masterpiece; God, now a much older and patriarchal deity, evokes Eve from Adam's rib; Adam and Eve eat the fruit of the tree, and are expelled from Eden; Noah and his sons prepare a sacrificial offering to God; the flood rises; Noah celebrates with too much wine. All in these panels is Old Testament, all is Hebraic; Michelangelo belongs to the prophets pronouncing doom, not to the evangelists expounding the gospel of love.

In the spandrels of alternate arches Angelo painted magnificent figures of Daniel, Isaiah, Zecharia, Joel, Ezekiel, Jeremiah, Jonah. In the other spandrels he pictured the pagan oracles that were believed to have foretold Christ: the graceful Libyan Sibyl, holding an open book of the future; the dark, unhappy, powerful Cumaean Sibyl; the studious Persian; the Delphic and Erythrean Sibyls; these too are such paintings as rival the sculptures of Pheidias; indeed, all these figures suggest sculpture; and Michelangelo, conscripted into an alien art, transforms it into his own. In the large triangle at one end of the ceiling, and in two others at the other end, the artist still stayed in the Old Testament, with the raising of the brazen serpent in the wilderness, the victory of David over Goliath, the hanging of Haman, the beheading of Holofernes by Judith. Finally, as if by concession and afterthought, in the lunettes and arched recesses above the windows, Angelo painted scenes expounding the genealogy of Mary and Christ.

No one of these pictures quite equals Raphael's *School of Athens* in conception, drawing, color, and technique; but taken all together, they constitute the greatest achievement of any man in the history of painting. The total effect of repeated and careful contemplation is far greater than in the case of the *Stanze*. There we feel a happy perfection of artistry, and an urbane union of pagan and Christian thought. Here we do not merely perceive technical accomplishment—in the perspective, the foreshortenings, the unrivaled variety of attitudes; we feel the sweep and breath of genius, almost as creative as in the wind-swept figure of the Almighty raising Adam out of the earth.

Here again Michelangelo has given his ruling passion free rein; and though the place was the chapel of the popes, the theme and object of his art was the human body. Like the Greeks, he cared less for the face and its expression than for the whole physical frame. On the Sistine ceiling are half a hundred male, a few female, nudes. There are no landscapes, no vegetation except in picturing the creation of plants, no decorative arabesques; as in Signorelli's frescoes at Orvieto, the body of man becomes the sole means of decoration as well as of representation. Signorelli was the one painter, as Iacopo della Quercia was the one sculptor, from whom Michelangelo cared to learn. Every little space left free in the ceiling by the general pictorial plan is occupied by a nude figure, not so much beautiful as athletic and strong. There is no sexual suggestion in them, only the persistent display of the human body as the highest embodiment of energy, vitality, life. Though some timid souls protested against this profusion of nudity in the house of God, Julius made no recorded objection; he was a man as broad as his hatreds, and he recognized great art when he saw it. Perhaps he understood that he had immortalized himself not by the wars that he had won, but by giving the strange and incalculable divinity fretting in Angelo freedom to disport itself on the papal chapel vault.

Julius died four months after the completion of the Sistine ceiling. Michelangelo was then nearing his thirty-eighth birthday. He had placed himself at the head of all Italian sculptors by his *David* and *Pietà;* by this ceiling he had equaled or surpassed Raphael in painting; there seemed no other world left for him to conquer. Surely even he hardly dreamed that he had over half a century yet to live, that his most famous painting, his most mature sculpture, were yet to be done. He mourned the passing of the great Pope, and wondered whether Leo would have as sure an instinct as Julius for the noble in art. He retired to his lodgings, and bided his time.

CHAPTER XVIII

Leo X

1513-21

I. THE BOY CARDINAL

THE Pope that gave his name to one of the most brilliant and immoral ages in the history of Rome owed his ecclesiastical career to the political strategy of his father. Lorenzo de' Medici had been almost destroyed by Sixtus IV; he hoped that the power of his family, and the security of his progeny in Florence, would be helped by having a Medici sitting in the college of cardinals, in the inner circles of the Church. He destined his second son for the ecclesiastical state almost from Giovanni's infancy. At seven (1482) the boy was given the tonsure; soon he was dowered with benefices *in commendam:* i.e., he was made absentee beneficiary of church properties, and received their surplus revenue. At the age of eight he was given the abbacy of Font Douce in France; at nine the rich abbey of Passignano, at eleven the historic abbey of Monte Cassino; before his election to the papacy Giovanni had collected sixteen such benefices.[1] At eight he was appointed protonotary apostolic; at fourteen he was made a cardinal.*

The young prelate was provided with all the education available to a millionaire's son. He grew up amid scholars, poets, statesmen, and philosophers; he was tutored by Marsilio Ficino; he learned Greek from Demetrius Chalcondyles, philosophy from Bernardo da Bibbiena, who became one of his cardinals. From the collections of art, and the conversations about art, in or around his father's palace he imbibed that taste for the beautiful which was almost a religion to him in his mature years. From his father, perhaps, he learned the profuse and sometimes reckless generosity, and the gay, almost epicurean, manner of life, which were to distinguish his cardinalate and his pontificate, with far-reaching results to the Christian world. At thirteen he entered the university that his father had re-established at Pisa; there, for three years, he studied philosophy and theology,

---

* It should be recalled that one might become a cardinal without being a priest, and that cardinals were chosen for their political ability and connections rather than for religious qualities.

477

canon and civil law. When, at sixteen, he was allowed openly to join the college of cardinals in Rome, Lorenzo sent him off (March 12, 1492) with one of the most interesting letters in history:

You, and all of us who are interested in your welfare, ought to esteem ourselves highly favored by Providence, not only for the many honors and benefits bestowed on our house, but more particularly for having conferred upon us, in your person, the greatest dignity we have ever enjoyed. This favor, in itself so important, is rendered still more so by the circumstances with which it is accompanied, and especially by the consideration of your youth and of our situation in the world. The first thing that I would therefore suggest to you is, that you ought to be grateful to God, and continually to recollect that it is not through your merits, your prudence, or your solicitude, that this event has taken place, but through His favor, which you can only repay by a pious, chaste, and exemplary life; and that your obligations to the performance of these duties are so much the greater, as in your early years you have given some reasonable expectation that your riper age may produce such fruits. . . . Endeavor, therefore, to alleviate the burden of your early dignity by the regularity of your life, and by your perseverance in those studies which are suitable to your profession. It gave me great satisfaction to learn that in the course of the past year you had frequently, of your own accord, gone to communion and confession; nor do I conceive that there is any better way of obtaining the favor of heaven than by habituating yourself to a performance of these and similar duties. . . .

I well know that as you are now to reside at Rome, that sink of all iniquity, the difficulty of conducting yourself by these admonitions will be increased. The influence of example is itself prevalent; but you will probably meet with those who will particularly endeavor to corrupt and incite you to vice; because, as you may yourself perceive, your early attainment to so great a dignity is not observed without envy, and those who could not prevent your receiving that honor will secretly endeavor to diminish it, by inducing you to forfeit the good estimation of the public; thereby precipitating you into that gulf into which they have themselves fallen; in which attempt the consideration of your youth will give them a confidence of success. To these difficulties you ought to oppose yourself with the greater firmness as there is at present less virtue amongst your brethren of the college. I acknowledge indeed that several of them are good and learned men, whose lives are exemplary,

and whom I would recommend to you as patterns of your conduct.
By emulating them you will be so much the more known and esteemed, in proportion as your age, and the peculiarity of your situation, will distinguish you from your colleagues. Avoid, however,
. . . the imputation of hypocrisy; guard against all ostentation, either
in your conduct or in your discourse; affect not austerity, nor even
appear too serious. This advice you will, I hope, in time understand and practise better than I can express it.

Yet you are not unacquainted with the great importance of the
character which you have to sustain, for you well know that all the
Christian world would prosper if the cardinals were what they ought
to be; because in such a case there would always be a good pope,
upon which the tranquillity of Christendom so materially depends.
Endeavor then to render yourself such that if all the rest resembled
you we might expect this universal blessing. To give you particular
directions as to your behavior and conversation would be a matter
of no small difficulty. I shall therefore only recommend that in
your intercourse with the cardinals and other men of rank your
language be unassuming and respectful. . . . On this your first visit
to Rome it will, however, be more advisable for you to listen to others than to speak much yourself. . . .

On public occasions let your equipage and dress be rather below
than above mediocrity. A handsome house and a well ordered family
will be preferable to a great retinue and a splendid residence. . . . Silk
and jewels are not suitable for persons in your station. Your taste
will be better shown in the acquisition of a few elegant remains of
antiquity, or in the collecting of handsome books, and by your attendants being learned and well bred rather than numerous. Invite
others to your house oftener than you receive invitations. Practise
neither too frequently. Let your own food be plain, and take sufficient exercise, for those who wear your habit are soon liable, without great caution, to contract infirmities. . . . Confide in others too
little rather than too much. There is one rule which I would recommend to your attention in preference to all others: Rise early in the
morning. This will not only contribute to your health, but will
enable you to arrange and expedite the business of the day; and as
there are various duties incident to your station, such as the performance of divine service, studying, giving audience, etc., you will find
the observance of this admonition productive of the greatest utility.
. . . You will probably be desired to intercede for the favors of the
Pope on particular occasions. Be cautious, however, that you trouble
him not too often; for his temper leads him to be most liberal to those

who weary him least with their solicitations. This you must observe, lest you should give him offense, remembering also at times to converse with him on more agreeable topics; and if you should be obliged to request some kindness from him, let it be done with that modesty and humility which are so pleasing to his disposition. Farewell.[2]

Lorenzo died less than a month later, and Giovanni had hardly reached the "sink of iniquity" when he hurried back to Florence to support his elder brother Piero in a precarious inheritance of political authority. It was one of Giovanni's rare misfortunes that he was again in Florence when Piero fell. To escape the indiscriminate wrath of the citizens against the Medici family he disguised himself as a Franciscan friar, made his way unrecognized through hostile crowds, and applied for admission to the monastery of San Marco, which his forebears had lavishly endowed, but which was at the time under the command of his father's enemy, Savonarola. The friars refused him admission. He hid for a time in a suburb, and then made his way over the mountains to join his brothers in Bologna. Disliking Alexander VI, he avoided Rome; for six years he lived as a fugitive or an exile, but apparently never out of funds. With his cousin Giulio (later Clement VII) and some friends he visited Germany, Flanders, and France. Finally, reconciling himself to Alexander, he took up his residence in Rome (1500).

Everybody there liked him. He was modest, affable, and unostentatiously generous. He sent substantial gifts to his old teachers Politian and Chalcondyles. He collected books and works of art, and even his ample income hardly sufficed for his aid to poets, artists, musicians, and scholars. He enjoyed all the arts and graces of life; nevertheless Guicciardini, who lost no love on the popes, described him as "having the reputation of a chaste person, and of unblameable manners";[3] and Aldus Manutius complimented him on his "pious and irreproachable life."[4]

His vicissitudes were resumed when Julius II appointed him papal legate to govern Bologna and the Romagna (1511). He accompanied the papal army to Ravenna; walked unarmed amid the battle, encouraging the soldiers; stayed too long on the field of defeat, administering the sacraments to the dying; and was captured by a Greek detachment in the service of the victorious French. Taken as a prisoner to Milan, he was pleased to note that even the French soldiers paid little attention to the schismatic cardinals and their peregrinating council, but came eagerly to him for his blessing, his absolution, perhaps his purse. He escaped from his lenient captors, joined the Spanish-papal forces that sacked Prato and took Florence, and shared with his brother Giuliano in the restoration of the Medici to power (1512). A few months later he was called to Rome to take part in selecting a successor to Julius.

He was still only thirty-seven, and could hardly have expected that he himself would be chosen pope. He entered the conclave in a litter, suffering from an anal fistula.[5] After a week of debate, and apparently without simony, Giovanni de' Medici was elected (March 11, 1513), and took the name of Leo X. He was not yet a priest, but this defect was remedied on March 15.

Everybody was surprised and delighted. After the dark intrigues of Alexander and Caesar Borgia, and the wars and turbulence and tantrums of Julius, it was a relief that a young man already distinguished for his easy-going good nature, his tact and courtesy, and his opulent patronage of letters and art, was now to lead the Church, presumably in the ways of peace. Alfonso of Ferrara, so relentlessly fought by Julius, had no fear in coming to Rome. Leo reinvested him with all his ducal dignities, and the grateful prince held the stirrup as Leo mounted a horse to ride in the coronation procession of March 17. These inauguration ceremonies were lavish beyond any precedent, costing 100,000 ducats.[6] The banker Agostino Chigi provided a float on which a Latin inscription proclaimed hopefully: "Once Venus" (Alexander) "reigned, then Mars" (Julius), "now Pallas" (Wisdom) "rules." A pithier epigram ran the rounds: "Mars was, Pallas is, I, Venus, will always be."[7] Poets, sculptors, painters, goldsmiths rejoiced; humanists promised themselves a revival of the Augustan Age. Never had a man mounted the pontifical chair under more favorable auspices of public approbation.

Leo himself, if we may believe the scribblers of the time, said pleasantly to his brother Giuliano: *Godiamoci il papato, poichè Dio ci l'ha dato*—"Let us enjoy the papacy, since God has given it to us."[8] The remark, possibly apocryphal, indicated no irreverence, but a blithe spirit, ready to be generous as well as happy, and ingenuously unaware, amid its good fortune, that half of Christendom was swelling with revolt against the Church.

II. THE HAPPY POPE

He began with excellent measures. He forgave the cardinals who had staged the anticouncil of Pisa and Milan; that threat of schism ended. He promised—and kept his promise—to refrain from touching the estates left by cardinals. He reopened the Lateran Council, and welcomed the delegates in his own graceful Latin. He effected some minor ecclesiastical reforms, and reduced taxes; but his edict calling for larger reforms (May 3, 1514) encountered so much opposition from the functionaries whose incomes it would abate that he made no strenuous effort to enforce it.[9] "I will think the matter over," he said, "and see how I can satisfy everybody."[10] This was his character, and his character was his fate.

Raphael's portrait of him (Pitti), painted between 1517 and 1519, is not as well known as that of Julius, but that was partly Leo's fault: there were in this case less depth of thought, heroism of action, and worth of inner soul to give majesty to the outward face and frame. The representation is merciless. A massive man, of more than medium height, and much more than medium weight—the indignity of obesity concealed under a fur-trimmed robe of velvet white and cape of scarlet red; hands soft and flabby, here shorn of the many rings that normally adorned them; a reading glass to help shortsighted eyes; round head and plump cheeks, full lips and double chin; large nose and ears; some lines of bitterness from the nose to the corners of the mouth; heavy eyes and slightly frowning brow: this is the Leo disillusioned with diplomacy, and perhaps soured with the unmannerly Reformation, rather than the lighthearted hunter and musician, the generous patron, the cultivated hedonist whose accession had so gladdened Rome. To do him justice the record must be added to the picture. A man is many men, to divers men and times; and not even the greatest portraitist can show all these features in one moment's face.

The basic quality in Leo, born of his fortunate life, was good nature. He had a pleasant word for everybody, saw the best side of everybody except the Protestants (whom he could not begin to understand), and gave so generously to so many that even this profuse philanthropy, involving heavy drafts on Christian purses, shared in causing the Reformation. We hear much of his courtesy, his tact, his amiability, his cheerful temper even in sickness and pain. (His fistula, repeatedly operated upon, always returned, and sometimes made locomotion an agony.) So far as he could, he let others lead their own lives. His initial moderation and kindliness yielded to severity when he discovered some cardinals plotting against his life. At times he was relentlessly hard, as with Francesco Maria della Rovere of Urbino and Gianpaolo Baglioni of Perugia.[11] He could lie like a diplomat when he had to, and now and then bettered the instruction of the treacherous statesmanship that enmeshed him. More often he was humane, as when he forbade (in vain) the enslavement of American Indians, and did his best to check the Inquisitorial ferocity of Ferdinand the Catholic.[12] Despite his general worldliness he fulfilled conscientiously all his religious duties, observed the fasts, and recognized no inherent contradiction between religion and gaiety. He has been charged with saying to Bembo: "It is well known to all ages how profitable this fable of Christ has been to us"; but the sole authority for this is a violent polemic work, *The Pageant of Popes*, written about 1574 by an obscure Englishman, John Bale; and the freethinking Bayle and the Protestant Roscoe alike reject the story as itself a fable.[13]

His enjoyments ranged from philosophy to buffoons. He had learned at his father's table to appreciate poetry, sculpture, painting, music, calligraphy, illumination, textiles, vases, glass—all the forms of the beautiful except perhaps their source and norm, woman; and though his enjoyment of the arts was too indiscriminate to be a guide to taste, his patronage of artists and poets carried on in Rome the magnanimous traditions of his ancestors in Florence. He was too easygoing to take philosophy to heart; he knew how precarious all conclusions are, and did not bother his head with metaphysics after his college days. At meals he had books read to him, usually of history, or he listened to music. There his taste was sure; he had a good ear and a melodious voice. He kept several musicians at his court, and paid them lavishly. The *improvisatore* Bernardo Accolti (called Unico Aretino because of his birth in Arezzo and his unequaled facility in impromptu poetry and music) was able, with the fees that Leo paid him, to buy the little duchy of Nepi; a Jewish lute player earned a castle and the title of count; the singer Gabriele Merino was made an archbishop.[14] Under Leo's care and encouragement the Vatican choir reached an unprecedented degree of excellence. Raphael rightly pictured the Pope as reading a book of sacred music. Leo collected musical instruments for their beauty as well as their tone. One was an organ adorned with alabaster, and judged by Castiglione to be the loveliest that he had ever seen or heard.

Leo liked also to keep at his court a number of jesters and buffoons. This accorded with the custom of his father and of contemporary kings, and did not altogether shock a Rome that loved laughter only next to wealth and venery; to our hindsight it seems offensive that jests light or coarse should have echoed through the papal court while the Reformation raged in Germany. It amused Leo to see one of his monk buffoons swallow a pigeon at a mouthful, or forty eggs in succession.[15] He received with pleasure from a Portuguese embassy a white elephant—brought from India—which genuflected thrice on meeting His Holiness.[16] To bring him a person whose wit, deformity, or imbecility could refresh his mirth was an open sesame to his heart.[17] He seems to have felt that to indulge in such diversions now and then would distract him from physical pain, relieve his mind of cosmic worries, and prolong his life.[18] There was something disarmingly childlike about him. Occasionally he would play cards with cardinals, allow the public to sit in as spectators, and then distribute gold pieces to the crowd.

Above all other amusements he loved to hunt. It controlled his tendency to corpulence, and allowed him to enjoy the open air and the countryside after being a prisoner of the Vatican. He kept a large stable, with a hundred grooms. It was his custom to devote nearly all of October to the chase. His physicians highly approved of his addiction, but his master of ceremonies, Paris de Grassis, complained that the Pope kept his heavy boots on so long that "no one can kiss his feet"—at which Leo laughed heartily.[19] We get a kindlier view of the Pope than in Raphael's picture when we read how the peasants and villagers would come to greet him as he passed along their roads, and would offer him their modest gifts—which were so handsomely returned by the pontiff that the people eagerly awaited his hunting trips. To the poor girls among them he gave marriage dowries; he paid the debts of the sick or aged, or the parents of large families.[20] These simple folk loved him more sincerely than the 2000 persons who made up his menage at the Vatican.*

But Leo's court was no mere focus of amusement and hilarity. It was also the meeting place of responsible statemen, and Leo was one of them; it was the center of the intellect and wit of Rome, the place where scholars, educators, poets, artists, and musicians were welcomed or housed; the scene of solemn ecclesiastical functions, ceremonious diplomatic receptions, costly banquets, dramatic or musical performances, poetical recitations, and exhibitions of art. It was without question the most refined court in the world at that time. The labors of popes from Nicholas V to Leo himself in the improvement and adornment of the Vatican, in the assemblage of literary and artistic genius, and of the ablest ambassadors in Europe, made the court of Leo the zenith not of the art (for that had come under Julius) but of the literature and brilliance of the Renaissance. In mere quantity of culture history had never seen its equal, not even in Periclean Athens or Augustan Rome.[22]

The city itself prospered and expanded as Leo's gathered gold flowed

---

* On these hunts Leo's favorite retreat was the Villa Magliana. Built for Sixtus IV, enlarged by Innocent VIII and Julius II, it was adorned for Julius with frescoes of Apollo and the Muses by the Umbrian Giovanni di Pietro (Lo Spagna). For its chapel Raphael (between 1513 and 1520) designed three frescoes, of which two survive in the Louvre; probably they were painted by Lo Spagna from Raphael's cartoons.[21]

along its economic arteries. In thirteen years after his accession, said the Venetian ambassador, ten thousand houses were built in Rome, chiefly by newcomers from northern Italy following the migration of the Renaissance. Florentines in particular crowded in to pick plums from a Florentine pontificate. Paolo Giovio, who moved in Leo's court, estimated the population of Rome at 85,000.[23] It was not yet so fair a city as Florence or Venice, but it was now by common consent the hub of Western civilization; Marcello Alberini, in 1527, called it "the rendezvous of the world."[24] Leo, amid amusements and foreign affairs, regulated the importation and price of food, abrogated monopolies and "corners," reduced taxes, administered justice impartially, struggled to drain the Pontine marshes, promoted agriculture in the Campagna, and continued the work of Alexander and Julius in opening or improving streets in Rome.[30] Like his father in Florence, he provided *circenses* as well as *panem*—engaged artists to plan gorgeous pageants, encouraged the masked festivities of Carnival, even allowed Borgian bullfights to be staged in St. Peter's square. He wished the people to share in the happiness and jollity of the new Golden Age.

The city took its cue from the Pope, and let joy be unconfined. Prelates, poets, parasites, panders, and prostitutes hurried to Rome to drink the golden rain. The cardinals—dowered by the pontiffs, and above all by Leo, with innumerable benefices that sent them revenues from all parts of Latin Christendom—were now far richer than the old nobility, which was sinking into economic and political decay. Some cardinals had an income of 30,000 ducats a year ($375,000,).[31] They lived in stately palaces manned by as many as three hundred servants[32] and adorned with every art and luxury known to the time. They did not quite think of themselves as ecclesiastics; they were statemen, diplomats, administrators; they were the Roman Senate of the Roman Church; and they proposed to live like senators. They smiled at those foreigners who expected of them the abstinence and continence of priests. Like so many men of their age, they judged conduct not by moral but by esthetic standards; a few commandments might be broken with impunity if it was done with courtesy and taste. They surrounded themselves with pages, musicians, poets, and humanists, and now and then dined with courtly courtesans.[33] They mourned that their salons were normally womanless; "all Rome," according to Cardinal Bibbiena, "says that nothing is wanting here but a Madonna to hold a court."[34] They envied Ferrara, Urbino, and Mantua, and rejoiced when Isabella d'Este came to spread her robes and feminine graces over their unisexual feast.

Manners, taste, good conversation, appreciation of art were now at their height, and patronage was opulent. There had been cultivated circles in the smaller capitals, and Castiglione preferred the quiet coterie of Urbino to the cosmopolitan, noisier, flashier civilization of Rome. But Urbino was a tiny island of culture; this was a stream, a sea. Luther came and saw it, and was shocked and repelled; Erasmus came and saw it, and was charmed to ecstasy.[35] A hundred poets proclaimed that the *Saturnia regna* had returned.

III. SCHOLARS

On November 5, 1513, Leo issued a bull uniting two impoverished institutions of learning: the *Studium sacri palatii*—the College of the Holy Palace, i.e., the Vatican—and the *Studium urbis*, or City College; these now became the University of Rome, and were housed in a building soon known as the Sapienza.[36] These schools had prospered under Alexander but languished under Julius, who diverted their funds to war, and preferred a sword to a book. Leo supported the new University handsomely until he too was enmeshed in the expensive game of competitive destruction. He brought in a bevy of devoted scholars, so that soon the institution had eighty-eight professors—fifteen in medicine alone—receiving from fifty to 530 florins ($625 to $6625?) a year. Leo, in these early years of his pontificate, did everything that he could to make the combined colleges the most scholarly and flourishing university in Italy.

It was one of his credits that he established the study of Semitic languages. A chair in the University of Rome was devoted to the teaching of Hebrew, and Teseo Ambrogio was appointed to teach Syriac and Chaldaic in the University of Bologna. Leo welcomed the dedication of a Hebrew grammar composed by Agacio Guidacerio. Learning that Sante Pagnini was translating the Old Testament from the original Hebrew into Latin, he asked to see a specimen, liked it, and undertook at once the expense of the laborious enterprise.

It was Leo, too, who restored Greek studies, which had begun to decline. He invited to Rome the old scholar John Lascaris, who had been teaching Greek in Florence, France, and Venice; and with him he organized a Greek Academy in Rome, distinct from the University. To Lascaris' pupil Marcus Musurus, chief aide to Manutius, Bembo wrote for Leo (August 7, 1513) a letter inviting the scholar to secure from Greece "ten young men, or as many more as you may think proper, of good education and virtuous disposition, who may compose a seminary of liberal studies, and from whom the Italians may derive the proper use and knowledge of the Greek tongue."[37] A month later Manutius published the edition of Plato that Musurus had completed, and the great printer dedicated the work to the Pope. Leo responded by granting to Aldus, for fifteen years, the exclusive privilege of reprinting the Greek or Latin books that Aldus had already issued, or would in that period publish; all who should encroach upon this privilege were by that deed excommunicated and subject to penalties; this *privilegium ad imprimendum solum* was the Renaissance way of giving to a printer a copyright on the editions that he had paid to prepare. Leo added to the privilege an earnest recommendation that the Aldine publications should be moderately priced; they were. The Greek college was established in the house of the Colocci on the Quirinal, and a press was set up there to print textbooks and scholia for the students. A similar "Medicean Academy" for Greek studies was about the same time founded in Florence. Under Leo's encouragement Varino Camerti, who Latinized his name as Favorinus, compiled the best Greek-Latin dictionary yet published in the Renaissance world.

The Pope's enthusiasm for the classics was almost a religion. He accepted from the Venetians "a shoulder bone of Livy" with the same piety as though it had been a relic of some major saint.[38] Soon after his accession he announced that he would amply reward any person who should procure for him unpublished manuscripts of ancient literature. Like his father, he directed his emissaries and appointees in foreign lands to seek and buy for him any manuscripts of ancient pagan or Christian authorship and value; and sometimes he dispatched envoys for that sole and special purpose, and gave them letters to kings and princes soliciting co-operation in the search. His agents seem on occasion to have stolen manuscripts when these could not be bought; this was apparently the case with the first six books of Tacitus' *Annals*, found in the monastery of Corvey in Westphalia, for we have a charming letter to the papal agent Heitmers, written by or for Leo after the *Annals* had been edited and published:

> We have sent a copy of the revised and printed books in a beautiful binding to the abbot and his monks, that they may place it in their library as a substitute for the one taken from it. But in order that they may understand that this purloining has done them far more good than harm, we have granted them for their church a plenary indulgence.[39]

Leo gave the purloined manuscript to Filippo Beroaldo, with instructions to correct and edit the text, and print it in an elegant but convenient form. Said Leo in this letter of instruction:

> We have been accustomed, even in our early years, to think that nothing more excellent or useful has been given by the Creator to mankind—if we except only the knowledge and true worship of Himself—than these studies, which not only lead to the ornament and guidance of human life, but are applicable and useful to every particular situation, consoling in adversity, pleasing and honorable in prosperity; insomuch that without them we should be deprived of all the grace of life and all the polish of society. The security and extension of these studies seem chiefly to depend on two circumstances: the number of learned men, and the ample supply of excellent texts. As to the first of these we hope, with the divine blessing, to show still more evidently our earnest desire and disposition to reward and honor their merits, this having been for a long time past our chief delight. . . . With respect to the acquisition of books, we return thanks to God that in this also an opportunity is now afforded us of promoting the advantage of mankind.[49]

Leo thought that the judgment of the Church should determine what literature would advantage mankind, for he renewed Alexander's edict for the episcopal censorship of books.

In the sack of the Medici Palace (1494) some of the books collected by Leo's ancestors had been dispersed. Most of them, however, had been bought by the monks of San Marco; and these salvaged volumes Leo, while still a cardinal, had repurchased for 2652 ducats ($33,150?), and had transferred to his palace in Rome. This Laurentian Library was returned to Florence after Leo's death; we shall see its further fortune later.

The Vatican Library had now swollen to such proportions as to need a corps of scholars for its care. When Leo acceded to the papacy the head librarian was Tommaso Inghirami—a nobleman and poet, a conversationalist noted for wit and brilliance in a society of brilliant wits, and an actor whose success in the part of Phaedra in Seneca's *Hippolytus* earned him the nickname of Fedra. When he died in a street accident in 1516 he was replaced as *bibliotecario* by Filippo Beroaldo, who divided his affections between Tacitus and the learned courtesan Imperia, and wrote such excellent Latin poetry as to receive six independent translations into French, one by Clément Marot. Girolamo Aleandro or Aleander, who became librarian in 1519, was a man of temper, learning, and ability. He spoke Latin and

Greek, and Hebrew so fluently that Luther mistakenly pronounced him a Jew. At the Diet of Augsburg (1520) he strove with more passion than wisdom to halt the Protestant tide. Paul III made him a cardinal (1538), but four years later Aleander died through too assiduous care of his health and too frequent use of medicine.[41] He was highly indignant at being taken off at sixty-two, and scandalized his friends with his exasperation at the ways of Providence.[42]

Private libraries were now numerous in Rome. Aleander himself had a considerable collection, which he bequeathed to Venice. Cardinal Grimani, envied by Erasmus, had eight thousand volumes, in a variety of languages; he willed these books to the church of San Salvador in Venice, where they were destroyed by fire. Cardinal Sadoleto had a precious library, which he put on a ship to send to France; it was lost at sea. Bembo's library was rich in Provençal poets and original manuscripts—e.g., of Petrarch; this collection passed to Urbino, thence to the Vatican. Rich laymen like Agostino Chigi and Bindo Altoviti imitated the popes and the cardinals in collecting books, engaging artists, and supporting poets and scholars.

These abounded in Leo's Rome beyond any precedent or later parallel. Many cardinals were themselves scholars; some, like Egidio Canisio, Sadoleto, and Bibbiena, had been made cardinals because they were scholars of long service to the Church. Most of the cardinals in Rome acted as patrons, usually by rewarding dedications; and the homes of Cardinals Riario, Grimani, Bibbiena, Alidosi, Petrucci, Farnese, Soderini, Sanseverino, Gonzaga, Canisio, and Giulio de' Medici were surpassed only by the papal court as meeting places for the intellectual and artistic talent of the city. Castiglione, whose genial nature made friends with both the amiable Raphael and the dour and unapproachable Michelangelo, maintained a modest salon of his own.

Leo, of course, was the patron par excellence. No one who could turn a good Latin epigram went away from him giftless. As in the days of Nicholas V, scholarship—but now also poetry—constituted a claim to some place in the vast officialdom of the Church. Lesser lights became apostolic scribes, *abbreviatores*, brief-writers; brighter luminaries rose to be canons, bishops, protonotaries; stars like Sadoleto and Bembo became secretaries to the Pope; some, like Sadoleto and Bibbiena, were made cardinals. Ciceronian oratory again resounded in Rome; epistles rose and fell in cadenced periods; Virgilian and Horatian verse flowed in a thousand rivulets into the Tiber as their final destination. Bembo set the stylistic standard pontifically; "far better to speak like Cicero," he wrote to Isabella d'Este, "than to be pope."[43] His friend and colleague, Iacopo Sadoleto, shamed most of the humanists by combining an impeccable Latin style with impeccable morals. There were many men of high integrity among the cardinals of this age, and Leo's humanists were, by and large, of finer temper and life than those of the preceding generation.[44] Some, however, remained pagan in everything but their professed creed. It was an unwritten law that whatever one believed or doubted, no gentleman would utter anything critical of a Church that was morally so tolerant, and so munificent a patron.

Bernardo Dovizi da Bibbiena was a composite of all these qualities—scholar, poet, dramatist, diplomat, connoisseur, conversationalist, pagan, priest, and cardinal. Raphael's portrait catches only a part of him—his sly eyes and sharp nose; it covers his baldness with a red hat, and his gaiety with an unwonted gravity. He was light of foot and word and spirit, escaping from every vicissitude with a smile. Employed by Lorenzo the Magnificent as secretary and tutor, he shared with Lorenzo's sons the flight of 1494; but he showed his cleverness by going to Urbino, charming that urbane circle with his epigrams, and using some of his leisure to write and stage a risqué play—*Calandra* (c. 1508), the oldest of Italian prose comedies. Julius II brought him to Rome. Bernardo managed Leo's election with so little fuss and friction that Leo at once made him apostolic protonotary, and the next day treasurer of the papal household, and six months later cardinal. His dignities did not prevent him from serving Leo as connoisseur of arts and organizer of festival pageantry. His play was performed before the Pope, who enjoyed it with a good stomach. Sent as papal nuncio to France, he fell in love with Francis I, and had to be recalled as too sensitive for a diplomat. When Raphael decorated his bathroom, it was, by the Cardinal's choice, with the *History of Venus and Cupid*, a series of pictures recounting the triumphs of love; nearly all done in true antique Pompeian style, and overleaping Christianity into a world that had never heard of Christ. Leo, pretending not to notice the Venus in Bibbiena, was faithful to him to the end.

Leo relished drama in all its comic forms and degrees, from the simplest farce to the subtlest *double-entendres* of Bibbiena and Machiavelli. In the first year of his pontificate he opened a theater on the Capitol. There, in 1518, he witnessed a performance of Ariosto's *I Suppositi*, and laughed heartily at the equivocal jests that stemmed from the plot—the effort of a youth to seduce a maiden.[45] Such gala performances were more than mere comedy; they included artistic stage settings (in this case the scenery was painted by Raphael), a ballet, and entr'acte music by a chorus and an orchestra of lutes, violas, cornets, bagpipes, fifes, and a small organ.

To Leo's pontificate belongs one of the major historical works of the Renaissance. Paolo Giovio was a native of Como. There, and in Milan and Rome, he practised medicine; but, inspired by the literary excitement that greeted Leo's accession, he gave his leisure hours to writing a Latin history of his own times—i.e., from the invasion of Italy by Charles VIII to Leo's pontificate. He was allowed to read the first sections to Leo, who, with his customary lavishness, pronounced it the most eloquent and elegant historical writing since Livy, and rewarded him at once with a pension. After Leo's death Giovio used what he called his "pen of gold" to write a eulogistic life of his dead patron, and his "pen of iron" to indict Pope Adrian VI, who ignored him. Meanwhile he continued to labor at his immense *Historiae sui temporis*, finally carrying it to 1547. When Rome was sacked in 1527 he hid his manuscript in a church; it was found by a soldier, who then asked the author to buy his own book; Paolo was saved from this indignity by Clement VII, who persuaded the thief to accept, in lieu of more immediate payment, a benefice in Spain; Giovio himself was made bishop of Nocera. His *History*, and the biographies that he added to it, were acclaimed for their fluent and vivid style, but were denounced for their careless inaccuracies and their flagrant prejudice. Giovio blithely confessed that he praised or condemned the persons of his story according as they or their relatives had or had not lubricated his palm.[46]

IV. POETS

The chief glory of this age was its poetry. As in samurai Japan everyone from peasant to emperor, so in Leo's Rome everyone from the pontiff to his clowns wrote verse; and nearly everybody insisted on reading his latest lines to the tolerant Pope. He loved clever improvisation, and was himself an expert in that game. Poets pursued him everywhere with outstretched rhymes; usually he rewarded them somehow; on occasion he would content himself by replying with an extempore Latin epigram. A thousand books were dedicated to him. For one he gave Angelo Colocci 400 ducats ($5,000?); but to Giovanni Augurelli, who presented him with a poetical treatise—*Chrysopoeia*, or the art of making gold by alchemy—he sent an empty purse. He did not have time to read all the books whose dedications he accepted; one such was an edition of the fifth-century Roman poet Rutilius Namatianus, who advocated the suppression of Christianity as an enervating poison, and demanded a return to the worship of the virile pagan gods.[47] To Ariosto—who may have seemed to Leo sufficiently cared for in Ferrara—he gave merely a bull forbidding the pirating of his verses. Ariosto was peeved, having hoped for a gift commensurate with the length of his epic.

Having lost Ariosto, Leo contented himself too readily with poets of duller radiance and shorter breath. His generosity often misled him into rewarding superficial talents as liberally as genius. Guido Postumo Silvestri, a noble of Pesaro, had fought vigorously, and written violently, against Alexander and Julius for seizing Pesaro and Bologna; now he addressed to Leo an elegant elegiac poem comparing the happiness of Italy under the new Pope with its turmoil and misery in the preceding reigns; the appreciative pontiff restored to him his confiscated estates, and made him a companion in the papal hunts; but Guido soon died (said some contemporaries) of eating too lavishly at Leo's table.[48] Antonio Tebaldeo, who had already made a name for himself as a poet in Naples, rushed to Rome on Leo's election, and (says an uncertain tradition) received five hundred ducats from Leo for an appetizing epigram;[49] in any case the Pope gave him the superintendence and tolls of the bridge of Sorga, so that "it may enable Tebaldeo to support himself in affluence."[50] But money, though it may finance the talent of scholars, seems rarely to feed the genius of poets. Tebaldeo wrote more epigrams, became dependent upon Bembo's charity after Leo's death, and took permanently to his bed, "having no other complaint," said a friend, "than the loss of his relish for wine." He lived a long time at ease on his back, and died at seventy-four.

Francesco Maria Molza of Modena acquired some proficiency in verse before Leo's elevation; but hearing of the Pope's poetic philanthropy, he left his parents, wife, and children, and migrated to Rome, where he forgot them in an infatuation for a Roman lady. He composed an eloquent pastoral *poemetto* entitled *La ninfa Tiberina* in praise of Faustina Mancini, and was severely wounded by an unknown assassin. He left Rome after Leo's death, and at Bologna joined the retinue of Cardinal Ippolito de' Medici, who was said to maintain three hundred poets, musicians, and wits at his court. Molza's Italian poems were the most elegant of the time, not excepting Ariosto's. His *Canzoni* equaled those of Petrarch in style, and surpassed them in fire; for Molza repeatedly fell out of one amorous conflagration into another, and perpetually burned. He died of syphilis in 1544.

Two major minor poets honored Leo's reign. The career of Marcantonio Flaminio shows the period in pleasant lights—the unfailing kindness of the Pope to men of letters, the unenvious friendship of Flaminio, Navagero, Fracastoro, and Castiglione, though all four were poets, and the clean lives led by these men in an age when sexual license was widely condoned. Flaminio was born at Serravalle in the Veneto, son of Gianantonio Flaminio, himself a poet. Violating a thousand precedents, the father trained and encouraged the boy to poetry, and sent him at sixteen to present to Leo a poem written by the youth urging a crusade against the Turks. Leo had no taste for crusades, but he liked the verses, and provided for the boy's further education in Rome. Castiglione took him in hand, and brought him to Urbino (1515); later the father sent his son to study philosophy at Bologna; finally the poet settled down at Viterbo under the patronage of the English Cardinal Reginald Pole. He had the distinction of declining two high appointments—as cosecretary, with Sadoleto, to Leo, and as secretary to the Council of Trent. Despite suspicion of sympathizing with the Protestant Reformation, he was handsomely supported by several cardinals. Through all his peregrinations he longed for the peaceful life and clean air of his father's villa near Imola. His poems—nearly all in Latin, and nearly all in the brief form of odes, eclogues, elegies, hymns, and Horatian epistles to friends—return again and again to his love of old rural haunts:

> Iam vos revisam, iam iuvabit arbores
> 　　manu paterna consitas
> videre, iam libebit in cubiculo
> 　　molles inire somnulos[51]—

"Now I shall see you again; now it will delight me to behold the trees planted by my father's hand; and I shall rejoice to woo a little quiet sleep in my little room." He complained of being a prisoner in the tumult of Rome, and envied a friend whom he pictured as hiding in a village retreat, reading "Socratic books," and "giving no thought to the shallow honors conferred by the vulgar crowd."[52] He dreamt of strolling in green valleys with the *Georgics* of Virgil and the idyls of Theocritus as his companions. His most touching lines were written to his dying father:

> Vixisti, genitor, bene ac beate,
> nec pauper, neque dives, eruditus
> satis, et satis eloquens, valente
> semper corpore, mente sana, amicis
> iucundus, pietate singulari.
> Nunc lustris bene sexdecism peractis
> ad divum proficisceris beatas
> oras; i, genitor, tuumque natum
> olympi cito siste tecum in arce.[53]

"You have lived, father, well and happily, neither poor nor rich, learned enough, eloquent enough, always of strong body and healthy mind; genial, and of unrivaled piety. Now, having completed eighty years, you move on to the blessed shores of the gods. Go, father, and soon take your son with you to the high seat of heaven."

Marco Girolamo Vida proved a more pliable poet for Leo's purposes. Born in Cremona, well schooled in Latin, he became so skilled in that language that he could write it gracefully even in didactic poems *De arte poetica*, or on the growth of silkworms, or on the game of chess. Leo was so pleased with this *Sacchiae ludus* that he sent for Vida, loaded him with emoluments, and begged him to crown the literature of the age with a Latin epic on the life of Christ. So Vida began his *Christiad*, which happy Leo died too soon to see. Clement VII continued Leo's patronage of Vida, giving him a bishopric to feed on, but Clement too died before the publication of the epic (1535). Though a monk when he began it, and a bishop when he finished it, Vida could not refrain from those classical mythological allusions that were in the very air of Leo's time, but may appear incongruous to those who are forgetting the mythology of Greece and Rome and are making Christianity a literary mythology in its turn. Vida speaks of God the Father as *Superum Pater nimbipotens*—"the cloud-compelling Father of the gods"—and as *Regnator Olympi*—"Ruler of Olympus"; he regularly describes Jesus as *heros;* he brings in gorgons, harpies, centaurs, and hydras to demand the death of Christ. So noble a theme deserved its own congenial poetic form rather than an adaptation of the *Aeneid*. The finest lines in Vida are addressed not to Christ in the *Christiad* but to Virgil in the *De arte poetica:*

> *O decus Italiae! lux o clarissima vatum!*
> *te colimus, tibi serta damus, tibi thura, tibi aras;*
> *et tibi rite sacrum semper dicemus honorem*
> *carminibus memores. Salve, sanctissime vates!*
> *Laudibus augeri tua gloria nil potis ultra,*
> *et nostrae nil vocis eget; nos aspice praesens,*
> *pectoribusque tuos castis infunde calores*
> *adveniens, pater, atque animis tete insere nostris.*[54]

Which may be hastily rendered:

> O glory of Italy! O brightest light
> Among the bards! We worship thee with wreaths,
> And give thee frankincense and shrines. To thee
> Of right we chant forever sacred paeans,
> Recalling you with hymns. Hail, holiest bard!
> Thy glory gains no increase from our praise,

Nor needs our voice. Come, look upon thy sons,
Pour thy warm spirit into our chaste hearts;
Come, father, place thine own self in our souls.

V. THE RECOVERY OF CLASSIC ART

The pagan spirit of the age was enhanced by the presence and salvaging of classic art. Poggio, Biondo, Pius II, and others had denounced the demolition of classic structures, but it persisted nevertheless, and probably increased as the influx of money enabled Rome to build new and larger edifices with the ruins of the old. Builders continued to throw ancient marbles into furnaces to produce lime. Paul II used the stone wall of the Colosseum for the palace of San Marco; Sixtus IV pulled down the temple of Hercules, and turned a Tiber bridge into cannon balls. The temple of the Sun provided the material for a chapel in Santa Maria Maggiore, for two public fountains, and for a papal palace in the Quirinal. Artists themselves were unconscious vandals; Michelangelo used one of the columns of the temple of Castor and Pollux to form a pedestal for the equestrian statue of Marcus Aurelius, and Raphael took part of another column from the same temple to make a statue of Jonah. The material for the Sistine Chapel was quarried from the mausoleum of Hadrian. Practically all the marble used in raising St. Peter's was taken from classic buildings; and to the same new shrine went the podium, steps, and pediment of the temple of Antoninus and Faustina, the triumphal arches of Fabius Maximus and Augustus, and the temple of Romulus, son of Maxentius. In just four years, 1546-9, the new builders destroyed or dismantled the temples of Castor and Pollux, Julius Caesar, and Augustus.[55] The destroyers argued that there were enough pagan monuments left; that the neglected ruins took up valuable space and interfered with the orderly rebuilding of the city; and that the appropriated materials were in most cases used to erect Christian churches just as beautiful as the ruins, and presumably more pleasing to God. Meanwhile the imperceptible inhumations of time had buried the Forum and other historic sites under successive layers of dust, debris, and vegetation, so that the Forum was at places forty-three feet below the level of the surrounding city; it was largely abandoned to pasturage, and was called Campo Vaccino—the cow field. Time is the greatest vandal of them all.

The influx of artists and humanists retarded the rate of demolition, and generated movements for the preservation of the old monuments. Popes collected pagan sculpture and architectural fragments into the Vatican and Capitoline Museums. Poggio, the Medici, Pomponius Laetus, bankers, cardinals gathered into private collections whatever of worth they could acquire of the ancient remains. Many classic sculptures found their way into private palaces and gardens, and stayed there till the nineteenth century; hence such names as the Barberini *Faun*, the Ludovisi *Throne*, the Farnese *Hercules*.

All Rome was thrilled when excavators unearthed (1506), near the Baths of Titus, a new and complex sculptural group. Julius II sent Giuliano da Sangallo to examine it, and Michelangelo went along. As soon as Giuliano saw the statue he cried out, "This is the *Laocoön* mentioned by Pliny." Julius bought it for the Belvedere Palace, paying the finder and his son a lifetime annuity of 600 ducats ($7,500?); so precious had classic sculptures become. Such rewards encouraged art prospectors. A year later one of these found another ancient group, *Hercules with the Infant Telephus*; soon afterward the *Sleeping Ariadne* was unearthed. The enthusiasm for recovering ancient manuscripts was now equaled by the eagerness to recover lost works of ancient art. Both of these sentiments were strong in Leo. It was in his pontificate that excavators found the so-called *Antinoüs*, and the statues of the Nile and the Tiber; and these were placed in the Vatican Museum. Leo bought back, whenever he could, the gems, cameos, and other dispersed works of art once possessed by the Medici, and placed these too in the Vatican. Supported by his patronage, and starting with the previous work of Fra Giocondo and others, Iacopo Mazochi and Francesco Albertini copied, through four years, all the inscriptions they could find on Roman remains, and published them as *Epigrammata antiquae urbis Romae* (1521)—an event in classical archeology.

In 1515 Leo appointed Raphael superintendent of antiquities. Helped by Mazochi, Andrea Fulvio, Fabio Calvo, Castiglione, and others, the young painter formed an ambitious archeological plan. In 1518 he addressed to Leo a letter adjuring the Pontiff to use the authority of the Church for the preservation of all classical remains. The words may be Castiglione's, the passion has the ring of Raphael:

> When we reflect upon the divinity of those antique souls, . . . when we see the corpse of this noble city, mother and queen of the world, so miserably mangled, . . . how many pontiffs have permitted the ruin and defacement of the ancient temples, statues, arches and other buildings, the glory of their founders! . . . I dare say that all this new Rome that we now behold, however grand it is and beautiful and adorned with palaces, churches, and other edifices, has been cemented with lime made from the ancient marbles. . . .

The letter recalls how much destruction has taken place even during Raphael's ten years in Rome. It surveys the history of architecture, denounces the crude barbarism of the Romanesque and Gothic styles (here called the Gothic and the Teutonic), and exalts the Greco-Roman orders as models of perfection and taste. Finally it proposes that a corps of experts should be formed, that Rome should be divided into the fourteen regions anciently designated by Augustus, and that in each of these regions a careful survey and record should be made of all classic remains. Raphael's early death, soon followed by Leo's, delayed for a long time this majestic enterprise.

The influence of the recovered relics was felt in every branch of art and thought. That influence worked on Brunellesco, Alberti, Bramante; now it became supreme, until in Palladio it completely and almost servilely copied ancient forms. Ghiberti and Donatello had tried to model classically. Michelangelo achieved the classic manner perfectly in his *Brutus*, but for the rest he remained his passionate and unclassic self. Literature transformed Christian theology into pagan mythology, and replaced paradise with Olympus. In painting the classic influence took the form of pagan subjects and—even in Christian themes—pagan nudes; Raphael himself, darling of the popes, painted Psyches, Venuses, and Cupids on palace walls; and classic designs and arabesques mounted the pillars and ran along the cornices and friezes of a thousand buildings in Rome.

The classical triumph expressed itself most clearly in the new St. Peter's. Leo kept Bramante as "master of the works" there as long as possible; but the old architect was crippled with gout, and Fra Giocondo was commissioned to help him design; however, Fra Giocondo was ten years older than Bramante, who was seventy. In January, 1514, Leo appointed Giuliano da Sangallo, also seventy, to direct the operations. Bramante, on his deathbed, urged the Pope to confide the enterprise to a younger man, specifically, Raphael. Leo compromised; in August, 1514, he made the young Raphael and the old Fra Giocondo comasters of the work. For a time Raphael worked enthusiastically in his uncongenial function as an architect; henceforth, he said, he would live nowhere but in Rome, and this "from love for the building of St. Peter's . . . the greatest building that man has ever yet seen." He continues, with characteristic modesty:

> The cost will amount to a million gold ducats; the Pope has ordered 60,000 for the works. He thinks of nothing else. He has associated me with an experienced monk who has passed his eightieth year. The Pope sees that the monk cannot live much longer, and His Holi-

ness has therefore determined that I should benefit by the instructions of this distinguished craftsman, and attain to greater proficiency
in the art of architecture, of the beauties of which the monk has
recondite knowledge. . . . The Pope gives us audience every day,
and keeps us long in conversation on the subject of the building.[56]

Fra Giocondo died July 1, 1515; and on the same day Giuliano da
Sangallo withdrew from the group of designers. Raphael, left supreme,
undertook to replace Bramante's ground plan with a Latin cross, of un-
equal arms, and sketched a cupola that Antonio da Sangallo (nephew of
Giuliano) proved too heavy for its supporting pillars. In 1517 Antonio was
appointed coarchitect with Raphael. Disputes arose now at every step, and
Raphael, burdened with pictorial engagements, lost interest in the undertaking. Meanwhile Leo ran short of funds, tried to raise more by issuing
indulgences, and as a result found a German Reformation on his hands
(1517). St. Peter's made no substantial progress until Michelangelo was
put in charge of it in 1546.

VI. MICHELANGELO AND LEO X

Julius II had left funds to his executors for the completion, on a smaller
scale, of the tomb that Michelangelo had designed for him. The artist
worked at this task through the first three years of Leo's pontificate, and
received from the executors, in those years, 6100 ducats ($76,250?). Most
of what remains of the monument was probably produced in this period,
along with the *Christ Risen* of Santa Maria sopra Minerva—a handsome
naked athlete whom later taste clothed in a loincloth of bronze. A letter
written by Michelangelo in May, 1518, tells how Signorelli came to his
studio and borrowed eighty *giulii* ($800?), which he never returned, and
adds: "He found me working on a marble statue four cubits in height,
which has the hands bound behind the back."[57] This was presumably one
of the *Prigioni* or *Captivi* intended to represent the cities or arts made captive by the warrior Pope. A statue in the Louvre fits the description: a
muscular figure wearing only a loincloth, and with arms so tightly bound
at the back that the cords eat into the flesh. Near it is a finer *Captive*, naked
except for a narrow band about the breast; here the musculature is not exaggerated; the body is a symphony of health and beauty; this is Greek
perfection. Four unfinished *Schiavi* or *Slaves* in the Florence Academy
were apparently intended as caryatids to support the superstructure of the
tomb. The aborted tomb is now in Julius' church of San Pietro in Vincoli:
a magnificent massive throne, pillars elegantly carved, and a seated *Moses*

—an ill-proportioned monster of beard and horns and wrathful brow, holding the Tables of the Law. If we choose to believe an improbable story in Vasari, Jews could be seen on any Saturday entering the Christian church "to worship this figure, not as a work of the human hand, but as something divine."[58] On Moses' left is a *Leah*, on his right a splendid *Rachel*—statues that Michael called "the Active and the Contemplative Life." The remaining figures of the tomb were indifferently carved by his aides: above the *Moses* a *Madonna*, and at her feet the half-recumbent effigy of Julius II, crowned with the papal tiara. The whole monument is a torso, the painfully interrupted work of scattered years from 1506 to 1545, confused, enormous, incongruous, and absurd.

While these figures were being chiseled out, Leo—perhaps during a stay in Florence—conceived the idea of finishing the church of San Lorenzo there. This was the shrine of the Medici, containing the tombs of Cosimo, Lorenzo, and many other members of the family. Brunellesco had built the church, but had left the façade unfinished. Leo asked Raphael, Giuliano da Sangallo, Baccio d'Agnolo, Andrea and Iacopo Sansovino to submit plans for completing the front. Michelangelo, apparently of his own accord, sent in a plan of his own, which Leo accepted as the best; hence the Pope cannot be blamed, as so many have blamed him, for diverting Michael from Julius' tomb. Leo sent him to Florence, whence he went to Carrara to quarry tons of marble. Back in Florence, he hired assistants for the work, quarreled with them, sent them packing, and brooded inactively in his uncongenial role as architect. Cardinal Giulio de' Medici, Leo's cousin, appropriated some of the idle marble for work on the cathedral; Michael fumed, but still dallied. At last (1520) Leo freed him from the contract, and required no accounting of the funds that had been advanced to the artist. When Sebastiano del Piombo asked the Pope to give Angelo further assignments, Leo excused himself. He recognized Michelangelo's supremacy in art, but, he said, "he is an alarming man, as you yourself see, and there is no getting on with him." Sebastiano reported the conversation to his friend, adding: "I told His Holiness that your alarming ways did no man any harm, and that it was only your devotion to the great work to which you have given yourself that made you seem terrible to others."[59]

What was this famous *terribilità*? It was, first of all, energy, a wild consuming force that tortured Michelangelo's body, but sustained it, for eighty-nine years; and second, a power of will that kept that energy harnessed and directed to one purpose—art—ignoring almost everything else. Now energy directed by a unifying will is almost the definition of genius. The energy that looked upon formless stone as a challenge, and clawed and hammered and chiseled it *con furia* till it took on a revealing significance, was the same force that swept angrily over the distracting trivialities of life, took no thought of clothing or cleanliness or superficial courtesies, and advanced to its end, if not blindly yet with blinders, over broken promises, broken friendships, broken health, at last over a broken spirit, leaving the body and mind shattered, but the work done—the greatest painting, the greatest sculpture, and some of the greatest architecture, of the time. "If God assist me," he said, "I shall produce the finest thing that Italy has ever seen."[60]

He was the least prepossessing figure in an age brilliant with proud beauty of person and splendor of dress. Middle height, broad shoulders, slim frame, large head, high brow, ears protruding beyond the cheeks, temples bulging out beyond the ears, drawn and somber face, crushed nose, sharp, small eyes, grizzly hair and beard—this was Michelangelo in his prime. He wore old clothing, and clung to it till it became almost part of his flesh; and he seems to have obeyed half of his father's advice: "See that you do not wash. Have yourself rubbed down, but do not wash."[61] Though rich, he lived like a poor man, not only frugally but penuriously. He ate whatever he found at hand, sometimes dining on a crust of bread. At Bologna he and his three workmen occupied one room, slept in one bed. "While he was in full vigor," says Condivi, "he usually went to bed with his clothes on, even to the tall boots, which he has always worn because of a chronic tendency to cramp. . . . At certain seasons he has kept these boots on for such a length of time that when he drew them off, the skin came away together with the leather."[62] As Vasari puts it, "he had no mind to undress merely that he might have to dress again."[63]

While he prided himself on his supposed noble lineage, he preferred the poor to the rich, the simple to the intellectual, the toil of a worker to the leisure and luxuries of wealth. He gave most of his earnings to maintain his shiftless relatives. He liked solitude; he found it intolerable to make small talk with third-rate minds; wherever he was, he followed his own train of thought. He cared little for beautiful women, and saved a fortune by continence. When a priest expressed regret that Michelangelo had not married and begotten children, he replied: "I have only too much of a wife in my art, and she has given me trouble enough. As to my children, they are the works that I shall leave; and if they are not worth much, they will at least live for some time."[64] He could not bear women about the house. He preferred males both for companionship and for art. He painted women, but always in their maternal maturity, not in the bright charm of their youth; it is remarkable that both he and Leonardo were apparently insensitive to the physical beauty of woman, who has seemed to most artists the very embodiment and fountainhead of beauty. There is no evidence that he was homosexual; apparently all the energy that might have gone into sex was in his case used up in work. At Carrara he spent the day, from early morn, in the saddle, directing the stonecutters and road makers; and the evening in his cabin by lamplight, studying plans, calculating costs, projecting the morrow's tasks. He had periods of apparent sluggishness, and then suddenly the fever of creation would possess him again, and everything else would be ignored, even the sack of Rome.

Absorbed in work, he gave himself little time for friendship, though he had devoted friends. "Rarely did any friend or other person eat at his table."[65] He was content with the company of his faithful servant Francesco degli Amadori, who for twenty-five years took care of him, and for many years shared his bed. Michael's gifts made Francesco a rich man, and the artist was heartbroken at his death (1555). For others he had a bad temper and a sharp tongue, criticized rudely, took offense readily, suspected everybody. He called Perugino a fool, and expressed his opinion about Francia's paintings by telling Francia's handsome son that his father made better forms by night than by day.[66] He was jealous of Raphael's success and popularity. Though the two artists respected each other, their supporters divided into feuding cabals; and Iacopo Sansovino sent Michael a letter of violent abuse, saying, "May the day be cursed on which you ever said any good about anybody on earth."[67] There were a few such days. Seeing Titian's portrait of Duke Alfonso of Ferrara, Michael remarked that he had not thought that art could perform so much, and that only Titian deserved the name of painter.[68] His bitter temper and somber mood were his lifelong tragedy. At times he was melancholy to the edge of madness; and in his old age the fear of hell so obsessed him that he thought of his art as a sin, and he dowered poor girls to propitiate an angry God.[69] A neurotic sensitivity brought him almost daily misery. As early as 1508 he wrote to his father: "It is now about fifteen years since I had a single hour of well-being."[70] He would not have many more, though he had still fifty-eight years to live.

VII. RAPHAEL AND LEO X: 1513-20

Leo neglected Michelangelo partly because he liked men and women of equable temper, and partly because he had no great love for architecture or the massive in art; he preferred a gem to a cathedral, and miniatures to monuments. He kept Caradosso, Santi de Cola Sabba, Michele Nardini, and many other goldsmiths busy making jewelry, cameos, medals, coins, sacred vessels. At his death he left a collection of precious stones, rubies, sapphires, emeralds, diamonds, pearls, tiaras, miters, and pectorals worth 204,655 ducats—over $2,500,000; we should remember, however, that most of these had been inherited from his predecessors, and that they constituted a portion of the papal treasury immune to depreciations of the currency.

He invited a score of painters to Rome, but Raphael was almost the only one that he really cared for. He tried Leonardo, and dismissed him as a dawdler. Fra Bartolommeo came to Rome in 1514, and painted a *St. Peter* and a *St. Paul;* but the air and excitement disagreed with him, and he soon returned to the peace of his Florentine monastery. Leo liked the work of Sodoma, but hardly dared let that reckless rake roam too freely about the Vatican. Sebastiano del Piombo was appropriated by Leo's cousin, Giulio de' Medici.

Raphael agreed with Leo in both temperament and taste. Both were amiable epicureans who made Christianity a pleasure and took their heaven here; but both worked as hard as they played. Leo plied the happy artist with tasks: the completion of the *stanze*, the designing of cartoons for the Sistine Chapel tapestries, the decoration of the Vatican Loggie, the building of St. Peter's, the preservation of classic art. Raphael accepted these commissions with good cheer and appetite, and found time, besides, to paint a score of religious pictures, several series of pagan frescoes, and half a hundred Madonnas and portraits any one of which would have assured him wealth and fame. Leo abused his complaisance by asking him to arrange fetes, to paint the scenery for a play, to make a portrait of a beloved elephant.[71] Perhaps overwork, as well as love, brought Raphael to an early death.

But he was now in the fullness of his powers and the bloom of his prosperity. In a letter (July 1, 1514) to his "dear Uncle Simone . . . who art dear to me as a father," and who had reproached him for persistent bachelorhood, he writes in a mood of happy self-confidence:

> As for a wife, I must tell you that I am daily thankful that I did not take the one you destined for me, or, indeed, any other. In this instance I have been wiser than you . . . and I am sure that you must now see that I am better as I am. I have capital in Rome worth 3000 ducats, and an assured income of fifty more. His Holiness allows me a salary of 300 ducats for superintending the rebuilding of St. Peter's,

which will not fail me as long as I live. . . . Besides this, they give me
whatever I ask for my works. I have commenced the decoration of
a large hall for His Holiness, for which I am to get 1200 golden
crowns. Thus you must see, my dear uncle, that I do honor to my
family as well as to my country.[72]

At thirty-one he was entering into conscious manhood. He had grown
a dark beard, perhaps to disguise his youth. He lived in comfort, even
splendor, in a palace built by Bramante and bought by Raphael for three
thousand ducats. He dressed in the style of a young aristocrat. On his visits
to the Vatican he was accompanied by a princely retinue of pupils and
clients. Michelangelo reproved him, saying, "You go about with a suite,
like a general"; to which Raphael replied, "And you go about alone, like
a hangman."[73] He was still a good-natured youth, free from envy but eager
with emulation, not quite as modest as before (how could he be?), but
always helpful to others, presenting masterpieces to his friends, and even
serving as Maecenas and patron to artists less fortunate or gifted than himself. But on occasion his wit could be sharp enough. When two cardinals,
visiting his studio, amused themselves by picking flaws in his pictures—saying, for example, that the faces of the Apostles were too red—he replied:
"Do not be surprised at that, your eminences; I painted them so deliberately; may we not think that they can blush in heaven when they see the
Church governed by such men as you?"[74] However, he could take correction without resentment, as in the plans for St. Peter's. He could flatter a
succession of artists by imitating their excellences, without ever losing his
own independence and originality. He did not need solitude in order to be
himself.

His morals were not quite up to his manners. He could not have painted
women so attractively had he not been powerfully attracted by their
charms. He wrote love sonnets on the back of his drawings for the *Disputa*.
He had a concatenation of mistresses, but everybody, including the Pope,
seemed to think that so great an artist had a right to such amusements. Vasari, after describing Raphael's sexual promiscuity, apparently saw no contradiction in remarking, two pages later, that "those who copy his virtuous
life will be rewarded in heaven."[75] When Castiglione asked Raphael where
he found the models for the beautiful women whom he painted, he replied
that he created them in his imagination out of the diverse elements of beauty
present in different women;[76] hence he needed a large variety of samples.
Nevertheless there is a healthy, life-enhancing tone in his character and his
works, a unity, peace, and serenity in his career, amid the conflicts, divi-

sions, envies, and recriminations of the age. He ignored the politics that were consuming Leo and Italy, perhaps feeling that the repetitious contentions of parties and states for power and privilege are the monotonous froth of history, and that nothing matters but devotion to goodness, beauty, and truth.

Raphael left the pursuit of truth to more reckless spirits, and contented himself with the service of beauty. In the first years of Leo's reign he continued the decoration of the *Stanza d'Eliodoro.* By some whim of circumstance—and to symbolize the expulsion of the *barbari* from Italy—Julius had chosen, for the second main mural of the room, the historic meeting of Attila and Leo I (452). Raphael's drawing had already given the first Leo the features of the second Julius when the tenth Leo came to the papal throne. The drawing was revised, and Leo became Leo. More successful than this vast assemblage is the smaller picture that Raphael painted in an arch over a window of the same room. Here the new Pope, perhaps to commemorate his escape from the French at Milan, suggested as topic the deliverance of Peter from prison by an angel. Raphael used all his compositional artistry to give unity and life to a story broken by the casement into three scenes: on the left the sleeping guards, at the top an angel waking Peter, at the right the angel leading the drowsy and bewildered Apostle to freedom. The radiance of the angel illuminating the cell, shining upon the soldiers' armor and blinding their eyes, and the crescent moon whitening the clouds, make this a model pictorial study of light.

The young artist was avid of every new technique. Bramante, without Michelangelo's permission, had secretly taken his friend to see the frescoes of the Sistine vault before they were finished. Raphael was deeply impressed; perhaps, with the modesty that still accompanied his pride, he felt himself in the presence of a genius more powerful, if less gracious, than his own. He let the new influence move him in the themes and forms of the ceiling frescoes in the room of Helidorus: *God Appearing to Noah, Abraham's Sacrifice, Jacob's Dream,* and *The Burning Bush.* It shows again in the *Prophet Isaiah* that he painted for the church of St. Augustine.

In 1514 he began work on the room known from its main picture as the *Stanza dell' Incendio del Borgo.* A medieval legend told how Pope Leo III (795-816), merely by making the sign of the cross, had put out a fire that threatened to consume the Borgo—i.e., the borough of Rome around the Vatican. Probably Raphael made only the cartoon for this mural, and assigned the painting of it to his pupil Gianfrancesco Penni. Even so it is a powerful composition, in Raphael's best episodic narrative style. Mingling classical and Christian story, Raphael showed, on the left, a handsome and muscular Aeneas carrying to safety his old but muscular father Anchises. Another nude male, perfectly drawn, hangs from the top of the wall of the burning building, ready to drop; the influence of Michelangelo is evident in these three nudes. More Raphaelesque is an excited mother leaning over the wall to hand her infant to a man stretching up on tiptoe from below. Between magnificent columns groups of women beseech the aid of the Pope, who from a balcony calmly bids the fire cease. Raphael here is still at the top of his line.

For the remaining pictures in the room Raphael drew the cartoons, perhaps helped even in this by his pupils. From these cartoons Perino del Vaga painted, over the window, *The Oath of Leo III* exculpating himself before Charlemagne (800); on the exit wall another and greater pupil, Giulio Romano—the only native Roman prominent in Renaissance art—pictured *The Battle of Ostia*, in which Leo IV (looking remarkably like Leo X) turned back the invading Saracens (849); and in other spaces the able pupils painted idealized portraits of sovereigns who had deserved well of the Church. In a final picture, *The Coronation of Charlemagne*, Leo X becomes Leo III; and Francis I, here painted as Charlemagne, achieves by proxy his ambition to be emperor. The picture echoed Leo's meeting with Francis at Bologna the year before (1516).

Raphael made some preliminary sketches for the fourth *stanza*, the *Sala di Costantino;* the paintings were executed after his death under the patronage of Clement VII. Meanwhile Leo X urged him to begin the decoration of the Loggie—i.e., the open galleries built by Bramante to surround the court of St. Damasus in the Vatican. Raphael himself had completed the construction of these galleries; now (1517-9) he designed for the ceiling of one gallery fifty-two frescoes retelling the Bible story from the Creation to the Last Judgment. The actual painting was delegated to Giulio Romano, Gianfrancesco Penni, Perino del Vaga, Polidoro Caldara da Caravaggio, and others; while Giovanni da Udine decorated pilasters and arch soffits with delightful pictures and arabesques in stucco and paint. These Loggie frescoes sometimes used themes already treated on the Sistine ceiling, but with a lighter hand and in a homelier and more cheerful spirit, seeking not grandeur or sublimity, but pleasant episodes like Adam and Eve and their children enjoying the fruits of Eden, Abraham visited by three angels, Isaac embracing Rebecca, Jacob and Rachel at the well, Joseph and Potiphar's wife, the finding of Moses, David and Bathsheba, the adoration of the shepherds. These little paintings, of course, cannot compare with Michelangelo's; they are in a different world and genre—a world of feminine grace, not of masculine strength; they are the sign of the lighthearted Raphael in his last five years, while the Sistine ceiling is Michelangelo in the culmination of his powers.

Perhaps Leo was a bit jealous of the ceiling and the glory that it had shed upon the reign of Julius. Soon after his accession he conceived the idea of commemorating his own pontificate by ad rning the walls of the Sistine Chapel with tapestries. There were no weavers in Italy who could match those of Flanders, and Leo thought there were no painters in Flanders who could equal Raphael. He commissioned the artist (1515) to draw ten cartoons describing scenes from the Acts of the Apostles. Seven of these cartoons were bought at Brussels by Rubens (1630) for Charles I of England, and are now in the Victoria and Albert Museum in London. They are among the most remarkable drawings ever made. Raphael lavished here all his knowledge of composition, anatomy, and dramatic effect; in the whole range of drawing few pieces surpass *The Miraculous Draught of Fishes, Christ's Charge to Peter, The Death of Ananias, Peter Healing the Lame Man,* or *Paul Preaching at Athens*—though in this last the fine figure of Paul is stolen from Masaccio's frescoes in Florence.

The ten cartoons were sent to Brussels, and there Bernaert van Orley, who had been a pupil of Raphael in Rome, superintended the transference of the designs to silk and wool. In the short space of three years seven of the tapestries were completed, and all ten were finished by 1520. On December 26, 1519, seven were hung on the Sistine walls, and the elite of Rome were invited to see them. They created a furore. Paris de Grassis noted in his diary: "The whole chapel was struck dumb by the sight of these hangings; by universal consent there is nothing more beautiful in the world."[77] Each tapestry had cost a total of 2000 ducats ($25,000); the expenditure for the ten helped to deplete Leo's finances, and to induce the further sale of indulgences and offices.* Leo must have felt that now he and Raphael had met Julius and Michelangelo in a battle of art in the same chapel, and had carried off the prize.

The amazing fertility of Raphael—greater in his thirty-seven years than

---

* At Leo's death the tapestries were pawned to ease the papal insolvency; at the sack of Rome they were seriously injured; one was cut into fragments, and two were sold to Constantinople. All were restored to the Sistine Chapel by 1554; and every year, on the feast of Corpus Christi, they were exhibited to the people in the Piazza di San Pietro. Louis XIV had them copied in oils. Seized by the French in 1798, they were again returned to the Vatican in 1808. They are now displayed there in a hall of their own, the Galleria degli Arazzi, or Hall of the Arrases.

Michelangelo's in eighty-nine—makes it difficult to summarize him justly, for nearly every product was a masterpiece deserving commemoration. He designed mosaics, woodwork, jewelry, medals, pottery, bronze vessels and reliefs, perfume boxes, statues, palaces. Michelangelo was disturbed when he heard that Raphael had made a model, and that from this the Florentine sculptor Lorenzetto Lotti had carved in marble, a statue of Jonah riding the whale; but the result reassured him—Raphael had strayed unwisely out of his pictorial element. He did better in architecture, for there his friend Bramante guided him. About 1514, when he was put in charge of St. Peter's, he had his friend Fabio Calvo translate Vitruvius for him into Italian; and from that time he was an ardent lover of classical architectural styles and forms. His continuation of Bramante's Loggie so pleased Leo that the Pope made him director of all the architectural and artistic departments of the Vatican. Raphael built some undistinguished palaces in Rome, and shared in designing the elegant Villa Madama for Cardinal Giulio de' Medici; this, however, was chiefly the work of Giulio Romano as architect and painter, and of Giovanni da Udine as decorator. Raphael's one surviving architectural masterpiece is the Palazzo Pandolfini, built from his plans after his death; it is still among the finest palaces in Florence. With sublime indifference he turned his talents to the service of his friend the banker Chigi, and built for him a chapel in the church of Santa Maria del Popolo, and for his horses such stables (Stalle Chigiane, 1514) as might have served for a palace. To understand Raphael, and Leo's Rome, we must pause for a moment and look at the egregious Chigi.

VIII. AGOSTINO CHIGI

He typified a new group in Rome: rich merchants or bankers, usually of non-Roman origin, whose wealth put the old Roman nobility in the shade, and whose generosity to artists and writers was exceeded only by that of popes and cardinals. Born in Siena, he had imbibed financial subtlety with his daily food. By the age of forty-three he was chief Italian moneylender to republics and kingdoms, Christian or infidel. He financed trade with a dozen countries including Turkey, and by lease from Julius II acquired a monopoly in alum and salt.[78] In 1511 he gave Julius an additional reason for war on Ferrara—Duke Alfonso had dared to sell salt at a lower price than Agostino could afford to take.[79] His firm had branch houses in every major Italian town, and in Constantinople, Alexandria, Cairo, Lyons, London, Amsterdam. A hundred vessels sailed under his flag; twenty thousand men were in his pay; a half-dozen sovereigns sent him gifts; his best horse was from the Sultan; when he visited Venice (to which he had lent 125,000 ducats), he was seated next to the doge.[80] Asked by Leo X to estimate his wealth, he answered, perhaps for reasons of tax, that it was impossible; however, his annual income was reckoned to be 70,000 ducats ($875,000). His silver plate and jewelry equaled in quantity that of all the Roman nobility combined. His bedstead was carved in ivory and encrusted with gold and precious stones. The fixtures of his bathroom were of solid silver.[81] He had a dozen palaces and villas, of which the most ornate was the Villa Chigi, on the west bank of the Tiber. Designed by Baldassare Peruzzi, adorned with paintings by Peruzzi, Raphael, Sodoma, Giulio Romano, and Sebastiano del Piombo, it was hailed by the Romans, on its completion in 1512, as the lordliest palace in Rome.

The Chigi banquets had almost the reputation that those of Lucullus had gained in Caesar's time. In the stables that Raphael had just completed, and before they were occupied by handsomer beasts than men, Agostino entertained Pope Leo and fourteen cardinals, in 1518, with a repast that proudly cost him 2000 ducats ($25,000?). At that distinguished function eleven massive silver plates were stolen, presumably by servants in the retinue of the guests. Chigi forbade any search, and expressed courteous astonishment that so little had been stolen.[82] When the feast was over, the silk carpet, the tapestries, and the fine furniture were removed, and a hundred horses filled the stalls.

A few months later the banker gave another dinner, this time in the loggia of the villa, projecting out over the river. After each course all the silver used in serving it was thrown into the Tiber before the eyes of the guests, to assure them that no plate would be used twice. After the banquet Chigi's servants drew up the silver from the net that had secretly been lowered into the stream beneath the windows of the loggia.[83] At a dinner given in the main hall of the villa on August 28, 1519, each guest—including Pope Leo and twelve cardinals—was served on silver or gold plate faultlessly engraved with his own motto, crest, and coat of arms, and was fed with special fish, game, vegetables, fruits, delicacies, and wines freshly imported for the occasion from his own country or locality.

Chigi tried to atone for this plebeian display of wealth by an openhanded support of literature and art. He financed the editing of Pindar by the scholar Cornelio Benigno of Viterbo, and set up in his own home a press for its printing; and the Greek type cut for that press excelled in beauty that which Aldus Manutius had used in publishing the *Odes* two years before. This was the first Greek text printed in Rome (1515). A year later the same press issued a correct edition of Theocritus. Though himself a man of modest education, Agostino prided himself on his friendship with Bembo, Giovio, even Aretino; in this last case the Roman adage, *pecunia non olet*—"money does not smell"—included a transitive verb. Next to money and his mistress, Chigi loved all the forms of beauty that art had fashioned. He rivaled Leo in commissions to artists, and led him a merry pace in the pagan interpretation of the Renaissance. He collected into his palaces and villas such quantities of art as would have furnished a museum. He seems to have thought of his villa as not merely his home, but as a public gallery of art, to which the public might occasionally be admitted.

In that villa, at the aforementioned dinner on August 28, 1519, Leo himself officiating, Chigi at last married the faithful mistress with whom he had lived for the preceding eight years. Eight months later he died, within a few days of the death of Raphael. His estate, valued at 800,000 ducats ($10,000,000?) was divided chiefly among his children. Lorenzo, the oldest son, led a life of dissipation, and was adjudged insane in 1553. The Villa Chigi was sold to the second Cardinal Alessandro Farnese for a small sum about 1580, and from that time bore the name of Farnesina.

IX. RAPHAEL: THE LAST PHASE

Raphael had accepted minor commissions from the jolly banker as early as 1510. In 1514 he painted a fresco for him in the church of Santa Maria della Pace. The space provided was narrow and irregular; Raphael made it seem adequate by distributing in it four sibyls—Cumaean, Persian, Phrygian, Tiburtine—pagan oracles here sterilized with attendant angels. They are graceful figures, since Raphael could hardly draw anything without grace; Vasari thought they were the young master's finest work. They are a weak imitation of Angelo's sibyls, except for the Tiburtine; here the priestess, haggard with age and frightened by the evil fortune she is foretelling, is a figure of original and dramatic power. According to a story not traceable beyond the seventeenth century, some misunderstanding arose between Raphael and Chigi's treasurer about the fee for these sibyls. Raphael had received five hundred ducats, but, when finished, claimed an additional payment. The treasurer thought the five hundred already paid were all that were due. Raphael suggested that the treasurer should appoint a competent artist to evaluate the frescoes; the official chose Michelangelo; Raphael agreed. Michelangelo, despite his supposed jealousy of Raphael, judged that each head in the picture was worth one hundred ducats. When the astonished treasurer brought this judgment to Chigi the banker ordered him to pay Raphael at once four hundred additional ducats. "Be tender with him," he cautioned, "so that he may be satisfied. If he makes me pay for the draperies I shall be ruined."[84]

Chigi had to be careful, for in that same year Raphael was painting for him a delectable fresco in the Villa Chigi—*The Triumph of Galatea*. The story was taken from Politian's *Giostra:* Polyphemus, the one-eyed Cyclops, tries to seduce the nymph Galatea by his songs and flute; she turns from him in disdain—as if to say, Who would marry an artist?—and gives the reins to two dolphins who pull her shell-like vessel out to sea. At her left a robust nymph is gaily seized by a powerful Triton, while from the clouds cupids shoot superfluous arrows to encourage love. Here the pagan Renaissance is in full swing, and Raphael enjoys himself picturing women as his bright imagination thought they should be formed.

In 1516 he adorned the bathroom of Cardinal Bibbiena with frescoes glorifying Venus and the triumphs of love. In 1517 he disported himself still more voluptuously in designs for the ceiling and pendentives of the Villa Chigi's central hall. Here he adapted his genial fancy to a tale from Apuleius' *Metamorphoses*. Psyche, daughter of a king, arouses by her beauty the envy of Venus; the spiteful goddess bids her son Cupid inspire Psyche with a passion for the most contemptible man to be found. Cupid descends to the earth to fulfill his mission, but falls in love with Psyche at first touch. He visits her in the dark, and bids her repress her curiosity as to who he is. Inevitably she rises from her bed one night, lights a lamp, and is delighted to see that she has been sleeping with the most handsome of the gods. In her excitement she lets a drop of hot oil fall upon his divine shoulder. He awakes, berates her for her curiosity, and leaves her in anger, not realizing that lack of curiosity by a woman in such cases would demoralize society. Psyche wanders over the earth disconsolate. Venus imprisons Cupid for disobeying his mother, and complains to Jupiter that celestial discipline is deteriorating. Jupiter sends Mercury to fetch Psyche, who then becomes the abused slave of Venus. Cupid escapes from his confinement, and begs Jove to grant him Psyche. The puzzled god, torn as usual between opposing prayers, summons the Olympian deities to debate the matter. He himself, susceptible to youthful male charms, sides with Cupid; the complaisant gods vote to free Psyche, to make her a goddess, and to give her to Cupid; and in the final scene they celebrate with an ambrosial banquet the nuptials of Cupid and Psyche. We are assured that the story is a pious allegory, in which Psyche represents the human soul, which, when purified by suffering, is admitted to paradise. But Raphael and Chigi saw in the myth no religious symbolism, but a chance to contemplate perfect male and female forms. Yet there is in Raphael's sensualism a refinement and grace that disarms puritan criticism; apparently the genial Leo found in them nothing to reprove. Only the figures and composition here are Raphael's; Giulio Romano and Francesco Penni painted the scenes from his designs, and Giovanni da Udine added enticing enclosing wreaths burgeoning with fruits and flowers. The school of Raphael had become a transmission belt whose end product was almost certain to be some form of loveliness.

Never were pagan and Christian so agreeably merged as in Raphael. This same worldly youth who lived like a prince and loved many women transiently, and (if one may venture such an anomaly) frolicked on ceilings with male and female nudes, painted in these same years (1513-20) some of the most appealing pictures in the gamut of history. With all his guileless sensualism he always returned to the Madonna as his favorite theme; fifty times he pictured her. Sometimes a pupil helped him, as in the *Madonna dell' Impannata;* but for the most part he worked on this type of painting with his own hand, and with a touch of the old Umbrian piety. Now (1515) he painted the *Sistine Madonna* for the convent of San Sisto at Piacenza:* a perfect pyramidal composition; the convincing realism of the old martyr St. Sixtus; the demure St. Barbara, a bit too beautiful and too splendidly gowned; the Virgin's green robe, over a touch of red, blown by heaven's winds; the Child quite human in His disheveled innocence; the simple rosy face of the Madonna, a little sad and wondering (as if La Fornarina, who may have posed for this picture, realized her disqualifications); the curtains drawn aside by angels behind the Virgin, admitting her to paradise: this is the favorite picture of all Christendom, the most widely loved product of Raphael's hand. Almost as fine, and perhaps more moving despite its traditional form, is *The Holy Family under the Oak Tree* (Prado), also called *La Perla*, "The Pearl Madonna." In the *Madonna della Sedia* or *Seggiola* (Pitti) the mood is less evangelical, more human; the Madonna is a young Italian mother, buxom and quietly passionate; clasping

---

* The picture was bought in 1753 for Frederick Augustus II of Saxony at a price of 60,000 thalers ($450,000?), and for almost two centuries it remained the chief treasure of the Dresden Gallery. Along with Correggio's *Holy Night*, Giorgione's *Venus*, and some 920,000 other art objects, it was taken from Germany by the victorious Russians after the Second World War.[85]

her fat babe with possessive and protective love, while he nestles timidly against her, as if he had heard some myth of massacred innocents. One such *Madonna* could atone for many Fornarinas.

Raphael painted relatively few pictures of Christ. His buoyant spirit shrank from the contemplation or portrayal of suffering; or perhaps, like Leonardo, he realized the impossibility of representing the divine. In 1517, probably with the collaboration of Penni, he painted *Christ Bearing the Cross* for the convent of Santa Maria dello Spasimo in Palermo, whence the picture came to be called *Lo Spasimo di Sicilia.* According to Vasari it had an adventurous career: the ship that carried it to Sicily was lost in a storm; the crated painting floated safely over the waters, and landed at Genoa; "even the fury of the winds and waves," said Vasari, "respected such painting." It was shipped again, and was set up in Palermo, where "it became more famous than the mountain of Vulcan."[86] In the seventeenth century Philip IV of Spain had it secretly transferred to Madrid. Christ in this picture is merely an exhausted and defeated man, conveying no sense of a mission accepted and fulfilled. Raphael succeeded better in suggesting divinity in *The Vision of Ezekiel,* though here again he borrows his majestic God from Michelangelo's *Creation of Adam.*

To this crowded period belongs the *St. Cecilia,* almost as popular as the *Sistine Madonna.* A Bolognese lady, in the fall of 1513, announced that she had heard heavenly voices bidding her dedicate a chapel to St. Cecilia in the church of San Giovanni del Monte. A relative undertook to build the chapel, and asked his uncle Cardinal Lorenzo Pucci to order from Raphael, for a thousand gold *scudi,* an appropriate picture for the altar. Delegating to Giovanni da Udine the representation of the musical instruments, Raphael finished the painting in 1516, and sent it to Bologna, as we have seen, with a kindly letter to Francia. We need not believe that Francia was mortally stricken by its beauty to feel the splendor of the work, its sense of music as something almost celestial, its St. Paul in a "brown study," its St. John in almost girlish ecstasy, its lovely Cecilia, its still lovelier Magdalen—here transformed into charming innocence—and the living lights and shadows on the drapery and on Magdalen's feet.

Now, too, came some masterly portraits. The *Baldassare Castiglione* (Louvre) is one of Raphael's most conscientious efforts, endlessly enticing, among his portraits second only to the *Julius II.* One sees first the strange fluffy headdress, then the furry robe and profuse beard, and imagines the man to be some Moslem poet or philosopher, or a rabbi seen by Rembrandt; then the soft eyes and mouth and clasped hands reveal the tender-minded, sentimental, bereaved minister of Isabella at Leo's court; one should linger over this portrait before reading *The Courtier*. The *Bibbiena* shows the Cardinal in his later years, tired of his Venuses and reconciled to Christianity.

La donna velata is not incontestably Raphael's, yet it is almost certainly the picture that Vasari describes as a portrait of Raphael's mistress. Her features are those that he used for the Magdalen, even the Cecilia, of *St. Cecilia*, perhaps for the *Sistine Madonna*—here dark and demure, a long veil falling from her head, a circlet of gems around her neck, and lucious robes wrapped loosely about her form. Probably by Raphael, but not so clearly representing his mistress as older views claimed, is *La Fornarina* in the Borghese Gallery. The word means a woman baker, or a baker's wife or daughter; but such names, like Smith or Carpenter, prove nothing of the bearer's occupation. This lady is not especially attractive; one misses in her the modest look that makes more charming such immodest revelations * It seems incredible that the modest *Veiled Lady* should be the same person as this bold dispenser of hurried joys; but, after all, Raphael had more mistresses than one.

Yet he was more faithful to his mistress than artists—who are more sensitive to beauty than to reason—can be expected to be. When Cardinal Bibbiena urged him to marry Maria Bibbiena, the Cardinal's niece, Raphael, indebted to him for rich commissions, gave unwilling consent (1514); but he delayed from month to month and from year to year the keeping of this troth; and tradition relates that Maria, so repeatedly put off, died of a broken heart.[87] Vasari suggests that Raphael delayed in hope of being made a cardinal; to such an elevation marriage was a major—a mistress a negligible —impediment. Meanwhile the artist seems to have kept his mistress within close reach of wherever he was working. When the distance between the Villa Chigi, where Raphael was designing the *History of Psyche*, and his mistress' dwelling led to much loss of time, the banker had the lady installed in an apartment of the villa; "that," says Vasari, "is why the work was finished."[88] We do not know if it was with this mistress that Raphael indulged in the "unusually wild debauch" to which Vasari ascribes his death.[89]

His last picture was one of his supreme interpretations of the Gospel story. In 1517 Cardinal Giulio de' Medici commissioned both Raphael and Sebastiano del Piombo to paint altarpieces for the cathedral of Narbonne, of which Francis I had made him bishop. Sebastiano had long felt

---

* Another and finer *Fornarina*, in the Uffizi, is by Sebastiano del Piombo.

that his talent was at least equal to Raphael's though so much less recognized; here was his chance to prove himself. He chose as subject the raising of Lazarus, and secured the help of Michelangelo in making his design. Spurred by the competition, Raphael rose to his final triumph. He took for his theme Matthew's account of the episode on Mt. Tabor:

> And after six days Jesus took Peter, James, and John his brother, and brought them up into a high mountain apart, and was transfigured before them; and his face did shine as the sun, and his raiment was white as the light. And behold, there appeared unto them Moses and Elias talking with him. . . . And when they returned to the multitude there came to him a certain man, kneeling down to him and saying, Lord, have mercy on my son, for he is a lunatic, and sore vexed; for ofttimes he falleth into the fire, and oft into the water. And I brought him to thy disciples, and they could not cure him.[90]

Raphael took both of these scenes and united them, with excessive strain on the unities of time and place. Above the mountain top the figure of Christ appears soaring in the air, His face transfigured with ecstasy, His garments made shining white by light from heaven; on one side of Him Moses, on the other Elias; and beneath them, lying on a plateau, the three favored Apostles. At the foot of the mountain a desperate father pushes forward his insane boy; the mother and another woman, both of them classic in their beauty, kneel beside the boy and beg a cure from the nine Apostles who are gathered at the left. One of these is startled out of his concentration on a book; another points to the transfigured Christ, and suggests that only He can cure the boy. It is usual to praise the splendor of the upper part of the picture, presumably finished by Raphael, and to deprecate a certain coarseness and violence in the lower group, which was painted by Giulio Romano; but two of the finest figures are in the lower foreground—the disturbed reader, and a kneeling woman with bare shoulder and gleaming drapery.

Raphael began work on the *Transfiguration* in 1517, but had not finished it when he died. We cannot say how much truth there is in Vasari's account, written some thirty years after the event:

> Raphael continued his secret pleasures beyond all measure. After an unusually wild debauch he returned home with a severe fever, and the doctors believed him to have caught a chill. As he did not confess the cause of his disorder, the doctors imprudently let blood,

thus enfeebling him when he needed restoratives. Accordingly he made his will, first sending his mistress out of the house like a Christian, leaving her the means to live honestly. He then divided his things among his pupils, Giulio Romano, of whom he was always very fond, Giovanni Francesco Penni of Florence, and some priest of Urbino, a relation. . . . Having confessed and shown penitence, he finished the course of his life on the day of his birth, Good Friday, at the age of thirty-seven (April 6, 1520).[91]

The priest who had come to shrive him refused to enter the sick room until Raphael's mistress had left the house; perhaps the priest felt that her continued presence would suggest on Raphael's part a lack of the contrition required before absolution. Driven away even from the funeral cortege, she fell into a melancholy that threatened insanity; and Cardinal Bibbiena persuaded her to become a nun. All the artists of Rome followed the dead youth to his grave. Leo mourned the loss of his beloved painter; and a papal secretary and poet, the Bembo who could be so eloquent in both Latin and Italian, put aside all rhetoric in writing an epitaph for Raphael's tomb in the Pantheon:

ILLE HIC EST RAPHAEL

—"He who is here is Raphael." It was enough.

In the opinion of his contemporaries he was the greatest painter of his age. He produced nothing equal in sublimity to the Sistine ceiling, but Michelangelo produced nothing equal in total beauty to the fifty Madonnas of Raphael. Michelangelo was the greater artist, because great in three fields, and deeper in thought and art. When he said of Raphael, "He is an example of what profound study can bring forth,"[92] he probably meant that Raphael had acquired by imitation the excellences of many other painters, and had combined them with assiduous talent into a perfected style; he did not feel, in Raphael, the creative fury that soon throws off guidance and cuts a path almost violently for its own way. Raphael appeared too happy to be a genius in the traditional frenzied sense; he had so solved his inner conflicts that he showed few signs of the demonic spirit or force that moves the greatest souls to creation and tragedy. Raphael's work was the product of finished skill, not of profound feeling or conviction. He adjusted himself to the needs and moods of Julius, then of Leo, then of Chigi, but remained always the guileless youth cheerfully oscillating between Madonnas and mistresses; this was his blithe way of reconciling paganism and Christianity.

As artist in the sense of technician, no one surpassed him; in the arrangement of elements in a picture, the rhythm of masses, the smooth flow of line, no one has equaled him. His life was a devotion to form. Consequently he tended to remain on the surface of things. Except in his portrait of Julius II, he did not probe into the mysteries or contradictions of life or creed; Leonardo's subtlety and Michelangelo's sense of tragedy were alike meaningless to him; the lust and joy of life, the creation and possession of beauty, the loyalty of friend and lover, were enough. Ruskin was right: there was now and then in Gothic sculpture and the "Pre-Raphaelite" painting of Italy and Flanders a simplicity, sincerity, and sublimity of faith and hope that sink deeper into the soul than the pretty Madonnas and voluptuous Venuses of Raphael. And yet the *Julius II* and the *Pearl Madonna* are anything but superficial; they reach to the heart of male ambition and female tenderness; the *Julius* is greater and profounder than the *Mona Lisa*.

Leonardo puzzles us, Michelangelo frightens us, Raphael gives us peace. He asks no questions, raises no doubts, evokes no terrors, but offers us the loveliness of life like an ambrosial drink. He admits no conflict between intellect and feeling, nor between body and soul; everything in him is a harmony of opposites, making a Pythagorean music. His art idealizes all that it touches: religion, woman, music, philosophy, history, even war. Himself fortunate and happy, he radiated serenity and grace. In the arbitrary analogies of genius he finds his place just below the greatest, but with them: Dante, Goethe, Keats; Beethoven, Bach, Mozart; Michelangelo, Leonardo, Raphael.

X. LEO POLITICUS

It was a pity that amid all this art and literature Leo had to play politics. But he was head of a state, and lived at a time when the powers beyond the Alps had ambitious leaders, large armies, and lusty generals; at any moment Louis XII of France and Ferdinand the Catholic might agree to divide Italy as they had agreed to divide the Kingdom of Naples. To meet these threats —and incidentally to strengthen the Papal States and aggrandize his family —Leo planned to combine Florence (which he already ruled through his brother Giuliano and his nephew Lorenzo) with Milan, Piacenza, Parma, Modena, Ferrara, and Urbino into a new and powerful federation to be ruled by loyal Medici; to unite these with the existing States of the Church as a barrier to aggression from the north; if possible, to secure by marriage, for some member of his house, the succession to the throne of Naples; and, with an Italy so welded into strength, to lead Europe in one more crusade against the ever threatening Turks. Machiavelli, who had no prejudice in favor of Christianity or the popes, warmly approved of this plan, at least so far as concerned the unification and protection of Italy; this was the leading idea of *The Prince*.

Pursuing these aims with very limited military means at his disposal, Leo used all the methods of statecraft and diplomacy employed by the princes of his day. It was inconvenient that the head of a Christian Church should have to lie, break faith, steal, and kill; but by the common consent of kings these procedures were indispensable to the preservation of a state. Leo, a Medici first and a pope afterward, played the game as well as his corpulence, his fistula, his hunts, his liberalities, and his finances would allow. All the kings denounced him, disappointed that he would not behave like a saint; "Leo," said Guicciardini, "deceived the expectations conceived of him at his accession, since he appeared to be endowed with greater prudence, but with much less goodness, than all had imagined."[93] For a long time his enemies thought that his Machiavellian subtlety was due to the influence of his cousin Giulio (the future Clement VII), or to Cardinal Bibbiena; but as events matured it became clear that they had to deal with Leo himself, not a lion but a fox, suave and slippery, cunning and incalculable, grasping and devious, sometimes frightened and often hesitant, but, in the last resort, capable of decision, resolution, and persistent policy.

Let us leave his relations with the transalpine states to a later chapter, confine ourselves here to Italian affairs, and deal with these summarily, for the art of Leo's time is a much more living thing than its politics. He had a great advantage over his predecessors, for Florence, which had opposed Alexander and Julius, was now happy to be part of his realm, since he gave its citizens many papal plums; and when he visited the city of his ancestors it raised a dozen artistic arches to welcome him. From that *point d'appui*, and from Rome, he deployed his diplomats and patronage and troops to swell his state. In 1514 he secured Modena. In 1515 Francis I prepared to invade Italy and take Milan; Leo organized an army and an Italian alliance to resist him, and ordered the Duke of Urbino, as a vassal of the Holy See and a general in the service of the Church, to join him at Bologna with all the forces he could muster. The Duke, Francesco Maria della Rovere, flatly refused to come, though Leo had recently advanced him money to pay his troops. The Pope with some reason suspected him of having a secret understanding with France.[94] As soon as his hands were freed from foreign entanglements, Leo summoned Francesco to Rome; the Duke instead fled to Mantua. Leo excommunicated him, and listened unmoved to the entreaties and messages of Elisabetta Gonzaga and Isabella d'Este, aunt and mother-in-law of the reckless prince; papal troops took Urbino unresisted, Francesco was declared deposed, and Leo's nephew Lorenzo became Duke of Urbino (1516). A year later the people of the city rose and expelled Lorenzo; Francesco organized an army and recaptured his duchy; Leo was hard put to it to raise funds and forces to recapture it in turn; he succeeded after eight months of war, but the cost exhausted the papal treasury, and turned the good will of Italy against the Pope and his grasping family.

Francis I took the opportunity to win the friendship of the Pope, and proposed a marriage between Lorenzo, the restored Duke of Urbino, and Madeleine de La Tour d'Auvergne, who had a charming income of 10,000 crowns ($125,000?) a year. Leo agreed; Lorenzo went to France (1518), like an echo of Borgia, and brought back Madeleine and her dowry. A year later she died in giving birth to a daughter Caterina, the future Queen Catherine de Médicis of France; and shortly thereafter Lorenzo himself died, allegedly of a sexual disease contracted in France.[95] Leo now declared Urbino a papal state, and sent a legate to govern it.

During these complications he had had to bear with two bitter signs of his political weakness and growing unpopularity. One of his generals, Gianpaolo Baglioni, ruler of Perugia by papal grace, had gone over to Francesco Maria, taking Perugia with him; Leo later lured Gianpaolo to Rome with a safe-conduct, and had him put to death (1520). Baglioni had shared also in a conspiracy, led by Alfonso Petrucci and other cardinals, to assassinate the Pope (1517). These cardinals had made such demands upon Leo as even his generosity could not meet; Petrucci, moreover, raged because his brother, with Leo's connivance, had been ousted from the government of Siena. He planned at first to kill Leo with his own hand, but was persuaded instead to bribe Leo's physician to poison the Pope while treating his fistula. The plot was discovered; the physician and Petrucci were executed, and several accomplice cardinals were imprisoned and deposed; some were released on paying enormous fines.

Leo's need for money was now souring his once happy reign. His gifts to relatives, friends, artists, writers, and musicians, his lavish maintenance of an unprecedented court, the insatiable demands of the new St. Peter's, the expense of the Urbino war and the preparation for a crusade, were leading him to bankruptcy. His regular revenue of 420,000 ducats ($5,250,000?) a year from fees, annates, and tithes was completely inadequate, and yet was always more difficult to secure from a Europe resentful of ecclesiastical collections flowing to Rome. To replenish his treasury Leo created 1353 new and saleable offices, for which the appointees paid a total of 889,000 ducats ($11,112,500?). We must not be too virtuous about this; most of the offices were sinecures whose modest toil could be delegated to subordinates; the sums paid for these appointments were in effect loans to the papacy; the salaries, averaging ten per cent per year on the initial payment, were interest on the loans; Leo was selling what we would now designate as government bonds;[96] and he would doubtless have urged that he paid a much handsomer return than governments pay today. However, he sold not only these sinecures, but even the highest offices, like that of papal chamberlain.[97] In July, 1517, he named thirty-one new cardinals, many of them men of ability, but most of them chosen frankly for their capacity to pay for the honor and power. So Cardinal Ponzetti—physician, scholar, author—paid 30,000 ducats; altogether Leo's pen on this occasion brought half a million ducats into the treasury.[98] Even blasé Italy was shocked; and in Germany the story of the transaction shared in the anger of Luther's revolt (October, 1517). When, in this momentous year, Sultan Selim conquered Egypt for the Ottoman Turks, Leo appealed in vain for a crusade. In his blind eagerness he sent agents throughout Christendom to offer extraordinary indulgences in return for contrition, confession, and contribution to the expenses of the proposed crusade.

Sometimes he borrowed money at forty per cent from the bankers of Rome, who charged him such rates because they feared that his careless administration of papal finances would ensure bankruptcy. As security for some of these loans he pledged his silver plate, his tapestries, his jewels. He rarely thought of economizing, and when he did it was by defaulting on the salaries of his Greek Academy and the University of Rome; as early as 1517 the former was closed for lack of funds. He continued his intemperate benevolence, sending rich subsidies to monasteries, hospitals, and charitable institutions throughout Christendom, heaping dignities and funds upon the Medici, and feeding his guests Lucullanly while himself eating and drinking in moderation.[99] All in all he spent during his pontificate 4,500,000 ducats ($56,250,000?), and died owing 400,000 more. A pasquinade expressed the opinion of Rome: "Leo has eaten up three pontificates: the treasury of Julius II, the revenues of Leo, and those of his successor."[100] When he died Rome experienced one of the worst financial crashes in its history.

His final year was rife with war. Having regained Urbino and Perugia, it seemed to him that control of Ferrara and the Po was indispensable to the security of the Papal States, and their capacity to check France at Milan. Duke Alfonso had given the requisite *casus belli* by sending troops and artillery to Francesco Maria for use against the Pope. Alfonso, though ill, and well-nigh exhausted after a generation of papal hostility, fought on with his usual courage, and was saved by Leo's death.

The Pope too was ill in August, 1521, partly from the pain of his fistula, partly from the worries and excitement of war. He recovered, but fell sick again in October. In November he was well enough to be taken out to his country villa at Magliana. There the news reached him that the papal-imperial army had captured Milan from the French. On the 25th he returned to Rome, and was given the wild reception accorded only to victors in war. He walked too much that day, perspiring till his clothes were drenched. The next morning he was put to bed with fever. Now he rapidly grew worse, and realized that his end was near. On December 1 he was cheered by intelligence that Piacenza and Parma had in their turn been taken by the papal forces; once he had declared that he would gladly give his life for the addition of those cities to the States of the Church. At midnight, December 1-2, 1521, he died, ten days before completing his forty-fifth year. Many of the attendants, and some members of the Medici family, carried off from the Vatican everything they could lay their hands on. Guicciardini, Giovio, and Castiglione thought that he had been poisoned, perhaps at the instigation of Alfonso or Francesco Maria; but apparently he died of malarial fever, like Alexander VI.[101]

Alfonso rejoiced at the news, and struck a new medal EX ORE LEONIS, "from the jaws of the lion." Francesco Maria returned to Urbino, and was once more restored to his throne. In Rome the bankers despoiled themselves. The Bini firm had lent Leo 200,000 ducats, the Gaddi 32,000, the Ricasoli 10,000; moreover, Cardinal Pucci had lent him 150,000, and Cardinal Salviati 80,000;[102] the cardinals would have first claim on anything salvaged; and Leo had died worse than bankrupt. Some others joined in condemning the dead Pope as a maladministrator of great wealth. But nearly all Rome mourned him as the most generous benefactor in its history. Artists, poets, and scholars knew that the heyday of their good fortune had passed, though they had no suspicion yet of the extent of their disaster. Said Paolo Giovio: "Knowledge, art, the common well-being, the joy of living—in a word, all good things—have gone down into the grave with Leo."[103]

He was a good man ruined by his virtues. Erasmus had rightly praised his kindness and humanity, his magnanimity and learning, his love and support of the arts, and had called Leo's pontificate an age of gold.[104] But Leo was too habituated to gold. Raised in a palace, he learned luxury as well as art; he never labored for his income, though he faced perils bravely; and when the revenues of the papacy were placed in his trust they slipped through his careless fingers while he basked in the happiness of recipients, or planned expensive wars. Proceeding on the lines laid down by Alexander and Julius, and inheriting their achievements, he made the Papal States stronger than ever, but he lost Germany by his extravagance and his exactions. He could see the beauty of a vase, but not the Protestant Reformation taking shape beyond the Alps; he paid no attention to a hundred warnings sent him, but asked for more gold from a nation already in revolt. He was a glory and a disaster to the Church.

He was the most generous, but not the most enlightened, of patrons. With all his patronage no great literature arose in his reign. Ariosto and Machiavelli were beyond him, though he could appreciate Bembo and Politian. His taste in art was not as sure and lordly as that of Julius; it was not to him that we owe St. Peter's or *The School of Athens*. He loved beautiful form too much, too little the revealing significance that great art clothes in beautiful form. He overworked Raphael, underestimated Leonardo, and could not, like Julius, find a way through Michelangelo's temper to his genius. He liked comfort too much to be great. It is a pity to judge him so harshly, for he was lovable.

The age received his name, and perhaps rightly; for though he rather took than gave its stamp, it was he who brought from Florence to Rome the Medicean heritage of wealth and taste, the princely patronage that he had seen in his father's house; and with that wealth, and papal sanction, he provided an exciting stimulus to such literature and art as excelled in style and form. His example stirred a hundred other men to seek out talent, support it, and set northern Europe a precedent and standard of appreciation and worth. He more than any other pope protected the remains of classic Rome, and encouraged men to rival them. He accepted the pagan enjoyment of life, and yet, in his own conduct, remained remarkably continent in an uninhibited age. His support of the Roman humanists helped to spread into France their cultivation of classic literature and form. Under his aegis Rome became the throbbing heart of European culture; thither the artists flocked to paint or carve or build, the scholars came to study, the poets to sing, the men of wit to sparkle. "Before I forget thee, Rome," wrote Erasmus, "I must plunge into the river of Lethe. . . . What precious freedom, what treasures in the way of books, what depths of knowledge among the learned, what beneficial social intercourse! Where else could one find such literary society, or such versatility of talent in one and the same place?"[105] The gentle Castiglione, the polished Bembo, the learned Lascaris, Fra Giocondo, Raphael, the Sansovini and Sangalli, Sebastiano and Michelangelo—where shall we find again, in one city and decade, such a company?

BOOK V

DEBACLE

CHAPTER XIX

The Intellectual Revolt

1300-1534

I. THE OCCULT

IN every age and nation civilization is the product, privilege, and responsibility of a minority. The historian acquainted with the pervasive
pertinacity of nonsense reconciles himself to a glorious future for superstition; he does not expect perfect states to arise out of imperfect men; he
perceives that only a small proportion of any generation can be so freed
from economic harassments as to have leisure and energy to think their own
thoughts instead of those of their forebears or their environment; and he
learns to rejoice if he can find in each period a few men and women who
have lifted themselves, by the bootstraps of their brains, or by some boon
of birth or circumstance, out of superstition, occultism, and credulity to an
informed and friendly intelligence conscious of its infinite ignorance.

So in Renaissance Italy civilization was of the few, by the few, and for
them. The simple common man, named legion, tilled and mined the earth,
pulled the carts or bore the burdens, toiled from dawn to dusk, and at
evening had no muscle left for thought. He took his opinions, his religion,
his answers to the riddles of life from the air about him, or inherited them
with the ancestral cottage; he let others think for him because others made
him work for them. He accepted not only the fascinating, comforting, inspiring, terrifying marvels of the traditional theology—which were daily
reimpressed upon him by contagion, inculcation, and art—but he added to
them, in his mental furniture, the demonology, sorcery, portents, magic,
divination, astrology, relic-worship, and miraclemongering that composed,
so to speak, a popular metaphysics unauthorized by the Church, which
deprecated them as a problem sometimes more troublesome then unbelief.
While the uncommon man in Italy was half a century or more ahead of his
class beyond the Alps in wealth and culture, the common man south of the
Alps shared equally with his transalpine peers the superstitions of the time.

Often the humanists themselves surrendered to the *genius* or *stultus loci*,
and sprinkled their Ciceronian pages with the spirit or foolishness of their

surroundings. Poggio revels in portents and prodigies like headless horse-men migrating from Como to Germany, or bearded Tritons rising from the sea to snatch fair women from the shore.[1] Machiavelli, so skeptical of re-ligion, suggested the possibility that "the air is peopled with spirits," and declared his belief that great events are heralded by prodigies, prophecies, revelations, and signs in the sky.[2] The Florentines, who liked to think that the air they breathed made them clever beyond compare, held that all im-portant events happened on Saturday, and that it was a sure misfortune to march out to war by certain streets.[3] Politian was so upset by the Pazzi conspiracy that he attributed to it a disastrous rainfall that followed it, and condoned the youths who, to end the rain, exhumed the corpse of the chief conspirator, paraded it through the city, and then flung it into the Arno.[4] Marsilio Ficino wrote in defense of divination, astrology, and demonology, and excused himself from visiting Pico della Mirandola on the ground that the stars were in an unfavorable conjunction[5]—or was it a whimsy? If humanists could believe so, how could the people, with no advantage of leisure or education, be blamed for thinking of the natural world as the shell and instrument of numberless supernatural powers?

The people of Italy reckoned so many objects as true relics of Christ or the Apostles that one might have furnished from Renaissance Roman churches alone all the scenes of the Gospels. One church claimed to have a swaddling cloth of the Infant Jesus; another, hay from the Bethlehem stall; another, fragments of the multiplied loaves and fishes; another, the table used at the Last Supper; another, the picture of the Virgin painted by angels for St. Luke.[6] Venetian churches displayed the body of St. Mark, an arm of St. George, an ear of St. Paul, some roasted flesh of St. Lawrence, some of the very stones that had killed St. Stephen.[7]

Nearly every object—every number and letter—was believed to have some magic power. According to Aretino some Roman harlots fed to their lovers, as an aphrodisiac, the rotting flesh of human corpses stolen from the cemeteries.[8] Incantations were used for a thousand purposes; by the proper one, said Apulian peasants, you could protect yourself from mad dogs. Spirits beneficent or malevolent peopled the air; Satan often appeared, in person or by deputy, to tempt or terrify, to seduce, empower or instruct; demons had a fund of mystic knowledge that could be tapped if one should properly propitiate them. Some Carmelite monks at Bologna (till Sixtus IV condemned them in 1474) taught that there was no harm in seeking knowl-edge from devils;[9] and professional sorcerers offered their expert charms in invoking the aid of demons for paying customers. Witches—sorcerers usually female—were believed to have special access to such helpful devils, whom they treated as lovers and gods; by delegated demonic power these women, in the belief of the people, could foresee the future, fly in a moment over long distances, pass through closed gates and doors, and wreak dire evils upon persons who offended them; they could induce love or hate, produce abortion, manufacture poisons, and cause death by a spell or a glance.

In 1484 a bull of Innocent VIII (*Summis desiderantes*) forbade resort to witches, took for granted the reality of some of their claimed powers, ascribed to them some storms and plagues, and complained that many Christians, falling away from orthodox worship, had contracted carnal union with devils, and, by spells and magic rhymes, curses and other diabolical arts, had done grievous harm to men, women, children, and beasts.[10] The Pope advised the officers of the Inquisition to be on the alert against such practices. The bull did not impose belief in witchcraft as the official doctrine of the Church, nor did it inaugurate the prosecution of witches; popular belief in witches, and occasional punishment of them, long antedated the bull. The Pope was here faithful to the Old Testament, which had commanded, "Thou shalt not suffer a witch to live."[11] The Church had for centuries maintained the possibility of demonic influences upon human beings;[12] but the Pope's assumption of the reality of witchcraft encouraged belief in it, and his admonition to the inquisitors played some part in the witchcraft persecution.[13] In the year following the promulgation of the bull forty-one women were burned for witchcraft in Como alone.[14] In 1486 the inquisitors at Brescia condemned several alleged witches to "the secular arm"—i.e., to death; but the government refused to execute the sentence, whereat Innocent was much peeved.[15] Matters went more harmoniously in 1510, when we hear of 140 persons burned at Brescia for witchcraft; and in 1514, in the pontificate of the gentle Leo, three hundred more were burned at Como.[16]

Whether through perverse stimulation by persecution, or from other causes, the number of persons who believed themselves, or were believed, to have practised witchcraft rapidly increased, especially in subalpine Italy; it took on the nature and proportions of an epidemic; popular report claimed that 25,000 persons had attended a "witches' sabbath" on a plain near Brescia. In 1518 the inquisitors burned seventy alleged witches from that region, and had thousands of suspects in their prisons. The Signory of Brescia protested against this wholesale detention, and interfered with further executions; whereupon Leo X, in a bull *Honestis* (February 15,

1521), ordered the excommunication of any officials, and the suspension of religious services in any community, that refused to execute, without examination or revision, the sentences of the inquisitors. The Signory, ignoring the bull, appointed two bishops, two Brescian physicians, and one inquisitor to supervise all further witchcraft trials, and to inquire into the justice of previous condemnations; only these men were to have the power to condemn the accused. The Signory admonished the papal legate to put an end to the condemnation of persons for the sake of confiscating their property.[16a] It was a brave procedure; but ignorance and sadism got the upper hand, and in the next two centuries, in Protestant as well as Catholic lands, in the New World as well as the old, burnings for witchcraft were to form the darkest spots in the history of mankind.

The mania to know the future supported the usual variety of fortune-tellers—palmists, dream interpreters, astrologers; these last were more numerous and powerful in Italy than in the rest of Europe. Almost every Italian government had an official astrologer, who determined the celestially propitious times when important enterprises should commence. Julius II would not leave Bologna till his astrologer marked the time as auspicious; Sixtus IV and Paul III let their stargazers fix the hours of their major conferences.[16b] So general was the belief that the stars governed human character and affairs that many university professors in Italy annually issued *iudicia*—predictions based on astrology;[16c] it was one of Aretino's humorous devices to parody these learned almanacs. When Lorenzo de' Medici reestablished the University of Pisa he made no arrangements for a course in astrology, but the students clamored for it, and he had to yield.[16d] In Lorenzo's erudite circle Pico della Mirandola wrote a powerful attack upon astrology, but Marsilio Ficino, still more learned, defended it. "How happy are the astrologers!" exclaimed Guicciardini, "who are believed if they tell one truth to a hundred lies, while other people lose all credit if they tell one lie to a hundred truths."[16e] Yet astrology had in it a certain groping toward a scientific view of the universe; it escaped in some measure from belief in a universe ruled by divine or demonic whim, and aimed to find a coordinating and universal natural law.

II. SCIENCE

The superstitions of the people, rather than the opposition of the Church, retarded the development of science. Censorship of publications did not become a substantial hindrance to science until the Counter Reformation that followed the Council of Trent (1545f). Sixtus IV brought to Rome (1463) the most famous astronomer of the fifteenth century, Johann Müller "Regiomontanus." During Alexander's pontificate Copernicus taught mathematics and astronomy in the University of Rome. Copernicus had not yet come to his world-shaking theory of the earth's orbital revolution, but Nicholas of Cusa had already suggested it; and both men were churchmen. Throughout the fourteenth and fifteenth centuries the Inquisition was relatively weak in Italy, partly through the absence of the popes in Avignon, their quarrels in the Schism, and their infection with the enlightenment of the Renaissance. In 1440 the materialist Amadeo de' Landi was tried by the Inquisition at Milan, and was acquitted; in 1497 Gabriele da Salò, a freethinking physician, was protected from the Inquisition by his patron, though "he was in the habit of maintaining that Christ was not God but the son of Joseph."[16f] Despite the Inquisition, thought was freer in Italy, and education more advanced, than in any other country in the fifteenth and early sixteenth centuries. Her schools of astronomy, law, medicine, and literature were the goals of students from a dozen lands. Thomas Linacre, English physician and scholar, after completing his university courses in Italy, set up an altar in the Italian Alps as he was returning to England, and, taking a last view of Italy, dedicated the altar to her as *Alma mater studiorum*, the fostering mother of studies, the postgraduate university of the Christian world.

If, in this atmosphere of superstition beneath and liberalism above, science made only modest advances in the two centuries before Vesalius (1514-64), it was largely because patronage and honor went to art, scholarship, and poetry, and there was as yet no clear call, in the economic or intellectual life of Italy, for scientific methods and ideas. A man like Leonardo could take a sweeping cosmic view, and touch a dozen sciences with eager curiosity; but there were no great laboratories, dissection was only beginning, no miscroscope could help biology or medicine, no telescope could yet enlarge the stars and bring the moon to the edge of the earth. The medieval love of beauty had matured into magnificent art; but there had been little medieval love of truth to grow into science; and the recovery of ancient literature stimulated a skeptical epicureanism idealizing antiquity rather than a stoic devotion to scientific research aiming to mold the future. The Renaissance gave its soul to art, leaving a little for literature, less for philosophy, least for science. In this sense it lacked the multiform mental activity of the Greek heyday from Pericles and Aeschylus to Zeno the Stoic and Aristarchus the astronomer. Science could not advance until philosophy had cleared the way.

Therefore it is natural that the same reader who knows by name a dozen Renaissance artists will find it hard to recall one Renaissance Italian scientist, barring Leonardo; even of Amerigo Vespucci he will have to be reminded; and Galileo (1564-1642) belongs to the seventeenth century. In truth there were no memorable names except in geography and medicine. Oderic of Pordenone went to India and China as a missionary (c. 1321), returned via Tibet and Persia, and wrote an account of what he had seen, adding much of value to what Marco Polo had reported a generation before. Paolo Toscanelli, astronomer, physician, and geographer, noted Halley's comet in 1456, and is reputed to have given Columbus knowledge and encouragement for his Atlantic venture.[16g] Amerigo Vespucci of Florence made four voyages to the New World (1497f), claimed to have been the first to discover the mainland, and prepared maps of it; Martin Waldseemüller, publishing them, suggested that the continent be called America; the Italians liked the idea, and popularized it in their writings.[16h]

The biological sciences were the last to develop, for the theory of the special creation of man—almost universally accepted—made it unnecessary and dangerous to inquire into his natural origin. For the most part these sciences limited themselves to practical pursuits and studies in medical botany, horticulture, floriculture, and agriculture. Pietro de' Crescenzi, at the age of seventy-six (1306), published *Ruralia commoda*, an admirable manual of agriculture, except that it ignored the still better writings of Spanish Moslems in this field. Lorenzo de' Medici had kept a semipublic garden of rare plants at Careggi; the first public botanical garden was founded by Luca Ghini at Pisa in 1544. Almost all rulers of style had zoological gardens; and Cardinal Ippolito de' Medici kept a human menagerie—a collection of barbarians of twenty different nationalities, all of splendid physique.

III. MEDICINE

The most prosperous science was medicine, for men will sacrifice anything but appetite for health. Physicians received a stimulating share of Italy's new wealth. Padua paid one of them two thousand ducats a year to serve as consultant, while leaving him free to charge for his private practice.[16i] Petrarch, standing on his benefices, indignantly denounced the high fees of physicians, their robes of scarlet and their miniver hoods,[161] their sparkling rings and golden spurs. He earnestly warned the sick Pope Clement VI against trusting physicians:

> I know that your bedside is beleaguered by doctors, and naturally this fills me with fear. Their opinions are always conflicting, and he who has nothing new to say suffers the shame of limping behind the others. As Pliny said, in order to make a name for themselves through some novelty, they traffic with our lives. With them—not as with other trades—it is sufficient to be called a physician to be believed to the last word, and yet a physician's lie harbors more danger than any other. Only sweet hope causes us not to think of the situation. They learn their art at our expense, and even our death brings them experience; the physician alone has the right to kill with impunity. Oh, Most Gentle Father, look upon their band as an army of enemies. Remember the warning epitaph which an unfortunate man had inscribed on his tombstone: "I died of too many physicians."[17]

In all civilized lands and times physicians have rivaled women for the distinction of being the most desirable and satirized of mankind.

The basis of progress in medicine was the renaissance of anatomy. Ecclesiastics, co-operating with physicians as well as with artists, sometimes provided corpses for dissection from the hospitals that they controlled. Mondino de' Luzzi dissected cadavers at Bologna, and wrote an *Anatomia* (1316) which remained a classic text for three centuries. Nevertheless corpses were hard to get. In 1319 some medical students at Bologna stole a corpse from a cemetery and brought it to a teacher at the University, who dissected it for their instruction. The students were prosecuted but acquitted, and from that time the civil authorities winked an eye at the use of executed and unclaimed criminals in "anatomies."[18] Berengario da Carpi (1470-1550), professor of anatomy at Bologna, was credited with having dissected over a hundred corpses.[19] Dissection was practised at the University of Pisa at least as early as 1341; soon it was permitted in all the medical schools of Italy, including the papal school of medicine in Rome. Sixtus IV (1471-84) officially authorized such dissections.[20]

Slowly Renaissance anatomy regained its forgotten classic heritage. Men like Antonio Benivieni, Alessandro Achillini, Alessandro Benedetti, and Marcantonio della Torre liberated anatomy from Arabic tutelage, went back to Galen and Hippocrates, questioned even these sacred authorities, and added, nerve by nerve, muscle by muscle, and bone by bone, to the scientific knowledge of the body. Benivieni directed his anatomies to find-

ing the internal causes of disease; his treatise *On Several Hidden and Wonderful Causes of Disease and Cures* (*De abditis nonnullis ac mirandis mor-
borum et sanationum causis*, 1507) founded pathological anatomy, and
made post-mortem examinations a main factor in the development of modern medicine. Meanwhile the new art of printing accelerated medical progress by facilitating the diffusion and international exchange of medical texts.

We may loosely estimate the medieval relapse of medical science in Latin
Christendom by noting that the most advanced anatomists and physicians
of this age had barely reached, by 1500, the knowledge possessed by Hippocrates, Galen, and Soranus in the period from 450 B.C. to A.D. 200. Treatment was still based on the Hippocratic theory of humors, and bloodletting
was a panacea. The first known transfusion of human blood was attempted
by a Jewish physician in the case of Pope Innocent VIII (1492); as we
have seen, it failed. Exorcists were still called in to treat impotence and
amnesia by religious incantations or the kissing of relics, perhaps because
such suggestive therapy was found occasionally helpful. Strange pills and
drugs were sold by apothecaries, who added to their incomes by including
stationery, varnish, confectionery, spices, and jewelry among their wares.[21]
Michele Savonarola, father of the fiery friar, wrote a *Practica medicinae*
(*c.* 1440), and some shorter treatises; one of these discussed the frequency
of mental pathology (*bizaria*) in great artists; another told of noted men
who had lived long by the daily use of alcoholic drinks.

Medical quacks were still numerous, but medical practice was now more
carefully regulated by law. Penalties were prescribed for persons who practised medicine without a medical degree; and this presumed a four-year
medical course (1500). No physician was allowed to prognose a grave
disease except by consultation with a colleague. Venetian legislation required physicians and surgeons to meet once a month to exchange clinical
notes, and to keep their knowledge up to date by attending a course on
anatomy at least once a year. The graduating medical student had to swear
that he would never protract the sickness of a patient, that he would supervise the preparation of his prescriptions, and that he would take no part of
the price charged by the apothecary for filling them. The same law (Venice, 1368) limited the apothecary's charge for filling a prescription to ten
soldi[22]—coins now impossible to evaluate. We hear of several cases in which
the medical fee, by a specific contract, was made conditional on cure.[23]

Surgery was rising rapidly in repute as its repertoire of operations and
instruments approached the variety and competence of ancient Egyptian
practice. Bernardo da Rapallo devised the perineal operation for stone

(1451), and Mariano Santo became famous for his many successful lithotomies by lateral incision (*c.* 1530). Giovanni da Vigo, surgeon to Julius II, developed better methods of ligature for arteries and veins. Plastic surgery, known to the ancients, reappeared in Sicily about 1450: mutilated noses, lips, and ears were repaired by grafts of skin from other parts of the body, and so well that the lines of adhesion could scarcely be detected.[24]

Public sanitation was improving. As Doge of Venice (1343-54), Andrea Dandolo established the first known municipal commission of public health;[25] other Italian cities followed the example. These *magistrati della sanità* tested all foods and drugs offered for public sale, and isolated the victims of some contagious diseases. As a result of the Black Death, Venice in 1374 excluded from her port all ships carrying persons or goods suspected of infection. At Ragusa (1377) such arrivals were detained for thirty days in special quarters before being admitted into the city. Marseille (1383) lengthened the detention period to forty days—*la quarantine*, and Venice followed suit in 1403.[26]

Hospitals were multiplying under the zeal of both laity and clergy. Siena built in 1305 a hospital famous for its size and services, and Francesco Sforza founded the Ospedale Maggiore in Milan (1456). In 1423 Venice converted the island of Santa Maria di Nazaret into a *lazaretto* to hospitalize infected persons; this is the first institution of its kind known in Europe.[27] Florence in the fifteenth century had thirty-five hospitals.[28] These establishments were generously supported by public and private donations. Some hospitals were notable examples of architecture, like the Ospedale Maggiore; some adorned their halls with inspiring works of art. The Ospedale del Ceppo at Pistoia engaged Giovanni della Robbia to mold for its walls terra-cotta reliefs vividly describing typical hospital scenes; and the façade of the Ospedale degli Innocenti at Florence, designed by Brunellesco, was signalized by the charming terra-cotta medallions placed in the spandrels of its portico arches by Andrea della Robbia. Luther, who was so shocked by the immorality that he found in Italy in 1511, was also impressed by its charitable and medical institutions. He described the hospitals in his *Table Talk:*

> In Italy the hospitals are handsomely built, and admirably provided with excellent food and drink, careful attendants, and learned physicians. The beds and bedding are clean, and the walls are covered with paintings. When a patient is brought in, his clothes are removed in the presence of a notary who makes a faithful inventory of them, and they are kept safely. A white smock is put on him,

and he is laid on a comfortable bed, with clean linen. Presently two doctors come to him, and servants bring him food and drink in clean vessels. . . . Many ladies take turns to visit the hospitals and tend the sick, keeping their faces veiled, so that no one knows who they are; each remains a few days and then returns home, another taking her place. . . . Equally excellent are the foundling asylums of Florence, where the children are well fed and taught, suitably clothed in a uniform, and altogether admirably cared for.[29]

It is often the fatality of medicine that its heroic advances in therapy are balanced—almost pursued—by new diseases. Smallpox and measles, hardly known in Europe before the sixteenth century, now came to the fore; Europe experienced its first recorded influenza epidemic in 1510; and epidemics of typhus—a disease not mentioned before 1477—swept Italy in 1505 and 1528. But it was the sudden appearance and rapid dissemination of syphilis in Italy and France toward the end of the fifteenth century that constituted the most startling phenomenon and test of Renaissance medicine. Whether syphilis existed in Europe before 1493, or was brought from America by the return of Columbus in that year, is a matter still debated by the well informed, and not to be settled here.

Certain facts support the theory of an indigenous European origin. On July 25, 1463, a prostitute testified in a court at Dijon that she had dissuaded an unwelcome suitor by telling him that she had *le gros mal*—not further described in the record.[30] On March 25, 1494, the town crier of Paris was directed to order from the city all persons afflicted with *la grosse verole*.[31] We do not know what this "great pox" was; it may have been syphilis. Late in 1494 a French army invaded Italy; on February 21, 1495, it occupied Naples; soon afterward a malady became rampant there, which the Italians called *il morbo gallico*, "the French disease," alleging that the French had brought it into Italy. Many of the French soldiers were infected with it; when they returned to France, in October, 1495, they scattered the disease among the people; in France, therefore, it was called *le mal de Naples*, on the assumption that the French army had contracted it there. On August 7, 1495, two months before the return of the French army from Italy, the Emperor Maximilian issued an edict in which mention was made of *malum francicum;* obviously this "French disease" could not be ascribed to the French army not yet returned from Italy. From 1500 on, the term *morbus gallicus* was used throughout Europe to mean syphilis.[32] We may conclude that there are suggestions, but no convincing evidence, that syphilis existed in Europe before 1493.

The case for an American origin is based upon a report written between 1504 and 1506 (but not published till 1539) by a Spanish physician, Ruy Diaz de l'Isla. He relates that on the return voyage of Columbus the pilot of the admiral's vessel was attacked by a severe fever, accompanied with frightful skin eruptions, and adds that he himself, at Barcelona, had treated sailors infected with this new disease, which, he says, had never been known there before. He identified it with what Europe was calling *morbus gallicus*, and contended that the infection had been brought from America.[33] Columbus, on his first return from the West Indies, reached Palos, Spain, on March 15, 1493. In that same month Pintor, physician to Alexander VI, noted the first appearance of the *morbus gallicus* in Rome.[34] Almost two years elapsed between the return of Columbus and the French occupation of Naples—sufficient time for the disease to spread from Spain to Italy; on the other hand, it is not certain that the plague that ravaged Naples in 1495 was syphilis.[35] Very few bones whose lesions may be interpreted as syphilitic have been found in pre-Columbian European remains; many such bones have been found among the relics of pre-Columbian America.*[36]

In any case the new disease spread with terrifying speed. Caesar Borgia apparently contracted it in France. Many cardinals, and Julius II himself, were infected; but we must allow the possibility, in such instances, of infection by innocent contact with persons or objects bearing the active germ. Skin pustules had long since been treated in Europe with mercurial ointment; now mercury became as popular as penicillin is in our day; surgeons and quacks were called alchemists because they turned mercury into gold. Prophylactic measures were taken. A law of 1496 in Rome forbade barbers to admit syphilitics, or to use instruments that had been employed by or on them. More frequent examination of prostitutes was established, and some cities tried to evade the problem by expelling courtesans; so Ferrara and Bologna banished such women in 1496, on the ground that they had "a secret kind of pox which others call the leprosy of St. Job."[38] The Church preached chastity as the one prophylaxis needed, and many churchmen practised it.

The name syphilis was first applied to the disease by Girolamo Fracastoro, one of the most varied and yet best integrated characters of the Renaissance. He had a good start: he was born at Verona (1483) of a

<hr />

* Sarton concludes: "As to syphilis, I have been thus far unable to discover a single description of it anterior to those which appeared in quick succession in 1495 and following years. In spite of frequent reaffirmations in recent years of the pre-Columbian antiquity of European syphilis, I remain unconvinced."[37]

patrician family that had already produced outstanding physicians. At Padua he studied almost everything. He had Copernicus as a fellow student, and Pomponazzi and Achillini to teach him philosophy and anatomy; at twenty-four he was himself professor of logic. Soon he retired to devote himself to scientific, above all medical, research, tempered with a fond study of classic literature. This association of science and letters produced a rounded personality, and a remarkable poem, written in Latin on the model of Virgil's *Georgics*, and entitled *Syphilis, sive de morbo gallico* (1521). Italians since Lucretius have excelled in writing poetical didactic poetry, but who would have supposed that the undulant spirochete would lend itself to fluent verse? Syphilus, in ancient mythology, was a shepherd who decided to worship not the gods, whom he could not see, but the king, the only visible lord of his flock; whereupon angry Apollo infected the air with noxious vapors, from which Syphilus contracted a disease fouled with ulcerous eruptions over his body; this is essentially the story of Job. Fracastoro proposed to trace the first appearance, epidemic spread, causes, and therapy of "a fierce and rare sickness, never before seen for centuries past, which ravished all of Europe and the flourishing cities of Asia and Libya, and invaded Italy in that unfortunate war whence from the Gauls it has its name." He doubted that the ailment had come from America, for it appeared almost simultaneously in many European countries far apart. The infection

> did not manifest itself at once, but remained latent for a certain time, sometimes for a month . . . even for four months. In the majority of cases small ulcers began to appear on the sexual organs. . . . Next, the skin broke out with encrusted pustules. . . . Then these ulcerated pustules ate away the skin, and . . . infected even the bones. . . . In some cases the lips or nose or eyes were eaten away, or, in others, the whole of the sexual organs.[39]

The poem goes on to discuss treatment by mercury or by guaiac—a "holy wood" used by the American Indians. In a later work, *De contagione*, Fracastoro dealt in prose with various contagious diseases—syphilis, typhus, tuberculosis—and the modes of contagion by which they could be spread. In 1545 he was called by Paul III to be head physician for the Council of Trent. Verona raised a noble monument to his memory, and Giovanni dal Cavino graved his likeness on a medallion which is one of the finest works of its kind.

Before 1500 it was usual to class all contagious diseases together under the indiscriminate name of "the plague." It was one measure of the progress of medicine that it now clearly distinguished and diagnosed the specific character of an epidemic, and was prepared to deal with so sudden and virulent an eruption as syphilis. Mere reliance on Hippocrates and Galen could never have sufficed in such a crisis; it was because the medical profession had learned the necessity of ever fresh and detailed study of symptoms, causes, and cures, in an ever widening and intercommunicated experience, that it could meet this unexpected test.

And it was because of such high qualifications, devotion, and practical success, that the better class of physicians was now recognized as belonging to the untitled aristocracy of Italy. Having completely secularized their profession, they made it more respected than the clergy. Several of them were not only the medical but as well the political advisers, and the frequent and favored companions, of princes, prelates, and kings. Many of them were humanists, familiar with classical literature, collecting manuscripts and works of art; often they were the close friends of great artists. Finally, many of them realized the Hippocratic ideal of adding philosophy to medicine; they passed with ease from one subject to another in their studies and their teaching; and they gave the professional philosophical fraternity a stimulus to subject Plato, Aristotle, and Aquinas—as they subjected Hippocrates, Galen, and Avicenna—to a fresh and fearless examination of reality.

IV. PHILOSOPHY

At first glance the Italian Renaissance does not seem to offer a reasonable harvest of philosophy. Its product cannot compare with the heyday of French Scholasticism from Abélard to Aquinas, not to speak of "the school of Athens." Its most famous name in philosophy (if we extend the time limit of the Renaissance) is Giordano Bruno (1548?-1600), whose work lies beyond the period of our study in this volume. Pomponazzi remains; but who now does reverence to his poor heroic skeptical squeak?

The humanists incubated a philosophical revolution by discovering, and cautiously revealing, the world of Greek philosophy; but, for the most part, and excepting Valla, they were too clever to lay their beliefs on the table. The university professors of philosophy were hobbled by the Scholastic tradition: after spending seven or eight years struggling through that wilderness, they either abandoned it for other fields of study, or drove another generation into it, glorifying the hurdles that had broken their wills and brought their intellects to a safe dead end. And who knows but many of them felt a certain mental and economic security in confining themselves to recondite problems carefully and fruitlessly phrased in unintelligible terminology? In most philosophical faculties Scholasticism was still *de rigueur*, and already stiffening with the approach of death. The old medieval questions were laboriously reviewed in the old medieval forms of disputation, and in the proud publications of the staff.

Two elements of life entered to revive philosophy: the conflict between Platonists and Aristotelians, and the division of Aristotelians into orthodox and Averroists. At Bologna and Padua these conflicts became veritable duels, literally matters of life and death. The humanists were mostly Platonists; under the influence of Gemistus Pletho, Bessarion, Theodorus Gaza, and other Greeks, they drank deeply of the wine of the *Dialogues*, and could hardly understand how anyone could bear the arid logic, impotent *Organon*, and leaden golden mean of the cautious Aristotle. But these Platonists were resolved to remain Christians; and it was, so to speak, as their representative and delegate that Marsilio Ficino devoted half his life to reconciling the two systems of thought. For this purpose he studied widely, going so far afield as to Zoroaster and Confucius. When he reached Plotinus, and himself translated the *Enneads*, he felt that he had found in mystic Neoplatonism the silken cord that would bind Plato to Christ. He tried to formulate this synthesis in his *Theologia platonica*, a confused medley of orthodoxy, occultism, and Hellenism, and arrived hesitantly at a pantheistic conclusion: God is the soul of the world. This became the philosophy of Lorenzo and his circle, of the Platonic Academies in Rome, Naples, and elswhere; from Naples it reached Giordano Bruno; from Bruno it passed to Spinoza and thence to Hegel; it is still alive.

But there was something to be said for Aristotle, especially if he could be misinterpreted. Was Aquinas right in understanding him to teach personal immortality, or was Averroes right in reading *De anima* as affirming the deathlessness of only the collective soul of mankind? The terrible Averroes, that ogre of an Arab, whom Italian art had long since pictured as prostrate under the feet of St. Thomas, was so active a competitor for the domination of the Aristotelians that both Bologna and Padua were hot with his heresy. It was at Padua that the Marsilius who took its name had lost his reverence for the Church;* at Padua that Filippo Algeri da Nola, the precursor of Nola-born Bruno, had imbibed those frightful errors for

---

* Marsilius of Padua belongs rather to the Reformation than to the Renaissance, and consideration of him is deferred accordingly.

which he was sorrowfully cast into a barrel of boiling pitch.[40] Nicoletto
Vernias, as professor of philosophy at Padua (1471-99), appears to have
taught there the doctrine that only the world-soul, not the individual soul,
is immortal;[41] and his pupil Agostino Nifo propounded the same notion in a
treatise *De intellectu et daemonibus* (1492). Usually the skeptics sought
to sooth the Inquisition by distinguishing (as Averroes had done) between
two kinds of truth—religious and philosophical: a proposition, they urged,
might be rejected in philosophy from the standpoint of reason, while still
accepted on faith in the word of Scripture or the Church. Nifo professed
the principle with reckless simplification: *Loquendum est ut plures, senti-
endum ut pauci*—"We must speak as the many do, we must think as
the few."[42] Nifo changed his mind or his speech as his hair changed, and
reconciled himself to orthodoxy. As professor of philosophy at Bologna
he drew lords, ladies, and multitudes to lectures dramatized with grimaces
and antics and salted with anecdotes and wit. He became socially the most
successful opponent of Pomponazzi.

Pietro Pomponazzi, the microscopic bombshell of Renaissance philosophy, was so diminutive that his familiars called him Peretto—"little Peter."
But he had a large head, a vast brow, a hooked nose, small, black, penetrating eyes: here was a man doomed to take life and thought with painful
seriousness. Born at Mantua (1462) of patrician stock, he studied philosophy and medicine at Padua, took both degrees at twenty-five, and was soon
himself a professor there. All the skeptical tradition of Padua descended
to him and culminated in him; as his admirer Vanini was to put it, "Pythagoras would have judged that the soul of Averroes had transmigrated into
the body of Pomponazzi."[43] Wisdom seems always a reincarnation or echo,
since it remains the same through a thousand varieties and generations of
error.

Pomponazzi continued to teach at Padua from 1495 to 1509; then the
winds of war swept through the city, and closed its historic University
halls. In 1512 we find him established at the University of Bologna. There
he remained to the end of his days, marrying thrice, always lecturing on
Aristotle, and modestly likening his relation to his master to that of an in-
sect exploring an elephant.[44] He thought it safer to offer his ideas not as his
own but as implied or explicit in Aristotle interpreted by Alexander of
Aphrodisias. His procedure seems at times too humble, apparently sub-
servient to a dead authority; but since the Church, following Aquinas,
claimed her doctrine to be that of Aristotle, Pomponazzi may have felt
that any demonstration of a heresy as truly Aristotelian would be one way,

short of the stake, of teasing the orthodox tail. The Fifth Council of the Lateran, under the presidency of Leo X (1513), condemned all who should assert that the soul is one and indivisible in all men, and that the individual soul is mortal. Three years later Pomponazzi published his major work, *De immortalitate animae*, in which he sought to show that the condemned view was precisely that of Aristotle. Mind, said Pietro's Aristotle, is at every step dependent upon matter; the most abstract knowledge is ultimately derived from sensation; only through the body can mind act upon the world; consequently a disembodied soul, surviving the mortal frame, would be a functionless and helpless wraith. As Christians and faithful sons of the Church, Pomponazzi concluded, we are warranted in believing in the immortality of the individual soul; as philosophers we are not. It seems never to have occurred to Pomponazzi that his argument had no validity against Catholicism, which taught the resurrection of the body as well as of the soul. Perhaps he did not take this doctrine seriously, and had no thought that his readers would. No one, so far as we know, urged it against him.

The book ran into a storm. The Fransciscan friars persuaded the doge of Venice to order all procurable copies to be publicly burned, which was done. Protests were made to the papal court, but Bembo and Bibbiena were then high in Leo's councils, and advised him that the conclusions of the book were perfectly orthodox; the conclusions were. Leo was not fooled; he knew quite well this little trick of the two truths; but he contented himself with ordering Pomponazzi to write a decent word of submission.[45] Pietro complied in *Apologiae libri tres* (1518), reasserting that as a Christian he accepted all the teaching of the Church. About the same time Leo commissioned Agostino Nifo to compose an answer to Pomponazzi's book; as Agostino loved controversy, he executed this assignment with pleasure and skill. It is remarkable, and perhaps illustrates a continuing antipathy between the universities and the clergy, that while Pomponazzi's head hung, so to speak, in this Inquisitorial balance, three universities competed for his services. Hearing that Pisa was seeking to lure him to her halls, the magistrates of Bologna, formally subject to the pope but deaf to the Franciscan furor, confirmed Pomponazzi's professorial tenure for eight years further, and raised his annual salary to 1600 ducats ($20,000?).[46]

In two minor books, which he did not publish in his lifetime, Pomponazzi continued his skeptical campaign. In *De incantatione* he reduced to natural causes many supposedly supernatural phenomena. A physician had written to him about cures allegedly due to incantations or charms; Pietro bade him doubt. "It would be ridiculous and absurd," he wrote, "to despise what is visible and natural in order to have recourse to an invisible cause the reality of which is not guaranteed to us by any solid probability."[47] As a Christian he accepts angels and spirits; as a philosopher he rejects them; all causes under God are natural. Reflecting his medical training, he laughs at the widespread belief in occult sources of cure: if spirits could cure the ills of the flesh they would have to be material, or use material means, to affect a material body; and he ironically pictures the healing spirits as rushing about with their paraphernalia of plasters, ointments, and pills.[48] However he admits certain curative powers in some plants and stones. He will accept the miracles of the Bible, but suspects that they were natural operations. The universe is governed by uniform and invariable laws. Miracles are unusual manifestations of natural forces whose powers and methods are only partly known to us; and what the people cannot understand they ascribe to spirits or to God.[49] Without contradicting this view of natural causation, Pomponazzi accepts much of astrology. Not only are the lives of men subject to the action of the heavenly bodies, but all human institutions, he thinks, even including religions, rise and flourish and decay according to celestial influences. This is true also of Christianity; at the present moment, says Pomponazzi, there are signs that Christianity is dying.[50] He adds that as a Christian he rejects all this as nonsense.

His final book, *De fato*, seems more orthodox, for it is a defense of free will. He admits its incompatibility with divine foreknowledge and omniscience, but stands on his consciousness of free activity, and on the necessity of assuming some freedom of choice if there is to be any moral responsibility in man. In his treatise on immortality he had faced the question whether a moral code could succeed without supernatural punishments and rewards. He held, with stoic pride, that the sufficient reward of virtue is virtue itself, not any post-mortem paradise;[51] but he confessed that most men can be induced to decency only by supernatural hopes and fears. Hence, he explained, great legislators have taught the belief in a future state as an economical substitute for ubiquitous police; and, like Plato, he justifies the inculcation of fables and myths if these can help to control the natural wickedness of men.[52]

> Therefore they have posited, for the virtuous, eternal reward in another life, but, for the sinful, eternal punishments, which frighten them very greatly. And the greater part of men, if they do good, do

it more from fear of eternal punishment than hope of eternal good, since the punishments are more known to us than those eternal goods. And since this last device can benefit all men, of whatever class they are, the legislator, seeing the proneness of men to evil, and intending the common good, has decreed that the soul is immortal, not caring for truth but only for righteousness, so that he may bring men to virtue.[52a]

Most men, he thinks, are so simple mentally and so brutish morally that they must be treated as children or invalids. It is not wise to teach them the doctrines of philosophy. "These things," he says of his own speculations, "are not to be communicated to common people, for they are incapable of receiving these secrets. We must beware even of holding discourse concerning them with ignorant priests."[53] He divides mankind into philosophers and religious persons, and innocently believes that "philosophers alone are the gods of the earth, and differ as much from all other men, of whatever rank and condition, as genuine men differ from those painted on canvas."[54]

In humbler moments he realized the narrow limits of human reason, and the honorable futility of metaphysics. He pictured himself in his later years as worn and haggard with thought about it and about, and likened the philosopher to Prometheus, who, because he wished to steal fire from heaven—i.e., snatch at divine knowledge—was condemned to be bound to a rock and to have his heart gnawed at by a vulture endlessly.[55] "The thinker who inquires into the divine mysteries is like Proteus. . . . The Inquisition persecutes him as a heretic, the multitude mocks him as a fool."[56]

The controversies in which he engaged wore him down and helped to ruin his health. He suffered from one illness after another, until finally he determined to die. He chose a hard form of suicide: he starved himself to death. Resisting every argument and every threat, and triumphing even over force, he refused either to eat or to speak. After seven days of this regimen he felt that he had won his battle for the right to die, and might now safely speak. "I depart gladly," he said. Some one asked him, "Where are you going?" "Where all mortals go," he answered. His friends made a final effort to persuade him to eat, but he preferred to die (1525).[57] Cardinal Gonzaga, who had been his pupil, had the remains transported to Mantua and buried there, and, with typical Renaissance tolerance, raised a statue to his memory.

Pomponazzi had put into philosophic form a skepticism that had for two

centuries been attacking the foundations of Christian belief. The failure
of the Crusades; the influx of Moslem ideas through Crusades, trade, and
Arab philosophy; the removal of the papacy to Avignon and its ridiculous
division in the Schism; the revelation of a pagan Greco-Roman world
full of wise men and great art and yet without the Bible or the Church; the
spread of education, and its increasing escape from ecclesiastical control;
the immorality and worldliness of the clergy, even of popes, suggesting
their private disbelief in the publicly professed creed; their use of the idea
of purgatory to raise funds for their purposes; the reaction of the rising
mercantile and moneyed classes against ecclesiastical domination; the transformation of the Church from a religious organization into a secular political power: all these factors, and many more, combined to make the Italian
middle and upper classes, in the late fifteenth and early sixteenth century,
"the most skeptical of European peoples."[58]

It is clear from the poetry of Politian and Pulci, and the philosophy of
Ficino, that the circle of Lorenzo had no actual belief in another life; and
the sentiment of Ferrara appears in the fun that Ariosto makes of the inferno
that to Dante had seemed so frightfully real. Almost half the literature of
the Renaissance is anticlerical. Many of the *condottieri* were open atheists;[59] the *cortigiani* or courtiers were far less religious than the *cortigiane*
or courtesans; and a polite skepticism was the mark and requisite of a
gentleman.[60] Petrarch lamented the fact that in the minds of many scholars
it was a sign of ignorance to prefer the Christian religion to pagan philosophy.[61] In Venice, 1530, it was found that most of the upper ranks neglected their Easter duty—i.e., did not go to confession and communion
even once a year.[62] Luther claimed to have found a saying current among
the educated classes in Italy on going to Mass: "Come, let us conform to
the popular error."[63]

As to the universities, a curious incident reveals the temper of professors
and students. Shortly after Pomponazzi's death his pupil Simone Porzio,
invited to lecture at Pisa, chose as his text Aristotle's *Meteorology*. The
audience did not like the subject. Several cried out impatiently: *Quid de
anima?*—"What about the soul?" Porzio had to set the *Meteorology* aside
and take up Aristotle's *De anima;* at once the audience was all attention.[64]
We do not know whether in that lecture Porzio expressed his belief that
the human soul differs in no essential point from the soul of a lion or a
plant; we do know that he so taught in his book *De mente humana—On
the Human Mind;*[65] and he seems to have escaped unharmed. Eugenio Tar-
ralba, indicted by the Spanish Inquisition in 1528, related that as a youth

he had studied in Rome under three teachers, all of whom taught that the soul was mortal.[66] Erasmus was astonished to find that at Rome the fundamentals of the Christian faith were topics of skeptical discussion among the cardinals. One ecclesiastic undertook to explain to him the absurdity of belief in a future life; others smiled at Christ and the Apostles; many, he assures us, claimed to have heard papal functionaries blaspheming the Mass.[67] The lower classes kept their faith, as we shall see; the thousands who heard Savonarola must have believed; and the example of Vittoria Colonna shows that piety could survive education. But the soul of the great creed had been pierced with the arrows of doubt; and the splendor of the medieval myth had been tarnished by its accumulated gold.

V. GUICCIARDINI

The mind of Guicciardini summarizes the skeptical disillusionment of the times. It was one of the sharpest minds of the age; too cynical for our taste, too pessimistic for our hopes, but penetrating as a roving searchlight in the skies, and candid with the frankness of a writer who has wisely resolved on solely posthumous publication.

Francesco Guicciardini had the initial advantage of aristocratic birth. From his childhood he heard educated conversation in good Italian, and learned to accept life with the realism and grace of a man confident of his footing. His great-uncle was several times gonfalonier of the republic; his grandfather held in turn most of the principal offices in the government; his father knew Latin and Greek, and filled several diplomatic posts; "my godfather," wrote Francesco, "was Messer Marsilio Ficino, the greatest Platonic philosopher then in the world"[68]—which did not prevent the historian from becoming an Aristotelian. He studied civil law, and at the age of twenty-three was appointed professor of law at Florence. He traveled widely, even to noting "the fantastic and bizarre inventions" of Hieronymus Bosch in Flanders.[69] At twenty-six he married Maria Salviati "because the Salviati, in addition to their wealth, surpassed other families in influence and power, and I had a great liking for these things."[70]

Nevertheless he had a passion for excellence, and the self-discipline to create works of literary art. His *Storia Fiorentina*, written at twenty-seven, is one of the most surprising products of an age when genius, swollen with its recovered heritage but loosened from tradition, flowed full and free in a dozen streams. The book limited itself to a short segment of Florentine history, from 1378 to 1509; but it treated that period with an accuracy of detail, a critical examination of sources, a penetrating analysis of causes, a maturity and impartiality of judgment, a command of vivid narrative in fine Italian, that were not matched by the *Storie Fiorentine* that Machiavelli wrote eleven years later in the sixth decade of his life.

In 1512, still a youth of thirty, Guicciardini was sent as ambassador to Ferdinand the Catholic. In quick succession Leo X and Clement VII made him governor of Reggio Emilia, Modena, and Parma, then governor general of all the Romagna, then lieutenant general of all papal troops. In 1534 he returned to Florence, and supported Alessandro de' Medici throughout that scoundrel's quinquennium of tyranny. In 1537 he was the chief agent in promoting the accession of Cosimo the Younger to be Duke of Florence. When his hopes of dominating Cosimo faded, Guicciardini retired to a rural villa to write in one year the ten volumes of his masterpiece, the *Storia d'Italia*.

It is inferior to his earlier work in freshness and vigor of style; Guicciardini had meanwhile studied the humanists, and slipped into formality and rhetoric; even so it is a stately style, presaging Gibbon's monumental prose. The subtitle, *History of the Wars*, limits the subject to matters military and political; at the same time the field is widened to all Italy, and to all Europe as related to Italy; this is the first history to view the European political system as a connected whole. Guicciardini writes of what for the most part he knew at first hand, and, toward the end, of events in which he had played a part. He collected documents sedulously, and is far more accurate and reliable than Machiavelli. If, like his more famous contemporary, he returns to the ancient custom of inventing speeches for the persons of his tale, he frankly states that they are true only in substance; some he specifies as authentic; and all are used effectively to state both sides of a debate, or to reveal the policies and diplomacy of the European states. Taken together, this massive history, and the brilliant *Storia Fiorentina*, constitute Guicciardini as the greatest historian of the sixteenth century. As Napoleon was anxious to see Goethe, so Charles V, at Bologna, kept lords and generals waiting in an anteroom while he conversed at length with Guicciardini. "I can create a hundred nobles in an hour," he said, "but I cannot produce such an historian in twenty years."[71]

As a man of the world he did not take too seriously the efforts of philosophers to diagnose the universe. He must have smiled at the excitement aroused by Pomponazzi, if he noticed it. Since the supernatural is beyond our ken, he considered it useless to war over rival philosophies. Doubtless all religions are based upon assumptions and myths, but these are forgivable if they help to maintain social order and moral discipline. For man, in Guicciardini's view, is by nature self-seeking, immoral, lawless; he has to be checked at every turn by custom, morals, law, or force; and religion is usually the least disagreeable means to these ends. But when a religion becomes so corrupt that it has a demoralizing rather than a moralizing influence, a society is in a bad way, for the religious supports of its moral code have been sapped. Guicciardini writes, in his secret record:

> To no man is it more displeasing than to me to see the ambition, covetousness, and excesses of priests, not only because all wickedness is hateful in itself, but because . . . such wickedness should find no place in men whose state of life implies a special relationship to God. . . . My relations with several popes have made me desire their greatness at the expense of my own interest. Had it not been for this consideration, I would have loved Martin Luther as myself; not that I might set myself free from the laws imposed upon us by Christianity . . . but that I might see this swarm of scoundrels (*questa caterva di scelerati*) confined within due limits, so that they might be forced to choose between a life without crime or a life without power.[72]

Nevertheless his own morality was hardly superior to that of the priests. His personal code was to adjust himself to whatever powers were at the moment supreme; his general principles he kept for his books. There, too, he could be as cynical as Machiavelli:

> Sincerity pleases and wins praise, dissimulation is censured and hated; the former, however, is more useful to others than to oneself. Therefore I should praise him whose usual mode of life was open and sincere, and who only used dissimulation in certain things of great importance; it then succeeds all the better, the more one has contrived to establish a reputation for sincerity.[73]

He saw through the shibboleths of the various political parties in Florence; each group, though it shouted for liberty, wanted power.

> It seems clear to me that the desire of dominating one's fellows and asserting superiority is natural to man, so that there are few so in love with liberty that they would not seize a favorable opportunity of ruling and lording it. Look closely at the behavior of the indwellers of the selfsame city; mark and examine their dissensions, and you shall find that the object is preponderance rather than freedom.

Those, then, who are the foremost citizens do not strive after liberty, though that be in their mouths; but the increase of their own sway and pre-eminence is really in their hearts. Liberty is a cant term with them, and disguises their lust of superiority in power and honor.[74]

He despised the Soderini merchant republic, accustomed to defend its liberties with gold instead of arms. And he had no faith in the people or democracy:

To speak of the people is to speak of madmen, for the people is a monster full of confusion ánd error, and its vain beliefs are as far from truth as is Spain from India. . . . Experience shows that things very rarely come to pass according to the expectations of the multitude. . . . The reason is that the effects . . . commonly depend on the will of a few, whose intentions and purposes are nearly always different from those of the many.[75]

Guicciardini was one of thousands in Renaissance Italy who had no faith whatever; who had lost the Christian idyl, had learned the emptiness of politics, expected no utopia, dreamed no dreams; and who sat back helpless while a world of war and barbarism swept over Italy; somber old men, emancipated in mind and broken in hope, who had discovered, too late, that when the myth dies only force is free.

VI. MACHIAVELLI

1. The Diplomat

One man remains, hard to classify: diplomat, historian, dramatist, philosopher; the most cynical thinker of his time, and yet a patriot fired with a noble ideal; a man who failed in everything that he undertook, but left upon history a deeper mark than almost any other figure of the age.

Niccolò Michiavelli was the son of a Florentine lawyer—a man of moderate means, who held a minor post in the government, and owned a small rural villa at San Casciano ten miles out of the city. The boy received the ordinary literary education; learned to read Latin readily, but no Greek. He took a fancy to Roman history, became enamored of Livy, and found for almost every political institution and event of his day an illuminating analogue in the history of Rome. He began, but seems never to have completed, the study of law. He cared little for the art of the Renaissance, and expressed no interest in the discovery of America; perhaps he felt that merely the theater of politics was now enlarged, while the plot and characters would remain unchanged. His one absorbing interest was politics, the technique of influence, the chess of power. In 1498, aged twenty-nine, he was appointed secretary to the Dieci della Guerra—a Council of Ten for War—and held that post for fourteen years.

It was at first a modest function—compiling minutes and records, summarizing reports, writing letters; but he was in government, he could watch the politics of Europe from an inside observation point, he could try to forecast developments by applying his knowledge of history. His eager, nervous, ambitious spirit felt that only time was needed before he would be at the top, playing the heady game of state against the duke of Milan, the Senate of Venice, the king of France, the king of Naples, the pope, the emperor. Soon he was sent on a mission to Caterina Sforza, Countess of Imola and Forlì (1498). She proved too subtle for him, and he came back empty-handed, chastened. Two years later he was tried again, accompanied Francesco della Casa as associate envoy to Louis XII of France; della Casa fell ill, and Machiavelli had to head the mission; he learned French, followed the court from château to château, and transmitted to the Signory such alert intelligence, such keen analyses, that on his return to Florence his friends acclaimed him as now a graduate diplomat.

The turning point in his intellectual development was his mission, as aide to Bishop Soderini, to Caesar Borgia at Urbino (1502). Called back to Florence for a personal report, he celebrated his rise in the world by taking a wife. In October he was again despatched to Caesar. He joined him at Imola, and arrived at Senigallia just in time to note Borgia's happiness at having successfully ensnared, and strangled or caged, the men who had conspired against him. These were events that stirred all Italy; to Machiavelli, meeting the brilliant ogre in the flesh, they were lessons in philosophy. The man of ideas found himself face to face with the man of action, and did him homage; envy burned in the young diplomat's soul as he realized the distance he had still to travel from analytical and theoretical thought to a magnificent crushing deed. Here was a man, six years younger than himself, who in two years had overthrown a dozen tyrants, given order to a dozen cities, and made himself the very meteor of his time; how weak words seemed before this youth who used them with such scornful scarcity! From that moment Caesar Borgia became the hero of Machiavelli's philosophy, as

Bismarck would be of Nietzsche's; here, in this embodied will to power, was a morality beyond good and evil, a model for supermen.

Back in Florence (1503), Machiavelli perceived that some members of the government suspected him of having been swept off his mental feet by the dashing Borgia. But his industrious scheming to advance the interests of his city regained for him the esteem of the Gonfalonier Soderini and the Council of Ten for War. In 1507 he saw the triumph of one of his basic ideas. No self-respecting state, he had long argued, could entrust its defense to mercenary troops; they could not be relied upon in a crisis; and they or their leader could almost always be bought by an enemy armed with sufficient gold. A national militia should be formed, said Machiavelli, composed of citizens, preferably of vigorous peasants used to hardship and the open air; it should be kept always in good equipment and training; and it should serve as the last firm line of the republic's defense. After long hesitation the government accepted the plan, and empowered Machiavelli to realize it in action. In 1508 he led his new *milizia* to the siege of Pisa, where it acquitted itself well; Pisa surrendered, and Machiavelli returned to Florence at the height of his arc.

On a second mission to France (1510) he passed through Switzerland; his enthusiasm was aroused by the armed independence of the Swiss Confederation, and he made it his ideal for Italy. Returning from France, he saw the problem of his country: how could its separate principalities unite to protect Italy if a united nation like France should decide to absorb the whole peninsula?

The supreme test of his militia came too soon. In 1512 Julius II, furious against Florence for having refused to join in expelling the French from Italy, ordered the armies of the Holy League to suppress the republic and restore the Medici; and Machiavelli's militia, assigned to defend the Florentine line at Prato, broke and fled before the trained mercenaries of the League. Florence was taken, the Medici triumphed; Machiavelli lost both his reputation and his governmental post. He made every effort to appease the victors, and might have succeeded; but two ardent youths, conspiring to re-establish the republic, were detected; among their papers was found a list of persons on whose support they had counted; it included Machiavelli. He was arrested and tortured with four turns of the rack; but no evidence of his complicity having been found, he was released. Fearing rearrest, he removed with his wife and four children to the ancestral villa at San Casciano. There he spent all but the last of his remaining fifteen years, fretting in hopeful poverty. But for this disaster we should never have heard of him, for it was in those hungry years that he wrote books that moved the world.

2. The Author and the Man

It was a dreary isolation for one who had lived at the very core of Florentine politics. Occasionally he would ride into Florence to talk with old friends and explore any chance of re-employment. Several times he wrote to the Medici, but he received no reply. In a celebrated letter to his friend Vettori, then Florentine ambassador in Rome, he described his life, and told how he came to write *The Prince:*

> Since my last misfortunes I have led a quiet country life. I rise with the sun, and go into one of the woods for a few hours to inspect yesterday's work; I pass some time with the woodcutters, who have always some troubles to tell me, either of their own or their neighbors'. On leaving the wood I go to a spring, and thence up to my bird-snaring enclosure, with a book under my arm—Dante, Petrarch, or one of the minor poets, such as Tibullus or Ovid. I read their amorous transports and the history of their loves, recalling my own to my mind, and time passes pleasantly in these meditations. Then I betake myself to the inn by the roadside, chat with passers-by, ask news of the places whence they come, hear various things, and note the varied tastes and diverse fancies of mankind. This carries me to the dinner hour, when, in the company of my brood, I swallow whatever fare this poor little place of mine, and my slender patrimony, can afford me. In the afternoon I go back to the inn. There I generally find the host, a butcher, a miller, and a couple of brickmakers. I mix with these boors the whole day, playing at *cricca* and *tric trac*, which games give rise to a thousand quarrels and much exchange of bad language; and we generally wrangle over farthings, and our shouts can be heard in San Casciano town. Steeped in this degradation my wits grow moldy, and I vent my rage at the indignity of fate. . . .
>
> At nightfall I return home and seek my writing room; and divesting myself on its threshold of my rustic garments, stained with mud and mire, I assume courtly attire; and thus suitably clothed, I enter within the ancient courts of ancient men, by whom, being cordially welcomed, I am fed with the food that alone is mine, and for which I was born, and am not ashamed to hold discourse with them and inquire the motives of their actions; and these men in their humanity

reply to me; and for the space of four hours I feel no weariness, remember no trouble, no longer fear poverty, no longer dread death;
my whole being is absorbed in them. And since Dante says that
there could be no science without retaining that which is heard, I
have recorded that which I have acquired from the conversation of
these worthies, and have composed a pamphlet *De principatibus*, in
which I plunge as deeply as I can into cogitations upon this subject,
discussing the nature of princedom, of how many species it consists,
how these are to be acquired, how they are maintained, why they are
lost; and if you ever cared for any of my scribbles, this one ought
not to displease you. And it should be especially welcome to a new
prince; for which reason I dedicate it to his Magnificence, Giuliano.
. . . (December 10, 1513)[76]

Probably Machiavelli has here simplified the story. Apparently he began by writing his *Discourses on the First Ten Books of Livy*, completing
his commentary on only the first three books. He dedicated these *Discorsi*
to Zanobi Buondelmonti and Cosimo Rucellai, saying: "I send you the
worthiest gift I have to offer, inasmuch as it comprises all that I have
learned from long experience and continuous study." He remarks that
classic literature and law and medicine have been revived to enlighten
modern writing and practice; he proposes likewise to resuscitate classic
principles of government, and apply them to contemporary politics. He
does not derive his political philosophy from history, but selects from history incidents supporting the conclusions to which he has been led by his
own experience and thought. He takes his examples almost entirely from
Livy, sometimes in his haste basing arguments on legends, and occasionally
helping himself to morsels from Polybius.

As he proceeded with the *Discourses*, he perceived that they would be
too long, and too long delayed in their completion, to serve as a practical
gift to one of the ruling Medici. Therefore he interrupted the work to
write a summary that would embody his conclusions; this would have
a better chance of being read, and of bringing a fair return in the
friendship of the powerful family that now (1513) ruled half of Italy. So
he composed *Il principe* (as he came to entitle the book) in a few months
of that year. He planned to dedicate it to Giuliano de' Medici, then ruling
Florence; but Giuliano died (1516) before Machiavelli could make up his
mind to send the book to him; so he rededicated it, and sent it, to Lorenzo,
Duke of Urbino, who made no acknowledgment of it. It circulated in
manuscript, and was surreptitiously copied; it was not printed till 1532,

five years after the author's death. Thereafter it was among the most frequently reprinted books in any language.

To his own description of himself we can add only the anonymous portrait of him in the Uffizi Gallery. It shows a slender figure with pale face, hollow cheeks, sharp dark eyes, thin lips tightly closed; obviously a man of thought rather than of action, and of keen intelligence rather than of amiable will. He could not be a good diplomat because he was too visibly subtle, nor a good statesman because he was too intense, grasping ideas fanatically as in the portrait he tightly clasps the gloves that affirm his semi-genteel rank. This man who so often wrote like a cynic, whose lips so often curled into sarcasm, who plumed himself on such perfect mendacity that he could make people think he lied when he spoke the truth,[77] was in his heart of hearts a flaming patriot, who made the *salus populi* the *suprema lex*, and subordinated all morality to the unification and redemption of Italy.

There were many unlikable qualities in him. When Borgia was up he idealized him; when Borgia was down he followed the crowd and denounced the broken Caesar as a criminal and "a rebel against Christ."[78] When the Medici were out he condemned them eloquently; when they were in he licked their boots for a post. He not only visited brothels before and after marriage, but sent his friends detailed descriptions of his adventures there.[79] Several of his letters are so coarse that not even his most voluminous and admiring biographer has dared to publish them. Nearing fifty, Machiavelli writes: "Cupid's nets still enthrall me. Bad roads cannot exhaust my patience, nor dark nights daunt my courage. . . . My whole mind is bent on love, for which I give Venus thanks."[80] These things are forgivable, for man was not made for monogamy; but less pardonable, though quite in harmony with the custom of the times, is the complete absence, from all of Machiavelli's considerable surviving correspondence, of any word of tenderness—of any word—about his wife.

Meanwhile he turned his able pen to divers forms of composition, and rivaled the masters in each. In a treatise on the art of war (*L'arte della guerra*, 1520) he announced to states and generals, from his ivory tower, the laws of military power and success. A nation that has lost the martial virtues is doomed. An army requires not gold but men; "gold alone will not procure good soldiers, but good soldiers will always procure gold";[81] gold will flow to the strong nation, but strength departs from the rich nation, for wealth makes for ease and decay. Consequently an army must be kept busy; a little war now and then will keep the martial muscles and apparatus in trim. Cavalry is beautiful, except when faced with sturdy pikes; the infantry must ever be regarded as the very nerve and foundation of an army.[82] Mercenary armies are the shame and sloth and ruin of Italy; each state should have a citizen militia, constituted of men who would be fighting for their own country, their own lands.

Trying his hand at fiction, Machiavelli wrote one of Italy's most popular *novelle*, *Belfagor arcidiavolo*, bursting with satiric wit on the institution of marriage. Turning to drama, he composed the outstanding comedy of the Italian Renaissance stage, *Mandragola*. The prologue struck a new note, making a novel curtsey to critics:

> Should anyone seek to cow the author by evil-speaking, I warn you that he, too, knows how to speak evil, and indeed excels in the art; and that he has no respect for anyone in Italy, though he bows and scrapes to those better dressed than himself.[83]

The play is an astounding revelation of Renaissance morals. The scene is laid in Florence. Callimaco, hearing an acquaintance praise the beauty of Lucrezia, wife of Nicias, decides—though he has never seen her—that he must seduce her if only to be able to sleep in peace. He is disturbed to learn that Lucrezia is as famous for her modesty as for her beauty; but he takes hope on being told that Nicias frets over her failure to conceive. He bribes a friend to introduce him to Nicias as a physician. He professes to have a potion that will make any woman fertile; but, alas, the first man who lies with her after she has taken it will soon afterward die. He offers to undertake this mortal adventure, and Nicias, with the traditional kindness of characters to their authors, consents to be replaced. But Lucrezia is obstinately virtuous; she hesitates to commit both adultery and murder in one night. All is not lost; her mother, lusting for progeny, bribes a friar to advise her in the confessional to go through with the plan. Lucrezia yields, drinks, lies with Callimaco, and becomes pregnant. The story ends with everybody happy: the friar purifies Lucrezia, Nicias rejoices in his vicarious parentage, and Callimaco can sleep. The play is excellent in structure, brilliant in dialogue, powerful in satire. What startles us is not the seductive theme, long hackneyed in classical comedy, nor even the merely physical interpretation of love, but the turn of the plot upon the readiness of a friar to counsel adultery for twenty-five ducats, and the fact that in 1520 the play was produced with great success before Leo X in

Rome. The Pope was so pleased with it that he asked Cardinal Giulio de' Medici to give Machiavelli some employment as a writer. Giulio suggested a history of Florence, and offered 300 ducats ($3,750?).

The resultant *Storie Fiorentine* (1520-5) was almost as decisive a revolution in historiography as *The Prince* in political philosophy. It is true that the book had vital defects: it was hastily inaccurate, it plagiarized substantial passages from previous historians, it was more interested in the strife of factions than in the development of institutions, and it totally ignored cultural history—as did nearly every historian before Voltaire. But it was the first major history written in Italian, and its Italian was clear, vigorous, and direct; it rejected the fables with which Florence had embellished her origins; it abandoned the usual chronicle year-by-year plan, and gave, instead, a smooth-flowing and logical narrative; it dealt not merely with events but with causes and effects; and it forced upon the chaos of Florentine politics a clarifying analysis of conflicting families, classes, and interests. It carried the tale along on two unifying themes: that the popes had kept Italy divided to preserve the temporal independence of the papacy; and that the great advances of Italy had come under princes like Theodoric, Cosimo, and Lorenzo. That a book with such tendencies should have been written by a man seeking papal ducats, and that Pope Clement VII accepted its dedication without complaint, illustrates the courage of the author and the mental and financial liberality of the Pope.

The *History of Florence* gave Machiavelli occupation for five years, but it did not satisfy his longing to swim again in the muddy stream of politics. When Francis I lost everything but honor and his skin at Pavia (1525), and Clement VII found himself helpless against Charles V, Machiavelli sent letters to the Pope and to Guicciardini, explaining what could yet be done against the imminent Spanish-German conquest of Italy; and perhaps his suggestion that the Pope should arm, empower, and finance Giovanni delle Bande Nere might have delayed destiny awhile. When Giovanni died, and the German horde advanced upon Florence as a rich and plunderable ally of the French, Machiavelli rushed to the city, and, at Clement's request, prepared a report on how the walls might be restored to make it defensible. On May 18, 1526, he was chosen by the Medicean government to head a board of five "Curators of the Walls." The Germans, however, by-passed Florence and headed for Rome. When that city was sacked, and Clement was a prisoner of the mob, the republican party in Florence once more expelled the Medici and restored the republic (May 16, 1527). Machiavelli rejoiced, and hopefully applied for his old post as secretary of the Ten for War. He was turned down (June 10, 1527); his dealings with the Medici had lost him the support of the republicans.

He did not long survive that blow. The vital spark of life and hope flickered out in him, and left the flesh spiritless. He fell ill, suffering violent spasms of the stomach. Wife, children, and friends gathered round his bedside. He confessed to a priest and died, twelve days after his rejection. He left his family in the utmost poverty, and the Italy that he had labored to unite was in ruins. He was buried in the church of Santa Croce, where a handsome monument, marked with the words, *Tanto nomini nullum par elogium*—"No eulogy would do justice to so great a name"—bears witness that an Italy at last united has forgiven his sins and remembered his dream.

3. The Philosopher

Let us examine the "Machiavellian" philosophy as impartially as we can. Nowhere else shall we find so much independent and fearless thinking on ethics and politics. Machiavelli was justified in claiming that he had opened new routes on relatively untraveled seas.

It is almost exclusively a political philosophy. There is no metaphysics here, no theology, no theism or atheism, no discussion of determinism or free will; and ethics itself is soon shoved aside as subordinate to, almost a tool of, politics. Politics he understands as the high art of creating, capturing, protecting, and strengthening a state. He is interested in states rather than in humanity. He sees individuals merely as members of a state; except as they help to determine its destiny, he pays no attention to the parade of egos across the landscape of time. He wishes to know why states rise and fall, and how they can be made to defer as long as possible their inevitable decay.

A philosophy of history, a science of government, are possible, he thinks, because human nature never changes.

> Wise men say, not without reason, that whoever wishes to foresee the future must consult the past; for human events ever resemble those of preceding times. This arises from the fact that they are produced by men who have been, and ever will be, animated by the same passions; and thus they must necessarily have the same results.[84] ... I believe that the world has always been the same, and has always contained as much good and evil, although variously distributed among the nations according to the times.[85]

Among the most instructive regularities of history are the phenomena of growth and decay in civilizations and states. Here Machiavelli meets a very complex problem with a very simple formula. "Valor produces peace; peace, repose; repose, disorder; disorder, ruin. From disorder order springs; from order, valor (*virtù*); and from this, glory and good fortune. Hence wise men have observed that the age of literary excellence is subsequent to that of distinction in arms; and that . . . great warriors are produced before philosophers."[86] In addition to the general factors in growth or decay may be the action and influence of leading individuals; so the excessive ambition of a ruler, blinding him to the inadequacy of his resources for his aims, may ruin his state by leading it into war with a stronger power. Fortune or chance also enters into the rise and fall of states. "Fortune is the arbiter of one half our actions, but she still leaves us to direct the other half."[87] The more *virtù* a man has, the less will he be subject to fortune or yield to it.

The history of a state follows general laws, determined by the natural wickedness of men. All men are by nature acquisitive, deceitful, pugnacious, cruel, and corrupt.

> Whoever wishes to found a state and give it laws, must start with assuming that all men are bad and ever ready to display their vicious nature whenever they find occasion for it. If their evil disposition remains concealed for a time, it must be attributed to some unknown reason; and we must assume that it lacked occasion to show itself; but time . . . does not fail to bring it to light. . . . The wish to acquire is in truth very natural and common, and men always acquire when they can; and for this they will be praised, not blamed.[88]

This being so, men can be made good—i.e., capable of living with order in a society—only by the application, in sequence, of force, deceit, and habit. This is the origin of a state: the organization of force through army and police, the establishment of rules and laws, and the gradual formation of habits, for the maintenance of leadership and order in a human group. The more developed a state, the less force will have to be used or visible in it; indoctrination and habit will suffice; for in the hands of a capable lawgiver or ruler the people are as soft clay in the hands of a sculptor.

The best means of habituating naturally wicked men to law and order is religion. Machiavelli, whom his admirer Paolo Giovio calls *irrisor et atheos*, a satirical atheist,[89] writes enthusiastically about religious institutions:

Although the founder of Rome was Romulus . . . yet the gods did not judge the laws of this prince sufficient . . . and therefore they inspired the Roman Senate to elect Numa Pompilius as his successor. . . . Numa, finding a very savage people, and wishing to reduce them to civil obedience by the arts of peace, had recourse to religion as the most necessary and assured support of any civil society; and he established it upon such foundations that for many centuries there was nowhere more fear of the gods than in that republic; which greatly facilitated all the enterprises which the Senate or its great men attempted. . . . Numa feigned that he held converse with a nymph, who dictated to him all that he wished to persuade the people to. . . . In truth there never was any remarkable lawgiver . . . who did not resort to divine authority, as otherwise his laws would not have been accepted by the people; for there are many good laws the importance of which is known to the sagacious lawgiver, but the reasons for which are not sufficiently evident to enable him to persuade others to submit to them; and therefore do wise men, to remove this difficulty, resort to divine authority.[90] . . . The observance of religious institutions is the cause of the greatness of republics; disregard of these institutions produces the ruin of states. For where the fear of God is wanting, there the country will be destroyed, unless it be sustained by fear of the prince, which may for a time supply the want of religion. But the lives of princes are short. . . .

Princes and republics who wish to maintain themselves . . . must above all things preserve the purity of religious observances, and treat them with proper reverence.[92] . . . Of all men who have been eulogized, those deserve it most who have been the authors and founders of religions. Next come such as have established republics or kingdoms. After these the most celebrated are those who have commanded armies and have extended the possessions of their country. To these may be added literary men. . . . Conversely, those men are doomed to infamy and universal execration who have destroyed religions, who have overturned republics and kingdoms, who are enemies of virtue or of letters.[93]

Having accepted religion in general, Machiavelli turns upon Christianity and excoriates it as having failed to make good citizens. It diverted too much attention to heaven, and enfeebled men by preaching the feminine virtues:

The Christian religion makes us hold of small account the love of this world, and renders us more gentle. The ancients, on the contrary, found their highest delight in this world . . . Their religion beatified none but men crowned with worldly glory, such as leaders of armies and founders of republics; whereas our religion has rather glorified meek and contemplative men than men of action. It has placed the supreme good in humility and poorness of spirit, and in contempt for worldly things; whereas the other placed it in greatness of mind, in bodily strength, and in all that gives men daring. . . . Thus the world has fallen a prey to the wicked, who have found men readier, for the sake of going to paradise, to submit to blows rather than to resent them.[94]. . .

Had the religion of Christianity been preserved according to the ordinances of its Founder, the states and commonwealths of Christendom would have been far more united and happy than they are. Nor can there be a greater proof of its decadence than the fact that the nearer people are to the Roman Church, the head of this religion, the less religious are they. And whoever examines the principles on which that religion is founded, and sees how widely different from those principles its present practice and application are, will judge that her ruin or chastisement is near at hand.[95]. . . Possibly the Christian religion would have been entirely extinguished by its corruption, had not St. Francis and St. Dominic . . . restored it to its original principles. . . . To ensure a long existence to religious sects or republics, it is necessary frequently to bring them back to their original principles.[96]

We do not know whether these words were written before news had reached Italy of the Protestant Reformation.

The rebellion of Machiavelli against Christianity is quite different from the rebellion of Voltaire, Diderot, Paine, Darwin, Spencer, Renan. These men rejected the theology of Christianity, but retained and admired the Christian moral code. This attitude continued till Nietzsche, and softened the "conflict between religion and science." Machiavelli is not bothered by the incredibility of the dogmas; he takes that for granted, but accepts the theology with a good stomach on the ground that some system of supernatural belief is an indispensable support of social order. What he rejects most decisively in Christianity is its ethic, its conception of goodness as gentleness, humility, nonresistance; its love of peace and its denunciation of war; its assumption that states, as well as citizens, are bound by the one moral code. For his part he prefers the Roman ethic, based upon the principle that the safety of the people or state is the supreme law. "Where it is an absolute question of the welfare of our country, we must admit of no considerations of justice or injustice, of mercy or cruelty, of praise or ignominy; but putting all else aside we must adopt whatever course will save the nation's existence and liberty."[97] Morality in general is a code of conduct given to the members of a society or state to maintain collective order, unity, and strength; the government of that state would fail in its duty if, in defending the state, it should allow itself to be restricted by the moral code that it must inculcate in its citizens. Hence a diplomat is not bound by the moral code of his people. "When the act accuses him the result should excuse him";[98] the end justifies the means. "No good man will ever reproach another who endeavors to defend his country, whatever be his mode of doing so."[99] Frauds, cruelties, and crimes committed in order to preserve one's country are "honorable frauds," "glorious crimes."[100] So Romulus did right in killing his brother; the young government had to have unity, or it would be torn to pieces.[101] There is no "natural law," no "right" universally agreed upon; politics, in the sense of statesmanship, must be held completely independent of morality.

If we apply these considerations to the ethics of war, Machiavelli is sure that they make Christian pacifism ridiculous and treasonable. War violates practically all the commandments of Moses: it swears, lies, steals, kills, commits adultery by the thousands; nevertheless, if it preserves the society, or strengthens it, it is good. When a state ceases to expand it begins to decay; when it loses the will to war it is finished. Peace too long maintained is enervating and disruptive; an occasional war is a national tonic, restoring discipline, vigor, and unity. The Romans of the Republic kept themselves ever ready for war; when they saw that they would have trouble with another state, they did nothing to avoid the war, but sent an army to attack Philip V in Macedon and Antiochus III in Greece rather than wait for them to bring the evils of war to Italy.[102] Virtue, to a Roman, was not humility or gentleness or peace, but virility, manliness, courage with energy and intelligence. This is what Machiavelli means by *virtù*.

From this point of view of a statesmanship quite freed of moral restraints, Machiavelli moves to meet what seems to him the basic problem of his time: to achieve for Italy the unity and strength indispensable to her collective liberty. He views with indignation the division, disorder, corruption, and weakness of his country; and here we find what in Petrarch's day was so rare—a man who loved his city not the less because he loved his country more. Who was responsible for keeping Italy so divided, and therefore so helpless against the foreigner?

A nation can never be united and happy except when it obeys only one government, whether a republic or a monarchy, as is the case in France and Spain; and the one cause why Italy is not in the same condition is the Church. For having acquired, and holding, a temporal dominion, yet she has never had sufficient power or courage to enable her to seize the rest of the country and make herself sole sovereign of all Italy.*[103]

We have a new idea here: Machiavelli condemns the Church not for protecting her temporal power, but for not having used all her resources to bring Italy under her political rule. So Machiavelli admired Caesar Borgia at Imola and Senigallia, because he thought he saw in that ruthless youth the conception and promise of a united Italy; and he was prepared to justify any means that the Borgias might use to accomplish this heroic consummation. When he turned against Caesar at Rome in 1503 it may have been through rage that his idol had allowed a cup of poison (as Machiavelli thought) to destroy the dream.

From two centuries of disunity Italy had fallen into such physical weakness and social decay that now (Machiavelli argued) only violent means could save her. Governments and people alike were corrupt. Sexual vice had come to replace military ardor and skill. As in the dying days of ancient Rome, the citizens had delegated to others—there to barbarians, here to mercenaries—the defense of their cities and their lands; but what did these mercenary bands, or their *condottieri,* care for the unity of Italy? They lived and thrived by its division. They had by mutual agreement made war a game almost as safe as politics; their soldiers had inconvenient objections to being killed; and when they met foreign armies they took to their heels and "brought Italy to slavery and contempt."[105]

Who, then, would make Italy one? How could it be done? Not by democratic suasion; men and cities were too individualistic, too partisan, and too corrupt, to accept union peaceably; it would have to be imposed upon them by all the methods of statecraft and war. Only a ruthless dictator

---

* Guicciardini wrote an important comment on this passage: "It is true that the Church has prevented the union of Italy in a single state; but I do not know whether this be a good or an evil. A single republic might certainly have made the name of Italy glorious, and been of the utmost profit to the capital city; but it would have proved the ruin of every other city. It is true that our divisions have brought many calamities upon us, although it should be remembered that the invasions of the barbarians began at the time of the Romans, precisely when Italy was united. And divided Italy has succeeded in having so many free cities that I believe a single republic would have caused her more misery than happiness. . . . This land has always desired liberty, and therefore has never been able to unite under one rule."—*Considerazioni interno ai Discorsi di Machiavelli,* i, 12.[104]

could do it; one who would not let conscience make a coward of him, but would strike with an iron hand, letting his great aim justify all means.

We are not sure that *The Prince* was written in this mood. In the very year 1513 in which it was apparently begun, Machiavelli wrote to a friend that "the idea of Italian union is laughable. Even if the heads of the states could agree, we have no soldiers but the Spaniards that are worth a farthing. Moreover, the people would never agree with the leaders."[106] But in that same 1513 Leo X, young and rich and clever, had reached the papacy; Florence and Rome, so long enemies, were united under the Medici. When Machiavelli transferred the dedication of the book to Lorenzo, Duke of Urbino, that state too had fallen to the Medici. The new Duke was only twenty-four in 1516; he had shown ambition and courage; Machiavelli might forgivably look to this reckless spirit as one who, under the guidance and diplomacy of Leo (and the instruction of Machiavelli) could accomplish what Caesar Borgia, under Alexander VI, had begun—could lead the Italian states, at least north of Naples and omitting proud Venice, into a federation strong enough to discourage foreign invasion. There is evidence that this was also Leo's hope. The dedication of *The Prince* to the Medici, though probably aiming first of all to win employment for the author, could sincerely think of that family as the possible creators of Italian unity.

The form of *Il principe* was traditional: it followed the outline and method of a hundred medieval treatises *De regimine principum*. But in content what a revolution! No idealistic charge here to a prince to be a saint, no appeal to him to apply the Sermon on the Mount to the problems of a throne. On the contrary:

> It being my intention to write something that shall be useful to him who comprehends it, it appears to me more appropriate to follow up the real truth of a matter than the imagination of it. Many have pictured republics and principalities which in fact have never been known or seen, for how one lives is so far distant from how one ought to live, that he who neglects what is done for what ought to be done, sooner effects his ruin than his preservation; a man who wishes to act entirely up to his professions of virtue soon meets with destruction amidst so much that is evil. Hence it is necessary for a prince who wishes to hold his own to know how to do wrong, and to make use of it or not according to necessity.[107]

The prince, therefore, must distinguish resolutely between morality and statesmanship, between his private conscience and the public good, and must be ready to do for the state what would be called wickedness in the relations of individuals. He must scorn half measures; enemies who cannot be won over must be crushed; contenders for his throne must be killed. He must have a strong army, for a statesman can speak no louder than his guns. He must keep his army in constant health, discipline, and equipment; and he must train himself for war by undertaking frequently the hardships and dangers of the hunt. At the same time he must study the arts of diplomacy, for sometimes cunning and deceit achieve more than force, and less expensively. Treaties are not to be honored when they have become a detriment to the nation; "a wise lord cannot, nor ought he, keep faith when such observance can be turned against him, and when the reasons that caused him to pledge it no longer exist."[108]

Some degree of public support is indispensable. But if a ruler must choose between being feared without love or being loved without fear, he must sacrifice the love.[109] On the other hand (say the *Discorsi*) "a multitude is more easily governed by humanity and gentleness than by haughtiness and cruelty. . . ."[110] Titus, Nerva, Trajan, Hadrian, Antoninus, and Marcus Aurelius did not require the pretorian guard nor the legions to defend them, because they were protected by their own good conduct, the good will of the people, and the love of the Senate."[111] To secure popular support the prince should patronize art and learning, provide public spectacles and games, and honor the guilds, always, however, maintaining the majesty of his rank.[112] He should not give the people liberty, but should comfort them as far as possible with the appearances of liberty. Subject cities, like Pisa and Arezzo in the case of Florence, must be dealt with vigorously, even cruelly, at the outset; then, when obedience has been established, their submission may be made habitual by gentler means. Indiscriminate and prolonged cruelty is suicidal.[113]

The ruler should support religion, and should himself appear to be religious, whatever his private beliefs.[114] Indeed, it is more important and profitable to the prince to seem to be virtuous than to be so.

> Though a prince need not possess all the virtues, to seem to have them is useful; as, for example, to seem merciful, loyal, humane, religious, and sincere; it is also useful to be so, but with a mind so flexible that if the need arise he can be the contrary. . . . He should be careful to let nothing fall from his lips that is not instinct with the five qualities mentioned, and must appear to those who see and hear him all compassion, all faith, all humanity, all religion, all integrity. . . . One must color his conduct, and be a great dissembler; and men are so simple, so absorbed in present necessities, that they are easily

deceived. . . . Everyone sees what you appear to be, few know what you are; and those few dare not oppose the opinion of the many.[115]

To these precepts Machiavelli adds examples. He notes the success of Alexander VI, and thinks it entirely due to marvelous lying. He admires Ferdinand the Catholic of Spain for always putting a religious front on his military enterprises. He praises the means—warlike courage and strategic skill mingled with diplomatic craft—by which Francesco Sforza rose to the throne of Milan. But above all he holds up as his supreme and almost perfect exemplar Caesar Borgia:

> When all the actions of the Duke are recalled, I do not know how to blame him; but rather it appears to me that I ought to offer him for imitation to all those who are . . . raised to government. . . . He was considered cruel; nevertheless his cruelty reconciled all the Romagna, unified it, and restored it to peace and loyalty. . . . Having a lofty spirit and far-reaching aims, he could not have regulated his conduct otherwise; and only the shortening of the life of Alexander, and his own sickness, frustrated his designs. Therefore he who considers it necessary to secure himself in his new principality, to gain friends, to overcome enemies by force or fraud, to make himself at once feared and loved by the people, to be followed and revered by the soldiers, to exterminate those who have power or reason to hurt him, to change the old order of things for new, to be severe and gracious, magnanimous and liberal, to destroy a disloyal soldiery and create new, to maintain friendship with kings and princes in such a way that they must help him with zeal and offend him with caution, cannot find a more lively example than the actions of this man.[116]

Machiavelli admired Borgia because he felt that his methods and character, had it not been for the simultaneous illness of Pope and son, would have gone far to unite Italy. Now, in concluding *The Prince*, he appeals to the young Duke Lorenzo, and through him to Leo and the Medici, to organize the union of the peninsula. He describes his countrymen as "more enslaved than the Hebrews, more oppressed than the Persians, more scattered than the Athenians; without head, without order, beaten, despoiled, pillaged, and torn, and overrun by foreign powers." "Italy, left as without life, waits for him who shall heal her wounds. . . . She entreats God to send some one who shall deliver her from these wrong and alien insolencies."[117] The situation is critical, but the opportunity is ripe. "Italy is ready and willing to follow a banner if only some one will raise it." And who better than the Medici, the most famous family in Italy, and now heading the Church?

> Who could express the love with which Italy would hail her liberator, with what thirst for revenge, what stubborn faith, what devotion, what tears? What door would be closed to him?—who would refuse him obedience? To all of us this barbarous dominion is a stench in the nostrils. Let therefore your illustrious house take up this charge, with that courage and hope with which all just enterprises are undertaken, so that under its standard our native country may be ennobled, and under its auspices may be verified those words of Petrarch:

> > *Virtù contr' al furore*
> > *Prendera l'arme e sia il combatter corto,*
> > *Che l'antico valore*
> > *Negl' Italici cuor non è ancor morto—*

"Manhood will take up arms against madness, and brief may the combat be, for the ancient valor is not yet dead in the veins of Italy."

4. Considerations

So the cry that Dante and Petrarch had sent up to alien emperors was here raised to the Medici; and indeed, had Leo lived longer and played less, Machiavelli might have seen the liberation begin. But young Lorenzo died in 1519, Leo in 1521; and in 1527, the year of Machiavelli's death, Italy's subjection to a foreign power was complete. Liberation would have to wait 343 years until Cavour would effect it by Machiavellian statesmanship.

Philosophers have been well nigh unanimous in condemning *The Prince*, and statesmen in practising its precepts. A thousand books began to appear against it on the morrow of its publication (1532). But Charles V studied it carefully, Catherine de' Medici brought it to France, Henry III and Henry IV of France had it with them at their death, Richelieu admired it, William of Orange kept it under his pillow as if to memorize it by osmosis.[118] Frederick the Great of Prussia wrote an *Anti-Machiavel* as a prelude to outprincing *The Prince*. To most rulers, of course, these precepts were no revelation, except as revealing injudiciously the secrets of their guild. Dreamers who thought to turn Machiavelli into a Jacobin fancied that he had written *The Prince* not to express his own philosophy but, by sarcastic indirection, to expose the ways and wiles of rulers; however,

the *Discourses* expound at greater length the same views. Francis Bacon
ventured a condoning word: "Our thanks are due to Machiavelli and similar writers, who have openly and without dissimulation shown us what
men are accustomed to do, not what they ought to do."[119] Hegel's judgment was intelligent and generous:

> *The Prince* has often been cast aside with horror as containing
> maxims of the most revolting tyranny; yet it was Machiavelli's high
> sense of the necessity of constituting a state which caused him to
> lay down the principles on which alone states could be formed under
> the circumstances. The isolated lords and lordships had to be en-
> tirely suppressed; and though our idea of Freedom is incompatible
> with the means which he proposes . . . including, as these do, the
> most reckless violence, all kinds of deception, murder, and the like—
> yet we must confess that the despots who had to be subdued were
> assailable in no other way.[120]

And Macaulay, in a famous essay, pictured the philosophy of Machiavelli
as a natural reflex of an Italy brilliant and de-moral-ized, and long since
accustomed, by her despots, to the principles of *The Prince*.

Machiavelli represents the ultimate challenge of a revived paganism to a
weakened Christianity. In his philosophy religion becomes again, as in
ancient Rome, the humble servant of a state which in effect is god. The
only virtues honored are pagan Roman virtues—courage, endurance, self-
reliance, intelligence; the only immortality is a fading fame. Perhaps Machiavelli exaggerated the enfeebling influence of Christianity; had he forgotten the lusty wars of medieval history, the campaigns of Constantine,
Belisarius, Charlemagne, the Templars, the Teutonic Knights, and Julius II
of recent memory? The Christian morality emphasized the feminine virtues because men had the opposite qualities in ruinous abundance; some
antidote and counterideal had to be preached to the sadistic Romans of the
amphitheater, to the rough barbarians entering Italy, to lawless peoples
striving to subside into civilization. The virtues that Machiavelli scorned
made for orderly and peaceful societies; those that he admired (and, like
Nietzsche, because he lacked them) made for strong and warlike states, and
for dictators capable of murdering by the million to enforce conformity,
and of incarnadining a planet to extend their rule. He confused the good
of the ruler with the good of the nation; he thought too much of the preservation, seldom of the obligations, never of the corruption, of power. He
ignored the stimulating rivalry and cultural fertility of the Italian city-

states; he cared little for the magnificent art of his time, or even for that of ancient Rome. He was lost in idolatry of the state. He helped to free the state from the Church, but he shared in setting up for worship an atomistic nationalism not visibly superior to the medieval notion of states subject to an international morality represented by the pope. Each ideal has broken down under the natural selfishness of men; and a candid Christian must admit that in preaching and practising the principle that no faith need be kept with a heretic (as in violating the safe-conduct of Huss at Constance and of Alfonso of Ferrara in Rome), the Church herself was playing a Machiavellian game fatal to her mission as a moral power.

And yet there is something stimulating in Machiavelli's forthrightness. Reading him, we are brought face to face, as nowhere else so vividly, with a question that few philosophers had dared discuss: is statesmanship bound by morality? We may come to at least one conclusion: that morality can exist only among the members of a society equipped to teach and enforce it; and that an interstate morality awaits the formation of an international organization dowered with the physical power and the public opinion to maintain an international law. Till then the nations will be as beasts in the jungle; and whatever principles their governments may profess, their practice will be that of *The Prince*.

Looking back upon two centuries of intellectual revolt in Italy from Petrarch to Machiavelli, we perceive that its essence and basis lay simply in lessened concern for another world, and a rising affirmation of life. Men were delighted to rediscover a pagan civilization whose citizens were not worried about original sin or a punitive hell, and in which the natural impulses were accepted as forgivable elements in a vibrant society. Asceticism, self-abnegation, and the sense of sin lost their hold, almost their meaning, in the upper strata of the Italian population; monasteries languished for lack of novices, and monks and friars and popes themselves sought the joys of the earth rather than the stigmata of Christ. The bonds of tradition and authority relaxed; the massive fabric of the Church weighed more lightly on the thoughts and purposes of men. Life became more extrovert, and though this often took the form of violence, it cleansed many souls of neurotic fears and disorders that had darkened the medieval mind. The unfettered intellect disported itself happily in every field but science; the exuberance of emancipation hardly comported, as yet, with the discipline of experiment and the patience of research; that would come in the constructive aftermath of liberation. Meanwhile, among the educated, the practices of piety made room for the worship of intellect and genius; the belief in immortality was commuted into the quest for enduring renown. Pagan ideals like Fortune, Fate, and Nature encroached upon the Christian conception of God.

For all this a price had to be paid. The brilliant enfranchisement of the mind sapped the supernatural sanctions of morality, and no others were found to effectually replace them. The result was such a repudiation of inhibitions, such a release of impulse and desire, so gay a luxuriance of immorality, as history had not known since the Sophists had shattered the myths, freed the mind, and loosened the morals, of ancient Greece.

CHAPTER XX

The Moral Release

1300-1534

V. THE FOUNTS AND FORMS OF IMMORALITY

NOWHERE are the prejudices of the historian so likely to mislead him as when he seeks to determine the moral level of an age—unless it be in the kindred inquiry into the decline of religious belief. In either case the dramatic exception will strike his eye and turn it from the unrecorded average. His vision will be further blurred if he approaches the problem with a thesis to prove—as, for example, that religious doubt brings moral decay. And the records themselves are ambivalent, capable, according to the selective bias, of proving almost anything. The works of Aretino, the autobiography of Cellini, the correspondence of Machiavelli and Vettori can be stressed to convey the odor of disintegration; the letters of Isabella and Beatrice d'Este, of Elisabetta Gonzaga and Alessandra Strozzi can be quoted to paint a picture of sisterly tenderness and ideal family life. The reader will have to be on his guard.

Many factors entered into the moral decline that accompanied the intellectual exaltation of the Renaissance. Probably the basic factor was the growth of wealth that resulted from Italy's strategic position on the routes of trade between western Europe and the East, and from the flow of tithes and annates out of a thousand Christian communities into Rome. Sin became more prevalent as more funds were provided to meet its costs. The spread of wealth weakened the ascetic ideal: men and women came to resent an ethic that had been born of poverty and fear, and that now ran counter to both their impulses and their means. They heard with rising sympathy the view of Epicurus that life should be enjoyed, and that all pleasures are to be accounted innocent until proved guilty. The charms of woman triumphed over the prohibitions of theology.

Perhaps next to wealth the main source of immorality was the political unsettlement of the times. The strife of factions, the frequency of war, the influx of foreign mercenaries, and, later, the invasion of Italy by foreign armies recognizing no moral restraints on Italian soil, the repeated disruption of agriculture and trade by the ravages of war, the destruction of freedom by despots who replaced peaceful legitimacy with autocratic force: all these disordered Italian life, and cracked the "cake of custom" that normally conserves morality. Men found themselves unmoored in a sea of violence. Neither state nor Church seemed able to protect them; they protected themselves as best they could, by arms or craft; lawlessness became the law. The despots, placed above the law and dedicated to a short but stirring life, indulged themselves in every pleasure; and their example was followed by the moneyed minority.

In assessing the role of religious unbelief in releasing the natural immorality of mankind, we must begin by distinguishing the skepticism of the lettered few from the persistent piety of the many. Enlightenment is of minorities, and emancipation is individual; minds are not freed *en masse*. A few skeptics might protest against false relics and bogus miracles and indulgences offering promissory notes for cash; but the people accepted them with awe and hope. In 1462 the scholar-Pope Pius II and some cardinals went out to the Milvian Bridge to meet the head of the Apostle Andrew, which was arriving from Greece; and the scholar-Cardinal Bessarion pronounced a solemn oration when the precious figment was deposited in St. Peter's. The people undertook pilgrimages to Loreto and Assisi, flocked to Rome in jubilee years, made the stations of the cross from church to church, and mounted on their knees the Scala Santa which, they were told, was the very stairway that Christ had climbed to the tribune of Pilate. Powerful characters might laugh at all this while their health was good, but rare was the Renaissance Italian who did not ask for the sacraments on his deathbed. Vitellozzo Vitelli, the rough *condottiere* who had fought Alexander VI and Caesar Borgia, begged a messenger to go to Rome and seek papal absolution for him before Caesar's handy man tightened the noose around his neck. Women especially worshiped Mary; almost every village had a miracle-working icon of her; now (*c.* 1524) the Rosary became a favorite form of prayer. Every decent house had a crucifix and a holy picture or two; and before one or more of these, in many homes, a lamp was kept burning endlessly. Village squares and city streets might be adorned with a statue of Jesus or the Virgin, placed in a separate tabernacle or a niche in a wall. The festivals of the religious calendar were celebrated with a pomp and magnificence that gave the people thrilling interruptions to their toil; and every decade or so the coronation of a pope offered processions and games that to antiquarians recalled the spectacles of ancient Rome. Never was a religion more beautiful than when the artists of the Renaissance housed and carved its shrines, and painted its heroes and legends, and drama, music, poetry, and incense joined in the colorful, odorous, sumptuous worship of God.

But this, again, is but one side of a scene too diverse and contradictory to be briefly described. In the cities many of the churches were left relatively empty of men then as now.[1] As to the countryside hear Archbishop Antonino of Florence describing the peasants of his diocese about 1430:

> In the churches themselves they sometimes dance and leap and sing with women. On holydays they spend little time on divine service or hearing the whole Mass, but most in games or taverns or contentions at the church doors. They blaspheme God and His saints on slender provocation. They are filled with lies and perjuries; they make no conscience of fornication, and of worse sins still. Very many of them do not confess even once a year; far fewer are those who take Communion. . . . They do little to instruct their families in the manner of faithful folk. They use enchantments for themselves and their beasts. Of God, or their own souls' health, they think not at all. . . . Their parish priests, caring not for the flock committed to them, but only for its wool and milk, do not instruct them through preaching and the confessional, or by private admonitions, but walk in the same error as their flocks, following their corrupt ways.[2]

We may reasonably conclude, from the existence and natural deaths of such men as Pomponazzi and Machiavelli, that a large section of the educated classes in the Italy of 1500 had lost faith in Catholic Christianity; and we may more precariously assume that even among the letterless religion had lost some of its power to control the moral life. An increasing proportion of the population had ceased to believe in the divine origin of the moral code. Once the Commandments appeared to be man-made, and were shorn of their supernatural sanctions in heaven and hell, the code lost its terrors and its efficacy. Tabus fell away, and a calculus of expediency took their place. The sense of sin, the gloom of guilt, waned; conscience was left comparatively free; and each man did what seemed to him convenient, even if not traditionally right. Men no longer wished to be good, but to be strong; many private individuals took to themselves, long before Machiavelli, those privileges of force and fraud—that principle of the end justifying the means—which he conceded to the rulers of states; perhaps his ethic was an after-image of the morals he had seen around him. Platina attributed to Pius II the remark that "even if the Christian faith had not been con-

firmed by miracles, it ought to be received because of its morality."³ But
men did not reason so philosophically. They said, simply: If there is no
hell or heaven, we must enjoy ourselves here, and we may indulge our
appetites without fear of punishment after death. Only a strong and intelligent public opinion could have taken the place of the lost supernatural
sanctions; but neither the clergy nor the humanists nor the universities rose
to this task.

The humanists were as morally corrupt as the clergy they criticized.
There were shining exceptions, scholars who found decency compatible
with intellectual liberation—Ambrogio Traversari, Vittorino da Feltre,
Marsilio Ficino, Aldus Manutius. . . . But an impressively large minority
of the men who resurrected Greek and Roman literature lived like pagans
who had never heard of Christianity. Their mobility deracinated them;
they passed from city to city seeking laurels and fees, and sank no roots in
stability. They were as fond of money as any moneylender or his wife.
They were vain of their genius, their income, their features, their dress.
They were coarse in their speech, ungenerous and disgraceful in their controversies, faithless in their friendships and transient in their loves. Ariosto,
as we have noted, dared not trust his son to a humanist tutor for fear of
moral contamination; probably he found it unnecessary to forbid the boy
to read *Orlando furioso*, which was salted with melodious obscenity. Valla,
Poggio, Beccadelli, Filelfo summarized in their loose lives one of the basic
problems of ethics and civilization: must a moral code, to function effectively, have supernatural sanctions—the belief in another life, or in the
divine origin of the moral code?

II. THE MORALS OF THE CLERGY

The Church might have sustained the supernatural sanctions provided by
the Hebraic Scriptures and the Christian tradition, if her personnel had led
lives of decency and devotion. But most of them accepted the bad as well
as the good in the morals of the time, and reflected the antithetical facets
of the laity. The parish priest was a simple ministrant, usually of slight
education, but normally (*pace* the good Antonino) leading an exemplary
life;⁴ ignored by the intelligentsia but welcomed by the people. Among the
bishops and abbots there were some high livers, but many good men; and
perhaps half the college of cardinals maintained a pious and Christian conduct that shamed the gay worldliness of their colleagues.⁵ All over Italy
there were hospitals, orphan asylums, schools, almshouses, *monti di pietà*

(loan offices), and other charitable institutions managed by the clergy. The Benedictine, Observantine, and Carthusian monks were honored for the relatively high moral level of their lives. Missionaries faced a thousand dangers to spread the faith in "heathen" lands and among the pagans of Christendom. Mystics hid themselves away from the violence of the times, and sought closer communion with God.

Amid this devotion there was so much laxity of morals among the clergy that a thousand testimonies could be adduced to prove it. The same Petrarch who remained faithful to Christianity to the end, and who drew a favorable picture of discipline and piety in the Carthusian monastery where his brother lived, repeatedly denounced the morals of the clergy in Avignon. From the *novelle* of Boccaccio in the fourteenth century, through those of Masuccio in the fifteenth, to those of Bandello in the sixteenth, the loose lives of the Italian clergy form a recurrent theme of Italian literature. Boccaccio speaks of "the lewd and filthy life of the clergy," in sins "natural or sodomitical."[6] Masuccio described the monks and friars as "ministers of Satan," addicted to fornication, homosexualism, avarice, simony, and impiety, and professed to have found a higher moral level in the army than in the clergy.[7] Aretino, familiar with all filth, railed at the errors of printers as rivaling in number the sins of the clergy; "truly it would be easier to find Rome sober and chaste than a correct book."[8] Poggio almost exhausts his vocabulary of vituperation in exposing the immorality, hypocrisy, cupidity, ignorance, and arrogance of monks and priests;[9] and Folengo's *Orlandino* tells the same tale. Apparently the nuns, who today are angels and ministers of grace, shared in the revelry. They were especially lively in Venice, where monasteries and nunneries were sufficiently close to each other to allow their inmates, now and then, to share a bed; the archives of the *Proveditori sopra monasteri* contain twenty volumes of trials for the cohabitation of monks and nuns.[10] Aretino speaks unquotably about the nuns of Venice.[11] And Guicciardini, usually temperate, loses his poise in describing Rome: "Of the Court of Rome it is impossible to speak with sufficient severity, for it is a standing infamy, an example of all that is most vile and shameful in the world."[12]

These testimonies seem exaggerated, and may be prejudiced. But hear St. Catherine of Siena:

> On whatever side you turn—whether to the secular clergy of priests and bishops, or to the religious orders, or to prelates small or great, old or young, . . . you see nothing but offenses; and all stink in my nostrils with a stench of mortal sin. Narrow, greedy, and ava-

ricious . . . they have abandoned the care of souls. . . . Making a god
of their belly, eating and drinking in disorderly feast, they fall thence
forthwith into filth, living in lasciviousness . . . feeding their children
with the substance of the poor. . . . They flee from choir service
as from poison.[13]

Here again we must discount something, since no saint can be trusted to
speak of human conduct without indignation. But we may accept the summing up of a candid Catholic historian:

It is not surprising, when the highest ranks of the clergy were in
such a state, that among the regular orders and secular priests vice
and irregularities of all sorts should have become more and more
common. The salt of the earth had lost its savor. . . . It was such
priests as these that gave occasion to the more or less exaggerated
descriptions of the clergy by Erasmus and Luther, who visited Rome
during the reign of Julius II. But it is a mistake to suppose that the
corruption of the clergy was worse in Rome than elsewhere; there
is documentary evidence of the immorality of the priests in almost
every town in the Italian peninsula. In many places—Venice, for
instance—matters were far worse than in Rome. No wonder, as
contemporary writers sadly testify, the influence of the clergy had
declined, and that in many places hardly any respect was shown for
the priesthood. Their immorality was so gross that suggestions in
favor of allowing priests to marry began to be heard. . . . Many of
the monasteries were in a deplorable condition. The three essential
vows of poverty, chastity, and obedience were in some convents
almost entirely disregarded. . . . The discipline of many convents of
nuns was equally lax.[14]

Less forgivable than irregularities of sex and festivities of diet were the
activities of the Inquisition. But these remarkably declined in Italy during
the fifteenth century. In 1440 Amadeo de' Landi, a mathematician, was
tried on a charge of materialism, but was acquitted. In 1478 Galeotto
Marcio was condemned to death for writing that any man who lived a
good life would go to heaven whatever his religion might be; but Pope
Sixtus IV saved him.[16] In 1497 the physician Gabriele da Salò was protected from the Inquisition by his patients, though he maintained that
Christ was not God, but was the son of Joseph and Mary, conceived in the
usual ridiculous way; that Christ's body was not in the consecrated wafer;
and that His miracles had been performed not by divine power but through
the influence of the stars;[17] so one myth drives out another. In 1500 Gior-

gio da Novara was burnt to death at Bologna, apparently for denying the divinity of Christ without having influential friends. In the same year the bishop of Aranda declared with impunity that there is neither heaven nor hell, and that indulgences were merely a means of raising funds.[18] In 1510, when Ferdinand the Catholic tried to introduce the Inquisition into Naples, he met with such determined resistance from all classes of the population that he had to abandon the attempt.[19]

Amid the ecclesiastical decay there were several centers of wholesome reform. Pius II deposed a general of the Dominicans, and disciplined lax monasteries in Venice, Brescia, Florence, and Siena. In 1517 Sadoleto, Giberti, Caraffa, and other churchmen founded the Oratory of the Divine Love as a center for pious men who desired some refuge from the pagan worldliness of Rome. In 1523 Caraffa organized the order of Theatines, in which secular priests lived under monastic rules of chastity, obedience, and poverty. Cardinal Caraffa resigned all his benefices and distributed his property among the poor; so did Saint Gaetano, another founder of the Theatines. These devotees, many of them men of noble lineage and great wealth, astonished Rome by strict adherence to their self-imposed rules, and their fearless visits to victims of the plague. In 1533 Antonio Maria Zaccaria established at Milan a similar community of priests, first called the Regular Clerics of St. Paul, but soon to be known as Barnabites from the church of St. Barnabas. Caraffa drew up a helpful program of reform for the clergy of Venice, and Giberti essayed similar reforms in the diocese of Verona (1528-31). Egidio Canisio reformed the Augustinian eremites, and Gregorio Cortese effected a similar betterment among the Benedictines at Padua.

The outstanding effort at monastic reform in this age was the foundation of the Capuchin Order. Matteo di Bassi, a friar of the Franciscan Observantines at Montefalcone, thought that he saw St. Francis in a vision, and that he heard him say: "I wish my rule to be observed to the letter, to the letter, to the letter." Learning that St. Francis had worn a four-cornered pointed hood, he adopted that headdress. Going to Rome, he secured from Clement VII (1528) permission to establish a new branch of the Franciscans, distinguished by the *cappuccio* or cowl, and by firm adherance to the final rule of St. Francis. They dressed in the coarsest cloth, went barefoot throughout the year, lived on bread, vegetables, fruit, and water, kept rigorous fasts, dwelt in narrow cells in poor cottages made of wood and loam, and never journeyed except on foot. The new order was not numerous, but it gave a stirring example and stimulus to the more widespread self-reform that came to the monastic and mendicant orders in the sixteenth and seventeenth centuries.[20]

Some of these reforms were undertaken in response to the Protestant Reformation. Many of them were of spontaneous generation, and indicated a saving vitality in Christianity and the Church.

III. SEXUAL MORALITY

Turning now to laic morals, and beginning with the relations of the sexes, we should remind ourselves at the outset that man is by nature polygamous, and that only the strongest moral sanctions, a helpful degree of poverty and hard work, and uninterrupted wifely supervision, can induce him to monogamy. It is not clear that adultery was less popular in the Middle Ages than in the Renaissance. And as medieval adultery was tempered with chivalry, so in the Renaissance it was softened, in the lettered classes, by an idealization of the refinement and spiritual charms of the educated woman. Greater equality of the sexes in education and social standing made possible a new intellectual comradeship between men and women. In Mantua, Milan, Urbino, Ferrara, and Naples life was graced and stirred by the prominence of attractive and cultivated women.

Girls of good family were kept in relative seclusion from men not of their own household. They were sedulously instructed in the advantages of premarital chastity; sometimes with such success that we hear of a young woman drowning herself after being raped. She was doubtless exceptional, for a bishop proposed to raise a statue to her.[21] In the Roman catacombs a young gentlewoman strangled herself to avoid seduction; her body was borne in triumph through the streets of Rome, with a laurel crown on her head.[22] Nevertheless there must have been considerable premarital adventure; otherwise it would be difficult to account for the extraordinary number of bastards to be found in any city of Renaissance Italy. Not to have bastards was a distinction; to have them was no serious disgrace; the man, on marrying, usually persuaded his wife to let his illegitimate progeny join the household and be brought up with her own children. To be a bastard was no great disability; the social stigma involved was almost negligible; legitimation could be obtained by lubricating an ecclesiastical hand. In default of legitimate and competent heirs bastard sons could succeed to an estate, even to a throne, as Ferrante I succeeded Alfonso I at Naples, and as Leonello d'Este succeeded Niccolò III at Ferrara. When Pius II came to Ferrara in 1459 he was received by seven princes, all illegitimate.[23] The rivalry of bastards with legitimate sons was a rich source of Renaissance violence. Half the *novelle* turn on seductions; and usually such stories were read or heard by women with only a momentary lowering of the eyes. Robert, Bishop of Aquino, toward the close of the fifteenth century, described the morals of the young men in his diocese as unashamedly corrupt; they explained to him, he tells us, that fornication was no sin, that chastity was an old-fashioned tabu, and that virginity was on the wane.[24] Even incest had its devotees.

As for homosexuality, it became almost an obligatory part of the Greek revival. The humanists wrote about it with a kind of scholarly affection, and Ariosto judged that they were all addicted to it. Politian, Filippo Strozzi, and the diarist Sanudo were reasonably suspected of it;[25] Michelangelo, Julius II, and Clement VII were less convincingly charged with it; San Bernardino found so much of it in Naples that he threatened the city with the fate of Sodom and Gomorrah.[26] Aretino described the aberration as quite popular in Rome,[27] and he himself, between one mistress and another, asked the duke of Mantua to send him an attractive boy.[28] In 1455 the Venetian Council of Ten took official note "how the abominable vice of sodomy multiplies in this city"; and "to avert the wrath of God," it appointed two men in each quarter of Venice to put down the practice.[29] The Council noted that some men had taken to wearing feminine garb, and that some women were adopting male attire, and it called this "a species of sodomy."[30] In 1492 a noble and a priest, convicted of homosexual acts, were beheaded in the Piazzetta, and their bodies were publicly burned.[31] These, of course, were exceptional cases, from which we must not generalize; but we may assume that homosexuality was more than normally present in Renaissance Italy until the Counter Reformation.

We may say likewise of prostitution. According to Infessura—who liked to load his statistics against papal Rome—there were 6,800 registered prostitutes in Rome in 1490, not counting clandestine practitioners, in a population of some 90,000.[32] In Venice the census of 1509 reported 11,654 prostitutes in a population of some 300,000.[33] An enterprising printer published a "Catalogue of all the principal and most honored courtesans of Venice, their names, addresses, and fees."[34] On the roads they frequented taverns; in the cities they were the favorite guests of young blades and fervent artists. Cellini recounts his night's lodging with a courtesan as an incident of no moment, and describes a dinner of artists, including Giulio Romano and himself, in which each man was required to bring a woman of low resistance. At a higher level the banker Lorenzo Strozzi gave a banquet in

1519 to fourteen persons, including four cardinals and three women of the demimonde.[35]

As wealth and refinement increased, a demand arose for courtesans with some education and social charm; and as in the Athens of Sophocles hetaerae rose to meet this demand, so in the Rome of the late fifteen century, and in the Venice of the sixteenth, a class of *cortigiane oneste*—genteel courtesans —developed, who rivaled the finest ladies in dress, manners, culture, even in hebdomadal piety. While the simpler prostitutes—*cortigiane di candela* —practised in brothels, these Roman hetaerae lived in their own homes, entertained lavishly, read and wrote poetry, sang and played music, and joined in educated conversation; some collected pictures and statuary, rare editions and the latest books; some maintained literary salons. To keep up with the humanists many of them took classical names—Camilla, Polyxena, Penthesilea, Faustina, Imperia, Tullia. One scandalous wit, in the pontificate of Alexander VI, wrote a series of epigrams beginning with a number in praise of the Virgin or the saints, and then, without a blush, continuing with several in honor of the distinguished courtesans of his time.[36] When one such, Faustina Mancina, died, half of Rome mourned her, and Michelangelo was one of many who wrote sonnets to her memory.[37]

The most renowned of these *cortigiane oneste* was Imperia de Cugnatis. Made rich by her patron Agostino Chigi, she adorned her home with luxurious furniture and choice art, and gathered about her a bevy of scholars, artists, poets, and churchmen; even the pious Sadoleto sang her praise.[38] Probably it was Imperia whom Raphael took as his model for the Sappho of his *Parnassus*. She died in the flower of her beauty at the age of twenty-six (1511), and received honorable burial in the church of San Gregorio, with a marble tomb engraved in the finest lapidary style; and half a hundred poets lamented her in classic elegies.[39] (Her daughter killed herself rather than submit to seduction.[40]) Almost as renowned was Tullia d'Aragona, illegitimate daughter of the Cardinal of Aragon. Admired for her golden hair and sparkling eyes, her generosity and carelessness with money, her grace of carriage and charm of conversation, she was received in Naples, Rome, Florence, and Ferrara like a visiting princess. The Mantuan ambassador at Ferrara described her entry in an undiplomatic letter to Isabella d'Este (1537):

> I have to record the arrival among us of a gentle lady, so modest
> in behavior, so fascinating in manners, that we cannot help consider-
> ing her something divine. She sings impromptu all kinds of airs and

motets. . . . There is not one lady in Ferrara, not even Vittoria Colonna the Duchess of Pescara, who can stand comparison with Tullia.[41]

Moretto da Brescia painted a bewitching portrait of her, looking as innocent as a novice nun. She made the mistake of outliving her charms; she died in a wretched hut near the Tiber; and her total belongings, at auction, brought a dozen crowns ($150?). But in all her poverty she had kept her lute and harpsichord to the last. She left also a book that she had composed *On the Infinity of Perfect Love.*[42]

Doubtless that title reflected the Renaissance fashion of talking and writing about Platonic love. If a woman could not commit adultery she might at least allow herself to arouse in a man a kind of poetic gallantry that made her the object of verses, courtesies, and dedications. The devotions of the troubadours, the *Vita Nuova* of Dante, and Plato's discourses on spiritual love had begotten in a few circles a fine sentiment of adoration toward woman—usually another man's wife. Most people paid no attention to the idea, preferring their love in a frankly sensual form; they might write sonnets, but their goal was coitus; and hardly once in a hundred cases, despite the novelists, did they marry the object of their love.

For marriage was an affair of property, and property could not be made dependent upon the passing whims of physical desire. Betrothals were arranged by family councils, and most young people accepted without effectual protest the mates so assigned to them. Girls could be betrothed at the age of three, though marriage had to be delayed till twelve. In the fifteenth century a daughter unmarried at fifteen was a family disgrace; in the sixteenth century the age of disgrace was deferred to seventeen, to allow time for higher education.[43] Men, who enjoyed all the privileges and facilities of promiscuity, could be lured into marriage only by brides bringing substantial dowries. In Savonarola's day there were many marriageable girls who, for lack of dowries, had failed to find a husband. Florence established a kind of state dowry insurance—*Monte delle fanciulle*, or fund of the maidens—from which marriage portions were given to girls that had paid small yearly premiums.[44] In Siena there were so many bachelors that the laws had to inflict legal disabilities upon them; in Lucca a decree of 1454 debarred from public office all unmarried men between twenty and fifty. "The times are not favorable to matrimony," wrote Alessandra Strozzi in 1455.[45] Raphael painted half a hundred Madonnas, but would not take a wife; and this was the one thing in which Michelangelo agreed with him.

Weddings themselves consumed enormous sums; Leonardo Bruni complained that his *matrimonium* had squandered his *patrimonium*.[46] Kings and queens, princes and princesses spent half a million dollars on a wedding while famine raged among the people.[47] When Alfonso the Magnificent of Naples married, he set up tables for 30,000 diners on the shores of the Bay. Lovelier was the reception that Urbino gave to Duke Guidobaldo when he brought from Mantua his bride Elisabetta Gonzaga: ranged on a hill slope stood the ladies of the city, beautifully dressed; before them their children carried olive branches; mounted choristers, in graceful formation, sang a cantata that had been composed for the occasion; and an especially comely matron, impersonating a goddess, offered the new Duchess the loyalty and affection of the people.[48]

After marriage the woman usually kept her own name; so Lorenzo's wife continued to be called Donna Clarice Orsini; sometimes, however, the wife might add her husband's name to her own—Maria Salviati de' Medici. In the medieval theory of marriage it was expected that love would develop between man and wife through the varied partnerships of marriage in joy and sorrow, prosperity and adversity; and apparently the expectation was fulfilled in the majority of cases. No love of youth for maiden could be deeper or truer than that of Vittoria Colonna for the Marquis of Pescara, to whom she had been engaged from the age of four; no loyalty could have been greater than that of Elisabetta Gonzaga, accompanying her crippled husband through all his misfortunes and exiles, and faithful to his memory till her death.

Nevertheless adultery was rampant.[49] Since most marriages among the upper classes were diplomatic unions of economic or political interests, many husbands felt warranted in having a mistress; and the wife, though she might mourn, usually closed her eyes—or her lips—to the offense. Among the middle classes some men assumed that adultery was a legitimate diversion; Machiavelli and his friends seem to have thought nothing of exchanging notes about their infidelities. When, in such cases, the wife avenged herself by imitation, the husband was as like as not to ignore it, and wear his horns with grace.[50] But the influx of Spaniards into Italy, via Naples and Alexander VI and Charles V, brought the Spanish "point of honor" into Italian life, and in the sixteenth century the husband felt called upon to punish his wife's adultery with death, while preserving his pristine privileges unimpaired. The husband might desert his wife and still prosper; the deserted wife had no remedy except to reclaim her dowry, return to her relatives, and live a lonely life; she was not allowed to marry again.

She might enter a convent, but it would expect a donation of her dowry.[51] In general, in the Latin countries, adultery is condoned as a substitute for divorce.

IV. RENAISSANCE MAN

The combination of intellectual enfranchisement and moral release produced "the man of the Renaissance." He was not typical enough to merit that title; there were a dozen types of man in that age as in any other; he was merely the most interesting, perhaps because he was exceptional. The Renaissance peasant was what peasants have always been until machinery made agriculture an industry. The Italian proletaire of 1500 was like those of Rome under the Caesars or Mussolini; occupation makes the man. The Renaissance businessman was like his past and present peers. The Renaissance priest, however, was different from the medieval or modern priest; he believed less and enjoyed more; he could make love and war. Amid these types was an arresting mutation, a sport of the species and the time, the kind of man we think of when we recall the Renaissance, a type unique in history, except that Alcibiades, seeing him, would have felt reborn.

The qualities of this type revolved about two foci: intellectual and moral audacity. A mind sharp, alert, versatile, open to every impression and idea, sensitive to beauty, eager for fame. It was a recklessly individualistic spirit, set on developing all its potential capacities; a proud spirit, scorning Christian humility, despising weakness and timidity, defying conventions, morals, tabus, popes, even, occasionally, God. In the city such a man might lead a turbulent faction; in the state, an army; in the Church he would gather a hundred benefices under his cassock, and use his wealth to climb to power. In art he was no longer an artisan working anonymously with others on a collective enterprise, as in the Middle Ages; he was "a single and separate person," who stamped his character upon his works, signed his name to his paintings, even, now and then, carved it on his statues, like Michelangelo on the *Pietà*. Whatever his achievements, this "Renaissance man" was always in motion and discontent, fretting at limits, longing to be a "universal man"—bold in conception, decisive in deed, eloquent in speech, skilled in art, acquainted with literature and philosophy, at home with women in the palace and with soldiers in the camp.

His immorality was part of his individualism. His goal being the successful expression of his personality, and his environment imposing upon him no standards of restraint either from the example of the clergy or from the terror of a supernatural creed, he allowed himself any means to his ends, and any pleasure on the way. None the less he had his own virtues. He was a realist, and seldom talked nonsense except to a reluctant woman. He had good manners when he was not killing, and even then he preferred to kill with grace. He had energy, force of character, direction and unity of will; he accepted the old Roman conception of virtue as manliness, but added to it skill and intelligence. He was not needlessly cruel, and he excelled the Romans in his capacity for pity. He was vain, but that was part of his sense of beauty and form. His appreciation of the beautiful in woman and nature, in art and crime, was a mainspring of the Renaissance. He replaced the moral with the esthetic sense; if his type had multiplied and prevailed, an irresponsible aristocracy of taste would have supplanted the aristocracies of birth or wealth.

But, again, he was only one of many kinds of Renaissance man. How different was the idealistic Pico, with his belief in the moral perfectibility of mankind—or the grim Savonarola, blind to beauty and absorbed in righteousness—or the gentle gracious Raphael, scattering beauty about him with an open hand—or the demonic Michelangelo, haunted with the Last Judgment long before he painted it—or the melodious Politian, who thought there would be pity even in hell—or the honest Vittorino da Feltre, so successfully binding Zeno to Christ—or the second Giuliano de' Medici, so kindly just that his brother the Pope considered him unfit for government! We perceive, after every effort to abbreviate and formulate, that there was no "man of the Renaissance." There were men, agreeing only in one thing: that life had never been lived so intensely before. The Middle Ages had said—or had pretended to say—No to life; the Renaissance, with all its heart and soul and might, said Yes.

V. RENAISSANCE WOMAN

The emergence of woman was one of the brightest phases of the period. Her status in European history has usually risen with wealth, though Periclean Greece, too near the Orient, was an exception. When hunger is no longer feared, the male quest turns to sex; and if man still despoils himself for gold, it is to lay it at a woman's feet, or before the children she has given him. If she resists him he idealizes her. Usually she has the good sense to resist him, and to make him pay dearly for the boons whose contemplated splendor swells his veins. If, moreover, she adds graces of mind and character to her body's charms, she gives man the highest satisfaction he can find this side of glory; and in return he raises her to an almost queenly dominance in his life.

We must not imagine that this was the pleasant role of the average woman in the Renaissance; it fell to a fortunate few, while the far greater number put off their bridal robes to carry domestic burdens and family headaches to their graves. Hear San Bernardino on the proper time for beating a wife:

> And I say to you men, never beat your wives while they are great with child, for therein would lie great peril. I say not that you should never beat them; but choose your time. . . . I know men who have more regard for a hen that lays a fresh egg daily than for their own wives. Sometimes the hen will break a pot or a cup, but the man will not beat her, for fear of losing the egg that is her fruit. How stark mad, then, are many that cannot suffer a word from their own lady who bears such fair fruit! For if she speak a word more than he thinks fit, forthwith he seizes a staff and begins to chastise her; and the hen, which cackles all day without ceasing, you suffer patiently for her egg's sake.[52]

A girl of good family was carefully trained for success in getting and keeping a prosperous mate; this was the major subject of her curriculum. Till a few weeks before marriage she was kept in relative seclusion in a convent or in the home, and received from her tutors or nuns an education as thorough as that which came to all but the scholars among the men of her class. Usually she learned some Latin, and became distantly acquainted with the leading figures of Greek and Roman history, literature, and philosophy. She practised some form of music, and sometimes played at sculpture or painting. A few women became scholars, and publicly debated problems of philosophy with men, like the learned Cassandra Fedeli of Venice; but this was highly exceptional. Several women wrote good verse, like Costanza Varano, Veronica Gambara, and Vittoria Colonna. But the educated woman of the Renaissance retained her femininity, her Christianity, and its moral code; and this gave her a union of culture and character that made her irresistible to the higher Renaissance man.

For the lettered men of that age felt her attractiveness intensely, even to writing and reading books that analyzed her charms in scholarly detail. Agnolo Firenzuola, a Vallombrosan monk, composed a dialogue *Sopra la bellezza delle donne*, on the beauty of women, and carried off this difficult subject with a skill and erudition hardly becoming a monk. Beauty itself

he defines after Plato and Aristotle as "an orderly concord, a harmony in-
scrutably resulting from the composition, union, and commission of divers
members, each of which shall itself be well proportioned and in a certain
sense beautiful, but which, before they combine to make one body, shall be
different and discrepant among themselves."[53] He proceeds to examine with
finesse every part of the feminine frame, laying down the standard of
beauty for each. The hair should be thick, long, and blonde—a soft yellow
nearing brown; the skin bright and clear, but not pale white; the eyes dark,
large, and full, with touches of blue in a white iris; the nose must not be
aquiline, for that is especially disconcerting in a woman; the mouth should
be small, but the lips full; the chin round and dimpled; the neck round and
rather long—but let not Adam's apple show; the shoulders should be broad,
the bosom full—with a gentle fall and swell; the hands white and plump and
soft; the legs long, the feet small.[54] We perceive that Firenzuola had spent
much time contemplating his subject, and had discovered an admirable new
topic for philosophy.

Not content with these gifts, Renaissance woman, like any other, dyed
her hair—almost always to blonde—and added false locks to fill it out;
peasant women, having spent their beauty, cut off their tresses and hung
them out for sale.[55] Perfumes were a mania in sixteenth-century Italy:
hair, hats, shirts, stockings, gloves, shoes, all had to be scented; Aretino
thanks Duke Cosimo for perfuming the roll of money he had sent him;
"some objects that date from that period have not yet lost their odor."[56] A
well-to-do woman's dressing table was a wilderness of cosmetics, usually in
fancy containers of ivory, silver, or gold. Rouge was applied not only to
the face but to the breasts, which in the larger cities were left mostly
bare.[57] Various preparations were used to remove blemishes, to polish the
fingernails, to render the skin soft and smooth. Flowers were placed in the
hair and on the dress. Pearls, diamonds, rubies, sapphires, emeralds, agates,
amethysts, beryls, topazes, or garnets adorned the fingers in rings, the arms
in bracelets, the head in tiaras, and (after 1525) the ears in earrings; besides
which jewelry might be studded into the headgear, the dress, the shoes, and
the fan.

Feminine dress, if we may judge from the portraits, was rich, heavy, and
uncomfortable. Velvets, silks, and furs hung in massive folds from the
shoulders or—when the shoulders were bare—from fastenings over the
breasts. Dresses were bound with a girdle at the waist, and swept the floor
behind the feet. The shoes of the well-to-do woman were high of both sole
and heel, to protect her feet from the filth of the streets; nevertheless the

upper portion was often of delicate brocade. Handkerchiefs were now in use in the upper classes; they were made of fine linen, often striped with gold thread or fringed with lace. Petticoats and lingerie were trimmed with lace and embroidered with silk. Sometimes the dress reached up around the neck in a ruff stiffened with metal ribs, and occasionally rising above the head. The headdress of the women took a hundred forms: turbans, tiaras, kerchiefs or veils bound with pearls, hoods stiffly shaped with wire, caps like a boy's or a forester's. . . . Frenchmen visiting Mantua were delightfully shocked to find the Marchioness Isabella wearing a fancy cap with jeweled feathers, and, beneath, shoulders and bosom bare almost to the nipples.[58] Preachers complained about the amount of female bosom that invited the male eye. Now and then the flair for nudity went out of bounds, and Sacchetti observed of some women that if they took off their shoes they would be naked.[59] Most women imprisoned themselves in corsets that could be tightened by turning a key, so that Petrarch pitied "their bellies so cruelly squeezed that they suffer as much pain from vanity as the martyrs suffered for religion."[60]

Armed with all these weapons, the Renaissance woman of the upper classes raised her sex out of medieval bondage and monastic contempt to be almost the equal of man. She conversed on equal terms with him about literature and philosophy; she governed states with wisdom, like Isabella, or with all-too-masculine force, like Caterina Sforza; sometimes, clad in armor, she followed her mate to the battlefield, and bettered the instruction of his violence. She refused to leave the room when rough stories came up; she had a good stomach, and could hear realistic language without losing her modesty or her charm. The Italian Renaissance is rich in women who made a high place for themselves by their intelligence or their virtue: Bianca Maria Visconti who, in the absence of her husband Francesco Sforza, governed Milan so capably that he used to say he had more confidence in her than in his whole army, and who at the same time was known for her "piety, compassion, charity, and beauty of person";[61] or Emilia Pio, whose husband died in her youth, but who so cherished his memory that she was never known, through all her remaining years, to encourage the attentions of any man; or Lucrezia Tornabuoni, mother and molder of Lorenzo the Magnificent; or Elisabetta Gonzaga, or Beatrice d'Este, or the maligned and gentle Lucrezia Borgia; or the Caterina Cornaro who made Asolo a school for poets, artists, and gentlemen; or Veronica Gambara, the poetess and *salonnière* of Correggio; or Vittoria Colonna, the untouched goddess of Michelangelo.

Vittoria recaptured, without proud display, all the quiet virtue of a Roman heroine of the Republic, and combined with it the noblest features of Christianity. She had distinguished ancestry: her father was Fabrizio Colonna, grand constable of the Kingdom of Naples; her mother, Agnese da Montefeltro, was a daughter of Federigo, the scholarly Duke of Urbino. Betrothed in childhood to Ferrante Francesco d'Ávalos, Marquis of Pescara, she married him at nineteen (1509); and the love that united them before and after marriage was a finer poem that any of the sonnets that they exchanged during his campaigns. At the battle of Ravenna (1512) he was wounded almost to death, and was taken prisoner; he took advantage of his captivity to compose *A Book of Loves*, which he dedicated to his wife. Meanwhile he had carried on a liaison with one of Isabella d'Este's maids of honor.[62] After his release he returned to Vittoria briefly, then sallied forth on one campaign after another, so that she seldom saw him again. He led the forces of Charles V at Pavia (1525), and won a decisive victory. Offered the crown of Naples if he would join a conspiracy against the Emperor, he thought it over for a while, then revealed the plot to Charles. When he died (November, 1525) he had not seen his wife for three years. Ignorant of, or ignoring, his infidelities, she spent her twenty-two years of widowhood in works of charity, piety, and devotion to his memory. When she was urged to marry again she replied: "My husband Ferdinand, who to you seems dead, is not dead to me."[63] She lived in quiet retirement at Ischia, then in convents at Orvieto and Viterbo, then in semiconventual privacy in Rome. There, while herself remaining apparently orthodox, she befriended several Italians who sympathized with the Reformation. For a time she was placed under the surveillance of the Inquisition, and to be her friend was to risk indictment for heresy. Michelangelo took the risk, and developed for her an intense spiritual affection that never dared go beyond poetry.

The educated women of the Renaissance emancipated themselves without any propaganda of emancipation, purely by their intelligence, character, and tact, and by the heightened sensitivity of men to their tangible and intangible charms. They influenced their time in every field: in politics by their ability to govern states for their absent husbands; in morals by their combination of freedom, good manners, and piety; in art by developing a matronly beauty which modeled a hundred Madonnas; in literature by opening their homes and their smiles to poets and scholars. There were innumerable satires on women, as in every age; but for every bitter or sarcastic line there were litanies of devotion and praise. The Italian Renaissance, like the French Enlightenment, was bisexual; women moved into every sphere of life; men ceased to be coarse and crude, and were molded to finer manners and speech; and civilization, with all its laxity and violence, took on a grace and refinement such as it had not known in Europe for a thousand years.

VI. THE HOME

The rising refinement showed itself in the form and life of the home. While the dwellings of the populace remained as before—unadorned white-washed stucco or plaster walls, flagstone floors, an inner court usually with a well, and around the court one or two stories of rooms furnished with the simple necessaries of life—the palaces of the nobles and *nouveaux riches* took on a splendor and luxury again recalling Imperial Rome. The wealth that in the Middle Ages had been concentrated on the cathedral now poured itself out into mansions equipped with such furniture, conveniences, delicacies, and ornaments as could hardly be found, north of the Alps, in the seats of princes and kings. The Villa Chigi and the Palazzo Massimi, both designed by Baldassare Peruzzi, enclosed a labyrinth of rooms, each ornate with columns and pilasters, or fretted cornice, or gilded coffered ceiling, or paintings on vault and walls, or sculptured chimney pieces, or stucco carvings and arabesques, or floors of marble or tile. Every mansion had elegant beds, tables, chairs, chests, and cabinets built for a century and cut to please the eye; its massive credences or buffets were loaded with silver plate and fancy pottery; it had soft and comfortable beds, fine carpets and handsome drapes, and linen abundant, enduring, and perfumed. Great fireplaces warmed the rooms, and lamps, torches, or chandeliers lighted them. All that was lacking in these palaces was children.

For family limitation rises as the means for supporting children mount. The Church and the Scriptures bade men increase and multiply, but comfort counseled infertility. Even in the countryside, where children were economic assets, families of six children were rare; in the city, where children were liabilities, families were small—the richer the smaller—and many homes had no children at all.[64] What lovely children Italian families could have appears in the *bambini* and *putti* of the artists, the *cantorie* of Donatello and Luca della Robbia, and such sculptural portraits as *The Young St. John* of Antonio Rossellino in the Washington National Gallery. The solidarity of the family, the mutual loyalty and love of parents and children, stand out all the more attractively amid the moral looseness of the times.

The family was still an economic, moral, and geographical unit. Usually the debts of one defaulting member were paid by the rest—a marked exception to the individualism of the age. Rarely did any member marry or leave the state without the family's consent. Servants were freeborn freespoken members of the family. Paternal authority was supreme, and was obeyed in all crises; but normally the mother ruled the household. Maternal love was as fond in the princesses as in the paupers. Beatrice d'Este writes about her baby boy to her sister Isabella: "I often wish that you could be here to see him, as I am quite sure that you would never be able to stop petting and kissing him."[65] Most families of the middle class kept a register of births, marriages, deaths, and interesting events, interspersed here and there with intimate comments. In one such family record Giovanni Rucellai (ancestor of the dramatist of the same name) wrote, toward the end of his life (c. 1460), these proud words of a Florentine:

> I thank God that he has created me a rational and immortal being; in a Christian country; close to Rome, the center of the Christian faith; in Italy, the noblest country in Christendom; and in Florence, the most beautiful city of the whole world. . . . I thank Our Lord for an excellent mother, who, though only in her twentieth year at the time of my father's death, refused all offers of marriage, and devoted herself wholly to her children; and also for an equally excellent wife, who loved me truly, and cared most faithfully for both household and children; who was spared to me for many years, and whose death has been the greatest loss that ever has or could have befallen me. Recalling all these innumerable favors and benefits, I now in my old age desire to detach myself from all earthly things in order to devote my whole soul to giving praise and thanks to Thee, my Lord, the living source of my being.[66]

Two men, who were perhaps one, wrote, about 1436, treatises on the family and its governance. Agnolo Pandolfini was probably the author of an eloquent *Trattato del governo della famiglia;* Leon Battista Alberti, soon afterward, composed a *Trattato della famiglia,* whose third book, "Economico," is so largely similar to the earlier treatise that some have thought the two works were different forms of one essay by Alberti. Perhaps they are both genuine, so alike because they both based themselves upon Xenophon's *Oeconomicus.* Pandolfini's performance is the better. Like the Rucellai, he was a man of means, serving Florence as diplomat, and contributing generously to public causes. He wrote his treatise toward the end of a long life, and cast it into the form of a dialogue with his three sons. They ask him should they seek public office; he advises against it, as necessitating acts of dishonesty, cruelty, and theft, and as exposing one to suspicion, envy, and abuse. The sources of a man's happiness lie not in public office or fame, but in his wife and children, his economic success, his good repute, and his friends. A man should marry a wife sufficiently younger than himself to submit to his instruction and molding; and he should teach her, in the early years of their marriage, the obligations of motherhood and the arts of household management. A prosperous life comes from the economical and orderly use of health, talent, time, and money: of health through continence, exercise, and a moderate diet; of talent through study and the formation of honest character by religion and example; of time through shunning idleness; and of money through a careful accounting and balancing of income, expenditure, and savings. The wise man will invest first of all in a farm or estate, so arranged as to provide him and his family not only with a country residence, but with corn, wine, oil, fowl, wood, and as many as possible of the other necessaries of life. It is well also to have a house in the city, so that the children may use the educational facilities there, and learn some of the industrial arts.[67] But the family should spend as much of the year as possible in the villa and the country:

> While every other possession causes work and danger, fear and disappointment, the villa brings a great and honorable advantage; the villa is always true and kind. . . . In spring the green trees and the song of the birds will make you joyful and hopeful; in autumn a moderate exertion will bring forth a hundredfold; all through the year melancholy will be banished from you. The villa is the spot where good and honest men love to congregate. . . . Hasten thither, and fly from the pride of the rich, and the dishonor of evil men.[68]

To which one Giovanni Campano answered for a million million peasants: "Had I not been born a rustic, I should readily have been touched with pleasure" by these descriptions of rural happiness; however, having been a farmer, "what to you are delights are to me a bore."[69]

VII. PUBLIC MORALITY

Pandolfini was right in at least one judgment—that commercial and public morality was the least attractive side of Renaissance life. Then, as now, success, not virtue, was the standard by which men were judged; even the righteous Pandolfino prays for wealth rather than for immortal life. Then, as now, men itched for money, and stretched their consciences to grasp it. Kings and princes betrayed their allies, and broke their most solemn pledges, at the call of gold. Artists were no better: many of them took advance payments, failed to finish or begin the work, but kept the money just the same. The papal court itself gave a high example of money lust; hear again the greatest historian of the papacy:

> A deep-rooted corruption had taken possession of nearly all the officials of the Curia. . . . The inordinate number of gratuities and exactions had passed all bounds. Moreover, on all sides deeds were dishonestly manipulated, and even falsified, by the officials. No wonder that there arose from all parts of Christendom the loudest complaints about the corruption and financial extortions of the papal officials. It was even said that in Rome everything had its price.[70]

The Church still condemned all taking of interest as usury. Preachers inveighed against it; cities—Piacenza, for example—sometimes forbade it under pain of exclusion from the sacraments and from Christian burial. But the lending of money at interest went on, because such loans were indispensable in an expanding commercial and industrial economy. Laws were passed prohibiting a higher rate than twenty per cent, but we hear of cases where thirty per cent was charged. Christians competed with Jews in moneylending, and the town council of Verona complained that the Christians exacted harder terms than the Jews;[71] public resentment, however, fell chiefly upon the Jews, and occasionally led to outbreaks of antisemitic violence. The Franciscans met the problem for the most helpless borrowers by establishing, through gifts and legacies, *monti di pietà*, funds (literally heaps) of charity, from which they made loans to the needy, at first without interest. The first of these was organized at Orvieto in 1463; soon every major city had one. Their growth involved expenditures of administration; and the Fifth Lateran Council (1515) granted the Franciscans the right to charge for each loan an amount necessary to cover the costs of management. Instructed by this experience, some theologians of the sixteenth century allowed a moderate interest on loans.[72] Through the competition of the *monti di pietà*, and probably more through the increasing competence and rivalry of the professional bankers, the rate of interest fell rapidly during the sixteenth century.

Industry became more ruthless with its size, and with the disappearance of a personal relationship between employer and employed. Under feudalism the serf had enjoyed certain rights along with his burdensome dues: in sickness, economic depression, war, and old age his lord was expected to take care of him. In the cities of Italy the guilds performed something of this function for the better class of labor; but in general the "free" laborer was free to starve when he could find no work. When he found it he had to take it on the employer's terms, and these were hard. Every invention and improvement in production and finance added to profits, rarely to wages. Businessmen were as severe with one another as with their employees; we hear of their many tricks in competition, their deceptive contracts, their innumerable frauds;[73] when they co-operated it was to ruin their competitors in another town. However, there were instances of a fine sense of honor among many Italian merchants; and the Italian financiers had the best reputation in Europe for integrity.[74]

Social morality was a blend of violence and chastity. In the correspondence of the times we find many evidences of a tender and kindly spirit; and the Italians could not compete with the Spaniards in ferocity, or with the French soldiery in wholesale butchery. Yet no nation in Europe could match the endless merciless slander that swept around all prominent persons in Rome; and who but the Italians of the Renaissance could have called Aretino divine? Private violence flourished. Family feuds were refreshed by the breakdown of custom and belief, and the inadequate administration of the laws; men took vengeance into their own hands, and families murdered one another for generations. At Ferrara, as late as 1537, dueling to the death was legal and practised; even boys were allowed to fight each other with knives in these legal lists.[75] The strife of parties was bitterer than anywhere else in Europe. Crimes of violence were innumerable. Assassins could be bought almost as cheaply as indulgences. The palaces of Roman nobles swarmed with *bravi*, thugs ready to kill at a nod from their lords. Everyone had a dagger, and brewers of poison found many customers; at last the people of Rome could hardly believe in the natural death of any man of prominence or wealth. Important personages required that all food or drink served to them should first be tasted by another in their presence. Strange stories were told in Rome of a *venenum atterminatum*, a poison that took effect only after an interval long enough to cover up the trail of the poisoner. A man had to live on the alert in those days; any evening, if he left the house, he might be ambushed and robbed, and be lucky not to be killed; even in church he was not safe; and on the highways he had to be ready for brigands. The Renaissance mind, living amid these dangers, had to be as sharp as an assassin's blade.

Sometimes cruelty was collective and contagious. At Arezzo, in 1502, a riot broke out against an oppressive Florentine commission; hundreds of Florentines in Arezzo were slain in the streets; whole families were wiped out. One victim was stripped naked and hanged, and a lighted torch was thrust between his buttocks; whereupon the jolly crowd nicknamed the corpse *il sodomita*.[76] Tales of violence, cruelty and lust were as popular as superstition. The court of Ferrara, brilliant with poetry and art, was ghastly with princely crimes and royal punishments. The irresponsibility of despots like the Visconti and the Malatestas provided a model and stimulus for the amateur violence of the people.

The morals of war worsened with time. In the early days of the Renaissance almost all battles were modest engagements of mercenaries, who fought without frenzy and knew when to stop; victory was judged won as soon as a few men had fallen; and a live ransomable prisoner was worth more than a dead enemy. As the *condottieri* became more powerful, and armies larger and more costly, troops were allowed to plunder captured cities in lieu of regular pay; resistance to plunder led to the massacre of the inhabitants, and ferocity grew at the smell of the blood it shed. Even so, the cruelty of the Italians in war was far exceeded by the invading Spanish and French. When the French took Capua in 1501, says Guicciardini, they "committed great slaughter . . . and women of all ranks and qualities, even such as were consecrated to the service of God . . . fell a sacrifice to their lust or avarice; many of these poor creatures were afterwards sold at Rome for a small price,"[77]—apparently to Christians. The enslavement of prisoners of war increased as the wars of the Renaissance progressed.

There were instances of fine loyalty of man to man, of citizen to state; but by and large the development of cunning put a premium on deceit. Generals sold themselves to the highest bidder, and then, in mid-campaign, negotiated with the enemy for a higher price. Governments too changed sides in the middle of a war, and allies became foes by the scratch of a pen. Princes and popes violated safe-conducts given by them;[78] governments consented to the secret assassination of their enemies in other states.[79] Traitors could be found in any city or camp: instance Bernardino del Corte, who sold Lodovico's Castello to France; the Swiss and Italians who betrayed Lodovico to the French; Francesco Maria della Rovere, who kept his papal troops from going to the rescue of the pope in 1527; Malatesta Baglioni, who sold out Florence in 1530. . . . As religious belief declined, the notion of right and wrong was replaced, in many minds, by that of practicality; and as governments seldom enjoyed the authority of legitimation by time, the habit of obedience to law lapsed, and custom had to be supplanted by force. Against the tyranny of governments the only recourse was tyrannicide.

Corruption ran through every department of administration. In Siena the bureau of finance had finally to be put into the hands of a saintly monk, since everybody else had embezzled. Except in Venice, the courts were notoriously venal. One of Sacchetti's stories tells of a judge who was bribed with the gift of an ox; but the opponent sent the judge a cow and a calf, and won his case.[80] Justice was expensive; the poor had to get along without it, and found it cheaper to kill than to litigate. Law itself was making some progress, but chiefly in theory. At Padua and Bologna, Pisa and Perugia, there were famous jurists—Cino da Pistoia, Bartolus of Sassoferrato, Baldo degli Ubaldi—whose reinterpretation of Roman law dominated jurisprudence for two centuries. Nautical and commercial law expanded as foreign trade increased. Giovanni da Legnano opened a path for Grotius with a *Tractatus de bello* (1360), the earliest known work on the laws of war.

But the practice of law was less excellent than its theory. Though police protection of life and property was taking form, especially in Florence, it could not keep abreast of crime. Lawyers abounded. Torture continued to be used in the examination of witnesses as well as of the accused. Punishments were barbarous. In Bologna a convict might be suspended in a cage from one of the leaning towers, and left to fester in the sun;[81] in Siena a condemned man was slowly torn to pieces with red-hot pincers while bound to a cart slowly moving through the streets;[82] in Milan, under Petrarch's host Giovanni Visconti, prisoners were subjected to piecemeal mutilation.[83] Early in the sixteenth century the custom began of condemning prisoners to pull the heavy oars of galleys; so the ships of Julius II were manned by galley slaves chained by the leg.[84]

Against these barbarities we may place the high development of organized charity. Every man who made a will left a sum to be distributed among the poor of his parish. Since beggars were numberless, some churches provided the equivalent of modern "soup kitchens"; so the church of Santa Maria in Campo Santo, at Rome, fed thirteen beggars daily, and two thousand on Mondays and Fridays.[85] Hospitals, lazarettos, asylums for incurables, for the poor, for orphans, for destitute pilgrims, for reformed prostitutes, were numerous in Renaissance as in medieval Italy. Pistoia and Viterbo were celebrated for the scope of their charities. At Mantua Lodovico Gonzaga established the Ospedale Maggiore for the care of the poor and infirm, and gave it three thousand ducats a year of governmental funds.[86] At Venice a society known as the Pellegrini, including in its membership Titian and the two Sansovini, provided mutual aid to its members, dowered poor girls, and practised other charities. Florence in 1500 had seventy-three civic organizations devoted to works of charity. The Confraternità della Misericordia, founded in 1244 but allowed to decay, was restored in 1475; its members were laymen who visited the sick, practised other charities, and earned the love of the people by their courageous attendance upon victims of the plague; their silent black-robed processions are still among the most impressive sights of Florence.[87] Venice had a similar Confraternità di San Rocco; Rome had a Sodality of the Dolorosa, now 504 years old; and Cardinal Giulio de' Medici founded in 1519 the Confraternità della Carità to take care of poor persons above the mendicant class, and to provide decent burial for the destitute. The private charity of unrecorded millions lent some mitigation to the struggle of man against man, nature, and death.

VIII. MANNERS AND AMUSEMENTS

Amid violence and dishonesty, and the boisterous life of university students, and the rough humor and kindliness of peasant and proletaire, good manners grew as one of the arts of the Renaissance. Italy now led Europe in personal and social hygiene, dress, table manners, cooking, conversation, and recreations; and in all of these except dress Florence claimed to lead Italy. Florence patriotically mourned the filth of other cities, and Italians made *Tedesco*, German, a synonym for coarseness of language and life.[88] The old Roman habit of frequent bathing continued in the educated classes; the well-to-do displayed their finery and "took the waters" at various spas, and drank sulphurous streams as an annual penance to purge digestive sins. Male dress was as ornate as female, except for jewelry: tight sleeves and colored hose, and such wondrous baggy bonnets as Raphael caught on Castiglione. Hose ran up the legs to the loins, splitting men into prancing absurdities; but above the hips a man could be elegant in velvet tunic and silk frills and ruffles of lace; even gloves and shoes sported wisps of lace. At a tournament given by Lorenzo de' Medici his brother Giuliano wore garments costing 8000 ducats.[89]

A revolution in table manners came in the fifteenth century with the increasing substitution of a fork for the fingers in carrying food to the mouth. Thomas Coryat, touring Italy about 1600, was struck by the novel custom, "which," he wrote, "is not used in any other country that I saw in my travels"; and he shared in introducing the idea into England.[90] Knives, forks, and spoons were of brass, sometimes of silver—which was lent out to neighbors preparing banquets. Meals were modest except on such outstanding occasions or at state functions; then excess was compulsory. Spices—pepper, cloves, nutmeg, cinnamon, juniper, ginger, etc.—were used in abundance to flavor food and stimulate thirst; hence every host offered his guests a variety of wines. The reign of garlic in Italy can be traced back to 1548, but doubtless had begun long before. There was very little drunkenness or gluttony; the Italians of the Renaissance, like the later French, were gourmets, not gourmands. When men ate apart from the women of their families they might invite a courtesan or two, as Aretino did when he entertained Titian. More careful people would grace the meal with music, poetic improvisations, and educated conversation.

The art of conversation—*bel parlare*—to speak with intelligence, urbanity, courtesy, clarity, and wit—was reinvented by the Renaissance. Greece and Rome had known it, and here and there in medieval Italy—as at the courts of Frederick II and Innocent III—it had been kept precariously alive. Now in Lorenzo's Florence, in Elisabetta's Urbino, in Leo's Rome, it flourished again: nobles and their ladies, poets and philosophers, generals and scholars, artists and musicians met in the companionship of minds, quoted famous authors, made an occasional obeisance to religion, graced their language with a light fantastic touch, and basked in one another's audience. Such conversation was so admired that many essays and treatises were cast in dialogue form to appropriate its elegance. In the end the game was carried to excess; language and thought became too precious and refined; an enervating dilettantism softened manliness. Urbino became Rambouillet in France, and Molière attacked *les précieuses ridicules* just in time to save the art of good converse for France.

Despite the preciosity of a few, Italian speech enjoyed a freedom of subject and epithet that would not be allowed by social manners today. Since general conversation was rarely heard by unmarried women of good character, it was assumed that sex might be openly discussed. But beyond this, and even in the highest male circles, there was a looseness of sexual jest, a gay freedom in poetry, a coarse obscenity in drama, that seem to us now among the less presentable aspects of the Renaissance. Educated men could scribble lewd verses on statuary, the refined Bembo wrote in praise of Priapus.[91] Youths competed in obscenity and profanity to prove their maturity. Men of all classes swore great oaths and curses, often involving blasphemy of the most sacred names in the Christian faith. And yet the phrases of courtesy had never been so flowery, forms of address had never been so gracious; women kissed the hand of any intimate male friend on meeting or leaving him, and men kissed the hand of a woman; presents were ever passing from friend to friend; and tact of word and deed reached a development that seemed unattainable in northern Europe. Italian manuals of manners became favored texts beyond the Alps.

The same was true of Italian handbooks of dancing, fencing, and other recreations; in recreation, as in conversation and profanity, Italy led the Christian world. On summer evenings girls danced in the squares of Florence, and the most graceful won a silver garland; in the villages young men and women danced on the green. In homes and at formal balls women danced with women or men, and men with men or women; in any case the aim was grace. In the Renaissance the ballet flourished; the poetry of motion was added to the arts.

Cardplaying was even more popular than dancing; in the fifteenth century it became a mania in all classes; Leo X was an addict. Often it involved gambling; recall how Cardinal Raffaello Riario won 14,000 ducats in two games with the son of Innocent VIII. Men gambled also with dice, and sometimes loaded them.[92] This too became a passion, which legislation vainly sought to moderate. In Venice gambling ruined so many noble families that the Council of Ten twice forbade the sale of cards or dice, and called upon servants to report masters violating these ordinances.[93] The *monte di pietà* established by Savonarola in 1495 required of borrowers a pledge to avoid gambling at least till the loan had been paid.[94] Sedate people brooded over chess, and fondled expensive sets; Giacomo Loredano at Venice had chessmen valued at 5000 ducats.

Young men had their special games, mostly in the open air. The upper-class Italian was trained to ride, wield sword and lance, and tilt in tournaments. For such contests the towns, on certain holidays, roped off space in a square, usually convenient to windows and balconies whence the ladies could encourage their knights. As these combats proved insufficiently mortal, some rash youths, in the Roman Colosseum in 1332, introduced the bullfight, with a man on foot armed only with a spear; on that occasion eighteen knights, all of old Roman families, were killed, and only eleven bulls.[95] Such contests were occasionally repeated in Rome and Siena, but never caught the Italian taste. Horse racing was more popular, and aroused the enthusiasm of Romans, Sienese, and Florentines alike. Hunting, falconry, foot races, boat regattas, tennis, and boxing rounded out the sports, and kept the Italians individually in form, while collectively the defense of the cities was left to mercenary aliens.

All in all it was a gay life despite its toils and risks, its natural and supernatural terrors. City folk had the pleasure of walking or riding out to the countryside, to the banks of the rivers or the shores of the sea; they cultivated flowers to adorn their homes and persons, and, by their villas, carved stately gardens into geometrical forms. The Church was generous with holydays, and the state added holidays of its own. Water festivals were held on the Venetian lagoons, on the Arno at Venice, the Mincio at Mantua, the Ticino at Milan. Or, on special days, great processions moved down the city streets, with floats and banners designed for the guilds by artists of international renown; bands played, pretty girls sang and danced, dignitaries marched; and in the evening fireworks shot their evanescent wonder into the sky. On Holy Saturday, in Florence, three flints brought from the Holy Sepulcher in Jerusalem lit a taper that lit a candle that—carried along a wire by a mechanical dove—reached and set off the fireworks in the *Carro* or emblematic car of state in the piazza before the cathedral. On Corpus Christi the parade would be halted to hear a cantata sung by a choir of girls and boys, or see an episode of Scriptural history or pagan mythology enacted by some confraternity. If a great dignitary came to town he might be received with a *trionfo*, a procession arranged with chariots in the manner of a Roman triumph for a victorious general. When Leo X visited his beloved Florence in 1513, all the city turned out to watch his triumphal car—decorated and painted by Pontormo—pass under great arches that spanned the central street; seven other chariots moved in that cavalcade, bearing impersonations of famous figures in Roman history; on the last a naked boy, covered with gilt, represented the coming, with Leo, of the Golden Age; but the boy died shortly afterward from the effect of the gilt.[96]

At carnival time the processional floats in Florence might symbolize some idea like Prudence, Hope, Fear, Death, or the elements, the winds, the seasons, or tell in pantomime a story like Paris and Helen, or Bacchus and Ariadne, with songs appropriate to each scene; for such a "masque" Lorenzo wrote his famous ode to youth and joy. On those carnival nights everyone from urchins to cardinals wore masks, played pranks, and made love, with a freedom that revenged itself in advance for the restraints of Lent. In 1512, when Florence seemed still prosperous, but unsuspected misfortunes were only a few months away, Piero di Cosimo and Francesco Granacci designed for a carnival pageant a "Masque of the Triumph of

Death": an enormous triumphal car, drawn by black buffaloes, was covered with a black cloth on which were painted skeletons and white crosses; in the car stood a colossal figure of Death with a scythe in his hand; around him were tombs, and lugubrious figures on whose black robes were painted white bones gleaming in the dark; and behind the car masked figures walked, whose black hoods were painted with death heads both in front and behind. From the tombs on the cars rose other figures, painted to seem only bones; and these skeletons chanted a song reminding men that all must die. Before and after the car came a cavalcade of decrepit horses, bearing the bodies of dead men.[97] So, at the height of carnival, Piero di Cosimo, echoing Savonarola, pronounced his judgment on the pleasures of Italy, and his prophecy of the doom to come.

IX. DRAMA

In such masques and carnival fetes the Italian drama had one of its progenitors. For often some scene, usually from sacred history, would be performed on one of the floats or cars, or on temporary stages at points on the procession route. But the primary source of the Italian drama was the *divozione*, an episode of the Christian story acted by the members of any guild, sometimes by professional players belonging to a confraternity that made a business of presenting such spectacles. The texts of several *divozioni* have come down through time, and show a surprising dramatic power; so the Virgin, finding Christ in Jerusalem and then again losing him, searches frantically for him, crying out: "O my so loving Son! O my Son, where have you gone? O my so gracious Son, through what gate have you gone? O my divine Son, you were so sorrowful when you left me! Tell me, for the love of God, where, where has my Son gone?"[98]

In the fifteenth century, especially in Florence, a more developed form of drama, the *sacra rappresentazione*, was played in the oratory of a guild, or in the refectory of a convent, or in a field or public square. The scenic arrangements for these performances were often complex and ingenious: skies were simulated by vast awnings painted with stars; clouds were represented by masses of wool suspended and swaying in the air; angels were impersonated by boys supported aloft on metal frames concealed in waving draperies. The libretto was usually in poetic form, accompanied with music on the viol or the lute. Lorenzo de' Medici and the Pulci were among the poets who wrote words for such religious plays. Politian, in his *Orfeo*, adapted the form of the *sacra rappresentazione* to a pagan theme.

Meanwhile other components of Italian life were sharing in the birth of Italian drama. The *farse* or farces that had long been played by passing mummers in the medieval towns contained the germ of Italian comedy. Some players excelled in improvising dialogue for simple scenarios or plots; this *commedia dell' arte* was a favorite vehicle of the Italian genius for satire and burlesque. In such farces the traditional masks or characters of popular comedy took form and name: Pantalone, Arlecchino, Pulcinella or Punchinello.

The humanists played their part in the complex of factors leading to the drama by restoring the texts, and arranging performances, of ancient Roman comedies. Twelve plays of Plautus were discovered in 1427, and served as an additional stimulus. At Venice, Ferrara, Mantua, Urbino, Siena, Rome the comedies of Plautus and Terence were staged, and the old classic tradition soared over centuries to form again a secular theater. In 1486 the *Menaechmi* of Plautus was for the first time presented in Italian, and the transition from ancient to Renaissance drama was fully prepared. Toward the end of the fifteenth century the religious drama lost its hold on educated audiences in Italy; pagan subjects increasingly replaced Christian themes; and when native dramatists like Bibbiena, Machiavelli, Ariosto, and Aretino wrote plays, it was in the ribald style of Plautus, a world away from the once-beloved stories of Mary and Christ. All the old scenes of Roman comedy, all the superficial plots turning on mistaken sex or identity or rank, all the stock characters, including panders and prostitutes, with which Plautus had pleased the groundlings, all the old plebian coarseness and rough play, reappeared in these Italian comedies.

Despite the preservation of Seneca's plays, and the recovery of the Greek drama, tragedy never acquired a standing on the Renaissance stage. Even the upper classes wished to be amused rather than deepened, and turned a cold eye upon Gian Trissino's *Sophonisba* (1515), and Giovanni Rucellai's *Rosamunda*, which in the same year was performed in the Rucellai gardens at Florence before Leo X.

It was the misfortune of Italian comedy that it took form when Italian morals were at nadir. That such plays as Bibbiena's *Calandra* and Machiavelli's *Mandragola* could satisfy the tastes of the Italian upper classes, even at refined Urbino, and could be performed before popes without arousing protest, reveals again how intellectual freedom can comport with moral deterioration. When the Counter Reformation came with the Council of Trent (1545f), the morals of clergy and laity were severely censored, and the comedy of the Renaissance was banished from the amusements of Italian society.

X. MUSIC

It was a redeeming feature of Italian comedy that ballets, pantomimes, and concerts were presented as intermezzi between the acts. For next to love itself, music was the chief recreation and consolation of every class in

Italy. Montaigne, traveling in Tuscany in 1581, was "astounded to see peasants with lutes in their hands, and, beside them, shepherds reciting Ariosto by heart"; but this, he adds, "is what we may see in all of Italy."[99] Renaissance painting has a thousand representations of people playing music, from the luting angels at the Madonna's feet in so many Coronations, and Melozzo's serenading seraphim, to the quiet exaltation of the man at the harpischord in *The Concert;* and note the boy—whom we can hardly believe to be the painter himself—in the center of Sebastiano del Piombo's *Three Ages of Man.* The literature likewise conveys a picture of a people singing or playing music in their homes, at their work, on the street, in music academies, monasteries, nunneries, churches, in processions, masques, *trionfi,* and pageants, in religious or secular plays, in the lyric passages and interludes of dramas, in such outings as Boccaccio imagined in the *Decameron.* Rich men kept a variety of musical instruments in their homes, and arranged private musicales. Women organized clubs for the study and performance of music. Italy was—is—mad about music.

Folk song flourished at all times, and learned music periodically rejuvenated itself at that fount; popular melodies were adapted for complex madrigals, for hymns, even for passages in music for the Mass. "In Florence," says Cellini, "people were wont to meet on the public streets of a summer night" to sing and dance.[100] Street singers—*cantori di piazza*—strummed their sad or merry notes on handsome lutes; people gathered to sing *laudes,* hymns of praise, to the Virgin before her street or roadside shrines; and in Venice mating songs rose to the moon from a hundred gondolas, or throaty lovers hopefully serenaded hesitant lasses in the mystic shadows of labyrinthine canals. Almost every Italian could sing, and nearly as many could sing in simple vertical harmony. Hundreds of these popular part songs have come down to us under the picturesque name of *frottole,* little fruits; usually short, usually amorous; arranged for a dominant soprano supported by tenor, alto, and bass. Whereas in previous centuries the tenor voice had "held" the melody and so derived its name, now in the fifteenth the air was carried by the soprano—so called because its music was written above the rest. This part did not need a female voice; as often as not it was sung by a boy, or by the falsetto of an adult male. (*Castrati* did not appear in the papal choir till 1562.)[101]

Among the educated classes considerable knowledge of music was required. Castiglione demands of his courtier or gentleman some amateur proficiency in music, "which not only doth make sweet the minds of men, but also many times doth wild beasts tame."[102] Every person of culture was expected to read simple music at sight, accompany himself on some instrument, and take part in an impromptu musicale.[103] Sometimes people joined in a *ballata* that involved a union of singing, dancing, and instrumental music. Universities after 1400 offered courses and degrees in music; there were hundreds of music academies; Vittorino da Feltre founded a school of music at Mantua about 1425; our "conservatories" of music are called so because in Naples many orphanages (*conservatori*) were used as music schools.[104] Music was further spread by the adaptation of printing to musical notation; about 1476 Ulrich Hahn printed at Rome a complete missal with movable type for notes and lines; and in 1501 Ottaviano de' Petrucci began at Venice the commercial printing of motets and *frottole*.

At the courts music was more prominent than any other art except those of personal adornment. Usually the ruler chose a favorite church, whose choir became the object of his care; he paid goodly sums to attract to it the finest available voices and instrumentalists from Italy, France, and Burgundy; he trained new singers from their childhood, as Federigo did at Urbino; and he expected the members of the choir to perform also for his state ceremonies and court festivities. Guillaume Dufay of Burgundy directed music at the court of the Malatestas in Rimini and Pesaro, and at the papal chapel in Rome, for a quarter of a century (1419-44). Galeazzo Maria Sforza about 1460 organized two chapel choirs, and brought to them from France Josquin Deprès, then the most famous composer in western Europe. When Lodovico Sforza welcomed Leonardo to Milan it was as a musician; and it is to be noted that Leonardo was accompanied, in going from Florence to Milan, by Atalante Migliorotti, a celebrated musician and maker of musical instruments. A still more famous maker of lyres, lutes, organs, and clavichords was Lorenzo Gusnasco of Pavia, who made Milan one of his homes. The court of Lodovico was flush with singers: Narcisso, Testagrossa, Cordier of Flanders, and Cristoforo Romano, chastely loved by Beatrice. Pedro Maria of Spain conducted concerts in the palace and for the public; and Franchino Gaffuri founded and taught in a famous private music school in Milan. Isabella d'Este was devoted to music, made it the chief theme of decoration in her inner sanctum, and herself played several instruments. When she ordered a clavichord from Lorenzo Gusnasco she specified that the keyboard should respond to a light touch, "for our hands are so delicate that we cannot play well if the keys are too stiff."[105] At her court lived the leading lutanist of his day, Marchetto Cara, and Bartolommeo Tromboncino, who composed such alluring madrigals that when he killed his unfaithful wife no punishment was meted out to him, and the matter was passed over as a discord soon to be resolved.

Finally the cathedrals and the churches, the monasteries and the nunneries resounded with music. In Venice, Bologna, Naples, Milan, the nuns sang Vespers so movingly that crowds flocked to hear them. Sixtus IV organized the famous Sistine Chapel choir; Julius II added, in St. Peter's, a *capella Iulia*, or Julian chapel choir, which trained singers for the Sistine choir. This was the summit of the Latin world's musical art in the Renaissance; to it came the greatest singers from all Roman Catholic countries. Plain chant was still the letter of canon law in church music; but here and there the *ars nova* of France—a form of complex counterpoint—made its way into the Roman choirs and prepared for Palestrina and Victoria. Once it had been held undignified to have any other musical instrument than the organ accompany a church choir; but in the sixteenth century a variety of instruments were brought in to give church music some of the grace and adornment of secular performances. At St. Mark's in Venice the Flemish master, Adrian Willaert of Bruges, presided over the choirs for thirty-five years, and trained them to such performances as made Rome envious. At Florence Antonio Squarcialupi organized a School of Harmony, of which Lorenzo was a member. For a generation Antonio reigned over the cathedral choir, and the great *duomo* rang with music that stilled all philosophic doubt. Leon Battista Alberti was a doubter, but when the choir sang he believed:

> All other modes of singing weary with repetition; only religious music never palls. I know not how others are affected; but for myself those hymns and psalms of the Church produce on me the very effect for which they were designed, soothing all disturbance of the soul, and inspiring a certain ineffable languor full of reverence toward God. What heart of man is so rude as not to be softened when he hears the rhythmic rise and fall of those voices, complete and true, in cadences so sweet and flexible? I assure you that I never listen . . . to the Greek words (*Kyrie eleison*) that call on God for aid against our human wretchedness, without weeping. Then, too, I ponder what power music brings with it to soften us and soothe.[106]

Despite all this popularity, music was the one art in which Italy lagged behind France during most of the Renaissance. Shorn of papal revenues by the flight of the popes to Avignon, and with the courts of the despots still culturally immature in the fourteenth century, Italy lacked then the means and the spirit for the higher grades of music. She produced lovely madrigals (a word of uncertain derivation), but these songs, modeled on those of the Provençal troubadours, were set to a musical frame of such strictly regulated polyphony that the form died of its own rigidity.

The pride of *trecento* music in Italy was Francesco Landini, organist of San Lorenzo in Florence. Though blind from his childhood, he became one of the finest and most loved musicians of his time, honored as an organist, lutanist, composer, poet, and philosopher. But even he took his lead from France; his two hundred secular compositions applied to Italian lyrics the *ars nova* that had captured France a generation before. The "new art" was doubly new: it accepted binary rhythms as well as the triple time previously required in the music of the Church; and it devised a more complex and flexible musical notation. Pope John XXII, who hurled his thunderbolts in all directions, aimed one at the *ars nova* as fanciful and degenerate, and his prohibition had some effect in discouraging musical development in Italy. However, John XXII could not live forever, though at times it seemed possible; after his death at the age of ninety (1334) the new art triumphed in the learned music of France, and shortly thereafter in Italy.

At Avignon French and Flemish singers and composers constituted the papal choir. When the papacy returned to Rome it brought with it a large number of French, Flemish, and Dutch composers and singers; and for a century these alien musicians and their successors dominated the music of Italy. As late as Sixtus IV all the voices in the papal choir were from beyond the Alps; and a like foreign supremacy ruled in the music of the courts in the fifteenth century. When Squarcialupi died (*c.* 1475), Lorenzo chose a Dutchman, Heinrich Ysaac, to succeed him as organist in the cathedral at Florence. Heinrich wrote music for some of the *canti carnascialeschi*, and for Politian's lyrics, and he taught the future Leo X to love—even to compose—French songs.[107] For a time the chansons of France were sung in Italy, as once Italy had recited the lays of the troubadours.

This invasion of Italy by French musicians, preceding by a century its invasion by French armies, produced toward 1520 a revolution in Italian music. For these men from the north—and the Italians whom they trained —were steeped in the *ars nova*, and applied it in setting to music the lyric poetry of Italy. In Petrarch, Ariosto, Sannazaro, and Bembo—later in Tasso and Guarini—they found delectable verses crying out for music; indeed, had not poetry always intended itself to be at least a recitative, if not a song? Petrarch's *canzoniere* had already lured musicians; now every line of it was set to music, some stanzas a dozen times or more; Petrarch is the most completely musicked poet in world literature. Or there were little lyrics of unknown authorship but simple and viable sentiment, that touched the chords of every heart, and invited the strings of every instrument. E.g.:

> One from the other borrowing leaves and flowers,
>   I saw fair maidens beneath summer trees,
>   Weaving bright garlands with low love ditties.
> Mid that sweet sisterhood the loveliest
>   Turned her soft eyes to me and whispered, "Take!"
>   Love-lost I stood, and not a word I spake.
> My heart she read, and her fair garland gave;
> Therefore I am her servant to the grave.[108]

To such verses the composers applied the full and complex music of the motet: polyphony in which all four parts—sung by four or eight voices—were of equal value, instead of three parts subserving one; and all the complex subtlety of counterpoint* and fugue wove the four independent rivulets of sound into a stream of harmony. So rose the Italian madrigal of the sixteenth century—one of the fairest flowers of Italian art. Whereas in Dante's time music had been a handmaid to poetry, now it became a full-fledged partner, not obscuring the words, not slurring the sentiment, but uniting them with a music that made them doubly stir the soul, while delighting with its technical skill the educated mind.

Almost all the great composers of sixteenth-century Italy, even Palestrina, turned their art now and then to the madrigal. Philippe Verdelot, a Frenchman living in Italy, and Costanza Festa, an Italian, contest the honor of having first developed the new form, between 1520 and 1530; soon after them came the Arcadelt—a Fleming in Rome—mentioned by Rabelais.[109] In Venice Adrian Willaert relaxed from his duties as choirmaster at San Marco to compose the finest madrigals of his time.

Usually the madrigal was sung without instrumental accompaniment. Musical instruments were innumerable , but only the organ dared compete with the human voice. Instrumental music slowly developed in the early sixteenth century out of music forms originally intended for dances or choruses; so the pavane, the *saltarello*, and the saraband graduated from dance accompaniments to instrumental pieces, alone or in suite; and the

---

* This term arose about 1300 as *punctum contra punctum*—point counter point, note against note; notes being then indicated by points.

music for a madrigal, played without song, became the instrumental *can-zone*, the distant progenitor of the sonata,[109a] and therefore of the symphony.

The organ was already in the fourteenth century almost as highly developed as today. The pedal board appeared in Germany and the Low Countries in that age, and was soon adopted in France and Spain; Italy delayed acceptance of it till the sixteenth century. By that time most large organs had two or three keyboards, with a variety of stops and couplers. Great church organs were themselves works of art, designed, carved, and painted by masters. The same love of form went into the making of other musical instruments. The lute—the favorite instrument of the home—was built of wood and ivory, shaped like a pear, pierced with sound holes in a graceful pattern, with a finger board divided by frets of silver or brass, and ending in a pegbox turned at a right angle to the neck. A pretty woman plucking the strings of a lute held in her lap made a picture that went to the head of many a sensitive Italian. Harps, citherns, psalters, dulcimers, and guitars were also favorites with musical fingers.

For those who preferred fiddling to plucking there were viols of diverse sizes, including the tenor *viola da braccio*, held on the arm, and the bass *viola da gamba*, resting against the leg. The latter became the later violoncello, and the viol, about 1540, became the violin. Wind instruments were less popular than the stringed; the Renaissance had the same objection that Alcibiades had raised to making music by puffing out the cheeks; nevertheless there were flutes and fifes ("pipes"), bagpipes, trumpets, horns, flageolets, and the shawm or oboe. Percussion instruments—drums, tabors, cymbals, tambourines, castanets—added their fury to the ensemble. All Renaissance musical instruments were of Oriental origin except for the keyboard that was added to other instruments besides the organ to indirectly strike or pluck the strings. The oldest of these keyboard instruments was the clavichord (*clavis* meaning key), which appeared in the twelfth century and had a sentimental resurrection in the days of Bach; here the strings were struck with little brass tangents operated by the keys. In the sixteenth century it was displaced by the *clavicembalo* or harpsichord, whose strings were plucked by points of quill or leather attached to wooden "jacks" that rose when the keys were depressed. The virginal was an English, the spinet an Italian, variant, of the harpsichord.

All these instruments were as yet subordinate to the voice; and the great virtuosos of the Renaissance were singers. But at the baptism of Alfonso of Ferrara in 1476 we hear of a feast in the Schifanoia Palace, at which a

concert was given by a hundred trumpeters, pipers, and tambourine players. In the sixteenth century the Signory of Florence employed a regular
band of musicians, of which Cellini was one. Performances by several
instruments in concert were given in this period, but they were still for the
aristocratic few. On the other hand solo instrumental performances were
almost fanatically popular. Men went to church not always to pray but
to hear a great organist like Squarcialupi or Orcagna. When Pietro Bono
played the lute at the court of Borso in Ferrara the souls of the listeners,
we are told, flew out of this world into another.[110] The great executants
were the happy favorites of a day, who asked no fame of posterity but
received all their renown before their deaths.

Musical theory lagged a generation behind practice: performers in-
novated, professors denounced, then debated, then approved. Meanwhile
the principles of polyphony, counterpoint, and fugue were formulated for
easier instruction and transmission. The great musical feature of the Renaissance was not theory, nor even technical advances; it was the increasing secularization of music. In the sixteenth century it was no longer religious music that made the advances and experiments; it was the music of
the madrigal and the courts. Side by side with philosophy and literature,
and reflecting the pagan aspect of Renaissance art and the relaxation of
morals, the music of sixteenth-century Italy escaped from ecclesiastical
control, and sought inspiration in the poetry of love; the old conflict between religion and sex was resolved for a time in the triumph of Eros. The
reign of the Virgin ended, the ascendancy of woman began. But under
either rule music was the handmaid of the queen.

XI. PERSPECTIVE

Were the morals of Renaissance Italy really worse than those of other
lands or times? It is difficult to make comparisons, since all evidence is a
selection. The age of Alcibiades in Athens displayed much of the immorality of the Renaissance in sexual relations and political chicanery; it
too practised abortion on a large scale, and cultivated erudite courtesans;
it too liberated simultaneously the intellect and the instincts; and, anticipating Machiavelli, Sophists like Thrasybulus in Plato's *Republic* attacked
morality as weakness. Perhaps (for in these matters we are limited to
vague impressions) there was less private violence in classic Greece than in
Renaissance Italy, and a bit less of corruption in religion and politics. During an entire century of Roman history—from Caesar to Nero—we find

greater corruption in government, and a worse breakdown of marriage, than in the Renaissance; but even in that epoch there remained many Stoic virtues in the Roman character; Caesar, with all his ambivalent capacity in bribery and love, was still the greatest general in a nation of generals.

The individualism of the Renaissance was another side of its intellectual vivacity, but compares unfavorably, in morals and politics, with the communal spirit of the Middle Ages. Political deceit, treachery, and crime were probably as rife in France, Germany, and England in the fourteenth and fifteenth centuries as in Italy, but those countries had the wisdom not to produce a Machiavelli to expound and expose the principles of their statecraft. Manners, not morals, were coarser north of the Alps than below them, except for a small class in France—exemplified by the Chevalier Bayard and Gaston de Foix—which still retained the better side of chivalry. Given equal opportunity, the French were as adept at adultery as the Italians; observe how readily they adopted syphilis; note the sexual melee in the *fabliaux;* count the twenty-four mistresses of Duke Philip of Burgundy, and the Agnès Sorels and Dianes de Poitiers of the French kings; read Brantôme.

Germany and England in the fourteenth and fifteenth centuries were too poor to rival Italy in immorality. Travelers from these countries were therefore astounded by the laxity of Italian life. Luther, visiting Italy in 1511, concluded that "if there is a hell, then Rome is built upon it; and this I have heard in Rome itself."[111] Everyone knows the shocked judgment of Roger Ascham, the English scholar who visited Italy about 1550:

> I was once in Italy myself; but I thank God my abode there was but nine days; and yet I saw in that little time, in one city, more liberty to sin than ever I heard tell in our noble city of London in nine years. I saw it was there as free to sin, not only without all punishment but also without any man's marking, as it is free in the city of London to choose without all blame whether a man lust to wear shoe or pantocle.[112]

And he quotes as an established proverb the saying, *Inglese Italianato è un diavolo incarnato:* "An Englishman Italianate is a devil incarnate."

We know the corruption of Italy better than that of transalpine Europe because we know more about Italy, and because the Italian laity made little effort to conceal its immorality, and sometimes wrote books defending it. However, Machiavelli, who wrote such a book, reckoned Italy as "more corrupt than all other countries; next come the French and the Spaniards";[113] he admired the Germans and the Swiss as still possessing many of the virile virtues of ancient Rome. We may diffidently conclude that Italy was more immoral because she was richer, weaker in government and the reign of law, and further advanced in that intellectual development which usually makes for a moral release.

The Italians made some laudable efforts to check license. The vainest of these efforts were the sumptuary regulations that in nearly every state forbade extravagance of immodesty of dress; the vanity of men and women overrode with sly persistence the occasional assiduity of the law. The popes inveighed against immorality, but were in some cases swept along with the stream; their attempts at reforming abuses in the Church were nullified by the inertia or vested interests of the clergy; they themselves were rarely as wicked as passionate history once painted them, but they were more concerned to re-establish the political power of the papacy than to restore the moral integrity of the Church. "In our corrupt times," said Guicciardini, "the goodness of a pontiff is commended when it does not surpass the wickedness of other men."[114] Valiant attempts at reform were made by the great preachers of the time, men like St. Bernardino of Siena, Roberto da Lecce, San Giovanni da Capistrano, and Savonarola. Their sermons and their audiences were part of the color and character of the age. They denounced vice with a vivid detail that contributed to their popularity; they persuaded feudists to forswear revenge and live in peace; they induced governments to release insolvent debtors and let exiles return home; they brought hardened sinners back to long neglected sacraments.

Even these powerful preachers failed. The instincts formed through a hundred thousand years of hunting and savagery had re-emerged through the cracked shell of a morality that had lost the support of religious belief, of respected authority, and established law. The great Church that had once ruled kings could no longer govern or cleanse itself. The destruction of political liberty in state after state had dulled the civic sense that had enfranchised and ennobled the medieval communes; where there had been citizens there were now only individuals. Excluded from government and flush with wealth, men turned to the pursuit of pleasure, and foreign invasion surprised them in siren arms. The city-states had for two centuries directed their forces, their subtlety, and their treachery against one another; it was now impossible for them to unite against a common foe. Preachers like Savonarola, rebuffed in all pleas for reform, called down the judgment of heaven upon Italy, and predicted the destruction of Rome and the break-up of the Church.[115] France, Spain, and Germany, weary of sending tribute to finance the wars of the Papal States and the luxuries of Italian life, looked with amazement and envy at a peninsula so shorn of will and power, so inviting in beauty and wealth. The birds of prey gathered to feast on Italy.

Fig. 47—RAPHAEL AND GIULIO ROMANO: *The Transfiguration;* Borghese Gallery, Rome

PAGE 514

Fig. 48—MICHELANGELO BUO-
NARROTI: *Tomb of Lorenzo
de' Medici*; New Sacristy,
San Lorenzo, Florence

PAGE 641

Fig. 49—TITIAN: *Portrait
of Aretino*; Frick
Gallery, New York

PAGE 659

Fig. 50—TITIAN: *Portrait of Pope Paul III;* Museum, Naples   PAGE 662

Fig.   51—TITIAN: *Portrait   of Charles V;* Alte Pinakothek, Munich   PAGE 662

Fig. 52—Titian: *Venus of Urbino;* Pitti Palace, Florence   PAGE 662

Fig. 53—Titian: *Portrait of a Young Englishman;* Pitti Palace, Florence   PAGE 666

Fig. 54—TITIAN: *Self-portrait*; Prado, Madrid   PAGE 666

Fig. 55—TINTORETTO: *The Miracle of St. Mark*; Academy, Venice   PAGE 670

Fig. 56—TINTORETTO: *Presentation of the Virgin;* Santa
Maria dell' Orto, Venice

PAGE 671

Fig. 57—PAOLO VERONESE: *Self-portrait;* Uffizi Gallery, Florence

PAGE 681

Fig. 58—PAOLO VERONESE: *Portrait of Daniele Barbaro;* Pitti Palace, Florence   PAGE 679

LIBRARY, METROPOLITAN MUSEUM OF ART

Fig. 59—PAOLO VERONESE: *The Rape of Europa;* Metropolitan Museum of Art, New York   PAGE 680

Fig. 60—PAOLO VERONESE: *Mars and Venus;* Metropolitan Museum of Art, New York

PAGE 680

Fig. 61—DANIELE DA VOLTERRA: Bust of Michelangelo Buonarroti; National Museum, Florence   PAGE 721

CHAPTER XXI

The Political Collapse

1494-1534

I. FRANCE DISCOVERS ITALY: 1494-5[1]

RECALL the situation of Italy in 1494. The city-states had grown through the rise of a middle class enriched by the development and management of commerce and industry. They had lost their communal freedom through the inability of semidemocratic governments to maintain order amid the feuds of families and the conflicts of classes. Their economy remained local in structure even while their fleets and products reached out to distant ports. They competed with one another more bitterly than with foreign states; they offered no concerted resistance to the expansion of French, German, and Spanish commerce into regions once dominated by Italy. Though Italy gave birth to the man who rediscovered America, it was Spain that financed him; trade followed in his wake, gold accompanied his return; the Atlantic nations flourished, and the Mediterranean ceased to be the favored home of the white man's economic life. Portugal was sending ships around Africa to India and China, avoiding Moslem hindrances in the Near and Middle East; even the Germans were shipping through the mouths of the Rhine rather than over the Alps to Italy. Countries that had for a century bought Italian woolen products were now making their own; nations that had paid interest to Italian bankers were nursing their own financiers. Tithes, annates, Peter's Pence, indulgence payments, and pilgrims' coins were now the chief economic contribution of transalpine Europe to Italy; and soon a third of Europe would divert that flow. In this generation when the stored-up wealth of Italy raised her cities to their supreme brilliance and art, Italy was economically doomed.

She was also politically doomed. While she remained divided into warring economies and states, the development of a national economy was compelling and financing, in other European societies, the transition from feudal principalities to the monarchical state. France unified herself under Louis XI, reducing her barons to courtiers and her burghers to patriots;

Spain unified herself by wedding Ferdinand of Aragon to Isabella of Castile, and conquering Granada, and cementing religious unity with blood; England unified herself under Henry VII; and though Germany was almost as fragmentary as Italy, it acknowledged one king and emperor, and occasionally gave him money and soldiers to make war upon one or another of the Italian states. England, France, Spain, and Germany raised national armies out of their own people, and their aristocracies provided cavalry and leadership; the Italian cities had small forces of mercenaries inspired only by plunder, led by purchasable *condottieri*, and prejudiced against sustaining mortal injuries. It needed only one engagement to reveal to Europe the defenselessness of Italy.

Half the courts of Europe now seethed with diplomatic intrigue as to which should seize the plum. France claimed the first right, and with many reasons. Giangaleazzo Visconti had given his daughter Valentina in marriage (1387) to Louis, first Duke of Orléans, and, as the price of this comforting connection with a royal family, had recognized her right, and the right of her male issue, to succeed to the duchy of Milan in case his own direct male line should fail; which it did when Filippo Maria Visconti died (1447). His son-in-law, Francesco Sforza, then took Milan by right of his wife Bianca, Filippo Maria's daughter; but Charles, Duke of Orléans, claimed Milan as Valentina's son, denounced the Sforzas as usurpers, and proclaimed his resolve, when opportunity should offer, to appropriate the Italian principality.

Moreover, said the French, Charles, Duke of Anjou, had received the Kingdom of Naples from Pope Urban IV (1266) as reward for defending the papacy against the Hohenstaufen kings; Joanna II had bequeathed the Kingdom to René of Anjou (1435); Alfonso I of Aragon had claimed it through her temporary adoption of him as her son, and had by force established the house of Aragon on the Neapolitan throne. René tried and failed to recapture the kingdom; his legal right to it passed at his death to Louis XI, King of France; and in 1482 Sixtus IV, at odds with Naples, invited Louis to come and conquer Naples, "which," said the Pope, "belongs to him." About this time Venice, hard pressed in war by a league of Italian states, called in desperation to Louis to attack either Naples or Milan, preferably both. Louis was busy unifying France; but his son Charles VIII inherited his claim to Naples, listened to the Angevin-Neapolitan exiles at his court, noted that the crown of Naples was joined to that of Sicily, which carried with it the crown of Jerusalem; he conceived, or was sold, the grandiose idea of capturing Naples and Sicily, getting himself crowned King of Jerusalem, and then leading a crusade against the Turks. In 1489 Innocent VIII, quarreling with Naples, offered the Kingdom to Charles if he would come and take it. Alexander VI (1494) forbade Charles, on pain of excommunication, to cross the Alps; but Alexander's enemy, Cardinal Giuliano della Rovere—who later, as Julius II, would war to drive the French from Italy—came to Charles at Lyons, and urged him to invade Italy and depose Alexander. Savonarola added another invitation, hoping that Charles would depose Piero de' Medici in Florence and Alexander in Rome; and many Florentines accepted the friar's lead. Finally, Lodovico of Milan, fearing attack from Naples, offered Charles unimpeded passage through the territory of Milan whenever Charles should undertake a campaign against Naples.

So encouraged by half of Italy, Charles prepared to invade. To protect his flanks he ceded Artois and Franche-Comté to Maximilian of Austria, and Roussillon and Cerdagne to Ferdinand of Spain, and paid a large sum to Henry VII for renouncing English claims on Brittany. In March, 1494, he assembled his army at Lyons: 18,000 cavalry, 22,000 infantry. A fleet was sent to keep Genoa safe for France; on September 8 it recaptured Rapallo from a Neapolitan force that had landed there; and the unrestrained bloodiness of this first encounter shocked an Italy accustomed to reasonable slaughter. In that month Charles and his army crossed the Alps, and paused at Asti. Lodovico of Milan and Ercole of Ferrara went there to meet him, and Lodovico lent him funds. Charles disrupted the schedule by getting smallpox. Recovering, he led his troops through the Milanese into Tuscany. The Florentine frontier fortresses at Sarzana and Pietrasanta might have resisted him, but Piero de' Medici came in person to surrender them, along with Pisa and Livorno. On November 17 Charles and half his army paraded through Florence; the populace admired the unprecedented cavalcade, grumbled at petty thefts by the soldiery, but noted with relief that they refrained from rape. In December Charles moved on toward Rome.

We have already looked at the meeting of King and Pope from Alexander's point of view. Charles behaved with moderation: he asked only a free passage through Latium for his army, the custody of the papal prisoner Djem (who might be used as a pretender and ally in a campaign against the Turks), and Caesar Borgia's company as a hostage. Alexander agreed; the army marched south (January 25, 1495), Borgia soon escaped, and Alexander was free to reform the lines of his diplomacy.

On February 22 Charles entered Naples in unresisted triumph, beneath a canopy of cloth of gold borne by four Neapolitan nobles, and acclaimed by the cheers of the populace. He showed his appreciation by reducing taxes and pardoning those who had opposed his coming; and at the request of the barons who ruled the hinterland he recognized the institution of slavery. Thinking himself secure, he relaxed to enjoy the climate and scenery; he wrote enthusiastically to the duke of Bourbon describing the gardens amid which he now lived, lacking only an Eve to be paradise; he marveled at the architecture, sculpture, and painting in the city, and planned to take a selection of Italian artists with him to France; meanwhile he dispatched to France a shipment of stolen art. Naples so charmed him that he forgot about Jerusalem and his crusade.

While he dallied in Naples, and his army enjoyed the women of the streets and the stews and caught or spread the "French disease," trouble was organizing behind him. The Neapolitan nobles, instead of being rewarded for helping depose their king, were in many cases deprived of their estates for the benefit of former Angevin possessors, or to pay Charles's debts to his servitors; all state offices were given to Frenchmen, and nothing could be obtained from them except by bribes offensively exceeding Neapolitan custom; the occupying army added insult to injury by their open contempt of the Italian people; in a few months the French had worn out their welcome, and earned a hatred that waited in fierce patience for a chance to expel the invaders.

On March 31, 1495, the resilient Alexander, the repentant Lodovico, the angry Ferdinand, the jealous Maximilian, the cautious Senate of Venice joined in a league for the united defense of Italy. King Charles, parading through Naples with a scepter in one hand and a ball—presumably the globe—in the other, took a month to realize that the new alliance was raising an army against him. On May 21 he left Naples in charge of his cousin the Count of Montpensier, and led half his army northward. At Fornovo, on the River Taro in the territory of Parma, his 10,000 troops found their passage blocked by an allied army of 40,000 men led by Gianfrancesco Gonzaga, Marquis of Mantua. There, on July 5, 1495, came the first real test of French vs. Italian arms and tactics. Gonzaga, though he himself fought bravely, mismanaged his forces, so that only half of them took part; the Italians were not mentally prepared to fight warriors who gave no quarter, and many of them fled; the Chevalier de Bayard, a lad of twenty, offered his men an inspiring example of reckless courage, and even the King fought valiantly. The battle was indecisive; both sides claimed victory; the French lost their baggage train, but remained masters of the field;

and during the night they marched unimpeded to Asti, where Louis, third Duke of Orléans, awaited them with reinforcements. In October Charles, with damaged repute but a whole skin, was back in France.

The territorial results of the invasion were slight. Gonzalo, the "Great Captain," drove the French out of Naples and Calabria, and restored the Aragonese dynasty in the person of Federigo III (1496). The indirect results of the invasion were endless. It proved the superiority of a national army to mercenary troops. The Swiss mercenaries were a temporary exception; armed with pikes eighteen feet long, and formed in solid battalions that presented a discouraging "hedgehog" to advancing cavalry, they were destined to many victories; but soon, at Marignano (1515), the invincibility of this revived Macedonian phalanx would be ended by improved artillery. It was probably in this war that cannon were first placed on carriages that allowed them to be readily manipulated for direction and range;[2] these carriages were drawn by horses, not (as hitherto in Italy) by oxen; and the French brought into action, says Guicciardini, such a number of "field pieces and battering cannon as Italy had never seen before."[3] The French knights, descendants of Froissart's heroes, fought magnificently at Fornovo; but the knights too would soon yield to cannon. In the Middle Ages the arts of defense had outrun the means of attack, and had discouraged war; now attack was gaining on defense, and war became bloodier. The wars of Italy had heretofore hardly engaged the people, and had afflicted their fields rather than their lives; now they were to see all Italy ravaged and incarnadined. The Swiss learned in this year of war how fertile were the plains of Lombardy; they would hereafter invade them repeatedly. The French learned that Italy was divided into fragments that awaited a conqueror. Charles VIII lost himself in amours, and almost ceased to think of Naples, but his cousin and heir was of sterner stuff. Louis XII would try again.

II. THE ATTACK RENEWED: 1496-1505

Maximilian, "King of the Romans"—i.e., of the Germans—provided an interlude. He fretted at the thought that his great enemy, France, should be strengthened, and outflank him, by capturing Italy; he had heard how rich and fair and weak that land was, not yet a country but only a peninsula. He too had claims on Italy; technically the cities of Lombardy were still imperial fiefs, and he, head of the Holy Roman Empire, might legally give them to whomever he wished; indeed, had not Lodovico bribed him,

with florins and another Bianca, to confer upon him the duchy of Milan?
Moreover, many Italians invited him: both Lodovico and Venice were appealing to him (1496) to enter Italy and help them resist a threatened
repetition of the French assault. Maximilian came, with a handful of troops;
Venetian subtlety persuaded him to attack Livorno, the final outlet of
Florence on the Mediterranean, and so weaken a Florence still allied with
France and always competing with Venice. Maximilian's campaign failed
through inadequate co-ordination and support, and he returned to Germany only slightly a wiser man (December, 1496).

In 1498 the Duke of Orléans became Louis XII. As the grandson of
Valentina Visconti he had not forgotten the claims of his family to Milan;
and as a cousin of Charles VIII he inherited the claims of the Anjous to
Naples. On the day of his coronation he assumed, among others, the titles
of Duke of Milan, King of Naples and Sicily, and Emperor of Jerusalem.
To clear his path he renewed a treaty of peace with England, and concluded another with Spain. By promising her Cremona and the lands east
of the Adda, he lured Venice into signing an alliance with him "for the
purpose of making war in common upon the Duke of Milan, Lodovico
Sforza, and against everyone save the Lord Pope of Rome, for the purpose
of restoring to the Most Christian King . . . the duchy of Milan as his
rightful and olden patrimony."[4] A month later (March, 1499) he made
an agreement with the Swiss cantons to supply him with soldiers in return
for an annual subsidy of 20,000 florins. In May he brought Alexander VI
into the alliance by giving to Caesar Borgia a French bride of royal blood,
the duchy of Valentinois, and a pledge of aid in reconquering the Papal
States for the papacy. Lodovico felt helpless against such a coalition; he
fled to Austria; in three weeks his duchy disappeared into the realms of
Venice and France; on October 6, 1499, Louis entered Milan in triumph,
welcomed by nearly all Italy except Naples.

Indeed, all Italy but Venice and Naples was now under French domination or influence. Mantua, Ferrara, and Bologna hastened to submit. Florence clung to her alliance with France as her only protection against
Caesar Borgia. Ferdinand of Spain, though so closely kin to the Aragonese
dynasty in Naples, entered into a secret compact at Granada (November
11, 1500) with the representatives of Louis, for the joint conquest of all
Italy south of the Papal States. Alexander VI, needing French aid in reconquering these States, co-operated by issuing a bull that deposed
Federigo III of Naples and confirmed the partition of the Kingdom between France and Spain.

In July, 1501, a French army under the Scot Stuart d'Aubigny, Caesar Borgia, and Lodovico's traitorous favorite Francesco di San Severino marched through Italy to Capua, took and plundered it, and advanced upon Naples. Federigo, abandoned by all, yielded the city to the French in return for a comfortable refuge and annuity in France. Meanwhile *el gran capitán*, Gonzalo de Córdoba, won Calabria and Apulia for Ferdinand and Isabella; and Federigo's son Ferrante, who surrendered Taranto after being promised his liberty by Gonzalo, was sent as a prisoner to Spain on Ferdinand's demand. When the Spanish army came into contact with the French on the borders between Apulia and the Abruzzi, disputes arose over the boundary line between the two thefts; and to Alexander's relief Spain and France went to war over the exact division of the spoils (July, 1502). "If the Lord had not put discord between France and Spain," said the Pope to the Venetian ambassador, "where should we be?"[5]

For a time the fortunes of the new war favored the French. D'Aubigny's forces overran almost all southern Italy, and Gonzalo shut up his troops in the fortified town of Barletta. There a medieval incident brightened a dismal war (February 13, 1503). Angered by the comment of a French officer that the Italians were an effeminate and dastardly people, the commander of an Italian regiment in the Spanish army challenged thirteen Frenchmen to fight thirteen Italians. It was agreed; the war was interrupted; and the hostile armies stood as spectators while the twenty-six combatants fought until all thirteen Frenchmen had been disabled by wounds and taken prisoner. Gonzalo, with the Spanish chivalry that often rivaled Spanish cruelty, paid from his own pocket the ransoms of the prisoners, and sent them back to their army.[6]

The incident restored the morale of the Great Captain's troops; they issued from Barletta, defeated and dispersed the besiegers, and defeated the French again at Cerignola. On May 16, 1503, Gonzalo entered Naples unresisted, and was acclaimed by the populace, which can always be relied upon to applaud the victor. Louis XII sent another army against Gonzalo; he met it on the banks of the Garigliano, and routed it (December 29, 1503); in that rout Piero de' Medici, fleeing with the French, was drowned. Gonzalo now laid siege to Gaeta, the last stronghold of the French in southern Italy. He offered them generous terms, which they soon accepted (January 1, 1504); and the fidelity with which he kept to these terms after the French had been disarmed led them—struck by so great a violation of precedents—to call him *le gentil capitaine*.[7] By the treaty of Blois (1505) Louis saved a bit of face by assigning his Neapolitan rights to his relative Germaine de Foix, who was, however, to marry the widowed Ferdinand and bring Naples to him as her dowry. The crowns of Naples and Sicily were added to those already on Ferdinand's insatiable head; and thereafter, till 1707, the Kingdom of Naples remained an appanage of Spain.

III. THE LEAGUE OF CAMBRAI: 1508-16

Italy was now half foreign: southern Italy was Spain's; northwestern Italy from Genoa through Milan to the outskirts of Cremona was in the power of France; the minor principalities accepted French influence; only Venice and the papacy were comparatively independent, and they were intermittently at war for the cities of the Romagna. Venice longed for additional mainland markets and resources to replace those lost to the Turks or threatened by Atlantic routes to India; she took advantage of Alexander's death, and Caesar Borgia's illness, to seize Faenza, Ravenna, and Rimini; Julius II proposed to recapture them. In 1504 he persuaded Louis and Maximilian to stop their unchristian quarreling and join him in attacking Venice and dividing among them the Venetian possessions on the mainland.[8] Maximilian's spirit was willing, but his treasury was weak, and nothing came of the plot. Julius kept on trying.

On December 10, 1508, a grand conspiracy was hatched against Venice at Cambrai. The Emperor Maximilian joined it because Venice had taken from imperial control Goriza, Trieste, Pordenone, and Fiume, because Venice ignored his imperial rights in Verona and Padua, and because Venice had refused him and his little army free passage toward Rome for the papal coronation upon which he had set his heart. Louis XII joined the League because disputes had arisen between France and Venice as to the division of northern Italy. Ferdinand of Spain joined it because Venice insisted on retaining Brindisi, Otranto, and other Apulian ports which for centuries had been part of the Kingdom of Naples, but had been seized by Venice during Naples' troubles in 1495. Julius joined the League (1509) because Venice not only refused to evacuate the Romagna, but made no secret of her ambition to acquire Ferrara—an acknowledged papal fief. The European powers now planned to absorb all the mainland holdings of Venice: Spain would recover her cities on the Adriatic; the Pope would regain the Romagna; Maximilian would get Padua, Vicenza, Treviso, Friuli, and Verona; Louis would receive Bergamo, Brescia, Crema, Cremona, and the valley of the Adda River. Had the plan succeeded, Italy would have ceased to exist; France and Germany would have reached down to the Po, Spain almost up to the Tiber; the Papal States would have been hemmed in helplessly; and the Venetian bulwark against the Turks would have been destroyed. In this crisis no Italian state offered Venice aid; she had provoked almost all of them by her rapacity; indeed, Ferrara, reasonably suspicious of her, joined the League. The noble Gonzalo, rudely retired by Ferdinand, offered his services as general to Venice; the Senate dared not accept, for its sole hope of survival lay in detaching one ally after another from the League.

Venice deserved sympathy now only because she stood alone against overwhelming power, and because her loyal rich and her conscripted poor alike fought with incredible pertinacity to a Pyrrhic victory. The Senate offered to restore Faenza and Rimini to the papacy, but the angry Julius responded with a blast of excommunication, and sent his troops to recapture the Romagna cities while the French advance compelled Venice to concentrate her forces in Lombardy. At Agnadello the French defeated the Venetians in one of the bloodiest battles of the Renaissance (May 14, 1509); six thousand men died there on that day. The desperate Signory recalled its remaining troops to Venice, allowed the French to occupy all Lombardy, evacuated Apulia and the Romagna, confessed to Verona, Vicenza, and Padua that she could no longer defend them, and gave them full freedom to surrender to the Emperor or resist him as they chose. Maximilian came down with the largest army—some 36,000 men—yet seen in those parts, and laid siege to Padua. The surrounding peasantry made all the trouble they could for his men; the Paduans fought with a bravery that attested the good government they had enjoyed under Venice. Maximilian, impatient and always pinched for funds, left in disgust for the Tirol; Julius suddenly ordered his troops to withdraw from the siege; Padua and Vicenza voluntarily returned to Venetian control. Louis XII, having obtained his share of the spoils, disbanded his army.

Julius had by this time realized that the full victory of the League would be a defeat for the papacy, since it would leave the popes at the mercy of northern powers among whom the Reformation was already beginning to find voice. When Venice again offered him all that he could ask, he, "vowing that he would ne'er consent, consented" (1510). Having reclaimed what he considered to be the just property of the Church, he was free to turn the fury of his spirit against the French who, controlling both Lombardy and Tuscany, were now unpleasant neighbors of the Papal States. At Mirandola he vowed never to shave till he had driven the

French from Italy; so grew the majestic beard of Raphael's portrait. Now the Pope gave to Italy, too late, a stirring motto, *Fuori i barbari!*—"Out with the barbarians!" In October, 1511, he formed a "League of Holy Union" with Venice and Spain; soon he won to it Switzerland and England. By the end of January, 1512, Venice had recaptured Brescia and Bergamo with the joyful co-operation of the inhabitants. France kept most of her troops at home to meet possible invasion from England and Spain.

One French force remained in Italy, under the command of a dashing and courtly youth of twenty-two years. Resenting inaction, Gaston de Foix led this army first to the relief of besieged Bologna, then to defeat the Venetians at Isola della Scala, then to retake Brescia, finally to win a brilliant but costly victory at Ravenna (April 11, 1512). Nearly 20,000 corpses fertilized that battlefield; and Gaston himself, fighting in the front, received mortal wounds.

Julius repaired with negotiation what had been lost by arms. He persuaded Maximilian to sign a truce with Venice, to join the Union against France, and to recall the 4000 German troops that had been part of the French army. On his urging, the Swiss marched down into Lombardy with 20,000 men. The French forces, decimated by victory and the loss of their German contingent, fell back before a converging mass of Swiss, Venetian, and Spanish soldiery, and retreated to the Alps, leaving ineffectual garrisons in Brescia, Cremona, Milan, and Genoa. Out of apparently complete disaster the "Holy Union" had in two months after the battle of Ravenna, through papal diplomacy, driven the French from Italian soil; and Julius was hailed as the liberator of Italy.

At the Congress of Mantua (August, 1512) the victors divided the spoils. On the insistence of Julius, Milan was given to Massimiliano Sforza, Lodovico's son; Switzerland received Lugano and the territory at the head of Lago Maggiore; Florence was forced to restore the Medici; the Pope regained all the Papal States won by the Borgias, and besides acquired Parma, Piacenza, Modena, and Reggio; only Ferrara still eluded the pontifical grasp. But Julius left many problems to his successor. He had not really driven out the foreigners: the Swiss held Milan as a guard for Sforza, the Emperor claimed Vicenza and Verona as his reward, and Ferdinand the Catholic, wiliest bargainer of them all, had consolidated the power of Spain in southern Italy. Only French power seemed finished in Italy. Louis XII sent another army to take Milan, but it was defeated by the Swiss at Novara with the loss of eight thousand Frenchmen (June 6,

1513). When Louis died (1515), nothing remained of his once extensive Italian empire except a precarious foothold at Genoa.

But Francis I proposed to recapture it all. Moreover (Brantôme assures us), he had heard that Signora Clerice of Milan was the most beautiful woman in Italy, and he desired her consumingly.[9] In August, 1515, he led over a new Alpine pass 40,000 men—the largest army yet seen in these campaigns. The Swiss came out to meet it; at Marignano, a few miles from Milan, a furious battle raged for two days (September 13-14, 1515); Francis himself fought like a Roland, and was knighted on the spot by the Chevalier de Bayard; the Swiss left 13,000 dead on the field; they and Sforza abandoned Milan, and the city became again a French prize.

The councilors of Leo X, vacillating, asked Machiavelli's advice. He warned against neutrality between King and Emperor, on the ground that the papacy would be as helpless before the victor as if it had taken part; and he recommended an entente with France as the lesser of two evils.[10] Leo so ordered; and on December 11, 1515, Francis and the Pope met at Bologna to arrange terms of concord. The Swiss signed a similar peace with France; the Spaniards retired to Naples; the Emperor, foiled again, surrendered Verona to Venice. So ended (1516) the wars of the League of Cambrai, in which the partners had changed as in a dance, and the last condition of affairs was essentially as the first, and nothing had been decided except that Italy was to be the battlefield on which the great powers would fight duel after duel for the mastery of Europe. The papacy yielded Parma and Piacenza to France; Venice rewon her possessions in northern Italy, but was financially exhausted. Italy was devastated; but art and literature continued to flourish, whether by the stimulus of tragic events, or by the impetus of a prosperous past. The worst was yet to come.

IV. LEO AND EUROPE: 1513-21

The conference at Bologna pitted prestige and diplomacy against audacity and power. The handsome young King, magnificent in gold-braided cloak and zibeline furs, came with victory in his plumes and armies at his back, eager to swallow all Italy, merely keeping the Pope as a policeman; against which Leo had nothing but the glamour of his office and the subtlety of a Medici. If Leo thereafter played King against Emperor, and veered from side to side elusively, and simultaneously signed treaties with each against the other, we mnst not be too righteous about it; he had no other weapons to wield, and he had the heritage of the Church to protect. His opponents also used those weapons, in addition to brandishing regiments and artillery.

The secret agreements made at this meeting have remained secret to this day. Apparently Francis tried to bring Leo into an alliance with him against Spain; Leo asked for time to think it over—diplomacy's way of saying no; it was contrary to the age-long policy of the Church to let the Papal States be hemmed in by one power on both north and south.[11] The one definite result of the Concordat of 1516 was the repeal of the Pragmatic Sanction of Bourges. This Sanction (1438) had asserted the superior authority of a general council over that of the popes, and had given the French king the right to appoint to all major ecclesiastical offices in France. Francis consented to annul the Sanction, provided the royal power of nomination remained; Leo agreed. It might seem a defeat for the Pope; but in so agreeing Leo was only accepting a custom centuries old in France; and without so planning it he was marrying Church and state in France in a way that left the French monarchy no fiscal reasons for supporting the Reformation. Meanwhile he ended the long conflict between France and the papacy over the relative power of councils and popes.

The conference concluded by the French leaders begging forgiveness of Leo for having warred against his predecessor. "Holy Father," said Francis, "you must not be surprised that we were such enemies to Julius II, since he was always the greatest enemy to us; insomuch that in our times we have not met with a more formidable adversary. For he was in fact a most excellent commander, and would have made a much better general than a pope."[12] Leo gave all these doughty penitents absolution and benediction, and they ended by almost kissing his feet away.[13]

Francis returned to France under a halo of glory, and for a time contented himself with Venus and mercury. When Ferdinand II died (1516) the French King planned again the conquest of Naples, perhaps as a glorious means of checking the excess population of France. Nevertheless he signed a treaty of peace with Ferdinand's grandson Charles I, the new King of Aragon, Castile, Naples, and Sicily. But when Maximilian died (1519), and his grandson Charles was put forward to succeed him as head of the Holy Roman Empire, Francis thought himself fitter to be Emperor than the nineteen-year-old King of Spain, and actively sought election. Leo was again in a dangerous position. He would have preferred to support Francis, for he foresaw that the union of Naples, Spain, Germany, Austria, and the Netherlands under one head would give that ruler such preponderance of territory, wealth, and men as would destroy the balance of power that had hitherto protected the Papal States. And yet the election of Charles over papal opposition would alienate the new emperor precisely when his aid was vitally needed to suppress the Protestant revolt. Leo hesitated too long to make his influence felt; Charles I was chosen emperor, and became Charles V. Still playing balance of power, the Pope offered Francis an alliance; when the King in turn hesitated, Leo abruptly signed an agreement with Charles (May 8, 1521). The young Emperor offered him almost everything: the return of Parma and Piacenza, aid against Ferrara and Luther, the reconquest of Milan for the Sforza family, and the protection of the Papal States and Florence from any attack.

In September, 1521, the duel was renewed. "My cousin Francis and I," said the Emperor, "are in perfect accord; he wants Milan, and so do I."[14] The French forces in Italy were led by Odet de Foix, Vicomte de Lautrec; Francis had appointed him at the solicitation of Lautrec's sister, who was for the moment the King's mistress. Louise of Savoy, the King's mother, resented the appointment, and secretly diverted to other uses the money provided for Lautrec's army by Francis;[15] and the Swiss in that army deserted for lack of pay. As a strong papal-imperial force—ably commanded by Prospero Colonna, the Marquis of Pescara, and the historian Guicciardini—approached Milan, the Ghibelline supporters of the Empire there raised a successful revolt of the overtaxed populace. Lautrec withdrew from the city into Venetian territory; the troops of Charles and Leo took Milan almost bloodlessly; Francesco Maria Sforza, another son of Lodovico, became Duke of Milan as an imperial vassal; and Leo could die (December 1, 1521) in the unction of victory.

V. ADRIAN VI: 1522-3

His successor was an anomaly in Renaissance Rome: a Pope who was resolved at all costs to be a Christian. Born of lowly folk in Utrecht (1459), Adrian Dedel imbibed piety and scholarship from the Brothers of the Common Life at Deventer, Scholastic philosophy and theology at Louvain. At thirty-four he was chancellor of that University; at forty-seven he was appointed tutor of the future Charles V. In 1515 he was sent on a mission to Spain, and so impressed Ferdinand with his administrative ability and moral integrity that he was made bishop of Tortosa. After Ferdinand's death Adrian helped Cardinal Ximenes to govern Spain in the absence of Charles; in 1520 he became regent of Castile. Through all this progress he remained modest in everything but certainty, lived simply, and pursued heretics with a zeal that endeared him to the people. The repute of his virtues reached Rome, and Leo made him a cardinal. In the conclave that met after Leo's death his name was put forward as a candidate for the papacy, apparently without his knowledge, and probably through the influence of Charles V. On January 2, 1522, for the first time since 1378 a non-Italian—for the first time since 1161 a Teuton—was chosen pope.

How could the Romans, who had hardly heard of Adrian, forgive such an affront? The populace denounced the cardinals as madmen, as "betrayers of Christ's blood"; pamphleteers demanded to know why the Vatican had been "surrendered to German fury."[16] Aretino composed a masterpiece of vituperation, termed the cardinals "filthy rabble," and prayed that they might be buried alive.[17] Pasquino's statue was covered with lampoons. The cardinals feared to show themselves in public; they ascribed the election to the Holy Ghost, who, they said, had so inspired them.[18] Many cardinals left Rome, fearing both the contumely of the people and the ax of ecclesiastical reform. For his part Adrian calmly completed his unfinished business in Spain, and notified the Curia that he could not reach Rome before August. Unaware of the splendor of the Vatican, he wrote to a Roman friend asking that a modest house and garden be rented for his residence. When at last he reached the city (which he had never seen before), his pale ascetic face and lean frame awed observers into some reverence; but when he spoke, and it appeared that he knew no Italian, and talked Latin with a guttural accent all the world away from Italian melody and grace, Rome fumed and despaired.

Adrian felt himself a prisoner in the Vatican, and pronounced it fit for the successors of Constantine rather than of Peter. He discontinued all further decoration of the Vatican chambers; the followers of Raphael, who had been working there, were dismissed. He sent away all but four of the hundred grooms that Leo had kept for his stable; he reduced his personal servants to two—both Dutch—and bade them bring his household expenses down to one ducat ($12.50) a day. He was horrified by the looseness of sex and tongue and pen in Rome, and agreed with Lorenzo and Luther that the capital of Christianity was a sink of iniquity. He cared nothing for the ancient art that the cardinals showed him; he denounced the statuary as relics of idolatry, and walled up the Belvedere Palace, which contained Europe's first collection of classical sculpture.[19] He had a mind to wall up the humanists too, and the poets, who seemed to him to live and write like pagans who had banished Christ. When Francesco Berni, in one of his bitterest *capitoli*, satirized him as a Dutch barbarian incapable of understanding the refinements of Italian art, literature, and life, Adrian threatened to have the whole tribe of satirists doused in the Tiber.[20]

To lead the Church back from Leo to Christ became the devout passion of Adrian's pontificate. He set himself with blunt directness to reform such ecclesiastical abuses as he could reach. He suppressed superfluous offices with sometimes inconsiderate and indiscriminate vigor. He canceled the contracts that Leo had signed to pay annuities to those who had bought church offices; 2550 persons who had purchased these as an investment lost, so to speak, both principal and interest; Rome resounded with their cries that they had been defrauded; and one of the victims tried to kill the Pope. Relatives who came to Adrian for sinecures were told to go back and earn an honest living. He put an end to simony and nepotism, scored the venality of the Curia, enacted severe penalties for bribery or embezzlement, and punished guilty cardinals with the same treatment as the humblest clerk. He bade bishops and cardinals go back to their sees, and read them lessons on the morality that he expected of them. The ill repute of Rome, he told them, was the talk of Europe. He would not accuse the cardinals themselves of vice, but he charged them with allowing vice to go unpunished in their palaces. He asked them to put an end to their luxuries, and to content themselves with a maximum income of 6000 ducats ($75,000) a year. All ecclesiastical Rome, wrote the Venetian ambassador, "is beside itself with terror, seeing what the Pope has done in the space of eight days."[21]

But the eight days were not enough, nor the brief thirteen months of Adrian's active pontificate. Vice hid its face for a while, but survived; reforms irked a thousand officials, and met with a sullen resistance and the hope for Adrian's early death. The Pope mourned to see how little one man could do to better men; "how much does a man's efficiency," he often said, "depend upon the age in which his work is cast!"—and he remarked wistfully to his old friend Heeze: "Dietrich, how much better it went with us when we were living quietly in Louvain!"[22]

Amid these domestic tribulations he faced as honorably as he could the critical problems of foreign policy. He restored Urbino to Francesco Maria della Rovere, and left Alfonso undisturbed in Ferrara. Ousted dictators took advantage of the pacific Pope and again seized power in Perugia, Rimini, and other Papal States. Adrian appealed to Charles and

Francis to make peace, or at least accept a truce, and to join in repelling the Turks, who were preparing to attack Rhodes. Instead, Charles signed with Henry VIII of England the Treaty of Windsor (June 19, 1522), which pledged them to make a concerted assault upon France. On December 21 the Turks took Rhodes, the last Christian stronghold in the Eastern Mediterranean, and it was rumored that they were planning to land in Apulia and conquer disorganized Italy. When Turkish spies were captured in Rome the trepidation mounted to a point that recalled the city's fear of invasion after Hannibal's victory at Cannae in 216 B.C. To quite fill Adrian's cup of gall, Cardinal Francesco Soderini, his chief minister and confidante, and a principal agent in his negotiations for a European peace, plotted with Francis a French attack upon Sicily. When Adrian discovered the plot, and learned that Francis was massing troops on the border of Italy, he abandoned neutrality and leagued the papacy with Charles V. Then, broken in body and spirit, he fell sick and died (September 14, 1523). His will left his property to the poor, and his last instructions were that he should be given a quiet and inexpensive funeral.

Rome greeted his death with more joy than if the city had been saved from capture by the Turks. Some believed that he had been poisoned for art's sake, and a wag attached to the door of the Pope's physician an inscription *Liberatori patriae SPQR*—expressing the gratitude of the "Senate and People of Rome to the Liberator of the Fatherland." The dead pontiff was blackened by a hundred satires; he was accused of greed, drunkenness, and the grossest immorality, and every act of his career was transformed into wickedness by malice and ridicule; now the surviving freedom of the "press" in Rome prepared by its excesses its own unmourned demise. It was a pity that Adrian could not understand the Renaissance; but it was a greater crime and folly that the Renaissance could not tolerate a Christian pope.

VI. CLEMENT VII: THE FIRST PHASE

The conclave that met on October 1, 1523, fought for seven weeks over the selection of Adrian's successor, and finally named a man who by universal opinion was the happiest possible choice. Giulio de' Medici was the illegitimate son of that amiable Giuliano who had fallen a victim to the Pazzi conspiracy, and of a mistress, Fioretta, who soon disappeared from history. Lorenzo took the boy into his family and had him brought up with his sons. These included Leo, who, as pope, dispensed Giulio from the canonical impediment of bastardy, made him archbishop of Florence, then a cardinal, then the able administrator of Rome and the chief minister of his pontificate. Now forty-five, Clement was tall and handsome, rich and learned, well mannered and of moral life, an admirer and patron of literature, learning, music, and art. Rome greeted his elevation with joy as the return of Leo's gulden age. Bembo prophesied that Clement VII would be the best and wisest ruler that the Church had ever known.[23]

He began most graciously. He distributed among the cardinals all the benefices that he had enjoyed, entailing a yearly revenue of 60,000 ducats. He won the hearts and dedications of scholars and scribes by drawing them into his service or supporting them with gifts. He dealt out justice justly, gave audience freely, bestowed charity with less than Leonine, but with wiser, generosity, and charmed all by his courtesy to every person and class. No pope ever began so well, or ended so miserably.

The task of steering a safe course between Francis and Charles in a war almost to the death, while the Turks were overrunning Hungary, and one third of Europe was in full revolt against the Church, proved too much for Clement's abilities, as for Leo's too. The magnificent portrait of Clement in his early pontificate, by Sebastiano del Piombo, is deceptive: he did not show in his actions the hard resolution that there seems limned in his face; and even in that picture a certain weak weariness shows in the tired eyelids drooping upon sullen eyes. Clement made irresolution a policy. He carried thought to excess, and mistook it as a substitute for action instead of its guide. He could find a hundred reasons for a decision, and a hundred against it; it was as if Buridan's ass sat on the papal throne. Berni satirized him in bitter lines prophetic of posterity's judgment:

> A papacy composed of compliment,
>   Debate, consideration, complaisance,
>   Of furthermore, then, but, yes, well, perchance,
> Haply, and such like terms inconsequent. . . .
> Of feet of lead, of tame neutrality. . . .
> To speak plain truth, you shall live to see
> Pope Adrian sainted through this papacy.[24]

He took as his chief counselors Gianmatteo Giberti who favored France, and Nikolaus von Schönberg who favored the Empire; he allowed his mind to be torn in two between them; and when he decided for France—only a few weeks before the French disaster at Pavia—he brought down upon his head and his city all the wiles and forces of Charles, and all the fury of a half-Protestant army unleashed upon Rome.

It was Clement's excuse that he feared the power of an Emperor holding both Lombardy and Naples; and he hoped, by siding with Francis, to secure a French veto on Charles's troublesome idea of a general council to adjudicate the affairs of the Church. When Francis came down over the Alps with a new army of 26,000 French, Italians, Swiss, and Germans, seized Milan, and besieged Pavia, Clement, while giving Charles assurances of loyalty and friendship, secretly signed an alliance with Francis (December 12, 1524), brought Florence and Venice into it, and reluctantly gave triumphant Francis permission to levy troops in the Papal States and to send an army through papal territory against Naples. Charles never forgave the deception. "I shall go into Italy," he vowed, "and revenge myself on those who have injured me, especially on that poltroon the Pope. Some day, perhaps, Martin Luther will become a man of weight."[25] At that moment some men thought that Luther would be made pope; and several of the Emperor's entourage advised him to contest the election of Clement on the ground of illegitimate birth.[26]

Charles sent a German army under Georg von Frundsberg and the Marquis of Pescara to attack the French outside Pavia. Poor tactics nullified the French artillery, while the hand firearms of the Spanish made a mockery of Swiss pikes; the French army was almost annihilated in one of the most decisive battles of history (February 24-5, 1525). Francis behaved gallantly: while his troops retreated he plunged forward into the enemy's ranks, making royal slaughter; his horse was killed under him, but he kept on fighting; at last, thoroughly exhausted, he could resist no more, and was taken prisoner along with several of his captains. From a tent among the victors he wrote to his mother the message so often half-quoted: "All is lost save honor—and my skin, which is safe." Charles, who was at this time in Spain, ordered him sent as a prisoner to a castle near Madrid.

Milan reverted to the Emperor. All Italy felt itself at his mercy, and one Italian state after another presented him with diverse bribes for permission to remain in existence. Clement, fearful of invasion by the imperial army, and of revolution against the Medici in Florence, abandoned his French alliance, and signed a treaty (April 1, 1525) with Charles de Lannoy, Viceroy of Naples for Charles, pledging Pope and Emperor to mutual aid; the Emperor would protect the Medici in Florence and accept Francesco Maria Sforza as imperial vicar in Milan; the Pope would pay Charles, for past affronts and futur : services, 100,000 ducats ($1,250,000?),[27] which were badly needed for the imperial troops. Shortly afterward Clement connived at a plot by Girolamo Morone to free Milan from the Emperor. The Marquis of Pescara revealed it to Charles, and Morone was jailed.

Charles treated captive Francis with feline procrastination. After soften-ing him with almost eleven months of courteous imprisonment, he agreed to free him on the impossible conditions that the King should surrender all French rights, actual or alleged, to Genoa, Milan, Naples, Flanders, Artois, Tournai, Burgundy, and Navarre; that Francis should supply Charles with ships and troops for an expedition against Rome or the Turks; that Francis should marry Charles's sister Eleonora; and that the King should surrender his eldest sons—Francis, ten, and Henry, nine years old—to Charles as hos-tages for the fulfillment of these terms. By the treaty of Madrid (Janu-ary 14, 1526) Francis agreed to all these conditions with solemn oaths and mental reservations. On March 17 he was allowed to return to France, leaving his sons in his place as prisoners. Arrived in France, he announced that he had no intention of honoring promises made under duress; Clement, with the support of canonical law, absolved him from his oaths; and on May 22 Francis, Clement, Venice, Florence, and Francesco Maria Sforza signed the League of Cognac, pledging them to restore Asti and Genoa to France, to give Milan to Sforza as a French fief, to return .to each Italian state all its prewar possessions, to ransom French prisoners for 2,000,000 crowns, and to bestow Naples upon an Italian prince who would pay a yearly tribute of 75,000 ducats to the king of France. The Emperor was cordially invited to sign this agreement; if he refused, the new League pro-posed to war upon him until he and all his forces were driven from Italy.[28]

Charles denounced the League as violating Francis' sacred oaths as well as the treaty that Clement had signed with Lannoy. Unable to go to Italy himself at this time, he commissioned Hugo de Moncada to win back Clem-ent by diplomacy, and, that failing, to stir up against the Pope a revolu-tion of the Colonna and the Roman populace. Moncada performed his mission nicely: he brought Clement into an amicable agreement with the Colonna, persuaded the Pope to disband the troops that were guarding him, and allowed the Colonna to continue organizing a conspiracy to capture Rome. While Christendom so exercised itself in treachery and war, the Turks under Suleiman the Magnificent overwhelmed the Hungarians at Mohacs (August 29, 1526), and captured Budapest (September 10). Clem-ent, alarmed less Europe should become not merely Protestant but Mo-hammedan, announced to the cardinals that he was thinking of going to

Barcelona in person to plead with Charles to make peace with Francis and join forces against the Turks. Charles at that time was equipping a fleet whose purpose, it was said in Rome, was to invade Italy and depose the Pope.[29]

On September 20 the Colonna entered Rome with five thousand men, and, overriding feeble resistance, plundered the Vatican, St. Peter's, and the neighboring Borgo Vecchio, while Clement fled to Castel Sant' Angelo. The papal palace was completely stripped, including Raphael's tapestries and the Pope's tiara; sacred vessels, treasured relics, and costly papal vestments were stolen; an hilarious soldier went about in the white robe and red cap of the Pope, distributing papal benedictions with mock solemnity.[30] On the following day Moncada restored to Clement the papal tiara, assured him that the Emperor had only the best intentions toward the papacy, and compelled the frightened Pope to sign an armistice with the Empire for four months, and to pardon the Colonna.

Moncada had hardly retired to Naples when Clement raised a new papal force of seven thousand troops. At the end of October he ordered it to march against the Colonna strongholds. At the same time he appealed to Francis I and Henry VIII for aid; Francis sent dilatory excuses; Henry, absorbed in the difficult task of begetting a son, sent nothing. Another papal army, in the north, was kept inactive by the apparently treacherous Fabianism of Francesco Maria della Rovere, Duke of Urbino, who could not forget that Leo X had ousted him from his duchy, and was not especially grateful that Adrian and Clement had let him return and stay. A braver leader was with that army—young Giovanni de' Medici, handsome son of Caterina Sforza, heir of her dauntless spirit, and called Giovanni delle Bande Nere because he and his troops had worn black bands of mourning when Leo died.[31] Giovanni was all for action against Milan, but Francesco Maria overruled him.

VII. THE SACK OF ROME: 1527

Charles, still remaining in Spain, and moving his pawns with magic remote control, commissioned his agents to raise a new army. They approached the Tirolese *condottiere*, Georg von Frundsberg, already famous for the exploits of the *Landsknechte*—German mercenaries—who fought under his lead. Charles could offer little money, but his agents promised rich plunder in Italy. Frundsberg was still nominally a Catholic, but he strongly sympathized with Luther, and hated Clement as a traitor to the

Empire. He pawned his castle, his other possessions, even the adornments of his wife; with the 38,000 gulden so obtained he collected some 10,000 men eager for adventure and pillage and not averse to breaking a lance over a papal head; some of them, it was said, carried a noose to hang the Pope.[32] In November, 1526, this impromptu army crossed the mountains and descended toward Brescia. Alfonso of Ferrara repaid the papacy for its many efforts to depose him, by sending Frundsberg four of his mightiest cannon. Near Brescia Giovanni delle Bande Nere was shot in a skirmish with the invaders; he died at Mantua on November 30, aged twenty-eight. No one remained to hinder the Duke of Urbino from doing nothing.

Frundsberg's rabble crossed the Po as Giovanni died, and ravaged the fertile fields of Lombardy so effectively that three years later English ambassadors described that terrain as "the most pitiable country that ever was in Christendom."[33] In Milan the imperial commander was now Charles, Duke of Bourbon; created constable of France for bravery at Marignano, he had turned against Francis when the King's mother, as he felt, had cheated him of his proper lands; he went over to the Emperor, shared in defeating Francis at Pavia, and was made Duke of Milan. Now, to raise and pay another army for Charles, he taxed the Milanese literally to death. He wrote to the Emperor that he had drained the city of its blood. His soldiers, quartered upon the inhabitants, so abused them with theft, brutality, and rape that many Milanese hanged themselves, or threw themselves from high places into the streets.[34] Early in February, 1527, Bourbon led his army out of Milan, and united it with Frundsberg's near Piacenza. The conglomerate horde, now numbering nearly 22,000 men, moved east along the Via Emilia, avoiding the fortified cities, but pillaging as it went, and leaving the countryside empty behind it.

When it became clear to Clement that he had no sufficient forces with which to stop these invaders, he appealed to Lannoy to arrange a truce. The Viceroy came up from Naples, and drew up terms for a truce of eight months: Clement and the Colonna ceased their war and exchanged their conquests, and the Pope provided 60,000 ducats with which to bribe Frundsberg's army to stay out of the Papal States. Then, nearing the end of his funds, and supposing that Frundsberg and Bourbon would honor an agreement signed by the imperial Viceroy, Clement reduced his Roman army to three hundred men. But Bourbon's brigands shrieked with fury when they heard the terms of the truce. For four months they had endured a thousand hardships only in the hope of plundering Rome; most of them were now in rags, many were shoeless, all were hungry, none was paid; they refused to be bought off with a miserable 60,000 ducats, of which they knew only a small part would trickle down to them. Fearing that Bourbon would sign the truce, they besieged his tent, crying, "Pay! pay!" He hid himself elsewhere, and they plundered his tent. Frundsberg tried to calm them, but was stricken with apoplexy in the course of his appeal; he played no further part in the campaign, and died a year later. Bourbon took command, but only by agreeing to march on Rome. On March 29 he sent messages to Lannoy and Clement that he could not hold back his men, and that the truce was perforce at an end.

Now at last Rome realized that it was the intended and helpless prey. On Holy Thursday (April 8), when Clement was giving his blessing to a crowd of 10,000 persons before St. Peter's, a fanatic clad only in a leather apron mounted the statue of St. Paul and shouted to the Pope: "Thou bastard of Sodom! For thy sins Rome shall be destroyed. Repent and turn thee! If thou wilt not believe me, in fourteen days thou shalt see." On Easter Eve this wild eremite—Bartolommeo Carosi, called Brandano—went through the streets crying, "Rome, do penance! They shall deal with thee as God dealt with Sodom and Gomorrah."[35]

Bourbon, perhaps hoping to satisfy his men with the enlarged sum, sent to Clement a demand for 240,000 ducats; Clement replied that he could not possibly raise such a ransom. The horde marched to Florence; but the Duke of Urbino, Guicciardini, and the Marquis of Saluzzo had brought in enough troops to man its fortifications effectively; the horde turned away baffled, and took the road to Rome. Clement, finding no salvation in truce, rejoined the League of Cognac against Charles, and implored the help of France. He appealed to the rich men of Rome to contribute to a fund for defense; they responded gingerly, and suggested that a better plan would be to sell red hats. Clement had not hitherto sold appointments to the college of cardinals, but when Bourbon's army reached Viterbo, only forty-two miles from Rome, he yielded, and sold six nominations. Before the nominees could pay, the Pope could see, from the windows of the Vatican, the hungry swarm advancing across the Neronian Fields. He had now some 4000 soldiers to protect Rome from an attacking host of 20,000 men.

On May 6 Bourbon's multitude approached the walls under cover of fog. They were repelled by a fusillade; Bourbon himself was hit, and died almost instantly. But the assailants could not be deterred from repeated attack; their alternatives were to capture Rome or starve. They found a weakly defended position; they broke through it, and poured into the city. The Roman militia and the Swiss Guards fought bravely, but were annihilated. Clement, most of the resident cardinals, and hundreds of officials fled to Sant' Angelo, whence Cellini and others tried to stop the invasion with artillery fire. But the swarm entered from a confusing variety of directions; some were hidden by the fog; others so mingled with fugitives that the Castle cannon could not strike them without killing the demoralized populace. Soon the invaders had the city at their mercy.

As they rushed on through the streets they killed indiscriminately any man, woman, or child that crossed their path. Their bloodthirst aroused, they entered the hospital and orphanage of Santo Spirito, and slaughtered nearly all the patients. They marched into St. Peter's and slew the people who had sought sanctuary there. They pillaged every church and monastery they could find, and turned some into stables; hundreds of priests, monks, bishops, and archbishops were killed. St. Peter's and the Vatican were rifled from top to bottom, and horses were tethered in Raphael's *stanze*.[36] Every dwelling in Rome was plundered, and many were burned, with two exceptions: the Cancelleria, occupied by Cardinal Colonna, and the Palazzo Colonna, in which Isabella d' Este and some rich merchants had sought asylum; these paid 50,000 ducats to leaders of the mob for freedom from attack, and then took two thousand refugees within their walls. Every palace paid ransoms for protection, only to face later attacks from other packs, and pay ransom again. In most houses all the occupants were required to ransom their lives at a stated price; if they did not pay they were tortured; thousands were killed; children were flung from high windows to pry parental savings from secrecy; some streets were littered with dead. The millionaire Domenico Massimi saw his sons slain, his daughter raped, his house burned, and then was himself murdered. "In the whole city," says one account, "there was not a soul above three years of age who had not to purchase his safety."[37]

Of the victorious mob half were Germans, of whom most had been convinced that the popes and cardinals were thieves, and that the wealth of the Church in Rome was a theft from the nations, and a scandal to the world. To reduce this scandal they seized all movable ecclesiastical valuables, including sacred vessels and works of art, and carried them off for melting or ransom or sale; relics, however, they left scattered on the floor. One soldier dressed himself as a pope; others put on cardinals' hats and kissed his feet; a crowd at the Vatican proclaimed Luther pope. The Lutherans among the invaders took especial delight in robbing cardinals, exacting high ransoms from them as the price of their lives, and teaching them new rituals. Some cardinals, says Guicciardini, "were set upon scrubby beasts, riding with their faces backward, in the habits and ensigns of their dignity, and were led about all Rome with the greatest derision and contempt. Some, unable to raise all the ransom demanded, were so tortured that they died there and then, or within a few days."[38] One cardinal was lowered into a grave and was told that he would be buried alive unless ransom were brought within a stated time; it came at the last moment.[39] Spanish and German cardinals, who thought themselves safe from their own country-men, were treated like the rest. Nuns and respectable women were vio-lated *in situ*, or were carried off to promiscuous brutality in the various shelters of the horde.[40] Women were assaulted before the eyes of their husbands or fathers. Many young women, despondent after being raped, drowned themselves in the Tiber.[41]

The destruction of books, archives, and art was immense. Philibert, Prince of Orange, who had succeeded to the quasi command of the undis-ciplined horde, saved the Vatican Library by making it his headquarters, but many monastic and private libraries went up in flames, and many pre-cious manuscripts disappeared. The University of Rome was ransacked, and its staff was scattered. The scholar Colocci saw his house burned to the ground with his collections of manuscripts and art. Baldus, a professor, saw his newly written commentary on Pliny used to light a camp fire for the pillagers. The poet Marone lost his poems, but was comparatively fortunate; the poet Paolo Bombasi was killed. The scholar Cristoforo Marcello was tortured by having one fingernail after another pulled out; the scholars Francesco Fortuno and Juan Valdes slew themselves in de-spair.[42] The artists Perino del Vaga, Marcantonio Raimondi, and many others were tortured and robbed of all that they had. The school of Raphael was finally dispersed.

The number of deaths cannot be calculated. Two thousand corpses were thrown into the Tiber from the Vatican side of Rome; 9800 dead were buried; there were unquestionably many more fatalities. A low esti-mate places the thefts at over a million ducats, the ransoms at three million; Clement judged the total loss at ten million ($125,000,000?).[43]

The sack lasted eight days, while Clement looked on from the towers of Sant' Angelo. He cried out to God like tortured Job: *Quare de vulva eduxisti me? qui utinam consumptus essem, ne oculus videret*—"Why didst Thou take me out of the womb? Would that I had been consumed, that no eye had seen me!"[44] He ceased to shave, and never shaved again. He remained a prisoner in the Castle from May 6 to December 7, 1527, hoping that rescue would come from the army of the Duke of Urbino, or from

Francis I, or Henry VIII. Charles, still in Spain, was glad to hear that Rome had been taken, but was shocked when he heard of the savagery of the sack; he disclaimed responsibility for the excesses, but took full advantage of the Pope's helplessness. On June 6 his representatives, possibly without his knowledge, compelled Clement to sign a humiliating peace. The Pope agreed to pay over to them and the imperialist army 400,000 ducats; to surrender to Charles the cities of Piacenza, Parma, and Modena, and the castles of Ostia, Città Vecchia, Città Castellana, and Sant' Angelo itself; he was to remain a prisoner there until the first 150,000 ducats had been delivered, and was then to be removed to Gaeta or Naples until Charles should determine what to do with him. All those in Sant' Angelo were allowed to depart except Clement and the thirteen cardinals who had accompanied him. Spanish and German soldiers were put in charge of the Castle, and kept the Pope nearly always confined in a narrow apartment. "They have not left him ten *scudi* worth of property," wrote Guicciardini on June 21.[45] All the silver and gold that he had salvaged in his flight was surrendered to his captors, to make up 100,000 ducats of his ransom.

In the meantime Alfonso of Ferrara seized Reggio and Modena (to which Ferrara had age-long rights), and Venice took Ravenna. Florence expelled the Medici a third time, and proclaimed Jesus Christ king of the new republic. The whole edifice of the papacy, material and spiritual, seemed to be collapsing into a tragic ruin that awoke the pity even of those who felt that some punishment was deserved by the infidelities of Clement, the sins of the papacy, the greed and corruption of the Curia, the luxury of the hierarchy, and the iniquity of Rome. Sadoleto, peaceful in Carpentras, heard with horror of Rome's fall, and mourned the passing of those halcyon days when Bembo and Castiglione and Isabella and a hundred scholars and poets and patrons had made the wicked city the home and summit of the thought and art of the age. And Erasmus wrote to Sadoleto: "Rome was not alone the shrine of the Christian faith, the nurse of noble souls, and the abode of the Muses, but the mother of nations. To how many was she not dearer and sweeter and more precious than their own land! . . . In truth this is not the ruin of one city, but of the whole world."[46]

VIII. CHARLES TRIUMPHANT: 1527-30

Plague had visited Rome in 1522, and had reduced its population to 55,000; murder, suicide, and flight must have reduced it below 40,000 in 1527; now, in July of that year, plague came back in the full heat of summer, and joined with famine and the continued presence of the ravaging horde to make Rome a city of horror, terror, and desolation. Churches and streets were littered anew with corpses; many of these were left to rot in the sun; the stench was so strong that the jailers and prisoners fled from the castle parapets to their rooms; even there many died of the infection, among them some servants of the Pope. The impartial plague struck the invaders too; 2500 Germans in Rome died by July 22, 1527; and malaria, syphilis, and malnutrition cut the horde in half.

The opponents of Charles began seriously to think of rescuing the Pope. Henry VIII, fearing that an imprisoned pontiff might not grant him a divorce from Catherine of Aragon, sent Cardinal Wolsey to France to confer with Francis on measures to liberate Clement. Early in August the two kings offered Charles peace and 2,000,000 ducats on condition that the Pope and the French princes should be freed, and that the Papal States should be restored to the Church. Charles refused. By the treaty of Amiens (August 18) Henry and Francis pledged themselves to war against Charles; soon Venice and Florence joined this new league. French forces captured Genoa and Pavia, and sacked the latter city almost as thoroughly as the imperialist army had sacked Rome. Mantua and Ferrara, dreading the present French more than the distant Charles, now joined the league. Nevertheless Lautrec, the French commander, unable to pay his troops, dared not march upon Rome.

The Emperor, hoping to restore his grace in Catholic Christendom, and to cool the ardor of the growing league, agreed to release the Pope, on condition that Clement should give no aid to the league, should at once pay the imperialist army in Rome 112,000 ducats, and should give hostages for his good behavior. Clement raised the money by selling red hats, and by granting the Emperor a tenth of ecclesiastical revenues in the Kingdom of Naples. On December 7, after seven months of confinement, Clement left Sant' Angelo, and, disguised as a servant, made his way humbly out of Rome to Orvieto, apparently a broken man.

At Orvieto he was lodged in a dilapidated palace whose roof had caved in, whose walls were bare and cracked, whose floors admitted a hundred draughts. English ambassadors visiting him to get Henry a divorce found him huddled in bed, his pale emaciated face half lost in a long and unkempt beard. He spent the winter there, and then moved to Viterbo. On February 17 the imperialist horde, having received from Clement all that he could pay, and fearing further decimation by disease, evacuated Rome and moved south to Naples. Lautrec now brought his army down with the hope of besieging Naples; but his own troops were thinned out by malaria, he himself died, and his disordered forces retreated to the north (August 29, 1528). Losing all hope of aid from the league, Clement offered his full surrender to Charles; and on October 6 he was allowed to re-enter Rome. Four fifths of the houses had been abandoned, thousands of buildings were in ruins; men were amazed to see what nine months of invasion had done to the capital of Christendom.

Charles seems to have thought for a while of deposing Clement, annexing the Papal States to the Kingdom of Naples, making Rome the seat of his empire, and reducing the pope to his primeval role as bishop of Rome and subject to the emperor.[47] But this would drive Charles into the arms of the Lutherans in Germany, would court civil war in Spain, and would arouse France, England, Poland, and Hungary to resist him with their full and united power. He abandoned the scheme, and turned to the idea of making the papacy his dependent ally and spiritual aid in dividing Italy between them. By the treaty of Barcelona (June 29, 1529) he made substantial concessions to the Pope: the principalities taken from the Church were to be restored; the Medici relatives of the Pope were to be re-established in Florence by diplomacy or force; even Ferrara was now promised to the Pope. In return the Pope agreed to give Charles the formal investiture of Naples, to allow the imperial armies free passage through the Papal States, and to meet the Emperor at Bologna in the following year to settle between them the peace and organization of Italy.

Shortly thereafter Margaret, aunt of Charles and Regent of the Netherlands, met with Louise of Savoy, mother of Francis, and, with the aid of various ambassadors and legates, formulated the treaty of Cambrai (August 3, 1529) between Emperor and King. Charles released the French princes for a ransom of 1,200,000 ducats; Francis renounced for France all claims to Italy, Flanders, Artois, Arras, and Tournai.[48] The allies of France in Italy were left to the mercy of the Emperor.

Charles and Clement met at Bologna on November 5, 1529, each now convinced that he needed the other. Strange to say, this was Charles's first visit to Italy; he had conquered it before seeing it. When he knelt before the Pope at Bologna, and kissed the foot of the man whom he had dragged in the dust, it was the first time that these two figures—the one representing the Church in decline, the other the rising and here victorious modern state—had ever seen each other. Clement swallowed all pride, forgave all offenses; he had to. He could no longer look to France; Charles had irresistible armies in both southern and northern Italy; Florence could not be recovered for the Medici without imperial troops; the aid of the Empire was needed against Luther in Germany, against Suleiman in the East. Charles was generous and prudent: he kept essentially to the terms of the Barcelona agreement made when he was not so unchallengeably strong. He forced Venice to restore all that she had taken from the Papal States. He allowed Francesco Maria Sforza, on paying a large indemnity, to keep ruined Milan under imperial watching; and he persuaded Clement to allow the cowardly or faithless Francesco Maria della Rovere to keep Urbino. He forgave Alfonso his recent association with France, and rewarded him for aiding the march on Rome by letting him retain his duchy as a papal fief, and giving him Modena and Reggio as imperial fiefs; in return Alfonso paid the Pope 100,000 badly needed ducats. To consolidate these settlements Charles summoned all the principalities to join in a union of Italy for common defense against foreign attack—except by Charles; that unity for which Dante had pled to the Emperor Henry VII, and Petrarch to the Emperor Charles IV, was now achieved through united subjection to a foreign power. Clement blessed it all, and crowned Charles Emperor with the iron crown of Lombardy and the imperial-papal crown of the Holy Roman Empire (February 22-24, 1530).

The alliance of Pope and Emperor was sealed with Florentine blood. Resolved to restore his family to power, Clement paid 70,000 ducats to Philibert, Prince of Orange (who had kept him prisoner), to organize an army and overturn the republic of rich men that had been set up there in 1527. Philibert sent on this mission 20,000 German and Spanish troops, many of whom had shared in the sack of Rome.[49] In December, 1529, this force occupied Pistoia and Prato, and laid siege to Florence. To expose the assailants to Florentine artillery the resolute burghers destroyed every house, garden, and wall for a mile around the city fortifications; and Michelangelo left his sculpture of the Medici tombs to build or rebuild the ramparts and forts. The siege continued mercilessly for eight months; food became so scarce in Florence that cats and rats brought some $12.50 apiece.[50] Churches surrendered their vessels, citizens their plate, women their jewelry, to be transformed into money for provisions or arms. Patriotic monks like Fra Benedetto da Foiano kept up the spirit of the people with fiery sermons. A courageous Florentine, Francesco Ferrucci, escaped from the city, organized a force of three thousand men, and attacked the besiegers. He was defeated with the loss of two thousand of his soldiers. He himself was captured and brought before Fabrizio Maramaldi, a Calabrian who commanded the imperial cavalry. Maramaldi had Ferrucci held helpless before him while he repeatedly drove a poignard into him until the hero died.[51] Meanwhile the general whom Florence had hired to lead its defense, Malatesta Baglioni, entered into a treacherous agreement with the besiegers; he let them into the city, and turned his guns upon the Florentines. Starving and disorganized, the republic surrendered (August 12, 1530).

Alessandro de' Medici became Duke of Florence, and disgraced his family by his rapacity and cruelty. Hundreds of those who had fought for the Republic were tortured, exiled, or slain. Fra Benedetto was sent to Clement, who ordered him imprisoned in Sant' Angelo; there, said an uncertain report, the monk was starved to death.[52] The Signory was disbanded; the Palazzo della Signoria now began to be called Palazzo Vecchio; and the great eleven-ton bell, La Vacca—the Cow—that had from the lovely tower called so many generations to *parlamento*, was taken down and broken to pieces, "in order," said a contemporary diarist, "that we should no more hear the sweet sound of liberty."[53]

IX. CLEMENT VII AND THE ARTS

The Pope's treatment of Florence confirmed the degeneration of the Medici; his efforts to restore Rome revealed a spark of the administrative genius and esthetic appreciation that had made the family great. Sebastiano del Piombo, who had portrayed him in maturity, painted him now as an old man, somber, deep-eyed, white-bearded, giving benediction; apparently suffering had chastened and in some measure strengthened him. He took vigorous action to protect Italy from the Turkish fleets that now commanded the Eastern Mediterranean; he fortified Ancona, Ascoli, and Fano, and paid the costs by persuading the consistory of June 21, 1532— over the opposition of the cardinals—to impose a levy of fifty per cent upon the incomes of the Italian clergy, including the cardinals.[54] Partly by selling ecclesiastical offices, he raised funds to rebuild the property of the Church, to restore the University of Rome, and to resume the patronage of scholarship and art. He took measures to ensure a proper supply of grain despite the raids of Barbary pirates upon shipping near Sicily. In a remarkably short time Rome was functioning again as the capital of the Western world.

The city was still rich in artists. Caradosso had come from Milan, Cellini from Florence, to raise the art of the goldsmith to its Renaissance zenith; they and many more were kept busy making gold roses and swords of honor as papal gifts, vessels for the altars, silver staffs for Church authorities and processions, seals for cardinals, tiaras and rings for the popes. Valerio Belli of Vicenza made for Clement a magnificent casket of rock crystal, engraved with scenes from the life of Christ. This, now one of the most precious objects in the Pitti Palace, was presented to Francis I at the marriage of his son to Catherine de' Medici.

The decoration of the Vatican *stanze* had been resumed in 1526. The greatest painting of Clement's pontificate was done in the Hall of Constantine: there Giulio Romano pictured *The Apparition of the Cross* and *The Battle of the Milvian Bridge;* Francesco Penni painted *The Baptism of Constantine*, and Raffaello del Colle portrayed *Rome Presented to Pope Sylvester by Constantine*.

After Michelangelo—and now that Giulio Romano had migrated to Mantua—the ablest painter in Rome was Sebastiano Luciano, who acquired his sobriquet del Piombo when he was appointed keeper and designer of the papal seals (1531). Born in Venice (*c.* 1485), he had the luck to be taught by Gian Bellini, Giorgione, and Cima. One of his earliest and finest pictures—*The Three Ages of Man*—shows him as a delectable youth between two famous foreign composers then in Venice—Jacob Obrecht and Philippe Verdelot. For the church of San Giovanni Crisostomo he painted —or finished for Giorgione—a vivid representation of that saint in the fever of composition; and about the same time (1510) he copied Giorgione's most voluptuous manner in a *Venus and Adonis* whose generous women seem to belong to a golden age before the birth of sin. Probably in Venice also Sebastiano painted his renowned *Portrait of a Lady*, long ascribed to Raphael as *La Fornarina*.

In 1511 Agostino Chigi invited Sebastiano to come to Rome and help adorn the Villa Chigi. There the young artist met Raphael, and for a time imitated his style of pagan ornament; in return he taught Raphael the Venetian secrets of warm coloring. Soon Sebastian became a devoted friend of Michelangelo, imbibed the Titan's muscular conception of man, and announced the aim of wedding Venetian color to Michelangelesque design. He had a chance to do this when Cardinal Giulio de' Medici asked him for a picture. Sebastiano chose as his subject *The Raising of Lazarus*, in deliberate competition with the *Transfiguration* that Raphael was painting at the time (1518). Critics did not unanimously contradict his judgment that he had equaled Leo's favorite.

He might have progressed further had he not been too readily content with his excellence. A passion for leisure kept him this side of genius. He was a jovial fellow who could not see why one should wear himself out either for superfluous gold or for such a will-o'-the-wisp as posthumous fame. After he had received his sinecure in the Vatican from his patron made pope, he confined himself for the most part to portraits, in which few painters have surpassed him.

Baldassare Peruzzi was more ambitious, and made his sonorous name ring for a generation across the mountains of Italy. He was the son of a weaver. (Artists are mostly of lowly stock: the middle classes seek utility first, hoping to have time for beauty in their senility; aristocrats, though they nourish art, prefer the art of life to the life of art.) Born in Siena (1481), Baldassare learned painting under Sodoma and Pinturicchio, and soon went off to Rome. Apparently it was he who painted the ceiling of the *Stanza d'Eliodoro* in the Vatican, and Raphael thought the work good enough to leave much of it unchanged. Meanwhile, like Bramante, he fell in love with the classic ruins, measured the ground plans of the ancient temples and palaces, and studied the diverse forms and arrangements of columns and capitals. He became a specialist in the application of perspective to architecture.

When Agostino Chigi decided to build the Villa Chigi, Peruzzi was invited to design it (1508). The banker was pleased with the result—the stately crowning of a Renaissance façade with classic moldings and cornices; and finding that Peruzzi could also paint, he gave the young artist freedom to decorate several rooms of the interior in competition with Sebastiano del Piombo and Raphael. In the entrance hall and the loggia Baldassare pictured Venus combing her hair, Leda and her swan, Europa and her bull, Danaë and her golden shower, Ganymede and his eagle, and other scenes calculated to raise the tired moneylender from the prose of his days to the poetry of his dreams. Peruzzi set off his frescoes with borders painted in such tricks of perspective that Titian thought them to be veritable reliefs in stone.[55] In the hall of the upper floor Baldassare made illusory architecture with his brush: cornices sustained by pictured caryatids, friezes supported by pictured pilasters, mimic windows opening upon pictured fields. Peruzzi had fallen in love with architecture, and made painting its handmaid, obeying all the builder's rules, but spiritless. Let us make an exception here for the Biblical scenes that he painted in a semidome of Santa Maria della Pace (1517), where Raphael had painted sibyls three years before. Baldassare's frescoes stood the comparison well, for these are his finest paintings, while Raphael's there were not his best.

Leo X must have been impressed by Peruzzi's versatility, for he appointed him to succeed Raphael as chief architect at St. Peter's (1520), and engaged him to paint the scenery for Bibbiena's comedy, *La Calandra* (1521). All that remains of Peruzzi's work on San Pietro is the ground plan that he drew; Symonds pronounced it "by far the most beautiful and interesting of those laid down for St. Peter's."⁵⁶ Leo's death, and the accession of a pope allergic to art, drove Peruzzi back to Siena, then to Bologna. There he designed the lovely Palazzo Albergati, and made a model for the never finished façade of San Petronio. He hurried back to Rome when Clement VII reopened the paradise of the arts, and resumed his work at St. Peter's. He was still there when the imperial mob sacked Rome. He suffered special tribulations, says Vasari, because "he was grave and noble of aspect, and they thought him some great prelate in disguise." They held him for a lordly ransom; but when he proved his lowly status by painting a masterly portrait, they contented themselves with taking from him all but the shirt on his back, and let him go. He made his way to Siena, and arrived there almost naked. The Sienese government, proud to recapture its prodigal son, engaged him to design fortifications; and the church of Fontegiusta commissioned him to paint a mural which was acclaimed by generous critics as his *chef-d'oeuvre*—a Sibyl announcing to a frightened Augustus the coming birth of Christ.

But Peruzzi's greatest success was the Palazzo Massimi delle Colonne, which he designed on his return to Rome (1530). The Massimi claimed descent, and derived their name, from Fabius Maximus, who had earned immortality by idling; they took their surname from the columned porch of their previous dwelling, which had been destroyed in the sack. It was Peruzzi's good fortune that the curved irregularity of the site forbade the usual dreary rectangular plan. He chose an oval form, with a Renaissance façade and a Doric portico; and while keeping the exterior simple, he gave the interior all the ornament and splendor of a Roman palace of Imperial days, with Greek refinements of proportion and decoration.

Despite his multiform ability Peruzzi died poor, not having had the heart to haggle with popes, cardinals, and bankers for fees commensurate with his skill. When Pope Paul III heard that he was dying he bethought himself that only Peruzzi and Michelangelo remained to raise St. Peter's from walls to dome. He sent the artist a hundred crowns ($1250?). Baldassare thanked him, and died nevertheless, at the age of fifty-four (1535). Vasari, after suggesting that a rival had poisoned him, relates that "all the painters, sculptors, and architects in Rome followed his body to the grave."

X. MICHELANGELO AND CLEMENT VII: 1520-34

It is one of the credits in Clement's account that through all his own misfortunes he bore with kindly patience the moods and revolts of Michelangelo, plied him with commissions, and accorded him all the privileges of genius. "When Buonarroti comes to see me," he said, "I always take a seat and bid him be seated, feeling sure that he will do so without leave."[57] Even before becoming pope he proposed (1519) what proved to be the artist's culminating sculptural assignment: to add to the church of San Lorenzo in Florence a "New Sacristy" as a mausoleum for famous Medici, to design their tombs, and to adorn these with appropriate statuary. Confident in the Titan's versatility, Clement also asked him to draw up architectural plans for the Laurentian Library, strong and spacious enough to safely house the literary collections of the Medici family. The stately stairway and pillared vestibule of this Biblioteca Laurenziana were completed (1526-7) under Angelo's supervision; the remainder of the building was later put up by Vasari and others from Buonarroti's designs.

The Nuova Sagrestia was hardly an architectural masterpiece. It was planned as a simple quadrangle, divided with pilasters and surmounted by a modest dome; its prime function was to receive statuary in the recesses left in the walls. This "Medici Chapel" was finished in 1524; and in 1525 Angelo began work on the tombs. Clement wrote to him in the latter year a gently impatient letter:

> Thou knowest that popes have no long life; and we cannot yearn more than we do to behold the chapel with the tombs of our kinsmen, or at any rate to hear that it is finished. And likewise as regards the Library. Wherefore we recommend both to thy diligence. Meanwhile we will betake us (in accord with your words) to a wholesome patience, praying God that He may put it into thy heart to push the whole enterprise forward together. Fear not that either commissions or rewards shall fail thee while we live. Farewell, with God's blessing and ours.—*Giulio*.[58]

There were to be six tombs: for Lorenzo the Magnificent, his assassinated brother Giuliano, Leo X, Clement VII, the younger Giuliano "too good to govern a state" (d. 1516), and the younger Lorenzo, Duke of Urbino (d. 1519). Only the tombs of the last two were completed, and even these not quite. Nevertheless they are the apogee of Renaissance sculpture, as the Sistine Chapel is the summit of Renaissance painting, and St. Peter's dome is the architectural pinnacle of the Renaissance. The tombs show the dead men in the prime of life, with no attempt to reproduce their real forms or features: Giuliano in the garb of a Roman commander, Lorenzo as *il Penseroso*, the thinker. When some incautious observer remarked this lack of realism, Michelangelo answered with words that revealed his sublime confidence in his artistic immortality: "Who will care, a thousand years hence, whether these are their features or not?"[59] Reclining on the sarcophagus of Giuliano are two nude figures: at the right a man allegedly symbolizing Day, at the left a woman supposedly representing Night. Similar recumbent figures on the tomb of Lorenzo have been named Twilight and Dawn. These interpretations are hypothetical, perhaps fanciful; probably the sculptor's aim was merely to carve again his secret fetish, the human body, in all the splendor of male strength and all the comely contours of the female form. As usual, he succeeded better with the male; the unfinished figure of Twilight, slowly surrendering an active and exhausting day to night, matches the noblest gods of the Parthenon.

War intervened upon art. When Rome fell to the *Landsknechte* (1527), Clement could no longer play patron, and Michelangelo's papal pension of fifty crowns ($625) a month ceased. Meanwhile Florence enjoyed two years of republican liberty. When Clement made up with Charles, and a German-Spanish army was despatched to overthrow the republic and reinstall the Medici, Florence appointed Angelo (April 6, 1529) to a Committee of Nine—Nove di Milizia—for the defense of the city. The Medicean artist became, by the hazard of circumstance, the anti-Medicean engineer feverishly engaged in designing and building forts and walls.

But as these works proceeded, Michelangelo became more and more convinced that the city could not be successfully defended. What single town, divided as Florence then was in heart and loyalties, could withstand the artillery and excommunications of Empire and papacy combined? On September 21, 1529, in a mood of panic, he fled from Florence, hoping to escape to France and its amiable King. Finding his way blocked by German-held terrain, he took temporary refuge in Ferrara, then in Venice. Thence he sent a message to his friend Battista della Palla, art agent of Francis I in Florence: Would he join Angelo in flight to France?[60] Battista refused to leave the post that had been assigned to him in the defense of the city; instead he wrote to Angelo a stirring appeal to return to his duty, warning him that otherwise the government would confiscate his property, leaving his impecunious relatives destitute. About November 20 the artist was back at his work on the Florentine fortifications.

According to Vasari he found time, even in those excited months, to continue work secretly on the tombs of the Medici, and also to paint, for Alfonso of Ferrara, the least characteristic of his works, *Leda and the Swan*. It was a strange product for a man so slightly sexual and so generally puritan; and perhaps it came from a temporarily disordered mind. It showed the swan copulating with Leda. Alfonso was something of a lecher between wars, but apparently he had not chosen the subject. The messenger whom he sent to secure the promised work expressed disappointment when he saw it, saying, "This is a mere trifle," and made no effort to secure it for the Duke. Angelo gave the picture to his servant Antonio Mini, who took it with him to France, where it passed into the collection of the omnivorous Francis I. It remained at Fontainebleau until the reign of Louis XIII, when a high official ordered it destroyed because of its indecency. How far this order was carried out, and what was the later history of this original, is unknown. A copy remains in the vaults of the London National Gallery.[61]

When Florence fell to the returning Medici, Battista della Palla and other republican leaders were put to death. Michelangelo hid himself for two months in the house of a friend, expecting at any moment a like fate. But Clement thought him worth more alive than dead. The Pope wrote to his ruling relatives in Florence bidding them seek out the artist, treat him with courtesy, and offer him the renewal of his pension if he would resume work on the tombs. Michael agreed. But again, as with the mausoleum of Julius, the mind of pontiff and artist had conceived more than the hand could execute, and the Pope could not live long enough to see the enterprise through. When Clement died (1534) Michelangelo, fearful that Alessandro de' Medici would do him harm now that his protector was gone, took the first opportunity to slip off to Rome.

A profound and somber sadness marks the tombs, and the solemn *Madonna de' Medici* that Angelo also carved for the Sacristy. Historians fond of democracy (and exaggerating its scope in Florence) have generally assumed that the recumbent figures symbolize a city mourning its forced surrender to tyranny. But this interpretation is probably fanciful: after all, they had been designed while the Medici ruled Florence reasonably well; they had been carved for a Medici Pope unfailingly kind to Angelo, and by an artist indebted to Medici from his youth; it is not clear that he intended to condemn the family whose tombs he was preparing; and his representations of Giuliano and Lorenzo have nothing derogatory about them. No, these figures express something deeper than the love of liberty by the rich few to rule the poor unhindered by a Medici house usually popular with the people. They express rather Michelangelo's weariness with life, the fatigue of a man all nerves and titanic uncompassable dreams, who found himself buffeted by a thousand tribulations, harassed in almost every enterprise by the dull recalcitrance of matter, the obtuseness of power, and the called-in loans of borrowed time. Angelo had enjoyed but few of life's delights: he had no friends on a par with his mind; woman seemed to him only a smooth anatomy threatening peace; and even his most majestic triumphs were the issue of exhausting toil and pain, the unfinishable symphonies of melancholy meditation and inescapable defeat.

But when Florence had fallen to her worst tyrants, and terror ruled where once Lorenzo had governed happily, the artist who had carved a criticism of life, and no mere theory of government, in the marbles of the Medici shrine, felt that those melancholy figures expressed, as well, the glory gone of the city that had nursed the Renaissance. On the unveiling of the statue of Night the poet Gianbattista Strozzi wrote a quatrain of literary exposition:

> The Night thous seest here, posed gracefully
> In act of slumber, was by an angel wrought
> Out of this stone. Sleeping, with life she's fraught.
> Wake her, incredulous wight; she'll speak to thee.

Michelangelo pardoned the complimentary pun on his name, but rejected the interpretation. He gave his own in four lines that are the most revealing in his poetry:

> *Caro m'è il sonno, e più l'esser di sasso*
> *Mentre che 'l danno e la vergogna dura.*
> *Non veder, non sentir m'è gran ventura;*
> *Però non mì destar; deh! parla basso.—*

> Dear is my sleep, but more to be mere stone,
> So long as ruin and dishonor reign.
> To see naught, to feel naught, is my great gain;
> Then wake me not; speak in an undertone.[62]

XI. THE END OF AN AGE: 1528-34

Clement did not die until he had made one more reversal of policy, and had crowned his disasters by losing England for the Church (1531). The spread of the Lutheran revolt in Germany had created for Charles V difficulties and dangers that might, he hoped, be eased by a general council. He urged this upon the Pope, and was angered by repeated excuses and delays. Irritated in turn by the Emperor's award of Reggio and Modena to Ferrara, Clement veered again toward France. He accepted a proposal of

Francis that Caterina de' Medici should marry the King's second son Henry, and he signed secret articles binding himself to help Francis recover Milan and Genoa (1531).[63] At a second conference in Bologna (1532) between Pope and Emperor, Charles again proposed a general council at which Catholics and Protestants might meet and find some formula of reconciliation; he was again rebuffed. He suggested a marriage of Catherine with Francesco Maria Sforza, imperial vicar in Milan; he found that the proposal came too late; Catherine was already sold. On October 12, 1533, Clement met Francis at Marseille, and there married his niece to Henry, Duke of Orléans. It was a prime defect of the Medici as popes that they thought of themselves as a royal dynasty, and sometimes rated the glory of their family above the fate of Italy or the Church. Clement tried to persuade Francis to make peace with Charles; Francis refused, and had the audacity to ask papal acquiescence to a temporary alliance of France with the Protestants and the Turks against the Emperor.[64] Clement thought that this was going a bit too far.

"Under these circumstances," says Pastor, "it must be considered fortunate for the Church that the Pope's days were numbered."[65] He had already lived too long. At his accession Henry VIII was still *Defensor fidei*, defender of the orthodox faith against Luther; and the Protestant revolt had as yet proposed no vital doctrinal changes, but only such ecclesiastical reforms as the Council of Trent would legislate for the Church in the next generation. At Clement's death (September 25, 1534) England, Denmark, Sweden, half of Germany, part of Switzerland had definitely broken away from the Church, and Italy had submitted to a Spanish domination fatal to the free thought and life that had for good or evil marked the Renaissance. It was beyond doubt the most disastrous pontificate in the history of the Church. Everyone had rejoiced at Clement's accession, everyone rejoiced at his death; and the rabble of Rome repeatedly defiled his tomb.[66]

BOOK VI

FINALE

1534-76

CHAPTER XXII

Sunset in Venice

1534-76

I. VENICE REBORN

IT is something of a mystery that this age of thralldom and decline for the rest of Italy was for Venice a golden age. She had suffered severely from the wars of the League of Cambrai; she had lost many of her Eastern possessions to the Turks; her trade with the Eastern Mediterranean was repeatedly disturbed with war and piracy; her commerce with India was passing to Portugal. Why, then, could she support in this period architects like Sansovino and Palladio, writers like Aretino, painters like Titian, Tintoretto, and Veronese? In this same age Andrea Gabrieli played the organ and led the choirs at San Marco, and wrote madrigals that sounded through Italy; music was a pampered passion of rich and poor; the palaces on the Grand Canal were rivaled in interior luxury and art only by those of bankers and cardinals in Rome; a hundred poets recited their verses in booths and taverns and public squares; a dozen companies of players performed comedies, permanent theaters were built, and Vittoria Piissimi, *la bella maga d'amore*, "the lovely sorceress of love," was the toast of the city as an actress, singer, and dancer as women replaced boys in female parts, and the reign of divas began.

Only the lamest explanation of the mystery will be given here. Though deeply injured by war, Venice had never been invaded; her homes and shops remained intact. She had recovered her mainland possessions, and included populous cities like Padua, Vicenza, and Verona among her tributaries in education, economy, and genius (Colombo and Cornaro at Padua, Palladio at Vicenza, Veronese from Verona). She still dominated large areas of trade in and near the Adriatic. Her leading families had still unspent treasures of nursed and inherited wealth. Old industries continued to flourish, and found new markets in Christendom; it was now, for example, that Venetian glass reached its tenuous crystalline perfection. The Venetian leadership in luxury products was maintained, and in this age Venetian lace first acquired fame. Despite religious censorship, Venice still gave

649

asylum to political refugees, and to intellectual refugees like Aretino, who fumigated his hilarious ribaldries with periodical contributions to the literature of piety.

Toward the end of this period Venice twice demonstrated her civic vigor and resilience. In 1571 she took a leading part, with Spain and the papacy, in equipping the armada of two hundred vessels that destroyed a Turkish fleet of 224 ships off Lepanto in the Gulf of Corinth. That victory, which may have saved western Europe for Christendom, was celebrated by Venice with three days of mad rejoicing: the region of the Rialto was hung with cloths of turquoise or gold; every window made the canals colorful with flags or tapestries; a great triumphal arch rose at the Rialto bridge; and paintings by the Bellini, Giorgione, Titian, and Michelangelo were displayed in the streets. The subsequent carnival was the wildest that Venice had ever known, setting the pace for many later carnivals; everyone masked and frolicked, laying a moratorium upon morality; and clowns like Pantalone and Zanni (i.e., Johnny) gave their names to a dozen languages.

And then, in 1574 and 1577, tragic fires in the Ducal Palace gutted several rooms; paintings by Gentile da Fabriano, the Bellini, the Vivarini, Titian, Pordenone, Tintoretto, and Veronese were destroyed; in two days the labor and art of a century disappeared. The spirit of the republic shone out in the rapidity and resolution with which the damaged interiors were restored. Giovanni da Ponte was commissioned to rebuild the chambers on their former lines; Cristoforo Sorte designed in twenty-nine divisions the marvelous ceiling of the Sala del Maggior Consiglio; and the walls were painted by Tintoretto, Veronese, Palma Giovane, and Francesco Bassano. In other rooms—the Collegio or meeting place of the Doge and his council, the Anticollegio or antechamber, the Sala de' Pregadi or Senate Hall— ceilings and doors and windows were designed by the greatest architects of the age—Iacopo Sansovino, Palladio, Antonio Scarpagnino, Alessandro Vittoria.

Iacopo d'Antonio di Iacopo Tatti was by birth (1486) a Florentine. He "went very reluctantly to school," says Vasari, but took eagerly to drawing. His mother encouraged this disposition; his father, who had hoped to make a merchant of him, was overruled. So Iacopo went to serve as apprentice to the sculptor Andrea Contucci di Monte San Savino, who loved the lad so well, and taught him so conscientiously, that Iacopo came to look upon him as a father, and adopted Andrea's cognomen, Sansovino, as his own. The youth had also the good fortune to make a friend of Andrea del Sarto, and perhaps learned from him the secrets of graceful and animated design. While in Florence the young sculptor carved the *Bacchus* now in the Bargello, famous for its perfect balance, and for the skill with which arm, hand, and vase—lightly poised on the finger tips—were cut from one piece of marble. Everyone (except Michelangelo) was kind to Andrea, and helped him up the hill to excellence. Giuliano da Sangallo took him to Rome and gave him lodging. Bramante commissioned him to make a wax copy of the *Laocoön;* it was so well done that it was cast in bronze for Cardinal Grimani. Perhaps through Bramante's influence Andrea turned from sculpture to architecture, and soon received lucrative commissions.

He was in Rome when the sack came, and, like many other artists, he lost all his possessions. He made his way to Venice, thinking to go to France; but the Doge Andrea Gritti begged him, instead, to strengthen the pillars and cupolas of St. Mark's. His work so pleased the Senate that he was made state architect (1529). For six years he labored to improve the Piazza San Marco, banishing the butchers' shops that had sullied the Piazzetta, opening new streets, and helping to make St. Mark's Square the spacious delight that it is today.

In 1536 he built the Zecca or mint, and began his most celebrated building, the Libreria Vecchia, facing the Palace of the Doges. He designed the façade with a stately double portico of Doric and Ionic columns, handsome cornices and balconies, and decorative statuary. Some have rated this Old Library "the most beautiful profane edifice in Italy";[1] but the multiplication of columns is excessive, and the structure can hardly compare with the Palace of the Doges. In any case the Procurators liked it, raised Sansovino's salary, and exempted him from war taxes. In 1544 one of the main arches collapsed, and the vault crashed down. Sansovino was thrown into jail and heavily fined, but Aretino and Titian persuaded the Procurators to release and pardon him. The arch and vault were repaired, and the building was successfully completed in 1553. Meanwhile (1540) Sansovino had designed the pretty Loggetta, or vestibule for police, on the eastern side of the Campanile, and had adorned it with bronze and terra-cotta sculptures. In St. Mark's he cast bronze doors for a sacristy, and took occasion to portray, among the reliefs, not only Aretino but Titian and himself.

The three men had now become firm friends, enviously known in Venetian art circles as "the Triumvirate." Many an evening they spent together, talking shop, or entertaining such beauty as could be engaged for the time. Iacopo rivaled Aretino in popularity with women, and Titian in longevity. He remained strong and healthy, and (we are assured) enjoyed perfect eyesight, till his eighty-fourth year.[2] For fifty years he never consulted a physician; during summers he lived almost entirely on fruit. When Paul III invited him to succeed Antonio da Sangallo as chief architect at St. Peter's, he refused, saying that he would not exchange his life in a republic for service under an absolute ruler.[3] Ercole II of Ferrara and Duke Cosimo of Florence in vain offered him large stipends to take up residence at their courts. He died peacefully in 1570, in the eighty-fifth year of his age.

In that year appeared an epoch-making work—*Four Books of Architecture*—by Andrea Palladio, who gave his name to a style that endured here and there into our own time. Like so many others, Andrea went to Rome and was thrilled by the ruined grandeur of the Forum. He came to love those broken columns and capitals as the finest conceptions that architecture had ever reached; he almost memorized Vitruvius; and his own book strove to restore to Renaissance building all those principles which, he thought, had created the glory of classic Rome. It seemed to him that the finest architecture would avoid all ornament that did not spring spontaneously from the constructive style itself; it would pledge itself to a strict proportion, connection, and congruity of the parts in an organic whole; it would be classically noble and strong, as chaste as a vestal virgin, and as dignified as an emperor.

His first major work was his best, and is one of the outstanding structures of secular Italy. Around the Palazzo della Ragione or Town Hall of his native Vicenza he built (1549f) magnificent and powerful arcades, transforming an undistinguished Gothic core into a Basilica Palladiana that might vie with the Basilica Iulia of the Roman Forum itself: a tier of arches sustaining Doric columns and pilasters, a massive architrave, a railing and balcony elegantly carved, a second tier of arches, on Ionic columns, a classic cornice and railing, and—above each spandrel—a statue rising to oversee the city and give it an exemplar of greatness. "I do not question," he wrote in his book twenty-one years later, "but that this fabric may be compared with the ancient edifices, and be looked upon as one of the most noble and beautiful buildings erected since the time of the ancients."[4] If he had confined his challenge to civic buildings the boast might stand.

Palladio became the hero of Vicenza, which felt that he had surpassed Sansovino's Libreria Vecchia. Rich men plied him with commissions for palaces and villas, ecclesiastics for churches; before he died (1580) he had transformed his city almost into an ancient Roman municipality. He built a loggia for the city administration, a pretty museum, a splendid Teatro Olimpico. Venice called him, and there he designed two of her finest churches—San Giorgio Maggiore and the Redentore. Even before his death

he had become a powerful influence in Italy. Early in the seventeenth century Inigo Jones brought the Palladian style into England; it spread through
Western Europe, and came to America.

Perhaps it was a misfortune. It never really captured the dignity of
Roman architecture; it confused its façades with a plethora of columns,
capitals, cornices, moldings, and statuary; the details detract from the simple lines and clarity of a classic edifice. And by reverting so humbly to an
ancient style, Palladio forgot that a living art should express its own epoch
and mood, not those of another age. That is why, when we think of the
Renaissance, we do not call to mind its architecture, nor even its sculpture,
but above all its painting, which bore lightly the traditions of Alexandria
and Rome, freed itself from cramping and uncongenial Byzantine molds,
and made itself the authentic voice and color of the time.

II. ARETINO: 1492-1556[5]

To make sure that 1492 would be memorable, Pietro Aretino, Scourge
of Princes and Prince of Blackmailers, came into the world on Good Friday
of that year. His father was a poor shoemaker of Arezzo, known to us only
as Luca. Like many other Italians, Pietro received in time the name of his
birthplace, and became Aretino. His enemies insisted that his mother was
a prostitute; he denied it, and claimed that his mother was a pretty girl
named Tita, who posed as a Madonna for painters, but in a careless moment conceived Pietro while in the arms of a casual but noble lover, Luigi
Bacci. Aretino did not mind being a bastard, having such distinguished
company in that class; and Luigi's legitimate sons, when Pietro became
famous, did not mind his calling them brothers. But his father was Luca.

Having attained the maturity of twelve years, he set out to make his
fortune. He found work as a bookbinder's assistant in Perugia, and there
he studied art sufficiently to become in later years an excellent critic and
connoisseur. He himself did some painting. In the chief square of Perugia
was a holy picture, fondly reverenced by the people, showing Magdalen
fervent at the feet of Christ. One night Aretino painted a lute in the arms
of the Magdalene, changing her prayer into a serenade. When the city
seethed with anger at the prank, Pietro slipped out of Perugia and examined
Italy. He earned his bread as a servant in Rome, as a street singer in
Vicenza, as an innkeeper in Bologna. He served a term in the galleys, became a hired man in a monastery, was discharged for lechery, and returned
to Rome (1516). There he labored as a lackey for Agostino Chigi. The
banker was not unkindly, but Aretino had discovered his own peculiar

genius, and fretted under servantry. He wrote a bitter satire describing a scullion's life: "cleaning privies, polishing chamberpots . . . performing lewd offices for cooks and stewards who soon see to it that he is all pricked out and embroidered with the French disease."[6] He showed his poems to some of Chigi's guests, and word went around that this Pietro was the sharpest and witties satirist in Rome. His pieces began to circulate. Pope Leo enjoyed them, sent for the author, laughed at his rough frank humor, and added him to the papal staff as a cross between poet and jester. For three years Pietro ate well.

Suddenly Leo died, and Aretino was afloat again. As the conclave dallied in choosing a successor, he wrote satires on the electors and the candidates, affixed the sheets to the statue of Pasquino, and poked fun at so many dignitaries that soon he had hardly a friend in the city. When Adrian VI was elected, and began a most unwelcome campaign of reform, Pietro fled to Florence, then to Mantua (1523), where Federigo took him on as court poet at a moderate salary. When the death of Adrian answered Rome's prayers, and a rich Medici sat again on the throne of thrones, Pietro, like a thousand other poets, artists, rascals, and rakes, hurried back to the capital.

Almost at once he ended his welcome there. Giulio Romano had painted twenty pictures describing various erotic attitudes; Marcantonio Raimondi made engravings for them; for each engraving, says Vasari, "Messer Pietro Aretino wrote an extremely lewd sonnet, so that I cannot say which is worse, the drawings or the words."[7] The pictures and sonnets went the rounds of the intelligentsia; they reached Pope Clement's datary, Giberti, who was known to be hostile to Aretino; Pietro heard of it, and took again to the road. At Pavia he charmed Francis I, who was on the verge of losing everything but honor. And now, by putting a different point on his pen, he turned a somersault that made Rome gasp. He wrote three laudatory poems—one about Clement, one about Giberti, one about Federigo. The Marquis said a good word for him to the Pope, Giberti relented, Clement sent for Aretino, and made him a pensioned Knight of Rhodes. Francesco Berni, his only rival among the satirists, described him at this period:

> He walks through Rome dressed like a duke. He takes part in all the wild doings of the lords. He pays his way with insults couched in tricked up words. He talks well, and he knows every libelous anecdote in the city. The Estes and the Gonzagas walk arm in arm with him, and listen to his prattle. He treats them with respect, and is haughty to everyone else. He lives on what they give him. His gifts as a satirist make people afraid of him, and he revels in hearing

himself called a cynical, impudent slanderer. All that he needed was a fixed pension. He got one by dedicating to the Pope a second-rate poem.[8]

Aretino would not have questioned any of this. As if to illustrate it, he asked the Mantuan ambassador to solicit for him from Federigo "two pairs of shirts worked with gold . . . two pairs worked in silk, together with two golden caps." When these took too much time in coming he threatened to annihilate the Marquis with a diatribe. The ambassador warned Federigo: "Your Excellency knows his tongue; therefore I will say no more." Soon four shirts worked in gold arrived, and four of silk, and two gold caps, and two silk hats. "Aretino," wrote the ambassador, "is satisfied." Pietro could now really dress like a duke.

This second period of Roman prosperity was ended by a cloak-and-dagger romance. Aretino composed an insulting sonnet on a young woman employed in the datary's kitchen. Another of Giberti's household, Achille della Volta, attacked Aretino in the street at two o'clock in the morning (1525), stabbed him twice in the chest, and so severely in the right hand that two fingers had to be cut off. The wounds were not mortal; Aretino healed rapidly. He demanded the arrest of Achille, but neither Clement nor his datary intervened. Pietro suspected the datary of planning to have him murdered, and he decided that the time had come for another Italian tour. He moved to Mantua, and resumed his service with Federigo (1525). A year later, hearing that Giovanni delle Bande Nere was marshaling a force to check Frundsberg's invasion, a secret atom of nobility stirred in him; he rode a hundred miles to join Giovanni at Lodi. All the ink in his veins tingled at the thought that he, the poor poet, might become a man of action, might even carve out for himself a principality, and be himself a prince, and no mere literary menial of a prince. And, indeed, the young commander, as generous as Don Quixote, promised to make him a marquis at least. But brave Giovanni was killed, and Aretino, putting aside the helmet he had received, returned to Mantua and his pen.

He composed now a mock *giudizio,* or almanac, for 1527, predicting absurd or evil fates for those he disliked. Furious against Clement for giving Giovanni delle Bande Nere inadequate and vacillating support, Aretino included the Pope among the victims of his satire. Clement expressed surprise that Federigo should harbor so irreverent an enemy of the papacy. Federigo gave Aretino a hundred crowns, and advised him to get out of the papal reach. "I will go to Venice," said Pietro; "only in Venice does justice hold the scales with an even balance." He arrived in March, 1527, and took a house on the Grand Canal. He was fascinated by the views across the lagoon, and by the teeming traffic of what he called "the fairest highway in the world." "I have determined," he wrote, "to live in Venice forever." He addressed a letter of lordly compliments to the Doge Andrea Gritti, praising the majestic beauty of Venice, the justice of her laws, the security of her people, the asylum she offered to political and intellectual refugees; and he added, magnificently: "I, who have stricken terror into kings . . . give myself to you, fathers of your people."[9] The Doge took him at his own estimate, assured him of protection, assigned him a pension, and interceded for him with the Pope. Though invitations were to come to Aretino from several foreign courts, he remained a loyal resident of Venice throughout his remaining twenty-nine years.

The furniture and art that he gathered into his new home attested the power of his pen, for they were given or made possible by the generosity or timidity of his patrons. Tintoretto himself painted the ceiling of Pietro's private apartments. Soon the walls shone with pictures by Titian, Sebastiano del Piombo, Giulio Romano, Bronzino, Vasari; there were statues by Iacopo Sansovino and Alessandro Vittoria. A rich ebony casket contained the letters received by Aretino from princes, prelates, captains, artists, poets, musicians, and noble dames; later he would publish these letters in two volumes totaling 875 closely printed pages. There were carved chests and chairs, and a walnut bed fit for Pietro's now ample form. Amid that art and luxury Aretino lived and dressed literally like a lord, dispersing charity to the neighborhood poor, entertaining a host of friends and a succession of mistresses.

Where did he get the means to support so lavish a life? Partly from the sale of his writings to publishers, partly from gifts and pensions sent him by men and women who feared his scorn and sought his praise. The satires, poems, letters, and plays that rushed from his pen were bought by the most alert or important people in Italy, all eager to see what he had to say about personalities and events, and delighting in his blasts at the corruption, hypocrisy, oppression, and immorality of the times. Ariosto inserted into the 1532 edition of *Orlando furioso* two lines that added two titles to Pietro's name:

Ecco il flagello
De' principi, il divin Pietro Aretino—[10]

"Behold the Scourge of Princes, the divine Pietro Aretino"; soon it became the fashion to speak of the coarsest and most scurrilous major writer of the age as divine.

His renown was Continental. His satires were at once translated into French; a bookseller on the Rue St. Jacques in Paris made a fortune retailing them.[11] They were welcomed in England, Poland, Hungary; Aretino and Machiavelli, said a contemporary, were the only Italian authors read in Germany. In Rome, where his favorite victims lived, his writings were sold out on the day of their publication. If we may take his own estimate, his receipts from his various publications amounted to a thousand crowns ($12,500?) a year. Moreover, in eighteen years, "the alchemy of my pen has drawn over 25,000 gold crowns from the entrails of various princes." Kings, emperors, dukes, popes, cardinals, sultans, pirates were among his tributaries. Charles V gave him a collar worth 300 crowns, Philip II another worth 400; Francis I a still more costly chain.[12] Francis and Charles competed for his favor with promises of fat pensions. Francis promised more than he gave; "I adored him," said Aretino, "but never to get money from the stirring of his liberality is enough to cool the furnaces of Murano" (the suburb where the glass industry of Venice was concentrated).[13] A knighthood was offered him, without income; he refused it, remarking that "a knighthood without revenue is like a wall without *Forbidden* signs; everybody commits nuisances there."[14] So Pietro pledged his pen to Charles, and served him with unwonted fidelity. He was invited to meet the Emperor at Padua; on reaching that city he was hailed by a crowd, like a modern celebrity. Charles, out of all those present, chose Aretino to ride beside him through the city, and told him: "Every gentleman in Spain knows all your writings; they read everything of yours as fast as it is printed." That night, at a state banquet, the son of the shoemaker sat at the Emperor's right hand. Charles invited him to Spain; Pietro refused, having discovered Venice. Sitting beside the conqueror of Italy, Aretino was the first example of what was later called the power of the press; nothing like his influence would appear again in literature until Voltaire.

His satires hardly hold our attention today, for their force lay mostly in pointed allusion to local events too tied to the time to have lasting significance. They were popular because it is hard for us not to enjoy the excoriation of others; because they exposed real abuses, and courageously attacked the great and powerful; and because they brought all the resources of the language of the streets to the uses of literature and gainful literary homicide. Aretino exploited the human interest in sex and sin by writing *Ragionamenti*—conversations—among prostitutes about the secrets and practices of nuns, wives, and courtesans. The title page announced the book as "The Dialogues of Nanna and Antonia . . . composed by the divine

Aretino for his pet monkey Capricio, and for the correction of the three states of women. Given to the printer in this month of April, 1533, in the illustrious city of Venice."[15] Aretino here anticipates the rollicking ribaldry and epithetic frenzy of Rabelais; he revels in four-letter words, and achieves some startling phrases ("I'd wager my soul against a pistachio nut"); and he indites such lively descriptions as that of the pretty wife of seventeen— the "finest little piece of flesh that I think I ever saw"—who, married to a man of sixty, took to sleepwalking as a way of "jousting with the lances of the night."[16] The conclusions to which the dialogues come is that courtesans are the most praiseworthy of the three classes of women, for the wives and nuns are faithless to their vows, while the courtesans live up to their professions and give an honest night's labor for their pay. Italy was not shocked; it laughed with delight.

Now, too, Aretino composed the most popular of his plays—*La cortigiana, The Courtesan*. Like most Italian comedies of the Renaissance, it followed the Plautine tradition of servants making fools of their masters, arranging intrigues for them, serving as their panders and their brains. But Aretino added something of his own: his burlesque and bawdy humor, his intimacy with prostitutes, his hatred of courts—above all, of the papal court —and his uninhibited transcript of life as he had seen it in the brothels and palaces of Rome. He laid bare the hypocrisies, timeserving, humiliations, flatteries required of the courtier; and in a famous line he defined slander as "telling the truth"; it was his pithy apologia for his life. In another Aretino comedy, *Talanta*, the title character is again a prostitute, and the story turns on the tricks she plays upon her four lovers, and her ways of squeezing money out of their agitation. Another play, *Ipocrita*, was an Italian *Tartuffe*; indeed, Molière is a French continuation of the Aretine comedies, deodorized and improved.

In the same year that produced these idyls of the stews, Aretino composed a long series of religious works—*The Humanity of Christ, The Seven Penitential Psalms, The Life of the Virgin Mary, The Life of the Virgin Catherine, The Life of St. Thomas, Lord of Aquino*, etc. They were largely compounded of fiction, and Pietro confessed that they were "poetical lies," but they won him the plaudits of the pious, even of the virtuous Vittoria Colonna. In some quarters he was regarded as a pillar of the Church. There was talk of making him a cardinal.

It was probably his letters that sustained his fame as well as his fortune. Many of these were eulogies addressed to the eulogized, or to persons near them. They were frankly intended to elicit gifts, pensions, or other favors;

sometimes they specified what was to be given, and when. Aretino published—printed—these letters almost as soon as he wrote them; this was necessary to their extractive power. Italy snapped them up because they provided an indirect intimacy with famous men and women, and because they were written with an originality, vivacity, and force unequaled by any other writer of the day. Aretino had style without seeking it. He laughed at the Bembos who polished their stanzas into perfect lifelessness; he ended the humanist idolatry of Latin, of correctness and grace. Pretending to be ignorant of literature, he felt free from cramping exemplars; he accepted in his writing one overruling rule: to enounce spontaneously, in direct and simple language, his experience and criticism of life, and the needs of his wardrobe and larder. Amid the mountain of hypocritical rubbish of these letters some diamonds can be found: tender epistles to a favorite ailing harlot, lusty accounts of his domestic history, a sunset described in a letter to Titian almost as brilliantly as Titian or Turner could paint it, and a letter to Michelangelo suggesting, for *The Last Judgment*, a design much more appropriate than that which the artist used.

Aretino's understanding and appreciation of art were among the better qualities of his character. His most intimate male friends were Titian and Sansovino. Together they had many a feast, usually graced with feminine company usually venal; and there, when the talk turned on art, Aretino could hold his own. His letters sang the praises of Titian to a host of possible patrons, and won Vecelli several lucrative commissions, in which Pietro may have shared. It was Aretino who persuaded the Doge, the Emperor, and the Pope to sit to Titian for portraits. Titian painted Aretino twice, and each time made a masterpiece of mountainous and vulgar vitality. Sansovino, pretending to carve an Apostle, placed the old satyr's head on a sacristy door in St. Mark's; and perhaps Michelangelo, in *The Last Judgment*, portrayed him as St. Bartholomew.

He was both better and worse than he was painted. He had almost every vice, and was accused of sodomy. His hypocrisy made his own Ipocrita seem by comparison sincere. His language, when he set his mind to it, could be a *cloaca maxima* of filth. He could be brutal and unmanly, as when he gloated over the fallen Clement; but he had the grace to write, later: "I am ashamed that in censuring him I did so in the depth of his afflictions."[17] He was physically an unabashed coward; but he had the courage to denounce powerful persons and highly cherished abuses. His most visible virtue was generosity. He gave to his friends and the poor a large part of what he received in pensions, earnings, gifts, and bribes. He waived royalties on his published letters, so that they might be sold more cheaply, and acquire wider fame and higher value. He was annually near bankruptcy with Christmas giving. Giovanni delle Bande Nere said to Guicciardini: "I yield to no man in generosity, unless it be to Messer Pietro, when he has means."[18] He helped his friends to sell their pictures and (as in the case of Sansovino) to get release from jail. "Everybody comes to me," he wrote, "as if I were a custodian of the royal treasury. Let a poor girl be confined, and my house pays the expenses. Let anyone be put into prison, and the cost falls upon me. Soldiers without equipment, strangers down on their luck, stray cavaliers without number, come to my house to refit."[19] If at times he had twenty-two women in his house, it was not that they constituted his harem; some were nursing unexpected infants, and found a refuge under his roof; we note that a bishop sent him shoes for one of these women. Many of the women whom he used or succored loved and honored him; six favorite courtesans proudly called themselves "Aretines."

He had whatever virtue is implied by abundant animal spirits; in private he was a good-natured animal who had never learned a moral code. He thought—with some excuse in those times—that no person of any consequence had any real moral code. He told Vasari that he had never seen a maiden whose features did not betray a touch of sensuality.[20] His own sensuality was gross, but to his friends it appeared to be merely the spontaneous exuberance of life. Hundreds of people found him lovable; princes and priests delighted in his conversation. He had no education, but he seemed to know everybody and everything. He became human in his love for Giovanni delle Bande Nere, for Caterina and the two children she bore him, and for frail, consumptive, gracious, faithless Pierina Riccia.

She came into his household as the fourteen-year-old wife of his secretary. They lived with him, and he played father to her; soon he loved her with a consuming and solicitous paternal affection. He reformed his morals, kept, of his mistresses, only Caterina and their babe Adria. Then, just as he was simmering down to respectability, a Venetian nobleman, whose wife he had charmed, accused him in court of blasphemy and sodomy. He denied the charges, but dared not face the exposures and chances of trial; conviction would have meant long imprisonment or death. He fled from his house, and hid for weeks with friends. They persuaded the court to dismiss the charges; Aretino returned to his home in triumph, cheered by crowds on both sides of the Grand Canal. But he was heartbroken to find in Pierina's eyes that she thought him guilty. Then Pierina's husband deserted her. When she came to Pietro for consolation he made her his mistress. She developed tuberculosis, and for thirteen months was near death; he nursed her with anxious tenderness, and brought her back to health. At the height of his devotion she left him for a younger lover. He tried to convince himself that it was better so, but from that day his spirit was broken, and old age advanced upon him triumphantly.

He grew fat, but never ceased to vaunt his sexual powers. He frequented brothels, and became more and more religious, he who in his youth had laughed at resurrections as "nonsense" which "only the rabble takes seriously."[21] In 1554 he went to Rome hoping to be crowned with a red hat, but Julius III could only make him a Knight of St. Peter. In that year he was evicted from the Casa Aretino for failure to pay his rent. He took more modest quarters, away from the Grand Canal. Two years later he died of apoplexy, aged sixty-four. He had confessed some fraction of his sins, and had received the Eucharist and Extreme Unction; and he was buried in the church of San Luca as if he had not been the very paragon and apostle of lechery. A wit composed for him a possible epitaph:

> Qui giace l'Aretin, poeta tosco,
> Chi disse mal d'ognun fuorche Dio,
> Scusandosi col dir, Non lo conosco;—

which is to say:

> Here lies the Tuscan poet Aretino,
> Who evil spoke of everyone but God,
> Giving as his excuse, "I never knew him."

III. TITIAN AND THE KINGS: 1530-76

In 1530, at Bologna, Aretino introduced Titian to Charles V. The Emperor, absorbed in reorganizing Italy, sat impatiently for a portrait, and paid the astonished artist a single ducat ($12.50). Federigo of Mantua, calling Titian "the best painter now living," added out of his own pocket a princely 150 ducats to the fee. Gradually the Duke brought Charles to his own point of view. In 1532 artist and Emperor met again. During the next sixteen years Titian painted a dazzling sequence of Imperial portraits: Charles in full armor (1532, now lost); Charles in brocaded coat, embroidered doublet, white breeches, stockings and shoes, and black cap with an inappropriate white feather (1533?); Charles with the Empress Isabella

(1538); Charles in shining armor on a prancing steed at the battle of Mühl-
berg (1548)—a glory of color and pride; Charles in somber black, seated
meditative on a balcony (1548). It is a credit to painter and King that
these portraits make no attempt to idealize their subject, except in costume; they show Charles's unprepossessing features, his bad skin, his
gloomy spirit, and a certain capacity for cruelty; and yet they reveal the
Emperor, a man of burdens and authority, a cold, hard mind that had
brought half of western Europe under its rule. He could be kind nevertheless, and atone handsomely for his initial miserliness. In 1533 he sent Titian
a patent making him a count palatine, and a Knight of the Golden Spur; and
from that year Titian was officially court painter to the most powerful
monarch in Christendom.

Meanwhile, presumably through Federigo, Titian had entered into correspondence with Francesco Maria della Rovere, Duke of Urbino, who had
married Eleonora Gonzaga, Federigo's sister and Isabella's daughter. Since
Francesco was now commander in chief of the Venetian armies, he and
his Duchess were frequently in Venice. There Titian painted their portraits: a man nine tenths mail (for Titian liked its sheen), a woman pale
and resigned after many illnesses. For them Titian painted on wood a
Magdalen attractive only for the remarkable variations of light and hue
that the artist gave to her auburn hair; and again for them a lovely portrait, in green and brown, known only as *La Bella*, and now in the Pitti
Gallery. For Federigo's successor, Duke Guidobaldo II, Titian made one
of art's most perfect nudes, the *Venus of Urbino* (*c.* 1538). Titian, we are
told, had put some finishing touches on Giorgione's *Sleeping Venus;* now
he imitated that masterpiece in all but the accompaniments and the features.
Here the face lacks the guileless peace of Giorgione's version; and instead
of a quiet landscape we see a rich interior of green curtain, brown drape,
and red couch, while two maids search for robes gorgeous enough to fitly
clothe the lady's golden flesh.

From Duke and Emperor Titian passed on to paint the Pope. Paul III
was also imperial: a man of virile character and subtle craft, with a face
that recorded two generations of history; here was a better opportunity
for Titian than he had found in the uncommunicative Emperor. At Bologna in 1535 Paul faced bravely the realism of Titian's portraiture. Aged
sixty-seven, tired but indomitable, he sat in his flowing papal robes, the long
head and large beard bent over a once powerful frame, the ring of authority conspicuous on his aristocratic hand; this and Raphael's *Julius II*
contest the distinction of being the finest, deepest portrait of the Italian

Renaissance. In 1545 the Pope invited Titian, himself now sixty-eight, to Rome. The artist was lodged in the Belvedere, and received all the honors of the city; Vasari acted as his cicerone in showing him the wonders of classic and Renaissance Rome; even Michelangelo welcomed him, and, in a moment of courtesy, concealed from him an opinion expressed to friends, that Titian would have been a greater painter had he learned to draw.[22] There Titian painted Paul again, older, more bent, more harassed than before, between two obsequious grandsons who were soon to rebel against the Pope; this, too, is among Titian's profoundest works. For one of these grandsons, Ottavio Farnese, he painted the voluptuous *Danaë* of the Naples Museum. After eight months in Rome he traveled slowly back via Florence to Venice (1546), hoping to spend his remaining days there in rest and peace.

But a year later the Emperor urgently called him over the Alps to Augsburg. There he stayed nine months, making two of the imperial portraits listed above, and immortalizing slim Spanish grandees and mountainous Teutons like the Elector Johann Friedrich of Saxony. On a second visit to Augsburg (1550) Titian met the future Philip II of Spain, and made several pictures of him; one of these, in the Prado, is among the master portraits of the Renaissance. Lovelier still is the likeness that he painted of Charles's Portuguese wife, the Empress Isabella. She had died in 1539, but the Emperor, four years later, gave Titian a middling representation of her by an obscure artist, and asked him to change it into a work of finished art. The result may not resemble the Empress, but even as an imaginary portrait this *Isabella of Portugal* must rank high among Titian's pictures: a refined and melancholy face, a most royal costume, a book of prayers to console her premonition of an early death, a distant landscape providing overtones of green and brown and blue. Titian many times over earned his noble rank.

After his return from Augsburg (1552) Titian felt that he had traveled enough. He was seventy-five, and doubtless thought that he had not much longer to live. Perhaps his busyness made for his longevity; absorbed in painting after painting, he forgot to die. In a long succession of religious pictures (1522-70) he gave his own colorful and dramatic rendering of the Christian creed and story from Adam to Christ.* He commemorated with

---

* E.g., *The Fall of Man* (c. 1570, Prado)—a frank apotheosis of the human form; *The Annunciation* (c. 1545, Scuola di San Rocco, Venice; still another in San Salvatore, Venice); *The Gypsy Madonna* (1510, Vienna); *Mater Dolorosa* (1554, Prado); *The Presentation* (1538, Venice)—a vast panorama (twenty-six by eleven and a half feet) of mountainous landscape, majestic architecture, and colorful figures, with Mary pictured as a girl diffidently ascending the Temple steps, two of Titian's loveliest women at the base, against the

powerful images the Apostles and the saints. The best and most unpleasant of these is *The Martyrdom of St. Lawrence* (1558, I Gesuiti, Venice): the saint is being roasted on a gridiron by Roman soldiers and slaves, who add to his discomfort with hot irons and flagellation. These religious pictures do not move us as deeply as the similar works of the Florentines; they excel in anatomy, but give no sense of piety; one look at the athletic figures of Christ and the Apostles makes it clear that Titian's interest was purely technical, that he was thinking of splendid bodies, not of ascetic saints. In the interval between the Bellini and Titian Christianity, while still proposing topics, had lost its spiritual hold on Venetian art.[23]

That sensual element which is one requisite of pictorial or plastic art remained strong in Titian for almost a century. He repeated his Farnese *Danaë* in several variations, and made many a *Venus* for defenders of the faith. Philip II of Spain was his best customer for these "mythologies"; the royal apartments in Madrid were adorned with a *Danaë*, *Venus and Adonis*, *Perseus and Andromeda*, *Jason and Medea*, *Actaeon and Diana*, *The Rape of Europa*, *Tarquin and Lucretia*, *Diana and Callisto*, and *Jupiter and Antiope* (also known as *The Venus of Pardo*); and all but the last of these were painted by Titian after 1553, when he was seventy-six or more. It is encouraging to find the Master's imagination creating in his eighties female nudes as perfect as those that he had portrayed in his prime. The Dianas,

---

wall an old woman realer than life, selling eggs; this is one of Titian's finest religious pictures. He painted Mary again in *The Virgin with the Rabbit* (c. 1530, Louvre). *The Transfiguration* (c. 1560, San Salvatore, Venice), the work of a man of eighty-three, is a vigorous conception of the astonished Apostles, with a glowing representation of the illuminated Christ. In *The Last Supper* (1564 Escorial) every figure is masterly except that of Christ—where Leonardo also failed; and in *Christ Crowned with Thorns* (1542, Louvre), Jesus, as in Michelangelo, is a gladiator rather than a saint. The *Ecce Homo* of the Vienna Gallery (c. 1543) still leaves Christ a massive and muscular divinity, whom Pilate (a humorous portrait of Aretino) offers to a crowd not of Jerusalem's rabble, but of such distinguished personalities as Charles V, Suleiman the Magnificent, Titian's daughter Lavinia, and Titian himself. A *Crucifixion* in Ancona (c. 1560) reduces the suffering Christ to more credible proportions; and another in the Escorial (c. 1565) effectively pictures the darkness, at the final hour, enveloping hills and sky and cross and the watchers at its foot. Twice—in 1529 (in the Louvre) and thirty years later (in the Prado)—Titian pictured *The Burial of Christ;* in the later—perhaps also in the earlier—painting he portrayed himself as Joseph of Arimathea. At an uncertain date he represented *The Supper at Emmaus* (Louvre), exquisite but too refined; Rembrandt would more successfully convey the awe felt in that moment of incredulous recognition. For Charles V Titian painted (1554) a picture variously called *The Trinity* or *The Last Judgment*, and labeled *La Gloria* in the Prado: a confusing mass of heads and legs, and, in a cloud, the First and Second Persons of the Trinity, with the Holy Ghost taking the form of light. It seems a little absurd, but the Emperor took it with him when he retired to a convent in 1557, and ordered it placed above the high altar after his death.

with their upswept auburn hair, are of the type that Veronese was using—blonde Venuses almost lovelier than any Aphrodite of the Greeks. Perhaps the same lady, grown ampler, appears in *Venus with the Mirror* (*c.* 1555, Washington); she is again the Venus who clings to Adonis in the Prado picture, struggling to woo him from his dogs. Not even in Correggio is there so frankly sensual a riot of feminine flesh. And there are still other Venuses scattered in the galleries, but once peopling Titian's brain: the *Venus Anadyomene* (*c.* 1520) of Bridgewater House, standing in the bath, and modestly concealed below the knees; the *Venus and Cupid* (*c.* 1545) of the Uffizi—a Germanic blonde with impeccable hands; the clothed Venus of *The Education of Cupid* (*c.* 1565) in the Borghese Gallery; the Prado *Venus with the Organ Player* (*c.* 1545), who cannot keep his mind on his music; and a *Venus with the Lute Player* (1560) in the Metropolitan Museum of Art. It must be said, however, that the women in these pictures are but part of their charm; Titian is interested in nature as well as women, and paints on several of these canvases splendid landscapes that are sometimes as lovely as the goddess herself.

Greater and deeper than these mythological pictures are the portraits. If the Venuses display a sense of form that never grew dull, the portraits reveal in Titian an ability to seize and convey human character with a force of art unequaled, in their total gallery, by the combined portraits of any other hand. What could be finer than the anonymous *Man with the Glove* (*c.* 1520, Louvre)?—whose gloved left hand and delicate white ruff about the neck harmonize so well with the sensitive spirit mirrored in the eyes. *Cardinal Ippolito de' Medici* (1533, Pitti) is a less searching portrayal, and yet in the face are the subtlety, the artistic sense, the love of power, that marked the Medici. The *Francis I* (*c.* 1538, Louvre) made the French King's features famous, sending over the world, in a hundred thousand reproductions, the feathered hat and jolly eye and rapier nose and handsome beard and scarlet shirt of the man who lost Italy but won Leonardo and Cellini and a hundred women. Titian's official post required him to paint portraits of various doges; nearly all these portraits are lost; three masterly figures remain: *Niccolò Marcello* (who died before Titan's birth)—an ugly face and a gorgeous robe; *Antonio Grimani* (in the picture of *Faith* in the Doges' Palace)—an ascetic face and a gorgeous robe; and *Andrea Gritti*—a less gorgeous robe, but a powerful face concentrating in itself all the resolute majesty of Venice. In an opposite vein is the delicate *Clarice Strozzi*, which Aretino praised too fully. The portraits of

Aretino, in the Pitti Gallery at Florence and in the Frick Collection in New York, are merciless evocations of a fascinating scoundrel by his dearest friend. Tenderer is Titian's commemoration of Bembo, the poet lover by this time (1542) become a cardinal. Among the greatest portraits in Titian's gallery is *The Jurist Ippolito Riminaldi* (1542), once known as *The Duke of Norfolk*—disheveled brown hair, high forehead, scanty mustache and beard, firm lips, fine nose, piercing glance; we begin to understand Italy and Venice better when we see that they had such men, in whom fine bodies and fine clothes were but the outward form of strong wills ready for any challenge, and penetrating minds alert to every facet of experience and art.

Titian's most interesting portraits were of himself. He pictured himself several times, finally at eighty-nine. Standing before this *autoritratto* in the Prado, we see a face lined and yet cleaned by the flow of countless days; a skullcap not quite enclosing the white hair; a red beard almost covering the face; a large nose breathing power; blue eyes a little somber, seeing death closer than it really was; the hand grasping a brush—the great artistic passion not yet spent. This—not the doges, not the senators, not the merchants—was the lord of Venice for half a century, giving immortality to transient aristocrats and kings, and raising his adopted city to a place beside Florence and Rome in the history of the Renaissance.

He was a rich man now, though the memory of early insecurity made him acquisitive to the end. Venice exempted him from certain taxes, "out of regard for his rare excellence."[24] He wore elegant clothing, and lived in a comfortable home with a spacious garden that overlooked the lagoon; we picture him there entertaining poets, artists, blue bloods, cardinals, and kings. The mistress whom he had married in 1525, after having two sons by her, died in 1530, and he resumed the baccalaureate liberty that he had enjoyed for almost half a century before. His daughter Lavinia was a joy and pride, and he made fond portraits of her, even in her matronly amplitude; but she too died a few years after his marriage. One son, Pomponio, became a worthless wastrel, saddening the old man's heart; the other, Orazio, painted some lost pictures, and probably shared in the works ascribed to his father's final years. Perhaps another of Titian's pupils—Domenico Theotocopoulos, "El Greco"—helped him then, though there is no sign of it in Titian's buxom figures and joyous scenes.

Far into old age he painted almost every day, and found in his art his only secure happiness. There he knew that he was master, that all the world acclaimed him, and that his hand had not lost its cunning, nor his eye its keenness; even his intellect, as well as his imagination, seemed to keep its power to the end. Some purchasers complained that these final paintings were sent to them unfinished; even so, they were miracles. Probably no other painter—excepting Raphael—ever possessed such technical facility, such control of color and texture, such wizardry of variegated light. His faults were those of rapid execution, sometimes of careless drawing; most of his preliminary designs were tentative; yet, when he cared to take the time, he could produce such a marvel as the pen drawing of *Medoro and Angelica* in the Musée Bonnat at Bayonne. In portraiture he had to work rapidly, for his subjects were too impatient and occupied to give him long or frequent sittings; therefore he made a quick sketch and painted from that, perhaps putting more into the subject's face and head than was really there. In paintings other than portraits he gave too much prominence to physical features, and seldom caught the spiritual essence; in depth of insight and feeling he could not match Leonardo or Michelangelo. But how healthy his art is compared with theirs! No abnormal introverted broodings, no volcanic grumblings at the nature of the world and man; Titian took the world as he found it, took men as he found them, took women when he found them, and enjoyed them all. He was a frank pagan, who contemplated the architecture of woman with delight through ninety years; even his Virgins are healthy, happy, and nubile. The poverty, grief, and insecurity of life found little room in Titian's art; except for a few martyrdoms and crucifixions, all is beauty and joy.

He grew old while painting, and lived a quarter century after the normal span of life. In his eighty-eighth year he traveled to Brescia, and accepted an arduous commission to paint a ceiling in the palace of the commune. Vasari, visiting him in his ninetieth year, found him at work, brush in hand. At ninety-one he painted a portrait of Iacopo da Strada (Vienna), brilliant with color, strong with character. But now at last his hand began to tremble, his eyes grew weak, and he felt that the time had come for piety. In 1576, aged ninety-nine, he agreed to paint a *Burial of Christ* for the church of the Frari, in exchange for a burial place there, where already two of his greatest works were hung. He did not finish it, and he fell a year short of living out a century. In that year plague broke out in Venice; on each day two hundred died; a fourth of the population succumbed to the pestilence. Titian himself died during the plague, probably not of it but from old age (August 26, 1576). The government set aside its prohibition of public gatherings in order to give him a state funeral. He was buried in Santa Maria Gloriosa de' Frari, as he had wished. It was the end of a magnificent life, and a wondrous age.

IV. TINTORETTO: 1518-94

It was not quite the end; for a power and spirit almost as great had still eighteen years to live, and had still to paint his *Paradise*.

Iacopo Robusti was the son of a dyer; hence the diminutive nickname by which the whimsical Italians have sent him down to history. He became indeed a *tintor* as a great colorist; but his family name fitted him well enough, for only a robust soul could have survived the long struggle that Iacopo had to fight for recognition.

Almost the first notice we have of him is that he was apprenticed to Titian at an unknown age, and was dismissed after a few days. Carlo Ridolfi, writing a century later, recounts the incident from the point of view of Tintoretto's descendants:

> When Titian came home and entered the place where his students were, he saw some papers sticking out from a desk; and seeing certain figures drawn on them, he asked who had done them. Iacopo said timidly that they were by his hand. Thereupon Titian, foreseeing from such beginnings that the lad would become a very able man, and would bring him some trouble in art, impatiently, as soon as he had gone upstairs and laid aside his mantle, bade Girolamo Dante, his chief pupil, to immediately forbid Iacopo the house. So a little tinge of jealousy works in human hearts.[25]

We should like to reject this story, but Aretino, Titian's bosom friend, alludes to the incident in a letter of 1549. The dismissal is a fact, the interpretation is problematic. It is hard to believe that Titian, who was already a painter to kings when Iacopo was only a lad of twelve, could be jealous of so hypothetical a competitor, or that he could see the future Tintoretto in the drawings of a student just admitted to his school. It is possible that the drawings offended Titian by their carelessness rather than by their excellence; careless drawing remained a fault in Tintoretto through many years. Iacopo throughout his life expressed great admiration for Titian, treasured a picture that Titian had given him, and put upon the wall of his studio a constant reminder of what he aspired to achieve in painting: "The design of Michelangelo and the color of Titian."[26]

According to Ridolfi and tradition, Iacopo had no instruction after leaving Titian, but taught himself by assiduous copying and experiment. He dissected bodies to learn anatomy. He observed almost every object in his experience with predatory eagerness, resolved to capture it in full detail in one or another of his paintings. He made models in wax, wood, or cardboard, dressed them, and drew them from every angle to find ways of portraying three dimensions in two. He had casts made and sent to him of ancient marbles in Florence and Rome, and of Michelangelo's statuary; he set up these casts in his studio, and painted images of them in divers shadows and lights. He was fascinated by the variations produced in the appearance of objects by changes in the quantity, character, and incidence of light; he made a hundred pictures by lamp or candle illumination; he grew too fond of dim backgrounds and heavy shadows; he became a specialist in picturing the play of light and shade upon hands and face and drapes, buildings and landscapes and clouds. He left no pebble unturned in his struggle for excellence.

Nevertheless there was an impatient haste, and lack of finish, in his work —possibly a penalty of self-instruction—which deferred the public recognition of his art. For years after reaching manhood he had to solicit opportunities. He painted furniture, frescoed house fronts, begged builders to get him decorative jobs at low fees, and tried to sell his pictures by displaying them in St. Mark's Square.[27] Everybody wanted Titian; and Titian and Aretino saw to it that nobody of extractable substance should get anyone but Titian, or, if Titian was busy, Bonifazio Veronese. Iacopo must have resented Aretino's pictorial pandering, but later, when the great Scourge came to him for a portrait, the artist pulled an impressive pistol from his pocket, pretended to measure with it Aretino's majestic dimensions, and enjoyed the mighty blackmailer's fright;[28] thereafter Pietro's pen was polite to Tintoretto. When Iacopo noted the vast unpainted walls—fifty feet high—of the choir in the church of the Madonna dell' Orto, he offered to cover their nakedness with frescoes for a total fee of 100 ducats ($1250?); whereupon the Venetian painters complained that he was "injuring the trade" by underselling art. But Tintoretto was resolved to paint.

He was thirty before his first triumph came. The Scuola di San Marco opened a competition for a painting of St. Mark delivering a slave. The story was in Iacopo de Voragine's *Golden Legend:* a Provençal servant had promised St. Mark to make a pilgrimage to his grave in Alexandria; his master refused him permission to go, but he went nevertheless. When he returned the master ordered his eyes to be gouged out, but the iron points pressed upon them failed to penetrate their surface. The master ordered the slave's limbs to be broken, but the iron rods failed to make any impression upon them. The master, recognizing the intervention of St. Mark, pardoned the slave. Tintoretto's picture told the tale with magnificent color, convincing realism, and dramatic intensity: the evangelist, clinging to his gospel, descends from heaven to rescue his devotee, who is about to be beheaded by a Moor, while a score of diverse figures look excitedly on. Iacopo seized every opportunity the story gave him: to limn powerful male and graceful female figures; to study the action of light upon Oriental velvets, silks, and turbans; to bathe the scene in colors learned from Giorgione and Titian. The directors of the Scuola were a bit frightened by the fleshly realism of the painting; they debated whether to place it on their walls; the impetuous Tintoretto proudly snatched it from their hands and took it home. They came and begged him to return it; he let them wait a chastening while, then yielded it. Aretino sent him a word of praise, and career was now open to his talent.

Soon commissions came in multitude. A dozen churches solicited him, a dozen lords, half a dozen princes and states. For these he told again, in a hundred paintings, the mighty epic of the Christian cosmology, theology, and eschatology, from the Creation to the Last Judgment. He was not a religious man; few artists were in this sixteenth-century Venice—half molded in soul and dominions by the heretical or Islamic East; art was his religion, to which he sacrificed night and day. But what finer subjects could a painter fancy than the legends of Adam and Eve, and the story of Mary and her Babe, and the tragedy of the God-man crucified, and the sufferings and marvels of the saints, and the awful climax of all history in the summoning of the quick and the dead to the judgment seat of Christ?*

---

* A selection from Tintoretto's religious paintings, excluding those at the Scuola di San Rocco (the churches named being all in Venice):
I. OLD TESTAMENT SCENES: *Creation of the Animals* (Venice); *Adam and Eve* (Venice)—a uniquely illumined landscape; *Cain and Abel* (Venice); *Abraham's Sacrifice* (Uffizi); *Joseph and Potiphar's Wife* (Prado); *Finding of Moses* (Escorial); *Golden Calf* (Madonna dell' Orto); *Gathering of the Manna* (San Giorgio Maggiore)—a remarkable mingling of nature, men, women, and animals.
II. MADONNAS: *Birth of the Virgin* (Mantua)—almost as gracious as a Correggio; *Annunciation* (Berlin); *Visitation* (Bologna); *Madonna and Child* (Cleveland); *Madonna and Saints* (Ferrara)—splendid, but the saints are Michelangelesque octogenarian gladiators; *Assumption* (I Gesuiti)—weak and pale compared with Titian's masterpiece in the Frari.
III. FROM THE LIFE OF CHRIST: *Circumcision* (Santa Maria del Carmine); *Baptism* (San Silvestro; a variant in the Prado); *Jesus in the House of Martha* (Munich)—exceptionally beautiful; *Marriage at Cana* (Madonna della Salute); *Christ at the Sea of Galilee* (Washington)—an almost impressionistic study in blue and green; *Woman Taken in Adultery* (Rome, Galleria Nazionale)—a pretty sinner in a too theatrical picture; *Christ*

The best of this long series is *The Presentation* (*c.* 1556), which Tintoretto painted for the church of Madonna dell' Orto: the Temple of Jerusalem pictured in classic splendor; a timid little Mary welcomed by the high priest with outstretched arms and beard; a woman, drawn with the majesty of Pheidias, pointing Mary out to her daughter; other women and their children, vividly realized; a prophet preaching enigmatic prophecies; beggars and cripples half naked, crouching on the Temple steps; this is a picture rivaling the best of Titian, one of the grand paintings of the Renaissance.

Tintoretto's success was confirmed when (1564) the Scuola di San Rocco, or the Confraternity of St. Roch, named him to decorate their *albergo* or assembly rooms. To choose a painter for the vast wall surfaces, the directors invited artists to submit drawings for a picture to fit into a ceiling oval, showing St. Roch in glory. While Paolo Veronese, Andrea Schiavone, and others made sketches, Tintoretto painted a finished picture, flaming with color and alive with action; had the canvas secretly pasted in the assigned place and covered; and, on the day when the others presented their drawings, had this painting uncovered, to the consternation of judges and competitors. He excused this unorthodox strategy on the ground that he could work best in this impulsive way, instead of following a cartoon. The other artists cried foul; Tintoretto withdrew from the contest, but left the painting as a gift to the Fraternity. The Scuola finally accepted it, made Tintoretto a member, gave him a salary of a hundred ducats a year for life, and required of him, in return, to paint for them three pictures per year.

In the next eighteen years (1564-81) he placed fifty-six scenes upon the *albergo* walls. The rooms were poorly lighted; Tintoretto had to work in semidarkness; he worked rapidly, laying on his colors coarsely, as to be

---

Washing the Apostles' Feet (Escorial); *Raising of Lazarus* (Leipzig); *Miracle of the Loaves and Fishes* (New York); *Christ and the Samaritan Woman* (Uffizi); *Last Supper* (San Trovaso; another in San Stefano and in San Giorgio Maggiore, and a magnificent drawing in the Uffizi); *Crucifixion* (San Cassiano); *Deposition* (Venice, Parma, Milan, Pitti Gallery); *Burial of Christ* (San Giorgio Maggiore); *Descent into Limbo* (San Cassiano); *Resurrection* (Farrer Collection); *Last Judgment* (Madonna dell' Orto)—a vain attempt to exceed the confusion and absurdities of Michelangelo's Sistine Chapel fresco.

IV. THE SAINTS: *St. Augustine Healing Victims of the Plague* (New York); *Miracle of St. Agnes* (Madonna dell' Orto); *St. George and the Dragon* (London)—a study in light and shade, as of a night engagement; *Marriage of St. Catherine* (Ducal Palace); *Martyrdom of St. Catherine* (Venice)—in both cases a lovely lady whom only a fool would want to kill; *Transportation of the Body of St. Mark* (Venice), and *Finding of the Body of St. Mark* (Milan)—a masterly perspective of a darkened nave, a kneeling patrician in holy terror, a charming lass whose knees are clasped by a youth pretending fright, and a splendid St. Mark standing erect over his own corpse.

seen from twenty feet below. These paintings became the most famous
one-man exhibition in Venetian history; and later artists came to study
them almost as students in Florence went to study Masaccio. Rain and
damp attacked the pictures through the years, but they are still impressive
in their scope and power. "Twenty or thirty years ago," wrote Ruskin a
hundred years ago, "they were taken down to be restored; but the man to
whom the task was committed providentially died, and only one of them
was spoiled."[29]

In this astonishing museum Tintoretto told the Christian story once
more, but as it had never been painted before, with an audacious realism
that took the episodes out of the world of ideal sentiment and placed them
in such natural surroundings that legend seemed transformed into the most
indubitable history. The capacity to see, to note every detail of a scene, to
feel these details as giving life, to dash them on to the wall with a stroke
or two of the brush—like the water visible through the laurel roots in the
Magdalen—these were sparks of Tintoretto's fire. He devoted the lower
floor of the *albergo* to Mary: her humble surprise in the *Annunciation*, her
modest grace in the *Visitation*, her simple awe at the precious Oriental gifts
in the *Adoration* of the Magi, her slow procession on donkeyback across
a peaceful landscape in *The Flight into Egypt*, safe from that "massacre of
the innocents" which provides the most powerful picture in this group.
On the walls of the main upper room Tintoretto recounted events in the
life of Christ: the baptism by John, the temptation by Satan, the miracles,
the Last Supper; this last was so unconventionally realistic that Ruskin
called it "the worst I know of Tintoretto":[30] Christ at the farther end, the
Apostles absorbed in eating or conversing, servants bustling about with
food, a dog inquiring when he too may eat. In an inner room of the upper
story Tintoretto painted two of his greatest paintings. *Christ Before Pilate*
shows an unforgettable figure clad in a white robe as if in a shroud, standing quietly in weariness and resignation, and yet in dignity, before a Pilate
trying to wash away the guilt of yielding to the bloodlust of a mob.
And last of all—judged by Tintoretto to be his best work—*The Crucifixion*, challenging and surpassing Michelangelo's *Last Judgment* in power
and range of composition, in artistry of execution; forty feet of wall, and
eighty figures, with horses, mountains, towers, trees, all with incredible
fidelity to detail; Christ in visualized agony of body and soul; one robber
being forced down upon a prostrate cross, and resisting to the last; another,
a Titan of strength and desperation, being raised to his death by rough
soldiers too angry at his weight to have a mind for pity; women huddled in

terrified groups; spectators crowding eager to watch men suffer and die; and, in the distance, a lowering sky offering no answer to the human tragedy but thunder and lightning and an indifferent rain. Here Tintoretto has reached his zenith, and equaled the best.

To all these masterpieces in the *albergo* Tintoretto added eight pictures for the church of the same Fraternity, chiefly concerning St. Roch himself. One of these paintings stands out, if only through its *terribilità—The Pool of Bethesda.* The artist takes his text from the fifth chapter of the Fourth Gospel: "a crowd of invalids used to lie" there, "the blind, the lame, and folk with shriveled limbs," waiting for a chance to bathe in the healing pool. Tintoretto sees not the miraculous healing of the cripple, but the variously diseased or stricken multitude, and he draws them unflinchingly as he sees them, in their malformations, their rags and filth, their hope and despair. It is a scene as from Dante's *Inferno* or Zola's *Lourdes.*

The same man who could so rage, with his art, against the ills that flesh is heir to, responded eagerly to the splendors of the flesh in the beauty of its health, and almost rivaled Titian and Correggio in portraying nudes. Though we might have expected his turbulent spirit and swift brush to fail in conveying the ancient sense of beauty in repose, we find, scattered over Europe, such delectable figures as the *Danaë* of the Lyons Museum, dressed in jewelry, the *Leda and Swan* of the Uffizi, the *Venus and Vulcan* of the Munich Pinacothek, the Dresden *Deliverance of Arsinoë*, the *Mercury and Graces* and *Bacchus and Ariadne* of the Doges' Palace. . . . Symonds thought this last "if not the greatest, at any rate the most beautiful, oil painting in existence."[31] And yet more perfect is the London Gallery's *Origin of the Milky Way* from Cupid's pressure upon Juno's breasts—as good an explanation as any. The Louvre, the Prado, Vienna, and the Washington Gallery have *Susanna and the Elders* in four Tintoretto versions. The Prado has a roomful of sensuous Tintorettos: *A Young Venetian Woman* drawing her robe aside to reveal her bosom; even in the *Battle of the Turks and Christians* two distracting breasts appear amid the gleam of arms. And in the Verona Museum is a *Concert* of nine women musicians, three of them bare to the waist—as if ears could hear when eyes had so much to see. These pictures are not the best of Tintoretto; his forte was in the massive representation of virile life and heroic death; but they show that he too, like Giorgione and Titian, could turn a perilous curve with a steady hand. And in all his nudes there is no immodesty; there is a healthy sensualism; these gods and goddesses take nudity as natural, and are not conscious of it; it is divine of them to greet the sun "all face," whole-bodily, and not be harassed and jailed with buttons and laces and bows.

After avoiding marriage for nearly forty years, Tintoretto took to wife Faustina de' Vescovi, who found him so disorderly and helpless that she achieved happiness in mothering him. She gave him eight children, three of whom became pardonable painters. They lived in a modest house not far from the church of Madonna dell' Orto; and the artist seldom wandered from that vicinity except to paint in a Venetian church, palace, or fraternity; consequently he can be appreciated in his variety and power only in the city of his birth. The Duke of Mantua offered him a place at his court; he refused. He was happy only in his studio, where he worked literally night and day. He was a good husband and father, but cared nothing for the social pleasures. He was almost as solitary, independent, moody, melancholy, nervous, vehement, and proud as the Michelangelo whom he ever worshiped and ever strove to surpass. There was no peace in his soul or his works. Like Angelo, he honored strength of body and mind and spirit above surface beauty; his Virgins are often as unprepossessing as the Doni *Madonna*. He has left us his own portrait (now in the Louvre), painted when he was seventy-two; it could have been the head and face of Angelo himself—a strong and somber face, profound and wondering, and bearing the marks of a hundred storms.

His own was his best portrait, but he painted some others that attest the depth of his insight and the integrity of his art. For there too he remained a realist, and no man dared sit for him who hoped to deceive posterity. Many a Venetian worthy has come down to us through Tintoretto's brush: doges, senators, procurators, three *proveditori* of the mint, six treasurers; above all, in this group, *Iacopo Soranzo*—one of the great portraits in Venetian art; here too, are Sansovino the architect and Cornaro the centenarian. Surpassed in Tintoretto's gallery of portraits only by the *Soranzo* are anonymous pictures of *The Man in a Cuirass* (Prado), the *Portrait of an Old Man* (Brescia), the *Portrait of a Man* (Hermitage, Leningrad) and *A Moor* in the Morgan Library in New York. In 1574 Tintoretto disguised himself as an attendant of Doge Alvise Mocenigo, secured entry to the Venetian flagship *Bucentaur*, and clandestinely made a pastel sketch of Henry III of France; later, in the corner of a chamber where Henry gave audience to notables, Tintoretto perfected the portrait. Henry liked it so much that he offered a knighthood to the artist, who begged to be excused.[32]

His acquaintance with the Venetian aristocracy had begun about 1556, when, with Veronese, he received a commission to paint canvases in the Ducal Palace. In the Sala del Maggior Consiglio he pictured *The Coronation of Frederick Barbarossa* and *Barbarossa Excommunicated by Alexander III;* in the Sala del Scrutinio he covered an entire wall with a *Last Judgment*. These so pleased the Senate that it chose him in 1572 to commemorate the great victory at Lepanto. All four of these paintings were destroyed in the fire of 1577. In 1574 the Senate engaged Tintoretto to decorate the Anticollegio (or antechamber); here the artist inspired the solons with *Mercury and the Graces, Ariadne and Bacchus,* the *Forge of Vulcan,* and *Mars Pursued by Minerva.* In the Sala de' Pregadi or Senate Hall Tintoretto painted (1574-85) a series of spacious panels celebrating the doges of his time, pictured against the background of the majestic Square: St. Mark's and its sparkling cupolas, or the Clock Tower, or the Campanile, or the stately façade of the Libreria Vecchia, or the radiant arcades of the Doges' Palace, or the misty or sunny vistas of the Grand Canal. Then, crowning this sequence to the taste of the proud government, he painted on the ceiling a triumphal picture of *Venice Queen of the Seas,* robed in splendor as a dogaressa, surrounded by circles of admiring divinities, and receiving from Tritons and Nereids the gifts of the waters—corals, shells, and pearls.

After the great fire the undiscourageable Senate called upon Tintoretto to redeem the ruined walls with pictures that would drown all memory of the loss. In the Hall of Scrutiny he painted a tremendous battle scene, *The Capture of Zara*. On a wall of the Great Council chamber he pictured the *Emperor Frederick Barbarossa Receiving Envoys from the Pope and the Doge,* and on the ceiling a masterpiece, *The Doge Niccolò da Ponte Receiving the Homage of Conquered Cities.*

When (1586) the Senate decided to cover the old fresco by Guariento on the east wall of the Council Chamber, they judged Tintoretto, then sixty-eight, to be too old for the task. They divided the assignment and the space between Paolo Veronese, then fifty-eight, and Francesco Bassano, thirty-seven. But Veronese died (1588) before the work was actually begun. Tintoretto offered to take his place, and proposed to cover the entire wall with one picture, *The Glory of Paradise*. The Senate agreed, and the old man, aided by his son Domenico and his daughter Marietta, laid out in the near-by Scuola della Misericordia the canvas sections that were to compose the picture. Many preliminary sketches were made; one, itself a *chef-d'oeuvre,* is in the Louvre. When all was set in place (1590) and Domenico had painted and concealed the seams, it constituted the largest oil painting that had yet been seen—seventy-two feet long by twenty-three feet high. The crowds that flocked to see it agreed with Ruskin that it was the culminating achievement of Venetian paint-ing—"the most wonderful piece of pure, manly, and masterly oil painting in the world."[33] The Senate offered Tintoretto so great a fee that he re-turned part of it, again to the scandal of his fellow artists.

Time has had its way with this *Paradise*, and today, when one enters the Hall of the Great Council, and turns back to the wall behind the doges' throne, he does not find the picture that Tintoretto left there, but a paint-ing so darkened by the smoke and damp of centuries that of the five hun-dred figures that filled it only a minority can now be made out distinctly by the eye. Circle within circle the figures vibrate—the simple blessed, the virgins, the confessors of the faith, the martyrs, the evangelists, the Apos-tles, the angels, the archangels—all concentered about Mary and her Son, as if these two, in some fitting recognition of woman as well as man, had become the real deities of Latin Christendom. And beyond the hundred figures that can be seen, Tintoretto makes us feel countless hundreds more. After all, even if only a few are chosen of the many called, there must have come to paradise, in sixteen Christian centuries, quite a happy host; and Tintoretto set himself to show their goodly number and their bliss. He did not deaden heaven with Dantesque solemnity; it was conceived as a place of joy, and only the radiantly happy were admitted there. It was the old artist's exorcism of his own misanthropy.

He had reason to be sad, for in the very year of the great picture's un-veiling his beloved daughter Marietta had died. Her skill in painting and music had been among the chief delights of his old age; and now that she was gone he seemed to think of nothing so much as of seeing her in another life. He went more frequently than before to Madonna dell' Orto—Our Lady of the Garden—and there spent hours in meditation and prayer, at last a humble man. He still painted, and produced in these concluding years a series on St. Catherine for the church of her name. But in his seventy-seventh year a stomach ailment gave him such pain that he could no longer sleep. He made his will, bade good-bye to his wife and children and friends, and died on May 31, 1594. Madonna dell' Orto received his remains.

If, after boating through Venice to stand face to face in every corner of the city with this Michelangelo of the lagoons, we try to clear our con-ception of his art, the first impression is one of size and multitude, of enormous walls pullulating with human and animal forms, in a thousand

degrees of beauty or ugliness, in a carnal confusion that has only this excuse, that it is life. This man who shunned and hated crowds saw them
everywhere, and reproduced them with fierce veracity. He seems to have
taken little interest in individuals; if he painted portraits it was frankly to
earn a fee. He saw humanity in the gross, interpreted life and history in
terms of masses of human beings struggling, competing, loving, enjoying,
suffering; virile and comely, diseased and crippled, saved or damned. He
covered canvases of awesome immensity, because only such expanses gave
him scope to picture what he saw. While never completely mastering, as
Titian did, the technique of pictorial art, he worked out for himself the
method of these gigantic paintings, and to him above all is due the grandeur
of the rooms in the Palace of the Doges. Therefore we must not ask of him
any finesse of finishing. He is crude, rough, hurried, and sometimes creates
a scene with a splash of the brush. His real fault is not this coarseness of
surface—for even a coarse surface may illuminate significance—but the
theatrical violence of the episodes he chooses, the unhealthy turbulence of
his moods, the gloom in which he bathes the life he shows, and the tiresome
repetition of his crowds; he was infatuated with number, as Michelangelo
with forms and Rubens with flesh. And yet even in these multitudes what
a wealth of meaningful detail, what accuracy and insight of observation,
what inexhaustible individualization of the parts, what courageous realism
where before there had only been imagination and sentiment!

Our final feeling in the presence of these pictures is one of affirmative
response: this is art in the grand style. Other artists have painted beauty,
like Raphael, or strength, like Michelangelo, or the depths of the soul, like
Rembrandt; but here in these cosmic canvases—as in the roar of a city, or
in mute masses at prayer, or in the troubled and affectionate intimacies of
a thousand homes—is humanity. No other artist has ever seen it so large or
pictured it so completely. Sometimes, silent before those fading walls in
the Palace of the Doges or in the Confraternity of St. Roch, the canvases
of better artists fall from our memory, and we feel that if he could have
finished like a jeweler after so conceiving like a giant, the little dyer would
have been the greatest painter of them all.

V. VERONESE: 1528-88

Let us honor, in passing, some stars of the second magnitude; they too
were part of the luminosity of Venice. Andrea Méldola was a Slavonian,
and received the name Schiavone. He studied with Titian, and made a

pretty *Galatea* on a chest in the Castello of Milan. In a *Jupiter and Antiope* (Leningrad) and a *Presentation of the Virgin* (Venice) he essayed a larger form, and produced canvases of brilliant coloring. Artists praised him, patrons ignored him, and Andrea had to carry his bearded dignity in rags. —Paris Bordone was the son of a saddler and the grandson of a shoemaker; but in the admirable democracy of genius—which appears in every rank— he made his way almost to the top in a Venice teeming with talent. Coming from Treviso to study under Titian, he matured so rapidly that at the age of thirty-eight he was invited to Paris by Francis I. He turned out some excellent religious pictures, like *The Baptism of Christ* (Washington) and *The Holy Family* (Milan), and reached his high point in *The Fisherman Presenting St. Mark's Ring to the Doge* (Venice); but the painting that has ferried him over the years is his *Venus and Eros* (Uffizi) —a stout blonde who uses a fine robe to reveal her breasts, while Cupid clamors for her attention.*—Iacopo da Ponte, called il Bassano from his birthplace, reached a modest fame and fortune when Titian bought his *Animals Going into the Ark;* he painted some good portraits—e.g., *The Bearded Man* (Chicago)—and managed to live to the age of eighty-two without leaving behind him any pictured humans not clothed from head to foot.

About 1553 there came from Verona to Venice a youth of twenty-five, Paolo Caliari, of a type contrasting sharply with Tintoretto: tranquil, friendly, sociable, self-critical, and only occasionally passionate. Like Tintoretto and nearly all educated Italians, he loved and practised music. He was generous and honorable, never offended a rival, never disappointed a patron. Venice called him il Veronese, and so the world knows him, though he adopted Venice as his home and one of his loves. He had many teachers in Verona, including his uncle Antonio Badile, who later gave him a daughter to wife; he was influenced by Giovanni Caroto and Brusasorci; but these factors in the development of his style soon faded in the warm brilliance of Venetian art and life. He never ceased to wonder at the changing skies playing their colors upon the Grand Canal; he marveled at the palaces and their tremulous reflections in the sea; he envied the aristocratic world of secure incomes, and artistic friendships, and gracious manners, and garments of silk and velvet almost more tempting to the touch than the beautiful women they enclosed. He wished himself an aristocrat; he dressed like one in lace and furs, and imitated the high code of honor

---

* This was one of many pictures taken from Italy by Hermann Goering during the Second World War, and recovered for Italy by the victory of the Allies.[84]

that he ascribed to the Venetian upper class. He hardly ever painted poor people, or poverty, or tragedy; his aim was to put this bright and fortunate world of the Venetian rich upon immortal canvas, and make it fairer and finer than wealth without art could ever be. The lords and ladies, the bishops and abbots, the doges and senators, took to him fondly; and soon he was working on a dozen commissions.

As early as 1553, when he was only twenty-five, he was asked to paint a ceiling for the Council of Ten in the Ducal Palace. There, likening the Council to Jove, he pictured *Jupiter Overthrowing the Vices*, now in the Louvre. It was not especially successful; the heavy figures cavorted precariously in the air; Paolo had not quite caught the spirit of Venice. But two years later he found himself, and touched mastery, in painting *The Triumph of Mordecai* on the ceiling of San Sebastiano; the face and figure of the Jewish hero were forcefully rendered, and the horses breathe reality. Titian himself may have been impressed, for when the Procurators of St. Mark's charged him to organize the decoration of the Libreria Vecchia with pictured medallions, he allotted three to Veronese, one each to other artists and himself. The Procurators offered a golden chain for the best medallion; Paolo won it with a representation of Music in the form of three young women—one playing a lute, another singing, a third intent upon her viola da gamba—and a Cupid at a harpsichord, and Pan puffing at his pipes. In some later pictures Veronese portrays himself wearing his golden chain.

Having acquired high repute for decorative painting, Paolo now received a lucrative assignment. The rich and lordly Barbaro family built in 1560 a luxurious villa at Macer, near that same Asolo where Caterina Cornaro played queen and Bembo played with Platonic love. The Barbari chose none but leading artists to make this "the finest pleasure house of the Renaissance":[35] Andrea Palladio to design it, Alessandro Vittoria to ornament it with sculptured stucco, Veronese to fresco the ceilings and walls, spandrels and lunettes with scenes from pagan and Christian mythology. On the vault of the central dome he pictured Olympus—the gods who knew all the joys of life but never grew old and never died. Amid ethereal scenes the impish artist introduced a hunter, a monkey, and a dog so perfect in its form and alert vitality as to be fit to be a hound of heaven. On one wall a painted page looked across a distance at a painted maid, and she at him, and for an immortal moment they too fed on ambrosia. It was such a pleasure palace as only the more refined taste of Kublai Khan's Chinese could have surpassed.

Inevitably, in this archipelago of Eros, Paolo received commissions to paint nudes. They were not his forte; he preferred rich, soft raiment covering semi-Rubensian forms topped with comely characterless faces crowned with upswept coiffures of golden hair. The *Mars and Venus* now in the Metropolitan Museum of Art shows a fat and ungainly goddess with an unshapely dropsical leg. But she is lovely in the *Venus and Adonis* of the Prado, outshone only by the dog at her feet; without a dog Paolo could not paint. The finest of Veronese's mythologies is *The Rape of Europa* in the Palace of the Doges: a landscape of dark trees, winged *putti* dropping garlands, Europa (the Phoenician princess) seating herself gaily upon the amorous bull, who licks one of her pretty feet, and turns out to be none other than Jupiter in a novel masquerade. The lucky Casanova of the skies here showed divine taste, for Europa, half robed in queenly array, is Veronese's most successful synthesis of feminine perfection, worth leaving heaven for. The distant background continues the story by showing the bull carrying Europa across the Sea to Crete, where, says a pretty legend, she gave her name to a continent.

Paolo himself took his time before surrendering to woman. He gathered samples till he was thirty-eight; then he married Elena Badile. She bore him two sons, Carlo and Gabriele; he trained both to be painters, and predicted, with more fondness than foresight, *Carletto mi vincera*—"Charlie will surpass me."[36] Like Correggio he bought a farm—at Sant' Angelo di Treviso—and spent most of his married years there, managing his finances thriftily, and seldom straying from the Veneto. He was at forty (1568) the most sought-for painter in Italy, with invitations coming even from foreign lands. When Philip II asked him to decorate the Escorial he appreciated the compliment, but resisted the lure.

Like his predecessors he was called upon to paint the sacred story for churches and worshipers.* After a thousand Madonnas we find every-

---

* Besides the pictures mentioned in the text the following are notable:
   I. FROM THE OLD TESTAMENT: *Creation of Eve* (Chicago); *Moses Saved from the Waters* (Prado); *Burning of Sodom* (Louvre); *Queen of Sheba Before Solomon* (Turin); *Bathsheba* (Lyons); *Judith Before Holofernes* (Tours); *Susanna and the Elders* (Louvre), where, for a change, the elders are more interesting than Susanna.
   II. OF THE VIRGIN: *Annunciation* (Venice); *Adoration of the Magi* (Vienna, Dresden, and London—all magnificent); *Holy Family* (Princeton); *Holy Family with St. Catherine and St. John* (Uffizi)—a major work; *Virgin, Child, and Saints*—superb (Venice); *Presentation* (Dresden); *Assumption* and *Coronation* (Venice).
   III. OF THE BAPTIST: *Preaching of St. John* (Borghese).
   IV. OF CHRIST: *Baptism* (Pitti, Brera, Washington); *Christ Disputing in the Temple* (Prado); *Jesus and the Centurion* (Prado); *Christ Revives the Daughter of Jairus* (Vienna); *Last Supper* (Brera); *Deposition* (Verona, Leningrad); *Maries at the Tomb* (Pitti).

thing fresh and attractive in the *Madonna of the Cuccino Family* (Dresden): the handsome black-bearded donors, the disconcertingly natural children, and the white-shawled figure of fate—a woman of such majestic beauty as even Venetian art seldom equaled. *The Marriage at Cana* (Louvre) was just the scene that Veronese liked to paint: Roman architecture for a background, a dog or two in the foreground, and a hundred persons in a hundred attitudes. He drew them all as if everyone were to be a major portrait, and placed among them Titian, Tintoretto, Bassano, and himself, each playing a stringed instrument. Paolo, unlike Tintoretto, cared nothing for realism; instead of making his feasters such men and women as a small Judean town might furnish, he made the host a Venetian millionaire, gave him a palace worthy of Augustus, and guests and dogs of pedigree, and provided the tables with delicate food and miraculous wine. If one should judge from Veronese, Christ had many a feast amid His tribulations: in the Louvre we see Him dining in the house of Simon the Pharisee, with Magdalen washing His feet, and splendid female figures moving about among Corinthian columns; in Turin He sups in the house of Simon the leper, and in the Venice Academy He dines in the house of Levi. But then, again, in Veronese's gallery, we see Christ fainting under the weight of the cross (Dresden), and crucified against a lowering sky, with the towers of Jerusalem dim in the distance below (Louvre). The end of the great drama is subdued: simple pilgrims supping with Christ at Emmaus, with charming children fondling the inevitable dog.

Greater than these illustrations of the New Testament are Veronese's pictures from the lives and legends of the saints: St. Helena robed in beauty, believing that she sees angels transporting the cross (London); St. Anthony tortured by a muscular youth and an angelic female (Caen); St. Jerome in the wilderness, comforted by his books (Chicago); St. George ecstatically welcoming martyrdom (San Giorgio, Venice); St. Anthony of Padua preaching to the fishes (Borghese)—a magnificent vista of sea and sky; St. Francis receiving the stigmata (Venice); St. Mennas brilliant in armor (Modena) and martyred (Prado); St. Catherine of Alexandria mystically married to the infant Christ (Santa Caterina, Venice); St. Sebastian flying the standard of faith and hope as he is led to martyrdom (San Sebastiano, Venice); St. Justina facing martyrdom with double jeopardy—in the Uffizi and in her church at Padua: all these are pictures not to be compared with the best of Titian or Tintoretto, but still meriting the name of masterpieces. Perhaps finer than any of these is *The Family of Darius Before Alexander* (London), with a somber queen and a lovely princess kneeling at the feet of the handsome and generous conqueror.

As Paolo had begun his Venetian career with painting in the Ducal Palace, so he ended it with grand murals there, fit to thrill every patriotic Venetian soul. After the fires of 1574 and 1577, the decoration of the rebuilt interiors was assigned chiefly to Tintoretto and Veronese, and the theme was to be Venice herself, undaunted by fire or war, Turks or Portuguese. In the Sala del Collegio (Audience Chamber) Paolo and his assistants painted on the carved and gilded ceiling eleven allegorical pictures of extraordinary elegance—Meekness with her lamb . . . Dialectics looking through a web of her own making . . . and Venice, a queen in ermine, with the Lion of St. Mark lying quietly at her feet, and receiving honors from Justice and Peace. In a great oval in the ceiling of the Sala del Maggior Consiglio he painted *The Triumph of Venice*, picturing the incomparable city as a goddess enthroned among pagan deities, receiving a crown of glory from the sky; at her feet the leading lords and ladies of the city, and some tributary Moors; and below these, prancing warriors ready for her defense, and pages holding hounds in leash. This was the zenith of Veronese.

In 1586 he was chosen to replace Guariento's faded fresco, *The Coronation of the Virgin*, in that same Hall of the Great Council. His sketch was made and approved, and he was preparing to paint the canvas when he was stricken with fever. Venice was shocked to learn, in April 1588, that the still young painter of her glories was dead. The fathers at San Sebastiano begged for his remains, and Paolo was buried there, beneath the pictures by which he had made that church a home of his religious art.

Time has reversed the judgment of his contemporaries, and ranks him below his robust contemporary. Technically he surpassed Tintoretto; in draftsmanship, composition, and color he was the culmination of Venetian painting. His crowded pictures are not confused; his scenes and episodes are clear, his backgrounds bright; Tintoretto seems a prince of darkness beside this idolater of light. Veronese was also the greatest decorative painter of the Italian Renaissance, ever ready to conceive some delightful turn or surprise of color and form, like the man suddenly stepping out from behind a curtain half drawn across a classic portal in a fresco at the Villa Macer. But he was too joyously intent upon surface melodies to hear the subtle overtones, tragic discords, and deeper harmonies that make the greatest paintings great. His eye was too quick, his art too eager to picture all that it saw, and more that it merely imagined—Turks at the baptism of Christ, Teutons in the house of Levi, Venetians at Emmaus, dogs everywhere. He must have loved dogs, he made so many of them. He wanted to portray the brightest aspects of the world, and did so with unmatched radiance; he pictured Venice in a sunset glow of the joy of life. In his world there are only handsome nobles, stately matrons, bewitching princesses, voluptuous blondes; and every second picture is a feast.

All the art world knows the story how the officers of the Inquisition—pursuant to a decree of the Council of Trent that all erroneous teaching must be avoided in art—summoned Veronese before them (1573), and demanded to know why he had introduced so many irreverent irrelevancies into *The Feast in the House of Levi* (Venice)—parrots, dwarfs, Germans, buffoons, halberdiers. . . . Paolo replied boldly that his "commission was to ornament the picture as seemed good to me. It was big, and with room for many figures. . . . Whenever an empty space in a picture needs filling up, I put in figures as the fancy takes me"—partly to balance the composition, and also, doubtless, to feast the observant eye. The Inquisition ordered him to amend the painting at his own cost, which he did.[37] That inquest marked the passage, in Venetian art, from the Renaissance to the Counter Reformation.

Veronese had no distinguished disciples, but his influence overleaped generations to share in molding the art of Italy, Flanders, and France. Tiepolo recaptured his decorative flair after a long intermission; Rubens studied him carefully, learned the secrets of Paolo's coloring, and inflated Veronese's plump females to Flemish amplitude. Nicolas Poussin and Claude Lorrain found in him a guide to the use of architectural ornament in their landscapes, and Charles Lebrun followed Veronese in designing vast murals. To Veronese and Correggio the painters of eighteenth-century France looked for inspiration in their idyls of *fêtes champêtres* and aristocratic lovers playing at Arcadia; here stemmed Watteau and Fragonard; here rose the rosy nudes of Boucher, the gracious children and women conceived by Greuze. Here, perhaps, Turner found something of the sunshine with which he illuminated London.

So, in Veronese's blaze of color, ended the Golden Age of the Adriatic Queen. Art could hardly go further in the direction that it had followed from Giorgione to Veronese. Technical perfection had been reached; the heights had been scaled; now there would be a slow descent until, in the eighteenth century, Tiepolo would rival Veronese in decorative painting, and Goldoni would be the Aristophanes of Venice in a last burst of splendor before the republic's death.

VI. PERSPECTIVE

As we look back across the heyday of Venetian art, and diffidently seek to assess its role in our heritage, we may say at once that only Florence and Rome rivaled it in excellence, splendor, and scope. It is true that the Venetian painters, even Titian, probed less deeply than the Florentines into the secret hopes and feelings, the despairs and tragedies of men, that often they loved the raiment and the flesh too keenly to reach the soul. Ruskin was right: after the Bellini, and excepting Lotto, real religion fades from Venetian art.[38] The Venetians could not help it if the collapse of the Crusades, the triumph and spread of Islam, the deterioration of the papacy at Avignon and in the Papal Schism, the secularization of the papacy under Sixtus IV and Alexander VI, and finally the secession of Germany and England from the Roman Church, had weakened the faith even of the faithful, and had left many vigorous spirits no better philosophy than to eat and drink and mate and disappear. But never elsewhere had Christian art and pagan art lived in such contented harmony. The same brush that painted a Virgin painted a Venus next, and no one effectively complained. Nor was it a sybaritic art or life of luxury and ease; the artists worked themselves to exhaustion, and the people whom they portrayed were often men who fought battles and governed states, or women who ruled such men.

The Venetian painters were too enamored of color to match the careful draftsmanship of the Florentine masters. But they were good draftsmen none the less. A Frenchman once said that *l'été c'est un coloriste, l'hiver c'est un dessinateur*—"summer is a colorist, winter is a designer";[39] the leafless trees reveal pure line. But those lines are still there under the green of spring, the brown of summer, and autumn's gold. Beneath the glory of color in Giorgione, Titian, Tintoretto, and Veronese there is line, but it is absorbed by the color, as the structural form of a symphony is concealed by its flow.

Venetian art and literature sang the glory of Venice even as her economy sank to ruin in a Mediterranean dominated at one end by the Turks and deserted at the other by a Europe seeking American gold. And perhaps the artists and poets were justified. No vicissitudes of trade or war could extinguish the proud memory of a marvelous century—1480-1580—during which the Mocenigo and Priuli and Loredani had made and saved imperial Venice, and the Lombardi and Leopardi had adorned her with statuary, and Sansovino and Palladio had crowned her waters with

churches and palaces, and the Bellini and Giorgione and Titian and Tintoretto and Veronese had lifted her to the art leadership of Italy, and Bembo
had sung impeccable songs, and Manutius had poured forth, to all who
cared, the literary heritage of Greece and Rome, and the irredeemable, ir-
repressible, Mephistophelean Scourge of Princes had sat enthroned on the
Grand Canal, judging and milking the world.

CHAPTER XXIII

The Waning of the Renaissance

1534-76

I. THE DECLINE OF ITALY

THE wars of invasion were not yet at an end, but they had already changed the face and character of Italy. The northern provinces had been so devastated that English envoys advised Henry VIII to leave them to Charles as a punishment. Genoa had been pillaged; Milan had been taxed to death. Venice had been subdued by the League of Cambrai and the opening of new trade routes. Rome, Prato, and Pavia had suffered sack, Florence had been starved and financially bled, Pisa had half destroyed herself in her struggle for freedom, Siena was exhausted with revolutions. Ferrara had impoverished herself in her long contest with the popes, and had dishonored herself by abetting the irresponsible attack upon Rome. The Kingdom of Naples, like Lombardy, had been ravaged and plundered by foreign armies, and had long languished under alien dynasties. Sicily was already the nursery of brigands. The only consolation of Italy was that its conquest by Charles V had probably saved it from spoliation by the Turks.

By the settlement of Bologna (1530) the control of Italy passed to Spain with two exceptions: cautious Venice retained her independence, and the chastened papacy was confirmed in its sovereignty over the States of the Church. Naples, Sicily, Sardinia, and Milan became Spanish dependencies, ruled by Spanish viceroys. Savoy and Mantua, Ferrara and Urbino, which had usually supported or connived with Charles, were allowed to keep their indigenous dukes subject to their good behavior. Genoa and Siena retained their republican forms, but as Spanish protectorates. Florence was compelled to accept another line of Medici rulers, who survived by cooperating with Spain.

The victory of Charles marked another triumph of the modern state over the Church. What Philip IV of France had begun in 1303 was completed by Charles and Luther in Germany, by Francis I in France, by Henry VIII in England, and all in Clement's pontificate. The powers of northern Europe had not only discovered the weakness of Italy, they had lost their fear of the papacy. The humiliation of Clement injured the respect that the transalpine populations had felt for the popes, and prepared them mentally for their secession from Catholic authority.

In some ways the Spanish hegemony was a boon to Italy. It put an end for a time to the wars of the Italian states against one another; and after 1559 it ended, till 1796, the battles of foreign powers on Italian soil. It gave the people some continuity of political order, and quieted the fierce individualism that had made and unmade the Renaissance. Those who craved order accepted the subjugation with relief; those who cherished freedom mourned. But soon the costs and penalties of peace by subjection damaged the economy and broke the spirit of Italy. The high taxes levied by the viceroys to sustain their pomp and soldiery, the severity of their laws, the state monopolies in grain and other necessaries, discouraged industry and commerce; and the native princes, competing in vain luxury, followed the same policy of taxing to frustration the economic activity that supported them. Shipping declined to a point where the surviving galleys could no longer protect themselves from Berber pirates, who raided ships and coasts and carried Italians off to serve Moslem dignitaries as slaves. Almost as irksome were the foreign troops quartered on Italian homes, openly despising a once unrivaled people and civilization, and contributing more than their share to the sexual laxity of the age.

Another misfortune befell Italy, more enduringly disastrous than the devastations of war and the subjection to Spain. The rounding of the Cape of Good Hope (1488) and the opening of an all-water route to India (1498) provided a cheaper means of transport between the Atlantic nations and Central Asia and the Far East than the troublesome route across the Alps to Genoa or Venice, thence to Alexandria, overland to the Red Sea, and again by ship to India. Moreover, the control of the eastern Mediterranean by the Turks made that route hazardous, subject to tribute, piracy, and war; and this was still more true of the route via Constantinople and the Black Sea. After 1498 Venetian and Genoese trade, and Florentine finance, declined. As early as 1502 the Portuguese bought so much of the available pepper in India that the Egyptian-Venetian merchants there found little left for export.[1] The price of pepper rose one third in a year on the Rialto, while in Lisbon it could be had for half the price that merchants had to charge in Venice;[2] the German traders began to desert their Fondaco on the Grand Canal and transfer their buying to Portugal. Venetian statesmanship almost solved the problem in 1504 by proposing to the

Mameluke government of Egypt a united enterprise to restore the old canal system between the Nile delta and the Red Sea; but the Turkish conquest of Egypt in 1517 blocked the plan.

In that year Luther pinned his rebel theses to the door of a Wittenberg church. The Reformation was both a cause and a result of the economic decline of Italy. It was a cause in so far as it diminished the movement of pilgrims and ecclesiastical revenues from the northern nations into Rome. It was an effect insomuch as the replacement of the Mediterranean-Egyptian route to India by the all-water route, and the development of European commerce with America, enriched the Atlantic countries while helping to impoverish Italy; German trade moved more and more down the Rhine to North Sea outlets, less and less over the mountains to Italy; Germany became commercially independent of Italy; a northward drift and pull of power wrenched Germany from the Italian web of trade and religion, and gave Germany the will and strength to stand alone.

The discovery of America had even more lasting effects upon Italy than the new route to India. Gradually the Mediterranean nations declined, left on a siding in the movement of men and goods; the Atlantic nations came to the fore, enriched with American trade and gold. This was a greater revolution in commercial routes than any that history had recorded since Greece, by her victory at Troy, had opened to her vessels the Black Sea route to Central Asia. It would be equaled and surpassed only by the airplane transformation of trade routes in the second half of the twentieth century.

The final factor in the fading of the Renaissance was the Counter Reformation. To Italy's own political disorder and moral decay, to her subjugation and desolation by foreign powers, to her loss of trade to the Atlantic nations, to her forfeiture of revenue in the Reformation, was now added a detrimental but natural change in the mood and conduct of the Church. The unformulated, perhaps unconscious, gentlemen's agreement by which the Church, while rich and apparently secure, had permitted considerable freedom of thought in the intellectual classes provided these made no attempt to disturb the faith of the people—to whom that faith was the vital poetry, discipline, and consolation of life—was ended by the German Reformation, the English secession, and the Spanish hegemony. When the people themselves began to reject the doctrines and authority of the Church, and the Reformation made converts even in Italy, the whole structure of Catholicism was threatened in its foundations, and the Church, considering herself a state, and behaving like any state imperiled in its very existence, reacted from tolerance and liberalism to a frightened conservatism that laid severe restraints upon thought, inquiry, publication, and speech. The Spanish domination affected religion as well as politics; it shared in transforming the lenient Catholicism of the Renaissance into the rigid orthodoxy of the Church after the Council of Trent (1545-63). The popes who followed Clement VII took over the Spanish system of uniting Church and state in strict control of religious and intellectual life.

Just as a Spaniard had been instrumental in establishing the Inquisition when, in the thirteenth century, the Albigensian revolt had vitally challenged the Church in southern France, and new religious orders had then been founded to serve the Church and renew the fervor of the Christian faith, so now in the sixteenth century the rigor of the Spanish Inquisition was imported into Italy, and a Spaniard founded the Jesuits (1534)—that remarkable Society of Jesus which would not only accept the old conventual vows of poverty, chastity, and obedience, but would go forth into the world to spread the orthodox faith, and to fight, everywhere in Christendom, against religious heresy or revolt. The intensity of religious debate in the age of the Reformation, the Calvinist intolerance, the mutual persecutions in England, encouraged a corresponding dogmatism in Italy;[3] the urbane Catholicism of Erasmus gave place to the militant orthodoxy of Ignatius Loyola. Liberalism is a luxury of security and peace.

That censorship of publications which had begun under Pope Sixtus IV was extended by the establishment of the *Index librorum prohibitorum* in 1559 and the Congregation of the Index in 1571. Printing facilitated censorship; it was easier to watch public printers than private copyists. So in Venice, which had been so hospitable to intellectual and political refugees, the state itself, feeling that religious division would damage social unity and order, instituted (1527) a censorship of the press, and joined with the Church in suppressing Protestant publications. Italians here and there resisted these policies; the Roman populace, on the death of Paul IV (1559), cast his statue into the Tiber, and burned the headquarters of the Inquisition to the ground.[4] But such resistance was sporadic, unorganized, and ineffectual. Authoritarianism triumphed, and a somber pessimism and resignation fell upon the spirit of the once joyous and exuberant Italian people. Even the dark Spanish dress—black cap, black doublet, black hose, black shoes—became the fashion in once colorful Italy, as if the people had put on mourning for glory departed and liberty dead.[5]

Some moral advance accompanied the intellectual retreat. The conduct of the clergy improved, now that competitive faiths put them on their mettle; and the popes and the Council of Trent reformed many ecclesiastical abuses. Whether a similar movement occured in the morals of the laity is hard to determine; apparently it is as easy to gather instances of sexual irregularity, illegitimacy, incest, obscene literature, political corruption, robbery, and brutal crime in the Italy of 1534-76 as before.[6] The *Autobiography* of Benvenuto Cellini indicates that fornication, adultery, brigandage, and murder tempered the orthodoxy of the age. Criminal law remained as severe as before: torture was frequently applied to innocent witnesses as well as to the accused, and murderers still had their flesh torn away by red-hot pincers before being hanged.[7] The restoration of slavery as a major economic institution belongs to this period. When Pope Paul III opened war upon England in 1535 he decreed that any English soldiers captured might lawfully be enslaved.[8] About 1550 the custom developed of using slaves and convicts to row the galleys of trade and war.

Nevertheless the popes of this period were men of relatively high morals in their personal life. Paul III was the greatest of them—that same Alessandro Farnese who had obtained the cardinalate through the effect of his sister's golden hair upon the spirits of Alexander VI. It is true that Paul had begotten two bastards;[9] but this had been an accepted custom in his youth, and Guicciardini could still describe him as "a man adorned with learning, and of unspotted character."[10] He had been trained as a humanist by Pomponius Laetus; his letters rivaled those of Erasmus in the classic elegance of their Latin; he was an accomplished conversationalist, and surrounded himself with capable and distinguished men. However, he was elected probably less for his talents and virtues than for his age and infirmities; he was sixty-six, and the cardinals could reasonable rely upon him to die soon and give them another chance to make bargains and receive more lucrative benefices.[11] He held them at bay for fifteen years.

For Rome his pontificate was among the happiest in the history of the city. Under his direction Latino Manetti, his *maestro delle strade*, drained, leveled, and widened streets, opened up many new public squares, replaced slum houses with handsome dwellings, and so improved one avenue—the Corso—that it became the Champs Elysées of Rome. As a diplomat Paul's greatest feat was to persuade Charles V and Francis I to a ten years' truce (1538). He almost achieved a greater aim—a reconciliation of the Church with the Protestants of Germany; but his efforts came too late. He had the courage—so lacking in Clement VII—to call a general council. Under his presidency and with his approval the Council of Trent restated the orthodox faith, reformed many ecclesiastical abuses, restored discipline and morality among the clergy, and shared with the Jesuits in saving the Latin nations for the Roman Church.

Paul's tragic failure was his nepotism. He gave Camerino to his grandson Ottavio, and he invested his son Pierluigi with Piacenza and Parma. Pierluigi was assassinated by discontented citizens, and Ottavio joined in a conspiracy against his grandfather. Paul lost his love of life, and died two years later of a heart stroke at eighty-three (1549). He was mourned by the Romans as no other pope since Pius II a century before.

II. SCIENCE AND PHILOSOPHY

In those sciences that did not affect theology Italy continued to make such moderate progress as could come from a nation predominantly disposed to art and literature, and in reaction against an intellect that had discarded conscience. Varoli, Eustachio, and Fallopio, whose names are imbedded in the terminology of modern anatomy, date from this brief age. Niccolò Tartaglia found a way to solve cubic equations; he confided his method to Jerome Cardan (Geronimo Cardano), who published it as his own (1545). Tartaglia challenged him to an algebraic duel, in which each was to propose thirty-one problems to be solved by the other. Cardan accepted, but disdainfully delegated one of his pupils to solve Tartaglia's problems. The pupil failed, Tartaglia succeeded, but Cardan wrote a strange and fascinating autobiography which has kept his head above the Lethe of time.

It begins with the startling candor that characterizes it to the end:

> Although various abortive medicines, as I have heard, were tried in vain, I was born on September 24, 1501. . . . Since Jupiter was in the ascendant and Venus ruled the horoscope, I was not maimed save in the genitals, so that from my twenty-first to my thirty-first year I was unable to lie with women; and many a time I lamented my fate, envying all other men their good fortune.[12]

This was only one of his disabilities. He stuttered, suffered all his life from hoarseness and catarrh of the throat, frequently from indigestion, palpitation of the heart, rupture, colic, dysentery, hemorrhoids, gout, itching skin, a cancerous growth on the left nipple, the plague, tertian fever, and "an annual period of sleeplessness lasting about eighty days." "In 1536 I was overtaken with an extraordinary discharge of urine; and although for nearly forty years I have been afflicted with this trouble, giving from sixty to a hundred ounces in a single day, I live well."[13]

Endowed with all this clinical experience, he became a successful physician, cured himself of almost everything except vanity, achieved the reputation of being the most sought-for physician in Italy, and was called as far afield as Scotland to cure an incurable archbishop, whom he cured. At thirty-four he gave public lectures in Milan on mathematics, and at thirty-five on medicine. In 1545, borrowing a title from Raymond Lully, he published a book, *Ars magna*, wherein he made substantial contributions to algebra—which still speaks of "Cardan's rule" for solving cubic equations. He was apparently the first to perceive that quadratic equations might have negative roots. With Tartaglia, and long before Descartes, he considered the application of algebra to geometry.[14] In *De subtilitate rerum* (1551) he discussed painting and color; in *De rerum varietate* (1557) he summarized the physical knowledge of his time; both of these books owed much to Leonardo's unpublished manuscripts.[15] Amid sickness, travels, and devastating tribulations, he wrote 230 books, of which 138 have been printed. Some he had the courage to burn.

He taught medicine in the universities of Pavia and Bologna, but so mingled his science with occultism and braggadocio that he forfeited the respect of his colleagues. He devoted a large volume to the relations between the planets and the human face. He was as expert and absurd as Freud in interpreting dreams, and as firm a believer in guardian angels as Fra Angelico. Yet he named, as the ten greatest intellects in history, men not overwhelmingly Christian: Archimedes, Aristotle, Euclid, Apollonius of Perga, Archytas of Tarentum, al-Khwarizmi, al-Kindi, Gebir, Duns Scotus, and Richard Swineshead—all scientists except Duns. Cardan made a hundred enemies, invited a thousand calumnies, married miserably, and fought unsucessfully to save his eldest son from being executed for poisoning an unfaithful wife. In 1570 he moved to Rome. He was arrested there for debt or heresy or both; but Gregory XIII released and pensioned him.

At seventy-four he wrote *De vita propria liber* (*A Book of My Own Life*)—one of three remarkable autobiographies composed in this period in Italy. With almost the garrulousness and fidelity of Montaigne, he analyzes himself—body, mind, character, habits, likes and dislikes, virtues and vices, honors and dishonors, errors and prophecies, illnesses, eccentricities, and dreams. He accuses himself of obstinacy, bitterness, unsociability, hasty judgment, pugnacity, cheating at gambling, vengefulness, and mentions "the debaucheries of the Sardanapalian life I led in the year when I was rector of the University of Padua."[16] He lists "things in which I feel that I have failed"—especially the proper rearing of his sons. But he lists also seventy-three books that mention him; tells of his many successful cures and predictions, and his invincibility in debate. He bemoans the persecutions to which he was subjected, and the hazards "that beset me on account of my unorthodox views."[17] He asks himself, "What animal do I find more treacherous, vile, and deceitful than man?" and offers no reply. But he records many things that give him happiness, including change, food, drink, sailing, music, puppies, cats, continence, and sleep. "Of all ends that man may attain, none seems more worthy or more pleasing than the recognition of truth."[18] His favorite pursuit was medicine, in which he achieved many surprising cures.

Medicine was the only science that made any significant progress in this period of Italy's decline. The greatest scientists of the age spent many years in Italy as students and teachers—Copernicus from 1496 to 1506, Vesalius from 1537 to 1546; but we must not steal them from Poland and Flanders to further honor Italy. Realdo Colombo, who succeeded Vesalius as professor of anatomy at Padua, expounded the pulmonary circulation of the blood in *De re anatomica* (1558), probably unaware that Servetus had proposed the same theory twelve years before. Colombo practised the dissection of human cadavers at Padua and Rome, apparently without ecclesiastical opposition;[19] he seems also to have vivisected dogs. Gabriele Fallopio, a pupil of Vesalius, discovered and described the semicircular canals and the *chorda tympani* of the ear, and the tubes, now named after him, that bear the ova from the ovaries to the uterus. Bartolommeo Eustachio described and gave his name to the Eustachian tube of the ear and the Eustachian valve of the heart; to him also we owe the discovery of the abducens nerve, the suprarenal bodies, and the thoracic duct. Costanzo Varoli studied the pons Varolii—a mass of nerves on the undersurface of the brain.

We have no figures as to the effects of medicine on human longevity in the Renaissance. Varoli died at thirty-two, Fallopio at forty, Colombo at forty-three, Eustachio at fifty; on the other hand Michelangelo lived to eighty-nine, Titian to ninety-nine, Luigi Cornaro to approximately a century. Born at Venice in 1467 or earlier, Luigi was rich enough to indulge in every luxury of food, drink, and love. These "excesses caused me to fall a prey to various ailments, such as pains in the stomach, frequent pains in the side, symptoms of gout . . . a low fever that was almost continuous . . .

and an unquenchable thirst. This evil condition left me nothing to hope for except that death should terminate my troubles." When he was forty his physicians abandoned all medicaments and advised him that his only hope of recovery lay in "a temperate and orderly life. . . . I was not to partake of any foods, either solid or liquid, save such as are prescribed for invalids; and of these in small quantities only." He was allowed to eat meat and drink wine, but always in moderation; and he soon reduced his total daily intake to twelve ounces of food and fourteen of wine. Within a year, he tells us, "I found myself entirely cured of all my complaints. . . . I grew most healthy, and have remained so from that time to this"[20]—i.e., age eighty-three. He found that this order and moderation of physical habits made for similar qualities and health of mind and character; his "brain remained constantly in a clear condition; . . . . melancholy, hatred, and the other passions" left him; even his esthetic sense was sharpened, and all lovely things seemed to him now more beautiful than ever before.

He spent a quiet and comfortable old age at Padua, undertook and financed public works, and wrote, at eighty-three, his autobiographical *Discorsi della vita sobria*. Tintoretto has pictured him for us in a delectable portrait: bald head but ruddy face, eyes clear and penetrating, wrinkles spelling benevolence, white beard thinned with years, hands still revealing, so near to death, an aristocratic youth. His octogenarian vivacity encourages us as he rallies those who thought life after seventy to be a meaningless valetudinarian procrastination:

> Let them come and see, and wonder at my good health, how I mount on horseback without help, how I run upstairs and uphill, how cheerful, amusing, and contented I am, how free from care and disagreeable thoughts. Peace and joy never quit me. . . . All my senses (thank God!) are in the best condition, including the sense of taste; for I enjoy more the simple food that I now take in moderation than all the delicacies that I ate in my years of disorder. . . . When I come home I see before me not one or two but eleven grandchildren. . . . I take delight in hearing them sing and play on different musical instruments. I sing myself, and find my voice better, clearer, and louder than ever. . . . . My life, therefore, is alive, not dead; nor would I exchange my old age for the youth of such as live in the service of their passions.[21]

At eighty-six, "full of health and strength," he wrote a second discourse, expressing his joy at the conversion of several friends to his way of life. At ninety-one he added a third essay, and told how "I constantly write, and with my own hand, eight hours a day, and. . . . in addition to this I walk and sing for many other hours . . . For I feel, when I leave the table, that I must sing. . . . Oh, how beautiful and sonorous my voice has become!" At ninety-two he composed "A loving exhortation . . . to all mankind to follow the orderly and temperate life."[22] He looked forward to completing a century, and to an easy death through the gradual diminution of his senses, feelings, and vital spirits. He died peacefully in 1566; some say at ninety-nine, others at one hundred and three or four. His wife, we are told, obeyed his precepts, lived to nearly a century, and died in "perfect ease of body and security of soul."[23]

We must not expect to find a major philosopher in so small a span of space and time. Iacopo Aconzio, an Italian Protestant, in a treatise *De methodo* (1558), prepared part of the way for Descartes; and in *De stratagematibus Satanae* (1565) he had the audacity to suggest that all Christianity might be reduced to a few doctrines held by all Christians, and not including the idea of the Trinity.[24] Mario Nizzoli made a path for Francis Bacon by inveighing against the continued reign of Aristotle in philosophy, appealing for direct observation against deductive reasoning, and denouncing logic as the art of proving the false to be true.[25] Bernardino Telesio of Cosenza, in *De rerum natura* (1565-86), joined Nizzoli and Pierre La Ramée in the spreading revolt against the authority of Aristotle, and called for empirical science: Nature must be explained in her own terms through the experience of our senses. What we see, said Telesio, is matter acted upon by two forces: heat coming from the sky, cold rising from the earth; heat producing expansion and motion, cold producing contraction and rest; in the conflict of these two principles lies the inner essence of all physical phenomena. These phenomena proceed according to natural causes and inherent laws, without the intervention of deity. Nature, however, is not inert; there is a soul in things as well as in man. Tommaso Campanella, Giordano Bruno, and Francis Bacon would all take something from these ideas. Some measure of liberalism must have survived in the Church to let Telesio die a natural death (1588). Twelve years later the Inquisition would burn Bruno at the stake.

III. LITERATURE

The great age of Italian scholarship was now ended: France took the torch when Julius Caesar Scaliger migrated from Verona to Agen in 1526.

Note the effect of war upon the book trade: in the last decade of the fifteenth century Florence published 179 books, Milan 228, Rome 460, Venice 1491; in the first decade of the sixteenth century Florence published 47, Milan 99, Rome 41, Venice 536.[26] The academies founded for classical scholarship—the Platonic Academy at Florence, the Roman Academy of Pomponius Laetus, the Neacademia at Venice, the Neapolitan Academy of Pontanus—died out in this period; the study of pagan philosophy was frowned upon except in a Scholastified Aristotle; and Latin gave place to Italian as the language of literature. New academies sprang up, chiefly devoted to literary and linguistic criticism, and serving as central exchanges of ears for the poets of the town. So Florence had the Della Crusca Academy (1572) and the Umidi; Venice had the Pellegrini, Padua the Eretei; and each new society took a sillier name. These academies encouraged talent and stifled genius; poets struggled to obey the rules laid down by the purists, and inspiration fled to airier haunts. Michelangelo belonged to no literary academy, and though he, like the rest, indulged his Muse in trite conceits, and forced his fire into cold Petrarchian molds, his sonnets, rough in form but warm in feeling and thought, are the best Italian poetry of the time. Luigi Alamanni fled from Florence to France, and composed a poem on agriculture—*La coltivazione*—which did not fall far short of Virgil's *Georgics* in combining tillage with poetry.* Bernardo Tasso rehearsed, in the misfortunes of his life, the vicissitudes of his famous son Torquato; his lyrics are among the choicest artificialities of the age; his epic, *Amadigi*, versified with heavy seriousness the chivalric romance, *Amadis de Gaul*. The Italian public, missing in it Ariosto's leavening humor, gave it a quiet burial.

The *novella*, or short story, had remained popular ever since *The Decameron* had given it a classic form. Written in simple language, and usually describing dramatic incidents or intimate scenes of Italian life, the *novelle* were welcomed by all ranks. Often they were read aloud to avid listeners, none more avid than the letterless, so that their audience was all Italy. We may marvel today at the broad tolerance of Renaissance women who heard these tales without reported blushing. Love, seduction, violence, adventure, humor, sentiment, descriptions of scenery, provided the material of the stories, and every class furnished types and characters.

Almost every city had a skilled practitioner of the form. At Salerno

---

* Alamanni shared with Trissino and Giovanni Rucellai the distinction of being among the first writers of blank verse—*versi sciolti*—in Italy.

Tommaso de' Guardati, known as Masuccio, published in 1476 his *Novellino* —fifty stories illustrating the generosity of princes, the incontinence of women, the vices of monks, and the hypocrisy of mankind. Less polished than Boccaccio's novelettes, they often surpass them in sincerity, power, and eloquence. At Siena the *novella* took on a highly sensuous quality, filling its pages with tales of unlicensed love. Florence had four famous *novellieri*. Franco Sacchetti, friend and imitator of Boccaccio, outwinded him by writing three hundred *novelle*, whose vulgarity and obscenity made them almost universally popular. Agnolo Firenzuola devoted many of his stories to satirizing the sins of the clergy; he described the goings-on in a dissolute convent, exposed the arts by which confessors induced pious women to leave legacies to monasteries, and himself became a monk of the Vallombrosan order. Antonfrancesco Grazzini, known to Italy as il Lasca, the Roach, excelled in comic stories, featuring the prankster Pilucca, but he could also season his dish with sex and blood, as when a husband, finding his wife in adultery with his son, cuts off their hands and feet, cuts out their eyes and tongues, and lets them bleed to death on their bed of love. Antonfrancesco Doni, a Servite monk and priest, was expelled from the cloister of the Annunciation (1540), apparently for sodomy; at Piacenza he joined a club of profligates devoted to Priapus; in Venice he became a devoted enemy of Aretino, against whom he wrote a pamphlet ominously entitled "Earthquake of Doni the Florentine, with the Ruin of the Great Colossus and Bestial Antichrist of Our Age"; meanwhile composing *novelle* noted for their pungent humor and style.

The best of the *novellieri* was Matteo Bandello, whose life spanned half a continent and most of a century (1480-1562). Born near Tortona, he was soon entered into the Dominican order, whose general was his uncle. He grew up in the monastery of Santa Maria delle Grazie in Milan; he was presumably there when Leonardo painted *The Last Supper* in the refectory, and when Beatrice d'Este was buried in the adjoining church. He lived at Mantua for six years as tutor in the ruling family, carried on a flirtation with Lucrezia Gonzaga, and saw Isabella fight with all her arts the coming of old age. Returning to Milan, he actively supported the French against the Spanish-German forces in Italy; after the French disaster at Pavia his house was burned and his library was almost totally destroyed, including a Latin dictionary which he had almost completed. He fled to France, served Cesare Fregoso, General of the Dominicans, well, and was made Bishop of Agen (1550). In his leisure hours he gathered together the 214 stories that he had written during the years, gave them their finished literary form, covered their mild indecency with his episcopal absolution, and had them printed in three volumes at Lucca (1554), and a fourth at Lyons (1573).

As in the other *novellieri*, so in Bandello the plots turn mostly on love or violence, or the morals of friars, monks, and priests. A sweet lass revenges herself upon a faithless lover by tearing him to pieces with pincers; a husband forces his adulterous wife to strangle her lover with her own hands; a convent abandoned to debauchery is described with tolerant good humor. Some of Bandello's stories provided material for exciting dramas, as when Webster took from one of them the plot for *The Duchess of Malfi*. Bandello tells with feeling and skill the romance of Romeo Montecchio and Giulietta Capelletti, and vividly conveys the passion of their love. Shall we sample him at his most romantic?

> Romeo, not daring to inquire who the damsel was, applied himself to feed his eyes on her lovely sight, and minutely considering all her movements, drank the sweet amorous poison, marvelously commending her every part and gesture. He was seated in a corner wherein, when dancing was toward, all passed before him. Giulietta (for so was the damsel called) was the daughter of the master of the house and giver of the feast. And she likewise, not knowing Romeo, but seeing withal that he was the handsomest and sprightliest youth that might be found, was marvelously pleased with his sight, and softly and furtively eyeing him a while askance, felt I know not what sweetness at heart, which all to-flooded her with exceeding delight; wherefore she would fain have had him join the dance, so she might the better see him and hear him speak, herseeming as much delight should issue from his speech as she still drank in at his eyes, what while she gazed on him; but he sat all alone and showed no wish to dance. All his study was to ogle the fair damsel, and she thought of nothing but to look upon him, and so they viewed each other on such wise that, their eyes bytimes encountering, and the flashing rays of the one and the other's glances mingling, they lightly perceived that they eyed each other amorously; more by token that, whenassoever their eyes met, both filled the air with amorous sighs, and it seemed they desired for the nonce no otherwhat than to discover one to other by speech their newborn flame.[27]

The climax in Bandello is subtler than in Shakespeare. Instead of Romeo dying before Juliet emerges from her coma, she awakes before Romeo feels the effect of the poison he has drunk in despair at her apparent death. In his joy at her recovery he forgets the poison, and the lovers have a few moments of delirious joy. When the poison wreaks its force and Romeo dies, Juliet stabs herself with his sword.*

IV. TWILIGHT IN FLORENCE: 1534-74

It is easier to rule a state in its decline than in its youth; diminished vitality almost welcomes subjugation. Florence, beaten down again by the Medici (1530), submitted wearily to domination by Clement VII; it rejoiced when the coarse tyrant Alessandro de' Medici was slain by his remote relative Lorenzino (1537); and, instead of seizing the opportunity to re-establish the republic, it accepted a second Cosimo, in hopes that he might show the wisdom and statesmanship of the first. The direct line of Cosimo *Pater Patriae* was now legally extinct; the younger Cosimo was descended from his older namesake's brother Lorenzo (1395-1440). Guicciardini manoeuvred the new ruler, then eighteen, into lordship in the hope of being the power behind the throne; but he forgot that the young Medici was the son of Giovanni delle Bande Nere and the grandson of Caterina Sforza, and therefore had at least two generations of iron in his blood. Cosimo took the reins in his own hands, and held them firmly for twenty-seven years.

His character and government mingled evil and good. He was as severe and cruel as unsentimental policy might dictate. He did not bother, like earlier Medici, to maintain republican forms and façade. He arranged a system of espionage that entered every family, and used parish priests as spies.[29] He enforced unanimity of professed religious belief, and co-operated with the Inquisition. He was greedy of wealth and power, exploited the state monopoly of grain, taxed his subjects avidly, overthrew the semi-republic of Siena to make that city, like Arezzo and Pisa, part of his dominions, and persuaded Pope Pius V to give him the title of grand duke of Tuscany (1569).

In partial compensation for the absolutism of his rule, he organized efficient administration, a reliable army and police, a competent and incorruptible judiciary. He lived simply, avoided costly ceremony and display, managed finances stringently, and left a full treasury to his son and heir. The order and safety that were now maintained on streets and highways

---

* Shakespeare took the story from Arthur Broke's *Tragical History of Romeus and Juliet* (1562); Broke took it from Masuccio or Bandello. Shakespeare also knew the tale in William Painter's *Palace of Pleasure* (1566), which took it from Bandello.[28]

revived the commerce and industry that had ailed under repeated revolutions. Cosimo brought in new manufactures, as of coral and glass; he invited and protected Portuguese Jews as a stimulus to industrial development; he enlarged Livorno (Leghorn) as a busy port. He had the marshes of the Maremma drained in an effort to free that region, and nearby Siena, from malaria. Under his conscientious despotism Siena, like Florence, became more prosperous than ever before. He used part of his levied wealth to support literature and art without extravagance and with discrimination. He raised the Accademia degli Umidi to an official position as the Accademia Fiorentina, and commissioned it to set norms for proper Tuscan usage. He befriended Vasari and Cellini, tried hard to win Michelangelo back to Florence, and founded, under his absent presidency, an Arte del Disegno, or Academy of Design. He established at Pisa (1544) a school of botany second only to Padua's in age and excellence. Doubtless Cosimo would have argued that he could not have accomplished this good had he not begun with a little evil and an iron fist.

At forty-five this iron Duke was already worn out with the strains of power and family tragedies. Within a few months, in 1562, his wife and two of his sons died from malarial fever caught during his efforts to drain the Maremma swamps. A year later he lost a daughter. In 1564 he resigned the actual government to his son Francesco. He tried to console himself with amours but found more boredom in promiscuity than in marriage. He died in 1574, aged fifty-five. He had lived up to the best and the worst in his ancestry.

Though Florence no longer produced Leonardos or Michelangelos, and had no artists to compare in this period with the urbane and universal Titian, the volcanic Tintoretto, or the festal Veronese, she experienced under her second Cosimo as vigorous a revival as could be expected from a generation that had grown up amid frustrated revolt and unsuccessful war. Even so, Cellini judged the artists employed by Cosimo to be "a band the like of which is not to be found at present in the world"[30]—which is a typically Florentine understatement of Venetian art. Benvenuto thought the Duke a patron with more taste than generosity, but perhaps this able governor considered economic reconstruction and political order more vital than the artistic decoration of his court. Vasari described Cosimo as "loving and favoring all artists, and indeed all men of genius." It was Cosimo who financed at Chiusi, Arezzo, and elsewhere the excavations that revealed a remarkable Etruscan culture, and unearthed the famous Etruscan bronze statues of *The Chimera, The Orator,* and *Minerva.* He bought back as many as he could locate of the art treasures looted from the Medici palace in 1494 and 1527, added his own collections to them, and housed the total in that palace-fortress that Luca Pitti had begun a hundred years before. Cosimo had this monstrous edifice enlarged by Bartolommeo Ammanati, and made it his official dwelling (1553).

Ammanati and Vasari were in Florence the leading architects of the age. It was Ammanati who laid out for Cosimo the famous Boboli Gardens behind the Pitti Palace, and spanned the Arno with the beautiful Santa Trinità Bridge (1567-70)—destroyed in the Second World War. He was also a painter and sculptor of quality; he won sculptural competitions from Cellini and Giovanni da Bologna, and carved the *Juno* that adorns the Bargello court. In his old age he apologized for having made many pagan figures. The Pagan Renaissance had now (1560) run its course, and Christianity was regaining its hold on the Italian mind.

Cosimo made Baccio Bandinelli his favorite sculptor, to the horror of Cellini. One of Cosimo's recreations was in hearing Cellini berate Bandinelli. Baccio was popular with himself; he proclaimed his intention to surpass Michelangelo, and was so critical of other artists that one of the gentlest, Andrea Sansovino, tried to kill him. Nearly everybody hated him, but his many commissions in Florence and Rome suggest that his talent was better than his character. When Leo X wished to duplicate the complex *Laocoön* group of the Belvedere as a gift to Francis I, Cardinal Bibbiena asked Bandinelli to undertake the assignment; Baccio promised to make a copy superior to the original. To the general dismay he almost succeeded. Clement VII was so pleased with the result that he sent authentic antiques to Francis and kept Baccio's copy for the Medici Palace in Florence, whence it passed to the Uffizi Gallery. For Clement and Alessandro de' Medici Bandinelli carved a gigantic group, *Hercules and Cacus*, which was set up on the porch of the Palazzo Vecchio beside Michelangelo's *David*. Cellini did not like it. "If your Hercules had his hair cropped," he told Bandinelli in Cosimo's presence, "he would not have skull enough to hold his brains. . . . His heavy shoulders remind one of the two baskets of a donkey's packsaddle. His chest and muscles are copied not from nature but from a bag of bad melons."[31] Clement, however, thought the *Hercules* a masterpiece, and rewarded the sculptor with a substantial property in addition to the promised fee. Baccio repaid the compliment by giving the name Clement to a bastard born to him soon after the Pope's death. His last work was a tomb prepared by him for himself and his father; as soon as it was finished he occupied it (1560). Probably he would have greater renown today had he not been invidiously immortalized by two artists who could write as well as design—Vasari and Cellini.

Giovanni da Bologna was a more genial competitor. Born at Douai, he made his way in youth to Rome (1561), resolved to be a sculptor. After a year of study there he brought a clay sample of his work to the aged Michelangelo. The old sculptor took it in his hands, pressed it here and there with his worn fingers and heavy thumbs, and in a few moments molded it to greater significance. Giovanni never forgot that visit; throughout the remainder of his eighty-four years he labored with unrelaxing ambition to equal the Titan. He started back to Flanders, but a Florentine nobleman advised him to study the art collected in Florence, and for three years maintained him in his palace. There were so many Italian artists in or near the city that it took the Fleming five years to win acceptance for his work. Then Francesco, son of Duke Cosimo, bought his *Venus*. He entered a competition to design a fountain for the Piazza della Signoria; Cosimo judged him too young for so responsible an assignment, but his model was rated best by many artists, and probably it won him an invitation to build a much larger fountain in Bologna. After that Giovanni was brought back to Florence as official sculptor for the Medici, and never lacked commissions. When he went to Rome again Vasari introduced him to the Pope as "the prince of the sculptors of Florence."[32] In 1583 he modeled a group, now in the Loggia dei Lanzi, and named in afterthought *The Rape of the Sabines:* a hero virile and muscular holds in his grasp a ravishing woman whose soft form is realistically compressed against his supporting hand, and whose back is the loveliest in the bronze sculpture of the Renaissance.

The sculptors surpassed the painters in Cosimo's galaxy and regard. Ridolfo Ghirlandaio strove but failed to maintain his father's excellence; we may sample him from his portrait of Lucrezia Summaria in Washington. Francesco Ubertini, nicknamed il Bachiacca, liked to paint historical scenes in great detail on a small scale. Iacopo Carrucci, called Pontormo from his birthplace, had every advantage and a good start; he received instruction from Leonardo, Piero di Cosimo, and Andrea del Sarto; and at nineteen (1513) he stirred the art world with a painting, now lost, that aroused the admiration of Michelangelo and was pronounced by Vasari "the finest fresco ever seen till then."[33] But soon afterward, to the disgust of the Italians, Pontormo fell in love with the engravings of Dürer, abandoned the smooth lines and harmonies of the Italian style, preferred crude and heavy Germanic forms, and pictured men and women in poses of physical or mental disturbance. In frescoes at the Certosa outside Florence Pontormo painted in this Teutonic style scenes from the passion of Christ. Vasari resented this imitation: "Was not Pontormo aware that Germans and Flemings come to learn the Italian style, which he made such effort to shake off as if it were bad?"[34] Even so, Vasari confessed the power of these frescoes. Pontormo further complicated his art by developing phobias. He never allowed death to be mentioned in his presence; he avoided feasts and crowds, lest he be crushed to death; though himself kind and gentle, he distrusted nearly everyone except his beloved pupil Bronzino. More and more he courted solitude, until he formed the habit of sleeping in an upper-story room reachable only by a ladder which he pulled up after him. On his final assignment—to fresco the main chapel of San Lorenzo—he worked for eleven years in isolation, boarding up the chapel and allowing none but himself to enter. He died (1556) before finishing the task; and when the frescoes were unveiled it was seen that the figures were badly disproportioned, the faces excited or melancholy. Let us remember him by a work of his saner maturity, the lovely portrait of Ugolino Martelli now in Washington—soft feathered hat, pensive eyes, luminous raiment, immaculate hands.

Agnolo di Cosimo di Mariano, renamed Bronzino, distinguished himself by a remarkable series of portraits, chiefly of the Medici. The Medici Palace contains a gallery of them, from Cosimo *Pater Patriae* to Duke Cosimo; and if we may judge from the pouchy face of his *Leo X*, they were often truthful. The best of them is of Giovanni delle Bande Nere (Uffizi) —a veritable Napoleon before Bonaparte—handsome, proud, and breathing fire.

Probably Duke Cosimo's favorite artist was the man to whom this and every book on the Italian Renaissance owes half its life—Giorgio Vasari. The family into which he was born at Arezzo already included several artists; he was distantly related to Luca Signorelli, and he has told us how the old painter, seeing Giorgio's boyhood drawings, encouraged him in studying design. In one of those innumerable acts of magnanimous and clairvoyant patronage that should be considered in judging the morals of the Renaissance, Cardinal Passerini, who had been appointed guardian of Ippolito and Alessandro de' Medici, took Giorgio to Florence; and there the lad of twelve shared the studies of the young heirs to wealth and power. He became a pupil of Andrea del Sarto and Michelangelo, and to the end of his life he revered Buonarroti—broken nose and all—as a god.

When the Medici were expelled from Florence in 1527, Giorgio returned to Arezzo. At eighteen, his father having died of plague, he found himself the chief support of his three sisters and two young brothers. Again kindness rescued him. His former fellow pupil, Ippolito de' Medici, invited him to Rome, where for three years Vasari sedulously studied ancient and Renaissance art; and in 1530 Alessandro, master of Florence after another restoration, called him to live and paint in the Palazzo Medici. There he made portraits of the family, including Lorenzo the Magnificent in a somber study, and the vivacious young Caterina—posing and opposing at whim, as if already conscious that she would be queen of France. When Alessandro was assassinated Vasari wandered for some time patronless. His paintings are rudely dealt with by modern critics, but they must have earned him some repute, for at Mantua he was housed by Giulio Romano, and at Venice Aretino was his burly chaperone. Wherever he went he carefully studied the local art, talked with artists or their descendants, collected drawings and made notes. Back in Rome, he painted for Bindo Altoviti a *Deposition from the Cross*, which, he tells us, "had the good fortune not to displease the greatest sculptor, painter, and architect that ever lived in our time."

It was this Michelangelo who introduced him to the second Cardinal Alessandro Farnese; and it was this cultivated prelate who, in 1546, suggested to Vasari that he should compose for the guidance of posterity the lives of the artists who had so distinguished the Italy of the preceding two hundred years. While busily serving as painter and architect in Rome, Rimini, Ravenna, Arezzo, and Florence, Giorgio devoted part of his time to the unremunerative labor of the *Lives*, "moved by love for these our artists." In 1550 he published the first edition of these *Vite de' più eccelenti pittori, scultori, ed architetti Italiani*, with an eloquent dedication to Duke Cosimo.

From 1555 to 1572 he was Cosimo's chief artist. He remodeled the interior of the Palazzo Vecchio and decorated many of its walls with paintings more immense than magnificent; he raised the vast administration building known from its governmental offices as the Uffizi, and now one of the great art galleries of the world. He led in completing the Laurentian Library, and he constructed the enclosed corridor that enabled Cosimo to pass under cover from the Palazzo Vecchio and the Uffizi across the Ponte Vecchio to the new ducal residence in the Pitti Palace. In 1567 he spent several months in travel and research, and a year later he brought out a new and much enlarged edition of the *Lives*. He died in Florence in 1574, and was buried with his ancestors in Arezzo.

He was not a great artist but he was a good man, an industrious investigator, and (barring a few bites at Bandinelli) a generous as well as intelligent critic. In simple, racy, almost colloquial Tuscan, and occasionally with the vividness of the *novelle*, he gave us one of the most interesting books of all time, from which a thousand other volumes have been cribbed. It is rich in inaccuracies, anachronisms, and contradictions, but richer still in fascinating information and judicious interpretation. It did for the artists of Renaissance Italy what Plutarch had done for the martial or civic heroes of Greece and Rome. It will remain for centuries to come one of the classics of the world's literature.

V. BENVENUTO CELLINI: 1500-71

There was in this age at the court of Cosimo a man who united in his character all the violence and sensitivity, all the mad pursuit of beauty in life and art, all the exhilarating pride of health, skill, or power, that distinguished the Renaissance; who, moreover, possessed the spontaneous capacity to pour forth his thoughts and feelings, vicissitudes and accomplishments, in one of the most engaging and unforgettable of all autobiographies. Benvenuto was not—no one man could be—completely typical of the Renaissance genius; he lacked the piety of Angelico, the craft of Machiavelli, the modesty of Castiglione, the blithe suavity of Raphael; and surely not all Italian artists of the time took the law into their own hands as Benvenuto did. Yet, as we read his turbulent narrative, we feel that his book, more than any other, more even than Vasari's *Lives*, takes us behind the scenes, and into the heart, of the Renaissance.

He begins disarmingly:

> All men, of whatsoever quality they be, who have done anything of excellence, or which may properly resemble excellence, ought, if they are persons of truth and honesty, to describe their life with their own hand; but they ought not to attempt so fine an enterprise till they have passed the age of forty. This duty occurs to my own mind, now that I am traveling beyond the term of fifty-eight years, and am in Florence, the city of my birth.

He is proud that he was "born humble" and made his family famous; at the same time he assures us that he was descended from a captain of Julius Caesar; "in a work like this," he warns us, "there will always be found occasion for natural bragging."[35] He was called Benvenuto—welcome—because his parents expected a girl and were pleasantly surprised. His grandfather (probably violating all of Cornaro's precepts) lived a hundred years; Cellini, inheriting his vitality, crowded as many into seventy-one. His father was an engineer, a worker in ivory, and a devotee of the flute; his fond hope was that Benvenuto would become a professional flutist and play in the band at the Medici court; in later years he seems to have derived more pleasure from hearing that his son had become a flutist in Pope Clement's private orchestra than from the goldsmithery by which the youth was earning florins and fame.

But Benvenuto was enamored of beautiful forms rather than of melodious sounds. He saw some of the work of Michelangelo, and caught the fever of art. He studied the cartoon for *The Battle of Pisa*, and was so impressed by it that even the Sistine Chapel ceiling seemed to him less marvelous. Against his father's pleading he apprenticed himself to a goldsmith, but in filial compromise he continued to practise the hated flute. In Filippino Lippi's house he found a book of drawings representing the art antiquities of Rome. He burned with desire to see those renowned exemplars with his own eyes, and often he talked with his friends about going to the capital. One day he and a young woodcarver, Giambattista Tasso, walking aimlessly and talking passionately, found themselves at the gate San Piero Gattolini; Benvenuto remarked that he felt himself already halfway from Florence to Rome; on a mutual dare they walked on, mile after mile, until they reached Siena, thirty-three miles away. There Gian's feet rebelled. Cellini had money enough to hire a horse; the two youths rode the one animal, and, "singing and laughing, we traveled the whole way to Rome. I had just nineteen years then, and so had the century."[36]

In Rome he found work as a goldsmith, studied the ancient remains, and earned enough to send his father consolatory sums. But the doting father pled so earnestly for his return that after two years Benvenuto went back to Florence. He had hardly domiciled himself there when he stabbed a youth in a quarrel. Thinking he had killed him, he fled again to Rome (1521). He pored over Michelangelo's paintings in the Sistine Chapel, Raphael's in the Villa Chigi and the Vatican; he noted all interesting forms and lines in men and women, metals and foliage; soon he was the best goldsmith in Rome. Clement took to him first as a flutist, then discovered his excellence in design. Cellini made such handsome coins for him that the Pope appointed him "stamp master of the papal mint"—i.e., designer of currency for the Papal States. Each cardinal had a seal, sometimes "as large as the head of a twelve-year-old child," which was used to impress the wax that sealed a letter; some such seals were worth a hundred crowns ($1250?).

Cellini engraved seals and coins, cut and set gems, modeled medallions, enameled cameos, made a hundred varieties of objects in silver and gold. These "various departments of art," he writes, "are very different from one another, so that a man who excels in one of them, if he undertakes another, hardly ever achieves the same success; whereas I strove with all my power to become equally versed in all of them; and in the proper place I shall demonstrate that I attained my object."[37]

Benvenuto brags on almost every page, but with such consistency and ardor that at last we come to believe him. He speaks of his "fine physiognomy and bodily symmetry," and we cannot deny it. "Nature bestowed on me a temperament so happy, and of such excellent parts, that I was freely able to accomplish whatever it pleased me to take in hand." Among these pleasant objects was "a girl of great beauty and grace, whom I used as a model. . . . I used frequently to pass the night with her. . . . After indulgence in sexual pleasure my slumber is sometimes very deep."[38] From one such slumber he woke to find himself host to the "French disease." In fifty days he was cured, and took another mistress.

We glimpse the lawlessness of Italian city life in the sixteenth century when we note with what easy conscience Cellini overrode the commandments of Church and state. Apparently the policing of Rome was lax and fragmentary; a man of strong instincts could be—sometimes had to be—a law unto himself. When provoked Benvenuto "felt a fever" which "would have been my death had I not resolved to give it vent";[39] when offended "I thought I ought to act as well as intone my *misereres*."[40] He fell into a hundred quarrels, and, he assures us, was in the right in all but one. He stuck a dagger into the neck of one offender, and with such matador precision that the man fell dead.[41] In another case "I stabbed him just beneath the ear. I gave him only two blows, for he fell stone dead at the second. I had not meant to kill him, but, as the saying goes, knocks are not dealt out by measure."[42]

His theology was as independent as his morality. Since he was always right (but once), he felt that God must be on his side, giving more power to his arm; he prayed to God for aid in his murders, and gave Him due credit for his success. However, when God failed to answer his prayers to help him find his lost love Angelica, he turned to devils for supplementary aid. A Sicilian sorcerer took him to the deserted Colosseum at night, drew a magic circle in the ground, lit a fire, sprinkled perfumes on the flames, and with Hebrew, Greek, and Latin invocations summoned demons to appear. Benvenuto was sure that hundreds of phantoms rose before him, and that they predicted his early reunion with Angelica. He returned to his house, and spent the rest of the night seeing devils.[43]

When the imperial army sacked Rome Cellini fled to the Castel Sant' Angelo, and served as a gunner; it was one of his shots, he avers, that killed the Duke of Bourbon; and it was his expert marksmanship that kept the besiegers at a distance from the Castle, so saving the Pope, the cardinals, and Benvenuto. We do not know how true this is; but we have it on the same authority that when Clement returned to Rome he made Cellini a mace-bearer with a salary of 200 crowns ($2500?) a year, and said: "Were I but a wealthy emperor, I would give Benvenuto as much land as my eyes could survey; yet, being now but a needy bankrupt, I will at any rate give him bread enough to satisfy his need."[44]

Paul III continued Clement's patronage. Probably exaggerating to his heart's delight, Cellini quotes Paul as saying, to one who protested his lenience with the artist: "Know then that men like Benvenuto, unique in their profession, stand above the law; and how far more, then, he who received the provocation I have heard of."[45] But Paul's son Pierluigi, as reckless a rascal as Benvenuto himself, turned the Pope against the artist. Even Cellini's arts proved inadequate to overcome such influence, and in 1537 he abandoned his shop in Rome and made for France. On the way he was handsomely entertained by Bembo at Padua, made a small portrait of him, and was in return presented with horses for himself and his two companions. They mounted and descended the Grisons, and rode through Zurich, Lausanne, Geneva, and Lyons to Paris. There too Benvenuto found enemies. Giovanni de' Rossi, Florentine painter, wanted no more rivals for the King's money; he put difficulties in the way of the newcomer; and when at last Cellini got to Francis he found him inextricably tangled in war. Ill and homesick, he climbed back over the Alps, made a pilgrimage to Loreto, and crossed the Apennines to Rome. To his dismay he found himself accused by Pierluigi of having embezzled papal jewelry. He was flung into the same Castello that he had helped to save, and suffered months of imprisonment. He escaped, but broke a leg in the process; captured, he was confined in an underground dungeon for two years. He was released at the request of Francis I, who now urgently solicited his services in France. Once more he clambered over the Alps (1540).

He found King and court at Fontana Belio—i.e., Fontainebleau; was warmly welcomed, and was assigned a castle in Paris for his workshop and home. When its occupants refused to leave he expelled them by force. The French did not like his manners or his language, and Mme d'Étampes, the

King's mistress, resented Cellini's lack of courtesy to her high estate. When she heard how he had thrown out of the castle windows the furniture of the tenants whom he had dispossessed, she warned Francis that "that devil will sack Paris one of these days."[46] The merry monarch enjoyed the story, forgave Cellini's violence for his artistry, and paid him 700 crowns a year ($8750?), 500 more for the expenses of his trip from Rome, and promised an additional sum for each work of art that Cellini should produce for him. Benvenuto was proud to learn that these were the same terms that had been given to Leonardo twenty-four years before.[47]

One of the dispossessed tenants sued him in court on a charge of stealing some effects. The court decided against Cellini. He reversed the judgment in his own striking way:

> When I perceived that my cause had been unjustly lost, I had recourse for my defense to a great dagger which I carried; for I have always taken pleasure in keeping fine weapons. The first man I attacked was the plaintiff who had sued me; and one evening I wounded him in the legs and arms so severely, taking care, however, not to kill him, that I deprived him of the use of both his legs.[48]

Apparently the plaintiff dared not press the matter further, and Cellini could turn his energies to other outlets. He had in his Paris studio "a poor young girl, Caterina; I keep her principally for my art's sake, since I cannot do without a model; but being a man also, I have used her for my pleasure."[49] However Caterina, with yielding largesse, slept also with his helper, Pagolo Micceri. Benvenuto, learning of it, beat her till he was exhausted. His servant Roberta reproved him for punishing so violently so ordinary an incident; did he not know that "there's not a husband in France without horns"? The next day he modeled from Caterina again, "during which occurred some amorous diversions; and at last, on the same hour as on the previous day, she irritated me to such a pitch that I gave her the same drubbing. So we went on for several days, repeating the same round. . . . Meanwhile I completed my work in a style which did me the greatest credit."[50] Another model, Jeanne, presented him with a daughter; he settled a dowry on the mother, "and from that time I had nothing more to do with her."[51] The child was later smothered by its nurse.

Francis bore patiently with all this lawlessness; but finally Benvenuto had so many enemies in Paris that he begged the King's permission to visit Italy. Consent was not given, but Cellini took French leave, and, after an arduous trip, found himself in his native Florence (1545). There he showed a better side of his nature, contributing materially to the support of his sister and her six daughters. He found Cosimo less openhanded than Francis. He made the usual enemies, but he cast a good portrait bust of the Duke (in the Bargello), and produced for him his most celebrated work—the *Perseus* that still stands in the Loggia dei Lanzi. He tells a vivid story of the casting. His anxieties, toil, and exposure to heat and cold culminated in a severe fever that compelled him to take to his bed just when the furnace that he had designed especially for this work was melting the metal, and this proved insufficient to fill the gigantic mold. The labor of months was about to be spoiled when Cellini rose from his bed and threw into the furnace a block of tin and two hundred pewter vessels. These proved enough; the casting was a complete success; and when the work was exposed to public view (1554) it was praised as highly as any statue made in Florence since Michelangelo's *David;* even Bandinelli said a good word for it.

From this climax the story descends to prosaic pages of haggling with the Duke about the fee for the *Perseus.* Benvenuto was long on expectations, Cosimo was short of funds. The narrative abruptly ends at 1562. It does not mention the fact, otherwise fairly well established, that in 1556 Benvenuto was twice imprisoned, apparently on charges of criminal immorality.[52] In these late years Cellini composed a treatise on the goldsmith's art—*Trattato . . . dell' Orificeria.* Having sown wild oats for half a century, he married in 1564, and had two legitimate children to add to one illegitimate child begotten in France and five generated in Florence after his return.

Of his works—usually small enough to be readily movable—only a few can now be located and identified. The Treasury of St. Peter's has an ornate silver candelabrum attributed to Cellini; the Bargello preserves his *Narcissus* and his *Ganymede,* both in marble, and both excellent; the Pitti has a salver and a pitcher in silver; the Louvre has his fine medallion of Bembo, and a lovely bronze relief called *The Nymph of Fontainebleau;* Vienna claims the saltcellar made for Francis I; the Gardner Collection in Boston has his bust of Altoviti; his large *Crucifixion* is in the Escorial. These scattered specimens hardly equip us to judge Cellini as an artist; they seem too slight for his fame, and even the *Perseus,* violent and overwrought, inclines to the baroque. Yet Clement VII (we have it on Benvenuto's word) rated him as "the greatest artist in his craft who was ever born";[53] and an extant letter of Michelangelo to Cellini reads: "I have known you all these years as the greatest goldsmith of whom the world has ever heard."[54] We may conclude that Cellini was a genius and a ruffian, a master craftsman and a murderer, whose spirited *Autobiography* outshines his silver and gold and cameos, and reconciles us to the morals of our time.

VI. LESSER LIGHTS

This age of decline for Italy was a resurrection for Savoy. As a lad of eight Emmanuel Philibert might have seen the French invade and conquer the duchy (1536). At twenty-five he inherited its crown but not its soil; at twenty-nine he played a leading part in the victory of the Spanish and the English over the French at St. Quentin (1557); and two years later France surrendered to him his ruined country and bankrupt throne. His regeneration of Savoy and Piedmont was a masterpiece of statesmanship. The Alpine slopes of his duchy were the haunts of Vaudois heretics, who were progressively transforming Catholic churches into whitewashed conventicles of Calvinist worship. Pope Pius IV offered him a year's ecclesiastical revenues to suppress the sect; Emmanuel took some drastic measures; but when these resulted in large-scale emigration he turned to a policy of tolerance, checked the ardor of the Inquisition, and gave asylum to Huguenot refugees. He founded a new university at Turin, and financed the compilation of an encyclopedia—*Teatro universale di tutte le scienze*. He was always courteous, and repeatedly unfaithful, to his wife, Margaret of Valois, who gave him wise counsel and diplomatic aid, and who presided over the bright social and intellectual life of Turin. When Emmanuel died (1580) his duchy was one of the best-governed lands in Europe. From his line in the nineteenth century would come the kings of united Italy.

Meanwhile Andrea Doria, who in the late wars had passed from the French to the Spanish side with timely treachery, maintained his leadership in Genoa. The bankers there had helped to finance the campaigns of Charles V, who repaid them by leaving undisturbed their domination of the city. Not as badly hurt as Venice by the movement of commerce out of the Mediterranean into the Atlantic, Genoa became again a great port and strategic citadel. Galeazzo Alessi of Perugia, a pupil of Michelangelo, built sumptuous churches and palaces in Genoa. Vasari described the Via Balbi as the most splendid street in Italy.*

When Francesco Maria Sforza, last of his line as rulers, died in 1535, Charles V appointed an imperial vicar to govern Milan. Subjection brought peace, and the ancient city prospered once more. Alessi built there the handsome Palazzo Marino; and Leone Leoni, engraver in the Milan mint, rivaled Cellini in the miniature plastic arts, but found no Cellini to publish his excellence. The most distinguished Milanese of the age was San Carlo Borromeo, who re-enacted at

---

* The Via Balbi was shattered in the Second World War.

the close of the Renaissance the role played by St. Ambrose in the decline of antiquity. He came of a rich patrician family; his uncle Pius IV made him a cardinal at twenty-one, and archbishop of Milan at twenty-two (1560). He was probably at that time the richest prelate in Christendom. But he renounced all his benefices except the archbishopric, gave the proceeds to charity, and consumed himself in almost fanatical devotion to the Church. He founded the order of Oblates of St. Ambrose, brought the Jesuits into Milan, and vigorously supported all movements for ecclesiastical reform that remained loyal to Catholicism. Accustomed to wealth and power, he insisted on the full medieval jurisdiction of his episcopal court, took into his hands much of the work of maintaining law and order, filled his archiepiscopal dungeons with criminals and heretics, and for twenty-four years was the real ruler of the city. Literature and art suffered under his passion for conformity and morality; but Pellegrino Tibaldi, architect and painter, flourished under his patronage, and designed the grandiose choir of the great cathedral. All the cardinal's severity was forgiven when, in the plague of 1576, while most notables fled, he stayed at his post and comforted the sick and bereaved with tireless visits, vigils, and prayers.

At Cernobbio, on Lake Como, Cardinal Tolomeo Gallio, perhaps not sure of another heaven, built the Villa d'Este (1568). At Brescia Giambattista Moroni, pupil of Moretto, painted some portraits worthy to stand beside most of Titian's.* In Cremona Vincenzo Campi carried on the family tradition of painting less than immortal pictures. At Ferrara Ercole II compromised the long quarrel of his state with the papacy by paying Paul III 180,000 ducats, and pledging 7,000 ducats tribute per year. Alfonso II gave the city another era of prosperity (1558-97), which culminated in the *Gerusalemme liberata* of Torquato Tasso and the *Pastor fido* of Giovanni Guarini. Girolamo da Carpi learned the art of painting from Garofolo, but (Vasari says) spent too much time on love and the lute, and married too soon, to indulge himself in the self-centeredness of genius.

Piacenza and Parma rose to excited prominence in this age. Though they had for centuries belonged to Milan, and that duchy was now a dependency of Charles V, Pope Paul III claimed the two cities as papal fiefs, and invested his son Pierluigi Farnese with them in 1545. Not quite two years later the new duke was assassinated at Piacenza by a revolt of nobles reconciled to his lechery but resenting his monopoly of power and plums. Paul rightly ascribed the initiative in the conspiracy to Ferrante Gonzaga, then ruling Milan as vicar for Charles; and noted that imperial troops, providentially at hand, at once took possession of Piacenza for the Emperor (1547). Soon after Paul's death Julius

---

* Notably *Portrait of an Old Gentleman* (Bergamo); *Antonio Navagero* (Milan); *Bartolommeo Bonga* (New York); *Old Man and Boy* (Boston); *Titian's Schoolmaster* (Washington); *Lodovico Madrazzo* (Chicago).

III appointed Pierluigi's son Ottavio Duke of Parma; and as Ottavio was also Charles's son-in-law, he was allowed to rule Parma till his death (1586).

No decline was visible in Bologna. Here Vignola designed the Portico de' Banchi for a group of traders; Antonio Morandi added to the University an Archiginnasio famous for its noble *cortile;* and Sebastiano Serlio wrote an architectural treatise that rivaled Palladio's in influence. In 1563 Pope Pius IV commissioned Tommaso Laureti of Palermo to set up a fountain in the Piazza di San Petronio. The sculptural part of the undertaking was offered to a young Flemish artist, who now came from Florence and perhaps received his name from the city in which he produced his greatest work. Giovanni da Bologna, or Gian Bologna, molded nine figures for the immense Fontana di Nettuno. At the summit of the group he raised a gigantic god of the waters, naked and strong; on the corners of the basin he cast in bronze four happy children in a game with leaping dolphins; at the feet of Neptune he placed four graceful maidens squeezing streams of water from their breasts. Bologna sent Gian back to Florence with florins and praise, and did not grudge the 70,000 florins ($875,-000?) that it had spent on the magnificent fountain. The spirit of civic art was still alive in Italy.

As we take our parting look at Renaissance Rome, we are struck by the rapidity of her recovery from the disaster of 1527. Clement VII had shown more skill in remedying the ruin than in preventing it. His surrender to Charles had saved the Papal States, and their revenues helped the papacy to finance the restoration of Church discipline and the partial reconstruction of Rome. The full effect of the Reformation in reduced income was not yet felt in the papal treasury; and under Paul III the spirit and splendor of the Renaissance seemed for a moment revived.

Some arts were dying, others were being born or changing form. Giulio Clovio, a Croatian domiciled with Cardinal Farnese, was almost the last of the great illuminators of manuscripts. But in 1567 Claudio Monteverdi was born at Cremona; soon opera and oratorio would be added to the arts; and the polyphonic masses of Palestrina were already celebrating the reinvigoration of the Church. The great age of Italian painting was ending; Perino del Vaga and Giovanni da Udine, epigoni of Raphael, turned the art toward decoration. Sculpture was becoming baroque; Raffaello da Montelupo and Giovanni da Montorsoli exaggerated the exaggerations of their master Michelangelo, and produced statues with limbs contorted into original but bizarre and ungainly poses.

Architecture was now the most flourishing of the arts. The Farnese Palace and Gardens on the Palatine were improved by Michelangelo (1547) and completed by Giacomo della Porta (1580). Antonio da Sangallo the Younger designed the Pauline Chapel of the Vatican (1540). In the Sala Regia—leading to the Pauline and Sistine Chapels—Pope Paul III had the marble floor and paneling designed by this Sangallo, the walls frescoed by Vasari and the Zuccari brothers, the ceiling beautifully carved in stucco by Daniele da Volterra and Perino del Vaga. The papal apartments in Sant' Angelo were embellished with frescoes and carvings by Perino, Giulio Romano, and Giovanni da Udine. The second Cardinal Ippolito d'Este built near Tivoli (1549) the earlier of two famous Villas d'Este; Pirro Ligorio prepared the plans, the Zuccari decorated the casino; and the terraced gardens still attest the fine taste and reckless wealth of the Renaissance cardinals.

The most popular architect in or about Rome in this age was Giacomo Barozzi da Vignola. Coming from Bologna to study the classic ruins, he formed his style by marrying the Pantheon of Agrippa to the Basilica of Julius Caesar, seeking to combine cupola and arches, columns and pediments; and, like Palladio, he wrote a book to propagate his principles. He achieved his first triumph at Caprarola, near Viterbo, by designing for Cardinal Farnese another vast and luxurious Palazzo Farnese (1547-9); and ten years later he built a third at Piacenza. But his most influential work was done at Rome in the Villa di Papa Giulio for Pope Julius III, the Porta del Popolo, and the church of the Gesù (1568-75). In this famous edifice, built for the rising Jesuits, Vignola designed a nave of impressive breadth and height, and converted the aisles into chapels; later architects would make this church the first clear manifestation of the baroque style—curved or contorted forms surfeited with ornament. In 1564 Vignola succeeded Michelangelo as chief architect at St. Peter's, and shared in the honor of raising the great dome that Angelo had designed.

VII. MICHELANGELO: THE LAST PHASE: 1534-64

Through all these years Michelangelo had survived as an unruly ghost from another age. He was fifty-nine when Clement died, but no one seemed to think that he had earned the right to rest. Paul III and Francesco Maria of Urbino fought over his living body. The Duke, as executor for Julius II, clamored for completion of his uncle's tomb, and flourished a contract long since signed by Angelo. But the imperious pontiff would not hear of it. "For thirty years," said Paul to Buonarroti, "I have wanted you to enter my service; and now that I am Pope will you disappoint me? That contract shall be torn up, and I'll have you work for me, come what may."[55] The Duke protested, but finally settled for a much smaller mausoleum than Julius had dreamed of. The knowledge that the tomb was an abortion shared in darkening the Titan's later years.

In 1535 the triumphant Pope issued a brief appointing Michelangelo chief architect, sculptor, and painter at the Vatican, and proclaiming his eminence in each field. The artist was made a member of the papal household, and was given a life pension of 1200 crowns ($15,000?) a year. Clement VII, shortly before his death, had asked him to paint a fresco of *The Last Judgment* behind the altar of the Sistine Chapel. Paul proposed that this commission should now be carried out. Michael was reluctant; he wanted to carve, not paint; he was happier with hammer and chisel than with the brush. The very size of the wall to be painted—sixty-six by thirty-three feet—might have given him pause. Nevertheless in September, 1535, aged sixty, he began his most famous picture.

Perhaps the repeated frustrations of his life—the maimed mausoleum of Julius, the destruction of his statue of that pope at Bologna, the unfinished façade of San Lorenzo, the unfinished Medici tombs—had accumulated in him a bitterness that poured itself into this consummation of divine wrath. Memories of Savonarola may have come back to him across forty years— those dire prophecies of doom, those denunciations of human wickedness, clerical corruption, Medicean tyranny, intellectual pride, and pagan joys, those blasts of hell-fire searing the soul of Florence; now the dead martyr would speak again, from the most intimate altar in Christendom. The somber artist whom Leonardo had called learned in Dante would soak himself anew in the brine of the *Inferno*, and put its horrors on the wall where for generations to come future popes might have that inescapable judgment before them as they read the Mass. And meanwhile, in this citadel of a religion that had till lately scorned and maligned the human body, he would be a sculptor even with the brush, and would paint that body in a hundred conditions and attitudes, in the contortions and grimaces of agony, in the drowsy then excited resurrection of the dead, in inflated angels blowing the fateful summons, in a Christ still showing His wounds, yet strong enough, with His titanic shoulders and Herculean arms, to hurl into hell those who had thought themselves superior to the commandments of God.

The sculptor in him ruined the painting. This stern puritan, who day by day became more religious, insisted on carving in color massive and muscular bodies, until the angels that art and poetry had conceived as happy children, gracious youths, or lithesome girls, became in his hands athletes racing through the skies, and damned and saved alike were worthy of salvation if only because they were made in the image and likeness of God, and even Christ Himself, in His majestic anger, became an incarnation of the *Adam* of the Sistine ceiling, a god made in the image and likeness of man. There is too much flesh here, there are too many arms and legs, biceps and swelling calves, to lift the spirit to contemplate the wages of sin. Even the lecherous Aretino thought these pullulating nudes were a bit out of place. Everyone knows how Paul III's master of ceremonies, Biagio da Cesena, complained that such a celebration of the human form would more fitly adorn a wineshop than the chapel of the popes; how Michelangelo avenged himself by painting Biagio among the damned; and how Paul, when Biagio begged him to order the erasure of the portrait, replied with excellent humor and theology that not even a pope can release a soul from hell.[56] Yielding to protests like Biagio's, Paul IV bade Daniele da Volterra paint breeches on the more glaring parts; whereupon Rome called the poor artist il Braghettone, the breeches tailor. The noblest figure in the dark panorama is completely clothed—Mary, whose raiment is the Master's last triumph in the painting of drapery, and whose look of horror and mercy is the one redeeming element in this apotheosis of human ferocity.

After six years of labor the picture was unveiled for the Christmas celebration of 1541. A Rome now entering upon a religious reaction against the Renaissance accepted *The Last Judgment* as good theology and great art. Vasari pronounced it the most wonderful of all paintings. Artists admired the anatomy, and were not offended by the muscular exaggerations, the bizarre attitudes, the carnal excess; on the contrary many painters imitated these mannerisms of the Master, and formed the mannerist school that began the decadence of Italian art. Even laymen marveled at the foreshortenings—which gave parts of the picture the semblance of relief—and the acute sense of perspective that had made the lower figures two meters in height, the middle figures three, the upper figures four. We who view the fresco today cannot judge it fairly; it has been injured by Daniele's tailoring, a further draping of some figures in 1762, and the dust and candle smoke and natural darkening of four centuries.

After some months of rest Michelangelo began (1542) work on two frescoes in the chapel that Antonio da Sangallo had built in the Vatican for Paul III. One represented the martyrdom of St. Peter, the other the conversion of St. Paul. Here again the aging artist lost himself in violent exaggerations of the human form. He was seventy-five when he completed these pictures, and he told Vasari that he painted them against his will, and with great effort and fatigue.[57]

He did not feel too old for sculpture; indeed, he said, the hammer and chisel kept him in health. Even during the painting of *The Last Judgment* he had sought refuge and consolation now and then with the marbles in his studio. In 1539 he carved his stern and powerful *Brutus* (in the Bargello), worthy of the greatest Roman portrait sculpture. Perhaps he meant it to sanction the recent tyrannicide of Alessandro de' Medici in Florence, and to serve as a reminder to future despots. Eleven years later, in a tenderer mood, he carved the *Pietà* that stands behind the high altar of the Florentine cathedral. He hoped to make this his own sepulchral monument, and he worked on it feverishly, often continuing his labor on it at night by the light of a candle fixed in his cap. But an overfurious blow of the hammer so injured the statue that he abandoned it as irrevocably spoiled. His servant Antonio Mini begged it as a gift, received it, and sold it to a Florentine. It is an astonishing product for a man of seventy-five years. The body of the dead Christ is represented without exaggeration; the figure of Mary, unfinished, is tenderness petrified; and the noble face of the hooded Nicodemus could well portray, as some have thought, Michelangelo himself, who now so often meditated on the Passion of Christ.

His religion was essentially medieval, darkened with mysticism, prophecy, and the thought of death and hell; he did not share the skepticism of Leonardo or the blithe indifference of Raphael; his favorite books were the Bible and Dante. Toward the end of his life his poetry turned more and more on religion:

> Now hath my life across a stormy sea,
>   Like a frail bark, reached that wide port where all
>   Are bidden, ere the final judgment fall,
> Of good and evil deeds to pay the fee.
> Now know I well how that fond phantasy,
>   Which made my soul the worshiper and thrall
>   Of earthly art, is vain; how criminal
> Is that which all men seek so willingly.
> These amorous thoughts which were so lightly dressed—
>   What are they when the double death is nigh?
>   The one I know for sure, the other dread.
> Painting nor sculpture now can lull to rest
>   My soul, that turns to His great love on high,
>   Whose arms to clasp us on the cross are spread.[58]

The old poet reproached himself for having composed in past years some sonnets to love. But these were apparently poetic exercises rather than passions of the flesh. The sincerest sonnets in Michelangelo's *Rime* are addressed to an elderly widow or a handsome youth. Tommaso Cavalieri was a Roman noble who played at painting. He came to Angelo (*c.* 1532) for instruction, and bewitched his teacher with the beauty of his face and form, the grace of his carriage and manners. Michael fell in love with him, and wrote to him sonnets of such frank admiration that some have been led to place Michelangelo with Leonardo among the famous homosexuals of history.[58a] Such fond expressions of man to man were common in the Renaissance, even among assiduous heterosexuals; their extreme language was part of the poetic and epistolary ritual of the time; we can draw no conclusions from them. We note, however, that—outside of poetry—Michelangelo seems to have been indifferent to women until he met Vittoria Colonna.

His friendship with her began about 1542, when she was fifty and he was sixty-seven. A woman of fifty can easily stir the embers of a sexagenarian, but Vittoria had no mind for it; she felt herself still bound to the Marquis of Pescara, now seventeen years dead. "Our friendship is stable," she wrote to Michelangelo, "and our affection very sure; it is tied with a Christian knot."[59] She sent him 143 sonnets, good but negligible; he replied in sonnets warm with admiration and devotion, but tarnished with literary conceits. When they met they talked about art and religion, and perhaps she confessed to him her sympathy with the men who were trying to reform the Church. Her influence upon him was profound; all the finest spiritual elements of life seemed gathered up in her piety, kindness, and fidelity. Something of his pessimism cleared away when she walked and talked with him; and he prayed that he might never again be the man he had been before they met. He was with her when she died (1547). For a long time thereafter he remained "downstricken as if deranged," and he reproached himself for not having kissed her face as well as her hand in those last moments.[60]

It was shortly before her death that he assumed his last and greatest responsibility in art. When Antonio da Sangallo passed away (1546), Paul III asked Michelangelo to undertake the completion of St. Peter's. The weary artist protested again that he was a sculptor, not an architect; perhaps he had not forgotten his failure with the façade of San Lorenzo. The Pope insisted, and Angelo yielded with "infinite regret"; but, Vasari adds, "I believe His Holiness was inspired by God." For this culminating task of his career the artist refused additional remuneration, though the Pope repeatedly pressed it upon him. He set to work with an energy hardly to be expected of a man in his seventy-second year.

As if St. Peter's were not burden enough he took upon himself in the same year two other major enterprises. To the Palazzo Farnese he added a third story, a cornice acclaimed by all for its beauty, and the two upper tiers of a court that Vasari judged the finest *cortile* in Europe. He designed a spacious flight of steps to the top of the Capitoline hill, and placed on the summit the ancient equestrian statue of Marcus Aurelius. Later, aged eighty-eight, he began to erect at the farther end of this plateau the Palazzo del Senatore, with its lordly double staircase; and he drew up plans for the Palazzo dei Conservatori at one side of the Senate Hall, and the Museo Capitolino at the other. Even he could not live long enough to carry out all these plans, but the structures were completed on his designs by Tommaso Cavalieri, Vignola, and Giacomo della Porta.

When Paul III died (1549) some doubt arose whether his successor, Julius III, would continue Angelo as architect-in-chief at St. Peter's. Michael had rejected Antonio da Sangallo's plan as making for so dark a church that (he said) it would have been dangerous to public morals.[61] The dead man's friends persuaded two cardinals to warn the Pope that Buonarroti was spoiling the edifice. Julius supported Angelo; but under a later pontiff, Paul IV (for popes came and went in quick succession in Michelangelo's life), the Sangallo faction returned to the attack, alleging that the artist, now eighty-one, was in his second childhood, was tearing down more than he built up, and was planning quite impossible things at San Pietro. Time and again Michael thought of resigning and accepting the repeated invitations of Duke Cosimo to resume residence in Florence; but he had conceived the dome, and would not leave his post until that conception was on the way to realization. In 1557, after years of thought on the problem, he constructed in clay a small model for the massive cupola, whose width and weight were the perilous ponderables of the enterprise. Another year was spent in making a large model in wood, and drawing up plans for construction and support. The dome was to be 138 feet in diameter and 151 feet in its own height, with its apex 334 feet from the ground; it was to rest on a corniced base upheld by four gigantic arches at the transept crossing of the church. A "lantern" or open-faced smaller cupola was to rise sixty-nine feet above the main dome, and a cross was to reach thirty-two feet higher still as the pinnacle of the whole majestic edifice, 435 feet in total height. The comparable dome that Brunellesco had raised over the cathedral of Florence, and whose beauty Michelangelo modestly pronounced unsurpassable, measured 138½ feet in width, 133 in its own height, 300 from ground to apex, 351 with its lantern. These two domes were the most audacious undertakings in the history of Renaissance architecture.

Pius IV succeeded Paul IV in 1569. Once again the enemies of the aging Titan sought to replace him. Worn out with a long war of dispute and recrimination, he submitted his resignation (1560). The Pope refused to accept it, and Michelangelo continued as chief architect of St. Peter's till his death. Then it became clear that his critics had not been wholly in the wrong. Just as in sculpture he often attacked the marble block with no other preparation than an idea in his head, so in architecture he seldom put his plans upon paper, rarely confided them even to his friends, but merely made blueprints for each part of the edifice as the time approached to build it. When he died he left no definite plans or models for any portion except the dome. Consequently his successors were free to adopt their own ideas. They changed his—and Bramante's—basic conception of a Greek cross to a Latin cross by elongating the eastern arm of the church, and fronting it with a high façade that made the cupola invisible on that side except from a quarter of a mile away. The only part of the building that is Angelo's is the cupola, which was erected from his plans, with no substantial change, by Giacomo della Porta in 1588. It is unquestionably the noblest architectural sight in Rome. Rising in stately curves from drum to lantern, it crowns with majesty the immense pile beneath, and gives to classic columns, pilasters, architraves, and pediments a comprehensive unity rivaling in splendor any known structure of the ancient world. Here again Christianity sought a reconciliation with antiquity: the temple of the worship of Christ placed the dome of the Pantheon (142 feet wide by 142 feet in total height) upon the Basilica of Constantine as Bramante had vowed to do, and dared to raise classic columns to a lofty stature unparalleled in the records of antiquity.

Michelangelo continued to work till his eighty-ninth year. In 1563, at the request of Pius IV, he transformed a part of the Baths of Diocletian into the church and convent of Santa Maria degli Angeli. He designed the Porta Pia, one of the city gates. He made for the Florentines in Rome a model for a church; Vasari, perhaps too enthusiastic about his old teacher and friend, pronounced the proposed building "as beautiful as ever man beheld";[62] but Florentine funds in Rome ran short, and the edifice was never built.

At last the Titan's incredible energy failed. About his seventy-third year he had begun to suffer from the stone. He seems to have found some palliative in medicine or mineral waters, but, he said, "I put more faith in prayers than in medicines." Twelve years later he wrote to a nephew: "As regards my condition, I am ill with all the troubles that are wont to afflict old men. The stone prevents me from passing water. My loins and back are so stiff that I often cannot climb upstairs."[63] Yet till his ninetieth year he went out in all weathers.

He took the approach of death with religious resignation and philosophical good humor. "I am so old," he remarked to Vasari, "that death often pulls me by the cape and bids me go with him."[64] A famous bronze relief by Daniele da Volterra shows a face lined with pain and haggard with age. In February, 1564, he grew weaker day by day, and spent most of the time sleeping in his old armchair. He made no will, but merely "left his soul to God, his body to the earth, and his goods to his nearest relations."[65] He died on February 18, 1564, aged eighty-nine. His body was taken to Florence and was buried in the church of Santa Croce, with ceremonies that lasted several days. Vasari devotedly designed for him a sumptuous tomb.

It was the judgment of some contemporaries, and has been the judgment of time, that despite a multitude of defects he was the greatest artist who ever lived. He exemplified fully the definition given by Ruskin of "the greatest artist"—as he "who has embodied, in the sum of his works, the greatest number of the greatest ideas"—i.e., ideas that "exercise and exalt the highest faculties of the mind."[66] He was, to begin with, a master draftsman whose drawings were among the most treasured gifts and thefts of his friends. We can see some of these drawings today in the Casa Buonarroti at Florence or in the Cabinet des Dessins of the Louvre: sketches for the façade of San Lorenzo, or for *The Last Judgment*, a lovely study for a sibyl, a *St. Anne* almost as subtly conceived as Leonardo's, and the strange drawing he made of Vittoria Colonna dead, with mystic countenance and wasted breasts. In one of the conversations reported by Francisco de Hollanda he reduced all arts to design:

> The science of design, or of fine drawing. . . . is the source and
> very essence of painting, sculpture, architecture, and of every form
> of representation, as well too as of all the sciences. He who has made
> himself a master in this art possesses a great treasure. . . . All the
> works of the human brain and hand are either design itself or a
> branch of that art.[67]

As a painter he remained a draftsman, far less interested in color than in line, seeking above all to draw an expressive form, to fix in art some human attitude, or to convey through a design a philosophy of life. The hand was that of Pheidias or Apelles, the voice was Jeremiah's or Dante's. On one of his passages between Florence and Rome he must have stopped at Orvieto and studied the nudes that Signorelli had painted there; these, and the frescoes of Giotto and Masaccio, gave some hints to a style that was nevertheless unlike anything else that history has preserved. Far beyond and above the others, even beyond Leonardo, Raphael, and Titian, he brought to his art, and brought out in his art, nobility. He did not dally with decoration or triviality; he cared nothing for prettiness, landscapes, architectural backgrounds, arabesques; he let his subject stand out stark and unadorned. His mind was caught by a high vision, to which he gave form, as well as the hand could, in the shape of sibyls, prophets, saints, heroes, and gods. His art used the human body as its medium, but those human forms were to him the tortured embodiments of his hopes and terrors, his confused philosophy, and his smoldering religious faith.

Sculpture was his favorite and characteristic art because it is the pre-eminent art of form. He never colored his statues, feeling that form was enough; even bronze had too much color for him, and he confined his sculpture to marble.[68] Whatever he painted or built was sculptural, even to St. Peter's dome. He failed as an architect (barring that sublime cupola) because he could hardly conceive a building except in terms and propor-tions of the human body, and could barely suffer it to be more than a re-ceptacle of statuary; he wanted to cover all surfaces, instead of making surfaces an element of form. Sculpture was a fever with him; the marble, he thought, obdurately hid a secret, which he was resolved to extricate; but the secret was in himself, and was too intimate for full revelation. Dona-tello helped him a little, della Quercia more, the Greeks less, in the struggle to give the inner vision outward form. He agreed with the Greeks in de-voting most of his art to the body, leaving the faces generalized and almost stereotyped, as in the female figures on the Medici tombs; but he never achieved—his temper would not let him care for—the unimpassioned repose of Greek statuary before the Hellenistic age. He had no use for a form that did not express feeling. He lacked the classic restraint and sense of proportion; he made shoulders too broad for the head, trunks too mighty for the limbs, and limbs knotted with muscles, as if all men and gods were wrestlers taut with strife. It must be admitted that in these dramatic exag-gerations of effort and emotion the art of the mannerists and the baroque was born.

Michelangelo did not found a school as Raphael did, but he trained some distinguished artists, and wielded pervasive influence. One pupil, Guglielmo della Porta, designed for Paul III, in St. Peter's, a mausoleum that could almost bear comparison with the tombs of the Medici. But generally the successors of Angelo in sculpture and painting imitated his excesses without redeeming them with his depth of thought and feeling and his technical mastery. Usually a supreme artist is the culmination of a tradition, method, style, and historical mood; his very superiority fulfills and exhausts a line of development, so that after him must come a period of helpless imitation and decline. Then slowly a new mood and tradition grow; a new conception, ideal, or technique struggles through a hundred bizarre experiments to find another discipline, some original and freshly revealing form.

The last word must be one of humility. We middling mortals, even while presuming to sit in judgment upon the gods, must not fail to recognize their divinity. We need not be ashamed to worship heroes, if our sense of discrimination is not left outside their shrines. We honor Michelangelo because through a long and tortured life he continued to create, and produced in each main field a masterpiece. We see these works torn, so to speak, out of his flesh and blood, out of his mind and heart, leaving him for a time weakened with birth. We see them taking form through a hundred thousand strokes of hammer and chisel, pencil and brush; one after another, like an immortal population, they take their place among the lasting shapes of beauty or significance. We cannot know what God is, nor understand a universe so mingled of apparent evil and good, of suffering and loveliness, destruction and sublimity; but in the presence of a mother tending her child, or of a genius giving order to chaos, meaning to matter, nobility to form or thought, we feel as close as we shall ever be to the life and mind and law that constitute the unintelligible intelligence of the world.

Envoi

IT has been a profound and grateful experience to study so many of the phases and personalities of these rich and vibrant centuries. How endless was the wealth of this Renaissance, which even in its waning produced men like Tintoretto and Veronese, Aretino and Vasari, Paul III and Palestrina, Sansovino and Palladio, Duke Cosimo and Cellini, and such art as the rooms of the Ducal Palace and St. Peter's dome! What frightening vitality there must have been in those Renaissance Italians, living amid violence, seduction, superstition, and war, yet eagerly alive to every form of beauty and artistry, and pouring forth—as if all Italy had been a volcano—the hot lava of their passions and their art, their architecture and assassinations, their sculpture and liaisons, their painting and brigandage, their Madonnas and grotesques, their hymns and macaronic verse, their obscenities and piety, their profanity and prayers! Has there ever been elsewhere such depth and intensity of Yea-saying life? To this day we feel the lifting breath of that afflatus, and our museums overflow with the spared surplus of that inspired and frenzied age.

It is difficult to judge it calmly, and we grudgingly rehearse the charges that have been brought against it. First of all, the Renaissance (limiting that term to Italy) was based materially upon the economic exploitation of the simple many by the clever few. The wealth of papal Rome came from the pious pennies of a million European homes; the splendor of Florence was the transmuted sweat of lowly proletaires who worked long hours, had no political rights, and were better off than medieval serfs only in sharing in the proud glory of civic art and the exciting stimulus of city life. Politically the Renaissance was the replacement of republican communes with mercantile oligarchies and military dictatorships. Morally it was a pagan revolt that sapped the theological supports of the moral code, and left human instincts grossly free to use as they pleased the new wealth of commerce and industry. Unchecked by censorship from a Church herself secularized and martial, the state declared itself above morality in government, diplomacy, and war.

Renaissance art (the indictment continues) was beautiful, but seldom sublime. It excelled Gothic art in detail, but fell short of it in grandeur, unity, and total effect; it rarely reached Greek perfection or Roman majesty. It was the voice of an aristocracy of wealth that divorced the artist from the artisan, uprooted him from the people, and made him dependent upon upstart princes and rich men. It lost its soul to a dead antiquity, and enslaved architecture and sculpture to ancient and alien forms. What an absurdity it was to put false Greco-Roman fronts upon Gothic churches, as Alberti did in Florence and Rimini! Perhaps the whole classical revival in art was a grievous mistake. A style once dead cannot properly be revitalized unless the civilization that it expressed can be restored; the vigor and health of the style lie in its harmony with the life and culture of its time. There was, in the great age of Greek and Roman art, a stoic restraint idealized by Greek thought and often realized in Roman character; but that restraint was quite foreign to the Renaissance spirit of freedom, passion, turbulence, and excess. What could be more contrary to the Italian temper in the fifteenth and sixteenth centuries than the flat roof and ceiling, the regular rectangular façade, the dreary rows of identical windows, that stigmatized the Renaissance palace? When Italian architecture tired of this monotony and artificial classicism, it let itself go, like a Venetian merchant robed for Titian, in excessive ornament and splendor, and fell from the classic into the baroque—*corruptio optimi pessima*.

Neither could classic sculpture express the Renaissance. For restraint is essential to sculpture; the enduring medium does not fitly embody a contortion or an agony that by its nature must be brief. Sculpture is motion immobilized, passion spent or controlled, beauty or form preserved from time by metal congealed or lasting stone. Perhaps for this reason the greatest sculptures of the Renaissance are mostly tombs or *pietàs*, in which restless man has at last achieved tranquillity. Donatello, try as he might to be classic, remained striving, aspiring, Gothic; Michelangelo was a law to himself, a Titan imprisoned in his temperament, struggling through *Slaves* and *Captives* to find esthetic peace, but ever too lawless and excited for repose. The recovered classic heritage was a burden as well as a boon; it enriched the modern soul with noble exemplars, but it almost smothered that youthful spirit—just come of age—under a falling multitude of columns, capitals, architraves, and pediments. Perhaps this resurrected antiquity, this idolatry of proportion and symmetry (even in gardens), halted the growth of a native and congenial art, precisely as the revival of Latin by the humanists impeded the development of literature in the vernacular.

Renaissance painting succeeded in expressing the color and passion of the time, and brought the art to a technical refinement never surpassed.

But it too had its faults. Its stress was on sensuous beauty, on lordly raiment and rosy flesh; even its religious pictures were a voluptuous senti-mentality, more intent upon corporeal forms than upon spiritual sig-nificance; and many a medieval crucifix reaches deeper into the soul than the demure Virgins of Renaissance art. Flemish and Dutch artists dared to picture unattractive faces and homely dress, and to seek behind these sim-ple features the secrets of character and the elements of life. How super-ficial the nudes of Venice—even the Madonnas of Raphael—seem beside the Van Eycks' *Adoration of the Lamb!* Raphael's *Julius II* is unexcelled, but is there anything in the hundred self-portraits by Italian artists that can compare with Rembrandt's honest mirrorings of himself? The popularity of portraiture in the sixteenth century suggests the rise of the *nouveaux riches*, and their hunger to see themselves in the glass of fame. The Renais-sance was a brilliant age, but through all its manifestations runs a strain of show and insincerity, a flaunting of costly costumes, a hollow fabric of precarious power unsupported by inner strength, and ready to fall into ruins at the touch of a merciless rabble, or at the distant cry of an obscure and angry monk.

Well, what shall we say to this harsh indictment of an epoch that we have loved with all the enthusiasm of youth? We shall not try to refute that indictment: though it is weighted with unfair comparisons, much of it is true. Refutations never convince, and to pit one half-truth against its opposite is vain unless the two can be merged into a larger and juster view. Of course the Renaissance culture was an aristocratic superstructure raised upon the backs of the laboring poor; but, alas, what culture has not been? Doubtless much of the literature and art could hardly have arisen without some concentration of wealth; even for righteous writers unseen toilers mine the earth, grow food, weave garments, and make ink. We shall not defend the despots; some of them deserved a Borgian garroting; many of them wasted in vain luxury the revenues drawn from their people; but neither shall we apologize for Cosimo and his grandson Lorenzo, whom the Florentines obviously preferred to a chaotic plutocracy. As for the moral laxity, it was the price of intellectual liberation; and heavy as the price was, that liberation is the invaluable birthright of the modern world, the very breath of our spirits today.

The devoted scholarship that resurrected classic letters and philosophy was chiefly the work of Italy. There the first modern literature arose, out of that resurrection and that liberation; and though no Italian writer of the age could match Erasmus or Shakespeare, Erasmus himself yearned for the clear free air of Renaissance Italy, and the England of Elizabeth owed to Italy—to "Englishmen Italianate"—the seeds of its flowering. Ariosto and Sannazaro were the models and progenitors of Spenser and Sidney, and Machiavelli and Castiglione were powerful influences in Elizabethan and Jacobean England. It is not certain that Bacon and Descartes could have done their work had not Pomponazzi and Machiavelli, Telesio and Bruno paved the way with their sweat and blood.

Yes, Renaissance architecture is depressingly horizontal, always excepting the lordly cupolas that rise over Florence and Rome. The Gothic style, ecstatically vertical, reflected a religion that pictured our terrestrial life as an exile for the soul, and placed its hopes and gods in the sky; classic architecture expressed a religion that lodged its deities in trees and streams and in the earth, and rarely higher than a mountain in Thessaly; it did not look upward to find divinity. That classic style, so cool and calm, could not fitly represent the turbulent Renaissance, but neither could it be allowed to die; rightly a generous emulation preserved its monuments, and transmitted its ideals and principals to be a part—a sharer but not a dictator —of our building art today. Italy could not equal Greek or Gothic architecture, nor Greek sculpture, nor, perhaps, the noblest flights of Gothic sculpture at Chartres and Reims; but it could produce an artist whose Medici tombs were worthy of Pheidias, and his *Pietà* of Praxiteles.

For Renaissance painting there shall be no word of apology; it is still the high point of that art in history. Spain approached that zenith in the halcyon days of Velásquez, Murillo, Ribera, Zurbarán, and El Greco; Flanders and Holland came not quite so close in Rubens and Rembrandt. Chinese and Japanese painters scale heights of their own, and at times their pictures impress us as especially profound, if only because they see man in a large perspective; yet their cold, contemplative philosophy or decorative elegance is outweighed by the richer range of complexity and power, and the warm vitality of color, in the pictorial art of the Florentines, of Raphael and Correggio and the Venetians. Indeed, Renaissance painting was a sensual art, though it produced some of the greatest religious paintings, and—as on the Sistine ceiling—some of the most spiritual and sublime. But that sensuality was a wholesome reaction. The body had been vilified long enough; woman had borne through ungracious centuries the abuse of a harsh asceticism; it was good that life should reaffirm, and art enhance, the loveliness of healthy human forms. The Renaissance had tired of original sin, breast-beating, and mythical post-mortem terrors; it turned its back upon death and its face to life; and long before Schiller and Beethoven it sang an exhilarating, incomparable ode to joy.

The Renaissance, by recalling classic culture, ended the thousand-year rule of the Oriental mind in Europe. From Italy by a hundred routes the good news of the great liberation passed over mountains and seas to France, Germany, Flanders, Holland, and England. Scholars like Aleandro and Scaliger, artists like Leonardo, del Sarto, Primaticcio, Cellini, and Bordone took the Renaissance to France; Italian painters, sculptors, architects took it to Pesth, Cracow, Warsaw; Michelozzo carried it to Cyprus; Gentile Bellini ventured with it to Istanbul. From Italy Colet and Linacre brought it back with them to England, Agricola and Reuchlin to Germany. The flow of ideas, morals, and arts continued to run northward from Italy for a century. From 1500 to 1600 all western Europe acknowledged her as the mother and nurse of the new civilization of science and art and the "humanities"; even the idea of the gentleman, and the aristocratic conception of life and government, came up from the south to mold the manners and states of the north. So the sixteenth century, when the Renaissance declined in Italy, was an age of exuberant germination in France, England, Germany, Flanders, and Spain.

For a time the tensions of Reformation and Counter Reformation, the debates of theology and the wars of religion, overlaid and overwhelmed the influence of the Renaissance; men fought through a bloody century for the freedom to believe and worship as they pleased, or as pleased their kings; and the voice of reason seemed stilled by the clash of militant faiths. But it was not altogether silent; even in that unhappy desolation men like Erasmus, Bacon, and Descartes echoed it bravely, gave it fresh and stronger utterance; Spinoza found for it a majestic formulation; and in the eighteenth century the spirit of the Italian Renaissance was reborn in the French Enlightenment. From Voltaire and Gibbon to Goethe and Heine, to Hugo and Flaubert, to Taine and Anatole France, the strain was carried on, through revolution and counterrevolution, through advance and reaction, somehow surviving war, and patiently ennobling peace. Everywhere today in Europe and the Americas there are urbane and lusty spirits—comrades in the Country of the Mind—who feed and live on this legacy of mental freedom, esthetic sensitivity, friendly and sympathetic understanding; forgiving life its tragedies, embracing its joys of sense, mind, and soul; and hearing ever in their hearts, amid hymns of hate and above the cannon's roar, the song of the Renaissance.

THANK YOU, FRIEND READER

Bibliographical Guide

to editions referred to in the Notes

Books starred are recommended for further study

ABRAHAMS, ISRAEL, Jewish Life in the Middle Ages, Philadelphia, 1896.
ADAMS, BROOKS, The New Empire, New York, 1903.
ADDISON, JOSEPH, *et al.*, The Spectator, New York, 1881, 8v.
ADDISON, JULIA D., Arts and Crafts in the Middle Ages, Boston, 1908.
ANDERSON, W. J., Architecture of the Renaissance in Italy, London, 1898.
ARETINO, PIETRO, Works: Dialogues, New York, 1926.
ARIOSTO, LODOVICO, Orlando furioso, Firenze, n.d.
ASCHAM, ROGER, The Scholemaster, London, 1863.
ASHLEY, W. J., Introduction to English Economic History and Theory, New
        York, 1894 and 1936, 2v.

*BACON, FRANCIS, Philosophical Works, ed. J. M. Robertson, London, 1905.
BAEDEKER, KARL, Northern Italy, London, 1913.
BALCARRES, LORD, Evolution of Italian Sculpture, London, 1909.
BANDELLO, MATTEO, Novels, tr. Payne, London, 1890, 6v.
*BARNES, H. E., History of Western Civilization, New York, 1935, 2v.
BASLER, E., Leonardo, Collection des maîtres, Braun, Paris, n.d.
BEARD, MIRIAM, History of the Business Man, New York, 1938.
BEAZLEY, C. R., The Dawn of Modern Geography, Oxford, 1906, 3v.
BERENSON, BERNARD, Florentine Painters of the Renaissance, New York, 1912.
BERENSON, BERNARD, North Italian Painters of the Renaissance, New York,
        1927.
BERENSON, BERNARD, Study and Criticism of Italian Art, London, 1901-17, 3v.
BERENSON, BERNARD, Venetian Painters of the Renaissance, New York, 1897.
BEUF, CARLO, Cesare Borgia, Oxford University Press, 1942.
BOCCACCIO, GIOVANNI, Amorous Fiammetta, New York, 1931.
BOCCACCIO, GIOVANNI, Decameron, New York, n.d.
BOISSONNADE, P., Life and Work in Medieval Europe, New York, 1927.
BRINTON, SELWYN, The Gonzaga Lords of Mantua, London, 1927.
*BURCKHARDT, JACOB, The Civilization of the Renaissance in Italy, London,
        1914.

CAMBRIDGE MEDIEVAL HISTORY, New York, 1924f, 8v.
CAMBRIDGE MODERN HISTORY, New York, 1907f, 12v.
CARDAN, JEROME, The Book of My Life (De vita propria liber), New York,
        1930.
CARLYLE, R. W., History of Medieval Political Theory in the West, Edin-
        burgh, 1928, 6v.

*Cartwright, Julia, Beatrice d'Este, London, 1928.
*Cartwright, Julia, Isabella d'Este, London, 1915, 2v.
*Cartwright, Julia, Baldassare Castiglione, London, 1908.
*Castiglione, Baldassare, The Courtier, Everyman's Library.
 Castiglioni, A., History of Medicine, New York, 1941.
*Cellini, Benvenuto, Autobiography, tr. J. A. Symonds, Garden City, New
          York, 1948.
*Chubb, Thomas C., Aretino, Scourge of Princes, New York, 1940.
 Commines, Philippe de, Memoirs, London, 1900, 2v.
*Cornaro, L., Art of Living Long (De vita sobria), Milwaukee, 1903.
 Coulton, G. G., The Black Death, New York, 1930.
 Coulton, G. G., Five Centuries of Religion, Cambridge University Press,
          1923f, 4v.
 Coulton, G. G., From St. Francis to Dante, a tr. of the Chronicle of Salim-
          bene, London, 1908.
 Coulton, G. G., Inquisition and Liberty, London, 1938.
 Coulton, G. G., Life in the Middle Ages, Cambridge University Press,
          1930, 4v.
 Coulton, G. G., Medieval Panorama, New York, 1944.
*Craven, Thomas, Treasury of Art Masterpieces, revised ed., New York, 1952.
*Creighton, Mandell, History of the Papacy during the Reformation, London,
          1882, 4v.
 Croce, Benedetto, Ariosto, Shakespeare, and Corneille, New York, 1920.
 Crowe, J. A., and Cavalcaselle, G. B., A New History of Painting in Italy,
          London, 1864, 3v.
 Crump, C. G., and Jacob, E. F., The Legacy of the Middle Ages, Oxford,
          1926.

 Dante, La commedia divina, ed. Paget Toynbee, London, 1900.
 Dillon, Edward, Glass, New York, 1907.
 Dopsch, Alfons, Economic and Social Foundations of European Civilization,
          New York, 1937.
 Duhem, P., Études sur Léonard de Vinci: Ceux qu'il a lus et ceux qui l'ont lu,
          Paris, 1906f, 3v.

 Einstein, Alfred, The Italian Madrigal, Princeton, 1949, 3v.
 Ellis, Havelock, Studies in the Psychology of Sex, Philadelphia, 1911, 6v.
*Emerton, Ephraim, The Defensor Pacis of Marsiglio of Padua, Harvard Uni-
          versity Press, 1920.
 Emporium: Rivista mensile d'arte e di cultura, LXXXIX, no. 534 (June, 1939),
          Bergamo.
 Encyclopaedia Britannica, 11th ed. when so specified.
 Encyclopaedia Britannica, 14th ed. when no edition is specified.

*Fattorusso, J., Wonders of Italy, Florence, 1930.
 Fattorusso, J., Florence Album, Florence, 1935. (Part of preceding)

*Faure, Élie, The Spirit of Forms, tr. Walter Pach, New York, 1937.
Ferrara, Orestes, The Borgia Pope, Alexander VI, New York, 1940.
Figgis, J. N., From Gerson to Grotius, Cambridge University Press, 1916.
Foligno, Cesare, The Story of Padua, London, 1910.
Freud, Sigmund, Leonardo da Vinci, New York, 1947.
Friedländer, L., Roman Life and Manners under the Early Empire, London,
    n.d., 4v.

Garrison, F., History of Medicine, Philadelphia, 1929.
Genoa, a Descriptive Booklet, Genoa, 1949.
*Gibbon, Edward, Decline and Fall of the Roman Empire, Everyman's Li-
    brary, 6v.
Gierke, Otto, Political Theories of the Middle Age, Cambridge University
    Press, 1922.
Gregorovius, Ferdinand, History of the City of Rome in the Middle Ages,
    London, 1900, 8v.
*Gregorovius, Ferdinand, Lucrezia Borgia, London, 1901.
Gronau, G., Titian, London, 1904.
Grove, Sir George, Dictionary of Music and Musicians, 3rd ed., New York,
    1928, 5v.
*Guicciardini, Francesco, History of the Wars in Italy, London, 1753, 10v.
Guizot, François Pierre, History of France, London, 1872, 8v.

Hallam, Henry, Introduction to the Literature of Europe in the 15th, 16th,
    and 17th Centuries, New York, 1880, 4v. in 2.
Hare, A. J. C., Walks in Rome, London, 1913.
Hearnshaw, F. J. C., ed., Medieval Contributions to Modern Civilization,
    New York, 1922.
Hegel, G. W. F., Philosophy of History, London, 1888.
Hollway-Calthrop, H. C., Petrarch, His Life and Times, New York, 1907.
Holzknecht, Karl, The Backgrounds of Shakespeare's Plays, New York,
    1950.
Huizinga, J., The Waning of the Middle Ages, London, 1948.
Huneker, James, Egoists, New York, 1910.
Hutton, Edward, Giovanni Boccaccio, London, 1910.

James, E. E. Coulson, Bologna, London, 1909.
Jusserand, J. J., English Wayfaring Life in the Middle Ages, London, 1891.

*Lacroix, Paul, Arts of the Middle Ages, London, n.d.
Lacroix, Paul, History of Prostitution, New York, 1931.
Lacroix, Paul, Science and Literature in the Middle Ages, London, n.d.
Lanciani, Rodolfo, Ancient Rome, Boston, 1889.
Lanciani, Rodolfo, The Golden Days of the Renaissance in Rome, Boston,
    1906.
*Lang, P. H., Music in Western Civilization, New York, 1941.

LA TOUR, P. IMBART DE, Les Origines de la Réforme, Paris, 1905f, 4v.
LEA, H. C., History of Agricular Confession, Philadelphia, 1896, 3v.
*LEA, H. C., History of the Inquisition in the Middle Ages, New York, 1888, 3v.
LEONARDO DA VINCI, Phaidon ed., London, 1943.
*LEONARDO DA VINCI, Notebooks, arranged, rendered into English, and introduced by Edward MacCurdy, New York, 1938, 2v.
LOMBARDIA: Vols. II and III of Attraverso l'Italia, issued by Touring Club Italiano, Milan, 1931, 2v.

*MACHIAVELLI, NICCOLÒ, Discourses, Modern Library.
MACHIAVELLI, NICCOLÒ, History of Florence, London, 1851.
*MACHIAVELLI, NICCOLÒ, The Prince, Modern Library.
MANTEGNA, ANDREA, L'oeuvre, Paris, 1911.
*MATHER, F. J., Venetian Painters, New York, 1936.
MATHER, F. J., Western European Painting of the Renaissance, New York, 1948.
MAULDE LA CLAVIÈRE, R. DE, The Women of the Renaissance, New York, 1905.
*MICHELET, JULES, Histoire de France, Paris, n.d., 5v.
*MICHELET, JULES, History of France, New York, 1880, 2v., an English tr. of first two volumes of preceding.
*MILMAN, H. H., History of Latin Christianity, New York, 1860, 8v.
MINIATURES OF THE RENAISSANCE, Catalogue de l'exposition du 5ème centenaire de la bibliothèque vaticane, Rome, 1950.
*MOLMENTI, POMPEO, Venice, London, 1906, 6v.
MONTALEMBERT, COMTE, DE, The Monks of the West, Boston, n.d., 2v.
*MOREY, C. R., Medieval Art, New York, 1942.
*MÜNTZ, EUGÈNE, Leonardo da Vinci, London, 1898, 2v.
*MÜNTZ, EUGÈNE, Raphael, London, 1882.

NOYES, ELLA, Story of Ferrara, London, 1904.
*NOYES, ELLA, Story of Milan, London, 1908.
NUSSBAUM, F. L., History of the Economic Institutions of Modern Europe, New York, 1937.

OGG, FREDERIC, Source Book of Medieval History, New York, 1907.
OWEN, JOHN, Sceptics of the Italian Renaissance, London, 1908.
OXFORD HISTORY OF MUSIC, Introductory Volume, Oxford University Press, 1929.

*PASTOR, LUDWIG VON, History of the Popes, St. Louis, Missouri, 1898, 14v.
*PATER, WALTER, The Renaissance, Modern Library.
PETRARCH, Sonnets and Other Poems, London, 1904.
*PETRARCH, Sonnets, tr. Joseph Auslander, New York, 1931.
PIRENNE, HENRI, Economic and Social History of Medieval Europe, New York, n.d.

POPHAM, A. E., Drawings of Leonardo da Vinci, London, 1947.

PORTIGLIOTTI, GIUSEPPE, The Borgia, New York, 1928.

*PRESCOTT, W. H., History of the Reign of Ferdinand and Isabella the Catholic, Philadelphia, 1890, 2v.

PUTNAM, GEORGE H., Books and Their Makers during the Middle Ages, New York, 1898.

*RANKE, LEOPOLD VON, History of the Popes, London, 1878, 3v.

RASHDALL, HASTINGS, The Universities of Europe in the Middle Ages, Oxford, 1936, 3v.

RÉNAN, ERNEST, Averroès et l'averroïsme, Paris, n.d.

RENARD, GEORGES, Guilds in the Middle Ages, London, 1918.

RICHTER, JEAN PAUL, Literary Works of Leonardo da Vinci, London, 1883, 2v.

ROBERTSON, J. M., Short History of Freethought, London, 1914, 2v.

*ROBINSON, J. H., and ROLF, H. W., Petrarch, New York, 1898.

*ROEDER, RALPH, The Man of the Renaissance, New York, 1935.

ROGERS, J. E. T., Economic Interpretation of History, London, 1891.

*ROSCOE, WILLIAM, Life and Pontificate of Leo X, London, 1853, 2v.

*ROSCOE, WILLIAM, Life of Lorenzo de' Medici, London, 1877.

RUSKIN, JOHN, Modern Painters, Boston, n.d., 5v.

RUSKIN, JOHN, Stones of Venice, Everyman's Library, 3v.

SACERDOTE, GUSTAVO, Cesare Borgia: La sua vita, la sua famiglia, i suoi tempi, Milan, 1950.

*SARTON, GEORGE, Introduction to the History of Science, Baltimore, 1930f, 3v. in 5.

*SCHEVILL, F., Siena, New York, 1909.

SISMONDI, J. C. L., History of the Italian Republics, London, n.d.

SIVIERO, R., Catalogue of the 2d National Exhibition of the Works of Art Recovered in Germany, Florence, 1950.

SOULIER, G., Le Tintoret, Paris, 1928.

SPECULUM: a Journal of Medieval Studies, Cambridge, Massachusetts.

*SPENGLER, OTTO, Decline of the West, New York, 1928.

STOECKLIN, PAUL DE, Le Corrège, Paris, 1928.

*SYMONDS, J. A., Life of Michelangelo Buonarroti, Modern Library.

*SYMONDS, J. A., The Renaissance in Italy, New York, 1883:
    Vol. I: The Age of the Despots;
    Vol. II: The Revival of Learning;
    Vol. III: The Fine Arts;
    Vol. IV: Italian Literature, Part I;
    Vol. V: Italian Literature, Part II;
    Vol. VI: The Catholic Reaction, Part I, London, 1914;
    Vol. VII: The Catholic Reaction, Part II.

SYMONDS, J. A., Sketches and Studies in Italy and Greece, London, 1898, 3v.

*TAINE, H. A., Italy: Florence and Venice, New York, 1869.

*TAINE, H. A., Italy: Rome and Naples, New York, 1889.

TAYLOR, RACHEL A., Leonardo the Florentine, New York, 1927.

THOMPSON, JAMES W., Economic and Social History of Europe in the Later
        Middle Ages, New York, 1931.

THORNDIKE, LYNN, History of Magic and Experimental Science, New York,
        1929f, 6v.

THORNDIKE, LYNN, History of Medieval Europe, Boston, 1949.

THORNDIKE, LYNN, Science and Thought in the Fifteenth Century, New York,
        1929.

TREITSCHKE, H. VON, Lectures on Politics, New York, n.d.

VARCHI, BENEDETTO, Storia fiorentina, Cologne, 1721.

*VASARI, GIORGIO, Lives of the Most Eminent Painters, Sculptors, and Archi-
        tects, Everyman's Library, 4v.

        Same, ed. E. H. & E. W. Blashfield, and A. A. Hopkins, New York,
        1907; references to Vol. IV are to this edition.

VASILIEV, A. A., History of the Byzantine Empire, Madison, 1921, 2v.

VENTURI, LIONELLO, and SKIRA-VENTURI, ROSABIANCA, Italian Painting: The
        Creators of the Renaissance, Geneva, 1950.

VILLARI, PASQUALE, Life and Times of Girolamo Savonarola. New York, 1896.

*VILLARI, PASQUALE, Life and Times of Niccolò Machiavelli, New York, n.d.,
        2v.

VILLARI, PASQUALE, The Two First Centuries of Florentine History, London,
        1908.

WALSH, JAMES J., The Popes and Science, New York, 1913.

WHITCOMB, M., Literary Source-Book of the Italian Renaissance, Philadelphia,
        1900.

WINCKELMANN, J., History of Ancient Art, Boston, 1880, 4v. in 2.

WOLF, A., History of Science, Technology, and Philosophy in the 16th and
        17th Centuries, New York, 1935.

WRIGHT, THOMAS, The Homes of Other Days, London, 1871.

YOUNG, G. F., The Medici, Modern Library.

Notes

CHAPTER I

1. Carlyle, R. W., *History of Medieval Political Theory*, VI, 85-6.
2. In Hollway-Calthrop, *Petrarch, His Life and Times*, 14.
2a. Robinson, J. H., and Rolf, H. W., *Petrarch*, 67, 82.
3. Marquis de Sade, *Mémoires pour la vie de Pétrarque*, III, 243, in Prescott, *Ferdinand and Isabella*, I, 328n.
4. Petrarch, *Sonnets and Other Poems*, sonnet 159.
5. Petrarch, *Sonnets*, tr. Jos. Auslander, 126.
6. *Epistolae variae*, no. 25, in Whitcomb, *Literary Source-book of the Italian Renaissance*, 13.
7. Renan, *Averroès*, 328.
8. Robinson and Rolf, 107.
9. Hutton, E., *Giovanni Boccaccio*, 3-5.
10. Ibid., 25, quoting the *Filocolo*.
11. *Encycl. Brit.*, III, 766b.
12. Boccaccio, *Filostrato*, iii, 32.
13. Gregorovius, F., *History of the City of Rome*, VI, 245.
14. Robinson and Rolf, 426.
15. Ibid., 137.
16. Ibid., 61, 97n.
17. *Speculum*, Apr., 1936, p. 267.
18. In Hollway-Calthrop, 21.
19. Owen, John, *Sceptics of the Italian Renaissance*, 110, 117.
20. Robinson and Rolf, 137.
21. *Epistolae rerum senilium*, i, 5, in Owen, 121.
22. Sismondi, *History of the Italian Republics*, 333.
23. Gregorovius, VI, 246.
24. Ibid., 252f.
25. Ibid., 271, 253.
26. Robinson and Rolf, 347.
27. Gregorovius, VI, 370-3; Sismondi, 340-1.
28. In Foligno, C., *Story of Padua*, 155.
29. Owen, 130.
30. Fattorusso, J., *Wonders of Italy*, 215.
31. Beard, Miriam, *History of the Business Man*, 141.
32. In Taylor, Rachel A., *Leonardo the Florentine*, 60.
33. Vasari, *Lives of the Painters*, Giotto, I, 66.
34. Dante, *La commedia divina*, Purgatorio, xi, 94.
35. Vasari, *Taddeo Gaddi*, I, 139.
36. Villari, Pasquale, *The Two First Centuries of Florentine History*, 50.
37. Boccaccio, *Amorous Fiammetta*, 39.
38. Castiglioni, *History of Medicine*, 355.
39. Coulton, G. G., *Black Death*, 10-11.
40. *Cambridge Modern History*, I, 501.
41. In Schevill, F., *Siena*, 210.
42. Machiavelli, *History of Florence*, ii, 9.
43. Boccaccio, *Decameron*, 2-7.
44. Ibid., 11.
45. Ibid., 13.
46. Dante, *Inferno*, xxviii, 22-42.
47. *Decameron*, Introd. to Sixth Day.
48. *Cambridge Medieval History*, VII, 756.
49. Hollway-Calthrop, 290.
50. Robinson and Rolf, 413.
51. Ibid., 119.
52. *Genoa, a Descriptive Booklet*, 6.
53. Crump and Jacob, *Legacy of the Middle Ages*, 442; *Cambridge Medieval History*, VI, 490.
54. In Sismondi, 527.
54a. Burckhardt, J., *Civilization of the Renaissance in Italy*, 79.
55. In Mather, F. J., *Venetian Painters*, 5.
56. Hutton, *Boccaccio*, 201.
57. Hollway-Calthrop, 257.
58. Ibid., 280.
59. Robinson and Rolf, 428.
60. Symonds, *Age of the Despots*, 73.
61. Hollway-Calthrop, 123.
62. Robinson and Rolf, 4.

CHAPTER II

1. Sismondi, 306; Coulton, G. G., *Life in the Middle Ages*, I, 205.
2. Milman, H. H., *History of Latin Christianity*, VII, 205.
3. Gregorovius, VI, 193.
4. Creighton, M., *History of the Papacy During the Reformation*, I, 42; Gregorovius, 192.
5. Milman, VII, 136.
6. Ibid., 137.
7. *Cambridge Medieval History*, VII, 273f; Rogers, J. E. T., *Economic Interpretation of History*, 75; Pastor, *History of the Popes*, I, 98.

8. Ibid., 66, 71.
9. Ibid.
10. Ibid., 92.
11. Coulton, *Life in the Middle Ages*, I, 205.
12. *Cambridge Medieval History*, VII, 288; Milman, VII, 138n.
13. Pastor, I, 107.
14. Sarton, G., *Introd. to the History of Science*, IIIb, 1034.
15. Pastor, I, 91.
16. Machiavelli, *History of Florence*, i, 6.
17. Sismondi, 328.
18. Gregorovius, VI, 436.
19. Ibid., 450.
20. Sismondi, 437.
21. Pastor, I, 100.
22. Ibid., 103.
23. Sismondi, 439.
24. In Pastor, I, 105.
25. Lanciani, R., *Golden Days of the Renaissance in Rome*, 1.
26. Lea, H. C., *History of the Inquisition in the Middle Ages*, III, 90-120; Milman, VII, 41-51.
27. Beazley, C. R., *Dawn of Modern Geography*, III, 181.
28. Coulton, G. G., *Medieval Panorama*, 650.
29. Sismondi, 458.
30. Gregorovius, VI, 522.
31. Pastor, I, 232.
32. Coulton, *Inquisition and Liberty*, 45.

CHAPTER III

1. Thompson, James W., *Economic and Social History of Europe in the Later Middle Ages*, 458.
2. Beard, Miriam, *History of the Business Man*, 134.
3. Cellini, B., *Autobiography*, i, 69.
4. *Cambridge Medieval History*, VI, 487.
5. Pirenne, Henri, *Economic and Social History of Medieval Europe*, 215.
6. Burckhardt, 76.
7. Nussbaum, F. L., *History of the Economic Institutions of Modern Europe*, 70.
8. Beard, M., 115.
9. Sarton, IIIa, 125.
10. Thompson, *Economic and Social History*, 406.
11. Symonds, *Age of the Despots*, 197; Sismondi, 573.
12. Machiavelli, *History*, iv, 3.
13. Beard, M., 152; Burckhardt, 80.
14. Machiavelli, *History*, iv, 6-7.

15. Beard, M., 152.
16. Villari, P., *Two First Centuries*, 358.
17. Sismondi, 598f; Beard, 152.
18. Burckhardt, 78.
19. Boissonnade, P., *Life and Work in Medieval Europe*, 299.
20. Roscoe, Wm., *Life of Lorenzo de' Medici*, 79.
21. Varchi, Benedetto, *Storia fiorentina*, end of book ix.
22. Ariosto, *Satires*, vii, 25.
23. *Cambridge Modern History*, I, 542.
24. Symonds, *Revival of Learning*, 104.
25. Ibid., 243.
26. Sismondi, 747.
27. Villari, *Machiavelli*, I, 89.
28. Pastor, I, 27.
29. Villari, *Machiavelli*, 83; Symonds, *Revival of Learning*, 234.
30. Villari, l.c.
31. Pastor, II, 201.
32. Symonds, *Revival*, 237.
33. Burckhardt, 503.
34. Symonds, *Revival*, 240.
35. In Dopsch, *Economic and Social Foundations of European Civilization*, 2.
36. Vasari, *Lives*, II, 270, *Andrea da Fiesole*.
37. Fattorusso, 209.
38. Vasari, *Lives*, II, 299, *Baldassare Peruzzi*.
39. Beard, 153.
40. Symonds, *Fine Arts*, 134; *Cambridge Modern History*, I, 548.
41. Vasari, II, 52, *The Bellini Family*.
42. Baedeker, *Northern Italy*, 567.
43. Vasari, II, 306, *Andrea del Sarto*.
44. Ibid.
45. Sarton, IIIb, 1132.
46. Vasari, II, 239, *Raphael*.
47. In Taylor, R. A., *Leonardo*, 60.
48. Morey, C. R., *Medieval Art*, 340.
49. Vasari, II, 3, *Fra Filippo Lippi*.
50. Crowe and Cavalcaselle, *New History of Painting in Italy*, II, 324.
51. Symonds, *Sketches and Studies in Italy and Greece*, 21-6.
52. Machiavelli, *History*, vii, 1.
53. Guicciardini, Fr., *History of the Wars in Italy*, I, 181.
54. Machiavelli, *History*, vii, 1.
55. In Young, G. F., *The Medici*, 77.

CHAPTER IV

1. Machiavelli, *History*, vii, 2.
2. Ibid.
3. *Cambridge Modern History*, I, 661; Roscoe, *Lorenzo*, 156-7.

4. Roscoe, 169.
5. Ibid., 278; Young, 220.
6. Sismondi, 659; Villari, *Life and Times of Savonarola*, 45; Beard, 156.
7. Machiavelli, viii, 7.
8. Guicciardini, I, 5.
9. Roscoe, *Lorenzo*, 235.
10. *Storia fiorentina*, ch. ix, in Villari, *Machiavelli*, I, 35.
11. Translation by Symonds, *Italian Literature*, I, 390.
12. Varchi, end of book ix.
13. Sellery, G. C., *The Renaissance*, 196.
14. Pastor, V, 154.
15. Villari, *Machiavelli*, I, 132.
16. Abrahams, I., *Jewish Life in the Middle Ages*, 421.
17. In Pater, W., *The Renaissance*, 32.
18. Translated from the Latin text as given in Burckhardt, 354-5.
19. Symonds, *Sketches*, II, 319-20.
20. Pulci, *Morgante maggiore*, i, 54f, in Owen, 151.
21. XVIII, 115f, in Symonds, *Italian Literature*, I, Appendix V.
22. Canto xxv.
23. XXV, 229-30, in Prescott, *Ferdinand and Isabella*, I, 496.
24. In Roscoe, *Lorenzo*, 311.
25. Vasari, *Life of Rustici*.
26. Vasari, II, 98, *Andrea Verrocchio*.
27. Müntz, E., *Raphael*, 146.
28. Berenson, B., *Study and Criticism of Italian Art*, 2.
29. Vasari, II, 23, *Benozzo Gozzoli*.
30. Berenson, *Florentine Painters of the Renaissance*, 63; Taine, H. A., *Italy: Florence and Venice*, 127.
31. In *The Martyrdom of St. Peter* in the Brancacci Chapel.
32. Vasari, II, 85, 87, *Botticelli*.
33. Crowe and Cavalcaselle, II, 431-3.
34. Von Reumont, *Lorenzo il Magnifico*, II, 590, Creighton, III, 296-8, and Roscoe, *Lorenzo*, 327, accept Politian's account; Villari, *Savonarola*, 168-72, prefers Pico's. Politian's third condition seems too innocuous to be historic.
35. Machiavelli, *History*, viii, 7; Guicciardini, I, 10.
36. Roscoe, *Lorenzo*, 334.

CHAPTER V

1. Noyes, *Ferrara*, 98.
2. In Roeder, R., *The Man of the Renaissance*, 6.
3. Ibid., 5.

4. Ibid.
5. Savonarola, 28th Sermon on Ezekiel.
6. In Villari, *Savonarola*, 126.
7. In Roeder, 25.
8. Villari, *Savonarola*, 129.
9. Symonds, *Italian Literature*, I, 386.
10. Villari, 183.
11. Ibid., 189.
12. Guicciardini, I, 173.
13. Villari, 343.
14. Roeder, 57.
15. Villari, 330.
16. Ibid., 329.
17. Guicciardini, II, 391.
18. *Cambridge Modern History*, I, 672 and ch. xix.
19. Villari, 393.
20. Ibid., 376.
21. Ibid., 390.
22. Ibid., 400.
23. Ibid., 401.
24. Ibid., 406.
25. Ibid., 410.
26. Ibid., 474.
27. *Cambridge Modern History*, I, 179.
28. Lenten sermons of 1497, no. 22, in Villari, 516-8.
29. Sermon no. 28, in Villari, 519-20.
30. Villari, 522.
31. *Cambridge Modern History*, I, 179.
32. Villari, 601.
33. Ibid., 645.
34. *Cambridge Modern History*, I, 182.
35. Vasari, II, 176, *Piero di Cosimo*.
36. Id., III, 319, *Lombard Artists*.
37. Crowe, III, 562.

CHAPTER VI

1. Beard, 134.
2. Boissonnade, 326.
3. Pastor, V, 126.
4. Sismondi, 746; Burckhardt, 296.
5. Ibid., 297.
6. Hollway-Calthrop, 14.
7. Thompson, J. W., *Economic and Social History*, 236.
8. Noyes, *Milan*, 132.
9. Thompson, 460; calculations made by Schmoller from governmental archives.
10. Burckhardt, 14; Symonds, *Age of the Despots*, 151.
11. Machiavelli, *History*, vii, 6; Sismondi, 620-1.
12. Cartwright, J., *Beatrice d'Este*, 260.
13. Müntz, E., *Leonardo da Vinci*, I, 103.
14. Taylor, R., *Leonardo*, 104.
15. In Cartwright, *Beatrice d'Este*, 165.

16. Cf., e.g., Cartwright, 78.
17. Sismondi, 741.
17a. In Noyes, *Milan,* 165.
18. Ibid., 183.
19. Cartwright, *Isabella d'Este,* I, 151.
20. Cartwright, *Beatrice d'Este,* 370-3.
21. Ibid., 141.
22. In Symonds, *Revival of Learning,* 273.
23. Ibid., 269.
24. Cellini, *Autobiography,* i, 26.

CHAPTER VII

1. *Leonardo da Vinci,* Phaidon, 21; Taylor, *Leonardo,* 49.
2. Ibid., 488.
3. *Codice Atlantico,* in Leonardo da Vinci, *Notebooks,* II, 502.
4. Fogli A 10r in *Notebooks,* I, 106.
5. Vasari, II, 160, *Leonardo da Vinci;* Paolo Giovio in Phaidon *Leonardo,* 5.
6. Vasari, II, 162; *Codice Atlantico,* 167 v.c. in *Notebooks,* II, 394.
7. Müntz, *Leonardo,* I, 192.
8. Matteo Bandelli in Müntz, *Leonardo,* I, 184.
9. Ibid., 187.
10. In Taylor, *Leonardo,* 231.
11. Müntz, I, 185; Cartwright, *Beatrice,* 138.
12. E.g., Müntz, II, 123.
13. MS. B 83 v in *Notebooks,* II, 204; illustration facing p. 212.
14. *Notebooks,* II, 212.
15. Popham, A. E., *Drawings of Leonardo da Vinci,* plate 309.
16. Ibid., plate 308.
17. Müntz, II, 96.
18. B. M. 35 r in *Notebooks,* II, 96.
19. Popham, plates 305, 298, 303.
20. Phaidon *Leonardo,* 19.
21. Ibid., 16, quoting a 1540 *Life of Leonardo.*
22. Müntz, II, 158.
23. Ibid., 124.
24. Vasari, II, 166, *Leonardo.*
24a. Phaidon *Leonardo,* 23.
25. Taylor, R. A., *Leonardo,* xii.
26. Andrea Corsali, writing to Giuliano de' Medici in 1515, in Müntz, I, 17.
27. Vasari, II, 157.
28. *Trattato della pittura,* 27 v, in *Notebooks,* II, 261.
29. MS 2037, Bibliothèque Nationale, 10 r in *Notebooks* II, 177.
30. A 56 in *Notebooks,* II, 24.
31. Berenson, *Florentine Painters,* 68.
32. Quaderni III, 12 v in *Notebooks,* II, 529.

33. Richter, J. P., *Literary Works of L. da V.,* II, 385-92; Müntz, I, 82-4.
34. In Müntz, II, 19.
35. *Notebooks,* I, 363; II, 13, 287-92.
36. *Trattato* 31 r and 30 v; *Notebooks,* 267-9.
37. Richter, I, #10.
38. *Trattato* 2 r; Bibl. Nat. ms. 2038; *Notebooks,* II, 235.
39. In Taylor, *Leonardo,* 355.
40. *Trattato,* 20 r; *Notebooks,* II, 245.
41. B 16 r and 15 v in *Notebooks,* II, 424.
42. Vasari, II, 157.
43. Usher, in Nussbaum, 80.
44. *Life* Magazine, July 17, 1939.
45. *Notebooks,* I, 25.
46. *Encyclopaedia Britannica,* 11th ed., XXI, 230c.
47. A 27 v.a.; *Notebooks,* II, 437.
48. *Codice Atlantico,* 381 v.a.; *Notebooks,* I, 515.
49. *Codice Atlantico,* 45 r.a.; *Notebooks,* I, 442.
50. *Sul volo,* in *Notebooks,* I, 436.
51. Ibid., 437.
52. *Codice Atlantico,* 161 r.a.; *Notebooks,* I, 511.
53. Popham, 317-8.
54. *Notebooks,* I, 427.
55. B 83 v; *Notebooks,* I, 517.
56. B 89 r; *Notebooks,* I, 519.
57. *Sul volo,* in *Notebooks,* I, 441.
58. *Codice Atlantico,* 318 v.a.; *Notebooks,* I, 513.
59. Taylor, *Leonardo,* 225.
60. *Trattato,* #10.
61. H 90 E 42 in *Notebooks,* II, 75.
62. Duhem, P., *Études sur Léonard de Vinci,* I, 20, 22, 30; III, 54f.
63. In Freud, *Leonardo da Vinci,* 102.
64. *Codice Atlantico,* 367 v.b. in *Notebooks,* II, 500.
65. Popham, plate 161.
66. G 96 v; *Notebooks,* I, 625.
67. Richter, I, 11, no. 3.
68. *Codice Atlantico,* 190 r.a.
69. Quaderni v., 25 r, and F 41 v; *Notebooks,* I, 310, 298.
70. *Codice Atlantico,* 303 v.b.
71. Duhem, I, 25f.
72. Ibid., 25, 30; *Notebooks,* I, 302.
73. F 79 r; *Notebooks,* I, 330-1.
74. About 1338. Cf. D. Müntz, II, 91.
75. *Codice Atlantico,* 155 r.b.; Leic 8 v, 9 r.v.
76. Richter, II, 265.
77. *Codice Atlantico,* 84 r.a.

78. Ibid., 160 v.a.
79. A 56 r; Leic 33 v; *Notebooks*, II, 21, 368.
80. Leic 36 r; *Notebooks*, II, 373.
81. E 8 v; *Notebooks*, I, 628.
82. B.M. 151 r; *Notebooks*, I, 602.
83. *Codice Atlantico*, 302 v.b.; *Notebooks*, I, 529; Müntz, II, 71.
84. Müntz, II, 79.
85. B 6 r; *Notebooks*, I, 284.
86. *Codice Atlantico*, 345 v.b.; *Notebooks*, I, 253.
87. *Codice Atlantico*, 244 r.a.; *Notebooks*, I, 248.
88. Richter, I, ##70-82.
89. Müntz, II, 78.
90. B.M. 57 v; *Notebooks*, II, 98.
91. Duhem, I, 204.
92. *Codice Atlantico*, 314, in Müntz, II, 75.
93. Vasari, II, 157.
94. Müntz, II, 87.
95. Ibid., 80.
96. *Notebooks*, I, 13.
97. Castiglioni, *History of Medicine*, 413-17.
98. Richter II, p. 132; Müntz, II, 84.
99. Fogli B, 10 v; *Notebooks*, I, 124.
100. Taylor, *Leonardo*, 406.
101. Humboldt, A. von, *Kosmos*, II, 324, in Müntz, II, 60.
102. In Garrison, *History of Medicine*, 216.
103. F 41 r; *Notebooks*, II, 47.
104. *Codice Atlantico*, 345 v.b.; *Notebooks*, I, 243.
105. In Müntz, II, 32n.
106. Richter, II, p. 302, 363-4.
107. Ibid., II, p. 369.
108. *Codice Atlantico*, B 70 r.a.; *Notebooks*, II, 504.
109. F 5 r and 4 v; *Notebooks*, I, 295.
110. Taylor, *Leonardo*, 22.
111. Ibid., 462.
112. Müntz, II, 31.
113. *Codice Atlantico*, 51 r.b.
114. A 24 r; *Notebooks*, I, 538; Richter, II, p. 285.
115. Taylor, 7.
116. Quoted in Müntz, II, 207.
117. Basler, *Leonardo*, 6.
118. Marcel Raymond in Taylor, 449-50.
119. *Notebooks*, I, 36.
120. Müntz, II, 22.
121. Taylor, 466.

CHAPTER VIII

1. Sismondi, 593.
2. Vasari, I, 183, *Spinello*.

3. Id., II, 147, *Signorelli*.
4. E.g., Symonds, *Sketches*, III, 151.
5. Allegretto Allegretti in Symonds, *Age of the Despots*, 616.
5a. Craven, *Treasury of Art Masterpieces*, 1952 ed., 6.
6. Vasari, III, 286, *Sodoma*.
7. Ibid., 285.
8. *Emporium* Magazine, June, 1939, 354.
9. Crowe, III, 104, 106.
10. Vasari, II, 18; *Gentile da Fabriano*.
11. Matarazzo, *Cronaca*, in Symonds, *Sketches*, III, 134-5.
12. In Villari, *Machiavelli*, I, 355.
13. Symonds, *Sketches*, III, 129.
14. Crowe, III, 293.
15. Ibid., 183.
16. Vasari, II, 133, *Perugino*.
17. Thorndike, L., *History of Medieval Europe*, 675-6.
18. Vasari, II, 132, *Perugino*; Crowe, III, 223.
19. Symonds, Fine Arts, 297n.

CHAPTER IX

1. Brinton, *The Gonzaga Lords of Mantua*, 91.
2. Mantegna, *L'oeuvre*, xiv.
3. Cartwright, *Isabella*, I, 362.
4. Ibid., 83.
5. Ibid., 152.
6. Ibid., 4.
7. Ibid., 288.
8. Maulde, *Women of the Renaissance*, 432.
9. Cartwright, *Isabella*, II, 381.

CHAPTER X

1. Gregorovius, *Lucrezia Borgia*, 267.
2. Noyes, *Ferrara*, 82.
3. Ibid., 136.
4. Burckhardt, 47.
5. Ariosto, *Orlando furioso*, xxxiii, 2.
6. Noyes, *Ferrara*, 83.
7. Ibid., 82-4.
8. Symonds, *Revival*, 298-301.
9. Burckhardt, 323.
10. Carducci in Villari, *Machiavelli*, I, 410.
11. Ariosto, *I Suppositi*, Prologue.
12. Cf. Symonds, *Italian Literature*, I, 496n, and Ariosto, Satire ii, 94-9.
13. *Orlando furioso*, x, 95-6.
13a. Cf. Croce, *Ariosto, Shakespeare, and Corneille*, 65.
14. *Orlando furioso*, x, 84.
15. Satire vii, tr. Symonds.
16. In Symonds, *Italian Literature*, II, 323.

17. Rabelais, *Pantagruel*, ii, 1, 7.
18. Gregorovius, *Lucrezia*, 362.

CHAPTER XI

1. Comines, *Memoirs*, vii, 17.
2. Molmenti, P., Part I, Vol. II, 62.
3. Young, *Medici*, 28.
4. Beazley, *Dawn of Modern Geography*, 474.
5. Thompson, J. W., *Economic and Social History*, 490.
6. Guicciardini, IV, 359.
7. Speech of Mocenigo, in Sismondi, 534n.
8. Molmenti, l.c., 42.
9. Ibid., 33.
10. Sismondi, 788.
11. Molmenti, 30.
12. Sismondi, 789.
13. Ibid.
14. Molmenti, 37-9.
15. Ibid., 94.
16. Burckhardt, 63.
17. *Cambridge Modern History*, I, 263; Molmenti, 12; Villari, *Machiavelli*, I, 464, 466; Foligno, *Padua*, 141.
18. Machiavelli, *History*, vi, 4.
19. Molmenti, Part I, Vol. II, 98.
20. Id., Part II, Vol. II, 240.
21. Ibid.
22. Petrarch, Letter of Sept. 21, 1373, in Foligno, 126.
23. Molmenti, Part I, Vol. II, 269.
24. Ibid., 22.
25. *Cambridge Modern History*, I, 269.
26. Molmenti, Part I, Vol. II, 21.
27. *Cambridge Modern History*, I, 268.
28. Vasari, I, 357, *Antonello da Messina*.
29. Ibid., 358.
30. Gronau, G., *Titian*, 6.
31. Vasari, II, 47, *The Bellini*.
32. Mather, F. J., *Venetian Painters*, 91.
33. Molmenti, Part I, Vol. II, 160.
34. Carlo Ridolfo in Mather, 195.
35. Mather, 206.
36. Gronau, 28.
37. Ibid., 38.
38. Ibid., 35.
39. Ibid., 62.
40. Mather, 300.
41. *Lombardia*, II, 85.
42. Renard, G., *Guilds of the Middle Ages*, 36; Dillon, E., *Glass*, 222.
43. Quoted by Alan Moorehead in *The New Yorker*, Feb. 24, 1951.
44. Symonds, *Revival*, 369.
45. Putnam, G. H., *Books*, I, 438.
46. Symonds, *Revival*, 381.

47. Ibid., 411; Gregorovius, *Lucrezia*, 305; Noyes, *Ferrara*, 163.
48. Pastor, VIII, 191.
49. *Cambridge Modern History*, I, 564; Symonds, *Revival*, 398.
50. Maulde, 366-7.
51. Berenson, B., *Venetian Painters*, 31.
52. Vasari, III, 48, *Veronese Artists*.
53. Ibid., 49.
54. Ibid., 30, *Giov. Fr. Caroto*.

CHAPTER XII

1. Stoecklin, *Le Corrège*, 21.
2. Vasari, II, 175, *Correggio*.
3. James, E. E. C., *Bologna*, 301.
4. Vasari, II, 118, *Francia*.
5. Ibid., 122
6. Berenson, *North Italian Painters*, 70.
7. James, E. E., 355.
8. Vasari, II, 123.
9. Sismondi, 737.
10. Symonds, *Sketches*, II, 17.
11. Burckhardt, 454.
12. Sismondi, 737.
13. Villari, *Machiavelli*, I, 117-8; Pastor, III, 117.
14. Symonds, *Sketches*, II, 20.
15. Burckhardt, 454.
16. Pastor, III, 117.
17. *Miniatures de la Renaissance*, 79.
18. Müntz, *Raphael*, 5.
19. Castiglione, *The Courtier*, 231.
20. Roeder, *Man of the Renaissance*, 175.
21. Cartwright, *Isabella*, I, 110.
22. Maulde, 294.
23. Roeder, 222.
24. Ibid., 397.
25. Castiglione, 188.
26. Ibid., 310.
27. Ibid., 304.
28. Ibid., 306.
29. Ibid., 286.
30. Cartwright, *Baldassare Castiglione*, II, 430.

CHAPTER XIII

1. Burckhardt, 226.
2. Pastor, I, 13-7; Villari, *Machiavelli*, I, 96-7; Symonds, *Revival*, 258.
3. Cf. Sellery, *Renaissance*, 202f.
4. Pastor, I, 19-21; Villari, *Machiavelli*, I, 98.
5. Pastor, V, 115; Burckhardt, 36-7; Villari, *Machiavelli*, I, 58; Sismondi, 739; Symonds, *Age of the Despots*, 570-2; but these rely on Paolo Giovio, an historian favorable to the popes.

6. Burckhardt, 267.
7. In Portogliotti, *The Borgias*, 60.
8. In Symonds, *Revival*, 469.

CHAPTER XIV

1. Pastor, I, 117; Creighton, I, 566-9.
2. In Pastor, I, 124.
3. Coulton, *Medieval Panorama*, 486.
4. Pastor, VII, 339; Creighton, I, 161.
5. Lea, H. C., *History of Auricular Confession*, III, 65.
6. Creighton, I, 147.
7. Ibid., 168.
8. Gierke, *Political Theories of the Middle Age*, 52, 59; Hearnshaw, *Medieval Contributions to Civilization*, 67.
9. Emerton, E., *Defensor Pacis of Marsiglio of Padua*, 70-2.
10. Pastor, I, 184.
11. Niem in Milman, VII, 235n.
12. Creighton, I, 273.
13. Milman, VII, 460.
14. Figgis, J. N., *From Gerson to Grotius*, 41.
15. In Ogg, F. A., *Source Book of Medieval History*, 391.
16. Creighton, I, 297.
17. *Cambridge Medieval History*, VIII, 8n.
18. Creighton, IV, 8.
19. In Pastor, I, 241.
20. Creighton, II, 272; Pastor I, 284.
21. Creighton, IV, 44.
22. Ogg, 393-7.
23. Pastor, II, 215.
24. *Cambridge Medieval History*, IV, 620f; Pastor, II, 258.
25. Creighton, IV, 71.

CHAPTER XV

1. Gibbon, *Decline and Fall*, VI, 558.
2. Lanciani, *Golden Days of the Renaissance*, 78-80.
3. Burckhardt, 105.
4. Roscoe, *Leo X*, I, 435.
5. Cf. Pastor, VII, 104.
6. Pastor, I, 169.
7. Pastor, II, 180; Hare, *Walks in Rome*, 167.
8. In Creighton, III, 111n.
9. Pastor, II, 14; Symonds, *Revival*, 222-5.
10. Ibid., 226.
11. Pastor, II, 193.
12. Pastor, II, 200.
13. Burckhardt, 188.
14. Pastor, II, 198.
15. Sismondi, 613.
16. Vasari, II, 31, *Bernardino Rossellino*.

17. Lea, *Auricular Confession*, III, 202.
18. Pastor, II, 102.
19. Creighton, II, 308f.
20. Pastor, II, 272f.
21. Ibid., 313.
21a. La Tour, P. Imbart de, *Les origines de la Réforme*, II, 7, 14.
22. Creighton, II, 245.
23. Ibid., 246.
24. Ibid., 247.
25. Platina, *In vitas summorum pontificum*, in Whitcomb, *Source Book*, 69.
26. Creighton, II, 483.
27. Ibid.
28. Burckhardt, 305.
29. Creighton, II, 483.
30. Sellery, 239.
31. Platina in Whitcomb, 65.
32. Creighton, II, 488.
33. Platina, l.c.
34. Ibid., 66.
35. Vasiliev, *History of the Byzantine Empire*, II, 442.
36. Pastor, III, 324.
37. Ibid., 256.
38. Creighton, IV, 209.
39. Thompson, J. W., 297.
40. Pastor, IV, 41-5; Villari, *Machiavelli*, I, 106-7; Burckhardt, 280, 505.
41. Ferrara, O., *The Borgia Pope*, 95.
42. Pastor IV, 238-44; Creighton, III, 63-6.
43. Ibid., 75.
44. Symonds, *Despots*, 388.
45. Ibid., 398n.
46. Cf. Creighton, III, 115, 285; Pastor, IV, 416.
47. Soriano in Symonds, *Despots*, 394n; Pastor, IV, 428.
48. Symonds, *Despots*, 394.
49. Pastor, V, 236-8.
50. Vespucci in *Cambridge Modern History*, I, 222.
51. Creighton, III, 120.
52. Ibid., 154-5; Pastor, V, 351.
53. Ibid., 352-4; Creighton, IV, 318.
54. Creighton, III, 126.
55. Ibid.
56. Burckhardt, 108; Pastor, V, 354.
57. Pastor, V, 317; Creighton, III, 126.
57a. La Tour, II, 13.
58. Pastor, V, 361-2.
59. Creighton, IV, 297-8.
60. Creighton, III, 126.
61. Ibid., 135.
62. In Taine, *Italy: Rome and Naples*, 171.
63. Creighton, III, 153; *Cambridge Modern History*, I, 225.

CHAPTER XVI

1. Ferrara, *Borgia Pope*, 55-62; Pastor, II, 541-2.
2. Creighton, III, 162.
3. Pastor, II, 455.
4. Beuf, *Cesare Borgia*, 19; Gregorovius, *Lucrezia*, 10.
5. Ibid., 18, 20.
6. Roscoe, *Leo X*, I, 24.
7. Gregorovius, *Lucrezia*, 352.
8. Id., IV, 324.
9. *Cambridge Modern History*, I, 225; Ferrara, 66; Creighton, III, 159.
10. Ferrara, 51; Pastor, V, 366; Gregorovius, 17.
11. Creighton, III, 160n.
12. *Cambridge Modern History*, I, 226.
13. Pastor, V, 385.
14. Sacerdote, G., *Cesare Borgia*, 94.
15. In Creighton, III, 47.
16. *Cambridge Modern History*, I, 234.
17. Vasari, II, 116, *Pinturicchio*.
18. Ferrara, 310.
18a. La Tour, II, 39.
19. Pastor, V, 396; Burckhardt, 109.
20. Portigliotti, 28f.
21. Guicciardini, I, 19-20.
22. Creighton, III, 168.
23. Ibid., 194-5, quoting the letters as given in Burckhard's *Diarium*.
24. Creighton, III, 196; Pastor, V, 429; *Cambridge Modern History*, I, 229.
24a. Guicciardini, I, 209.
25. Creighton, III, 206; *Cambridge Modern History*, I, 231.
26. Ibid., 230.
27. Pastor, V, 381.
28. Ferrara, 163.
29. Roscoe, *Leo X*, I, 394.
30. Guicciardini, I, 29.
31. Gregorovius, 75.
32. Creighton, III, 175; Gregorovius, 39, 62; Portigliotti, 47.
33. Ferrara, 164.
34. Creighton, III, 176; Gregorovius, 65.
35. Portigliotti, 45, 48, 61.
36. Burckhard, *Diarium*, iii, 227, in Creighton, IV, 49n.
37. Boccaccio, Ferrarese ambassador, in Symonds, *Despots*, 417; Portigliotti, 56.
38. Gregorovius, 75.
39. Lea, *Auricular Confession*, III, 211f.
40. Guicciardini, III, 26; Pastor, VI, 153-4.
41. Guicciardini, III, 26; Creighton, IV, 13-4.
42. Portigliotti, 66.

43. In Villari, *Machiavelli*, I, 321.
44. Portigliotti, 66.
45. Ferrara, 318.
46. Villari, l.c.
47. Cf. Ferrara, ch. xxi.
48. Ibid., 309.
49. Ferrara, 246; Sacerdote, 198f.
50. Ibid., 221.
51. Ibid., 202.
52. Ferrara, 246; Pastor, V, 512, and Roscoe, Leo X, I, 154, acquit Caesar Borgia; Gregorovius, *Lucrezia*, 106; Beuf, 76-8; and Symonds, *Despots*, 425 accuse him; Creighton, III, 258, concludes that "it is impossible to pronounce any certain opinion."
53. Pastor, V, 501.
54. Gregorovius, 220; Burckhardt, 110.
55. Beuf, 41.
56. Gregorovius, 57.
57. Beuf, 97.
58. Cartwright, *Isabella*, I, 178.
59. Beuf, 7; Sacerdote, 207.
60. Ferrara, 291.
61. Burckhardt, 112; Creighton, IV, 3-4.
62. Id., III, 6n; Ferrara, 293.
63. Richard Garnett in *Cambridge Modern History*, I, 238.
64. In Beuf, 155.
65. Ferrara, 308.
66. Beuf, 194.
67. Ibid., 223.
68. Creighton, IV, 27.
69. Ibid.
70. Ibid., 29; Sacerdote, 806.
71. Guicciardini, III, 137; Machiavelli, *Relation of the Murder of Vitellezzo*, in Appendix to *History of Florence*, pp. 491-6.
72. Beuf, 292.
73. Ibid.
74. Ibid and 296.
75. Creighton, IV, 36.
76. Ibid., 40.
77. Beuf, 290.
78. Beuf, 252-8.
79. Beuf, 131.
80. Beuf, 66, 177; Guicciardini, III, 129.
81. Portigliotti, 83.
82. Villari, *Machiavelli*, I, 323.
83. Burckhardt, 116.
84. Pastor, VI, 128.
85. Beuf, 305-7.
86. Ferrara, 326.
87. Burckhardt, 115; Villari, *Machiavelli*, I, 323.
88. Cartwright, *Isabella*, I, 327.

89. Creighton, IV, 30, 40; *Cambridge Modern History*, I, 242; Beuf, 307.
90. Symonds, *Despots*, 426.
91. Burckhard, *Diarium*, ed. Celani, II, 303, in Portigliotti, 54.
92. Ferrara, 337; Gregorovius, *Lucrezia*, 178.
93. Ferrara, 337.
94. Gregorovius, 177; Ferrara, 336. Creighton, IV, 50n, accepts the tale.
95. Gregorovius, 189.
96. Ferrara, 252.
97. Ibid., 251.
98. Gregorovius, 108, **330.**
99. Creighton, III, 264.
100. There are different accounts of Alfonso's death; the text follows the despatches of the Venetian ambassador Capello as given in Creighton, IV, 257-62. Pastor (VI, 77) suggests that Alfonso was slain by his own bodyguard.
101. Cf. Gregorovius, *Lucrezia*, 175.
102. Cartwright, *Isabella*, I, 205.
103. Creighton, IV, 21; Pastor, V, 399; Gregorovius, 175.
104. Ibid., 167.
105. Ibid., 213.
106. Ibid., 222; Friedländer, L., *Roman Life and Manners*, II, 176.
107. Gregorovius, 246-8.
108. Ibid., 290.
109. *Cambridge Modern History*, I, 241; Pastor, VI, 132; Sacerdote, 683; Villari, *Machiavelli*, I, 327; Lanciani, 76; Ferrara, 400; Roscoe, *Leo X*, I, 469; Beuf, 318. Portigliotti, 129-37, defends the poison theory.
110. Lanciani, 76.
111. Portigliotti, 127.
112. Gregorovius, 289.
113. Guicciardini, III, 228.
114. Machiavelli, *Prince*, ch. xviii.
115. Pastor, VI, 137.
116. Roscoe, *Leo X*, I, 195.
117. Creighton, IV, 44-50.
118. *Cambridge Modern History*, I, 241-2.
119. Creighton, IV, 57.
120. Pastor, VI, 208.
121. Gregorovius, *Lucrezia*, 310.
122. Ibid., 31.
123. Roscoe, *Leo X*, I, 404.

CHAPTER XVII

1. Pastor, V, 369.
2. Paris de Grassis in Roscoe, *Leo X*, I, 300.
3. Pastor, l.c.

4. Villari, *Machiavelli*, I, 367.
5. Pastor, VI, 215.
6. Ibid., 223.
7. Beuf, 364.
8. Machiavelli, *Discourses*, i, 27.
9. Creighton, IV, 117.
10. Ibid., 123.
11. Ibid., 124.
12. Ibid., 127.
13. Guicciardini, V, 90.
14. Creighton, IV, 163n.
15. Ibid., 130n.
16. Guicciardini, VI, 111.
17. Müntz, *Raphael*, 293.
18. Symonds, *Michelangelo*, 92-4.
19. Pastor, VI, 469f.
20. New York *World*, May 12, 1928.
21. Nietzsche, Letter to Brandes, in Huneker, *Egoists*, 251.
22. Vasari, ed., Blashfield and Hopkins, IV, 37n, *Michelangelo.*
23. Ibid., 38.
24. In Symonds, *Michelangelo*, 7.
25. Cellini, *Autobiography*, i, 13.
26. Symonds, *Mich.*, 134.
27. Ibid., 44.
28. Ibid., 45.
29. Maulde, 313.
30. Symonds, *Mich.*, 58.
31. Vasari, IV, 59.
32. Symonds, 70.
33. Ibid., 100.
34. Cellini, i, 12.
35. Condivi in Symonds, 111.
36. Symonds, 125.
37. Vasari, IV, 89.
38. Condivi in Symonds, 139.
39. Faure, E., *Spirit of Forms*, 139.
40. Vasari, IV, 91.

CHAPTER XVIII

1. Montalembert, *Monks of the West*, I, 81.
2. Roscoe, *Lorenzo*, 285.
3. Guicciardini, VI, 114.
4. Roscoe, *Leo X*, I, 344.
5. Guicciardini, VII, 68.
6. Ibid., VI, 117.
7. Creighton, IV, 182.
8. *Cambridge Modern History*, II, 14; Gregorovius, *History of City of Rome*, VIIIa, 294; Creighton, IV, 181n. All these rest on the *Relazione* of Marino Giorgio, the Venetian ambassador, and on Prato's *Storia Milanese;* probable but inconclusive evidence, since Gior-

gio did not take up residence in Rome till 1515.

9. Pastor, VIII, 391.
10. Ibid.
11. Ibid., 84.
12. Roscoe, *Leo X*, II, 259.
13. Ibid., 388; Pastor, VIII, 79.
14. Müntz, *Raphael*, 409.
15. Taine, *Italy: Rome and Naples*, 185.
16. Pastor, VIII, 74.
17. Roscoe, II, 391.
18. Burckhardt, 185.
19. Pastor, VIII, 160, 162.
20. Ibid., 163-4.
21. Lanciani, *Golden Days of the Renaissance in Rome*, 321.
22. Burckhardt, 387.
23. Gregorovius, VIIIa, 407.
24. Lanciani, 58.
30. Roscoe, II, 82; Pastor, VIII, 127.
31. Gregorovius, VIIIa, 302.
32. Lanciani, 108.
33. Pastor, VIII, 121.
34. Cartwright, *Isabella*, II, 116.
35. Gregorovius, VIIIa, 309, 311.
36. Rashdall, H., *Universities of Europe in the M.A.*, II, 39.
37. Roscoe, I, 342.
38. Huizinga, *Waning of the Middle Ages*, 62.
39. Pastor, VIII, 268.
40. Roscoe, I, 357.
41. Ibid., 287.
42. Ibid.
43. Maulde, 432.
44. Roscoe, II, 173.
45. Müntz, *Raphael*, 405; Symonds, *Italian Literature*, II, 147.
46. Roscoe, II, 299-302; Pastor, VIII, 238.
47. Ibid., 270.
48. Roscoe, II, 176.
49. Ibid., 110; Pastor, VIII, 184.
50. Roscoe, II, 110.
51. In Symonds, *Revival*, 499.
52. Ibid., 500.
53. Ibid., 503.
54. Ibid., 476.
55. Lanciani, *Ancient Rome*, 154f.
56. In Pastor, VIII, 362.
57. Symonds, *Michelangelo*, 195.
58. Vasari, IV, 75.
59. Pastor, VIII, 435.
60. Symonds, 219.
61. Ibid., 51.
62. Ibid., 52.
63. Vasari, IV, 213.
64. Ibid., 218.

65. Ibid., 212.
66. Symonds, *Fine Arts*, 268.
67. Symonds, *Michel.*, 203.
68. Ibid., 529.
69. 535.
70. 149.
71. Müntz, *Raphael*, 421.
72. Ibid., 422.
73. 420.
74. Ibid.
75. Vasari, II, 247-9, *Raphael*.
76. Winckelmann, *History of Ancient Art*, II, 316.
77. Müntz, *Raphael*, 462.
78. Roscoe, *Leo X*, I, 347.
79. Lanciani, *Golden Days*, 279-80.
80. Friedländer, II, 136; Pastor, VIII, 117.
81. Friedländer, l.c.
82. Ibid., 157.
83. Lanciani, *Golden Days*, 302.
84. Müntz, *Raphael*, 491.
85. *Time* Magazine, April 30, 1951, p. 29.
86. Vasari, II, 238.
87. Lanciani, 230.
88. Vasari, II, 241.
89. Ibid., 247.
90. Matt. 17:1-3, 14f.
91. Vasari, II, 247.
92. In Mantegna, *L'oeuvre*, Introd., x.
93. Guicciardini, VII, 287; VIII, 11.
94. Ibid., VI, 412.
95. Ibid., VII, 129; Roscoe, *Leo X*, II, 200.
96. Cf. Ranke, *History of the Popes*, I, 309.
97. Pastor, VIII, 2.
98. Thompson, J. W., 423.
99. Pastor, VIII, 81, 151.
100. Ibid., 102.
101. 63-5.
102. Thompson, 423.
103. Pastor, VIII, 460.
104. Young, *Medici*, 296.
105. Pastor, VIII, 139.

CHAPTER XIX

1. Poggio, *Facetiae*, in Burckhardt, 521.
2. Machiavelli, *Discourses*, i, 56.
3. Burckhardt, 519.
4. Ibid., 520.
5. Thorndike, Lynn, *History of Magic and Experimental Science*, IV, 562.
6. Jusserand, J. J., *English Wayfaring Life in the M.A.*, 377.
7. Ibid.
8. Aretino, *Ragionamenti del Zoppino*, in Burckhardt, 529; Sismondi, 744.
9. Ibid.
10. Pastor, V, 348.

11. Ibid., 349; Exodus, xxii, 18.
12. Pastor, V, 349.
13. Lea, H. C., *History of the Inquisition in the M.A.*, III, 540.
14. Sismondi, 745; Burckhardt, 528.
15. Lea, op. cit., 547.
16. Ibid.
16a. Ibid., 548.
16b. Burckhardt, 508.
16c. Thorndike, IV, 761.
16d. Ibid., 435.
16e. Guicciardini, *Ricordi*, 57, in Burckhardt, 518.
16f. Robertson, J. M., *Short History of Freethought*, I, 369.
16g. Roscoe, *Leo X*, II, 253.
16h. Lacroix, Paul, *Science and Literature in the Middle Ages*, 290.
16i. Burckhardt, 211.
16j. Boccaccio, *Decameron*, viii, 9.
17. In Castiglioni, *History of Medicine*, 399.
18. Walsh, J. J., *The Popes and Science*, 75.
19. Ibid., 115.
19a. Cornaro, L., *Art of Living Long*, 43f.
20. Castiglioni, 368.
20a. Cornaro, 92, 103.
20b. Ibid., Introd., 31.
20c. Ibid.
21. Lanciani, *Golden Days*, 87.
22. Molmenti, Part II, Vol. I, 159f.
23. Lanciani, 86.
24. Thorndike, *Science and Thought in the Fifteenth Century*, 221.
24. Sarton, IIIb, 1658.
25. Garrison, 187.
27. Molmenti, Part I, Vol. II, 54.
28. Pastor, V, 61.
29. Luther, *Table Talk*, in Pastor, V, 65.
30. Garrison, 191.
31. Ibid.
32. Lacroix, Paul, *History of Prostitution*, II, 1119.
33. Castiglioni, 454.
34. Lanciani, *Golden Days*, 84.
35. Sudhoff in Garrison, 191.
36. Castiglioni, 453.
37. Sarton, IIIa, 274.
38. Castiglioni, 465.
39. Ibid., 459; Lacroix, *Prostitution*, II, 951.
40. Molmenti, Part I, Vol. II, 262.
41. Robertson, *Freethought*, I, 369.
42. Ibid.
43. Owen, *Skeptics*, 215.
44. *Cambridge Modern History*, II, 703.
45. Pastor, V, 157.
46. Owen, 208.
47. Ibid.

48. 209.
49. *De incantatione*, ch. iii, in Symonds, *Italian Literature*, II, 476.
50. Ibid., ch. xii, in Symonds, op. cit., 477.
51. Owen, 201.
52. *De immortalitate animae*, ch. xiv.
52a. Ibid.
53. In Owen, 204.
54. Ibid.
55. *De fato*, iii, 7.
56. In *Cambridge Modern History*, II, 703.
57. Pastor, V, 157.
58. Molmenti, Part I, Vol. II, 1.
59. Burckhardt, 453.
60. Ranke, *History of the Popes*, I, 56.
61. Pastor, I, 27.
62. Pastor, X, 422.
63. *Encyclopaedia Britannica*, 11th ed., XXIII, 85a.
64. Symonds, *Italian Lit.*, II, 479.
65. Ibid.
66. Lea, *Inquisition in the M.A.*, III, 576.
67. Erasmus, Epistle xxvi, 34, in Robertson, J. M., *Freethought*, I, 370.
68. Guicciardini, I, 4.
69. Mather, F. J., *Western European Painting of the Renaissance*, 150.
70. In Villari, *Machiavelli*, I, 417.
71. Guicciardini, I, Introd. xvi.
72. Guicciardini, *Ricordi*, xxviii, in Burckhardt, 464, Pastor, VIII, 178, and Villari, *Machiavelli*, II, 86.
73. *Ricordi* civ and cclxvii, in Villari, *Machiavelli*, II, 86.
74. *Opere inedite*, ii, 51, in Sismondi, 389.
75. *Ricordi*, cccxlvi, in Villari, II, 85; Guicciardini, *History*, III, 104.
76. Villari, II, 158-9.
77. Ibid., 325.
78. In Roeder, 209.
79. Cf. the letters in Villari, I, 469 and II, 48.
80. In Pastor, V, 160.
81. Machiavelli, *Discourses*, ii, 10.
82. Ibid., ii, 18.
83. In Villari, II, 344.
84. *Discourses*, iii, 43.
85. Ibid., proem to book ii.
86. Machiavelli, *History*, v, 1.
87. Machiavelli, *The Prince*, ch. xxv.
88. *Discourses*, i, 3; *Prince*, iii.
89. Robertson, I, 374.
90. *Discourses*, i, 11.
91. I, 12.
92. I, 11-12.
93. I, 10.
94. II, 2; iii, 1.

95. I, 12.
96. III, 1.
97. III, 41.
98. I, 9.
99. *History*, v, 2.
100. In Villari, II, 143.
101. *Discourses*, i, 9.
102. *Prince*, i.
103. *Discourses*, i, 12.
104. In Villari, II, 151.
105. *Prince*, xi-xii; *History*, vi, 1.
106. In Pastor, V, 164.
107. *Prince*, xv.
108. *Prince*, xviii.
109. Ibid., xvii.
110. *Discourses*, iii, 19.
111. Ibid., i, 10.
112. *Prince*, xxi.
113. Ibid., viii.
114. XVIII.
115. Ibid.
116. VII, xvii.
117. XXVI.
118. Villari, II, 193; Treitschke, H. von, *Lectures on Politics*, 29.
119. Bacon, F., *De augmentis scientiarum*, vii, 2.
120. Hegel, *Philosophy of History*, in Symonds, *Despots*, 367.

CHAPTER XX

1. Burckhardt, 485.
2. Coulton, *Medieval Panorama*, 192.
3. Platina, *Vitae*, in Burckhardt, 501.
4. Sismondi, 468.
5. Pastor, V, 84.
6. *Decameron*, i, 2 and 7.
7. Symonds, *Despots*, 458n.
8. In Roeder, 512.
9. Pastor, I, 31.
10. Molmenti, Part I, Vol. II, 222.
11. Aretino, *Dialogues*, p. 82.
12. Guicciardini, *Considerazione* on Machiavelli's *Discourses* (i, 12), in Villari, II, 151.
13. St. Catherine of Siena in Coulton, *Five Centuries of Religion*, II, 399.
14. Pastor, V, 171-3.
16. Robertson, I, 369.
17. Burckhardt, 502.
18. Robertson, I, 369.
19. Pastor, VI, 443.
20. Pastor, X, 457-76.
21. Bandello, *Novels*, Vol. I, Part I, Story I; Maulde, 178.
22. Ibid.
23. Pastor, V, 113.

24. Lea, *Auricular Confession*, III, 417.
25. Pastor, V, 133; Symonds, *Despots*, 477.
26. Pastor, V, 132.
27. Aretino, *La cortigiana*, Act. iii, p. 219 of *Works*.
28. Chubb, T. C., *Aretino*, 216.
29. Pastor, I, 26.
30. Molmenti, Part II, Vol. II, 239.
31. Ibid., 238.
32. Castiglioni, 464; Burckhardt, 400, who considers the estimate exaggerated.
33. Castiglioni, 464.
34. Molmenti, 250n.
35. Pastor, VIII, 121.
36. Gregorovius, *Lucrezia*, 96.
37. Symonds, *Italian Lit.*, II, 225.
38. Maulde, 361.
39. Gregorovius, VIIIa, 306.
40. Lanciani, *Golden Days*, 67.
41. Ibid., 64.
42. Maulde, 360, 164.
43. Ibid., 27, 98.
44. Villari, I, 315.
45. Pastor, V, 105, 127.
46. Burckhardt, 416.
47. An example in Cartwright, *Isabella*, II, 288.
48. Maulde, 43.
49. Burckhardt, 456.
50. Maulde, 353; Sismondi, 747.
51. Ibid., 456.
52. Coulton, *From St. Francis to Dante*, 14.
53. In Symonds, *Italian Lit.*, II, 86.
54. Burckhardt, 346.
55. Molmenti, II, II, 92.
56. Burckhardt, 374.
57. Molmenti, 94; Taylor, *Leonardo*, 484.
58. Ibid.
59. Sismondi, 452.
60. Addison, Julia, *Development of Arts and Crafts in the Middle Ages*, 192.
61. Cagnola in Noyes, Milan, 133.
62. Cartwright, *Isabella*, II, 115.
63. Maulde, 131.
64. Ibid., 70-1.
65. Cartwright, *Beatrice*, 172.
66. Pastor, V, 17-9.
67. Symonds, *Despots*, 240f.
68. In Burckhardt, 404.
69. Ibid.
70. Pastor, VIII, 124.
71. Pastor, V, 107.
72. Ashley, W. J., *Introd. to English Economic History*, 447.
73. Pastor, V, 106.
74. *Cambridge Modern History*, I, 250; Symonds, *Despots*, 474.

75. Taine: *Rome and Naples*, 172.
76. Chubb, 23.
77. Guicciardini, III, 59.
78. Ibid., VII, 69; Machiavelli, *History*, vi, 4.
79. Pastor, V, 134.
80. Sismondi, 456.
81. James, *Bologna*, 138.
82. Schevill, *Siena*, 223.
83. Robinson and Rolf, 123.
84. Cartwright, *Isabella*, II, 59.
85. Lanciani, 99.
86. Brinton, *The Gonzaga Lords*, 88.
87. Fattorusso, 247.
88. Thorndike, *Science and Thought in the Fifteenth Century*, 53; Burckhardt, 374.
89. Friedländer, II, 176.
90. Wright, T., *Homes of Other Days*, 462.
91. Molmenti, II, II, 162.
92. *Decameron*, i, 1.
93. Molmenti, 231.
94. Villari, *Savonarola*, 246.
95. Gibbon, VI, 562.
96. Symonds, *Italian Lit.*, I, 397-8.
97. Vasari, II, 178-9, *Piero di Cosimo*.
98. Pastor, V, 48.
99. In Lang, P. H., *Music in Western Civilization*, 299.
100. Cellini, i, 32.
101. Lang, 302.
102. Castiglione, B., *The Courtier*, p. 76.
103. Ibid.; *Oxford History of Music*, Introd. Volume, 215; Lang, 300.
104. *Oxford History*, Introd., 188.
105. In Einstein, Alfred, *The Italian Madrigal*, I, 39.
106. Symonds, *Ital. Lit.*, I, 217.
107. Einstein, 7.
108. Tr. Symonds, *Sketches*, II, 332.
109. Rabelais, *Pantagruel*, bk. iv, Prologue.
109a. Grove, *Dictionary of Music*, IV, 809.
110. Einstein, 6, 8.
111. Luther, in Gregorovius, VIIIa, 249.
112. Ascham, *The Scholemaster*, 87.
113. Machiavelli, *Discourses*, i, 12.
114. Guicciardini, VIII, 354.
115. Pastor, V, 181.

CHAPTER XXI

1. The phrase is from Michelet, *Histoire de France*, III, i, 2, p. 5.
2. Lacroix, Paul, *Arts of the M.A.*, 99.
3. Guicciardini, I, 147.
4. Guizot, *History of France*, II, 554.
5. *Cambridge Modern History*, I, 240.
6. Roscoe, *Leo X*, I, 200-1.
7. Prescott, II, 307.
8. Guizot, II, 511; Sismondi, 676.
9. Lacroix, *Prostitution*, II, 1130.
10. Pastor, VII, 105.
11. Ibid., 141; Roscoe, *Leo X*, II, 39; Guicciardini, VI, 382, however, thought that Leo agreed.
12. De Grassis in Roscoe, *Leo X*, II, 40.
13. Pastor, VII, 139.
14. Beuf, 222.
15. Guicciardini, VII, 266.
16. Pastor, IX, 27.
17. Chubb, 76.
18. Symonds, *Despots*, 440.
19. Pastor, IX, 73.
20. Burckhardt, 162.
21. Pastor, IX, 91-113.
22. Ibid., 125.
23. Cartwright, *Isabella*, II, 232.
24. Tr. Symonds, *Ital. Lit.*, II, 368.
25. Pastor, IX, 266.
26. Ibid., 271.
27. Guicciardini, VIII, 230f.
28. Pastor, IX, 304.
29. Ibid., 328.
30. 331.
31. Sismondi, 687.
32. Young, 330.
33. In Cartwright, II, 272.
34. Guicciardini, IX, 98, 113.
35. Pastor, IX, 362.
36. Ibid., 390-405; Cartwright, II, 260.
37. Pastor, IX, 400, 413.
38. Guicciardini, IX, 305; Lanciani, 108.
39. Ibid., 107.
40. Guicciardini, IX, 307.
41. Pastor, IX, 400.
42. Symonds, *Revival*, 444-5.
43. Guicciardini, IX, 308; Pastor, IX, 413.
44. Symonds, *Despots*, 444; Job, x, 18.
45. Guicciardini, IX, 320-2; Pastor, IX, 424.
46. In Cartwright, *Isabella*, II, 270.
47. Burckhardt, 123; Symonds, *Despots*, 445.
48. Guicciardini, X, 139.
49. Sismondi, 729; Symonds, *Despots*, 446.
50. Fattorusso, *Florence*, 192.
51. Sismondi, 731.
52. Symonds, *Michelangelo*, 279.
53. Young, 351.
54. Pastor, X, 199.
55. Vasari, II, 295, *Peruzzi*.
56. Symonds, *Michelangelo*, 441.
57. Ibid., 372.
58. 255.
59. Vasari, IV, 119n.
60. Symonds, *Michelangelo*, 267.
61. Ibid., 282.

62. 324.
63. *Cambridge Modern History*, II, 67.
64. Pastor, X, 235.
65. Ibid., 322.
66. Letter of Gregorio da Casale, Oct., 1534, in Young, 358.

CHAPTER XXII

1. Burckhardt, *Cicerone*, in Vasari, IV, 320n.
2. Vasari, IV, 327.
3. Ibid., 329.
4. In Anderson, *Architecture of the Renaissance in Italy*, 145.
5. This section is especially indebted to Thomas Caldecott Chubb's *Aretino*.
6. Chubb, 46.
7. Vasari, III, 77, *Marcantonio Bolognese*.
8. In Chubb, 117.
9. Symonds, *Ital. Lit.*, II, 395.
10. Ariosto, *Orlando furioso*, xlvi, 14.
11. Maulde, 391.
12. Symonds, *Lit.*, II, 399-400.
13. Ibid., 404.
14. Chubb, 205.
15. Aretino, *Dialogues*, p. 55.
16. Aretino, 108, 83.
17. Roeder, 498.
18. Ibid., 441.
19. Taine, *Italy: Florence and Venice*, 289.
20. In Gronau, *Titian*, 46.
21. Chubb, 437.
22. Vasari, IV, 286.
23. Ruskin, *Stones of Venice*, I, 10.
24. Vasari, IV, 298.
25. In Mather, *Venetian Painters*, 340.
26. Soulier, G., *Le Tintoret*, 12.
27. Ibid., 19; Mather, 342.
28. Soulier, 115.
29. Ruskin, *Stones*, III, 285.
30. Ibid., 295.
31. Symonds, *Fine Arts*, 377.
32. Soulier, 75-6.
33. Ruskin, *Stones*, II, 243.
34. Siviero, R., *Catalogue of the Second National Exhibition of the Works of Art Recovered in Germany*, 45.
35. Mather, *Venetian Painters*, 396.
36. Ibid., 168.
37. 416; Venturi and Skira-Venturi, *Italian Painting: The Creators of the Renaissance*, 164.
38. Ruskin, *Stones*, II, 10.
39. Quoted by E. Herriot in a lecture at Cannes, Jan., 1951.

CHAPTER XXIII

1. Thompson, J. W., 376.
2. Adams, Brooks, *The New Empire*, 90.
3. Cf. Barnes, H. E., *History of Western Civilization*, I, 867.
4. Robertson, J. M., I, 469.
5. Symonds, *Catholic Reaction*, I, 33.
6. Ibid., 38, 234-334; Sismondi, 763.
7. Symonds, *Catholic Reaction*, I, 273.
8. Coulton, *Medieval Panorama*, 679.
9. Ranke, *History of the Popes*, I, 181.
10. Guicciardini, X, 257.
11. Ibid., 258.
12. Cardan, Jerome, *Book of My Life*, ch. ii.
13. Ibid., ch. vi.
14. Hallam, H., *Literature of Europe*, I, 451-2.
15. Duhem, *Leonardo*, I, 229f; Wolf, A., *History of Science, Technology, and Philosophy in the Sixteenth and Seventeenth Centuries*, 537.
16. Cardan, ch. xiii.
17. Ch. xiv.
18. Prologue.
19. Walsh, *The Popes and Science*, 116.
20. Cornaro, 43-7.
21. Ibid., 66-72.
22. Ibid., 79, 92, 103.
23. Ibid., Introd., 31. Addison, in No. 195 of *The Spectator*, III, 328, makes good use of Cornaro's treatise.
24. Hallam, II, 88.
25. Ibid., 119; Robertson, I, 470.
26. Hallam, II, 260.
27. Bandello, III, 123.
28. Holzknecht, *Backgrounds of Shakespeare*, 243.
29. *Cambridge Modern History*, III, 400-4.
30. Cellini, ii, 99.
31. Ibid., ii, 70.
32. James, *Bologna*, 317.
33. Vasari, III, 237, *Pontormo*.
34. Ibid., 245.
35. Cellini, i, 2.
36. Ibid., i, 14.
37. I, 26.
38. I, 52.
39. II, 33.
40. II, 50.
41. I, 51.
42. I, 73.
43. I, 64.
44. I, 55.
45. I, 74.
46. II, 26.

47. II, 12.
48. II, 28.
49. Ibid.
50. II, 34-5.
51. II, 37.
52. Notes by Symonds, p. 415.
53. I, 58.
54. Symonds, *Michelangelo*, 484.
55. Vasari, IV, 134, *Michelangelo*.
56. Ibid., 140.
57. 148.
58. Symonds, *Michelangelo*, 501.
58a. Ellis, H., *Studies in the Psychology of Sex*, Vol. II, *Sexual Inversion*, 19.

59. Maulde, 182.
60. Symonds, 377; Taine, *Italy: Rome and Naples*, 188.
61. Symonds, 442.
62. Vasari, IV, 198.
63. Symonds, 490.
64. Vasari, IV, 219.
65. Ibid., 203.
66. Ruskin, *Modern Painters*, Part I, ch. ii, end.
67. Symonds, 372.
68. Balcarres, Lord, *Evolution of Italian Sculpture*, 271; Spengler, O., *Decline of the West*, I, 276.

Index

Most abbreviations are self-explanatory. A single date indicates a *floruit* or, at least, a focal point mentioned in the text; if two dates constitute a *floruit*, they are preceded by *fl.* A footnote is indicated by an asterisk (*). All dates of male rulers, lay and ecclesiastical, are regnal. The index is to be used in conjunction with the Table of Contents (xi-xiv), where discussions of the major arts are indicated by section.

About the Authors

WILL DURANT was born in North Adams, Massachusetts, in 1885. He was educated in the Catholic parochial schools there and in Kearny, New Jersey, and thereafter in St. Peter's (Jesuit) College, Jersey City, New Jersey, and Columbia University, New York. For a summer he served as a cub reporter on the New York *Journal*, in 1907, but finding the work too strenuous for his temperament, he settled down at Seton Hall College, South Orange, New Jersey, to teach Latin, French, English, and geometry (1907–11). He entered the seminary at Seton Hall in 1909, but withdrew in 1911 for reasons which he has described in his book *Transition*. He passed from this quiet seminary to the most radical circles in New York, and became (1911–13) the teacher of the Ferrer Modern School, an experiment in libertarian education. In 1912 he toured Europe at the invitation and expense of Alden Freeman, who had befriended him and now undertook to broaden his borders.

Returning to the Ferrer School, he fell in love with one of his pupils, resigned his position, and married her (1913). For four years he took graduate work at Columbia University, specializing in biology under Morgan and Calkins and in philosophy under Woodbridge and Dewey. He received the doctorate in philosophy in 1917, and taught philosophy at Columbia University for one year. In 1914, in a Presbyterian church in New York, he began those lectures on history, literature, and philosophy which, continuing twice weekly for thirteen years, provided the initial material for his later works.

The unexpected success of *The Story of Philosophy* (1926) enabled him to retire from teaching in 1927. Thenceforth, except for some incidental essays, Mr. and Mrs. Durant gave nearly all their working hours (eight to fourteen daily) to *The Story of Civilization*. To better prepare themselves they toured Europe in 1927, went around the world in 1930 to study Egypt, the Near East, India, China, and Japan, and toured the globe again in 1932 to visit Japan, Manchuria, Siberia, Russia, and Poland. These travels provided the background for *Our Oriental Heritage* (1935) as the first volume in *The Story of Civilization*. Several further visits to Europe prepared for Volume II, *The Life of Greece* (1939) and Volume III, *Caesar and Christ* (1944). In 1948, six months in Turkey, Iraq, Iran, Egypt, and Europe provided perspective for Volume IV, *The Age of Faith* (1950). In 1951 Mr. and Mrs. Durant returned to Italy to add to a lifetime of gleanings for Volume V, *The Renaissance* (1953); and in 1954 further studies in Italy, Switzerland, Germany, France, and England opened new vistas for Volume VI, *The Reformation* (1957).

Mrs. Durant's share in the preparation of these volumes became more and more substantial with each year, until in the case of Volume VII, *The Age of Reason Begins* (1961), it was so pervasive that justice required the union of both names on the title page. The name Ariel was first applied to his wife by Mr. Durant in his novel *Transition* (1927) and in his *Mansions of Philosophy* (1929) —now reissued as *The Pleasures of Philosophy*.

With the publication of Volume X, *Rousseau and Revolution*, the Durants have concluded over four decades of work.

HB3J

Tivoli
Tagliacozzo
Chieti

STATES OF THE CHURCH

Tremiti Is.

Adriatic Sea

Termoli
Larino

Mt. Gargano

Campobasso
Lucera
Foggia

Manfredonia
Barletta
Trani

KINGDOM

Grandella
Capua
Gaeta
Benevento
Cerignola

Bari

Monopoli

Naples
Melfi

OF

Vesuvius
Pompei
Salerno

Ischia
Capri
Amalfi
Sorrento

Potenza

NAPLES

Matera

Taranto

Policastro

Gulf of Taranto

Sibari

Corigliano

Tyrrhenian Sea

Cosenza

Catanzaro
Catrone

LIPARI or AEOLIAN Is.
Ustica

Stromboli

Tropea

Ionian Sea

Filicudi
Salina
Panaria
Alicudi
Lipari
Vulcano
Messina
Gerace
Patti

Palermo

Cefalu
Mt. Etna

Reggio

SICILY

Taormina

Enna
Caltanissetta
Catania
Lentini

Agrigento

Ragusa
Syracuse
Noto

Southern **ITALY** *in the* XV *and* XVI *Centuries*